W9-BZD-177

Visit Our Web Site
www.precisiontype.com

A price list for the products shown in this Font Reference Guide can be printed or downloaded from our web site. Go to the bottom of the Font Reference Guide information page and click on the link labeled Font Reference Guide Price List (1MB-PDF-39 Pages)

Precision Type
Font Reference Guide
version 5.0

Precision Type
Commack · New York

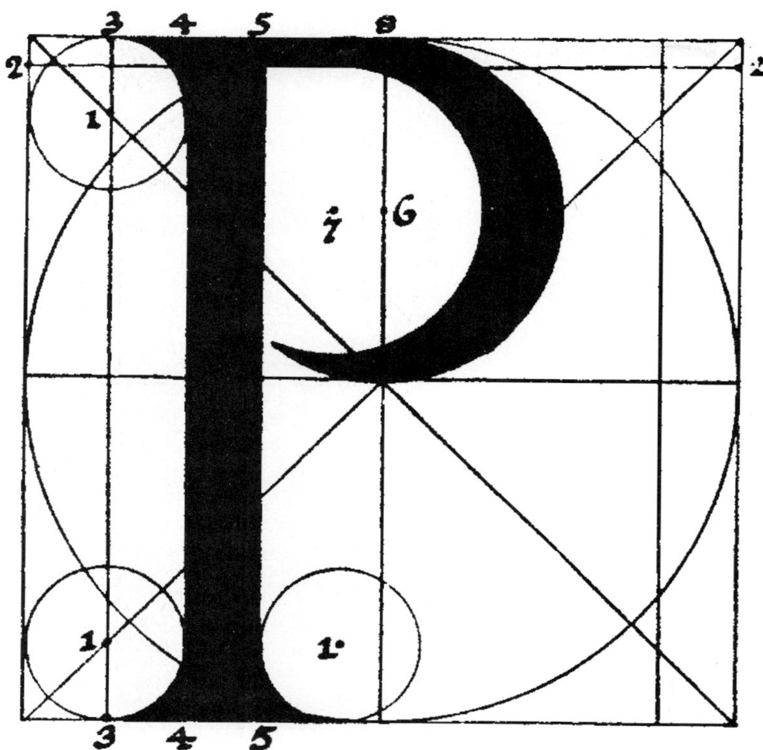
3 4 5 8
2 2
1
7 6
1 1
3 4 5

A B C D E F G

H I J K L M N O P Q R S T U V

W X Y Z & Ξ ff ? . . .

Precision Type Font Reference Guide

version 5.0

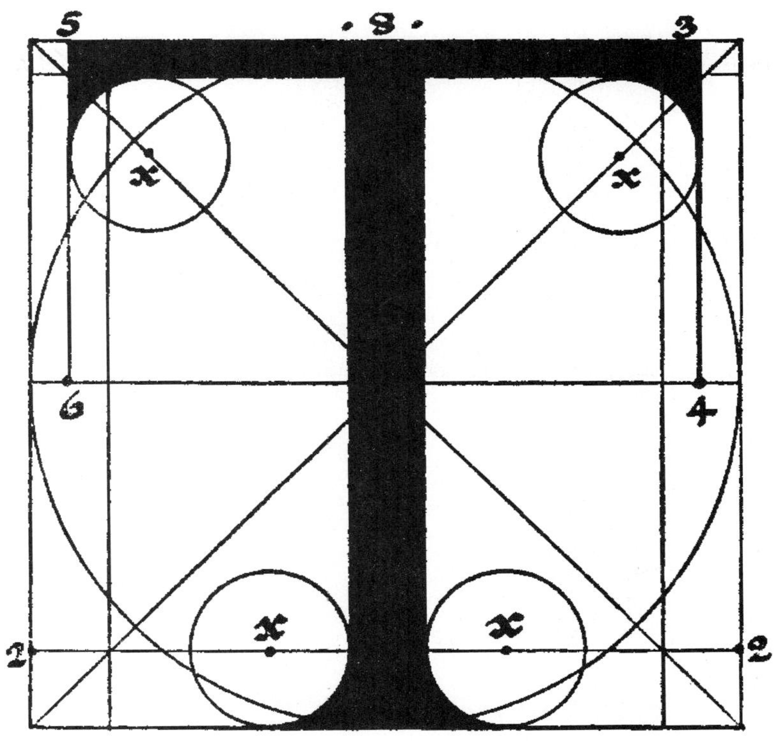

5
8
3
x
x
6
4
x
x
2
2

Jeff Level · Bruce Newman · Brenda Newman

ISBN 0-9646252-0-2

Printed in USA.

Contents

1495

1595

1695

1795

1895

1995

Foreword

A type specimen book is a remarkable resource.

Its obvious purpose, of course, is to display an inventory of available types – the more the better. Certainly, this particular book fulfills that obligation very well, and users will be pleased to see the large number and variety of type designs now obtainable in digital form. Specimen books also do much more. The small and modest ones can be used to study changing tastes and fashions, while those that aspire to comprehensiveness, as this one does, open a window onto five-hundred-plus years of type history. Even a cursory tour through these pages reveals the seemingly inexhaustible number of ways in which type designers have wooed the alphabet. Some have treated it with affection and reverence, others with ingenuity and inventiveness, while still others have wrestled its familiar characters into barely recognizable forms. Looking through this book, produced in the closing years of the twentieth century, during a time of digital wonders, we can't help but applaud the benefits of a technology that provides us with such a cornucopia of historic and contemporary typefaces. All these faces now, we marvel, where once there were so few. . .

FIVE HUNDRED YEARS AGO, the fifteenth century was drawing to a close, and the art of *printing* books had very nearly displaced the art of *writing* books. Just as scribes had developed a broad variety of scripts and explored the limits of the quill pen, printers, in their turn, now made characters out of metal, usually following manuscript models, but also probing the potentials of a new technology. But profound changes occurred over the next hundred years. Printers no longer cut and cast their own type, but turned instead to type founders who specialized in the design, manufacture and trade of punches, matrices and fonts of type. The types of Garamond and Granjon could be found throughout Europe, and publishers like Christopher Plantin of Antwerp conducted an international trade in books.

By the 1690s the revolutionary spirit that animated the art of printing in its early years had been replaced by a more pragmatic attitude: making books was a business like any other. On the other hand, new type design, which had withered for so long in the shadow of Garamond, had finally begun to flower again. It was the time of the sturdy types of Van Dijck and Voskens, owing something of their forms to Garamond, but much more suited to everyday use. These were the types that inspired Fell and Caslon, and sparked a revival of printing in England. The late seventeenth century was also a time of experimentation as the great *Romain du roi* of the French academicians took shape on the rack of geometry, but was soothed into more natural forms by the punchcutter Grandjean. The mathematical description of letterforms would not emerge again for almost 300 years, but when it did the results were almost as extraordinary as Gutenberg's perfection of movable type.

THERE WAS AN ABUNDANCE OF TYPE by the end of the eighteenth century. Fournier and Baskerville had come and gone, Bodoni had purged the last vestiges of the oldstyle model from his work, and the Caslon, Enschedé and Didot foundries, to name just three, supplied huge quantities of type to the world. The Americans, for their part, after importing thousands of pounds of metal during the Colonial period, were finally making decent type of their own; before long they had become leaders in the manufacture of display type.

The 1890s saw printers and the public – particularly in the United States – suffering from type exhaustion. American foundries had shown a distinct aptitude for introducing faces that ranged from innovative to just plain hideous. The good, the bad, and the ugly clawed out claims on a lawless type design frontier that seemed to have no bounds. With no copyright legislation to protect original designs, printers had their choice of not just one freakish face, but nine copies of it, all trotted out for view in the specimen books that grew larger and more lavish as the century neared its end. Faced with intense competition, revolt by a printing community unhappy with an industry that had no common manufacturing standards, and abandoned by a reading public satiated with type gimcrackery, American type manufacturers made significant changes. First, they agreed on a common point system for measuring and manufacturing type. Then, in 1892, a majority of them consolidated their operations, banished obsolete faces from their specimen books, and began anew as the American Type Founders Company. The welcome result of standardization was that printers could buy type from mulitple foundries and freely mix it. Consolidation brought fairer prices and a host of sensible new designs.

Today, as the twentieth century draws to a close, parallels can be drawn between the modern type industry and each of the eras just described. For example, digital techniques for designing and manufacturing type have virtually eliminated earlier technologies. Where letterforms were once described by the path of the pen and metal faces sculpted with files and gravers, modern digital types are products of mathematically-defined outlines. Once Adobe Systems' PostScript language became the standard for typeface manufacturers, the design, production and distribution of type was democratized. Anyone who now wants to make type can do so – with inexpensive, easy-to-use professional tools. The results are an extraordinary variety of new types and a new flowering of type design.

Emancipation, however, often brings chaos. Just as the nineteenth-century public appetite for new and unconventional faces led to unrestrained aesthetics, designers once again seem intent on breaking or ignoring all the rules. To be sure, many new digital releases are offshoots of traditional models, but others are far more experimental and take advantage of increasing sophistication in outline geometry and the manipulation of design axes. A huge number of digital typefaces now exist – over 13,000 are shown in this specimen book alone. These faces are gathered from more than sixty different manufacturing sources and are presented here in a single specimen book in the hope that comprehensiveness, insistence on high standards, convenience, and prompt service will persuade typographers to buy their type from one source.

DISPLAYING A COMPREHENSIVE COLLECTION of typefaces, however, presents vexing problems. In the 1730s, Caslon could show all of his types on a single broadsheet; two hundred years later the American Type Founders' specimen book of 1923 contained 1,148 carefully designed pages in which 8,096 ATF types were displayed in various arrangements. Needless to say, it was an enormously expensive and time-consuming book to produce and was almost the last of its kind. Sadly, but inevitably, the delightful practice of showing types in use has all but ceased. The original objective for including stylish exemplars in a specimen book was to inspire compositors with little training. Surely, it might be argued, the same situation is no different today amongst the huge untutored mass of desktop publishers. But good typographic guides now abound, leaving specimen books to forgo the instructive part of their duties in the interest of a wide selection and an affordable format. They should, however, incorporate (as this one efficiently does) certain essential elements: full alphabets for each member of a typeface family, including any special characters, along with information about the type designers and manufacturers. Additionally, it is useful to have a separate section with one-line showings of every typeface organized alphabetically by manufacturer since the typefaces displayed here come from multiple sources in many different versions.

Type is now more affordable, more varied, more easily available, and more transportable than at any time in its long history. The classic and the contemporary, as well as the shocking, illegible, and bizarre so beloved of today's hip designers, are all available for study in this concise, thorough and well-designed specimen. Choose what types you like and use them as you will. Instruct or provoke, but above all make your type communicate.

. . . .

DAVID PANKOW, *Curator*
Cary Graphic Arts Collection
Rochester Institute of Technology

. . .of what good is our Art & Craft if the director does not
oversee with Clear Vision and keep the business in order,
and Show the Clients throughout the land the Latest Products,
so that the Finished Fonts find their way into the world. . . .

'The Type Sales Manager,' by Rudolf Koch,
from his portfolio of woodcuts,
The Type Foundry in Silhouette, *1918.*

Introduction

I'm very pleased to introduce version 5.0 of the Precision Type Font Reference Guide.

You have in your hands the most comprehensive type specimen book of font software for electronic publishing ever produced – the result of an enormous amount of time and effort by a group of very dedicated individuals, and the continuing support and assistance of all the foundries whose fonts are displayed.

Within these pages you will find an unprecedented number of fonts from over sixty different sources. The type libraries of all the larger, well-known names in the business are here, plus the collections of many smaller companies from around the world. In total, there are more than 13,000 fonts of all kinds: from classic to contemporary, traditional to trend-setting, simply unusual to absolutely bizarre. The display formats have been designed to give you as much information as possible about the fonts themselves as well as their designers, manufacturers and availability.

Throughout the long, painstaking process of collating, organizing, and finally composing all of the fonts in this book, everyone involved has remained committed to the goal of producing a type specimen book that was unrivaled in scope, accuracy and, most importantly, practicality and ease of use; I'm happy to say that our goal has been achieved.

All of the fonts in this book are available directly from Precision Type or from any one of our *TypeOnSite* remarketers around the world.

I hope that this book provides you with information, assistance and inspiration in your pursuit of typographic excellence.

Bruce Newman, *President & CEO*, Precision Type

Notes on Contents & Organization

AS DAVID PANKOW SAYS SO WELL IN HIS FOREWORD, “displaying a comprehensive collection of typefaces. . . presents vexing problems.” There has never been, by our reckoning, a type specimen book of *any kind* that has shown in its pages the number of fonts that this one does. And the sheer number of fonts involved has meant that every step in the planning, design, and production of this book had to be thoroughly researched, checked and cross-referenced at several stages in the overall process. Vexing problems, indeed. More than 13,000 of them. . .

This version of the Font Reference Guide displays every font available from every foundry represented by Precision Type – up to the point in time when we had to ‘close the book’ to facilitate its completion. Early on in the research and design process we had to decide the best way to show all of these fonts within the constraints of a finite number of pages, a reasonable schedule and a cost-effective budget.

In Section One: Font.Family Reference, you’ll find some 5,500 fonts displayed as either comprehensive character sets or as complete upper- and lowercase alphabets, figures and some punctuation. Organized alphabetically, A – Z, followed by Pi, Symbol, Logo, Ornament & Image Fonts and Fonts for World-wide Languages, the range of fonts displayed was selected – on a proportional basis – from all of the foundries in this book. Included are fonts that have been standards for many years, those that have proven popular in recent times and a large number of fonts that we feel deserve more attention. In the case of duplicate offerings from two or more foundries, our selection of which foundries version to display was based on several factors: the font’s originator in whatever form, the first foundry to issue the font(s) in PostScript format, and the completeness of the offering.

Section Two: Font Foundry Reference, is organized alphabetically by foundry and every font from that foundry is shown in a one-line setting – usually set as the name of the font. There is also a brief paragraph or two with notes and information about each foundry.

Both sections have ‘Keys’ at their beginnings that explain all of the details, definitions and symbols used. Lastly, there is a comprehensive index – with page numbers and foundry references for both sections – following the end of Section Two.

About Precision Type. . .

PRECISION TYPE, INC. OF COMMACK, NEW YORK, *was one of the first independent font software distributors to market a wide range of typeface libraries in the PostScript language format to the professional graphic arts market. Created as an independent business with unique growth opportunities, the company was formally incorporated in 1992. The font software distribution activities had previously been a part of Precision Type & Form, Inc, a commercial typography and pre-press service company.*

In the years since its incorporation, Precision Type and the font software market have experienced explosive growth. The company now operates exclusively as a licensor and distributor for the products of over sixty font software developers and is recognized as one of the largest suppliers of font software products in the world.

Precision Type has an established reputation for typographic and technical expertise, excellent customer service, and competitive pricing. Its customers include professional typographers and designers, novice desktop publishers, and numerous corporate clients.

In addition to direct sales, Precision Type distributes the products of many of the companies it represents through its growing world-wide TypeOnSite *remarketer network, an on-demand order fulfilment system for fast and efficient retail sales. And, the company's* FontLink CD-ROM *makes a vast number of fonts available for sale to end-users almost instantly, 24 hours a day.*

Character References

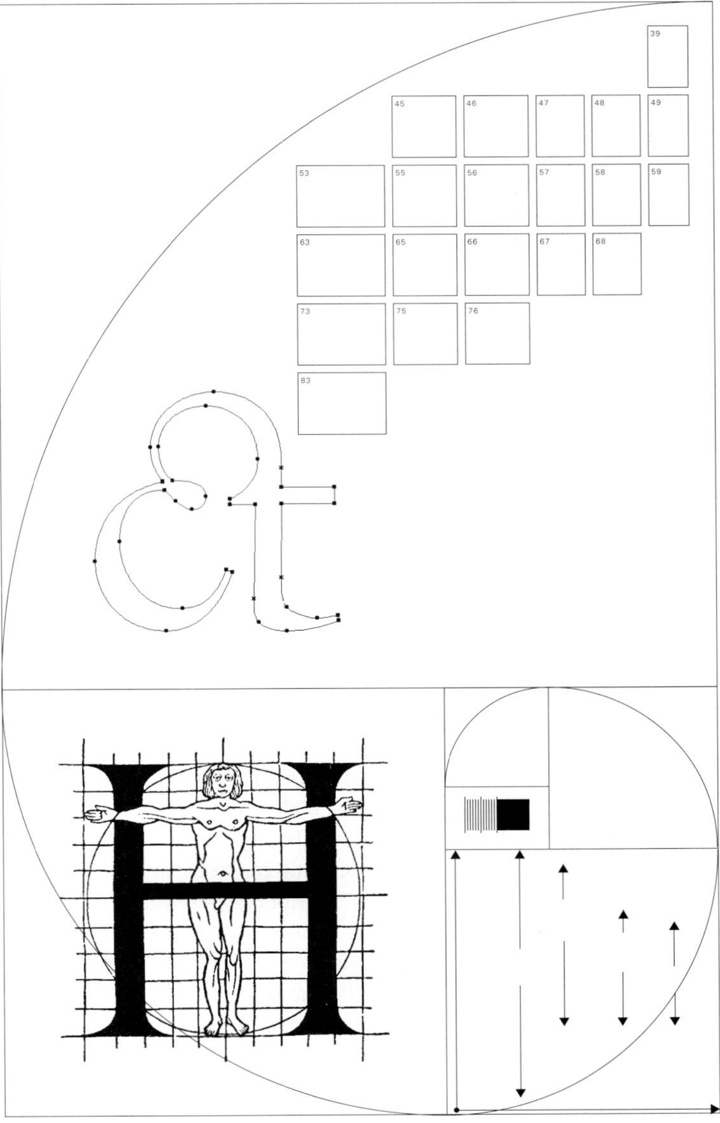
39
45
46
47
48
49
53
55
56
57
58
59
63
65
66
67
68
73
75
76
83

Typefaces, Fonts & Font Formats

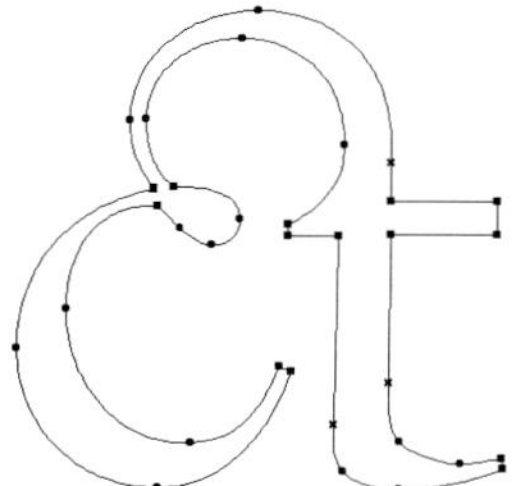

An PostScript font outline illustrating the character contour and the 'control points' which are used to manipulate and, ultimately, define the final shape of the character.

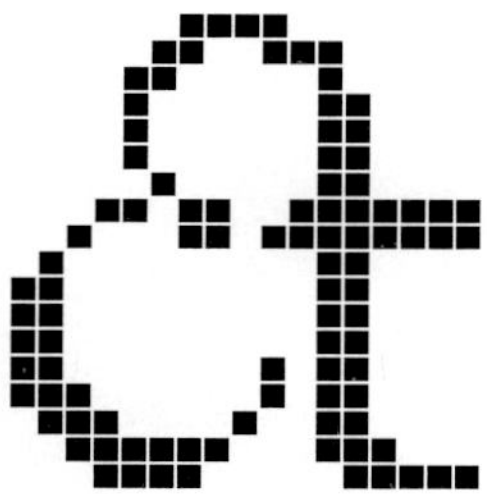

A bitmap character generated from the outline above. This one is intended for use at 24-point on a 72 dot-per-inch resolution video display.

The final result: the character genererated from the PostScript font; set here at 126-point.

Typefaces & Fonts

In present-day terminology, typeface and font are often used interchangably and are generally understood to mean the same thing: one set of characters of one design. In the past, the two words had distinctly different meanings and were, indeed, two distinctly different things because of the technology employed.

When type was made of metal and each size was a separate unit, the complete range of sizes of one design was a *typeface* and each individual size was a *font*. And, a *typeface family* was all of the variants in weight and style of a particular typeface design (such as roman, italic, bold, etc.) in all of their various sizes.

Today's type technologies no longer require separate sets of characters for each size and the distinction between typefaces and fonts has become blurred. Font, rather than typeface, has gained favor in recent years as the generally accepted and understood term, and it has been employed – for most purposes – in this book.

PostScript Fonts

All of the fonts in this book are available in Adobe System's PostScript language format. PostScript fonts (also known as Type1 fonts) are a specialized form of computer software containing mathematical descriptions, or outlines, of the contours of all the characters in a typeface design. These outlines are size and resolution independent and can be used with any PostScript or PostScript compatible output device. PostScript fonts can also be used with a number of graphics applications to produce various transformations and special effects.

Bitmap Fonts

A bitmap font is a set of digital information that describes characters as a series of black or white dots. In some of the earliest digital output devices all of the fonts were bitmaps. They are still used today in low resolution printers and for on-screen representations in many video display units.

A bitmap font is one size in one style and weight of a typeface design, as in the traditional meaning of the word font. In contemporary usage, it is one size built for one resolution: the number of dots per inch of the device it will be used with.

Bitmap fonts are also used on the Macintosh computer to identify and access PostScript outline fonts and, in that instance, are usually called screen fonts.

MultipleMaster Fonts

The MultipleMaster format is a specialized form of Adobe's PostScript Type1 font format. Each MultipleMaster font contains two or more sets of outlines, or master designs. By selectively merging, or interpolating, these master designs, a vast number of intermediate variations can be generated. These variations can encompass changes in weight, width, style and optical size depending on the definitions incorporated into the master designs. The format offers the opportunity to have access to an almost infinite number of design permutations from one font.

Other Outline Font Formats

Although there are a number of outline font formats in use today, many of them are tied to specific software applications and/or hardware platforms and are distributed on a selective basis. An exception is the TrueType format developed by Apple Computer for use with Macintosh operating systems and also used in Microsoft Windows.

Apple has also developed a new format called TrueTypeGX. In conjunction with Macintosh system software, it allows a variety of character transformations and composition functions to be performed that have usually required separate fonts and/or specialized applications.

A GX font can contain many thousands of characters enabling access to alternate designs, special ligatures, fractions, swash characters and other forms without changing fonts. The format can automatically generate true small capitals and properly weighted and sized superior and inferior characters. In some GX fonts, features similar to MultipleMaster fonts enable the generation of intermediate weights, widths, styles and other design variants.*

*To find about more about the GX format, see the Linotype-Hell pages in the *FontFoundryFocus* section.

A CHARACTER SET is the complete group (or a subset of the complete group) of characters in a font. The following is a summary of most of the character sets referred to in this book. *Note that the character sets shown here are a subset of those available on Macintosh computers using System 7 (mathematical and other little-used, miscellaneous characters are not shown).*

'Standard'

Adobe Systems has defined their standard character set as a superset of ISOLatin1.*
Most other foundries adhere to this standard.

All-Caps, Display, Headline, etc.

Any number of variants on the 'Standard' set... used for fonts that have no lowercase and/or were designed for use at large sizes.

Character Sets

Expert

An Adobe standard... contains Small Capitals, Oldstyle Figures, Em-Fractions, Superior and Inferior Figures, Superior Lowercase, additional f-ligatures and other specialized characters.

SCOSF

Small Capitals & Oldstyle Figures... Small Capitals in place of lowercase, Oldstyle Figures (with ascenders and descenders) in place of regular figures.

OSF

Oldstyle Figures... in place of regular figures.

Dfr and other Alternates

DeutschFraktur... a specialized subset for German Blackletter, or *Fraktur*, fonts. Other Alternate Character Sets encompass any number of varieties... some created for specialized applications, some for Pi, Symbol, Logo, Ornament & Image fonts, and many others that do not fit any sort of standard.

* ISOLatin1 is a character set defined and agreed to by the International Standards Organization. It is intended to be the global *lingua franca* for printed and electronic communications using the Latin alphabet.

'Standard' Character Set

abcdefghijklmnopqrstuvwyxzfiflß-(".;'!*?':,")»...«‹,¡·¿„›
áâäåãàæçéêëèíîïìñóôöõòœøúûüùÿ ´ ˆ ¨ ˚ ˇ ˜ ` ˘ ¯ ˙ ˝ ¸ ˛
$1234567890¢–¥£#'@"ƒ/—/°\{%_‰} ®™©
ABCDEFGHIJKLMNOPQRSTUVWXYZ [¶§•†‡]
ÁÂÄÅÃÀÆÇÉÊËÈÍÎÏÌÑÓÔÖÕÒŒØÚÛÜÙŸ

All-Caps, Display, Headline, etc. Character Set

ABCDEFGHIJKLMNOPQRSTUVWYXZ
(".;'!*?':,")»...«‹,¡·¿„› ´ ˆ ¨ ˚ ˇ ˜ ` ˘ ¯ ˙ ˝ ¸ ˛ ®™©[•]
ÁÂÄÅÃÀÆÇÉÊËÈÍÎÏÌÑÓÔÖÕÒŒØ
-ÚÛÜÙŸ$1234567890¢–¥£ƒ—/ {%_}

Expert Character Set

ABCDEFGHIJKLMNOPQRSTUVWXYZ-(.,!?:,)..·
ÁÂÄÅÃÀÆÇÐÉÊËÈÍÎÏÌŁÑÓÔÖÕÒŒØÞŠÚÛÜÙÝŸŽ ´ ˆ ¨ ˚ ˇ ˜ ` ˘ ¯ ˙ ˝ ¸ ˛
$1234567890¢ – ⅛ ¼ ⅓ ⅜ ½ ⅝ ⅔ ¾ ⅞ ₡Rp 1
$12345-67890¢/$12345-67890¢., — ff fi fl ffi ffl (abdeilmnorst.,)

SCOSF Character Set

ABCDEFGHIJKLMNOPQRSTUVWYXZ-(".;'!*?':,")»...«‹,¡·¿„›
ÁÂÄÅÃÀÆÇÉÊËÈÍÎÏÌÑÓÔÖÕÒŒØÚÛÜÙŸ ´ ˆ ¨ ˚ ˇ ˜ ` ˘ ¯ ˙ ˝ ¸ ˛
$1234567890¢–¥£#'@"ƒ/—/°\{%_‰} ®™©
ABCDEFGHIJKLMNOPQRSTUVWXYZ [¶§•†‡]
ÁÂÄÅÃÀÆÇÉÊËÈÍÎÏÌÑÓÔÖÕÒŒØÚÛÜÙŸ

OSF Character Set

abcdefghijklmnopqrstuvwyxzfiflß-(".;'!*?':,")»...«‹,¡·¿„›
áâäåãàæçéêëèíîïìñóôöõòœøúûüùÿ ´ ˆ ¨ ˚ ˇ ˜ ` ˘ ¯ ˙ ˝ ¸ ˛
$1234567890¢–¥£#'@"ƒ/—/°\{%_‰} ®™©
ABCDEFGHIJKLMNOPQRSTUVWXYZ [¶§•†‡]
ÁÂÄÅÃÀÆÇÉÊËÈÍÎÏÌÑÓÔÖÕÒŒØÚÛÜÙŸ

Dfr Character Set

ch ck ff ft ll ſ s ſi ſſ ß tz — ä ö ü Ä Ö Ü

Alternate Character Set

I V X st nd rd th ¼ ⅓ ½ ¾ D c r c s O rs s & %

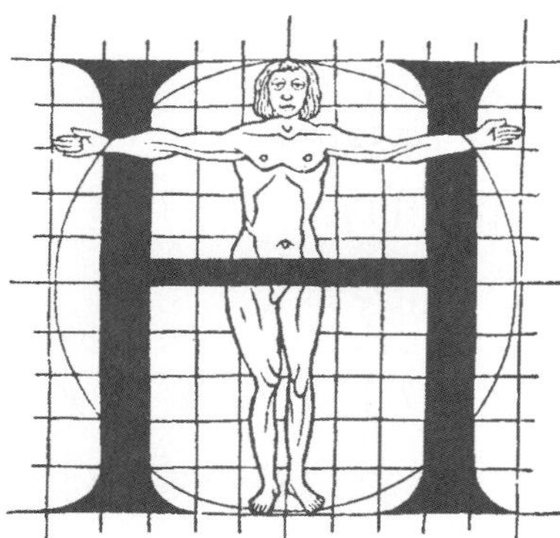

Geofroy Tory's depiction of the relationship between the proportions of the human body and those of roman capitals. From his book Champ Fleury, *1527.*

Character Dimensions & Anatomy

THE CHARACTERS OF A TYPEFACE DESIGN may not be quite so pleasant to look at as the human body but they have many features in common: height and girth, arms and legs, spines, shoulders and ears. And like the parts of the human body, some parts of typeface characters figure prominently in their overall appearance while others have a more subtle influence on the whole.

Since all typefaces are basically the same thing – the letters A through Z, etc. in one form or another – it would be easy to conclude (and many might agree) that no one typeface design is any different from another, *i.e.* they all look the same. But few would disagree with the fact that while every human body is essentially the same, each human being has a very distinct and unique appearance. The same is true of typeface designs: as a species they're all about the same; as individuals, each one has its very own distinguishing details.

To understand and appreciate the differences between typeface designs one needs to become familiar with the characteristics and features they share in common and those that make them stand apart. Each typeface does, indeed, possess unique qualities – qualities out of the ordinary or mundane, beautiful or ugly, obvious or elusive – as does the body and the face of every human being.

'Habit d'Imprimeur en Lettres' (The Clothes of the Printer of Letters). Etching by Bonnart for Les Métiers, *c.1680.*

Body Size
An archaic – yet still appropriate – term that describes the height of the piece of lead on which a character is cast. Equal to the type's point size, it includes room for ascenders and descenders plus the white space above and below them.

Baseline
An imaginary line where the bottoms of characters without descenders sit, or align.

Cap Height
The distance from the Baseline to the top of the capitals.

x-height
The distance from the Baseline to the top of the lowercase *x*.

Ascender Height
The distance between the top of the x-height and the tops of lowercase characters such as *b, d, f,* and *k*. Also stated as the distance from the Baseline to the tops of the ascenders.

Descender Depth
The distance between the Baseline and the bottoms of lowercase characters such as *g, j, p* and *y*. Also stated as the distance from the top of the x-height to the bottoms of the descenders.

Small Cap Height
The distance from the Baseline to the top of the small cap *x*.

Figure Height
The height of the figures 1–0; usually it is approximately equivalent to the Cap Height.

Em Square
Describes a square that has a height and width equal to the Body Size.

Em Space
Defines a distance equal to the Body Size.

Unit Width
Total width of a character including any white space on either side, *not including* any Kerns.

Kern
Any portion of a character which extends to the left and/or right of the Unit Width.

Figure Width/En Space
A fixed width for the figures 1–0. Usually one-half of the Em Space.

Cap Height Line
Imaginary line where the tops of capitals align.

x-height line
Imaginary line where the tops of lowercase characters without ascenders align.

Ascender Line
Imaginary line where the tops of ascenders align.

Descender Line
Imaginary line where the bottoms of descenders align.

Small Cap Height Line
Imaginary line where the tops of small capitals align.

Accent Line (Uppercase)
Imaginary line where the tops of uppercase accents align, usually above and beyond the upper extreme of the Body Size.

Stem or Stroke
The principal vertical or oblique element(s) of a character. . . except for curved characters when they are always called Strokes. And, in diagonal characters such as *W*, Stem usually refers to the secondary diagonal element(s).

Serif
The beginning or end of a Stem or Stroke, Arm, Leg or Tail drawn at a right angle or at an oblique to the Stem or Stroke.

Brackets or Fillets
The join between a Serif and a Stem or Stroke.

Terminal
Stem or Stroke ending other than a Serif.

Hairline
The thinner part of a curved Stroke, usually located on the Stress or Axis.

Bowl
A curved Stroke enclosing a Counter.

Counter
An area enclosed by a Bowl or a Crossbar.

Stress or Axis
The inclination of curved Strokes – either vertical or oblique – which implies the path of a pen. . . were a pen to be used.

Crossbar
A horizontal element connecting two vertical or diagonal Stems or Strokes.

Ascender
The part of a lowercase character above the x-height.

Descender
The part of a lowercase character below the Baseline.

Cross-stroke or Bar
Horizontal element crossing a Stem or Stroke.

Apex
The Point where two diagonal Stems or Strokes meet.

Arm
A projecting horizontal or diagonal Stem or Stroke.

Leg
A projecting diagonal Stem or Stroke extending downward; sometimes called a Tail.

Tail
A Stem or Stroke – usually extending below the Baseline – in characters such as *Q* and *j*.

Shoulder
The portion of a curved Stroke, but not the hairline, connecting two vertical Stems or Strokes.

Spine
The diagonal portion of the Stroke in *S*.

Loop
The Descender of *g* when it is entirely enclosed (otherwise it is a Tail).

Ear
The small Stroke attached to the Bowl of *g*.

Link
The Stroke which connects the Bowl and the Loop of *g*.

Spur
A small, pointed projection from a Stem or Stroke, such as those found on *G* or *t*.

Beak
A vertical or oblique Serif that terminates a horizontal Stem or Stroke.

Tie or Connecting Stroke
A Stroke that joins two characters together to make a ligature or tied character.

Swash
A flourished Terminal, Stem or Stroke added to a character in any number of places.

Character Dimensions:

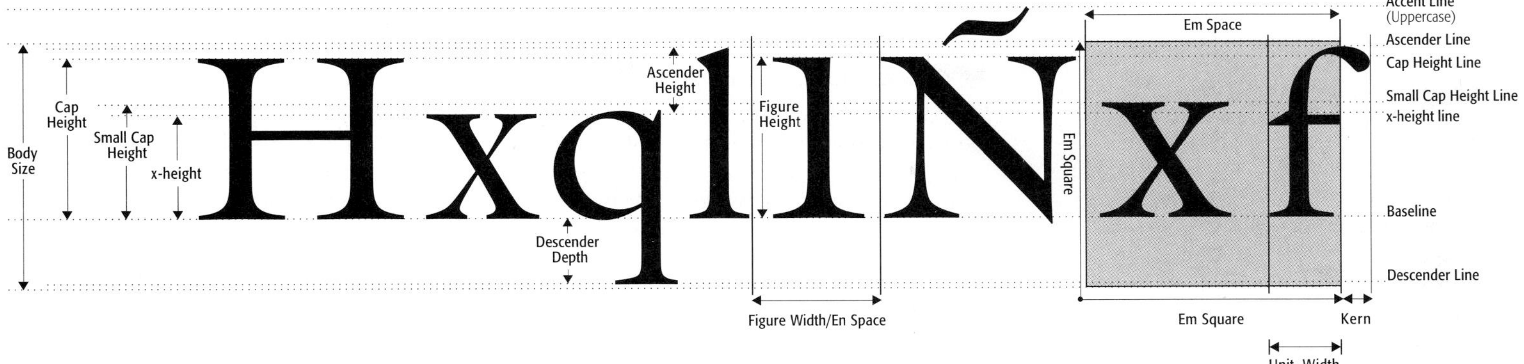
Hxql1Ñxf
Accent Line (Uppercase)
Ascender Line
Cap Height Line
Small Cap Height Line
x-height line
Baseline
Descender Line
Body Size
Cap Height
Small Cap Height
x-height
Ascender Height
Descender Depth
Figure Height
Figure Width/En Space
Em Space
Em Square
Em Square
Kern
Unit Width

Systems for Measuring Type

There are three principal systems in use today for measuring the size of type, two based on traditional 'printer's points', the other on the metric system.

The American-British Point System was developed by Nelson C. Hawks in the 1870s. Standard units are the Pica and the Point measuring .166 and .01383 inches, respectively. There are 12 Points in one Pica and approximately six picas, or 72 Points, in one inch.

height of cap H above is 63 American-British Points

Twelve Points = One Pica

The Didot Point System was progressively developed by P. S. Fournier and F. A. Didot in the eighteenth century. Standard units are the Cicero and the Corps (or, Didot Point), measuring .178 and .01483 inches, respectively. There are 12 Didot Points in one Cicero.

height of cap H above is 59 Didot Points

Twelve Didot Points = One Cicero

In Europe, **The Metric System** has been applied to the measurement of type in recent years. Millimeters (.001 meter, .1 centimeter, .0394 inch) are the standard units of measure. One Millimeter is equal to approximately 2.85 American-British Points.

height of cap H above is 22.1 Millimeters

Five Millimeters = One-Half Centimeter

Character Anatomy:

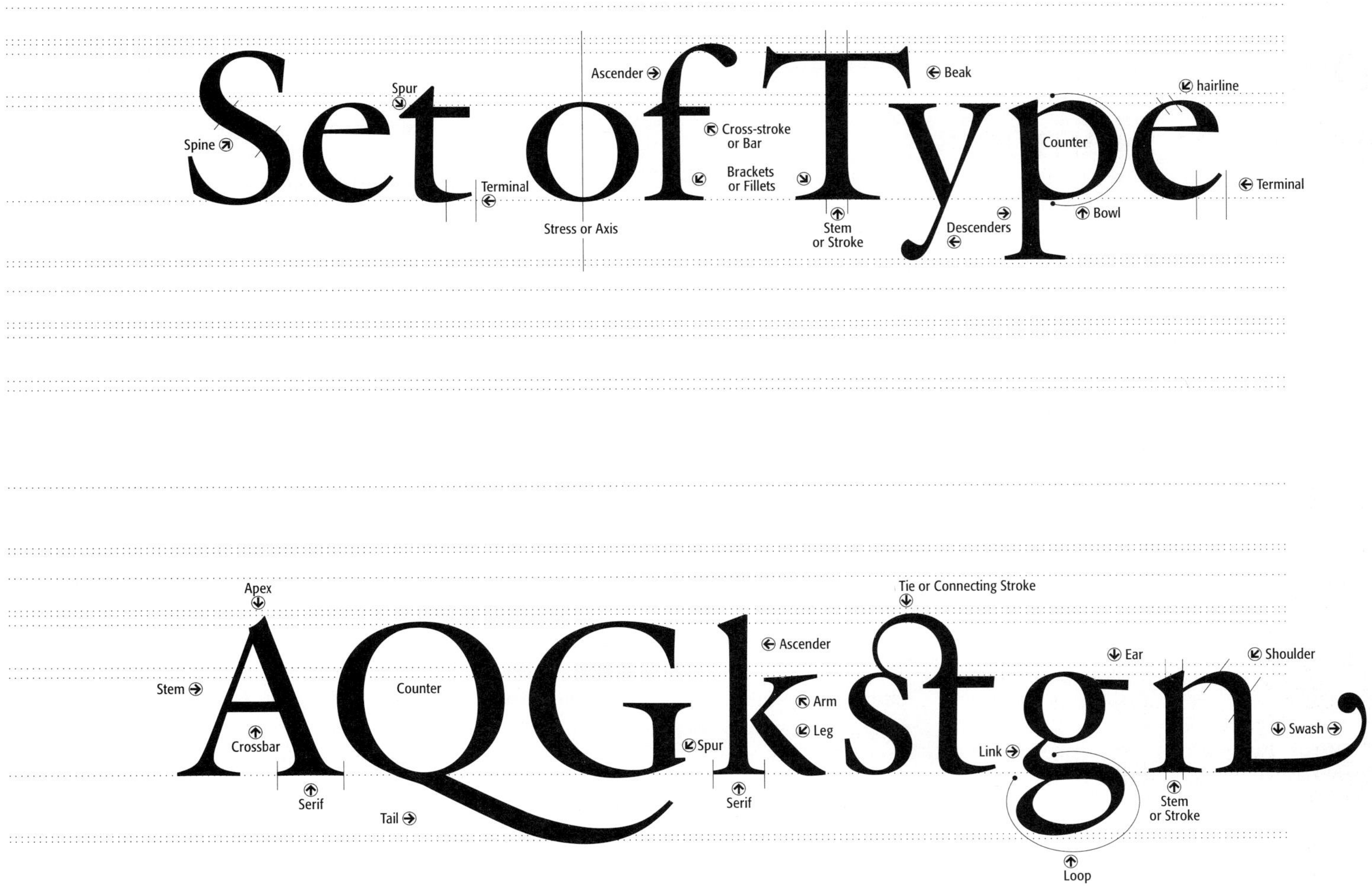

Set of Type

Spine, Spur, Terminal, Ascender, Stress or Axis, Cross-stroke or Bar, Brackets or Fillets, Beak, Stem or Stroke, Descenders, Counter, Bowl, hairline, Terminal

AQGkstgn

Apex, Stem, Crossbar, Serif, Counter, Tail, Spur, Serif, Ascender, Arm, Leg, Tie or Connecting Stroke, Link, Loop, Ear, Stem or Stroke, Shoulder, Swash

Neue Helvetica 25 - Ultra Light
Neue Helvetica 26 - Ultra Light Italic
Neue Helvetica 35 - Thin
Neue Helvetica 36 - Thin Italic
Neue Helvetica 45 - Light
Neue Helvetica 46 - Light Italic
Neue Helvetica 55 - Regular
Neue Helvetica 56 - Italic
Neue Helvetica 65 - Medium
Neue Helvetica 66 - Medium Italic
Neue Helvetica 75 - Bold
Neue Helvetica 76 - Bold Italic
Neue Helvetica 85 - Heavy
Neue Helvetica 86 - Heavy Italic
Neue Helvetica 95 - Black
Neue Helvetica 96 - Black Italic
Neue Helvetica 75 - Bold Outline
Neue Helvetica 27 - Ultra Light Condensed
Neue Helvetica 27 - Ultra Light Condensed Oblique
Neue Helvetica 37 - Thin Condensed
Neue Helvetica 37 - Thin Condensed Oblique
Neue Helvetica 47 - Light Condensed
Neue Helvetica 47 - Light Condensed Oblique

Typeface Families: Weights, Widths, Styles & Numbers

Neue Helvetica 57 - Condensed
Neue Helvetica 57 - Condensed Oblique
Neue Helvetica 67 - Medium Condensed
Neue Helvetica 67 - Medium Condensed Oblique
Neue Helvetica 77 - Bold Condensed
Neue Helvetica 77 - Bold Condensed Oblique
Neue Helvetica 87 - Heavy Condensed
Neue Helvetica 87 - Heavy Condensed Oblique
Neue Helvetica 97 - Black Condensed
Neue Helvetica 97 - Black Condensed Oblique
Neue Helvetica 107 - Extra Black Condensed
Neue Helvetica 107 - Extra Black Condensed Oblique
Neue Helvetica 23 - Ultra Light Extended
Neue Helvetica 23 - Ultra Light Extended Oblique
Neue Helvetica 33 - Thin Extended
Neue Helvetica 33 - Thin Extended Oblique
Neue Helvetica 43 - Light Extended
Neue Helvetica 43 - Light Extended Oblique
Neue Helvetica 53 - Extended
Neue Helvetica 53 - Extended Oblique
Neue Helvetica 63 - Medium Extended
Neue Helvetica 63 - Medium Extended Oblique
Neue Helvetica 73 - Bold Extended
Neue Helvetica 73 - Bold Extended Oblique
Neue Helvetica 83 - Heavy Extended
Neue Helvetica 83 - Heavy Extended Oblique
Neue Helvetica 93 - Black Extended
Neue Helvetica 93 - Black Extended Oblique

The Neue (New) Helvetica *typeface family introduced by Linotype AG in the late 1980s. A revised and rationalized version of the original* Helvetica *of 1957, the complete family is made up of more than fifty different fonts.*

Typeface Families

Only in the mid-sixteenth century – 100 years after the invention of movable types – were roman and italic seen as a mated pair instead of separate entities. And prior to the 1850s, the idea that a roman and italic should have a bold or semibold companion face was a novelty. It was not until the early years of the twentieth century that most new typeface designs began to appear in the range of weights, widths and styles that we now think of as a family of types.

A typeface family is a group of fonts related to each other by an overall, unifying design theme. Its purpose is to provide the means to produce typography that is diverse, dynamic and harmonious. Typeface families range in scope from the most basic – one weight and width of roman and italic – to the immense variety found in an 'extended' or 'super' family that may contain fifty or more different fonts. While all the members of a typeface family share a common identity, each font has its own unique attributes of weight, width, form, inclination, surface treatment and, sometimes, design.

Weights & Widths

Changing the weight of a typeface design is one method used to produce variations between different members of a family. The range of weights can extend from a stroke that is almost invisible to one so heavy that the legibility of a typeface may suffer – neither are of much use for anything but the most unusual of applications. The most useful (and most commonly used) weights tend to be those closest to the norm.

Varying a typeface's width is another method used to introduce diversity and functionality into a typeface family. The 'normal' width can be made narrower (condensed) or wider (extended or expanded); of the two, condensed versions are more prevalent and more useful. As with radical changes in the weight of a typeface design, the usefulness of fonts exhibiting extreme variations in width is limited.

Styles

In addition to variations in weight and width, the diversity of a typeface family is most often apparent, and its utility increased, by the range of styles it contains, the most common variant being italic (or cursive). Although most italics differ from roman in their inclination from the vertical, it is the form of the italic letter, not its angle, which most clearly distinguishes it. While most seriffed typeface families contain *true italics* for use with the romans, in sans serif designs obliques (which are or almost appear to be slanted romans) are often found instead.

Outlines, inlines, shadows, shadings, and other surface treatements are styles found in some typeface families. Such variations are usually intended, and only useful, for display purposes.

Ideally, any typeface family intended for text should have fonts with both small capitals and oldstyle figures. Also useful are fonts that have been properly weighted and proportioned for use at large sizes.

Design

A recent development in typeface families is the concept of integrating serif, sans serif and other design variants into a cohesive whole. Proposed in the 1930s by Jan Van Krimpen, the idea was not fully implemented until the late 1970s by Gerard Unger with his designs *Demos*, *Praxis* and *Flora*. Such multi-faceted families provide tools to satisfy complex graphic requirements while maintaining typographic unity.

Type by the Numbers

Type nomenclature is inconsistent and often imprecise, and style names like *Extra Bold Extra Condensed Outline Shaded* are not unheard of. A solution to this problem was developed and implemented by Adrian Frutiger in the late 1950s for his *Univers* typeface family.

Frutiger devised a system assigning a two-digit code to each font. The first digit denoted weight – from 3 to 8, light to heavy, the second denoted width – 3 to 9, extended to condensed. The second digit also described inclination – even digits for roman fonts, odd for italic.

The system, while logical and practical, was not well received by the typographic community and, while still used, it is rarely found without the addition of names qualifying the numbers.

Roman & *Italic*
& **Semibold**

SMALL CAPITALS
& 1234·567·890

Italic
SWASH CAPITALS

1234567890 . . . SUPERIOR FIGURES

. . . ORNAMENTS

Condensed & *Condensed Italic*
& **Semibold Condensed**

CONDENSED
SMALL CAPITALS & 1234·567·890

Condensed Italic
SWASH CAPITALS

1234567890 . . . CONDENSED SUPERIOR FIGURES

An 'idealized' family of fonts for book and magazine work that should satisfy most of the requirements for good typography. Above, fonts for text in wide or narrow column widths; below, fonts for display use. Examples selected from Adobe Systems' Minion MultipleMaster family.

Roman & *Italic*

SMALL CAPS

& 1234567890

SWASH

Adrian Frutiger's Univers palette: the original family of 21 variations in weight, width and orientation (black) plus additions made by several foundries over the years (grey).

						39 univers
		45 univers	46 *univers*	47 univers	48 *univers*	49 univers
53 univers	54 *univers*	55 univers	56 *univers*	57 univers	58 *univers*	59 univers
63 univers	64 *univers*	65 univers	66 *univers*	67 univers	68 *univers*	
73 univers	74 *univers*	75 univers	76 *univers*			
83 univers		85 univers	86 *univers*			
93 univers	94 *univers*					

Demos · Praxis · *Flora*

Lucida · Lucida Sans · Lucida Sans Typewriter

ITC Stone Serif · ITC Stone Sans · ITC Stone Informal

ITC Officina Serif · ITC Officina Sans

Charlotte · Charlotte Sans

Five examples of 'extended' or 'super' typeface families where styles such as serif, sans serif, cursives and others are integrated and unified by repeating design features and common weights, widths, sizes and alignments.

11 Bureau Grotesque
13 Bureau Grotesque
15 Bureau Grotesque
17 Bureau Grotesque
31 Bureau Grotesque
33 Bureau Grotesque
35 Bureau Grotesque
37 Bureau Grotesque
51 Bureau Grotesque
53 Bureau Grotesque
55 Bureau Grotesque
79 Bureau Grotesque

Another numbering system for weight and width. The first digit designates width – from 1 to 9, narrow to wide; the second digit is for weight – 1 to 9, light to heavy. Italics (if they were available) would use even digits in the same manner of progression. Developed by David Berlow of The Font Bureau.

Vox Classification : ...1954
1. Humane
2. Garalde
3. Réale
4. Didone
5. Incise
6. Linéale
7. Mécane
8. Scripte
9. Manuaire

ATypI Classification : ...1961
1. Humane
2. Garalde
3. Réale
4. Didone
5. Incise
6. Linéale
7. Mécane
8. Scripte
9. Manuaire
10. Fractura

DIN Classification : ...1964
1.1 Roman
1.2 Baroque
1.3 Classical
1.4 Free Roman
1.5 Linear Roman
1.6 Block
1.7 Script
2. Blackletter
3. Non-Roman

British Standards Classification : ...1965
1. Graphic
2. Humanist
3. Garalde
4. Transitional
5. Didone
6. Lineale
7. Slab-Serif
8. Glyphic
9. Script

Typeface Classification

Lawson.RIT Classification : ...1971
1. Blackletter
2. Oldstyle
   a. Venetian
   b. Aldine-French
   c. Dutch-English
3. Transitional
4. Modern
5. Square Serif
6. Sans Serif
7. Script-Cursive
8. Display-Decorative

Bitstream Classification : ...1986
1. Oldstyle
2. Transitional
3. Modern
4. Clarendon
5. Slabserif
6. Latin
7. Freeform
8. Sanserif
9. Engravers
10. Stencil
11. Strike-On
12. Computer
13. Decorated
14. Script
15. Exotic
16. Pi
... Non-Roman

Linotype Classification : ...1988
1. Old Face
2. Transitional
3. Modern Face
4. Slab Serif
5. Sans Serif
6. Decorative & Display
7. Script & Brush
8. Blackletter.Broken
9. Non-Roman
10. Pi

Adobe Classification : ...1991
1. Venetian
2. Garalde
3. Transitional
4. Didone
5. Slab Serif
6. Sans Serif
7. Glyphic
8. Script
9. Display
10. Blackletter
11. Symbol
12. Non-Latin

THERE ARE THOUSANDS OF TYPE DESIGNS and over 13,000 individual fonts displayed in this book. Hundreds of them will be familiar and immediately recognized by many users of type; hundreds of others – be they obscure revivals from the past or new arrivals on the typographic scene – may be less well known. Confronted with such a vast array of choices, deciding how any one of these fonts might fulfill a particular need or be used in place of another design can be perplexing. One method of becoming better acquainted with typeface designs old and new, as well as understanding their potential uses, is to learn and employ a method of typeface classification.

Accuracy & Practicality

All typeface classification systems share a common goal: accurate classification of type designs in logical groupings. Most, if not all, systems attempt to achieve this goal by using the historical development of type – from the mid-fifteenth century to the present day – as an underlying structure. Having this principle in common, the differences between various classification systems are manifested in their degrees of accuracy and their practicality in everyday use.

It would be rather easy to classify typeface designs into three categories: serif, sans serif and scripts – but it wouldn't be a very useful system. It would be also be easy (but much more time consuming) to create a system with hundreds of type classifications that would be very accurate... and extremely impractical.

The requirements for a good typeface classification system are logical, accurate categories that can be easily understood and practically utilized. Such a system will have about ten categories, some of which may be further sub-dividied, and the system will be based on the historical development of type.*

In the last 40 years a number of typeface classification systems have been developed, proposed and debated – then sometimes employed and sometimes forgotten. Some have been very accurate but difficult to learn and utilize; others not so specific are quite practical. A system suited to the exacting requirements of a typographic scholar or historian may be quite inappropriate to the more basic, though no less important, needs of a practicing typographer.

No two systems of typeface classification agree in their categorization of *every* type design. Nor is it likely that every typographer will agree on which category a particular type design should be placed in. But typeface classification systems still provide a useful framework for identifying and utilizing the ever-increasing variety and number of typefaces available today.

A Simplified Approach :

The classification system outlined below is intended to be a simplified, practical tool for everyday use that can be easily understood. It borrows from several existing systems, is less detailed in some aspects, and expands or attempts to clarify in others. It is accurate within its own limitations and it's primary intent is to be a useful guide to typeface classification – not a definitive treatment.

Multiple examples of each category and a brief description of historical development and characteristic features are given on the following pages.

- *Oldstyle*
- *Transitional*
- *Modern*
- *Slab Serif*
- *Sans Serif*
- *Script. Cursive. Brush*
- *Graphic. Display. Decorative*
- *Blackletter*
- *Polyglot*
- *Pi, Symbol, Logo, Ornament & Image*

* Using the principle of historical development does not exclude typefaces designed in later periods from a category; a typeface of 1995 can incorporate features from one designed in 1495.

Oldstyle

Historical Development:
The Oldstyle category of type begins with the first romans used in Venice by Nicolas Jenson about 1470 and extends into the early years of the 18th century with the Dutch-influenced designs of William Caslon.

After Jenson came the types of Aldus cut by Francesco Griffo in the 1490s, also in Venice. These types then influenced French designers such as Garamond, Granjon and Jannon in the 16th century whose own tastes and sensibilities produced vibrant, new expressions of style in the Oldstyle form.

Finally, the types produced in Holland by Van Dijck and Voskens, and in England by Caslon, tending to be heavier and sturdier than those of the French, represent the fullest extension in the development of Oldstyle type.

Characteristic Features:
In varying degrees, most Oldstyle types do not exhibit strong contrasts in stroke weights and the stress of curved strokes is noticably inclined to the left. The types of Jenson, and revivals based on his work, usually have a diagonal crossbar on the lowercase e; in later Oldstyles this crossbar is usually horizontal. In the earliest Oldstyle types, ascenders are about the same height as capitals; in later expressions, the ascenders tend to be taller.

Aurelia & *Aurelia*

Bembo & *Bembo*

ITC Berkeley Oldstyle & *ITC Berkeley Oldstyle*

Cartier & *Cartier*

Caslon Oldstyle No. 337 & *Caslon Oldstyle No. 337*

Centaur & *Centaur*

FC Cooper Old Style & *FC Cooper Old Style*

ITC Galliard & *ITC Galliard*

Stempel Garamond & *Stempel Garamond*

Granjon & *Granjon*

ITC Golden Type

Bitstream Iowan Old Style & *Bitstream Iowan Old Style*

Meno & *Meno*

Minion & *Minion*

Poliphilus Roman & *Blado Italic*

Van Dijck & *Van Dijck*

Vendome & *Vendome*

Village & *Village*

Yan Series 333 & *Yan Series 333*

Transitional

Historical Development:
At the end of the 17th century, a committee, under the auspices of the French Académie des Sciences, *was formed to create a new, improved style of type for use by the royal printing office. Designed on a grid of 2,304 tiny squares, the result was a typeface named* Romain du Roi *(The King's Roman) that exhibited some features that set it apart from Oldstyle types: a stronger contrast in stroke weights and serifs that were almost straight and quite sharp. At about the same time, the Hungarian type designer Nikolas Kis was cutting types in Holland with similar characteristics.*

Fifty years after the design of the Romain du Roi, *Pierre Simon Fournier introduced types with similar features. And, in 1757, John Baskerville printed his first book in a new type of his own design cut by John Handy that displayed even more contrast between thick and thin strokes, sharp serifs, and curves with vertical stress.*

Towards the end of the 18th century, two other English types, know today as Bell and Bulmer showed further refinements in the style called Transitional (between Oldstyle and Modern).

Characteristic Features:
As noted above, Transitional types have greater stroke contrasts than Oldstyles and their serifs tend to be sharper. The stress of curved strokes is vertical or almost nearly so.

Albertan & *Albertan*

Monotype Baskerville & *Monotype Baskerville*

Bell & *Bell*

Monotype Bulmer & *Monotype Bulmer*

New Caledonia & *New Caledonia*

Ehrhardt & *Ehrhardt*

Electra & *Electra*

Fairfield & *Fairfield*

Fournier & *Fournier*

Janson Text & *Janson Text*

Life & *Life*

Meridien & *Meridien*

Photina & *Photina*

Spectrum & *Spectrum*

ITC Stone Serif & *ITC Stone Serif*

Swift & *Swift*

Times New Roman & *Times New Roman*

Versailles & *Versailles*

Wessex & *Wessex*

Modern

Historical Development: *The Modern style is epitomized by the late 17th- and early 18th-century typeface designs of Giambattista Bodoni in Italy and Firmin Didot in France. Both produced types that were quite different from any that had come before. While these types are now seen as a logical step in the evolution of letterforms in type that began with Oldstyle and became Transitional, in their day they were considered extremely radical departures and were both reviled and admired in equal measure.*

After the types of Bodoni and Didot, the Modern style was employed in the types of the German, Justus Erich Walbaum, and by a number of English and Scottish type founders. Lastly, it became the point of departure for a variety of sometimes unique, but often hideously distorted display types produced throughout the 1800s.

Characteristic Features: *The most prominent characteristic of Modern types is their extreme contrast in stroke weights. In some Moderns the light strokes verge on hairline weight while the heavier elements are thickened to an almost excessive degree. The serifs of Modern types are usually quite thin and completely flat displaying little if any bracketing. The stress of Modern types is almost invariably vertical.*

Basilia & *Basilia*

Bauer Bodoni & *Bauer Bodoni*

ITC Bodoni Twelve & *ITC Bodoni Twelve*

Linotype Centennial & *Linotype Centennial*

Century 725 & *Century 725*

Craw Modern & *Craw Modern*

De Vinne & *De Vinne*

Linotype Didot & *Linotype Didot*

Firmin Didot

ITC Fenice & *ITC Fenice*

Marconi & *Marconi*

Melior & *Melior*

Monotype Modern & *Monotype Modern*

Modern 880 & *Modern 880*

ITC Modern No. 216 & *ITC Modern No. 216*

Monotype Scotch Roman & *Monotype Scotch Roman*

Monotype Walbaum & *Monotype Walbaum*

Slab Serif

Historical Development: *The first Slab Serif designs were produced by the English typefounder Vincent Figgins in the early 19th century. Called* Antiques, *these types were completely monotone in weight including the serifs, which were also unbracketed. These early Slab Serif designs were only available as capitals.*

Later versions of the Slab Serif style – with lowercase and bracketed serifs – were called Egyptians, *and finally, in the mid-19th century, versions with some differentiation in stroke weights called* Clarendons *were introduced.*

In the 20th century, the Slab Serif style has been utilized extensively in designs for typewriter composition as well as for many typefaces created to be used in newspapers.

Characteristic Features: *Like the Modern style, the stress of Slab Serif typefaces is almost always vertical. They exhibit moderate to negligible contrasts in stroke weights, sometimes appearing to be almost completely monotone. Serifs are weighty, sometimes as heavy as the main strokes.*

ITC American Typewriter

PMN Caecilia & *PMN Caecilia*

Candida & *Candida*

ITC Charter & *ITC Charter*

Cheltenham & *Cheltenham*

Berthold City & *Berthold City*

Clarendon

Congress & *Congress*

Egyptienne F & *Egyptienne F*

Egyptian 505

ITC Lubalin Graph & *ITC Lubalin Graph*

Memphis & *Memphis*

ITC Officina Serif & *ITC Officina Serif*

Prestige Elite & *Prestige Elite*

Rockwell & *Rockwell*

Schadow & *Schadow*

Serifa & *Serifa*

Silica

Stymie

Sans Serif

Historical Development: *The first Sans Serif type, a set of monotone capitals without serifs, appeared in a type specimen issued in 1816 by William Caslon IV. The term 'sans surryph' was applied to the style in 1833, ultimately becoming Sans (French for 'without') Serif. Also know as* Grotesques *and* Gothics, *the Sans Serif style was popular throughout the 19th century in England and Germany. It flourished in the early 20th century, becoming widely used throughout the world.*

Notable interpretations of the Sans Serif style are the 'Geometric' Sans Serifs Futura, Kabel and Erbar, the 'Neo-Grotesques' Helvetica and Univers, and the 'Humanistic' Sans Serifs Gill Sans, Optima, and Frutiger.

Characteristic Features: *Clearly, the distinguishing feature of Sans Serifs is their lack of serifs. Stroke contrast tends toward the monotone although moderate contrasts are not uncommon. The italic versions of the Sans Serif types most often appear to be slanted romans or 'obliques' but italic forms can be found in some.*

Berthold Akzidenz Grotesk & *Berthold Akzidenz Grotesk*

ITC Avant Garde Gothic & *ITC Avant Garde Gothic*

Charlotte Sans & *Charlotte Sans*

Congress Sans & *Congress Sans*

Frutiger & *Frutiger*

Futura & *Futura*

Gill Sans & *Gill Sans*

Monotype Grotesque

Bureau Grotesque

Neue Helvetica & *Neue Helvetica*

ITC Highlander & *ITC Highlander*

Berthold Imago & *Berthold Imago*

Maiandra

Ocean Sans MultipleMaster & *Ocean Sans MultipleMaster*

ITC Officina Sans & *ITC Officina Sans*

DV Simplix & *DV Simplix*

ITC Stone Sans & *ITC Stone Sans*

Syntax & *Syntax*

Univers & *Univers*

Script Cursive Brush

Historical Development: *If one considers the chancery cursives used as models for the first italic types as scripts (which is the case in this classification system), then the first Script types were produced in Italy at the end of the 15th century. But the kind of type most often thought of as Script or Cursive was first cut by Robert Granjon (called 'lettre courante' in France and 'secretary hand' in England) in the mid- 16th century.*

This category also includes the Copperplate and Spencerian scripts of the 18th century and any number of other styles, connecting or non-connecting, all of which appear to have been written with some kind of pen or brush.

Characteristic Features: *Formal or informal, upright or cursive, displaying strong contrasts in thick and thin or consistently light or heavy, letters that connect with each other or stand alone. . . all the styles in this category have in common the appearance of being written rather than sculpted or drawn.*

Berthold Script

Byron

Caflisch Script MultipleMaster

Cascade Script

Bitstream Cataneo

Citadel

COMICBOOK
& COMICBOOK

Corsiva

Hurry

ITC Isadora

Katfish

Künstler Script

Laser

Matura

Mistral

Monoline Script

Original Script

Script 12-Pitch

Snell Roundhand

Sloop Script

Tomboy

Ulysses

ITC Zapf Chancery

Historical Development: Setting aside the decorative initial caps used in many early printed books (usually wood engravings, not types), the first decorative typeface was probably Union Pearl, cut in England about 1690.

Decorative letters were made available by many French and English type founders in the 18th century and, in response to the need for advertising types, the 19th century saw a plethora of such styles introduced – a trend which continued unabated into the 20th century to the present.

Graphic Display Decorative

HF American Diner

Arriba-Arriba

Arcadia

Auriol & *Auriol*

A*I Barrel

ITC Beesknees

Boca Raton

Broadway

Cardboard Cutout

CASTELLAR

Eckmann

Empire & *Empire*

ENTROPY

FAITHFUL FLY

fobia

Gill Sans

GRECOADORNADO

TF Guestcheck

HIBISCUS

HipHop

TF Hôtelmoderne

IRONMONGER

Janaki

KRYPTIC

LASER CHROME

Lino Cut

MO' FUNKY FRESH

HF Modular Stencil

Old Dreadful No.7

OSPREY

ITC Ozwald

PAJAMAS

A*I Parma Petit & *A*I Parma Petit*

Publicity Gothic

A*I QuasiModo

Roughedge

TF Roux

Characteristic Features: There is only one feature which all the types in this category share: they are intended for limited use at large sizes rather than for text.

Typefaces included in this category vary widely in style: versions from other categories which have had white or black inline or outline modeling added to them, designs which appear to have been cut from paper and/or stencilled, outlines, shadows, inlines, reverses, etc.

Not included in this category are typefaces from other categories which have been specifically proportioned and weighted for use at large sizes.

SOPHIA
TATTOO
UMBRA
VARIATOR

Zeitgeist

ZOMBIE

Blackletter

Strictly speaking, this category (regardless of what it might be called) should come first in any classification system based on the principle of the historical development of type. But, because of the relatively small number of types in this category, and the fact that they are not widely used, it has been placed here.

This category includes types of the German Fraktura *style,* Uncials, *and any number of others based on manuscript hands pre-dating the invention of printing with movable types.*

Alte Schwabacher

Agincourt

Cloister Black

Duc De Berry

Fette Fraktur

Goudy Text

Goudy Thirty

Libra

Linotext

Monotype Old English Text

Ondine

San Marco

Uncial

Wilhelm Klingspor Gotisch

Wittenberger Fraktur

Polyglot

Polyglot: speaking, writing, written in, or composed of several languages.

Types in this category have specialized, language-specific character sets or are those that use scripts other than the Latin alphabet.

Stempel Garamond East A

ąbçđęfghîjĄBČĐĘFGHÎJK

Neue Helvetica East A

ąbçđęfghîjĄBČĐĘFGHÎJK

Minion Cyrillic

абвгдежзикАБВГДЕЖЗИК

Times New Roman Cyrillic

абвгдежзикАБВГДЕЖЗИК

New Century Schoolbook Monotonic Greek

άβγδέζήθίκΑΒΓΔΕΖΗΘΙΚ

Times New Roman Greek

άβγδέζήθίκΑΒΓΔΕΖΗΘΙΚ

Rashi

Script Hebrew

NewSeoul

ㄱㄴㄷㄹㅁㅂㅅㅇㅈㅊㅋㅌㅍㅎㅏㅑㅓㅕㅗ

Pi, Symbol, Logo, Ornament & Image

This category includes typeface designs which contain specialized character sets for mathematical, phonetic, and other specialized applications and fonts composed of symbols and signs, logotypes, ornaments, images, and other non-alphabetic characters.

While most of these fonts are not, by any means, typefaces, they are included as a category in this classification system in recognition of the important role they play as an adjunct to type in graphic communications.

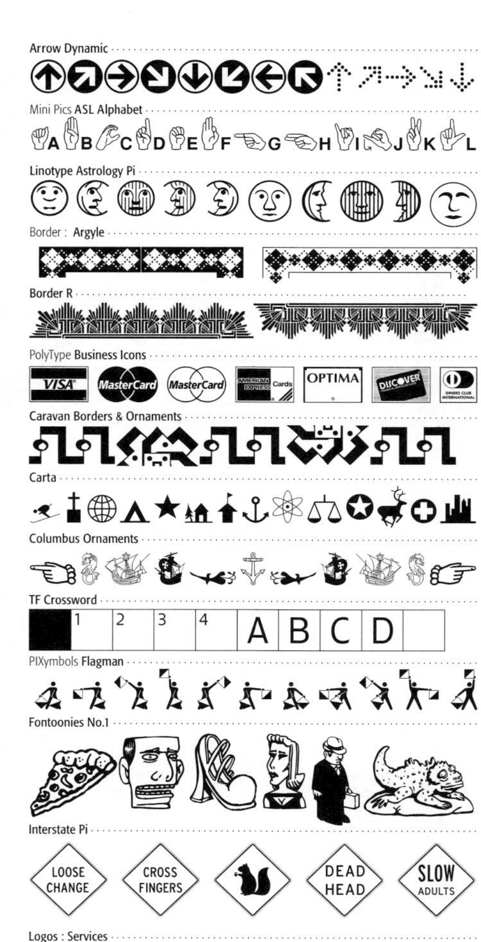
Arrow Dynamic
Mini Pics ASL Alphabet
A B C D E F G H I J K L
Linotype Astrology Pi
Border : Argyle
Border R
PolyType Business Icons
VISA
MasterCard
MasterCard
OPTIMA
DISCOVER
Caravan Borders & Ornaments
Carta
Columbus Ornaments
TF Crossword
1 2 3 4 A B C D
PIXymbols Flagman
Fontoonies No.1
Interstate Pi
LOOSE CHANGE
CROSS FINGERS
DEAD HEAD
SLOW ADULTS
Logos : Services

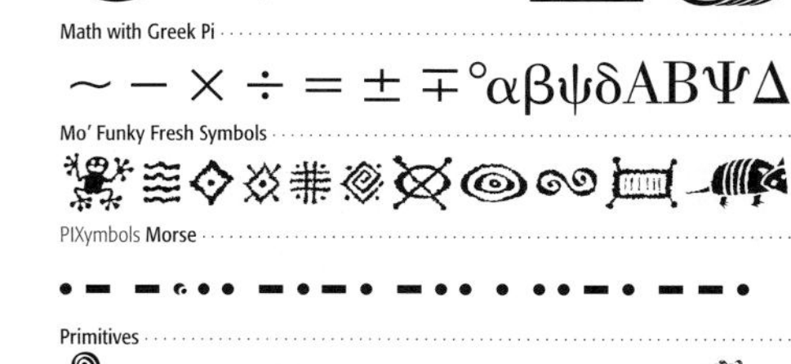
Math with Greek Pi
~ − × ÷ = ± ∓ °αβψδΑΒΨΔ
Mo' Funky Fresh Symbols
PIXymbols Morse

Primitives
NIMX Quirks
Sign Pix
ITC Stone Phonetic IPA Sans
Type Embellishments
ITC Zapf Dingbats

Section One: Font Family Reference

A B C D E F G H I J K L M N O P Q R S T U V W XYZ & Ξ

Aaaaaaaargh Caps
Aachen
Administer
AG Old Face
AG Old Face Shaded
AG Book Stencil
AG Book Rounded
AG Schoolbook
Bureau Agency
Agenda
Agincourt
Albertan
Albertus
Algerian
Alhambra
Allegro
Alternate Gothic
Alte Schwabacher
Alys
Amasis
Amazone
HF American Diner
American Text
ITC American Typewriter
American Uncial
Americana
Bitstream Amerigo
Amigo
Andrich Minerva
ITC Anna
Antikva Margaret
A*I Antique Condensed
Antique Roman
Sackers Antique Roman
Antique Olive
Aquitane
Arabia Felix
Ariadne
Arial
Aristocrat
Armada
Arquitectura
Arriba
Arriba-Arriba
Bitstream Arrus
Arta
FC Artcraft
Artisan Roman
Artiste
Ashley Script
New Aster
Athenaeum
Augustea
Aurelia
Auriol
ITC Avant Garde Gothic
ITC Avant Garde Gothic MM
Avenida
Avenir
Avery Jean
Barbedor
ITC Barcelona
Barmeno
PL Barnum Block
A*I Barrel
Basilia
Basilica
Monotype Baskerville
Fry's Baskerville
ITC New Baskerville
Berthold Baskerville
Berthold Baskerville Book
Basque
Bassuto
ITC Bauhaus
FC Beacon
Becka Script
Beckenham
Beebopp
ITC Beesknees
Bell
Bell Gothic
Bell Centennial
Bellevue
BeLucian
Belwe

Belwe Mono
Bembo
Berlin Sans
Berliner Grotesk
Berling
Bernhard Modern
Bernhard Fashion
Bernhard Bold Condensed
Bernhard Tango
PL Bernhardt
Berthold Script
Bertram
Birch
Bitmax
Blackboard
Blackletter 686
Blackoak
Black Rocks
Black Tents
Blado Italic
Blast-O-Rama
Berthold Block
Blueprint
Bluntz
Boca Raton
Bodega Sans
Bodega Serif
Bodoni
Berthold Bodoni Antiqua
Bauer Bodoni
Bodoni 26
WTC Our Bodoni
Berthold Bodoni Old Face
ITC Bodoni
Boink
Bookman Old Style
Bordeaux
Boton
Boulevard
Brighton
MN Brio
PL Britannia
Broadway
TC Broadway
Bronx
Brophy Script
Bruce Old Style
Brush 445
Brush Script
TF Bryn Mawr
Bubbalove
FC Bulmer
Monotype Bulmer
Burin Roman
Burin Sans
Burlington
Byron
Cabaret
Cafeteria
Calisto
Calvert
Campaign
Cancellaresca Script
Cantoria
Cardboard Cutout
Bitstream Carmina
Carnival
Carolina
Cartier
FC Cartoon
Cascade Script
Caslon 540
Caslon 3
Caslon Open Face
Caslon Oldstyle No.337
Caslon Bold No.537
Caslon Bold No.637
Caslon Antique
ITC Caslon No. 224
ITC Caslon Headline
Adobe Caslon
Big Caslon
Berthold Caslon Book
Castellar
Castle
Bitstream Cataneo
Catastrophe

Catull
Cavalier
Caxton
Centaur
ITC Century
Century 725
Century Gothic
ITC Cerigo
Challenge
Champagne
Champers
A*I Chaotiqua
Charlemagne
Charlotte
Cirkulus
Citadel
Citation
Berthold City
Clairvaux
Clarendon
Classic Roman
Sackers Classic Roman
Claude Sans
ITC Clearface
Clearface Gothic
Cloister Black
Cloister Open Face
Cochin
Colmcille
Colonna
Colossalis
Columbus
Columna Solid
FC Contemporary Brush
FC Cooper Old Style
Cooper Black
Bitstream Cooper
Copperplate Gothic
Corinthian
Corona
Coronet
Corsiva
Cosmos
Cottonwood
Courier
Monotype Courier Twelve
FC Craw Modern
Cremona
Crillee Italic
ITC Cushing
Jaeger Daily News
Dante
De Vinne
Devit
ITC Didi
Linotype Didot
FC Firmin Didot
TF Dierama
Digitek
DIN Schriften
Diotima
FC Disco
Dolmen
Dom Casual
HF Doodle
Dorchester Script
Doric
DV Drukpa
Duc De Berry
Durango
Dynamo
Bureau Eagle
Eaglefeather
Earthquake
East Bloc
Eckmann

Economist
Ecru
Edison
Edwardian
Egizio
Monotype Egyptian 72 Extended
Egyptian 505
A*I Egyptian
Egyptienne F
Ehrhardt
Einhorn
El Grande
ITC Élan
Electra
Elefont
DV Elevator
Elli
Ellington
Elysium
Embassy
Emphasis
Bureau Empire
Engravers' Gothic
Entropy
Epitaph
Epokha
Equinox
ITC Eras
Erasmus
Erbar
Escalido
ITC Esprit
Estro
Etruscan
Eurostile
Excelsior
HF Exposition
eXposure
Fairfield
Faithful Fly
Fajita
Fine Hand
PL Fiorello Condensed
Flaco
Flamme
Flemish Script 2
Flexure
Flicker
ITC Flora
Florens
Florentine Script 2
Floridian Script
Fluidum
Flyer
Fobia
Folio
Follies
Fontoon
Footlight
TF Forever
A*I FranklySpoken
Freakshow
FreeBe Caps
FreeDom
Freehand 521
Freehand 575
Freehand 591
Freestyle Script
A*I French XXX Condensed
French Script
Friz Quadrata
Frutiger
MN Fumo DropShadow
Futura
Futura Black
Futura Stencil
PL Futura Maxi
Gadzooks
Galadriel
MN Galba
Gallia
ITC Galliard
ITC Gamma
Gando

Garage Gothic
Stempel Garamond
Garamond 3
Monotype Garamond
Bureau Garamond
Simoncini Garamond
Berthold Garamond
ITC Garamond
Adobe Garamond
Garbage
Garth Graphic
Geometric 415
Gill Sans
Gill Kayo
Gillies Gothic
ITC Giovanni
Giza
Glypha
Glyphic Series
ITC Golden Type
ITC Gorilla
Sackers Gothic
Gothic Blond
Gothic 13
Goudy
Goudy Handtooled
Goudy Cloister Initials
Monotype Goudy Modern
Monotype Goudy Text & Lombardic Capitals
Goudy 38
Goudy Thirty
ITC Goudy Sans
Graffiti
Granjon
Graphite
Greco
Greyton Script
Monotype Grotesque
Bureau Grotesque
Grove Script
Guardi
TF Guestcheck
TF Habitat
Hadfield
Hadriano
Hamilton
Handle Oldstyle
Handwrite Inkblot
Harting
Harvey
Hazel
HipHop
Hiroshige
Hobo
Hoffmann
Hogarth Script
Holland Seminar
Hollander
Honduras
Horley Old Style
TF Hôtelmoderne
Hurry
Huxley
Huxley Vertical
Ice Age
Ignatius
Berthold Imago
Impact
Imperial
Impressum
Industria
Monotype Ionic
Bitstream Iowan Old Style
Iris
Ironmonger
Ironwood
Isabella
ITC Isadora
ITC Isbell
Isis
Italia
Monotype Italian Old Style
Sackers Italian Script
Jacobean Initials
NIMX Jacoby
ITC Jamille
Janaki
Janson Text
Monotype Janson
Jasper
Javelin
Jazz
Jenson Old Style
Joanna
John Handy
Jonas
Jubilee
Judy Finckel
A*I Juliana

Juniper
Kaatskill
Kabel
ITC Kabel
Katfish
Kaufmann
Kennerley
KidTYPE
Kiilani
Kindergarten
Kino
Klang
Klee
Kniff
A*I Koch Antiqua
FC Koloss
ITC Korinna
Kristen
Kryptic
Kufi Script
Künstler Script
La Bamba
Lambada
Langer
Laser
Laser Chrome
Latienne
Latin Condensed
Latin Wide
MN Latina
HF LaVardera
FC LeAsterix
ITC Leawood
ITC Legacy Serif
ITC Legacy Sans
Le Griffe
Lemonade
Letter Gothic
Liberty
Libra
HF Libris
Life
Lightnin'
Limehouse Script
Lindsay
Lino Cut
LinoLetter
Linoscript
Linotext
Litera
Lithos
Little Louis
Locarno
Berthold Lo-Type
ITC Lubalin Graph
Lucia
Bitstream Lucian
Lucida
Lucida Sans
Lucida Sans Typewriter
Lydian
ITC Machine
Madame
Madrone
Mahogany Script
Maiandra
MalakaLaka-LakaLakaLaka
Malibu
TF Maltby Antique
ITC/LSC Manhattan
Manito
Mantinia
FC Marcato
Marconi
Marguerita
Marigold
Mastercard
Mata
Matt Antique
Matura
ITC Mendoza
Meridien
Mesopotamia
Mesquite
Metro
Mezz MultipleMaster
Midway
Mill Harrow
Minion
Minion MultipleMaster
Minister
Mirarae
Missive
Mister Earl
Mistral
ITC Mixage
Monotype Modern
Modern 880
PL Modern Heavy Condensed
ITC Modern No. 216
HF Modular Stencil
Mo' Funky Fresh
ITC Mona Lisa
Monoline Script
Montauk

ITC Motter Corpus
Munich
Murray Hill
Myriad MultipleMaster
Agfa Nadianne
Narrowband Prime
National Oldstyle
Neo Bold
Neographik
Neon
A*I Neptune Serif
A*I Neuland
Neuzeit S
Nevison Casual Script
New Berolina
New Geneva Nine
News Gothic
ITC Newtext
Nimrod
Nofret
Notre Dame
Nouveau Riche
ITC Novarese
Numskill
Nuptial Script
Nutcracker
Oberon
Ocean Sans MultipleMaster
OCR-A
OCR-B
Octavian
Odessa
ITC Officina
Old Claude
Old Dreadful No.7
Old English
Monotype Old English Text
Old Fashion Script
Monotype Old Style
Old Style No.7
Olympian
Omnia
Ondine
Onyx
Optima
Bitstream Oranda
Orator
Oreana
Original Script
Osprey
Outhaus
Oxford
A*I Oz Brush
Bitstream Oz Handicraft
A*I Oz Poster
ITC Ozwald
ITC Pacella
Pacifica Condensed
A*I Painter
Paisley
Pajamas
Palace Script
Palatino
ITC Panache
Papyrus
Paris Flash
Parisian
Park Avenue
Parkinson
A*I ParmaPetit
A*I Pacrsons
Party
Peignot
Pelican
Pendry Script
Pepita
Pepperwood
Perky
Perpetua
Perrywood
Photina
Piranesi Italic
Placard
Plak
Plantin
Playbill
Plaza
Pleasure
Pneuma
Pointille
Poliphilus Roman
FC Polonaise
Pompeijana
Ponderosa
Poplar
Poppl-Laudatio
Poppl-Pontifex
Poppl-Residenz
Portobello
Poseidon
Post-Antiqua
Post-Mediäval
HF Poster
Poster Black
Prague
Praxis
Premier
Present Script
Prestige Elite
Pristina
Pritchard
A*I Prospera II
P.T. Barnum

Publicity Gothic
Quadrus
A*I Quanta
Quartz
A*I QuasiModo
ITC Quay Sans
Quill Script
Quixley
ITC Quorum
Rage Italic
Ragtime
TF Raincheck
Raleigh
Raleigh Gothic
Ramiz
Raphael
Rapier
Rebeca
Recess
Refracta
Regatta Condensed
Reiner Script
Relief
Renault
Reporter No. 2
Retro
Revue
Ribbit
Riot
Ritmo
Riviera Script
Rivoli Initials
NIMX Robust
Robotik
Rockwell
Roman
Sackers Roman
Romeo
Romic
Rosewood
Rotation
Agfa Rotis
Roughedge
Roundy
TF Roux
Roxy
Ru'ach
Rubaya Inline
Rubber Stamp
Ruling Script
Rumble
Rundfunk
Monotype Runic Condensed
A*I Russell Oblique
Russell Square
Rusticana
Ruzicka Freehand
Sabon
Saginaw
Sam Sans
San Marco
Santa Fe
Sanvito MultipleMaster
Sassoon Primary
Savoye
Scamp
Schadow
Stempel Schneidler
Scorpio
Monotype Scotch Roman
Scotty
Scratch
Scrawl
Scriba
Script 12-Pitch
Scriptek
Seagull
HF Secede
ITC Serif Gothic
Serifa
Serlio
Shaman
Shannon
Shatter
Shelley
Sho
Showcard Gothic
Sierra
Signature
Silica
DV Simplix
Sinaloa
Sinclair Script
Skid Row
NIMX Skinny
Skreetch Caps
Skyline
ITC Slimbach
Slipstream
Slogan
Sloop Script
Smaragd
Smudger
Snell Roundhand
Sophia
ITC Souvenir
Spartan Classified
Spectrum
Spike
Spotlight
Spring
Spumoni
Sputnik
Sackers Square Gothic

MN Squash
Squire
Staccato 555
Stencil
Stentor
Stereo
ITC Stone
Stone Print
Stop
Story
Strobos
Sturbridge Twisted
Stuyvesant
Stymie
MN Sully Jonquieres
Swift
ITC Symbol
Synchro
ITC Syndor
Syntax
A*I Szene
Tag
Tangient
Tannhäuser
Tattoo
Teknik
NIMX Tekno
Tekton
Tekton Multiple Master
Tempo
ITC Tiepolo
ITC Tiffany
Tiger Rag
FC Timbre
Times New Roman
Times
Times Europa
Tiranti
Tomboy
Tommy's Type
PL Torino Open
A*I Toskana
Trade Gothic
Trajan
CG Triumvirate
PL Trophy Oblique
Truesdell
Trump Mediäval
A*I Tuscan Egyptian
Twang
Twist
Typewriter
Typewriter Elite
Typewriter Gothic
Typo Upright
Ulysses
Umbra
Uncial
Univers
University Roman
DV Upright
ITC Usherwood
Utopia
VAG Rounded
Van Dijck
Van Dijk
Varga
Variator
Vario
Vectora
ITC Veljovic
Vendome
A*I Venezia
Vermont
Versailles
Victoria Titling Condensed
Vienna Extended
Goudy Village No. 2
Village
Visage
Visigoth
Viva MultipleMaster
Vivaldi
Vladimir Script
Wade Sans
Wakefield
Monotype Walbaum
Berthold Walbaum Book
Wanted
Waterloo Bold
Wave
Wedding Text
ITC Weidemann
Weiss
A*I Weissenau
Wendy
Werkman
Wessex
Westwood
Wiesbaden Swing
Agfa Wile Roman
Wilhelm Klingspor Gotisch
Wilke
Willow
Windsor
Wittenberger Fraktur
Xylo
Yan Series 333
Young Baroque
MN Zambesi
ITC Zapf Book
ITC Zapf International
ITC Zapf Chancery
Zebrawood
Zeitgeist
Zinjaro

Zombie
PIXymbols ADA Symbols
PolyType Allure
PIXymbols AlphaBox
PIXymbols AlphaCircle
PIXymbols Ameslan
A*I Ampersands
Animals
PolyType Animals
PIXymbols Apothecary
Arabesque Borders & Ornaments
Arrow Dynamic
PolyType ArrowTek
PolyType Art Deco
Mini Pics Art Jam
Artifact
Mini Pics ASL Alphabet
Astrology
Linotype Astrology Pi
PIXymbols Astrology
Attitudes
Linotype Audio Pi
Auriol Flowers
PIXymbols Backstitch
PrintBar Code 39
PrintBar UPC EAN ISBN
PrintBar Interleaved 2 of 5
PrintBar PostNET & FIM
A*I BeforeTheAlphabet-1
Berlin Sans Bold Dingbats
PolyType Birds
Blackfoot
Border Pi
General Glyphics Border Fonts
Key Borders Border Fonts
Borders & Ornaments
PIXymbols Boxkey
PIXymbols BoxnLines
PIXymbols Braille Grade 2
TF Bridgette
BulletsNStuff
Bundebahn Pi
Business & Services
PolyType Business Icons
Calligraphic Ornaments
Caravan Borders & Ornaments
Carta
Adobe Caslon Ornaments
Celebrations
Chemistra Pi
Cheq
PIXymbols Chess
Monotype Christmas Ornaments
City Ornaments
Mini Pics Classic
Colmcille Ornaments
Columbus Ornaments
PIXymbols Command Key
Commercial
Commercial Pi
Commercials
Communications
Monotype Contemporary Ornaments
PolyType Corners
Credit Cards
TF Crossword
PIXymbols Crossword
Deco Numbers
Linotype Decoration Pi
Delectables
Linotype Didot Ornaments
PIXymbols Digits & Clocks
PIXymbols Dingbats
DingBRATS
Dingura
Mini Pics Directional
Diversions
PIXymbols DOSscreen
A*I EclecticOne
Ecology
Linotype EEC Pi
European Pi
PIXymbols FabriCare
PIXymbols FARmarks
PIXymbols Flagman
Fleurons : Folio One
Fleurons : Granjon Folio
A*I Flighty
Fontoonies No.1
Fournier Ornaments
Linotype Fraction Pi
PolyType Fruits
Linotype Game Pi
Games & Sports
General Symbols
PIXymbols GridMaker
A*I HeadToHead
PIXymbols Highway Signs
Linotype Holiday Pi
Holidays
PolyType Holidays
PIXymbols Hospital & Safety
Stempel Hot Metal Borders
Incidentals
Industrials
Industry & Engineering
Mini Pics International
International Symbols
Interstate Pi
Journeys
Kurusu
PIXymbols LCD
Leaves One
Legal Trademarks
PolyType Leisure

Mini Pics Lil' Critters
Mini Pics Lil' Faces
Logos : Company
Logos : Services
Lucida Math
PIXymbols Luna
Math with Greek Pi
Math & Technical
Mathematical Pi
Medical & Pharmaceutical
PIXymbols Meeting
PIXymbols MenuFonts
MICR
Military & Patriotic
Minion Ornaments
Minion MultipleMaster Ornaments
Mo' Funky Fresh Symbols
Moderns
PIXymbols Morse
PIXymbols Musica
Musical
Naturals
Newspaper Pi
Notre Dame Ornaments
Nucleus One
Numerics
PolyType Optyx
Organics
PolyType Ornaments

Linotype Textile Pi
Thingbat
Thornforms
Times Phonetic
PIXymbols Tolerances
Town Ornaments
Transportation
PIXymbols Travel & Hotel
Truesdell Sorts
PIXymbols TV Listings
Type Embellishments
PIXymbols Unikey
Universal Greek with Math Pi
Universal Math 1
Universal News with Commercial Pi
PIXymbols US Map
Utopia Ornaments
PolyType Vegetables
Village Ornaments
Vine Leaves
Linotype Warning Pi
Water Garden
Wildlifes
Adobe Wood Type Ornaments 1
Adobe Wood Type Ornaments 2
PIXymbols Xcharting
Linotype X-Mas Pi
PIXymbols Xstitch

Cyrillic II : Monospaced
Excelsior Cyrillic
Fat Man Cyrillic
Garamond No.4 Cyrillic
Helvetica Cyrillic
Magna Cyrillic
Maxima Cyrillic
Minion Cyrillic
Mystic Cyrillic
Northern Cyrillic
Osho Cyrillic Script
Oval Cyrillic
Rome Cyrillic
Socrates Cyrillic Heavy
St. Petersburg Cyrillic
Times New Roman Cyrillic
Times Ten Cyrillic
TransCyrillic : Serif
TransCyrillic : Sans Serif
Arial Greek
Baskerville Monotonic Greek
Baskerville Polytonic Greek
New Century Schoolbook Monotonic Greek
New Century Schoolbook Polytonic Greek
Courier Greek
Graeca
Greek Sans
Helvetica Monotonic Greek

✍ David Lance Goines, 1982

PIXymbols Passkey
PIXymbols Patchwork
PolyType Patterns
Petroglyph Hawaii
Phonetics
Poetica Ornaments
Pompeijana Borders
Primitives
NIMX Quirks
Radicals
PIXymbols Recycle
Religious
Rococo Borders & Ornaments
TF Roux Borders
Rusticana Borders
Scorpio Dingbats
Scorpio Tribal
SignPix
Sonata
Monotype Sorts
Special Alphabets
PIXymbols Squared
TF Squiggle
ITC Stone Phonetic
PIXymbols Stylekey
Symbol Monospace
Symbol Proportional
Linotype Technical Pi
Television

ITC Zapf Dingbats
Zenzuous Pi
Antique Olive EastA
Arial Efo
Arial Narrow Efo
ITC Avant Garde Gothic PS Efo
ITC Bookman PS Efo
Century Schoolbook PS Efo
Courier PS Efo
Excelsior EastA
Stempel Garamond EastA
Neue Helvetica EastA
Optima EastA
Times New Roman PS Efo
Times Ten EastA
TransRoman : Chan
TransRoman : Gara
TransRoman : Pala
TransRoman : Serif
TransRoman : Sans Serif
Z-Antiqua Efo
ITC Zapf Chancery PS Efo
Arial Cyrillic
Baskerville Cyrillic
Book Cyrillic
Brush Cyrillic
Courier Cyrillic
Cyrillic II : Serif
Cyrillic II : Sans Serif

Helvetica Polytonic Greek
ITC Souvenir Monotonic Greek
ITC Souvenir Polytonic Greek
Symbol Greek
Times New Roman Greek
Times Ten Monotonic Greek
Times Ten Polytonic Greek
Uncial LS
Acheneli
Arad Level VI
Aztor
Bethel
Broadweli
Busoreli
Careli
Coopereli
David
Frank
Frizeli
Galed
Gilgal Ultra
Hadas
Hebraica
Hebras
Hobeli
Ivricana
Kabelim
Lublineli
Mehandes

Meiri
Nekoshet
Optimeli
Optwo
Peigneli
Rashi
Revieli
ScriptHebrew
Sofer
Uncieli
Vilna
Yavaneli
HiGwangJu
HiInchon
NewHiPusan
NewJeju
NewSeoul

(A) AGFA ROTIS SERIF & SEMISERIF

(B) AGP ADO AGA LIN MAE abcdefghijklmnopqrstuvwxyz(".;'!*?':,")
$1234567890&fifl ß-äöüåçèîñóæøœ
(C) ABCDEFGHIJKLMNOPQRSTUVWXYZ
ÄÖÜÅÇÈÎÑÓÆØŒ»„«[¶§•†‡]‹¡·¿›…

(D) Agfa Rotis Serif & Semiserif …

• Serif, 55-Roman abcdefghijklmnopqrstuvwxyzABCDEFGHIJKLMNOPQRSTUVWXYZ–$1234567890(".;

(E) Serif, 56-Italic *abcdefghijklmnopqrstu (F) vwxyzABCDEFGHIJKLMNOPQRSTUVWXYZ–$1234567890(".*

Serif, 65-Bold **abcdefghijklmnopqrstuvwxyzABCDEFGHIJKLMNOPQRSTUVWXYZ–$1234567890**

Semiserif, 55-Regular abcdefghijklmnopqrstuvwxyzABCDEFGHIJKLMNOPQRSTUVWXYZ–$1234567890(".;'!*?'

Semiserif, 65-Bold **abcdefghijklmnopqrstuvwxyzABCDEFGHIJKLMNOPQRSTUVWXYZ–$1234567890(".**

(G) Roughedge

(H) Robert J. Howell • 1994 abcdefghijklmnopqrstuvwxyz(.;!*?:,)$1234567890
RJH ▲16 ¢-ABCDEFGHIJKLMNOPQRSTUVWXYZ[]

ROUNDY
(I) Linotype DisplaySet 4
LIN abcdefghijklmnopqrstuvwxyz(".;'!*?':,")
$1234567890&fifl ß-äöüåçèîñóæøœ
ABCDEFGHIJKLMNOPQRSTUVWXYZ
ÄÖÜÅÇÈÎÑÓÆØŒ»„«[¶§•†‡]‹¡·¿›…

Roundy …

• Regular abcdefghijklmnopqrstuvwxyzABCDEFGHIJKLMNOPQRSTUVWXYZ–$12

Swash Capitals ABCDEFGHIJKLMNOPQRSTUVWXYZÆŒ

TF ROUX
Joseph Treacy • 1973 **abcdefghijklmnopqrstuvwxyz(".;'!*?':,")**
TRE MTD
(J) ▲22 **$1234567890&fifl ß-äöüåçèîñóæøœ**
ABCDEFGHIJKLMNOPQRSTUVWXYZ
ÄÖÜÅÇÈÎÑÓÆØŒ»„«[¶§•†‡]‹¡·¿›… ▷ 123579/23 (K)

TF Roux …

Shaded abcdefghijklmnopqrstuvwxyzABCDEFG

• Extra Bold **abcdefghijklmnopqrstuvwxyzABCDEFGHIJ**

(L) *Linotype DisplaySet 4:* Madame Letters, Numericals & Accents, Roundy Regular & Swash Capitals.
TF Roux ▶ TF Roux Borders

R

A B C D E F G H I J K L M N O P Q R S T U V W XYZ & Ξ

Key to Section One

Font Displays & Information

Ⓐ Font.Family Name
The principal identifier for a group of fonts related to each other by an overall, unifying design theme. A font family may include multiple variations such as condensed, extended, outline, small capitals, etc. or it may be so simple as to consist of only a basic roman and italic. Large families are often sub-divided into several packages (see Ⓓ below).

Ⓑ Font Foundry Codes
A listing of the font foundries that offer the fonts shown. The first code, in **bold type**, indicates the source foundry for the fonts displayed. Font package contents and configurations may differ from one foundry to another. To examine each foundry's particular offering, see Section Two.

Ⓒ Primary Font Display
A representative character set display. For font families this is usually the normal weight and width font of the family (roman or regular). This display is repeated in large font families to show variants such as condensed, extended, expert sets, etc. The standard size is 14-point; fonts intended for display or other uses are shown at larger or smaller sizes (see Ⓙ below). The Primary Font Display is also used to show individual font designs (see Ⓖ and Ⓘ below).

Ⓓ Font.Family Package Name
Identifier for a group of fonts as they are configured for sale. Usually the same as, or, an extension of the Font.Family Name. Package contents may differ from one foundry to another.

Ⓔ Font Names
Names for each font in the family identifying the style/weight/width, etc. The name of the font used for the Primary Font Display is indicated with a bullet (•).

Ⓕ Font.Family Package Display
A one-line showing for each font in a package. Display fonts are sometimes shown on two lines.

Ⓖ Individual Font Name
Identifier for a font that is only available in the version shown and/or is only sold separately.

Ⓗ Design Information
Name of the font designer(s) and date of original design or first release. Additional information regarding historical precedents, previous versions, etc. is provided as appropriate and available.

Ⓘ Multi-Font Package Name
Identifier for a font package that contains two or more individual fonts of different design and/or style. Each font in a Multi-Font Package is shown in it's appropriate alphabetical sub-section. Complete contents of Multi-FontPackages are detailed at the bottom of the page. (see Ⓛ below).

Ⓙ Point-Size Information
Size of the font display if other than 14-point.

Ⓚ Alternate Characters
Display of characters not usually included in a standard character set.

Ⓛ Notes
Information on Multi-Font Packages, Additional Fonts and associated fonts of the same design that are shown elsewhere.

Ⓜ Page Contents
Names of the first and last font families and/or individual fonts shown on the page.

Symbols, Definitions, Abbreviations

✍ **Design Information**
Name of the font designer(s) and date of original design or first release. Additional information regarding historical precedents, previous versions, etc. is provided as appropriate and available.

❖ **Multi-Font Package**
A font package that contains two or more individual fonts of different design and/or style. Complete contents of Multi-Font Packages are detailed in the notes at the bottom of each page.

▲ **Point-Size Information**
Size of the font display if other than 14-point.

Additional Fonts. . . Fonts shown in the Pi, Symbol, Logo, Ornament & Image Font sub-section that are part of the Font.Family Packages displayed in sub-sections A–xYz. Additional Fonts are indicated by one of the following symbols:
- π Additional Pi Font
- Σ Additional Symbol Font
- λ Additional Logo Font
- ❦ Additional Ornament/Border Font
- i Additional Image Font

▶ **Additional Font Names**
Listed in the notes at the bottom of the page. . . indicates the name of one or more fonts shown in the Pi, Symbol, Logo, Ornament & Image Font sub-section that are part of a Font.Family Package.

▷ **Alternate Characters/Alternate Font**
Indicates characters not usually included in a standard character set or a separate font with alternate characters.*

☞ Font display is continued on the facing page.

☞ Font display is continued on the following page.

☜ Font display is continued from the preceding page.

Ξ **World-wide Language Font**
Identifies fonts with specialized character sets and/or fonts using scripts other than the Latin alphabet.

👁 **Associated Font**
Indicates that fonts of the same design for different applications are shown elsewhere; the font names are detailed. Associated Fonts are packaged separately.

⊕ **Source Package Information**
Used only in the Pi, Symbold, Logo, Ornament & Image Font sub-section; indicates that a font is part of a package shown elsewhere in Section One.

◀ **Source Package Name**
Used only in the Pi, Symbol, Logo, Ornament & Image Font sub-section; indicates the name of the package a font is contained in.

MM
MultipleMaster fonts.

SC
Small Capitals character set.

OSF
Oldstyle Figures character set.*

SCOSF
Small Capitals and Oldstyle Figures character set.*

SC&OSF
Small Capitals & Oldstyle Figures character set.

SCLF
Small Capitals and Lining Figures character set.

SCSLF
Small Capitals and Small Lining Figures character set.

SD
Short Descenders.

SA/D
Short Ascenders and Descenders.

Dfr
Dfr (DeutschFraktur) character set.*

*see page xv for examples

Font Foundry Codes

Adobe Systems	ADO
Agfa	AGP AGA AGL
Alphabets Inc	ALP
Andersen Agency	AND
Bear Rock Technologies	BEA
Bitstream	BIT
Carter & Cone Type	CAR
Diehl.Volk	DVT
Elsner+Flake	LEF
EmDash	EMD
Famous Fonts	FAM
The Font Bureau	FBU
The Font Company	TFC
Franklin Type Founders	FRA
Galápagos Design Group	GAL
Handcrafted Fonts	HAN
Harris Design	HAR
Headliners International	HEA
Image Club	IMA
Intecsas	INT
International Typeface Corporation	ITC
Isis Imaging	ISI
Key Borders	KEY
Lanston Type Company	LAN
Letraset	LET
Letter Perfect	LPT
Linguist's Software	LSI
Linotype-Hell	LIN
Monotype Typography	MCL MAE MTD
New York Design Studio	NYD
NIMX Graphics	NIM
Page Studio	PAG
PolyType	POL
Red Rooster Typefounders	RED
RJH Productions	RJH
Russian Type Foundry	RUS
Christian Schwartz Design	CHR
Stone Type Foundry	STO
Torah	TOR
Treacyfaces	TRE
[T-26]	T26
URW	URW
Vanguard Media	VAN
Jack Yan & Associates	JAC

✍ Anonymous, c. 1450

A

Aaaaaaaargh Caps

INT

▲36

ABCDEFGHIJKLMNOPQRSTUVWXYZ
(".;'!?':,")$1234567890&-ÆŒ

Aachen Bold
Adobe DisplaySet 1
Colin Brignall • 1969

ADO AGA BIT LET LIN MAE URW

▲24

abcdefghijklmnopqrstuvwxyz(".;'!*?':,")
$1234567890&ﬁﬂß-äöüåçèîñóæøœ
ABCDEFGHIJKLMNOPQRSTUVWXYZ
ÄÖÜÅÇÈÎÑÓÆØŒ»,,«[•]‹¡•¿›...

Aarcover

INT

▲36

ABCDEFGHIJKLMNOPQRSTUVWXYZ
(.:!*?:,)$1234567890-
ÄÖÜÅÇÈÎÑÓÆØŒ

AARDVARK

John Benson & Jill Pichotta • 1991

FBU AGP MTD

▲36

ABCDEFGHIJKLMNOPQRSTUVWXYZ(".;'!*?':,")
$1234567890&-ÄÖÜÅÇÈÎÑÓÆØŒ
»,,«[¶|§•†‡]‹¡•¿›...

Aardvark ...

• Regular

ABCDEFGHIJKLMNOPQRSTUVWXYZ–$1234567

Bold

ABCDEFGHIJKLMNOPQRSTUVWXYZ–$1

Adobe DisplaySet 1: Aachen Bold, Freestyle Script, Revue, University Roman.

ABADI

Ong Chong Wah • 1987 abcdefghijklmnopqrstuvwxyz(".;'!*?':,")

MCL $1234567890&fiflß-äöüåçèîñóæøœ

ABCDEFGHIJKLMNOPQRSTUVWXYZ

ÄÖÜÅÇÈÎÑÓÆØŒ»„«[¶§•†‡]‹¡·¿›...

Abadi 1 ...

Extra Light abcdefghijklmnopqrstuvwxyzABCDEFGHIJKLMNOPQRSTUVWXYZ–$1234567890(".;'!*?':,"

Extra Light Italic *abcdefghijklmnopqrstuvwxyzABCDEFGHIJKLMNOPQRSTUVWXYZ–$1234567890(".;'!*?':,*

• Regular abcdefghijklmnopqrstuvwxyzABCDEFGHIJKLMNOPQRSTUVWXYZ–$1234567890(".

Italic *abcdefghijklmnopqrstuvwxyzABCDEFGHIJKLMNOPQRSTUVWXYZ–$1234567890(".;*

Bold **abcdefghijklmnopqrstuvwxyzABCDEFGHIJKLMNOPQRSTUVWXYZ–$123456789**

Bold Italic ***abcdefghijklmnopqrstuvwxyzABCDEFGHIJKLMNOPQRSTUVWXYZ–$123456789***

Abadi 2 ...

Light abcdefghijklmnopqrstuvwxyzABCDEFGHIJKLMNOPQRSTUVWXYZ–$1234567890(".;'!

Light Italic *abcdefghijklmnopqrstuvwxyzABCDEFGHIJKLMNOPQRSTUVWXYZ–$1234567890(".;'!*?*

Extra Bold **abcdefghijklmnopqrstuvwxyzABCDEFGHIJKLMNOPQRSTUVWXYZ–$1234567**

Extra Bold Italic ***abcdefghijklmnopqrstuvwxyzABCDEFGHIJKLMNOPQRSTUVWXYZ–$1234567***

ABADI 3

MCL abcdefghijklmnopqrstuvwxyz(".;'!*?':,")

▲16 $1234567890&fiflß-äöüåçèîñóæøœ

ABCDEFGHIJKLMNOPQRSTUVWXYZ

ÄÖÜÅÇÈÎÑÓÆØŒ»„«[¶§•†‡]‹¡·¿›...

Abadi 3 ...

Light Condensed abcdefghijklmnopqrstuvwxyzABCDEFGHIJKLMNOPQRSTUVWXYZ–$1234567890(".;'!*?':,")&fi

• Condensed abcdefghijklmnopqrstuvwxyzABCDEFGHIJKLMNOPQRSTUVWXYZ–$1234567890(".;'!*?':

Bold Condensed **abcdefghijklmnopqrstuvwxyzABCDEFGHIJKLMNOPQRSTUVWXYZ–$1234567890(".;'!**

Extra Bold Condensed **abcdefghijklmnopqrstuvwxyzABCDEFGHIJKLMNOPQRSTUVWXYZ–$1234567890("**

FC ABBEY

TFC abcdefghijklmnopqrstuvwxyz(".;'!*?':,")

▲18 $1234567890&fiflß-äöüåçèîñóæøœ

ABCDEFGHIJKLMNOPQRSTUVWXYZ

ÄÖÜÅÇÈÎÑÓÆØŒ»„«[¶§•†‡]‹¡·¿›...

FC Abbey ...

• Regular abcdefghijklmnopqrstuvwxyzABCDEFGHIJKLMNOPQRSTUVWXYZ–$123456

Medium abcdefghijklmnopqrstuvwxyzABCDEFGHIJKLMNOPQRSTUVWXYZ–$12345

Bold **abcdefghijklmnopqrstuvwxyzABCDEFGHIJKLMNOPQRSTUVWXYZ–$1234**

A

FC Accent

TFC ▲18

abcdefghijklmnopqrstuvwxyz(".;'!*?':,")
$1234567890&fiflß-äöüåçèîñóæøœ
ABCDEFGHIJKLMNOPQRSTUVWXYZ
ÄÖÜÅÇÈÎÑÓÆØŒ»„«[•]‹¡·¿›...

Ad Lib

Freeman Craw • 1961

BIT ▲24

abcdefghijklmnopqrstuvwxyz(".;'!*?':,")
$1234567890&fiflß-äöüåçèîñóæøœ
ABCDEFGHIJKLMNOPQRSTUVWXYZ
ÄÖÜÅÇÈÎÑÓÆØŒ»„«[§•†‡]‹¡·¿›...

TF Adepta A Extra Bold

TF DisplaySet 2

Joseph Treacy • 1992

TRE MTD ▲24

abcdefghijklmnopqrstuvwxyz(".;'!*?':,")
$1234567890&fiflß-äöüåçèîñóæøœ
ABCDEFGHIJKLMNOPQRSTUVWXYZ ÄÖÜ
ÅÇÈÎÓÆØŒ»„«[§•†‡]‹¡·¿›... ▷123579/234816■□

ADMINISTER

Leslie Usherwood • 1980

AGP RED

abcdefghijklmnopqrstuvwxyz(".;'!*?':,")
$1234567890&fiflß-äöüåçèîñóæøœ
ABCDEFGHIJKLMNOPQRSTUVWXYZ
ÄÖÜÅÇÈÎÑÓÆØŒ»„«[¶§•†‡]‹¡·¿›...

Administer ...

Light abcdefghijklmnopqrstuvwxyzABCDEFGHIJKLMNOPQRSTUVWXYZ-$12345678

Light Italic *abcdefghijklmnopqrstuvwxyzABCDEFGHIJKLMNOPQRSTUVWXYZ-$1234567890(".*

• Book abcdefghijklmnopqrstuvwxyzABCDEFGHIJKLMNOPQRSTUVWXYZ-$123456

Book Italic *abcdefghijklmnopqrstuvwxyzABCDEFGHIJKLMNOPQRSTUVWXYZ-$1234567890(*

Bold **abcdefghijklmnopqrstuvwxyzABCDEFGHIJKLMNOPQRSTUVWXYZ-$1**

TF DisplaySet 2: TF Adepta A Extra Bold & TF Guestcheck Heavy.

AG OLD FACE

Günter Gerhard Lange • 1980
Berthold AG. . . 1900
ADO AGA MAE

abcdefghijklmnopqrstuvwxyz(“.;‘!*?’:,”)
$1234567890&fiflß-äöüåçèîñóæøœ
ABCDEFGHIJKLMNOPQRSTUVWXYZ
ÄÖÜÅÇÈÎÑÓÆØŒ»„«[¶§•†‡]‹¡·¿›...

AG Old Face . . .

• Regular abcdefghijklmnopqrstuvwxyzABCDEFGHIJKLMNOPQRSTUVWXYZ–$12345678

Medium abcdefghijklmnopqrstuvwxyzABCDEFGHIJKLMNOPQRSTUVWXYZ–$1234567

Bold abcdefghijklmnopqrstuvwxyzABCDEFGHIJKLMNOPQRSTUVWXYZ–$1234

Shaded ▲16 abcdefghijklmnopqrstuvwxyzABCDEFGHIJKLMNOPQRSTUVWXYZ–

Outline ▲16 abcdefghijklmnopqrstuvwxyzABCDEFGHIJKLMNOPQRSTUVWXYZ–$12

Bold Outline ▲16 abcdefghijklmnopqrstuvwxyzABCDEFGHIJKLMNOPQRSTUVWXY

AG Old Face Shaded
Berthold DisplaySet 1
Günter Gerhard Lange • 1984
ADO AGA MAE
▲24

abcdefghijklmnopqrstuvwxyz(“.;‘!*?’:,”)
$1234567890&fiflß-äöüåçèîñóæøœ
ABCDEFGHIJKLMNOPQRSTUVWXYZ
ÄÖÜÅÇÈÎÑÓÆØŒ»„«[•]‹¡·¿›...

AG Book Stencil
Berthold DisplaySet 1
Günter Gerhard Lange • 1985
ADO AGA MAE
▲24

abcdefghijklmnopqrstuvwxyz(“.;‘!*?’:,”)
$1234567890&fiflß-äöüåçèîñóæøœ
ABCDEFGHIJKLMNOPQRSTUVWXYZ
ÄÖÜÅÇÈÎÑÓÆØŒ»„«[•]‹¡·¿›...

AG BOOK ROUNDED

Günter Gerhard Lange • 1980
ADO AGA MAE
▲16

abcdefghijklmnopqrstuvwxyz(“.;‘!*?’:,”)
$1234567890&fiflß-äöüåçèîñóæøœ
ABCDEFGHIJKLMNOPQRSTUVWXYZ
ÄÖÜÅÇÈÎÑÓÆØŒ»„«[•]‹¡·¿›...

AG Book Rounded . . .

• Regular abcdefghijklmnopqrstuvwxyzABCDEFGHIJKLMNOPQRSTUVWXYZ–$1

Berthold DisplaySet 1: AG Book Stencil, AG Old Face Shaded, Barmeno Extra Bold, Cosmos Extra Bold, Formata Outline.

A

... AG Book Rounded

Medium abcdefghijklmnopqrstuvwxyzABCDEFGHIJKLMNOPQRSTUVWXYZ–$1

Bold abcdefghijklmnopqrstuvwxyzABCDEFGHIJKLMNOPQRSTUVWXYZ

Bold Condensed abcdefghijklmnopqrstuvwxyzABCDEFGHIJKLMNOPQRSTUVWXYZ–$1234567890(

Medium Outline abcdefghijklmnopqrstuvwxyzABCDEFGHIJKLMNOPQRSTUVWXYZ–$

Bold Outline abcdefghijklmnopqrstuvwxyzABCDEFGHIJKLMNOPQRSTUVWXYZ

Bold Condensed Outline abcdefghijklmnopqrstuvwxyzABCDEFGHIJKLMNOPQRSTUVWXYZ–$1234567890(

AG SCHOOLBOOK

ADO AGA MAE abcdefghijklmnopqrstuvwxyz(".;'!*?':;")
$1234567890&fiflß-äöüåçèîñóæøœ
ABCDEFGHJJKLMNOPQRSTUVWXYZ
ÄÖÜÅÇÈĴÑÓÆØŒ»„«[¶§•†‡]‹i·¿›... ▹ kßtuyGIJKMR

AG Schoolbook ...

• Regular abcdefghijklmnopqrstuvwxyzABCDEFGHJJKLMNOPQRSTUVWXYZ–$123456

Medium abcdefghijklmnopqrstuvwxyzABCDEFGHJJKLMNOPQRSTUVWXYZ–$123456

Regular & Medium Alternate ▹ kßtuyGIJKMR **kßtuyGIJKMR**

BUREAU AGENCY

David Berlow • 1990 (Morris Fuller Benton, 1933)

FBU AGP MTD

▲30

abcdefghijklmnopqrstuvwxyz(".;'!*?':;")
$1234567890&fiflß-äöüåçèîñóæøœ
ABCDEFGHIJKLMNOPQRSTUVWXYZ
ÄÖÜÅÇÈÎÑÓÆØŒ»„«[¶§•†‡]‹i·¿› ▹ ff ffi ffl

Bureau Agency ...

• Regular abcdefghijklmnopqrstuvwxyzABCDEFGHIJKLMNOPQRS

Bold abcdefghijklmnopqrstuvwxyzABCDEFGHIJKLMNOPQRST

AGENDA

Greg Thompson • 1992 abcdefghijklmnopqrstuvwxyz(".;'!*?':;")
FBU $1234567890&fiflß-äöüåçèîñóæøœ
ABCDEFGHIJKLMNOPQRSTUVWXYZ
ÄÖÜÅÇÈÎÑÓÆØŒ»„«[¶§•†‡]‹i·¿›... ▹ ff ffi ffl

A

... Agenda 1 ...

Thin Ultra Condensed ▲36 abcdefghijklmnopqrstuvwxyzABCDEFGHIJKLMNOPQRSTUVWXYZ–$1234567890(".;'!*?':,")&

Light abcdefghijklmnopqrstuvwxyzABCDEFGHIJKLMNOPQRSTUVWXYZ–$1234567890(".;'!*?':,")

Light Italic *abcdefghijklmnopqrstuvwxyzABCDEFGHIJKLMNOPQRSTUVWXYZ–$1234567890(".;'!*?':,")&*

Light Condensed abcdefghijklmnopqrstuvwxyzABCDEFGHIJKLMNOPQRSTUVWXYZ–$1234567890(".;'!*?':,")&fifIß-äöüÄÖÜåçèÅÇ

Light Extra Condensed ▲16 abcdefghijklmnopqrstuvwxyzABCDEFGHIJKLMNOPQRSTUVWXYZ–$1234567890(".;'!*?':,")&fifIß-äöüÄÖÜåçèÅÇÈîñóÎÑÓæøœ

Light Ultra Condensed ▲18 abcdefghijklmnopqrstuvwxyzABCDEFGHIJKLMNOPQRSTUVWXYZ–$1234567890(".;'!*?':,")&fifIß-äöüÄÖÜåçèÅÇÈîñóÎÑÓæøœÆØŒ»„«[¶§•†‡]‹¡·¿›...

Agenda 2 ...

• Medium abcdefghijklmnopqrstuvwxyzABCDEFGHIJKLMNOPQRSTUVWXYZ–$1234567890(".;'!*?':,

Medium Italic *abcdefghijklmnopqrstuvwxyzABCDEFGHIJKLMNOPQRSTUVWXYZ–$1234567890(".;'!*?':,"*

Medium Condensed abcdefghijklmnopqrstuvwxyzABCDEFGHIJKLMNOPQRSTUVWXYZ–$1234567890(".;'!*?':,")&fifIß-äöüÄÖÜåç

Medium Extra Condensed ▲16 abcdefghijklmnopqrstuvwxyzABCDEFGHIJKLMNOPQRSTUVWXYZ–$1234567890(".;'!*?':,")&fifIß-äöüÄÖÜåçèÅÇÈîñóÎÑ

Medium Ultra Condensed ▲18 **abcdefghijklmnopqrstuvwxyzABCDEFGHIJKLMNOPQRSTUVWXYZ–$1234567890(".;'!*?':,")&fifIß-äöüÄÖÜåçèÅÇÈîñóÎÑÓæøœÆØŒ»„«[¶§•†‡]‹¡·¿**

Agenda 3 ...

Bold **abcdefghijklmnopqrstuvwxyzABCDEFGHIJKLMNOPQRSTUVWXYZ–$1234567890(".;'!**

Bold Condensed **abcdefghijklmnopqrstuvwxyzABCDEFGHIJKLMNOPQRSTUVWXYZ–$1234567890(".;'!*?':,")&fifIß-äöü**

Bold Extra Condensed ▲16 **abcdefghijklmnopqrstuvwxyzABCDEFGHIJKLMNOPQRSTUVWXYZ–$1234567890(".;'!*?':,")&fifIß-äöüÄÖÜåçè**

Bold Ultra Condensed ▲18 **abcdefghijklmnopqrstuvwxyzABCDEFGHIJKLMNOPQRSTUVWXYZ–$1234567890(".;'!*?':,")&fifIß-äöüÄÖÜåçèÅÇÈîñóÎÑÓæøœÆØ**

Black ▲18 **abcdefghijklmnopqrstuvwxyzABCDEFGHIJKLMNOPQRSTUVWX**

Agincourt

✍ *David Quay • 1983* abcdefghijklmnopqrstuvwxyz(".;'!*?':,")

LET $1234567890&fifIß-äöüåçèîñóæøœ

▲18 ABCDEFGHIJKLMNOPQRSTUVWXYZ

ÄÖÜÅÇÈÎÑÓ»„«[•]‹¡·¿›... ▷ aerso Th

TF AKIMBO

✍ *Joseph Treacy • 1992* abcdefghijklmnopqrstuvwxyz(".;'!*?':,")

TRE MTD $1234567890&fifIß-äöüåçèîñóæøœ

▲30 ABCDEFGHIJKLMNOPQRSTUVWXYZ

ÄÖÜÅÇÈÎÑÓÆØŒ»„«[¶§·†‡]‹¡·¿›... ▷ 123579/234816

TF Akimbo A ...

Light abcdefghijklmnopqrstuvwxyzABCDEFGHIJKLMNOPQRSTUVWX

A

... TF Akimbo A

Demibold abcdefghijklmnopqrstuvwxyzABCDEFGHIJKLMNOPQRSTUVW

Extra Bold abcdefghijklmnopqrstuvwxyzABCDEFGHIJKLMNOPQRSTUV

TF Akimbo B ...

Medium abcdefghijklmnopqrstuvwxyzABCDEFGHIJKLMNOPQRSTUVW

Bold abcdefghijklmnopqrstuvwxyzABCDEFGHIJKLMNOPQRSTUV

• Heavy abcdefghijklmnopqrstuvwxyzABCDEFGHIJKLMNOPQRSTU

TF Akimbo Medium
TF DisplaySet 1
Joseph Treacy • 1992
TRE MTD
▲30

abcdefghijklmnopqrstuvwxyz(".;'!*?':;")
$1234567890&fiflß-äöüåçèîñóæøœ
ABCDEFGHIJKLMNOPQRSTUVWXYZ
ÄÖÜÅÇÈÎÑÓÆØŒ»„«[¶§·†‡]‹¡·¿›...

▷ 12357⁹/2 3 4 8 16

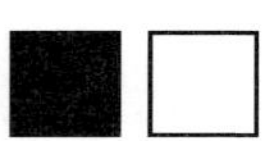

BERTHOLD AKZIDENZ GROTESK

H. Berthold AG • 1900...
ADO AGA MAE

abcdefghijklmnopqrstuvwxyz(".;'!*?':;")
$1234567890&fiflß-äöüåçèîñóæøœ
ABCDEFGHIJKLMNOPQRSTUVWXYZ
ÄÖÜÅÇÈÎÑÓÆØŒ»„«[¶§•†‡]‹¡·¿›...

Berthold Akzidenz Grotesk 1 ...

Light abcdefghijklmnopqrstuvwxyzABCDEFGHIJKLMNOPQRSTUVWXYZ–$1234567890

Light OSF abcdefghijklmnopqrstuvwxyzABCDEFGHIJKLMNOPQRSTUVWXYZ–$1234567890(".

• Regular abcdefghijklmnopqrstuvwxyzABCDEFGHIJKLMNOPQRSTUVWXYZ–$12345678

Italic *abcdefghijklmnopqrstuvwxyzABCDEFGHIJKLMNOPQRSTUVWXYZ–$1234567*

Medium **abcdefghijklmnopqrstuvwxyzABCDEFGHIJKLMNOPQRSTUVWXYZ–$1234567**

Medium Italic ***abcdefghijklmnopqrstuvwxyzABCDEFGHIJKLMNOPQRSTUVWXYZ–$12345678***

Bold **abcdefghijklmnopqrstuvwxyzABCDEFGHIJKLMNOPQRSTUVWXYZ–$123**

Bold Italic ***abcdefghijklmnopqrstuvwxyzABCDEFGHIJKLMNOPQRSTUVWXYZ–$12***

Super
▲16 **abcdefghijklmnopqrstuvwxyzABCDEFGHIJKLMNOPQRSTUV**

....
TF DisplaySet 1: TF Akimbo Medium & TF Avian Extra Bold.

BERTHOLD AKZIDENZ GROTESK 2

ADO AGA MAE abcdefghijklmnopqrstuvwxyz(".;'!*?':,")
▲16 $1234567890&fiflß-äöüåçèîñóæøœ
ABCDEFGHIJKLMNOPQRSTUVWXYZ
ÄÖÜÅÇÈÎÑÓÆØŒ»„«[¶§•†‡]‹¡·¿›...

Berthold Akzidenz Grotesk 2 ...

Light Condensed abcdefghijklmnopqrstuvwxyzABCDEFGHIJKLMNOPQRSTUVWXYZ–$1234567890(".;'!*?':,")&fiflß-äöüÄÖÜåçèÅÇÈîñó

• Condensed abcdefghijklmnopqrstuvwxyzABCDEFGHIJKLMNOPQRSTUVWXYZ–$1234567890(".;'!*?':,")&fiflß-äöü

Medium Condensed abcdefghijklmnopqrstuvwxyzABCDEFGHIJKLMNOPQRSTUVWXYZ–$1234567890(".;'!*?':,")&fiflß-äöüÄÖÜåçèÅÇÈîñóÎÑ

Medium Condensed Italic *abcdefghijklmnopqrstuvwxyzABCDEFGHIJKLMNOPQRSTUVWXYZ–$1234567890(".;'!*?':,")&fiflß-äöüÄÖÜåçèÅÇÈîñóÎ*

Bold Condensed **abcdefghijklmnopqrstuvwxyzABCDEFGHIJKLMNOPQRSTUVWXYZ–$1234567890(".;'!*?':,")&**

Extra Bold Condensed **abcdefghijklmnopqrstuvwxyzABCDEFGHIJKLMNOPQRSTUVWXYZ–$123456789**

Extra Bold Condensed Italic ***abcdefghijklmnopqrstuvwxyzABCDEFGHIJKLMNOPQRSTUVWXYZ–$1234567***

Extra Bold **abcdefghijklmnopqrstuvwxyzABCDEFGHIJKLMNOPQRSTUVWXYZ–$123456**

BERTHOLD AKZIDENZ GROTESK EXTENDED

ADO AGA MAE abcdefghijklmnopqrstuvwxyz(".;'!*?':,")
$1234567890&fiflß-äöüåçèîñóæøœ
ABCDEFGHIJKLMNOPQRSTUVWXYZ
ÄÖÜÅÇÈÎÑÓÆØŒ»„«[¶§•†‡]‹¡·¿›...

Berthold Akzidenz Grotesk Extended ...

Light Extended abcdefghijklmnopqrstuvwxyzABCDEFGHIJKLMNOPQRSTUVWX

• Extended abcdefghijklmnopqrstuvwxyzABCDEFGHIJKLMNOPQRSTUVW

Medium Extended **abcdefghijklmnopqrstuvwxyzABCDEFGHIJKLMNOPQRSTUV**

Bold Extended **abcdefghijklmnopqrstuvwxyzABCDEFGHIJKLMNOPQRS**

Bold Italic Extended ***abcdefghijklmnopqrstuvwxyzABCDEFGHIJKLMNOPQRS***

ALBERTAN

✍ *Jim Rimmer* • 1987 abcdefghijklmnopqrstuvwxyz(".;'!*?':,")
LAN $1234567890&fiflß-äöüåçèîñóæøœ
▲16 ABCDEFGHIJKLMNOPQRSTUVWXYZ
ÄÖÜÅÇÈÎÑÓÆØŒ»„«[¶§·†] ‹¡·¿›... ▷ ctffffifflst

Albertan ...

• Roman abcdefghijklmnopqrstuvwxyzABCDEFGHIJKLMNOPQRSTUVWXYZ–$12345

Italic *abcdefghijklmnopqrstuvwxyzABCDEFGHIJKLMNOPQRSTUVWXYZ–$1234567*

Roman OSF abcdefghijklmnopqrstuvwxyzABCDEFGHIJKLMNOPQRSTUVWXYZ–$123456

Italic OSF *abcdefghijklmnopqrstuvwxyzABCDEFGHIJKLMNOPQRSTUVWXYZ–$12345678*

Roman SCOSF ABCDEFGHIJKLMNOPQRSTUVWXYZABCDEFGHIJKLMNOPQRSTUVWXYZ–$12345

Italic SCOSF *ABCDEFGHIJKLMNOPQRSTUVWXYZABCDEFGHIJKLMNOPQRSTUVWXYZ–$12345*

A

ALBERTAN BOLD

LAN abcdefghijklmnopqrstuvwxyz(“.;‘!*?’:,”)
▲16 $1234567890&fifl߬-äöüåçèîñóæøœ
ABCDEFGHIJKLMNOPQRSTUVWXYZ
ÄÖÜÅÇÈÎÑÓÆØŒ»„«[¶§•†]‹¡·¿›... ▷ ct ff ffi ffl st

Albertan Bold ...

• Bold abcdefghijklmnopqrstuvwxyzABCDEFGHIJKLMNOPQRSTUVWXYZ–$
Bold Italic *abcdefghijklmnopqrstuvwxyzABCDEFGHIJKLMNOPQRSTUVWXYZ–$12*
Bold SD abcdefghijklmnopqrstuvwxyzABCDEFGHIJKLMNOPQRSTUVWXYZ–$
Italic SD *abcdefghijklmnopqrstuvwxyzABCDEFGHIJKLMNOPQRSTUVWXYZ–$12*

ALBERTAN INLINE & TITLING

LAN ABCDEFGHIJKLMNOPQRSTUVWXYZ(“.;‘!*?’:,”)
▲24 $1234567890&-ÄÖÜÅÇÈÎÑÓÆØŒ«„»[¶§•†]‹¡¿›

Albertan Inline & Titling ...

• Inline ABCDEFGHIJKLMNOPQRSTUVWXYZ(“.;‘!*?’:,”)
Inline Italic *ABCDEFGHIJKLMNOPQRSTUVWXYZ(“.;‘!*?’:,*
Titling ABCDEFGHIJKLMNOPQRSTUVWXYZ(“.;‘!*?’:,”
Titling Italic *ABCDEFGHIJKLMNOPQRSTUVWXYZ(“.;‘!*?’:,*

ALBERTUS
Monotype Headliners 6
Berthold Wolpe • 1932
MCL ADO AGA LIN MAE
▲16

abcdefghijklmnopqrstuvwxyz(“.;‘!*?’:,”)
$1234567890&fifl߬-äöüåçèîñóæøœ
ABCDEFGHIJKLMNOPQRSTUVWXYZ
ÄÖÜÅÇÈÎÑÓÆØŒ»„«[¶§•†‡]‹¡·¿›...

Albertus ...

Light abcdefghijklmnopqrstuvwxyzABCDEFGHIJKLMNOPQRSTUVWXYZ–$123
• Regular abcdefghijklmnopqrstuvwxyzABCDEFGHIJKLMNOPQRSTUVWXYZ–$12
Italic *abcdefghijklmnopqrstuvwxyzABCDEFGHIJKLMNOPQRSTUVWXYZ–$1234567890(“.;‘!*

....
Monotype Headliners 6: Albertus Light, Albertus Regular, Albertus Italic, Castellar.

URW ALCUIN

Gudrun Zapf-Von Hesse • 1992 abcdefghijklmnopqrstuvwxyz(".;'!*?':,")

URW $1234567890&fiflß-äöüåçèîñóæøœ

ABCDEFGHIJKLMNOPQRSTUVWXYZ

ÄÖÜÅÇÈÎÑÓÆØŒ»„«[¶§•†‡]‹¡·¿›...

URW Alcuin 1 ...

Light abcdefghijklmnopqrstuvwxyzABCDEFGHIJKLMNOPQRSTUVWXYZ–$123456789

Light SCOSF ABCDEFGHIJKLMNOPQRSTUVWXYZABCDEFGHIJKLMNOPQRSTUVWXYZ–$1234567890(

Bold **abcdefghijklmnopqrstuvwxyzABCDEFGHIJKLMNOPQRSTUVWXYZ–$12345**

Bold SCOSF **ABCDEFGHIJKLMNOPQRSTUVWXYZABCDEFGHIJKLMNOPQRSTUVWXYZ–$1234**

URW Alcuin 2 ...

• Regular abcdefghijklmnopqrstuvwxyzABCDEFGHIJKLMNOPQRSTUVWXYZ–$1234567

Regular SCOSF ABCDEFGHIJKLMNOPQRSTUVWXYZABCDEFGHIJKLMNOPQRSTUVWXYZ–$12345678

Extra Bold **abcdefghijklmnopqrstuvwxyzABCDEFGHIJKLMNOPQRSTUVWXYZ–$123**

Extra Bold SCOSF **ABCDEFGHIJKLMNOPQRSTUVWXYZABCDEFGHIJKLMNOPQRSTUVWXYZ–$12**

ALDUS + SCOSF

Hermann Zapf • 1954 abcdefghijklmnopqrstuvwxyz(".;'!*?':,")

LIN ADO AGA MAE $1234567890&fiflß-äöüåçèîñóÿæøœ

ABCDEFGHIJKLMNOPQRSTUVWXYZ

ÄÖÜÅÇÈÎÑÓÆØŒ»„«[¶§•†‡]‹¡·¿›...

Aldus + SCOSF ...

• Roman abcdefghijklmnopqrstuvwxyzABCDEFGHIJKLMNOPQRSTUVWXYZ–$1234567890

Italic *abcdefghijklmnopqrstuvwxyzABCDEFGHIJKLMNOPQRSTUVWXYZ–$1234567890*

Roman SCOSF ABCDEFGHIJKLMNOPQRSTUVWXYZABCDEFGHIJKLMNOPQRSTUVWXYZ–$12345678

Italic OSF *abcdefghijklmnopqrstuvwxyzABCDEFGHIJKLMNOPQRSTUVWXYZ–$1234567890*

ALEKSEI

Lewis Tsalis • 1994 **abcdefghijklmnopqrstuvwxyz(".;'!*?':,")**

T26 **$1234567890&fiflß-äöüåçèîñóæøœ**

▲18 **ABCDEFGHIJKLMNOPQRSTUVWXYZ**

ÄÖÜÅÇÈÎÑÓÆØŒ»„«[¶§•†‡]‹¡·¿›...

Aleksei ...

• Solid **abcdefghijklmnopqrstuvwxyzABCDEFGHIJKLMNOPQRSTUVWXYZ–$1234567890(".;'!***

Disturbed **abcdefghijklmnopqrstuvwxyzABCDEFGHIJKLMNOPQRSTUVWXYZ~$123456789**

Inline ▲24 abcdefghijklmnopqrstuvwxyzABCDEFGHIJKLMNOPQRSTUVWXY

A

A*I ALEXIA

✍ *Philip Bouwsma • 1994* abcdefghijklmnopqrstuvwxyz(".;'!*?':,")

ALP $1234567890&fiflß-äöüåçèîñóæøœ

▲16 ABCDEFGHIJKLMNOPQRSTUVWXYZ

ÄÖÜÅÇÈÎÑÓÆØŒ»„«[¶§•†‡]‹¡·¿›...

A*I Alexia ...

• Regular abcdefghijklmnopqrstuvwxyzABCDEFGHIJKLMNOPQRSTUVWXYZ–$12345678

Italic *abcdefghijklmnopqrstuvwxyzABCDEFGHIJKLMNOPQRSTUVWXYZ–$1234567890(".;'!*?':,*

Algerian Condensed

✍ *Phillip Kelly • 1988* ABCDEFGHIJKLMNOPQRSTUVWXYZ(".;'!*?':,")

LET URW

▲30 $1234567890&-ÄÖÜÅÇÈÎÑÓÆØŒ»„«[•]‹¡·¿›...

▷ AHKMNRS

Alhambra

✍ *Richard Lipton • 1993* ABCDEFGHIJKLMNOPQRSTUVWXYZ

FBU

▲22 (".;'!*?':,")$1234567890&-ÄÖÜÅÇÈÎÑÓÆØŒ

ABCDEFGHIJKLMNOPQRSTUVWXYZ

ÄÖÜÅÇÈÎÑÓÆØŒ»„«[¶§•†‡]‹¡·¿›... ▷

Allegro

✍ *Hans Bohn • 1936* abcdefghijklmnopqrstuvwxyz(".;'!*?':,")

BIT

▲24 $1234567890&fiflß-äöüåçèîñóæøœ

ABCDEFGHIJKLMNOPQRSTUVWXYZ

ÄÖÜÅÇÈÎÑÓÆØŒ»„«[¶§•†‡]‹¡·¿›...

A*I ALPHAKID

Manfred Klein • 1994

ALP

▲24

ABCDEFGHIJKLMNOPQRSTUVWXYZ(".;'!*?':,")

$1234567890&ß–ÄÖÜÇÈÎÑÓ

ABCDEFGHIJKLMNOPQRSTUVWXYZ

ÄÖÜÇÈÎÑÓ€ »„«**

A*I AlphaKid …

• Plain ABCDEFGHIJKLMNOPQRSTUVWXYZABCDEFG

Black ABCDEFGHIJKLMNOPQRSTUVWXYZABCDE

Extra Black ABCDEFGHIJKLMNOPQRSTUVWXYZABCD

ALTERNATE GOTHIC

Morris Fuller Benton • 1903

LEF BIT URW

▲18

abcdefghijklmnopqrstuvwxyz(".;'!*?':,")

$1234567890&fiflß-äöüåçèîñóæøœ

ABCDEFGHIJKLMNOPQRSTUVWXYZ

ÄÖÜÅÇÈÎÑÓÆØŒ»„«[¶§ • †‡]‹¡·¿›…

Alternate Gothic …

No. 1 abcdefghijklmnopqrstuvwxyzABCDEFGHIJKLMNOPQRSTUVWXYZ–$1234567890(".;'!*?':,")&fiflß-äöüÄÖÜåçè

• No. 2 abcdefghijklmnopqrstuvwxyzABCDEFGHIJKLMNOPQRSTUVWXYZ–$1234567890(".;'!*?':,")&fiflß-

No. 3 abcdefghijklmnopqrstuvwxyzABCDEFGHIJKLMNOPQRSTUVWXYZ–$1234567890(".;'!*?'

Alte Schwabacher

URW

▲24

abcdefghijklmnopqrſtuvwxyz(".;'!*?':,")

$1234567890&fiflß-äöüåçèîñóæøœ

ABCDEFGHIJKLMNOPQRSTUVWXYZ

ÄÖÜÅÇÈÎÑÓÆØŒ»„«[¶§ • †‡]‹¡·¿›…

▷ S

A

ALYS

Pat Hickson • 1994 abcdefghijklmnopqrstuvwxyz(“.;‘!*?’:,”)

RED $1234567890&ﬁﬂß-äöüåçèîñóæøœ

▲16 ABCDEFGHIJKLMNOPQRSTUVWXYZ

ÄÖÜÅÇÈÎÑÓÆØŒ»„«[§•†‡]‹¡·¿›…

Alys …

Light abcdefghijklmnopqrstuvwxyzABCDEFGHIJKLMNOPQRSTUVWXYZ–$1234567890(“.;‘!*?’:,

• Medium abcdefghijklmnopqrstuvwxyzABCDEFGHIJKLMNOPQRSTUVWXYZ–$1234567890(“.;‘!

Bold abcdefghijklmnopqrstuvwxyzABCDEFGHIJKLMNOPQRSTUVWXYZ–$1234567890(

AMASIS

Ron Carpenter • 1990 abcdefghijklmnopqrstuvwxyz(“.;‘!*?’:,”)

MCL $1234567890&ﬁﬂß-äöüåçèîñóæøœ

ABCDEFGHIJKLMNOPQRSTUVWXYZ

ÄÖÜÅÇÈÎÑÓÆØŒ»„«[¶§•†‡]‹¡·¿›…

Amasis 1 …

• Roman abcdefghijklmnopqrstuvwxyzABCDEFGHIJKLMNOPQRSTUVWXYZ–$123456789

Italic *abcdefghijklmnopqrstuvwxyzABCDEFGHIJKLMNOPQRSTUVWXYZ–$1234567890(“.;‘!*

Bold **abcdefghijklmnopqrstuvwxyzABCDEFGHIJKLMNOPQRSTUVWXYZ–$1234**

Bold Italic ***abcdefghijklmnopqrstuvwxyzABCDEFGHIJKLMNOPQRSTUVWXYZ–$1234567***

Amasis 2 …

Light abcdefghijklmnopqrstuvwxyzABCDEFGHIJKLMNOPQRSTUVWXYZ–$1234567890(“.

Light Italic *abcdefghijklmnopqrstuvwxyzABCDEFGHIJKLMNOPQRSTUVWXYZ–$1234567890(“.;‘!*?’:,*

Medium **abcdefghijklmnopqrstuvwxyzABCDEFGHIJKLMNOPQRSTUVWXYZ–$123456**

Medium Italic ***abcdefghijklmnopqrstuvwxyzABCDEFGHIJKLMNOPQRSTUVWXYZ–$1234567890***

Black **abcdefghijklmnopqrstuvwxyzABCDEFGHIJKLMNOPQRSTUVWXYZ–$1**

Black Italic ***abcdefghijklmnopqrstuvwxyzABCDEFGHIJKLMNOPQRSTUVWXYZ–$1234***

Amazone

Leonard H. D. Smit • 1959 abcdefghijklmnopqrstuvwxyz(“.;‘!*?’:,”)

BIT $1234567890&ﬁﬂß-äöüåçèîñóæøœ

▲16 ABCDEFGHIJKLMNOPQRSTUVWXYZ

ÄÖÜÅÇÈÎÑÓÆÉŒ«„»[§•†‡]‹¡·¿›…

HF AMERICAN-DINER
Jonathan Macagba • 1993
HAN MTD
▲30

abcdefghijklmnopqrstuvwxyz(“.:;‘!*?’:,”)
$1234567890&fiß-äöüåçèîñóæøœ
ABCDEFGHIJKLMNOPQRSTUVWXYZ
ÄÖÜÅÇÈÎÑÓÆØŒ»«‹¡·¿› ▷ aeGwAMRTr

HF AmericanDiner ...

Solid abcdefghijklmnopqrstuvwxyzABCDEF
• Inline abcdefghijklmnopqrstuvwxyzABCDEF
Narrow abcdefghijklmnopqrstuvwxyzABCDEFGHIJKLMN

American Text
Morris Fuller Benton • 1932
BIT
▲18

abcdefghijklmnopqrstuvwxyz(“.:;‘!*?’:,”)
$1234567890&fiflſ-äöüåçèîñóæøœ
ABCDEFGHIJKLMNOPQRSTUVWXYZ
ÄÖÜÅÇÈÎÑÓÆØŒ»„«[§•†‡]‹¡·¿›...

ITC AMERICAN TYPEWRITER
Joel Kadan & Tony Stan • 1974
ADO AGA BIT LEF FAM LIN MAE URW

abcdefghijklmnopqrstuvwxyz(“.:;‘!*?’:,”)
$1234567890&fiflß-äöüåçèîñóæøœ
ABCDEFGHIJKLMNOPQRSTUVWXYZ
ÄÖÜÅÇÈÎÑÓÆØŒ»„«[¶§•†‡]‹¡·¿›... ▷ eR$&

ITC American Typewriter ...

Light abcdefghijklmnopqrstuvwxyzABCDEFGHIJKLMNOPQRSTUVWXYZ-$12
• Medium abcdefghijklmnopqrstuvwxyzABCDEFGHIJKLMNOPQRSTUVWXYZ–$1
Bold **abcdefghijklmnopqrstuvwxyzABCDEFGHIJKLMNOPQRSTUVWXYZ**
Light, Medium, Bold Alternate ▷ eR$& eR$& **eR$&**
Light Condensed abcdefghijklmnopqrstuvwxyzABCDEFGHIJKLMNOPQRSTUVWXYZ-$1234567890(“.:;‘!*?’:,”)
Medium Condensed abcdefghijklmnopqrstuvwxyzABCDEFGHIJKLMNOPQRSTUVWXYZ-$1234567890(“.:;‘!*?’:,
Bold Condensed **abcdefghijklmnopqrstuvwxyzABCDEFGHIJKLMNOPQRSTUVWXYZ-$1234567890(“.:;‘!***
Light, Medium, Bold Condensed Alternate ▷ eR$& eR$& **eR$&**

A

American Uncial

Victor Hammer • 1953

URW

▲24

abcdefghijklmnopqrstuvwxyz
("·;'!*?':,")$1234567890
&-äöüåçèîñóæøœ»„«[¶§•†‡]‹¡·¿›...

AMERICANA

Richard Isbell • 1965

BIT ADO AGA FRA LIN MAE

abcdefghijklmnopqrstuvwxyz(".;'!*?':,")
$1234567890&fiflß-äöüåçèîñóæøœ
ABCDEFGHIJKLMNOPQRSTUVWXYZ
ÄÖÜÅÇÈÎÑÓÆØŒ»„«[¶§•†‡]‹¡·¿›...

Americana ...

• Roman abcdefghijklmnopqrstuvwxyzABCDEFGHIJKLMNOPQRSTUVWYZ–$123

Italic *abcdefghijklmnopqrstuvwxyzABCDEFGHIJKLMNOPQRSTUVWXYZ–$123*

Bold abcdefghijklmnopqrstuvwxyzABCDEFGHIJKLMNOPQRSTUVWXYZ–$1

Extra Bold **abcdefghijklmnopqrstuvwxyzABCDEFGHIJKLMNOPQRSTUVWXYZ–$**

Extra Bold Condensed **abcdefghijklmnopqrstuvwxyzABCDEFGHIJKLMNOPQRSTUVWXYZ–$123456**

BITSTREAM AMERIGO

Gerard Unger • 1987

BIT

abcdefghijklmnopqrstuvwxyz(".;'!*?':,")
$1234567890&fiflß-äöüåçèîñóæøœ
ABCDEFGHIJKLMNOPQRSTUVWXYZ
ÄÖÜÅÇÈÎÑÓÆØŒ»„«[¶§•†‡]‹¡·¿›...

Bitstream Amerigo ...

• Roman abcdefghijklmnopqrstuvwxyzABCDEFGHIJKLMNOPQRSTUVWXYZ–$1234567890(".;'!*?':

Italic *abcdefghijklmnopqrstuvwxyzABCDEFGHIJKLMNOPQRSTUVWXYZ–$1234567890(".;'!*?':,")&*

Medium abcdefghijklmnopqrstuvwxyzABCDEFGHIJKLMNOPQRSTUVWXYZ–$1234567890(".;'!*?'

Medium Italic *abcdefghijklmnopqrstuvwxyzABCDEFGHIJKLMNOPQRSTUVWXYZ–$1234567890(".;'!*?':,")&*

Bold **abcdefghijklmnopqrstuvwxyzABCDEFGHIJKLMNOPQRSTUVWXYZ–$1234567890(".;'!*?**

Bold Italic ***abcdefghijklmnopqrstuvwxyzABCDEFGHIJKLMNOPQRSTUVWXYZ–$1234567890(".;'!*?':,")***

Amigo

Baker Calligraphy

Arthur Baker • 1989

AGP ADO AGA LIN MAE

▲16

abcdefghijklmnopqrstuvwxyz(".;'!*?':,")
$1234567890 &fiflß-äöüåçèîñóæøœ
ABCDEFGHIJKLMNOPQRSTUVWXYZ
ÄÖÜÅÇÈÎÑÓÆØŒ»„«[¶§•†‡]‹¡·¿›...

Baker Calligraphy: Amigo, Marigold, Oxford, Pelican, Visigoth.

A

ANDRICH MINERVA

✍ Vladimir Andrich • ... abcdefghijklmnopqrstuvwxyz(“.;‘!*?’:,”)

IMA $1234567890&ß-äöüåçèîñóæøœ

ABCDEFGHIJKLMNOPQRSTUVWXYZ

ÄÖÜÅÇÈÎÑÓÆØŒ»„«[¶§•†]¡·¿...

Andrich Minerva ...

• Roman abcdefghijklmnopqrstuvwxyzABCDEFGHIJKLMNOPQRSTUVWXY

Italic *abcdefghijklmnopqrstuvwxyzABCDEFGHIJKLMNOPQRSTUVWXYZ-$*

ITC Anna
❖ *ITC Typographica*
✍ *Daniel Pelavin • 1991*
ADO AGA AGP LEF ITC LIN MAE URW

ABCDEFGHIJKLMNOPQRSTUVWXYZ

(“.;‘!*?’:,”)$1234567890

▲48

&-ÄÖÜÅÇÈÎÑÓÆØŒ»„«[§•†‡]‹i·¿›...

ANTIKVA MARGARET

IMA abcdefghijklmnopqrstuvwxyz(“.;‘!*?’:,”)

$1234567890&ß-äöüåçèîñóæøœ

ABCDEFGHIJKLMNOPQRSTUVWXYZ

ÄÖÜÅÇÈÎÑÓÆØŒ»„«[¶§·†]¡·¿...

Antikva Margaret ...

• Roman abcdefghijklmnopqrstuvwxyzABCDEFGHIJKLMNOPQRSTUVWXY

Italic *abcdefghijklmnopqrstuvwxyzABCDEFGHIJKLMNOPQRSTUVW*

A*I Antique Condensed
❖ *A*I Wood Type*
✍ *A*I Design Staff • 1990*
ALP MTD

ABCDEFGHIJKLMNOPQRS

TUVWXYZ(.;!*?:,)$1234567

▲40

890&-ABCDEFGHIJKLMN

OPQRSTUVWXYZ[]¡¿

....
❖ *ITC Typographica:* ITC Anna, ITC Beesknees, ITC Mona Lisa Recut & Solid, ITC Ozwald.
❖ *A*I Wood Type:* A*I Antique Condensed, A*I Barrel, A*I Box Gothic, A*I French XXX Condensed, A*I Painter, A*I Tuscan Egyptian.

A

Antique Roman Solid
✣ *Agfa Engravers 1*

AGP abcdefghijklmnopqrstuvwxyz(".;'!*?':,")

▲24 $1234567890&ß-äöüåçèîñó

ABCDEFGHIJKLMNOPQRSTUVWXYZ

ÄÖÜÅÇÈÎÑÓ»«[.]‹› ▹I V X st nd rd th ∽ 1/4 1/3 1/2 3/4 ∼ D' c r. 'c 's O'

Antique Roman Slanted
✣ *Agfa Engravers 1*

AGP *abcdefghijklmnopqrstuvwxyz(".;'!*?':,")*

▲20 *$1234567890äöüåçèîñó*

ABCDEFGHIJKLMNOPQRSTUVWXYZ

ÄÖÜÅÇÈÎÑÓ»«[.]‹› ▹I V X st nd rd th ∽ 1/4 1/3 1/2 3/4 ∼ D' c r. 'c 's O' rs. s. & %

Sackers Antique Roman Open
✣ *Agfa Engravers 2*

AGP abcdefghijklmnopqrstuvwxyz(".;'!*?':,")

▲24 $1234567890äöüåçèîñó

ABCDEFGHIJKLMNOPQRSTUVWXYZ

ÄÖÜÅÇÈÎÑÓ»«[.]‹› ▹I V X st nd rd th ∽ 1/4 1/3 1/2 3/4 ∽ D' c r. 'c 's O'

Sackers Antique Roman Solid
✣ *Agfa Engravers 2*

AGP abcdefghijklmnopqrstuvwxyz(".;'!*?':,")

▲24 $1234567890&ß-äöüåçèîñó

ABCDEFGHIJKLMNOPQRSTUVWXYZ

ÄÖÜÅÇÈÎÑÓ»«[.]‹›▹I V X st nd rd th ∽ 1/4 1/3 1/2 3/4 ∽ D' c r. 'c 's O'

✣ *Agfa Engravers 1*: Antique Roman Solid & Slanted, Artisan Roman, Burin Roman & Sans, Classic Roman Light & Regular, Handle Oldstyle, Roman Light & Medium.

✣ *Agfa Engravers 2*: Sackers Antique Roman Open & Solid, Sackers Light Classic Roman, Sackers English Script, Sackers Gothic Light, Medium & Heavy, Sackers Italian Script, Sackers Roman Light, Sackers Square Gothic.

A

ANTIQUE OLIVE

Roger Excoffon • 1962 abcdefghijklmnopqrstuvwxyz(".;'!*?':,")

LIN ADO AGA AGP MAE URW $1234567890&fifIß-äöüåçèîñóæøœ

ABCDEFGHIJKLMNOPQRSTUVWXYZ

ÄÖÜÅÇÈÎÑÓÆØŒ»„«[¶§•†‡]‹¡·¿›...

Antique Olive 1 ...

Light abcdefghijklmnopqrstuvwxyzABCDEFGHIJKLMNOPQRSTUVWXYZ–$1234567890

• Regular abcdefghijklmnopqrstuvwxyzABCDEFGHIJKLMNOPQRSTUVWXYZ–$12345

Italic *abcdefghijklmnopqrstuvwxyzABCDEFGHIJKLMNOPQRSTUVWXYZ–$12345*

Bold **abcdefghijklmnopqrstuvwxyzABCDEFGHIJKLMNOPQRSTUVWXYZ–$1234**

Black **abcdefghijklmnopqrstuvwxyzABCDEFGHIJKLMNOPQRSTUVWXYZ–$12**

Antique Olive 2 ...

Bold Condensed ▲16 **abcdefghijklmnopqrstuvwxyzABCDEFGHIJKLMNOPQRSTUVWXYZ–$1234567890(".;'!*?':,**

Compact ▲16 **abcdefghijklmnopqrstuvwxyzABCDEFGHIJKLMNOPQ**

Nord ▲16 **abcdefghijklmnopqrstuvwxyzABCDEFGHI**

Nord Italic ▲16 ***abcdefghijklmnopqrstuvwxyzABCDEFGHIJKLM***

APOLLO + EXPERT & SCOSF

Adrian Frutiger • 1964 abcdefghijklmnopqrstuvwxyz(".;'!*?':,")

MAE ADO AGA LIN MCL $1234567890&fiflß-äöüåçèîñóæøœ

ABCDEFGHIJKLMNOPQRSTUVWXYZ

ÄÖÜÅÇÈÎÑÓÆØŒ»„«[¶§•†‡]‹¡·¿›...

Apollo + Expert & SCOSF ...

• Roman abcdefghijklmnopqrstuvwxyzABCDEFGHIJKLMNOPQRSTUVWXYZ–$1234567890(".;'!

Italic *abcdefghijklmnopqrstuvwxyzABCDEFGHIJKLMNOPQRSTUVWXYZ–$1234567890(".;'!*

Semibold **abcdefghijklmnopqrstuvwxyzABCDEFGHIJKLMNOPQRSTUVWXYZ–$1234567890**

Expert Roman ABCDEFGHIJKLMNOPQRSTUVWXYZ–$1234567890.;!?:,&-fffiflffiffl ⅛ ¼ ⅓ ⅜ ½ $12345/67890¢

Expert Italic *$1234567890.;:,–fffiflffiffl ⅛ ¼ ⅓ ⅜ ½ $12345/67890¢ (abdeilmnorst) ⅝ ⅔ ¾ ⅞ ₡Rp*

Expert Semibold **$1234567890.;:,–fffiflffiffl ⅛ ¼ ⅓ ⅜ ½ $12345/67890¢ (abdeilmnorst) ⅝ ⅔ ¾ ⅞ ₡Rp**

Roman SCOSF ABCDEFGHIJKLMNOPQRSTUVWXYZABCDEFGHIJKLMNOPQRSTUVWXYZ–$1234567890(".;

Italic OSF *abcdefghijklmnopqrstuvwxyzABCDEFGHIJKLMNOPQRSTUVWXYZ–$1234567890(".;'!*

Semibold OSF **abcdefghijklmnopqrstuvwxyzABCDEFGHIJKLMNOPQRSTUVWXYZ–$1234567890**

Aquinas

David Quay • 1989 abcdefghijklmnopqrstuvwxyz(".;'!*?':,")

LET $1234567890&fiflß-äöüåçèîñóæøœ

▲16 ABCDEFGHIJKLMNOPQRSTUVWXYZ

ÄÖÜÅÇÈÎÑÓÆØŒ»„«[•]‹¡·¿›...

▷ b ff ffi ffl h k l th y Th

Antique Olive 1 · Antique Olive EastA.

A

Aquitane Initials

Steven Albert • 1987

LET

▲24

ABCDEFGHIJKLMNOPQRSTUVWXYZ

(".;'!*?':,")$1234567890

&-ÄÖÜÅÇÈÎÑÓÆØŒ»,,«[•]‹¡·¿›... ▷AAAAAA

▷BBCEEEFGHHHLMMNNQRRRSGTTWG

Arabia Felix

Group Arabia

Judith Sutcliffe • 1992

MTD

▲24

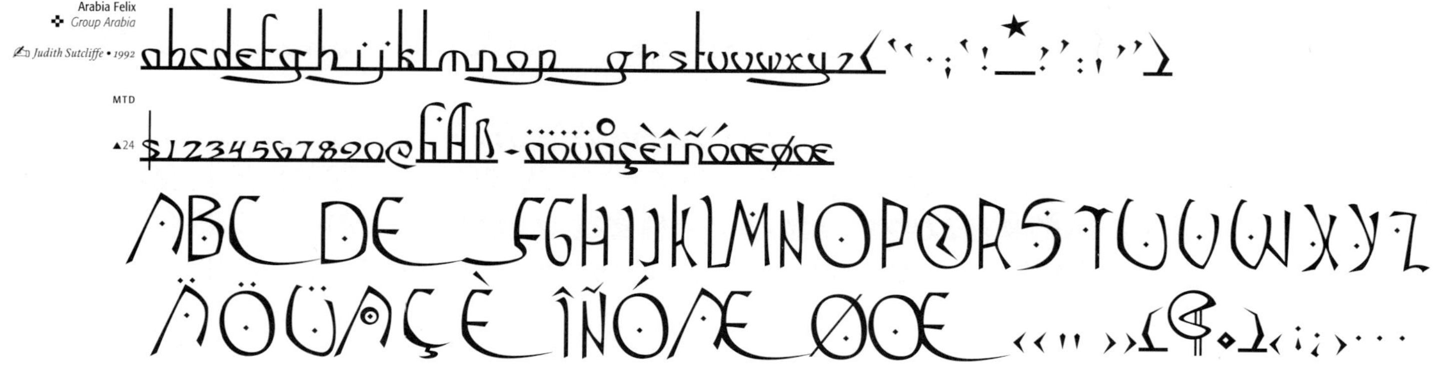

Arcadia

Brody DisplaySet 1

Neville Brody • 1990

LIN ADO AGA MAE

▲60

abcdefghijklmnopqrstuvwxyz(".:'!*?':,")

$1234567890£fiflß-äöüåçèîñóæøœ

ABCDEFGHIJKLMNOPQRSTUVWXYZ

ÄÖÜÅÇÈÎÑÓÆØŒ»,,«[¶$●†‡]‹¡·¿› . . . ▷bdhpq

ARCHI·TEXT

Marshall Bohlin • 1989

EMD

▲12

abcdefghijklmnopqrstuvwxyz(".:'!*?':,")

$1234567890&fifIß-äöüåçèîñóæøœ

ABCDEFGHIJKLMNOPQRSTUVWXYZ

ÄÖÜÅÇÈÎÑÓÆØŒ»«[¶§°†]¡·¿...

Group Arabia: Arabia Felix, Black Rocks, Black Tents, Kufi Script, Mesopotamia.

Brody DisplaySet 1: Arcadia, Industria Inline & Solid, Insignia.

A

... ArchiText ...

• Regular abcdefghijklmnopqrstuvwxyzABCDEFGHIJKLMNOPQRSTUVWXYZ–$1234

Bold abcdefghijklmnopqrstuvwxyzABCDEFGHIJKLMNOPQRSTUVWXYZ–$1

TF ARDENT

Joseph Treacy • 1991 abcdefghijklmnopqrstuvwxyz(".;'!*?':;")

TRE MTD $1234567890&fiflß-äöüåçèîñóæøœ

ABCDEFGHIJKLMNOPQRSTUVWXYZ

ÄÖÜÅÇÈÎÑÓÆØŒ»„«[¶§•†‡]‹¡·¿›... ▷123579⁄234816■□

TF Ardent ...

• Regular abcdefghijklmnopqrstuvwxyzABCDEFGHIJKLMNOPQRSTUVWXYZ– $123456789

Italic abcdefghijklmnopqrstuvwxyzABCDEFGHIJKLMNOPQRSTUVWXYZ– $1234567890(".;'!*?':;")&fiflß-äöüÄ

Extra Bold abcdefghijklmnopqrstuvwxyzABCDEFGHIJKLMNOPQRSTUVWXYZ–$1

Extra Bold Italic abcdefghijklmnopqrstuvwxyzABCDEFGHIJKLMNOPQRSTUVWXYZ–$1234567890(".;'!*?':

Ariadne

GudrunSchrift

Gudrun Zapf-Von Hesse • 1954 ABCDEFGHIJKLMNOPQRSTUVWXYZ

LIN ADO AGA MAE ".;'!?':;"&-ÄÖÜÅÇÈÎÑÓÆØŒ„¡¿ ▷LRVZ

▲24

ARIAL

Monotype Design Staff • 1982 abcdefghijklmnopqrstuvwxyz(".;'!*?':;")

MCL $1234567890&fiflß-äöüåçèîñóæøœ

ABCDEFGHIJKLMNOPQRSTUVWXYZ

ÄÖÜÅÇÈÎÑÓÆØŒ»„«[¶§•†‡]‹¡·¿›...

Arial 1 ...

• Regular abcdefghijklmnopqrstuvwxyzABCDEFGHIJKLMNOPQRSTUVWXYZ–$1234567

Italic abcdefghijklmnopqrstuvwxyzABCDEFGHIJKLMNOPQRSTUVWXYZ–$1234567

Bold abcdefghijklmnopqrstuvwxyzABCDEFGHIJKLMNOPQRSTUVWXYZ–$1234

Bold Italic abcdefghijklmnopqrstuvwxyzABCDEFGHIJKLMNOPQRSTUVWXYZ–$1234

Arial 2 ...

Light abcdefghijklmnopqrstuvwxyzABCDEFGHIJKLMNOPQRSTUVWXYZ–$12345678

Light Italic abcdefghijklmnopqrstuvwxyzABCDEFGHIJKLMNOPQRSTUVWXYZ–$12345678

Black abcdefghijklmnopqrstuvwxyzABCDEFGHIJKLMNOPQRSTUVWXY

Black Italic abcdefghijklmnopqrstuvwxyzABCDEFGHIJKLMNOPQRSTUVWXY

Arial 3 ...

Medium abcdefghijklmnopqrstuvwxyzABCDEFGHIJKLMNOPQRSTUVWXYZ–$123456

Medium Italic abcdefghijklmnopqrstuvwxyzABCDEFGHIJKLMNOPQRSTUVWXYZ–$123456

GudrunSchrift: Ariadne, Diotima Roman, Italic, Roman SCOSF, Roman OSF, Italic OSF, Smaragd.

Arial 1 Arial Cyrillic, Arial Efo, Arial Greek.

A

... Arial 2

Extra Bold **abcdefghijklmnopqrstuvwxyzABCDEFGHIJKLMNOPQRSTUVWXYZ–$1**

Extra Bold Italic ***abcdefghijklmnopqrstuvwxyzABCDEFGHIJKLMNOPQRSTUVWXYZ–$1***

ARIAL 4

MCL abcdefghijklmnopqrstuvwxyz(“.;‘!*?’:,”)
▲16 $1234567890&fiflß-äöüåçèîñóæøœ
ABCDEFGHIJKLMNOPQRSTUVWXYZ
ÄÖÜÅÇÈÎÑÓÆØŒ»„«[¶§•†‡]‹¡·¿›...

Arial 4 ...

Light Condensed abcdefghijklmnopqrstuvwxyzABCDEFGHIJKLMNOPQRSTUVWXYZ–$1234567890(“.;‘!*?’

• Condensed abcdefghijklmnopqrstuvwxyzABCDEFGHIJKLMNOPQRSTUVWXYZ–$12345678

Bold Condensed **abcdefghijklmnopqrstuvwxyzABCDEFGHIJKLMNOPQRSTUVWXYZ–$1234567**

Extra Bold Condensed **abcdefghijklmnopqrstuvwxyzABCDEFGHIJKLMNOPQRSTUVWXYZ–$12345678**

ARIAL ROUNDED

MCL abcdefghijklmnopqrstuvwxyz(“.;‘!*?’:,”)
$1234567890&fiflß-äöüåçèîñóæøœ
ABCDEFGHIJKLMNOPQRSTUVWXYZ
ÄÖÜÅÇÈÎÑÓÆØŒ»„«[¶§•†‡]‹¡·¿›...

Arial Rounded ...

Light abcdefghijklmnopqrstuvwxyzABCDEFGHIJKLMNOPQRSTUVWXYZ–$12345678

• Regular abcdefghijklmnopqrstuvwxyzABCDEFGHIJKLMNOPQRSTUVWXYZ–$123456

Bold **abcdefghijklmnopqrstuvwxyzABCDEFGHIJKLMNOPQRSTUVWXYZ–$1234**

Extra Bold **abcdefghijklmnopqrstuvwxyzABCDEFGHIJKLMNOPQRSTUVWXYZ–$1**

ARIAL NARROW

MCL abcdefghijklmnopqrstuvwxyz(“.;‘!*?’:,”)
$1234567890&fiflß-äöüåçèîñóæøœ
ABCDEFGHIJKLMNOPQRSTUVWXYZ
ÄÖÜÅÇÈÎÑÓÆØŒ»„«[¶§•†‡]‹¡·¿›...

Arial Narrow ...

• Regular abcdefghijklmnopqrstuvwxyzABCDEFGHIJKLMNOPQRSTUVWXYZ–$1234567890(“.

Italic *abcdefghijklmnopqrstuvwxyzABCDEFGHIJKLMNOPQRSTUVWXYZ–$1234567890(“.*

Bold **abcdefghijklmnopqrstuvwxyzABCDEFGHIJKLMNOPQRSTUVWXYZ–$123456789**

Bold Italic ***abcdefghijklmnopqrstuvwxyzABCDEFGHIJKLMNOPQRSTUVWXYZ–$123456789***

Arial Narrow Arial Narrow Efo.

Aristocrat

Donald Stevens • 1994 abcdefghijklmnopqrstuvwxyz(".;'!*?':,")

LET $1234567890&fiflß-äöüåçèîñóæøœ

▲18 ABCDEFGHIJKLMNOPQRSTUVWXYZ

ÄÖÜÅÇÈÎÑÓÆØŒ»„«[•]‹i·¿›...

ARMADA

Tobias Frere-Jones • 1994 abcdefghijklmnopqrstuvwxyz(".;'!*?':,")

FBU $1234567890&fiflß-äöüåçèîñóæøœ

ABCDEFGHIJKLMNOPQRSTUVWXYZ

ÄÖÜÅÇÈÎÑÓÆØŒ»„«[¶§•†‡]‹i·¿›...

Armada 1 ...

Thin abcdefghijklmnopqrstuvwxyzABCDEFGHIJKLMNOPQRSTUVWXYZ-$12345

Light abcdefghijklmnopqrstuvwxyzABCDEFGHIJKLMNOPQRSTUVWXYZ-$123

• Regular abcdefghijklmnopqrstuvwxyzABCDEFGHIJKLMNOPQRSTUVWXYZ-$12

Bold abcdefghijklmnopqrstuvwxyzABCDEFGHIJKLMNOPQRSTUVWXYZ

Black ▲16 abcdefghijklmnopqrstuvwxyzABCDEFGHIJKLMNOPQR

ARMADA 2

FBU abcdefghijklmnopqrstuvwxyz(".;'!*?':,")

▲18 $1234567890&fiflß-äöüåçèîñóæøœ

ABCDEFGHIJKLMNOPQRSTUVWXYZ

ÄÖÜÅÇÈÎÑÓÆØŒ»„«[¶§•†‡]‹i·¿›...

Armada 2 ...

Thin Condensed abcdefghijklmnopqrstuvwxyzABCDEFGHIJKLMNOPQRSTUVWXYZ-$1234567890(".;'!*?':,)&fiflß-äöüÄÖ

Light Condensed abcdefghijklmnopqrstuvwxyzABCDEFGHIJKLMNOPQRSTUVWXYZ-$1234567890(".;'!*?':,)&fiflß-

• Condensed abcdefghijklmnopqrstuvwxyzABCDEFGHIJKLMNOPQRSTUVWXYZ-$1234567890(".;'!*?':,

Bold Condensed abcdefghijklmnopqrstuvwxyzABCDEFGHIJKLMNOPQRSTUVWXYZ-$1234567

Black Condensed ▲20 abcdefghijklmnopqrstuvwxyzABCDEFGHIJKLMNOPQRSTUVW

ARMADA 3

FBU ▲48 abcdefghijklmnopqrstuvwxyz(".;'!*?':,")

$1234567890&fiflß-äöüåçèîñóæøœ

ABCDEFGHIJKLMNOPQRSTUVWXYZÄÖÜÅÇÈÎÑÓÆØŒ»„«[¶§•†‡]‹i·¿›...

A

Armada 3 . . .
Thin Compressed
Light Compressed
• Compressed
Bold Compressed
Black Compressed

Arnold Böcklin
Linotype DisplaySet 1
LIN ADO AGA MAE MTD URW
▲24

abcdefghijklmnopqrstuvwxyz(".:;'!*?':,")
$1234567890&fifIß-äöüåçèîñóæøœ
ABCDEFGHIJKLMNOPQRSTUVWXYZ
ÄÖÜÅÇÈÎÑÓÆØŒ»„«[¶§•†‡]‹¡·¿›...

Arquitectura
IMA
▲16

abcdefghijklmnopqrstuvwxyz(".:;'!*?':,")
$1234567890&ß-äöüåçèîñóœøæ
ABCDEFGHIJKLMNOPQRSTUVWXYZ
ÄÖÜÅÇÈÎÑÓÆØŒ>>„<<[¶§•†]¡·¿...

Arriba
Phill Grimshaw • *1993*
LET
▲18

abcdefghijklmnopqrstuvwxyz(".:;'!*?':,")
$1234567890 &fifIß-äöüåçèîñóæøœ
ABCDEFGHIJKLMNOPQRSTUVWXYZ
ÄÖÜÅÇÈÎÑÓÆØŒ»„«[•]‹¡·¿›...
▷aabddfhijknoprsttuyzzASU6ff

Linotype DisplaySet 1: Arnold Böcklin, Fette Fraktur, Helvetica Inserat, Present Script.

Arriba-Arriba

✍ Phill Grimshaw • 1993 abcdefghijklmnopqrstuvwxyz(“.;‘!*?’:,”)
LET $1234567890 &fiflß-äöüåçèîñóæøœ
▲18 ABCDEFGHIJKLMNOPQRSTUVWXYZ
ÄÖÜÅÇÈÎÑÓÆØŒ»„«[•]‹i·¿›...
▷aabddfhijknoprsttuyzzASUGff

BITSTREAM ARRUS

✍ Richard Lipton • 1991 abcdefghijklmnopqrstuvwxyz(“.;‘!*?’:,”)
BIT $1234567890&fiflß-äöüåçèîñóæøœ
ABCDEFGHIJKLMNOPQRSTUVWXYZ
ÄÖÜÅÇÈÎÑÓÆØŒ»„«[¶§•†‡]‹i·¿›...

Bitstream Arrus ...

• Roman abcdefghijklmnopqrstuvwxyzABCDEFGHIJKLMNOPQRSTUVWXYZ–$123
Italic *abcdefghijklmnopqrstuvwxyzABCDEFGHIJKLMNOPQRSTUVWXYZ–$1234567*
Bold **abcdefghijklmnopqrstuvwxyzABCDEFGHIJKLMNOPQRSTUVWXYZ–$**
Bold Italic ***abcdefghijklmnopqrstuvwxyzABCDEFGHIJKLMNOPQRSTUVWXYZ–$123***
Black **abcdefghijklmnopqrstuvwxyzABCDEFGHIJKLMNOPQRSTUVWXY**
Black Italic ***abcdefghijklmnopqrstuvwxyzABCDEFGHIJKLMNOPQRSTUVWXYZ***

ARTA

✍ David Quay • 1991 abcdefghijklmnopqrstuvwxyz(“.;‘!*?’:,”)
AGP $1234567890&fiflß-äöüåçèîñóæøœ
▲16 ABCDEFGHIJKLMNOPQRSTUVWXYZ
ÄÖÜÅÇÈÎÑÓÆØŒ»„«[¶§•†‡]‹i·¿›...

Arta ...

Light abcdefghijklmnopqrstuvwxyzABCDEFGHIJKLMNOPQRSTUVWXYZ–$1234
Light Italic *abcdefghijklmnopqrstuvwxyz*ABCDEFGHIJKLMNOPQRSTUVWXYZ–$1234567890
• Book abcdefghijklmnopqrstuvwxyzABCDEFGHIJKLMNOPQRSTUVWXYZ–$123
Book Italic *abcdefghijklmnopqrstuvwxyz*ABCDEFGHIJKLMNOPQRSTUVWXYZ–$123456789
Medium **abcdefghijklmnopqrstuvwxyzABCDEFGHIJKLMNOPQRSTUVWXYZ–$**
Medium Italic ***abcdefghijklmnopqrstuvwxyz*ABCDEFGHIJKLMNOPQRSTUVWXYZ–$123456**
Bold **abcdefghijklmnopqrstuvwxyzABCDEFGHIJKLMNOPQRSTUVWXY**
Bold Italic ***abcdefghijklmnopqrstuvwxyz*ABCDEFGHIJKLMNOPQRSTUVWXYZ–$123**

A

FC ARTCRAFT

Robert Wiebking • 1912 abcdefghijklmnopqrstuvwxyz(".;'!*?':,")

TFC $1234567890&fiflß-äöüåçêîñóæøœ

▲16 ABCDEFGHIJKLMNOPQRSTUVWXYZ

ÄÖÜÅÇÈÎÑÓÆØŒ»„«[¶§·†‡]‹¡·¿›... ▷ wg

FC Artcraft ...

• Regular abcdefghijklmnopqrstuvwxyzABCDEFGHIJKLMNOPQRSTUVWXYZ–$12

Bold **abcdefghijklmnopqrstuvwxyzABCDEFGHIJKLMNOPQRSTUVWXYZ–$123**

Artisan Roman
Agfa Engravers 1

AGP abcdefghijklmnopqrstuvwxyz(".;'!*?':,")

▲24 $1234567890äöüåçèîñó

ABCDEFGHIJKLMNOPQRSTUVWXYZ

ÄÖÜÅÇÈÎÑÓ»«[·]‹› ▷ I V X st nd rd th 1/4 1/3 1/2 3/4 D' c r. 'c 's O'

Artiste

Martin Wait • 1991 ABCDEFGHIJKLMNOPQRSTUVWXYZ

LET (".;'!*?':,")$1234567890

▲28 &-ÄÖÜÅÇÈÎÑÓÆØŒ»„«[•]‹¡·¿›...

Ashley Script
Monotype Scripts 2

Ashley Havinden • 1955 *abcdefghijklmnopqrstuvwxyz(".;'!*?':,")*

MCL ADO AGA LIN MAE *$1234567890&fiflß-äöüåçèîñóæøœ*

▲16 *ABCDEFGHIJKLMNOPQRSTUVWXYZ*

ÄÖÜÅÇÈÎÑÓÆØŒ»„«[§•†‡]‹¡·¿›...

NEW ASTER

Francesco Simoncini • 1958 (Linotype Design Staff, 1982) abcdefghijklmnopqrstuvwxyz(".;'!*?':,")

LIN ADO AGA MAE $1234567890&fiflß-äöüåçèîñóæøœ

ABCDEFGHIJKLMNOPQRSTUVWXYZ

ÄÖÜÅÇÈÎÑÓÆØŒ»„«[¶§•†‡]‹¡·¿›...

New Aster ...

• Regular abcdefghijklmnopqrstuvwxyzABCDEFGHIJKLMNOPQRSTUVWXYZ–$1234

Italic *abcdefghijklmnopqrstuvwxyzABCDEFGHIJKLMNOPQRSTUVWXYZ–$123456*

Agfa Engravers 1: Antique Roman Solid & Slanted, Artisan Roman, Burin Roman & Sans, Classic Roman Light & Regular, Handle Oldstyle, Roman Light & Medium.
Monotype Scripts 2: Ashley Script, Monoline Script, New Berolina, Palace Script Regular & Semibold.

A

. . . New Aster

Semibold abcdefghijklmnopqrstuvwxyzABCDEFGHIJKLMNOPQRSTUVWXYZ–$123
Semibold Italic *abcdefghijklmnopqrstuvwxyzABCDEFGHIJKLMNOPQRSTUVWXYZ–$1234*
Bold **abcdefghijklmnopqrstuvwxyzABCDEFGHIJKLMNOPQRSTUVWXYZ–$1**
Bold Italic ***abcdefghijklmnopqrstuvwxyzABCDEFGHIJKLMNOPQRSTUVWXYZ–$12***
Black **abcdefghijklmnopqrstuvwxyzABCDEFGHIJKLMNOPQRSTUVWXYZ–**
Black Italic ***abcdefghijklmnopqrstuvwxyzABCDEFGHIJKLMNOPQRSTUVWXYZ–$***

ATHENAEUM
Agfa Typographer's Edition 5
Alessandro Butti & Aldo Novarese • 1945
AGP
▲16

abcdefghijklmnopqrstuvwxyz(".;'!*?':,")
$1234567890&fifl-äöüåçèîñóæøœ
ABCDEFGHIJKLMNOPQRSTUVWXYZ
ÄÖÜÅÇÈÎÑÓÆØŒ»„«[¶§•†‡]‹¡·¿›... ▷ ff ffi ffl

Athenaeum . . .

• Regular abcdefghijklmnopqrstuvwxyzABCDEFGHIJKLMNOPQRSTUVWXYZ–$12345678
Italic *abcdefghijklmnopqrstuvwxyzABCDEFGHIJKLMNOPQRSTUVWXYZ–$1234567890("*
Bold **abcdefghijklmnopqrstuvwxyzABCDEFGHIJKLMNOPQRSTUVWXYZ–$**

Initials Positive ▲30
Initials Negative ▲30

Augustea Open
Alessandro Butti & Aldo Novarese • 1951
LET
▲30

ABCDEFGHIJKLMNOPQRSTUVW
XYZ(".;'!*?':,")$1234567890
&-ÄÖÜÅÇÈÎÑÓÆØŒ»„«[•]‹¡·¿›... ▷

AURELIA
Hermann Zapf • 1983
LEF

abcdefghijklmnopqrstuvwxyz(".;'!*?':,")
$1234567890&fiflß-äöüåçèîñóæøœ
ABCDEFGHIJKLMNOPQRSTUVWXYZ
ÄÖÜÅÇÈÎÑÓÆØŒ»„«[¶§•†‡]‹¡·¿›...

Aurelia . . .

Light abcdefghijklmnopqrstuvwxyzABCDEFGHIJKLMNOPQRSTUVWXYZ–$1234567
Light Italic *abcdefghijklmnopqrstuvwxyzABCDEFGHIJKLMNOPQRSTUVWXYZ–$1234567890(".;'!*?':,*

Agfa Typographer's Edition 5: Athenaeum Roman, Italic & Bold, Athenaeum Initials Positive & Negative.

A

... Aurelia

• Roman abcdefghijklmnopqrstuvwxyzABCDEFGHIJKLMNOPQRSTUVWXYZ–$123456

Italic *abcdefghijklmnopqrstuvwxyzABCDEFGHIJKLMNOPQRSTUVWXYZ–$1234567890(".;*

Bold **abcdefghijklmnopqrstuvwxyzABCDEFGHIJKLMNOPQRSTUVWXYZ–$12345**

AURIOL

Georges Auriol • 1901 abcdefghijklmnopqrstuvwxyz(".;'!*?':,")

LIN ADO AGA MAE $1234567890&fiflß-äöüåçèîñóæøœ

▲16 ABCDEFGHIJKLMNOPQRSTUVWXYZ

ÄÖÜÅÇÈÎÑÓÆØŒ»„«[¶§•†‡]‹¡·¿›...

Auriol ...

• Regular abcdefghijklmnopqrstuvwxyzABCDEFGHIJKLMNOPQRSTUVWXYZ–

Italic *abcdefghijklmnopqrstuvwxyzABCDEFGHIJKLMNOPQRSTUVWXYZ–$1234*

Bold **abcdefghijklmnopqrstuvwxyzABCDEFGHIJKLMNOPQRSTUVWXY**

Bold Italic ***abcdefghijklmnopqrstuvwxyzABCDEFGHIJKLMNOPQRSTUVWXYZ–***

Black **abcdefghijklmnopqrstuvwxyzABCDEFGHIJKLMNOPQRSTUVW**

Black Italic ***abcdefghijklmnopqrstuvwxyzABCDEFGHIJKLMNOPQRSTUVW***

ITC AVANT GARDE GOTHIC

Herb Lubalin & Tom Carnase • 1970 André Gürtler, Christian Mengelt & Erich Gschwind • 1977

abcdefghijklmnopqrstuvwxyz(".;'!*?':,")

$1234567890&fiflß-äöüåçèîñóæøœ

ADO AGA BIT LEF FAM LIN MAE URW ABCDEFGHIJKLMNOPQRSTUVWXYZ

ÄÖÜÅÇÈÎÑÓÆØŒ»„«(¶§•†‡)‹¡·¿›...

ITC Avant Garde Gothic 1 ...

• Book abcdefghijklmnopqrstuvwxyzABCDEFGHIJKLMNOPQRSTUVWXYZ–$123456

Book Oblique *abcdefghijklmnopqrstuvwxyzABCDEFGHIJKLMNOPQRSTUVWXYZ–$123456*

Demi **abcdefghijklmnopqrstuvwxyzABCDEFGHIJKLMNOPQRSTUVWXYZ–$123456**

Demi Oblique ***abcdefghijklmnopqrstuvwxyzABCDEFGHIJKLMNOPQRSTUVWXYZ–$123456***

ITC Avant Garde Gothic 2 ...

Extra Light abcdefghijklmnopqrstuvwxyzABCDEFGHIJKLMNOPQRSTUVWXYZ–$12345678

Extra Light Oblique *abcdefghijklmnopqrstuvwxyzABCDEFGHIJKLMNOPQRSTUVWXYZ–$12345678*

Medium abcdefghijklmnopqrstuvwxyzABCDEFGHIJKLMNOPQRSTUVWXYZ–$123456

Medium Oblique *abcdefghijklmnopqrstuvwxyzABCDEFGHIJKLMNOPQRSTUVWXYZ–$123456*

Bold **abcdefghijklmnopqrstuvwxyzABCDEFGHIJKLMNOPQRSTUVWXYZ–$12**

Bold Oblique ***abcdefghijklmnopqrstuvwxyzABCDEFGHIJKLMNOPQRSTUVWXYZ–$12***

Auriol Auriol Flowers.

ITC AVANT GARDE GOTHIC CONDENSED

Ed Benguiat • 1974

ADO AGA BIT LEF FAM LIN MAE URW

abcdefghijklmnopqrstuvwxyz(".;'!*?':,")
$1234567890&fiflß-äöüåçèîñóœøœ
ABCDEFGHIJKLMNOPQRSTUVWXYZ
ÄÖÜÅÇÈÎÑÓÆØŒ»„«[¶§•†‡]‹¡·¿›...

ITC Avant Garde Gothic Condensed ...

• Book Condensed abcdefghijklmnopqrstuvwxyzABCDEFGHIJKLMNOPQRSTUVWXYZ–$1234567890(".;'!*?':,"

Medium Condensed abcdefghijklmnopqrstuvwxyzABCDEFGHIJKLMNOPQRSTUVWXYZ–$1234567890(".;'!*?':,"

Demi Condensed abcdefghijklmnopqrstuvwxyzABCDEFGHIJKLMNOPQRSTUVWXYZ–$1234567890(".;'!*?'

Bold Condensed abcdefghijklmnopqrstuvwxyzABCDEFGHIJKLMNOPQRSTUVWXYZ–$1234567890(".;'!*

ITC AVANT GARDE GOTHIC MULTIPLE-MASTER

(two axes : weight & width)

ADO AGA MAE

abcdefghijklmnopqrstuvwxyz(".;'!*?':,")
$1234567890&fiflß-äöüåçèîñóœøœ
ABCDEFGHIJKLMNOPQRSTUVWXYZ
ÄÖÜÅÇÈÎÑÓÆØŒ»„«[¶§•†‡]‹¡·¿›...

ITC Avant Garde Gothic MultipleMaster ...

Extra Light abcdefghijklmnopqrstuvwxyzABCDEFGHIJKLMNOPQRSTUVWXYZ–$12345678

Extra Light Oblique *abcdefghijklmnopqrstuvwxyzABCDEFGHIJKLMNOPQRSTUVWXYZ–$12345678*

Light abcdefghijklmnopqrstuvwxyzABCDEFGHIJKLMNOPQRSTUVWXYZ–$123456

Light Oblique *abcdefghijklmnopqrstuvwxyzABCDEFGHIJKLMNOPQRSTUVWXYZ–$123456*

• Regular abcdefghijklmnopqrstuvwxyzABCDEFGHIJKLMNOPQRSTUVWXYZ–$12345

Oblique *abcdefghijklmnopqrstuvwxyzABCDEFGHIJKLMNOPQRSTUVWXYZ–$12345*

Semibold **abcdefghijklmnopqrstuvwxyzABCDEFGHIJKLMNOPQRSTUVWXYZ–$1234**

Semibold Oblique ***abcdefghijklmnopqrstuvwxyzABCDEFGHIJKLMNOPQRSTUVWXYZ–$1234***

Bold **abcdefghijklmnopqrstuvwxyzABCDEFGHIJKLMNOPQRSTUVWXYZ–$12**

Bold Oblique ***abcdefghijklmnopqrstuvwxyzABCDEFGHIJKLMNOPQRSTUVWXYZ–$12***

Extra Light Condensed abcdefghijklmnopqrstuvwxyzABCDEFGHIJKLMNOPQRSTUVWXYZ–$1234567890(".;'!*?':,")&fiflß-ä

Extra Light Condensed Oblique *abcdefghijklmnopqrstuvwxyzABCDEFGHIJKLMNOPQRSTUVWXYZ–$1234567890(".;'!*?':,")&fiflß-ä*

Light Condensed abcdefghijklmnopqrstuvwxyzABCDEFGHIJKLMNOPQRSTUVWXYZ–$1234567890(".;'!*?':,")&fi

Light Condensed Oblique *abcdefghijklmnopqrstuvwxyzABCDEFGHIJKLMNOPQRSTUVWXYZ–$1234567890(".;'!*?':,")&fi*

Condensed abcdefghijklmnopqrstuvwxyzABCDEFGHIJKLMNOPQRSTUVWXYZ–$1234567890(".;'!*?':,")

Condensed Oblique *abcdefghijklmnopqrstuvwxyzABCDEFGHIJKLMNOPQRSTUVWXYZ–$1234567890(".;'!*?':,")*

Semibold Condensed **abcdefghijklmnopqrstuvwxyzABCDEFGHIJKLMNOPQRSTUVWXYZ–$1234567890(".;'!*?':,**

Semibold Condensed Oblique ***abcdefghijklmnopqrstuvwxyzABCDEFGHIJKLMNOPQRSTUVWXYZ–$1234567890(".;'!*?':,***

Bold Condensed **abcdefghijklmnopqrstuvwxyzABCDEFGHIJKLMNOPQRSTUVWXYZ–$1234567890(".;'!***

Bold Condensed Oblique ***abcdefghijklmnopqrstuvwxyzABCDEFGHIJKLMNOPQRSTUVWXYZ–$1234567890(".;'!****

A

Avenida

John Chippindale • 1994

LET

▲30

ABCDEFGHIJKLMNOPQRSTUVWXYZ(“.;‘!*?’:,”)
$1234567890&-ÄÖÜÅÇÈÎÑÓÆØŒ
ABCDEFGHIJKLMNOPQRSTUVWXYZ
ÄÖÜÅÇÈÎÑÓÆØŒ»„«[•]‹¡·¿›...
▷ıºRS·ıºRS&1234567890oº

AVENIR

Adrian Frutiger • 1988

LIN ADO AGA MAE

abcdefghijklmnopqrstuvwxyz(“.;‘!*?’:,”)
$1234567890&fiflß-äöüåçèîñóæøœ
ABCDEFGHIJKLMNOPQRSTUVWXYZ
ÄÖÜÅÇÈÎÑÓÆØŒ»„«[¶§•†‡]‹¡·¿›...

Avenir 1 ...

35-Light abcdefghijklmnopqrstuvwxyzABCDEFGHIJKLMNOPQRSTUVWXYZ–$123456789

35-Light Oblique *abcdefghijklmnopqrstuvwxyzABCDEFGHIJKLMNOPQRSTUVWXYZ–$123456789*

• 55-Regular abcdefghijklmnopqrstuvwxyzABCDEFGHIJKLMNOPQRSTUVWXYZ–$12345678

55-Oblique *abcdefghijklmnopqrstuvwxyzABCDEFGHIJKLMNOPQRSTUVWXYZ–$12345678*

85-Heavy **abcdefghijklmnopqrstuvwxyzABCDEFGHIJKLMNOPQRSTUVWXYZ–$12345**

85-Heavy Oblique ***abcdefghijklmnopqrstuvwxyzABCDEFGHIJKLMNOPQRSTUVWXYZ–$12345***

Avenir 2 ...

45-Book abcdefghijklmnopqrstuvwxyzABCDEFGHIJKLMNOPQRSTUVWXYZ–$12345678

45-Book Oblique *abcdefghijklmnopqrstuvwxyzABCDEFGHIJKLMNOPQRSTUVWXYZ–$12345678*

65-Medium abcdefghijklmnopqrstuvwxyzABCDEFGHIJKLMNOPQRSTUVWXYZ–$1234567

65-Medium Oblique *abcdefghijklmnopqrstuvwxyzABCDEFGHIJKLMNOPQRSTUVWXYZ–$1234567*

95-Black **abcdefghijklmnopqrstuvwxyzABCDEFGHIJKLMNOPQRSTUVWXYZ–$1234**

95-Black Oblique ***abcdefghijklmnopqrstuvwxyzABCDEFGHIJKLMNOPQRSTUVWXYZ–$1234***

Avery Jean

INT

▲18

abcdefghijklmnopqrstuvwxyz(“.;‘!*?’:,”)
$1234567890&fiflß-äöüåçèîñóæøœ
ABCDEFGHIJKLMNOPQRSTUVWXYZ
ÄÖÜÅÇÈÎÑÓÆØŒ»„«[¶§•†‡]‹¡·¿›...

TF Avian Extra Bold
TF DisplaySet 1
Joseph Treacy • 1991

TRE MTD

▲18

abcdefghijklmnopqrstuvwxyz

("".;:'!*?':;")$1234567890&fifl ß-

äöüåçèîñóœøœ

ABCDEFGHIJKLMNOPQRSTUV

WXYZÄÖÜ ÅÇÈÎÑÓ ÆØŒ

»„«[¶ § • † ‡]‹¡ · ¿›...

▷ 123579/234816■□

TF DisplaySet 1: TF Akimbo Medium & TF Avian Extra Bold.

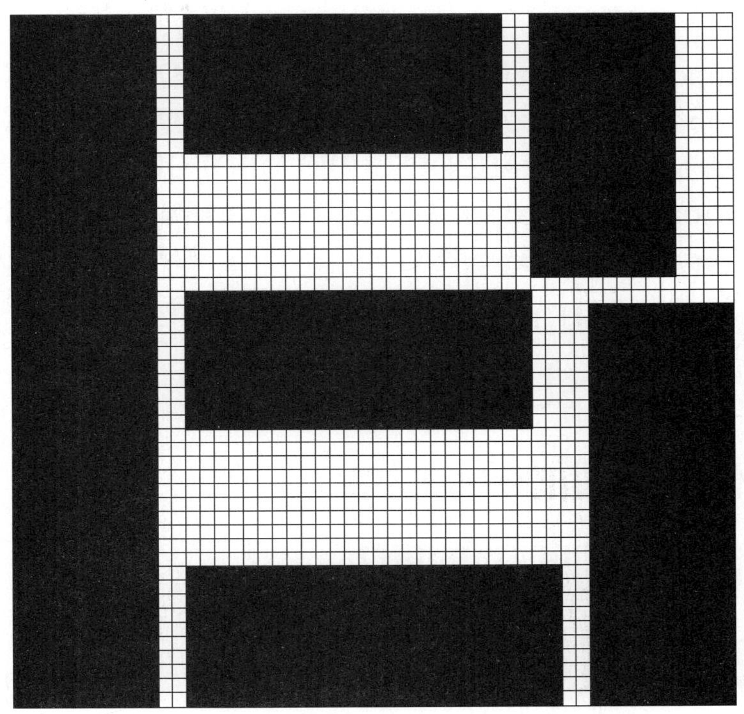

✍ Bart Van der Leck, 1942

B

BADGER

Pat Hickson • 1993

RED

abcdefghijklmnopqrstuvwxyz(".;'!*?':,")
$1234567890&ß-äöüåçèîñóæøœ
ABCDEFGHIJKLMNOPQRSTUVWXYZ
ÄÖÜÅÇÈÎÑÓÆØŒ»„«[¶§•†‡]‹¡·¿›...

Badger 1 ...

Light abcdefghijklmnopqrstuvwxyzABCDEFGHIJKLMNOPQRSTUVWXYZ-$1234567890(".;'!*?':,")&
Light Italic *abcdefghijklmnopqrstuvwxyzABCDEFGHIJKLMNOPQRSTUVWXYZ-$1234567890(".;'!*?':,")&*
Light SCOSF ABCDEFGHIJKLMNOPQRSTUVWXYZABCDEFGHIJKLMNOPQRSTUVWXYZ-$1234567890(".;'!*?':,")&-
Bold **abcdefghijklmnopqrstuvwxyzABCDEFGHIJKLMNOPQRSTUVWXYZ-$1234567890(".;**
Bold Italic ***abcdefghijklmnopqrstuvwxyzABCDEFGHIJKLMNOPQRSTUVWXYZ-$1234567890(".;***

Badger 2 ...

• Medium abcdefghijklmnopqrstuvwxyzABCDEFGHIJKLMNOPQRSTUVWXYZ-$1234567890(".;'!*?'
Medium Italic *abcdefghijklmnopqrstuvwxyzABCDEFGHIJKLMNOPQRSTUVWXYZ-$1234567890(".;'!*?'*
Medium SCOSF ABCDEFGHIJKLMNOPQRSTUVWXYZABCDEFGHIJKLMNOPQRSTUVWXYZ-$1234567890(".;'!*?':
Extra Bold **abcdefghijklmnopqrstuvwxyzABCDEFGHIJKLMNOPQRSTUVWXYZ-$123456789**
Extra Bold Italic ***abcdefghijklmnopqrstuvwxyzABCDEFGHIJKLMNOPQRSTUVWXYZ-$123456789***

BADLOC

Grant Hutchinson • 1989

IMA

▲24

abcdefghijklmnopqrstuvwxyz[".;'!?':,"]
$1234567890ß-äöüåçèîñóæøœ
ABCDEFGHIJKLMNOPQRSTUVWXYZ
ÄÖÜÅÇÈÎÑÓÆØŒ»„«[ ]¡·¿

Badloc ...

• Regular abcdefghijklmnopqrstuvwxyzABCDEFGHIJKLMNOPQRSTUVWXYZ-$12345
Bevel abcdefghijklmnopqrstuvwxyzABCDEFGHIJKLMNOPQRSTUVWXYZ-$12345
Compression
▲48 abcdefghijklmnopqrstuvwxyzABCDEF

B

BadTyp
Leslie Cabarga • 1993
FBU
▲24

ABCDeFGHiJKLMNOPQRSTUVWXYZ(".;'!*?':,")$1234567890&ß-ÄÖÜÅÇèÎÑÓÆØŒ
ABCDEFGHIJKLMNOPQRSTUVWXYZ
ÄÖÜÅÇÈÎÑÓÆØŒ»„«[¶§•]‹i•¿›...

▷

Baker Signet
Adobe DisplaySet 2
Arthur Baker • 1965
ADO AGA BIT TFC LIN MAE
▲16

abcdefghijklmnopqrstuvwxyz(".;'!*?':,")
$1234567890&fiflß-äöüåçèîñóæøœ
ABCDEFGHIJKLMNOPQRSTUVWXYZ
ÄÖÜÅÇÈÎÑÓÆØŒ»„«[¶§•†‡]‹¡·¿›...

BALLOON
M. R. Kaufmann • 1939
BIT TFC MTD URW
▲16

ABCDEFGHIJKLMNOPQRSTUVWXYZ(".;'!*?':,")
$1234567890&-ÄÖÜÅÇÈÎÑÓÆØŒ»„«[§•†‡]‹¡·¿›...

Balloon ...

Light ABCDEFGHIJKLMNOPQRSTUVWXYZ–$1234567890(".;'!*?':,")&-ÄÖÜÅÇÈÎÑÓÆØŒ«„»[§•†‡]‹¡·¿›...

• Bold ABCDEFGHIJKLMNOPQRSTUVWXYZ–$1234567890(".;'!*?':,")&-ÄÖÜÅÇÈÎÑÓÆØŒ«„»[§•†‡]‹

Extra Bold ABCDEFGHIJKLMNOPQRSTUVWXYZ–$1234567890(".;'!*?':,")&-ÄÖÜÅÇÈÎÑÓÆ

Balmoral
Martin Wait • 1978
LET URW
▲20

abcdefghijklmnopqrstuvwxyz(".;'!*?':,")
$1234567890&fiflß-äöüåçèîñóæøœ
ABCDEFGHIJKLMNOPQRSTUVWXYZ
Ç»„«[•]‹¡·¿›... ▷b g j y

Banco
Linotype DisplaySet 2
Roger Excoffon • 1951
ADO AGA LIN MAE
▲24

ABCDEFGHIJKLMNOPQRSTUVWXYZ(".;'!*?':,")
$1234567890&-ÄÖÜÅÇÈÎÑÓÆØŒ»„«[•]‹¡·¿›...

Adobe DisplaySet 2: Baker Signet, Impact.
Linotype DisplaySet 2: Banco, Charme, Flyer Black Condensed & Extra Black Condensed, Wilhelm Klingspor Gotisch.

B

BANK GOTHIC

Morris Fuller Benton • 1930 ABCDEFGHIJKLMNOPQRSTUVWXYZ(".;'!*?':,")

BIT $1234567890&-ÄÖÜÅÇÈÎÑÓÆØŒ

▲16 ABCDEFGHIJKLMNOPQRSTUVWXYZ

ÄÖÜÅÇÈÎÑÓÆØŒ»„«[§•†‡]‹¡·¿›...

Bank Gothic ...

Light ABCDEFGHIJKLMNOPQRSTUVWXYZABCDEFGHIJKLMNOPQRSTU

• Medium ABCDEFGHIJKLMNOPQRSTUVWXYZABCDEFGHIJKLMNOPQRS

BARBEDOR

Hans Eduard Meier • 1985 abcdefghijklmnopqrstuvwxyz(".;'!*?':,")

URW LEF $1234567890&fifl ß-äöüåçèîñóæøœ

ABCDEFGHIJKLMNOPQRSTUVWXYZ

ÄÖÜÅÇÈÎÑÓÆØŒ»„«[¶§•†‡]‹¡·¿›...

Barbedor 1 ...

• Regular abcdefghijklmnopqrstuvwxyzABCDEFGHIJKLMNOPQRSTUVWXYZ–$1234567890(".;'!*?':,

Italic *abcdefghijklmnopqrstuvwxyzABCDEFGHIJKLMNOPQRSTUVWXYZ–$1234567890(".;'!*?':,")&fifl*

Regular SCOSF ABCDEFGHIJKLMNOPQRSTUVWXYZABCDEFGHIJKLMNOPQRSTUVWXYZ–$1234567890(".;'!*?':,

Medium abcdefghijklmnopqrstuvwxyzABCDEFGHIJKLMNOPQRSTUVWXYZ–$1234567890(".;'

Medium Italic *abcdefghijklmnopqrstuvwxyzABCDEFGHIJKLMNOPQRSTUVWXYZ–$1234567890(".;'!*?':*

Medium SCOSF ABCDEFGHIJKLMNOPQRSTUVWXYZABCDEFGHIJKLMNOPQRSTUVWXYZ–$1234567890(".;"

Barbedor 2 ...

Bold **abcdefghijklmnopqrstuvwxyzABCDEFGHIJKLMNOPQRSTUVWXYZ–$1234567890**

Bold Italic ***abcdefghijklmnopqrstuvwxyzABCDEFGHIJKLMNOPQRSTUVWXYZ–$1234567890(".***

Heavy **abcdefghijklmnopqrstuvwxyzABCDEFGHIJKLMNOPQRSTUVWXYZ–$12345678**

Heavy Italic ***abcdefghijklmnopqrstuvwxyzABCDEFGHIJKLMNOPQRSTUVWXYZ–$12345678***

ITC BARCELONA

Ed Benguiat • 1981 abcdefghijklmnopqrstuvwxyz(".;'!*?':,")

LEF FRA $1234567890&fifl ß-äöüåçèîñóæøœ

ABCDEFGHIJKLMNOPQRSTUVWXYZ

ÄÖÜÅÇÈÎÑÓÆØŒ»„«[¶§•†‡]‹¡·¿›...

ITC Barcelona 1 ...

• Book abcdefghijklmnopqrstuvwxyzABCDEFGHIJKLMNOPQRSTUVWXYZ–$1

Book Italic *abcdefghijklmnopqrstuvwxyzABCDEFGHIJKLMNOPQRSTUVWXYZ–$12*

Bold **abcdefghijklmnopqrstuvwxyzABCDEFGHIJKLMNOPQRSTUVWXYZ–$123**

Bold Italic ***abcdefghijklmnopqrstuvwxyzABCDEFGHIJKLMNOPQRSTUVWXYZ–$1234***

B

ITC Barcelona 2 . . .

Medium abcdefghijklmnopqrstuvwxyzABCDEFGHIJKLMNOPQRSTUVWXYZ–$1

Medium Italic *abcdefghijklmnopqrstuvwxyzABCDEFGHIJKLMNOPQRSTUVWXYZ–$12*

Heavy **abcdefghijklmnopqrstuvwxyzABCDEFGHIJKLMNOPQRSTUVWXYZ–$1**

Heavy Italic ***abcdefghijklmnopqrstuvwxyzABCDEFGHIJKLMNOPQRSTUVWXYZ–$12***

Barclay Open
✣ *Agfa Typographer's Edition 3*
AGP

abcdefghijklmnopqrstuvwxyz(“.;‘!*?’:,”)

▲20 $1234567890&-äöüåçèîñóæøœ

ABCDEFGHIJKLMNOPQRSTUVWXYZ

ÄÖÜÅÇÈÎÑÓÆØŒ»„«[•]‹¿·¿›...

BARMENO

✍ *Hans Reichel • 1983* abcdefghijklmnopqrstuvwxyz(“.;‘!*?’:,”)

ADO AGA MAE $1234567890&fiflß-äöüåçèîñóæøœ

ABCDEFGHIJKLMNOPQRSTUVWXYZ

ÄÖÜÅÇÈÎÑÓÆØŒ»„«[¶§•†‡]‹¡·¿›...

Barmeno . . .

• Regular abcdefghijklmnopqrstuvwxyzABCDEFGHIJKLMNOPQRSTUVWXYZ–$1234567890(“.;‘!*?

Medium abcdefghijklmnopqrstuvwxyzABCDEFGHIJKLMNOPQRSTUVWXYZ–$1234567890(“.;‘!

Bold **abcdefghijklmnopqrstuvwxyzABCDEFGHIJKLMNOPQRSTUVWXYZ–$1234567890(“.;‘!***

Extra Bold ▲18 **abcdefghijklmnopqrstuvwxyzABCDEFGHIJKLMNOPQRSTUVWXYZ–**

Barmeno Extra Bold
✣ *Berthold DisplaySet 1*
ADO AGA MAE

abcdefghijklmnopqrstuvwxyz(“.;‘!*?’:,”)

▲24 **$1234567890&fiflß-äöüåçèîñóæøœ**

ABCDEFGHIJKLMNOPQRSTUVWXYZ

ÄÖÜÅÇÈÎÑÓÆØŒ»„«[¶§•†‡]‹¡·¿›...

✣ *Agfa Typographer's Edition 3*: Barclay Open, PL Bernhardt Light, Medium & Bold, PL Britannia Bold, Delphian Open, PL Fiorello Condensed, Fluidium Bold, PL Modern Heavy Condensed, PL Torino Open.
✣ *Berthold DisplaySet 1*: AG Book Stencil, AG Old Face Shaded, Barmeno Extra Bold, Cosmos Extra Bold, Formata Outline.

B

PL Barnum Block
✣ *Agfa Typographer's Edition 2*
AGP
▲30

abcdefghijklmnopqrstuvwxyz
(".;'!*?':,")$1234567890&ß-äöüåçèî
ñóæøœABCDEFGHIJKLMNOPQRSTU
VWXYZÄÖÜÅÇÈÎÑÓÆØŒ»„«[§•†‡]‹¡

A*I Barrel
✣ *A*I Wood Type*
✍ *A*I Design Staff • 1990*
ALP MTD
▲36

ABCDEFGHIJKLMNOPQRS
TUVWXYZ(.;!*?:,)$12345678
90&-ABCDEFGHIJKLMNO
PQRSTUVWXYZ[]

BASILIA
✍ *André Gürtler • 1978*
AGP

abcdefghijklmnopqrstuvwxyz(".;'!*?':,")
$1234567890&fiflß-äöüåçèîñóæøœ
ABCDEFGHIJKLMNOPQRSTUVWXYZ
ÄÖÜÅÇÈÎÑÓÆØŒ»„«[¶§•†‡]‹¡·¿›…

Basilia …

• Roman abcdefghijklmnopqrstuvwxyzABCDEFGHIJKLMNOPQRSTUVWXYZ–$123456

Italic *abcdefghijklmnopqrstuvwxyzABCDEFGHIJKLMNOPQRSTUVWXYZ–$123456*

Medium abcdefghijklmnopqrstuvwxyzABCDEFGHIJKLMNOPQRSTUVWXYZ–$12345

Medium Italic *abcdefghijklmnopqrstuvwxyzABCDEFGHIJKLMNOPQRSTUVWXYZ–$1234*

Bold **abcdefghijklmnopqrstuvwxyzABCDEFGHIJKLMNOPQRSTUVWXYZ–$123**

Bold Italic ***abcdefghijklmnopqrstuvwxyzABCDEFGHIJKLMNOPQRSTUVWXYZ–$123***

Black **abcdefghijklmnopqrstuvwxyzABCDEFGHIJKLMNOPQRSTUVWXYZ–$12**

Black Italic ***abcdefghijklmnopqrstuvwxyzABCDEFGHIJKLMNOPQRSTUVWXYZ–$1***

✣ *Agfa Typographer's Edition 2*: PL Barnum Block, PL Benguiat Frisky Bold, TC Broadway, PL Davison Zip Bold, PL Fiedler Gothic Bold, PL Futura Maxi Book & Bold, Neon Extra Condensed, Ritmo Bold, PL Trophy Oblique.
✣ *A*I Wood Type*: A*I Antique Condensed, A*I Barrel, A*I Box Gothic, A*I French XXX Condensed, A*I Painter, A*I Tuscan Egyptian.

B

Basilica
Agfa ScriptSet 1
AGP ▲18

abcdefghijklmnopqrstuvwxyz(".;'!?':,")*
$1234567890&ß-äöüåçèîñóœøœ
ABCDEFGHIJKLMNOPQRSTUVWXYZ
ÄÖÜÅÇÈÎÑÓÆØŒ»„«[§•†‡]‹¡·¿›...

MONOTYPE BASKERVILLE

Monotype Design Staff • 1923
... John Baskervile, 1757
MCL

abcdefghijklmnopqrstuvwxyz(".;'!*?':,")
$1234567890&fiflß-äöüåçèîñóæøœ
ABCDEFGHIJKLMNOPQRSTUVWXYZ
ÄÖÜÅÇÈÎÑÓÆØŒ»„«[¶§•†‡]‹¡·¿›...

Monotype Baskerville ...

• Roman abcdefghijklmnopqrstuvwxyzABCDEFGHIJKLMNOPQRSTUVWXYZ–$123456789

Italic *abcdefghijklmnopqrstuvwxyzABCDEFGHIJKLMNOPQRSTUVWXYZ–$1234567890(".;'!*?':,"*

Semibold **abcdefghijklmnopqrstuvwxyzABCDEFGHIJKLMNOPQRSTUVWXYZ–$1234**

Semibold Italic ***abcdefghijklmnopqrstuvwxyzABCDEFGHIJKLMNOPQRSTUVWXYZ–$1234567***

Bold **abcdefghijklmnopqrstuvwxyzABCDEFGHIJKLMNOPQRSTUVWXYZ–$123**

Bold Italic ***abcdefghijklmnopqrstuvwxyzABCDEFGHIJKLMNOPQRSTUVWXYZ–$12345***

MONOTYPE BASKERVILLE EXPERT

MCL

ABCDEFGHIJKLMNOPQRSTUVWXYZ.;!?:,
$1234567890&ffffiflffiffl–ÄÖÜÅÇÈÎÑÓÆØŒ
(abdeilmnorst) 1/8 1/4 1/3 3/8 1/2 5/8 2/3 3/4 7/8 $12345/67890¢ ₡Rp

Monotype Baskerville Expert ...

• Expert Roman ABCDEFGHIJKLMNOPQRSTUVWXYZ–$1234567890.;!?:,&-ffffiflffiffl 1/8 1/4 1/3 3/8 1/2 $12345/67890¢ (abdei

Expert Italic *$1234567890.;:,–ffffiflffiffl 1/8 1/4 1/3 3/8 1/2 $12345/67890¢ (abdeilmnorst) 5/8 2/3 3/4 7/8 ₡Rp*

Expert Semibold **$1234567890.;:,–ffffiflffiffl 1/8 1/4 1/3 3/8 1/2 $12345/67890¢ (abdeilmnorst) 5/8 2/3 3/4 7/8 ₡Rp**

Expert Semibold Italic ***$1234567890.;:,–ffffiflffiffl 1/8 1/4 1/3 3/8 1/2 $12345/67890¢ (abdeilmnorst) 5/8 2/3 3/4 7/8 ₡Rp***

Expert Bold **$1234567890.;:,–ffffiflffiffl 1/8 1/4 1/3 3/8 1/2 $12345/67890¢ (abdeilmnorst) 5/8 2/3 3/4 7/8 ₡Rp**

Expert Bold Italic ***$1234567890.;:,–ffffiflffiffl 1/8 1/4 1/3 3/8 1/2 $12345/67890¢ (abdeilmnorst) 5/8 2/3 3/4 7/8 ₡Rp***

Fry's Baskerville

Isaac Moore • 1764
... John Baskervile, 1757
BIT ▲24

abcdefghijklmnopqrstuvwxyz(".;'!*?':,")
$1234567890&fiflß-äöüåçèîñóæøœ
ABCDEFGHIJKLMNOPQRSTUVWXYZ
ÄÖÜÅÇÈÎÑÓÆØŒ»„«[§•†‡]‹¡·¿›...

Agfa ScriptSet 1: Basilica, Floridian Script, Jasper, Liberty.

B

ITC NEW BASKERVILLE

Linotype Design Staff • 1978
... John Baskervile, 1757
LIN ADO AGA BIT LEF FAM MAE URW

abcdefghijklmnopqrstuvwxyz(“.;‘!*?’:,”)
$1234567890&fiflß-äöüåçèîñóæøœ
ABCDEFGHIJKLMNOPQRSTUVWXYZ
ÄÖÜÅÇÈÎÑÓÆØŒ»„«[¶§•†‡]‹¡·¿›...

ITC New Baskerville ...

• Roman abcdefghijklmnopqrstuvwxyzABCDEFGHIJKLMNOPQRSTUVWXYZ–$123456789

Italic *abcdefghijklmnopqrstuvwxyzABCDEFGHIJKLMNOPQRSTUVWXYZ–$1234567890(“.;‘!**

Bold **abcdefghijklmnopqrstuvwxyzABCDEFGHIJKLMNOPQRSTUVWXYZ–$12345678**

Bold Italic ***abcdefghijklmnopqrstuvwxyzABCDEFGHIJKLMNOPQRSTUVWXYZ–$1234567890(“.;‘!***

ITC NEW BASKERVILLE SCOSF

LIN ADO AGA MAE

ABCDEFGHIJKLMNOPQRSTUVWXYZ(“.;‘!*?’:,”)
$1234567890&-ÄÖÜÅÇÈÎÑÓÆØŒ
ABCDEFGHIJKLMNOPQRSTUVWXYZ
ÄÖÜÅÇÈÎÑÓÆØŒ»„«[¶§•†‡]‹¡·¿›...

ITC New Baskerville SCOSF ...

• Roman SCOSF ABCDEFGHIJKLMNOPQRSTUVWXYZABCDEFGHIJKLMNOPQRSTUVWXYZ–$12345

Italic OSF *abcdefghijklmnopqrstuvwxyzABCDEFGHIJKLMNOPQRSTUVWXYZ–$1234567890(“.;‘!*

Bold SCOSF **ABCDEFGHIJKLMNOPQRSTUVWXYZABCDEFGHIJKLMNOPQRSTUVWXYZ–$123**

Bold Italic OSF ***abcdefghijklmnopqrstuvwxyzABCDEFGHIJKLMNOPQRSTUVWXYZ–$1234567890(“.;***

BERTHOLD BASKERVILLE

Günter Gerhard Lange • 1980
... John Baskervile, 1757
ADO AGA MAE

abcdefghijklmnopqrstuvwxyz(“.;‘!*?’:,”)
$1234567890&fiflß-äöüåçèîñóæøœ
ABCDEFGHIJKLMNOPQRSTUVWXYZ
ÄÖÜÅÇÈÎÑÓÆØŒ»„«[¶§•†‡]‹¡·¿›...

Berthold Baskerville ...

• Roman abcdefghijklmnopqrstuvwxyzABCDEFGHIJKLMNOPQRSTUVWXYZ–$12345

Italic *abcdefghijklmnopqrstuvwxyzABCDEFGHIJKLMNOPQRSTUVWXYZ–$1234567890(“.;*

Medium **abcdefghijklmnopqrstuvwxyzABCDEFGHIJKLMNOPQRSTUVWXYZ–$12**

Medium Italic ***abcdefghijklmnopqrstuvwxyzABCDEFGHIJKLMNOPQRSTUVWXYZ–$12345678***

Bold **abcdefghijklmnopqrstuvwxyzABCDEFGHIJKLMNOPQRSTUVWXYZ**

BERTHOLD BASKERVILLE BOOK

Günter Gerhard Lange • 1980
... John Baskervile, 1757
ADO AGA MAE

abcdefghijklmnopqrstuvwxyz(“.;‘!*?’:,”)
$1234567890&fiflß-äöüåçèîñóæøœ
ABCDEFGHIJKLMNOPQRSTUVWXYZ
ÄÖÜÅÇÈÎÑÓÆØŒ»„«[¶§•†‡]‹¡·¿›...

B

... Berthold Baskerville Book ...

• Roman abcdefghijklmnopqrstuvwxyzABCDEFGHIJKLMNOPQRSTUVWXYZ–$1234567

Italic *abcdefghijklmnopqrstuvwxyzABCDEFGHIJKLMNOPQRSTUVWXYZ–$1234567890(".;'!**

Medium **abcdefghijklmnopqrstuvwxyzABCDEFGHIJKLMNOPQRSTUVWXYZ–$123**

Medium Italic ***abcdefghijklmnopqrstuvwxyzABCDEFGHIJKLMNOPQRSTUVWXYZ–$1234567***

Basque
Agfa DisplaySet 3

AGP abcdefghijklmnopqrstuvwxyz(".;'!*?':,")

▲18 $1234567890&ß-äöüåçèîñóæøœ

ABCDEFGHIJKLMNOPQRSTUVWXYZ

ÄÖÜÅÇÈÎÑÓÆØŒ»„«[¶§•†‡]‹¡·¿›...

Bassuto

Paul Hickson • 1994 (Stephenson Blake, 1927)

RED

▲24

ABCDEFGHIJKLMNOPQRSTUVWXYZ

(".;'!*?':,")$1234567890

&-ÄÖÜÅÇÈÎÑÓÆØŒ»„«[¶·†‡]‹¡·¿›...

ITC BAUHAUS

Ed Benguiat & Victor Caruso • 1975 (Herbert Bayer, 1925)

LIN ADO AGA AGP BIT LEF MAE URW

▲16

abcdefghijklmnopqrstuvwxyz(".;'!*?':,")

$1234567890&fiflß-äöüåçèîñóæøœ

ABCDEFGHIJKLMNOPQRSTUVWXYZ

ÄÖÜÅÇÈÎÑÓÆØŒ»„«[¶§•†‡]‹¡·¿›...

ITC Bauhaus ...

Light abcdefghijklmnopqrstuvwxyzABCDEFGHIJKLMNOPQRSTUVWXYZ–$123456

• Medium abcdefghijklmnopqrstuvwxyzABCDEFGHIJKLMNOPQRSTUVWXYZ–$123456

Demi **abcdefghijklmnopqrstuvwxyzABCDEFGHIJKLMNOPQRSTUVWXYZ–$12345**

Bold **abcdefghijklmnopqrstuvwxyzABCDEFGHIJKLMNOPQRSTUVWXYZ–$123**

Heavy **abcdefghijklmnopqrstuvwxyzABCDEFGHIJKLMNOPQRSTUVWXYZ–$**

FC BEACON

TFC abcdefghijklmnopqrstuvwxyz(".;'!*?':,")

$1234567890&ß-äöüèîñó

ABCDEFGHIJKLMNOPQRSTUVWXYZ

ÄÖÜÈÎÑÓ»„«[¶§·†‡]‹¡·¿›...

FC Beacon ...

Light abcdefghijklmnopqrstuvwxyzABCDEFGHIJKLMNOPQRSTUVWXYZ–$1234567890(".;'!*?'

Agfa DisplaySet 3: Basque, Brophy Script, Chevalier, Uncial.

B

... FC Beacon

• Medium abcdefghijklmnopqrstuvwxyzABCDEFGHIJKLMNOPQRSTUVWXYZ–$1234567890(".

Bold abcdefghijklmnopqrstuvwxyzABCDEFGHIJKLMNOPQRSTUVWXYZ–$123456789

Becka Script

David Harris • 1985

LET

abcdefghijklmnopqrstuvwxyz(".;'!*?':,")
$1234567890&fiflß-äöüåçèîñóæøœ
ABCDEFGHIJKLMNOPQRSTUVWXYZ
ÄÖÜÅÇÈÎÑÓÆØŒ»„«[•]‹¡·¿›...

BECKENHAM

Leslie Usherwood • ....

RED

abcdefghijklmnopqrstuvwxyz(".;'!*?':,")
$1234567890&fiflß-äöüåçèîñóæøœ
ABCDEFGHIJKLMNOPQRSTUVWXYZ
ÄÖÜÅÇÈÎÑÓÆØŒ»„«[¶§·†‡]‹¡·¿›...

Beckenham ...

Light abcdefghijklmnopqrstuvwxyzABCDEFGHIJKLMNOPQRSTUVWXYZ–$1234567890(".;'!*?':,")&fiflß-äöüÄÖÜå

• Medium abcdefghijklmnopqrstuvwxyzABCDEFGHIJKLMNOPQRSTUVWXYZ–$1234567890(".;'!*?'

Bold abcdefghijklmnopqrstuvwxyzABCDEFGHIJKLMNOPQRSTUVWXYZ–$1234567890(".;

Extra Bold abcdefghijklmnopqrstuvwxyzABCDEFGHIJKLMNOPQRSTUVWXYZ–$123456789

Beebopp

Greg Kolodziejzyk • 1989

IMA

▲30

ABCDEFGHIJKLMNOPQRSTU
VWXYZ(".;'!*?':,")$1234567890
&-ÄÖÜÅÇÈÎÑÓÆØŒ[•]¡·¿...

ITC Beesknees
ITC Typographica

David Farey • 1990

ADO AGA AGP LEF ITC LIN MAE URW

▲36

ABCDEFGHIJKLMNOPQRSTU
VWXYZ(".;'!*?':,")$123456
7890&-ÄÖÜÅÇÈÎÑÓÆØŒ»

ITC Typographica: ITC Anna, ITC Beesknees, ITC Mona Lisa Recut & Solid, ITC Ozwald.

BELL

✍ *Monotype Design Staff • 1930*
… Richard Austin, 1788
MCL URW

abcdefghijklmnopqrstuvwxyz(“.;‘!*?’:,”)
$1234567890&fiflß-äöüåçèîñóæøœ
ABCDEFGHIJKLMNOPQRSTUVWXYZ
ÄÖÜÅÇÈÎÑÓÆØŒ»„«[¶§•†‡]‹¡·¿›…

Bell …

• Roman abcdefghijklmnopqrstuvwxyzABCDEFGHIJKLMNOPQRSTUVWXYZ–$123456789
Italic *abcdefghijklmnopqrstuvwxyzABCDEFGHIJKLMNOPQRSTUVWXYZ–$1234567890(“.;‘*
Semibold abcdefghijklmnopqrstuvwxyzABCDEFGHIJKLMNOPQRSTUVWXYZ–$12345678
Semibold Italic *abcdefghijklmnopqrstuvwxyzABCDEFGHIJKLMNOPQRSTUVWXYZ–$1234567890(*
Bold **abcdefghijklmnopqrstuvwxyzABCDEFGHIJKLMNOPQRSTUVWXYZ–$123456**
Bold Italic ***abcdefghijklmnopqrstuvwxyzABCDEFGHIJKLMNOPQRSTUVWXYZ–$1234567***

BELL EXPERT

MCL ABCDEFGHIJKLMNOPQRSTUVWXYZ.;!?:,
$1234567890&ff fi fl ffi ffl–ÄÖÜÅÇÈÎÑÓÆØŒ
(abdeilmnorst) ⅛ ¼ ⅓ ⅜ ½ ⅝ ⅔ ¾ ⅞ $12345/67890¢ ₡Rp ▷JKQR

Bell Expert …

• Expert Roman ABCDEFGHIJKLMNOPQRSTUVWXYZ–$1234567890.;!?:,&–ff fi fl ffi ffl ⅛ ¼ ⅓ ⅜ ½ $12345/67890¢ (abdeil
Expert Italic *$1234567890.; :,–ff fi fl ffi ffl ⅛ ¼ ⅓ ⅜ ½ $12345/67890¢ (abdeilmnorst) ⅝ ⅔ ¾ ⅞ ₡Rp*
Expert Roman, Roman & Italic Alternate ▷JKQR k JKQR *h k A J J K N Q R T V Y Æ*
Expert Semibold ABCDEFGHIJKLMNOPQRSTUVWXYZ–$1234567890.;!?:,&–ff fi fl ffi ffl ⅛ ¼ ⅓ ⅜ ½ $12345/67890¢ (abd
Expert Semibold Italic *$1234567890.; :,–ff fi fl ffi ffl ⅛ ¼ ⅓ ⅜ ½ $12345/67890¢ (abdeilmnorst) ⅝ ⅔ ¾ ⅞ ₡Rp*
Expert Semibold, Semibold & Semibold Italic Alternate ▷JKQR k JKQR *h k A J J K N Q R T V Y Æ*
Expert Bold **$1234567890.; :,–ff fi fl ffi ffl ⅛ ¼ ⅓ ⅜ ½ $12345/67890¢ (abdeilmnorst) ⅝ ⅔ ¾ ⅞ ₡Rp**
Expert Bold Italic ***$1234567890.; :,–ff fi fl ffi ffl ⅛ ¼ ⅓ ⅜ ½ $12345/67890¢ (abdeilmnorst) ⅝ ⅔ ¾ ⅞ ₡Rp***

BELL GOTHIC

✍ *C. H. Griffith • 1938*
LIN ADO AGA BIT MAE

abcdefghijklmnopqrstuvwxyz(“.;‘!*?’:,”)
$1234567890&fiflß-äöüåçèîñóæøœ
ABCDEFGHIJKLMNOPQRSTUVWXYZ
ÄÖÜÅÇÈÎÑÓÆØŒ»„«[¶§•†‡]‹¡·¿›…

Bell Gothic …

Light abcdefghijklmnopqrstuvwxyzABCDEFGHIJKLMNOPQRSTUVWXYZ–$1234567890
• Bold abcdefghijklmnopqrstuvwxyzABCDEFGHIJKLMNOPQRSTUVWXYZ–$123456789
Black **abcdefghijklmnopqrstuvwxyzABCDEFGHIJKLMNOPQRSTUVWXYZ–$1234567**

B

BELL CENTENNIAL

Matthew Carter • 1978
LIN ADO AGA BIT MAE

abcdefghijklmnopqrstuvwxyz(".;'!*?':,")
$1234567890&fiflß-äöüåçèîñóæøœ
ABCDEFGHIJKLMNOPQRSTUVWXYZ
ÄÖÜÅÇÈÎÑÓÆØŒ»„«[¶§•†‡]‹¡·¿›...

Bell Centennial ...

• Name & Number abcdefghijklmnopqrstuvwxyzABCDEFGHIJKLMNOPQRSTUVWXYZ–$1234567890(
Address abcdefghijklmnopqrstuvwxyzABCDEFGHIJKLMNOPQRSTUVWXYZ–$1234567890(".;'!*?':,")&fiflß-ä
Sub Caption abcdefghijklmnopqrstuvwxyzABCDEFGHIJKLMNOPQRSTUVWXYZ–$1234567890(".;'!*?':,
Bold Listing ABCDEFGHIJKLMNOPQRSTUVWXYZABCDEFGHIJKLMNOPQRSTUVWXYZ-$1
Bold Listing Alternate ABCDEFGHIJKLMNOPQRSTUVWXYZABCDEFGHIJKLMNOPQRSTUVWXYZ-$1

Bellevue
Berthold ScriptSet 1
Gustav Jaeger • 1986
ADO AGA MAE URW

abcdefghijklmnopqrstuvwxyz(".;'!?':,")*
$1234567890&fiflß-äöüåçèîñóæøœ
ABCDEFGHIJKLMNOPQRSTUVWXYZ
ÄÖÜÅÇÈÎÑÓÆØŒ»„«[•]‹¡·¿›...

BELUCIAN

David Berlow • 1988
... Lucian Bernhard, 1937
FBU AGP MTD

abcdefghijklmnopqrstuvwxyz(".;'!*?':,")
$1234567890&fiflß-äöüåçèîñóæøœ
▲16 ABCDEFGHIJKLMNOPQRSTUVWXYZ
ÄÖÜÅÇÈÎÑÓÆØŒ»„«[¶§•†‡]‹¡·¿›...

▷ ff ffi ffl ft

BeLucian ...

• Book abcdefghijklmnopqrstuvwxyzABCDEFGHIJKLMNOPQRSTUVWXYZ–$
Book Italic *abcdefghijklmnopqrstuvwxyzABCDEFGHIJKLMNOPQRSTUVWXYZ–$12345*
Demi abcdefghijklmnopqrstuvwxyzABCDEFGHIJKLMNOPQRSTUVWXYZ–
Ultra **abcdefghijklmnopqrstuvwxyzABCDEFGHIJKLMNOPQRSTUVW**

BELWE

Georg Belwe • 1926
LEF ADO AGA BIT FAM LIN MAE URW

abcdefghijklmnopqrstuvwxyz(".;'!*?' ,")
$1234567890&fiflß-äöüåçèîñóæøœ
▲16 ABCDEFGHIJKLMNOPQRSTUVWXYZ
ÄÖÜÅÇÈÎÑÓÆØŒ»„«[•]‹¡·¿›...

Belwe ...

Light abcdefghijklmnopqrstuvwxyzABCDEFGHIJKLMNOPQRSTUVWXYZ$1234567
Light Italic *abcdefghijklmnopqrstuvwxyzABCDEFGHIJKLMNOPQRSTUVWXYZ$123456*
• Medium **abcdefghijklmnopqrstuvwxyzABCDEFGHIJKLMNOPQRSTUVWXYZ$12**

...
Berthold ScriptSet 1: Bellevue, Berthold Script Regular & Medium, Boulevard.

B

... Belwe

Bold abcdefghijklmnopqrstuvwxyzABCDEFGHIJKLMNOPQRSTUVWXYZ

Bold Condensed abcdefghijklmnopqrstuvwxyzABCDEFGHIJKLMNOPQRSTUVWXYZ$123456789

Belwe Mono

Alan Meeks • 1989 ... Georg Belwe, 1926

LET ▲16

abcdefghijklmnopqrstuvwxyz(".;'!*?':,")
$1234567890&fiflß-äöüåçèîñóæøœ
ABCDEFGHIJKLMNOPQRSTUVWXYZ
ÄÖÜÅÇÈÎÑÓÆØŒ»„«[•]‹¡·¿›...

Belwe Mono Italic

LET ▲16

abcdefghijklmnopqrstuvwxyz(".;'!?':,")*
$1234567890&fiflß-äöüåçèîñóæøœ
ABCDEFGHIJKLMNOPQRSTUVWXYZ
ÄÖÜÅÇÈÎÑÓÆØŒ»„«[•]‹¡·¿›...

BEMBO

Monotype Design Staff • 1929 (Francesco Griffo, 1495 – Giovantonio Tagliente, 1524)

MCL ADO AGA LIN MAE

abcdefghijklmnopqrstuvwxyz(".;'!★?':,")
$1234567890&fiflß-äöüåçèîñóæøœ
ABCDEFGHIJKLMNOPQRSTUVWXYZ
ÄÖÜÅÇÈÎÑÓÆØŒ»„«[¶§•†‡]‹¡·¿›...

Bembo 1 ...

• Roman abcdefghijklmnopqrstuvwxyzABCDEFGHIJKLMNOPQRSTUVWXYZ–$1234567890(

Italic *abcdefghijklmnopqrstuvwxyzABCDEFGHIJKLMNOPQRSTUVWXYZ–$1234567890(".;'*

Bold **abcdefghijklmnopqrstuvwxyzABCDEFGHIJKLMNOPQRSTUVWXYZ–$12345**

Bold Italic ***abcdefghijklmnopqrstuvwxyzABCDEFGHIJKLMNOPQRSTUVWXYZ–$1234567890(***

Bembo 2 ...

Semibold abcdefghijklmnopqrstuvwxyzABCDEFGHIJKLMNOPQRSTUVWXYZ–$1234567

Semibold Italic *abcdefghijklmnopqrstuvwxyzABCDEFGHIJKLMNOPQRSTUVWXYZ–$1234567890("*

Extra Bold **abcdefghijklmnopqrstuvwxyzABCDEFGHIJKLMNOPQRSTUVWXYZ–$12**

Extra Bold Italic ***abcdefghijklmnopqrstuvwxyzABCDEFGHIJKLMNOPQRSTUVWXYZ–$1234567***

BEMBO EXPERT

MCL ADO AGA MAE

ABCDEFGHIJKLMNOPQRSTUVWXYZ.;!?:,
$1234567890&ffﬁﬂﬃﬄ–ÄÖÜÅÇÈÎÑÓÆØŒ
(abdeilmnorst) ⅛ ¼ ⅓ ⅜ ½ ⅝ ⅔ ¾ ⅞ $12345/67890¢ ₡Rp

▷ R

Bembo Expert 1 ...

• Expert Roman ABCDEFGHIJKLMNOPQRSTUVWXYZ–$1234567890.;!?:,&-ffﬁﬂﬃﬄ ⅛ ¼ ⅓ ⅜ ½ $12345/67890¢ (abdeil

Expert Italic *$1234567890.;:,–ffﬁﬂﬃﬄ ⅛ ¼ ⅓ ⅜ ½ $12345/67890¢ (abdeilmnorst) ⅝ ⅔ ¾ ⅞ ₡Rp*

Expert Bold **$1234567890.;:,–ffﬁﬂﬃﬄ ⅛ ¼ ⅓ ⅜ ½ $12345/67890¢ (abdeilmnorst) ⅝ ⅔ ¾ ⅞ ₡Rp**

B

... Bembo Expert 1

Expert Bold Italic $1234567890.;:,–ﬀﬁﬂﬃﬄ 1/8 1/4 1/3 3/8 1/2 $12345/67890¢ (abdeilmnorst) 5/8 2/3 3/4 7/8 ₡Rp

Roman, Italic, Bold & Bold Italic Alternate ▷ R R R R

Bembo Expert 2 ...

Expert Semibold ABCDEFGHIJKLMNOPQRSTUVWXYZ–$1234567890.;!?:,&–ﬀﬁﬂﬃﬄ 1/8 1/4 1/3 3/8 1/2 $12345/67890¢ (abd

Expert Semibold Italic $1234567890.;:,–ﬀﬁﬂﬃﬄ 1/8 1/4 1/3 3/8 1/2 $12345/67890¢ (abdeilmnorst) 5/8 2/3 3/4 7/8 ₡Rp

Expert Extra Bold $1234567890.;:,–ﬀﬁﬂﬃﬄ 1/8 1/4 1/3 3/8 1/2 $12345/67890¢ (abdeilmnorst) 5/8 2/3 3/4 7/8 ₡Rp

Expert Extra Bold Italic $1234567890.;:,–ﬀﬁﬂﬃﬄ 1/8 1/4 1/3 3/8 1/2 $12345/67890¢ (abdeilmnorst) 5/8 2/3 3/4 7/8 ₡Rp

Semibold, Semibold Italic & Bold Alternate ▷ R R R

Bendigo

Phill Grimshaw • 1993 abcdefghijklmnopqrstuvwxyz(“.;‘!*?’:,”)

LET $1234567890&ﬁﬂß-äöüåçèîñóæøœ

▲16 ABCDEFGHIJKLMNOPQRSTUVWXYZ

ÄÖÜÅÇÈÎÑÓÆØŒ»„«[•]‹¡·¿›...

▷ cdegikkmnoqrsttvyyzffffft thtt——— KLQRYZ

A*I Benedict Uncial

Philip Bouwsma • 1994 ABCDEFGHIJKLMNOPQRSTUVWXYZ(“.;‘!*?’:,”)

ALP $1234567890&ß-ÄÖÜÅÇÈÎÑÓÆØŒ

▲16 ABCDEFGHIJKLMNOPQRSTUVWXYZ

ÄÖÜÅÇÈÎÑÓÆØŒ»„«[¶§•†‡]‹¡·¿›...

ITC BENGUIAT

Ed Benguiat • 1978 abcdefghijklmnopqrstuvwxyz(“.;‘!*?’:,”)

BIT ADO AGA LEF LIN MAE URW $1234567890&ﬁﬂß-äöüåçèîñóæøœ

ABCDEFGHIJKLMNOPQRSTUVWXYZ

ÄÖÜÅÇÈÎÑÓÆØŒ»„«[§•†‡]‹¡·¿›...

ITC Benguiat ...

• Book abcdefghijklmnopqrstuvwxyzABCDEFGHIJKLMNOPQRSTUVWXYZ–$1234567

Book Italic *abcdefghijklmnopqrstuvwxyzABCDEFGHIJKLMNOPQRSTUVWXYZ–$123456*

Medium abcdefghijklmnopqrstuvwxyzABCDEFGHIJKLMNOPQRSTUVWXYZ–$12345

Medium Italic *abcdefghijklmnopqrstuvwxyzABCDEFGHIJKLMNOPQRSTUVWXYZ–$12345*

Bold **abcdefghijklmnopqrstuvwxyzABCDEFGHIJKLMNOPQRSTUVWXYZ–$12**

Bold Italic ***abcdefghijklmnopqrstuvwxyzABCDEFGHIJKLMNOPQRSTUVWXYZ–$1***

B

ITC BENGUIAT CONDENSED

Ed Benguiat • 1978 abcdefghijklmnopqrstuvwxyz(".;'!*?':,")
BIT ADO AGA LEF LIN MAE URW $1234567890&fiflß-äöüåçèîñóæøœ
ABCDEFGHIJKLMNOPQRSTUVWXYZ
ÄÖÜÅÇÈÎÑÓÆØŒ»„«[§•†‡]‹¡·¿›...

ITC Benguiat Condensed ...

• Book Condensed abcdefghijklmnopqrstuvwxyzABCDEFGHIJKLMNOPQRSTUVWXYZ–$1234567890(".;'!*?':,")
Book Condensed Italic *abcdefghijklmnopqrstuvwxyzABCDEFGHIJKLMNOPQRSTUVWXYZ–$1234567890(".;'!*?':,*
Medium Condensed abcdefghijklmnopqrstuvwxyzABCDEFGHIJKLMNOPQRSTUVWXYZ–$1234567890(".;'!*?
Medium Condensed Italic *abcdefghijklmnopqrstuvwxyzABCDEFGHIJKLMNOPQRSTUVWXYZ–$1234567890(".;'!**
Bold Condensed **abcdefghijklmnopqrstuvwxyzABCDEFGHIJKLMNOPQRSTUVWXYZ–$1234567890(**
Bold Condensed Italic ***abcdefghijklmnopqrstuvwxyzABCDEFGHIJKLMNOPQRSTUVWXYZ–$1234567890***

PL Benguiat Frisky Bold
Afga Typographer's Edition 2
Ed Benguiat • 1960 **abcdefghijklmnopqrstuvwxyz(".;'!*?':,")**
AGP **$1234567890&ß-äöüåçèîñóæøœ**
▲16 **ABCDEFGHIJKLMNOPQRSTUVWXYZ**
ÄÖÜÅÇÈÎÑÓÆØŒ »„« ‹¡·¿›...

ITC BENGUIAT GOTHIC

Ed Benguiat • 1979 abcdefghijklmnopqrstuvwxyz(".;'!*?':,")
BIT ADO AGA AGP LEF LIN MAE URW $1234567890&fiflß-äöüåçèîñóæøœ
ABCDEFGHIJKLMNOPQRSTUVWXYZ
ÄÖÜÅÇÈÎÑÓÆØŒ»„«[§•†‡]‹¡·¿›...

ITC Benguiat Gothic 1 ...

• Book abcdefghijklmnopqrstuvwxyzABCDEFGHIJKLMNOPQRSTUVWXYZ–$1234567890(".;'
Book Italic *abcdefghijklmnopqrstuvwxyzABCDEFGHIJKLMNOPQRSTUVWXYZ–$1234567890(".;*
Bold **abcdefghijklmnopqrstuvwxyzABCDEFGHIJKLMNOPQRSTUVWXYZ–$1234567890(**
Bold Italic ***abcdefghijklmnopqrstuvwxyzABCDEFGHIJKLMNOPQRSTUVWXYZ–$1234567890***

ITC Benguiat Gothic 2 ...

Medium abcdefghijklmnopqrstuvwxyzABCDEFGHIJKLMNOPQRSTUVWXYZ–$1234567890("
Medium Italic *abcdefghijklmnopqrstuvwxyzABCDEFGHIJKLMNOPQRSTUVWXYZ–$1234567890("*
Heavy **abcdefghijklmnopqrstuvwxyzABCDEFGHIJKLMNOPQRSTUVWXYZ–$123456789**
Heavy Italic ***abcdefghijklmnopqrstuvwxyzABCDEFGHIJKLMNOPQRSTUVWXYZ–$12345678***

Agfa Typographer's Edition 2: PL Barnum Block, PL Benguiat Frisky Bold, TC Broadway, PL Davison Zip Bold, PL Fiedler Gothic Bold, PL Futura Maxi Book & Bold, Neon Extra Condensed, Ritmo Bold, PL Trophy Oblique.

B

Bergell

Thomas Finke • 1991 abcdefghijklmnopqrstuvwxyz(“.;‘!*?’:,”)

LET $1234567890&fiflß-äöüåçèîñóæøœ

▲16 ABCDEFGHIJKLMNOPQRSTUVWXYZ Ç»„«[•]‹i·¿›...

▷ a r

ITC BERKELEY OLDSTYLE

Tony Stan • 1983 ... Frederic W. Goudy, 1938 abcdefghijklmnopqrstuvwxyz(“.;‘!*?’:,”)

AGP ADO AGA BIT LEF FAM LIN MAE URW $1234567890&fiflß-äöüåçèîñóæøœ

ABCDEFGHIJKLMNOPQRSTUVWXYZ

ÄÖÜÅÇÈÎÑÓÆØŒ»„«[¶§•†‡]‹¡·¿›...

ITC Berkeley Oldstyle 1 ...

• Book abcdefghijklmnopqrstuvwxyzABCDEFGHIJKLMNOPQRSTUVWXYZ–$1234567890(“.;‘!

Book Italic *abcdefghijklmnopqrstuvwxyzABCDEFGHIJKLMNOPQRSTUVWXYZ–$1234567890(“.;‘!*?’:,”)*

Bold **abcdefghijklmnopqrstuvwxyzABCDEFGHIJKLMNOPQRSTUVWXYZ–$1234567890(**

Bold Italic ***abcdefghijklmnopqrstuvwxyzABCDEFGHIJKLMNOPQRSTUVWXYZ–$1234567890(“.;‘!***

ITC Berkeley Oldstyle 2 ...

Medium abcdefghijklmnopqrstuvwxyzABCDEFGHIJKLMNOPQRSTUVWXYZ–$1234567890(“.;‘

Medium Italic *abcdefghijklmnopqrstuvwxyzABCDEFGHIJKLMNOPQRSTUVWXYZ–$1234567890(“.;‘!*?’:*

Black **abcdefghijklmnopqrstuvwxyzABCDEFGHIJKLMNOPQRSTUVWXYZ–$123456789**

Black Italic ***abcdefghijklmnopqrstuvwxyzABCDEFGHIJKLMNOPQRSTUVWXYZ–$1234567890(***

BERLIN SANS

David Berlow • 1992 ... Lucien Bernhard ... abcdefghijklmnopqrstuvwxyz(“.;‘!*?’:,”)

FBU $1234567890&fiflß-äöüåçèîñóœøœ

ABCDEFGHIJKLMNOPQRSTUVWXYZ

ÄÖÜÅÇÈÎÑÓÆØŒ»„«[¶§•†‡]‹i·¿›...

▷ a g s ch ck ff ffi ffl ft rf rt st tz S Th

Berlin Sans 1 ...

• Regular ▲16 abcdefghijklmnopqrstuvwxyzABCDEFGHIJKLMNOPQRSTUVWXYZ–$12345

Bold ▲18 **abcdefghijklmnopqrstuvwxyzABCDEFGHIJKLMNOPQRST**

Regular Alternate Capitals OSF ▲16 ABCDEFGHIJKLMNOOPQRSTUVWXYZABCDEFGHIJKLMNOPQRSTUV...$1234

Bold Alternate Capitals OSF ▲18 **ABCDEFGHIJKLMNOOPQRSTUVWXYZABCDEFG...$123456**

Berlin Sans 2 ...

▲16 Light abcdefghijklmnopqrstuvwxyzABCDEFGHIJKLMNOPQRSTUVWXYZ–$1234567890

Demi **abcdefghijklmnopqrstuvwxyzABCDEFGHIJKLMNOPQRSTUVWXYZ–$1**

Light Alternate Capitals OSF ABCDEFGHIJKLMNOOPQRSTUVWXYZABCDEFGHIJKLMNOPQRSTUVWXYZ–$123

Demi Alternate Capitals OSF **ABCDEFGHIJKLMNOOPQRSTUVWXYZABCDEFGHIJKLMNOP...$1234567**

Berlin Sans 1 ▶ Berlin Sans Bold Dingbats.

B

BERLINER GROTESK

✍ Erik Spiekermann • 1979
... H. Berthold AG, 1913
ADO AGA MAE URW
▲16

abcdefghijklmnopqrstuvwxyz(".;'!*?':,")
$1234567890&fiflß-äöüåçèîñóæøœ
ABCDEFGHIJKLMNOPQRSTUVWXYZ
ÄÖÜÅÇÈÎÑÓÆØŒ»„«[•]‹i·¿›...

Berliner Grotesk ...

Light abcdefghijklmnopqrstuvwxyzABCDEFGHIJKLMNOPQRSTUVWXYZ–$123456789
• Medium abcdefghijklmnopqrstuvwxyzABCDEFGHIJKLMNOPQRSTUVWXYZ–$12345678

BERLING

✍ Karl Erik Forsberg • 1951
LIN ADO AGA AGP LEF MAE URW

abcdefghijklmnopqrstuvwxyz(".;'!*?':,")
$1234567890&fiflß-äöüåçèîñóæøœ
ABCDEFGHIJKLMNOPQRSTUVWXYZ
ÄÖÜÅÇÈÎÑÓÆØŒ»„«[¶§•†‡]‹¡·¿›...

Berling ...

• Roman abcdefghijklmnopqrstuvwxyzABCDEFGHIJKLMNOPQRSTUVWXYZ–$12345
Italic *abcdefghijklmnopqrstuvwxyzABCDEFGHIJKLMNOPQRSTUVWXYZ–$12345678*
Bold **abcdefghijklmnopqrstuvwxyzABCDEFGHIJKLMNOPQRSTUVWXYZ–$12345**
Bold Italic ***abcdefghijklmnopqrstuvwxyzABCDEFGHIJKLMNOPQRSTUVWXYZ–$12345***

BERNHARD MODERN

✍ Lucian Bernhard • 1937
BIT ADO AGA AGP TFC LIN MAE
▲16

abcdefghijklmnopqrstuvwxyz(".;'!*?':,")
$1234567890&fiflß-äöüåçèîñóæøœ
ABCDEFGHIJKLMNOPQRSTUVWXYZ
ÄÖÜÅÇÈÎÑÓÆØŒ»„«[¶§•†‡]‹¡·¿›...

Bernhard Modern ...

• Roman abcdefghijklmnopqrstuvwxyzABCDEFGHIJKLMNOPQRSTUVWXYZ–$1
Italic *abcdefghijklmnopqrstuvwxyzABCDEFGHIJKLMNOPQRSTUVWXYZ–$123*
Bold **abcdefghijklmnopqrstuvwxyzABCDEFGHIJKLMNOPQRSTUVWXY**
Bold Italic ***abcdefghijklmnopqrstuvwxyzABCDEFGHIJKLMNOPQRSTUVWXYZ–***

Bernhard Fashion

✍ Lucian Bernhard • 1929
BIT AGP LEF URW
▲24

abcdefghijklmnopqrstuvwxyz(".;'!*?':,")
$1234567890&fiflß-äöüåçèîñóæøœ
ABCDEFGHIJKLMNOPQRSTUVWXYZ
ÄÖÜÅÇÈÎÑÓÆØŒ»„«[§•†‡]‹i·¿›...

B

Bernhard Bold Condensed

Lucian Bernhard • 1912
BIT TFC
▲24

abcdefghijklmnopqrstuvwxyz(".;'!*?':,")$1234567890&fiflß-
äöüåçèîñóæøœABCDEFGHIJKLMNOPQRSTUVWXYZÄÖÜÅÇÈÎÑÓ
ÆØŒÄÖÜÅÇÈÎÑÓÆØŒ»„«[§•†‡]‹¡·¿›...

Bernhard Tango

Lucian Bernhard • 1934
BIT
▲16

abcdefghijklmnopqrstuvwxyz(".;'!?':,")*
$1234567890&fiflß-äöüåçèîñóæøœ
ABCDEFGHIJKLMNOPQRSTUVWXYZ
ÄÖÜÅÇÈÎÑÓÆØŒ»„«[§•†‡]‹¡·¿›...

PL BERNHARDT
Agfa Typographer's Edition 3
Lucian Bernhard • 1929
AGP

abcdefghijklmnopqrstuvwxyz(".;'!*?':,")
$1234567890&-äöüåçèîñóæøœ
ABCDEFGHIJKLMNOPQRSTUVWXYZ
ÄÖÜÅÇÈÎÑÓÆØŒ»„«[¶•†‡]‹¡·¿›...

PL Bernhardt ...

Light abcdefghijklmnopqrstuvwxyzABCDEFGHIJKLMNOPQRSTUVWXYZ–$1234567890(".;'!
• Medium abcdefghijklmnopqrstuvwxyzABCDEFGHIJKLMNOPQRSTUVWXYZ–$123456789
Bold abcdefghijklmnopqrstuvwxyzABCDEFGHIJKLMNOPQRSTUVWXYZ–$12345

BERTHOLD SCRIPT
Berthold ScriptSet 1
Günter Gerhard Lange • 1977
ADO AGA MAE
▲15

abcdefghijklmnopqrstuvwxyz(".;'!?':,")*
$1234567890&fiflß-äöüåçèîñóæøœ
ABCDEFGHIJKLMNOPQRSTUVWXYZ
ÄÖÜÅÇÈÎÑÓÆØŒ»„«[•]‹¡·¿›...

Berthold Script ...

• Regular *abcdefghijklmnopqrstuvwxyzABCDEFGHIJKLMNOPQRSTUVWXYZ–$*
Medium *abcdefghijklmnopqrstuvwxyzABCDEFGHIJKLMNOPQRSTUVW*

Agfa Typographer's Edition 3: Barclay Open, PL Bernhardt Light, Medium & Bold, PL Britannia Bold, Delphian Open, PL Fiorello Condensed, Fluidium Bold, PL Modern Heavy Condensed, PL Torino Open.
Berthold ScriptSet 1: Bellevue, Berthold Script Regular & Medium, Boulevard.

Bertie

Alan Meeks • 1985

LET

▲24

abcdefghijklmnopqrstuvwxyz(".;'!*?':,")
$1234567890&fiflß-äöüåçèîñóæøœ
ABCDEFGHIJKLMNOPQRSTUVWXYZ
ÄÖÜÅÇÈÎÑÓÆØŒ»„«[•]‹i•¿›...

Bertram

Martin Wait • 1991

LET

▲30

ABCDEFGHIJKLMNOPQRSTUVWXYZ
(".;'!*?':,")$1234567890
&-ÄÖÜÅÇÈÎÑÓÆØŒ»„«[•]‹i•¿›...

Bible Script

Richard Bradley • 1979

LET

abcdefghijklmnopqrstuvwxyz(".;'!*?':,")
$1234567890&fiflß-äöüåçèîñóæøœ
ABCDEFGHIJKLMNOPQRSTUVWXYZ
ÄÖÜÅÇÈÎÑÓÆØŒ»„«[•]‹i•¿›...
▷ b d e e g k k l p r t t v A A B C D E F G J L M M N P Q R R S V W Y
▷

Bickley Script

Alan Meeks • 1986

LET

▲20

abcdefghijklmnopqrstuvwxyz(".;'!*?':,")
$1234567890&fiflß-äöüåçèîñóæøœ
ABCDEFGHIJKLMNOPQRSTUVWXYZ Ç»„«[•]‹i•¿›...

Biffo Script

Monotype Scripts 1

MCL ADO AGA LIN MAE

▲16

abcdefghijklmnopqrstuvwxyz(".;'!*?':,")
$1234567890&fiflß-äöüåçèîñóæøœ
ABCDEFGHIJKLMNOPQRSTUVWXYZ
ÄÖÜÅÇÈÎÑÓÆØŒ»„«(§•†‡)¡•¿...

Monotype Scripts 1: Biffo Script, Dorchester Script, Pepita, Monotype Script Bold, Swing Bold.

B

Big Black

FRA

▲36

ABCDEFGHIJKLMNOPQR
STUVWXYZ“.;‘!?’:,”$12345
67890-ÄÖÜÅÇÈÎÑÓÆØŒ

BINNY OLD STYLE

MCL

abcdefghijklmnopqrstuvwxyz(“.;‘!*?’:,”)
$1234567890&ﬁﬂß-äöüåçèîñóæøœ
ABCDEFGHIJKLMNOPQRSTUVWXYZ
ÄÖÜÅÇÈÎÑÓÆØŒ»„«[¶§•†‡]‹¡·¿›…

Binny Old Style …

• Roman abcdefghijklmnopqrstuvwxyzABCDEFGHIJKLMNOPQRSTUVWXY

Italic *abcdefghijklmnopqrstuvwxyzABCDEFGHIJKLMNOPQRSTUVWXYZ–$1*

Birch

Adobe Wood Type 2

Kim Buker, Barbara Lind & Joy Redick • 1990

ADO AGA LIN MAE

▲36

abcdefghijklmnopqrstuvwxyz(“.;‘!*?’:,”)
$1234567890&ﬁﬂß-äöüåçèîñóæøœ
ABCDEFGHIJKLMNOPQRSTUVWXYZ
ÄÖÜÅÇÈÎÑÓÆØŒ»„«[·]‹¡·¿›…

Bitmax

Alan Birch • 1990

LET

▲36

ABCDEFGHIJKLMNOPQRSTUVWXYZ
(“.;‘!*?’:,”)$1234567890
&-ÄÖÜÅÇÈÎÑÓÆØŒ»„«[•]‹¡·¿›…

Adobe Wood Type 2: Birch, Blackoak, Madrone, Poplar, Willow, Adobe Wood Type Ornaments 2.
Birch ▶ Adobe Wood Type Ornaments 2.

B

Blackboard
FTF ChalkBoard
FRA abcdefghijklmnopqrstuvwxyz(.:!*?:,)$1234567890&-
▲18 ABCDEFGHIJKLMNOPQRSTUVWXYZ

Blackletter 686
BIT abcdefghijklmnopqrstuvwxyz(“.;‘!*?’:,”)
▲24 $1234567890&fiflß-äöüåçèîñóæøœ
ABCDEFGHIJKLMNOPQRSTUVWXYZ
ÄÖÜÅÇÈÎÑÓÆØŒ»„«[§•†‡]‹¡·¿›...

Blackmoor
David Quay • 1983 abcdefghijklmnopqrstuvwxyz(“.;‘!*?’:,”)
LET $1234567890&fiflß-äöüåçèîñóæøœ
▲18 ABCDEFGHIJKLMNOPQRSTUVWXYZ
ÄÖÜÅÇÈÎÑÓÆØŒ»„«[•]‹¡·¿›... ▷ Th

Blackoak
Adobe Wood Type 2
Kim Buker, Barbara Lind & Joy Redick • 1990
ADO AGA LIN MAE
abcdefghijklmnopqrstuvwxyz
(“.;‘!*?’:,”)$1234567890&fiflß-
äöüåçèîñóæøœABCDEFGHIJ
KLMNOPQRSTUVWXYZ
ÄÖÜÅÇÈÎÑÓÆØŒ»„«[•]‹¡·¿›...

Black Rocks
Group Arabia
Judith Sutcliffe • 1992
abcdefghijklmnopqrstuvwxyz(“.;‘!?’:,”)$1234567890&fiflß·äöüåçèîñóæøœ
MTD
▲24 ABCDEFGHIJKLMNOPQRSTUVWXYZÄÖÜÅÇÈÎÑÓÆØŒ » « [§•] ‹¡¿›
▷ ff ◂ ▸

Black Tents
Group Arabia
Judith Sutcliffe • 1992
abcdefghijklmnopqrstuvwxyz(“.;‘!?’:,”)$1234567890&fiflß·äöüåçèîñóæøœ
MTD
▲24 ABCDEFGHIJKLMNOPQRSTUVWXYZÄÖÜÅÇÈÎÑÓÆØŒ »«« [§•] ‹¡¿›
▷ ff ◂ ▸

FTF Chalkboard: Blackboard, Recess.
Adobe Wood Type 2: Birch, Blackoak, Madrone, Poplar, Willow, Adobe Wood Type Ornaments 2.
Blackoak ▶ Adobe Wood Type Ornaments 2.

Group Arabia: Arabia Felix, Black Rocks, Black Tents, Kufi Script, Mesopotamia.

B

Blado Italic
Monotype AldineDutch
Monotype Design Staff • 1923
... Ludovico degli Arrighi, 1526
MCL
▲16

abcdefghijklmnopqrstuvwxyz(“.;‘!?’:,”)*
$1234567890&fiflß-äöüåçèîñóæøœ
ABCDEFGHIJKLMNOPQRSTUVWXYZ
ÄÖÜÅÇÈÎÑÓÆØŒ»„«[§•†‡]‹¡·¿›...

Blado Italic Expert ...
Monotype AldineDutch Expert
MCL
▲16

$1234567890.;:,ffffiflffiffl (abdeilmnorst)
— 1/8 1/4 1/3 3/8 1/2 5/8 2/3 3/4 7/8 $12345/67890¢ ₡Rp

BLAST-O-RAMA
Todd Brei • 1993
T26

abcdefghijklmnopqrstuvwxyz(“.;‘!*?’:,”)
$1234567890&fiflß-äöüåçèîñóæøœ
ABCDEFGHIJKLMNOPQRSTUVWXYZ
ÄÖÜÅÇÈÎÑÓÆØŒ»„«[¶§•†‡]‹¡·¿›...

Blast-O-Rama ...
Regular abcdefghijklmnopqrstuvwxyzABCDEFGHIJKLMNOPQRSTUVWXYZ-$123
Bold **abcdefghijklmnopqrstuvwxyzABCDEFGHIJKLMNOPQRSTUV**
• Beat abcdefghijklmnopqrstuvwxyzABCDEFGHIJKLMNOPQRSTUVWXYZ-

BERTHOLD BLOCK
H. Hoffmann • 1908
ADO AGA MAE
▲18

abcdefghijklmnopqrstuvwxyz(“.;‘!*?’:,”)
$1234567890&fiflß-äöüåçèîñóæøœ
ABCDEFGHIJKLMNOPQRSTUVWXYZ
ÄÖÜÅÇÈÎÑÓÆØŒ»„«[•]‹¡·¿›...

Berthold Block ...
• Regular **abcdefghijklmnopqrstuvwxyzABCDEFGHIJKLMNOPQRSTUVWXYZ–**
Italic ***abcdefghijklmnopqrstuvwxyzABCDEFGHIJKLMNOPQRSTUVWXY***
Heavy **abcdefghijklmnopqrstuvwxyzABCDEFGHIJKLMNOPQ**
Condensed **abcdefghijklmnopqrstuvwxyzABCDEFGHIJKLMNOPQRSTUVWXYZ–$1234567**
Extra Condensed **abcdefghijklmnopqrstuvwxyzABCDEFGHIJKLMNOPQRSTUVWXYZ–$1234567890(“.;‘!*?’:**
Extra Condensed Italic ***abcdefghijklmnopqrstuvwxyzABCDEFGHIJKLMNOPQRSTUVWXYZ–$1234567890(“.;‘!*?’:***

BLUEPRINT
Steve Matteson • 1993
MCL
▲16

abcdefghijklmnopqrstuvwxyz(“.;‘!*?’:,”)
$1234567890&fiflß-äöüåçèîñóæøœ
ABCDEFGHIJKLMNOPQRSTUVWXYZ
ÄÖÜÅÇÈÎÑÓÆØŒ»„«[¶§•†‡]‹¡·¿›...

Monotype AldineDutch: Poliphilus Roman & Blado Italic, Van Dijck Roman & Italic.
Monotype AldineDutch Expert: Poliphilus Roman Expert & Blado Italic Expert, Van Dijck Expert Roman & Expert Italic.

B

... Blueprint ...

• Regular abcdefghijklmnopqrstuvwxyzABCDEFGHIJKLMNOPQRSTUVWXYZ–$123456

Italic *abcdefghijklmnopqrstuvwxyzABCDEFGHIJKLMNOPQRSTUVWXYZ–$123456*

Bold **abcdefghijklmnopqrstuvwxyzABCDEFGHIJKLMNOPQRSTUVWXYZ–$1234**

Bold Italic ***abcdefghijklmnopqrstuvwxyzABCDEFGHIJKLMNOPQRSTUVWXYZ–$123***

BLUNTZ

David Sagorski • 1994

LET

▲24

ABCDEFGHIJKLMNOPQRSTUVWXYZ(".;'!*?':,")

$1234567890&-ÄÖÜÅÇÈÎÑÓÆØŒ»«[•]‹¡·¿›...

BOCA RATON

Grant Hutchinson • 1993

IMA

▲24

abcdefghijklmnopqrstuvwxyz(".;'!*?':,")

$1234567890&fifIß-äöüåçèîñóæøœ

ABCDEFGHIJKLMNOPQRSTUVWXYZ

ÄÖÜÅÇÈÎÑÓÆØŒ»„«[¶§•†‡]‹¡·¿›...

Boca Raton ...

• Engraved abcdefghijklmnopqrstuvwxyzABCDEFGHIJK

Solid **abcdefghijklmnopqrstuvwxyzABCDEFGHIJK**

BODEGA SANS

Greg Thompson • 1991

FBU AGP MTD

▲24

abcdefghijklmnopqrstuvwxyz(".;'!*?':,")

$1234567890&fifIß-äöüåçèîñóæøœ

ABCDEFGHIJKLMNOPQRSTUVWXYZ

ÄÖÜÅÇÈÎÑÓÆØŒ»„«[¶§-†‡]‹¡·¿›...

Bodega Sans Light ...

Light abcdefghijklmnopqrstuvwxyzABCDEFGHIJKLMNOPQRSTUVWXYZ–$1234567890(".;'!*?':,")&fifl

Light Oldstyle abcdefghijklmnopqrstuvwxyzABCDEFGHIJKLMNOPQRSTUVWXYZ–$1234567890(".;'!*?':,")&fifl

Light SCOSF ABCDEFGHIJKLMNOPQRSTUVWXYZABCDEFGHIJKLMNOPQRSTUVWXYZ–$1234567890(".;'!*?':,")&–ÄÖÜ

B

Bodega Sans Medium . . .

• Medium abcdefghijklmnopqrstuvwxyzABCDEFGHIJKLMNOPQRSTUVWXYZ–$12345678

Medium Oldstyle abcdefghijklmnopqrstuvwxyzABCDEFGHIJKLMNOPQRSTUVWXYZ–$1234567

Medium SCOSF ABCDEFGHIJKLMNOPQRSTUVWXYZABCDEFGHIJKLMNOPQRSTUVWXYZ–$1234567

Bodega Sans Black . . .

Black abcdefghijklmnopqrstuvwxyzABCDEFGHIJKLMNOPQRSTUVWXY

Black Oldstyle abcdefghijklmnopqrstuvwxyzABCDEFGHIJKLMNOPQRS...$12345

Black SCOSF ABCDEFGHIJKLMNOPQRSTUVWXYZABCDEFGHIJKLMNOPQRS...$12345

BODEGA SERIF

Greg Thompson • 1991

FBU

▲24

abcdefghijklmnopqrstuvwxyz(".;'!*?':,")

$1234567890&fiflß-äöüåçèîñóæøœ

ABCDEFGHIJKLMNOPQRSTUVWXYZ

ÄÖÜÅÇÈÎÑÓÆØŒ»„«[¶§-†‡]‹¡·¿›...

▷

Bodega Serif Light . . .

Light abcdefghijklmnopqrstuvwxyzABCDEFGHIJKLMNOPQRSTUVWXYZ–$1234567890(".;'!*?':,")&fi

Light Oldstyle abcdefghijklmnopqrstuvwxyzABCDEFGHIJKLMNOPQRSTUVWXYZ–$1234567890(".;'!*?':,")&fifl

Light SCOSF ABCDEFGHIJKLMNOPQRSTUVWXYZABCDEFGHIJKLMNOPQRSTUVWXYZ–$1234567890(".;'!*?':,")&-Ä

Bodega Serif Medium . . .

• Medium abcdefghijklmnopqrstuvwxyzABCDEFGHIJKLMNOPQRSTUVWXYZ–$123456

Medium Oldstyle abcdefghijklmnopqrstuvwxyzABCDEFGHIJKLMNOPQRSTUVWXYZ–$123456

Medium SCOSF ABCDEFGHIJKLMNOPQRSTUVWXYZABCDEFGHIJKLMNOPQRSTUVWXYZ–$123456

Bodega Serif Black . . .

Black abcdefghijklmnopqrstuvwxyzABCDEFGHIJKLMNOPQRSTUVWX

Black Oldstyle abcdefghijklmnopqrstuvwxyzABCDEFGHIJKLMNOPQRS...$1234

Black SCOSF ABCDEFGHIJKLMNOPQRSTUVWXYZABCDEFGHIJKLMNOPQRS...$1234

BODONI 1

Morris Fuller Benton • 1910...
... Giambattista Bodoni, 1798...
LIN ADO AGA BIT FAM LAN MAE

abcdefghijklmnopqrstuvwxyz(“.;‘!*?’:,”)
$1234567890&fifl ß-äöüåçèîñóæøœ
ABCDEFGHIJKLMNOPQRSTUVWXYZ
ÄÖÜÅÇÈÎÑÓÆØŒ»„«[¶§•†‡]‹¡·¿›...

Bodoni 1 ...

• Roman abcdefghijklmnopqrstuvwxyzABCDEFGHIJKLMNOPQRSTUVWXYZ–$12345678

Italic *abcdefghijklmnopqrstuvwxyzABCDEFGHIJKLMNOPQRSTUVWXYZ–$123456789*

Bold **abcdefghijklmnopqrstuvwxyzABCDEFGHIJKLMNOPQRSTUVWXYZ–$123456**

Bold Italic ***abcdefghijklmnopqrstuvwxyzABCDEFGHIJKLMNOPQRSTUVWXYZ–$1234567***

Poster Black ▲18 **abcdefghijklmnopqrstuvwxyzABCDEFGHIJKLMN**

BODONI 2

Morris Fuller Benton • 1910...
... Giambattista Bodoni, 1798...
LIN ADO AGA BIT FAM LAN MAE

abcdefghijklmnopqrstuvwxyz(“.;‘!*?’:,”)
$1234567890&fifl ß-äöüåçèîñóæøœ
ABCDEFGHIJKLMNOPQRSTUVWXYZ
ÄÖÜÅÇÈÎÑÓÆØŒ»„«[¶§•†‡]‹¡·¿›...

Bodoni 2 ...

• Book abcdefghijklmnopqrstuvwxyzABCDEFGHIJKLMNOPQRSTUVWXYZ–$1234567890(“.;‘!

Book Italic *abcdefghijklmnopqrstuvwxyzABCDEFGHIJKLMNOPQRSTUVWXYZ–$1234567890(“.;‘!*?’*

Bold Condensed ▲16 **abcdefghijklmnopqrstuvwxyzABCDEFGHIJKLMNOPQRSTUVWXYZ–$1234567890(“.;‘!*?’:,”)**

Poster Compressed ▲18 **abcdefghijklmnopqrstuvwxyzABCDEFGHIJKLMNOPQRSTUVWXYZ–$1234567890(“.;‘!*?’:,”)&fifl ß-**

Poster Black Italic ▲18 ***abcdefghijklmnopqrstuvwxyzABCDEFGHIJKLMN***

BERTHOLD BODONI ANTIQUA

H. Berthold AG • 1930
... Giambattista Bodoni, 1798...
ADO AGA MAE

abcdefghijklmnopqrstuvwxyz(“.;‘!*?’:,”)
$1234567890&fifl ß-äöüåçèîñóæøœ
ABCDEFGHIJKLMNOPQRSTUVWXYZ
ÄÖÜÅÇÈÎÑÓÆØŒ»„«[¶§•†‡]‹¡·¿›...

Berthold Bodoni Antiqua ...

Light abcdefghijklmnopqrstuvwxyzABCDEFGHIJKLMNOPQRSTUVWXYZ–$1234567890(“

Light Italic *abcdefghijklmnopqrstuvwxyzABCDEFGHIJKLMNOPQRSTUVWXYZ–$1234567890(*

• Roman abcdefghijklmnopqrstuvwxyzABCDEFGHIJKLMNOPQRSTUVWXYZ–$1234567890(“

Italic *abcdefghijklmnopqrstuvwxyzABCDEFGHIJKLMNOPQRSTUVWXYZ–$1234567890(“*

Medium **abcdefghijklmnopqrstuvwxyzABCDEFGHIJKLMNOPQRSTUVWXYZ–$123456**

Medium Italic ***abcdefghijklmnopqrstuvwxyzABCDEFGHIJKLMNOPQRSTUVWXYZ–$123456***

Bold **abcdefghijklmnopqrstuvwxyzABCDEFGHIJKLMNOPQRSTUVWXYZ–**

Bold Italic ***abcdefghijklmnopqrstuvwxyzABCDEFGHIJKLMNOPQRSTUVWXYZ–***

B

BERTHOLD BODONI ANTIQUA EXPERT & SCOSF

ADO AGA MAE ABCDEFGHIJKLMNOPQRSTUVWXYZ.;!?:,
$1234567890&ff fi fl ffi ffl – ÄÖÜÅÇÈÎÑÓÆØŒ
(abdeilmnorst) 1/8 1/4 1/3 3/8 1/2 5/8 2/3 3/4 7/8 $12345/67890¢ ₡Rp

Berthold Bodoni Antiqua Expert & SCOSF …

Expert Light ABCDEFGHIJKLMNOPQRSTUVWXYZ–$1234567890.;!?:,&-ff fi fl ffi ffl 1/8 1/4 1/3 3/8 1/2 $12345/67890¢ (abd
Expert Light Italic *$1234567890.;:,–ff fi fl ffi ffl 1/8 1/4 1/3 3/8 1/2 $12345/67890¢ (abdeilmnorst) 5/8 2/3 3/4 7/8 ₡Rp*
• Expert Roman ABCDEFGHIJKLMNOPQRSTUVWXYZ–$1234567890.;!?:,&-ff fi fl ffi ffl 1/8 1/4 1/3 3/8 1/2 $12345/67890¢ (abd
Expert Italic *$1234567890.;:,–ff fi fl ffi ffl 1/8 1/4 1/3 3/8 1/2 $12345/67890¢ (abdeilmnorst) 5/8 2/3 3/4 7/8 ₡Rp*
Expert Medium **ABCDEFGHIJKLMNOPQRSTUVWXYZ–$1234567890.;!?:,&-ff fi fl ffi ffl 1/8 1/4 1/3 3/8 1/2 $12345/67890¢**
Expert Medium Italic ***$1234567890.;:,–ff fi fl ffi ffl 1/8 1/4 1/3 3/8 1/2 $12345/67890¢ (abdeilmnorst) 5/8 2/3 3/4 7/8 ₡Rp***
Expert Bold **$1234567890.;:,–ff fi fl ffi ffl 1/8 1/4 1/3 3/8 1/2 $12345/67890¢ (abdeilmnorst) 5/8 2/3 3/4 7/8 ₡**
Expert Bold Italic ***$1234567890.;:,–ff fi fl ffi ffl 1/8 1/4 1/3 3/8 1/2 $12345/67890¢ (abdeilmnorst) 5/8 2/3 3/4 7/8***
Light SCOSF ABCDEFGHIJKLMNOPQRSTUVWXYZABCDEFGHIJKLMNOPQRSTUVWXYZ–$1234567890(
Light Italic OSF *abcdefghijklmnopqrstuvwxyzABCDEFGHIJKLMNOPQRSTUVWXYZ–$1234567890(“.*
Roman SCOSF ABCDEFGHIJKLMNOPQRSTUVWXYZABCDEFGHIJKLMNOPQRSTUVWXYZ–$1234567890(“
Italic OSF *abcdefghijklmnopqrstuvwxyzABCDEFGHIJKLMNOPQRSTUVWXYZ–$1234567890(“.*
Medium SCOSF **ABCDEFGHIJKLMNOPQRSTUVWXYZABCDEFGHIJKLMNOPQRSTUVWXYZ–$123456**
Medium Italic OSF ***abcdefghijklmnopqrstuvwxyzABCDEFGHIJKLMNOPQRSTUVWXYZ–$1234567***
Bold OSF **abcdefghijklmnopqrstuvwxyzABCDEFGHIJKLMNOPQRS…$12345678**
Bold Italic OSF ***abcdefghijklmnopqrstuvwxyzABCDEFGHIJKLMNOPQRS…$12345678***

BERTHOLD BODONI ANTIQUA CONDENSED

ADO AGA MAE abcdefghijklmnopqrstuvwxyz(“.;‘!*?’:,”)
▲16 $1234567890&fiflß-äöüåçèîñóæøœ
ABCDEFGHIJKLMNOPQRSTUVWXYZ
ÄÖÜÅÇÈÎÑÓÆØŒ»„«[§•†‡]‹·¿›…

Berthold Bodoni Antiqua Condensed …

• Condensed abcdefghijklmnopqrstuvwxyzABCDEFGHIJKLMNOPQRSTUVWXYZ-$1234567890(“.;‘!*?’:,”)&fiflß-äö
Condensed Italic *abcdefghijklmnopqrstuvwxyzABCDEFGHIJKLMNOPQRSTUVWXYZ-$1234567890(“.;‘!*?’:,”)&fiflß-ä*
Medium Condensed **abcdefghijklmnopqrstuvwxyzABCDEFGHIJKLMNOPQRSTUVWXYZ-$1234567890(“.;‘!*?’:**
Medium Condensed Italic ***abcdefghijklmnopqrstuvwxyzABCDEFGHIJKLMNOPQRSTUVWXYZ-$1234567890(“.;‘!*?***
Bold Condensed **abcdefghijklmnopqrstuvwxyzABCDEFGHIJKLMNOPQRSTUVWXYZ-$123456789**
Bold Condensed Italic ***abcdefghijklmnopqrstuvwxyzABCDEFGHIJKLMNOPQRSTUVWXYZ-$12345678***

BAUER BODONI

Heinrich Jost • 1926
. . . Giambattista Bodoni, 1798. . .
ADO AGA AGP BIT LEF LIN MAE URW

abcdefghijklmnopqrstuvwxyz(“.;‘!*?’:,”)
$1234567890&fiflß-äöüåçèîñóæøœ
ABCDEFGHIJKLMNOPQRSTUVWXYZ
ÄÖÜÅÇÈÎÑÓÆØŒ»„«[¶§•†‡]‹¡·¿›...

Bauer Bodoni 1 ...

• Roman abcdefghijklmnopqrstuvwxyzABCDEFGHIJKLMNOPQRSTUVWXYZ–$12345678
Italic *abcdefghijklmnopqrstuvwxyzABCDEFGHIJKLMNOPQRSTUVWXYZ–$1234567890*
Bold **abcdefghijklmnopqrstuvwxyzABCDEFGHIJKLMNOPQRSTUVWXYZ–$1234**
Bold Italic ***abcdefghijklmnopqrstuvwxyzABCDEFGHIJKLMNOPQRSTUVWXYZ–$123456***

Bauer Bodoni 2 ...

Black **abcdefghijklmnopqrstuvwxyzABCDEFGHIJKLMNOPQRSTUVWXYZ–$12**
Black Italic ***abcdefghijklmnopqrstuvwxyzABCDEFGHIJKLMNOPQRSTUVWXYZ–***
Bold Condensed ▲16 **abcdefghijklmnopqrstuvwxyzABCDEFGHIJKLMNOPQRSTUVWXYZ–$123456789**
Black Condensed ▲16 **abcdefghijklmnopqrstuvwxyzABCDEFGHIJKLMNOPQRSTUVWXYZ–$123456789**

BAUER BODONI SCOSF

ADO AGA LIN MAE

ABCDEFGHIJKLMNOPQRSTUVWXYZ(“.;‘!*?’:,”)
$1234567890&-ÄÖÜÅÇÈÎÑÓÆØŒ
ABCDEFGHIJKLMNOPQRSTUVWXYZ
ÄÖÜÅÇÈÎÑÓÆØŒ»„«[¶§•†‡]‹¡·¿›...

Bauer Bodoni SCOSF ...

• Roman SCOSF ABCDEFGHIJKLMNOPQRSTUVWXYZABCDEFGHIJKLMNOPQRSTUVWXYZ–$123456789
Italic OSF *abcdefghijklmnopqrstuvwxyzABCDEFGHIJKLMNOPQRSTUVWXYZ–$1234567890(“*
Bold OSF **abcdefghijklmnopqrstuvwxyzABCDEFGHIJKLMNOPQRSTUVWXYZ–$12345**
Bold Italic OSF ***abcdefghijklmnopqrstuvwxyzABCDEFGHIJKLMNOPQRSTUVWXYZ–$12345678***

BAUER BODONI TITLING

Heinrich Jost • 1926
. . . Giambattista Bodoni, 1798. . .
BIT URW

▲30

ABCDEFGHIJKLMNOPQRSTUV
WXYZ(“.;‘!*?’:,”)$1234567890
&-ÄÖÜÅÇÈÎÑÓŸÆØŒ»„«[§•†‡]‹

Bauer Bodoni Titling ...

• No. 1 ABCDEFGHIJKLMNOPQRSTUV
No. 2 ABCDEFGHIJKLMNOPQRSTUV

B

BODONI 26

Bradbury Thompson • 1960
abcdefghijklmnopqrstuvwxyz(“.;‘!*?’:,”)
LAN $1234567890&-äöüåçèîñóæøœ
aBCDeFGHIJKLmnOPQRSTUVWXYZ
äöüåçèîñóæøœ»«[¶§•†]‹¡¿›...

WTC OUR BODONI

Massimo Vignelli & Tom Carnase • 1989 ... Giambattista Bodoni, 1798...
abcdefghijklmnopqrstuvwxyz(“.;‘!*?’:,”)
$1234567890&fiflß-äöüåçèîñóæøœ
AGP ABCDEFGHIJKLMNOPQRSTUVWXYZ
ÄÖÜÅÇÈÎÑÓÆØŒ»„«[¶§•†‡]‹¡·¿›...

WTC Our Bodoni ...

Light abcdefghijklmnopqrstuvwxyzABCDEFGHIJKLMNOPQRSTUVWXYZ–$1234567890(“
Light Italic *abcdefghijklmnopqrstuvwxyzABCDEFGHIJKLMNOPQRSTUVWXYZ–$1234567890(“.;‘!*
• Roman abcdefghijklmnopqrstuvwxyzABCDEFGHIJKLMNOPQRSTUVWXYZ–$12345678
Italic *abcdefghijklmnopqrstuvwxyzABCDEFGHIJKLMNOPQRSTUVWXYZ–$1234567890*
Medium **abcdefghijklmnopqrstuvwxyzABCDEFGHIJKLMNOPQRSTUVWXYZ–$1234**
Medium Italic ***abcdefghijklmnopqrstuvwxyzABCDEFGHIJKLMNOPQRSTUVWXYZ–$123456***
Bold **abcdefghijklmnopqrstuvwxyzABCDEFGHIJKLMNOPQRSTUVWXYZ–$**
Bold Italic ***abcdefghijklmnopqrstuvwxyzABCDEFGHIJKLMNOPQRSTUVWXYZ–$12***

BERTHOLD BODONI OLD FACE

Günter Gerhard Lange • 1983 ... Giambattista Bodoni, 1798...
abcdefghijklmnopqrstuvwxyz(“.;‘!*?’:,”)
ADO AGA MAE $1234567890&fiflß-äöüåçèîñóæøœ
ABCDEFGHIJKLMNOPQRSTUVWXYZ
ÄÖÜÅÇÈÎÑÓÆØŒ»„«[¶§•†‡]‹¡·¿›...

Berthold Bodoni Old Face ...

• Roman abcdefghijklmnopqrstuvwxyzABCDEFGHIJKLMNOPQRSTUVWXYZ–$1234567
Italic *abcdefghijklmnopqrstuvwxyzABCDEFGHIJKLMNOPQRSTUVWXYZ–$1234567890*
Medium **abcdefghijklmnopqrstuvwxyzABCDEFGHIJKLMNOPQRSTUVWXYZ–$1234**
Medium Italic ***abcdefghijklmnopqrstuvwxyzABCDEFGHIJKLMNOPQRSTUVWXYZ–$123456***
Bold **abcdefghijklmnopqrstuvwxyzABCDEFGHIJKLMNOPQRSTUVWXYZ–$1**
Bold Italic ***abcdefghijklmnopqrstuvwxyzABCDEFGHIJKLMNOPQRSTUVWXYZ–$***

BERTHOLD BODONI OLD FACE
EXPERT & SCOSF

ADO AGA MAE ABCDEFGHIJKLMNOPQRSTUVWXYZ.;!?:,
$1234567890&ff fi fl ffi ffl–ÄÖÜÅÇÈÎÑÓÆØŒ
(abdeilmnorst) 1/8 1/4 1/3 3/8 1/2 5/8 2/3 3/4 7/8 $12345/67890¢ ₡Rp

... Berthold Bodoni Old Face Expert & SCOSF ...

• Expert Roman ABCDEFGHIJKLMNOPQRSTUVWXYZ–$1234567890.;!?:,&-fffiflffiffl 1/8 1/4 1/3 3/8 1/2 $12345/67890

Expert Italic *$1234567890.;!?:,–fffiflffiffl 1/8 1/4 1/3 3/8 1/2 $12345/67890¢ (abdeilmnorst) 5/8 2/3 3/4 7/8 ₡Rp*

Expert Medium ABCDEFGHIJKLMNOPQRSTUVWXYZ–$1234567890.;!?:,&-fffiflffiffl 1/8 1/4 1/3 3/8 1/2 $12345/67

Expert Medium Italic *$1234567890.;:,–fffiflffiffl 1/8 1/4 1/3 3/8 1/2 $12345/67890¢ (abdeilmnorst) 5/8 2/3 3/4 7/8 ₡Rp*

Expert Bold **$1234567890.;:,–fffiflffiffl 1/8 1/4 1/3 3/8 1/2 $12345/67890¢ (abdeilmnorst) 5/8 2/3 3/4 7/8 ₡Rp**

Expert Bold Italic ***$1234567890.;:,–fffiflffiffl 1/8 1/4 1/3 3/8 1/2 $12345/67890¢ (abdeilmnorst) 5/8 2/3 3/4 7/8 ₡***

Roman SCOSF ABCDEFGHIJKLMNOPQRSTUVWXYZABCDEFGHIJKLMNOPQRSTUVWXYZ–$123456

Italic SCOSF *ABCDEFGHIJKLMNOPQRSTUVWXYZABCDEFGHIJKLMNOPQRSTUVWXYZ–$12345678*

Medium SCOSF ABCDEFGHIJKLMNOPQRSTUVWXYZABCDEFGHIJKLMNOPQRSTUVWXYZ–$1234

Medium Italic OSF *abcdefghijklmnopqrstuvwxyzABCDEFGHIJKLMNOPQRSTUVWXYZ–$1234567*

Bold OSF **abcdefghijklmnopqrstuvwxyzABCDEFGHIJKLMNOPQRSTUVWXYZ–$12**

Bold Italic OSF ***abcdefghijklmnopqrstuvwxyzABCDEFGHIJKLMNOPQRSTUVWXYZ–$1***

ITC BODONI SIX + SCOSF

Grupo Bodoniana • 1994 ... Giambattista Bodoni, 1798...* abcdefghijklmnopqrstuvwxyz(“.;‘!*?’:,”)

ITC $1234567890&fiflß-äöüåçèîñóæøœ

** Janice Prescott Fishman, Holly Goldsmith, Allan Haley, Jim Parkinson, Sumner Stone, Ilene Strizver* ABCDEFGHIJKLMNOPQRSTUVWXYZ

ÄÖÜÅÇÈÎÑÓÆØŒ»„«[¶§•†‡]‹¡·¿›...

ITC Bodoni Six + SCOSF ...

• Book abcdefghijklmnopqrstuvwxyzABCDEFGHIJKLMNOPQRSTUVWXYZ-$123

Book Italic *abcdefghijklmnopqrstuvwxyzABCDEFGHIJKLMNOPQRSTUVWXYZ-$12*

Bold **abcdefghijklmnopqrstuvwxyzABCDEFGHIJKLMNOPQRSTUVWXYZ**

Bold Italic ***abcdefghijklmnopqrstuvwxyzABCDEFGHIJKLMNOPQRSTUVWXY***

Book SCOSF ABCDEFGHIJKLMNOPQRSTUVWXYZABCDEFGHIJKLMNOPQRSTUVWXYZ-$123

Book OSF abcdefghijklmnopqrstuvwxyzABCDEFGHIJKLMNOPQRSTUVWXYZ-$123

Book Italic OSF *abcdefghijklmnopqrstuvwxyzABCDEFGHIJKLMNOPQRSTUVWXYZ-$123*

Bold OSF **abcdefghijklmnopqrstuvwxyzABCDEFGHIJKLMNOPQRS...$123456**

Bold Italic OSF ***abcdefghijklmnopqrstuvwxyzABCDEFGHIJKLMNOPQRS...$1234567***

ITC BODONI TWELVE + SCOSF

ITC abcdefghijklmnopqrstuvwxyz(“.;‘!*?’:,”)

$1234567890&fiflß-äöüåçèîñóæøœ

ABCDEFGHIJKLMNOPQRSTUVWXYZ

ÄÖÜÅÇÈÎÑÓÆØŒ»„«[¶§•†‡]‹¡·¿›...

ITC Bodoni Twelve + SCOSF ...

• Book abcdefghijklmnopqrstuvwxyzABCDEFGHIJKLMNOPQRSTUVWXYZ-$123456789

Book Italic *abcdefghijklmnopqrstuvwxyzABCDEFGHIJKLMNOPQRSTUVWXYZ-$12345678*

Bold **abcdefghijklmnopqrstuvwxyzABCDEFGHIJKLMNOPQRSTUVWXYZ-$123**

B

. . . ITC Bodoni Twelve
+ SCOSF

Bold Italic ***abcdefghijklmnopqrstuvwxyzABCDEFGHIJKLMNOPQRSTUVWXYZ–$123***

Book SCOSF ABCDEFGHIJKLMNOPQRSTUVWXYZABCDEFGHIJKLMNOPQRSTUVWXYZ–$123456789

Book OSF abcdefghijklmnopqrstuvwxyzABCDEFGHIJKLMNOPQRSTUVWXYZ–$123456789

Book Italic OSF *abcdefghijklmnopqrstuvwxyzABCDEFGHIJKLMNOPQRSTUVWXYZ–$123456789*

Bold OSF **abcdefghijklmnopqrstuvwxyzABCDEFGHIJKLMNOPQRSTUVWXYZ–$1234**

Bold Italic OSF ***abcdefghijklmnopqrstuvwxyzABCDEFGHIJKLMNOPQRSTUVWXYZ–$1234***

ITC BODONI SEVENTY-TWO
+ SCOSF

ITC abcdefghijklmnopqrstuvwxyz(“.;‘!*?’:,”)

▲30 $1234567890&fiflß-äöüåçèîñóæøœ

ABCDEFGHIJKLMNOPQRSTUVWXYZ

ÄÖÜÅÇÈÎÑÓÆØŒ»„«[¶§•†‡]‹¡·¿›...

ITC Bodoni Seventy-Two
+ SCOSF . . .

• Book abcdefghijklmnopqrstuvwxyzABCDEFGHIJ

Book Italic *abcdefghijklmnopqrstuvwxyzABCDEFGHI*

Bold **abcdefghijklmnopqrstuvwxyzABCDEFG**

Bold Italic ***abcdefghijklmnopqrstuvwxyzABCDEFGH***

Book SCOSF ABCDEFGHIJKLMNOPQRSTUVWXYZABC...$1234

Book OSF abcdefghijklmnopqrstuvwxyzABC...$123456

Book Italic OSF *abcdefghijklmnopqrstuvwxyzABC...$123456*

Bold OSF **abcdefghijklmnopqrstuvwxyzABC...$123**

Bold Italic OSF ***abcdefghijklmnopqrstuvwxyzABC...$1234***

B

Boink

Robert Petrick • 1994

LET

▲24

ABCDEFGHIJKLMNOPQRSTUVWXYZ(“.;‘!*?’:,”)

$1234567890&-ÄÖÜÅÇÈÎÑÓÆØŒ»«[•]‹¡·¿›...

▷ I J Q ! ¡

ITC BOOKMAN

Ed Benguiat • 1975

ADO AGA BIT LEF FAM FRA LIN MAE URW

abcdefghijklmnopqrstuvwxyz(“.;‘!*?’:,”)
$1234567890&fifl ß-äöüåçèîñóæøœ
ABCDEFGHIJKLMNOPQRSTUVWXYZ
ÄÖÜÅÇÈÎÑÓÆØŒ»„«[¶§•†‡]‹¡·¿›...

ITC Bookman 1 ...

Light abcdefghijklmnopqrstuvwxyzABCDEFGHIJKLMNOPQRSTUVWXYZ–$123

Light Italic *abcdefghijklmnopqrstuvwxyzABCDEFGHIJKLMNOPQRSTUVWXYZ–$1234*

Demi **abcdefghijklmnopqrstuvwxyzABCDEFGHIJKLMNOPQRSTUVWXYZ–$**

Demi Italic ***abcdefghijklmnopqrstuvwxyzABCDEFGHIJKLMNOPQRSTUVWXYZ–$***

ITC Bookman 2 ...

• Medium abcdefghijklmnopqrstuvwxyzABCDEFGHIJKLMNOPQRSTUVWXYZ–$12

Medium Italic *abcdefghijklmnopqrstuvwxyzABCDEFGHIJKLMNOPQRSTUVWXYZ–$12*

Bold **abcdefghijklmnopqrstuvwxyzABCDEFGHIJKLMNOPQRSTUVWXYZ**

Bold Italic ***abcdefghijklmnopqrstuvwxyzABCDEFGHIJKLMNOPQRSTUVWXY***

BOOKMAN OLD STYLE

Ong Chong Wah • 1991

MCL

abcdefghijklmnopqrstuvwxyz(“.;‘!*?’:,”)
$1234567890&fifl ß-äöüåçèîñóæøœ
ABCDEFGHIJKLMNOPQRSTUVWXYZ
ÄÖÜÅÇÈÎÑÓÆØŒ»„«[¶§•†‡]‹¡·¿›...

Bookman Old Style ...

• Roman abcdefghijklmnopqrstuvwxyzABCDEFGHIJKLMNOPQRSTUVWXYZ–$123

Italic *abcdefghijklmnopqrstuvwxyzABCDEFGHIJKLMNOPQRSTUVWXYZ–$1234*

Bold **abcdefghijklmnopqrstuvwxyzABCDEFGHIJKLMNOPQRSTUVWXYZ–$**

Bold Italic ***abcdefghijklmnopqrstuvwxyzABCDEFGHIJKLMNOPQRSTUVWXYZ–$***

Bordeaux Roman

David Quay • 1987

LET FRA

▲30

abcdefghijklmnopqrstuvwxyz(“.;‘!*?’:,”)$1234567890&fifl ß-äöüåçèîñóæøœ
ABCDEFGHIJKLMNOPQRSTUVWXYZÄÖÜÅÇÈÎÑÓÆØŒ»„«[•]‹¡·¿› . . .

B

Bordeaux Italic
LET FRA
▲30
abcdefghijklmnopqrstuvwxyz(“.;‘!?’:,”)$1234567890&fiflß-äöüåçèîñóæøœ
ABCDEFGHIJKLMNOPQRSTUVWXYZÄÖÜÅÇÈÎÑÓÆØŒ»„«[•]‹¡·¿›. . .

Bordeaux Bold
LET
▲30
abcdefghijklmnopqrstuvwxyz(“.;‘!*?’:,”)$1234567890&fiflß-äöüåçèîñóæøœ
ABCDEFGHIJKLMNOPQRSTUVWXYZÄÖÜÅÇÈÎÑÓÆØŒ»„«[•]‹¡·¿›. . . ▷ ch ct ffi ffl sh st

Bordeaux Display
LET
▲30
abcdefghijklmnopqrstuvwxyz(“.;‘!*?’:,”)$1234567890&fiflß-
äöüåçèîñóæøœABCDEFGHIJKLMNOPQRSTUVWXYZ ÄÖÜ
ÅÇÈÎÑÓÆØŒ»„«[•]‹¡·¿› . . .

Bordeaux Script
LET FRA
▲30
abcdefghijklmnopqrstuvwxyz(“.;‘!*?’:,”)$1234567890&fiflß-äöüåçèîñóæøœ ▷ ch ct ffi ffl sh st
ABCDEFGHIJKLMNOPQRSTUVWXYZ Ç»„«[•]‹¡·¿›. . .

BOTON

Albert Boton • 1986
ADO AGA MAE
abcdefghijklmnopqrstuvwxyz(“.;‘!*?’:,”)
$1234567890&fiflß-äöüåçèîñóæøœ
ABCDEFGHIJKLMNOPQRSTUVWXYZ
ÄÖÜÅÇÈÎÑÓÆØŒ»„«[¶§•†‡]‹¡·¿›...

Boton ...

Light abcdefghijklmnopqrstuvwxyzABCDEFGHIJKLMNOPQRSTUVWXYZ–$1234567890(“.;‘!

Light Italic *abcdefghijklmnopqrstuvwxyzABCDEFGHIJKLMNOPQRSTUVWXYZ–$1234567890(“.;‘!*

• Regular abcdefghijklmnopqrstuvwxyzABCDEFGHIJKLMNOPQRSTUVWXYZ–$1234567890(

Italic *abcdefghijklmnopqrstuvwxyzABCDEFGHIJKLMNOPQRSTUVWXYZ–$1234567890*

Medium **abcdefghijklmnopqrstuvwxyzABCDEFGHIJKLMNOPQRSTUVWXYZ–$1234567**

Medium Italic ***abcdefghijklmnopqrstuvwxyzABCDEFGHIJKLMNOPQRSTUVWXYZ–$1234567***

Bold **abcdefghijklmnopqrstuvwxyzABCDEFGHIJKLMNOPQRSTUVWXYZ–$12345**

Bold Italic ***abcdefghijklmnopqrstuvwxyzABCDEFGHIJKLMNOPQRSTUVWXYZ–$1234***

B

Boulevard
Berthold ScriptSet 1
Günter Gerhard Lange • 1955 abcdefghijklmnopqrstuvwxyz(".;'!*?':,")
ADO AGA MAE $1234567890&fifl ß-äöüåçèîñóæøœ
▲15 ABCDEFGHIJKLMNOPQRSTUVWXYZ
ÄÖÜÅÇÈÎÑÓÆØŒ»„«[•]‹i·¿›...

A*I Bouwsma Script
Philip Bouwsma • 1994 abcdefghijklmnopqrstuvwxyz(".;'!*?':,")
ALP $1234567890&-fifl ß-äöüåçèîñóæøœ
ABCDEFGHIJKLMNOPQRSTUVWXYZ
ÄÖÜÅÇÈÎÑÓÆØŒ »„«[¶§•†‡]‹¡·¿›...

A*I Box Gothic
A*I Wood Type
A*I Design Staff • 1990 ABCDEFGHIJKLMNOPQRSTUVWXYZ
ALP MTD (.;!*?:,)$1234567890&-
▲36 ABCDEFGHIJKLMNOPQRSTUVWXYZ[]

DV BOY
Mike Diehl • 1986 abcdefghijklmnopqrstuvwxyz(".;'!*?':,")
DVT $1234567890&-äöüçèîñó
▲36 ABCDEFGHIJKLMNOPQRSTUVWXYZ ÇÑ[]¡¿...
▷

DV Boy ...
Wide ▲18 abcdefghijklmnopqrstuvwxyzABCDEFGH
In ABCDEFGHIJKLMNOPQRSTUVWXYZ-$1234567890.!?,&-
• Out abcdefghijklmnopqrstuvwxyzABCDEFGHIJKLMNOPQRSTUVWXYZ-$1234567890(".;'!*

Berthold ScriptSet 1: Bellevue, Berthold Script Regular & Medium, Boulevard.
A*I Wood Type: A*I Antique Condensed, A*I Barrel, A*I Box Gothic, A*I French XXX Condensed, A*I Painter, A*I Tuscan Egyptian.

B

Braggadocio
Monotype Headliners 3
W. A. Woolley • 1930
MCL
▲24

abcdefghijklmnopqrstuvwxyz
(“.;‘!*?’:,”)$1234567890&fiflß-
äöüåçèîñóæøœABCDEFGHIJKL
MNOPQRSTUVWXYZÄÖÜ
ÅÇÈÎÑÓÆØŒ»„«[¶§·†‡]‹¡·¿›…

BRAMLEY
Alan Meeks • 1980
URW AGP

abcdefghijklmnopqrstuvwxyz(“.;‘!*?’:,”)
$1234567890&fiflß-äöüåçèîñóæøœ
ABCDEFGHIJKLMNOPQRSTUVWXYZ
ÄÖÜÅÇÈÎÑÓÆØŒ»„«[¶§•†‡]‹¡·¿›…

Bramley …

Light abcdefghijklmnopqrstuvwxyzABCDEFGHIJKLMNOPQRSTUVWXYZ-$1234567890(“.;‘!
Light SCOSF ABCDEFGHIJKLMNOPQRSTUVWXYZABCDEFGHIJKLMNOPQRSTUVWXYZ-$1234567890(“.;
• Medium abcdefghijklmnopqrstuvwxyzABCDEFGHIJKLMNOPQRSTUVWXYZ-$1234567890(“
Medium SCOSF ABCDEFGHIJKLMNOPQRSTUVWXYZABCDEFGHIJKLMNOPQRSTUVWXYZ-$1234567890
Bold abcdefghijklmnopqrstuvwxyzABCDEFGHIJKLMNOPQRSTUVWXYZ-$123456789
Extra Bold abcdefghijklmnopqrstuvwxyzABCDEFGHIJKLMNOPQRSTUVWXYZ-$1234567

Branding Iron
Agfa DisplaySet 4
AGP
▲36

abcdefghijklmnopqrstuvwxyz(“.;‘!*?’:,”)
$1234567890&fiflß-äöüåçèîñóæøœ
ABCDEFGHIJKLMNOPQRSTUVWXYZ
ÄÖÜÅÇÈÎÑÓÆØŒ»„«[§•†‡]‹¡·¿›…

Monotype Headliners 3: Braggadocio, Figaro, Forte, Klang.
Agfa DisplaySet 4: Branding Iron, Isabella, McCollough, Raphael.

B

BREMEN

Richard Lipton • 1992

FBU BIT

▲24

ABCDEFGHIJKLMNOPQRSTUVWXYZ(“.;‘!*?’:,”)
$1234567890&-ÄÖÜÅÇÈÎÑÓÆØŒ
ABCDEFGHIJKLMNOPQRSTUVWXYZ
ÄÖÜÅÇÈÎÑÓÆØŒ»„«[¶§·†‡]‹¡·¿›...

Bremen ...

• Light ABCDEFGHIJKLMNOPQRSTUVWXYZABCDEFGHIJKL

Bold ABCDEFGHIJKLMNOPQRSTUVWXYZABCDEFG

Black ABCDEFGHIJKLMNOPQRSTUVWXYZABCD

Brighton Light

Alan Bright • 1979

LET URW

▲16

abcdefghijklmnopqrstuvwxyz(“.;‘!*?’:,”)
$1234567890&ﬁﬂß-äöüåçèîñóæøœ
ABCDEFGHIJKLMNOPQRSTUVWXYZ
ÄÖÜÅÇÈÎÑÓÆØŒ»„«[•]‹¡·¿›...

▷ ktKLR

Brighton Medium

LET URW

▲16

abcdefghijklmnopqrstuvwxyz(“.;‘!*?’:,”)
$1234567890&ﬁﬂß-äöüåçèîñóæøœ
ABCDEFGHIJKLMNOPQRSTUVWXYZ
ÄÖÜÅÇÈÎÑÓÆØŒ»„«[•]‹¡·¿›...

▷ ktKLR

Brighton Bold

LET URW

▲16

abcdefghijklmnopqrstuvwxyz(“.;‘!*?’:,”)
$1234567890&ﬁﬂß-äöüåçèîñóæøœ
ABCDEFGHIJKLMNOPQRSTUVWXYZ
ÄÖÜÅÇÈÎÑÓÆØŒ»„«[•]‹¡·¿›...

▷ ktKLR

MN Brio

MTD

▲16

abcdefghijklmnopqrstuvwxyz(“.;‘!*?’:,”)
$1234567890&ß-äöüåçèîñóæøœ
ABCDEFGHIJKLMNOPQRSTUVWXYZ
ÄÖÜÅÇÈÎÑÓÆØŒ»„«[·]‹¡¿›...

B

PL Britannia Bold
✤ *Agfa Typographer's Edition 3*
AGP ▲16

abcdefghijklmnopqrstuvwxyz(".;'!*?':,")
$1234567890&ß-äöüåçèîñóæøœ
ABCDEFGHIJKLMNOPQRSTUVWXYZ
ÄÖÜÅÇÈÎÑÓÆØŒ»,,«[•†‡]‹¡·¿›…

BROADWAY
✍ *Morris Fuller Benton • 1927*
Sol Hess, 1928
BIT URW ▲22

abcdefghijklmnopqrstuvwxyz(".;'!*?':,")
$1234567890&fiflß-äöüåçèîñóæøœ
ABCDEFGHIJKLMNOPQRSTUVWXYZ
ÄÖÜÅÇÈÎÑÓÆØŒ»,,«[§•†‡]‹¡·¿›…

Broadway …

Solid abcdefghijklmnopqrstuvwxyzABCDEFG

• Engraved abcdefghijklmnopqrstuvwxyzABCDEFGH

TC Broadway
✤ *Agfa Typographer's Edition 2*
AGP ▲24

abcdefghijklmnopqrstuvwxyz(".;'!*?':,")
$1234567890&ß-äöüåçèîñóæøœ
ABCDEFGHIJKLMNOPQRSTUVWXYZ
ÄÖÜÅÇÈÎÑÓÆØŒ»,,«[•†‡]‹¡·¿›…

Bronx
✍ *David Quay • 1986*
LET ▲16

abcdefghijklmnopqrstuvwxyz(".;'!?':,")
$1234567890&fiflß-äöüåçèîñóæøœ
ABCDEFGHIJKLMNOPQRSTUVWXYZ Ç»„«[•]‹¡·¿›…

Brophy Script
✤ *Agfa DisplaySet 3*
✍ *Harold Broderson • 1953*
AGP ▲16

abcdefghijklmnopqrstuvwxyz(".;'!*?':,")
$1234567890&fiflß-äöüåçèîñóæøœ
ABCDEFGHIJKLMNOPQRSTUVWXYZ
ÄÖÜÅÇÈÎÑÓÆØŒ»„«[§•†‡]‹¡·¿›…

✤ *Agfa Typographer's Edition 3*: Barclay Open, PL Bernhardt Light, Medium & Bold, PL Britannia Bold, Delphian Open, PL Fiorello Condensed, Fluidium Bold, PL Modern Heavy Condensed, PL Torino Open.

✤ *Agfa Typographer's Edition 2*: PL Barnum Block, PL Benguiat Frisky Bold, TC Broadway, PL Davison Zip Bold, PL Fiedler Gothic Bold, PL Futura Maxi Book & Bold, Neon Extra Condensed, Ritmo Bold, PL Trophy Oblique.

✤ *Agfa DisplaySet 3*: Basque, Brophy Script, Chevalier, Uncial.

B

BRUCE OLD STYLE

✍ Sol Hess • 1907 abcdefghijklmnopqrstuvwxyz(".;'!*?':,")
BIT $1234567890&fiflß-äöüåçèîñóæøœ
ABCDEFGHIJKLMNOPQRSTUVWXYZ
ÄÖÜÅÇÈÎÑÓÆØŒ»„«[§•†‡]‹¡·¿›...

Bruce Old Style ...

• Roman abcdefghijklmnopqrstuvwxyzABCDEFGHIJKLMNOPQRSTUVWXYZ–$1234
Italic *abcdefghijklmnopqrstuvwxyzABCDEFGHIJKLMNOPQRSTUVWXYZ–$123456*

Brush 445

✍ Martin Wilke • 1950 abcdefghijklmnopqrstuvwxyz(".;'!*?':,")
BIT $1234567890&fiflß-äöüåçèîñóæøœ
ABCDEFGHIJKLMNOPQRSTUVWXYZ
ÄÖÜÅÇÈÎÑÓÆØŒ»„«[§•†‡]‹¡·¿›...

Brush Script
✣ Adobe DisplaySet 4
✍ Robert E. Smith • 1942 abcdefghijklmnopqrstuvwxyz(".;'!*?':,")
ADO AGA BIT LIN MAE MCL MTD URW $1234567890&fiflß-äöüåçèîñóæøœ
▲16 ABCDEFGHIJKLMNOPQRSTUVWXYZ
ÄÖÜÅÇÈÎÑÓÆØŒ»„«[•]‹¡·¿›...

TF BRYN MAWR

✍ Joseph Treacy • 1983 abcdefghijklmnopqrstuvwxyz(".;'!*?':,")
TRE $1234567890&fiflß-äöüåçèîñóæøœ
ABCDEFGHIJKLMNOPQRSTUVWXYZ
ÄÖÜÅÇÈÎÑÓÆØŒ»„«[¶§•†‡]‹¡·¿›... ▷123579/234816■□

TF Bryn Mawr A ...

Light abcdefghijklmnopqrstuvwxyzABCDEFGHIJKLMNOPQRSTUVWXYZ–$123456789(".;'!*?':,")
Light Italic *abcdefghijklmnopqrstuvwxyzABCDEFGHIJKLMNOPQRSTUVWXYZ–$1234567890(".;'!*?':*
Medium **abcdefghijklmnopqrstuvwxyzABCDEFGHIJKLMNOPQRSTUVWXYZ–$1234567890**
Medium Italic ***abcdefghijklmnopqrstuvwxyzABCDEFGHIJKLMNOPQRSTUVWXYZ–$123456789***

TF Bryn Mawr B ...

• Book abcdefghijklmnopqrstuvwxyzABCDEFGHIJKLMNOPQRSTUVWXYZ–$1234567890(".;'!
Book Italic *abcdefghijklmnopqrstuvwxyzABCDEFGHIJKLMNOPQRSTUVWXYZ–$1234567890(".;'*
Bold **abcdefghijklmnopqrstuvwxyzABCDEFGHIJKLMNOPQRSTUVWXYZ–$123456**
Bold Italic ***abcdefghijklmnopqrstuvwxyzABCDEFGHIJKLMNOPQRSTUVWXYZ–$123456***

✣ *Adobe DisplaySet 4*: Brush Script, Hobo, Stencil.

B

BUBBALOVE

Todd Brei • 1993

T26

▲24

abcdefghijklmnopqrstuvwxyz(".;'!*?':,")$1234567890&fifl-äöüåçèîñóæøœ
ABCDEFGHIJKLMNOPQRSTUVWXYZÄÖÜÅÇÈÎÑÓÆØŒ»„«[¶§•†‡]‹¡·¿›...

Bubbalove ...

Light abcdefghijklmnopqrstuvwxyzABCDEFGHIJKLMNOPQRSTUVWXYZ—$1234567890(".;'!*?':

• Medium abcdefghijklmnopqrstuvwxyzABCDEFGHIJKLMNOPQRSTUVWXYZ—$1234567890(".;'!*?':

Bold abcdefghijklmnopqrstuvwxyzABCDEFGHIJKLMNOPQRSTUVWXYZ—$12

FC BULMER

Morris Fuller Benton • 1928
... William Martin, 1790

TFC

abcdefghijklmnopqrstuvwxyz(".;'!*?':,")
$1234567890&fifl-äöüåçèîñóæøœ
ABCDEFGHIJKLMNOPQRSTUVWXYZ
ÄÖÜÅÇÈÎÑÓÆØŒ»„«[•]‹¡·¿›...

▷ ff ffi ffl

FC Bulmer ...

• Roman abcdefghijklmnopqrstuvwxyzABCDEFGHIJKLMNOPQRSTUVWXYZ—$12345678

Italic *abcdefghijklmnopqrstuvwxyzABCDEFGHIJKLMNOPQRSTUVWXYZ—$1234567890("*

Roman SCOSF ABCDEFGHIJKLMNOPQRSTUVWXYZABCDEFGHIJKLMNOPQRSTUVWXYZ—$123456

Italic OSF *abcdefghijklmnopqrstuvwxyzABCDEFGHIJKLMNOPQRSTUVWXYZ—$1234567890(*

MONOTYPE BULMER

Ron Carpenter • 1994
... William Martin, 1790

MCL

abcdefghijklmnopqrstuvwxyz(".;'!*?':,")
$1234567890&fiflß-äöüåçèîñóæøœ
ABCDEFGHIJKLMNOPQRSTUVWXYZ
ÄÖÜÅÇÈÎÑÓÆØŒ»„«[¶§•†‡]‹¡·¿›...

Monotype Bulmer ...

• Roman abcdefghijklmnopqrstuvwxyzABCDEFGHIJKLMNOPQRSTUVWXYZ-$1234567890(".;'!*

Italic *abcdefghijklmnopqrstuvwxyzABCDEFGHIJKLMNOPQRSTUVWXYZ-$1234567890(".;'!*?':,*

Semibold **abcdefghijklmnopqrstuvwxyzABCDEFGHIJKLMNOPQRSTUVWXYZ-$1234567890(".;'**

Semibold Italic ***abcdefghijklmnopqrstuvwxyzABCDEFGHIJKLMNOPQRSTUVWXYZ-$1234567890(".;'!****

Bold **abcdefghijklmnopqrstuvwxyzABCDEFGHIJKLMNOPQRSTUVWXYZ-$1234567890(".**

Bold Italic ***abcdefghijklmnopqrstuvwxyzABCDEFGHIJKLMNOPQRSTUVWXYZ-$1234567890(".;'!****

Display Roman

▲30

abcdefghijklmnopqrstuvwxyzABCDEFGHIJKL
MNOPQRSTUVWXYZ-$1234567890(".;'!*?':,

B

... Monotype Bulmer Display Italic

▲30 *abcdefghijklmnopqrstuvwxyzABCDEFGHIJKLMN OPQRSTUVWXYZ-$1234567890(".;'!*?':,")&fifl*

Display Bold

▲30 **abcdefghijklmnopqrstuvwxyzABCDEFGHIJ KLMNOPQRSTUVWXYZ-$1234567890("**

Display Bold Italic

▲30 ***abcdefghijklmnopqrstuvwxyzABCDEFGHIJK LMNOPQRSTUVWXYZ-$1234567890(".;'!****

MONOTYPE BULMER EXPERT & SCOSF

MCL ABCDEFGHIJKLMNOPQRSTUVWXYZ.;!?:,
$1234567890&ﬀﬁﬂﬃﬄ–ÄÖÜÅÇÈÎÑÓÆØŒ
(abdeilmnorst) ⅛ ¼ ⅓ ⅜ ½ ⅝ ⅔ ¾ ⅞ $12345/67890¢ ₡Rp ▷J$1234567890' "

Monotype Bulmer Expert & SCOSF ...

• Expert Roman ABCDEFGHIJKLMNOPQRSTUVWXYZ–$1234567890.;!?:,&-ﬀﬁﬂﬃﬄ ⅛ ¼ ⅓ ⅜ ½ $12345/67890¢ (abdeilmnor

Expert Italic *$1234567890.; :,–ﬀﬁﬂﬃﬄ ⅛ ¼ ⅓ ⅜ ½ $12345/67890¢ (abdeilmnorst) ⅝ ⅔ ¾ ⅞ ₡Rp*

Roman & Italic Alternative ▷J$1234567890' " *JJKNOQTY$1234567890' "ÑÒØ*

Expert Semibold **ABCDEFGHIJKLMNOPQRSTUVWXYZ–$1234567890.;!?:,&-ﬀﬁﬂﬃﬄ ⅛ ¼ ⅓ ⅜ ½ $12345/67890¢ (abdeil**

Expert Semibold Italic ***$1234567890.; :,–ﬀﬁﬂﬃﬄ ⅛ ¼ ⅓ ⅜ ½ $12345/67890¢ (abdeilmnorst) ⅝ ⅔ ¾ ⅞ ₡Rp***

Semibold & Semibold Italic Alternative ▷**J$1234567890' "** ***JJKNOQTY$1234567890' "ÑÒØ***

Expert Bold **$1234567890.; :,–ﬀﬁﬂﬃﬄ ⅛ ¼ ⅓ ⅜ ½ $12345/67890¢ (abdeilmnorst) ⅝ ⅔ ¾ ⅞ ₡Rp**

Expert Bold Italic ***$1234567890.; :,–ﬀﬁﬂﬃﬄ ⅛ ¼ ⅓ ⅜ ½ $12345/67890¢ (abdeilmnorst) ⅝ ⅔ ¾ ⅞ ₡Rp***

Bold & Bold Italic Alternative ▷**J$1234567890' "** ***JJKNOQTY$1234567890' "ÑÒØ***

Roman SCOSF ABCDEFGHIJKLMNOPQRSTUVWXYZABCDEFGHIJKLMNOPQRSTUVWXYZ–$1234567890(".;'!

Semibold SCOSF **ABCDEFGHIJKLMNOPQRSTUVWXYZABCDEFGHIJKLMNOPQRSTUVWXYZ–$1234567890(".;**

Display Roman Alternative

▲30 ﬁ ﬂ ﬀ ﬃ ﬄ J$1234567890' "$1234567890 ⅛ ¼ ⅓

Display Italic Alternative

▲30 *ﬁﬂﬀﬃﬄJJKNOQTY$1234567890' "$1234567890*

Display Bold Alternative

▲30 **ﬁ ﬂ ﬀ ﬃ ﬄ J$1234567890' "$1234567890 ⅛ ¼**

Display Bold Italic Alternative

▲30 ***ﬁﬂﬀﬃﬄJJKNOQTY$1234567890' "$1234567***

B

Burin Roman
Agfa Engravers 1
AGP abcdefghijklmnopqrstuvwxyz(“.;‘!*?’:,”)
▲16 $1234567890&ß-äöüåçèîñó
ABCDEFGHIJKLMNOPQRSTUVWXYZ
ÄÖÜÅÇÈÎÑÓ»«[·]‹› ▹I V X st nd rd th ¼ ⅓ ½ ¾ D’ C r. ’c ’s O’ rs. s. & %

Burin Sans
Agfa Engravers 1
AGP abcdefghijklmnopqrstuvwxyz(“.;‘!*?’:,”)
▲16 $1234567890&ß-äöüåçèîñó
ABCDEFGHIJKLMNOPQRSTUVWXYZ
ÄÖÜÅÇÈÎÑÓ»«[·]‹› ▹I V X st nd rd th ¼ ⅓ ½ ¾ D’ C r. ’c ’s O’ rs. s. & %

Burlington
Alan Meeks • 1985
LET
▲30
abcdefghijklmnopqrstuvwxyz(“.;‘!*?’:,”)
$1234567890&ß-äöüåçèîñóæøœ
ABCDEFGHIJKLMNOPQRSTUVWXYZ
ÄÖÜÅÇÈÎÑÓÆØŒ»«[•]‹›

BYRON
Pat Hickson • 1993
RED
▲16
abcdefghijklmnopqrstuvwxyz(“.;‘!*?’:,”)
$1234567890&fiflß-äöüåçèîñóæøœ
ABCDEFGHIJKLMNOPQRSTUVWXYZ
ÄÖÜÅÇÈÎÑÓÆØŒ»„«[·]‹¡·¿›…

Byron …

Light abcdefghijklmnopqrstuvwxyzABCDEFGHIJKLMNOPQRSTUVWXYZ–

Light Swash OSF e f g h k l m n q r s t u v w x y z A B C E M P Q R S –$1234567890(“.;‘!*?’:,”)&fiflß-äöü

• Medium abcdefghijklmnopqrstuvwxyzABCDEFGHIJKLMNOPQRSTUVWXY

Medium Swash OSF e f g h k l m n q r s t u v w x y z A B C E M P Q R S –$1234567890(“.;‘!*?’:,”)&fiflß-

Bold abcdefghijklmnopqrstuvwxyzABCDEFGHIJKLMNOPQRSTUVWX

Bold Swash OSF e f g h k l m n q r s t u v w x y z A B C E M P Q R S –$1234567890(“.;‘!*?’:,”)&fi

Agfa Engravers 1: Antique Roman Solid & Slanted, Artisan Roman, Burin Roman & Sans, Classic Roman Light & Regular, Handle Oldstyle, Roman Light & Medium.

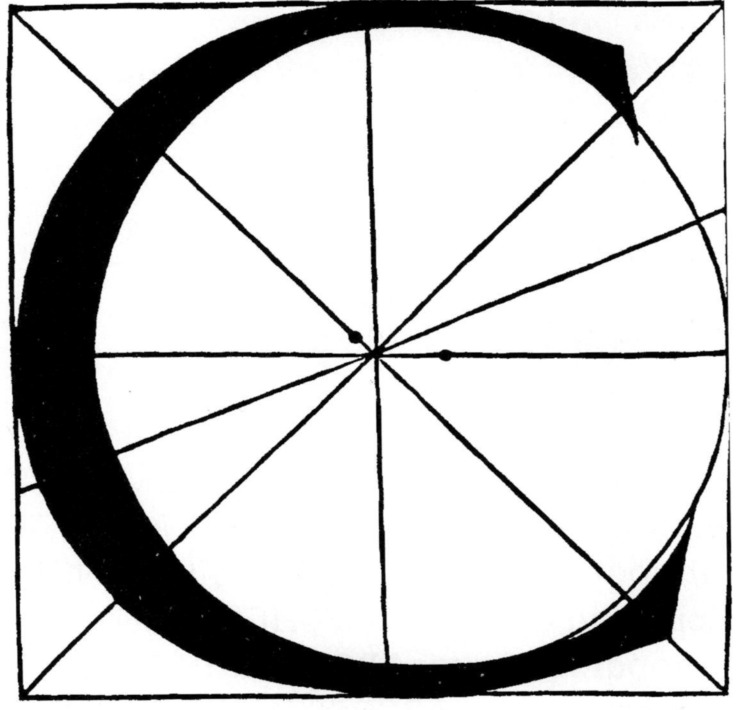

✍ Luca de Pacioli, 1509

C

Cabaret

Alan Meeks • 1980

LET LEF FRA

▲30

abcdefghijklmnopqrstuvwxyz(".;'!*?':,")
$1234567890&-fifl ß-äöüåçèîñóæøœ
ABCDEFGHIJKLMNOPQRSTUVWXYZ
ÄÖÜÅÇÈÎÑÓÆØŒ»„«[•]‹¡·¿›...

Cabarga Cursiva

Demetrio E. & Leslie Cabarga • 1982

LET

▲16

abcdefghijklmnopqrstuvwxyz(".;'!*?':,")
$1234567890&fiflß-äöüåçèîñóæøœ
ABCDEFGHIJKLMNOPQRSTUVWXYZ
ÄÖÜÅÇÈÎÑÓ»„«[•]‹¡·¿›...

▷h m n s

PMN CAECILIA

Peter Matthias Noordzij • 1991

LIN ADO AGA MAE

abcdefghijklmnopqrstuvwxyz(".;'!*?':,")
$1234567890&fiflß-äöüåçèîñóæøœ
ABCDEFGHIJKLMNOPQRSTUVWXYZ
ÄÖÜÅÇÈÎÑÓÆØŒ»„«[¶§•†‡]‹¡·¿›...

PMN Caecilia + OSF ...

45-Light abcdefghijklmnopqrstuvwxyzABCDEFGHIJKLMNOPQRSTUVWXYZ–$12345
46-Light Italic *abcdefghijklmnopqrstuvwxyzABCDEFGHIJKLMNOPQRSTUVWXYZ–$123456789*
• 55-Roman abcdefghijklmnopqrstuvwxyzABCDEFGHIJKLMNOPQRSTUVWXYZ–$1234
56-Italic *abcdefghijklmnopqrstuvwxyzABCDEFGHIJKLMNOPQRSTUVWXYZ–$12345678*
75-Bold **abcdefghijklmnopqrstuvwxyzABCDEFGHIJKLMNOPQRSTUVWXYZ–$123**
76-Bold Italic ***abcdefghijklmnopqrstuvwxyzABCDEFGHIJKLMNOPQRSTUVWXYZ–$123456***
85-Heavy **abcdefghijklmnopqrstuvwxyzABCDEFGHIJKLMNOPQRSTUVWXYZ–$12**
86-Heavy Italic ***abcdefghijklmnopqrstuvwxyzABCDEFGHIJKLMNOPQRSTUVWXYZ–$12345***
45-Light OSF abcdefghijklmnopqrstuvwxyzABCDEFGHIJKLMNOPQRSTUVWXYZ–$12345
46-Light Italic OSF *abcdefghijklmnopqrstuvwxyzABCDEFGHIJKLMNOPQRSTUVWXYZ–$123456789*
55-Roman OSF abcdefghijklmnopqrstuvwxyzABCDEFGHIJKLMNOPQRSTUVWXYZ–$1234
56-Italic OSF *abcdefghijklmnopqrstuvwxyzABCDEFGHIJKLMNOPQRSTUVWXYZ–$12345678*
75-Bold OSF **abcdefghijklmnopqrstuvwxyzABCDEFGHIJKLMNOPQRSTUVWXYZ–$123**
76-Bold Italic OSF ***abcdefghijklmnopqrstuvwxyzABCDEFGHIJKLMNOPQRSTUVWXYZ–$123456***
85-Heavy OSF **abcdefghijklmnopqrstuvwxyzABCDEFGHIJKLMNOPQRSTUVWXYZ–$12**
86-Heavy Italic OSF ***abcdefghijklmnopqrstuvwxyzABCDEFGHIJKLMNOPQRSTUVWXYZ–$12345***

C

PMN CAECILIA SCOSF

LIN ADO AGA MAE ABCDEFGHIJKLMNOPQRSTUVWXYZ(".;'!*?':,")
$1234567890&-ÄÖÜÅÇÈÎÑÓÆØŒ
ABCDEFGHIJKLMNOPQRSTUVWXYZ
ÄÖÜÅÇÈÎÑÓÆØŒ»„«[¶§•†‡]‹¡·¿›...

PMN Caecilia SCOSF ...

45-Light SCOSF ABCDEFGHIJKLMNOPQRSTUVWXYZABCDEFGHIJKLMNOPQRSTUVWXYZ–$1234
46-Light Italic SCOSF *ABCDEFGHIJKLMNOPQRSTUVWXYZABCDEFGHIJKLMNOPQRSTUVWXYZ–$1234567*
• 55-Roman SCOSF ABCDEFGHIJKLMNOPQRSTUVWXYZABCDEFGHIJKLMNOPQRSTUVWXYZ–$123
56-Italic SCOSF *ABCDEFGHIJKLMNOPQRSTUVWXYZABCDEFGHIJKLMNOPQRSTUVWXYZ–$123456*
75-Bold SCOSF **ABCDEFGHIJKLMNOPQRSTUVWXYZABCDEFGHIJKLMNOPQRSTUVWXYZ–$12**
76-Bold Italic SCOSF ***ABCDEFGHIJKLMNOPQRSTUVWXYZABCDEFGHIJKLMNOPQRSTUVWXYZ–$12345***
85-Heavy SCOSF **ABCDEFGHIJKLMNOPQRSTUVWXYZABCDEFGHIJKLMNOPQRSTUVWXYZ–$1**
86-Heavy Italic SCOSF ***ABCDEFGHIJKLMNOPQRSTUVWXYZABCDEFGHIJKLMNOPQRSTUVWXYZ–$1234***

CAFETERIA

Tobias Frere-Jones • 1993 abcdefghijklmnopqrstuvwxyz(".;'!*?':,")
FBU $1234567890&fiflß-äöüåçèîñóæøœ
▲18 ABCDEFGHIJKLMNOPQRSTUVWXYZ
ÄÖÜÅÇÈÎÑÓÆØŒ»„«[¶§•†‡]‹¡·¿›...

▷

Cafeteria ...

Light abcdefghijklmnopqrstuvwxyzABCDEFGHIJKLMNOPQRSTUVWXYZ-$1234567890(".;'!*?':,")&fiflß-äöüÄÖÜåçè
• Regular abcdefghijklmnopqrstuvwxyzABCDEFGHIJKLMNOPQRSTUVWXYZ-$1234567890(".;'!*?':,")&fiflß-äöü
Bold **abcdefghijklmnopqrstuvwxyzABCDEFGHIJKLMNOPQRSTUVWXYZ-$1234567890(".;'!*?':,")&fi**
Black **abcdefghijklmnopqrstuvwxyzABCDEFGHIJKLMNOPQRSTUVWXYZ-$1234567890(".;'!*?'**

CAFLISCH SCRIPT MULTIPLE·MASTER
(one axis : weight)
Robert Slimbach • 1993
... Max Caflisch

abcdefghijklmnopqrstuvwxyz(".;'!?':,")*
ADO AGA MAE *$1234567890&fiflß-äöüåçèîñóæøœ*
▲16 *ABCDEFGHIJKLMNOPQRSTUVWXYZ*
ÄÖÜÅÇÈÎÑÓÆØŒ»„«[¢§·†‡]‹¡·¿›...

Caflisch Script MultipleMaster ...

Light *abcdefghijklmnopqrstuvwxyzABCDEFGHIJKLMNOPQRSTUVWXYZ–$1234567890(".;'!*?':,")*
Light Swash *abcdefghijklmnopqrstuvwxyzABCDEFGHIJKLMNOPQRSTUVWXYZ–$1234567890(*
Light Alternate *ch ck ct d ff ffi ffl ft g g k q st tf tt y z z*
• Regular *abcdefghijklmnopqrstuvwxyzABCDEFGHIJKLMNOPQRSTUVWXYZ–$1234567890(".;'!*?':*
Regular Swash *abcdefghijklmnopqrstuvwxyzABCDEFGHIJKLMNOPQRSTUVWXYZ–$123456789*
Regular Alternate *ch ck ct d ff ffi ffl ft g g k q st tf tt y z z*

C

... Caflisch Script MultipleMaster

Semibold abcdefghijklmnopqrstuvwxyzABCDEFGHIJKLMNOPQRSTUVWXYZ–$1234567890(“.;‘!

Semibold Swash abcdefghijklmnopqrstuvwxyzABCDEFGHIJKLMNOPQRSTUVWXYZ–$123456

Semibold Alternate ch ck ct d ff ffi ffl ft g g k q st tf tt y z z

Bold abcdefghijklmnopqrstuvwxyzABCDEFGHIJKLMNOPQRSTUVWXYZ–$1234567890(“.

Bold Swash abcdefghijklmnopqrstuvwxyzABCDEFGHIJKLMNOPQRSTUVWXYZ–$12345

Bold Alternate ch ck ct d ff ffi ffl ft g g k q st tf tt y z z

NEW CALEDONIA

John Quaranta • 1978 *(William Addison Dwiggins, 1938)* abcdefghijklmnopqrstuvwxyz(“.;‘!*?’:,”)

LIN ADO AGA MAE $1234567890&fiflß-äöüåçèîñóæøœ

ABCDEFGHIJKLMNOPQRSTUVWXYZ

ÄÖÜÅÇÈÎÑÓÆØŒ»„«[¶§•†‡]‹¡·¿›...

New Caledonia ...

• Regular abcdefghijklmnopqrstuvwxyzABCDEFGHIJKLMNOPQRSTUVWXYZ–$1234567890

Italic *abcdefghijklmnopqrstuvwxyzABCDEFGHIJKLMNOPQRSTUVWXYZ–$1234567890(*

Semibold abcdefghijklmnopqrstuvwxyzABCDEFGHIJKLMNOPQRSTUVWXYZ–$12345678

Semibold Italic *abcdefghijklmnopqrstuvwxyzABCDEFGHIJKLMNOPQRSTUVWXYZ–$123456789*

Bold **abcdefghijklmnopqrstuvwxyzABCDEFGHIJKLMNOPQRSTUVWXYZ–$12345**

Bold Italic ***abcdefghijklmnopqrstuvwxyzABCDEFGHIJKLMNOPQRSTUVWXYZ–$123456***

Black **abcdefghijklmnopqrstuvwxyzABCDEFGHIJKLMNOPQRSTUVWXYZ–$1**

Black Italic ***abcdefghijklmnopqrstuvwxyzABCDEFGHIJKLMNOPQRSTUVWXYZ–$12***

NEW CALEDONIA SCOSF

LIN ADO AGA MAE ABCDEFGHIJKLMNOPQRSTUVWXYZ(“.;‘!*?’:,”)

$1234567890&-ÄÖÜÅÇÈÎÑÓÆØŒ

ABCDEFGHIJKLMNOPQRSTUVWXYZ

ÄÖÜÅÇÈÎÑÓÆØŒ»„«[¶§•†‡]‹¡·¿›...

New Caledonia SCOSF ...

• Regular SCOSF ABCDEFGHIJKLMNOPQRSTUVWXYZABCDEFGHIJKLMNOPQRSTUVWXYZ–$1234

Italic OSF *abcdefghijklmnopqrstuvwxyzABCDEFGHIJKLMNOPQRSTUVWXYZ–$1234567890(*

Bold SCOSF **ABCDEFGHIJKLMNOPQRSTUVWXYZABCDEFGHIJKLMNOPQRSTUVWXYZ–$12**

Bold Italic OSF ***abcdefghijklmnopqrstuvwxyzABCDEFGHIJKLMNOPQRSTUVWXYZ–$123456***

CALISTO

Ron Carpenter • 1987 abcdefghijklmnopqrstuvwxyz(“.;‘!*?’:,”)

MCL $1234567890&fiflß-äöüåçèîñóæøœ

ABCDEFGHIJKLMNOPQRSTUVWXYZ

ÄÖÜÅÇÈÎÑÓÆØŒ»„«[¶§•†‡]‹¡·¿›...

C

... Calisto ...

• Roman abcdefghijklmnopqrstuvwxyzABCDEFGHIJKLMNOPQRSTUVWXYZ–$123456

Italic *abcdefghijklmnopqrstuvwxyzABCDEFGHIJKLMNOPQRSTUVWXYZ–$1234567890(".;'!*

Bold **abcdefghijklmnopqrstuvwxyzABCDEFGHIJKLMNOPQRSTUVWXYZ–$12345**

Bold Italic ***abcdefghijklmnopqrstuvwxyzABCDEFGHIJKLMNOPQRSTUVWXYZ–$1234567890(***

Calligraphic 421

Georg Trump • 1954 abcdefghijklmnopqrstuvwxyz(".;'!*?':,")

BIT $1234567890&fiflß-äöüåçèîñóæøœ

▲16 ABCDEFGHIJKLMNOPQRSTUVWXYZ

ÄÖÜÅÇÈÎÑÓÆØŒ»„«[§•†‡]‹¡·¿›...

CALVERT

Margaret Calvert • 1980 abcdefghijklmnopqrstuvwxyz(".;'!*?':,")

MCL ADO AGA LIN MAE $1234567890&fiflß-äöüåçèîñóæøœ

▲16 ABCDEFGHIJKLMNOPQRSTUVWXYZ

ÄÖÜÅÇÈÎÑÓÆØŒ»„«[¶§•†‡]‹¡·¿›...

Calvert ...

Light abcdefghijklmnopqrstuvwxyzABCDEFGHIJKLMNOPQRSTUVWXYZ

• Medium abcdefghijklmnopqrstuvwxyzABCDEFGHIJKLMNOPQRSTUVWXY

Bold **abcdefghijklmnopqrstuvwxyzABCDEFGHIJKLMNOPQRSTUVWXY**

Campaign

Alan Meeks • 1987 ABCDEFGHIJKLMNOPQRSTUVWXYZ

LET (".;'!*?':,")$1234567890

▲30 &-ÄÖÜÅÇÈÎÑÓÆØŒ»„«[•]‹¡·¿›...

Cancellaresca Script

Alan Meeks • 1982 *abcdefghijklmnopqrstuvwxyz(".;'!*?':,")*

LET *$1234567890&fiflß-äöüåçèîñóæøœ*

▲17 *ABCDEFGHIJKLMNOPQRSTUVWXYZ*

Ç»„«[•]‹¡·¿›...

C

CANDIDA

Jakob Erbar • 1936 abcdefghijklmnopqrstuvwxyz(".;'!*?':,")

BIT ADO AGA LIN MAE URW $1234567890&fiflß-äöüåçèîñóæøœ

ABCDEFGHIJKLMNOPQRSTUVWXYZ

ÄÖÜÅÇÈÎÑÓÆØŒ»,,«[¶§•†‡]‹¡·¿›...

Candida ...

• Roman abcdefghijklmnopqrstuvwxyzABCDEFGHIJKLMNOPQRSTUVWXYZ–$1234

Italic *abcdefghijklmnopqrstuvwxyzABCDEFGHIJKLMNOPQRSTUVWXYZ–$123456*

Bold **abcdefghijklmnopqrstuvwxyzABCDEFGHIJKLMNOPQRSTUVWXYZ–$123**

CANTERBURY OLD STYLE

Morris Fuller Benton • 1926 abcdefghijklmnopqrstuvwxyz(".;'!*?':,")

RED

▲30 $1234567890&flß-äöüåçèîñóæøœ

ABCDEFGHIJKLMNOPQRSTUVWXYZ

ÄÖÜÅÇÈÎÑÓÆØŒ»,,«[¶§•†‡]‹¡·¿›...

Canterbury Old Style ...

• Regular abcdefghijklmnopqrstuvwxyzABCDEFGHIJKLMNOPQRS

Bold **abcdefghijklmnopqrstuvwxyzABCDEFGHIJKLMNOPQR**

CANTORIA

Ron Carpenter • 1986 abcdefghijklmnopqrstuvwxyz(".;'!*?':,")

MCL ADO AGA LIN MAE $1234567890&-fiflß-äöüåçèîñóæøœ

ABCDEFGHIJKLMNOPQRSTUVWXYZ

ÄÖÜÅÇÈÎÑÓÆØŒ»,,«[¶§•†‡]‹¡·¿›...

Cantoria 1 ...

• Regular abcdefghijklmnopqrstuvwxyzABCDEFGHIJKLMNOPQRSTUVWXYZ–$123456

Italic *abcdefghijklmnopqrstuvwxyzABCDEFGHIJKLMNOPQRSTUVWXYZ–$1234567890(*

Bold **abcdefghijklmnopqrstuvwxyzABCDEFGHIJKLMNOPQRSTUVWXYZ–$1**

Bold Italic ***abcdefghijklmnopqrstuvwxyzABCDEFGHIJKLMNOPQRSTUVWXYZ–$1234***

Cantoria 2 ...

Light abcdefghijklmnopqrstuvwxyzABCDEFGHIJKLMNOPQRSTUVWXYZ–$1234567890

Light Italic *abcdefghijklmnopqrstuvwxyzABCDEFGHIJKLMNOPQRSTUVWXYZ–$1234567890(".;'*

Semibold **abcdefghijklmnopqrstuvwxyzABCDEFGHIJKLMNOPQRSTUVWXYZ–$1234**

C

. . . Cantoria 2

Semibold Italic *abcdefghijklmnopqrstuvwxyzABCDEFGHIJKLMNOPQRSTUVWXYZ–$1234567*

Extra Bold **abcdefghijklmnopqrstuvwxyzABCDEFGHIJKLMNOPQRSTUVWXYZ–**

Extra Bold Italic ***abcdefghijklmnopqrstuvwxyzABCDEFGHIJKLMNOPQRSTUVWXYZ–$12***

Cardboard Cutout

INT

▲24

ABCDEFGHIJKLMNOPQRSTUV
WXYZ(.:;!?,)1234567890-

BITSTREAM CARMINA

✍ *Gudrun Zapf-Von Hesse • 1987*

BIT

abcdefghijklmnopqrstuvwxyz(“.;‘!*?’:,”)
$1234567890&fiflß-äöüåçèîñóæøœ
ABCDEFGHIJKLMNOPQRSTUVWXYZ
ÄÖÜÅÇÈÎÑÓÆØŒ»„«[¶§•†‡]‹i·¿›...

Bitstream Carmina 1 . . .

• Medium abcdefghijklmnopqrstuvwxyzABCDEFGHIJKLMNOPQRSTUVWXYZ–$12345

Medium Italic *abcdefghijklmnopqrstuvwxyzABCDEFGHIJKLMNOPQRSTUVWXYZ–$123456789*

Bold **abcdefghijklmnopqrstuvwxyzABCDEFGHIJKLMNOPQRSTUVWXYZ–$12**

Bold Italic ***abcdefghijklmnopqrstuvwxyzABCDEFGHIJKLMNOPQRSTUVWXYZ–$1234***

Bitstream Carmina 2 . . .

Light abcdefghijklmnopqrstuvwxyzABCDEFGHIJKLMNOPQRSTUVWXYZ–$123456

Light Italic *abcdefghijklmnopqrstuvwxyzABCDEFGHIJKLMNOPQRSTUVWXYZ–$1234567890(“*

Black **abcdefghijklmnopqrstuvwxyzABCDEFGHIJKLMNOPQRSTUVWXYZ–**

Black Italic ***abcdefghijklmnopqrstuvwxyzABCDEFGHIJKLMNOPQRSTUVWXYZ–***

Carnival

✍ *Jim Marcus • 1994*

T26

▲30

abcdefghijklmnopqrstuvwxyz(.;!*?:,)$1234567890
&–ABCDEFGHIJKLMNOPQRSTUVWXYZ[]

Carolina

✣ *Type Before Gutenberg 2*

✍ *Gottfried Pott • 1991*

LIN ADO AGA MAE

abcdefghijklmnopqrstuvwxyz(“.;‘!*?’:,”)
$1234567890&fiflß-äöüåçèîñóæøœ
ABCDEFGHIJKLMNOPQRSTUVWXYZ
ÄÖÜÅÇÈÎÑÓÆØŒ»„«[¶§•†‡]‹¡·¿›...

▹ch ck ff ft ll ſ s fi ff ß tz – äöüÄÖÜ

✣ *Type Before Gutenberg 2*: Carolina, Clairvaux, San Marco.

C

CARTIER
Agfa TextSet 1
Carl Dair • 1967
AGP
▲16

abcdefghijklmnopqrstuvwxyz(".;'!*?':,")
$1234567890&fiflß-äöüåçèîñóæøœ
ABCDEFGHIJKLMNOPQRSTUVWXYZ
ÄÖÜÅÇÈÎÑÓÆØŒ»„«[¶§•†‡]‹¡·¿›...

Cartier ...
• Roman abcdefghijklmnopqrstuvwxyzABCDEFGHIJKLMNOPQRSTUVWXYZ–$1234567890("
Italic *abcdefghijklmnopqrstuvwxyz*ABCDEFGHIJKLMNOPQRSTUVWXYZ–*$1234567890(".;'!*?':,")*

FC Cartoon
Howard Allen Trafton • 1936
TFC
▲18

ABCDEFGHIJKLMNOPQRSTUVWXYZ(".;'!*' ':,")
$1234567890&-ÄÖÜÅÇÈÎÑÓÆØŒ
ABCDEFGHIJKLMNOPQRSTUVWXYZ
ÄÖÜÅÇÈÎÓÆØŒ»„«[•]‹¡·¿›...

Cascade Script
Linotype ScriptSet 1
Matthew Carter • 1967
LIN ADO AGA MAE
▲16

abcdefghijklmnopqrstuvwxyz (".;'!*?':,")
$1234567890&fiflß-äöüåçèîñóæøœ
ABCDEFGHIJKLMNOPQRSTUVWXYZ
ÄÖÜÅÇÈÎÑÓÆØŒ»„«[¶§•†‡]‹¡·¿›...

CASLON 540 & CASLON 3
ATF, Linotype • 1900, 1965 (William Caslon, 1725)
LIN ADO AGA BIT FAM MAE

abcdefghijklmnopqrstuvwxyz(".;'!*?':,")
$1234567890&fiflß-äöüåçèîñóæøœ
ABCDEFGHIJKLMNOPQRSTUVWXYZ
ÄÖÜÅÇÈÎÑÓÆØŒ»„«[¶§•†‡]‹¡·¿›...

Caslon 540 & Caslon 3 ...
• Caslon 540 Roman abcdefghijklmnopqrstuvwxyzABCDEFGHIJKLMNOPQRSTUVWXYZ–$1234567
Caslon 540 Italic *abcdefghijklmnopqrstuvwxyzABCDEFGHIJKLMNOPQRSTUVWXYZ–$1234567890(".;'*
Caslon 3 Roman **abcdefghijklmnopqrstuvwxyzABCDEFGHIJKLMNOPQRSTUVWXYZ–**
Caslon 3 Italic ***abcdefghijklmnopqrstuvwxyzABCDEFGHIJKLMNOPQRSTUVWXYZ–$12345***

CASLON 540 & CASLON 3 SCOSF
LIN ADO AGA MAE

ABCDEFGHIJKLMNOPQRSTUVWXYZ(".;'!*?':,")
$1234567890&-ÄÖÜÅÇÈÎÑÓÆØŒ
ABCDEFGHIJKLMNOPQRSTUVWXYZ
ÄÖÜÅÇÈÎÑÓÆØŒ»„«[¶§•†‡]‹¡·¿›...

Caslon 540 & Caslon 3 SCOSF ...
• Caslon 540 Roman SCOSF ABCDEFGHIJKLMNOPQRSTUVWXYZABCDEFGHIJKLMNOPQRSTUVWXYZ–$123456

Agfa TextSet 1: Cartier, Cartier Italic, Holland Seminar, Holland Seminar Italic.
Linotype ScriptSet 1: Cascade Script, Medici Script, Nuptial Script.

C

... Caslon 540 & Caslon 3 SCOSF

Caslon 540 Italic OSF *abcdefghijklmnopqrstuvwxyzABCDEFGHIJKLMNOPQRSTUVWXYZ–$1234567890(".;'*

Caslon 3 SCOSF ABCDEFGHIJKLMNOPQRSTUVWXYZABCDEFGHIJKLMNOPQRSTUVWX

Caslon 3 Italic OSF ***abcdefghijklmnopqrstuvwxyzABCDEFGHIJKLMNOPQRSTUVWXYZ–$12345***

Caslon 540 Italic with Swashes

Freda Sack • 1981 (William Caslon, 1725) *abcdefghijklmnopqrstuvwxyz(".;'!*?':,")*

LET *$1234567890&fiflß-äöüåçèîñóæøœ* ▷ *ctefgy ksp st wz*

▲16 *ABCDEFGHIJKLMNOPQRSTUVWXYZ*

ÄÖÜÅÇÈÎÑÓÆØŒ»„«[•]¡¿... ▷ *ABCCDEFFGHHIJKKLLMNOPQ*

Caslon Open Face

... • 1915 abcdefghijklmnopqrstuvwxyz(".;'!*?':,")

LIN ADO AGA BIT MAE

▲30 $1234567890&fiflß-äöüåçèîñóæøœ

ABCDEFGHIJKLMNOPQRSTUV

WXYZÄÖÜÅÇÈÎÑÓÆØŒ»„«|¶§•

CASLON OLDSTYLE NO.337

Sol Hess • 1915 (William Caslon, 1725) abcdefghijklmnopqrstuvwxyz(".;'!*?':,")

LAN $1234567890&fiflß-äöüåçèîñóÿæøœ

ABCDEFGHIJKLMNOPQRSTUVWXYZ

ÄÖÜÅÇÈÎÑÓÆØŒ»„«[¶§•†]¡¿... ▷ ct ff ffi ffl st

Caslon Oldstyle No. 337 ...

• Roman abcdefghijklmnopqrstuvwxyzABCDEFGHIJKLMNOPQRSTUVWXYZ-$12345

Italic *abcdefghijklmnopqrstuvwxyzABCDEFGHIJKLMNOPQRSTUVWXYZ-$1234567*

Italic Swash *ctffffiflffiffl ft st h k v w z ABCDGKLMNPRTVWY(".;'!*?':,")-$1234567890abcdefgh*

Roman OSF abcdefghijklmnopqrstuvwxyzABCDEFGHIJKLMNOPQRSTUVWXYZ-$12345

Italic OSF *abcdefghijklmnopqrstuvwxyzABCDEFGHIJKLMNOPQRSTUVWXYZ-$1234567*

Italic Swash OSF *ctffffiflffiffl ft st h k v w z ABCDGKLMNPRTVWY(".;'!*?':,")-$1234567890abcdefgh*

Roman SCOSF ABCDEFGHIJKLMNOPQRSTUVWXYZABCDEFGHIJKLMNOPQRSTUVWXYZ-$12

Italic SCOSF *ABCDEFGHIJKLMNOPQRSTUVWXYZABCDEFGHIJKLMNOPQRSTUVWXYZ-$12*

Roman & Italic Quaints ſſ ſb ſh ſi ſk ſl ſſ ſſi ſſl ſt *ſſ ſb ſh ſi ſk ſl ſſ ſſi ſſl ſt*

Roman SD abcdefghijklmnopqrstuvwxyzABCDEFGHIJKLMNOPQRSTUVWXYZ-$12345

Italic SD *abcdefghijklmnopqrstuvwxyzABCDEFGHIJKLMNOPQRSTUVWXYZ-$1234567*

Roman OSF SD abcdefghijklmnopqrstuvwxyzABCDEFGHIJKLMNOPQRSTUVWXYZ-$12345

... Caslon Oldstyle No. 337

Italic OSF SD *abcdefghijklmnopqrstuvwxyzABCDEFGHIJKLMNOPQRSTUVWXYZ-$1234567*

Roman SCOSF SD ABCDEFGHIJKLMNOPQRSTUVWXYZABCDEFGHIJKLMNOPQRSTUVWXYZ-$123

Italic SCOSF SD *ABCDEFGHIJKLMNOPQRSTUVWXYZABCDEFGHIJKLMNOPQRSTUVWXYZ-$123*

Italic Swash & Quaints *hkſſbſhſiſkſlſſſſiſſlſtvwzABCDEFGHIJKLMNOPQRSTUVWXYZ*

CASLON BOLD 537 & 637

Sol Hess • 1915 (William Caslon, 1725) abcdefghijklmnopqrstuvwxyz(“.;‘!*?’:,”)

LAN $1234567890&fiflß-äöüåçèîñóæøœ

ABCDEFGHIJKLMNOPQRSTUVWXYZ

ÄÖÜÅÇÈÎÑÓÆØŒ»,,«[¶§·†]¡¿...

▷ ctffffiffl st

Caslon Bold 537 & 637 ...

• 537 Bold abcdefghijklmnopqrstuvwxyzABCDEFGHIJKLMNOPQRSTUVWXYZ-$123

537 Bold Italic *abcdefghijklmnopqrstuvwxyzABCDEFGHIJKLMNOPQRSTUVWXYZ-$123456789*

537 Bold OSF abcdefghijklmnopqrstuvwxyzABCDEFGHIJKLMNOPQRSTUVWXYZ-$123

537 Bold Italic OSF *abcdefghijklmnopqrstuvwxyzABCDEFGHIJKLMNOPQRSTUVWXYZ-$1234567*

637 Bold SD abcdefghijklmnopqrstuvwxyzABCDEFGHIJKLMNOPQRSTUVWXYZ-$123

637 Bold Italic SD *abcdefghijklmnopqrstuvwxyzABCDEFGHIJKLMNOPQRSTUVWXYZ-$123456789*

637 Bold OSF SD abcdefghijklmnopqrstuvwxyzABCDEFGHIJKLMNOPQRSTUVWXYZ-$123

637 Bold Italic OSF SD *abcdefghijklmnopqrstuvwxyzABCDEFGHIJKLMNOPQRSTUVWXYZ-$1234567*

CASLON ANTIQUE

Berne Nadall • 1896 abcdefghijklmnopqrstuvwxyz(“.;‘!*?’:,”)

IMA FAM MTD

▲30 $1234567890&ß-äöüåçèîñóæøœ

ABCDEFGHIJKLMNOPQRSTUVWXYZ

ÄÖÜÅÇÈÎÑÓÆØŒ»,,«[¶§·†]¡¿...

Caslon Antique ...

• Roman abcdefghijklmnopqrstuvwxyzABCDEFGHIJ

Italic *abcdefghijklmnopqrstuvwxyzABCDEFGHIJ*

C

ITC CASLON NO. 224

Ed Benguiat • 1982 abcdefghijklmnopqrstuvwxyz(“.;‘!*?’:,”)

BIT ADO AGA AGP LEF LIN MAE URW $1234567890&fifIß-äöüåçèîñóæøœ

ABCDEFGHIJKLMNOPQRSTUVWXYZ

ÄÖÜÅÇÈÎÑÓÆØŒ»„«[¶§•†‡]‹¡·¿›...

ITC Caslon No. 224 One ...

• Book abcdefghijklmnopqrstuvwxyzABCDEFGHIJKLMNOPQRSTUVWXYZ–$123456789

Book Italic *abcdefghijklmnopqrstuvwxyzABCDEFGHIJKLMNOPQRSTUVWXYZ–$12345678*

Bold **abcdefghijklmnopqrstuvwxyzABCDEFGHIJKLMNOPQRSTUVWXYZ–$123456**

Bold Italic ***abcdefghijklmnopqrstuvwxyzABCDEFGHIJKLMNOPQRSTUVWXYZ–$123456***

ITC Caslon No. 224 Two ...

Medium abcdefghijklmnopqrstuvwxyzABCDEFGHIJKLMNOPQRSTUVWXYZ–$1234567

Medium Italic *abcdefghijklmnopqrstuvwxyzABCDEFGHIJKLMNOPQRSTUVWXYZ–$1234567*

Black **abcdefghijklmnopqrstuvwxyzABCDEFGHIJKLMNOPQRSTUVWXYZ–$123**

Black Italic ***abcdefghijklmnopqrstuvwxyzABCDEFGHIJKLMNOPQRSTUVWXYZ–$123***

ITC Caslon Headline

FAM **abcdefghijklmnopqrstuvwxyz(“.;‘!*?’:,”)**

▲30 **$1234567890&ß-äöüåçèñæøœ**

ABCDEFGHIJKLMNOPQRSTUVWXYZ

ÄÖÜÅÇÈÑÆØŒ»„«[¶§•†]¡·¿...

ADOBE CASLON

Carol Twombly • 1990 (William Caslon, 1725) abcdefghijklmnopqrstuvwxyz(“.;‘!*?’:,”)

ADO AGA LIN MAE $1234567890&fifIß-äöüåçèîñóæøœ

ABCDEFGHIJKLMNOPQRSTUVWXYZ

ÄÖÜÅÇÈÎÑÓÆØŒ»„«[¶§•†‡]‹¡·¿›...

Adobe Caslon ...

• Roman abcdefghijklmnopqrstuvwxyzABCDEFGHIJKLMNOPQRSTUVWXYZ–$123456789

Italic *abcdefghijklmnopqrstuvwxyzABCDEFGHIJKLMNOPQRSTUVWXYZ–$1234567890(“.;‘*

Semibold **abcdefghijklmnopqrstuvwxyzABCDEFGHIJKLMNOPQRSTUVWXYZ–$1234567**

Semibold Italic ***abcdefghijklmnopqrstuvwxyzABCDEFGHIJKLMNOPQRSTUVWXYZ–$1234567890(“***

Bold **abcdefghijklmnopqrstuvwxyzABCDEFGHIJKLMNOPQRSTUVWXYZ–$1234567**

Bold Italic ***abcdefghijklmnopqrstuvwxyzABCDEFGHIJKLMNOPQRSTUVWXYZ–$1234567890(***

C

ADOBE CASLON
EXPERT & SCOSF

ADO AGA LIN MAE ABCDEFGHIJKLMNOPQRSTUVWXYZ.;!?:,
$1234567890&ﬀﬁﬂﬃﬄ-ÄÖÜÅÇÈÎÑÓÆØŒ
(abdeilmnorst) ⅛ ¼ ⅓ ⅜ ½ ⅝ ⅔ ¾ ⅞ $12345/67890¢ ₡Rp

Adobe Caslon
Expert & SCOSF . . .

• Expert Roman ABCDEFGHIJKLMNOPQRSTUVWXYZ–$1234567890.;!?:,&-ﬀﬁﬂﬃﬄ ⅛ ¼ ⅓ ⅜ ½ $12345/67890¢ (ab

Expert Italic *$1234567890.;:,–ﬀﬁﬂﬃﬄ ⅛ ¼ ⅓ ⅜ ½ $12345/67890¢ (abdeilmnorst) ⅝ ⅔ ¾ ⅞ ₡Rp*

Expert Semibold **ABCDEFGHIJKLMNOPQRSTUVWXYZ–$1234567890.;!?:,&-ﬀﬁﬂﬃﬄ ⅛ ¼ ⅓ ⅜ ½ $12345/67890¢ (**

Expert Semibold Italic ***$1234567890.;:,–ﬀﬁﬂﬃﬄ ⅛ ¼ ⅓ ⅜ ½ $12345/67890¢ (abdeilmnorst) ⅝ ⅔ ¾ ⅞ ₡Rp***

Expert Bold **$1234567890.;:,–ﬀﬁﬂﬃﬄ ⅛ ¼ ⅓ ⅜ ½ $12345/67890¢ (abdeilmnorst) ⅝ ⅔ ¾ ⅞ ₡Rp**

Expert Bold Italic ***$1234567890.;:,–ﬀﬁﬂﬃﬄ ⅛ ¼ ⅓ ⅜ ½ $12345/67890¢ (abdeilmnorst) ⅝ ⅔ ¾ ⅞ ₡Rp***

Roman SCOSF ABCDEFGHIJKLMNOPQRSTUVWXYZABCDEFGHIJKLMNOPQRSTUVWXYZ–$123456

Italic OSF *abcdefghijklmnopqrstuvwxyzABCDEFGHIJKLMNOPQRSTUVWXYZ–$1234567890(".;'!*?*

Semibold SCOSF **ABCDEFGHIJKLMNOPQRSTUVWXYZABCDEFGHIJKLMNOPQRSTUVWXYZ–$12345**

Semibold Italic OSF ***abcdefghijklmnopqrstuvwxyzABCDEFGHIJKLMNOPQRSTUVWXYZ–$1234567890(".;'!***

Bold OSF **abcdefghijklmnopqrstuvwxyzABCDEFGHIJKLMNOPQRSTUVWXYZ–$12345678**

Bold Italic OSF ***abcdefghijklmnopqrstuvwxyzABCDEFGHIJKLMNOPQRSTUVWXYZ–$1234567890("***

Roman & Italic Alternate ctkſſhſiſlſſſtſtvw *ctkſſhſiſlſſſtſtvw*

Semibold & Semibold Italic Alternate **ctkſſhſiſlſſſtſtvw** ***ctkſſhſiſlſſſtſtvw***

Bold & Bold Italic Alternate **ctkſſhſiſlſſſtſtvw** ***ctkſſhſiſlſſſtſtvw***

Italic Swash Caps *ABCDEFGHIJKLMNOPQR STUVWXYZ*

Semibold Italic Swash Caps ***ABCDEFGHIJKLMNOPQR STUVWXYZ***

Bold Italic Swash Caps ***ABCDEFGHIJKLMNOPQR STUVWXYZ***

BIG CASLON

Matthew Carter • 1993
(William Caslon, 1725)

CAR

▲30

abcdefghijklmnopqrstuvwxyz(".;'!*?':,")
$1234567890&ﬁﬂß-äöüåçèîñóæøœ
ABCDEFGHIJKLMNOPQRSTUV
WXYZÄÖÜÅÇÈÎÑÓÆØŒ»„«[¶§•†‡]

Big Caslon . . .

• Roman abcdefghijklmnopqrstuvwxyzABCDEF

Expert Roman ABCDEFGHIJKLMNOPQRSTUVWXYZ-$1234

Adobe Caslon Expert & SCOSF ▶ Adobe Caslon Ornaments.

C

... Big Caslon

Roman Alternate ctfbffffhffiffifftfhfifjfkftQQſſbſhſiſjſkſlſſſt

Roman SCOSF ABCDEFGHIJKLMNOPQRSTUVWXYZABC

BERTHOLD CASLON BOOK

Günter Gerhard Lange • 1977 (William Caslon, 1725) abcdefghijklmnopqrstuvwxyz(".;'!*?':,")

ADO AGA MAE $1234567890&fiflß-äöüåçèîñóæøœ

ABCDEFGHIJKLMNOPQRSTUVWXYZ

ÄÖÜÅÇÈÎÑÓÆØŒ»„«[¶§•†‡]‹¡·¿›...

Berthold Caslon Book ...

• Roman abcdefghijklmnopqrstuvwxyzABCDEFGHIJKLMNOPQRSTUVWXYZ–$123456789

Italic *abcdefghijklmnopqrstuvwxyzABCDEFGHIJKLMNOPQRSTUVWXYZ–$1234567890(".*

Medium **abcdefghijklmnopqrstuvwxyzABCDEFGHIJKLMNOPQRSTUVWXYZ–$123456**

Bold **abcdefghijklmnopqrstuvwxyzABCDEFGHIJKLMNOPQRSTUVWXYZ–$123**

BERTHOLD CASLON BOOK EXPERT & SCOSF

ADO AGA MAE ABCDEFGHIJKLMNOPQRSTUVWXYZ.;!?:,

$1234567890&fffiflffiffl-ÄÖÜÅÇÈÎÑÓÆØŒ

(abdeilmnorst) 1/8 1/4 1/3 3/8 1/2 5/8 2/3 3/4 7/8 $12345/67890¢ ₡Rp

Berthold Caslon Book Expert & SCOSF ...

• Expert Roman ABCDEFGHIJKLMNOPQRSTUVWXYZ–$1234567890.;!?:,&-fffiflffiffl 1/8 1/4 1/3 3/8 1/2 $12345/67890¢ (abde

Expert Italic *$1234567890.;:,-fffiflffiffl 1/8 1/4 1/3 3/8 1/2 $12345/67890¢ (abdeilmnorst) 5/8 2/3 3/4 7/8 ₡Rp*

Expert Medium **ABCDEFGHIJKLMNOPQRSTUVWXYZ–$1234567890.;!?:,&-fffiflffiffl 1/8 1/4 1/3 3/8 1/2 $12345/67890¢ (a**

Expert Bold **$1234567890.;:,-fffiflffiffl 1/8 1/4 1/3 3/8 1/2 $12345/67890¢ (abdeilmnorst) 5/8 2/3 3/4 7/8 ₡Rp**

Roman SCOSF ABCDEFGHIJKLMNOPQRSTUVWXYZABCDEFGHIJKLMNOPQRSTUVWXYZ–$1234567

Italic OSF *abcdefghijklmnopqrstuvwxyzABCDEFGHIJKLMNOPQRSTUVWXYZ–$1234567890(".;'!*

Medium SCOSF **ABCDEFGHIJKLMNOPQRSTUVWXYZABCDEFGHIJKLMNOPQRSTUVWXYZ–$12345**

Bold OSF **abcdefghijklmnopqrstuvwxyzABCDEFGHIJKLMNOPQRSTUVWXYZ–$1234**

Castellar
Monotype Headliners 6
John Peters • 1957

MCL ADO AGA LIN MAE
▲30

ABCDEFGHIJKLMNOPQRSTUV

WXYZ(".;'!*?':,")$1234567890

&-ÄÖÜÅÇÈÎÑÓÆØŒ»„«[•]‹¡·¿›...

Monotype Headliners 6: Albertus Light, Albertus Regular, Albertus Italic, Castellar.

CASTLE

URW LEF FRA abcdefghijklmnopqrstuvwxyz(".;'!*?':,")
▲16 $1234567890&fiflß-äöüåçèîñóæøœ
ABCDEFGHIJKLMNOPQRSTUVWXYZ
ÄÖÜÅÇÈÎÑÓÆØŒ»„«[¶§•†‡]‹¡·¿›...

Castle ...

Light abcdefghijklmnopqrstuvwxyzABCDEFGHIJKLMNOPQRSTUVWXYZ–$123456789
• Book abcdefghijklmnopqrstuvwxyzABCDEFGHIJKLMNOPQRSTUVWXYZ–$123456
Bold **abcdefghijklmnopqrstuvwxyzABCDEFGHIJKLMNOPQRSTUVWXYZ–$123**
Ultra **abcdefghijklmnopqrstuvwxyzABCDEFGHIJKLMNOPQRSTUVWXYZ–$**

BITSTREAM CATANEO

✍ *Jacqueline Sakwa & Richard Lipton • 1993 (Bernardino Cataneo, 1545)*

abcdefghijklmnopqrstuvwxyz(".;'!?':,")*
$1234567890&fiflß-äöüåçèîñóæøœ
BIT *ABCDEFGHIJKLMNOPQRSTUVWXYZ*
ÄÖÜÅÇÈÎÑÓÆØŒ»„«[§•†‡]‹¡·¿›...

Bitstream Cataneo 1 ...

Light *abcdefghijklmnopqrstuvwxyzABCDEFGHIJKLMNOPQRSTUVWXYZ–$1234567890(".;'!*?':,")*
• Regular *abcdefghijklmnopqrstuvwxyzABCDEFGHIJKLMNOPQRSTUVWXYZ–$1234567890(".;'!*?'*
Bold ***abcdefghijklmnopqrstuvwxyzABCDEFGHIJKLMNOPQRSTUVWXYZ–$1234567890(".;***

Bitstream Cataneo 2 ...

Light Swash *a d e g h k n p q r t v w y z A B C D E F G H I J K L M N O P Q R S T U V W X Y Z $1234567*
Regular Swash *a d e g h k n p q r t v w y z A B C D E F G H I J K L M N O P Q R S T U V W X Y Z $12345*
Bold Swash ***a d e g h k n p q r t v w y z A B C D E F G H I J K L M N O P Q R S T U V W X Y Z $12***
Light Extension *Th ct d ll sp & st ff ffi ffl abdeilmnorst $1234567890¢ 1/8 1/4 1/3 3/8 1/2 5/8 2/3 3/4 7/8*
Regular Extension *Th ct d ll sp & st ff ffi ffl abdeilmnorst $1234567890¢ 1/8 1/4 1/3 3/8 1/2 5/8 2/3 3/4 7/8*
Bold Extension ***Th ct d ll sp & st ff ffi ffl abdeilmnorst $1234567890¢ 1/8 1/4 1/3 3/8 1/2 5/8 2/3 3/4 7/8***

Catastrophe
✤ *Group Cats*

✍ *Judith Sutcliffe • 1993*

MTD ABCDEFGHIJKLMNOPQRS
▲30 TUVWXYZ .!?, ▷

✤ *Group Cats*: Catastrophe & Tommys Type.

CATULL

Gustav Jaeger • 1982 abcdefghijklmnopqrstuvwxyz(“.;‘!*?’:,”)

ADO AGA MAE $1234567890&fiflß-äöüåçèîñóæøœ

ABCDEFGHIJKLMNOPQRSTUVWXYZ

ÄÖÜÅÇÈÎÑÓÆØŒ»„«[¶§•†‡]‹i·¿›...

Catull ...

• Regular abcdefghijklmnopqrstuvwxyzABCDEFGHIJKLMNOPQRSTUVWXYZ-$123456789

Italic *abcdefghijklmnopqrstuvwxyzABCDEFGHIJKLMNOPQRSTUVWXYZ-$123456789*

Medium **abcdefghijklmnopqrstuvwxyzABCDEFGHIJKLMNOPQRSTUVWXYZ-$1**

Bold **abcdefghijklmnopqrstuvwxyzABCDEFGHIJKLMNOPQRSTUVWXYZ**

CAVALIER

HEA abcdefghijklmnopqrstuvwxyz(“.;‘!*?’:,”)

▲18 $1234567890&ß-äöüåçèîñóæøœ

ABCDEFGHIJKLMNOPQRSTUVWXYZ

ÄÖÜÅÇÈÎÑÓÆØŒ»„«[¶§•†‡]‹i·¿›...

Cavalier ...

Light abcdefghijklmnopqrstuvwxyzABCDEFGHIJKLMNOPQRSTUVWXYZ-$1234567890(“.;‘!*?’:,”)&

• Regular abcdefghijklmnopqrstuvwxyzABCDEFGHIJKLMNOPQRSTUVWXYZ-$1234567890(“.;‘!*

Bold **abcdefghijklmnopqrstuvwxyzABCDEFGHIJKLMNOPQRSTUVWXYZ-$123456789**

Extra Bold **abcdefghijklmnopqrstuvwxyzABCDEFGHIJKLMNOPQRSTUVWXYZ-$123456789**

Black **abcdefghijklmnopqrstuvwxyzABCDEFGHIJKLMNOPQRSTUVWXYZ-$12345**

CAXTON

Leslie Usherwood • 1981 abcdefghijklmnopqrstuvwxyz(“.;‘!*?’:,”)

URW ADO AGA AGP BIT FAM LET LIN MAE $1234567890&fiflß-äöüåçèîñóæøœ

ABCDEFGHIJKLMNOPQRSTUVWXYZ

ÄÖÜÅÇÈÎÑÓÆØŒ»„«[¶§•†‡]‹i·¿›...

Caxton 1 ...

• Book abcdefghijklmnopqrstuvwxyzABCDEFGHIJKLMNOPQRSTUVWXYZ-$123456789

Book Italic *abcdefghijklmnopqrstuvwxyzABCDEFGHIJKLMNOPQRSTUVWXYZ-$12345678*

Bold **abcdefghijklmnopqrstuvwxyzABCDEFGHIJKLMNOPQRSTUVWXYZ-$123456**

Bold Italic ***abcdefghijklmnopqrstuvwxyzABCDEFGHIJKLMNOPQRSTUVWXYZ-$12345***

Bold Condensed **abcdefghijklmnopqrstuvwxyzABCDEFGHIJKLMNOPQRSTUVWXYZ-$1234567890(“.;‘!*?**

Caxton 2 ...

Light abcdefghijklmnopqrstuvwxyzABCDEFGHIJKLMNOPQRSTUVWXYZ-$1234567890(

Light Italic *abcdefghijklmnopqrstuvwxyzABCDEFGHIJKLMNOPQRSTUVWXYZ-$1234567890*

Extra Bold **abcdefghijklmnopqrstuvwxyzABCDEFGHIJKLMNOPQRSTUVWXYZ-$123**

... Caxton 2

Extra Bold Italic *abcdefghijklmnopqrstuvwxyzABCDEFGHIJKLMNOPQRSTUVWXYZ-$123*

Extra Bold Condensed **abcdefghijklmnopqrstuvwxyzABCDEFGHIJKLMNOPQRSTUVWXYZ-$1234567890(".;'**

C

CENTAUR

Bruce Rogers & Frederic Warde • 1928 abcdefghijklmnopqrstuvwxyz(".;'!*?':,")

MCL ADO AGA LIN MAE $1234567890&fiflß-äöüåçèîñóæøœ

▲16 ABCDEFGHIJKLMNOPQRSTUVWXYZ

ÄÖÜÅÇÈÎÑÓÆØŒ»„«[¶§•†‡]‹¡·¿›...

Centaur ...

• Roman abcdefghijklmnopqrstuvwxyzABCDEFGHIJKLMNOPQRSTUVWXYZ–$1234

Italic *abcdefghijklmnopqrstuvwxyzABCDEFGHIJKLMNOPQRSTUVWXYZ–$1234567890(".;'!*?':*

Bold **abcdefghijklmnopqrstuvwxyzABCDEFGHIJKLMNOPQRSTUVWXYZ–$1234**

Bold Italic ***abcdefghijklmnopqrstuvwxyzABCDEFGHIJKLMNOPQRSTUVWXYZ–$1234567890(".***

CENTAUR EXPERT

MCL ADO AGA LIN MAE ABCDEFGHIJKLMNOPQRSTUVWXYZ.;!?:,

▲16 $1234567890&ff fi fl ffi ffl -ÄÖÜÅÇÈÎÑÓÆØŒ

(abdeilmnorst) 1/8 1/4 1/3 3/8 1/2 5/8 2/3 3/4 7/8 $12345/67890¢ ₡Rp

Centaur Expert ...

• Expert Roman ABCDEFGHIJKLMNOPQRSTUVWXYZ—$1234567890.;!?:,&-ff fi fl ffi ffl 1/8 1/4 1/3 3/8 1/2 $12345/67890¢ (ab

Expert Italic *$1234567890.;:,–ff fi fl ffi ffl 1/8 1/4 1/3 3/8 1/2 $12345/67890¢ (abdeilmnorst) 5/8 2/3 3/4 7/8 ₡Rp*

Expert Bold **$1234567890.;:,–ff fi fl ffi ffl 1/8 1/4 1/3 3/8 1/2 $12345/67890¢ (abdeilmnorst) 5/8 2/3 3/4 7/8 ₡Rp**

Expert Bold Italic ***$1234567890.;:,–ff fi fl ffi ffl 1/8 1/4 1/3 3/8 1/2 $12345/67890¢ (abdeilmnorst) 5/8 2/3 3/4 7/8 ₡Rp***

Roman, Italic, Bold & Bold Italic Alternate »QRQR&« *»ghzQ«* **»QR«** ***»ghzQ«***

Italic Swash *a e g k r sp st v w z & ABCDEFGHIJKLMNOPQRSTUVWXYZ&*

LINOTYPE CENTENNIAL

Adrian Frutiger • 1986 abcdefghijklmnopqrstuvwxyz(".;'!*?':,")

LIN ADO AGA MAE $1234567890&fiflß-äöüåçèîñóæøœ

ABCDEFGHIJKLMNOPQRSTUVWXYZ

ÄÖÜÅÇÈÎÑÓÆØŒ»„«[¶§•†‡]‹¡·¿›...

Linotype Centennial ...

45-Light abcdefghijklmnopqrstuvwxyzABCDEFGHIJKLMNOPQRSTUVWXYZ–$123456

46-Light Italic *abcdefghijklmnopqrstuvwxyzABCDEFGHIJKLMNOPQRSTUVWXYZ–$123456*

• 55-Roman abcdefghijklmnopqrstuvwxyzABCDEFGHIJKLMNOPQRSTUVWXYZ–$12345

56-Italic *abcdefghijklmnopqrstuvwxyzABCDEFGHIJKLMNOPQRSTUVWXYZ–$123456*

75-Bold **abcdefghijklmnopqrstuvwxyzABCDEFGHIJKLMNOPQRSTUVWXYZ–$123**

76-Bold Italic ***abcdefghijklmnopqrstuvwxyzABCDEFGHIJKLMNOPQRSTUVWXYZ–$1234***

C

... Linotype Centennial

95-Black **abcdefghijklmnopqrstuvwxyzABCDEFGHIJKLMNOPQRSTUVWXYZ–$1**
96-Black Italic ***abcdefghijklmnopqrstuvwxyzABCDEFGHIJKLMNOPQRSTUVWXYZ–$123***

LINOTYPE CENTENNIAL SCOSF

LIN ADO AGA MAE ABCDEFGHIJKLMNOPQRSTUVWXYZ(".;'!*?':,")
$1234567890&-ÄÖÜÅÇÈÎÑÓÆØŒ
ABCDEFGHIJKLMNOPQRSTUVWXYZ
ÄÖÜÅÇÈÎÑÓÆØŒ»„«[¶§•†‡]‹¡·¿›...

Linotype Centennial SCOSF ...

45-Light SCOSF ABCDEFGHIJKLMNOPQRSTUVWXYZABCDEFGHIJKLMNOPQRSTUVWXYZ–$1234
46-Light Italic OSF *abcdefghijklmnopqrstuvwxyzABCDEFGHIJKLMNOPQRSTUVWXYZ–$123456*
• 55-Roman SCOSF ABCDEFGHIJKLMNOPQRSTUVWXYZABCDEFGHIJKLMNOPQRSTUVWXYZ–$123
56-Italic OSF *abcdefghijklmnopqrstuvwxyzABCDEFGHIJKLMNOPQRSTUVWXYZ–$123456*
75-Bold OSF **abcdefghijklmnopqrstuvwxyzABCDEFGHIJKLMNOPQRSTUVWXYZ–$123**
76-Bold Italic OSF ***abcdefghijklmnopqrstuvwxyzABCDEFGHIJKLMNOPQRSTUVWXYZ–$1234***
95-Black OSF **abcdefghijklmnopqrstuvwxyzABCDEFGHIJKLMNOPQRSTUVWXYZ–$1**
96-Black Italic OSF ***abcdefghijklmnopqrstuvwxyzABCDEFGHIJKLMNOPQRSTUVWXYZ–$123***

CENTURY EXPANDED

Morris Fuller Benton • 1900
... Linn Boyd Benton
& Thomas Maitland Cleland, 1896

BIT ADO AGA TFC FAM LIN MAE MCL URW

abcdefghijklmnopqrstuvwxyz(".;'!*?':,")
$1234567890&fiflß-äöüåçèîñóæøœ
ABCDEFGHIJKLMNOPQRSTUVWXYZ
ÄÖÜÅÇÈÎÑÓÆØŒ»„«[¶§•†‡]‹¡·¿›...

Century Expanded ...

• Roman abcdefghijklmnopqrstuvwxyzABCDEFGHIJKLMNOPQRSTUVWXYZ–$123456
Italic *abcdefghijklmnopqrstuvwxyzABCDEFGHIJKLMNOPQRSTUVWXYZ–$123456*
Bold **abcdefghijklmnopqrstuvwxyzABCDEFGHIJKLMNOPQRSTUVWXYZ–$1234**
Bold Italic ***abcdefghijklmnopqrstuvwxyzABCDEFGHIJKLMNOPQRSTUVWXYZ–$12345***

CENTURY OLD STYLE

Morris Fuller Benton • 1906

ADO AGA BIT FAM LIN MAE MCL URW

abcdefghijklmnopqrstuvwxyz(".;'!*?':,")
$1234567890&fiflß-äöüåçèîñóæøœ
ABCDEFGHIJKLMNOPQRSTUVWXYZ
ÄÖÜÅÇÈÎÑÓÆØŒ»„«[¶§•†‡]‹¡·¿›...

Century Old Style ...

• Roman abcdefghijklmnopqrstuvwxyzABCDEFGHIJKLMNOPQRSTUVWXYZ–$123456789
Italic *abcdefghijklmnopqrstuvwxyzABCDEFGHIJKLMNOPQRSTUVWXYZ–$1234567890(*
Bold **abcdefghijklmnopqrstuvwxyzABCDEFGHIJKLMNOPQRSTUVWXYZ–$123**

NEW CENTURY SCHOOLBOOK

Linotype Design Staff • 1980
. . . *Morris Fuller Benton,* 1919

LIN ADO AGA FAM MAE

abcdefghijklmnopqrstuvwxyz(“.;‘!*?’:,”)
$1234567890&fiflß-äöüåçèîñóæøœ
ABCDEFGHIJKLMNOPQRSTUVWXYZ
ÄÖÜÅÇÈÎÑÓÆØŒ»„«[¶§•†‡]‹¡·¿›...

New Century Schoolbook . . .

• Roman abcdefghijklmnopqrstuvwxyzABCDEFGHIJKLMNOPQRSTUVWXYZ–$123
Italic *abcdefghijklmnopqrstuvwxyzABCDEFGHIJKLMNOPQRSTUVWXYZ–$1234*
Bold **abcdefghijklmnopqrstuvwxyzABCDEFGHIJKLMNOPQRSTUVWXYZ**
Bold Italic ***abcdefghijklmnopqrstuvwxyzABCDEFGHIJKLMNOPQRSTUVWXYZ–***

ITC CENTURY

Tony Stan • 1975

BIT ADO AGA LEF FAM LIN MAE URW

abcdefghijklmnopqrstuvwxyz(“.;‘!*?’:,”)
$1234567890&fiflß-äöüåçèîñóæøœ
ABCDEFGHIJKLMNOPQRSTUVWXYZ
ÄÖÜÅÇÈÎÑÓÆØŒ»„«[¶§•†‡]‹¡·¿›...

ITC Century 1 . . .

• Book abcdefghijklmnopqrstuvwxyzABCDEFGHIJKLMNOPQRSTUVWXYZ–$12345678
Book Italic *abcdefghijklmnopqrstuvwxyzABCDEFGHIJKLMNOPQRSTUVWXYZ–$12345*
Bold **abcdefghijklmnopqrstuvwxyzABCDEFGHIJKLMNOPQRSTUVWXYZ–$123**
Bold Italic ***abcdefghijklmnopqrstuvwxyzABCDEFGHIJKLMNOPQRSTUVWXYZ–$12***

ITC Century 2 . . .

Light abcdefghijklmnopqrstuvwxyzABCDEFGHIJKLMNOPQRSTUVWXYZ–$12345678
Light Italic *abcdefghijklmnopqrstuvwxyzABCDEFGHIJKLMNOPQRSTUVWXYZ–$1234567*
Ultra **abcdefghijklmnopqrstuvwxyzABCDEFGHIJKLMNOPQRSTUVW**
Ultra Italic ***abcdefghijklmnopqrstuvwxyzABCDEFGHIJKLMNOPQRSTUV***

ITC CENTURY CONDENSED

BIT ADO AGA LEF FAM LIN MAE URW

abcdefghijklmnopqrstuvwxyz(“.;‘!*?’:,”)
$1234567890&fiflß-äöüåçèîñóæøœ
ABCDEFGHIJKLMNOPQRSTUVWXYZ
ÄÖÜÅÇÈÎÑÓÆØŒ»„«[¶§•†‡]‹¡·¿›...

ITC Century Condensed 1 . . .

• Book Condensed abcdefghijklmnopqrstuvwxyzABCDEFGHIJKLMNOPQRSTUVWXYZ–$1234567890(“.;‘!*?’:,”)&fi
Book Condensed Italic *abcdefghijklmnopqrstuvwxyzABCDEFGHIJKLMNOPQRSTUVWXYZ–$1234567890(“.;‘!*?’:,”)*
Bold Condensed **abcdefghijklmnopqrstuvwxyzABCDEFGHIJKLMNOPQRSTUVWXYZ–$1234567890(“.;‘!*?’:**
Bold Condensed Italic ***abcdefghijklmnopqrstuvwxyzABCDEFGHIJKLMNOPQRSTUVWXYZ–$1234567890(“.;‘!*?’***

ITC Century Condensed 2 . . .

Light Condensed abcdefghijklmnopqrstuvwxyzABCDEFGHIJKLMNOPQRSTUVWXYZ–$1234567890(“.;‘!*?’:,”)&fiflß-

New Century Schoolbook Linotype Fraction Pi.
New Century Schoolbook New Century Schoolbook Monotonic & Polytonic Greek.

C

Champagne

IMA abcdefghijklmnopqrstuvwxyz(“.;‘!*?’:,”)

▲16 $1234567890&ß-äöüåçèîñóæøœ

ABCDEFGHIJKLMNOPQRSTUVWXYZ

ÄÖÜÅÇÈÎÓÆØŒ„[·];¿...

Champers

Alan Meeks • 1991 abcdefghijklmnopqrstuvwxyz(“.;‘!*?’:,”)

LET $1234567890&fiflß-äöüåçèîñóæøœ

▲18 ABCDEFGHIJKLMNOPQRSTUVWXYZ

ÄÖÜÅÇÈÎÑÓÆØŒ»„«[•]‹¡·¿›...

A*I CHAOTIQUA

Manfred Klein • 1994 abcdefghijklmnopqrstuvwxyz(“.;‘!*?’:,”)

ALP

▲24 $1234567890&ß-äöüåçèîñó

ABCDEFGHIJKLMNOPQRSTUVWXYZ

ÄÖÜÅÇÈÎÑÓ»„«[¶§•†]¡¿

A*I Chaotiqua ...

• Regular abcdefghijklmnopqrstuvwxyzABCDEFGHIJK

Bold abcdefghijklmnopqrstuvwxyzABCDEFG

CHARLEMAGNE

Adobe TitlingSet 1

Carol Twombly • 1989 ABCDEFGHIJKLMNOPQRSTUVWXYZ

ADO AGA LIN MAE

▲24 (“.;‘!*?’:,”)$1234567890

&-ÄÖÜÅÇÈÎÑÓÆØŒ»„«[•]‹¡·¿›...

Charlemagne ...

• Regular ABCDEFGHIJKLMNOPQRSTUVWXYZ(“.;

Bold ABCDEFGHIJKLMNOPQRSTUVWXYZ(“.

Adobe TitlingSet 1: Charlemagne Regular & Bold, Trajan Regular & Bold.

CHARLOTTE

Michael Gills • 1992 abcdefghijklmnopqrstuvwxyz(“.;‘!*?’:,”)
LET $1234567890&fiflß-äöüåçèîñóæøœ
ABCDEFGHIJKLMNOPQRSTUVWXYZ
ÄÖÜÅÇÈÎÑÓÆØŒ»„«[¶§•†‡]‹i·¿›...

Charlotte ...

• Book abcdefghijklmnopqrstuvwxyzABCDEFGHIJKLMNOPQRSTUVWXYZ–$123456789
Book Italic *abcdefghijklmnopqrstuvwxyzABCDEFGHIJKLMNOPQRSTUVWXYZ–$1234567890(“.;‘*
Book SCOSF ABCDEFGHIJKLMNOPQRSTUVWXYZABCDEFGHIJKLMNOPQRSTUVWXYZ–$1234567890
Medium **abcdefghijklmnopqrstuvwxyzABCDEFGHIJKLMNOPQRSTUVWXYZ–$1234567**
Bold **abcdefghijklmnopqrstuvwxyzABCDEFGHIJKLMNOPQRSTUVWXYZ–$1234567**

CHARLOTTE SANS

Michael Gills • 1992 abcdefghijklmnopqrstuvwxyz(“.;‘!*?’:,”)
LET $1234567890&fiflß-äöüåçèîñóæøœ
ABCDEFGHIJKLMNOPQRSTUVWXYZ
ÄÖÜÅÇÈÎÑÓÆØŒ»„«[¶§•†‡]‹i·¿›...

Charlotte Sans ...

• Book abcdefghijklmnopqrstuvwxyzABCDEFGHIJKLMNOPQRSTUVWXYZ–$1234567890(“.;‘!
Book Italic *abcdefghijklmnopqrstuvwxyzABCDEFGHIJKLMNOPQRSTUVWXYZ–$1234567890(“.;‘!*?’:*
Book SCOSF ABCDEFGHIJKLMNOPQRSTUVWXYZABCDEFGHIJKLMNOPQRSTUVWXYZ–$1234567890(“.;‘!*
Medium **abcdefghijklmnopqrstuvwxyzABCDEFGHIJKLMNOPQRSTUVWXYZ–$1234567890(“**
Bold **abcdefghijklmnopqrstuvwxyzABCDEFGHIJKLMNOPQRSTUVWXYZ–$1234567890**

Charme
Linotype DisplaySet 2
Helmut Matheis • 1958 *abcdefghijklmnopqrstuvwxyz(“.;‘!*?’:,”)*
LIN ADO AGA MAE *$1234567890&fiflß-äöüåçèîñóæøœ*
▲18 *ABCDEFGHIJKLMNOPQRSTUVWXYZ*
ÄÖÜÅÇÈÎÑÓÆØŒ»„«[¶§•†‡]‹¡·¿›...

ITC CHARTER

Matthew Carter • 1987 abcdefghijklmnopqrstuvwxyz(“.;‘!*?’:,”)
BIT ITC URW $1234567890&fiflß-äöüåçèîñóæøœ
ABCDEFGHIJKLMNOPQRSTUVWXYZ
ÄÖÜÅÇÈÎÑÓÆØŒ»„«[¶§•†‡]‹¡·¿›...

... ITC Charter ...

• Roman abcdefghijklmnopqrstuvwxyzABCDEFGHIJKLMNOPQRSTUVWXYZ–$123456789
Italic *abcdefghijklmnopqrstuvwxyzABCDEFGHIJKLMNOPQRSTUVWXYZ–$1234567890(“.*
Bold **abcdefghijklmnopqrstuvwxyzABCDEFGHIJKLMNOPQRSTUVWXYZ–$1234567**

Linotype DisplaySet 2: Banco, Charme, Flyer Black Condensed & Extra Black Condensed, Wilhelm Klingspor Gotisch.

... ITC Charter

Bold Italic *abcdefghijklmnopqrstuvwxyzABCDEFGHIJKLMNOPQRSTUVWXYZ–$12345678*

Black **abcdefghijklmnopqrstuvwxyzABCDEFGHIJKLMNOPQRSTUVWXYZ–$1**

Black Italic ***abcdefghijklmnopqrstuvwxyzABCDEFGHIJKLMNOPQRSTUVWXYZ–$12***

CHELTENHAM

Morris Fuller Benton • 1904 ... Bertram G. Goodhue, 1896

BIT

▲16

abcdefghijklmnopqrstuvwxyz(“.;‘!*?’:,”)
$1234567890&fiflß-äöüåçèîñóæøœ
ABCDEFGHIJKLMNOPQRSTUVWXYZ
ÄÖÜÅÇÈÎÑÓÆØŒ»„«[¶§•†‡]‹¡·¿›...

Cheltenham 1 ...

• Roman abcdefghijklmnopqrstuvwxyzABCDEFGHIJKLMNOPQRSTUVWXYZ–$12

Italic *abcdefghijklmnopqrstuvwxyzABCDEFGHIJKLMNOPQRSTUVWXYZ–$1234*

Bold **abcdefghijklmnopqrstuvwxyzABCDEFGHIJKLMNOPQRSTUVWXYZ**

Bold Italic ***abcdefghijklmnopqrstuvwxyzABCDEFGHIJKLMNOPQRSTUVWXYZ–***

Cheltenham 2 ...

Bold Condensed **abcdefghijklmnopqrstuvwxyzABCDEFGHIJKLMNOPQRSTUVWXYZ–$1234567890(“.;‘!*?’:,”)**

Bold Condensed Italic ***abcdefghijklmnopqrstuvwxyzABCDEFGHIJKLMNOPQRSTUVWXYZ–$1234567890(“.;‘!*?’:,”)***

Bold Extra Condensed **abcdefghijklmnopqrstuvwxyzABCDEFGHIJKLMNOPQRSTUVWXYZ–$1234567890(“.;‘!*?’:,’)&fiflß-äöüÄ**

Bold Headline ▲24 **abcdefghijklmnopqrstuvwxyzABCDEFGHIJKL**

Bold Italic Headline ▲24 ***abcdefghijklmnopqrstuvwxyzABCDEFGHIJKLM***

ITC CHELTENHAM

Tony Stan • 1975

LIN ADO AGA BIT LEF FAM MAE URW

abcdefghijklmnopqrstuvwxyz(“.;‘!*?’:,”)
$1234567890&fiflß-äöüåçèîñóæøœ
ABCDEFGHIJKLMNOPQRSTUVWXYZ
ÄÖÜÅÇÈÎÑÓÆØŒ»„«[¶§•†‡]‹¡·¿›...

ITC Cheltenham 1 ...

Light abcdefghijklmnopqrstuvwxyzABCDEFGHIJKLMNOPQRSTUVWXYZ–$1234567890(“.;

Light Italic *abcdefghijklmnopqrstuvwxyzABCDEFGHIJKLMNOPQRSTUVWXYZ–$1234567890(“.;*

Ultra **abcdefghijklmnopqrstuvwxyzABCDEFGHIJKLMNOPQRSTUVWXYZ**

Ultra Italic ***abcdefghijklmnopqrstuvwxyzABCDEFGHIJKLMNOPQRSTUVWXYZ–***

ITC Cheltenham 2 ...

• Book abcdefghijklmnopqrstuvwxyzABCDEFGHIJKLMNOPQRSTUVWXYZ–$12345678

Book Italic *abcdefghijklmnopqrstuvwxyzABCDEFGHIJKLMNOPQRSTUVWXYZ–$1234567890(*

Bold **abcdefghijklmnopqrstuvwxyzABCDEFGHIJKLMNOPQRSTUVWXYZ–$12345**

. . . ITC Cheltenham 2

Bold Italic *abcdefghijklmnopqrstuvwxyzABCDEFGHIJKLMNOPQRSTUVWXYZ–$12345*

C

ITC CHELTENHAM CONDENSED

LIN ADO AGA LEF FAM MAE URW abcdefghijklmnopqrstuvwxyz(“.;‘!*?’:,”)
$1234567890&fiflß-äöüåçèîñóæøœ
ABCDEFGHIJKLMNOPQRSTUVWXYZ
ÄÖÜÅÇÈÎÑÓÆØŒ»„«[¶§•†‡]‹¡·¿›...

ITC Cheltenham Condensed . . .

Light Condensed abcdefghijklmnopqrstuvwxyzABCDEFGHIJKLMNOPQRSTUVWXYZ–$1234567890(“.;‘!*?’:,”)&fiflß-äöüÄ

Light Condensed Italic *abcdefghijklmnopqrstuvwxyzABCDEFGHIJKLMNOPQRSTUVWXYZ–$1234567890(“.;‘!*?’:,”)&fiflß-äöüÄ*

• Book Condensed abcdefghijklmnopqrstuvwxyzABCDEFGHIJKLMNOPQRSTUVWXYZ–$1234567890(“.;‘!*?’:,”)&fi

Book Condensed Italic *abcdefghijklmnopqrstuvwxyzABCDEFGHIJKLMNOPQRSTUVWXYZ–$1234567890(“.;‘!*?’:,”)&fifl*

Bold Condensed **abcdefghijklmnopqrstuvwxyzABCDEFGHIJKLMNOPQRSTUVWXYZ–$1234567890(“.;‘!***

Bold Condensed Italic ***abcdefghijklmnopqrstuvwxyzABCDEFGHIJKLMNOPQRSTUVWXYZ–$1234567890(“.;‘!*?’***

Ultra Condensed **abcdefghijklmnopqrstuvwxyzABCDEFGHIJKLMNOPQRSTUVWXYZ–$1234567890(**

Ultra Condensed Italic ***abcdefghijklmnopqrstuvwxyzABCDEFGHIJKLMNOPQRSTUVWXYZ–$1234567890(***

ITC CHELTENHAM HANDTOOLED

Ed Benguiat • 1993 (Tony Stan, 1975)

ITC URW

▲24

abcdefghijklmnopqrstuvwxyz(“.;‘!*?’:,”)
$1234567890&fiflß-äöüåçèîñóæøœ
ABCDEFGHIJKLMNOPQRSTUVWXYZ
ÄÖÜÅÇÈÎÑÓÆØŒ»„«[¶§•†‡]‹¡·¿›...

ITC Cheltenham Handtooled . . .

• Regular abcdefghijklmnopqrstuvwxyzABCDEFGH

Regular OSF abcdefghijklmnopqrstuvwxyzABC...$1234

Italic *abcdefghijklmnopqrstuvwxyzABCDEFGH*

Italic OSF *abcdefghijklmnopqrstuvwxyzABC...$1234*

C

Chevalier
Agfa DisplaySet 3
AGP URW

ABCDEFGHIJKLMNOPQRSTU
VWXYZ(“.;‘!*?’:,”)$1234567890
&-ÄÖÜÅÇÈÎÑÓÆØŒ»„«[§•†‡]‹¿›
▲24

FC Chevalier
TFC

abcdefghijklmnopqrstuvwxyz(“.;‘!*?’:,”)
$1234567890&fiflß-äöüåçèîñóœøœ
ABCDEFGHIJKLMNOPQRSTUVWXYZ
ÄÖÜÅÇÈÎÑÓÆŒ»„«[·]‹i·¿›...
▲24

Chinese Menu
INT

abcdefghijklmnopqrstuvwxyz(“.;‘!*?’:,”)
$1234567890&ß-äöüåçèîñóœøœ
ABCDEFGHIJKLMNOPQRSTUVWXYZ
ÄÖÜÅÇÈÎÑÓÆØŒ»„«[¶§•]¡·¿
▲18

CHRISTIANA
+ EXPERT & SCOSF
Gustav Jaeger • 1992
ADO AGA MAE

abcdefghijklmnopqrstuvwxyz(“.;‘!*?’:,”)
$1234567890&fiflß-äöüåçèîñóæøœ
ABCDEFGHIJKLMNOPQRSTUVWXYZ
ÄÖÜÅÇÈÎÑÓÆØŒ»„«[¶§•†‡]‹i·¿›...

Christiana + Expert & SCOSF ...

• Regular abcdefghijklmnopqrstuvwxyzABCDEFGHIJKLMNOPQRSTUVWXYZ–$1234567890(“.

Italic *abcdefghijklmnopqrstuvwxyzABCDEFGHIJKLMNOPQRSTUVWXYZ–$1234567890(“.;‘!*

Medium **abcdefghijklmnopqrstuvwxyzABCDEFGHIJKLMNOPQRSTUVWXYZ–$12345678**

Medium Italic ***abcdefghijklmnopqrstuvwxyzABCDEFGHIJKLMNOPQRSTUVWXYZ–$123456789***

Bold **abcdefghijklmnopqrstuvwxyzABCDEFGHIJKLMNOPQRSTUVWXYZ–$12345**

Bold Italic ***abcdefghijklmnopqrstuvwxyzABCDEFGHIJKLMNOPQRSTUVWXYZ–$123456***

Expert Regular ABCDEFGHIJKLMNOPQRSTUVWXYZ–$1234567890.;!?:,&–ff fi fl ffi ffl 1/8 1/4 1/3 3/8 1/2 $12345/67890¢ (

Regular SCOSF ABCDEFGHIJKLMNOPQRSTUVWXYZABCDEFGHIJKLMNOPQRSTUVWXYZ–$1234567890(

Agfa DisplaySet 3 : Basque, Brophy Script, Chevalier, Uncial.

CHRISTMAS GIFT SCRIPT

Andy Hullinger • 1993 abcdefghijklmnopqrstuvwxyz(“.:!?’;,”)

T26 $1234567890&ffifl-äöüåçèîñó

▲16 ABCDEFGHIJKLMNOPQRSTUVWXYZ

ÄÖÜÅÈÎÓÆŒ »« [§] i¿...

Christmas Gift Script . . .

• Regular abcdefghijklmnopqrstuvwxyzABCDEFGHIJKLMNOPQRSTUVWXYZ–$1234

Bold abcdefghijklmnopqrstuvwxyzABCDEFGHIJKLMNOPQRSTUVWXYZ–$1234

Chromium One

David Harris • 1983 ABCDEFGHIJKLMNOPQRSTUVWXYZ

LET

▲30 (“.;‘!*?’:,”)$1234567890

&-ÄÖÜÅÇÈÎÑÓÆØŒ»„«[•]‹¡·¿›...

Chwast Buffalo Black Condensed
✣ Linotype Headliners

Seymour Chwast • . . . . abcdefghijklmnopqrstuvwxyz(“.:‘!*?’;,”)

LIN

▲24 $1234567890&fiflß-äöüåçèîñóæøœ

ABCDEFGHIJKLMNOPQRSTUVWXYZ

ÄÖÜÅÇÈÎÑÓÆØŒ»„«[¶§•†‡]‹¡·¿›...

Cirkulus

Michael Neugebauer • 1970 abcdefghijklmnopqrstuvwxyz(“.:‘!*?’;,”)

LEF URW

▲24 $1234567890&fiflss-äöüåçèîñóæøœ»„«[•]‹¡·¿›...

Citadel
✣ Agfa Scripts 2

AGP abcdefghijklmnopqrstuvwxyz(“.;‘!*?’:,”)

▲16 $1234567890&ß-äöüåçèîñó

ABCDEFGHIJKLMNOPQRSTUVWXYZ

ÄÖÜÅÇÈÎÑÓŸ»«[•]‹› ▷ IVX st nd rd th 1/4 1/3 1/2 3/4 D c r c s O rs s & %

✣ *Linotype Headliners*: Chwast Buffalo Black Condensed, Erbar Condensed & Bold Condensed, Metrolite, Metromedium, Metroblack, Plak Black, Black Condensed & Extra Black Condensed, Stop, Times Eighteen Roman & Bold
✣ *Agfa Scripts 2*: Citadel, Flemish Script 2, Florentine Script 2, French Script, Mahogany Script, Old Fashion Script, Riviera Script.

C

Citation
Trevor Loan • 1990
LET
▲24

ABCDEFGHIJKLMNOPQRSTUVWXYZ
(“.;‘!*?’:,”)$1234567890
&-ÄÖÜÅÇÈÎÑÓÆØŒ»„«[•]‹¡·¿›...

BERTHOLD CITY
Georg Trump • 1930
ADO AGA MAE
▲16

abcdefghijklmnopqrstuvwxyz(".;'!*?':,")
$1234567890&fifl ß-äöüåçèîñóæøœ
ABCDEFGHIJKLMNOPQRSTUVWXYZ
ÄÖÜÅÇÈÎÑÓÆØŒ»„«[¶§•†‡]‹¡·¿›...

Berthold City ...

Light abcdefghijklmnopqrstuvwxyzABCDEFGHIJKLMNOPQRSTUVWXYZ–$1234567890(".;'!
Light Italic *abcdefghijklmnopqrstuvwxyzABCDEFGHIJKLMNOPQRSTUVWXYZ–$1234567890(".;'!*
• Medium abcdefghijklmnopqrstuvwxyzABCDEFGHIJKLMNOPQRSTUVWXYZ–$12345678
Medium Italic *abcdefghijklmnopqrstuvwxyzABCDEFGHIJKLMNOPQRSTUVWXYZ–$12345678*
Bold **abcdefghijklmnopqrstuvwxyzABCDEFGHIJKLMNOPQRSTUVWXYZ–$1234**
Bold Italic ***abcdefghijklmnopqrstuvwxyzABCDEFGHIJKLMNOPQRSTUVWXYZ–$1234***

Clairvaux
Type Before Gutenberg 2
Herbert Maring • 1981
LIN ADO AGA MAE
▲16

abcdefghijklmnopqrstuvwxyz(“.;‘!*?’:,”)
$1234567890&fifl ß-äöüåçèîñóæøœ
ABCDEFGHIJKLMNOPQRSTUVWXYZ
ÄÖÜÅÇÈÎÑÓÆØŒ»„«[¶§•†‡]‹¡·¿›...

▷ ch ck ff ft ll ſ s ſi ſſ ß tz — äöü ÄÖÜ

CLARENDON
Hermann Eidenbenz • 1951
BIT ADO AGA AGP LIN MAE MCL URW

abcdefghijklmnopqrstuvwxyz(“.;‘!*?’:,”)
$1234567890&fiflß-äöüåçèîñóæøœ
ABCDEFGHIJKLMNOPQRSTUVWXYZ
ÄÖÜÅÇÈÎÑÓÆØŒ»„«[¶§•†‡]‹¡·¿›...

Clarendon 1 ...

Light abcdefghijklmnopqrstuvwxyzABCDEFGHIJKLMNOPQRSTUVWXYZ–$1
• Roman **abcdefghijklmnopqrstuvwxyzABCDEFGHIJKLMNOPQRSTUVWXYZ–$**
Bold **abcdefghijklmnopqrstuvwxyzABCDEFGHIJKLMNOPQRSTUVWXYZ–**

Clarendon 2 ...

Condensed ▲16 **abcdefghijklmnopqrstuvwxyzABCDEFGHIJKLMNOPQRSTUVWXYZ–$1234567890(“.;‘!*?’:,**
Bold Condensed ▲16 **abcdefghijklmnopqrstuvwxyzABCDEFGHIJKLMNOPQRSTUVWXYZ–$1234567890(“.**

Type Before Gutenberg 2: Carolina, Clairvaux, San Marco.

... Clarendon 2

Heavy abcdefghijklmnopqrstuvwxyzABCDEFGHIJKLMNOPQRSTUVWXYZ–$

Black ▲16 abcdefghijklmnopqrstuvwxyzABCDEFGHIJKLMNOPQRST

C

CLASSIC ROMAN
Agfa Engravers 1

AGP ABCDEFGHIJKLMNOPQRSTUVWXYZ(".;'!*?':,")

▲18 $1234567890&-ÄÖÜÅÇÈÎÑÓ

ABCDEFGHIJKLMNOPQRSTUVWXYZ

ÄÖÜÅÇÈÎÑÓ»«[·]‹› ▹I V X ST ND RD TH ~ 1/4 1/3 1/2 3/4 D' C R. 'C 'S

Classic Roman ...

Light ABCDEFGHIJKLMNOPQRSTUVWXYZABCDEFGHIJKLMNOPQRSTUVW

• Regular ABCDEFGHIJKLMNOPQRSTUVWXYZABCDEFGHIJKLMNOPQRSTUVWXY

Sackers Light Classic Roman
Agfa Engravers 2

AGP ABCDEFGHIJKLMNOPQRSTUVWXYZ(".;'!*?':,")

▲18 $1234567890&-ÄÖÜÅÇÈÎÑÓ

ABCDEFGHIJKLMNOPQRSTUVWXYZ

ÄÖÜÅÇÈÎÑÓ»«[•]‹› ▹I V X ST ND RD TH 1/4 1/3 1/2 3/4 D' C

CLAUDE SANS

Alan Meeks • 1988 abcdefghijklmnopqrstuvwxyz(".;'!*?':,")

LET $1234567890&fiflß-äöüåçèîñóæøœ

▲16 ABCDEFGHIJKLMNOPQRSTUVWXYZ

ÄÖÜÅÇÈÎÑÓÆØŒ»„«[•]‹¡·¿›...

▹ *as ct e et fr gy is k ll m nt sp ta us v A B C D E F G H J K M N P Q R T U*

Claude Sans ...

• Regular abcdefghijklmnopqrstuvwxyzABCDEFGHIJKLMNOPQRSTUVWXYZ–$1234567890(

• Italic *abcdefghijklmnopqrstuvwxyzABCDEFGHIJKLMNOPQRSTUVWXYZ–$1234567890(".;'!*

Bold Italic ***abcdefghijklmnopqrstuvwxyzABCDEFGHIJKLMNOPQRSTUVWXYZ–$1234567890***

ITC CLEARFACE

Victor Caruso • 1978 (Morris Fuller Benton, 1907) abcdefghijklmnopqrstuvwxyz(".;'!*?':,")

BIT ADO AGA AGP LEF LIN MAE URW $1234567890&fiflß-äöüåçèîñóæøœ

ABCDEFGHIJKLMNOPQRSTUVWXYZ

ÄÖÜÅÇÈÎÑÓÆØŒ»„«[¶§•†‡]‹¡·¿›...

ITC Clearface 1 ...

• Roman abcdefghijklmnopqrstuvwxyzABCDEFGHIJKLMNOPQRSTUVWXYZ–$1234567890(".;'!*

Italic *abcdefghijklmnopqrstuvwxyzABCDEFGHIJKLMNOPQRSTUVWXYZ–$1234567890(".;'*

Agfa Engravers 1: Antique Roman Solid & Slanted, Artisan Roman, Burin Roman & Sans, Classic Roman Light & Regular, Handle Oldstyle, Roman Light & Medium.

Agfa Engravers 2: Sackers Antique Roman Open & Solid, Sackers Light Classic Roman, Sackers English Script, Sackers Gothic Light, Medium & Heavy, Sackers Italian Script, Sackers Roman Light, Sackers Square Gothic.

... ITC Clearface 1

Heavy abcdefghijklmnopqrstuvwxyzABCDEFGHIJKLMNOPQRSTUVWXYZ–$1234567890

Heavy Italic *abcdefghijklmnopqrstuvwxyzABCDEFGHIJKLMNOPQRSTUVWXYZ–$123456789*

ITC Clearface 2 ...

Bold abcdefghijklmnopqrstuvwxyzABCDEFGHIJKLMNOPQRSTUVWXYZ–$1234567890(".;

Bold Italic *abcdefghijklmnopqrstuvwxyzABCDEFGHIJKLMNOPQRSTUVWXYZ–$1234567890("*

Black abcdefghijklmnopqrstuvwxyzABCDEFGHIJKLMNOPQRSTUVWXYZ–$123456

Black Italic *abcdefghijklmnopqrstuvwxyzABCDEFGHIJKLMNOPQRSTUVWXYZ–$12345*

Contour ▲30 abcdefghijklmnopqrstuvwxyzABCDE

CLEARFACE GOTHIC

✍ *Morris Fuller Benton • 1908* abcdefghijklmnopqrstuvwxyz(".;'!*?':,")

LIN ADO AGA AGP LEF MAE MCL URW $1234567890&fiflß-äöüåçèîñóæøœ

▲16 ABCDEFGHIJKLMNOPQRSTUVWXYZ

ÄÖÜÅÇÈÎÑÓÆØŒ»„«[¶§•†‡]‹¡·¿›...

Clearface Gothic ...

45-Light abcdefghijklmnopqrstuvwxyzABCDEFGHIJKLMNOPQRSTUVWXYZ–$1234567890(".;'!*?

• 55-Regular abcdefghijklmnopqrstuvwxyzABCDEFGHIJKLMNOPQRSTUVWXYZ–$1234567890(

65-Medium abcdefghijklmnopqrstuvwxyzABCDEFGHIJKLMNOPQRSTUVWXYZ–$123456789

75-Bold abcdefghijklmnopqrstuvwxyzABCDEFGHIJKLMNOPQRSTUVWXYZ–$123456

95-Black abcdefghijklmnopqrstuvwxyzABCDEFGHIJKLMNOPQRSTUVWXYZ–$123

Cloister Black

✍ *Morris Fuller Benton • 1904* *... Joseph W. Phinney* abcdefghijklmnopqrstuvwxyz(".;'!*?':,")

BIT $1234567890&fiflß-äöüåçèîñóæøœ

▲16 ABCDEFGHIJKLMNOPQRSTUVWXYZ

ÄÖÜÅÇÈÎÑÓÆØŒ»„«[§•†‡]‹¡·¿›...

Cloister Open Face

✍ *Robert Hunter Middleton • 1920* abcdefghijklmnopqrstuvwxyz(".;'!*?':,")

BIT ▲30 $1234567890&fiflß-äöüåçèîñóæøœ

ABCDEFGHIJKLMNOPQRSTUVW

XYZÄÖÜÅÇÈÎÑÓÆØŒ»„«[§•†‡]‹¡·¿›

C

COCHIN

Matthew Carter • 1977 abcdefghijklmnopqrstuvwxyz(".;'!*?':,")

LIN ADO AGA MAE $1234567890&fifl ß-äöüåçèîñóæøœ

ABCDEFGHIJKLMNOPQRSTUVWXYZ

ÄÖÜÅÇÈÎÑÓÆØŒ»„«[¶§•†‡]‹¡·¿›...

Cochin ...

• Roman abcdefghijklmnopqrstuvwxyzABCDEFGHIJKLMNOPQRSTUVWXYZ–$123456

Italic *abcdefghijklmnopqrstuvwxyzABCDEFGHIJKLMNOPQRSTUVWXYZ–$1234567890(".;'!*?':*

Bold **abcdefghijklmnopqrstuvwxyzABCDEFGHIJKLMNOPQRSTUVWXYZ–$12345**

Bold Italic ***abcdefghijklmnopqrstuvwxyzABCDEFGHIJKLMNOPQRSTUVWXYZ–$1234567890("***

COLMCILLE

Dara Ó Lochlainn • 1992 (Colm Ó Lochlainn & Karl Uhlemann, 1934) abcdefghijklmnopqrstuvwxyz(".;'!*?':,")

$1234567890–&fifl ß-äöüåçèîñóæøœ

MCL ABCDEFGHIJKLMNOPQRSTUVWXYZ

ÄÖÜÅÇÈÎÑÓÆØŒ»„«[¶§•†‡]‹¡·¿›...

Colmcille ...

• Regular abcdefghijklmnopqrstuvwxyzABCDEFGHIJKLMNOPQRSTUVWXYZ–$12345678

Regular Alternate ḃċḋḟġṁṗṡṫ ſfffiffl ⁊ ḂĊḊḞĠṀṖṠṪ

Italic *abcdefghijklmnopqrstuvwxyzABCDEFGHIJKLMNOPQRSTUVWXYZ–$1234567890(".;'!*?':,*

Italic Alternate *ḃċḋḟġṁṗṡṫ ſfffiffl ⁊ ḂĊḊḞĠṀṖṠṪ*

Bold **abcdefghijklmnopqrstuvwxyzABCDEFGHIJKLMNOPQRSTUVWXYZ–$1234567**

Bold Alternate **ḃċḋḟġṁṗṡṫ ſfffiffl ⁊ ḂĊḊḞĠṀṖṠṪ**

Bold Italic ***abcdefghijklmnopqrstuvwxyzABCDEFGHIJKLMNOPQRSTUVWXYZ–$1234567890(".;'!***

Bold Italic Alternate ***ḃċḋḟġṁṗṡṫ ſfffiffl ⁊ ḂĊḊḞĠṀṖṠṪ***

Colonna
Monotype Handtooled

MCL abcdefghijklmnopqrstuvwxyz(".;'!*?':,")

▲30 $1234567890&fifl ß-äöüåçèîñóæøœ

ABCDEFGHIJKLMNOPQRSTUVWXYZ

ÄÖÜÅÇÈÎÑÓÆØŒ»„«[•]‹¡·¿›...

Colmcille ▶ Colmcille Borders & Ornaments.
Monotype Handtooled: Colonna, Imprint Shadow, Imprint Shadow Italic.

C

COLOSSALIS

Aldo Novarese • 1984 abcdefghijklmnopqrstuvwxyz(“.;‘!*?’:,”)
ADO AGA MAE $1234567890&fiflß-äöüåçèîñóæøœ
▲16 ABCDEFGHIJKLMNOPQRSTUVWXYZ
ÄÖÜÅÇÈÎÑÓÆØŒ»„«[¶§•†‡]‹i·¿›...

Colossalis ...

• Regular abcdefghijklmnopqrstuvwxyzABCDEFGHIJKLMNOPQRSTUVWXYZ–$1234567890(“.;‘!*
Medium abcdefghijklmnopqrstuvwxyzABCDEFGHIJKLMNOPQRSTUVWXYZ–$123456
Bold abcdefghijklmnopqrstuvwxyzABCDEFGHIJKLMNOPQRSTUVWXYZ–$1
Black abcdefghijklmnopqrstuvwxyzABCDEFGHIJKLMNOPQRSTUVW

COLUMBUS

Patricia Saunders • 1992 abcdefghijklmnopqrstuvwxyz(“.;‘!*?’:,”)
MCL $1234567890&fiflß-äöüåçèîñóæøœ
ABCDEFGHIJKLMNOPQRSTUVWXYZ
ÄÖÜÅÇÈÎÑÓÆØŒ»„«[¶§•†‡]‹¡·¿›...

Columbus ...

• Roman abcdefghijklmnopqrstuvwxyzABCDEFGHIJKLMNOPQRSTUVWXYZ–$1234567890(“.;‘!*
Italic *abcdefghijklmnopqrstuvwxyzABCDEFGHIJKLMNOPQRSTUVWXYZ–$1234567890(“.;‘!*?’:,”)&*
Semibold **abcdefghijklmnopqrstuvwxyzABCDEFGHIJKLMNOPQRSTUVWXYZ–$1234567890(**
Semibold Italic ***abcdefghijklmnopqrstuvwxyzABCDEFGHIJKLMNOPQRSTUVWXYZ–$1234567890(“.;‘!*?’:,”)***
Bold **abcdefghijklmnopqrstuvwxyzABCDEFGHIJKLMNOPQRSTUVWXYZ–$12345678**
Bold Italic ***abcdefghijklmnopqrstuvwxyzABCDEFGHIJKLMNOPQRSTUVWXYZ–$1234567890(“.;‘!*?’***

COLUMBUS EXPERT

MCL ABCDEFGHIJKLMNOPQRSTUVWXYZ.;!?:,
$1234567890&ff fi fl ffi ffl-ÄÖÜÅÇÈÎÑÓÆØŒ
(abdeilmnorst) 1/8 1/4 1/3 3/8 1/2 5/8 2/3 3/4 7/8 $12345/67890¢ ₡Rp

Columbus Expert ...

• Expert Roman ABCDEFGHIJKLMNOPQRSTUVWXYZ–$1234567890.;!?:,&-ff fi fl ffi ffl 1/8 1/4 1/3 3/8 1/2 $12345/67890¢ (abdeilmnor
Expert Italic *$1234567890.;:,–ff fi fl ffi ffl 1/8 1/4 1/3 3/8 1/2 $12345/67890¢ (abdeilmnorst) 5/8 2/3 3/4 7/8 ₡Rp*
Expert Semibold **$1234567890.;:,–ff fi fl ffi ffl 1/8 1/4 1/3 3/8 1/2 $12345/67890¢ (abdeilmnorst) 5/8 2/3 3/4 7/8 ₡Rp**
Expert Semibold Italic ***$1234567890.;:,–ff fi fl ffi ffl 1/8 1/4 1/3 3/8 1/2 $12345/67890¢ (abdeilmnorst) 5/8 2/3 3/4 7/8 ₡Rp***
Expert Bold **$1234567890.;:,–ff fi fl ffi ffl 1/8 1/4 1/3 3/8 1/2 $12345/67890¢ (abdeilmnorst) 5/8 2/3 3/4 7/8 ₡Rp**
Expert Bold Italic ***$1234567890.;:,–ff fi fl ffi ffl 1/8 1/4 1/3 3/8 1/2 $12345/67890¢ (abdeilmnorst) 5/8 2/3 3/4 7/8 ₡Rp***

Columbus Expert ▶ Columbus Ornaments One & Two.

C

Columna Solid
Max Caflisch • 1955
URW
▲30

ABCDEFGHIJKLMNOPQRSTUVWXYZ
(“.;‘!*?’:,”)$1234567890
&-ÄÖÜÅÇÈÎÑÓÆØŒ»„«[¶§•†‡]‹¡·¿›...

COMENIUS ANTIQUA
Hermann Zapf • 1980
ADO AGA MAE

abcdefghijklmnopqrstuvwxyz(“.;‘!*?’:,”)
$1234567890&fiflß-äöüåçèîñóæøœ
ABCDEFGHIJKLMNOPQRSTUVWXYZ
ÄÖÜÅÇÈÎÑÓÆØŒ»„«[¶§•†‡]‹¡·¿›...

Comenius Antiqua ...

• Roman abcdefghijklmnopqrstuvwxyzABCDEFGHIJKLMNOPQRSTUVWXYZ–$1234
Italic *abcdefghijklmnopqrstuvwxyzABCDEFGHIJKLMNOPQRSTUVWXYZ–$1234*
Medium **abcdefghijklmnopqrstuvwxyzABCDEFGHIJKLMNOPQRSTUVWXYZ–**
Bold **abcdefghijklmnopqrstuvwxyzABCDEFGHIJKLMNOPQRSTUVWX**

COMICBOOK
Nicholas D. Kent • 1992
VAN
▲16

ABCDEFGHIJKLMNOPQRSTUVWXYZ(“.;‘!*?’:,”)
$1234567890&-ÄÖÜÅÇÈÎÑÓÆØŒ»„«[¶•†‡]‹¡·¿›... ▹★

Comicbook ...

• Book ABCDEFGHIJKLMNOPQRSTUVWXYZ(“.;‘!*?’:,”)&–$123456
Book Italic *ABCDEFGHIJKLMNOPQRSTUVWXYZ(“.;‘!*?’:,”)&–$123456*
Demi **ABCDEFGHIJKLMNOPQRSTUVWXYZ(“.;‘!*?’:,”)&–$1**
Demi Italic ***ABCDEFGHIJKLMNOPQRSTUVWXYZ(“.;‘!*?’:,”)&–$1***
Bold **ABCDEFGHIJKLMNOPQRSTUVWXYZ(“.;‘!*?’:,”)&–$12**
Bold Italic ***ABCDEFGHIJKLMNOPQRSTUVWXYZ(“.;‘!*?’:,”)***

COMIC BOOK
Greg Kolodziejzyk • 1987
IMA
▲16

ABCDEFGHIJKLMNOPQRSTUVWXYZ(“.;‘!*?’:,”)
$1234567890&-ÄÖÜÅÇÈÎÑÓÆØŒ
ABCDEFGHIJKLMNOPQRSTUVWXYZ
ÄÖÜÅÇÈÎÑÓÆØŒ»„«[¶§°†]¡·¿...

Comic Book ...

• Comic Book Regular ABCDEFGHIJKLMNOPQRSTUVWXYZABCDEFGHIJKLMNOPQRSTUVWXYZ–
Comic Book Two **ABCDEFGHIJKLMNOPQRSTUVWXYZABCDEFGHIJKLMNOPQRSTUVWXYZ-**
Comic Book Two Outline ABCDEFGHIJKLMNOPQRSTUVWXYZABCDEFGHIJKLMNOPQRSTUVWXYZ-

C

MN Comic Strip

MTD ABCDEFGHIJKLMNOPQRSTUVWXYZ(".;'!*?':,")

▲16 $1234567890&-ÄÖÜÅÇÈÎÑÓÆØŒ»,,«[•]‹¡¿›...

COMMERCE

Rick Valicenti & Greg Thompson • 1991 abcdefghijklmnopqrstuvwxyz(".;'!*?':,")

FBU AGP MTD $1234567890&fifIß-äöüåçèîñóæøœ

▲16 ABCDEFGHIJKLMNOPQRSTUVWXYZ

ÄÖÜÅÇÈÎÑÓÆØŒ»,,«[¶§•†‡]‹¡·¿›...

Commerce ...

• Lean abcdefghijklmnopqrstuvwxyzABCDEFGHIJKLMNOPQRSTUVWXYZ–$

Fat abcdefghijklmnopqrstuvwxyzABCDEFGHIJKLMNOPQRSTUVWXY

Commercial Script
Agfa Scripts 1

Morris Fuller Benton • 1908 abcdefghijklmnopqrstuvwxyz(".;'!*?':,")

AGP BIT LEF LET MCL MTD URW $1234567890&ß-äöüåçèîñó

▲16 ABCDEFGHIJKLMNOPQRSTUVWXYZ

ÄÖÜÅÇÈÎÑÓ»«[·]‹›   ▷ I V X st nd rd th 1/4 1/3 1/2 3/4 D' c/o 'c 's O' rs & %

COMPACTA

Fred Lambert • 1963 abcdefghijklmnopqrstuvwxyz(".;'!*?':,")

BIT LEF LET MCL MTD URW $1234567890&fifIß-äöüåçèîñóæøœ

▲16 ABCDEFGHIJKLMNOPQRSTUVWXYZ

ÄÖÜÅÇÈÎÑÓÆØŒ»,,«[§ • †‡]‹¡·¿›...

Compacta ...

Light abcdefghijklmnopqrstuvwxyzABCDEFGHIJKLMNOPQRSTUVWXYZ–$1234567890(".;'!*?':,")&fifIß-äöüÄÖÜåçèÅÇÈîñóÎÑÓæøœÆØŒ»,,«[§

• Regular abcdefghijklmnopqrstuvwxyzABCDEFGHIJKLMNOPQRSTUVWXYZ–$1234567890(".;'!*?':,")&fifIß-äöüÄÖÜåçèÅÇ

Italic abcdefghijklmnopqrstuvwxyzABCDEFGHIJKLMNOPQRSTUVWXYZ–$1234567890(".;'!*?':,")&fifIß-äöüÄÖÜåçèÅÇÉ

Bold abcdefghijklmnopqrstuvwxyzABCDEFGHIJKLMNOPQRSTUVWXYZ–$1234567890(".;'!*?':,")&

Bold Italic abcdefghijklmnopqrstuvwxyzABCDEFGHIJKLMNOPQRSTUVWXYZ–$1234567890(".;'!*?':,")&

Black abcdefghijklmnopqrstuvwxyzABCDEFGHIJKLMNOPQRSTUV

Agfa Scripts 1: Commercial Script, Helinda Rook, Old English, Original Script, Quill Script, Stuyvesant, Wedding Text.

C

CONCORDE

Günter Gerhard Lange • 1968

ADO AGA LIN MAE

abcdefghijklmnopqrstuvwxyz(".;'!*?':,")
$1234567890&fiflß-äöüåçèîñóæøœ
ABCDEFGHIJKLMNOPQRSTUVWXYZ
ÄÖÜÅÇÈÎÑÓÆØŒ»„«[¶§•†‡]‹¡·¿›...

Concorde ...

• Roman abcdefghijklmnopqrstuvwxyzABCDEFGHIJKLMNOPQRSTUVWXYZ–$123
Italic *abcdefghijklmnopqrstuvwxyzABCDEFGHIJKLMNOPQRSTUVWXYZ–$1234*
Medium **abcdefghijklmnopqrstuvwxyzABCDEFGHIJKLMNOPQRSTUVWXYZ–$12**
Medium Italic ***abcdefghijklmnopqrstuvwxyzABCDEFGHIJKLMNOPQRSTUVWXYZ–$1234567***

CONCORDE EXPERT & SCOSF

ADO AGA MAE

ABCDEFGHIJKLMNOPQRSTUVWXYZ.;!?:,
$1234567890&fffiflffiffl-ÄÖÜÅÇÈÎÑÓÆØŒ
(abdeilmnorst) 1/8 1/4 1/3 3/8 1/2 5/8 2/3 3/4 7/8 $12345/67890¢ ₡Rp

Concorde Expert & SCOSF ...

• Expert Roman ABCDEFGHIJKLMNOPQRSTUVWXYZ–$1234567890.;!?:,&-fffiflffiffl 1/8 1/4 1/3 3/8 1/2 $12345/
Expert Italic *$1234567890.;:,–fffiflffiffl 1/8 1/4 1/3 3/8 1/2 $12345/67890¢ (abdeilmnorst) 5/8 2/3 3/4 7/8 ₡Rp*
Expert Medium **ABCDEFGHIJKLMNOPQRSTUVWXYZ–$1234567890.;!?:,&-fffiflffiffl 1/8 1/4 1/3 3/8 1/2 $1**
Expert Medium Italic ***$1234567890.;:,–fffiflffiffl 1/8 1/4 1/3 3/8 1/2 $12345/67890¢ (abdeilmnorst) 5/8 2/3 3/4 7/8 ₡Rp***
Roman SCOSF ABCDEFGHIJKLMNOPQRSTUVWXYZABCDEFGHIJKLMNOPQRSTUVWXYZ–$12
Italic OSF *abcdefghijklmnopqrstuvwxyzABCDEFGHIJKLMNOPQRSTUVWXYZ–$12345*
Medium SCOSF **ABCDEFGHIJKLMNOPQRSTUVWXYZABCDEFGHIJKLMNOPQRSTUVWXYZ–$**
Medium Italic OSF ***abcdefghijklmnopqrstuvwxyzABCDEFGHIJKLMNOPQRSTUVWXYZ–$12345678***

CONCORDE CONDENSED

ADO AGA MAE

abcdefghijklmnopqrstuvwxyz(".;'!*?':,")
$1234567890&fiflß-äöüåçèîñóæøœ
ABCDEFGHIJKLMNOPQRSTUVWXYZ
ÄÖÜÅÇÈÎÑÓÆØŒ»„«[¶§•†‡]‹¡·¿›...

Concorde Condensed ...

• Condensed abcdefghijklmnopqrstuvwxyzABCDEFGHIJKLMNOPQRSTUVWXYZ–$1234567890(".;'!*?':,"
Medium Condensed **abcdefghijklmnopqrstuvwxyzABCDEFGHIJKLMNOPQRSTUVWXYZ–$1234567890(".;'!**
Bold Condensed **abcdefghijklmnopqrstuvwxyzABCDEFGHIJKLMNOPQRSTUVWXYZ–$1234567890(".;'**
Bold Condensed Outline ▲18 abcdefghijklmnopqrstuvwxyzABCDEFGHIJKLMNOPQRSTUVWXY

C

CONCORDE NOVA
+ EXPERT & SCOSF

Günter Gerhard Lange • 1975 abcdefghijklmnopqrstuvwxyz(“.;‘!*?’:,”)

ADO AGA MAE $1234567890&fiflß-äöüåçèîñóæøœ

ABCDEFGHIJKLMNOPQRSTUVWXYZ

ÄÖÜÅÇÈÎÑÓÆØŒ»„«[¶§•†‡]‹i·¿›...

Concorde Nova
+ Expert & SCOSF ...

• Roman abcdefghijklmnopqrstuvwxyzABCDEFGHIJKLMNOPQRSTUVWXYZ–$1234567890(“.;‘!*?’:,”)&

Italic *abcdefghijklmnopqrstuvwxyzABCDEFGHIJKLMNOPQRSTUVWXYZ–$1234567890(“.;‘!*?’:,”)&*

Medium **abcdefghijklmnopqrstuvwxyzABCDEFGHIJKLMNOPQRSTUVWXYZ–$1234567890(“.;‘!***

Expert Roman ABCDEFGHIJKLMNOPQRSTUVWXYZ–$1234567890.;!?:,&-ff fi fl ffi ffl 1/8 1/4 1/3 3/8 1/2 $12345/67890¢ (abdeilmnorst)

Expert Italic *$1234567890(.;:,)–ff fi fl ffi ffl 1/8 1/4 1/3 3/8 1/2 $12345/67890¢ (abdeilmnorst) 5/8 2/3 3/4 7/8 ₡Rp*

Expert Medium **ABCDEFGHIJKLMNOPQRSTUVWXYZ–$1234567890.;!?:,&-ff fi fl ffi ffl 1/8 1/4 1/3 3/8 1/2 $12345/67890¢ (ab**

Roman SCOSF ABCDEFGHIJKLMNOPQRSTUVWXYZABCDEFGHIJKLMNOPQRSTUVWXYZ–$1234567890(“.;‘!*?’:,”)&-

Italic OSF *abcdefghijklmnopqrstuvwxyzABCDEFGHIJKLMNOPQRSTUVWXYZ–$1234567890(“.;‘!*?’:,”)&fi*

Medium SCOSF **ABCDEFGHIJKLMNOPQRSTUVWXYZABCDEFGHIJKLMNOPQRSTUVWXYZ–$1234567890(“.;**

CONGRESS

Adrian Williams • 1980 abcdefghijklmnopqrstuvwxyz(“.;‘!*?’:,”)

URW AGP $1234567890&fiflß-äöüåçèîñóæøœ

ABCDEFGHIJKLMNOPQRSTUVWXYZ

ÄÖÜÅÇÈÎÑÓÆØŒ»„«[¶§•†‡]‹i·¿›...

Congress ...

Light abcdefghijklmnopqrstuvwxyzABCDEFGHIJKLMNOPQRSTUVWXYZ–$1234567890(

• Regular abcdefghijklmnopqrstuvwxyzABCDEFGHIJKLMNOPQRSTUVWXYZ–$1234567890(

Italic *abcdefghijklmnopqrstuvwxyzABCDEFGHIJKLMNOPQRSTUVWXYZ–$1234567890(*

Medium abcdefghijklmnopqrstuvwxyzABCDEFGHIJKLMNOPQRSTUVWXYZ–$1234567890

Bold **abcdefghijklmnopqrstuvwxyzABCDEFGHIJKLMNOPQRSTUVWXYZ–$123456789**

Black **abcdefghijklmnopqrstuvwxyzABCDEFGHIJKLMNOPQRSTUVWXYZ–$123456789**

CONGRESS SANS

Adrian Williams • 1985 abcdefghijklmnopqrstuvwxyz(“.;‘!*?’:,”)

MTD $1234567890&fiflß-äöüåçèîñóæøœ

ABCDEFGHIJKLMNOPQRSTUVWXYZ

ÄÖÜÅÇÈÎÑÓÆØŒ»„«[¶§•†‡]‹i·¿›...

Congress Sans ...

Light abcdefghijklmnopqrstuvwxyzABCDEFGHIJKLMNOPQRSTUVWXYZ–$1234567890(“.;‘!*

Light Italic *abcdefghijklmnopqrstuvwxyzABCDEFGHIJKLMNOPQRSTUVWXYZ–$1234567890(“.;‘!**

• Regular abcdefghijklmnopqrstuvwxyzABCDEFGHIJKLMNOPQRSTUVWXYZ–$1234567890(“

Italic *abcdefghijklmnopqrstuvwxyzABCDEFGHIJKLMNOPQRSTUVWXYZ–$1234567890(“*

C

... Congress Sans

Bold abcdefghijklmnopqrstuvwxyzABCDEFGHIJKLMNOPQRSTUVWXYZ–$12345678

Bold Italic *abcdefghijklmnopqrstuvwxyzABCDEFGHIJKLMNOPQRSTUVWXYZ–$12345678*

Extra Bold **abcdefghijklmnopqrstuvwxyzABCDEFGHIJKLMNOPQRSTUVWXYZ–$12345**

Extra Bold Italic ***abcdefghijklmnopqrstuvwxyzABCDEFGHIJKLMNOPQRSTUVWXYZ–$12345***

Constructivist

INT ABC DEFG HIJKLM NOPQRSTUVWXYZ

▲30 ("".;'?*?':,"")$1234567890&-

FC CONTEMPORARY BRUSH

TFC abcdefghijklmnopqrstuvwxyz(".;'!*?':,")

▲16 $1234567890&fifl ß-äöüåçèîñóæøœ

ABCDEFGHIJKLMNOPQRSTUVWXYZ

ÄÖÜÅÇÈÎÑÓÆØŒ»„«[¶§•†‡]‹¡·¿›...

FC Contemporary Brush ...

• Regular abcdefghijklmnopqrstuvwxyzABCDEFGHIJKLMNOPQRSTUVWXYZ–$1234567890("

Bold **abcdefghijklmnopqrstuvwxyzABCDEFGHIJKLMNOPQRSTUVWXYZ–$123456789**

Extra Bold **abcdefghijklmnopqrstuvwxyzABCDEFGHIJKLMNOPQRSTUVWXYZ–$12345678**

FC COOPER OLD STYLE

Oswald Cooper • 1918 abcdefghijklmnopqrstuvwxyz(".;'!*?':,")

TFC $1234567890&fifl ß-äöüåçèîñóæøœ

ABCDEFGHIJKLMNOPQRSTUVWXYZ

ÄÖÜÅÇÈÎÑÓÆØŒ»„«[•]‹¡·¿›...

FC Cooper Old Style 1 ...

Light abcdefghijklmnopqrstuvwxyzABCDEFGHIJKLMNOPQRSTUVWXYZ–$12345

Light Italic *abcdefghijklmnopqrstuvwxyzABCDEFGHIJKLMNOPQRSTUVWXYZ–$12345678*

Demi **abcdefghijklmnopqrstuvwxyzABCDEFGHIJKLMNOPQRSTUVWXYZ–$1234**

Demi Italic ***abcdefghijklmnopqrstuvwxyzABCDEFGHIJKLMNOPQRSTUVWXYZ–$1234***

FC Cooper Old Style 2 ...

• Medium abcdefghijklmnopqrstuvwxyzABCDEFGHIJKLMNOPQRSTUVWXYZ–$12345

Medium Italic *abcdefghijklmnopqrstuvwxyzABCDEFGHIJKLMNOPQRSTUVWXYZ–$1234567*

Bold **abcdefghijklmnopqrstuvwxyzABCDEFGHIJKLMNOPQRSTUVWXYZ–$1234**

COOPER BLACK

Ozwald Cooper • 1924

LIN ADO AGA LEF MAE MTD URW

▲18

abcdefghijklmnopqrstuvwxyz(".;'!*?':,")
$1234567890&fiflß-äöüåçèîñóæøœ
ABCDEFGHIJKLMNOPQRSTUVWXYZ
ÄÖÜÅÇÈÎÑÓÆØŒ»„«[¶§•†‡]‹¡·¿›...

Cooper Black ...

• Black abcdefghijklmnopqrstuvwxyzABCDEFGHIJKLMNO

Black Italic *abcdefghijklmnopqrstuvwxyzABCDEFGHIJKLMNOPQ*

BITSTREAM COOPER

Bitstream Design Staff • 1986 (Ozwald Cooper, 1924)

BIT

abcdefghijklmnopqrstuvwxyz(".;'!*?':,")
$1234567890&fiflß-äöüåçèîñóæøœ
ABCDEFGHIJKLMNOPQRSTUVWXYZ
ÄÖÜÅÇÈÎÑÓÆØŒ»„«[¶§•†‡]‹¡·¿›...

Bitstream Cooper 1 ...

Light abcdefghijklmnopqrstuvwxyzABCDEFGHIJKLMNOPQRSTUVWXYZ–$12345678

Light Italic *abcdefghijklmnopqrstuvwxyzABCDEFGHIJKLMNOPQRSTUVWXYZ–$1234567890*

Bold **abcdefghijklmnopqrstuvwxyzABCDEFGHIJKLMNOPQRSTUVWXYZ–$1**

Bold Italic ***abcdefghijklmnopqrstuvwxyzABCDEFGHIJKLMNOPQRSTUVWXYZ–$123***

Bitstream Cooper 2 ...

• Medium abcdefghijklmnopqrstuvwxyzABCDEFGHIJKLMNOPQRSTUVWXYZ–$1234

Medium Italic *abcdefghijklmnopqrstuvwxyzABCDEFGHIJKLMNOPQRSTUVWXYZ–$123456*

Black **abcdefghijklmnopqrstuvwxyzABCDEFGHIJKLMNOPQRSTUVWX**

Black Italic ***abcdefghijklmnopqrstuvwxyzABCDEFGHIJKLMNOPQRSTUVWXYZ–***

Bitstream Cooper 3 ...

Black Headline ▲18 **abcdefghijklmnopqrstuvwxyzABCDEFGHIJKLMN**

Black Headline Italic ▲18 ***abcdefghijklmnopqrstuvwxyzABCDEFGHIJKLMNOP***

Black Outline ▲18 abcdefghijklmnopqrstuvwxyzABCDEFGHIJKLM

COPPERPLATE GOTHIC

Frederic W. Goudy • 1901

LIN ADO AGA BIT MAE

ABCDEFGHIJKLMNOPQRSTUVWXYZ(".;'!*?':,")
$1234567890&-ÄÖÜÅÇÈÎÑÓÆØŒ
ABCDEFGHIJKLMNOPQRSTUVWXYZ
ÄÖÜÅÇÈÎÑÓÆØŒ»„«[¶§•†‡]‹¡·¿›...

Copperplate Gothic ...

29 B-C ABCDEFGHIJKLMNOPQRSTUVWXYZABCDEFGHIJKLMNOPQRSTUVWXYZ–$1234567890(".;'!*?':,")

29 A-B ABCDEFGHIJKLMNOPQRSTUVWXYZABCDEFGHIJKLMNOPQRSTUVWXYZ–$123456

• 30 B-C ABCDEFGHIJKLMNOPQRSTUVWXYZABCDEFGHIJKLMNOPQRSTUVWXYZ–$1234567890(".;'!*?':,"

C

... Copperplate Gothic

30 A-B ABCDEFGHIJKLMNOPQRSTUVWXYZABCDEFGHIJKLMNOPQRSTUVWXYZ–$1234
31 B-C ABCDEFGHIJKLMNOPQRSTUVWXYZABCDEFGHIJKLMNOPQRSTUVWXYZ–$12
31 A-B ABCDEFGHIJKLMNOPQRSTUVWXYZABCDEFGHIJKLMNOPQRS
32 B-C ABCDEFGHIJKLMNOPQRSTUVWXYZABCDEFGHIJKLMNOPQRSTUVWXYZ–$123
32 A-B ABCDEFGHIJKLMNOPQRSTUVWXYZABCDEFGHIJKLMNOPQRST
33 B-C ABCDEFGHIJKLMNOPQRSTUVWXYZABCDEFGHIJKLMNOPQRSTUVWXYZ–$1

CORINTHIAN

Colin Brignall • *1981* abcdefghijklmnopqrstuvwxyz(“.;‘!*?’:,”)
URW LET $1234567890&fiflß-äöüåçèîñóæøœ
▲16 ABCDEFGHIJKLMNOPQRSTUVWXYZ
ÄÖÜÅÇÈÎÑÓÆØŒ»,,«[¶§•†‡]‹¡·¿...

Corinthian ...

Light abcdefghijklmnopqrstuvwxyzABCDEFGHIJKLMNOPQRSTUVWXYZ-$1234567
• Medium abcdefghijklmnopqrstuvwxyzABCDEFGHIJKLMNOPQRSTUVWXYZ-$12345
Bold **abcdefghijklmnopqrstuvwxyzABCDEFGHIJKLMNOPQRSTUVWXYZ-$123**
Extra Bold **abcdefghijklmnopqrstuvwxyzABCDEFGHIJKLMNOPQRSTUVWXYZ-$**

CORONA

C. H. Griffith • *1940* abcdefghijklmnopqrstuvwxyz(“.;‘!*?’:,”)
LIN ADO AGA MAE $1234567890&fiflß-äöüåçèîñóæøœ
ABCDEFGHIJKLMNOPQRSTUVWXYZ
ÄÖÜÅÇÈÎÑÓÆØŒ»,,«[¶§•†‡]‹¡·¿›...

Corona ...

• Roman abcdefghijklmnopqrstuvwxyzABCDEFGHIJKLMNOPQRSTUVWXYZ–
Italic *abcdefghijklmnopqrstuvwxyzABCDEFGHIJKLMNOPQRSTUVWXYZ–$12*
Bold **abcdefghijklmnopqrstuvwxyzABCDEFGHIJKLMNOPQRSTUVWXYZ–**

Coronet Bold
Monotype Scripts 3

Robert Hunter Middleton • *1937* *abcdefghijklmnopqrstuvwxyz(“.;‘!*?’:,”)*
MCL AGP *$1234567890&fiflß-äöüåçèîñóæøœ*
▲16 *ABCDEFGHIJKLMNOPQRSTUVWXYZ*
ÄÖÜÅÇÈÎÑÓÆØŒ»,,«[§•†‡]‹¡¿›...

Monotype Scripts 3: Coronet Bold, Mercurius Script Bold.

C

π Corsiva
Monotype PlusSet 6
Patricia Saunders • 1991
MCL
▲16

abcdefghijklmnopqrstuvwxyz(".;'!?':,")*
$1234567890&fiflß-äöüåçèîñóæøœ
ABCDEFGHIJKLMNOPQRSTUVWXYZ
ÄÖÜÅÇÈÎÑÓÆØŒ»„«[¶§•†‡]‹¡·¿›...

COSMOS
Gustav Jaeger • 1982
ADO AGA MAE

abcdefghijklmnopqrstuvwxyz(".;'!*?':,")
$1234567890&fiflß-äöüåçèîñóæøœ
ABCDEFGHIJKLMNOPQRSTUVWXYZ
ÄÖÜÅÇÈÎÑÓÆØŒ»„«[¶§•†‡]‹¡·¿›...

Cosmos ...
Light abcdefghijklmnopqrstuvwxyzABCDEFGHIJKLMNOPQRSTUVWXYZ–$12345678
Light Italic *abcdefghijklmnopqrstuvwxyzABCDEFGHIJKLMNOPQRSTUVWXYZ–$123456789*
• Medium abcdefghijklmnopqrstuvwxyzABCDEFGHIJKLMNOPQRSTUVWXYZ–$12345
Extra Bold ▲16 **abcdefghijklmnopqrstuvwxyzABCDEFGHIJKLMNOPQRSTU**

Cosmos Extra Bold
Berthold DisplaySet 1
Gustav Jaeger • 1982
ADO AGA MAE
▲24

abcdefghijklmnopqrstuvwxyz(".;'!*?':,")
$1234567890&fiflß-äöüåçèîóÿæøœ
ABCDEFGHIJKLMNOPQRSTUVWXYZ
ÄÖÜÅÇÈÎÑÓÆØŒ»„«[¶§•†‡]‹¡·¿›...

Cottonwood
Adobe Wood Type 1
Kim Buker, Barbara Lind & Joy Redick • 1990
ADO AGA LIN MAE
▲48

ABCDEFGHIJKLMNOP
QRSTUVWXYZ(".;'!*?':,")
$1234567890&-ÄÖÜ
ÅÇÈÎÑÓÆØŒ»„«[•]‹¡·¿›...

Monotype PlusSet 6: Corsiva & Monotype Sorts.
π Corsiva ▶ Monotype Sorts.
Berthold DisplaySet 1: AG Book Stencil, AG Old Face Shaded, Barmeno Extra Bold, Cosmos Extra Bold, Formata Outline.

Adobe Wood Type 1: Cottonwood, Ironwood, Juniper, Mesquite, Ponderosa, Adobe Wood Type Ornaments 1.
Cottonwood ▶ Adobe Wood Type Ornaments 1.

C

COURIER 10 PITCH

Howard Kettler • 1956 abcdefghijklmnopqrstuvwxyz(“.;‘!*?’:,”)

BIT $1234567890&ß-äöüåçèîñóæøœ

▲12 ABCDEFGHIJKLMNOPQRSTUVWXYZ

ÄÖÜÅÇÈÎÑÓÆØŒ»„«[¶§·†‡]‹¡·¿›…

Courier 10 Pitch …

• Regular abcdefghijklmnopqrstuvwxyzABCDEFGHIJKLMNOPQRSTUVWXYZ–$1234567890(“.;‘

Italic *abcdefghijklmnopqrstuvwxyzABCDEFGHIJKLMNOPQRSTUVWXYZ–$1234567890(“.;‘*

Bold **abcdefghijklmnopqrstuvwxyzABCDEFGHIJKLMNOPQRSTUVWXYZ–$1234567890(“.;‘**

Bold Italic ***abcdefghijklmnopqrstuvwxyzABCDEFGHIJKLMNOPQRSTUVWXYZ-$1234567890(".;'***

Monotype Courier Twelve
Monotype Typewriter Faces

Howard Kettler • 1956 abcdefghijklmnopqrstuvwxyz(“.;‘!*?’:,”)

MCL $1234567890&ß-äöüåçèîñóæøœ

▲12 ABCDEFGHIJKLMNOPQRSTUVWXYZ

ÄÖÜÅÇÈÎÑÓÆØŒ»„«[¶§•†‡]‹¡·¿›…

FC CRAW MODERN

Freeman Craw • 1958 abcdefghijklmnopqrstuvwxyz(“.;‘!*?’:,”)

TFC

▲22 $1234567890&fiflß-äöüåçèîñóæøœ

ABCDEFGHIJKLMNOPQRSTUVWXYZ

ÄÖÜÅÇÈÎÑÓÆØŒ»„«[¶§·†‡]‹¡·¿›…

FC Craw Modern …

• Roman abcdefghijklmnopqrstuvwxyzABCDEF

Italic *abcdefghijklmnopqrstuvwxyzABCDEFGH*

Bold **abcdefghijklmnopqrstuvwxyzABCD**

CREMONA

Vladimir Andrich • 1982 abcdefghijklmnopqrstuvwxyz(“.;‘!*?’:,”)

ADO AGA MAE $1234567890&fiflß-äöüåçèîñóæøœ

ABCDEFGHIJKLMNOPQRSTUVWXYZ

ÄÖÜÅÇÈÎÑÓÆØŒ»„«[¶§•†‡]‹¡·¿›…

Monotype Typewriter Faces: Monotype Courier Twelve, Typewirter, Typewriter Elite, Typewriter Gothic.

C

... Cremona ...

• Roman abcdefghijklmnopqrstuvwxyzABCDEFGHIJKLMNOPQRSTUVWXYZ–$123456789

Italic *abcdefghijklmnopqrstuvwxyzABCDEFGHIJKLMNOPQRSTUVWXYZ–$1234567890(*

Bold **abcdefghijklmnopqrstuvwxyzABCDEFGHIJKLMNOPQRSTUVWXYZ–$12345**

Bold Italic ***abcdefghijklmnopqrstuvwxyzABCDEFGHIJKLMNOPQRSTUVWXYZ–$1234567***

Crillee Italic

Dick Jones • 1980

LET AGP LEF URW

▲16

abcdefghijklmnopqrstuvwxyz(".;'!?':,")*
$1234567890&ﬁﬂß-äöüåçèîñóæøœ
ABCDEFGHIJKLMNOPQRSTUVWXYZ
ÄÖÜÅÇÈÎÑÓÆØŒ»„«[•]‹i·¿›...

Crillee Italic Inline Shadow

▲18

abcdefghijklmnopqrstuvwxyz(".;'!?':,")*
$1234567890&ﬁﬂß-äöüåçèîñóæøœ
ABCDEFGHIJKLMNOPQRSTUVWXYZ
ÄÖÜÅÇÈÎÑÓÆØŒ»„«[•]‹i·¿›...

Crillee Bold Italic

▲16

abcdefghijklmnopqrstuvwxyz(".;'!*?':,")
$1234567890&ﬁﬂß-äöüåçèîñóæøœ
ABCDEFGHIJKLMNOPQRSTUVWXYZ
ÄÖÜÅÇÈÎÑÓÆØŒ»„«[•]‹i·¿›...

Crillee Extra Bold Italic

▲16

abcdefghijklmnopqrstuvwxyz(".;'!*?':,")
$1234567890&ﬁﬂß-äöüåçèîñóæøœ
ABCDEFGHIJKLMNOPQRSTUVWXYZ
ÄÖÜÅÇÈÎÑÓÆØŒ»„«[•]‹i·¿›...

ITC CUSHING

Vincent Pacella • 1982 (J. Stearns & F. W. Goudy, 1897–1904)

LIN ADO AGA BIT LEF MAE URW

abcdefghijklmnopqrstuvwxyz(".;'!*?':,")
$1234567890&ﬁﬂß-äöüåçèîñóæøœ
ABCDEFGHIJKLMNOPQRSTUVWXYZ
ÄÖÜÅÇÈÎÑÓÆØŒ»„«[¶§•†‡]‹¡·¿›...

ITC Cushing ...

• Book abcdefghijklmnopqrstuvwxyzABCDEFGHIJKLMNOPQRSTUVWXYZ–$1234567890(".;'

Book Italic *abcdefghijklmnopqrstuvwxyzABCDEFGHIJKLMNOPQRSTUVWXYZ–$1234567890(".;'!**

Medium abcdefghijklmnopqrstuvwxyzABCDEFGHIJKLMNOPQRSTUVWXYZ–$1234567890(

Medium Italic *abcdefghijklmnopqrstuvwxyzABCDEFGHIJKLMNOPQRSTUVWXYZ–$1234567890(".;*

Bold **abcdefghijklmnopqrstuvwxyzABCDEFGHIJKLMNOPQRSTUVWXYZ–$123456789**

☞

... ITC Cushing

Bold Italic *abcdefghijklmnopqrstuvwxyzABCDEFGHIJKLMNOPQRSTUVWXYZ–$1234567890*

Heavy **abcdefghijklmnopqrstuvwxyzABCDEFGHIJKLMNOPQRSTUVWXYZ–$123456**

Heavy Italic ***abcdefghijklmnopqrstuvwxyzABCDEFGHIJKLMNOPQRSTUVWXYZ–$1234567***

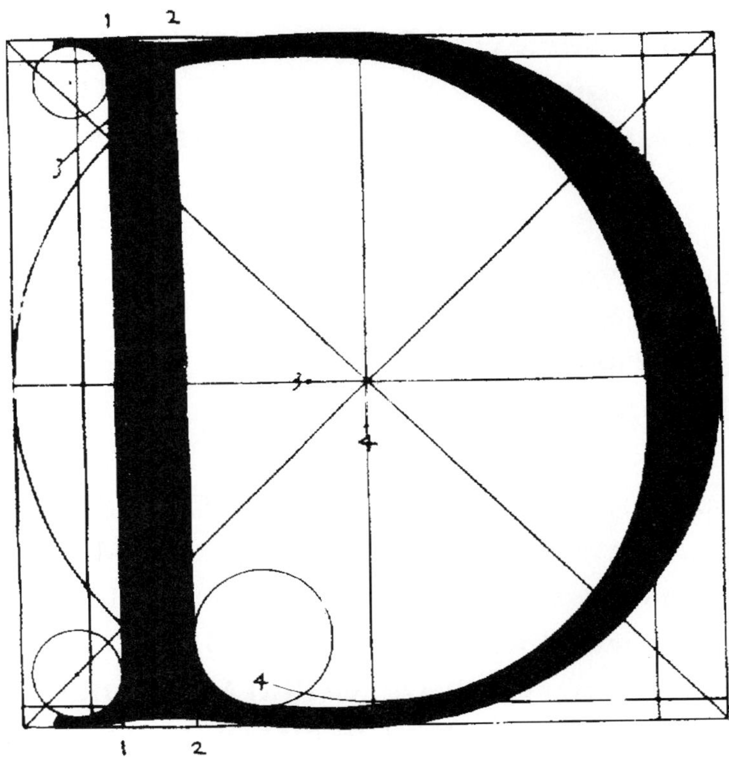
1
2
3
3
4
4
1
2

✍ Marco Antonio Rossi, 1598

D

JAEGER DAILY NEWS

Gustav Jaeger • 1985 abcdefghijklmnopqrstuvwxyz(".;'!*?':,")

ADO AGA MAE $1234567890&fiflß-äöüåçèîñóæøœ

ABCDEFGHIJKLMNOPQRSTUVWXYZ

ÄÖÜÅÇÈÎÑÓÆØŒ»„«[¶§•†‡]‹¡·¿›...

Jaeger Daily News ...

• Roman abcdefghijklmnopqrstuvwxyzABCDEFGHIJKLMNOPQRSTUVWXYZ–$123456789

Italic *abcdefghijklmnopqrstuvwxyzABCDEFGHIJKLMNOPQRSTUVWXYZ–$1234567890(".;'*

Medium **abcdefghijklmnopqrstuvwxyzABCDEFGHIJKLMNOPQRSTUVWXYZ–$1234**

Medium Italic ***abcdefghijklmnopqrstuvwxyzABCDEFGHIJKLMNOPQRSTUVWXYZ–$1234567***

Bold **abcdefghijklmnopqrstuvwxyzABCDEFGHIJKLMNOPQRSTUVWXYZ–$1**

Bold Italic ***abcdefghijklmnopqrstuvwxyzABCDEFGHIJKLMNOPQRSTUVWXYZ–$123***

Extra Bold **abcdefghijklmnopqrstuvwxyzABCDEFGHIJKLMNOPQRSTUVWXYZ**

Extra Bold Italic ***abcdefghijklmnopqrstuvwxyzABCDEFGHIJKLMNOPQRSTUVWXYZ–$***

DANTE

Ron Carpenter • 1991 ... Giovanni Mardersteig & Charles Malin, 1952 abcdefghijklmnopqrstuvwxyz(".;'!*?':,")

$1234567890&fiflß-äöüåçèîñóæøœ

MCL ABCDEFGHIJKLMNOPQRSTUVWXYZ

ÄÖÜÅÇÈÎÑÓÆØŒ»„«[¶§•†‡]‹¡·¿›...

Dante ...

• Roman abcdefghijklmnopqrstuvwxyzABCDEFGHIJKLMNOPQRSTUVWXYZ–$1234567890(".;'!*?

Italic *abcdefghijklmnopqrstuvwxyzABCDEFGHIJKLMNOPQRSTUVWXYZ–$1234567890(".;'!*?':,")&fifl*

Medium **abcdefghijklmnopqrstuvwxyzABCDEFGHIJKLMNOPQRSTUVWXYZ–$1234567890(".;'!**

Medium Italic ***abcdefghijklmnopqrstuvwxyzABCDEFGHIJKLMNOPQRSTUVWXYZ–$1234567890(".;'!*?':,")&***

Bold **abcdefghijklmnopqrstuvwxyzABCDEFGHIJKLMNOPQRSTUVWXYZ–$1234567890(".**

Bold Italic ***abcdefghijklmnopqrstuvwxyzABCDEFGHIJKLMNOPQRSTUVWXYZ–$1234567890(".;'!*?':,"***

DANTE EXPERT

MCL ABCDEFGHIJKLMNOPQRSTUVWXYZ.;!?:,

1234567890&fffiflffiffl–ÄÖÜÅÇÈÎÑÓÆØŒ

(abdeilmnorst) 1/8 1/4 1/3 3/8 1/2 5/8 2/3 3/4 7/8 $12345/67890¢ ₡Rp ▷1 £ g gg gg z zy £ , ;

Dante Expert ...

Dante Titling ▲36 ABCDEFGHIJKLMNOPQRSTU VWXYZ–$1234567890(".;'!*?':,")

• Expert Roman ABCDEFGHIJKLMNOPQRSTUVWXYZ–$1234567890.;!?:,&-fffiflffiffl 1/8 1/4 1/3 3/8 1/2 $12345/67890¢ (abdeilmno

Expert Italic *$1234567890.; :,–fffiflffiffl 1/8 1/4 1/3 3/8 1/2 $12345/67890¢ (abdeilmnorst) 5/8 2/3 3/4 7/8 ₡Rp*

D

... Dante Expert

Expert Roman, Roman & Italic Alternate ▷ 1 £ g gg gg z zy £ , ;

Expert Medium $1234567890.; :,–ff fi fl ffi ffl ⅛ ¼ ⅓ ⅜ ½ $12345/67890¢ (abdeilmnorst) ⅝ ⅔ ¾ ⅞ ₡Rp

Expert Medium Italic *$1234567890.; :,–ff fi fl ffi ffl ⅛ ¼ ⅓ ⅜ ½ $12345/67890¢ (abdeilmnorst) ⅝ ⅔ ¾ ⅞ ₡Rp*

Expert Medium, Medium & Italic Alternate ▷ 1 £ g gg gg z zy £ , ;

Expert Bold **$1234567890.; :,–ff fi fl ffi ffl ⅛ ¼ ⅓ ⅜ ½ $12345/67890¢ (abdeilmnorst) ⅝ ⅔ ¾ ⅞ ₡Rp**

Expert Bold Italic ***$1234567890.; :,–ff fi fl ffi ffl ⅛ ¼ ⅓ ⅜ ½ $12345/67890¢ (abdeilmnorst) ⅝ ⅔ ¾ ⅞ ₡Rp***

Expert Bold, Bold & Bold Italic Alternate ▷ 1 £ g gg gg z zy £ , ;

PL Davison Zip Bold
✜ *Agfa Typographer's Edition 2*
AGP

ABCDEFGHIJKLMNOPQRSTUVWXYZ

▲24 ("".;'!*?':,")$1234567890&-ÄÖÜÅÇÈÎÑÓÆØŒ

»„«[•†‡]‹¡·¿›... ▷ ADGHIKOPRTUWYÄÖÜÅÎÓ

DECCO MODERN
✍ *Andy Hullinger • 1993*
T26

abcdefghijklmnopqrstuvwxyz("".;!?':,)

▲42 $1234567890&fifl-äöåèîñó

ABCDEFGHIJKLMNOPQRSTUVWXYZ

ÄÖÜÅÈÎÑÓÆ[•]i¿...   ▷ ct ffl ft h i st 0

Decco Modern ...

• Regular
abcdefghijklmnopqrstuvwxyzABCDEFGHIJKLMNOPQRSTUV

Organic
abcdefghijklmnopqrstuvwxyzABCDEFGHIJKLMNOPQRSTUV

✜ *Agfa Typographer's Edition 2*: PL Barnum Block, PL Benguiat Frisky Bold, TC Broadway, PL Davison Zip Bold, PL Fiedler Gothic Bold, PL Futura Maxi Book & Bold, Neon Extra Condensed, Ritmo Bold, PL Trophy Oblique.

D

DECOTURA

Noel Rubin • 1992

IMA

▲36

ABCDEFGHIJKLMNOPQRSTUVWXYZ(“.;‘!*?’:,”)
$1234567890&-ÄÖÜÅÇÈÎÑÓÆØŒ
ABCDEFGHIJKLMNOPQRSTUVWXYZ
ÄÖÜÅÇÈÎÑÓÆØŒ»„«[¶§•†‡]‹¡·¿›...

Decotura ...

• Inline ABCDEFGHIJKLMNOPQRSTUVWXYZABCDEFGHIJKLMNOP

Solid ABCDEFGHIJKLMNOPQRSTUVWXYZABCDEFGHIJKLMNOP

DEEPDENE

Frederic W. Goudy • 1927

LAN TFC

abcdefghijklmnopqrstuvwxyz(“.;‘!*?’:,”)
$1234567890&fiflß-äöüåçèîñóæøœ
ABCDEFGHIJKLMNOPQRSTUVWXYZ
ÄÖÜÅÇÈÎÑÓÆØŒ»„«[¶§•†]‹¡¿›...

▷ ct ff ffi ffl st

Deepdene ...

• Roman abcdefghijklmnopqrstuvwxyzABCDEFGHIJKLMNOPQRSTUVWXYZ–$1234567890

Italic *abcdefghijklmnopqrstuvwxyzABCDEFGHIJKLMNOPQRSTUVWXYZ–$1234567890(“.;‘!*?’:,”)&fi*

Roman OSF abcdefghijklmnopqrstuvwxyzABCDEFGHIJKLMNOPQRSTUVWXYZ–$1234567890

Italic OSF *abcdefghijklmnopqrstuvwxyzABCDEFGHIJKLMNOPQRSTUVWXYZ–$1234567890(“.;‘!*?’:,”)&fi*

Roman SCOSF ABCDEFGHIJKLMNOPQRSTUVWXYZABCDEFGHIJKLMNOPQRSTUVWXYZ–$1234567890

Italic SCOSF *ABCDEFGHIJKLMNOPQRSTUVWXYZABCDEFGHIJKLMNOPQRSTUVWXYZ–$1234567890(“.;‘!**

Italic Swash *abcdefghijklmnopqrstuvwxyzABCDEFGHIJKLMNOPQRSTUVWXYZ–$1234567890(“.;‘!*?’:,”*

Italic Swash OSF *abcdefghijklmnopqrstuvwxyzABCDEFGHIJKLMNOPQRSTUVWXYZ–$1234567890(“.;‘!*?’:,*

Italic Swash Alternate *abcdefghijklmnopqrstuvwxyzABCDEFGHIJKLMNOPQRSTUVWXYZ–$1234567890(“.;‘!*?’:,*

Italic Swash OSF Alternate *abcdefghijklmnopqrstuvwxyzABCDEFGHIJKLMNOPQRSTUVWXYZ–$1234567890(“.;‘!*?’*

Italic Swash SCOSF *ABCDEFGHIJKLMNOPQRSTUVWXYZABCDEFGHIJKLMNOPQRSTUVWXYZ–$1234567890*

Italic Swash SCOSF Alternate *ABCDEFGHIJKLMNOPQRSTUVWXYZABCDEFGHIJKLMNOPQRSTUVWXYZ–$1234567890*

DELIMA

Ong Chong Wah • 1993

MCL

abcdefghijklmnopqrstuvwxyz(“.;‘!*?’:,”)
$1234567890&fiflß-äöüåçèîñóæøœ
ABCDEFGHIJKLMNOPQRSTUVWXYZ
ÄÖÜÅÇÈÎÑÓÆØŒ»„«[¶§•†‡]‹¡·¿›...

D

... Delima 1 ...

Light abcdefghijklmnopqrstuvwxyzABCDEFGHIJKLMNOPQRSTUVWXYZ–$123456

Light Italic *abcdefghijklmnopqrstuvwxyzABCDEFGHIJKLMNOPQRSTUVWXYZ–$12345678*

• Roman abcdefghijklmnopqrstuvwxyzABCDEFGHIJKLMNOPQRSTUVWXYZ–$12345

Italic *abcdefghijklmnopqrstuvwxyzABCDEFGHIJKLMNOPQRSTUVWXYZ–$123456*

Bold **abcdefghijklmnopqrstuvwxyzABCDEFGHIJKLMNOPQRSTUVWXYZ–$12**

Bold Italic ***abcdefghijklmnopqrstuvwxyzABCDEFGHIJKLMNOPQRSTUVWXYZ–$123***

Delima 2 ...

Semibold **abcdefghijklmnopqrstuvwxyzABCDEFGHIJKLMNOPQRSTUVWXYZ–$123**

Semibold Italic ***abcdefghijklmnopqrstuvwxyzABCDEFGHIJKLMNOPQRSTUVWXYZ–$12345***

Extra Bold **abcdefghijklmnopqrstuvwxyzABCDEFGHIJKLMNOPQRSTUVWXYZ–$1**

Extra Bold Italic ***abcdefghijklmnopqrstuvwxyzABCDEFGHIJKLMNOPQRSTUVWXYZ–$1***

DELLA ROBBIA

Thomas Maitland Cleland • 1902
BIT
▲16

abcdefghijklmnopqrstuvwxyz(“.;‘!*?’:,”)
$1234567890&-fiflß-äöüåçèîñóæøœ
ABCDEFGHIJKLMNOPQRSTUVWXYZ
ÄÖÜÅÇÈÎÑÓÆØŒ»„«[¶§•†‡]‹¡·¿›...

Della Robbia ...

• Roman abcdefghijklmnopqrstuvwxyzABCDEFGHIJKLMNOPQRSTUVWXYZ–$12

Bold **abcdefghijklmnopqrstuvwxyzABCDEFGHIJKLMNOPQRSTUVWXYZ–$**

DELTA·FONT

Marshall Gisser • 1994
NYD
▲24

abcdefghijklmnopqrstuvwxyz(“.;‘!*?’:,”)
$1234567890¢–
ABCDEFGHIJKLMNOPQRSTUVWXYZ [ ]

DeltaFont ...

• Regular abcdefghijklmnopqrstuvwxyzABCDEFGHIJKLMNOPQRSTUVWXYZ$123456789

Italic *abcdefghijklmnopqrstuvwxyzABCDEFGHIJKLMNOPQRSTUVWXYZ$123456789*

Extended abcdefghijklmnopqrstuvwxyzABCDEF

D

DELTA JAEGER

Gustav Jaeger • 1983 abcdefghijklmnopqrstuvwxyz(".;'!*?':,")

ADO AGA MAE $1234567890&fiflß-äöüåçèîñóæøœ

▲16 ABCDEFGHIJKLMNOPQRSTUVWXYZ

ÄÖÜÅÇÈÎÑÓÆØŒ»„«[¶§•†‡]‹i·¿›...

Delta Jaeger ...

Light abcdefghijklmnopqrstuvwxyzABCDEFGHIJKLMNOPQRSTUVWXYZ–$123

Light Italic *abcdefghijklmnopqrstuvwxyzABCDEFGHIJKLMNOPQRSTUVWXYZ–$1234*

• Book abcdefghijklmnopqrstuvwxyzABCDEFGHIJKLMNOPQRSTUVWXYZ–$

Book Italic *abcdefghijklmnopqrstuvwxyzABCDEFGHIJKLMNOPQRSTUVWXYZ–$*

Medium **abcdefghijklmnopqrstuvwxyzABCDEFGHIJKLMNOPQRSTUVWXY**

Medium Italic ***abcdefghijklmnopqrstuvwxyzABCDEFGHIJKLMNOPQRSTUVWXY***

Bold **abcdefghijklmnopqrstuvwxyzABCDEFGHIJKLMNOPQRSTUVWX**

Bold Italic ***abcdefghijklmnopqrstuvwxyzABCDEFGHIJKLMNOPQRSTUVWX***

Outline ▲18 abcdefghijklmnopqrstuvwxyzABCDEFGHIJKLMNOPQRS

Delphian Open

Agfa Typographer's Edition 3

Robert Hunter Middleton • 1928

AGP

▲30

ABCDEFGHIJKLMNOPQRSTUVWXYZ

(".;'!*?':,")$1234567890

&-ÄÖÜÅÇÈÎÑÓÆØŒ»„«[•]‹i·¿›...

Demian

Jan Van Dijk • 1984 abcdefghijklmnopqrstuvwxyz(".;'!*?':,")

LET $1234567890&fiflß-äöüåçèîñóæøœ

▲16 ABCDEFGHIJKLMNOPQRSTUVWXYZ

ÄÖÜÅÇÈÎÑÓÆØŒ»„«[•]‹i·¿›...

Demian Bold

LET abcdefghijklmnopqrstuvwxyz(".;'!*?':,")

▲16 $1234567890&fiflß-äöüåçèîñóæøœ

ABCDEFGHIJKLMNOPQRSTUVWXYZ

ÄÖÜÅÇÈÎÑÓÆØŒ»„«[•]‹i·¿›...

Agfa Typographer's Edition 3: Barclay Open, PL Bernhardt Light, Medium & Bold, PL Britannia Bold, Delphian Open, PL Fiorello Condensed, Fluidium Bold, PL Modern Heavy Condensed, PL Torino Open.

D

DEMOS

✍ Gerard Unger • 1976 abcdefghijklmnopqrstuvwxyz(".;'!*?':,")

LEF $1234567890&fiflß-äöüåçèîñóæøœ

ABCDEFGHIJKLMNOPQRSTUVWXYZ

ÄÖÜÅÇÈÎÑÓÆØŒ»„«[¶§•†‡]‹i·¿›...

Demos ...

• Medium abcdefghijklmnopqrstuvwxyzABCDEFGHIJKLMNOPQRSTUVWXYZ–$12345678

Medium Italic *abcdefghijklmnopqrstuvwxyzABCDEFGHIJKLMNOPQRSTUVWXYZ–$1234567890(".;'*

Medium SCOSF ABCDEFGHIJKLMNOPQRSTUVWXYZABCDEFGHIJKLMNOPQRSTUVWXYZ–$1234567

Semibold **abcdefghijklmnopqrstuvwxyzABCDEFGHIJKLMNOPQRSTUVWXYZ–$12345**

DESTIJL

✍ Neville Burtis • 1989 ABCDEFGHIJKLMNOPQRSTUVWXYZ(".;'!*?':,")

LPT MTD $1234567890&fiflß-äöüåçèîñóÆØŒ

▲24 ABCDEFGHIJKLMNOPQRSTUVWXYZ

ÄÖÜÅÇÈÎÑÓÆØŒ»„«[¶§•†‡]‹i·¿›...

DeStijl ...

• Regular ABCDEFGHIJKLMNOPQRSTUVWXYZABCDEFGHIJKLMNOPQRSTUVWXYZ–$12345

Alternate ABCDEFGHIJKLMNOPQRSTUVWXYZABCDEFGHIJKLMNOPQRSTUVWXYZ–$123456

DE VINNE

BIT AGP URW abcdefghijklmnopqrstuvwxyz(".;'!*?':,")

▲16 $1234567890&fiflß-äöüåçèîñóæøœ

ABCDEFGHIJKLMNOPQRSTUVWXYZ

ÄÖÜÅÇÈÎÑÓÆØŒ»„«[§•†‡]‹i·¿›...

De Vinne ...

• Text Roman abcdefghijklmnopqrstuvwxyzABCDEFGHIJKLMNOPQRSTUVWXYZ–$1

Text Italic *abcdefghijklmnopqrstuvwxyzABCDEFGHIJKLMNOPQRSTUVWXYZ–$123*

Display Roman ▲24 abcdefghijklmnopqrstuvwxyzABCDEFGHIJKLM

NOPQRSTUVWXYZ–$1234567890(".;'!*?':,")&fi

Display Italic ▲24 *abcdefghijklmnopqrstuvwxyzABCDEFGHIJKLMN*

OPQRSTUVWXYZ–$1234567890(".;'!?':,")&fiflß-*

D

Devit
Lewis Tsalis • 1993
T26
▲36

ABCDEFGHIJKLMNOPQRSTUVWXYZ(".;'!*?':,")
$1234567890&-ÄÖÜÅÇÊÎÑÓÆØŒ
ABCDEFGHIJKLMNOPQRSTUVWXYZ
ÄÖÜÅÇÊÎÑÓÆØŒ»„«[¶§•†‡]‹¡·¿›...

▷ 

ITC Didi
FAM
▲24

abcdefghijklmnopqrstuvwxyz(".;'!*?':,")
$1234567890&fiflß-äöüåçèñæøœ
ABCDEFGHIJKLMNOPQRSTUVWXYZ
ÄÖÜÅÇÈÑÆØŒ»„«[¶§•†‡]‹¡·¿›...

LINOTYPE DIDOT
Adrian Frutiger • 1991
... Firmin Didot, 1784
LIN ADO AGA MAE

abcdefghijklmnopqrstuvwxyz(".;'!*?':,")
$1234567890&fiflß-äöüåçèîñóæøœ
ABCDEFGHIJKLMNOPQRSTUVWXYZ
ÄÖÜÅÇÈÎÑÓÆØŒ»„«[¶§•†‡]‹¡·¿›...

Linotype Didot ...

• Roman	abcdefghijklmnopqrstuvwxyzABCDEFGHIJKLMNOPQRSTUVWXYZ–$1234
Italic	*abcdefghijklmnopqrstuvwxyzABCDEFGHIJKLMNOPQRSTUVWXYZ–$12345678*
Bold	**abcdefghijklmnopqrstuvwxyzABCDEFGHIJKLMNOPQRSTUVWXYZ–$123**
Roman SCOSF	ABCDEFGHIJKLMNOPQRSTUVWXYZABCDEFGHIJKLMNOPQRSTUVWXYZ–$12345
Roman OSF	abcdefghijklmnopqrstuvwxyzABCDEFGHIJKLMNOPQRSTUVWXYZ–$12345
Italic OSF	*abcdefghijklmnopqrstuvwxyzABCDEFGHIJKLMNOPQRSTUVWXYZ–$123456789*
Bold OSF	**abcdefghijklmnopqrstuvwxyzABCDEFGHIJKLMNOPQRSTUVWXYZ–$123**

Headline
▲30

abcdefghijklmnopqrstuvwxyzABCDE
FGHIJKLMNOPQRSTUVWXYZ–$1

Headline OSF
▲30

abcdefghijklmnopqrstuvwxyzABCDE
FGHIJKLMNOPQRSTUVW...$123456

Linotype Didot ▶ Didot Ornaments One & Two.

D

... Linotype Didot
Initials
▲30

ABCDEFGHIJKLMNOPQRSTUVWX

FC FIRMIN DIDOT
... *Firmin Didot • 1784*
TFC
▲30

abcdefghijklmnopqrstuvwxyz(".;'!*?':,")
$1234567890&fiflß-äöüåçèîñóæøœ
ABCDEFGHIJKLMNOPQRSTUVWXYZ
ÄÖÜÅÇÈÎÑÓÆØŒ»„«[•]‹¡·¿›...

FC Firmin Didot ...
• Roman
abcdefghijklmnopqrstuvwxyzABCDEFGH
Bold
abcdefghijklmnopqrstuvwxyzABCD

TF DIERAMA
Joseph Treacy • 1991
TRE MTD

abcdefghijklmnopqrstuvwxyz(".;'!*?':,")
$1234567890&fiflß-äöüåçèîñóæøœ
ABCDEFGHIJKLMNOPQRSTUVWXYZ
ÄÖÜÅÇÈÎÑÓÆØŒ»„«[¶§•†‡]‹¡·¿›...

▷ 123579/234816■□

TF Dierama ...
• Regular
abcdefghijklmnopqrstuvwxyzABCDEFGHIJKLMNOPQRSTUVWXYZ–$123
Extra Bold
abcdefghijklmnopqrstuvwxyzABCDEFGHIJKLMNOPQRSTUVWXYZ–

Digitek
David Quay • 1990
LET
▲36

abcdefghijklmnopqrstuvwxyz(".;'!*?':,") $1234567890&fiflß-äöüåçèîñóæøœ
ABCDEFGHIJKLMNOPQRSTUVWXYZ ÄÖÜÅÇÈÎÑÓÆØŒ»„«[•]‹¡·¿› . . .

DIN SCHRIFTEN
LIN ADO AGA LEF MAE

abcdefghijklmnopqrstuvwxyz(".;'!*?':,")
$1234567890&fiflß-äöüåçèîñóæøœ
ABCDEFGHIJKLMNOPQRSTUVWXYZ
ÄÖÜÅÇÈÎÑÓÆØŒ»„«[¶§•†‡]‹¡·¿›...

▷ 6 9

DIN Schriften ...
Engschrift
abcdefghijklmnopqrstuvwxyzABCDEFGHIJKLMNOPQRSTUVWXYZ–$1234567890(".;'!*?':,")&fiflß-äöüÄÖÜåçèÅÇÈîñóÎÑ

D

. . . DIN Schriften

• Mittelschrift abcdefghijklmnopqrstuvwxyzABCDEFGHIJKLMNOPQRSTUVWXYZ–$1234567890(“.;‘!*?

Engschrift & Mittelschrift Alternate ▷ 6 9 6 9

Neuzeit Grotesk Light abcdefghijklmnopqrstuvwxyzABCDEFGHIJKLMNOPQRSTUVWXYZ–$123456

Neuzeit Grotesk Bold Condensed abcdefghijklmnopqrstuvwxyzABCDEFGHIJKLMNOPQRSTUVWXYZ–$1234567890(“.;‘!*?’:,”)&fiflß-äöüÄÖÜåçèÅ

DIOTIMA

GudrunSchrift

Gudrun Zapf-Von Hesse • 1954

LIN ADO AGA MAE

abcdefghijklmnopqrstuvwxyz(“.;‘!*?’:,”)

$1234567890&fiflß-äöüåçèîñóæøœ

ABCDEFGHIJKLMNOPQRSTUVWXYZ

ÄÖÜÅÇÈÎÑÓÆØŒ»„«[¶§•†‡]‹¡·¿›...

Diotima . . .

• Roman abcdefghijklmnopqrstuvwxyzABCDEFGHIJKLMNOPQRSTUVWXYZ–$12345

Italic *abcdefghijklmnopqrstuvwxyzABCDEFGHIJKLMNOPQRSTUVWXYZ–$1234567890(“.;‘*

Roman SCOSF ABCDEFGHIJKLMNOPQRSTUVWXYZABCDEFGHIJKLMNOPQRSTUVWXYZ–$123456

Roman OSF abcdefghijklmnopqrstuvwxyzABCDEFGHIJKLMNOPQRSTUVWXYZ–$123456

Italic OSF *abcdefghijklmnopqrstuvwxyzABCDEFGHIJKLMNOPQRSTUVWXYZ–$1234567890(“.;‘!*?*

FC Disco

TFC

▲24

abcdefghijklmnopqrstuvwxyz(“.;‘!*?’:,”)

$1234567890&fiflß-äöüåçèîñóæøœ

ABCDEFGHIJKLMNOPQRSTUVWXYZ

ÄÖÜÅÇÈÎÑÓÆØŒ»„«[•]‹¡·¿›...

Dolmen

Letraset Design Staff • 1987

. . . Max Salzmann, 1922

LET

▲24

abcdefghijklmnopqrstuvwxyz(“.;‘!*?’:,”)

$1234567890&fiflß-äöüåçèîñóæøœ

ABCDEFGHIJKLMNOPQRSTUVWXYZ

ÄÖÜÅÇÈÎÑÓÆØŒ»„«[•]‹¡·¿›... ▷ R

GudrunSchrift: Ariadne, Diotima Roman, Italic, Roman SCOSF, Roman OSF, Italic OSF, Smaragd.

D

DOM CASUAL

✍ Peter Dom • 1951 abcdefghijklmnopqrstuvwxyz(".;'!*?':,")

LIN ADO AGA BIT LEF MAE URW $1234567890&fiflß-äöüåçèîñóæøœ

▲16 ABCDEFGHIJKLMNOPQRSTUVWXYZ

ÄÖÜÅÇÈÎÑÓÆØŒ»„«[§•†‡]‹¡·¿›...

Dom Casual ...

• Regular abcdefghijklmnopqrstuvwxyzABCDEFGHIJKLMNOPQRSTUVWXYZ–$1234567890(".;'!*?':,"

Bold abcdefghijklmnopqrstuvwxyzABCDEFGHIJKLMNOPQRSTUVWXYZ–$1234567890(".;'

HF DOODLE

✍ Jonathan Macagba • 1994 abcdefghijklmnopqrstuvwxyz(".;'!*?':,")

HAN MTD $1234567890&fiflß-äöüåçèîñóæøœ

▲16 ABCDEFGHIJKLMNOPQRSTUVWXYZ

ÄÖÜÅÇÈÎÑÓÆØŒ»«•‹¡¿›...

HF Doodle ...

• Medium abcdefghijklmnopqrstuvwxyzABCDEFGHIJKLMNOPQRSTUVWXYZ–$123

Medium Italic abcdefghijklmnopqrstuvwxyzABCDEFGHIJKLMNOPQRSTUVWXYZ–$123

Bold abcdefghijklmnopqrstuvwxyzABCDEFGHIJKLMNOPQRSTUVWXYZ

Bold Italic abcdefghijklmnopqrstuvwxyzABCDEFGHIJKLMNOPQRSTUVWXYZ

Dorchester Script
✤ Monotype Scripts 1

✍ ... • 1939 abcdefghijklmnopqrstuvwxyz(".;'!*?':,")

MCL ADO AGA LIN MAE $1234567890&fiflß-äöüåçèîñóæøœ

▲18 ABCDEFGHIJKLMNOPQRSTUVWXYZ

ÄÖÜÅÇÈÎÑÓÆØŒ»„«[§•†‡]‹¡·¿›...

Doric Bold
✤ Linotype ClassAdSet 1

LIN ADO AGA MAE abcdefghijklmnopqrstuvwxyz(".;'!*?':,")

▲12 $1234567890&fiflß-äöüåçèîñóæøœ

ABCDEFGHIJKLMNOPQRSTUVWXYZ

ÄÖÜÅÇÈÎÑÓÆØŒ»„«[¶§•†‡]‹¡·¿›...

✤ *Monotype Scripts 1*: Biffo Script, Dorchester Script, Pepita, Monotype Script Bold, Swing Bold.
✤ *Linotype ClassAdSet 1*: Doric Bold & Maximus.

D

DV DRUKPA
Diehl.Volk • 1990
DVT
▲30

abcdefghijklmnopqrstuvwxyz(".;'!*?':,")
$1234567890¢-äöüçèîñóæ
ABCDEFGHIJKLMNOPQRSTUVWXYZ
ÄÖÜÇÈÎÑÓ»«[¶•]¡¿...
▷ w M W

DV Drukpa . . .
• Regular
abcdefghijklmnopqrstuvwxyzABCDEFGHIJKLMNOPQ
Bold
abcdefghijklmnopqrstuvwxyzABCDEFGHIJKLM

Duc De Berry
Type Before Gutenberg 1
Gottfried Pott • 1990
LIN ADO AGA MAE
▲16

abcdefghijklmnopqrstuvwxyz(".;'!*?':,")
$1234567890&fiflß-äöüåçèîñóæøœ
ABCDEFGHIJKLMNOPQRSTUVWXYZ
ÄÖÜÅÇÈÎÑÓÆØŒ»„«[¶§•†‡]‹¡·¿›...
▷ ch ck ff ft ll ſs ſi ſſ ß tz äöü ÄÖÜ

Durango
FRA
▲16

abcdefghijklmnopqrstuvwxyz(".;'!?':,")
$1234567890&fiflß-äöüåçèîñóæøœ
ABCDEFGHIJKLMNOPQRSTUVWXYZ
ÄÖÜÅÇÈÎÑÓÆØŒ„•

DYNAMO
K. Sommer • 1930
URW AGP LEF LET MTD
▲24

abcdefghijklmnopqrstuvwxyz(".;'!*?':,")
$1234567890&fiflß-äöüåçèîñóæøœ
ABCDEFGHIJKLMNOPQRSTUVWXYZ
ÄÖÜÅÇÈÎÑÓÆØŒ»„«[•]‹¡·¿›...

Dynamo . . .
• Medium
abcdefghijklmnopqrstuvwxyzABCDEFGHIJKLMNOP
Bold
abcdefghijklmnopqrstuvwxyzABCDEFGHIJKLMN

. . .
Type Before Gutenberg 1: Duc De Berry, Herculanum, Omnia.

. . . Dynamo

Bold Condensed abcdefghijklmnopqrstuvwxyzABCDEFGHIJKLMNOPQRST

Bold Shadow abcdefghijklmnopqrstuvwxyzABCDEFGH

E

Bureau Eagle
Eaglefeather
Earthquake
East Bloc
Eckmann
Economist
Ecru
Edison
Edwardian
Egizio
Monotype Egyptian 72 Extended
Egyptian 505
A*I Egyptian
Egyptienne F
Ehrhardt
Einhorn
El Grande
ITC Élan
Electra
Elefont
DV Elevator
Elli
Ellington
Else NPL
Elysium
Embassy
Emphasis
Bureau Empire
EndsMeansMends
Sackers English Script
Engravers' Old English
Monotype Engravers Old English
Engravers' Roman
Monotype Engravers
Engravers Bold Face
Engravers' Gothic
Entropy
Epitaph
Epokha
Equinox
ITC Eras
Erasmus
Erbar
Escalido
ITC Esprit
Estro
Etruscan
Eurostile
Excelsior
HF Exposition
eXposure

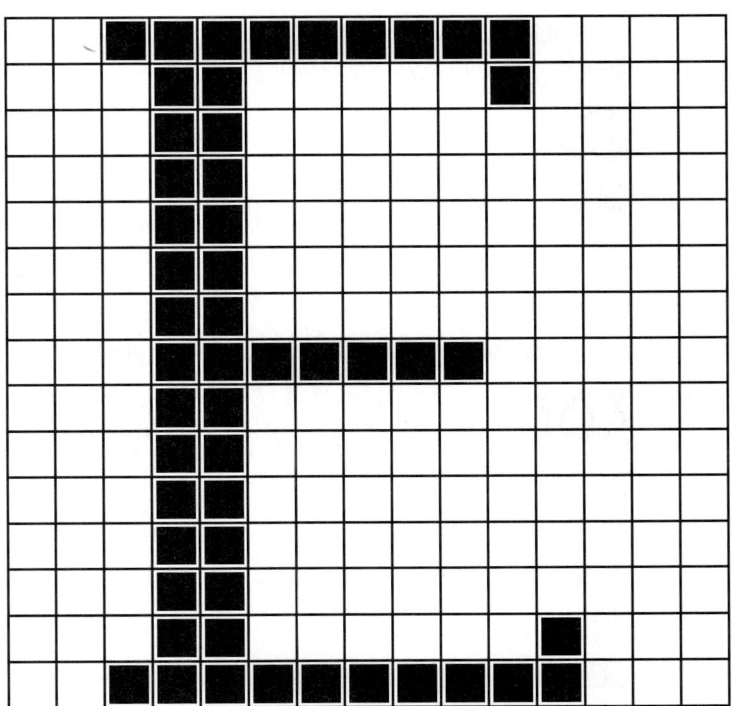

✍ Chuck Bigelow & Kris Holmes, 1984

E

BUREAU EAGLE

David Berlow • 1989
... Morris Fuller Benton, 1933
FBU AGP MTD
▲18

abcdefghijklmnopqrstuvwxyz(".;'!*?':,")
$1234567890&fiflß-äöüåçèîñóœøœ
ABCDEFGHIJKLMNOPQRSTUVWXYZ
ÄÖÜÅÇÈÎÑÓÆØŒ»,,«[¶§•†‡]‹¡·¿›...

▷ ff ffi ffl

Bureau Eagle ...

• Book abcdefghijklmnopqrstuvwxyzABCDEFGHIJKLMNOPQRSTU
Bold abcdefghijklmnopqrstuvwxyzABCDEFGHIJKLMNOPQR

EAGLEFEATHER FORMAL

David Siegel
& Carol Toriumi-Lawrence • 1994
(Frank Lloyd Wright, 1920)
AGP
▲18

abcdefghijklmnopqrstuvwxyz(".;'!*?':,")
$1234567890&fiflß-äöüåçèîñóœøœ
ABCDEFGHIJKLMNOPQRSTUVWXYZ
ÄÖÜÅÇÈÎÑÓÆØŒ»,,«[¶§•†‡]‹¡·¿›...

Eaglefeather Formal ...

Light abcdefghijklmnopqrstuvwxyzABCDEFGHIJKLMNOPQRSTUVWXYZ–$123456
Light Italic *abcdefghijklmnopqrstuvwxyzABCDEFGHIJKLMNOPQRSTUVWXYZ–$12345678*
• Regular abcdefghijklmnopqrstuvwxyzABCDEFGHIJKLMNOPQRSTUVWXYZ–$12345
Italic *abcdefghijklmnopqrstuvwxyzABCDEFGHIJKLMNOPQRSTUVWXYZ–$1234567*
Bold **abcdefghijklmnopqrstuvwxyzABCDEFGHIJKLMNOPQRSTUVWXYZ–$1**
Bold Italic ***abcdefghijklmnopqrstuvwxyzABCDEFGHIJKLMNOPQRSTUVWXYZ–$123***

EAGLEFEATHER INFORMAL

AGP
▲18

abcdefghijklmnopqrstuvwxyz(".;'!*?':,")
$1234567890&fiflß-äöüåçèîñóœøœ
ABCDEFGHIJKLMNOPQRSTUVWXYZ
ÄÖÜÅÇÈÎÑÓÆØŒ»,,«[¶§•†‡]‹¡·¿›...

Eaglefeather Informal ...

Light abcdefghijklmnopqrstuvwxyzABCDEFGHIJKLMNOPQRSTUVWXYZ–$1234567
Light Italic *abcdefghijklmnopqrstuvwxyzABCDEFGHIJKLMNOPQRSTUVWXYZ–$12345678*
• Regular abcdefghijklmnopqrstuvwxyzABCDEFGHIJKLMNOPQRSTUVWXYZ–$123456
Italic *abcdefghijklmnopqrstuvwxyzABCDEFGHIJKLMNOPQRSTUVWXYZ–$1234567*
Bold **abcdefghijklmnopqrstuvwxyzABCDEFGHIJKLMNOPQRSTUVWXYZ–$123**
Bold Italic ***abcdefghijklmnopqrstuvwxyzABCDEFGHIJKLMNOPQRSTUVWXYZ–$123***

EAGLEFEATHER SCOSF

AGP
▲18

ABCDEFGHIJKLMNOPQRSTUVWXYZ(".;'!*?':,")
$1234567890&-ÄÖÜÅÇÈÎÑÓÆØŒ
ABCDEFGHIJKLMNOPQRSTUVWXYZ
ÄÖÜÅÇÈÎÑÓÆØŒ»,,«[¶§•†‡]‹¡·¿›...

... Eaglefeather SCOSF ...

Light SCOSF ABCDEFGHIJKLMNOPQRSTUVWXYZABCDEFGHIJKLMNOPQRSTUVWXYZ–$123456

• Regular SCOSF ABCDEFGHIJKLMNOPQRSTUVWXYZABCDEFGHIJKLMNOPQRSTUVWXYZ–$1234

Bold SCOSF ABCDEFGHIJKLMNOPQRSTUVWXYZABCDEFGHIJKLMNOPQRSTUVWXYZ–$1

Earthquake

✣ [T-26] FontSet 1

✍ Michael Polydoris • 1993

abcdefghijklmnopqrstuvwxyz(.;!*?:,)$1234567890

T26

▲24

& -ABCDEFGHIJKLMNOPQRSTUVWXYZ[·]

E

EAST BLOC

✍ Grant Hutchinson • 1993

ABCDEFGHIJKLMNOPQRSTUVWXYZ(".;'!*?':,")

IMA

$1234567890&fifl ß-äöüåçèîñóœøœ

▲16

ABCDEFGHIJKLMNOPQRSTUVWXYZ

ÄÖÜÅÇÈÎÑÓŒØŒ»„«[¶§•†‡]‹¡·¿›...

East Bloc ...

• Open ABCDEFGHIJKLMNOPQRSTUVWXYZABCDEFGHIJKLMNOPQRS

Closed ABCDEFGHIJKLMNOPQRSTUVWXYZABCDEFGHIJKLMNOPQRS

Open Alternate ABCDEFGHiJKLMNOPQRSTUVWXYZAbcdEFGhiJHLMNopqR

Closed Alternate ABCDEFGHiJKLMNOPQRSTUVWXYZAbcdEFGhiJHLMNopqR

Eckmann

✍ Otto Eckmann • 1900

abcdefghijklmnopqrstuvwxyz(".;'!*?':,")

URW

$1234567890&fifl ß-äöüåçèîñóœøœ

▲18

ABCDEFGHIJKLMNOPQRSTUVWXYZ

ÄÖÜÅÇÈÎÑÓÆØŒ»„«[¶§•†‡]‹¡·¿›...

ECONOMIST

✍ Gunnlaugur S. E. Briem & A. Patel • 1991

abcdefghijklmnopqrstuvwxyz(".;'!*?':,")

MTD

$1234567890&fifl ß-äöüåçèîñóæøœ

ABCDEFGHIJKLMNOPQRSTUVWXYZ

ÄÖÜÅÇÈÎÑÓÆØŒ „ [¶§•†‡] ¡·¿ ...

▷ ff ffi ffl 1/8 1/4 1/3 3/8 1/2 5/8 2/3 3/4 7/8

Economist ...

• 101 Roman abcdefghijklmnopqrstuvwxyzABCDEFGHIJKLMNOPQRSTUVWXYZ–$1234567890(".;

102 Italic *abcdefghijklmnopqrstuvwxyzABCDEFGHIJKLMNOPQRSTUVWXYZ–$1234567890(".;'*

401 Roman SC & OSF ABCDEFGHIJKLMNOPQRSTUVWXYZ–1234567890".;'?':,"&-ÄÖÜÅÇÈÎÑÓÆØŒ

201 Demi **abcdefghijklmnopqrstuvwxyzABCDEFGHIJKLMNOPQRSTUVWXYZ–$123456789**

202 Demi Italic ***abcdefghijklmnopqrstuvwxyzABCDEFGHIJKLMNOPQRSTUVWXYZ–$123456789***

✣ [T-26] FontSet 1: Earthquake & Outhaus.

... Economist

301 Bold abcdefghijklmnopqrstuvwxyzABCDEFGHIJKLMNOPQRSTUVWXYZ–$123456

302 Bold Italic *abcdefghijklmnopqrstuvwxyzABCDEFGHIJKLMNOPQRSTUVWXYZ–$1234567*

Ecru

Richard Lipton • 1993 ... Margo Chase

FBU ▲30

abcdefghijklmnopqrstuvwxyz(".;'!*?':,")
$1234567890&fiflß-äöüåçèîñóæøœ
ABCDEFGHIJKLMNOPQRSTUVWXYZ
ÄÖÜÅÇÈÎÑÓÆØŒ»„«[¶§•†‡]‹¡·¿›... ▷ff ffi ffl

EDISON

Hermann Zapf • 1978

LEF

abcdefghijklmnopqrstuvwxyz(".;'!*?':,")
$1234567890&fiflß-äöüåçèîñóæøœ
ABCDEFGHIJKLMNOPQRSTUVWXYZ
ÄÖÜÅÇÈÎÑÓÆØŒ»„«[¶§•†‡]‹¡·¿›...

Edison ...

• Book abcdefghijklmnopqrstuvwxyzABCDEFGHIJKLMNOPQRSTUVWXYZ–$12

Book Italic *abcdefghijklmnopqrstuvwxyzABCDEFGHIJKLMNOPQRSTUVWXYZ–$1234*

Semibold abcdefghijklmnopqrstuvwxyzABCDEFGHIJKLMNOPQRSTUVWXYZ–

Semibold Italic *abcdefghijklmnopqrstuvwxyzABCDEFGHIJKLMNOPQRSTUVWXYZ–$12*

Bold Condensed ▲18 **abcdefghijklmnopqrstuvwxyzABCDEFGHIJKLMNOPQRSTUVW**

EDWARDIAN

Colin Brignall • 1983

URW LET

abcdefghijklmnopqrstuvwxyz(".;'!*?':,")
$1234567890&fiflß-äöüåçèîñóæøœ
ABCDEFGHIJKLMNOPQRSTUVWXYZ
ÄÖÜÅÇÈÎÑÓÆØŒ»„«[¶§•†‡]‹¡·¿›...

Edwardian 1 ...

• Medium abcdefghijklmnopqrstuvwxyzABCDEFGHIJKLMNOPQRSTUVWXYZ–$12

Medium Italic *abcdefghijklmnopqrstuvwxyzABCDEFGHIJKLMNOPQRSTUVWXYZ–$*

Bold abcdefghijklmnopqrstuvwxyzABCDEFGHIJKLMNOPQRSTUVWXYZ–

Bold Italic *abcdefghijklmnopqrstuvwxyzABCDEFGHIJKLMNOPQRSTUVWXY*

Edwardian 2 ...

Light abcdefghijklmnopqrstuvwxyzABCDEFGHIJKLMNOPQRSTUVWXYZ–$1234

Light Italic *abcdefghijklmnopqrstuvwxyzABCDEFGHIJKLMNOPQRSTUVWXYZ–$123*

... Edwardian 2

Extra Bold abcdefghijklmnopqrstuvwxyzABCDEFGHIJKLMNOPQRSTUVWX

Extra Bold Italic *abcdefghijklmnopqrstuvwxyzABCDEFGHIJKLMNOPQRSTUVW*

E

Egizio Condensed

Aldo Novarese • 1955
URW
▲18

abcdefghijklmnopqrstuvwxyz(".;'!*?':,")
$1234567890&fiflß-äöüåçèîñóæøœ
ABCDEFGHIJKLMNOPQRSTUVWXYZ
ÄÖÜÅÇÈÎÑÓÆØŒ»„«[¶§•†‡]‹¡·¿›...

Monotype Egyptian 72 Extended
Monotype Headliners 1
MCL
▲18

abcdefghijklmnopqrstuvwxyz(".;'!*?':,")
$1234567890&fiflß-äöüåçèîñóæøœ
ABCDEFGHIJKLMNOPQRSTUVWXYZ
ÄÖÜÅÇÈÎÑÓÆØŒ»„«[§•†‡]‹¡·¿›...

EGYPTIAN 505

André Gürtler, et al. • 1966
BIT AGP FRA

abcdefghijklmnopqrstuvwxyz(".;'!*?':,")
$1234567890&fiflß-äöüåçèîñóæøœ
ABCDEFGHIJKLMNOPQRSTUVWXYZ
ÄÖÜÅÇÈÎÑÓÆØŒ»„«[§•†‡]‹¡·¿›...

Egyptian 505 ...

Light abcdefghijklmnopqrstuvwxyzABCDEFGHIJKLMNOPQRSTUVWXYZ–$1234567890(

• Roman abcdefghijklmnopqrstuvwxyzABCDEFGHIJKLMNOPQRSTUVWXYZ–$1234567890

Medium abcdefghijklmnopqrstuvwxyzABCDEFGHIJKLMNOPQRSTUVWXYZ–$123456789

Bold abcdefghijklmnopqrstuvwxyzABCDEFGHIJKLMNOPQRSTUVWXYZ–$12345678

A*I EGYPTIAN BOLD CONDENSED

Robert McCamant • 1990
ALP

abcdefghijklmnopqrstuvwxyz(".;'!*?':,")
$1234567890&fiflß-äöüåçèîñóæøœ
ABCDEFGHIJKLMNOPQRSTUVWXYZ
ÄÖÜÅÇÈÎÑÓÆØŒ»„«[¶§•†‡]‹¡·¿›...

A*I Egyptian Bold Condensed ...

• Text ▲16 abcdefghijklmnopqrstuvwxyzABCDEFGHIJKLMNOPQRSTUVWXYZ–$1234

Display ▲30 abcdefghijklmnopqrstuvwxyzABCDEFGHIJKL
MNOPQRSTUVWXYZ$1234567890(".;'!*?':,")&

Monotype Headliners 1: Monotype Clarendon, Monotype New Clarendon Roman & Bold, Monotype Egyptian 72 Extended.

E

EGYPTIENNE F

Adrian Frutiger • 1955 abcdefghijklmnopqrstuvwxyz(".;'!*?':,")

LIN ADO AGA MAE $1234567890&fiflß-äöüåçèîñóæøœ

ABCDEFGHIJKLMNOPQRSTUVWXYZ

ÄÖÜÅÇÈÎÑÓÆØŒ»„«[¶§•†‡]‹¡·¿›...

Egyptienne F ...

• Roman abcdefghijklmnopqrstuvwxyzABCDEFGHIJKLMNOPQRSTUVWXYZ–$12345

Italic *abcdefghijklmnopqrstuvwxyzABCDEFGHIJKLMNOPQRSTUVWXYZ–$12345*

Bold **abcdefghijklmnopqrstuvwxyzABCDEFGHIJKLMNOPQRSTUVWXYZ–$123**

Black **abcdefghijklmnopqrstuvwxyzABCDEFGHIJKLMNOPQRSTUVWXYZ–$1**

EHRHARDT

Monotype Design Staff • 1938 abcdefghijklmnopqrstuvwxyz(".;'!*?':,")

MCL ADO AGA LIN MAE $1234567890&fiflß-äöüåçèîñóæøœ

ABCDEFGHIJKLMNOPQRSTUVWXYZ

ÄÖÜÅÇÈÎÑÓÆØŒ»„«[¶§•†‡]‹¡·¿›...

Ehrhardt ...

• Roman abcdefghijklmnopqrstuvwxyzABCDEFGHIJKLMNOPQRSTUVWXYZ–$1234567890(

Italic *abcdefghijklmnopqrstuvwxyzABCDEFGHIJKLMNOPQRSTUVWXYZ–$1234567890(".*

Semibold **abcdefghijklmnopqrstuvwxyzABCDEFGHIJKLMNOPQRSTUVWXYZ–$1234567**

Semibold Italic ***abcdefghijklmnopqrstuvwxyzABCDEFGHIJKLMNOPQRSTUVWXYZ–$123456789***

EHRHARDT EXPERT

MCL ABCDEFGHIJKLMNOPQRSTUVWXYZ.;!?:,

1234567890&ff fi fl ffi ffl–ÄÖÜÅÇÈÎÑÓÆØŒ

(abdeilmnorst) ⅛ ¼ ⅓ ⅜ ½ ⅝ ⅔ ¾ ⅞ $12345/67890¢ ₡Rp

Ehrhardt Expert ...

• Expert Roman ABCDEFGHIJKLMNOPQRSTUVWXYZ–$1234567890.;!?:,&–ff fi fl ffi ffl ⅛ ¼ ⅓ ⅜ ½ $12345/67890¢ (abdeilmno

Expert Italic *$1234567890.;:,–ff fi fl ffi ffl ⅛ ¼ ⅓ ⅜ ½ $12345/67890¢ (abdeilmnorst) ⅝ ⅔ ¾ ⅞ ₡Rp*

Expert Semibold **$1234567890.;:,–ff fi fl ffi ffl ⅛ ¼ ⅓ ⅜ ½ $12345/67890¢ (abdeilmnorst) ⅝ ⅔ ¾ ⅞ ₡Rp**

Expert Semibold Italic ***$1234567890.;:,–ff fi fl ffi ffl ⅛ ¼ ⅓ ⅜ ½ $12345/67890¢ (abdeilmnorst) ⅝ ⅔ ¾ ⅞ ₡Rp***

Einhorn

Alan Meeks • 1980 abcdefghijklmnopqrstuvwxyz(".;'!*?':,")

URW LEF FRA $1234567890&fiflß-äöüåçèîñóæøœ

▲18 ABCDEFGHIJKLMNOPQRSTUVWXYZ

ÄÖÜÅÇÈÎÑÓÆØŒ»„«[•]‹¡·¿›...

El Grande

Jim Parkinson • 1993

FBU

▲24

ABCDEFGHIJKLMNOPQRSTUVWXYZ
("•;'!*?':,")$1234567890
&-ÄÖÜÅÇÈÎÑÓÆØŒ»„«[¶§•]‹¡·¿›...

ITC ÉLAN

Albert Boton • 1985

URW AGP LEF

▲16

abcdefghijklmnopqrstuvwxyz(".;'!*?':,")
$1234567890&fiflß-äöüåçèîñóæøœ
ABCDEFGHIJKLMNOPQRSTUVWXYZ
ÄÖÜÅÇÈÎÑÓÆØŒ»„«[¶§•†‡]‹¡·¿›...

ITC Élan 1 ...

• Book abcdefghijklmnopqrstuvwxyzABCDEFGHIJKLMNOPQRSTUVWXYZ–$12

Book Italic *abcdefghijklmnopqrstuvwxyzABCDEFGHIJKLMNOPQRSTUVWXYZ–$1*

Book SCOSF ABCDEFGHIJKLMNOPQRSTUVWXYZABCDEFGHIJKLMNOPQRSTUVWXYZ–$123

Bold **abcdefghijklmnopqrstuvwxyzABCDEFGHIJKLMNOPQRSTUVWXYZ–**

Bold Italic ***abcdefghijklmnopqrstuvwxyzABCDEFGHIJKLMNOPQRSTUVWXYZ***

ITC Élan 2 ...

Medium abcdefghijklmnopqrstuvwxyzABCDEFGHIJKLMNOPQRSTUVWXYZ–$

Medium Italic *abcdefghijklmnopqrstuvwxyzABCDEFGHIJKLMNOPQRSTUVWXYZ–$*

Medium SCOSF ABCDEFGHIJKLMNOPQRSTUVWXYZABCDEFGHIJKLMNOPQRSTUVWXYZ–$123

Black **abcdefghijklmnopqrstuvwxyzABCDEFGHIJKLMNOPQRSTUVWXY**

Black Italic ***abcdefghijklmnopqrstuvwxyzABCDEFGHIJKLMNOPQRSTUVWX***

ELECTRA 1

Alex Kaczun • 1993
...William Addison Dwiggins, 1935

LIN ADO AGA MAE

abcdefghijklmnopqrstuvwxyz(".;'!*?':,")
$1234567890&fiflß-äöüåçèîñóæøœ
ABCDEFGHIJKLMNOPQRSTUVWXYZ
ÄÖÜÅÇÈÎÑÓÆØŒ»„«[¶§•†‡]‹¡·¿›...

Electra 1 ...

• Roman abcdefghijklmnopqrstuvwxyzABCDEFGHIJKLMNOPQRSTUVWXYZ–$1234567890

Cursive *abcdefghijklmnopqrstuvwxyzABCDEFGHIJKLMNOPQRSTUVWXYZ–$1234567890("*

Bold **abcdefghijklmnopqrstuvwxyzABCDEFGHIJKLMNOPQRSTUVWXYZ–$12345678**

Bold Cursive ***abcdefghijklmnopqrstuvwxyzABCDEFGHIJKLMNOPQRSTUVWXYZ–$12345678***

Electra 1 Caravan Ornaments.

E

ELECTRA 2
LIN ADO AGA MAE

abcdefghijklmnopqrstuvwxyz(“.;‘!*?’:,”)
$1234567890&fiflß-äöüåçèîñóæøœ
ABCDEFGHIJKLMNOPQRSTUVWXYZ
ÄÖÜÅÇÈÎÑÓÆØŒ»„«[¶§•†‡]‹¡·¿›…

Electra 2 …

Roman SCOSF ABCDEFGHIJKLMNOPQRSTUVWXYZABCDEFGHIJKLMNOPQRSTUVWXYZ–$12345678

Roman OSF abcdefghijklmnopqrstuvwxyzABCDEFGHIJKLMNOPQRSTUVWXYZ–$1234567890(“

Cursive OSF *abcdefghijklmnopqrstuvwxyzABCDEFGHIJKLMNOPQRSTUVWXYZ–$1234567890(“.;*

Bold SCOSF **ABCDEFGHIJKLMNOPQRSTUVWXYZABCDEFGHIJKLMNOPQRSTUVWXYZ–$123456**

Bold OSF **abcdefghijklmnopqrstuvwxyzABCDEFGHIJKLMNOPQRSTUVWXYZ–$123456789**

Bold Cursive OSF ***abcdefghijklmnopqrstuvwxyzABCDEFGHIJKLMNOPQRSTUVWXYZ–$123456789***

• Display Roman
▲30 abcdefghijklmnopqrstuvwxyzABCDEFGHIJK
LMNOPQRSTUVWXYZ–$1234567890(“.;‘!*

Display Cursive
▲30 *abcdefghijklmnopqrstuvwxyzABCDEFGHIJK*
LMNOPQRSTUVWXYZ–$1234567890(“.;‘!

Display Bold
▲30 **abcdefghijklmnopqrstuvwxyzABCDEFGHI**
JKLMNOPQRSTUVWXYZ–$1234567890

Display Bold Cursive
▲30 ***abcdefghijklmnopqrstuvwxyzABCDEFGHIJ***
KLMNOPQRSTUVWXYZ–$1234567890

Electra 2 Caravan Ornaments.

E

ELEFONT
URW LEF
▲30

ABCDEFGHIJKLMNOPQRSTUVWXYZ
(“.;‘!*?’:,”)$1234567890
&-ÄÖÜÅÇÈÎÑÓÆØŒ»„«[¶§ • †‡]‹¡·¿›…

Elefont …
• Poster ABCDEFGHIJKLMNOPQRSTUVWXYZ–$12345
Poster Outline ABCDEFGHIJKLMNOPQRSTUVWXYZ–$12345

DV ELEVATOR
Diehl.Volk • 1990
DVT
▲24

abcdefghijklmnopqrstuvwxyz(“.;‘!*?’:,”)
$1234567890¢-äöüèîñó
ABCDEFGHIJKLMNOPQRSTUVWXYZ Ñ[•]… ▷ekmnpqr suwy5

DV Elevator …
• Regular abcdefghijklmnopqrstuvwxyzABCDEFGHIJKLMNOPQRSTUVWXYZ–$1234567890(“.;
Wide abcdefghijklmnopqrstuvwxyzABCDEFGH

Elli
Jean Evans • 1993
FBU
▲18

abcdefghijklmnopqrstuvwxyz(“.;‘!*?’:,”)
$1234567890&fiflß-äöüåçèîñóæøœ
ABCDEFGHIJKLMNOPQRSTUVWXYZ
ÄÖÜÅÇÈÎÑÓÆØŒ»„«[¶§·]‹¡·¿›… ▷d e e ff ffi ffl k ll ll p a t y

ELLINGTON
Michael Harvey • 1990
MCL ADO AGA LIN MAE
▲16

abcdefghijklmnopqrstuvwxyz(“.;‘!*?’:,”)
$1234567890&fiflß-äöüåçèîñóæøœ
ABCDEFGHIJKLMNOPQRSTUVWXYZ
ÄÖÜÅÇÈÎÑÓÆØŒ»„«[¶§·†‡]‹¡·¿›…

Ellington …
Light abcdefghijklmnopqrstuvwxyzABCDEFGHIJKLMNOPQRSTUVWXYZ–$123456
Light Italic *abcdefghijklmnopqrstuvwxyzABCDEFGHIJKLMNOPQRSTUVWXYZ–$12345678*
• Regular abcdefghijklmnopqrstuvwxyzABCDEFGHIJKLMNOPQRSTUVWXYZ–$1234

... Ellington

Italic *abcdefghijklmnopqrstuvwxyzABCDEFGHIJKLMNOPQRSTUVWXYZ–$12345*

Bold **abcdefghijklmnopqrstuvwxyzABCDEFGHIJKLMNOPQRSTUVWXYZ–$1**

Bold Italic ***abcdefghijklmnopqrstuvwxyzABCDEFGHIJKLMNOPQRSTUVWXYZ–$1***

Extra Bold **abcdefghijklmnopqrstuvwxyzABCDEFGHIJKLMNOPQRSTUVWXYZ**

Extra Bold Italic ***abcdefghijklmnopqrstuvwxyzABCDEFGHIJKLMNOPQRSTUVWXY***

E

ELSE NPL

Robert Norton • 1982 abcdefghijklmnopqrstuvwxyz(".;'!*?':,")

LIN ADO AGA MAE $1234567890&fiflß-äöüåçèîñóæøœ

ABCDEFGHIJKLMNOPQRSTUVWXYZ

ÄÖÜÅÇÈÎÑÓÆØŒ»„«[¶§•†‡]‹¡·¿›...

Else NPL ...

Light abcdefghijklmnopqrstuvwxyzABCDEFGHIJKLMNOPQRSTUVWXYZ–$123456

• Medium abcdefghijklmnopqrstuvwxyzABCDEFGHIJKLMNOPQRSTUVWXYZ–$123456

Semibold **abcdefghijklmnopqrstuvwxyzABCDEFGHIJKLMNOPQRSTUVWXYZ–$1234567**

Bold **abcdefghijklmnopqrstuvwxyzABCDEFGHIJKLMNOPQRSTUVWXYZ–$1234567**

ELYSIUM

Michael Gills • 1992 abcdefghijklmnopqrstuvwxyz(".;'!*?':,")

LET $1234567890&fiflß-äöüåçèîñóæøœ

ABCDEFGHIJKLMNOPQRSTUVWXYZ

ÄÖÜÅÇÈÎÑÓÆØŒ»„«[¶§•†‡]‹¡·¿›...

Elysium ...

• Book abcdefghijklmnopqrstuvwxyzABCDEFGHIJKLMNOPQRSTUVWXYZ–$1234567

Book Italic *abcdefghijklmnopqrstuvwxyzABCDEFGHIJKLMNOPQRSTUVWXYZ–$1234567890(".;'*

Book SCOSF ABCDEFGHIJKLMNOPQRSTUVWXYZABCDEFGHIJKLMNOPQRSTUVWXYZ–$12345

Medium **abcdefghijklmnopqrstuvwxyzABCDEFGHIJKLMNOPQRSTUVWXYZ–$123**

Bold **abcdefghijklmnopqrstuvwxyzABCDEFGHIJKLMNOPQRSTUVWXYZ–**

Embassy

BIT *abcdefghijklmnopqrstuvwxyz(".;'!*?':,")*

▲16 *$1234567890&fiflß-äöüåçèîñóæøœ*

ABCDEFGHIJKLMNOPQRSTUVWXYZ

ÄÖÜÅÇÈÎÑÓÆØŒ»„«[§•†‡]‹¡·¿›...

E

Emphasis

Martin Wait • 1989

LET

▲24

ABCDEFGHIJKLMNOPQRSTUVWXYZ

(“.;‘!*?’:,”)$1234567890

&-ÄÖÜÅÇÈÎÑÓÆØŒ»„«[•]‹‡•&›...

BUREAU EMPIRE

David Berlow • 1989
... Morris Fuller Benton • 1937

FBU AGP MTD

▲36

abcdefghijklmnopqrstuvwxyz(“.;‘!*?’:,”)

$1234567890&fifl ß-äöüåçèîñóæøœ

ABCDEFGHIJKLMNOPQRSTUVWXYZ

ÄÖÜÅÇÈÎÑÓÆØŒ»„«[¶§•†‡]‹¡·¿›...

▷ ff ffi ffl

Bureau Empire 1 ...

• Regular abcdefghijklmnopqrstuvwxyzABCDEFGHIJKLMNOPQRSTUVWXYZ–$1234567890(“.;‘!*?’:,”)&fiflß

Italic *abcdefghijklmnopqrstuvwxyzABCDEFGHIJKLMNOPQRSTUVWXYZ–$1234567890(“.;‘!*?’:,”)&fiflß*

Regular SCOSF ABCDEFGHIJKLMNOPQRSTUVWXYZABCDEFGHIJKLMNOPQRSTUVWXYZ–$1234567890(“.;‘!*?’:,”)&-ÄÖÜÅ

Bureau Empire 2 ...

Bold **abcdefghijklmnopqrstuvwxyzABCDEFGHIJKLMNOPQRSTUVWXYZ–$1234567890(“.;**

Bold SCOSF **ABCDEFGHIJKLMNOPQRSTUVWXYZABCDEFGHIJKLMNOPQRSTUVWXYZ–$1234567890(“.;‘!***

Black **abcdefghijklmnopqrstuvwxyzABCDEFGHIJKLMNOPQRSTUVWXYZ–$12345**

Black SCOSF **ABCDEFGHIJKLMNOPQRSTUVWXYZABCDEFGHIJKLMNOPQRSTUVWXYZ–$1234567**

ENDS MEANS MENDS
Sumner Stone • 1992
STO
▲30

ABCDEFGHIJKLMNOPQRSTUVWXYZ
"".;'!?':,"$1234567890
&-ÄÖÜÅÇÈÎÑÓZ„

E

EndsMeansMends ...

Ends ABCDEFGHIJKLMNOPQRSTUVWXYZ
• Means ABCDEFGHIJKLMNOPQRSTUVWXYZ
Mends ABCDEFGHIJKLMNOPQRSTUVWXYZ

Sackers English Script
Agfa Engravers 2
AGP
▲18

abcdefghijklmnopqrstuvwxyz(".;'!*?':,")
$1234567890&ß-äöüåçèîñó
ABCDEFGHIJKLMNOPQRSTUVWXYZ
ÄÖÜÅÇÈÎÑÓ»«[·]‹› ▷ I V X st nd rd th ∞ 1/4 1/3 1/2 3/4 ∞ D c ° %

ENGRAVERS' OLD ENGLISH
Morris Fuller Benton • 1901
BIT
▲16

abcdefghijklmnopqrstuvwxyz(".;'!*?':,")
$1234567890&fiflß-äöüåçèîñóæøœ
ABCDEFGHIJKLMNOPQRSTUVWXYZ
ÄÖÜÅÇÈÎÑÓÆØŒ»„«[§•†‡]‹¡·¿›...

Engravers' Old English ...

• Regular abcdefghijklmnopqrstuvwxyzABCDEFGHIJKLMNOPQRSTUVWXYZ–$12
Bold abcdefghijklmnopqrstuvwxyzABCDEFGHIJKLMNOPQRSTUV

Monotype Engravers Old English
Monotype Engravers
MCL
▲16

abcdefghijklmnopqrstuvwxyz(".;'!*?':,")
$1234567890&fiflß-äöüåçèîñóæøœ
ABCDEFGHIJKLMNOPQRSTUVWXYZ
ÄÖÜÅÇÈÎÑÓ ÆØŒ»„«[§•†‡](¡·¿)...

Agfa Engravers 2: Sackers Antique Roman Open & Solid, Sackers Light Classic Roman, Sackers English Script, Sackers Gothic Light, Medium & Heavy, Sackers Italian Script, Sackers Roman Light & Heavy, Sackers Square Gothic.
Monotype Engravers: Monotype Engravers Old English, Monotype Engravers Roman & Bold.

ENGRAVERS' ROMAN

BIT ABCDEFGHIJKLMNOPQRSTUVWXYZ(".;'!*?':,")
$1234567890&-ÄÖÜÅÇÈÎÑÓÆØŒ
ABCDEFGHIJKLMNOPQRSTUVWXYZ
ÄÖÜÅÇÈÎÑÓÆØŒ»„«[§•†‡]‹¡·¿›...

Engravers' Roman ...

• Regular ABCDEFGHIJKLMNOPQRSTUVWXYZABCDEFGHIJKLMNOPQRSTUVWXYZ–$

Bold ABCDEFGHIJKLMNOPQRSTUVWXYZABCDEFGHIJKLMNOPQRSTUVWXYZ–$12345

E °

MONOTYPE ENGRAVERS
Monotype Engravers

MCL ABCDEFGHIJKLMNOPQRSTUVWXYZ
(".;'!*?':,")$1234567890
ÄÖÜÅÇÈÎÑÓÆØŒ»„«[•]‹¡·¿›...

Monotype Engravers ...

• Roman ABCDEFGHIJKLMNOPQRSTUVWXYZ–$1234567890(".;'!*?'

Bold ABCDEFGHIJKLMNOPQRSTUVWXYZ–$1234567890(

Engravers Bold Face
Linotype Engravers Set 1

LIN ADO AGA MAE ABCDEFGHIJKLMNOPQRSTUVWXYZ(".;'!*?':,")
$1234567890&-ÄÖÜÅÇÈÎÑÓÆØŒ
ABCDEFGHIJKLMNOPQRSTUVWXYZ
ÄÖÜÅÇÈÎÑÓÆØŒ»„«[¶§•†‡]‹¡·¿›...

Engravers' Gothic

BIT ABCDEFGHIJKLMNOPQRSTUVWXYZ(".;'!*?':,")
$1234567890&-ÄÖÜÅÇÈÎÑÓÆØŒ
ABCDEFGHIJKLMNOPQRSTUVWXYZ
ÄÖÜÅÇÈÎÑÓÆØŒ»„«[§•†‡]‹¡·¿›...

Entropy

Stephen Farrell • 1993

T26

▲42

ABCDEFGHIJKLMNOPQR
STUVWXYZ(".;'!*?':,")&-
ÄÖÜÅÇÈÎÑÓÆØŒ»„«[¶§†‡]

Monotype Engravers: Monotype Engravers Old English, Monotype Engravers Roman & Bold.
Linotype Engravers Set 1: Engravers Bold Face, Serlio.

Epitaph
Tobias Frere-Jones • 1993
FBU
▲28

ABCDEFGHIJKLMNOPQRSTUVWXYZ
(".;'!*?':,")$1234567890&-ÄÖÜÅÇÈÎÑÓÆØŒ
ABCDEFGHIJKLMNOPQRSTUVWXYZ
ÄÖÜÅÇÈÎÑÓÆØŒ»,„«[¶§•]‹i·¿›… ▷

Epokha
Colin Brignall • 1992
LET
▲24

ABCDEFGHIJKLMNOPQRSTUVWXYZ
(".;'!*?':,")$1234567890
&-ÄÖÜÅÇÈÎÑÓÆØŒ»„«[•]‹i·¿› ▷CEGILNSY

Equinox
Vince Whitlock • 1988
LET
▲16

abcdefghijklmnopqrstuvwxyz(".;'!*?':,")
$1234567890&fiflß-äöüåçèîñóæøœ
ABCDEFGHIJKLMNOPQRSTUVWXYZ
ÄÖÜÅÇÈÎÑÓÆØŒ»„«[•]‹i·¿›…
▷abcdefghpqstyз235ABEGKLPRYZ

ITC ERAS
Albert Boton & Albert Hollenstein • 1976
BIT ADO AGA LEF FAM LIN MAE URW
▲16

abcdefghijklmnopqrstuvwxyz(".;'!*?':,")
$1234567890&fiflß-äöüåçèîñóæøœ
ABCDEFGHIJKLMNOPQRSTUVWXYZ
ÄÖÜÅÇÈÎÑÓÆØŒ»„«[§•†‡]‹i·¿›…

ITC Eras …

Light abcdefghijklmnopqrstuvwxyzABCDEFGHIJKLMNOPQRSTUVWXYZ–$1234567
• Book abcdefghijklmnopqrstuvwxyzABCDEFGHIJKLMNOPQRSTUVWXYZ–$12345
Medium abcdefghijklmnopqrstuvwxyzABCDEFGHIJKLMNOPQRSTUVWXYZ–$1234
Demi **abcdefghijklmnopqrstuvwxyzABCDEFGHIJKLMNOPQRSTUVWXYZ–$1**
Bold **abcdefghijklmnopqrstuvwxyzABCDEFGHIJKLMNOPQRSTUVWX**
Ultra **abcdefghijklmnopqrstuvwxyzABCDEFGHIJKLMNOPQRSTUV**
Outline abcdefghijklmnopqrstuvwxyzABCDEFGHIJKLMNOPQ

E

ERASMUS

Sjoerd Hendrick de Roos • 1923 abcdefghijklmnopqrstuvwxyz(".;'!*?':,")
RED $1234567890&ß-äöüåçèîñóæøœ
ABCDEFGHIJKLMNOPQRSTUVWXYZ
ÄÖÜÅÇÈÎÑÓÆØŒ»„«[¶§•†‡]‹¡·¿›...

Erasmus ...

Light abcdefghijklmnopqrstuvwxyzABCDEFGHIJKLMNOPQRSTUVWXYZ-$1234567890(".;'!*
Light SCOSF ABCDEFGHIJKLMNOPQRSTUVWXYZABCDEFGHIJKLMNOPQRSTUVWXYZ-$1234567890(".;
• Medium abcdefghijklmnopqrstuvwxyzABCDEFGHIJKLMNOPQRSTUVWXYZ-$1234567890(
Medium SCOSF ABCDEFGHIJKLMNOPQRSTUVWXYZABCDEFGHIJKLMNOPQRSTUVWXYZ-$12345678
Bold abcdefghijklmnopqrstuvwxyzABCDEFGHIJKLMNOPQRSTUVWXYZ-$12345678
Extra Bold abcdefghijklmnopqrstuvwxyzABCDEFGHIJKLMNOPQRSTUVWXYZ-$12

ERBAR
Linotype Headliners
Jakob Erbar • 1922 abcdefghijklmnopqrstuvwxyz(".;'!*?':,")
LIN AGP $1234567890&fiflß-äöüåçèîñóæøœ
▲16 ABCDEFGHIJKLMNOPQRSTUVWXYZ
ÄÖÜÅÇÈÎÑÓÆØŒ»„«[¶§•†‡]‹¡·¿›...

Erbar ...

• Light Condensed abcdefghijklmnopqrstuvwxyzABCDEFGHIJKLMNOPQRSTUVWXYZ–$1234567890(".;'!*?':,")&fiflß-äöüÄÖ
Bold Condensed abcdefghijklmnopqrstuvwxyzABCDEFGHIJKLMNOPQRSTUVWXYZ–$1234567890(".;'!*?':,")&fiflß-äöüÄ

ESCALIDO
Jim Marcus • 1993 abcdefghijklmnopqrstuvwxyz(.;!*?:,)
T26 $1234567890&ß-–çœø
▲30 ABCDEFGHIJKLMNOPQRSTUVWXYZ [†]

Escalido ...

• Gothico abcdefghijklmnopqrstuvwxyzABCDEFGHIJKLMNO
Streak abcdefghijklmnopqrstuvwxyzABCDEFG

...
Linotype Headliners: Chwast Buffalo Black Condensed, Erbar Light Condensed & Bold Condensed, Metrolite, Metromedium, Metroblack, Plak Black, Black Condensed & Extra Black Condensed, Stop, Times Eighteen Roman & Bold.

E

ITC ESPRIT

Jovica Veljovic • 1985 abcdefghijklmnopqrstuvwxyz(".;'!*?':,")
URW ADO AGA AGP LEF LIN MAE $1234567890&fiflß-äöüåçèîñóæøœ
ABCDEFGHIJKLMNOPQRSTUVWXYZ
ÄÖÜÅÇÈÎÑÓÆØŒ»„«[¶§ • †‡]‹¡·¿›...

ITC Esprit 1 ...

• Book abcdefghijklmnopqrstuvwxyzABCDEFGHIJKLMNOPQRSTUVWXYZ-$12345678
Book Italic *abcdefghijklmnopqrstuvwxyzABCDEFGHIJKLMNOPQRSTUVWXYZ-$1234567890(*
Book SCOSF ABCDEFGHIJKLMNOPQRSTUVWXYZABCDEFGHIJKLMNOPQRSTUVWXYZ-$1234567
Bold **abcdefghijklmnopqrstuvwxyzABCDEFGHIJKLMNOPQRSTUVWXYZ-$123**
Bold Italic ***abcdefghijklmnopqrstuvwxyzABCDEFGHIJKLMNOPQRSTUVWXYZ-$12345***

ITC Esprit 2 ...

Medium abcdefghijklmnopqrstuvwxyzABCDEFGHIJKLMNOPQRSTUVWXYZ-$12345
Medium Italic *abcdefghijklmnopqrstuvwxyzABCDEFGHIJKLMNOPQRSTUVWXYZ-$12345678*
Medium SCOSF ABCDEFGHIJKLMNOPQRSTUVWXYZABCDEFGHIJKLMNOPQRSTUVWXYZ-$12345
Black **abcdefghijklmnopqrstuvwxyzABCDEFGHIJKLMNOPQRSTUVWXYZ-$1**
Black Italic ***abcdefghijklmnopqrstuvwxyzABCDEFGHIJKLMNOPQRSTUVWXYZ-$12***

Estro

Aldo Novarese • 1961 abcdefghijklmnopqrstuvwxyz(".;'!*?':,")
IMA MTD $1234567890&ß-äöüåçèîñóœøœ
▲16 ABCDEFGHIJKLMNOPQRSTUVWXYZ
ÄÖÜÅÇÈÎÑÓÆØŒ »„« [·] ¡·¿...

Etruscan

Tim Donaldson • 1995 abcdefghijklmnopqrstuvwxyz(".;'!*?':,")$1234567890⊙
LET &fiflß-äöüåçèîñóæøœABCDEFGHIJKLMNOPQRSTUVWXYZ
▲36 ÄÖÜÅÇÈÎÑÓÆØŒ»„«[•]‹¡·¿›... ▷

EUROSTILE

Aldo Novarese • 1962 abcdefghijklmnopqrstuvwxyz(".;'!*?':,")
LIN ADO AGA LEF MAE MTD URW $1234567890&fiflß-äöüåçèîñóæøœ
▲16 ABCDEFGHIJKLMNOPQRSTUVWXYZ
ÄÖÜÅÇÈÎÑÓÆØŒ»„«[¶§•†‡]‹¡·¿›...

Eurostile 1 ...

• Regular abcdefghijklmnopqrstuvwxyzABCDEFGHIJKLMNOPQRSTUVWXYZ-

... Eurostile 1

Oblique *abcdefghijklmnopqrstuvwxyzABCDEFGHIJKLMNOPQRSTUVWXYZ–*
Demi **abcdefghijklmnopqrstuvwxyzABCDEFGHIJKLMNOPQRSTUVWXY**
Demi Oblique ***abcdefghijklmnopqrstuvwxyzABCDEFGHIJKLMNOPQRSTUVWX***
Bold **abcdefghijklmnopqrstuvwxyzABCDEFGHIJKLMNOPQRSTUVW**
Bold Oblique ***abcdefghijklmnopqrstuvwxyzABCDEFGHIJKLMNOPQRSTUVW***

Eurostile 2 ...

Condensed abcdefghijklmnopqrstuvwxyzABCDEFGHIJKLMNOPQRSTUVWXYZ–$12345678
Bold Condensed **abcdefghijklmnopqrstuvwxyzABCDEFGHIJKLMNOPQRSTUVWXYZ–$1234567890("**
Extended No. 2 abcdefghijklmnopqrstuvwxyzABCDEFGHIJKLMN
Bold Extended No. 2 **abcdefghijklmnopqrstuvwxyzABCDEFGHIJKLM**

EXCELSIOR

C. H. Griffith • 1931 abcdefghijklmnopqrstuvwxyz(".;'!*?':,")
LIN ADO AGA MAE $1234567890&fiflß-äöüåçèîñóæøœ
ABCDEFGHIJKLMNOPQRSTUVWXYZ
ÄÖÜÅÇÈÎÑÓÆØŒ»„«[¶§•†‡]‹¡·¿›...

Excelsior ...

• Roman abcdefghijklmnopqrstuvwxyzABCDEFGHIJKLMNOPQRSTUVWXYZ–$1
Italic *abcdefghijklmnopqrstuvwxyzABCDEFGHIJKLMNOPQRSTUVWXYZ–$12*
Bold **abcdefghijklmnopqrstuvwxyzABCDEFGHIJKLMNOPQRSTUVWXYZ–$1**

HF EXPOSITION

Jonathan Macagba • 1992 (Leopoldo Metlicovitz, 1906) abcdefghijklmnopqrstuvwxyz(".;'!*?':,")
HAN MTD $1234567890&fiflß-äöüåçèîñóæøœ
▲18 ABCDEFGHIJKLMNOPQRSTUVWXYZ
ÄÖÜÅÇÈÎÑÓÆØŒ»«·‹¡¿›... ▷abcdepq&ff ffi ffl A C G & J R S LA Po To

HF Exposition ...

• One abcdefghijklmnopqrstuvwxyzABCDEFGHIJKLMNOPQRSTUVWXYZ-$123456789
Two abcdefghijklmnopqrstuvwxyzABCDEFGHIJKLMNOPQRSTUVWXYZ-$123456789

HF EXPOSITION ROUNDED

HAN MTD **abcdefghijklmnopqrstuvwxyz(".;'!*?':,")**
▲18 **$1234567890&fiflß-äöüåçèîñóæøœ**
ABCDEFGHIJKLMNOPQRSTUVWXYZ
ÄÖÜÅÇÈÎÑÓÆØŒ»«·‹¡¿›... ▷**abdegps ffi ffl A J R LA Po To**

HF Exposition Rounded ...

• Medium **abcdefghijklmnopqrstuvwxyzABCDEFGHIJKLMNOPQRSTUVWXYZ-$1234567890(**
Demi **abcdefghijklmnopqrstuvwxyzABCDEFGHIJKLMNOPQRSTUVWXYZ-$1234567**

Excelsior · Excelsior Cyrillic & Excelsior EastA.

... HF Exposition Rounded

Bold abcdefghijklmnopqrstuvwxyzABCDEFGHIJKLMNOPQRSTUVWXYZ-$1234

eXPOSURE

Marshall Gisser • 1994

NYD

▲24

abcdefghijklmnopqrstuvwxyz
("; '!*?':")$1234567890&-
ABCDEFGHIJKLMNOPQRSTUVWXYZ[]

eXposure ...

• Regular abcdefghijklmnopqrstuvwxyz ABCDEFGHIJKLMNOP

Bloated abcdefghijklmnopqrstuvwxyz ABCDEFGHIJKLMNOPQR

Wide abcdefghijklmnopqrstuvwxyz ABCDEFGHIJKLM

E

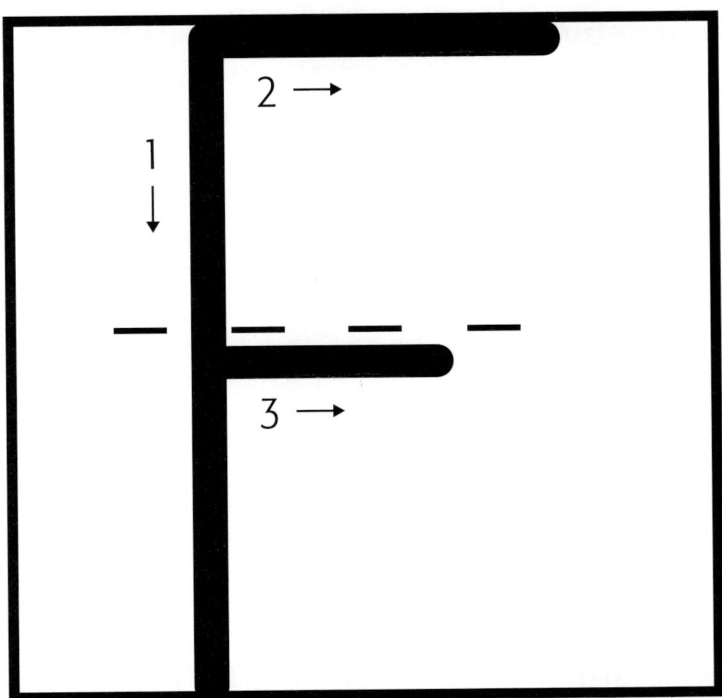
2 →
1 ↓
3 →

✍ Bill Andersen, 1993

FAIRFIELD

✍ *Alex Kaczun • 1991* abcdefghijklmnopqrstuvwxyz(“.;‘!*?’:,”)
... Rudolph Ruzicka, 1939
LIN ADO AGA MAE $1234567890&fiflß-äöüåçèîñóæøœ
ABCDEFGHIJKLMNOPQRSTUVWXYZ
ÄÖÜÅÇÈÎÑÓÆØŒ»„«[¶§•†‡]‹¡·¿›...

Fairfield 1 ...

Light abcdefghijklmnopqrstuvwxyzABCDEFGHIJKLMNOPQRSTUVWXYZ–$1234567890(
Light Italic *abcdefghijklmnopqrstuvwxyzABCDEFGHIJKLMNOPQRSTUVWXYZ–$1234567890(“.;*
• Medium abcdefghijklmnopqrstuvwxyzABCDEFGHIJKLMNOPQRSTUVWXYZ–$12345678
Medium Italic *abcdefghijklmnopqrstuvwxyzABCDEFGHIJKLMNOPQRSTUVWXYZ–$12345678*
Bold **abcdefghijklmnopqrstuvwxyzABCDEFGHIJKLMNOPQRSTUVWXYZ–$1234**
Bold Italic ***abcdefghijklmnopqrstuvwxyzABCDEFGHIJKLMNOPQRSTUVWXYZ–$12345***
Heavy **abcdefghijklmnopqrstuvwxyzABCDEFGHIJKLMNOPQRSTUVWXYZ–$1**
Heavy Italic ***abcdefghijklmnopqrstuvwxyzABCDEFGHIJKLMNOPQRSTUVWXYZ–$1***

FAIRFIELD 2

LIN ADO AGA MAE ABCDEFGHIJKLMNOPQRSTUVWXYZ(“.;‘!*?’:,”)
$1234567890&-ÄÖÜÅÇÈÎÑÓÆØŒ
ABCDEFGHIJKLMNOPQRSTUVWXYZ
ÄÖÜÅÇÈÎÑÓÆØŒ»„«[¶§•†‡]‹¡·¿›...

Fairfield 2 ...

Light SCOSF ABCDEFGHIJKLMNOPQRSTUVWXYZABCDEFGHIJKLMNOPQRSTUVWXYZ–$123456789
Light Italic Swash Caps OSF *abcdefghijklmnopqrstuvwxyzABCDEFGHIJKLMNOPQRSTUVWXYZ–$12345*
• Medium SCOSF ABCDEFGHIJKLMNOPQRSTUVWXYZABCDEFGHIJKLMNOPQRSTUVWXYZ–$1234567
Medium Italic Swash Caps OSF *abcdefghijklmnopqrstuvwxyzABCDEFGHIJKLMNOPQRSTUVWXYZ–$12*
Bold SCOSF **ABCDEFGHIJKLMNOPQRSTUVWXYZABCDEFGHIJKLMNOPQRSTUVWXYZ–$123**
Bold Italic Swash Caps OSF ***abcdefghijklmnopqrstuvwxyzABCDEFGHIJKLMNOPQRSTUVWXY***
Heavy SCOSF **ABCDEFGHIJKLMNOPQRSTUVWXYZABCDEFGHIJKLMNOPQRSTUVWXYZ–**
Heavy Italic Swash Caps OSF ***abcdefghijklmnopqrstuvwxyzABCDEFGHIJKLMNOPQRSTUVW***
Light Caption abcdefghijklmnopqrstuvwxyzABCDEFGHIJKLMNOPQRSTUVWXYZ–$1234567890(
Medium Caption abcdefghijklmnopqrstuvwxyzABCDEFGHIJKLMNOPQRSTUVWXYZ–$1234567
Bold Caption **abcdefghijklmnopqrstuvwxyzABCDEFGHIJKLMNOPQRSTUVWXYZ–$1234**
Heavy Caption **abcdefghijklmnopqrstuvwxyzABCDEFGHIJKLMNOPQRSTUVWXYZ–$1**

F

Faithful Fly
David Sagorski • 1994
LET
▲30

ABCDEFGHIJKLMNOPQRSTUVWXYZ
(".;'!*?':,")$1234567890
&-ÄÖÜÅÇÈÎÑÓÆØŒ»,,«[•]‹¡·¿›...

FAJITA
Noel Rubin • 1993
IMA
▲18

ABCDEFGHIJKLMNOPQRSTUVWXYZ(".;'!*?':,")
$1234567890&-ÄÖÜÅÇÈÎÑÓÆØŒ
ABCDEFGHIJKLMNOPQRSTUVWXYZ
ÄÖÜÅÇÈÎÑÓÆØŒ»,,«[¶§•†‡]‹¡·¿›...

Fajita ...
• Mild ABCDEFGHIJKLMNOPQRSTUVWXYZABCDEFGHIJKLMNOPQRS
Picante ABCDEFGHIJKLMNOPQRSTUVWXYZABCDEFGHIJKLMNOPQRS

Falstaff
Monotype Headliners 2
Monotype Design Staff • 1935
MCL ADO AGA LIN MAE
▲18

abcdefghijklmnopqrstuvwxyz(".;'!*?':,")
$1234567890&fiflß-äöüåçèîñóæøœ
ABCDEFGHIJKLMNOPQRSTUVWXYZ
ÄÖÜÅÇÈÎÑÓÆØŒ»,,«[§•†‡]‹¡·¿›...

FC Fanfare Condensed
Louis Oppenhiem • 1927
TFC
▲30

abcdefghijklmnopqrstuvwxyz(".;'!*?':,")
$1234567890&ß-äöüåçèîñóæøœ
ABCDEFGHIJKLMNOPQRSTUVWXYZ
ÄÖÜÅÇÈÎÑÓÆØŒ»,,«[§•†‡]‹¡·¿›...

FARFELL
Noel Rubin • 1992
IMA

ABCDEFGHIJKLMNOPQRSTUVWXYZ
(".;'!*?':,")$1234567890
&-ÄÖÜÅÇÈÎÑÓÆØŒ»,,«[¶§•†‡]‹¡·¿›...

Farfell ...
• Pencil ABCDEFGHIJKLMNOPQRSTUVWXYZ—$1234567890(".;'!*?':
Felt Tip ABCDEFGHIJKLMNOPQRSTUVWXYZ—$1234567890(".;'!*?':

Monotype Headliners 2: Falstaff, Headline Bold, Placard Condensed & Bold Condensed.

Fashion Compressed

Alan Meeks • 1986

LET

▲30

abcdefghijklmnopqrstuvwxyz(".;'!*?':,")
$1234567890&fiflß-äöüåçèîñóæøœ
ABCDEFGHIJKLMNOPQRSTUVWXYZ
ÄÖÜÅÇÈÎÑÓÆØŒ»„«[•]‹¡·¿›...

F

Fashion Engraved

Alan Meeks • 1991

LET

▲30

abcdefghijklmnopqrstuvwxyz(".;'!*?':,")
$1234567890&fiflß-äöüåçèîñóæøœ
ABCDEFGHIJKLMNOPQRSTUVWXYZ
ÄÖÜÅÇÈÎÑÓÆØŒ»„«[•]‹¡·¿›...

FAUST

Albert Kapr • 1959

RED

abcdefghijklmnopqrstuvwxyz(".;'!*?':,")
$1234567890&fiflß-äöüåçèîñóæøœ
ABCDEFGHIJKLMNOPQRSTUVWXYZ
ÄÖÜÅÇÈÎÑÓÆØŒ»„«[¶§•†‡]‹¡·¿›...

Faust 1 ...

Light abcdefghijklmnopqrstuvwxyzABCDEFGHIJKLMNOPQRSTUVWXYZ-$1234

Light Italic *abcdefghijklmnopqrstuvwxyzABCDEFGHIJKLMNOPQRSTUVWXYZ-$1234*

Light SCOSF ABCDEFGHIJKLMNOPQRSTUVWXYZABCDEFGHIJKLMNOPQRSTUVWXYZ-$1234567

• Medium abcdefghijklmnopqrstuvwxyzABCDEFGHIJKLMNOPQRSTUVWXYZ-$123

Bold **abcdefghijklmnopqrstuvwxyzABCDEFGHIJKLMNOPQRSTUVWXYZ-$12**

Extra Bold **abcdefghijklmnopqrstuvwxyzABCDEFGHIJKLMNOPQRSTUVWXYZ-$1**

Faust 2 ...

Light OSF abcdefghijklmnopqrstuvwxyzABCDEFGHIJKLMNOPQRSTUVWXYZ-$1234

Light Italic OSF *abcdefghijklmnopqrstuvwxyzABCDEFGHIJKLMNOPQRSTUVWXYZ-$1234*

Medium OSF abcdefghijklmnopqrstuvwxyzABCDEFGHIJKLMNOPQRSTUVWXYZ-$123

Bold OSF **abcdefghijklmnopqrstuvwxyzABCDEFGHIJKLMNOPQRSTUVWXYZ-$12**

Extra Bold OSF **abcdefghijklmnopqrstuvwxyzABCDEFGHIJKLMNOPQRSTUVWXYZ-$1**

Felix Titling
Monotype Classic Titling
Monotype Design Staff • 1934 (Felice Feliciano, 1463)
MCL
▲28

ABCDEFGHIJKLMNOPQRSTUVWXYZ
(“.;‘!*?’:,”)$1234567890
&-ÄÖÜÅÇÈÎÑÓÆØŒ»„«[•]‹¡·¿›...

ITC FENICE
Aldo Novarese • 1980
URW ADO AGA AGP BIT LEF FAM LIN MAE
▲16

abcdefghijklmnopqrstuvwxyz(“.;‘!*?’:,”)
$1234567890&fiflß-äöüåçèîñóæøœ
ABCDEFGHIJKLMNOPQRSTUVWXYZ
ÄÖÜÅÇÈÎÑÓÆØŒ»„«[¶§•†‡]‹¡·¿›...

ITC Fenice 1 ...
• Roman abcdefghijklmnopqrstuvwxyzABCDEFGHIJKLMNOPQRSTUVWXYZ-$1234567
Italic *abcdefghijklmnopqrstuvwxyzABCDEFGHIJKLMNOPQRSTUVWXYZ-$1234567*
Bold **abcdefghijklmnopqrstuvwxyzABCDEFGHIJKLMNOPQRSTUVWXYZ-$123**
Bold Italic ***abcdefghijklmnopqrstuvwxyzABCDEFGHIJKLMNOPQRSTUVWXYZ-$123***

ITC Fenice 2 ...
Light abcdefghijklmnopqrstuvwxyzABCDEFGHIJKLMNOPQRSTUVWXYZ-$1234567890(“.
Light Italic *abcdefghijklmnopqrstuvwxyzABCDEFGHIJKLMNOPQRSTUVWXYZ-$1234567890(“*
Ultra **abcdefghijklmnopqrstuvwxyzABCDEFGHIJKLMNOPQRSTUVWX**
Ultra Italic ***abcdefghijklmnopqrstuvwxyzABCDEFGHIJKLMNOPQRSTUVWXY***

Festival Titling
Monotype Crazy Headlines
Phillip Boydell • 1951
MCL
▲30

ABCDEFGHIJKLMNOPQRSTUVWXYZ
(“.;‘!*?’:,”)$1234567890
&-ÄÖÜÅÇÈÎÑÓÆØŒ»„«[•]‹¡·¿›...

Fette Fraktur
Linotype DisplaySet 1
C. E. Weber • 1875
LIN ADO AGA MAE URW
▲16

abcdefghijklmnopqrstuvwxyz(“.;‘!*?’:,”)
$1234567890&fiflß-äöüåçèîñóæøœ
ABCDEFGHIJKLMNOPQRSTUVWXYZ
ÄÖÜÅÇÈÎÑÓÆØŒ»„«[¶§•†‡]‹¡·¿›... ▷ch ck ff ft ll ſ s ſi ſſ ß tz-äöüÄÖÜ

Monotype Classic Titling: Felix Titling, Perpetua Titling Light, Regular & Bold.
Monotype Crazy Headlines: Festival Titling, Kino, Matura, Matura Scriptorial Capitals, Victoria Titling Condensed.
Linotype DisplaySet 1: Arnold Böcklin, Fette Fraktur, Helvetica Inserat, Present Script.

PL Fiedler Gothic
Agfa Typographers's Edition 2
Hal Fiedler • ....
AGP
▲16

abcdefghijklmnopqrstuvwxyz(".;'!*?':,")
$1234567890&ß-äöüåçèîñóæøœ
ABCDEFGHIJKLMNOPQRSTUVWXYZ
ÄÖÜÅÇÈÎÑÓÆŒ»„«[¶§•†‡]‹¡·¿›... ▹ d g

Figaro
Monotype Headliners 3
Monotype Design Staff • 1940
MCL
▲24

abcdefghijklmnopqrstuvwxyz(".;'!*?':,")$1234567890&fiflß-äöüåçèîñóæøœ
ABCDEFGHIJKLMNOPQRSTUVWXYZÄÖÜÅÇÈÎÑÓÆØŒ»„«[§•†‡]‹¡·¿›...

FIGURAL
Michael Gills • 1992
... Oldrich Menhart, 1940
LET

abcdefghijklmnopqrstuvwxyz(".;'!*?':,")
$1234567890&fiflß-äöüåçèîñóæøœ
ABCDEFGHIJKLMNOPQRSTUVWXYZ
ÄÖÜÅÇÈÎÑÓÆØŒ»„«[¶§•†‡]‹¡·¿›...

Figural ...

• Book abcdefghijklmnopqrstuvwxyzABCDEFGHIJKLMNOPQRSTUVWXYZ–$1234567
Book Italic *abcdefghijklmnopqrstuvwxyzABCDEFGHIJKLMNOPQRSTUVWXYZ–$1234567890(*
Book SCOSF ABCDEFGHIJKLMNOPQRSTUVWXYZABCDEFGHIJKLMNOPQRSTUVWXYZ–$123456
Medium abcdefghijklmnopqrstuvwxyzABCDEFGHIJKLMNOPQRSTUVWXYZ–$12345
Bold **abcdefghijklmnopqrstuvwxyzABCDEFGHIJKLMNOPQRSTUVWXYZ–$12**

Fine Hand
Richard Bradley • 1987
LET
▲12

abcdefghijklmnopqrstuvwxyz(".;'!*?':,")
$1234567890&fiflß-äöüåçèîñóæøœ
ABCDEFGHIJKLMNOPQRSTUVWXYZ
Ç»„«[·]‹¡·¿›... ▹ ct d e ff g g k r t v w
▹ A B C D E F G H J K L M N O P Q R S T V W & Th

PL Fiorello Condensed
Agfa Typographer's Edition 3
AGP
▲30

abcdefghijklmnopqrstuvwxyz(".;'!*?':,")$1234567890
&-äöüåçèîñóæøœABCDEFGHIJKLMNOPQRSTUVWXYZ
ÄÖÜÅÇÈÎÑÓÆØŒ»„«[¶•†‡]‹¡·¿›

Agfa Typographer's Edition 2: PL Barnum Block, PL Benguiat Frisky Bold, TC Broadway, PL Davison Zip Bold, PL Fiedler Gothic Bold, PL Futura Maxi Book & Bold, Neon Extra Condensed, Ritmo Bold, PL Trophy Oblique.
Monotype Headliners 3: Braggadocio, Figaro, Forte, Klang.

Agfa Typographer's Edition 3: Barclay Open, PL Bernhardt Light, Medium & Bold, PL Britannia Bold, Delphian Open, PL Fiorello Condensed, Fluidum Bold, PL Modern Heavy Condensed, PL Torino Open.

F

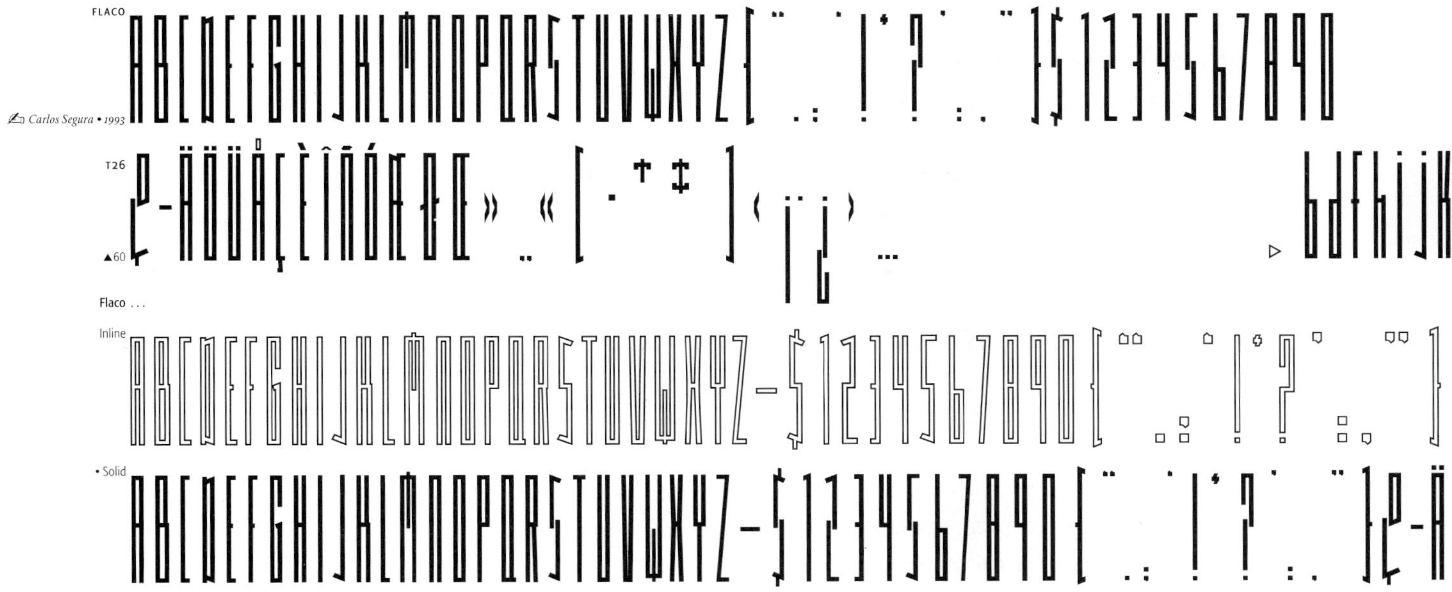
FLACO
Carlos Segura • 1993
T26
▲60
Flaco . . .
Inline
• Solid

Flamme

Alan Meeks • 1993
. . . Schelter & Giesecke, 1933

LET

▲24

abcdefghijklmnopqrstuvwxyz(“.;‘!*?’:,”)
$1234567890&fiflß-äöüåçèîñóæøœ
ABCDEFGHIJKLMNOPQRSTUVWXYZ
ÄÖÜÅÇÈÎÑÓÆØŒ»„«[•]‹¡·¿›...

Flemish Script 2
Agfa Scripts 2

AGP BIT

▲18

abcdefghijklmnopqrstuvwxyz(“.;‘!*?’:,”)
$1234567890&ß-äöüåçèîñó
ABCDEFGHIJKLMNOPQRSTUVWXYZ
ÄÖÜÅÇÈÎÑÓ»«[•]‹› ▷I V X st nd rd th 1/4 1/3 1/2 3/4 & %

Flexure

Stephen Farrell • 1993

T26

▲16

abcdefghijklmnopqrstuvwxyz(".;'!*?':,")
$1234567890&fiflß-äöüåçèîñóæøœ
ABCDEFGHIJKLMNOPQRSTUVWXYZ
ÄÖÜÅÇÈÎÑÓÆØŒ»„«[¶§•†‡]‹¡·¿›...

Flicker

INT

▲30

ABCDEFGHIJKLMNOPQRSTUVWXYZ
".:'!?':,"$1234567890

Agfa Scripts 2: Citadel, Flemish Script 2, Florentine Script 2, French Script, Mahogany Script, Old Fashion Script, Riviera Script.

ITC FLORA

Gerard Unger • 1980
LIN ADO AGA AGP LEF MAE URW
▲16

abcdefghijklmnopqrstuvwxyz(“.;‘!*?’:,”)
$1234567890&fiflß-äöüåçèîñóæøœ
ABCDEFGHIJKLMNOPQRSTUVWXYZ
ÄÖÜÅÇÈÎÑÓÆØŒ»„«[¶§•†‡]‹¡·¿›...

ITC Flora ...

• Medium abcdefghijklmnopqrstuvwxyzABCDEFGHIJKLMNOPQRSTUVWXYZ–$123456789
Bold **abcdefghijklmnopqrstuvwxyzABCDEFGHIJKLMNOPQRSTUVWXYZ–$1234**

F

FLORENS

Garrett Boge • 1989
LPT MTD
▲16

abcdefghijklmnopqrstuvwxyz(“.;‘!*?’:,”)
$1234567890&fiflß-äöüåçèîñóæøœ
ABCDEFGHIJKLMNOPQRSTUVWXYZ
ÄÖÜÅÇÈÎÑÓÆØŒ»„«[•]‹¡·¿›...

Florens ...

• Regular abcdefghijklmnopqrstuvwxyzABCDEFGHIJKLMNOPQRSTUVWXYZ–$1234567890(“.
Swash OSF abcdefghijklmnopqrstuvwxyzABCDEFGHIJKLMNOPQR...123456

Florentine Script 2
Agfa Scripts 2

AGP abcdefghijklmnopqrstuvwxyz(“.;‘!*?’:,”)
▲16 $1234567890&ß-äöüåçèîñó
ABCDEFGHIJKLMNOPQRSTUVWXYZ
ÄÖÜÅÇÈÎÑÓ»«[.]‹›
▷ I V X st nd rd th 1/4 1/3 1/2 3/4 D c r c s O rs & %

Floridian Script
Agfa ScriptSet 1

AGP abcdefghijklmnopqrstuvwxyz(“.;‘!*?’:,”)
▲16 $1234567890&fiflß-äöüåçèîñóæøœ
ABCDEFGHIJKLMNOPQRSTUVWXYZ
ÄÖÜÅÇÈÎÑÓÆØŒ»„«[§•†‡]‹¡·¿›...

Fluidum Bold
Agfa Typographer's Edition 3
Aldo Novarese • 1951

abcdefghijklmnopqrstuvwxyz(“.;‘!*?’:,”)
AGP $1234567890&-äöüåçèîñóæøœ
▲24 ABCDEFGHIJKLMNOPQRSTUVWXYZ
ÄÖÜÅÇÈÎÑÓÆØŒ»„«[•†‡]‹¡·¿›...

Agfa Scripts 2: Citadel, Flemish Script 2, Florentine Script 2, French Script, Mahogany Script, Old Fashion Script, Riviera Script.
Agfa ScriptSet 1: Basilica, Floridian Script, Jasper, Liberty.

Agfa Typographer's Edition 3: Barclay Open, PL Bernhardt Light, Medium & Bold, PL Britannia Bold, Delphian Open, PL Fiorello Condensed, Fluidum Bold, PL Modern Heavy Condensed, PL Torino Open.

FLYER
Linotype DisplaySet 2
LIN ADO AGA MAE
▲18

abcdefghijklmnopqrstuvwxyz(“.;‘!*?’:,”)
$1234567890&fiflß-äöüåçèîñóæøœ
ABCDEFGHIJKLMNOPQRSTUVWXYZ
ÄÖÜÅÇÈÎÑÓÆØŒ»„«[¶§•†‡]‹¡·¿›...

Flyer ...
• Black Condensed abcdefghijklmnopqrstuvwxyzABCDEFGHIJKLMNOPQRSTUVWXYZ–$12
Extra Black Condensed abcdefghijklmnopqrstuvwxyzABCDEFGHIJKLMNOPQRSTUVWXYZ–$1234567890(“.;‘!*?

F

Fobia
Daryl Roske • 1994
FBU
▲24

abcdefghijklmnopqrstuvwxyz(“.;‘!*?’:,”)
$1234567890&-äöüåçèîñóæøœ
ABCDEFGHIJKLMNOPQRSTUVWXYZ
ÄÖÜÅÇÈÎÑÓÆØŒ»„«[¶§•†•]‹¡·¿›...

▷ ©

FOLIO
Konrad Bauer & Walter Baum • 1957
BIT ADO AGA AGP LEF FRA LIN MAE MTD URW

abcdefghijklmnopqrstuvwxyz(“.;‘!*?’:,”)
$1234567890&fiflß-äöüåçèîñóæøœ
ABCDEFGHIJKLMNOPQRSTUVWXYZ
ÄÖÜÅÇÈÎÑÓÆØŒ»„«[¶§•†‡]‹¡·¿›...

Folio ...
Light abcdefghijklmnopqrstuvwxyzABCDEFGHIJKLMNOPQRSTUVWXYZ–$12345678
Light Italic *abcdefghijklmnopqrstuvwxyzABCDEFGHIJKLMNOPQRSTUVWXYZ–$12345678*
• Book abcdefghijklmnopqrstuvwxyzABCDEFGHIJKLMNOPQRSTUVWXYZ–$1234567
Medium abcdefghijklmnopqrstuvwxyzABCDEFGHIJKLMNOPQRSTUVWXYZ–$12345
Bold **abcdefghijklmnopqrstuvwxyzABCDEFGHIJKLMNOPQRSTUVWXYZ–**
Extra Bold **abcdefghijklmnopqrstuvwxyzABCDEFGHIJKLMNOPQRSTUVWXY**
Bold Condensed **abcdefghijklmnopqrstuvwxyzABCDEFGHIJKLMNOPQRSTUVWXYZ–$1234567890(“.;‘!*?’:,”**

Follies
Alan Meeks • 1991
LET
▲30

ABCDEFGHIJKLMNOPQRSTUVWXYZ
(“.;‘!*?’:,”)$1234567890
&-ÄÖÜÅÇÈÎÑÓÆØŒ»„«[•]‹¡·¿›...

Linotype DisplaySet 2: Banco, Charme, Flyer Black Condensed & Extra Black Condensed, Wilhelm Klingspor Gotisch.

i Fontoon

Steve Zafarana • 1994 abcdefghijklmnopqrstuvwxyz(“.;‘!*?’:,”)
GAL $1234567890&fiflß-äöüåçéîñóœøœ
▲16 ABCDEFGHIJKLMNOPQRSTUVWXYZ
ÄÖÜÅÇÈÎÑÓÆØŒ»„«[¶§●†‡]‹i·¿›…

FOOTLIGHT

F

Ong Chong Wah • 1986 abcdefghijklmnopqrstuvwxyz(“.;‘!*?’:,”)
MCL $1234567890&fiflß-äöüåçèîñóæøœ
▲16 ABCDEFGHIJKLMNOPQRSTUVWXYZ
ÄÖÜÅÇÈÎÑÓÆØŒ»„«[¶§•†‡]‹i·¿›…

Footlight 1 …

• Regular abcdefghijklmnopqrstuvwxyzABCDEFGHIJKLMNOPQRSTUVWXYZ–$12
Italic *abcdefghijklmnopqrstuvwxyzABCDEFGHIJKLMNOPQRSTUVWXYZ–$12*
Bold **abcdefghijklmnopqrstuvwxyzABCDEFGHIJKLMNOPQRSTUVWXYZ–**
Bold Italic ***abcdefghijklmnopqrstuvwxyzABCDEFGHIJKLMNOPQRSTUVWXYZ–$***

Footlight 2 …

Light abcdefghijklmnopqrstuvwxyzABCDEFGHIJKLMNOPQRSTUVWXYZ–$1234
Light Italic *abcdefghijklmnopqrstuvwxyzABCDEFGHIJKLMNOPQRSTUVWXYZ–$12345*
Extra Bold **abcdefghijklmnopqrstuvwxyzABCDEFGHIJKLMNOPQRSTUVWXYZ**
Extra Bold Italic ***abcdefghijklmnopqrstuvwxyzABCDEFGHIJKLMNOPQRSTUVWXYZ***

TF FOREVER

Joseph Treacy • 1985 abcdefghijklmnopqrstuvwxyz(“.;‘!*?’:,”)
TRE MTD $1234567890&fiflß-äöüåçèîñóæøœ
ABCDEFGHIJKLMNOPQRSTUVWXYZ
ÄÖÜÅÇÈÎÑÓÆØŒ»„«[¶§•†‡]‹¡ · ¿›… ▷123579/234816■□

TF Forever A …

• Regular abcdefghijklmnopqrstuvwxyzABCDEFGHIJKLMNOPQRSTUVWXYZ–$1234567890(“.;‘!*?’:,
Italic *abcdefghijklmnopqrstuvwxyzABCDEFGHIJKLMNOPQRSTUVWXYZ–$1234567890(“.;‘!*?’:,”)&*
Extra Bold **abcdefghijklmnopqrstuvwxyzABCDEFGHIJKLMNOPQRSTUVWXYZ–$12345678**
Extra Bold Italic ***abcdefghijklmnopqrstuvwxyzABCDEFGHIJKLMNOPQRSTUVWXYZ–$1234567890***

TF Forever B …

Thin abcdefghijklmnopqrstuvwxyzABCDEFGHIJKLMNOPQRSTUVWXYZ–$1234567890(“.;‘!*?’:,
Thin Italic *abcdefghijklmnopqrstuvwxyzABCDEFGHIJKLMNOPQRSTUVWXYZ–$1234567890(“.;‘!*?’:,”)&*
Medium abcdefghijklmnopqrstuvwxyzABCDEFGHIJKLMNOPQRSTUVWXYZ–$1234567890(“.;‘!*
Medium Italic *abcdefghijklmnopqrstuvwxyzABCDEFGHIJKLMNOPQRSTUVWXYZ–$1234567890(“.;‘!*?’:,*

i Foontoon Foontoonie No.1

F

TF Forever C . . .

Extra Light abcdefghijklmnopqrstuvwxyzABCDEFGHIJKLMNOPQRSTUVWXYZ–$1234567890(“.;‘!*?’:,

Extra Light Italic *abcdefghijklmnopqrstuvwxyzABCDEFGHIJKLMNOPQRSTUVWXYZ–$1234567890(“.;‘!*?’:,”)&*

Demi **abcdefghijklmnopqrstuvwxyzABCDEFGHIJKLMNOPQRSTUVWXYZ–$1234567890(“.**

Demi Italic ***abcdefghijklmnopqrstuvwxyzABCDEFGHIJKLMNOPQRSTUVWXYZ–$1234567890(“.;‘!****

TF Forever D . . .

Light abcdefghijklmnopqrstuvwxyzABCDEFGHIJKLMNOPQRSTUVWXYZ–$1234567890(“.;‘!*?’:,

Light Italic *abcdefghijklmnopqrstuvwxyzABCDEFGHIJKLMNOPQRSTUVWXYZ–$1234567890(“.;‘!*?’:,”)&*

Bold **abcdefghijklmnopqrstuvwxyzABCDEFGHIJKLMNOPQRSTUVWXYZ–$1234567890**

Bold Italic ***abcdefghijklmnopqrstuvwxyzABCDEFGHIJKLMNOPQRSTUVWXYZ–$1234567890(“***

TF FOREVER TWO
(alternate lowercase g and uppercase M)
✍ *Joseph Treacy* • 1993
TRE MTD

abcdefghijklmnopqrstuvwxyz(“.;‘!*?’:,”)
$1234567890&ﬁﬂß-äöüåçèîñóæøœ
ABCDEFGHIJKLMNOPQRSTUVWXYZ
ÄÖÜÅÇÈÎÑÓÆØŒ»,„«[¶§•†‡]‹¡ · ¿›...

▷123579/234816■□

TF Forever Two A . . .

• Regular abcdefghijklmnopqrstuvwxyzABCDEFGHIJKLMNOPQRSTUVWXYZ–$1234567890(“.;‘!*?’:,

Italic *abcdefghijklmnopqrstuvwxyzABCDEFGHIJKLMNOPQRSTUVWXYZ–$1234567890(“.;‘!*?’:,”)&*

Extra Bold **abcdefghijklmnopqrstuvwxyzABCDEFGHIJKLMNOPQRSTUVWXYZ–$12345678**

Extra Bold Italic ***abcdefghijklmnopqrstuvwxyzABCDEFGHIJKLMNOPQRSTUVWXYZ–$1234567890***

TF Forever Two B . . .

Thin abcdefghijklmnopqrstuvwxyzABCDEFGHIJKLMNOPQRSTUVWXYZ–$1234567890(“.;‘!*?’:,

Thin Italic *abcdefghijklmnopqrstuvwxyzABCDEFGHIJKLMNOPQRSTUVWXYZ–$1234567890(“.;‘!*?’:,”)&*

Medium **abcdefghijklmnopqrstuvwxyzABCDEFGHIJKLMNOPQRSTUVWXYZ–$1234567890(“.;‘!***

Medium Italic ***abcdefghijklmnopqrstuvwxyzABCDEFGHIJKLMNOPQRSTUVWXYZ–$1234567890(“.;‘!*?’:,***

TF Forever Two C . . .

Extra Light abcdefghijklmnopqrstuvwxyzABCDEFGHIJKLMNOPQRSTUVWXYZ–$1234567890(“.;‘!*?’:,

Extra Light Italic *abcdefghijklmnopqrstuvwxyzABCDEFGHIJKLMNOPQRSTUVWXYZ–$1234567890(“.;‘!*?’:,”)&*

Demi **abcdefghijklmnopqrstuvwxyzABCDEFGHIJKLMNOPQRSTUVWXYZ–$1234567890(“.**

Demi Italic ***abcdefghijklmnopqrstuvwxyzABCDEFGHIJKLMNOPQRSTUVWXYZ–$1234567890(“.;‘!****

TF Forever Two D . . .

Light abcdefghijklmnopqrstuvwxyzABCDEFGHIJKLMNOPQRSTUVWXYZ–$1234567890(“.;‘!*?’:,

Light Italic *abcdefghijklmnopqrstuvwxyzABCDEFGHIJKLMNOPQRSTUVWXYZ–$1234567890(“.;‘!*?’:,”)&*

Bold **abcdefghijklmnopqrstuvwxyzABCDEFGHIJKLMNOPQRSTUVWXYZ–$1234567890**

Bold Italic ***abcdefghijklmnopqrstuvwxyzABCDEFGHIJKLMNOPQRSTUVWXYZ–$1234567890(“***

Formal 436

✍ Georg Trump • 1954 abcdefghijklmnopqrstuvwxyz(".;'!*?':,")

BIT $1234567890&fiflß-äöüåçèîñóœøœ

▲16 ABCDEFGHIJKLMNOPQRSTUVWXYZ

ÄÖÜÅÇÈÎÑÓÆØŒ»„«[§•†‡]‹i·¿›...

Formal Script 421

✍ Adrian Frutiger • 1954 abcdefghijklmnopqrstuvwxyz(".;'!*?':,")

BIT $1234567890&fiflß-äöüåçèîñóæøœ

▲16 ABCDEFGHIJKLMNOPQRSTUVWXYZ

ÄÖÜÅÇÈÎÑÓÆØŒ»„«[§•†‡]‹i·¿›...

FORMATA

✍ Bernd Möllenstädt • 1984 abcdefghijklmnopqrstuvwxyz(".;'!*?':,")

ADO AGA MAE $1234567890&fiflß-äöüåçèîñóæøœ

ABCDEFGHIJKLMNOPQRSTUVWXYZ

ÄÖÜÅÇÈÎÑÓÆØŒ»„«[¶§•†‡]‹i·¿›...

Formata ...

Light abcdefghijklmnopqrstuvwxyzABCDEFGHIJKLMNOPQRSTUVWXYZ–$1234567890(".;'!

Light Italic *abcdefghijklmnopqrstuvwxyzABCDEFGHIJKLMNOPQRSTUVWXYZ–$1234567890(".;'!*

• Regular abcdefghijklmnopqrstuvwxyzABCDEFGHIJKLMNOPQRSTUVWXYZ–$1234567890

Italic *abcdefghijklmnopqrstuvwxyzABCDEFGHIJKLMNOPQRSTUVWXYZ–$123456789*

Medium **abcdefghijklmnopqrstuvwxyzABCDEFGHIJKLMNOPQRSTUVWXYZ–$1234567**

Medium Italic ***abcdefghijklmnopqrstuvwxyzABCDEFGHIJKLMNOPQRSTUVWXYZ–$123456***

Bold **abcdefghijklmnopqrstuvwxyzABCDEFGHIJKLMNOPQRSTUVWXYZ–$12345**

Bold Italic ***abcdefghijklmnopqrstuvwxyzABCDEFGHIJKLMNOPQRSTUVWXYZ–$1234***

FORMATA CONDENSED

ADO AGA MAE abcdefghijklmnopqrstuvwxyz(".;'!*?':,")

$1234567890&fiflß-äöüåçèîñóæøœ

ABCDEFGHIJKLMNOPQRSTUVWXYZ

ÄÖÜÅÇÈÎÑÓÆØŒ»„«[¶§•†‡]‹i·¿›...

Formata Condensed ...

Light Condensed abcdefghijklmnopqrstuvwxyzABCDEFGHIJKLMNOPQRSTUVWXYZ–$1234567890(".;'!*?':,")&fiflß-äöüÄ

Light Condensed Italic *abcdefghijklmnopqrstuvwxyzABCDEFGHIJKLMNOPQRSTUVWXYZ–$1234567890(".;'!*?':,")&fiflß-äöüÄ*

• Condensed abcdefghijklmnopqrstuvwxyzABCDEFGHIJKLMNOPQRSTUVWXYZ–$1234567890(".;'!*?':,")&fiflß-ä

Condensed Italic *abcdefghijklmnopqrstuvwxyzABCDEFGHIJKLMNOPQRSTUVWXYZ–$1234567890(".;'!*?':,")&fiflß-*

Medium Condensed **abcdefghijklmnopqrstuvwxyzABCDEFGHIJKLMNOPQRSTUVWXYZ–$1234567890(".;'!*?':,")**

Medium Condensed Italic ***abcdefghijklmnopqrstuvwxyzABCDEFGHIJKLMNOPQRSTUVWXYZ–$1234567890(".;'!*?':,")***

. . . Formata Condensed

Bold Condensed **abcdefghijklmnopqrstuvwxyzABCDEFGHIJKLMNOPQRSTUVWXYZ–$1234567890(“.;‘!***

Bold Condensed Italic ***abcdefghijklmnopqrstuvwxyzABCDEFGHIJKLMNOPQRSTUVWXYZ–$1234567890(“.;‘!****

Condensed Outline ▲18 abcdefghijklmnopqrstuvwxyzABCDEFGHIJKLMNOPQRSTUVWXYZ–

FORMATA EXPERT & SCOSF

ADO AGA MAE ABCDEFGHIJKLMNOPQRSTUVWXYZ.;!?:,
1234567890&ff fi fl ffi ffl –ÄÖÜÅÇÈÎÑÓÆØŒ
(abdeilmnorst) 1/8 1/4 1/3 3/8 1/2 5/8 2/3 3/4 7/8 $12345/67890¢ ₡Rp

F

Formata Expert & SCOSF . . .

Expert Light ABCDEFGHIJKLMNOPQRSTUVWXYZ–$1234567890.;!?:,&-ff fi fl ffi ffl 1/8 1/4 1/3 3/8 1/2 $12345/67890¢ (ab

Expert Light Italic *ABCDEFGHIJKLMNOPQRSTUVWXYZ–$1234567890.;!?:,&-ff fi fl ffi ffl 1/8 1/4 1/3 3/8 1/2 $12345/67890¢ (ab*

• Expert Regular ABCDEFGHIJKLMNOPQRSTUVWXYZ–$1234567890.;!?:,&-ff fi fl ffi ffl 1/8 1/4 1/3 3/8 1/2 $12345/6789

Expert Italic *ABCDEFGHIJKLMNOPQRSTUVWXYZ–$1234567890.;!?:,&-ff fi fl ffi ffl 1/8 1/4 1/3 3/8 1/2 $12345/6789*

Expert Light Condensed ABCDEFGHIJKLMNOPQRSTUVWXYZ–$1234567890.;!?:,&-ff fi fl ffi ffl 1/8 1/4 1/3 3/8 1/2 $12345/67890¢ (abdeilmnorst) 5/8 2/3

Expert Light Condensed Italic *ABCDEFGHIJKLMNOPQRSTUVWXYZ–$1234567890.;!?:,&-ff fi fl ffi ffl 1/8 1/4 1/3 3/8 1/2 $12345/67890¢ (abdeilmnorst) 5/8 2/3*

Expert Condensed **ABCDEFGHIJKLMNOPQRSTUVWXYZ–$1234567890.;!?:,&-ff fi fl ffi ffl 1/8 1/4 1/3 3/8 1/2 $12345/67890¢ (abdeilmnorst)**

Expert Condensed Italic ***ABCDEFGHIJKLMNOPQRSTUVWXYZ–$1234567890.;!?:,&-ff fi fl ffi ffl 1/8 1/4 1/3 3/8 1/2 $12345/67890¢ (abeilmnorst)***

Light SCOSF ABCDEFGHIJKLMNOPQRSTUVWXYZABCDEFGHIJKLMNOPQRSTUVWXYZ–$1234567890(“.;‘!*?

Light Italic SCOSF *ABCDEFGHIJKLMNOPQRSTUVWXYZABCDEFGHIJKLMNOPQRSTUVWXYZ–$1234567890(“.;‘!*?*

Regular SCOSF **ABCDEFGHIJKLMNOPQRSTUVWXYZABCDEFGHIJKLMNOPQRSTUVWXYZ–$1234567890(**

Italic SCOSF ***ABCDEFGHIJKLMNOPQRSTUVWXYZABCDEFGHIJKLMNOPQRSTUVWXYZ–$1234567890(***

Light Condensed SCOSF ABCDEFGHIJKLMNOPQRSTUVWXYZABCDEFGHIJKLMNOPQRSTUVWXYZ–$1234567890(“.;‘!*?’:,”)&-ÄÖÜÄÖÜÅ

Light Condensed Italic SCOSF *ABCDEFGHIJKLMNOPQRSTUVWXYZABCDEFGHIJKLMNOPQRSTUVWXYZ–$1234567890(“.;‘!*?’:,”)&-ÄÖÜÄÖÜ*

Condensed SCOSF **ABCDEFGHIJKLMNOPQRSTUVWXYZABCDEFGHIJKLMNOPQRSTUVWXYZ–$1234567890(“.;‘!*?’:,”)&-ÄÖÜ**

Condensed Italic SCOSF abcdefghijklmnopqrstuvwxyzABCDEFGHIJKLMNOPQRSTUVWXYZ–$1234567890(“.;‘!*?’:,”)&-äö

Formata Outline
✥ *Berthold DisplaySet 1*
ADO AGA MAE abcdefghijklmnopqrstuvwxyz(“.;‘!*?’:,”)

▲24 $1234567890&fiflß-äöüåçèîñóæøœ

ABCDEFGHIJKLMNOPQRSTUVWXYZ

ÄÖÜÅÇÈÎÑÓÆØŒ»„«[·]‹i·¿›. . .

. . . .
✥ *Berthold DisplaySet 1*: AG Book Stencil, AG Old Face Shaded, Barmeno Extra Bold, Cosmos Extra Bold, Formata Outline.

Forte
Monotype Headliners 3
Carl Reissberger • 1962
MCL ADO AGA LIN MAE
▲16

abcdefghijklmnopqrstuvwxyz(".;'!*?':,")
$1234567890&fiflß-äöüåçèîñóæøœ
ABCDEFGHIJKLMNOPQRSTUVWXYZ
ÄÖÜÅÇÈÎÑÓÆØŒ»„«[§•†‡]‹¡·¿›...

FORUM TITLING
Frederic W. Goudy • 1912
RED LAN
▲24

ABCDEFGHIJKLMNOPQRSTUVWXYZ(".;'!*?':,")
$1234567890&-ÄÖÜÅÇÈÎÑÓÆØŒ
ABCDEFGHIJKLMNOPQRSTUVWXYZ
ÄÖÜÅÇÈÎÑÓÆØŒ»„«[¶§•†‡]‹¡·¿›...

Forum Titling ...

Light ABCDEFGHIJKLMNOPQRSTUVWXYZABCDEFGHIJK
• Medium ABCDEFGHIJKLMNOPQRSTUVWXYZABCDEFGHIJ
Bold **ABCDEFGHIJKLMNOPQRSTUVWXYZABCDEFGH**
Light OSF ABCDEFGHIJKLMNOPQRSTUVWXYZABC...$1234567890
Medium OSF ABCDEFGHIJKLMNOPQRSTUVWXYZABC...$123456789
Bold OSF **ABCDEFGHIJKLMNOPQRSTUVWXYZABC...$123456**

FOURNIER
Monotype Design Staff • 1925
... Pierre Simon Fournier, c.1740
MCL

abcdefghijklmnopqrstuvwxyz(".;'!*?':,")
$1234567890&fiflß-äöüåçèîñóæøœ
ABCDEFGHIJKLMNOPQRSTUVWXYZ
ÄÖÜÅÇÈÎÑÓÆØŒ»„«[¶§•†‡]‹¡·¿›...

Fournier ...

• Roman abcdefghijklmnopqrstuvwxyzABCDEFGHIJKLMNOPQRSTUVWXYZ–$1234567890(".;'!*?':,
Italic *abcdefghijklmnopqrstuvwxyzABCDEFGHIJKLMNOPQRSTUVWXYZ–$1234567890(".;'!*?':,")*
Roman Tall Capitals abcdefghijklmnopqrstuvwxyzABCDEFGHIJKLMNOPQRSTUVWXYZ–$1234567890(".;'!*?':,
Italic Tall Capitals *abcdefghijklmnopqrstuvwxyzABCDEFGHIJKLMNOPQRSTUVWXYZ–$1234567890(".;'!*?':*

Monotype Headliners 3: Braggadocio, Figaro, Forte, Klang.
Fournier ▶Fournier Ornaments

... Fournier

Alternates ct fb fh fj fk st w J J J Q Q $ £ *ct fb fh fj fk st z J J Q Q $ £*

Expert Roman ABCDEFGHIJKLMNOPQRSTUVWXYZ–$1234567890.;!?:,&-ff fi fl ffi ffl ⅛ ¼ ⅓ ⅜ ½ $12345⁄67890¢ (abdeilmnorst)

Expert Italic *$1234567890.;:,–ff fi fl ffi ffl ⅛ ¼ ⅓ ⅜ ½ $12345⁄67890¢ (abdeilmnorst) ⅝ ⅔ ¾ ⅞ ₵Rp*

A*I Fragment

Manfred Klein • 1994

ALP

a bcd ef gh ij k l mno pq r s t uvwxyz

(“.;‘!*?’:,”) $1234567890&fifl¢-

ä ö ü æ ø abcdefghijklmnopqrstuvwxyz

ä ö ü ... „“ $ @ ! ▷ 1234567890

A*I Frakt Konstruct

Manfred Klein • 1994

ALP

▲36

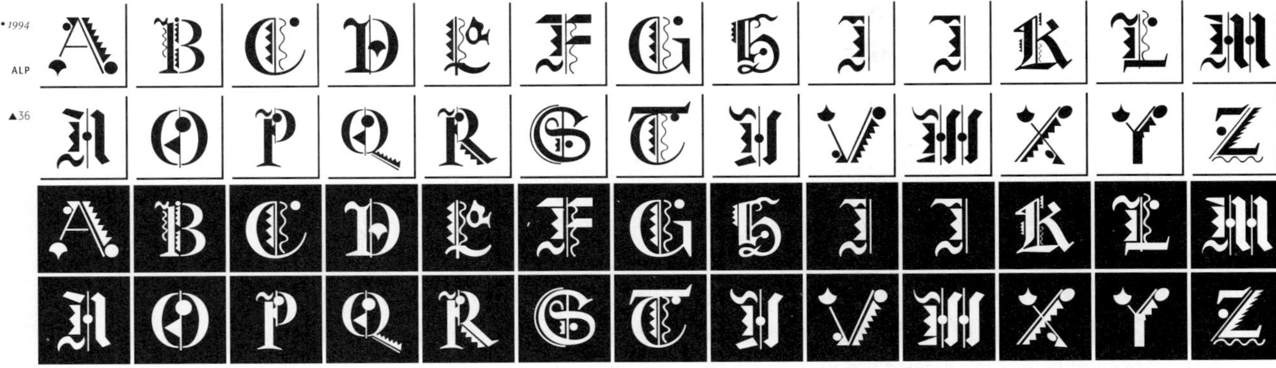

Frances Uncial

Michael Gills • 1995

LET

▲24

abcdefghijklmnopqrstuvwxyz

(“.;‘!*?’:,”) $1234567890

&-äöüåçèîÑóæøœ»„«[•]‹¡·¿›...

▷ ðhıkʀʏfjftŧt•ĿĿ Ŀo¢✠ ¶

Frankfurter

Bob Newman • 1970

LET LEF URW

▲30

ABCDEFGHIJKLMNOPQRSTUVWXYZ

(“.;‘!*?’:,”)$1234567890

&-ÄÖÜÅÇÈÎÑÓÆØŒ»„«[•]‹¡·¿›...

Frankfurter Highlight

LET LEF URW

▲30

ABCDEFGHIJKLMNOPQRSTUVWXYZ
(“.;‘!*?’:,”)$1234567890
&-ÄÖÜÅÇÈÎÑÓÆØŒ»„«[•]‹¡·¿›...

F

Frankfurter Inline

LET LEF TFC URW

▲30

ABCDEFGHIJKLMNOPQRSTUVWXYZ
(“.;‘!*?’:,”)$1234567890
&-ÄÖÜÅÇÈÎÑÓÆØŒ»„«[•]‹¡·¿›...

Frankfurter Medium

LET LEF URW

▲18

abcdefghijklmnopqrstuvwxyz(“.;‘!*?’:,”)
$1234567890&fifl ß-äöüåçèîñóæøœ
ABCDEFGHIJKLMNOPQRSTUVWXYZ
ÄÖÜÅÇÈÎÑÓÆØŒ»„«[•]‹¡·¿›...

FRANKLIN GOTHIC

Morris Fuller Benton • 1903

BIT ADO LEF LIN MAE URW

abcdefghijklmnopqrstuvwxyz(“.;‘!*?’:,”)
$1234567890&fifl ß-äöüåçèîñóæøœ
ABCDEFGHIJKLMNOPQRSTUVWXYZ
ÄÖÜÅÇÈÎÑÓÆØŒ»„«[¶§•†‡]‹¡·¿›...

Franklin Gothic ...

• Regular abcdefghijklmnopqrstuvwxyzABCDEFGHIJKLMNOPQRSTUVWXYZ–$12

Italic *abcdefghijklmnopqrstuvwxyzABCDEFGHIJKLMNOPQRSTUVWXYZ–$12345*

Condensed abcdefghijklmnopqrstuvwxyzABCDEFGHIJKLMNOPQRSTUVWXYZ–$1234567890(“.;‘!*?’

Extra Condensed abcdefghijklmnopqrstuvwxyzABCDEFGHIJKLMNOPQRSTUVWXYZ–$1234567890(“.;‘!*?’:,”)&fifl ß-äöüÄÖÜåçèÅÇÈîñóÎ

ITC FRANKLIN GOTHIC

Victor Caruso • 1980
... Morris Fuller Benton, 1903

URW ADO AGA BIT LEF FAM LIN MAE

abcdefghijklmnopqrstuvwxyz(“.;‘!*?’:,”)
$1234567890&fifl ß-äöüåçèîñóæøœ
ABCDEFGHIJKLMNOPQRSTUVWXYZ
ÄÖÜÅÇÈÎÑÓÆØŒ»„«[¶§•†‡]‹¡·¿›...

ITC Franklin Gothic ...

• Book abcdefghijklmnopqrstuvwxyzABCDEFGHIJKLMNOPQRSTUVWXYZ–$1234567890(“.;‘!

Book Italic *abcdefghijklmnopqrstuvwxyzABCDEFGHIJKLMNOPQRSTUVWXYZ–$1234567890(“.;‘*

. . . ITC Franklin Gothic

Medium abcdefghijklmnopqrstuvwxyzABCDEFGHIJKLMNOPQRSTUVWXYZ-$1234567890(".

Medium Italic *abcdefghijklmnopqrstuvwxyzABCDEFGHIJKLMNOPQRSTUVWXYZ-$1234567890(".;*

Demi **abcdefghijklmnopqrstuvwxyzABCDEFGHIJKLMNOPQRSTUVWXYZ-$1234567890(**

Demi Italic ***abcdefghijklmnopqrstuvwxyzABCDEFGHIJKLMNOPQRSTUVWXYZ-$1234567890(***

Heavy **abcdefghijklmnopqrstuvwxyzABCDEFGHIJKLMNOPQRSTUVWXYZ-$1234567**

Heavy Italic ***abcdefghijklmnopqrstuvwxyzABCDEFGHIJKLMNOPQRSTUVWXYZ-$12345678***

F

ITC FRANKLIN GOTHIC CONDENSED

David Berlow • 1991
. . . Victor Caruso, 1980
. . . Morris Fuller Benton, 1903
URW LEF

abcdefghijklmnopqrstuvwxyz(".;'!*?':,")
$1234567890&fiflß-äöüåçèîñóæøœ
ABCDEFGHIJKLMNOPQRSTUVWXYZ
ÄÖÜÅÇÈÎÑÓÆØŒ»„«[¶§•†‡]‹¡·¿›...

ITC Franklin Gothic Condensed . . .

• Book Condensed abcdefghijklmnopqrstuvwxyzABCDEFGHIJKLMNOPQRSTUVWXYZ-$1234567890(".;'!*?':,")&fiflß-ä

Book Condensed Italic *abcdefghijklmnopqrstuvwxyzABCDEFGHIJKLMNOPQRSTUVWXYZ-$1234567890(".;'!*?':,")&fiflß-ä*

Book Condensed SCOSF ABCDEFGHIJKLMNOPQRSTUVWXYZABCDEFGHIJKLMNOPQRSTUVWXYZ-$1234567890(".;'!*?':,")&-ÄÖÜÄ

Medium Condensed abcdefghijklmnopqrstuvwxyzABCDEFGHIJKLMNOPQRSTUVWXYZ-$1234567890(".;'!*?':,")&fiflß

Medium Condensed Italic *abcdefghijklmnopqrstuvwxyzABCDEFGHIJKLMNOPQRSTUVWXYZ-$1234567890(".;'!*?':,")&fiflß*

Medium Condensed SCOSF ABCDEFGHIJKLMNOPQRSTUVWXYZABCDEFGHIJKLMNOPQRSTUVWXYZ-$1234567890(".;'!*?':,")&-ÄÖÜ

Demi Condensed **abcdefghijklmnopqrstuvwxyzABCDEFGHIJKLMNOPQRSTUVWXYZ-$1234567890(".;'!*?':,")&**

Demi Condensed Italic ***abcdefghijklmnopqrstuvwxyzABCDEFGHIJKLMNOPQRSTUVWXYZ-$1234567890(".;'!*?':,")&fi***

ITC FRANKLIN GOTHIC COMPRESSED

David Berlow • 1991
. . . Victor Caruso, 1980
. . . Morris Fuller Benton, 1903
URW LEF
▲16

abcdefghijklmnopqrstuvwxyz(".;'!*?':,")
$1234567890&fiflß-äöüåçèîñóæøœ
ABCDEFGHIJKLMNOPQRSTUVWXYZ
ÄÖÜÅÇÈÎÑÓÆØŒ»„«[¶§•†‡]‹¡·¿›...

ITC Franklin Gothic Compressed . . .

• Book Compressed abcdefghijklmnopqrstuvwxyzABCDEFGHIJKLMNOPQRSTUVWXYZ-$1234567890(".;'!*?':,")&fiflß-äöü

Book Compressed Italic *abcdefghijklmnopqrstuvwxyzABCDEFGHIJKLMNOPQRSTUVWXYZ–$1234567890(".;'!*?':,")&fiflß-*

Demi Compressed **abcdefghijklmnopqrstuvwxyzABCDEFGHIJKLMNOPQRSTUVWXYZ-$1234567890(".;'!*?':,")&fifl**

Demi Compressed Italic ***abcdefghijklmnopqrstuvwxyzABCDEFGHIJKLMNOPQRSTUVWXYZ–$1234567890(".;'!*?':,")&***

ITC FRANKLIN GOTHIC EXTRA COMPRESSED

David Berlow • 1991
. . . Victor Caruso, 1980
. . . Morris Fuller Benton, 1903
URW LEF
▲18

abcdefghijklmnopqrstuvwxyz(".;'!*?':,")
$1234567890&fiflß-äöüåçèîñóæøœ
ABCDEFGHIJKLMNOPQRSTUVWXYZ
ÄÖÜÅÇÈÎÑÓÆØŒ»„«[¶§•†‡]‹¡·¿›...

ITC Franklin Gothic Extra Compressed . . .

• Book Extra Compressed abcdefghijklmnopqrstuvwxyzABCDEFGHIJKLMNOPQRSTUVWXYZ-$1234567890(".;'!*?':,")&fiflß-äöüÄÖÜåçèÅÇÈîñóÎÑ

. . . ITC Franklin Gothic
Extra Compressed
Demi Extra Compressed

abcdefghijklmnopqrstuvwxyzABCDEFGHIJKLMNOPQRSTUVWXYZ-$1234567890(".;'!*?':,")&fiflß-äöüÄÖÜåçèÅÇÈîñó

A*I FranklySpoken
Manfred Klein • 1994
ALP

abcdefghijklmnopqrstuvwxyz(".;' !*?' :,")
$1234567890&fiflß-äöüåçèîñóæøœ
ABCDEFGHIJKLMNOPQRSTUVWXYZ
ÄÖÜÅÇÈÎÑÓÆØŒ»„«[§•†‡]‹ ¡ · ¿› ...

FREAKSHOW
Todd Brei • 1993
T26
▲26

abcdefghijklmnopqrstuvwxyz(".;'!*?':,")$1234567890&fiflß-äöüåçèîñóæøœ
ABCDEFGHIJKLMNOPQRSTUVWXYZÄÖÜÅÇÈÎÑÓÆØŒ»„«[¶§·†‡]‹¡·¿›...

Freakshow . . .
• Scary
abcdefghijklmnopqrstuvwxyzABCDEFGHIJKLMNOPQRSTUVWXYZ-$1234

Real Scary
abcdefghijklmnopqrstuvwxyzABCDEFGHIJKLMNOPQRSTUVWXYZ-$12

FreeDom
[T-26] FontSet 2
Carlos Segura • 1993
T26

abcdefghijklmnopqrstuvwxyz(".;'!*?':,")
$1234567890&fiflß-äöüåçèîñóæøœ
ABCDEFGHIJKLMNOPQRSTUVWXYZ
ÄÖÜÅÇÈÎÑÓÆØŒ»„«[¶§·†‡]‹¡·¿›...

FreeBe Caps
[T-26] FontSet 2
Carlos Segura • 1993
T26
▲24

ABCDEFGHIJKLMNOPQRSTUVWXYZ
(".;'!*?':,")$1234567890&-[•†]¿

Freehand 521
Robert Hunter Middleton • 1934
BIT

abcdefghijklmnopqrstuvwxyz(".;'!?':,")*
$1234567890&fiflß-äöüåçèîñóæøœ
ABCDEFGHIJKLMNOPQRSTUVWXYZ
ÄÖÜÅÇÈÎÑÓÆØŒ»„«[§•†‡]‹¡·¿›...

Freehand 575
BIT
▲18

abcdefghijklmnopqrstuvwxyz(".;'!?':,")*
$1234567890&fiflß-äöüåçèîñóæøœ
ABCDEFGHIJKLMNOPQRSTUVWXYZ
ÄÖÜÅÇÈÎÑÓÆØŒ»„«[§•†‡]‹¡·¿›...

[T-26] FontSet 2: FreeDom & FreeBe Caps.

F

Freehand 591

BIT abcdefghijklmnopqrstuvwxyz(".;'!*?':,")
$1234567890&fiflß-äöüåçèîñóæøœ
ABCDEFGHIJKLMNOPQRSTUVWXYZ
ÄÖÜÅÇÈÎÑÓÆØŒ»„«[§•†‡]‹¡·¿›...

Freestyle Script
Adobe DisplaySet 1
Martin Wait • 1981
ADO AGA LET LIN MAE URW
▲16

abcdefghijklmnopqrstuvwxyz(".;'!*?':,")
$1234567890&fiflß-äöüåçèîñóæøœ
ABCDEFGHIJKLMNOPQRSTUVWXYZ
ÄÖÜÅÇÈÎÑÓÆØŒ»„«[•]¡·¿›...

A*I French XXX Condensed
A*I Wood Type
A*I Design Staff • 1990
ALP MTD
▲96

ABCDEFGHIJKLMNOPQRSTUVWXYZ(.,!*?:,)$1234567890
&-ABCDEFGHIJKLMNOPQRSTUVWXYZ[]

French Script
Agfa Scripts 2
William Schraubstädter • 1905
AGP MCL
▲16

abcdefghijklmnopqrstuvwxyz(".;'!*?':,")
$1234567890&ß-äöüåçèîñó
ABCDEFGHIJKLMNOPQRSTUVWXYZ
ÄÖÜÅÇÈÎÑÓ»«[•]‹›
▷I V X st nd rd th 1/4 1/3 1/2 3/4 D'c r. 'c's O'rs. s. &%

FRIZ QUADRATA
Ernst Friz & Victor Caruso • 1973
Thierry Puyfoulhoux • 1994
ITC ADO AGA BIT LEF FAM LIN MAE URW

abcdefghijklmnopqrstuvwxyz(".;'!*?':,")
$1234567890&fiflß-äöüåçèîñóæøœ
ABCDEFGHIJKLMNOPQRSTUVWXYZ
ÄÖÜÅÇÈÎÑÓÆØŒ»„«[¶§•†‡]‹¡·¿›...

Friz Quadrata ...

• Regular abcdefghijklmnopqrstuvwxyzABCDEFGHIJKLMNOPQRSTUVWXYZ-$12345

Italic *abcdefghijklmnopqrstuvwxyzABCDEFGHIJKLMNOPQRSTUVWXYZ-$123456789*

Regular SCOSF ABCDEFGHIJKLMNOPQRSTUVWXYZABCDEFGHIJKLMNOPQRSTUVWXYZ-$12345

Adobe DisplaySet 1: Aachen Bold, Freestyle Script, Revue, University Roman.
*A*I Wood Type*: A*I Antique Condensed, A*I Barrel, A*I Box Gothic, A*I French XXX Condensed, A*I Painter, A*I Tuscan Egyptian.
Agfa Scripts 2: Citadel, Flemish Script 2, Florentine Script 2, French Script, Mahogany Script, Old Fashion Script, Riviera Script.

... Friz Quadrata

Regular OSF abcdefghijklmnopqrstuvwxyzABCDEFGHIJKLMNOPQRSTUVWXYZ-$123456

Italic OSF *abcdefghijklmnopqrstuvwxyzABCDEFGHIJKLMNOPQRSTUVWXYZ-$1234567890*

Bold **abcdefghijklmnopqrstuvwxyzABCDEFGHIJKLMNOPQRSTUVWXYZ-$1234**

Bold Italic ***abcdefghijklmnopqrstuvwxyzABCDEFGHIJKLMNOPQRSTUVWXYZ-$123456***

Bold OSF **abcdefghijklmnopqrstuvwxyzABCDEFGHIJKLMNOPQRSTUVWXYZ-$12345**

Bold Italic OSF ***abcdefghijklmnopqrstuvwxyzABCDEFGHIJKLMNOPQRSTUVWXYZ-$1234567***

F

FRUTIGER

Adrian Frutiger • 1976 abcdefghijklmnopqrstuvwxyz(".;'!*?':,")

LIN ADO AGA MAE $1234567890&fiflß-äöüåçèîñóæøœ

ABCDEFGHIJKLMNOPQRSTUVWXYZ

ÄÖÜÅÇÈÎÑÓÆØŒ»„«[¶§•†‡]‹¡·¿›...

Frutiger 1 ...

45-Light abcdefghijklmnopqrstuvwxyzABCDEFGHIJKLMNOPQRSTUVWXYZ–$1234567890(".

46-Light Italic *abcdefghijklmnopqrstuvwxyzABCDEFGHIJKLMNOPQRSTUVWXYZ–$1234567890(".*

65-Bold **abcdefghijklmnopqrstuvwxyzABCDEFGHIJKLMNOPQRSTUVWXYZ–$123456**

66-Bold Italic ***abcdefghijklmnopqrstuvwxyzABCDEFGHIJKLMNOPQRSTUVWXYZ–$123456***

Frutiger 2 ...

• 55-Regular abcdefghijklmnopqrstuvwxyzABCDEFGHIJKLMNOPQRSTUVWXYZ–$1234567

56-Italic *abcdefghijklmnopqrstuvwxyzABCDEFGHIJKLMNOPQRSTUVWXYZ–$1234567*

75-Black **abcdefghijklmnopqrstuvwxyzABCDEFGHIJKLMNOPQRSTUVWXYZ–$12**

76-Black Italic ***abcdefghijklmnopqrstuvwxyzABCDEFGHIJKLMNOPQRSTUVWXYZ–$12***

95-Ultra Black **abcdefghijklmnopqrstuvwxyzABCDEFGHIJKLMNOPQRSTUVWXY**

FRUTIGER CONDENSED

LIN ADO AGA MAE abcdefghijklmnopqrstuvwxyz(".;'!*?':,")

$1234567890&fiflß-äöüåçèîñóæøœ

ABCDEFGHIJKLMNOPQRSTUVWXYZ

ÄÖÜÅÇÈÎÑÓÆØŒ»„«[¶§•†‡]‹¡·¿›...

Frutiger Condensed ...

47-Light Condensed abcdefghijklmnopqrstuvwxyzABCDEFGHIJKLMNOPQRSTUVWXYZ–$1234567890(".;'!*?':,")&fiflß

• 57-Condensed abcdefghijklmnopqrstuvwxyzABCDEFGHIJKLMNOPQRSTUVWXYZ–$1234567890(".;'!*?':,")&

67-Bold Condensed **abcdefghijklmnopqrstuvwxyzABCDEFGHIJKLMNOPQRSTUVWXYZ–$1234567890(".;'!***

77-Black Condensed **abcdefghijklmnopqrstuvwxyzABCDEFGHIJKLMNOPQRSTUVWXYZ–$1234567890("**

87-Extra Black Condensed **abcdefghijklmnopqrstuvwxyzABCDEFGHIJKLMNOPQRSTUVWXYZ–$123456789**

MN Fumo DropShadow
MTD
▲30

abcdefghijklmnopqrstuvwxyz
(".:'!°?':,")$1234567890
&fifllß-äöüåçèîñóæøœ
ABCDEFGHIJKLMNOPQRSTUVWXYZ
ÄÖÜÅÇÈÎÑÓÆØŒ»„«[•]‹¡¿›...

F

FUTURA

Paul Renner • 1928
ADO AGA BIT LEF FAM LIN MAE URW

abcdefghijklmnopqrstuvwxyz(".;'!*?':,")
$1234567890&fiflß-äöüåçèîñóæøœ
ABCDEFGHIJKLMNOPQRSTUVWXYZ
ÄÖÜÅÇÈÎÑÓÆØŒ»„«[¶§•†‡]‹¡·¿›...

Futura 1 ...

Light abcdefghijklmnopqrstuvwxyzABCDEFGHIJKLMNOPQRSTUVWXYZ–$1234567890("

Light Oblique *abcdefghijklmnopqrstuvwxyzABCDEFGHIJKLMNOPQRSTUVWXYZ–$1234567890("*

Book abcdefghijklmnopqrstuvwxyzABCDEFGHIJKLMNOPQRSTUVWXYZ–$123456789

Book Oblique *abcdefghijklmnopqrstuvwxyzABCDEFGHIJKLMNOPQRSTUVWXYZ–$123456789*

Bold **abcdefghijklmnopqrstuvwxyzABCDEFGHIJKLMNOPQRSTUVWXYZ–$**

Bold Oblique ***abcdefghijklmnopqrstuvwxyzABCDEFGHIJKLMNOPQRSTUVWXYZ–$***

Futura 2 ...

• Medium abcdefghijklmnopqrstuvwxyzABCDEFGHIJKLMNOPQRSTUVWXYZ–$1234567890(

Medium Oblique *abcdefghijklmnopqrstuvwxyzABCDEFGHIJKLMNOPQRSTUVWXYZ–$1234567890(*

Heavy **abcdefghijklmnopqrstuvwxyzABCDEFGHIJKLMNOPQRSTUVWXYZ–$1234567890**

Heavy Oblique ***abcdefghijklmnopqrstuvwxyzABCDEFGHIJKLMNOPQRSTUVWXYZ–$1234567890***

Extra Bold **abcdefghijklmnopqrstuvwxyzABCDEFGHIJKLMNOPQRSTUVWX**

Extra Bold Oblique ***abcdefghijklmnopqrstuvwxyzABCDEFGHIJKLMNOPQRSTUVWX***

FUTURA CONDENSED

Paul Renner • 1930
ADO AGA BIT LEF FAM LIN MAE URW
▲16

abcdefghijklmnopqrstuvwxyz(".;'!*?':,")
$1234567890&fiflß-äöüåçèîñóæøœ
ABCDEFGHIJKLMNOPQRSTUVWXYZ
ÄÖÜÅÇÈÎÑÓÆØŒ»„«[¶§•†‡]‹¡·¿›...

Futura Condensed ...

Light Condensed abcdefghijklmnopqrstuvwxyzABCDEFGHIJKLMNOPQRSTUVWXYZ–$1234567890(".;'!*?':,")&fiflß-äöüÄÖÜ

Light Condensed Oblique *abcdefghijklmnopqrstuvwxyzABCDEFGHIJKLMNOPQRSTUVWXYZ–$1234567890(".;'!&?':,")&fiflß-äöüÄÖ*

... Futura Condensed

• Medium Condensed abcdefghijklmnopqrstuvwxyzABCDEFGHIJKLMNOPQRSTUVWXYZ–$1234567890(".;'!*?':,")&fiflß-äö

Medium Condensed Oblique *abcdefghijklmnopqrstuvwxyzABCDEFGHIJKLMNOPQRSTUVWXYZ–$1234567890(".;'!*?':,")&fiflß-äö*

Bold Condensed **abcdefghijklmnopqrstuvwxyzABCDEFGHIJKLMNOPQRSTUVWXYZ–$1234567890(".;'**

Bold Condensed Oblique ***abcdefghijklmnopqrstuvwxyzABCDEFGHIJKLMNOPQRSTUVWXYZ–$1234567890(".;'***

Extra Bold Condensed **abcdefghijklmnopqrstuvwxyzABCDEFGHIJKLMNOPQRSTUVWXYZ–$12**

Extra Bold Condensed Oblique ***abcdefghijklmnopqrstuvwxyzABCDEFGHIJKLMNOPQRSTUVWXYZ–$12***

F

Futura Black

Paul Renner • 1929

BIT AGP MTD URW

▲30

abcdefghijklmnopqrstuvwxyz(".;'!*?':,")
$1234567890&fiflß-äöüåçèîñóæøœ
ABCDEFGHIJKLMNOPQRSTUVWXYZ
ÄÖÜÅÇÈÎÑÓÆØŒ»„«[§•†‡]‹¡·¿›...

Futura Stencil

Paul Renner • ....

IMA

▲24

ABCDEFGHIJKLMNOPQRSTUVWXYZ
(".;'!*?':,")$1234567890
&-ÄÖÜÅÇÈÎÑÓÆØŒ»„«[•]‹¡·¿›...

PL FUTURA MAXI

Agfa Typographer's Edition 2

Victor Caruso • 1960
... Paul Renner • 1928

AGP

abcdefghijklmnopqrstuvwxyz(".;'!*?':,")
$1234567890&ß-äöüåçèîñóæøœ
ABCDEFGHIJKLMNOPQRSTUVWXYZ
ÄÖÜÅÇÈÎÑÓÆØŒ»„«[•]‹¡·¿›...

PL Futura Maxi ...

• Book abcdefghijklmnopqrstuvwxyzABCDEFGHIJKLMNOPQRSTUVWXYZ–$1234

Bold **abcdefghijklmnopqrstuvwxyzABCDEFGHIJKLMNOPQRSTUVWXY**

Agfa Typographer's Edition 2: PL Barnum Block, PL Benguiat Frisky Bold, TC Broadway, PL Davison Zip Bold, PL Fiedler Gothic Bold, PL Futura Maxi Book & Bold, Neon Extra Condensed, Ritmo Bold, PL Trophy Oblique.

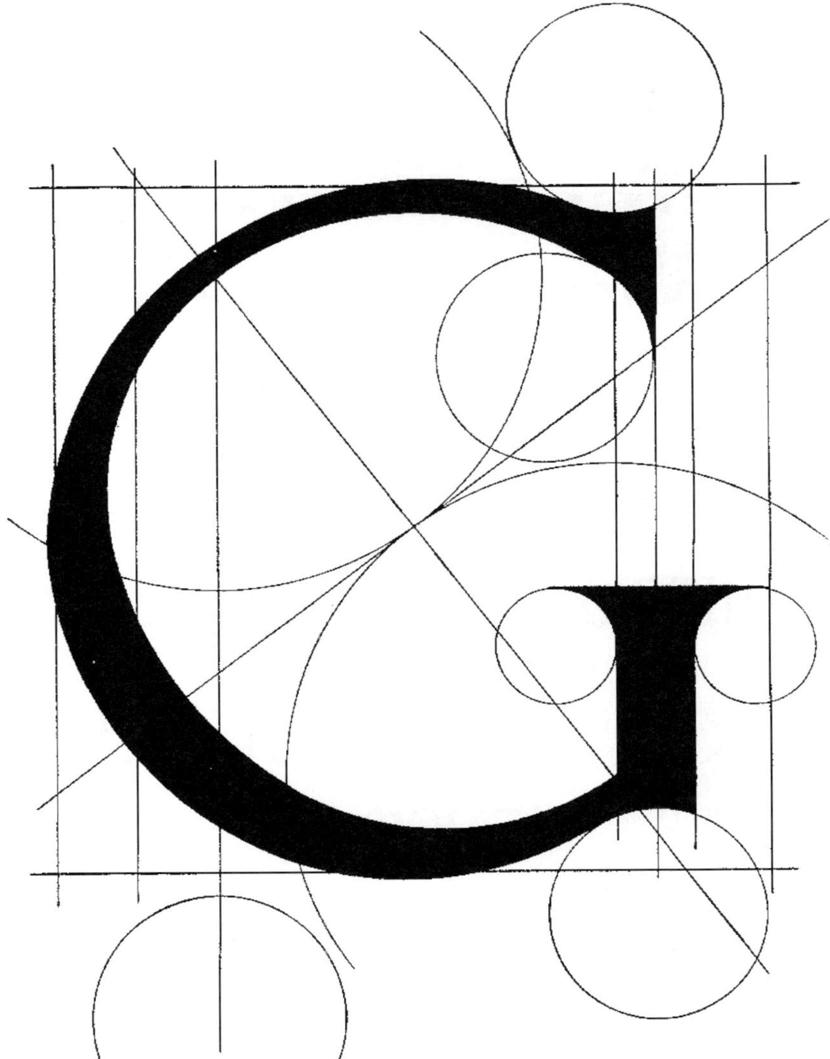

✍ Anonymous, c.1490

GADZOOKS

Todd Brei • 1993

T26

▲18

abcdefghijklmnopqrstuv
wxyz("".;'!*?':,"")$12345678
90fiflß-äöüåçèîñóæøœ
ABCDEFGHIJKLMNOPQRST
UVWXYZÄÖÜÅÇÈÎÑÓÆØŒ
»,,«[¶§•†‡]‹¡·¿›...

Gadzooks . . .

• Regular

abcdefghijklmnopqrstuv
wxyzABCDEFGHIJKLMNO

Sans

abcdefghijklmnopqrstuvwx
yzABCDEFGHIJKLMNOPQRST

Square

abcdefghijklmnopqrstuv
wxyzABCDEFGHIJKLMNOP

Galadriel

URW LEF

▲30

ABCDEFGHIJKLMNOPQRSTUVWXYZ
(".;'!*?':,")$1234567890
&-ÄÖÜÅÇÈÎÑÓÆØŒ»,,«[¶§ • †‡]‹¡·¿›...

MN Galba

MTD

▲30

ABCDEFGHIJKLMNOPQRSTUVWXYZ
(".;'!*?':,")$1234567890
&-ÄÖÜÅÇÈÎÑÓÆØŒ»,,«[•]‹¡¿›...

Gallia

Wadsworth A. Parker • 1927

IMA AGP

▲24

ABCDEFGHIJKLMNOPQRSTUV
WXYZ(".;'!*?':,")$1234567890
&-ÄÖÜÅÇÈÎÑÓÆØŒ»,,«[¶§•†]¡·¿...

ITC GALLIARD

Matthew Carter • 1978 abcdefghijklmnopqrstuvwxyz(“.;‘!*?’:,”)

BIT ADO AGA CAR LEF FRA LIN MAE $1234567890&fiflß-äöüåçèîñóæøœ

ABCDEFGHIJKLMNOPQRSTUVWXYZ

ÄÖÜÅÇÈÎÑÓÆØŒ»„«[¶§•†‡]‹¡·¿›...

ITC Galliard 1 ...

• Roman abcdefghijklmnopqrstuvwxyzABCDEFGHIJKLMNOPQRSTUVWXYZ–$123456

Italic *abcdefghijklmnopqrstuvwxyzABCDEFGHIJKLMNOPQRSTUVWXYZ–$1234567890*

Bold **abcdefghijklmnopqrstuvwxyzABCDEFGHIJKLMNOPQRSTUVWXYZ–$12**

Bold Italic ***abcdefghijklmnopqrstuvwxyzABCDEFGHIJKLMNOPQRSTUVWXYZ–$1234567***

ITC Galliard 2 ...

Black **abcdefghijklmnopqrstuvwxyzABCDEFGHIJKLMNOPQRSTUVWXYZ–$**

Black Italic ***abcdefghijklmnopqrstuvwxyzABCDEFGHIJKLMNOPQRSTUVWXYZ–$123***

Ultra **abcdefghijklmnopqrstuvwxyzABCDEFGHIJKLMNOPQRSTUVWXY**

Ultra Italic ***abcdefghijklmnopqrstuvwxyzABCDEFGHIJKLMNOPQRSTUVWXYZ–$***

ITC GALLIARD [CC]

Matthew Carter • 1978 abcdefghijklmnopqrstuvwxyz(“.;‘!*?’:,”)

CAR $1234567890&fiflß-äöüåçèîñóæøœ

ABCDEFGHIJKLMNOPQRSTUVWXYZ

ÄÖÜÅÇÈÎÑÓÆØŒ»„«[¶§•†‡]‹¡·¿›...

ITC Galliard CC ...

• Roman abcdefghijklmnopqrstuvwxyzABCDEFGHIJKLMNOPQRSTUVWXYZ–$123456

Italic *abcdefghijklmnopqrstuvwxyzABCDEFGHIJKLMNOPQRSTUVWXYZ–$1234567890*

Expert Roman ABCDEFGHIJKLMNOPQRSTUVWXYZ–$1234567890.;!?:,&-ff fi fl ffi ffl 1/8 1/4 1/3 3/8 1/2 $123

Expert Italic *$1234567890.;:,–ff fi fl ffi ffl 1/8 1/4 1/3 3/8 1/2 $12345/67890¢ (abdehilmnorstv) 5/8 2/3 3/4 7/8 ₡Rp 1/8 1/4 1/3 3/8*

Roman SCOSF ABCDEFGHIJKLMNOPQRSTUVWXYZABCDEFGHIJKLMNOPQRSTUVWXYZ–$123

Roman OSF abcdefghijklmnopqrstuvwxyzABCDEFGHIJKLMNOPQRSTUVWXYZ–$12345678

Italic OSF *abcdefghijklmnopqrstuvwxyzABCDEFGHIJKLMNOPQRSTUVWXYZ–$1234567890(“.;‘*

Roman Alternates a à ä å d e é è h m n r t t z & ct ct fj & st st Q Q R

Italic Alternates *a à ä å d e é è g k m n t v z & as ct fj fr ij is nt sp st st us Q*

Roman Fractions & Figures 1/8 1/6 1/5 1/4 1/3 3/8 2/5 1/2 3/5 5/8 2/3 3/4 4/5 5/6 7/8 ,.-1234567890/1234567890,.- 1234567890 -1234567890,. 123456789

Italic Fractions & Figures *1/8 1/4 1/3 3/8 1/2 5/8 2/3 3/4 7/8 ,.-1234567890/1234567890,.- -1234567890,. 1234567890*

ITC GAMMA

Jovica Veljovic • 1986 abcdefghijklmnopqrstuvwxyz(".;'!*?':,")

URW LEF $1234567890&fiflß-äöüåçèîñóæøœ

ABCDEFGHIJKLMNOPQRSTUVWXYZ

ÄÖÜÅÇÈÎÑÓÆØŒ»„«[¶§•†‡]‹¡·¿›...

ITC Gamma 1 ...

• Book abcdefghijklmnopqrstuvwxyzABCDEFGHIJKLMNOPQRSTUVWXYZ-$1234567890(".

Book Italic *abcdefghijklmnopqrstuvwxyzABCDEFGHIJKLMNOPQRSTUVWXYZ-$1234567890(".;'!**

Book SCOSF ABCDEFGHIJKLMNOPQRSTUVWXYZABCDEFGHIJKLMNOPQRSTUVWXYZ-$1234567890("

Bold **abcdefghijklmnopqrstuvwxyzABCDEFGHIJKLMNOPQRSTUVWXYZ-$1234567**

Bold Italic ***abcdefghijklmnopqrstuvwxyzABCDEFGHIJKLMNOPQRSTUVWXYZ-$123456789***

ITC Gamma 2 ...

Medium abcdefghijklmnopqrstuvwxyzABCDEFGHIJKLMNOPQRSTUVWXYZ-$123456789

Medium Italic *abcdefghijklmnopqrstuvwxyzABCDEFGHIJKLMNOPQRSTUVWXYZ-$1234567890("*

Medium SCOSF ABCDEFGHIJKLMNOPQRSTUVWXYZABCDEFGHIJKLMNOPQRSTUVWXYZ-$1234567890

Black **abcdefghijklmnopqrstuvwxyzABCDEFGHIJKLMNOPQRSTUVWXYZ-$12345**

Black Italic ***abcdefghijklmnopqrstuvwxyzABCDEFGHIJKLMNOPQRSTUVWXYZ-$1234567***

Gando

Matthew Carter & Hans-Jorg Hunziker • 1970 abcdefghijklmnopqrstuvwxyz(".;'!*?':,")

BIT $1234567890&fiflß-äöüåçèîñóæøœ

▲16 ABCDEFGHIJKLMNOPQRSTUVWXYZ

ÄÖÜÅÇÈÎÑÓÆØŒ»„«[§•†‡]‹¡·¿›...

GARAGE GOTHIC

Tobias Frere-Jones • 1992 abcdefghijklmnopqrstuvwxyz(".;'!*?':,")$1234567890&fiflß-äöüåçèîñóæøœ

FBU AGP MTD

▲30 ABCDEFGHIJKLMNOPQRSTUVWXYZÄÖÜÅÇÈÎÑÓÆØŒ»„«[¶§•†‡]‹¡·¿›... ▷¢

Garage Gothic ...

• Regular abcdefghijklmnopqrstuvwxyzABCDEFGHIJKLMNOPQRSTUVWXYZ–$1234567

Bold **abcdefghijklmnopqrstuvwxyzABCDEFGHIJKLMNOPQRSTUVWXY**

Black **abcdefghijklmnopqrstuvwxyzABCDEFGHIJKLMNOPQR**

G

STEMPEL GARAMOND

Stempel Design Staff • *1924* (*. . . Claude Garamont, c.1530*)
LIN ADO AGA MAE

abcdefghijklmnopqrstuvwxyz(“.;‘!*?’:,”)
$1234567890&fiflß-äöüåçèîñóæøœ
ABCDEFGHIJKLMNOPQRSTUVWXYZ
ÄÖÜÅÇÈÎÑÓÆØŒ»„«[¶§•†‡]‹¡·¿›…

Stempel Garamond . . .

• Roman abcdefghijklmnopqrstuvwxyzABCDEFGHIJKLMNOPQRSTUVWXYZ–$12345
Italic *abcdefghijklmnopqrstuvwxyzABCDEFGHIJKLMNOPQRSTUVWXYZ–$123456*
Bold **abcdefghijklmnopqrstuvwxyzABCDEFGHIJKLMNOPQRSTUVWXYZ–$1234**
Bold Italic ***abcdefghijklmnopqrstuvwxyzABCDEFGHIJKLMNOPQRSTUVWXYZ–$123456***

G

STEMPEL GARAMOND SCOSF

LIN ADO AGA MAE

ABCDEFGHIJKLMNOPQRSTUVWXYZ(“.;‘!*?’:,”)
$1234567890&-ÄÖÜÅÇÈÎÑÓÆØŒ
ABCDEFGHIJKLMNOPQRSTUVWXYZ
ÄÖÜÅÇÈÎÑÓÆØŒ»„«[¶§•†‡]‹¡·¿›…

Stempel Garamond SCOSF . . .

• Roman SCOSF ABCDEFGHIJKLMNOPQRSTUVWXYZABCDEFGHIJKLMNOPQRSTUVWXYZ–$123
Roman OSF abcdefghijklmnopqrstuvwxyzABCDEFGHIJKLMNOPQRSTUVWXYZ–$12345
Italic OSF *abcdefghijklmnopqrstuvwxyzABCDEFGHIJKLMNOPQRSTUVWXYZ–$123456*
Bold OSF **abcdefghijklmnopqrstuvwxyzABCDEFGHIJKLMNOPQRSTUVWXYZ–$1234**
Bold Italic OSF ***abcdefghijklmnopqrstuvwxyzABCDEFGHIJKLMNOPQRSTUVWXYZ–$123456***

GARAMOND 3

Linotype Design Staff • *1922* (*. . . Jean Jannon, c.1615*)
LIN ADO AGA MAE

abcdefghijklmnopqrstuvwxyz(“.;‘!*?’:,”)
$1234567890&fiflß-äöüåçèîñóæøœ
ABCDEFGHIJKLMNOPQRSTUVWXYZ
ÄÖÜÅÇÈÎÑÓÆØŒ»„«[¶§•†‡]‹¡·¿›…

Garamond 3 . . .

• Roman abcdefghijklmnopqrstuvwxyzABCDEFGHIJKLMNOPQRSTUVWXYZ–$1234567890(“.;‘
Italic *abcdefghijklmnopqrstuvwxyzABCDEFGHIJKLMNOPQRSTUVWXYZ–$1234567890(“.;‘!*?’:*
Bold **abcdefghijklmnopqrstuvwxyzABCDEFGHIJKLMNOPQRSTUVWXYZ–$12345678**
Bold Italic ***abcdefghijklmnopqrstuvwxyzABCDEFGHIJKLMNOPQRSTUVWXYZ–$1234567890(***

GARAMOND 3 SCOSF

LIN ADO AGA MAE

ABCDEFGHIJKLMNOPQRSTUVWXYZ(“.;‘!*?’:,”)
$1234567890&-ÄÖÜÅÇÈÎÑÓÆØŒ
ABCDEFGHIJKLMNOPQRSTUVWXYZ
ÄÖÜÅÇÈÎÑÓÆØŒ»„«[¶§•†‡]‹¡·¿›…

... Garamond 3 SCOSF ...

• Roman SCOSF ABCDEFGHIJKLMNOPQRSTUVWXYZABCDEFGHIJKLMNOPQRSTUVWXYZ–$123456789

Italic OSF *abcdefghijklmnopqrstuvwxyzABCDEFGHIJKLMNOPQRSTUVWXYZ–$1234567890(".;'!*?':*

Bold SCOSF **ABCDEFGHIJKLMNOPQRSTUVWXYZABCDEFGHIJKLMNOPQRSTUVWXYZ–$1234567**

Bold Italic SCOSF ***abcdefghijklmnopqrstuvwxyzABCDEFGHIJKLMNOPQRSTUVWXYZ–$1234567890(***

MONOTYPE GARAMOND

Monotype Design Staff • 1923 (... Jean Jannon, c.1615) abcdefghijklmnopqrstuvwxyz(".;'!*?':;")

MCL $1234567890&fiflß-äöüåçèîñóæøœ

ABCDEFGHIJKLMNOPQRSTUVWXYZ

ÄÖÜÅÇÈÎÑÓÆØŒ»„«[¶§•†‡]‹¡·¿›...

Monotype Garamond ...

• Roman abcdefghijklmnopqrstuvwxyzABCDEFGHIJKLMNOPQRSTUVWXYZ–$1234567890(".;'

Italic No. 156 *abcdefghijklmnopqrstuvwxyzABCDEFGHIJKLMNOPQRSTUVWXYZ–$1234567890(".;'!*?':;")*

Italic No. 174 *abcdefghijklmnopqrstuvwxyzABCDEFGHIJKLMNOPQRSTUVWXYZ–$1234567890(".;'!*?':;")*

Bold **abcdefghijklmnopqrstuvwxyzABCDEFGHIJKLMNOPQRSTUVWXYZ–$123456789**

Bold Italic ***abcdefghijklmnopqrstuvwxyzABCDEFGHIJKLMNOPQRSTUVWXYZ–$1234567890(".***

MONOTYPE GARAMOND EXPERT

MCL ABCDEFGHIJKLMNOPQRSTUVWXYZ.;!?:,

1234567890&ff fi fl ffi ffl–ÄÖÜÅÇÈÎÑÓÆØŒ

(abdeilmnorst) 1/8 1/4 1/3 3/8 1/2 5/8 2/3 3/4 7/8 $12345/67890¢ ₡Rp

Monotype Garamond Expert ...

• Expert Roman ABCDEFGHIJKLMNOPQRSTUVWXYZ–$1234567890.;!?:,&-ff fi fl ffi ffl 1/8 1/4 1/3 3/8 1/2 $12345/67890¢ (abdeil

Expert Italic *$1234567890.;:,–fffiflffiffl 1/8 1/4 1/3 3/8 1/2 $12345/67890¢ (abdeilmnorst) 5/8 2/3 3/4 7/8 ₡Rp*

Expert Bold **$1234567890.;:,–ff fi fl ffi ffl 1/8 1/4 1/3 3/8 1/2 $12345/67890¢ (abdeilmnorst) 5/8 2/3 3/4 7/8 ₡Rp**

Expert Bold Italic ***$1234567890.;:,–fffiflffiffl 1/8 1/4 1/3 3/8 1/2 $12345/67890¢ (abdeilmnorst) 5/8 2/3 3/4 7/8 ₡Rp***

BUREAU GARAMOND

Robert Hunter Middleton • 1929 (... Claude Garamont, c.1530) abcdefghijklmnopqrstuvwxyz(".;'!*?':;")

$1234567890&fiflß-äöüåçèîñóæøœ

FBU ABCDEFGHIJKLMNOPQRSTUVWXYZ

ÄÖÜÅÇÈÎÑÓÆØŒ»„«[¶§•†‡]‹¡·¿›...

▹ff ffi ffl ❊ ❈

Bureau Garamond ...

• Roman abcdefghijklmnopqrstuvwxyzABCDEFGHIJKLMNOPQRSTUVWXYZ–$1234567890(".;'!*?':;")

Italic *abcdefghijklmnopqrstuvwxyzABCDEFGHIJKLMNOPQRSTUVWXYZ–$1234567890(".;'!*?':;")&fiflß-ä*

SIMONCINI GARAMOND

Francesco Simoncini • 1958
(. . . Jean Jannon, c.1615)

ADO AGA LIN MAE

abcdefghijklmnopqrstuvwxyz(".;'!*?':,")
$1234567890&fifl ß-äöüåçèîñóæøœ
ABCDEFGHIJKLMNOPQRSTUVWXYZ
ÄÖÜÅÇÈÎÑÓÆØŒ»„«[¶§•†‡]‹¡·¿›...

Simoncini Garamond . . .

• Roman abcdefghijklmnopqrstuvwxyzABCDEFGHIJKLMNOPQRSTUVWXYZ–$123456789

Italic *abcdefghijklmnopqrstuvwxyzABCDEFGHIJKLMNOPQRSTUVWXYZ–$1234567890("*

Bold **abcdefghijklmnopqrstuvwxyzABCDEFGHIJKLMNOPQRSTUVWXYZ–$12345678**

G

BERTHOLD GARAMOND

Günther Gerard Lange • 1972
(. . .Claude Garamont, c.1530)

ADO AGA MAE

abcdefghijklmnopqrstuvwxyz(".;'!*?':,")
$1234567890&fifl ß-äöüåçèîñóæøœ
ABCDEFGHIJKLMNOPQRSTUVWXYZ
ÄÖÜÅÇÈÎÑÓÆØŒ»„«[¶§•†‡]‹¡·¿›...

Berthold Garamond . . .

• Roman abcdefghijklmnopqrstuvwxyzABCDEFGHIJKLMNOPQRSTUVWXYZ–$123456789

Italic *abcdefghijklmnopqrstuvwxyzABCDEFGHIJKLMNOPQRSTUVWXYZ–$1234567890(".*

Medium **abcdefghijklmnopqrstuvwxyzABCDEFGHIJKLMNOPQRSTUVWXYZ–$12345**

Medium Italic ***abcdefghijklmnopqrstuvwxyzABCDEFGHIJKLMNOPQRSTUVWXYZ–$123456789***

Bold **abcdefghijklmnopqrstuvwxyzABCDEFGHIJKLMNOPQRSTUVWXYZ–$1234567**

Condensed abcdefghijklmnopqrstuvwxyzABCDEFGHIJKLMNOPQRSTUVWXYZ–$1234567890(".;'!*?':,")&fifl ß-ä

Medium Condensed **abcdefghijklmnopqrstuvwxyzABCDEFGHIJKLMNOPQRSTUVWXYZ–$1234567890(".;'!*?':,")&**

BERTHOLD GARAMOND
EXPERT & SCOSF

ADO AGA MAE

ABCDEFGHIJKLMNOPQRSTUVWXYZ.;!?:,
1234567890&ff fi fl ffi ffl –ÄÖÜÅÇÈÎÑÓÆØŒ
(abdeilmnorst) 1/8 1/4 1/3 3/8 1/2 5/8 2/3 3/4 7/8 $12345/67890¢ ₡Rp

Berthold Garamond
Expert & SCOSF . . .

• Expert Roman ABCDEFGHIJKLMNOPQRSTUVWXYZ–$1234567890.;!?:,&-ff fi fl ffi ffl 1/8 1/4 1/3 3/8 1/2 $12345/67890¢ (ab

Expert Italic *$1234567890.;:,–ff fi fl ffi ffl 1/8 1/4 1/3 3/8 1/2 $12345/67890¢ (abdeilmnorst) 5/8 2/3 3/4 7/8 ₡Rp*

Expert Medium **ABCDEFGHIJKLMNOPQRSTUVWXYZ–$1234567890.;!?:,&-ff fi fl ffi ffl 1/8 1/4 1/3 3/8 1/2 $12345/67890¢**

Expert Medium Italic ***$1234567890.;:,–ff fi fl ffi ffl 1/8 1/4 1/3 3/8 1/2 $12345/67890¢ (abdeilmnorst) 5/8 2/3 3/4 7/8 ₡Rp***

Expert Bold **$1234567890.;:,–ff fi fl ffi ffl 1/8 1/4 1/3 3/8 1/2 $12345/67890¢ (abdeilmnorst) 5/8 2/3 3/4 7/8 ₡Rp**

Expert Condensed ABCDEFGHIJKLMNOPQRSTUVWXYZ–$1234567890.;!?:,&-ff fi fl ffi ffl 1/8 1/4 1/3 3/8 1/2 $12345/67890¢ (abdeilmnorst) 5/8 2/3 3/4

Expert Medium Condensed **$1234567890.;:,–ff fi fl ffi ffl 1/8 1/4 1/3 3/8 1/2 $12345/67890¢ (abdeilmnorst) 5/8 2/3 3/4 7/8 ₡Rp**

Roman SCOSF ABCDEFGHIJKLMNOPQRSTUVWXYZABCDEFGHIJKLMNOPQRSTUVWXYZ–$123456789

Italic OSF *abcdefghijklmnopqrstuvwxyzABCDEFGHIJKLMNOPQRSTUVWXYZ–$1234567890(".;'!*

Medium SCOSF **ABCDEFGHIJKLMNOPQRSTUVWXYZABCDEFGHIJKLMNOPQRSTUVWXYZ–$12345**

... Berthold Garamond Expert & SCOSF

Medium Italic OSF *abcdefghijklmnopqrstuvwxyzABCDEFGHIJKLMNOPQRSTUVWXYZ–$1234567890(*

Bold OSF **abcdefghijklmnopqrstuvwxyzABCDEFGHIJKLMNOPQRSTUVWXYZ–$123456789**

Condensed SCOSF ABCDEFGHIJKLMNOPQRSTUVWXYZABCDEFGHIJKLMNOPQRSTUVWXYZ–$1234567890(".;'!*?':,")&-ÄÖÜ

Medium Condensed OSF abcdefghijklmnopqrstuvwxyzABCDEFGHIJKLMNOPQRSTUVWXYZ–$1234567890(".;'!*?':,")&fi

Italic Swash Caps OSF *abcdefghijklmnopqrstuvwxyzABCDEFGHIJKLMNOPQRSTUVWXYZ–$12*

ITC GARAMOND

Tony Stan • 1975 abcdefghijklmnopqrstuvwxyz(".;'!*?':,")

ADO AGA BIT LEF FAM LIN MAE URW $1234567890&fiflß-äöüåçèîñóæøœ

ABCDEFGHIJKLMNOPQRSTUVWXYZ

ÄÖÜÅÇÈÎÑÓÆØŒ»„«[¶§•†‡]‹¡·¿›...

ITC Garamond 1 ...

Light abcdefghijklmnopqrstuvwxyzABCDEFGHIJKLMNOPQRSTUVWXYZ–$1234567890(

Light Italic *abcdefghijklmnopqrstuvwxyzABCDEFGHIJKLMNOPQRSTUVWXYZ–$1234567890("*

Bold **abcdefghijklmnopqrstuvwxyzABCDEFGHIJKLMNOPQRSTUVWXYZ–$12345**

Bold Italic ***abcdefghijklmnopqrstuvwxyzABCDEFGHIJKLMNOPQRSTUVWXYZ–$12345***

ITC Garamond 2 ...

• Book abcdefghijklmnopqrstuvwxyzABCDEFGHIJKLMNOPQRSTUVWXYZ-$1234567890(

Book Italic *abcdefghijklmnopqrstuvwxyzABCDEFGHIJKLMNOPQRSTUVWXYZ-$123456789*

Ultra **abcdefghijklmnopqrstuvwxyzABCDEFGHIJKLMNOPQRSTUVWXYZ-$**

Ultra Italic ***abcdefghijklmnopqrstuvwxyzABCDEFGHIJKLMNOPQRSTUVWXYZ-***

ITC GARAMOND CONDENSED

Tony Stan • 1977 abcdefghijklmnopqrstuvwxyz(".;'!*?':,")

ADO AGA BIT LEF FAM LIN MAE URW $1234567890&fiflß-äöüåçèîñóæøœ

▲16 ABCDEFGHIJKLMNOPQRSTUVWXYZ

ÄÖÜÅÇÈÎÑÓÆØŒ»„«[¶§•†‡]‹¡·¿›...

ITC Garamond Condensed ...

Light Condensed abcdefghijklmnopqrstuvwxyzABCDEFGHIJKLMNOPQRSTUVWXYZ–$1234567890(".;'!*?':,")&fiflß

Light Condensed Italic *abcdefghijklmnopqrstuvwxyzABCDEFGHIJKLMNOPQRSTUVWXYZ–$1234567890(".;'!*?':,")*

• Book Condensed abcdefghijklmnopqrstuvwxyzABCDEFGHIJKLMNOPQRSTUVWXYZ–$1234567890(".;'!*?':,"

Book Condensed Italic *abcdefghijklmnopqrstuvwxyzABCDEFGHIJKLMNOPQRSTUVWXYZ–$1234567890(".;'!*?':*

Bold Condensed **abcdefghijklmnopqrstuvwxyzABCDEFGHIJKLMNOPQRSTUVWXYZ–$1234567890**

Bold Condensed Italic ***abcdefghijklmnopqrstuvwxyzABCDEFGHIJKLMNOPQRSTUVWXYZ–$12345678***

Ultra Condensed **abcdefghijklmnopqrstuvwxyzABCDEFGHIJKLMNOPQRSTUVWXYZ–$12345678**

Ultra Condensed Italic ***abcdefghijklmnopqrstuvwxyzABCDEFGHIJKLMNOPQRSTUVWXYZ–$123456***

G

ITC GARAMOND HANDTOOLED

Ed Benguiat • 1994 (Tony Stan, 1975)
ITC URW
▲24

abcdefghijklmnopqrstuvwxyz(".;'!*?':,")
$1234567890&fiflß-äöüåçèîñóæøœ
ABCDEFGHIJKLMNOPQRSTUVWXYZ
ÄÖÜÅÇÈÎÑÓÆØŒ»„«[¶§•†‡]‹¡·¿›...

ITC Garamond Handtooled ...

• Regular abcdefghijklmnopqrstuvwxyzABCDEFGH
Italic *abcdefghijklmnopqrstuvwxyzABCDEFGH*
Regular OSF abcdefghijklmnopqrstuvwxyzABC...$1234
Italic OSF *abcdefghijklmnopqrstuvwxyzABC...$1234*

ITC GARAMOND NARROW

Bitstream Design Staff • 1991 (Tony Stan, 1977)
BIT
▲16

abcdefghijklmnopqrstuvwxyz(".;'!*?':,")
$1234567890&fiflß-äöüåçèîñóæøœ
ABCDEFGHIJKLMNOPQRSTUVWXYZ
ÄÖÜÅÇÈÎÑÓÆØŒ»„«[¶§•†‡]‹¡·¿›...

ITC Garamond Narrow ...

Light Narrow abcdefghijklmnopqrstuvwxyzABCDEFGHIJKLMNOPQRSTUVWXYZ–$1234567890(".;'!*?':,")
Light Italic Narrow *abcdefghijklmnopqrstuvwxyzABCDEFGHIJKLMNOPQRSTUVWXYZ–$1234567890(".;'!*?':,")&*
• Book Narrow abcdefghijklmnopqrstuvwxyzABCDEFGHIJKLMNOPQRSTUVWXYZ–$1234567890(".;'!*?'
Book Italic Narrow *abcdefghijklmnopqrstuvwxyzABCDEFGHIJKLMNOPQRSTUVWXYZ–$1234567890(".;'!*?':*
Bold Narrow **abcdefghijklmnopqrstuvwxyzABCDEFGHIJKLMNOPQRSTUVWXYZ–$1234567890(**
Bold Italic Narrow ***abcdefghijklmnopqrstuvwxyzABCDEFGHIJKLMNOPQRSTUVWXYZ–$1234567890(***

ADOBE GARAMOND

Robert Slimbach • 1989 (...Claude Garamont, c.1530)
ADO AGA LIN MAE

abcdefghijklmnopqrstuvwxyz(".;'!*?':,")
$1234567890&fiflß-äöüåçèîñóæøœ
ABCDEFGHIJKLMNOPQRSTUVWXYZ
ÄÖÜÅÇÈÎÑÓÆØŒ»„«[¶§•†‡]‹¡·¿›...

Adobe Garamond ...

• Roman abcdefghijklmnopqrstuvwxyzABCDEFGHIJKLMNOPQRSTUVWXYZ–$1234567890(".;

. . . Adobe Garamond

Italic *abcdefghijklmnopqrstuvwxyzABCDEFGHIJKLMNOPQRSTUVWXYZ–$1234567890(".;'!*?':*

Semibold **abcdefghijklmnopqrstuvwxyzABCDEFGHIJKLMNOPQRSTUVWXYZ–$1234567890(**

Semibold Italic ***abcdefghijklmnopqrstuvwxyzABCDEFGHIJKLMNOPQRSTUVWXYZ–$1234567890(".;'***

Bold **abcdefghijklmnopqrstuvwxyzABCDEFGHIJKLMNOPQRSTUVWXYZ–$1234567890**

Bold Italic ***abcdefghijklmnopqrstuvwxyzABCDEFGHIJKLMNOPQRSTUVWXYZ–$1234567890(***

ADOBE GARAMOND
EXPERT & SCOSF

ADO AGA LIN MAE ABCDEFGHIJKLMNOPQRSTUVWXYZ.;!?:,
1234567890&ﬀﬁﬂﬃﬄ–ÄÖÜÅÇÈÎÑÓÆØŒ
(abdeilmnorst) 1/8 1/4 1/3 3/8 1/2 5/8 2/3 3/4 7/8 $12345/67890¢ ₡Rp

Adobe Garamond
Expert & SCOSF . . .

• Expert Roman ABCDEFGHIJKLMNOPQRSTUVWXYZ–$1234567890.;!?:,&-ﬀﬁﬂﬃﬄ 1/8 1/4 1/3 3/8 1/2 $12345/67890¢ (abd

Expert Italic *$1234567890.;:,–ﬀﬁﬂﬃﬄ 1/8 1/4 1/3 3/8 1/2 $12345/67890¢ (abdeilmnorst) 5/8 2/3 3/4 7/8 ₡Rp*

Expert Semibold **ABCDEFGHIJKLMNOPQRSTUVWXYZ–$1234567890.;!?:,&-ﬀﬁﬂﬃﬄ 1/8 1/4 1/3 3/8 1/2 $12345/67890¢**

Expert Semibold Italic ***$1234567890.;:,–ﬀﬁﬂﬃﬄ 1/8 1/4 1/3 3/8 1/2 $12345/67890¢ (abdeilmnorst) 5/8 2/3 3/4 7/8 ₡Rp***

Expert Bold **$1234567890.;:,–ﬀﬁﬂﬃﬄ 1/8 1/4 1/3 3/8 1/2 $12345/67890¢ (abdeilmnorst) 5/8 2/3 3/4 7/8 ₡Rp**

Expert Bold Italic ***$1234567890.;:,–ﬀﬁﬂﬃﬄ 1/8 1/4 1/3 3/8 1/2 $12345/67890¢ (abdeilmnorst) 5/8 2/3 3/4 7/8 ₡Rp***

Roman SCOSF ABCDEFGHIJKLMNOPQRSTUVWXYZABCDEFGHIJKLMNOPQRSTUVWXYZ–$1234567890(

Italic OSF *abcdefghijklmnopqrstuvwxyzABCDEFGHIJKLMNOPQRSTUVWXYZ–$1234567890(".;'!*?':,")*

Semibold SCOSF **ABCDEFGHIJKLMNOPQRSTUVWXYZABCDEFGHIJKLMNOPQRSTUVWXYZ–$123456789**

Semibold Italic OSF ***abcdefghijklmnopqrstuvwxyzABCDEFGHIJKLMNOPQRSTUVWXYZ–$1234567890(".;'!****

Bold OSF **abcdefghijklmnopqrstuvwxyzABCDEFGHIJKLMNOPQRSTUVWXYZ–$1234567890(**

Bold Italic OSF ***abcdefghijklmnopqrstuvwxyzABCDEFGHIJKLMNOPQRSTUVWXYZ–$1234567890(".***

Roman Alternate a e n r t t z & Q

Italic Alternate & Swash *v & & & ABCDEFGHIJKLMNOPQRSTUVWXYZ*

Roman Titling
▲30 ABCDEFGHIJKLMNOPQRSTUVWXY

GARBAGE

Michael Polydoris • 1993 abcdefghijklmnopqrstuvwxyz(";!*?':,")$1234567890

T26
▲30 & -ABCDEFGHIJKLMNOPQRSTUVWXYZ [·]

Garbage . . .

• Normal abcdefghijklmnopqrstuvwxyzABCDEFGHIJKLMN

Italic *abcdefghijklmnopqrstuvwxyzABCDEFGHIJKLMNOPQRSTUV*

GARTH GRAPHIC

✍ Constance Blanchard & Renee Le Winter • 1979 . . John Matt, c.1965

AGP ADO AGA LIN MAE

abcdefghijklmnopqrstuvwxyz(".;'!*?':,")
$1234567890&fifl ß-äöüåçèîñóæøœ
ABCDEFGHIJKLMNOPQRSTUVWXYZ
ÄÖÜÅÇÈÎÑÓÆØŒ»„«[¶§•†‡]‹¡·¿›...

Garth Graphic ...

• Roman abcdefghijklmnopqrstuvwxyzABCDEFGHIJKLMNOPQRSTUVWXYZ-$12345
Italic *abcdefghijklmnopqrstuvwxyzABCDEFGHIJKLMNOPQRSTUVWXYZ-$123456789*
Bold **abcdefghijklmnopqrstuvwxyzABCDEFGHIJKLMNOPQRSTUVWXYZ-**
Bold Italic ***abcdefghijklmnopqrstuvwxyzABCDEFGHIJKLMNOPQRSTUVWXYZ-$123***
Extra Bold **abcdefghijklmnopqrstuvwxyzABCDEFGHIJKLMNOPQRSTUVWXYZ**
Black **abcdefghijklmnopqrstuvwxyzABCDEFGHIJKLMNOPQRSTUVWXY**
Condensed abcdefghijklmnopqrstuvwxyzABCDEFGHIJKLMNOPQRSTUVWXYZ-$1234567890(".;'!*?':,")&fi
Bold Condensed **abcdefghijklmnopqrstuvwxyzABCDEFGHIJKLMNOPQRSTUVWXYZ-$1234567890(".;'!*?':**

GARTH GRAPHIC PREMIER

AGP ABCDEFGHIJKLMNOPQRSTUVWXYZ.;!?:,
1234567890&ff fi fl ffi ffl -ÄÖÜÅÇÈÎÑÓÆØŒ
(abdeilmnorst) 1/8 1/4 1/3 3/8 1/2 5/8 2/3 3/4 7/8 $12345/67890¢ ₡ Rp

Garth Graphic Premier ...

• Premier Roman ABCDEFGHIJKLMNOPQRSTUVWXYZ-$1234567890.;!?:,&-ff fi fl ffi ffl 1/8 1/4 1/3 3/8 1/2 $12345/678
Premier Italic *$1234567890.;:,-ff fi fl ffi ffl 1/8 1/4 1/3 3/8 1/2 $12345/67890¢ (abdeilmnorst) 5/8 2/3 3/4 7/8 ₡ Rp*
Premier Bold **$1234567890.;:,-ff fi fl ffi ffl 1/8 1/4 1/3 3/8 1/2 $12345/67890¢ (abdeilmnorst) 5/8 2/3 3/4 7/8 ₡ Rp**
Premier Bold Italic ***$1234567890.;:,-ff fi fl ffi ffl 1/8 1/4 1/3 3/8 1/2 $12345/67890¢ (abdeilmnorst) 5/8 2/3 3/4 7/8 ₡ Rp***
Premier Extra Bold **$1234567890.;:,-ff fi fl ffi ffl 1/8 1/4 1/3 3/8 1/2 $12345/67890¢ (abdeilmnorst) 5/8 2/3 3/4**
Premier Black **$1234567890.;:,-ff fi fl ffi ffl 1/8 1/4 1/3 3/8 1/2 $12345/67890¢ (abdeilmnorst) 5/8 2/3**
Premier Condensed $1234567890.;:,-ff fi fl ffi ffl 1/8 1/4 1/3 3/8 1/2 $12345/67890¢ (abdeilmnorst) 5/8 2/3 3/4 7/8 ₡ Rp
Premier Bold Condensed **$1234567890.;:,-ff fi fl ffi ffl 1/8 1/4 1/3 3/8 1/2 $12345/67890¢ (abdeilmnorst) 5/8 2/3 3/4 7/8 ₡ Rp**

GEOMETRIC 415

✍ William Addison Dwiggins • 1929

BIT

abcdefghijklmnopqrstuvwxyz(".;'!*?':,")
$1234567890&fifl ß-äöüåçèîñóæøœ
ABCDEFGHIJKLMNOPQRSTUVWXYZ
ÄÖÜÅÇÈÎÑÓÆØŒ»„«[¶§•†‡]‹¡·¿›...

Geometric 415 ...

Lite abcdefghijklmnopqrstuvwxyzABCDEFGHIJKLMNOPQRSTUVWXYZ–$1234567890
Lite Italic *abcdefghijklmnopqrstuvwxyzABCDEFGHIJKLMNOPQRSTUVWXYZ–$1234567890(*
• Medium **abcdefghijklmnopqrstuvwxyzABCDEFGHIJKLMNOPQRSTUVWXYZ–$123456789**
Medium Italic ***abcdefghijklmnopqrstuvwxyzABCDEFGHIJKLMNOPQRSTUVWXYZ–$123456789***

... Geometric 415

Black abcdefghijklmnopqrstuvwxyzABCDEFGHIJKLMNOPQRSTUVWXYZ–$12345678

Black Italic *abcdefghijklmnopqrstuvwxyzABCDEFGHIJKLMNOPQRSTUVWXYZ–$12345678*

GILL SANS

Eric Gill • 1928 abcdefghijklmnopqrstuvwxyz(“.;‘!*?’:,”)

MCL ADO AGA FAM LIN MAE $1234567890&fiflß-äöüåçèîñóæøœ

ABCDEFGHIJKLMNOPQRSTUVWXYZ

ÄÖÜÅÇÈÎÑÓÆØŒ»,„«[¶§•†‡]‹¡·¿›...

G

Gill Sans 1 ...

Light abcdefghijklmnopqrstuvwxyzABCDEFGHIJKLMNOPQRSTUVWXYZ–$1234567890(“.;‘!*?’

Light Italic *abcdefghijklmnopqrstuvwxyzABCDEFGHIJKLMNOPQRSTUVWXYZ–$1234567890(“.;‘!*?’:,”)&fi*

• Regular abcdefghijklmnopqrstuvwxyzABCDEFGHIJKLMNOPQRSTUVWXYZ–$1234567890(“.;‘

Italic *abcdefghijklmnopqrstuvwxyzABCDEFGHIJKLMNOPQRSTUVWXYZ–$1234567890(“.;‘!*?’:,”)&*

Bold **abcdefghijklmnopqrstuvwxyzABCDEFGHIJKLMNOPQRSTUVWXYZ–$123**

Bold Italic ***abcdefghijklmnopqrstuvwxyzABCDEFGHIJKLMNOPQRSTUVWXYZ–$123456789***

Gill Sans 2 ...

▲16 Extra Bold **abcdefghijklmnopqrstuvwxyzABCDEFGHIJKLMNOPQRST**

Ultra Bold **abcdefghijklmnopqrstuvwxyzABCDEFGHIJKLMNO**

Condensed abcdefghijklmnopqrstuvwxyzABCDEFGHIJKLMNOPQRSTUVWXYZ–$1234567890(“.;‘!*?’:,”)&fiflß-äöüÄÖÜåçèÅÇÈÎ

Bold Condensed **abcdefghijklmnopqrstuvwxyzABCDEFGHIJKLMNOPQRSTUVWXYZ–$123456**

Ultra Bold Condensed **abcdefghijklmnopqrstuvwxyzABCDEFGHIJKLMNOPQRSTUVWXYZ–$1234**

Gill Sans 3 ...

Book abcdefghijklmnopqrstuvwxyzABCDEFGHIJKLMNOPQRSTUVWXYZ–$1234567890(“.;‘!

Book Italic *abcdefghijklmnopqrstuvwxyzABCDEFGHIJKLMNOPQRSTUVWXYZ–$1234567890(“.;‘!*?’:,”)*

Heavy **abcdefghijklmnopqrstuvwxyzABCDEFGHIJKLMNOPQRSTUVWXYZ–**

Heavy Italic ***abcdefghijklmnopqrstuvwxyzABCDEFGHIJKLMNOPQRSTUVWXYZ–$1234***

GILL SANS DISPLAY

MCL ADO AGA MAE abcdefghijklmnopqrstuvwxyz(“.;‘!*?’:,”)$1234567890&fiflß-äöüåçèîñóæøœ

ABCDEFGHIJKLMNOPQRSTUVWXYZÄÖÜÅÇÈÎÑÓÆØŒ»,„«[¶§•†‡]‹¡·¿›...

Gill Sans Display 1 ...

Light Shadowed ▲24 abcdefghijklmnopqrstuvwxyzABCDEFGHIJK

Shadow ▲30 ABCDEFGHIJKLMNOPQRSTUVWXY

• Bold Extra Condensed ▲30 abcdefghijklmnopqrstuvwxyzABCDEFGHIJKLMNOPQRSTUVWXYZ–$123456

Gill Sans Display 2 . . .

▲18

Display Bold abcdefghijklmnopqrstuvwxyzABCDEFGHIJKLMNOPQRSTUV

Display Extra Bold abcdefghijklmnopqrstuvwxyzABCDEFGHIJKLMNOPQ

Display Bold Condensed abcdefghijklmnopqrstuvwxyzABCDEFGHIJKLMNOPQRSTUVWXYZ–$12

GILL SANS ALTERNATE

(alternate figure 1)

Eric Gill • 1928 abcdefghijklmnopqrstuvwxyz(“.;‘!*?’:,”)

MCL $1234567890&ﬁﬂß-äöüåçèîñóæøœ

ABCDEFGHIJKLMNOPQRSTUVWXYZ

ÄÖÜÅÇÈÎÑÓÆØŒ»„«[¶§•†‡]‹¡·¿›…

Gill Sans Alternate 1 . . .

Light abcdefghijklmnopqrstuvwxyzABCDEFGHIJKLMNOPQRSTUVWXYZ–$1234567890(“.;‘!*?’

Light Italic *abcdefghijklmnopqrstuvwxyzABCDEFGHIJKLMNOPQRSTUVWXYZ–$1234567890(“.;‘!*?’:,”)&ﬁ*

• Regular abcdefghijklmnopqrstuvwxyzABCDEFGHIJKLMNOPQRSTUVWXYZ–$1234567890(“.;‘

Italic *abcdefghijklmnopqrstuvwxyzABCDEFGHIJKLMNOPQRSTUVWXYZ–$1234567890(“.;‘!*?’:,”)&*

Bold **abcdefghijklmnopqrstuvwxyzABCDEFGHIJKLMNOPQRSTUVWXYZ–$123**

Bold Italic ***abcdefghijklmnopqrstuvwxyzABCDEFGHIJKLMNOPQRSTUVWXYZ–$123456789***

Gill Sans Alternate 3 . . .

Book abcdefghijklmnopqrstuvwxyzABCDEFGHIJKLMNOPQRSTUVWXYZ–$1234567890(“.;‘!

Book Italic *abcdefghijklmnopqrstuvwxyzABCDEFGHIJKLMNOPQRSTUVWXYZ–$1234567890(“.;‘!*?’:,”)*

Heavy **abcdefghijklmnopqrstuvwxyzABCDEFGHIJKLMNOPQRSTUVWX…$1**

Heavy Italic ***abcdefghijklmnopqrstuvwxyzABCDEFGHIJKLMNOPQRSTUVWXYZ–$1234***

Gill Kayo Condensed

Eric Gill • 1928 **abcdefghijklmnopqrstuvwxyz(“.;‘!*?’:,”)**

LET **$1234567890&ﬁﬂß-äöüåçèîñóæøœ**

▲30

ABCDEFGHIJKLMNOPQRSTUVWXYZ

ÄÖÜÅÇÈÎÑÓÆØŒ»„«[•]‹¡·¿›…

GILLIES GOTHIC

William S. Gillies • 1935 *abcdefghijklmnopqrstuvwxyz(“.;‘!*?’:,”)*

URW AGP LEF LET MTD *$1234567890&ﬁﬂß-äöüåçèîñóæøœ*

ABCDEFGHIJKLMNOPQRSTUVWXYZ

ÄÖÜÅÇÈÎÑÓÆØŒ»„«[¶§•†‡]‹¡·¿›…

Gillies Gothic . . .

Light *abcdefghijklmnopqrstuvwxyzABCDEFGHIJKLMNOPQRSTUVWXYZ–$123456789*

... Gillies Gothic

• Bold abcdefghijklmnopqrstuvwxyzABCDEFGHIJKLMNOPQRSTUVWXYZ–$12
Extra Bold abcdefghijklmnopqrstuvwxyzABCDEFGHIJKLMNOPQRSTUVWXYZ–$12
Shaded abcdefghijklmnopqrstuvwxyzABCDEFGHIJKLMNOPQRSTUVWXYZ–

ITC GIOVANNI

Robert Slimbach • 1989 abcdefghijklmnopqrstuvwxyz(“.;‘!*?’:,”)
ADO AGA AGP LEF LIN MAE URW $1234567890&fiflß-äöüåçèîñóæøœ
ABCDEFGHIJKLMNOPQRSTUVWXYZ
ÄÖÜÅÇÈÎÑÓÆØŒ»„«[¶§•†‡]‹¡·¿›...

G

ITC Giovanni ...

• Book abcdefghijklmnopqrstuvwxyzABCDEFGHIJKLMNOPQRSTUVWXYZ–$123456789
Book Italic *abcdefghijklmnopqrstuvwxyzABCDEFGHIJKLMNOPQRSTUVWXYZ–$1234567890(“.;*
Bold **abcdefghijklmnopqrstuvwxyzABCDEFGHIJKLMNOPQRSTUVWXYZ–$1234567**
Bold Italic ***abcdefghijklmnopqrstuvwxyzABCDEFGHIJKLMNOPQRSTUVWXYZ–$1234567890(***
Black **abcdefghijklmnopqrstuvwxyzABCDEFGHIJKLMNOPQRSTUVWXYZ–$123456**
Black Italic ***abcdefghijklmnopqrstuvwxyzABCDEFGHIJKLMNOPQRSTUVWXYZ–$123456789***

GIZA 1

David Berlow • 1994 **abcdefghijklmnopqrstuvwxyz(“.;‘!*?’:,”)**
FBU **$1234567890&fiflß-äöüåçèîñóæøœ**
▲16 **ABCDEFGHIJKLMNOPQRSTUVWXYZ**
ÄÖÜÅÇÈÎÑÓÆØŒ»„«[¶§•†‡]‹¡·¿›... ▷ **ff ffi ffl**

Giza 1 ...

15- **abcdefghijklmnopqrstuvwxyzABCDEFGHIJKLMNOPQR**
35- **abcdefghijklmnopqrstuvwxyzABCDEFGHIJKLMNOPQR**
• 55- **abcdefghijklmnopqrstuvwxyzABCDEFGHIJKLMNOPQR**
75- **abcdefghijklmnopqrstuvwxyzABCDEFGHIJKLMNOPQR**
95- ▲18 **abcdefghijklmnopqrstuvwxyzABCDEFGHIJKLMN**

GIZA 2

FBU **abcdefghijklmnopqrstuvwxyz(“.;‘!*?’:,”)**
▲16 **$1234567890&fiflß-äöüåçèîñóæøœ**
ABCDEFGHIJKLMNOPQRSTUVWXYZ
ÄÖÜÅÇÈÎÑÓÆØŒ»„«[¶§•†‡]‹¡·¿›... ▷ **ff ffi ffl**

Giza 2 ...

11- ▲18 **abcdefghijklmnopqrstuvwxyzABCDEFGHIJKLMNOPQRSTUVWXYZ–$1234567890(“.;‘!*?’**
31- ▲18 **abcdefghijklmnopqrstuvwxyzABCDEFGHIJKLMNOPQRSTUVWXYZ–$12345678**
91- ▲18 **abcdefghijklmnopqrstuvwxyzABCDEFGHIJKLMNOPQRSTUVWXYZ–$1**

... Giza 2

13- abcdefghijklmnopqrstuvwxyzABCDEFGHIJKLMNOPQRSTUVWXYZ–$12
33- abcdefghijklmnopqrstuvwxyzABCDEFGHIJKLMNOPQRSTUVWXYZ–$
• 53- abcdefghijklmnopqrstuvwxyzABCDEFGHIJKLMNOPQRSTUVWXYZ
73- abcdefghijklmnopqrstuvwxyzABCDEFGHIJKLMNOPQRSTUVWXY
93- ▲18 abcdefghijklmnopqrstuvwxyzABCDEFGHIJKLMNOPQRST

GIZA 3

FBU abcdefghijklmnopqrstuvwxyz(".;'!*?':,")
▲16 $1234567890&ﬁﬂß-äöüåçèîñóæøœ
ABCDEFGHIJKLMNOPQRSTUVWXYZ
ÄÖÜÅÇÈÎÑÓÆØŒ»„«[¶§•†‡]‹¡·¿›... ▷ ﬀ ﬃ ﬄ

G

Giza 3 ...

• 57- abcdefghijklmnopqrstuvwxyzABCDEFGHIJKLMNO
77- abcdefghijklmnopqrstuvwxyzABCDEFGHIJKLMNO
79- abcdefghijklmnopqrstuvwxyzABCDEFGHIJKL

GLYPHA

✍ *Adrian Frutiger • 1979* abcdefghijklmnopqrstuvwxyz(".;'!*?':,")
LIN ADO AGA MAE $1234567890&ﬁﬂß-äöüåçèîñóæøœ
ABCDEFGHIJKLMNOPQRSTUVWXYZ
ÄÖÜÅÇÈÎÑÓÆØŒ»„«[¶§▪†‡]‹¡·¿›...

Glypha 1 ...

• 55-Regular abcdefghijklmnopqrstuvwxyzABCDEFGHIJKLMNOPQRSTUVWXYZ–$1234
55-Oblique *abcdefghijklmnopqrstuvwxyzABCDEFGHIJKLMNOPQRSTUVWXYZ–$1234*
65-Bold **abcdefghijklmnopqrstuvwxyzABCDEFGHIJKLMNOPQRSTUVWXYZ–$123**
65-Bold Oblique ***abcdefghijklmnopqrstuvwxyzABCDEFGHIJKLMNOPQRSTUVWXYZ–$123***

Glypha 2 ...

35-Thin abcdefghijklmnopqrstuvwxyzABCDEFGHIJKLMNOPQRSTUVWXYZ–$1234567890(".;'
35-Thin Oblique *abcdefghijklmnopqrstuvwxyzABCDEFGHIJKLMNOPQRSTUVWXYZ–$1234567890(".;'*
45-Light abcdefghijklmnopqrstuvwxyzABCDEFGHIJKLMNOPQRSTUVWXYZ–$1234567890(
45-Light Oblique *abcdefghijklmnopqrstuvwxyzABCDEFGHIJKLMNOPQRSTUVWXYZ–$1234567890(*
75-Black **abcdefghijklmnopqrstuvwxyzABCDEFGHIJKLMNOPQRSTUVWXYZ–$**
75-Black Oblique ***abcdefghijklmnopqrstuvwxyzABCDEFGHIJKLMNOPQRSTUVWXYZ–$***

G

GLYPHIC SERIES

R. Schlatter • 1972

IMA

▲18

ABCDEFGHIJKLMNOPQRSTUVWXYZ
(".;'!*?':,")$1234567890
&fiß-äöüåçèîñóæøœ»„«[¶§•†]¡·¿...

Glyphic Series ...

• Regular ABCDEFGHIJKLMNOPQRSTUVWXYZ-$123456789

Italic ABCDEFGHIJKLMNOPQRSTUVWXYZ-$123456789

Outline ABCDEFGHIJKLMNOPQRSTUVWXYZ-$123456789

Italic Outline ABCDEFGHIJKLMNOPQRSTUVWXYZ-$123456789

ITC GOLDEN TYPE

Englemann, Jorgensen, Newton • 1989 ... William Morris & Edward Prince, 1890 (Nicolas Jenson, c.1470)

URW LEF

abcdefghijklmnopqrstuvwxyz(".;'!*?':,")
$1234567890&fiflß-äöüåçèîñóæøœ
ABCDEFGHIJKLMNOPQRSTUVWXYZ
ÄÖÜÅÇÈÎÑÓÆØŒ»„«[¶§•†‡]‹¡·¿›...

ITC Golden Type ...

• Original abcdefghijklmnopqrstuvwxyzABCDEFGHIJKLMNOPQRSTUVWXYZ-$123456789

Original SCOSF ABCDEFGHIJKLMNOPQRSTUVWXYZABCDEFGHIJKLMNOPQRSTUVWXYZ-$12345678

Bold abcdefghijklmnopqrstuvwxyzABCDEFGHIJKLMNOPQRSTUVWXYZ-$123456789

Bold SCOSF ABCDEFGHIJKLMNOPQRSTUVWXYZABCDEFGHIJKLMNOPQRSTUVWXYZ-$1234567

Black abcdefghijklmnopqrstuvwxyzABCDEFGHIJKLMNOPQRSTUVWXYZ-$123456

ITC Gorilla

Tom Carnase & Ronne Bonder • 1970

BIT

▲16

abcdefghijklmnopqrstuvwxyz(".;'!*?':,")
$1234567890&fiflß-äöüåçèîñóæøœ
ABCDEFGHIJKLMNOPQRSTUVWXYZ
ÄÖÜÅÇÈÎÑÓÆØŒ»„«[§•†‡]‹¡·¿›...

SACKERS GOTHIC

✣ Agfa Engravers 2

AGP

ABCDEFGHIJKLMNOPQRSTUVWXYZ(".;'!*?':,")
$1234567890&-ÄÖÜÅÇÈÎÑÓ
ABCDEFGHIJKLMNOPQRSTUVWXYZ
ÄÖÜÅÇÈÎÑÓ»«[·]‹›
▷I V X ST ND RD TH ¼ ⅓ ½ ¾ D'C R. 'C 'S O' RS. S. & %

Sackers Gothic ...

Light ABCDEFGHIJKLMNOPQRSTUVWXYZABCDEFGHIJKLMNOPQRST

• Medium ABCDEFGHIJKLMNOPQRSTUVWXYZABCDEFGHIJKLMNOPQRST

Heavy ABCDEFGHIJKLMNOPQRSTUVWXYZABCDEFGHIJKLMNOPQRST

✣ *Agfa Engravers 2*: Sackers Antique Roman Open & Solid, Sackers Light Classic Roman, Sackers English Script, Sackers Gothic Light, Medium & Heavy, Sackers Italian Script, Sackers Roman Light & Heavy, Sackers Square Gothic.

G

GOTHIC BLOND

Todd Brei • 1993 abcdefghijklmnopqrstuvwxyz(“.;‘!*?’:,”)
T26 $1234567890&fifl ß-äöüåçèîñóœøœ
▲16 ABCDEFGHIJKLMNOPQRSTUVWXYZ
ÄÖÜÅÇÈÎÑÓÆØŒ»„«[¶§•†‡]‹¡•¿›…

Gothic Blond …

• Slim abcdefghijklmnopqrstuvwxyzABCDEFGHIJKLMNOPQRSTUVWXYZ-$1234567890(“.;‘!
Husky abcdefghijklmnopqrstuvwxyzABCDEFGHIJKLMNOPQRSTUVWXYZ-$1234567890(“.;‘!

Gothic 13
Linotype DisplaySet 3
LIN ADO AGA BIT MAE abcdefghijklmnopqrstuvwxyz(“.;‘!*?’:,”)
▲16 $1234567890&fifl ß-äöüåçèîñóæøœ
ABCDEFGHIJKLMNOPQRSTUVWXYZ
ÄÖÜÅÇÈÎÑÓÆØŒ»„«[¶§•†‡]‹¡·¿›…

GOUDY

Frederic W. Goudy • 1915 abcdefghijklmnopqrstuvwxyz(“.;‘!*?’:,”)
ADO AGA AGP BIT FAM FRA LAN LIN MAE URW $1234567890&fifl ß-äöüåçèîñóæøœ
ABCDEFGHIJKLMNOPQRSTUVWXYZ
ÄÖÜÅÇÈÎÑÓÆØŒ»„«[¶§•†‡]‹¡·¿›…

Goudy 1 …

• Old Style Roman abcdefghijklmnopqrstuvwxyzABCDEFGHIJKLMNOPQRSTUVWXYZ–$1234567890(
Old Style Italic *abcdefghijklmnopqrstuvwxyzABCDEFGHIJKLMNOPQRSTUVWXYZ–$1234567890(“.;‘*
Bold **abcdefghijklmnopqrstuvwxyzABCDEFGHIJKLMNOPQRSTUVWXYZ–$1234567**
Bold Italic ***abcdefghijklmnopqrstuvwxyzABCDEFGHIJKLMNOPQRSTUVWXYZ–$12345678***

Goudy 2 …

Extra Bold **abcdefghijklmnopqrstuvwxyzABCDEFGHIJKLMNOPQRSTUVWXYZ–$1234**
Heavyface **abcdefghijklmnopqrstuvwxyzABCDEFGHIJKLMNOPQRSTU**
Heavyface Italic ***abcdefghijklmnopqrstuvwxyzABCDEFGHIJKLMNOPQRST***

GOUDY SCOSF

ADO AGA LAN LIN MAE ABCDEFGHIJKLMNOPQRSTUVWXYZ(“.;‘!*?’:,”)
$1234567890&-ÄÖÜÅÇÈÎÑÓÆØŒ
ABCDEFGHIJKLMNOPQRSTUVWXYZ
ÄÖÜÅÇÈÎÑÓÆØŒ»„«[¶§•†‡]‹¡·¿›…

Goudy SCOSF …

• Old Style Roman SCOSF ABCDEFGHIJKLMNOPQRSTUVWXYZABCDEFGHIJKLMNOPQRSTUVWXYZ–$12345678
Old Style Italic OSF *abcdefghijklmnopqrstuvwxyzABCDEFGHIJKLMNOPQRSTUVWXYZ–$1234567890(“.;‘*
Bold OSF **abcdefghijklmnopqrstuvwxyzABCDEFGHIJKLMNOPQRSTUVWXYZ–$12345678**

Linotype DisplaySet 3: Gothic 13, Tempo Heavy Condensed & Heavy Condensed Italic.

... Goudy SCOSF

Bold Italic OSF *abcdefghijklmnopqrstuvwxyzABCDEFGHIJKLMNOPQRSTUVWXYZ–$12345678*

Goudy Handtooled

Morris Fuller Benton • 1922 (Frederic W. Goudy)

BIT LEF FAM FRA URW

▲24

abcdefghijklmnopqrstuvwxyz(“.;‘!*?’:,”)
$1234567890&fiflß-äöüåçèîñóæøœ
ABCDEFGHIJKLMNOPQRSTUVWX
YZÄÖÜÅÇÈÎÑÓÆØŒ»„«[§•†‡]‹¡·¿›

Goudy Cloister Initials
(26 Encapsulated PostScript Files)

Fredric W. Goudy • 1918

LAN

▲≈66

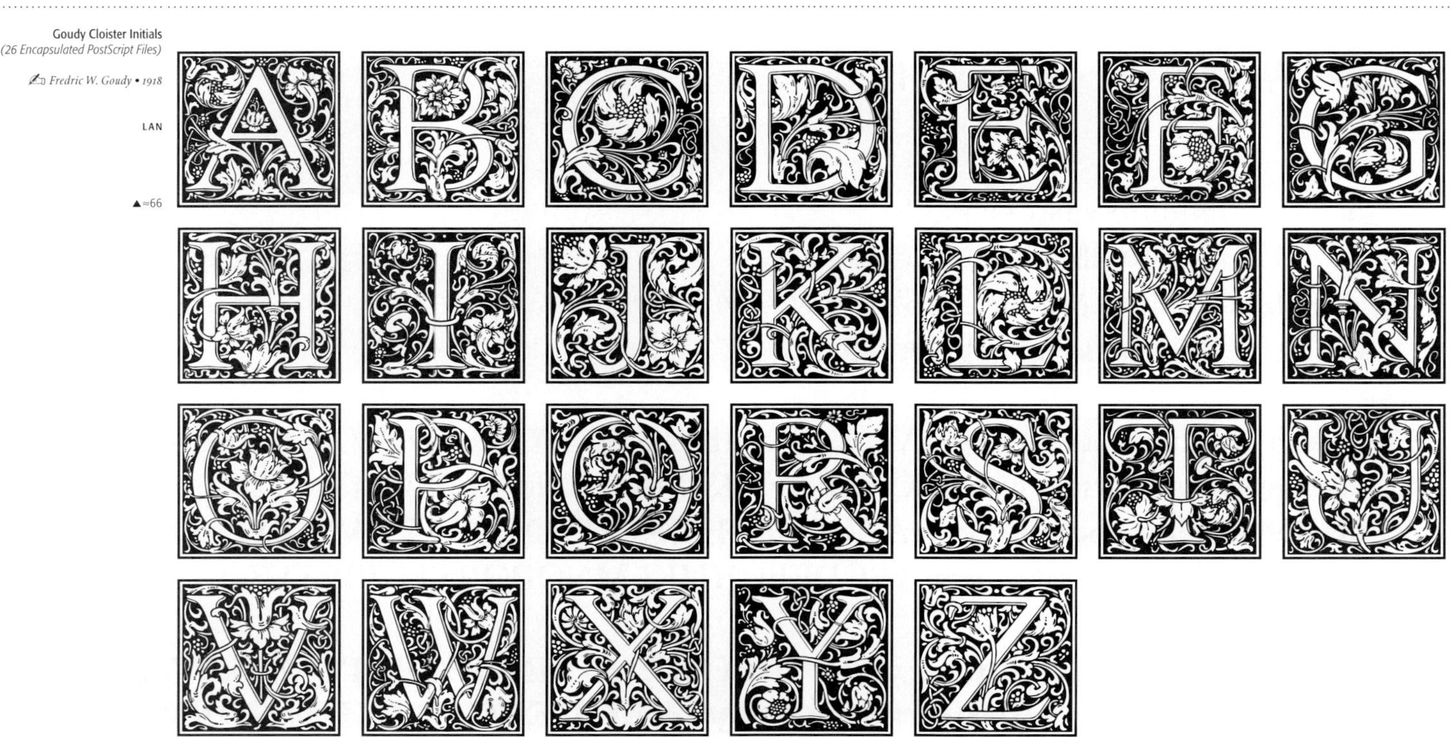

MONOTYPE GOUDY MODERN
Monotype TextSet 1

Frederic W. Goudy • 1918

MCL ADO AGA LIN MAE

abcdefghijklmnopqrstuvwxyz(“.;‘!*?’:,”)
$1234567890&fiflß-äöüåçèîñóæøœ
ABCDEFGHIJKLMNOPQRSTUVWXYZ
ÄÖÜÅÇÈÎÑÓÆØŒ»„«[¶§•†‡]‹¡·¿›...

Monotype Goudy Modern ...

• Roman abcdefghijklmnopqrstuvwxyzABCDEFGHIJKLMNOPQRSTUVWXYZ–$1234567890(“.;‘!*?

Italic *abcdefghijklmnopqrstuvwxyzABCDEFGHIJKLMNOPQRSTUVWXYZ–$1234567890(“.*

...
Monotype TextSet 1: Monotype Goudy Modern Roman & Italic, Monotype Scotch Roman Regular & Italic.

MONOTYPE GOUDY TEXT & LOMBARDIC CAPITALS

Frederic W. Goudy • 1927-29 abcdefghijklmnopqrstuvwxyz(".;'!*?':;")

MCL ADO AGA LIN MAE $1234567890&fiflß-äöüåçèîñóæøœ

ABCDEFGHIJKLMNOPQRSTUVWXYZ

ÄÖÜÅÇÈÎÑÓÆØŒ»„«[¶§•†‡]‹¡·¿›... ▷ ch ck ff ft ll ſ s ſi ſſ ß tz—äöüÄÖÜ

Monotype Goudy Text & Lombardic Capitals ...

• Goudy Text abcdefghijklmnopqrstuvwxyzABCDEFGHIJKLMNOPQRSTUVWXYZ

Goudy Text with Lombardic Capitals abcdefghijklmnopqrst...ABCDEFGHIJKLMNOPQRSTUVWXYZ

Alternates ff fi fl ffi ffl ı ſh ſl ct st B G J T

G

GOUDY 38

Frederic W. Goudy • 1905 abcdefghijklmnopqrstuvwxyz(".;'!*?':;")

RED $1234567890&fiflß-äöüåçèîñóæøœ

ABCDEFGHIJKLMNOPQRSTUVWXYZ

ÄÖÜÅÇÈÎÑÓÆØŒ»„«[¶§•†‡]‹¡·¿›...

Goudy 38 One ...

Light abcdefghijklmnopqrstuvwxyzABCDEFGHIJKLMNOPQRSTUVWXYZ–$1234567890(".;

Light Italic *abcdefghijklmnopqrstuvwxyzABCDEFGHIJKLMNOPQRSTUVWXYZ–$1234567890(".;'!**

Medium abcdefghijklmnopqrstuvwxyzABCDEFGHIJKLMNOPQRSTUVWXYZ–$1234567890

Extra Bold **abcdefghijklmnopqrstuvwxyzABCDEFGHIJKLMNOPQRSTUVWXYZ–$1234567**

Goudy 38 Two ...

• Book abcdefghijklmnopqrstuvwxyzABCDEFGHIJKLMNOPQRSTUVWXYZ–$1234567890("

Book Italic *abcdefghijklmnopqrstuvwxyzABCDEFGHIJKLMNOPQRSTUVWXYZ–$1234567890(".;'!*

Bold **abcdefghijklmnopqrstuvwxyzABCDEFGHIJKLMNOPQRSTUVWXYZ–$123456789**

GOUDY THIRTY

Frederic W. Goudy • 1943 abcdefghijklmnopqrstuvwxyz(".;'!*?':;")

LAN $1234567890&fiflß-äöüåçèîñóæøœ

ABCDEFGHIJKLMNOPQRSTUVWXYZ

ÄÖÜÅÇÈÎÑÓÆØŒ»„«[¶§•†]‹¡¿›... ▷ ct ff ffi ffl st

Goudy Thirty ...

• Regular abcdefghijklmnopqrstuvwxyzABCDEFGHIJKLMNOPQRSTUVWXYZ–$12345678

Alternate abcdefghijklmnopqrstuvwxyzABCDEFGHIJKLMNOPQRSTUVWXYZ–$1234567

G

ITC GOUDY SANS

ITC Design Staff • 1986
. . . Frederic W. Goudy, 1929
AGP BIT LEF URW

abcdefghijklmnopqrstuvwxyz(“.;‘!*?’:,”)
$1234567890&fifl ß-äöüåçèîñóæøœ
ABCDEFGHIJKLMNOPQRSTUVWXYZ
ÄÖÜÅÇÈÎÑÓÆØŒ»„«[¶§•†‡]‹¡·¿›...

ITC Goudy Sans . . .

• Book abcdefghijklmnopqrstuvwxyzABCDEFGHIJKLMNOPQRSTUVWXYZ–$1234567890(“.;‘!*?’:,”
Book Italic *abcdefghijklmnopqrstuvwxyzABCDEFGHIJKLMNOPQRSTUVWXYZ–$1234567890(“.;‘!*?’:,”*
Medium abcdefghijklmnopqrstuvwxyzABCDEFGHIJKLMNOPQRSTUVWXYZ–$1234567890(“.;‘!
Medium Italic *abcdefghijklmnopqrstuvwxyzABCDEFGHIJKLMNOPQRSTUVWXYZ–$1234567890(“.;‘!*?*
Bold **abcdefghijklmnopqrstuvwxyzABCDEFGHIJKLMNOPQRSTUVWXYZ–$123456**
Bold Italic ***abcdefghijklmnopqrstuvwxyzABCDEFGHIJKLMNOPQRSTUVWXYZ–$1234567890(“***
Black **abcdefghijklmnopqrstuvwxyzABCDEFGHIJKLMNOPQRSTUVWXYZ–$12**
Black Italic ***abcdefghijklmnopqrstuvwxyzABCDEFGHIJKLMNOPQRSTUVWXYZ–$123***

Graffiti

Leslie Cabarga • 1993
FBU
▲24

abcdefghijklmnopqrstuvwxyz(‘.;“!*?”:,’)
$1234567890+ß-äöüåçèîñóæøœ
ABCDEFGHIJKLMNOPQRSTUVWXYZ
ÄÖÜÅÇÈÎÑÓÆØŒ»„«[¶§•†‡]‹¡·¿›...

GRANJON

George W. Jones • 1928
(. . .Claude Garamont, c.1530)
LIN ADO AGA MAE

abcdefghijklmnopqrstuvwxyz(“.;‘!*?’:,”)
$1234567890&fifl ß-äöüåçèîñóæøœ
ABCDEFGHIJKLMNOPQRSTUVWXYZ
ÄÖÜÅÇÈÎÑÓÆØŒ»„«[¶§•†‡]‹¡·¿›...

Granjon . . .

• Roman abcdefghijklmnopqrstuvwxyzABCDEFGHIJKLMNOPQRSTUVWXYZ–$1234567890(“.
Italic *abcdefghijklmnopqrstuvwxyzABCDEFGHIJKLMNOPQRSTUVWXYZ–$1234567890(“.;‘!*?’:*
Bold **abcdefghijklmnopqrstuvwxyzABCDEFGHIJKLMNOPQRSTUVWXYZ–$1234567890(“**

GRANJON SCOSF

LIN ADO AGA MAE

ABCDEFGHIJKLMNOPQRSTUVWXYZ(“.;‘!*?’:,”)
$1234567890&-ÄÖÜÅÇÈÎÑÓÆØŒ
ABCDEFGHIJKLMNOPQRSTUVWXYZ
ÄÖÜÅÇÈÎÑÓÆØŒ»„«[¶§•†‡]‹¡·¿›...

... Granjon SCOSF ...

• Roman SCOSF ABCDEFGHIJKLMNOPQRSTUVWXYZABCDEFGHIJKLMNOPQRSTUVWXYZ–$1234567890(

Italic OSF *abcdefghijklmnopqrstuvwxyzABCDEFGHIJKLMNOPQRSTUVWXYZ–$1234567890(".;'!*?':*

Bold OSF **abcdefghijklmnopqrstuvwxyzABCDEFGHIJKLMNOPQRSTUVWXYZ–$1234567890("**

GRAPHITE NORMAL

David Siegel • 1993 abcdefghijklmnopqrstuvwxyz(".;'!*?':,")

MTD AGP $1234567890₵ﬁﬂß-äöüåçèîñóœøœ

ABCDEFGHIJKLMNOPQRSTUVWXYZ

ÄÖÜÅÇÈÎÑÓÆØŒ»„«[¶§•†‡]‹¡·¿›...

G

Graphite Normal ...

Light abcdefghijklmnopqrstuvwxyzABCDEFGHIJKLMNOPQRSTUVWXYZ-$12345678

Light Oblique *abcdefghijklmnopqrstuvwxyzABCDEFGHIJKLMNOPQRSTUVWXYZ-$12345678*

• Regular abcdefghijklmnopqrstuvwxyzABCDEFGHIJKLMNOPQRSTUVWXYZ-$12345

Oblique *abcdefghijklmnopqrstuvwxyzABCDEFGHIJKLMNOPQRSTUVWXYZ-$12345*

Demi abcdefghijklmnopqrstuvwxyzABCDEFGHIJKLMNOPQRSTUVWXYZ-$1234

Demi Oblique *abcdefghijklmnopqrstuvwxyzABCDEFGHIJKLMNOPQRSTUVWXYZ-$1234*

Bold **abcdefghijklmnopqrstuvwxyzABCDEFGHIJKLMNOPQRSTUVWXYZ-$12**

Bold Oblique ***abcdefghijklmnopqrstuvwxyzABCDEFGHIJKLMNOPQRSTUVWXYZ-$12***

Black **abcdefghijklmnopqrstuvwxyzABCDEFGHIJKLMNOPQRSTUVWXYZ-$1**

Black Oblique ***abcdefghijklmnopqrstuvwxyzABCDEFGHIJKLMNOPQRSTUVWXYZ-$1***

GRAPHITE CONDENSED

MTD AGP abcdefghijklmnopqrstuvwxyz(".;'!*?':,")

$1234567890₵ﬁﬂß-äöüåçèîñóœøœ

ABCDEFGHIJKLMNOPQRSTUVWXYZ

ÄÖÜÅÇÈÎÑÓÆØŒ»„«[¶§•†‡]‹¡·¿›...

Graphite Condensed ...

Light Condensed abcdefghijklmnopqrstuvwxyzABCDEFGHIJKLMNOPQRSTUVWXYZ-$1234567890(".;'!*?':,")₵ﬁﬂß-äöüÄÖÜåçè

Light Condensed Oblique *abcdefghijklmnopqrstuvwxyzABCDEFGHIJKLMNOPQRSTUVWXYZ-$1234567890(".;'!*?':,")₵ﬁﬂß-äöüÄÖÜåçè*

• Condensed abcdefghijklmnopqrstuvwxyzABCDEFGHIJKLMNOPQRSTUVWXYZ-$1234567890(".;'!*?':,")₵ﬁﬂß-äöüÄÖ

Condensed Oblique *abcdefghijklmnopqrstuvwxyzABCDEFGHIJKLMNOPQRSTUVWXYZ-$1234567890(".;'!*?':,")₵ﬁﬂß-äöüÄÖ*

Demi Condensed abcdefghijklmnopqrstuvwxyzABCDEFGHIJKLMNOPQRSTUVWXYZ-$1234567890(".;'!*?':,")₵ﬁﬂß-äöü

Demi Condensed Oblique *abcdefghijklmnopqrstuvwxyzABCDEFGHIJKLMNOPQRSTUVWXYZ-$1234567890(".;'!*?':,")₵ﬁﬂß-äöü*

Bold Condensed **abcdefghijklmnopqrstuvwxyzABCDEFGHIJKLMNOPQRSTUVWXYZ-$1234567890(".;'!*?':,")₵ﬁﬂß-**

Bold Condensed Oblique ***abcdefghijklmnopqrstuvwxyzABCDEFGHIJKLMNOPQRSTUVWXYZ-$1234567890(".;'!*?':,")₵ﬁﬂß-***

Black Condensed **abcdefghijklmnopqrstuvwxyzABCDEFGHIJKLMNOPQRSTUVWXYZ-$1234567890(".;'!*?':,")₵ﬁ**

Black Condensed Oblique ***abcdefghijklmnopqrstuvwxyzABCDEFGHIJKLMNOPQRSTUVWXYZ-$1234567890(".;'!*?':,")₵ﬁ***

GRAPHITE EXTENDED

MTD AGP abcdefghijklmnopqrstuvwxyz(".;'!*?':,")
$1234567890&fiflß-äöüåçèîñóæøœ
ABCDEFGHIJKLMNOPQRSTUVWXYZ
ÄÖÜÅÇÈÎÑÓÆØŒ»,,«[¶§•†‡]‹¡·¿›...

Graphite Extended ...

Light Extended abcdefghijklmnopqrstuvwxyzABCDEFGHIJKLMNOPQRSTUVWXY
Light Extended Oblique abcdefghijklmnopqrstuvwxyzABCDEFGHIJKLMNOPQRSTUVWXY
• Extended abcdefghijklmnopqrstuvwxyzABCDEFGHIJKLMNOPQRSTUVW
Extended Oblique abcdefghijklmnopqrstuvwxyzABCDEFGHIJKLMNOPQRSTUVW
Demi Extended abcdefghijklmnopqrstuvwxyzABCDEFGHIJKLMNOPQRSTUV
Demi Extended Oblique abcdefghijklmnopqrstuvwxyzABCDEFGHIJKLMNOPQRSTUV
Bold Extended abcdefghijklmnopqrstuvwxyzABCDEFGHIJKLMNOPQRSTU
Bold Extended Oblique abcdefghijklmnopqrstuvwxyzABCDEFGHIJKLMNOPQRSTU
Black Extended abcdefghijklmnopqrstuvwxyzABCDEFGHIJKLMNOPQRSTU
Black Extended Oblique abcdefghijklmnopqrstuvwxyzABCDEFGHIJKLMNOPQRSTU

GRECO

FRA abcdefghijklmnopqrstuvwxyz(".;'!*?':,")
$1234567890&fiflß-äöüåçèîñóæøœ
ABCDEFGHIJKLMNOPQRSTUVWXYZ
ÄÖÜÅÇÈÎÑÓÆØŒ»,,« §•†‡ ‹¡·¿›...

▷ ff ffi ffl

Greco ...

• Roman abcdefghijklmnopqrstuvwxyzABCDEFGHIJKLMNOPQRSTUVWXYZ–$1
Italic *abcdefghijklmnopqrstuvwxyzABCDEFGHIJKLMNOPQRSTUVWXYZ–$12*
Negra **abcdefghijklmnopqrstuvwxyzABCDEFGHIJKLMNOPQRSTUVWXYZ–$**
Negra Italic ***abcdefghijklmnopqrstuvwxyzABCDEFGHIJKLMNOPQRSTUVWXYZ–$1***
Bold **abcdefghijklmnopqrstuvwxyzABCDEFGHIJKLMNOPQRSTUV**
Bold Italic ***abcdefghijklmnopqrstuvwxyzABCDEFGHIJKLMNOPQRSTUV***

Greco Adornado
FRA ABCDEFGHIJKLMNOPQRSTUV
▲24 WXYZ(".;'!?':,")$1234567890
&-ÄÖÜÅÇÈÎÑÓÆØŒ ,, •†‡ ¡ ¿ ...

Greyton Script

Gerhard Schwekendiek • 1991 abcdefghijklmnopqrstuvwxyz(“.;‘!*?’:,”)

LET $1234567890&fiflß-äöüåçèîñóæøœ

▲18 ABCDEFGHIJKLMNOPQRSTUVWXYZÇ»„«[•]‹¡·¿›...

▷ e f g k l m n r s & t t v w y y M N V W

MONOTYPE GROTESQUE

Monotype Design Staff •.... abcdefghijklmnopqrstuvwxyz(“.;‘!*?’:,”)

MCL ADO AGA LIN MAE $1234567890&fiflß-äöüåçèîñóæøœ

ABCDEFGHIJKLMNOPQRSTUVWXYZ

ÄÖÜÅÇÈÎÑÓÆØŒ»„«[¶§•†‡]‹¡·¿›...

Monotype Grotesque 1 ...

Light No. 126 abcdefghijklmnopqrstuvwxyzABCDEFGHIJKLMNOPQRSTUVWXYZ–$12345678

Light Italic No. 126 *abcdefghijklmnopqrstuvwxyzABCDEFGHIJKLMNOPQRSTUVWXYZ–$1234567890(“*

• Regular No. 215 abcdefghijklmnopqrstuvwxyzABCDEFGHIJKLMNOPQRSTUVWXYZ–$12345

Italic No. 215 *abcdefghijklmnopqrstuvwxyzABCDEFGHIJKLMNOPQRSTUVWXYZ–$123456789*

Bold No. 216 **abcdefghijklmnopqrstuvwxyzABCDEFGHIJKLMNOPQRSTUVWXYZ–**

Black **abcdefghijklmnopqrstuvwxyzABCDEFGHIJKLMNOPQRSTUVWXYZ–$12345678**

Monotype Grotesque 2 ...

Extra Condensed abcdefghijklmnopqrstuvwxyzABCDEFGHIJKLMNOPQRSTUVWXYZ–$1234567890(“.;‘!*?’:,”)&fiflß-äöüÄÖÜåçè

Light Condensed abcdefghijklmnopqrstuvwxyzABCDEFGHIJKLMNOPQRSTUVWXYZ–$1234567890(“.;‘!*?’:,”)

Condensed abcdefghijklmnopqrstuvwxyzABCDEFGHIJKLMNOPQRSTUVWXYZ–$1234567890(“.;‘!*?’:,”

Black **abcdefghijklmnopqrstuvwxyzABCDEFGHIJKLMNOPQRSTUVWXYZ–$12345678**

Bold Extended **abcdefghijklmnopqrstuvwxyzABCDEFGHIJKLMNOPQRSTUV**

BUREAU GROTESQUE

David Berlow & Jonathan Hoefler • 1989 abcdefghijklmnopqrstuvwxyz(“.;‘!*?’:,”)

FBU AGP MTD $1234567890&fiflß-äöüåçèîñóæøœ

ABCDEFGHIJKLMNOPQRSTUVWXYZ

ÄÖÜÅÇÈÎÑÓÆØŒ»„«[¶§•†‡]‹¡·¿›... ▷ ff ffi ffl ⊙

Bureau Grotesque 1 ...

No. 13 abcdefghijklmnopqrstuvwxyzABCDEFGHIJKLMNOPQRSTUVWXYZ–$1234567890(“.;‘!*?’:,”)&fiflß-äöüÄÖÜåçèÅÇÈîñóÎÑÓ

No. 15 **abcdefghijklmnopqrstuvwxyzABCDEFGHIJKLMNOPQRSTUVWXYZ–$1234567890(“.;‘!*?’:,”)&fiflß-äöüÄ**

No. 17 **abcdefghijklmnopqrstuvwxyzABCDEFGHIJKLMNOPQRSTUVWXYZ–$1234567890(“.;‘!*?’:,”)&fi**

No. 37 **abcdefghijklmnopqrstuvwxyzABCDEFGHIJKLMNOPQRSTUVWXYZ–$1234567890(“.;‘!*?’:,”)&fi**

• No. 53 abcdefghijklmnopqrstuvwxyzABCDEFGHIJKLMNOPQRSTUVWXYZ–$12345678

No. 79 **abcdefghijklmnopqrstuvwxyzABCDEFGHIJKLMNOPQRSTU**

Bureau Grotesque 2 . . .

No. 11 abcdefghijklmnopqrstuvwxyzABCDEFGHIJKLMNOPQRSTUVWXYZ–$1234567890(“.;‘!*?’:,”)&fiflß-äöüÄÖÜåçèÅÇÈîñóÎÑÒæøœÆØŒ»„«[¶§•†‡]‹¡·¿›

No. 31 abcdefghijklmnopqrstuvwxyzABCDEFGHIJKLMNOPQRSTUVWXYZ–$1234567890(“.;‘!*?’:,”)&fiflß-äöüÄÖÜåçèÅÇÈîñóÎÑÒæøœÆØŒ

No. 33 abcdefghijklmnopqrstuvwxyzABCDEFGHIJKLMNOPQRSTUVWXYZ–$1234567890(“.;‘!*?’:,”)&fiflß-äöüÄÖÜåç

No. 35 abcdefghijklmnopqrstuvwxyzABCDEFGHIJKLMNOPQRSTUVWXYZ–$1234567890(“.;‘!*?’:,”)&fiflß-äö

No. 51 abcdefghijklmnopqrstuvwxyzABCDEFGHIJKLMNOPQRSTUVWXYZ–$1234567890(“.;‘!*?’:,

No. 55 abcdefghijklmnopqrstuvwxyzABCDEFGHIJKLMNOPQRSTUVWXYZ–$123

G

GROVE SCRIPT

Pat & Paul Hickson • 1994 abcdefghijklmnopqrstuvwxyz(“.;‘!*?’:,”)

RED $1234567890&ß-äöüåçèîñóæøœ

ABCDEFGHIJKLMNOPQRSTUVWXYZ

ÄÖÜÅÇÈÎÑÓÆØŒ»„«[§•†‡]‹¡·¿›...

Grove Script . . .

Light abcdefghijklmnopqrstuvwxyzABCDEFGHIJKLMNOPQRSTUVWXYZ-$1234567890(“.;‘!*

• Medium abcdefghijklmnopqrstuvwxyzABCDEFGHIJKLMNOPQRSTUVWXYZ-$1234567890(“.;‘!

Bold abcdefghijklmnopqrstuvwxyzABCDEFGHIJKLMNOPQRSTUVWXYZ-$1234567890(“.;‘!

GUARDI

Reinhard Haus • 1986 abcdefghijklmnopqrstuvwxyz(“.;‘!*?’:,”)

LIN ADO AGA MAE $1234567890&fiflß-äöüåçèîñóæøœ

ABCDEFGHIJKLMNOPQRSTUVWXYZ

ÄÖÜÅÇÈÎÑÓÆØŒ»„«[¶§•†‡]‹¡·¿›…

Guardi . . .

• 55-Roman abcdefghijklmnopqrstuvwxyzABCDEFGHIJKLMNOPQRSTUVWXYZ–$1234

56-Italic *abcdefghijklmnopqrstuvwxyzABCDEFGHIJKLMNOPQRSTUVWXYZ–$1234567890*

75-Bold **abcdefghijklmnopqrstuvwxyzABCDEFGHIJKLMNOPQRSTUVWXYZ–$**

76-Bold Italic ***abcdefghijklmnopqrstuvwxyzABCDEFGHIJKLMNOPQRSTUVWXYZ–$12345***

95-Black **abcdefghijklmnopqrstuvwxyzABCDEFGHIJKLMNOPQRSTUVWXY**

96-Black Italic ***abcdefghijklmnopqrstuvwxyzABCDEFGHIJKLMNOPQRSTUVWXYZ–***

TF Guestcheck Heavy
TF DisplaySet 2

Joseph Treacy • 1992 abcdefghijklmnopqrstuvwxyz

TRE MTD (“.;‘!*?’:,”)$1234567890&fiflß-äöü

▲16 åçèîñóæøœABCDEFGHIJKLMNOPQR

STUVWXYZÄÖÜÅÇÈÎÑÓÆØŒ

»„«[¶§•†‡]‹¡ - ¿›… ▷ 123579/2 34 8 16

TF DisplaySet 2: TF Adepta A Extra Bold & TF Guestcheck Heavy.

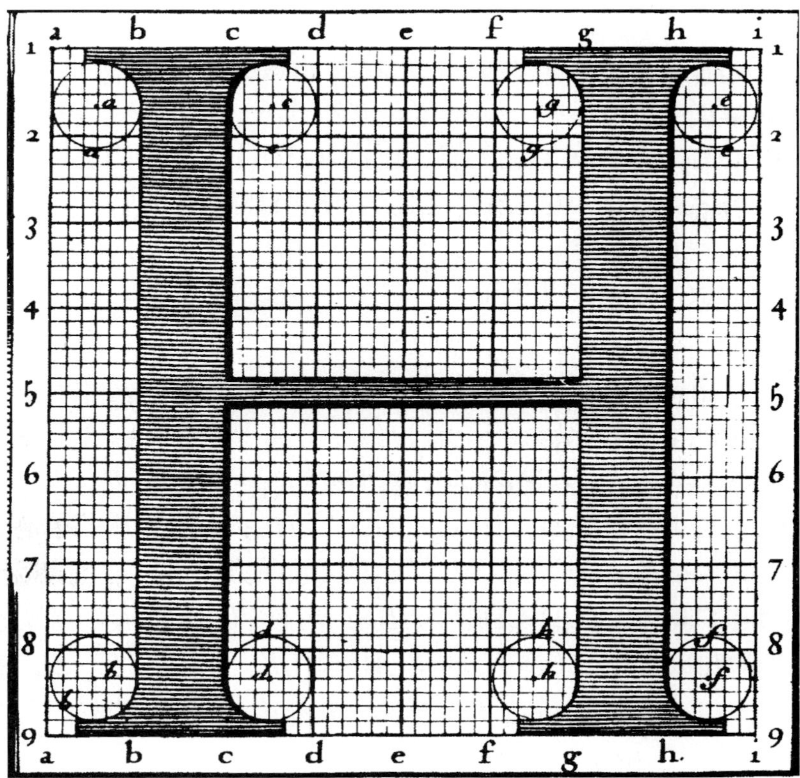
a b c d e f g h i
1 2 3 4 5 6 7 8 9

✍ Nicolas Jaugeon, Louis Simonneau *et al.*, 1700

TF HABITAT

Joseph Treacy • 1985 abcdefghijklmnopqrstuvwxyz(".;'!*?':;")

TRE MTD $1234567890&fiflß-äöüåçèîñóæøœ

ABCDEFGHIJKLMNOPQRSTUVWXYZ

ÄÖÜÅÇÈÎÑÓÆØŒ»,,«[¶§•†‡]‹¡ · ¿›... ▷ 123579/234816■□

TF Habitat A ...

Regular abcdefghijklmnopqrstuvwxyzABCDEFGHIJKLMNOPQRSTUVWXYZ-$123456789

Italic *abcdefghijklmnopqrstuvwxyzABCDEFGHIJKLMNOPQRSTUVWXYZ-$1234567890(".;'!*?':,)*

Bold **abcdefghijklmnopqrstuvwxyzABCDEFGHIJKLMNOPQRSTUVWXYZ-$12345**

Bold Italic ***abcdefghijklmnopqrstuvwxyzABCDEFGHIJKLMNOPQRSTUVWXYZ-$1234567890("***

H

TF Habitat B ...

• Book abcdefghijklmnopqrstuvwxyzABCDEFGHIJKLMNOPQRSTUVWXYZ-$12345678

Book Italic *abcdefghijklmnopqrstuvwxyzABCDEFGHIJKLMNOPQRSTUVWXYZ-$1234567890(".;'!*?'*

Demi Bold **abcdefghijklmnopqrstuvwxyzABCDEFGHIJKLMNOPQRSTUVWXYZ-$123456**

Demi Bold Italic ***abcdefghijklmnopqrstuvwxyzABCDEFGHIJKLMNOPQRSTUVWXYZ-$1234567890(".;***

TF HABITAT CONDENSED

Joseph Treacy • 1987 abcdefghijklmnopqrstuvwxyz(".;'!*?':;")

TRE MTD $1234567890&fiflß-äöüåçèîñóæøœ

ABCDEFGHIJKLMNOPQRSTUVWXYZ

ÄÖÜÅÇÈÎÑÓÆØŒ»,,«[¶§•†‡]‹¡ · ¿›... ▷ 123579/234816■□

TF Habitat Condensed A ...

• Condensed abcdefghijklmnopqrstuvwxyzABCDEFGHIJKLMNOPQRSTUVWXYZ-$1234567890(".;'!*?':;")&fiflß-

Condensed Italic *abcdefghijklmnopqrstuvwxyzABCDEFGHIJKLMNOPQRSTUVWXYZ-$1234567890(".;'!*?':;")&fiflß-äöüÄÖÜ*

Bold Condensed **abcdefghijklmnopqrstuvwxyzABCDEFGHIJKLMNOPQRSTUVWXYZ-$1234567890(".;'!*?':**

Bold Condensed Italic ***abcdefghijklmnopqrstuvwxyzABCDEFGHIJKLMNOPQRSTUVWXYZ-$1234567890(".;'!*?':;")&fiflß-***

TF Habitat Bold Contour A

Joseph Treacy • 1992 abcdefghijklmnopqrstuvwxyz(".;'!*?':;")

TRE MTD

▲24 $1234567890&fiflß-äöüåçèîñóæøœ

ABCDEFGHIJKLMNOPQRSTUVWXYZ

ÄÖÜÅÇÈÎÑÓÆØŒ»,,«[¶§•†‡]‹¡ · ¿›... ▷ 123579/2

TF Habitat Bold Contour B

Joseph Treacy • 1993

TRE MTD

▲24

abcdefghijklmnopqrstuvwxyz(“.;‘!*?’:;”)

$1234567890&fiflß-äöüåçèîñóæøœ

ABCDEFGHIJKLMNOPQRSTUVWXYZ

ÄÖÜÅÇÈÎÑÓÆØŒ»„«[¶§•†‡]‹¡·¿›… ▷123579/2

TF HABITAT BOLD CAMEO INITIALS ONE & TWO

Joseph Treacy • 1994

TRE MTD

▲30

ABCDEFGHIJKLMNOPQR

STUVWXYZ•!?’$12345

67890&-ÄÖÜÅÇÈÎÑÓÆØ

Œ•¡•¿ ABCDEF

GHIJKLMNOPQRSTUVWX

YZ•!?’$1234567890&

-ÄÖÜÅÇÈÎÑÓÆØŒ•¡•¿

Hadfield

Martin Wait • 1980

LET LEF URW

▲16

abcdefghijklmnopqrstuvwxyz(“.;‘!*?’:;”)

$1234567890&fiflß-äöüåçèîñóæøœ

ABCDEFGHIJKLMNOPQRSTUVWXYZ

ÄÖÜÅÇÈÎÑÓÆØŒ»„«[•]‹¡·¿›…

HADRIANO STONECUT

Sol Hess • 1932

… Frederic W. Goudy, 1918

LAN

▲24

ABCDEFGHIJKLMNOPQRSTUVWXYZ(“.;‘!*?’:;”)

$1234567890&-ÄÖÜÅÇÈÎÑÓÆØŒ

ABCDEFGHIJKLMNOPQRSTUVWXYZ

ÄÖÜÅÇÈÎÑÓÆØŒ»„«¶§•†‡‹¡¿›… ▷Q Q

HADRIANO TITLING

Frederic W. Goudy • 1918

LAN

▲24

ABCDEFGHIJKLMNOPQRSTUVWXYZ(".;'!*?':,")

$1234567890&-ÄÖÜÅÇÈÎÑÓÆØŒ

ABCDEFGHIJKLMNOPQRSTUVWXYZ

ÄÖÜÅÇÈÎÑÓÆØŒ»,,«¶§•†‡‹¡¿›... ▷ Q Q

HAMILTON

H

Tom Rickner • 1993 (William Hamilton Page)

FBU

▲36

abcdefghijklmnopqrstuvwxyz(".;'!*?':,")

$1234567890&fifl ß-äöüåçèîñóæøœ

ABCDEFGHIJKLMNOPQRSTUVWXYZ

ÄÖÜÅÇÈÎÑÓÆØŒ»,,«[¶§•†‡]‹¡·¿›... ▷ ff fi ffl

Hamilton ...

Light

abcdefghijklmnopqrstuvwxyzABCDEFGHIJKLMNOPQR

• Medium

abcdefghijklmnopqrstuvwxyzABCDEFGHIJ

Bold

abcdefghijklmnopqrstuvwxyzABC

Handle Oldstyle

Agfa Engravers 1

AGP

▲18

ABCDEFGHIJKLMNOPQRSTUVWXYZ(".;'!*?':,")

$1234567890&-ÄÖÜÅÇÈÎÑÓ

ABCDEFGHIJKLMNOPQRSTUVWXYZ

ÄÖÜÅÇÈÎÑÓ»«[·]‹› ▷ I V X ST ND RD TH 1/4 1/3 1/2 3/4 D' C R. 'C 'S O' RS. S. & %

Handwrite Inkblot

Todd Brei • 1993

T26

▲16

abcdefghijklmnopqrstuvwxyz(".;'!*?':,")

$1234567890&fiflß–äöüåçèîñóæøœ

ABCDEFGHIJKLMNOPQRSTUVWXYZ

ÄÖÜÅÇÈÎÑÓÆØŒ»,,«[¶§•†‡]‹¡·¿›...

....

Agfa Engravers 1: Antique Roman Solid & Slanted, Artisan Roman, Burin Roman & Sans, Classic Roman Light & Regular, Handle Oldstyle, Roman Light & Medium.

HARTING

INT abcdefghijklmnopqrstuvwxyz(".;'!*?':,")
$1234567890&ß-äöüåçèîñóæøœ
ABCDEFGHIJKLMNOPQRSTUVWXYZ
ÄÖÜÅÇÈÎÑÓÆØŒ»„«[]‹¡¿›

Harting ...

• Regular abcdefghijklmnopqrstuvwxyzABCDEFGHIJKLMNOPQRSTUVWXYZ-
Alternate abcdefghijklmnopqrstuvwxyzABCDEFGHIJKLMNOPQRSTUVWXYZ-

Harvey

Dale R. Kramer • 1989 ABCDEFGHIJKLMNOPQRSTUVWXYZ(".;'!*?':,")$1234567890

LET

▲24 &-ÄÖÜÅÇÈÎÑÓÆØŒ»„«[•]‹¡·¿›... ▷EFHNUY79

Hazel

Phil Grimshaw • 1992 ABCDEFGHIJKLMNOPQRSTUVWXYZ

LET

▲30 (".;'!*?':,")$1234567890&-
ÄÖÜÅÇÈÎÑÓÆØŒ»„«[•]‹¡·¿›... ▷

Headline Bold
Monotype Headliners 2

MCL abcdefghijklmnopqrstuvwxyz(".;'!*?':,")

▲24 $1234567890&fiflß-äöüåçèîñóæøœ
ABCDEFGHIJKLMNOPQRSTUVWXYZ
ÄÖÜÅÇÈÎÑÓÆØŒ»„«[¶§•†‡]‹¡·¿›...

Helinda Rook
Agfa Scripts 1

AGP abcdefghijklmnopqrstuvwxyz(".;'!*?':,")

▲18 $1234567890&ß-äöüåçèîñó
ABCDEFGHIJKLMNOPQRSTUVWXYZ
ÄÖÜÅÇÈÎÑÓ»«[·]‹› ▷I V X st nd rd th 1/4 1/8 1/2 3/4 D c r c s C rs s &%

...
Monotype Headliners 2: Falstaff, Headline Bold, Placard Condensed & Bold Condensed.
Agfa Scripts 1: Commercial Script, Helinda Rook, Old English, Original Script, Quill Script, Stuyvesant, Wedding Text.

HELIOS ROUNDED

FAM abcdefghijklmnopqrstuvwxyz(".;'!*?':,")
$1234567890&fiflß-äöüåçèîñóæøœ
ABCDEFGHIJKLMNOPQRSTUVWXYZ
ÄÖÜÅÇÈÎÑÓÆØŒ»„«[¶§•†‡]‹¡·¿›...

Helios Rounded ...

• Regular abcdefghijklmnopqrstuvwxyzABCDEFGHIJKLMNOPQRSTUVWXYZ–$1234567890(".
Semibold **abcdefghijklmnopqrstuvwxyzABCDEFGHIJKLMNOPQRSTUVWXYZ–$1234567890("**
Bold **abcdefghijklmnopqrstuvwxyzABCDEFGHIJKLMNOPQRSTUVWXYZ–$12345678**

H

Heliotype
Lee McAuley • 1991
LET
▲36

abcdefghijklmnopqrstuvwxyz(".;'!*?':,")
$1234567890&fiflß-äöüåçèîñóæøœ
ABCDEFGHIJKLMNOPQRSTUVWXYZ
ÄÖÜÅÇÈÎÑÓÆØŒ»„«[•]‹¡·¿›...

▷ g n w x y a e g N U W X Y

HELVETICA

Max Miedinger & Edouard Hoffman • 1957

abcdefghijklmnopqrstuvwxyz(".;'!*?':,")
$1234567890&fiflß-äöüåçèîñóæøœ
LIN ADO AGA MAE ABCDEFGHIJKLMNOPQRSTUVWXYZ
ÄÖÜÅÇÈÎÑÓÆØŒ»„«[¶§•†‡]‹¡·¿›...

π Ξ Helvetica ...

• Light abcdefghijklmnopqrstuvwxyzABCDEFGHIJKLMNOPQRSTUVWXYZ–$12345678
Light Oblique *abcdefghijklmnopqrstuvwxyzABCDEFGHIJKLMNOPQRSTUVWXYZ–$12345678*
Black **abcdefghijklmnopqrstuvwxyzABCDEFGHIJKLMNOPQRSTUVWXY**
Black Oblique ***abcdefghijklmnopqrstuvwxyzABCDEFGHIJKLMNOPQRSTUVWXY***

HELVETICA CONDENSED

LIN ADO AGA LET MAE abcdefghijklmnopqrstuvwxyz(".;'!*?':,")
$1234567890&fiflß-äöüåçèîñóæøœ
ABCDEFGHIJKLMNOPQRSTUVWXYZ
ÄÖÜÅÇÈÎÑÓÆØŒ»„«[¶§•†‡]‹¡·¿›...

Helvetica Condensed ...

Light Condensed abcdefghijklmnopqrstuvwxyzABCDEFGHIJKLMNOPQRSTUVWXYZ–$1234567890(".;'!*?':,")&fiflß-äöü
Light Condensed Oblique *abcdefghijklmnopqrstuvwxyzABCDEFGHIJKLMNOPQRSTUVWXYZ–$1234567890(".;'!*?':,")&fiflß-äöü*
• Condensed abcdefghijklmnopqrstuvwxyzABCDEFGHIJKLMNOPQRSTUVWXYZ–$1234567890(".;'!*?':,

π Helvetica ⊛ Linotype Fraction Pi.
Ξ Helvetica ⊛ Helvetica Cyrillic & Greek.

. . . Helvetica Condensed

Condensed Oblique *abcdefghijklmnopqrstuvwxyzABCDEFGHIJKLMNOPQRSTUVWXYZ–$1234567890(".;'!*?':,*

Bold Condensed **abcdefghijklmnopqrstuvwxyzABCDEFGHIJKLMNOPQRSTUVWXYZ–$1234567890(".;'!*?**

Bold Condensed Oblique ***abcdefghijklmnopqrstuvwxyzABCDEFGHIJKLMNOPQRSTUVWXYZ–$1234567890(".;'!*?***

Black Condensed **abcdefghijklmnopqrstuvwxyzABCDEFGHIJKLMNOPQRSTUVWXYZ–$1234567890(".;'!*?':**

Black Condensed Oblique ***abcdefghijklmnopqrstuvwxyzABCDEFGHIJKLMNOPQRSTUVWXYZ–$1234567890(".;'!*?':***

HELVETICA COMPRESSED

LIN ADO AGA MAE **abcdefghijklmnopqrstuvwxyz(".;'!*?':,")**
$1234567890&fiflß-äöüåçèîñóæøœ
ABCDEFGHIJKLMNOPQRSTUVWXYZ
ÄÖÜÅÇÈÎÑÓÆØŒ»„«[¶§•†‡]‹¡·¿›...

H

Helvetica Compressed . . .

• Compressed ▲16 **abcdefghijklmnopqrstuvwxyzABCDEFGHIJKLMNOPQRSTUVWXYZ–$1234567890(".;'!*?':,**

Extra Compressed ▲16 **abcdefghijklmnopqrstuvwxyzABCDEFGHIJKLMNOPQRSTUVWXYZ–$1234567890(".;'!*?':,")&fiflß-äöüÄÖÜåçèÅ**

Ultra Compressed ▲18 **abcdefghijklmnopqrstuvwxyzABCDEFGHIJKLMNOPQRSTUVWXYZ–$1234567890(".;'!*?':,")&fiflß-äöüÄÖÜåçèÂÇÊÎ**

Helvetica Inserat
Linotype DisplaySet 1

LIN ADO AGA MAE **abcdefghijklmnopqrstuvwxyz(".;'!*?':,")**
▲16 **$1234567890&fiflß-äöüåçèîñóæøœ**
ABCDEFGHIJKLMNOPQRSTUVWXYZ
ÄÖÜÅÇÈÎÑÓÆØŒ»„«[¶§•†‡]‹¡·¿›...

HELVETICA ROUNDED

LIN ADO AGA MAE **abcdefghijklmnopqrstuvwxyz(".;'!*?':,")**
$1234567890&fiflß-äöüåçèîñóæøœ
ABCDEFGHIJKLMNOPQRSTUVWXYZ
ÄÖÜÅÇÈÎÑÓÆØŒ»„«[¶§•†‡]‹¡·¿›...

Helvetica Rounded . . .

• Bold **abcdefghijklmnopqrstuvwxyzABCDEFGHIJKLMNOPQRSTUVWXYZ–$1234**

Bold Oblique ***abcdefghijklmnopqrstuvwxyzABCDEFGHIJKLMNOPQRSTUVWXYZ–$1234***

Black **abcdefghijklmnopqrstuvwxyzABCDEFGHIJKLMNOPQRSTUVWXYZ–**

Black Oblique ***abcdefghijklmnopqrstuvwxyzABCDEFGHIJKLMNOPQRSTUVWXYZ–***

Bold Condensed ▲16 **abcdefghijklmnopqrstuvwxyzABCDEFGHIJKLMNOPQRSTUVWXYZ–$1234567890(".;**

Bold Condensed Oblique ▲16 ***abcdefghijklmnopqrstuvwxyzABCDEFGHIJKLMNOPQRSTUVWXYZ–$1234567890(".;***

. . .

Linotype DisplaySet 1: Arnold Böcklin, Fette Fraktur, Helvetica Inserat, Present Script.
Helvetica Inserat ⟶ Helvetica Inserat Cyrillic.

NEUE HELVETICA

Linotype Design Staff • 1983 . . . Max Miedinger & Edouard Hoffman, 1957

abcdefghijklmnopqrstuvwxyz(".;'!*?':,")
$1234567890&fiflß-äöüåçèîñóæøœ
LIN ADO AGA MAE ABCDEFGHIJKLMNOPQRSTUVWXYZ
ÄÖÜÅÇÈÎÑÓÆØŒ»„«[¶§•†‡]‹¡·¿›...

Neue Helvetica 1 . . .

25-Ultra Light abcdefghijklmnopqrstuvwxyzABCDEFGHIJKLMNOPQRSTUVWXYZ–$1234567890(".;'!*?'
26-Ultra Light Italic *abcdefghijklmnopqrstuvwxyzABCDEFGHIJKLMNOPQRSTUVWXYZ–$1234567890(".;'!*?'*
95-Black **abcdefghijklmnopqrstuvwxyzABCDEFGHIJKLMNOPQRSTUVWXYZ–$1**
96-Black Italic ***abcdefghijklmnopqrstuvwxyzABCDEFGHIJKLMNOPQRSTUVWXYZ–$1***

H

Neue Helvetica 2 . . .

35-Thin abcdefghijklmnopqrstuvwxyzABCDEFGHIJKLMNOPQRSTUVWXYZ–$1234567890(".;
36-Thin Italic *abcdefghijklmnopqrstuvwxyzABCDEFGHIJKLMNOPQRSTUVWXYZ–$1234567890(".;*
• 55-Regular abcdefghijklmnopqrstuvwxyzABCDEFGHIJKLMNOPQRSTUVWXYZ–$1234567
56-Italic *abcdefghijklmnopqrstuvwxyzABCDEFGHIJKLMNOPQRSTUVWXYZ–$12345678*
75-Bold **abcdefghijklmnopqrstuvwxyzABCDEFGHIJKLMNOPQRSTUVWXYZ–$1234**
76-Bold Italic ***abcdefghijklmnopqrstuvwxyzABCDEFGHIJKLMNOPQRSTUVWXYZ–$12345***

Neue Helvetica 3 . . .

45-Light abcdefghijklmnopqrstuvwxyzABCDEFGHIJKLMNOPQRSTUVWXYZ–$1234567890
46-Light Italic *abcdefghijklmnopqrstuvwxyzABCDEFGHIJKLMNOPQRSTUVWXYZ–$1234567890*
65-Medium **abcdefghijklmnopqrstuvwxyzABCDEFGHIJKLMNOPQRSTUVWXYZ–$123456**
66-Medium Italic ***abcdefghijklmnopqrstuvwxyzABCDEFGHIJKLMNOPQRSTUVWXYZ–$123456***
85-Heavy **abcdefghijklmnopqrstuvwxyzABCDEFGHIJKLMNOPQRSTUVWXYZ–$12**
86-Heavy Italic ***abcdefghijklmnopqrstuvwxyzABCDEFGHIJKLMNOPQRSTUVWXYZ–$12***

Neue Helvetica 75-Bold Outline

LIN ADO AGA MAE abcdefghijklmnopqrstuvwxyz(".;'!*?':,")
▲18 $1234567890&fiflß-äöüåçèîñóæøœ
ABCDEFGHIJKLMNOPQRSTUVWXYZ
ÄÖÜÅÇÈÎÑÓÆØŒ»„«[•]‹¡·¿›...

NEUE HELVETICA CONDENSED

LIN ADO AGA MAE abcdefghijklmnopqrstuvwxyz(".;'!*?':,")
$1234567890&fiflß-äöüåçèîñóæøœ
ABCDEFGHIJKLMNOPQRSTUVWXYZ
ÄÖÜÅÇÈÎÑÓÆØŒ»„«[¶§•†‡]‹¡·¿›...

Neue Helvetica Condensed 1 . . .

27-Ultra Light Condensed abcdefghijklmnopqrstuvwxyzABCDEFGHIJKLMNOPQRSTUVWXYZ–$1234567890(".;'!*?':,")&fiflß-äöüÄÖÜåçè
27-Ultra Light Condensed Oblique *abcdefghijklmnopqrstuvwxyzABCDEFGHIJKLMNOPQRSTUVWXYZ–$1234567890(".;'!*?':,")&fiflß-äöüÄÖÜåçè*
97-Black Condensed **abcdefghijklmnopqrstuvwxyzABCDEFGHIJKLMNOPQRSTUVWXYZ–$1234567890(".;'!*?'**

Neue Helvetica 2 Neue Helvetica EastA.

.. Neue Helvetica Condensed 1

97-Black Condensed Oblique *abcdefghijklmnopqrstuvwxyzABCDEFGHIJKLMNOPQRSTUVWXYZ–$1234567890(“.;‘!*?’*

107-Extra Black Condensed **abcdefghijklmnopqrstuvwxyzABCDEFGHIJKLMNOPQRSTUVWXYZ–$1234567890(“.;‘!*?**

107-Extra Black Condensed Oblique ***abcdefghijklmnopqrstuvwxyzABCDEFGHIJKLMNOPQRSTUVWXYZ–$1234567890(“.;‘!*?***

Neue Helvetica Condensed 2 ...

37-Thin Condensed abcdefghijklmnopqrstuvwxyzABCDEFGHIJKLMNOPQRSTUVWXYZ–$1234567890(“.;‘!*?’:,”)&fiflß-äöüÄÖÜ

37-Thin Condensed Oblique *abcdefghijklmnopqrstuvwxyzABCDEFGHIJKLMNOPQRSTUVWXYZ–$1234567890(“.;‘!*?’:,”)&fiflß-äöüÄÖÜ*

• 57-Condensed abcdefghijklmnopqrstuvwxyzABCDEFGHIJKLMNOPQRSTUVWXYZ–$1234567890(“.;‘!*?’:,”)&fiflß-

57-Condensed Oblique *abcdefghijklmnopqrstuvwxyzABCDEFGHIJKLMNOPQRSTUVWXYZ–$1234567890(“.;‘!*?’:,”)&fiflß-*

77-Bold Condensed **abcdefghijklmnopqrstuvwxyzABCDEFGHIJKLMNOPQRSTUVWXYZ–$1234567890(“.;‘!*?’:,”)**

77-Bold Condensed Oblique ***abcdefghijklmnopqrstuvwxyzABCDEFGHIJKLMNOPQRSTUVWXYZ–$1234567890(“.;‘!*?’:,”)***

H

Neue Helvetica Condensed 3 ...

47-Light Condensed abcdefghijklmnopqrstuvwxyzABCDEFGHIJKLMNOPQRSTUVWXYZ–$1234567890(“.;‘!*?’:,”)&fiflß-äöü

47-Light Condensed Oblique *abcdefghijklmnopqrstuvwxyzABCDEFGHIJKLMNOPQRSTUVWXYZ–$1234567890(“.;‘!*?’:,”)&fiflß-äöü*

67-Medium Condensed **abcdefghijklmnopqrstuvwxyzABCDEFGHIJKLMNOPQRSTUVWXYZ–$1234567890(“.;‘!*?’:,”)&fi**

67-Medium Condensed Oblique ***abcdefghijklmnopqrstuvwxyzABCDEFGHIJKLMNOPQRSTUVWXYZ–$1234567890(“.;‘!*?’:,”)&fi***

87-Heavy Condensed **abcdefghijklmnopqrstuvwxyzABCDEFGHIJKLMNOPQRSTUVWXYZ–$1234567890(“.;‘!*?**

87-Heavy Condensed Oblique ***abcdefghijklmnopqrstuvwxyzABCDEFGHIJKLMNOPQRSTUVWXYZ–$1234567890(“.;‘!*?***

NEUE HELVETICA EXTENDED

LIN ADO AGA MAE abcdefghijklmnopqrstuvwxyz(“.;‘!*?’:,”)
$1234567890&fiflß-äöüåçèîñóæøœ
ABCDEFGHIJKLMNOPQRSTUVWXYZ
ÄÖÜÅÇÈÎÑÓÆØŒ»„«[¶§•†‡]‹¡·¿›…

Neue Helvetica Extended 1 ...

23-Ultra Light Extended abcdefghijklmnopqrstuvwxyzABCDEFGHIJKLMNOPQRSTUVWXYZ–$123456

23-Ultra Light Extended Oblique *abcdefghijklmnopqrstuvwxyzABCDEFGHIJKLMNOPQRSTUVWXYZ–$123456*

93-Black Extended **abcdefghijklmnopqrstuvwxyzABCDEFGHIJKLMNOP**

93-Black Extended Oblique ***abcdefghijklmnopqrstuvwxyzABCDEFGHIJKLMNOP***

Neue Helvetica Extended 2 ...

33-Thin Extended abcdefghijklmnopqrstuvwxyzABCDEFGHIJKLMNOPQRSTUVWXYZ–$1234

33-Thin Extended Oblique *abcdefghijklmnopqrstuvwxyzABCDEFGHIJKLMNOPQRSTUVWXYZ–$1234*

• 53-Extended abcdefghijklmnopqrstuvwxyzABCDEFGHIJKLMNOPQRSTUVWXYZ–

53-Extended Oblique *abcdefghijklmnopqrstuvwxyzABCDEFGHIJKLMNOPQRSTUVWXYZ–*

73-Bold Extended **abcdefghijklmnopqrstuvwxyzABCDEFGHIJKLMNOPQRSTU**

73-Bold Extended Oblique ***abcdefghijklmnopqrstuvwxyzABCDEFGHIJKLMNOPQRSTU***

Neue Helvetica Extended 3 ...

43-Light Extended abcdefghijklmnopqrstuvwxyzABCDEFGHIJKLMNOPQRSTUVWXYZ–$1

43-Light Extended Oblique *abcdefghijklmnopqrstuvwxyzABCDEFGHIJKLMNOPQRSTUVWXYZ–$1*

. . . Neue Helvetica Extended 3

63-Medium Extended abcdefghijklmnopqrstuvwxyzABCDEFGHIJKLMNOPQRSTUVW

63-Medium Extended Oblique *abcdefghijklmnopqrstuvwxyzABCDEFGHIJKLMNOPQRSTUVW*

83-Heavy Extended **abcdefghijklmnopqrstuvwxyzABCDEFGHIJKLMNOPQR**

83-Heavy Extended Oblique ***abcdefghijklmnopqrstuvwxyzABCDEFGHIJKLMNOPQR***

Herculanum
Type Before Gutenberg 1
Adrian Frutiger • 1990

LIN ADO AGA MAE

▲30

ABCDEFGHIJKLMNOPQRSTUVWXYZ
(“.;‘!*?’:,”)$1234567890
&-ÄÖÜÅÇÈÎÑÓÆØŒ»„«[§•†‡]‹¡·¿›…

Σ Hibiscus
Group Hawaii
Judith Sutcliffe • 1993

MTD

▲30

ABCDEFGHIJKLMNO
PQRSTUVWXYZ

ITC HIGHLANDER

Dave Farey • 1993
(Ozwald Cooper, c.1930)

ITC ADO URW

abcdefghijklmnopqrstuvwxyz(“.;‘!*?’:,”)
$1234567890&fiflß-äöüåçèîñóæøœ
ABCDEFGHIJKLMNOPQRSTUVWXYZ
ÄÖÜÅÇÈÎÑÓÆØŒ»„«[¶§•†‡]‹¡·¿›…

ITC Highlander . . .

• Book abcdefghijklmnopqrstuvwxyzABCDEFGHIJKLMNOPQRSTUVWXYZ–$1234567890(“.;‘!*?’:

Book Italic *abcdefghijklmnopqrstuvwxyzABCDEFGHIJKLMNOPQRSTUVWXYZ–$1234567890(“.;‘!*?’*

Medium abcdefghijklmnopqrstuvwxyzABCDEFGHIJKLMNOPQRSTUVWXYZ–$1234567890(“.

Medium Italic *abcdefghijklmnopqrstuvwxyzABCDEFGHIJKLMNOPQRSTUVWXYZ–$1234567890(“.;*

Bold **abcdefghijklmnopqrstuvwxyzABCDEFGHIJKLMNOPQRSTUVWXYZ–$12345678**

Bold Italic ***abcdefghijklmnopqrstuvwxyzABCDEFGHIJKLMNOPQRSTUVWXYZ–$1234567***

Book SCOSF ABCDEFGHIJKLMNOPQRSTUVWXYZABCDEFGHIJKLMNOPQRSTUVWXYZ–$1234567890(“.;‘!*?’:

Book OSF abcdefghijklmnopqrstuvwxyzABCDEFGHIJKLMNOPQRSTUVWXYZ–$1234567890(“.;‘!*?’:,

Book Italic OSF *abcdefghijklmnopqrstuvwxyzABCDEFGHIJKLMNOPQRSTUVWXYZ–$1234567890(“.;‘!*?’:,*

Medium SCOSF ABCDEFGHIJKLMNOPQRSTUVWXYZABCDEFGHIJKLMNOPQRSTUVWXYZ–$1234567890(“

Medium OSF abcdefghijklmnopqrstuvwxyzABCDEFGHIJKLMNOPQRSTUVWXYZ–$1234567890(“.;

Medium Italic OSF *abcdefghijklmnopqrstuvwxyzABCDEFGHIJKLMNOPQRSTUVWXYZ–$1234567890(“.;‘*

Bold OSF **abcdefghijklmnopqrstuvwxyzABCDEFGHIJKLMNOPQRSTUVWXYZ–$123456789**

Type Before Gutenberg 1: Duc De Berry, Herculanum, Omnia.
Group Hawaii: Hibiscus, Kiilani, Petroglyph Hawaii.
Σ Hibiscus ▶ Petroglyph Hawaii.

... ITC Highlander

Bold Italic OSF abcdefghijklmnopqrstuvwxyzABCDEFGHIJKLMNOPQRSTUVWXYZ–$12345678

HIP·HOP

✍ Jill Pichotta • 1993

FBU

▲24

abcdefghijklmnopqrstuvwxyz

("·;'!*?':,")$1234567890&ß-äöüåçèîñó

æøœABCDEFGHIJKLMNOPQRSTUVWXYZ

ÄÖÜÅÇÈÎÑÓÆØŒ»„«[¶§•†x]‹¡·¿›...

HipHop ...

Demi abcdefghijklmnopqrstuvwxyzABCDEFGHI

• Inline abcdefghijklmnopqrstuvwxyzABCDE

HIROSHIGE

✍ Cynthia Hollandsworth • 1986

URW ADO AGA LIN MAE

abcdefghijklmnopqrstuvwxyz("·;'!*?':,")

$1234567890&fifl ß-äöüåçèîñóæøœ

ABCDEFGHIJKLMNOPQRSTUVWXYZ

ÄÖÜÅÇÈÎÑÓÆØŒ»„«[¶§•†‡]‹¡·¿›...

Hiroshige 1 ...

• Book abcdefghijklmnopqrstuvwxyzABCDEFGHIJKLMNOPQRSTUVWXYZ–$12345678

Book Italic *abcdefghijklmnopqrstuvwxyzABCDEFGHIJKLMNOPQRSTUVWXYZ–$1234567890(*

Bold **abcdefghijklmnopqrstuvwxyzABCDEFGHIJKLMNOPQRSTUVWXYZ–$123**

Bold Italic ***abcdefghijklmnopqrstuvwxyzABCDEFGHIJKLMNOPQRSTUVWXYZ-$1234***

Hiroshige 2 ...

Medium abcdefghijklmnopqrstuvwxyzABCDEFGHIJKLMNOPQRSTUVWXYZ–$123456

Medium Italic *abcdefghijklmnopqrstuvwxyzABCDEFGHIJKLMNOPQRSTUVWXYZ-$1234567*

Black **abcdefghijklmnopqrstuvwxyzABCDEFGHIJKLMNOPQRSTUVWXYZ–$**

Black Italic ***abcdefghijklmnopqrstuvwxyzABCDEFGHIJKLMNOPQRSTUVWXYZ-$1***

Hobo

❖ Adobe DisplaySet 4

✍ Morris Fuller Benton • 1910

ADO AGA BIT TFC LIN MAE URW

▲16

abcdefghijklmnopqrstuvwxyz("·;'!*?':,")

$1234567890&fifl ß-äöüåçèîñóæøœ

ABCDEFGHIJKLMNOPQRSTUVWXYZ

ÄÖÜÅÇÈÎÑÓÆØŒ»„«[•]‹¡·¿›...

❖ *Adobe DisplaySet 4*: Brush Script, Hobo, Stencil.

H

HOFFMANN

✍ Richard Lipton • 1993 abcdefghijklmnopqrstuvwxyz(".;'!*?':,")

FBU $1234567890&fiflß-äöüåçèîñóæøœ

ABCDEFGHIJKLMNOPQRSTUVWXYZ

ÄÖÜÅÇÈÎÑÓÆØŒ»„«[¶§•†‡]‹¡·¿›... ▹ff fi ffl

Hoffmann 1 ...

Light abcdefghijklmnopqrstuvwxyzABCDEFGHIJKLMNOPQRSTUVWXYZ–$1234567890(

Light SCOSF ABCDEFGHIJKLMNOPQRSTUVWXYZABCDEFGHIJKLMNOPQRSTUVWXYZ–$1234567890(

Roman abcdefghijklmnopqrstuvwxyzABCDEFGHIJKLMNOPQRSTUVWXYZ–$12345

Roman SCOSF ABCDEFGHIJKLMNOPQRSTUVWXYZABCDEFGHIJKLMNOPQRSTUVWXYZ–$123

H

Hoffmann 2 ...

• Book abcdefghijklmnopqrstuvwxyzABCDEFGHIJKLMNOPQRSTUVWXYZ–$12345678

Book SCOSF ABCDEFGHIJKLMNOPQRSTUVWXYZABCDEFGHIJKLMNOPQRSTUVWXYZ–$123456

Bold abcdefghijklmnopqrstuvwxyzABCDEFGHIJKLMNOPQRSTUVWXYZ–$123

Bold SCOSF ABCDEFGHIJKLMNOPQRSTUVWXYZABCDEFGHIJKLMNOPQRSTUVWXYZ–$

Black Titling

▲30 ABCDEFGHIJKLMNOPQRSTUV

WXYZ–$1234567890(".;'!*?':,")

Hogarth Script

URW LEF *abcdefghijklmnopqrstuvwxyz(".;'!*?':,")*

▲16 *$1234567890&fiflß-äöüåçèîñóæøœ*

ABCDEFGHIJKLMNOPQRSTUVWXYZ

ÄÖÜÅÇÈÎÑÓÆØŒ»„«[¶§•†‡]‹¡·¿›...

HOLLAND SEMINAR
✤ Agfa TextSet 1

✍ Hollis Holland • 1974 abcdefghijklmnopqrstuvwxyz(".;'!*?':,")

AGP $1234567890&fiflß-äöüåçèîñóæøœ

ABCDEFGHIJKLMNOPQRSTUVWXYZ

ÄÖÜÅÇÈÎÑÓÆØŒ»„«[¶§•†‡]‹¡·¿›...

Holland Seminar ...

• Roman abcdefghijklmnopqrstuvwxyzABCDEFGHIJKLMNOPQRSTUVWXYZ–$1234567890(".;'!*?':,

Italic *abcdefghijklmnopqrstuvwxyzABCDEFGHIJKLMNOPQRSTUVWXYZ–$1234567890(".;'!*?':,")&fiflß-*

✤ *Agfa TextSet 1*: Cartier Roman & Italic, Holland Seminar Roman & Italic.

HOLLANDER

Gerard Unger • 1983 abcdefghijklmnopqrstuvwxyz(".;'!*?':,")
LEF $1234567890&fiflß-äöüåçèîñóæøœ
ABCDEFGHIJKLMNOPQRSTUVWXYZ
ÄÖÜÅÇÈÎÑÓÆØŒ»„«[¶§•†‡]‹i·¿›...

Hollander ...

• Roman abcdefghijklmnopqrstuvwxyzABCDEFGHIJKLMNOPQRSTUVWXYZ–$1234567
Italic *abcdefghijklmnopqrstuvwxyzABCDEFGHIJKLMNOPQRSTUVWXYZ–$1234567890(".;'!*
Bold **abcdefghijklmnopqrstuvwxyzABCDEFGHIJKLMNOPQRSTUVWXYZ–$12345**
Roman SCOSF ABCDEFGHIJKLMNOPQRSTUVWXYZABCDEFGHIJKLMNOPQRSTUVWXYZ–$123456

H

HONDURAS

Paul Hickson • 1993 ... Albert Auspurg, 1936 ABCDEFGHIJKLMNOPQRSTUVWXYZ
RED (".;'!*?':,")$1234567890
▲24 &-ÄÖÜÅÇÈÎÑÓÆØŒ»„«[•]‹i·¿›... ▷KRVWY

Honduras ...

Solid **ABCDEFGHIJKLMNOPQRSTUVWXYZ–$1**
• Inline ABCDEFGHIJKLMNOPQRSTUVWXYZ–$1

HORLEY OLD STYLE

Monotype Design Staff • 1925 abcdefghijklmnopqrstuvwxyz(".;'!*?':,")
MCL ADO AGA LIN MAE $1234567890&fiflß-äöüåçèîñóæøœ
ABCDEFGHIJKLMNOPQRSTUVWXYZ
ÄÖÜÅÇÈÎÑÓÆØŒ»„«[¶§•†‡]‹¡·¿›...

Horley Old Style 1 ...

• Roman abcdefghijklmnopqrstuvwxyzABCDEFGHIJKLMNOPQRSTUVWXYZ–$1234567
Italic *abcdefghijklmnopqrstuvwxyzABCDEFGHIJKLMNOPQRSTUVWXYZ–$1234567890*
Bold **abcdefghijklmnopqrstuvwxyzABCDEFGHIJKLMNOPQRSTUVWXYZ–$1**
Bold Italic ***abcdefghijklmnopqrstuvwxyzABCDEFGHIJKLMNOPQRSTUVWXYZ–$12345***

Horley Old Style 2 ...

Light abcdefghijklmnopqrstuvwxyzABCDEFGHIJKLMNOPQRSTUVWXYZ–$1234567890
Light Italic *abcdefghijklmnopqrstuvwxyzABCDEFGHIJKLMNOPQRSTUVWXYZ–$1234567890("*
Semibold **abcdefghijklmnopqrstuvwxyzABCDEFGHIJKLMNOPQRSTUVWXYZ–$1234**
Semibold Italic ***abcdefghijklmnopqrstuvwxyzABCDEFGHIJKLMNOPQRSTUVWXYZ–$1234567***

TF HÔTELMODERNE

Joseph Treacy • 1992

TRE MTD

▲30

abcdefghijklmnopqrstuvwxyz(".:'!*?';")$1234567890&fifl ß-äöüåçéîñóœøœ

ABCDEFGHIJKLMNOPQRSTUVWXYZÄÖÜÅÇÊÎÑÓÆØŒ» „ «[¶§•†‡]‹¡·¿›… ▷ 123579/2

TF Hôtelmoderne A . . .

• Medium abcdefghijklmnopqrstuvwxyzABCDEFGHIJKLMNOPQRSTUVWXYZ—$12345678

Demi abcdefghijklmnopqrstuvwxyzABCDEFGHIJKLMNOPQRSTUVWXYZ—$1234567

Bold abcdefghijklmnopqrstuvwxyzABCDEFGHIJKLMNOPQRSTUVWXYZ—$12345

Heavy abcdefghijklmnopqrstuvwxyzABCDEFGHIJKLMNOPQRSTUVWXYZ—$1234

TF Hôtelmoderne A Two . . .
(alternate lowercase a and f)

• Medium abcdefghijklmnopqrstuvwxyzABCDEFGHIJKLMNOPQRSTUVWXYZ—$12345678

Demi abcdefghijklmnopqrstuvwxyzABCDEFGHIJKLMNOPQRSTUVWXYZ—$1234567

Bold abcdefghijklmnopqrstuvwxyzABCDEFGHIJKLMNOPQRSTUVWXYZ—$12345

Heavy abcdefghijklmnopqrstuvwxyzABCDEFGHIJKLMNOPQRSTUVWXYZ—$1234

TF HÔTELMODERNE SERIF

TRE MTD

▲30

abcdefghijklmnopqrstuvwxyz(".:'!*?';")$1234567890&fifl ß-

äöüåçéîñóœøœABCDEFGHIJKLMNOPQRSTUVWXYZ

ÄÖÜÅÇÊÎÑÓÆØŒ» „ «[¶§•†‡]‹¡·¿›… ▷ 123579/2 4 8 16 ■ □

TF Hôtelmoderne Serif . . .

Regular abcdefghijklmnopqrstuvwxyzABCDEFGHIJKLMNOPQRSTUVWXY

• Shaded abcdefghijklmnopqrstuvwxyzABCDEFGHIJKLMNOPQRSTUVWXY

H

HURRY

✍ Marshall Bohlin • 1994 abcdefghijklmnopqrstuvwxyz(".;'!*?':,")
EMD $1234567890&fiflß-äöüåçèîñóæøœ
▲16 ABCDEFGHIJKLMNOPQRSTUVWXYZ
ÄÖÜÅÇÈÎÑÓÆØŒ[¶§•†];¿...

Hurry ...

• Regular abcdefghijklmnopqrstuvwxyzABCDEFGHIJKLMNOPQRSTUVWXYZ–$12
Bold abcdefghijklmnopqrstuvwxyzABCDEFGHIJKLMNOPQRSTUVWXYZ–$12

HUXLEY HIGH

✍ ... Walter Huxley, 1935 abcdefghijklmnopqrstuvwxyz(".;'!*?':,")$1234567890&fiflß-äöüåçèîñóæøœ
HEA ABCDEFGHIJKLMNOPQRSTUVWXYZÄÖÜÅÇÈÎÑÓÆØŒ»„«[¶§•†‡]‹¡·¿›...
▲30

Huxley High ...

Light abcdefghijklmnopqrstuvwxyzABCDEFGHIJKLMNOPQRSTUVWXYZ–$1234567890(".;'!*?':,")&fiflß-
• Medium abcdefghijklmnopqrstuvwxyzABCDEFGHIJKLMNOPQRSTUVWXYZ–$1234567890(".;'!*?':,")&fi
Bold abcdefghijklmnopqrstuvwxyzABCDEFGHIJKLMNOPQRSTUVWXYZ–$1234567890(".;'!*
Black abcdefghijklmnopqrstuvwxyzABCDEFGHIJKLMNOPQRSTUVWXYZ–$1234567890(".;'

HUXLEY LOW

✍ ... Walter Huxley, 1935 abcdefghijklmnopqrstuvwxyz(".;'!*?':,")$1234567890&fiflß-äöüåçèîñóæøœ
HEA ABCDEFGHIJKLMNOPQRSTUVWXYZÄÖÜÅÇÈÎÑÓÆØŒ»„«[¶§•†‡]‹¡·¿›...
▲30

Huxley Low ...

Light abcdefghijklmnopqrstuvwxyzABCDEFGHIJKLMNOPQRSTUVWXYZ–$1234567890(".;'!*?':,")&fiflß-
• Medium abcdefghijklmnopqrstuvwxyzABCDEFGHIJKLMNOPQRSTUVWXYZ–$1234567890(".;'!*?':,")&fi
Bold abcdefghijklmnopqrstuvwxyzABCDEFGHIJKLMNOPQRSTUVWXYZ–$1234567890(".;'!*
Black abcdefghijklmnopqrstuvwxyzABCDEFGHIJKLMNOPQRSTUVWXYZ–$1234567890(".;'

HUXLEY VERTICAL ABCDEFGHIJKLMNOPQRSTUVWXYZ(".;'!*?':,")$1234567890

Walter Huxley • 1935

IMA BIT TFC &-ÄÖÜÅÇÈÎÑÓÆØŒ»„«[§•†‡]‹Ì·¿›. . .

▲30

Huxley Vertical . . .

• Regular ABCDEFGHIJKLMNOPQRSTUVWXYZ-$1234567890(".;'!*?':,")&-ÄÖÜÅÇÈÎÑÓÆØŒ»„

Alternate ABCDEFGHIJKLMNOPQRSTUVWXYZ-$1234567890(".;'!*?':,")&-ÄÖÜÅÇÈÎÑÓÆØŒ»„«

Bold ABCDEFGHIJKLMNOPQRSTUVWXYZ-$1234567890(".;'!*?':,")&-ÄÖÜÅÇÈÎÑÓÆØ

Bold Alternate ABCDEFGHIJKLMNOPQRSTUVWXYZ-$1234567890(".;'!*?':,")&-ÄÖÜÅÇÈÎÑÓÆØŒ

H

Ice Age
Ignatius
Berthold Imago
Impact
Imperial
Impressum
Imprint
Impulse
Industria
Indy Italic
Informal Roman
Inscription
Insignia
Interstate
Monotype Ionic
Bitstream Iowan Old Style
Iris
Ironmonger
Ironwood
Isabella
ITC Isadora
ITC Isbell
Isis
Italia
Monotype Italian Old Style
Sackers Italian Script

```
+                  Any serif like                  +
                     this at or
                     across the
                     top of any
                     high plain
                     column can
                     fully make
                     capital of
                     miniscules
                     or bear up
                     under such
                     burdens as
                     that which
                     I carry on
                     about as I
                     weigh this
                     head heavy
                     and dulled
                     with being
                     bearer and
                     borne both
                     Self a god
                     can make a
                     propter of
                     a post and
                     out of one
                     an I which
                     will speak
                     thundering
                     of I alone
                     I not some
                     angel no I
+                  not any seraph                  +
```

✍ John Hollander, 1987

Ice Age

URW FRA ▲16
abcdefghijklmnopqrstuvwxyz(“.;‘!*?’:,”)
$1234567890&fifl ß-äöüåçèîñóæøœ
ABCDEFGHIJKLMNOPQRSTUVWXYZ
ÄÖÜÅÇÈÎÑÓÆØŒ»„«[¶§•†‡]‹¡·¿›…

Ignatius

Freda Sack • 1987
LET ▲24
abcdefghijklmnopqrstuvwxyz(“.;‘!*?’:,”)
$1234567890&fifl ß-äöüåçèîñóæøœ
ABCDEFGHIJKLMNOPQRSTUVWXYZ
ÄÖÜÅÇÈÎÑÓÆØŒ»„«[•]‹¡·¿›…

BERTHOLD IMAGO

Günter Gerhard Lange • 1982
ADO AGA MAE
abcdefghijklmnopqrstuvwxyz(“.;‘!*?’:,”)
$1234567890&fifl ß-äöüåçèîñóæøœ
ABCDEFGHIJKLMNOPQRSTUVWXYZ
ÄÖÜÅÇÈÎÑÓÆØŒ»„«[¶§•†‡]‹¡·¿›…

Berthold Imago …

Light abcdefghijklmnopqrstuvwxyzABCDEFGHIJKLMNOPQRSTUVWXYZ–$1234567890(“.;‘!*?’
Light Italic *abcdefghijklmnopqrstuvwxyzABCDEFGHIJKLMNOPQRSTUVWXYZ–$1234567890(“.;‘!*?’:,*
• Book abcdefghijklmnopqrstuvwxyzABCDEFGHIJKLMNOPQRSTUVWXYZ–$1234567890(“.;‘
Book Italic *abcdefghijklmnopqrstuvwxyzABCDEFGHIJKLMNOPQRSTUVWXYZ–$1234567890(“.;‘!**
Medium **abcdefghijklmnopqrstuvwxyzABCDEFGHIJKLMNOPQRSTUVWXYZ–$123456**
Medium Italic ***abcdefghijklmnopqrstuvwxyzABCDEFGHIJKLMNOPQRSTUVWXYZ–$123456***
Extra Bold **abcdefghijklmnopqrstuvwxyzABCDEFGHIJKLMNOPQRSTUVWXYZ–$12**
Extra Bold Italic ***abcdefghijklmnopqrstuvwxyzABCDEFGHIJKLMNOPQRSTUVWXYZ–$12***

Impact

✣ Adobe DisplaySet 2
Geoffrey Lee • 1965
ADO AGA TFC LIN MAE ▲30
abcdefghijklmnopqrstuvwxyz(“.;‘!*?’:,”)
$1234567890&fifl ß-äöüåçèîñóæøœ
ABCDEFGHIJKLMNOPQRSTUVWXYZ
ÄÖÜÅÇÈÎÑÓÆØŒ»„«[¶§•†‡]‹¡·¿›…

✣ *Adobe DisplaySet 2*: Baker Signet & Impact.

IMPERIAL

Edwin Sharr • 1957 abcdefghijklmnopqrstuvwxyz(“.;‘!*?’:,”)

BIT $1234567890&fiflß-äöüåçèîñóæøœ

ABCDEFGHIJKLMNOPQRSTUVWXYZ

ÄÖÜÅÇÈÎÑÓÆØŒ»„«[¶§•†‡]‹i·¿›...

Imperial ...

• Roman abcdefghijklmnopqrstuvwxyzABCDEFGHIJKLMNOPQRSTUVWXYZ–$12

Italic *abcdefghijklmnopqrstuvwxyzABCDEFGHIJKLMNOPQRSTUVWXYZ–$12*

Bold **abcdefghijklmnopqrstuvwxyzABCDEFGHIJKLMNOPQRSTUVWXYZ–$**

IMPRESSUM

Konrad Bauer & Walter Baum • 1963 abcdefghijklmnopqrstuvwxyz(“.;‘!*?’:,”)

LIN ADO AGA AGP MAE URW $1234567890&fiflß-äöüåçèîñóæøœ

ABCDEFGHIJKLMNOPQRSTUVWXYZ

ÄÖÜÅÇÈÎÑÓÆØŒ»„«[¶§•†‡]‹¡·¿›...

Impressum ...

• Roman abcdefghijklmnopqrstuvwxyzABCDEFGHIJKLMNOPQRSTUVWXYZ–

Italic *abcdefghijklmnopqrstuvwxyzABCDEFGHIJKLMNOPQRSTUVWXYZ–$*

Bold **abcdefghijklmnopqrstuvwxyzABCDEFGHIJKLMNOPQRSTUVWXYZ–**

IMPRINT

Gerard Meynell, Edward Johnston, J. H. Mason, Ernest Jackson... Monotype Design Staff • 1913 abcdefghijklmnopqrstuvwxyz(“.;‘!*?’:,”)

$1234567890&fiflß-äöüåçèîñóæøœ

MCL ABCDEFGHIJKLMNOPQRSTUVWXYZ

ÄÖÜÅÇÈÎÑÓÆØŒ»„«[¶§•†‡]‹¡·¿›...

Imprint ...

• Roman abcdefghijklmnopqrstuvwxyzABCDEFGHIJKLMNOPQRSTUVWXYZ–$123

Italic *abcdefghijklmnopqrstuvwxyzABCDEFGHIJKLMNOPQRSTUVWXYZ–$1234*

Bold **abcdefghijklmnopqrstuvwxyzABCDEFGHIJKLMNOPQRSTUVWXYZ–$12**

Bold Italic ***abcdefghijklmnopqrstuvwxyzABCDEFGHIJKLMNOPQRSTUVWXYZ–***

IMPRINT EXPERT

MCL ABCDEFGHIJKLMNOPQRSTUVWXYZ.;!?:,

1234567890&ﬀﬁﬂﬃﬄ–ÄÖÜÅÇÈÎÑÓÆØŒ

(abdeilmnorst) 1/8 1/4 1/3 3/8 1/2 5/8 2/3 3/4 7/8 $12345/67890¢ ₡Rp

Imprint Expert ...

• Expert Roman ABCDEFGHIJKLMNOPQRSTUVWXYZ–$1234567890.;!?:,&-ﬀﬁﬂﬃﬄ 1/8 1/4 1/3 3/8 1/2 $12345/67890

Expert Italic *$1234567890.;:,–ﬀﬁﬂﬃﬄ 1/8 1/4 1/3 3/8 1/2 $12345/67890¢ (abdeilmnorst) 5/8 2/3 3/4 7/8 ₡Rp*

Expert Bold **$1234567890.;:,–ﬀﬁﬂﬃﬄ 1/8 1/4 1/3 3/8 1/2 $12345/67890¢ (abdeilmnorst) 5/8 2/3 3/4 7/8 ₡Rp**

I

... Imprint Expert

Expert Bold Italic $1234567890.;:,–ﬀﬁﬂﬃﬄ 1/8 1/4 1/3 3/8 1/2 $12345/67890¢ (abdeilmnorst) 5/8 2/3 3/4 7/8 ₡Rp

IMPRINT SHADOW
Monotype Handtooled
Monotype Design Staff • 1935

abcdefghijklmnopqrstuvwxyz(".;'!*?':,")

MCL $1234567890&ﬁﬂß-äöüåçèîñóæøœ

▲24 ABCDEFGHIJKLMNOPQRSTUVWXYZ

ÄÖÜÅÇÈÎÑÓÆØŒ»„«[•]‹¡·¿›...

I

Imprint Shadow ...

• Roman abcdefghijklmnopqrstuvwxyzABCDEFGHIJKL

Italic *abcdefghijklmnopqrstuvwxyzABCDEFGHIJKL*

Impuls

Paul Zimmerman • 1945 abcdefghijklmnopqrstuvwxyz(".;'!*?':,")

BIT $1234567890&ﬁﬂß-äöüåçèîñóæøœ

▲16 ABCDEFGHIJKLMNOPQRSTUVWXYZ

ÄÖÜÅÇÈÎÑÓÆØŒ»„«[§•†‡]‹¡·¿›...

INDUSTRIA
Brody DisplaySet 1

abcdefghijklmnopqrstuvwxyz(".;'!*?':,")

Neville Brody • 1990

$1234567890&ﬁﬂß-äöüåçèîñóæøœ

LIN ADO AGA MAE

ABCDEFGHIJKLMNOPQRSTUVWXYZ

▲36

ÄÖÜÅÇÈÎÑÓÆØŒ»„«[●]‹¡·¿›... ▷Q l t

Industria ...

Inline abcdefghijklmnopqrstuvwxyzABCDEFGHIJKLMNOPQRSTUVW

• Solid abcdefghijklmnopqrstuvwxyzABCDEFGHIJKLMNOPQRSTUVW

....
Monotype Handtooled: Colonna, Imprint Shadow Roman & Italic.
Brody DisplaySet 1: Arcadia, Industria Inline & Solid, Insignia.

Indy Italic

✍ Charles Hughes • 1990 abcdefghijklmnopqrstuvwxyz(“.;‘!*?’:,”)
LET $1234567890&fiflß-äöüåçèîñóæøœ
▲16 ABCDEFGHIJKLMNOPQRSTUVWXYZ
ÄÖÜÅÇÈÎÑÓÆØŒ»„«[•]‹¡·¿›... ▷ abcefijklmnooprssuvwxzffflolorquttveEHVWY

Informal Roman

✍ Martin Wait • 1989 abcdefghijklmnopqrstuvwxyz(“.;‘!*?’:,”)
LET $1234567890&fiflß-äöüåçèîñóæøœ
▲18 ABCDEFGHIJKLMNOPQRSTUVWXYZ
ÄÖÜÅÇÈÎÑÓÆØŒ»„«[•]‹¡·¿›...

Inscription

✍ Alan Meeks • 1983 abcdefghijklmnopqrstuvwxyz(“.;‘!*?’:,”)
LET
▲24 $1234567890&fiflß-äöüåçèîñóæøœ
ABCDEFGHIJKLMNOPQRSTUVWXYZ
ÄÖÜÅÇÈÎÑÓÆØŒ»„«[•]‹¡·¿›... ▷ r

INSIGNIA
✤ Brody DisplaySet 1
✍ Neville Brody • 1990 abcdefghijklmnopqrstuvwxyz(“.;‘!*?’:,”)
LIN ADO AGA MAE $1234567890&fiflß-äöüåçèîñóœøœ
▲18 ABCDEFGHIJKLMNOPQRSTUVWXYZ
ÄÖÜÅÇÈÎÑÓÆØŒ»„«[¶§•†‡]‹¡·¿›... ▷ s t J S Z

INTERSTATE

✍ Tobias Frere-Jones • 1993 abcdefghijklmnopqrstuvwxyz(“.;‘!*?’:,”)
FBU $1234567890&fiflß-äöüåçèîñóæøœ
▲16 ABCDEFGHIJKLMNOPQRSTUVWXYZ
ÄÖÜÅÇÈÎÑÓÆØŒ»„«[¶§•†‡]‹¡·¿›... ▷ a ← → ↑ ↓ ↕ ↔ ✥

i Interstate ...

Light abcdefghijklmnopqrstuvwxyzABCDEFGHIJKLMNOPQRSTUVWXYZ-$1
• Regular abcdefghijklmnopqrstuvwxyzABCDEFGHIJKLMNOPQRSTUVWXYZ-
Bold **abcdefghijklmnopqrstuvwxyzABCDEFGHIJKLMNOPQRSTUVWXY**
Black **abcdefghijklmnopqrstuvwxyzABCDEFGHIJKLMNOPQRSTUVWX**

✤ *Brody DisplaySet 1*: Arcadia, Industria Inline & Solid, Insignia.
i Interstate ▶Interstate Pi

INTERSTATE CONDENSED

FBU abcdefghijklmnopqrstuvwxyz(“.;‘!*?’:,”)
▲16 $1234567890&fiflß-äöüåçèîñóæøœ
ABCDEFGHIJKLMNOPQRSTUVWXYZ
ÄÖÜÅÇÈÎÑÓÆØŒ»,„«[¶§•†‡]‹i·¿›... ▷a ← → ↑ ↓ ↕ ↔ ✥

i Interstate Condensed ...

Light Condensed abcdefghijklmnopqrstuvwxyzABCDEFGHIJKLMNOPQRSTUVWXYZ-$1234567890(“.;‘!*?’:,”)&fi
• Condensed abcdefghijklmnopqrstuvwxyzABCDEFGHIJKLMNOPQRSTUVWXYZ-$1234567890(“.;‘!*?’
Bold Condensed abcdefghijklmnopqrstuvwxyzABCDEFGHIJKLMNOPQRSTUVWXYZ-$1234567890(“.;
Black Condensed abcdefghijklmnopqrstuvwxyzABCDEFGHIJKLMNOPQRSTUVWXYZ-$1234567890

INTERSTATE COMPRESSED

FBU abcdefghijklmnopqrstuvwxyz(“.;‘!*?’:,”)
▲18 $1234567890&fiflß-äöüåçèîñóæøœ
ABCDEFGHIJKLMNOPQRSTUVWXYZ
ÄÖÜÅÇÈÎÑÓÆØŒ»,„«[¶§•†‡]‹i·¿›... ▷a ← → ↑ ↓ ↕ ↔ ✥

i Interstate Compressed ...

Light Compressed abcdefghijklmnopqrstuvwxyzABCDEFGHIJKLMNOPQRSTUVWXYZ-$1234567890(“.;‘!*?’:,”)&fiflß-äöüÄÖÜå
• Compressed abcdefghijklmnopqrstuvwxyzABCDEFGHIJKLMNOPQRSTUVWXYZ-$1234567890(“.;‘!*?’:,”)&fiflß-äöü
Bold Compressed abcdefghijklmnopqrstuvwxyzABCDEFGHIJKLMNOPQRSTUVWXYZ-$1234567890(“.;‘!*?’:,”)&fiflß-äö
Black Compressed abcdefghijklmnopqrstuvwxyzABCDEFGHIJKLMNOPQRSTUVWXYZ-$1234567890(“.;‘!*?’:,”)&fiflß-

MONOTYPE IONIC

MCL abcdefghijklmnopqrstuvwxyz(“.;‘!*?’:,”)
$1234567890&fiflß-äöüåçèîñóæøœ
ABCDEFGHIJKLMNOPQRSTUVWXYZ
ÄÖÜÅÇÈÎÑÓÆØŒ»,„«[¶§•†‡]‹¡·¿›...

Monotype Ionic ...

• Roman abcdefghijklmnopqrstuvwxyzABCDEFGHIJKLMNOPQRSTUVWXY
Italic *abcdefghijklmnopqrstuvwxyzABCDEFGHIJKLMNOPQRSTUVWXYZ–$*
Bold **abcdefghijklmnopqrstuvwxyzABCDEFGHIJKLMNOPQRSTUVWXYZ–**

BITSTREAM IOWAN OLD STYLE

✍ John Downer • 1990 abcdefghijklmnopqrstuvwxyz(“.;‘!*?’:,”)
BIT $1234567890&fiflß-äöüåçèîñóæøœ
ABCDEFGHIJKLMNOPQRSTUVWXYZ
ÄÖÜÅÇÈÎÑÓÆØŒ»,„«[¶§•†‡]‹i·¿›...

Bitstream Iowan Old Style ...

• Roman abcdefghijklmnopqrstuvwxyzABCDEFGHIJKLMNOPQRSTUVWXYZ–$123456

i Interstate Condensed & Compressed ▶ Interstate Pi

. . . Bitstream Iowan Old Style

Italic *abcdefghijklmnopqrstuvwxyzABCDEFGHIJKLMNOPQRSTUVWXYZ–$1234567890("*

Bold **abcdefghijklmnopqrstuvwxyzABCDEFGHIJKLMNOPQRSTUVWXYZ–$12**

Bold Italic ***abcdefghijklmnopqrstuvwxyzABCDEFGHIJKLMNOPQRSTUVWXYZ–$1234567***

Black **abcdefghijklmnopqrstuvwxyzABCDEFGHIJKLMNOPQRSTUVWX**

Black Italic ***abcdefghijklmnopqrstuvwxyzABCDEFGHIJKLMNOPQRSTUVWXYZ–$1***

IRIS

Letraset Design Staff • 1994

LET

▲54

ABCDEFGHIJKLMNOPQRSTUVWXYZ(".:'!*?':;")

$1234567890&-ÄÖÜÅÇÈÎÑÓÆØŒ»„«[•] . . .

IRONMONGER

John Downer • 1991

FBU AGP MTD

▲30

ABCDEFGHIJKLMNOPQ

RSTUVWXYZ("„;'!*?':;")

$1234567890&-ÄÖÜÅÇÈ

ÎÑÓÆØÆØŒ»„«[¶§•†‡]...

Ironmonger . . .

Extra Condensed ABCDEFGHIJKLMNOPQRSTUVWXYZ-$1234567890(".:'!*?':;")&-ÄÖÖÅÇÈÎÑÓÆØŒ»„«[¶§•†‡]•

Black ABCDEFGHIJKLMNOPQ

Extended ABCDEFGHIJKLMNOPQ

• Inlaid ABCDEFGHIJKLMNOPQ

Ironmonger 3-D

John Downer • 1993

FBU

▲30

ABCDEFGHIJKLMNOPQ

RSTUVWXYZ("„;'!*?':;")

$1234567890&-ÄÖÜÅÇÈ

ÎÑÓÆØÆØŒ»„«[¶§•†‡]...

Ironwood
Adobe Wood Type 1
Kim Buker, Barbara Lind & Joy Redick • 1991
ADO AGA LIN MAE
▲48

ABCDEFGHIJKLMNOPQRSTUVWXYZ
(".;'!*?':,")$1234567890
&-ÄÖÜÅÇÊÎÑÓÆØŒ»„«[•]‹¡·¿›...

Isabella
Agfa DisplaySet 4
Herman Ihlenburg • 1892
AGP
▲18

abcdefghijklmnopqrstuvwxyz(".;'!*?':,")
$1234567890&fiflß-äöüåçèîñóœøœ
ABCDEFGHIJKLMNOPQRSTUVWXYZ
ÄÖÜÅÇÈÎÑÓŒØŒ»„«[¶§•†‡]‹¡·¿›...

ITC ISADORA
Kris Holmes • 1985
LIN ADO AGA AGP LEF FRA MAE URW
▲16

abcdefghijklmnopqrstuvwxyz(".;'!?':,")*
$1234567890& fiflß-äöüåçèîñóæøœ
ABCDEFGHIJKLMNOPQRSTUVWXYZ
ÄÖÜÅÇÈÎÑÓÆØŒ»„«[¶§•†‡]‹¡·¿›...

ITC Isadora ...
• Regular *abcdefghijklmnopqrstuvwxyzABCDEFGHIJKLMNOPQRSTUVWXY*
Bold ***abcdefghijklmnopqrstuvwxyzABCDEFGHIJKLMNOPQRSTUVW***

ITC ISBELL
Richard Isbell & Jerry Campbell • 1981
BIT AGP LEF FRA

abcdefghijklmnopqrstuvwxyz(".;'!*?':,")
$1234567890&fiflß-äöüåçèîñóæøœ
ABCDEFGHIJKLMNOPQRSTUVWXYZ
ÄÖÜÅÇÈÎÑÓÆØŒ»„«[¶§•†‡]‹¡·¿›...

ITC Isbell 1 ...
• Book abcdefghijklmnopqrstuvwxyzABCDEFGHIJKLMNOPQRSTUVWXYZ–$1234567
Book Italic *abcdefghijklmnopqrstuvwxyzABCDEFGHIJKLMNOPQRSTUVWXYZ–$12345678*
Bold **abcdefghijklmnopqrstuvwxyzABCDEFGHIJKLMNOPQRSTUVWXYZ–$12**
Bold Italic ***abcdefghijklmnopqrstuvwxyzABCDEFGHIJKLMNOPQRSTUVWXYZ–$123***

ITC Isbell 2 ...
Medium abcdefghijklmnopqrstuvwxyzABCDEFGHIJKLMNOPQRSTUVWXYZ–$12345
Medium Italic *abcdefghijklmnopqrstuvwxyzABCDEFGHIJKLMNOPQRSTUVWXYZ–$123456*

Adobe Wood Type 1: Cottonwood, Ironwood, Juniper, Mesquite, Ponderosa, Adobe Wood Type Ornaments 1.
Ironwood ▶ Adobe Wood Type Ornaments 1.
Agfa DisplaySet 4: Branding Iron, Isabella, McCollough, Raphael.

... ITC Isbell 2

Heavy abcdefghijklmnopqrstuvwxyzABCDEFGHIJKLMNOPQRSTUVWXYZ–$

Heavy Italic *abcdefghijklmnopqrstuvwxyzABCDEFGHIJKLMNOPQRSTUVWXYZ–$*

Isis

Michael Gills • 1990 ABCDEFGHIJKLMNOPQRSTUVWXYZ

LET [“.;‘!*?’:,”]$1234567890

▲24 &-ÄÖÜÅÇÈÎÑÓÆØŒ»„«[•]‹¡·¿›...

ITALIA

Colin Brignall • 1975 abcdefghijklmnopqrstuvwxyz(“.;‘!*?’:,”)

BIT ADO AGA LEF LIN MAE URW $1234567890&fiflß-äöüåçèîñóæøœ

ABCDEFGHIJKLMNOPQRSTUVWXYZ

ÄÖÜÅÇÈÎÑÓÆØŒ»„«[¶§•†‡]‹¡·¿›...

Italia ...

• Book abcdefghijklmnopqrstuvwxyzABCDEFGHIJKLMNOPQRSTUVWXYZ–$1234567890

Medium abcdefghijklmnopqrstuvwxyzABCDEFGHIJKLMNOPQRSTUVWXYZ–$123456789

Bold **abcdefghijklmnopqrstuvwxyzABCDEFGHIJKLMNOPQRSTUVWXYZ–$12345678**

MONOTYPE ITALIAN OLD STYLE

MCL ADO AGA LIN MAE abcdefghijklmnopqrstuvwxyz(“.;‘!*?’:,”)

$1234567890&fiflß-äöüåçèîñóæøœ

ABCDEFGHIJKLMNOPQRSTUVWXYZ

ÄÖÜÅÇÈÎÑÓÆØŒ»„«[¶§•†‡]‹¡·¿›...

Monotype Italian Old Style ...

• Roman abcdefghijklmnopqrstuvwxyzABCDEFGHIJKLMNOPQRSTUVWXYZ–$123456

Italic *abcdefghijklmnopqrstuvwxyzABCDEFGHIJKLMNOPQRSTUVWXYZ–$1234567890(*

Bold **abcdefghijklmnopqrstuvwxyzABCDEFGHIJKLMNOPQRSTUVWXYZ–$1234**

Bold Italic ***abcdefghijklmnopqrstuvwxyzABCDEFGHIJKLMNOPQRSTUVWXYZ–$1234567890(***

Sackers Italian Script
Agfa Engravers 2

AGP *abcdefghijklmnopqrstuvwxyz(“.;‘!*?’:,”)*

▲18 *$1234567890&ß-äöüåçèîñó*

ABCDEFGHIJKLMNOPQRSTUVWXYZ

ÄÖÜÅÇÈÎÑÓ»«[.]‹› ▷ *I V X st nd rd th ¼ ⅓ ½ ¾ % %*

Agfa Engravers 2: Sackers Antique Roman Open & Solid, Sackers Light Classic Roman, Sackers English Script, Sackers Gothic Light, Medium & Heavy, Sackers Italian Script, Sackers Roman Light & Heavy, Sackers Square Gothic.

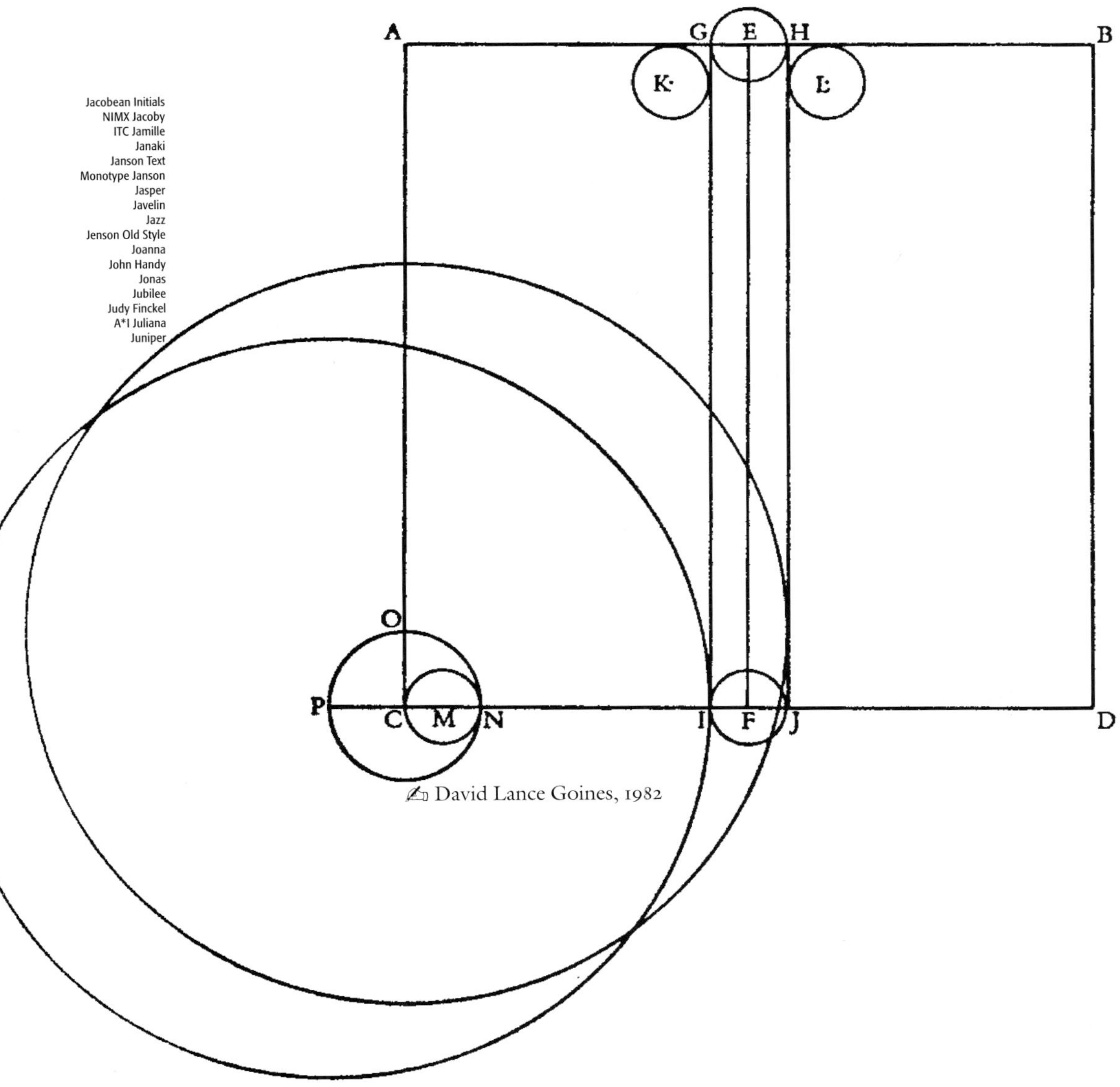
A
G
E
H
B
K·
L·
O
P
C
M
N
I
F
J
D

✍ David Lance Goines, 1982

JACOBEAN INITIALS SET 1

Designer Name • DATE

LAN

▲30

Jacobean Initials Set 1 . . .

Alphabet Fill

Alphabet Pattern

Alphabet Matrix

• Composite

JACOBEAN INITIALS SET 2

LAN

▲30

Jacobean Initials Set 2 . . .

Square Frame Positive

Square Frame Alphabet Fill

• Square Frame Negative

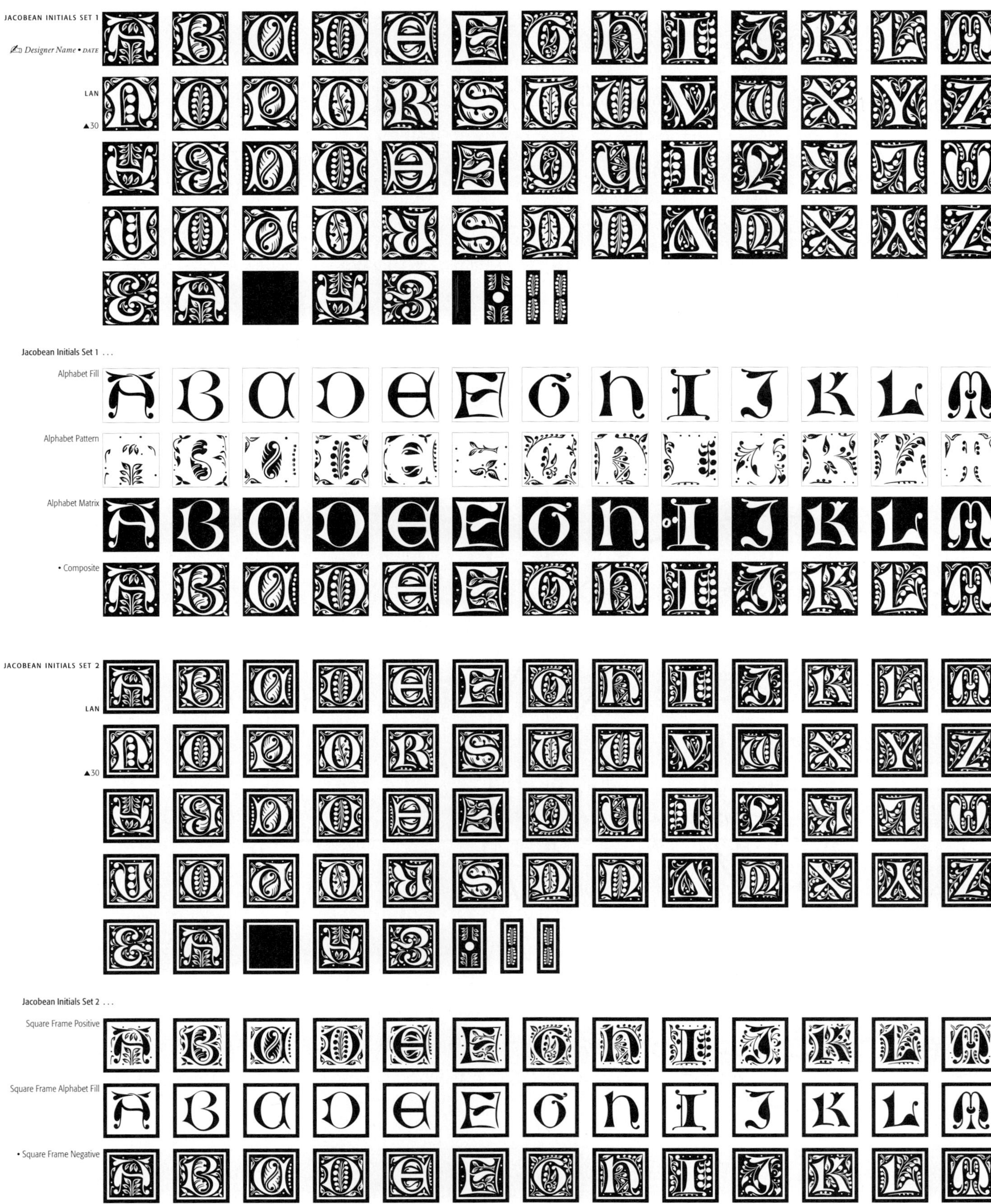

NIMX JACOBY

✍ *Calvin Glenn • 1993* abcdefghijklmnopqrstuvwxyz(“.;‘!*?’:,”)
NIM $1234567890&fiflß-äöüåçèîñóæøœ
ABCDEFGHIJKLMNOPQRSTUVWXYZ
ÄÖÜÅÇÈÎÑÓÆØŒ»„«[¶§•†‡]‹¡·¿›...

NIMX Jacoby ...

Extra Light abcdefghijklmnopqrstuvwxyzABCDEFGHIJKLMNOPQRSTUVWXYZ–$1234567890(“.;‘!
• Light abcdefghijklmnopqrstuvwxyzABCDEFGHIJKLMNOPQRSTUVWXYZ–$1234567890(“.;‘!
Black **abcdefghijklmnopqrstuvwxyzABCDEFGHIJKLMNOPQRSTUVWXYZ–$1234567890(“.;‘**

ITC JAMILLE

✍ *Mark Jamra • 1988* abcdefghijklmnopqrstuvwxyz(“.;‘!*?’:,”)
AGP LEF URW $1234567890&fiflß-äöüåçèîñóæøœ
ABCDEFGHIJKLMNOPQRSTUVWXYZ
ÄÖÜÅÇÈÎÑÓÆØŒ»„«[¶§•†‡]‹¡·¿›...

ITC Jamille ...

• Book abcdefghijklmnopqrstuvwxyzABCDEFGHIJKLMNOPQRSTUVWXYZ–$123456789
Book Italic *abcdefghijklmnopqrstuvwxyzABCDEFGHIJKLMNOPQRSTUVWXYZ–$1234567890(*
Bold **abcdefghijklmnopqrstuvwxyzABCDEFGHIJKLMNOPQRSTUVWXYZ–$1234567**
Bold Italic ***abcdefghijklmnopqrstuvwxyzABCDEFGHIJKLMNOPQRSTUVWXYZ–$1234567***
Black **abcdefghijklmnopqrstuvwxyzABCDEFGHIJKLMNOPQRSTUVWXYZ–$1234**
Black Italic ***abcdefghijklmnopqrstuvwxyzABCDEFGHIJKLMNOPQRSTUVWXYZ–$12345***

JANAKI

✍ *Mouli Marur • 1993* abcdefghijklmnopqrstuvwxyz(“.;‘!*?’:,”)
T26 $1234567890&fiflß-äöüåçèîñóæøœ
▲16 ABCDEFGHIJKLMNOPQRSTUVWXYZ
ÄÖÜÅÇÈÎÑÓÆØŒ»„«[¶§•†‡]‹¡·¿›...

Janaki ...

• Regular abcdefghijklmnopqrstuvwxyzABCDEFGHIJKLMNOPQRSTUVWXYZ–$12
Italic abcdefghijklmnopqrstuvwxyzABCDEFGHIJKLMNOPQRSTUVWXYZ–$12
Bold abcdefghijklmnopqrstuvwxyzABCDEFGHIJKLMNOPQRSTUVWXYZ–$
Bold Italic abcdefghijklmnopqrstuvwxyzABCDEFGHIJKLMNOPQRSTUVWXYZ–
Black abcdefghijklmnopqrstuvwxyzABCDEFGHIJKLMNOPQRSTUVWXYZ–$

J

JANSON TEXT

Linotype Design Staff, Horst Heiderhoff & Adrian Frutiger • 1985

abcdefghijklmnopqrstuvwxyz(“.;‘!*?’:,”)
$1234567890&fiflß-äöüåçèîñóæøœ

LIN ADO AGA MAE ABCDEFGHIJKLMNOPQRSTUVWXYZ
ÄÖÜÅÇÈÎÑÓÆØŒ»„«[¶§•†‡]‹¡·¿›…

Janson Text …

• 55-Roman abcdefghijklmnopqrstuvwxyzABCDEFGHIJKLMNOPQRSTUVWXYZ–$123456

56-Italic *abcdefghijklmnopqrstuvwxyzABCDEFGHIJKLMNOPQRSTUVWXYZ–$1234567890(*

75-Bold **abcdefghijklmnopqrstuvwxyzABCDEFGHIJKLMNOPQRSTUVWXYZ–$123**

76-Bold Italic ***abcdefghijklmnopqrstuvwxyzABCDEFGHIJKLMNOPQRSTUVWXYZ–$12345***

JANSON TEXT SCOSF

LIN ADO AGA MAE ABCDEFGHIJKLMNOPQRSTUVWXYZ(“.;‘!*?’:,”)
$1234567890&-ÄÖÜÅÇÈÎÑÓÆØŒ
ABCDEFGHIJKLMNOPQRSTUVWXYZ
ÄÖÜÅÇÈÎÑÓÆØŒ»„«[¶§•†‡]‹¡·¿›…

Janson Text SCOSF …

• 55-Roman SCOSF ABCDEFGHIJKLMNOPQRSTUVWXYZABCDEFGHIJKLMNOPQRSTUVWXYZ–$1234

56-Italic OSF *abcdefghijklmnopqrstuvwxyzABCDEFGHIJKLMNOPQRSTUVWXYZ–$1234567890(*

75-Bold OSF **abcdefghijklmnopqrstuvwxyzABCDEFGHIJKLMNOPQRSTUVWXYZ–$123**

76-Bold Italic OSF ***abcdefghijklmnopqrstuvwxyzABCDEFGHIJKLMNOPQRSTUVWXYZ–$12345***

MONOTYPE JANSON

Monotype Design Staff • 1986

abcdefghijklmnopqrstuvwxyz(“.;‘!*?’:,”)

MCL $1234567890&fiflß-äöüåçèîñóæøœ
ABCDEFGHIJKLMNOPQRSTUVWXYZ
ÄÖÜÅÇÈÎÑÓÆØŒ»„«[¶§•†‡]‹¡·¿›…

Monotype Janson …

• Roman abcdefghijklmnopqrstuvwxyzABCDEFGHIJKLMNOPQRSTUVWXYZ–$1234567890(“.

Italic *abcdefghijklmnopqrstuvwxyzABCDEFGHIJKLMNOPQRSTUVWXYZ–$1234567890(“.;‘!*?’:,”)&fi*

Bold **abcdefghijklmnopqrstuvwxyzABCDEFGHIJKLMNOPQRSTUVWXYZ–$12345678**

Bold Italic ***abcdefghijklmnopqrstuvwxyzABCDEFGHIJKLMNOPQRSTUVWXYZ–$1234567890(“.;‘!*?***

MONOTYPE JANSON EXPERT

MCL ABCDEFGHIJKLMNOPQRSTUVWXYZ.;!?:,
1234567890&fffiflffiffl–ÄÖÜÅÇÈÎÑÓÆØŒ
(abdeilmnorst) 1/8 1/4 1/3 3/8 1/2 5/8 2/3 3/4 7/8 $12345/67890¢ ₡Rp

Monotype Janson Expert …

• Expert Roman ABCDEFGHIJKLMNOPQRSTUVWXYZ–$1234567890.;!?:,&-fffiflffiffl 1/8 1/4 1/3 3/8 1/2 $12345/67890¢ (abdeilmnor

Expert Italic *$1234567890.;:,–fffiflffiffl 1/8 1/4 1/3 3/8 1/2 $12345/67890¢ (abdeilmnorst) 5/8 2/3 3/4 7/8 ₡Rp*

... Monotype Janson Expert

Expert Bold $1234567890.;:,–ff fi fl ffi ffl ⅛ ¼ ⅓ ⅜ ½ $12345/67890¢ (abdeilmnorst) ⅝ ⅔ ¾ ⅞ ₡Rp

Expert Bold Italic *$1234567890.;:,–ff fi fl ffi ffl ⅛ ¼ ⅓ ⅜ ½ $12345/67890¢ (abdeilmnorst) ⅝ ⅔ ¾ ⅞ ₡Rp*

Jasper
Agfa ScriptSet 1

AGP *abcdefghijklmnopqrstuvwxyz(“.;‘!*?’:,”)*

▲16 *$1234567890&fiflß-äöüåçèîñóæøœ*

ABCDEFGHIJKLMNOPQRSTUVWXYZ

ÄÖÜÅÇÈÎÑÓÆØŒ»„«[¶§•†‡]‹¡·¿›...

JAVELIN

Pat Hickson • c.1978 abcdefghijklmnopqrstuvwxyz(“.;‘!*?’:,”)

RED $1234567890&fiflß-äöüåçèîñóæøœ

ABCDEFGHIJKLMNOPQRSTUVWXYZ

ÄÖÜÅÇÈÎÑÓÆØŒ»„«[¶·†‡]‹¡·¿›...

▷ _ _

Javelin ...

Light abcdefghijklmnopqrstuvwxyz ABCDEFGHIJKLMNOPQRSTUVWXYZ–$1234567890(“.;‘!*?’:,”)&fiflß-

• Medium abcdefghijklmnopqrstuvwxyz ABCDEFGHIJKLMNOPQRSTUVWXYZ–$1234567890(“.;

Bold abcdefghijklmnopqrstuvwxyz ABCDEFGHIJKLMNOPQRSTUVWXYZ–$1234567

Extra Bold abcdefghijklmnopqrstuvwxyz ABCDEFGHIJKLMNOPQRSTUVWXYZ–$1234

Jazz

Alan Meeks • 1992 abcdefghijklmnopqrstuvwxyz(“.;‘!*?’:,”)

LET

▲24 $1234567890&fiflß-äöüåçèîñóæøœ

ABCDEFGHIJKLMNOPQRSTUVWXYZ

ÄÖÜÅÇÈÎÑÓÆØŒ»„«[•]‹¡·¿›...

Jenson Old Style
Bold Condensed

URW LEF FRA abcdefghijklmnopqrstuvwxyz(“.;‘!*?’:,”)

▲24 $1234567890&fiflß-äöüåçèîñóæøœ

ABCDEFGHIJKLMNOPQRSTUVWXYZ

ÄÖÜÅÇÈÎÑÓÆØŒ»„«[¶§•†‡]‹¡·¿›...

Agfa ScriptSet 1: Basilica, Floridian Script, Jasper, Liberty.

J

JOANNA

Eric Gill • 1930 abcdefghijklmnopqrstuvwxyz(".;'!*?':,")

MCL ADO AGA LIN MAE $1234567890&fiflß-äöüåçèîñóæøœ

▲16 ABCDEFGHIJKLMNOPQRSTUVWXYZ

ÄÖÜÅÇÈÎÑÓÆØŒ»„«[¶§•†‡]‹¡·¿›...

Joanna ...

• Roman abcdefghijklmnopqrstuvwxyzABCDEFGHIJKLMNOPQRSTUVWXYZ–$1234567

Italic *abcdefghijklmnopqrstuvwxyzABCDEFGHIJKLMNOPQRSTUVWXYZ–$1234567890(".;'!*?':,")*

Semibold **abcdefghijklmnopqrstuvwxyzABCDEFGHIJKLMNOPQRSTUVWXYZ–$1234**

Semibold Italic ***abcdefghijklmnopqrstuvwxyzABCDEFGHIJKLMNOPQRSTUVWXYZ–$1234567890(".;'!***

Bold **abcdefghijklmnopqrstuvwxyzABCDEFGHIJKLMNOPQRSTUVWXYZ–$123**

Bold Italic ***abcdefghijklmnopqrstuvwxyzABCDEFGHIJKLMNOPQRSTUVWXYZ–$1234567890(".;'!***

Extra Bold **abcdefghijklmnopqrstuvwxyzABCDEFGHIJKLMNOPQRSTUVWXYZ–$**

JOANNA OSF

MCL abcdefghijklmnopqrstuvwxyz(".;'!*?':,")

▲16 $1234567890&fiflß-äöüåçèîñóæøœ

ABCDEFGHIJKLMNOPQRSTUVWXYZ

ÄÖÜÅÇÈÎÑÓÆØŒ»„«[¶§•†‡]‹¡·¿›...

Joanna OSF ...

• Roman OSF abcdefghijklmnopqrstuvwxyzABCDEFGHIJKLMNOPQRSTUVWXYZ–$1234567

Italic OSF *abcdefghijklmnopqrstuvwxyzABCDEFGHIJKLMNOPQRSTUVWXYZ–$1234567890(".;'!*?':,"*

Bold OSF **abcdefghijklmnopqrstuvwxyzABCDEFGHIJKLMNOPQRSTUVWXYZ–$123**

Bold Italic OSF ***abcdefghijklmnopqrstuvwxyzABCDEFGHIJKLMNOPQRSTUVWXYZ–$1234567890("***

John Handy

Tim Donaldson • 1995 abcdefghijklmnopqrstuvwxyz(".;'!*?':,")

LET $1234567890&fiflß-äöüåçèîñóæøœ

ABCDEFGHIJKLMNOPQRSTUVWXYZ

ÄÖÜÅÇÈÎÑÓÆØŒ»„«[•]‹¡·¿›...

JONAS

Johannes Birkenbach • 1994

MTD

▲30

abcdefghijklmnopqrstuvwxyz(“.;‘!*?’:,”)

$1234567890&fiflß-äöüåçèîñóæøœ

ABCDEFGHIJKLMNOPQRSTUVWXYZ

ÄÖÜÅÇÈÎÑÓÆØŒ»,,«[¶§•†‡]‹¡·¿›...

Jonas ...

• Body abcdefghijklmnopqrstuvwxyzABCDEFGHIJKLMN

Head abcdefghijklmnopqrstuvwxyzABCDEFGHIJKLMN

JUBILEE

Eric Gill • 1934

RED

▲28

abcdefghijklmnopqrstuvwxyz(“.;‘!*?’:,”)

$1234567890&fiflß-äöüåçèîñóæøœ

ABCDEFGHIJKLMNOPQRSTUVWXYZ

ÄÖÜÅÇÈÎÑÓÆØŒ»,,«[¶§•†‡]‹¡·¿›...

Jubilee ...

Light abcdefghijklmnopqrstuvwxyzABCDEFGHIJK

• Medium abcdefghijklmnopqrstuvwxyzABCDEFGHIJ

Bold abcdefghijklmnopqrstuvwxyzABCDEFG

JudyFinckel

INT

▲16

abcdefghijklmnopqrstuvwxyz(“.;‘!*?’:,”)

$1234567890&ß-äöüåçèîñóæøœ

ABCDEFGHIJKLMNOPQRSTUVWXYZ

ÄÖÜÅÇÈÎÑÓÆØŒ»,,«[§]‹¡·¿›

A*I Juliana

Philip Bouwsma • 1994 abcdefghijklmnopqrstuvwxyz(“.;'!*?':,”)

ALP $1234567890&fiflß-äöüåçèîñóæøœ

▲18 ABCDEFGHIJKLMNOPQRSTUVWXYZ

ÄÖÜÅÇÈÎÑÓÆØŒ»„«[¶§•†‡]‹¡·¿›...

Juniper

Adobe Wood Type 1

Kim Buker, Barbara Lind & Joy Redick • 1991

ADO AGA LIN MAE

▲48

ABCDEFGHIJKLMNOPQRST

UVWXYZ(“.;‘!*?’:,”)$12345

67890&-ÄÖÜÅÇÈÎÑÓÆØ...

Adobe Wood Type 1: Cottonwood, Ironwood, Juniper, Mesquite, Ponderosa, Adobe Wood Type Ornaments 1.

Juniper ▶Adobe Wood Type Ornaments 1.

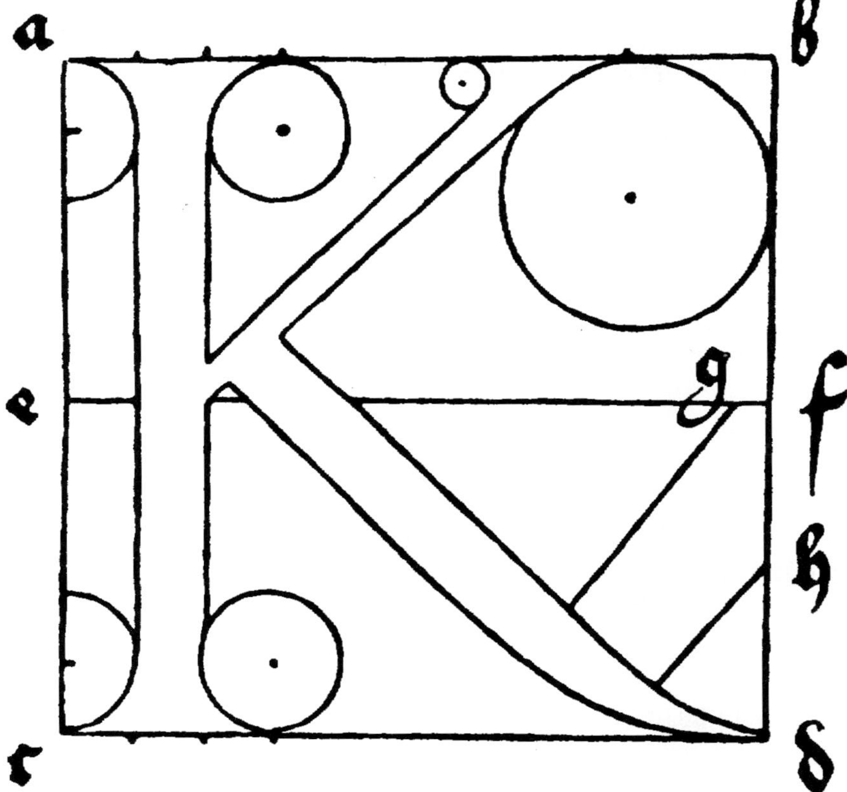
a
b
e
g
f
h
c
d

✍ Albrecht Dürer, 1525

KAATSKILL

Frederic W. Goudy • 1929 abcdefghijklmnopqrstuvwxyz(“.;‘!*?’:,”)

LAN $1234567890&fiflß-äöüåçèîñóæøœ

ABCDEFGHIJKLMNOPQRSTUVWXYZ

ÄÖÜÅÇÈÎÑÓÆØŒ»„«[¶§•†‡]‹¡¿›…

▹ ct ff ffi ffl st

Kaatskill …

• Roman abcdefghijklmnopqrstuvwxyzABCDEFGHIJKLMNOPQRSTUVWXYZ–$1234567890(“.;‘!*?”:

Italic *abcdefghijklmnopqrstuvwxyzABCDEFGHIJKLMNOPQRSTUVWXYZ–$1234567890(“.;‘!*?’:,”)&fi*

Roman SCOSF ABCDEFGHIJKLMNOPQRSTUVWXYZABCDEFGHIJKLMNOPQRSTUVWXYZ–$1234567890(“.;‘!*?’:

Roman OSF abcdefghijklmnopqrstuvwxyzABCDEFGHIJKLMNOPQRSTUVWXYZ–$1234567890(“.;‘!*?’:,

Italic SCOSF *ABCDEFGHIJKLMNOPQRSTUVWXYZABCDEFGHIJKLMNOPQRSTUVWXYZ–$1234567890(“.;‘!*?’:*

Italic OSF *abcdefghijklmnopqrstuvwxyzABCDEFGHIJKLMNOPQRSTUVWXYZ–$1234567890(“.;‘!*?’:,”)&fi*

KABEL

Rudolph Koch • 1927 abcdefghijklmnopqrstuvwxyz(″.;′!*?′:,″)

LIN ADO AGA MAE $1234567890&fiflß-äöüåçèîñóæøœ

▲16 ABCDEFGHIJKLMNOPQRSTUVWXYZ

ÄÖÜÅÇÈÎÑÓÆØŒ»„«[¶§•†‡]‹¡·¿›…

K

Kabel …

Light abcdefghijklmnopqrstuvwxyzABCDEFGHIJKLMNOPQRSTUVWXYZ–$1234567890(″.;′

• Book abcdefghijklmnopqrstuvwxyzABCDEFGHIJKLMNOPQRSTUVWXYZ–$1234567890(″.

Heavy **abcdefghijklmnopqrstuvwxyzABCDEFGHIJKLMNOPQRSTUVWXYZ–$1234567890(**

Black **abcdefghijklmnopqrstuvwxyzABCDEFGHIJKLMNOPQRSTUVWXYZ–$12345**

ITC KABEL

ITC Design Staff • 1976 … Rudolph Koch, 1927 abcdefghijklmnopqrstuvwxyz(“.;‘!*?’:,”)

BIT ADO AGA LEF FAM LIN MAE URW $1234567890&fiflß-äöüåçèîñóæøœ

ABCDEFGHIJKLMNOPQRSTUVWXYZ

ÄÖÜÅÇÈÎÑÓÆØŒ»„«[¶§•†‡]‹¡·¿›…

ITC Kabel …

• Book abcdefghijklmnopqrstuvwxyzABCDEFGHIJKLMNOPQRSTUVWXYZ–$1234567890(“.;‘!*?’:,

Medium abcdefghijklmnopqrstuvwxyzABCDEFGHIJKLMNOPQRSTUVWXYZ–$1234567890(“.;‘!*

Demi **abcdefghijklmnopqrstuvwxyzABCDEFGHIJKLMNOPQRSTUVWXYZ–$1234567890(“.;‘**

Bold **abcdefghijklmnopqrstuvwxyzABCDEFGHIJKLMNOPQRSTUVWXYZ–$1234567890(**

Ultra **abcdefghijklmnopqrstuvwxyzABCDEFGHIJKLMNOPQRSTUVWXYZ–$123456789**

Katfish

Michael Gills • 1994 abcdefghijklmnopqrstuvwxyz(“.;‘!*?’:,”)

LET $1234567890&fiflß-äöüåçèîñóæøœ

▲16 ABCDEFGHIJKLMNOPQRSTUVWXYZ

ÄÖÜÅÇÈÎÑÓÆØŒ»„«[•]‹¡·¿›...

▷ a b c d d e e e g g i j k l m o p q r r r s s s t v w w x y z z z ff Fi Th

KAUFMANN

M. R. Kaufmann • 1936 abcdefghijklmnopqrstuvwxyz(“.;‘!*?’:,”)

BIT ADO AGA LEF LIN MAE URW $1234567890&fiflß-äöüåçèîñóæøœ

▲16 ABCDEFGHIJKLMNOPQRSTUVWXYZ

ÄÖÜÅÇÈÎÑÓÆØŒ»„«[§•†‡]‹¡·¿›...

Kaufmann ...

• Regular abcdefghijklmnopqrstuvwxyzABCDEFGHIJKLMNOPQRSTUVWXYZ–$1234567

Bold **abcdefghijklmnopqrstuvwxyzABCDEFGHIJKLMNOPQRSTUVWXYZ–$1**

K

KENNERLEY

Frederic W. Goudy • 1911 abcdefghijklmnopqrstuvwxyz(“.;‘!*?’:,”)

LAN TFC $1234567890&fiflßäöüåçèîñóæøœ

ABCDEFGHIJKLMNOPQRSTUVWXYZ

ÄÖÜÅÇÈÎÑÓÆØŒ»«[(C·†‡]‹¡¿›...

▷ ct ff ffi ffl st

Kennerley ...

• Roman abcdefghijklmnopqrstuvwxyzABCDEFGHIJKLMNOPQRSTUVWXYZ–$1234567890

Italic *abcdefghijklmnopqrstuvwxyzABCDEFGHIJKLMNOPQRSTUVWXYZ-$1234567890(“*

Roman SCOSF ABCDEFGHIJKLMNOPQRSTUVWXYZABCDEFGHIJKLMNOPQRSTUVWXYZ–$12345678

Roman OSF abcdefghijklmnopqrstuvwxyzABCDEFGHIJKLMNOPQRSTUVWXYZ–$1234567890

Italic SCOSF *ABCDEFGHIJKLMNOPQRSTUVWXYZABCDEFGHIJKLMNOPQRSTUVWXYZ–$12345678*

Italic OSF *abcdefghijklmnopqrstuvwxyzABCDEFGHIJKLMNOPQRSTUVWXYZ-$1234567890(“*

Italic Swash Caps *abcdefghijklmnopqrstuvwxyzABCDEFGHIJKLMNOPQRSTUVWXYZ–$1234567*

Italic Swash Caps OSF *abcdefghijklmnopqrstuvwxyzABCDEFGHIJKLMNOPQRSTUVWXYZ–$1234567*

KIDTYPE

Jake & Scott Scarano • 1994 abcdefghijklmnopqrstuvwxyz(.;!?:,)

MTD $1234567890&–?

ABCDEFGHIJKLMNOPQRSTUVWXYZ

Σ KidTYPE ...

• Crayon abcdefghijklmnopqrstuvwxyzABCDEFGHIJKLMNOPQRSTUVWX

Marker abcdefghijklmnopqrstuvwxyzABCDEFGHIJKLMNOPQRSTUVWXYZ$1234567890(“.;!

Σ KidType DingBRATS.

... KidTYPE

Paint abcdefghijklmnopqrstuvwxyzABCDEFGHIJKLMNOPQR

Σ KidTYPE Ruled abcdefghijklmnopqrstuvwxyz

Jake & Scott Scarano • 1994

MTD ▲36 (.;!*?:,)$1234567890&–çèñABCDE

FGHIJKLMNOPQRSTUVWXYZÇÈÎÑ

Σ Kiilani
Group Hawaii
Judith Sutcliffe • 1993
ABCDEFGHIJKLMNOPQRSTUVWXYZ

MTD ▲20 $1234567890&–ÄÖÜÅÈÎÑÓÆØŒ

ABCDEFGHIJKLMNOPQRSTUVWXYZ

ÄÖÜÅÈÎÑÓÆØŒ»«¶

KINDERGARTEN

Bill Andersen • 1993 abcdefghijklmnopqrstuvwxyz

AND (".;!*?:,")$1234567890&fiflß–

äöüåçèîñóœøœABCDEFGHI

JKLMNOPQRSTUVWXYZ

ÄÖÜÅÇÈÎÑÓÆØŒ»„«[¶§•...

Kindergarten ...

Regular ▲16 abcdefghijklmnopqrstuvwxyzABCDEFGHIJKLMNOPQRSTUVWXYZ–$1234567890(".;!*?:

Σ KidType DingBRATS.
Group Hawaii: Hibiscus, Kiilani, Petroglyph Hawaii.
Σ Kiilani ▶ Petroglyph Hawaii.

. . . Kindergarten

Bold ▲16 abcdefghijklmnopqrstuvwxyzABCDEFGHIJKLMNOPQRSTUVWXYZ-$1234567890(".;'!*?

Teach Ruled ▲42 abcdefghijklmnopqrstuvwxyz

• Teach ▲42 abcdefghijklmnopqrstuvwxyz

Kino

Monotype Crazy Headlines

M. Dovey • 1937

MCL ADO AGA LIN MAE

▲18

abcdefghijklmnopqrstuvwxyz(".;'!*?':,")
$1234567890&fifl ß-äöüåçèîñóæøœ
ABCDEFGHIJKLMNOPQRSTUVWXYZ
ÄÖÜÅÇÈÎÑÓÆØŒ»,,«[•]‹¡·¿›...

Klang

Monotype Headliners 3

Will Carter • 1955

MCL ADO AGA LIN MAE

▲16

abcdefghijklmnopqrstuvwxyz(".;'!*?':,")
$1234567890&fiflß-äöüåçèîñóæøœ
ABCDEFGHIJKLMNOPQRSTUVWXYZ
ÄÖÜÅÇÈÎÑÓÆØŒ»,,«[¶§•†‡]‹¡·¿›...

Klee

Tim Donaldson • 1992

LET

▲24

abcdefghijklmnopqrstuvwxyz(".;'!*?':,")
$1234567890&fiflß-äöüåçèîñóæøœ
ABCDEFGHIJKLMNOPQRSTUVWXYZ
ÄÖÜÅÇÈÎÑÓÆØŒ»,,«[•]‹¡·¿›...

▷ a b d

Kniff

Emo Risaliti • 1993

FBU

▲36

abcdefghijklmnopqrstuvwxyz(".;'!*?':,")
$1234567890&fiflß-äöüåçèîñóæøœ
ABCDEFGHIJKLMNOPQRSTUVWXYZ
ÄÖÜÅÇÈÎÑÓÆØŒ»,,«[¶§•†‡]‹¡·¿›...

▷ 

. . .

Monotype Crazy Headlines: Festival Titling, Kino, Matura, Matura Scriptorial Capitals, Victoria Titling Condensed.
Monotype Headliners 3: Braggadocio, Figaro, Forte, Klang.

A*I KOCH ANTIQUA

✍ Randall Jones • 1991 … Rudolph Koch, 1922
ALP MTD
▲16

abcdefghijklmnopqrstuvwxyz(“.;‘!*?’:,”)
$1234567890&fifl-äöüåçèîñóæøœ
ABCDEFGHIJKLMNOPQRSTUVWXYZ
ÄÖÜÅÇÈÎÑÓÆØŒ»«[•]¡¿…

A*I Koch Antiqua …

Light abcdefghijklmnopqrstuvwxyzABCDEFGHIJKLMNOPQRSTUVWXYZ–$123456
• Demi abcdefghijklmnopqrstuvwxyzABCDEFGHIJKLMNOPQRSTUVWXYZ–$12345
Extra Bold abcdefghijklmnopqrstuvwxyzABCDEFGHIJKLMNOPQRSTUVWXYZ–$12345

FC Koloss

✍ Jakob Erbar • 1923
TFC AGP LEF
▲24

abcdefghijklmnopqrstuvwxyz
(“.;‘!*?’:,”)$1234567890&ß-äöüåçèîñó
æøœABCDEFGHIJKLMNOPQRSTUVWXYZ
ÄÖÜÅÇÈÎÑÓÆØŒ»„«[•]‹¡·¿›…▹bdgijqpBKKP

ITC KORINNA

✍ Ed Benguiat • 1984 … H. Berthold AG, 1904
BIT ADO AGA LEF FAM LIN MAE URW

abcdefghijklmnopqrstuvwxyz(“.;‘!*?’:,”)
$1234567890&fiflß-äöüåçèîñóæøœ
ABCDEFGHIJKLMNOPQRSTUVWXYZ
ÄÖÜÅÇÈÎÑÓÆØŒ»„«[¶§•†‡]‹¡·¿›…

ITC Korinna 1 …

• Regular abcdefghijklmnopqrstuvwxyzABCDEFGHIJKLMNOPQRSTUVWXYZ–$1234567890(
Kursiv *abcdefghijklmnopqrstuvwxyzABCDEFGHIJKLMNOPQRSTUVWXYZ–$123456789*
Bold **abcdefghijklmnopqrstuvwxyzABCDEFGHIJKLMNOPQRSTUVWXYZ–$1234567**
Bold Kursiv ***abcdefghijklmnopqrstuvwxyzABCDEFGHIJKLMNOPQRSTUVWXYZ–$123456***

ITC Korinna 1 …

Extra Bold **abcdefghijklmnopqrstuvwxyzABCDEFGHIJKLMNOPQRSTUVWXYZ–$123**
Extra Bold Kursiv ***abcdefghijklmnopqrstuvwxyzABCDEFGHIJKLMNOPQRSTUVWXYZ–$1234***
Heavy **abcdefghijklmnopqrstuvwxyzABCDEFGHIJKLMNOPQRSTUVWXYZ–**
Heavy Kursiv ***abcdefghijklmnopqrstuvwxyzABCDEFGHIJKLMNOPQRSTUVWXYZ–$***
Bold Outline ▲18 abcdefghijklmnopqrstuvwxyzABCDEFGHIJKLMNOPQRST

KRISTEN

George Ryan • 1994 abcdefghijklmnopqrstuvwxyz(".;'!*?':,")

GAL $1234567890&fifl ß-äöüåçèîñóæøœ

ABCDEFGHIJKLMNOPQRSTUVWXYZ

ÄÖÜÅÇÈÎÑÓÆØŒ»„«[¶§•†‡]‹¡·¿›...

Kristen ...

• Normal abcdefghijklmnopqrstuvwxyzABCDEFGHIJKLMNOPQRSTUVWXYZ–$

Not So Normal abcdefghijklmnopqrstuvwxyzABCDEFGHIJKLMNOPQRSTUVWXYZ–$1234567890(".;'

Kryptic

Garrett Boge • 1986 abcdefghijklmnopqrstuv

LPT MTD wxyz[·;!?:,]&–$1234567890

▲24

Kufi Script

Group Arabia

Judith Sutcliffe • 1993 abcdefghijklmnopqrstuvwxyz(".;'!*?':,")

MTD

▲24 $1234567890&fifl ß-äöüåçèîñóæøœ

ABCDEFGHIJKLMNOPQRSTUVWXYZ

ÄÖÜÅÇÈÎÑÓÆØŒ»„«[¶§•†‡]‹¡·¿›...

KÜNSTLER SCRIPT

Hans Bohn • 1957 abcdefghijklmnopqrstuvwxyz(".;'!*?':,")

LIN ADO AGA MAE $1234567890&fifl ß-äöüåçèîñóæøœ

▲16 ABCDEFGHIJKLMNOPQRSTUVWXYZ

ÄÖÜÅÇÈÎÑÓÆØŒ»„«[¶§•†‡]‹¡·¿›...

Künstler Script ...

• Regular abcdefghijklmnopqrstuvwxyzABCDEFGHIJKLMNOPQRSTU

No. 2 Bold abcdefghijklmnopqrstuvwxyzABCDEFGHIJKLMNOPQRSTUVWX

Black abcdefghijklmnopqrstuvwxyzABCDEFGHIJKLMNOPQR

Group Arabia: Arabia Felix, Black Rocks, Black Tents, Kufi Script, Mesopotamia.

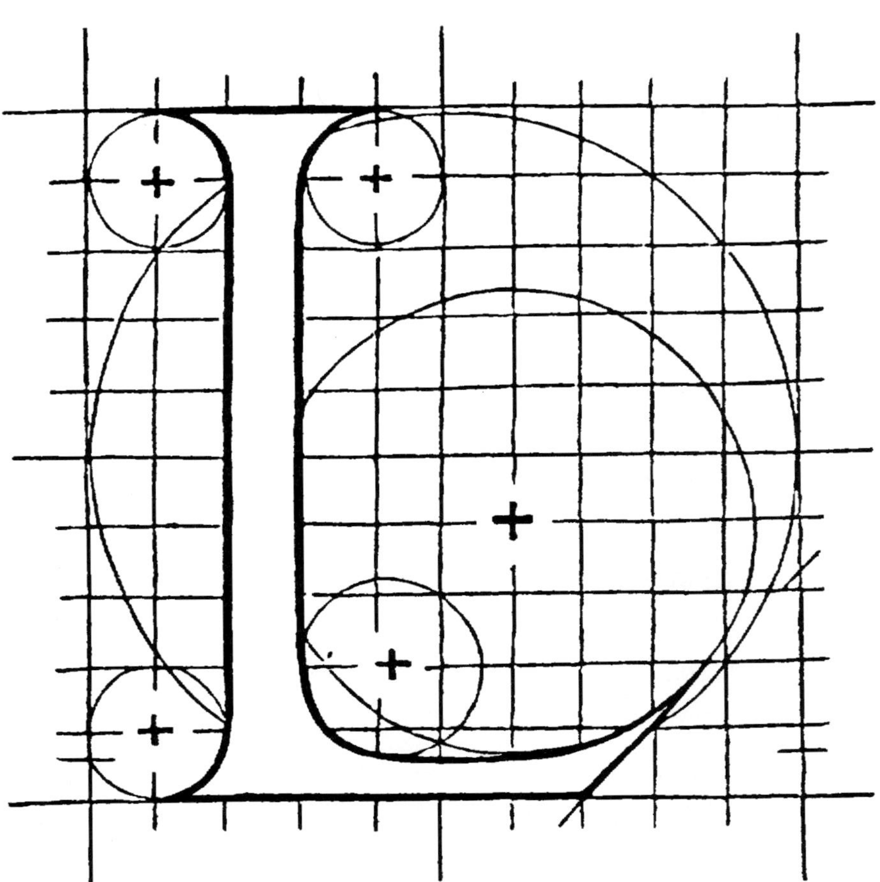

✍ Geofroy Tory, 1527

La Bamba

David Quay • 1992 abcdefghijklmnopqrstuvwxyz(".;'!*?':,")
LET $1234567890&fiflß-äöüåçèîñóæøœ
▲18 ABCDEFGHIJKLMNOPQRSTUVWXYZ
ÄÖÜÅÇÈÎÑÓÆØŒ»„«[•]‹i·¿›...
▷ ABCDEFGHIJKLMNOPQRSTUVWXYZ

Lambada

David Quay • 1992 abcdefghijklmnopqrstuvwxyz(".;'!*?':,")
LET $1234567890&fiflß-äöüåçèîñóæøœ
▲18 ABCDEFGHIJKLMNOPQRSTUVWXYZ
ÄÖÜÅÇÈÎÑÓÆØŒ»„«[•]‹i·¿›... ▷ DT

LANGER

Paul Lang • 1993 abcdefghijklmnopqrstuvwxyz(".;'!*?':,")
MTD $1234567890&fiflß-äöüåçèîñóæøœ
ABCDEFGHIJKLMNOPQRSTUVWXYZ
ÄÖÜÅÇÈÎÑÓÆØŒ»„«[¶•]‹i¿›... ▷ ⅛ ¼ ⅜ ½ ⅝ ¾ ⅞ □

Langer ...

• Regular abcdefghijklmnopqrstuvwxyzABCDEFGHIJKLMNOPQRSTUVWXYZ-$12345678
Italic *abcdefghijklmnopqrstuvwxyzABCDEFGHIJKLMNOPQRSTUVWXYZ-$12345678*
Bold **abcdefghijklmnopqrstuvwxyzABCDEFGHIJKLMNOPQRSTUVWXYZ-$1234**
Bold Italic ***abcdefghijklmnopqrstuvwxyzABCDEFGHIJKLMNOPQRSTUVWXYZ-$12345678***
Alternate abcdefghijklmnopqrstuvwxyzABCDEFGHIJKLMNOPQRSTUVWXYZ-$1234567
Alternate Italic *abcdefghijklmnopqrstuvwxyzABCDEFGHIJKLMNOPQRSTUVWXYZ-$12345*
Alternate Bold **abcdefghijklmnopqrstuvwxyzABCDEFGHIJKLMNOPQRSTUVWXYZ-$12345**
Alternate Bold Italic ***abcdefghijklmnopqrstuvwxyzABCDEFGHIJKLMNOPQRSTUVWXYZ-$12345***

Laser

Martin Wait • 1987 *abcdefghijklmnopqrstuvwxyz(".;'!*?':,")*
LET *$1234567890&fiflß-äöüåçèîñóæøœ*
▲18 *ABCDEFGHIJKLMNOPQRSTUVWXYZ*
ÄÖÜÅÇÈÎÑÓÆØŒ»„«[•]‹i·¿›... ▷ *f j x*

Laser Chrome

Martin Wait • 1988 *abcdefghijklmnopqrstuvwxyz(".;'!*?':,")*
LET *$1234567890&fiflß-äöüåçèîñóæøœ*
▲18 *ABCDEFGHIJKLMNOPQRSTUVWXYZ*
ÄÖÜÅÇÈÎÑÓÆØŒ»„«[•]‹i·¿›... ▷ *f j x*

LATIENNE

Mark Jamra • 1991 abcdefghijklmnopqrstuvwxyz(".;'!*?':,")

URW LEF $1234567890&fiflß-äöüåçèîñóæøœ

ABCDEFGHIJKLMNOPQRSTUVWXYZ

ÄÖÜÅÇÈÎÑÓÆØŒ»„«[¶§•†‡]‹¡·¿›...

Latienne 1 ...

• Roman abcdefghijklmnopqrstuvwxyzABCDEFGHIJKLMNOPQRSTUVWXYZ-$12345678

Italic *abcdefghijklmnopqrstuvwxyzABCDEFGHIJKLMNOPQRSTUVWXYZ-$1234567890(".;'!*

Roman SCOSF ABCDEFGHIJKLMNOPQRSTUVWXYZABCDEFGHIJKLMNOPQRSTUVWXYZ-$123456789

Italic SCOSF *ABCDEFGHIJKLMNOPQRSTUVWXYZABCDEFGHIJKLMNOPQRSTUVWXYZ-$1234567890(".;'!**

Roman Swash Caps abcdefghijklmnopqrstuvwxyzABCDEFGHIJKLMNOPQRSTUVWXYZ-$12

Italic Swash Caps *abcdefghijklmnopqrstuvwxyzABCDEFGHIJKLMNOPQRSTUVWXYZ-$123456*

Latienne 2 ...

Medium **abcdefghijklmnopqrstuvwxyzABCDEFGHIJKLMNOPQRSTUVWXYZ-$12345**

Medium Italic ***abcdefghijklmnopqrstuvwxyzABCDEFGHIJKLMNOPQRSTUVWXYZ-$1234567890***

Medium SCOSF **ABCDEFGHIJKLMNOPQRSTUVWXYZABCDEFGHIJKLMNOPQRSTUVWXYZ-$12345**

Medium Swash Caps **abcdefghijklmnopqrstuvwxyzABCDEFGHIJKLMNOPQRSTUVWXYZ-**

Medium Italic Swash Caps ***abcdefghijklmnopqrstuvwxyzABCDEFGHIJKLMNOPQRSTUVWXYZ-$123***

Latienne 3 ...

Bold **abcdefghijklmnopqrstuvwxyzABCDEFGHIJKLMNOPQRSTUVWXYZ-$1**

Bold Italic ***abcdefghijklmnopqrstuvwxyzABCDEFGHIJKLMNOPQRSTUVWXYZ-$12345***

Bold Swash Caps **abcdefghijklmnopqrstuvwxyzABCDEFGHIJKLMNOPQRSTUVW**

Bold Italic Swash Caps ***abcdefghijklmnopqrstuvwxyzABCDEFGHIJKLMNOPQRSTUVWXYZ***

Latin Condensed
Monotype DisplaySet 4
MCL ADO AGA LIN MAE

abcdefghijklmnopqrstuvwxyz(".;'!*?':,")

▲30 $1234567890&fiflß-äöüåçèîñóæøœ

ABCDEFGHIJKLMNOPQRSTUVWXYZ

ÄÖÜÅÇÈÎÑÓÆØŒ»„«[•]‹¡·¿›...

Latin Wide

URW **abcdefghijklmnopqrstuvwxyz(".;'!*?':,")**

▲18 **$1234567890&fiflß-äöüåçèîñóæøœ**

ABCDEFGHIJKLMNOPQRSTUVWXYZ

ÄÖÜÅÇÈÎÑÓÆØŒ»„«[•†‡]‹¡·¿›...

....
Monotype DisplaySet 4: Latin Condensed, Onyx, Runic Condensed.

MN Latina

✍ Jean Larcher • 1990 abcdefghijklmnopqrstuvwxyz(".;'!*?':,")
MTD $1234567890&fiflß-äöüåçèîñóæøœ
▲18 ABCDEFGHIJKLMNOPQRSTUVWXYZ
ÄÖÜÅÇÈÎÑÓÆØŒ»„«[¶§•]‹¡¿›...

LA·VARDERA

✍ Greg La Vardera • 1993 abcdefghijklmnopqrstuvwxyz(".;'!*?':,")
HAN MTD $1234567890&fiflß-äöüåçèîñóæøœ
ABCDEFGHIJKLMNOPQRSTUVWXYZ
ÄÖÜÅÇÈÎÑÓÆØŒ [¶•†] ¡¿...
▷ ff ffi ffl

LaVardera ...

• Book abcdefghijklmnopqrstuvwxyzABCDEFGHIJKLMNOPQRSTUVWXYZ–$1234567
Bold abcdefghijklmnopqrstuvwxyzABCDEFGHIJKLMNOPQRSTUVWXYZ–$1234567
Extra Bold abcdefghijklmnopqrstuvwxyzABCDEFGHIJKLMNOPQRSTUVWXYZ–$1234567

L

FC LeAsterix

TFC ABCDEFGHIJKLMNOPQRSTUVWXYZ(".;'!*?':,")
▲16 $1234567890&ß-ÄÖÜÅÇÈÎÑÓÆØŒ
ABCDEFGHIJKLMNOPQRSTUVWXYZ
ÄÖÜÅÇÈÎÑÓÆŒ»„«[¶§·†‡]‹¡·¿›...

ITC LEAWOOD

✍ Les Usherwood • 1985 abcdefghijklmnopqrstuvwxyz(".;'!*?':,")
BIT ADO AGA LEF LIN MAE URW $1234567890&fiflß-äöüåçèîñóæøœ
ABCDEFGHIJKLMNOPQRSTUVWXYZ
ÄÖÜÅÇÈÎÑÓÆØŒ»„«[¶§•†‡]‹¡·¿›...

ITC Leawood 1 ...

• Book abcdefghijklmnopqrstuvwxyzABCDEFGHIJKLMNOPQRSTUVWXYZ–$1234567890(
Book Italic *abcdefghijklmnopqrstuvwxyzABCDEFGHIJKLMNOPQRSTUVWXYZ–$1234567890("*
Bold **abcdefghijklmnopqrstuvwxyzABCDEFGHIJKLMNOPQRSTUVWXYZ–$123**
Bold Italic ***abcdefghijklmnopqrstuvwxyzABCDEFGHIJKLMNOPQRSTUVWXYZ–$1234***

ITC Leawood 2 ...

Medium abcdefghijklmnopqrstuvwxyzABCDEFGHIJKLMNOPQRSTUVWXYZ–$123456
Medium Italic *abcdefghijklmnopqrstuvwxyzABCDEFGHIJKLMNOPQRSTUVWXYZ–$1234567*
Black **abcdefghijklmnopqrstuvwxyzABCDEFGHIJKLMNOPQRSTUVWXYZ–$1**
Black Italic ***abcdefghijklmnopqrstuvwxyzABCDEFGHIJKLMNOPQRSTUVWXYZ–$123***

ITC LEGACY SERIF

Ron Arnholm • 1992 abcdefghijklmnopqrstuvwxyz(“.;‘!*?’:,”)

URW ADO AGA ITC LIN MAE $1234567890&fiflß-äöüåçèîñóæøœ

ABCDEFGHIJKLMNOPQRSTUVWXYZ

ÄÖÜÅÇÈÎÑÓÆØŒ»„«[¶§•†‡]‹¡·¿›...

ITC Legacy Serif ...

• Book abcdefghijklmnopqrstuvwxyzABCDEFGHIJKLMNOPQRSTUVWXYZ-$1234567

Book Italic *abcdefghijklmnopqrstuvwxyzABCDEFGHIJKLMNOPQRSTUVWXYZ-$1234567890(“.;‘*

Medium abcdefghijklmnopqrstuvwxyzABCDEFGHIJKLMNOPQRSTUVWXYZ-$12345

Medium Italic *abcdefghijklmnopqrstuvwxyzABCDEFGHIJKLMNOPQRSTUVWXYZ-$1234567890(*

Bold **abcdefghijklmnopqrstuvwxyzABCDEFGHIJKLMNOPQRSTUVWXYZ-$12**

Bold Italic ***abcdefghijklmnopqrstuvwxyzABCDEFGHIJKLMNOPQRSTUVWXYZ-$12345678***

Ultra **abcdefghijklmnopqrstuvwxyzABCDEFGHIJKLMNOPQRSTUVWXYZ-$**

ITC LEGACY SANS

Ron Arnholm • 1992 abcdefghijklmnopqrstuvwxyz(“.;‘!*?’:,”)

URW ADO AGA ITC LIN MAE $1234567890&fiflß-äöüåçèîñóæøœ

ABCDEFGHIJKLMNOPQRSTUVWXYZ

ÄÖÜÅÇÈÎÑÓÆØŒ»„«[¶§•†‡]‹¡·¿›...

ITC Legacy Sans ...

• Book abcdefghijklmnopqrstuvwxyzABCDEFGHIJKLMNOPQRSTUVWXYZ-$1234567890

Book Italic *abcdefghijklmnopqrstuvwxyzABCDEFGHIJKLMNOPQRSTUVWXYZ-$1234567890(“.;‘!**

Medium abcdefghijklmnopqrstuvwxyzABCDEFGHIJKLMNOPQRSTUVWXYZ-$12345678

Medium Italic *abcdefghijklmnopqrstuvwxyzABCDEFGHIJKLMNOPQRSTUVWXYZ-$1234567890(“.;*

Bold **abcdefghijklmnopqrstuvwxyzABCDEFGHIJKLMNOPQRSTUVWXYZ-$1234567**

Bold Italic ***abcdefghijklmnopqrstuvwxyzABCDEFGHIJKLMNOPQRSTUVWXYZ-$123456789***

Ultra **abcdefghijklmnopqrstuvwxyzABCDEFGHIJKLMNOPQRSTUVWXYZ-$123**

LE GRIFFE

Andre-Michel Lubac • 1973 abcdefghijklmnopqrstuvwxyz(“.;‘!*?’:,”)

LEF FRA LET $1234567890&fiflß-äöüåçèîñóæøœ

A B C D E F G H I J K L M N O P Q R S T U V W X Y Z

Ä Ö Ü Å Ç È Î Ñ Ó Æ Ø Œ »„«[•]·¡·¿...

Le Griffe ...

• Regular abcdefghijklmnopqrstuvwxyzA B C D E F G H I J K L M N O P Q R S T U V W X Y Z $12345678

Alternate One a b c d e f g h i j k l m n o p q r s t u v w x y z A B C D E F G H I J K L M N O P Q R S T

Alternate Two a b c d e f g h i j k l m n o p q r s t u v w x y z A B C D E F G H I J K L M N O P Q R

LEMONADE

Ty Semaka • 1991 abcdefghijklmnopqrstuvwxyz(“.;‘!*?’:,”)

IMA $1234567890&fiflß-äöüåçèîñóœøœ

▲16 ABCDEFGHIJKLMNOPQRSTUVWXYZ

ÄÖÜÅÇÈÎÑÓÆØŒ»„«[¶§•†‡]‹¡·¿›...

Lemonade ...

• Regular abcdefghijklmnopqrstuvwxyzABCDEFGHIJKLMNOPQRSTUVWXYZ-$1234567890

Bold abcdefghijklmnopqrstuvwxyzABCDEFGHIJKLMNOPQRSTUVWXYZ-$1234567890

LETTER GOTHIC

Roger Robertson • 1962 abcdefghijklmnopqrstuvwxyz(“.;‘!*?’:,”)

ADO AGA BIT FRA LIN MAE MCL URW $1234567890&fiflß-äöüåçèîñóæøœ

▲12 ABCDEFGHIJKLMNOPQRSTUVWXYZ

ÄÖÜÅÇÈÎÑÓÆØŒ»„«[¶§•†‡]‹¡·¿›...

Letter Gothic ...

• Regular abcdefghijklmnopqrstuvwxyzABCDEFGHIJKLMNOPQRSTUVWXYZ-$1234567890(“.;‘

Slanted abcdefghijklmnopqrstuvwxyzABCDEFGHIJKLMNOPQRSTUVWXYZ-$1234567890(“.;‘

Bold abcdefghijklmnopqrstuvwxyzABCDEFGHIJKLMNOPQRSTUVWXYZ-$1234567890(“.;‘

Bold Slanted abcdefghijklmnopqrstuvwxyzABCDEFGHIJKLMNOPQRSTUVWXYZ-$1234567890(“.;‘

L

Liberty

Agfa ScriptSet 1

Willard T. Sniffin • 1927 abcdefghijklmnopqrstuvwxyz(“.;‘!*?’:,”)

AGP BIT $1234567890&fiflß-äöüåçèîñóœøœ

▲18 ABCDEFGHIJKLMNOPQRSTUVWXYZ

ÄÖÜÅÇÈÎÑÓÆØŒ»„«[¶§•†‡]‹¡·¿›...

Libra

Sjoerd Hendrick de Roos • 1938 abcdefghijklmnopqrstuvwxyz(“.;‘!*?’:,”)

BIT

▲24 $1234567890&-äöüåçèîñóæøœ»„«[§•†‡]‹¡·¿›...

HF Libris

Jonathan Macagba • 1991 ABCDEFGHIJKLMNOPQRSTUVWXYZ(“.;‘!*?’:,”)$1234567890

HAN MTD &-ÄÖÜÅÇÈÎÑÓÆØŒABCDEFGHIJKLMNOPQRSTUVWXYZ

▲30 ÄÖÜÅÇÈÎÑÓÆØŒ»« ‹¡¿›... ALMMW LALEP

Agfa ScriptSet 1: Basilica, Floridian Script, Jasper, Liberty.

LIFE

Francesco Simoncini & W. Bilz • 1965

URW ADO AGA BIT LIN MAE

abcdefghijklmnopqrstuvwxyz(".;'!*?':,")
$1234567890&fiflß-äöüåçèîñóæøœ
ABCDEFGHIJKLMNOPQRSTUVWXYZ
ÄÖÜÅÇÈÎÑÓÆØŒ»„«[¶§•†‡]‹¡·¿›...

Life ...

• Roman abcdefghijklmnopqrstuvwxyzABCDEFGHIJKLMNOPQRSTUVWXYZ-$1234567890(
Italic *abcdefghijklmnopqrstuvwxyzABCDEFGHIJKLMNOPQRSTUVWXYZ-$1234567890(".;'*
Bold **abcdefghijklmnopqrstuvwxyzABCDEFGHIJKLMNOPQRSTUVWXYZ-$1234567890(**
Roman SCOSF ABCDEFGHIJKLMNOPQRSTUVWXYZABCDEFGHIJKLMNOPQRSTUVWXYZ-$123456789

Lightnin'

Alan Meeks • 1994

LET

▲16

abcdefghijklmnopqrstuvwxyz(".;'!*?':,")
$1234567890&fiflß-äöüåçèîñóæøœ
ABCDEFGHIJKLMNOPQRSTUVWXYZ
ÄÖÜÅÇÈÎÑÓÆØŒ»„«[•]‹¡·¿›...

▷ r s w

Limehouse Script

Alan Meeks • 1986

LET

▲18

abcdefghijklmnopqrstuvwxyz(".;'!*?':,")
$1234567890&fiflß-äöüåçèîñóæøœ
ABCDEFGHIJKLMNOPQRSTUVWXYZ
ÄÖÜÅÇÈÎÑÓÆØŒ»„«[•]‹¡·¿›...

▷ k v w

Lindsay

URW LEF FRA

▲18

abcdefghijklmnopqrstuvwxyz(".;'!*?':,")
$1234567890&fiflß-äöüåçèîñóæøœ
ABCDEFGHIJKLMNOPQRSTUVWXYZ
ÄÖÜÅÇÈÎÑÓÆØŒ»„«[¶§•†‡]‹¡·¿›...

Lino Cut

Bob Anderton • 1990

LET

▲24

abcdefghijklmnopqrstuvwxyz(".;'!*?':,")
$1234567890&fiflß-äöüåçèîñóæøœ
ABCDEFGHIJKLMNOPQRSTUVWXYZ
ÄÖÜÅÇÈÎÑÓÆØŒ»„«[•]‹¡·¿›...

L

LINO·LETTER

André Gürtler, et al. • 1991 abcdefghijklmnopqrstuvwxyz(".;'!*?':,")

LIN ADO AGA MAE $1234567890&fiflß-äöüåçèîñóæøœ

ABCDEFGHIJKLMNOPQRSTUVWXYZ

ÄÖÜÅÇÈÎÑÓÆØŒ»„«[¶§•†‡]‹¡·¿›...

LinoLetter ...

• Roman abcdefghijklmnopqrstuvwxyzABCDEFGHIJKLMNOPQRSTUVWXYZ–$1

Italic *abcdefghijklmnopqrstuvwxyzABCDEFGHIJKLMNOPQRSTUVWXYZ–$1234*

Medium abcdefghijklmnopqrstuvwxyzABCDEFGHIJKLMNOPQRSTUVWXYZ–$

Medium Italic *abcdefghijklmnopqrstuvwxyzABCDEFGHIJKLMNOPQRSTUVWXYZ–$12*

Bold **abcdefghijklmnopqrstuvwxyzABCDEFGHIJKLMNOPQRSTUVWXYZ**

Bold Italic ***abcdefghijklmnopqrstuvwxyzABCDEFGHIJKLMNOPQRSTUVWXYZ–$***

Black **abcdefghijklmnopqrstuvwxyzABCDEFGHIJKLMNOPQRSTUVWX**

Black Italic ***abcdefghijklmnopqrstuvwxyzABCDEFGHIJKLMNOPQRSTUVWXY***

LINO·LETTER SCOSF

LIN ADO AGA MAE ABCDEFGHIJKLMNOPQRSTUVWXYZ(".;'!*?':,")

$1234567890&-ÄÖÜÅÇÈÎÑÓÆØŒ

ABCDEFGHIJKLMNOPQRSTUVWXYZ

ÄÖÜÅÇÈÎÑÓÆØŒ»„«[¶§•†‡]‹¡·¿›...

LinoLetter SCOSF ...

• Roman SCOSF ABCDEFGHIJKLMNOPQRSTUVWXYZABCDEFGHIJKLMNOPQRSTUV...$123456

Roman OSF abcdefghijklmnopqrstuvwxyzABCDEFGHIJKLMNOPQRSTUV...$123456

Italic OSF *abcdefghijklmnopqrstuvwxyzABCDEFGHIJKLMNOPQRSTUV...$12345678*

Medium SCOSF ABCDEFGHIJKLMNOPQRSTUVWXYZABCDEFGHIJKLMNOPQRSTUV...$12345

Medium OSF abcdefghijklmnopqrstuvwxyzABCDEFGHIJKLMNOPQRSTUV...$12345

Medium Italic OSF *abcdefghijklmnopqrstuvwxyzABCDEFGHIJKLMNOPQRSTUV...$1234567*

Bold SCOSF **ABCDEFGHIJKLMNOPQRSTUVWXYZABCDEFGHIJKLMNOPQRSTUV...$123**

Bold OSF **abcdefghijklmnopqrstuvwxyzABCDEFGHIJKLMNOPQRSTUV...$123**

Bold Italic OSF ***abcdefghijklmnopqrstuvwxyzABCDEFGHIJKLMNOPQRSTUV...$12345***

Black SCOSF **ABCDEFGHIJKLMNOPQRSTUVWXYZABCDEFGHIJKLMNOPQRS...$1234**

Black OSF **abcdefghijklmnopqrstuvwxyzABCDEFGHIJKLMNOPQRS...$1234**

Black Italic OSF ***abcdefghijklmnopqrstuvwxyzABCDEFGHIJKLMNOPQRS...$12345***

Linoscript

✣ *Linotype ScriptSet 2*

Morris Fuller Benton • 1905 abcdefghijklmnopqrstuvwxyz(".;'!*?':,")

LIN ADO AGA MAE $1234567890 &fiflß-äöüåçèîñóæøœ

▲18 ABCDEFGHIJKLMNOPQRSTUVWXYZ

ÄÖÜÅÇÈÎÑÓÆØŒ»„«[¶§•†‡]‹¡·¿›...

✣ *Linotype ScriptSet 2*: Linoscript & Linotext.

Linotext
Linotype ScriptSet 2
Morris Fuller Benton • 1901
LIN ADO AGA MAE
▲16

abcdefghijklmnopqrstuvwxyz(".;'!*?':,")
$1234567890&fiflß-äöüåçèîñóæøœ
ABCDEFGHIJKLMNOPQRSTUVWXYZ
ÄÖÜÅÇÈÎÑÓÆØŒ»„«[¶§•†‡]‹¡·¿›… ▷ chckfffftll[sſi[[ß–äöüÄÖÜ

LITERA
Michael Neugebauer • 1983
URW

abcdefghijklmnopqrstuvwxyz(".;'!*?':,")
$1234567890&fiflß-äöüåçèîñóæøœ
ABCDEFGHIJKLMNOPQRSTUVWXYZ
ÄÖÜÅÇÈÎÑÓÆØŒ»„«[¶§•†‡]‹¡·¿›…

Litera …

Light abcdefghijklmnopqrstuvwxyzABCDEFGHIJKLMNOPQRSTUVWXYZ–$1234567890(".;'!
• Regular abcdefghijklmnopqrstuvwxyzABCDEFGHIJKLMNOPQRSTUVWXYZ–$1234567890(".;
Medium abcdefghijklmnopqrstuvwxyzABCDEFGHIJKLMNOPQRSTUVWXYZ–$1234567890("
Heavy abcdefghijklmnopqrstuvwxyzABCDEFGHIJKLMNOPQRSTUVWXYZ–$1234567890(

L

LITHOS
Carol Twombly • 1989
ADO AGA LIN MAE
▲24

ABCDEFGHIJKLMNOPQRSTUVWXYZ
(".;'!*?':,")$1234567890
&-ÄÖÜÅÇÈÎÑÓÆØŒ»„«[·]‹¡·¿›…

Lithos …

Extra Light ABCDEFGHIJKLMNOPQRSTUVWXYZ–$12
Light ABCDEFGHIJKLMNOPQRSTUVWXYZ–$1
• Regular ABCDEFGHIJKLMNOPQRSTUVWXYZ–$1
Bold ABCDEFGHIJKLMNOPQRSTUVWXYZ–$
Black ABCDEFGHIJKLMNOPQRSTUVWXYZ–

Linotype ScriptSet 2: Linoscript & Linotext.

Little Louis

FRA ABCDEFGHIJKLMNOPQRSTUVWXYZ(".;'!*?':,")
▲16 $1234567890&fiflß-ÄÖÜÅÇÈÎÑÓÆØŒ
ABCDEFGHIJKLMNOPQRSTUVWXYZ
ÄÖÜÅÇÈÎÑÓÆØŒ»„«•†<>

▷ 0 0 ʃ 6 9

Locarno Light

Alan Meeks • 1985 ... Rudolph Koch, 1922 abcdefghijklmnopqrstuvwxyz(".;'!*?':,")
LET $1234567890&fiflß-äöüåçèîñóæøœ
▲16 ABCDEFGHIJKLMNOPQRSTUVWXYZ
ÄÖÜÅÇÈÎÑÓÆØŒ»„«[•]‹¡·¿›...

Locarno Italic

Alan Meeks • 1985 ... Rudolph Koch, 1922 *abcdefghijklmnopqrstuvwxyz(".;'!*?':,")*
LET *$1234567890&fiflß-äöüåçèîñóæøœ*
▲16 *ABCDEFGHIJKLMNOPQRSTUVWXYZ*
ÄÖÜÅÇÈÎÑÓÆØŒ»„«[•]‹¡·¿›...

BERTHOLD LO-TYPE

Erik Spiekermann • 1980 ... Louis Oppenheim, 1913 **abcdefghijklmnopqrstuvwxyz(".;'!*?':,")**
ADO AGA MAE **$1234567890&fiflß-äöüåçèîñóæøœ**
▲18 **ABCDEFGHIJKLMNOPQRSTUVWXYZ**
ÄÖÜÅÇÈÎÑÓÆØŒ»„«[•]‹¡·¿›...

Berthold Lo-Type ...

Light abcdefghijklmnopqrstuvwxyzABCDEFGHIJKLMNOPQRSTUVWX
• Regular abcdefghijklmnopqrstuvwxyzABCDEFGHIJKLMNOPQRSTUVW
Medium **abcdefghijklmnopqrstuvwxyzABCDEFGHIJKLMNOPQRSTU**
Medium Italic ***abcdefghijklmnopqrstuvwxyzABCDEFGHIJKLMNOPQRST***
Medium Condensed **abcdefghijklmnopqrstuvwxyzABCDEFGHIJKLMNOPQRSTUVWXYZ–$1234567890(".;'!***
Bold **abcdefghijklmnopqrstuvwxyzABCDEFGHIJKLM**

ITC LUBALIN GRAPH

Herb Lubalin, et al. • 1974 abcdefghijklmnopqrstuvwxyz(".;'!*?':,")
URW ADO AGA BIT LEF LIN MAE $1234567890&fiflß-äöüåçèîñóœøœ
ABCDEFGHIJKLMNOPQRSTUVWXYZ
ÄÖÜÅÇÈÎÑÓÆØŒ»„«[¶§•†‡]‹¡·¿›...

ITC Lubalin Graph 1 ...

• Book abcdefghijklmnopqrstuvwxyzABCDEFGHIJKLMNOPQRSTUVWXYZ–$1234567
Book Oblique *abcdefghijklmnopqrstuvwxyzABCDEFGHIJKLMNOPQRSTUVWXYZ–$123456789*

... ITC Lubalin Graph 1

Demi abcdefghijklmnopqrstuvwxyzABCDEFGHIJKLMNOPQRSTUVWXYZ–$123456

Demi Oblique *abcdefghijklmnopqrstuvwxyzABCDEFGHIJKLMNOPQRSTUVWXYZ–$1234567*

ITC Lubalin Graph 2 ...

Light abcdefghijklmnopqrstuvwxyzABCDEFGHIJKLMNOPQRSTUVWXYZ–$1234567

Light Oblique *abcdefghijklmnopqrstuvwxyzABCDEFGHIJKLMNOPQRSTUVWXYZ–$12345678*

Medium abcdefghijklmnopqrstuvwxyzABCDEFGHIJKLMNOPQRSTUVWXYZ–$123456

Medium Oblique *abcdefghijklmnopqrstuvwxyzABCDEFGHIJKLMNOPQRSTUVWXYZ–$12345678*

Bold **abcdefghijklmnopqrstuvwxyzABCDEFGHIJKLMNOPQRSTUVWXYZ–$12345**

Bold Oblique ***abcdefghijklmnopqrstuvwxyzABCDEFGHIJKLMNOPQRSTUVWXYZ–$123456***

ITC LUBALIN GRAPH CONDENSED

Helga Jörgenson & Sigrid Englemann • 1992 ... Herb Lubalin, et al., 1974

abcdefghijklmnopqrstuvwxyz(".;'!*?':,")

$1234567890&fiflß-äöüåçèîñóœøœ

URW LEF ABCDEFGHIJKLMNOPQRSTUVWXYZ

ÄÖÜÅÇÈÎÑÓÆØŒ»„«(¶§•†‡)‹¡·¿›...

ITC Lubalin Graph Condensed 1 ...

• Book Condensed abcdefghijklmnopqrstuvwxyzABCDEFGHIJKLMNOPQRSTUVWXYZ-$1234567890(".;'!*?':,")

Book Condensed Oblique *abcdefghijklmnopqrstuvwxyzABCDEFGHIJKLMNOPQRSTUVWXYZ-$1234567890(".;'!*?':,")&*

Demi Condensed **abcdefghijklmnopqrstuvwxyzABCDEFGHIJKLMNOPQRSTUVWXYZ-$1234567890(".;'!*?':,"**

Demi Condensed Oblique ***abcdefghijklmnopqrstuvwxyzABCDEFGHIJKLMNOPQRSTUVWXYZ-$1234567890(".;'!*?':,"***

ITC Lubalin Graph Condensed 2 ...

Medium Condensed abcdefghijklmnopqrstuvwxyzABCDEFGHIJKLMNOPQRSTUVWXYZ-$1234567890(".;'!*?':,")

Medium Condensed Oblique *abcdefghijklmnopqrstuvwxyzABCDEFGHIJKLMNOPQRSTUVWXYZ-$1234567890(".;'!*?':,")*

Bold Condensed **abcdefghijklmnopqrstuvwxyzABCDEFGHIJKLMNOPQRSTUVWXYZ-$1234567890(".;'!*?':,**

Bold Condensed Oblique ***abcdefghijklmnopqrstuvwxyzABCDEFGHIJKLMNOPQRSTUVWXYZ-$1234567890(".;'!*?':,***

Lucia

BIT *abcdefghijklmnopqrstuvwxyz(".;'!*?':,")*

▲16 *$1234567890&fiflß-äöüåçèîñóœøœ*

ABCDEFGHIJKLMNOPQRSTUVWXYZ

ÄÖÜÅÇÈÎÑÓÆØŒ»„«[§•†‡]‹¡·¿›...

L

BITSTREAM LUCIAN

Lucian Bernhard • 1937 abcdefghijklmnopqrstuvwxyz(“.;‘!*?’:,”)

BIT $1234567890&fiflß-äöüåçèîñóæøœ

▲16 ABCDEFGHIJKLMNOPQRSTUVWXYZ

ÄÖÜÅÇÈÎÑÓÆØŒ»„«[¶§•†‡]‹¡·¿›...

Bitstream Lucian ...

• Roman abcdefghijklmnopqrstuvwxyzABCDEFGHIJKLMNOPQRSTUVWXYZ–$1

Bold **abcdefghijklmnopqrstuvwxyzABCDEFGHIJKLMNOPQRSTUVWXYZ**

LUCIDA

Charles Bigelow & Kris Holmes • 1985 abcdefghijklmnopqrstuvwxyz(“.;‘!*?’:,”)

ADO AGA FRA LIN MAE URW $1234567890&fiflß-äöüåçèîñóæøœ

ABCDEFGHIJKLMNOPQRSTUVWXYZ

ÄÖÜÅÇÈÎÑÓÆØŒ»„«[¶§•†‡]‹¡·¿›...

π Lucida ...

• Roman abcdefghijklmnopqrstuvwxyzABCDEFGHIJKLMNOPQRSTUVWXYZ–$123

Italic *abcdefghijklmnopqrstuvwxyzABCDEFGHIJKLMNOPQRSTUVWXYZ–$1234*

Bold **abcdefghijklmnopqrstuvwxyzABCDEFGHIJKLMNOPQRSTUVWXY**

Bold Italic ***abcdefghijklmnopqrstuvwxyzABCDEFGHIJKLMNOPQRSTUVWXYZ***

LUCIDA SANS

ADO AGA FRA LIN MAE abcdefghijklmnopqrstuvwxyz(“.;‘!*?’:,”)

$1234567890&fiflß-äöüåçèîñóæøœ

ABCDEFGHIJKLMNOPQRSTUVWXYZ

ÄÖÜÅÇÈÎÑÓÆØŒ»„«[¶§▪†‡]‹¡·¿›...

π Lucida Sans ...

• Regular abcdefghijklmnopqrstuvwxyzABCDEFGHIJKLMNOPQRSTUVWXYZ–$12345

Italic *abcdefghijklmnopqrstuvwxyzABCDEFGHIJKLMNOPQRSTUVWXYZ–$12345*

Bold **abcdefghijklmnopqrstuvwxyzABCDEFGHIJKLMNOPQRSTUVWXYZ–**

Bold Italic ***abcdefghijklmnopqrstuvwxyzABCDEFGHIJKLMNOPQRSTUVWXYZ–***

LUCIDA SANS TYPEWRITER

URW TFC abcdefghijklmnopqrstuvwxyz(“.;‘!*?’:,”)

$1234567890&fiflß-äöüåçèîñóæøœ

ABCDEFGHIJKLMNOPQRSTUVWXYZ

ÄÖÜÅÇÈÎÑÓÆØŒ»„«[¶§·†‡]‹¡·¿›...

Lucida Sans Typewriter ...

• Regular abcdefghijklmnopqrstuvwxyzABCDEFGHIJKLMNOPQRSTUVWXYZ-$12345

Bold **abcdefghijklmnopqrstuvwxyzABCDEFGHIJKLMNOPQRSTUVWXYZ-$12345**

π Lucida Lucida Math.

LYDIAN

✍ Warren Chappell • 1938 abcdefghijklmnopqrstuvwxyz(".;'!*?':,")

BIT MCL $1234567890&fiflß-äöüåçèîñóæøœ

▲16 ABCDEFGHIJKLMNOPQRSTUVWXYZ

ÄÖÜÅÇÈÎÑÓÆØŒ»„«[¶§•†‡]‹¡·¿›...

Lydian ...

• Regular abcdefghijklmnopqrstuvwxyzABCDEFGHIJKLMNOPQRSTUVWXYZ–$12345678

Italic *abcdefghijklmnopqrstuvwxyzABCDEFGHIJKLMNOPQRSTUVWXYZ–$12345678*

Cursive *abcdefghijklmnopqrstuvwxyzABCDEFGHIJKLMNOPQRSTUVWXYZ–$123*

Bold **abcdefghijklmnopqrstuvwxyzABCDEFGHIJKLMNOPQRSTUVWXYZ–$1234567**

Bold Italic ***abcdefghijklmnopqrstuvwxyzABCDEFGHIJKLMNOPQRSTUVWXYZ–$123456***

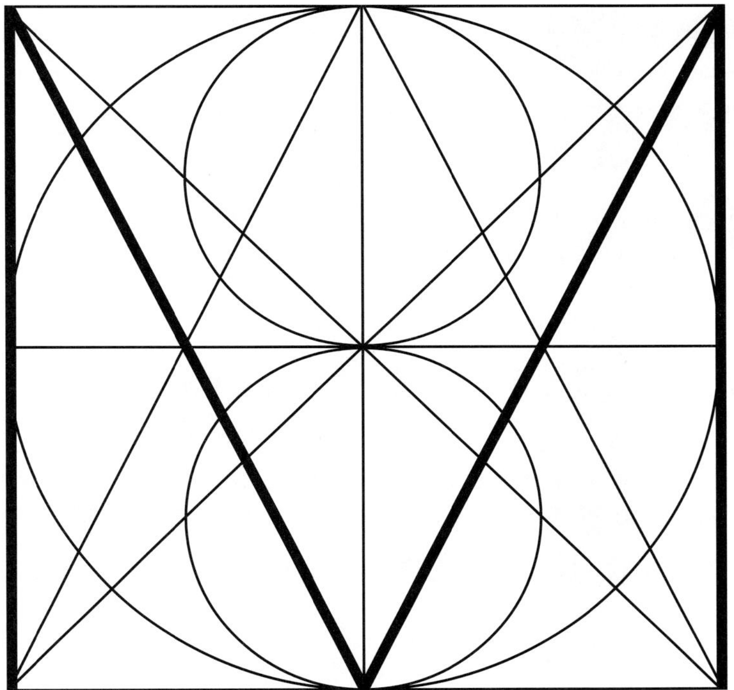

✍ John Howard Benson & Arthur Graham Carey, 1940

ITC MACHINE

Tom Carnase & Renne Bonder • 1970

ADO AGA BIT LEF LIN MAE URW

▲30

ABCDEFGHIJKLMNOPQRSTUVWXYZ(“.;‘!*?’:,”)
$1234567890&-ÄÖÜÅÇÈÎÑÓÆØŒ»„«[¶§•†‡]...

ITC Machine ...

• Medium

ABCDEFGHIJKLMNOPQRSTUVWXYZ–$123456789

Bold

ABCDEFGHIJKLMNOPQRSTUVWXYZ–$123456789

Madame

Linotype DisplaySet 4

LIN

▲36

• Letters, Numericals & Accents

ABCDEFGHIJKLMNOPQRS
TUVWXYZ(“.;‘!?’:,”)$123456
7890&-ÄÖÜÅÈÎÑÔÆŒ

Madrone

Adobe Wood Type 2

Kim Buker, Barbara Lind & Joy Redick • 1991

ADO AGA LIN MAE

▲16

abcdefghijklmnopqrstuvwxy
z(“.;‘!*?’:,”)$1234567890&fiflß-
äöüåçèîñóæøœABCDEFGHIJ
KLMNOPQRSTUVWXYZÄÖÜ
ÅÇÈÎÑÓÆØŒ»„«[•]‹i-¿›...

Mahogany Script

Agfa Scripts 2

E. J. Klumpp • 1956

AGP

▲16

abcdefghijklmnopqrstuvwxyz(“.;‘!*?’:,”)
$1234567890&ß-äöüåçèîñó
ABCDEFGHIJKLMNOPQRSTUVWXYZ
ÄÖÜÅÇÈÎÑÓ»«[.]‹›

▷ I V X st nd rd th ¼ ⅓ ½ ¾ D & %

MAIANDRA

Dennis Pasternak • 1994 (Oswald Cooper, c. 1924)

GAL

abcdefghijklmnopqrstuvwxyz(“.;‘!*?’:,”)
$1234567890&fiflß-äöüåçèîñóæøœ
ABCDEFGHIJKLMNOPQRSTUVWXYZ
ÄÖÜÅÇÈÎÑÓÆØŒ»„«[¶§•†‡]‹i·¿›...

▷

Maiandra ...

• Regular

abcdefghijklmnopqrstuvwxyzABCDEFGHIJKLMNOPQRSTUVWXYZ–$123456789

....

Adobe Wood Type 2: Birch, Blackoak, Madrone, Poplar, Willow, Adobe Wood Type Ornaments 2.
Madrone ▶Adobe Wood Type Ornaments 2.
Linotype DisplaySet 4: Madame Letters, Numericals & Accents, Roundy Regular & Swash Caps.

Agfa Scripts 2: Citadel, Flemish Script 2, Florentine Script 2, French Script, Mahogany Script, Old Fashion Script, Riviera Script.

M

... Maiandra

Bold abcdefghijklmnopqrstuvwxyzABCDEFGHIJKLMNOPQRSTUVWXYZ–$123

Ultra abcdefghijklmnopqrstuvwxyzABCDEFGHIJKLMNOPQRSTUVWXYZ–$1

MalakaLaka-LakaLakaLaka

INT abcdefghijklmnopqrstuvwxyz(".;'!*?':,")

▲16 $1234567890&fiflß-äöüåçèîñóæøœ

ABCDEFGHIJKLMNOPQRSTUVWXYZ

ÄÖÜÅÇÈÎÑÓÆØŒ¶•¡¿ ▷ adfhilprstxyemorsTWXY

Malibu

Alan Meeks • 1992 abcdefghijklmnopqrstuvwxyz(".;'!*?':,")

LET $1234567890&fiflß-äöüåçèîñóæøœ

▲16 ABCDEFGHIJKLMNOPQRSTUVWXYZ

ÄÖÜÅÇÈÎÑÓÆØŒ»„«[•]‹¡·¿›...

TF MALTBY ANTIQUE

Joseph Treacy • 1993 abcdefghijklmnopqrstuvwxyz(".;'!*?':,")

TRE MTD $1234567890&fiflß-äöüåçèîñóæøœ

ABCDEFGHIJKLMNOPQRSTUVWXYZ

ÄÖÜÅÇÈÎÑÓÆØŒ»„«[¶§•†‡]‹¡·¿›... ▷ 123579/234816

TF Maltby Antique A ...

Regular abcdefghijklmnopqrstuvwxyzABCDEFGHIJKLMNOPQRSTUVWXYZ–$1234567890(".;'!*?':

Medium abcdefghijklmnopqrstuvwxyzABCDEFGHIJKLMNOPQRSTUVWXYZ–$1234567890(".;'!*

Extra Bold abcdefghijklmnopqrstuvwxyzABCDEFGHIJKLMNOPQRSTUVWXYZ–$1234567890(".;

Heavy abcdefghijklmnopqrstuvwxyzABCDEFGHIJKLMNOPQRSTUVWXYZ–$1234567890(

TF Maltby Antique B ...

• Book abcdefghijklmnopqrstuvwxyzABCDEFGHIJKLMNOPQRSTUVWXYZ–$1234567890(".;'!*?

Bold abcdefghijklmnopqrstuvwxyzABCDEFGHIJKLMNOPQRSTUVWXYZ–$1234567890(".;'!

Black abcdefghijklmnopqrstuvwxyzABCDEFGHIJKLMNOPQRSTUVWXYZ–$1234567890("

Ragged ▲18 abcdefghijklmnopqrstuvwxyzABCDEFGHIJKLMNOPQRSTUVWXY

TF Maltby Antique Ragged Initials

Joseph Treacy • 1994

TRE MTD

▲24

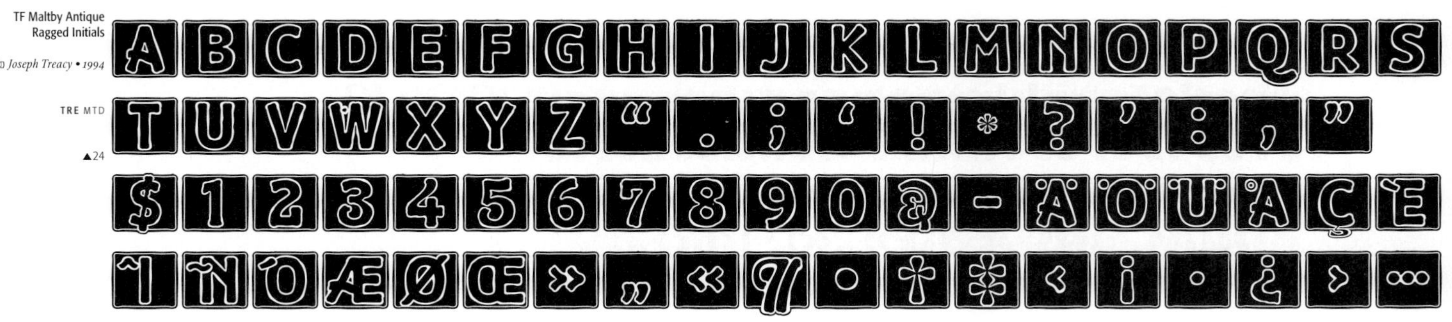

M

ITC/LSC Manhattan

URW

▲24

abcdefghijklmnopqrstuvwxyz("•.;•!*?•:,")

$1234567890&fiflß-äöüåçèîñóæøœ

ABCDEFGHIJKLMNOPQRSTUVWXYZ

ÄÖÜÅÇÈÎÑÓÆØŒ»„«[¶§•†‡]‹¿•¿›…

Manito

Garrett Boge • 1990

LPT MTD

▲24

ABCDEFGHIJKLMNOPQRSTUVWXYZ

(".,'!*?':,")$1234567890&-ÄÖÜÅÇÈÎÑÓ

ÆØŒABCDEFGHIJKLMNOPQRSTUVWXYZ

ÄÖÜÅÇÈÎÑÓÆØŒ»„«[¶§-†‡]‹¡-¿›…

M

Mantinia

Matthew Carter • 1993

CAR

▲30

ABCDEFGHIJKLMNOPQRSTUVWXYZ(".;'!*?':,")

$1234567890&-ÄÖÜÅÇÈÎÑÓÆØŒ

ABCDEFGHIJKLMNOPQRSTUV

WXYZÄÖÜÅÇÈÎÑÓÆØŒ»„«[]‹¡·¿›

▷ QR QRTYILTYCTHELAMBMDME

▷ MPHETTTUTWTYUPV ♠ ♤ &ACEHIORS

FC Marcato

Herbert Post • 1963

TFC

▲18

abcdefghijklmnopqrstuvwxyz(".;'!*?':,")

$1234567890&fiflß-äöüåçèîñóœøœ

ABCDEFGHIJKLMNOPQRSTUVWXYZ

ÄÖÜÅÇÈÎÑÓÆØŒ»„«[•]‹i.¿›…

MARCONI

Hermann Zapf • 1975 abcdefghijklmnopqrstuvwxyz(“.;‘!*?’:,”)
LEF $1234567890&fiflß-äöüåçèîñóæøœ
ABCDEFGHIJKLMNOPQRSTUVWXYZ
ÄÖÜÅÇÈÎÑÓÆØŒ»„«[¶§•†‡]‹¡·¿›...

Marconi ...

• Book abcdefghijklmnopqrstuvwxyzABCDEFGHIJKLMNOPQRSTUVWXYZ-$123456
Book Italic *abcdefghijklmnopqrstuvwxyzABCDEFGHIJKLMNOPQRSTUVWXYZ-$1234567*
Book SCOSF ABCDEFGHIJKLMNOPQRSTUVWXYZABCDEFGHIJKLMNOPQRSTUVWXYZ-$123456
Semibold **abcdefghijklmnopqrstuvwxyzABCDEFGHIJKLMNOPQRSTUVWXYZ-$12**
Semibold Italic ***abcdefghijklmnopqrstuvwxyzABCDEFGHIJKLMNOPQRSTUVWXYZ-$1***

Marguerita

David Quay • 1993 *abcdefghijklmnopqrstuvwxyz(“.;‘!*?’:,”)*
LET *$1234567890&fiflß-äöüåçèîñóæøœ*
▲16 *ABCDEFGHIJKLMNOPQRSTUVWXYZ*
ÄÖÜÅÇÈÎÑÓ»„«[•]‹¡·¿›... ▷ *b d g h i k s y et of st th E G S & Th –*

Marigold
Agfa Baker Calligraphy
Arthur Baker • 1989 abcdefghijklmnopqrstuvwxyz(“.;‘!*?’:,”)
AGP ADO AGA LIN MAE $1234567890&fiflß-äöüåçèîñóæøœ
▲20 ABCDEFGHIJKLMNOPQRSTUVWXYZ
ÄÖÜÅÇÈÎÑÓÆØŒ»„«[¶§•†‡]‹¡·¿›...

Mastercard

ABCDEFGHIJKLMNOPQRSTUVWXYZ
John Hamon • 1984
LET (".;'!*?':,")$1234567890
▲42 &-ÄÖÜÅÇÈÎÑÓÆØŒ»„«[•]‹¡·¿›...

Agfa Baker Calligraphy: Amigo, Marigold, Oxford, Pelican, Visigoth.

MATA

Greg Semata • 1993

T26

▲20

ABCDEFGHIJKLMNOP
QRSTUVWXYZ(".;'!*?':,")
$1234567890&-ÄÖÜÅ
ÇÈÎÑÓØABCDEFGHIJKL
MNOPQRSTUVWXYZÄÖÜ
ÅÇÑÆŒ»«[•]i¿...

Mata ...

• Regular ABCDEFGHIJKLMNOP QRSTUVWXYZABCDEFGH

Bold ABCDEFGHIJKLMNOP QRSTUVWXYZABCDEFGH

Condensed ABCDEFGHIJKLMNOPQRS TUVWXYZABCDEFGHIJKLMN

Bold Condensed ABCDEFGHIJKLMNOPQRS TUVWXYZABCDEFGHIJKLMN

M

MATT ANTIQUE

John Matt • 1965

BIT

abcdefghijklmnopqrstuvwxyz(".;'!*?':,")
$1234567890&fiflß-äöüåçèîñóæøœ
ABCDEFGHIJKLMNOPQRSTUVWXYZ
ÄÖÜÅÇÈÎÑÓÆØŒ»„«[¶§•†‡]‹¡·¿›...

Matt Antique ...

• Roman abcdefghijklmnopqrstuvwxyzABCDEFGHIJKLMNOPQRSTUVWXYZ–$123456

Italic *abcdefghijklmnopqrstuvwxyzABCDEFGHIJKLMNOPQRSTUVWXYZ–$1234567*

Bold **abcdefghijklmnopqrstuvwxyzABCDEFGHIJKLMNOPQRSTUVWXYZ–$1234**

MATURA

✤ *Monotype Crazy Headlines*

Imre Reiner • 1938

MCL ADO AGA LIN MAE

▲16

abcdefghijklmnopqrstuvwxyz(".;'!*?':,")
$1234567890&fiflß-äöüåçèîñóæøœ
ABCDEFGHIJKLMNOPQRSTUVWXYZ
ÄÖÜÅÇÈÎÑÓÆØŒ»„«[¶§•†‡]‹¡·¿›...

Matura ...

• Regular **abcdefghijklmnopqrstuvwxyzABCDEFGHIJKLMNOPQRSTUVWXYZ–$1234**

Scriptorial Capitals **abc...ABCDEFGHIJKLMNOPQRSTUVWXYZ**

✤ *Monotype Crazy Headlines*: Festival Titling, Kino, Matura, Matura Scriptorial Capitals, Victoria Titling Condensed.

Maximus
Linotype ClassAdSet 1
Walter Tracy • 1967
LIN ADO AGA MAE
▲12

abcdefghijklmnopqrstuvwxyz(".;'!*?':,")
$1234567890&fiflß-äöüåçèîñóæøœ
ABCDEFGHIJKLMNOPQRSTUVWXYZ
ÄÖÜÅÇÈÎÑÓÆØŒ»,,«[¶§•†‡]‹¡·¿›...

Maximus Display
BIT
▲30

ABCDEFGHIJKLMNOPQRSTUVWXYZ
(".;'!*?':,")$1234567890
&-ÄÖÜÅÇÈÎÑÓÆØŒ»,,«[§•†‡]‹¡·¿›...

McCollough
Agfa DisplaySet 4
Gustaf F. Schroeder • ....
AGP
▲24

abcdefghijklmnopqrstuvwxyz(".;'!*?':,")$1234567890
&fiflß-äöüåçèîñóæøœABCDEFGHIJKLMNOPQRSTUVWXYZ
ÄÖÜÅÇÈÎÑÓÆØŒ»,,«[¶§•†‡]‹¡·¿›...

McGarey Fractured
INT
▲16

abcdefghijklmnopqrstuvwxyz(".;'!*?':,")
$1234567890&ß-äöüåçèîñóæøœ
ABCDEFGHIJKLMNOPQRSTUVWXYZ
ÄÖÜÅÇÈÎÑÓÆØŒ»,,«[]‹¡¿›

MEAD
Steve Matteson • 1993
MTD
▲18

abcdefghijklmnopqrstuvwxyz(".;'!*?':,")
$1234567890&fiflß-äöüåçèîñóæøœ
ABCDEFGHIJKLMNOPQRSTUVWXYZ
ÄÖÜÅÇÈÎÑÓÆØŒ»,,«[¶§•†‡]‹¡·¿›...

Mead ...

• Regular abcdefghijklmnopqrstuvwxyzABCDEFGHIJKLMNOPQRSTUVWXYZ–$1234567890(".;'!

Bold **abcdefghijklmnopqrstuvwxyzABCDEFGHIJKLMNOPQRSTUVWXYZ–$1**

....
Linotype ClassAdSet 1: Doric Bold & Maximus.
Agfa DisplaySet 4: Branding Iron, Isabella, McCollough, Raphael.

M

Medici Script
Linotype ScriptSet 1
Hermann Zapf • 1971
LIN ADO AGA MAE
▲16

abcdefghijklmnopqrstuvwxyz(“.;‘!*?’:,”)
$1234567890&fiflß-äöüåçèîñóæøœ
ABCDEFGHIJKLMNOPQRSTUVWXYZ
ÄÖÜ ÅÇÈÎÑÓÆØŒ»„«[¶§•†‡]‹¡·¿›...

Mekanik
David Quay • 1988
LET
▲30

abcdefghijklmnopqrstuvwxyz(“.;‘!*?’:,”)$1234567890&fiflß-äöüåçèîñóæøœ
ABCDEFGHIJKLMNOPQRSTUVWXYZÄÖÜÅÇÈÎÑÓÆØŒ»„«[•]‹¡·¿›... ▷ mEEFFJLLTZ

Mekanik Italic
LET
▲30

abcdefghijklmnopqrstuvwxyz(“.;‘!*?’:,”)$1234567890&fiflß-äöüåçèîñóæøœ
ABCDEFGHIJKLMNOPQRSTUVWXYZÄÖÜÅÇÈÎÑÓÆØŒ»„«[•]‹¡·¿›... ▷ mEEFFJLLTZ

MELIOR
Hermann Zapf • 1952
LIN ADO AGA MAE

abcdefghijklmnopqrstuvwxyz(“.;‘!*?’:,”)
$1234567890&fiflß-äöüåçèîñóæøœ
ABCDEFGHIJKLMNOPQRSTUVWXYZ
ÄÖÜÅÇÈÎÑÓÆØŒ»„«[¶§•†‡]‹¡·¿›...

Melior ...

• Roman abcdefghijklmnopqrstuvwxyzABCDEFGHIJKLMNOPQRSTUVWXYZ–$12345
Italic *abcdefghijklmnopqrstuvwxyzABCDEFGHIJKLMNOPQRSTUVWXYZ–$123456*
Bold **abcdefghijklmnopqrstuvwxyzABCDEFGHIJKLMNOPQRSTUVWXYZ–$1234**
Bold Italic ***abcdefghijklmnopqrstuvwxyzABCDEFGHIJKLMNOPQRSTUVWXYZ–$123***

MEMPHIS
Rudolf Weiss • 1929
LIN ADO AGA MAE URW

abcdefghijklmnopqrstuvwxyz(“.;‘!*?’:,”)
$1234567890&fiflß-äöüåçèîñóæøœ
ABCDEFGHIJKLMNOPQRSTUVWXYZ
ÄÖÜÅÇÈÎÑÓÆØŒ»„«[¶§•†‡]‹¡·¿›...

Memphis ...

Light abcdefghijklmnopqrstuvwxyzABCDEFGHIJKLMNOPQRSTUVWXYZ–$1234567
Light Italic *abcdefghijklmnopqrstuvwxyzABCDEFGHIJKLMNOPQRSTUVWXYZ–$1234567*
• Medium abcdefghijklmnopqrstuvwxyzABCDEFGHIJKLMNOPQRSTUVWXYZ–$123456
Medium Italic *abcdefghijklmnopqrstuvwxyzABCDEFGHIJKLMNOPQRSTUVWXYZ–$123456*
Bold **abcdefghijklmnopqrstuvwxyzABCDEFGHIJKLMNOPQRSTUVWXYZ–$123456**

Linotype ScriptSet 1: Cascade Script, Medici Script, Nuptial Script.

... Memphis

Bold Italic *abcdefghijklmnopqrstuvwxyzABCDEFGHIJKLMNOPQRSTUVWXYZ–$123456*

Extra Bold **abcdefghijklmnopqrstuvwxyzABCDEFGHIJKLMNOPQRSTUVW**

ITC MENDOZA ROMAN

José Mendoza y Almeida • 1990

URW ADO AGA AGP LEF ITC LIN MAE

abcdefghijklmnopqrstuvwxyz(".;'!*?':,")
$1234567890&fiflß-äöüåçèîñóæøœ
ABCDEFGHIJKLMNOPQRSTUVWXYZ
ÄÖÜÅÇÈÎÑÓÆØŒ»„«[¶§•†‡]‹¡·¿›...

ITC Mendoza Roman ...

• Book abcdefghijklmnopqrstuvwxyzABCDEFGHIJKLMNOPQRSTUVWXYZ–$1234567890("

Book Italic *abcdefghijklmnopqrstuvwxyzABCDEFGHIJKLMNOPQRSTUVWXYZ–$1234567890(".;!*

Medium **abcdefghijklmnopqrstuvwxyzABCDEFGHIJKLMNOPQRSTUVWXYZ–$12345678**

Medium Italic ***abcdefghijklmnopqrstuvwxyzABCDEFGHIJKLMNOPQRSTUVWXYZ–$1234567890(***

Bold **abcdefghijklmnopqrstuvwxyzABCDEFGHIJKLMNOPQRSTUVWXYZ–$12345**

Bold Italic ***abcdefghijklmnopqrstuvwxyzABCDEFGHIJKLMNOPQRSTUVWXYZ–$12345678***

Book SCOSF ABCDEFGHIJKLMNOPQRSTUVWXYZABCDEFGHIJKLMNOPQRSTUVWXYZ–$1234567890(

Book Italic OSF *abcdefghijklmnopqrstuvwxyzABCDEFGHIJKLMNOPQRSTUVWXYZ–$1234567890(".;'!*

Medium SCOSF **ABCDEFGHIJKLMNOPQRSTUVWXYZABCDEFGHIJKLMNOPQRSTUVWXYZ–$1234567**

M

MENO

Richard Lipton • 1994

FBU

abcdefghijklmnopqrstuvwxyz(".;'!*?':,")
$1234567890&fiflß-äöüåçèîñóæøœ
ABCDEFGHIJKLMNOPQRSTUVWXYZ
ÄÖÜÅÇÈÎÑÓÆØŒ»„«[¶§•†‡]‹¡·¿›...

▷ ff fi ffl

Meno 1 ...

• Roman abcdefghijklmnopqrstuvwxyzABCDEFGHIJKLMNOPQRSTUVWXYZ–$12345

Italic *abcdefghijklmnopqrstuvwxyzABCDEFGHIJKLMNOPQRSTUVWXYZ–$12345678*

Bold **abcdefghijklmnopqrstuvwxyzABCDEFGHIJKLMNOPQRSTUVWXYZ–$12**

Bold Italic ***abcdefghijklmnopqrstuvwxyzABCDEFGHIJKLMNOPQRSTUVWXYZ–$12345***

Black **abcdefghijklmnopqrstuvwxyzABCDEFGHIJKLMNOPQRSTUVWXYZ–**

Black Italic ***abcdefghijklmnopqrstuvwxyzABCDEFGHIJKLMNOPQRSTUVWXYZ–$1***

Meno 2 ...

Roman SCOSF ABCDEFGHIJKLMNOPQRSTUVWXYZABCDEFGHIJKLMNOPQRSTUVWXYZ–$123456

Roman OSF & Extras $1234567890.;:, ⅛ ¼ ⅓ ⅜ ½ ⅝ ⅔ ¾ ⅞ $12345/67890¢ (abdehilmnorst)

Italic OSF & Extras *$1234567890.;:, ⅛ ¼ ⅓ ⅜ ½ ⅝ ⅔ ¾ ⅞ $12345/67890¢ (abdehilmnorst)*

Bold OSF & Extras **$1234567890.;:, ⅛ ¼ ⅓ ⅜ ½ ⅝ ⅔ ¾ ⅞ $12345/67890¢ (abdehilmnorst)**

Bold Italic OSF & Extras ***$1234567890.;:, ⅛ ¼ ⅓ ⅜ ½ ⅝ ⅔ ¾ ⅞ $12345/67890¢ (abdehilmnorst)***

... Meno 2

Black OSF & Extras $1234567890.;:, 1/8 1/4 1/3 3/8 1/2 5/8 2/3 3/4 7/8 $12345/67890¢ (abdehilmnorst)

Black Italic OSF & Extras *$1234567890.;:, 1/8 1/4 1/3 3/8 1/2 5/8 2/3 3/4 7/8 $12345/67890¢ (abdehilmnorst)*

Italic Swash Caps *ABCDEFGHIJKLMNOPQRSTUVWXYZ*

Display Roman SCLF

▲30 ABCDEFGHIJKLMNOPQRSTUVWXYZABC DEFGHIJKLMNOPQRSTUV...$1234

Mercurius Script Bold
Monotype Scripts 3
Imre Reiner • 1957
MCL ADO AGA LIN MAE
▲16

abcdefghijklmnopqrstuvwxyz(".;'!*?':,")
$1234567890&fiflß-äöüåçèîñóæøœ
ABCDEFGHIJKLMNOPQRSTUVWXYZ
ÄÖÜÅÇÈÎÑÓÆØŒ»„«[·]‹¡·¿›...

MERIDIEN
Adrian Frutiger • 1957
LIN ADO AGA FAM MAE

abcdefghijklmnopqrstuvwxyz(".;'!*?':,")
$1234567890&fiflß-äöüåçèîñóæøœ
ABCDEFGHIJKLMNOPQRSTUVWXYZ
ÄÖÜÅÇÈÎÑÓÆØŒ»„«[¶§•†‡]‹¡·¿›...

Meridien ...

• Roman abcdefghijklmnopqrstuvwxyzABCDEFGHIJKLMNOPQRSTUVWXYZ–$1234567

Italic *abcdefghijklmnopqrstuvwxyzABCDEFGHIJKLMNOPQRSTUVWXYZ–$1234567890(".;'*

Medium abcdefghijklmnopqrstuvwxyzABCDEFGHIJKLMNOPQRSTUVWXYZ–$1234

Medium Italic *abcdefghijklmnopqrstuvwxyzABCDEFGHIJKLMNOPQRSTUVWXYZ–$1234567890(".;'*

Bold **abcdefghijklmnopqrstuvwxyzABCDEFGHIJKLMNOPQRSTUVWXYZ–$**

Bold Italic ***abcdefghijklmnopqrstuvwxyzABCDEFGHIJKLMNOPQRSTUVWXYZ–$1234567***

Mesopotamia
Group Arabia
Judith Sutcliffe • 1992
MTD
▲24

abcdefghijklmnopqrstuvwxyz(".;'!*?':,")
$1234567890&fiflß-äöüåçèîñóæøœ
ABCDEFGHIJKLMNOPQRSTUVWXYZ
ÄÖÜÅÇÈÎÑÓÆØŒ»„«[§•]‹¡·¿›...

M

....
Monotype Scripts 3: Coronet Bold & Mercurius Script.
Group Arabia: Arabia Felix, Black Rocks, Black Tents, Kufi Script, Mesopotamia.

Mesquite
Adobe Wood Type 1
Kim Buker, Barbara Lind & Joy Redick • 1990
ADO AGA LIN MAE
▲54

ABCDEFGHIJKLMNOPQRSTUVWXYZ(“.;‘!*?’:,”)
$1234567890&ÄÖÜÅÇÈÎÑÓÆØŒ»„«[•]‹¡·¿›...

METRO
Linotype Headliners
William Addison Dwiggins • 1929
LIN
▲18

abcdefghijklmnopqrstuvwxyz(“.;‘!*?’:,”)
$1234567890&fiflß-äöüåçèîñóæøœ
ABCDEFGHIJKLMNOPQRSTUVWXYZ
ÄÖÜÅÇÈÎÑÓÆØŒ»„«[¶§•†‡]‹¡·¿›...

Metro ...

MetroLite No. 2 abcdefghijklmnopqrstuvwxyzABCDEFGHIJKLMNOPQRSTUVW
• MetroMedium No. 2 abcdefghijklmnopqrstuvwxyzABCDEFGHIJKLMNOPQRSTUVW
MetroBlack No. 2 abcdefghijklmnopqrstuvwxyzABCDEFGHIJKLMNOPQRSTUV

M

MEZZ MULTIPLE·MASTER
(one axis: weight)
Michael Harvey • 1993
ADO AGA MAE
▲24

abcdefghijklmnopqrstuvwxyz(“.;‘!*?’:,”)
$1234567890&fiflß-äöüåçèîñóæøœ
ABCDEFGHIJKLMNOPQRSTUVWXYZ
ÄÖÜÅÇÈÎÑÓÆØŒ»„«[·]‹¡·¿›...

Mezz MultipleMaster ...

Light abcdefghijklmnopqrstuvwxyzABCDEFGHIJKLMNOPQRSTUVWXYZ–$1234567890(“.;‘!*?’:,”)&fiflß-äöü
• Regular abcdefghijklmnopqrstuvwxyzABCDEFGHIJKLMNOPQRSTUVWXYZ–$1234567890(“.;‘!*?’:,”
Semibold abcdefghijklmnopqrstuvwxyzABCDEFGHIJKLMNOPQRSTUVWXYZ–$123456789
Bold abcdefghijklmnopqrstuvwxyzABCDEFGHIJKLMNOPQRSTUVWXYZ–$123
Black abcdefghijklmnopqrstuvwxyzABCDEFGHIJKLMNOPQRSTUVW

MIDWAY
Stephen Herron • 1993
(Frank Lloyd Wright, 1913)
ISI
▲16

abcdefghijklmnopqrstuvwxyz(“.;‘!*?’:,”)
$1234567890&fiflß-äöüåçèîñóæøœ
ABCDEFGHIJKLMNOPQRSTUVWXYZ
ÄÖÜÅÇÈÎÑÓÆØŒ»„«[¶§•†‡]‹¡·¿›... ▷G◆

... Midway ...

• Book abcdefghijklmnopqrstuvwxyzABCDEFGHIJKLMNOPQRSTUVWXYZ–$1234567
Book Italic *abcdefghijklmnopqrstuvwxyzABCDEFGHIJKLMNOPQRSTUVWXYZ–$123456*
Bold **abcdefghijklmnopqrstuvwxyzABCDEFGHIJKLMNOPQRSTUVWXYZ–$1**

Adobe Wood Type 1: Cottonwood, Ironwood, Juniper, Mesquite, Ponderosa, Adobe Wood Type Ornaments 1.
Mesquite ▶Adobe Wood Type Ornaments 1.

Linotype Headliners: Chwast Buffalo Black Condensed, Erbar Light Condensed & Bold Condensed, Metrolite, Metromedium, Metroblack, Plak Black, Black Condensed & Extra Black Condensed, Stop, Times Eighteen Roman & Bold.

... Midway

Bold Italic abcdefghijklmnopqrstuvwxyzABCDEFGHIJKLMNOPQRSTUVWXYZ–$1234567890

Heavy abcdefghijklmnopqrstuvwxyzABCDEFGHIJKLMNOPQRSTUVWXYZ–$1234

Heavy Italic abcdefghijklmnopqrstuvwxyzABCDEFGHIJKLMNOPQRSTUVWXYZ–$1234

Book SCOSF ABCDEFGHIJKLMNOPQRSTUVWXYZABCDEFGHIJKLMNOPQRSTUVWXYZ–$1234567890(".;'!*?'

Book Italic OSF abcdefghijklmnopqrstuvwxyzABCDEFGHIJKLMNOPQRSTUVWXYZ–$1234567890(".;'!*?'

Bold SCOSF ABCDEFGHIJKLMNOPQRSTUVWXYZABCDEFGHIJKLMNOPQRSTUVWXYZ–$1234567890(

Bold Italic OSF abcdefghijklmnopqrstuvwxyzABCDEFGHIJKLMNOPQRSTUVWXYZ–$1234567890

MILL HARROW

Marcus Burlile • 1993 abcdefghijklmnopqrstuvwxyz(".;'!*?';,")$1234567890 and fifl ß–äöüåçè

T26 ▲30 îñóæøœabcdefghijklmnopqrstuvwxyzäöüåçèîñóæøœ»„«

[¶§•†‡]‹¡·¿›...

▷ Θ

Mill Harrow ...

• Mill Harrow abcdefghijklmnopqrstuvwxyzabcdefghijklmnopqrstuvwxyz–$12345

Mill Harrow Knob a b c d e f g h i j k l m n o

p q r s t u v w x y z a b c d

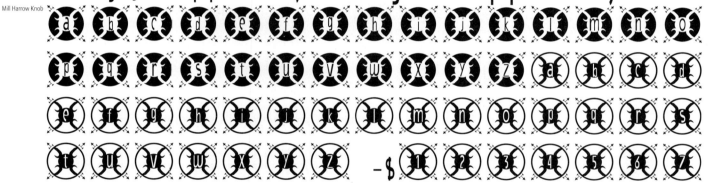

e f g h i j k l m n o p q r s

t u v w x y z –$ 1 2 3 4 5 6 7

MINION

Robert Slimbach • 1989 abcdefghijklmnopqrstuvwxyz(".;'!*?';,")

ADO AGA LIN MAE $1234567890&fiflß-äöüåçèîñóæøœ

ABCDEFGHIJKLMNOPQRSTUVWXYZ

ÄÖÜÅÇÈÎÑÓÆØŒ»„«[¶§•†‡]‹¡·¿›...

Minion ...

• Roman abcdefghijklmnopqrstuvwxyzABCDEFGHIJKLMNOPQRSTUVWXYZ–$1234567890(".;'

Italic *abcdefghijklmnopqrstuvwxyzABCDEFGHIJKLMNOPQRSTUVWXYZ–$1234567890(".;'!*?*

Semibold **abcdefghijklmnopqrstuvwxyzABCDEFGHIJKLMNOPQRSTUVWXYZ–$1234567890(".**

Semibold Italic ***abcdefghijklmnopqrstuvwxyzABCDEFGHIJKLMNOPQRSTUVWXYZ–$1234567890(".;'***

Bold **abcdefghijklmnopqrstuvwxyzABCDEFGHIJKLMNOPQRSTUVWXYZ–$1234567890(**

Minion Minion Cyrillic.

... Minion

Bold Italic *abcdefghijklmnopqrstuvwxyzABCDEFGHIJKLMNOPQRSTUVWXYZ–$1234567890(".;*

Black **abcdefghijklmnopqrstuvwxyzABCDEFGHIJKLMNOPQRSTUVWXYZ–$1234567890**

Display Roman ▲30 abcdefghijklmnopqrstuvwxyzABCDEFGH IJKLMNOPQRSTUVWXYZ–$123456789

Display Italic ▲30 *abcdefghijklmnopqrstuvwxyzABCDEFGHIJ KLMNOPQRSTUVWXYZ–$1234567890(*

MINION EXPERT & SCOSF

ADO AGA LIN MAE ABCDEFGHIJKLMNOPQRSTUVWXYZ.;!?:, 1234567890&ff fi fl ffi ffl-ÄÖÜÅÇÈÎÑÓÆØŒ (abdeilmnorst) 1/8 1/4 1/3 3/8 1/2 5/8 2/3 3/4 7/8 $12345/67890¢ ₡Rp

Minion Expert & SCOSF ...

• Expert Roman ABCDEFGHIJKLMNOPQRSTUVWXYZ-$1234567890.;!?:,&-ff fi fl ffi ffl 1/8 1/4 1/3 3/8 1/2 $12345/67890¢ (a

Expert Italic *ABCDEFGHIJKLMNOPQRSTUVWXYZ-$1234567890.;!?:,&-ff fi fl ffi ffl 1/8 1/4 1/3 3/8 1/2 $12345/67890¢ (ab*

Expert Semibold **ABCDEFGHIJKLMNOPQRSTUVWXYZ-$1234567890.;!?:,&-ff fi fl ffi ffl 1/8 1/4 1/3 3/8 1/2 $12345/67890¢ (**

Expert Semibold Italic ***ABCDEFGHIJKLMNOPQRSTUVWXYZ-$1234567890.;!?:,&-ff fi fl ffi ffl 1/8 1/4 1/3 3/8 1/2 $12345/67890¢ (***

Expert Bold **$1234567890.;:,-ff fi fl ffi ffl 1/8 1/4 1/3 3/8 1/2 $12345/67890¢ (abdeilmnorst) 5/8 2/3 3/4 7/8 ₡Rp**

Expert Bold Italic ***$1234567890.;:,-ff fi fl ffi ffl 1/8 1/4 1/3 3/8 1/2 $12345/67890¢ (abdeilmnorst) 5/8 2/3 3/4 7/8 ₡Rp***

Expert Black **$1234567890.;:,-ff fi fl ffi ffl 1/8 1/4 1/3 3/8 1/2 $12345/67890¢ (abdeilmnorst) 5/8 2/3 3/4 7/8 ₡Rp**

Expert Display Roman ▲30 ABCDEFGHIJKLMNOPQRSTUVWXYZ-$12345 67890.;!?:,&-ff fi fl ffi ffl 1/8 1/4 1/3 3/8 1/2 $12345/6

Expert Display Italic ▲30 *ABCDEFGHIJKLMNOPQRSTUVWXYZ-$123456 7890.;!?:,&-ff fi fl ffi ffl 1/8 1/4 1/3 3/8 1/2 $12345/678*

Roman SCOSF ABCDEFGHIJKLMNOPQRSTUVWXYZABCDEFGHIJKLMNOPQRSTUVWXYZ–$1234567890

Italic SCOSF *ABCDEFGHIJKLMNOPQRSTUVWXYZABCDEFGHIJKLMNOPQRSTUVWXYZ–$1234567890("*

Semibold SCOSF **ABCDEFGHIJKLMNOPQRSTUVWXYZABCDEFGHIJKLMNOPQRSTUVWXYZ–$123456789**

Semibold Italic SCOSF ***ABCDEFGHIJKLMNOPQRSTUVWXYZABCDEFGHIJKLMNOPQRSTUVWXYZ–$1234567890***

Bold OSF **abcdefghijklmnopqrstuvwxyzABCDEFGHIJKLMNOPQRSTUVWXYZ–$1234567890(".**

Bold Italic OSF ***abcdefghijklmnopqrstuvwxyzABCDEFGHIJKLMNOPQRSTUVWXYZ–$1234567890(".;'***

Minion Expert & SCOSF ▶Minion Ornaments.

M

... Minion Expert & SCOSF

Black OSF **abcdefghijklmnopqrstuvwxyzABCDEFGHIJKLMNOPQRSTUVWXYZ–$1234567890(**

Display Roman SCOSF
▲30 ABCDEFGHIJKLMNOPQRSTUVWXYZABCDE
FGHIJKLMNOPQRSTUVWXYZ–$12345

Display Italic SCOSF
▲30 *ABCDEFGHIJKLMNOPQRSTUVWXYZABCDE*
FGHIJKLMNOPQRSTUVWXYZ–$123456

Italic Swash Caps *ABCDEFGHIJKLMNOPQRSTUVWXYZ*

Semibold Italic Swash Caps ***ABCDEFGHIJKLMNOPQRSTUVWXYZ***

Display Italic Swash Caps
▲30 *ABCDEFGHIJKLMNOPQRSTU*

MINION MULTIPLE·MASTER
(three axes: weight, width, optical size)
Robert Slimbach • 1991
ADO AGA MAE

abcdefghijklmnopqrstuvwxyz(".;'!*?':,")
$1234567890&fiflß-äöüåçèîñóæøœ
ABCDEFGHIJKLMNOPQRSTUVWXYZ
ÄÖÜÅÇÈÎÑÓÆØŒ»„«[¶§•†‡]‹¡·¿›...

Minion MultipleMaster ...

• Roman abcdefghijklmnopqrstuvwxyzABCDEFGHIJKLMNOPQRSTUVWXYZ–$1234567890(".;'

Italic *abcdefghijklmnopqrstuvwxyzABCDEFGHIJKLMNOPQRSTUVWXYZ–$1234567890(".;'!*?*

Semibold **abcdefghijklmnopqrstuvwxyzABCDEFGHIJKLMNOPQRSTUVWXYZ–$1234567890("**

Semibold Italic ***abcdefghijklmnopqrstuvwxyzABCDEFGHIJKLMNOPQRSTUVWXYZ–$1234567890(".;'!***

Bold **abcdefghijklmnopqrstuvwxyzABCDEFGHIJKLMNOPQRSTUVWXYZ–$1234567890**

Bold Italic ***abcdefghijklmnopqrstuvwxyzABCDEFGHIJKLMNOPQRSTUVWXYZ–$1234567890(".***

Display Roman
▲30 abcdefghijklmnopqrstuvwxyzABCDEFGHI
JKLMNOPQRSTUVWXYZ–$1234567890

Display Italic
▲30 *abcdefghijklmnopqrstuvwxyzABCDEFGHIJK*
LMNOPQRSTUVWXYZ–$1234567890(".;'

Condensed Roman abcdefghijklmnopqrstuvwxyzABCDEFGHIJKLMNOPQRSTUVWXYZ–$1234567890(".;'!*?':,")&fiflß-

M

... Minion MultipleMaster

Condensed Italic *abcdefghijklmnopqrstuvwxyzABCDEFGHIJKLMNOPQRSTUVWXYZ–$1234567890(".;'!*?':;")&fiflß-ä*

Semibold Condensed abcdefghijklmnopqrstuvwxyzABCDEFGHIJKLMNOPQRSTUVWXYZ–$1234567890(".;'!*?':;")&fi

Semibold Condensed Italic ***abcdefghijklmnopqrstuvwxyzABCDEFGHIJKLMNOPQRSTUVWXYZ–$1234567890(".;'!*?':;")&fifl***

Bold Condensed **abcdefghijklmnopqrstuvwxyzABCDEFGHIJKLMNOPQRSTUVWXYZ–$1234567890(".;'!*?':;")**

Bold Condensed Italic ***abcdefghijklmnopqrstuvwxyzABCDEFGHIJKLMNOPQRSTUVWXYZ–$1234567890(".;'!*?':;")&***

MINION MULTIPLE-MASTER EXPERT & SCOSF

ADO AGA MAE ABCDEFGHIJKLMNOPQRSTUVWXYZ.;!?:,
1234567890&ﬀﬁﬂﬃﬄ-ÄÖÜÅÇÈÎÑÓÆØŒ
(abdeilmnorst) 1/8 1/4 1/3 3/8 1/2 5/8 2/3 3/4 7/8 $12345/67890¢ ₡Rp

Minion MultipleMaster Expert & SCOSF ...

• Expert Roman ABCDEFGHIJKLMNOPQRSTUVWXYZ-$1234567890.;!?:,&-ﬀﬁﬂﬃﬄ 1/8 1/4 1/3 3/8 1/2 $12345/67890¢

Expert Italic *ABCDEFGHIJKLMNOPQRSTUVWXYZ-$1234567890.;!?:,&-ﬀﬁﬂﬃﬄ 1/8 1/4 1/3 3/8 1/2 $12345/67890¢ (a*

Expert Semibold **ABCDEFGHIJKLMNOPQRSTUVWXYZ-$1234567890.;!?:,&-ﬀﬁﬂﬃﬄ 1/8 1/4 1/3 3/8 1/2 $12345/678**

Expert Semibold Italic ***ABCDEFGHIJKLMNOPQRSTUVWXYZ-$1234567890.;!?:,&-ﬀﬁﬂﬃﬄ 1/8 1/4 1/3 3/8 1/2 $12345/67890***

Expert Bold **ABCDEFGHIJKLMNOPQRSTUVWXYZ-$1234567890.;!?:,&-ﬀﬁﬂﬃﬄ 1/8 1/4 1/3 3/8 1/2 $12345/6**

Expert Bold Italic ***ABCDEFGHIJKLMNOPQRSTUVWXYZ-$1234567890.;!?:,&-ﬀﬁﬂﬃﬄ 1/8 1/4 1/3 3/8 1/2 $12345/67***

Expert Display Roman

▲30 ABCDEFGHIJKLMNOPQRSTUVWXYZ-$123456
7890.;!?:,&-ﬀﬁﬂﬃﬄ 1/8 1/4 1/3 3/8 1/2 $12345/678

Expert Display Italic

▲30 *ABCDEFGHIJKLMNOPQRSTUVWXYZ-$1234567
890.;!?:,&-ﬀﬁﬂﬃﬄ 1/8 1/4 1/3 3/8 1/2 $12345/6789*

Roman SCOSF ABCDEFGHIJKLMNOPQRSTUVWXYZABCDEFGHIJKLMNOPQRSTUVWXYZ–$123456789

Italic SCOSF *ABCDEFGHIJKLMNOPQRSTUVWXYZABCDEFGHIJKLMNOPQRSTUVWXYZ–$1234567890(".*

Semibold SCOSF **ABCDEFGHIJKLMNOPQRSTUVWXYZABCDEFGHIJKLMNOPQRSTUVWXYZ–$1234567**

Semibold Italic SCOSF ***ABCDEFGHIJKLMNOPQRSTUVWXYZABCDEFGHIJKLMNOPQRSTUVWXYZ–$123456789***

Bold SCOSF **ABCDEFGHIJKLMNOPQRSTUVWXYZABCDEFGHIJKLMNOPQRSTUVWXYZ–$123456**

Bold Italic SCOSF ***ABCDEFGHIJKLMNOPQRSTUVWXYZABCDEFGHIJKLMNOPQRSTUVWXYZ–$12345678***

Display Roman SCOSF

▲30 ABCDEFGHIJKLMNOPQRSTUVWXYZABCDEF
GHIJKLMNOPQRSTUVWXYZ–$1234567

Minion MultipleMaster Expert & SCOSF ▶ Minion MultipleMaster Ornaments.

... Minion MultipleMaster
Expert & SCOSF

Display Italic SCOSF ▲30 *ABCDEFGHIJKLMNOPQRSTUVWXYZABCDEF GHIJKLMNOPQRSTUVWXYZ–$12345678*

Italic Swash Caps *ABCDEFGHIJKLMNOPQRSTUVWXYZ*

Semibold Italic Swash Caps *ABCDEFGHIJKLMNOPQRSTUVWXYZ*

Bold Italic Swash Caps ***ABCDEFGHIJKLMNOPQRSTUVWXYZ***

Display Italic Swash Caps ▲30 *ABCDEFGHIJKLMNOPQRSTU*

Expert Condensed Roman ABCDEFGHIJKLMNOPQRSTUVWXYZ-$1234567890.;!?:,&-fffiflffiffl 1/8 1/4 1/3 3/8 1/2 $12345/67890¢ (abdilmnor

Expert Condensed Italic *ABCDEFGHIJKLMNOPQRSTUVWXYZ-$1234567890.;!?:,&-fffiflffiffl 1/8 1/4 1/3 3/8 1/2 $12345/67890¢ (abdeilmnorst)*

Expert Semibold Condensed **ABCDEFGHIJKLMNOPQRSTUVWXYZ-$1234567890.;!?:,&-fffiflffiffl 1/8 1/4 1/3 3/8 1/2 $12345/67890¢ (abdeil**

Expert Semibold Condensed Italic ***ABCDEFGHIJKLMNOPQRSTUVWXYZ-$1234567890.;!?:,&-fffiflffiffl 1/8 1/4 1/3 3/8 1/2 $12345/67890¢ (abdeilm***

Expert Bold Condensed **ABCDEFGHIJKLMNOPQRSTUVWXYZ-$1234567890.;!?:,&-fffiflffiffl 1/8 1/4 1/3 3/8 1/2 $12345/67890¢ (ab**

Expert Bold Condensed Italic ***ABCDEFGHIJKLMNOPQRSTUVWXYZ-$1234567890.;!?:,&-fffiflffiffl 1/8 1/4 1/3 3/8 1/2 $12345/67890¢ (abd***

Condensed Roman SCOSF ABCDEFGHIJKLMNOPQRSTUVWXYZABCDEFGHIJKLMNOPQRSTUVWXYZ–$1234567890(".;'!*?':,")&

M

Condensed Italic SCOSF *ABCDEFGHIJKLMNOPQRSTUVWXYZABCDEFGHIJKLMNOPQRSTUVWXYZ–$1234567890(".;'!*?':,")&-Ä*

Semibold Condensed SCOSF **ABCDEFGHIJKLMNOPQRSTUVWXYZABCDEFGHIJKLMNOPQRSTUVWXYZ–$1234567890(".;'!*?':**

Semibold Condensed Italic SCOSF ***ABCDEFGHIJKLMNOPQRSTUVWXYZABCDEFGHIJKLMNOPQRSTUVWXYZ–$1234567890(".;'!*?':,")***

Bold Condensed SCOSF **ABCDEFGHIJKLMNOPQRSTUVWXYZABCDEFGHIJKLMNOPQRSTUVWXYZ–$1234567890(".;'!**

Bold Condensed Italic SCOSF ***ABCDEFGHIJKLMNOPQRSTUVWXYZABCDEFGHIJKLMNOPQRSTUVWXYZ–$1234567890(".;'!*?'***

Condensed Italic Swash Caps *ABCDEFGHIJKLMNOPQRSTUVWXYZ*

Semibold Condensed Italic Swash Caps ***ABCDEFGHIJKLMNOPQRSTUVWXYZ***

Bold Condensed Italic Swash Caps ***ABCDEFGHIJKLMNOPQRSTUVWXYZ***

MINISTER

M. Fahrenwaldt • 1929

LIN ADO AGA MAE URW

abcdefghijklmnopqrstuvwxyz(".;'!*?':,")
$1234567890&fiflß-äöüåçèîñóæøœ
ABCDEFGHIJKLMNOPQRSTUVWXYZ
ÄÖÜÅÇÈÎÑÓÆØŒ»,,«[¶§•†‡]‹¡·¿›...

Minister ...

Light abcdefghijklmnopqrstuvwxyzABCDEFGHIJKLMNOPQRSTUVWXYZ–$1234

Light Italic *abcdefghijklmnopqrstuvwxyzABCDEFGHIJKLMNOPQRSTUVWXYZ–$12345678*

• Book abcdefghijklmnopqrstuvwxyzABCDEFGHIJKLMNOPQRSTUVWXYZ–$12

Book Italic *abcdefghijklmnopqrstuvwxyzABCDEFGHIJKLMNOPQRSTUVWXYZ–$1234*

Bold **abcdefghijklmnopqrstuvwxyzABCDEFGHIJKLMNOPQRSTUVWXYZ–**

... Minister

Bold Italic *abcdefghijklmnopqrstuvwxyzABCDEFGHIJKLMNOPQRSTUVWXYZ–$1*

Black **abcdefghijklmnopqrstuvwxyzABCDEFGHIJKLMNOPQRSTUVWX**

Black Italic ***abcdefghijklmnopqrstuvwxyzABCDEFGHIJKLMNOPQRSTUVWXY***

MIRARAE

Carol Twombly • 1989 abcdefghijklmnopqrstuvwxyz(".;'!*?':,")

BIT $1234567890&fiflß-äöüåçèîñóæøœ

ABCDEFGHIJKLMNOPQRSTUVWXYZ

ÄÖÜÅÇÈÎÑÓÆØŒ»„«[¶§•†‡]‹i·¿›...

Mirarae ...

• Regular abcdefghijklmnopqrstuvwxyzABCDEFGHIJKLMNOPQRSTUVWXYZ–$1234567

Bold **abcdefghijklmnopqrstuvwxyzABCDEFGHIJKLMNOPQRSTUVWXYZ–$1234**

Missive

Stephen Farrell • 1993 abcdefghijklmnopqrstuvwxyz(".;'!*?':,")

T26 $1234567890&fiflß-äöüåçèîñóæøœ

▲16 ABCDEFGHIJKLMNOPQRSTUVWXYZ

ÄÖÜÅÇÈÎÑÓÆØŒ»„«[¶§•†‡]‹¡·¿›...

Mister Earl

Jenny Maestre • 1991 **abcdefghijklmnopqrstuvwxyz(".;'!*?':,")$1234567890&fiflß-äöüåçèîñó**

BIT

▲24 **æøœABCDEFGHIJKLMNOPQRSTUVWXYZÄÖÜÅÇÈÎÑÓÆØŒ»„«[¶§•†‡]‹i·¿›...**

Mistral

✤ *Adobe ScriptSet 1*

Roger Excoffon • 1953 abcdefghijklmnopqrstuvwxyz(".;'!*?':,")

ADO AGA LET LIN MAE MTD URW $1234567890&fiflß-äöüåçèîñóæøœ

▲16 ABCDEFGHIJKLMNOPQRSTUVWXYZ

ÄÖÜÅÇÈÎÑÓÆØŒ»„«[•]‹¡·¿›...

ITC MIXAGE

Aldo Novarese • 1985 abcdefghijklmnopqrstuvwxyz(".;'!*?':,")

BIT LEF URW $1234567890&fiflß-äöüåçèîñóæøœ

ABCDEFGHIJKLMNOPQRSTUVWXYZ

ÄÖÜÅÇÈÎÑÓÆØŒ»„«[¶§•†‡]‹i·¿›...

ITC Mixage 1 ...

• Book abcdefghijklmnopqrstuvwxyzABCDEFGHIJKLMNOPQRSTUVWXYZ–$123456789

✤ *Adobe ScriptSet 1*: Mistral & Reporter No. 2.

M

... ITC Mixage 1

Book Italic *abcdefghijklmnopqrstuvwxyzABCDEFGHIJKLMNOPQRSTUVWXYZ–$1234567890*

Bold **abcdefghijklmnopqrstuvwxyzABCDEFGHIJKLMNOPQRSTUVWXYZ–$123**

Bold Italic ***abcdefghijklmnopqrstuvwxyzABCDEFGHIJKLMNOPQRSTUVWXYZ–$123***

ITC Mixage 2 ...

Medium abcdefghijklmnopqrstuvwxyzABCDEFGHIJKLMNOPQRSTUVWXYZ–$123456

Medium Italic *abcdefghijklmnopqrstuvwxyzABCDEFGHIJKLMNOPQRSTUVWXYZ–$1234567*

Black **abcdefghijklmnopqrstuvwxyzABCDEFGHIJKLMNOPQRSTUVWXYZ–$**

Black Italic ***abcdefghijklmnopqrstuvwxyzABCDEFGHIJKLMNOPQRSTUVWXYZ–$1***

MONOTYPE MODERN

MCL ADO AGA LIN MAE abcdefghijklmnopqrstuvwxyz(“.;‘!*?’:,”)

▲16 $1234567890&fiflß-äöüåçèîñóæøœ

ABCDEFGHIJKLMNOPQRSTUVWXYZ

ÄÖÜÅÇÈÎÑÓÆØŒ»„«[¶§•†‡]‹¡·¿›...

Monotype Modern ...

Condensed abcdefghijklmnopqrstuvwxyzABCDEFGHIJKLMNOPQRSTUVWXYZ–$123456

Condensed Italic *abcdefghijklmnopqrstuvwxyzABCDEFGHIJKLMNOPQRSTUVWXYZ–$12345678*

• Extended abcdefghijklmnopqrstuvwxyzABCDEFGHIJKLMNOPQRSTUVWXY

Extended Italic *abcdefghijklmnopqrstuvwxyzABCDEFGHIJKLMNOPQRSTUVWXYZ–$*

Bold **abcdefghijklmnopqrstuvwxyzABCDEFGHIJKLMNOPQRSTUVWXYZ–$**

Bold Italic ***abcdefghijklmnopqrstuvwxyzABCDEFGHIJKLMNOPQRSTUVWXY***

Wide abcdefghijklmnopqrstuvwxyzABCDEFGHIJKLMNOPQRS

Wide Italic *abcdefghijklmnopqrstuvwxyzABCDEFGHIJKLMNOPQRST*

M

MODERN 880

Walter Tracy • 1969 abcdefghijklmnopqrstuvwxyz(“.;‘!*?’:,”)

BIT $1234567890&fiflß-äöüåçèîñóæøœ

ABCDEFGHIJKLMNOPQRSTUVWXYZ

ÄÖÜÅÇÈÎÑÓÆØŒ»„«[¶§•†‡]‹¡·¿›...

Modern 880 ...

• Roman abcdefghijklmnopqrstuvwxyzABCDEFGHIJKLMNOPQRSTUVWXYZ–$12345

Italic *abcdefghijklmnopqrstuvwxyzABCDEFGHIJKLMNOPQRSTUVWXYZ–$123456*

Bold **abcdefghijklmnopqrstuvwxyzABCDEFGHIJKLMNOPQRSTUVWXYZ–$123**

PL Modern Heavy Condensed
Agfa Typographer's Edition 3
Robert Hunter Middleton • 1936
AGP
▲16

abcdefghijklmnopqrstuvwxyz(".;'!*?':,")
$1234567890&ß-äöüåçèîñóæøœ
ABCDEFGHIJKLMNOPQRSTUVWXYZ
ÄÖÜÅÇÈÎÑÓÆØŒ»„«[¶•†‡]‹¡·¿›...

ITC MODERN NO. 216
Ed Benguiat • 1982
LEF FRA

abcdefghijklmnopqrstuvwxyz(".;'!*?':,")
$1234567890&fiflß-äöüåçèîñóæøœ
ABCDEFGHIJKLMNOPQRSTUVWXYZ
ÄÖÜÅÇÈÎÑÓÆØŒ»„«[¶§•†‡]‹¡·¿›...

ITC Modern No. 216 One ...

Light abcdefghijklmnopqrstuvwxyzABCDEFGHIJKLMNOPQRSTUVWXYZ-$123
Light Italic *abcdefghijklmnopqrstuvwxyzABCDEFGHIJKLMNOPQRSTUVWXYZ-$1234*
Bold **abcdefghijklmnopqrstuvwxyzABCDEFGHIJKLMNOPQRSTUVWXYZ-$**
Bold Italic ***abcdefghijklmnopqrstuvwxyzABCDEFGHIJKLMNOPQRSTUVWXYZ-$***

ITC Modern No. 216 Two ...

• Medium abcdefghijklmnopqrstuvwxyzABCDEFGHIJKLMNOPQRSTUVWXYZ-$12
Medium Italic *abcdefghijklmnopqrstuvwxyzABCDEFGHIJKLMNOPQRSTUVWXYZ-$12*
Heavy **abcdefghijklmnopqrstuvwxyzABCDEFGHIJKLMNOPQRSTUVWXY**
Heavy Italic ***abcdefghijklmnopqrstuvwxyzABCDEFGHIJKLMNOPQRSTUVWXY***

HF MODULAR STENCIL
Greg La Vardera • 1994
HAN MTD
▲24

abcdefghijklmnopqrstuvwxyz(".;'!*?':,")
$1234567890&fiflß-äöüåçèîñóæøœ
ABCDEFGHIJKLMNOPQRSTUVWXYZ
ÄÖÜÅÇÈÎÑÓÆØŒ[·]¡¿ ▷ff ffi ffl fi ft

HF Modular Stencil ...

• Regular abcdefghijklmnopqrstuvwxyzABCDE
Italic *abcdefghijklmnopqrstuvwxyzABCDE*
Outline abcdefghijklmnopqrstuvwxyzABCDE

M

Agfa Typographer's Edition 3: Barclay Open, PL Bernhardt Light, Medium & Bold, PL Britannia Bold, Delphian Open, PL Fiorello Condensed, Fluidum Bold, PL Modern Heavy Condensed, PL Torino Open.

... HF Modular Stencil

Italic Outline abcdefghijklmnopqrstuvwxyzABCDE

Mo' Funky Fresh

David Sagorski • 1993

LET

▲30

ABCDEFGHIJKLMNOPQRSTUVWXYZ

(".;'!*?':,")$1234567890

&-ÄÖÜÅÇÈÎÑÓÆØŒ»„«[•]‹¡·¿›... ▷ ABCDEFGHI

▷ JKLMNOPQRSTUVWXYZ

ITC MONA LISA

ITC Typographica

Pat Hickson • 1991

... Albert Auspurg, 1930

ADO AGA AGP LEF ITC LIN MAE URW

▲30

abcdefghijklmnopqrstuvwxyz(".;'!*?':,")

$1234567890&fifl ß-äöüåçèîñóæøœ

ABCDEFGHIJKLMNOPQRSTUVWXYZ

ÄÖÜÅÇÈÎÑÓÆØŒ»„«[¶§·†‡]‹¡·¿›...

ITC Mona Lisa ...

• Recut abcdefghijklmnopqrstuvwxyzABCDEFGHIJKLM

Solid abcdefghijklmnopqrstuvwxyzABCDEFGHIJKLM

Monoline Script

Monotype Scripts 2

.... • 1933

MCL ADO AGA LIN MAE

▲16

abcdefghijklmnopqrstuvwxyz(".;'!*?':,")

$1234567890&fiflß-äöüåçèîñóæøœ

ABCDEFGHIJKLMNOPQRSTUVWXYZ

ÄÖÜÅÇÈÎÑÓÆØŒ»„«[§•†‡]‹¡·¿›...

MONTAUK

HEA

▲16

abcdefghijklmnopqrstuvwxyz(".;'!*?':,")

$1234567890&-äöüåçèîñóø

ABCDEFGHIJKLMNOPQRSTUVWXYZ

ÄÖÜÅÇÈÎÑÓØ»„«[¶§•]‹¡·¿›... ▷ a

Σ Mo' Funky Fresh Mo' Funky Fresh Symbols.

ITC Typographica: ITC Anna, ITC Beesknees, ITC Mona Lisa Recut & Solid, ITC Ozwald.

Monotype Scripts 2: Ashley Script, Monoline Script, New Berolina, Palace Script Regular & Semibold.

... Montauk ...

Light abcdefghijklmnopqrstuvwxyzABCDEFGHIJKLMNOPQRSTUVWXYZ–$
• Medium abcdefghijklmnopqrstuvwxyzABCDEFGHIJKLMNOPQRSTUVWXYZ–
Bold abcdefghijklmnopqrstuvwxyzABCDEFGHIJKLMNOPQRSTUVWXY

ITC MOTTER CORPUS

Othmar Motter • 1993
ITC URW

abcdefghijklmnopqrstuvwxyz(".;'!*?':,")
$1234567890&fiflß-äöüåçèîñóæøœ
ABCDEFGHIJKLMNOPQRSTUVWXYZ
ÄÖÜÅÇÈÎÑÓÆØŒ»„«[¢§•†‡]‹i·¿›...

ITC Motter Corpus ...

• Bold abcdefghijklmnopqrstuvwxyzABCDEFGHIJKLMNOPQRSTUVW
Bold OSF abcdefghijklmnopqrstuvwxyzABCDEFGHIJKLMNOP...$12345
Bold Condensed abcdefghijklmnopqrstuvwxyzABCDEFGHIJKLMNOPQRSTUVWXYZ–$123457890(".;'!*?
Bold Condensed OSF abcdefghijklmnopqrstuvwxyzABCDEFGHIJKLMNOPQRSTUVWXYZ–$1234567890(".;'!*

MUNICH

Richard Lipton • 1993 (Ludwig Holwein)
FBU
▲18

ABCDEFGHIJKLMNOPQRSTUVWXYZ(".;'!*?':,")
$1234567890&-ÄÖÜÅÇÈÎÑÓÆØŒ
ABCDEFGHIJKLMNOPQRSTUVWXYZ
ÄÖÜÅÇÈÎÑÓÆØŒ»„«[¶§•†‡]‹i·¿›...

Munich ...

Light ABCDEFGHIJKLMNOPQRSTUVWXYZABCDEFGHIJKLMNOPQRSTUVW
• Bold ABCDEFGHIJKLMNOPQRSTUVWXYZABCDEFGHIJKLMNOPQR
Black ABCDEFGHIJKLMNOPQRSTUVWXYZABCDEFGHIJKLMNO

MURRAY HILL

E. J. Klumpp • 1956
BIT LEF URW
▲16

abcdefghijklmnopqrstuvwxyz(".;'!*?':,")
$1234567890&fiflß-äöüåçèîñóæøœ
ABCDEFGHIJKLMNOPQRSTUVWXYZ
ÄÖÜÅÇÈÎÑÓÆØŒ»„«[§•†‡]‹i·¿›...

Murray Hill ...

• Regular abcdefghijklmnopqrstuvwxyzABCDEFGHIJKLMNOPQRSTUVWXYZ–$12345
Bold abcdefghijklmnopqrstuvwxyzABCDEFGHIJKLMNOPQRSTUVWXY

MYRIAD MULTIPLE-MASTER
(two axes: weight & width)

Robert Slimbach & Carol Twombly • 1991

ADO AGA MAE

abcdefghijklmnopqrstuvwxyz(".;'!*?':,")
$1234567890&fiflß-äöüåçèîñóæøœ
ABCDEFGHIJKLMNOPQRSTUVWXYZ
ÄÖÜÅÇÈÎÑÓÆØŒ»„«[¶§•†‡]‹¡·¿›…

Myriad MultipleMaster …

Light abcdefghijklmnopqrstuvwxyzABCDEFGHIJKLMNOPQRSTUVWXYZ–$1234567890(".;'!*?':,")&

Light Italic *abcdefghijklmnopqrstuvwxyzABCDEFGHIJKLMNOPQRSTUVWXYZ–$1234567890(".;'!*?':,")&fiflß*

• Regular abcdefghijklmnopqrstuvwxyzABCDEFGHIJKLMNOPQRSTUVWXYZ–$1234567890(".;'!*

Italic *abcdefghijklmnopqrstuvwxyzABCDEFGHIJKLMNOPQRSTUVWXYZ–$1234567890(".;'!*?':,")*

Semibold **abcdefghijklmnopqrstuvwxyzABCDEFGHIJKLMNOPQRSTUVWXYZ–$1234567890("**

Semibold Italic ***abcdefghijklmnopqrstuvwxyzABCDEFGHIJKLMNOPQRSTUVWXYZ–$1234567890(".;'!****

Bold **abcdefghijklmnopqrstuvwxyzABCDEFGHIJKLMNOPQRSTUVWXYZ–$123456789**

Bold Italic ***abcdefghijklmnopqrstuvwxyzABCDEFGHIJKLMNOPQRSTUVWXYZ–$1234567890("***

Black **abcdefghijklmnopqrstuvwxyzABCDEFGHIJKLMNOPQRSTUVWXYZ–$1234567**

Black Italic ***abcdefghijklmnopqrstuvwxyzABCDEFGHIJKLMNOPQRSTUVWXYZ–$123456789***

Light Condensed abcdefghijklmnopqrstuvwxyzABCDEFGHIJKLMNOPQRSTUVWXYZ–$1234567890(".;'!*?':,")&fiflß-äöüÄÖÜåçèÅÇÈîñóÎÑÓæøœ

Light Condensed Italic *abcdefghijklmnopqrstuvwxyzABCDEFGHIJKLMNOPQRSTUVWXYZ–$1234567890(".;'!*?':,")&fiflß-äöüÄÖÜåçèÅÇÈîñóÎÑÓæøœÆØ*

Condensed abcdefghijklmnopqrstuvwxyzABCDEFGHIJKLMNOPQRSTUVWXYZ–$1234567890(".;'!*?':,")&fiflß-äöüÄÖÜåçèÅÇÈîñóÎ

Condensed Italic *abcdefghijklmnopqrstuvwxyzABCDEFGHIJKLMNOPQRSTUVWXYZ–$1234567890(".;'!*?':,")&fiflß-äöüÄÖÜåçèÅÇÈîñóÎÑÓ*

Semibold Condensed **abcdefghijklmnopqrstuvwxyzABCDEFGHIJKLMNOPQRSTUVWXYZ–$1234567890(".;'!*?':,")&fiflß-äöüÄÖÜåçèÅ**

Semibold Condensed Italic ***abcdefghijklmnopqrstuvwxyzABCDEFGHIJKLMNOPQRSTUVWXYZ–$1234567890(".;'!*?':,")&fiflß-äöüÄÖÜåçèÅÇÈ***

Bold Condensed **abcdefghijklmnopqrstuvwxyzABCDEFGHIJKLMNOPQRSTUVWXYZ–$1234567890(".;'!*?':,")&fiflß-äöüÄÖÜ**

Bold Condensed Italic ***abcdefghijklmnopqrstuvwxyzABCDEFGHIJKLMNOPQRSTUVWXYZ–$1234567890(".;'!*?':,")&fiflß-äöüÄÖÜåç***

Black Condensed **abcdefghijklmnopqrstuvwxyzABCDEFGHIJKLMNOPQRSTUVWXYZ–$1234567890(".;'!*?':,")&fiflß-äöü**

Black Condensed Italic ***abcdefghijklmnopqrstuvwxyzABCDEFGHIJKLMNOPQRSTUVWXYZ–$1234567890(".;'!*?':,")&fiflß-äöüÄÖ***

Light Semi-Extended abcdefghijklmnopqrstuvwxyzABCDEFGHIJKLMNOPQRSTUVWXYZ–$1234567890(".

Light Semi-Extended Italic *abcdefghijklmnopqrstuvwxyzABCDEFGHIJKLMNOPQRSTUVWXYZ–$1234567890(".;'!*?':,*

Semi-Extended abcdefghijklmnopqrstuvwxyzABCDEFGHIJKLMNOPQRSTUVWXYZ–$12345678

Semi-Extended Italic *abcdefghijklmnopqrstuvwxyzABCDEFGHIJKLMNOPQRSTUVWXYZ–$1234567890(".*

Semibold Semi-Extended **abcdefghijklmnopqrstuvwxyzABCDEFGHIJKLMNOPQRSTUVWXYZ–$123456**

Semibold Semi-Extended Italic ***abcdefghijklmnopqrstuvwxyzABCDEFGHIJKLMNOPQRSTUVWXYZ–$12345678***

Bold Semi-Extended **abcdefghijklmnopqrstuvwxyzABCDEFGHIJKLMNOPQRSTUVWXYZ–$1234**

Bold Semi-Extended Italic ***abcdefghijklmnopqrstuvwxyzABCDEFGHIJKLMNOPQRSTUVWXYZ–$123456***

Black Semi-Extended **abcdefghijklmnopqrstuvwxyzABCDEFGHIJKLMNOPQRSTUVWXYZ–$12**

Black Semi-Extended Italic ***abcdefghijklmnopqrstuvwxyzABCDEFGHIJKLMNOPQRSTUVWXYZ–$1234***

M

✍ Juan Yciar, 1548

AGFA NADIANNE

Aldo Novarese • 1990 abcdefghijklmnopqrstuvwxyz(".;'!*?':,")
AGP $1234567890&fiflß-äöüåçèîñóæøœ
ABCDEFGHIJKLMNOPQRSTUVWXYZ
ÄÖÜÅÇÈÎÑÓÆØŒ»„«[¶§•†‡]‹¡·¿›...

Agfa Nadianne ...

• Book abcdefghijklmnopqrstuvwxyzABCDEFGHIJKLMNOPQRSTUVWXYZ–$12345678
Medium abcdefghijklmnopqrstuvwxyzABCDEFGHIJKLMNOPQRSTUVWXYZ–$1234
Bold abcdefghijklmnopqrstuvwxyzABCDEFGHIJKLMNOPQRSTUVWXYZ

AGFA NADIANNE CONDENSED

AGP abcdefghijklmnopqrstuvwxyz(".;'!*?':,")
$1234567890&fiflß-äöüåçèîñóæøœ
ABCDEFGHIJKLMNOPQRSTUVWXYZ
ÄÖÜÅÇÈÎÑÓÆØŒ»„«[¶§•†‡]‹¡·¿›...

Agfa Nadianne Condensed ...

• Book Condensed abcdefghijklmnopqrstuvwxyzABCDEFGHIJKLMNOPQRSTUVWXYZ–$1234567890(".;'!*?':,")&fiflß-äöüÄ
Medium Condensed abcdefghijklmnopqrstuvwxyzABCDEFGHIJKLMNOPQRSTUVWXYZ–$1234567890(".;'!*?':,")&fi
Bold Condensed abcdefghijklmnopqrstuvwxyzABCDEFGHIJKLMNOPQRSTUVWXYZ–$123456789

N

NARROWBAND PRIME

IMA ▲42 abcdefghijklmnopqrstuvwxyz(".;'!*?':,")$1234567890&fiflß-äöüåçèîñóæøœ
ABCDEFGHIJKLMNOPQRSTUVWXYZÄÖÜÅÇÈÎÑÓÆØŒ»„«[¶§•†‡]‹¡·¿›...

Narrowband Prime ...

• Regular abcdefghijklmnopqrstuvwxyzABCDEFGHIJKLMNOPQRSTUVWXYZ–$1234567890(".;
Bold abcdefghijklmnopqrstuvwxyzABCDEFGHIJKLMNOPQRSTUVWXYZ–$1

NATIONAL OLDSTYLE

Frederic W. Goudy • 1916 abcdefghijklmnopqrstuvwxyz(".;'!*?':,")
FRA $1234567890&fiflß-äöüåçèîñóæøœ
ABCDEFGHIJKLMNOPQRSTUVWXYZ
ÄÖÜÅÇÈÎÑÓÆØŒ»„«¶§•†‹¡¿›

▷ ct ff fi ffl

... National Oldstyle ...

• Roman abcdefghijklmnopqrstuvwxyzABCDEFGHIJKLMNOPQRSTUVWXYZ$12

Italic OSF *abcdefghijklmnopqrstuvwxyzABCDEFGHIJKLMNOPQRSTUVWXYZ$12*

Neo Bold

Carlos Segura • 1993

T26

▲30

ABCDEFGHIJKLMNOPQRSTUVWXYZ

$1234567890&-[·]

Neographik

❖ *Monotype Headliners 5*

MCL

▲24

abcdefghijklmnopqrstuvwxyz(".;'!*?':,")

$1234567890&fiflß-äöüåçèîñóæøœ

ABCDEFGHIJKLMNOPQRSTUVWXYZ

ÄÖÜÅÇÈÎÑÓÆØŒ»,,«[·]‹¡·¿›...

Neon Extra Condensed

❖ *Agfa Typographer's Edition 2*

G. de Milano • 1935

AGP

▲54

ABCDEFGHIJKLMNOPQRSTUVWXYZ(".;'!*?':,")

$1234567890&-ÄÖÜÅÇÈÎÑÓŒØŒ»,,«[¶§•†‡]‹¡·¿›...

A*I Neptune Serif

Manfred Klein • 1994

ALP

▲24

ABCDEFGHIJKLMNOPQRSTUVWXYZ

(".;'!*?':,")$1234567890&-ÄÖÜÅÇÈÎÑÓ

ABCDEFGHIJKLMNOPQRSTUVWXYZ

ÄÖÜÅÇÈÎÑÓ»,,«¶§•...

N

❖ *Agfa Typographer's Edition 2*: PL Barnum Block, PL Benguiat Frisky Bold, TC Broadway, PL Davison Zip Bold, PL Fiedler Gothic Bold, PL Futura Maxi Book & Bold, Neon Extra Condensed, Ritmo Bold, PL Trophy Oblique.

❖ *Monotype Headliners 5*: Monotype Bernhard Condensed, Compacta Bold, Neographik, Monotype Runic Condensed.

A*I Neuland

Lester Doré • 1991
... Rudolph Koch, 1923

ALP FRA MTD

▲24

ABCDEFGHIJKLMNOPQRSTUVWXYZ

(.;!*?:,)$1234567890&-ÄÖÜÅÇÊÑÆØŒ

[¶·] ▷ABCDEFGHIJKLMNOPQRSTUVWXY

▷Z

▷

▷

NEUZEIT S

Linotype Design Staff • 1966

LIN ADO AGA MAE

abcdefghijklmnopqrstuvwxyz(".;'!*?':,")
$1234567890&fiflß-äöüåçèîñóæøœ
ABCDEFGHIJKLMNOPQRSTUVWXYZ
ÄÖÜÅÇÈÎÑÓÆØŒ»„«[¶§•†‡]‹¡·¿›...

Neuzeit S ...

• Book Regular abcdefghijklmnopqrstuvwxyzABCDEFGHIJKLMNOPQRSTUVWXYZ–$1234567

Book Heavy **abcdefghijklmnopqrstuvwxyzABCDEFGHIJKLMNOPQRSTUVWXYZ–$1234**

Nevison Casual Script

T. Nevison • 1967

IMA

▲18

abcdefghijklmnopqrstuvwxyz(".;'!*?':,")
$1234567890&ß-äöüåçèîñóæøœ
ABCDEFGHIJKLMNOPQRSTUVWXYZ
ÄÖÜÅÇÈÎÑÓÆØŒ»„«[§·†]¡·¿...

New Berolina
✤ *Monotype Scripts 2*

Martin Wilke • 1965

MCL ADO AGA LIN MAE

▲16

abcdefghijklmnopqrstuvwxyz(".;'!?':,")*
$1234567890&fiflß-äöüåçèîñóæøœ
ABCDEFGHIJKLMNOPQRSTUVWXYZ
ÄÖÜÅÇÈÎÑÓÆØŒ»„«[§•†‡]‹¡·¿›...

N

✤ *Monotype Scripts 2*: Ashley Script, Monoline Script, New Berolina, Palace Script Regular & Semibold.

NEW GENEVA NINE

Grant Hutchinson • 1991 abcdefghijklmnopqrstuvwxyz(".;'!*?':,")

IMA $1234567890&fiflß-äöüåçèîñóœøœ

▲16 ABCDEFGHIJKLMNOPQRSTUVWXYZ

ÄÖÜÅÇÈÎÑÓÆØŒ»„«[¶§•†‡]‹¡·¿›...

New Geneva Nine ...

• Regular abcdefghijklmnopqrstuvwxyzABCDEFGHIJKLMNOPQRSTUVWXYZ–$123

Point Five abcdefghijklmnopqrstuvwxyzABCDEFGHIJKLMNOPQRSTUVWXYZ–$1234567890(".;'!*?':,")&fiflß–äöüÄÖÜåçèÅÇÈîñóÎÑÓœøœÆØ

NEWS GOTHIC

Morris Fuller Benton & H. R. Freund • 1908... ... Frank Bartuska, 1958 abcdefghijklmnopqrstuvwxyz(".;'!*?':,")

$1234567890&fiflß-äöüåçèîñóæøœ

BIT ADO AGA LIN MAE MCL URW ABCDEFGHIJKLMNOPQRSTUVWXYZ

ÄÖÜÅÇÈÎÑÓÆØŒ»„«[¶§•†‡]‹¡·¿›...

News Gothic 1 ...

• Regular abcdefghijklmnopqrstuvwxyzABCDEFGHIJKLMNOPQRSTUVWXYZ–$1234567890(

Italic *abcdefghijklmnopqrstuvwxyzABCDEFGHIJKLMNOPQRSTUVWXYZ–$1234567890(*

Bold **abcdefghijklmnopqrstuvwxyzABCDEFGHIJKLMNOPQRSTUVWXYZ–$123456789**

Bold Italic ***abcdefghijklmnopqrstuvwxyzABCDEFGHIJKLMNOPQRSTUVWXYZ–$1234567890(***

News Gothic 2 ...

Light abcdefghijklmnopqrstuvwxyzABCDEFGHIJKLMNOPQRSTUVWXYZ–$1234567890("

Light Italic *abcdefghijklmnopqrstuvwxyzABCDEFGHIJKLMNOPQRSTUVWXYZ–$1234567890("*

Demi **abcdefghijklmnopqrstuvwxyzABCDEFGHIJKLMNOPQRSTUVWXYZ–$1234567890**

Demi Italic ***abcdefghijklmnopqrstuvwxyzABCDEFGHIJKLMNOPQRSTUVWXYZ–$1234567890(***

NEWS GOTHIC CONDENSED

BIT MCL abcdefghijklmnopqrstuvwxyz(".;'!*?':,")

$1234567890&fiflß-äöüåçèîñóæøœ

ABCDEFGHIJKLMNOPQRSTUVWXYZ

ÄÖÜÅÇÈÎÑÓÆØŒ»„«[¶§•†‡]‹¡·¿›...

News Gothic Condensed ...

• Condensed abcdefghijklmnopqrstuvwxyzABCDEFGHIJKLMNOPQRSTUVWXYZ–$1234567890(".;'!*?':,")&fiflß-äöüÄÖÜåçè

Condensed Italic *abcdefghijklmnopqrstuvwxyzABCDEFGHIJKLMNOPQRSTUVWXYZ–$1234567890(".;'!*?':,")&fiflß-äöüÄÖÜå*

Bold Condensed **abcdefghijklmnopqrstuvwxyzABCDEFGHIJKLMNOPQRSTUVWXYZ–$1234567890(".;'!*?':,")&fiflß-äöüÄÖ**

Bold Condensed Italic ***abcdefghijklmnopqrstuvwxyzABCDEFGHIJKLMNOPQRSTUVWXYZ–$1234567890(".;'!*?':,")&fiflß-äöüÄ***

Extra Condensed ▲16 abcdefghijklmnopqrstuvwxyzABCDEFGHIJKLMNOPQRSTUVWXYZ–$1234567890(".;'!*?':,")&fiflß-äöüÄÖÜåçèÅÇ

Bold Extra Condensed ▲16 **abcdefghijklmnopqrstuvwxyzABCDEFGHIJKLMNOPQRSTUVWXYZ–$1234567890(".;'!*?':,")&fiflß-äöü**

N

ITC NEWTEXT

Ray Baker • 1974 abcdefghijklmnopqrstuvwxyz(".;'!*?':,")

BIT LEF FRA ITC $1234567890&fiflß-äöüåçèîñóæøœ

ABCDEFGHIJKLMNOPQRSTUVWXYZ

ÄÖÜÅÇÈÎÑÓÆØŒ»„«[§•†‡]‹¡·¿›...

ITC Newtext 1 ...

• Book abcdefghijklmnopqrstuvwxyzABCDEFGHIJKLMNOPQRSTUVWXYZ–$123

Book Italic *abcdefghijklmnopqrstuvwxyzABCDEFGHIJKLMNOPQRSTUVWXYZ–$1234*

Demi **abcdefghijklmnopqrstuvwxyzABCDEFGHIJKLMNOPQRSTUVWXYZ–$12**

Demi Italic ***abcdefghijklmnopqrstuvwxyzABCDEFGHIJKLMNOPQRSTUVWXYZ–$123***

ITC Newtext 2 ...

Light abcdefghijklmnopqrstuvwxyzABCDEFGHIJKLMNOPQRSTUVWXYZ–$123

Light Italic *abcdefghijklmnopqrstuvwxyzABCDEFGHIJKLMNOPQRSTUVWXYZ–$1234*

Regular **abcdefghijklmnopqrstuvwxyzABCDEFGHIJKLMNOPQRSTUVWXYZ–$12**

Italic ***abcdefghijklmnopqrstuvwxyzABCDEFGHIJKLMNOPQRSTUVWXYZ–$123***

NIMROD

Robin Nicholas • 1980 abcdefghijklmnopqrstuvwxyz(".;'!*?':,")

MCL $1234567890&fiflß-äöüåçèîñóæøœ

ABCDEFGHIJKLMNOPQRSTUVWXYZ

ÄÖÜÅÇÈÎÑÓÆØŒ»„«[¶§•†‡]‹¡·¿›...

Nimrod ...

• Roman abcdefghijklmnopqrstuvwxyzABCDEFGHIJKLMNOPQRSTUVWXYZ–$12

Italic *abcdefghijklmnopqrstuvwxyzABCDEFGHIJKLMNOPQRSTUVWXYZ–$12*

Bold **abcdefghijklmnopqrstuvwxyzABCDEFGHIJKLMNOPQRSTUVWXY**

Bold Italic ***abcdefghijklmnopqrstuvwxyzABCDEFGHIJKLMNOPQRSTUVWXYZ***

NOFRET

Gudrun Zapf-Von Hesse • 1986 abcdefghijklmnopqrstuvwxyz(".;'!*?':,")

ADO AGA MAE $1234567890&fiflß–äöüåçèîñóæøœ

ABCDEFGHIJKLMNOPQRSTUVWXYZ

ÄÖÜÅÇÈÎÑÓÆØŒ»„«[¶§•†‡]‹¡·¿›...

Nofret ...

Light abcdefghijklmnopqrstuvwxyzABCDEFGHIJKLMNOPQRSTUVWXYZ–$1234567890

Light Italic *abcdefghijklmnopqrstuvwxyzABCDEFGHIJKLMNOPQRSTUVWXYZ–$1234567890(".;'!*?':,")*

• Roman abcdefghijklmnopqrstuvwxyzABCDEFGHIJKLMNOPQRSTUVWXYZ–$123456

Italic *abcdefghijklmnopqrstuvwxyzABCDEFGHIJKLMNOPQRSTUVWXYZ–$1234567890(".;'!*

Medium **abcdefghijklmnopqrstuvwxyzABCDEFGHIJKLMNOPQRSTUVWXYZ–**

N

... Nofret

Medium Italic *abcdefghijklmnopqrstuvwxyzABCDEFGHIJKLMNOPQRSTUVWXYZ–$123*

Bold **abcdefghijklmnopqrstuvwxyzABCDEFGHIJKLMNOPQRSTUV**

Bold Italic ***abcdefghijklmnopqrstuvwxyzABCDEFGHIJKLMNOPQRSTUVW***

NOFRET EXPERT & SCOSF

ADO AGA MAE ABCDEFGHIJKLMNOPQRSTUVWXYZ.;!?:,
1234567890&ff fi fl ffi ffl–ÄÖÜÅÇÈÎÑÓÆØŒ
(abdeilmnorst) 1/8 1/4 1/3 3/8 1/2 5/8 2/3 3/4 7/8 $12345/67890¢ ₡Rp

Nofret Expert & SCOSF ...

Expert Light ABCDEFGHIJKLMNOPQRSTUVWXYZ–$1234567890.;!?:,&–ff fi fl ffi ffl 1/8 1/4 1/3 3/8 1/2 $12345/67890¢ (

Expert Light Italic *$1234567890.;:,–ff fi fl ffi ffl 1/8 1/4 1/3 3/8 1/2 $12345/67890¢ (abdeilmnorst) 5/8 2/3 3/4 7/8 ₡Rp*

• Expert Roman ABCDEFGHIJKLMNOPQRSTUVWXYZ–$1234567890.;!?:,&–ff fi fl ffi ffl 1/8 1/4 1/3 3/8 1/2 $12345/67

Expert Italic *$1234567890.;:,–ff fi fl ffi ffl 1/8 1/4 1/3 3/8 1/2 $12345/67890¢ (abdeilmnorst) 5/8 2/3 3/4 7/8 ₡Rp*

Expert Medium **ABCDEFGHIJKLMNOPQRSTUVWXYZ–$1234567890.;!?:,&–ff fi fl ffi ffl 1/8 1/4 1/3**

Expert Medium Italic ***$1234567890.;:,–ff fi fl ffi ffl 1/8 1/4 1/3 3/8 1/2 $12345/67890¢ (abdeilmnorst) 5/8 2/3 3/4 7/8 ₡Rp***

Expert Bold **$1234567890.;:,–ff fi fl ffi ffl 1/8 1/4 1/3 3/8 1/2 $12345/67890¢ (abdeilmnorst) 5/8 2/3**

Expert Bold Italic ***$1234567890.;:,–ff fi fl ffi ffl 1/8 1/4 1/3 3/8 1/2 $12345/67890¢ (abdeilmnorst) 5/8 2/3***

Light SCOSF ABCDEFGHIJKLMNOPQRSTUVWXYZABCDEFGHIJKLMNOPQRSTUVWXYZ–$12345678

Light Italic OSF *abcdefghijklmnopqrstuvwxyzABCDEFGHIJKLMNOPQRSTUVWXYZ–$1234567890(".;'!*?':,")&*

Roman SCOSF ABCDEFGHIJKLMNOPQRSTUVWXYZABCDEFGHIJKLMNOPQRSTUVWXYZ–$12345

Italic OSF *abcdefghijklmnopqrstuvwxyzABCDEFGHIJKLMNOPQRSTUVWXYZ–$1234567890(".;'!**

Medium SCOSF **ABCDEFGHIJKLMNOPQRSTUVWXYZABCDEFGHIJKLMNOPQRSTUV...$123**

Medium Italic OSF ***abcdefghijklmnopqrstuvwxyzABCDEFGHIJKLMNOPQRSTUVWXYZ–$1234***

Bold OSF **abcdefghijklmnopqrstuvwxyzABCDEFGHIJKLMNOPQRS...$12**

Bold Italic OSF ***abcdefghijklmnopqrstuvwxyzABCDEFGHIJKLMNOPQRS...$1234***

N

Notre Dame
Type Before Gutenberg 3
Karlgeorg Hoefer • 1993

abcdefghijklmnopqrstuvwxyz(".;'!*?':,")
LIN ADO AGA MAE $1234567890&fiflß–äöüåçèîñóæøœ
▲16 A B C D E F G H I J K L M N O P Q R S T U V W X Y Z
Ä Ö Ü Å Ç È Î Ñ Ó Æ Ø Œ »„«[¶§•†‡]‹¡·¿›...
▷ ch ck ff ft ll ſ s ſi ſſ ß – ä ö ü Ä Ö Ü

Type Before Gutenberg 3: Notre Dame, Notre Dame Ornaments, Pompeijana, Pompeijana Borders, Rusticana, Rusticana Borders.
Notre Dame ▶ Notre Dame Ornaments.

NOUVEAU RICHE
HEA
▲60

abcdefghijklmnopqrstuvwxyz(".;'!*?':,")$1234567890£fifl ß-äöüåçèîñóæøœ
ABCDEFGHIJKLMNOPQRSTUVWXYZÄÖÜÅÇÈÎÑÓÆØŒ»,„«[¶§•†‡]‹¡·¿›... ▷ ∫ ∫

Nouveau Riche . . .

Light
abcdefghijklmnopqrstuvwxyzABCDEFGHIJKLMNOPQRSTUVWXYZ-$1234567890(".;'!*?

• Medium
abcdefghijklmnopqrstuvwxyzABCDEFGHIJKLMNOPQRSTUVWXYZ-$1234567890(".;'

Bold
abcdefghijklmnopqrstuvwxyzABCDEFGHIJKLMNOPQRSTUVWXYZ-$1234567890(

NOUVEAU RICHE CONDENSED
HEA
▲60

abcdefghijklmnopqrstuvwxyz(".;'!*?':,")$1234567890£fifl ß-äöüåçèîñóæøœ
ABCDEFGHIJKLMNOPQRSTUVWXYZÄÖÜÅÇÈÎÑÓÆØŒ»,„«[¶§•†‡]‹¡·¿›... ▷ ∫ ∫

Nouveau Riche Condensed . . .

Light Condensed
abcdefghijklmnopqrstuvwxyzABCDEFGHIJKLMNOPQRSTUVWXYZ-$1234567890(".;'!*?':,")£fiflß-äöüÄÖÜåçèÅÇÈîñóÎ

• Medium Condensed
abcdefghijklmnopqrstuvwxyzABCDEFGHIJKLMNOPQRSTUVWXYZ-$1234567890(".;'!*?':,")£fiflß-äöüÄÖÜåçèÅÇÈî

Bold Condensed
abcdefghijklmnopqrstuvwxyzABCDEFGHIJKLMNOPQRSTUVWXYZ-$1234567890(".;'!*?':,")£fiflß-äöüÄÖÜå

N

ITC NOVARESE

Aldo Novarese • 1980 abcdefghijklmnopqrstuvwxyz(".;'!*?':,")

BIT ADO AGA AGP LEF FRA FAM LIN MAE URW $1234567890&fiflß-äöüåçèîñóæøœ

ABCDEFGHIJKLMNOPQRSTUVWXYZ

ÄÖÜÅÇÈÎÑÓÆØŒ»„«[¶§•†‡]‹¡·¿›...

ITC Novarese ...

• Book abcdefghijklmnopqrstuvwxyzABCDEFGHIJKLMNOPQRSTUVWXYZ–$1234567890(".;'!*?

Book Italic *abcdefghijklmnopqrstuvwxyz*ABCDEFGHIJKLMNOPQRSTUVWXYZ–$1234567890(".;'!*?':,")

Medium abcdefghijklmnopqrstuvwxyzABCDEFGHIJKLMNOPQRSTUVWXYZ–$1234567890(".;

Medium Italic *abcdefghijklmnopqrstuvwxyz*ABCDEFGHIJKLMNOPQRSTUVWXYZ–$1234567890(".;'!*?'

Bold **abcdefghijklmnopqrstuvwxyzABCDEFGHIJKLMNOPQRSTUVWXYZ–$12345678**

Bold Italic ***abcdefghijklmnopqrstuvwxyz*ABCDEFGHIJKLMNOPQRSTUVWXYZ–$1234567890(**

Ultra **abcdefghijklmnopqrstuvwxyzABCDEFGHIJKLMNOPQRSTUVWXYZ–$12**

Numskill

David Berlow • 1990 **abcdefghijklmnopqrstuvwxyz(".;'!*?':,")**

FBU AGP MTD

▲24 **$1234567890&fiflß-äöüåçèîñóæøœ**

ABCDEFGHIJKLMNOPQRSTUVWXYZ

ÄÖÜÅÇÈÎÑÓÆØŒ»„«[¶§•†‡]‹¡·¿›...

Nuptial Script
Linotype ScriptSet 1

Edwin Shaar • 1952 *abcdefghijklmnopqrstuvwxyz(".;'!*?':,")*

LIN ADO AGA BIT MAE *$1234567890&fiflß-äöüåçèîñóæøœ*

▲18 *ABCDEFGHIJKLMNOPQRSTUVWXYZ*

ÄÖÜÅÇÈÎÑÓÆØŒ»„«[¶§•†‡]‹¡·¿›...

Nutcracker

Richard Lipton • 1993 abcdefghijklmnopqrstuvwxyz(".;'!*?':,")

FBU

▲30 $1234567890&fiflß-äöüåçèîñóæøœ

ABCDEFGHIJKLMNOPQRSTUVWXYZ

ÄÖÜÅÇÈÎÑÓÆØŒ»„«[¶§•†‡]‹¡·¿›... ff ffi ffl

N

Linotype ScriptSet 1: Cascade Script, Medici Script, Nuptial Script.

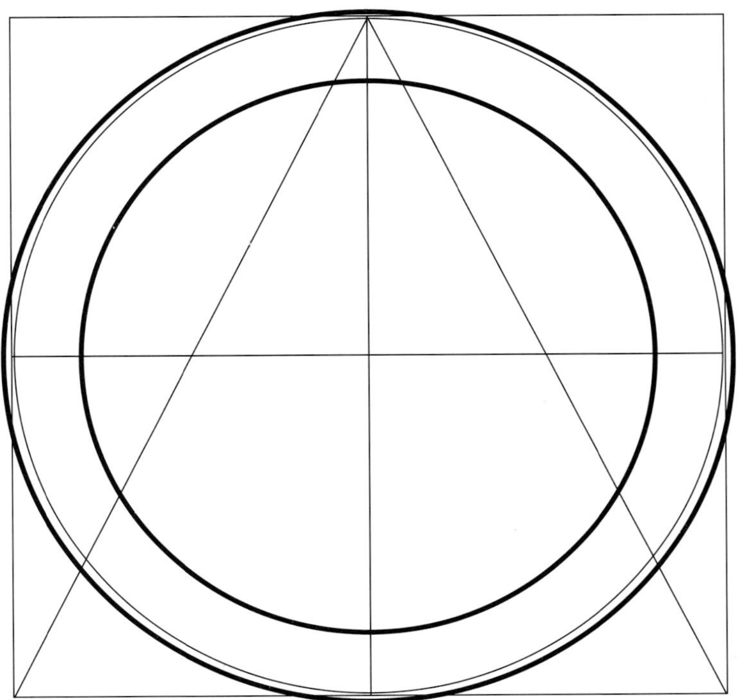

✍ Paul Renner, 1927

Oberon

✍ Phill Grimshaw • 1986 abcdefghijklmnopqrstuvwxyz(“.;‘!*?’:,”)

LET $1234567890&fifl ß-äöüåçèîñóæøœ

▲18 ABCDEFGHIJKLMNOPQRSTUVWXYZ

ÄÖÜÅÇÈÎÑÓÆØŒ»„«[•]‹¡·¿›... ▷ bdhklqruvwxyz ff ffl Th

OCEAN SANS MULTIPLE·MASTER (two axes: weight & width) abcdefghijklmnopqrstuvwxyz(“.;‘!*?’:,”)

✍ Ong Chong Wah • 1993 $1234567890&fiflß-äöüåçèîñóæøœ

MCL ABCDEFGHIJKLMNOPQRSTUVWXYZ

ÄÖÜÅÇÈÎÑÓÆØŒ»„«[¶§•†‡]‹¡·¿›...

Ocean Sans MultipleMaster ...

Light abcdefghijklmnopqrstuvwxyzABCDEFGHIJKLMNOPQRSTUVWXYZ–$1234567890(“.;‘!*?’:,”)&fi

Light Italic *abcdefghijklmnopqrstuvwxyzABCDEFGHIJKLMNOPQRSTUVWXYZ–$1234567890(“.;‘!*?’:,”)&fi*

• Book abcdefghijklmnopqrstuvwxyzABCDEFGHIJKLMNOPQRSTUVWXYZ–$1234567890(“.;‘!*?’:,”)

Book Italic *abcdefghijklmnopqrstuvwxyzABCDEFGHIJKLMNOPQRSTUVWXYZ–$1234567890(“.;‘!*?’:,”)&*

Semibold **abcdefghijklmnopqrstuvwxyzABCDEFGHIJKLMNOPQRSTUVWXYZ–$1234567890(“.;‘!*?’:,**

Semibold Italic ***abcdefghijklmnopqrstuvwxyzABCDEFGHIJKLMNOPQRSTUVWXYZ–$1234567890(“.;‘!*?’:,”***

Bold **abcdefghijklmnopqrstuvwxyzABCDEFGHIJKLMNOPQRSTUVWXYZ–$1234567890(“.;‘!***

Bold Italic ***abcdefghijklmnopqrstuvwxyzABCDEFGHIJKLMNOPQRSTUVWXYZ–$1234567890(“.;‘!*?’***

Extra Bold **abcdefghijklmnopqrstuvwxyzABCDEFGHIJKLMNOPQRSTUVWXYZ–$1234567890(“.;‘**

Extra Bold Italic ***abcdefghijklmnopqrstuvwxyzABCDEFGHIJKLMNOPQRSTUVWXYZ–$1234567890(“.;‘!***

Book Semi-Extended abcdefghijklmnopqrstuvwxyzABCDEFGHIJKLMNOPQRSTUVWXYZ–$1234567890(“.;‘!*

Book Semi-Extended Italic *abcdefghijklmnopqrstuvwxyzABCDEFGHIJKLMNOPQRSTUVWXYZ–$1234567890(“.;‘!*?*

Bold Semi-Extended **abcdefghijklmnopqrstuvwxyzABCDEFGHIJKLMNOPQRSTUVWXYZ–$1234567890(**

Bold Semi-Extended Italic ***abcdefghijklmnopqrstuvwxyzABCDEFGHIJKLMNOPQRSTUVWXYZ–$1234567890(“***

Light Extended abcdefghijklmnopqrstuvwxyzABCDEFGHIJKLMNOPQRSTUVWXYZ–$123457

Light Extended Italic *abcdefghijklmnopqrstuvwxyzABCDEFGHIJKLMNOPQRSTUVWXYZ–$1234578*

Book Extended abcdefghijklmnopqrstuvwxyzABCDEFGHIJKLMNOPQRSTUVWXYZ–$12345

Book Extended Italic *abcdefghijklmnopqrstuvwxyzABCDEFGHIJKLMNOPQRSTUVWXYZ–$123456*

Semibold Extended **abcdefghijklmnopqrstuvwxyzABCDEFGHIJKLMNOPQRSTUVWXYZ–$1234**

Semibold Extended Italic ***abcdefghijklmnopqrstuvwxyzABCDEFGHIJKLMNOPQRSTUVWXYZ–$12345***

Bold Extended **abcdefghijklmnopqrstuvwxyzABCDEFGHIJKLMNOPQRSTUVWXYZ–$12**

Bold Extended Italic ***abcdefghijklmnopqrstuvwxyzABCDEFGHIJKLMNOPQRSTUVWXYZ–$123***

Extra Bold Extended **abcdefghijklmnopqrstuvwxyzABCDEFGHIJKLMNOPQRSTUVWXYZ–$**

Extra Bold Extended Italic ***abcdefghijklmnopqrstuvwxyzABCDEFGHIJKLMNOPQRSTUVWXYZ–$12***

OCR-A
OCR Set 1
United States Bureau of Standards • 1966
ADO AGA BIT FRA LIN MAE URW
▲12

abcdefghijklmnopqrstuvwxyz(".;'!*?':,")
$1234567890&ﬁﬂß-äöüåçæøœ
ABCDEFGHIJKLMNOPQRSTUVWXYZ
ÄÖÜÅÇÑÆØŒ>„<[•†‡]¡·¿… ▷ ⑁ ⑂ ⑃ ' ⑀ . ?

OCR-B …
OCR Set 1
Adrian Frutiger • 1968
ADO AGA BIT LEF FRA LIN MAE URW
▲12

abcdefghijklmnopqrstuvwxyz(".;'!*?':,")
$1234567890&ﬁﬂß-äöüåçæøœ
ABCDEFGHIJKLMNOPQRSTUVWXYZ
ÄÖÜÅÇÑÆØŒ»„«[•†‡]¡·¿… ▷ m ij ¤ —— | _

OCTAVIAN + EXPERT & SCOSF
Will Carter & David Kindersley • 1961
MCL ADO AGA LIN MAE

abcdefghijklmnopqrstuvwxyz(".;'!*?':,")
$1234567890&ﬁﬂß-äöüåçèîñóæøœ
ABCDEFGHIJKLMNOPQRSTUVWXYZ
ÄÖÜÅÇÈÎÑÓÆØŒ»„«[¶§•†‡]‹¡·¿›…

Octavian + Expert & SCOSF …

• Roman abcdefghijklmnopqrstuvwxyzABCDEFGHIJKLMNOPQRSTUVWXYZ–$1234567890(".;'!*?':,")&
Italic *abcdefghijklmnopqrstuvwxyzABCDEFGHIJKLMNOPQRSTUVWXYZ–$1234567890(".;'!*?':,")&ﬁ*
Expert Roman ABCDEFGHIJKLMNOPQRSTUVWXYZ–$1234567890.;!?:,&-ﬀﬁﬂﬃﬄ ⅛ ¼ ⅓ ⅜ ½ $12345/67890¢ (abdeilmnorst)
Expert Italic *$1234567890.;:,–ﬀﬁﬂﬃﬄ ⅛ ¼ ⅓ ⅜ ½ $12345/67890¢ (abdeilmnorst) ⅝ ⅔ ¾ ⅞ ₡Rp*
Roman SCOSF ABCDEFGHIJKLMNOPQRSTUVWXYZABCDEFGHIJKLMNOPQRSTUVWXYZ–$1234567890(".;'!*?':,
Italic OSF *abcdefghijklmnopqrstuvwxyzABCDEFGHIJKLMNOPQRSTUVWXYZ–$1234567890(".;'!*?':,")&ﬁ*

O

Odessa
Peter O'Donnell • 1988
LET
▲36

abcdefghijklmnopqrstuvwxyz(".;'!*?':,")
$1234567890&ﬁﬂß-äöüåçèîñóæøœ
ABCDEFGHIJKLMNOPQRSTUVWXYZ
ÄÖÜÅÇÈÎÑÓÆØŒ»„«[•]‹¡·¿›…

OCR Set 1: OCR-A, OCR-B, MICR.
OCR-A & OCR-B ▶MICR.

ITC OFFICINA SERIF

Erik Spiekermann • 1990 abcdefghijklmnopqrstuvwxyz(".;'!*?':,")

LIN ADO AGA AGP LEF ITC MAE URW $1234567890&fiflß-äöüåçèîñóæøœ

ABCDEFGHIJKLMNOPQRSTUVWXYZ

ÄÖÜÅÇÈÎÑÓÆØŒ»„«[¶§•†‡]‹¡·¿›...

ITC Officina Serif ...

• Book abcdefghijklmnopqrstuvwxyzABCDEFGHIJKLMNOPQRSTUVWXYZ–$1234567890(".;'!*?':,

Book Italic *abcdefghijklmnopqrstuvwxyzABCDEFGHIJKLMNOPQRSTUVWXYZ–$1234567890(".;'!*?':,"*

Bold **abcdefghijklmnopqrstuvwxyzABCDEFGHIJKLMNOPQRSTUVWXYZ–$1234567890(**

Bold Italic ***abcdefghijklmnopqrstuvwxyzABCDEFGHIJKLMNOPQRSTUVWXYZ–$1234567890(".***

ITC OFFICINA SANS

Erik Spiekermann • 1990 abcdefghijklmnopqrstuvwxyz(".;'!*?':,")

LIN ADO AGA AGP LEF ITC MAE URW $1234567890&fiflß-äöüåçèîñóæøœ

ABCDEFGHIJKLMNOPQRSTUVWXYZ

ÄÖÜÅÇÈÎÑÓÆØŒ»„«[¶§•†‡]‹¡·¿›...

ITC Officina Sans ...

• Book abcdefghijklmnopqrstuvwxyzABCDEFGHIJKLMNOPQRSTUVWXYZ–$1234567890(".;'!*?':,")

Book Italic *abcdefghijklmnopqrstuvwxyzABCDEFGHIJKLMNOPQRSTUVWXYZ–$1234567890(".;'!*?':,")&*

Bold **abcdefghijklmnopqrstuvwxyzABCDEFGHIJKLMNOPQRSTUVWXYZ–$1234567890(".;'!**

Bold Italic ***abcdefghijklmnopqrstuvwxyzABCDEFGHIJKLMNOPQRSTUVWXYZ–$1234567890(".;'!****

O

OLD CLAUDE

Garrett Boge • 1993 ... Claude Garamont, c.1530 abcdefghijklmnopqrstuvwxyz(".;'!*?':,")

LPT MTD $1234567890&fiflß-äöüåçèîñóæøœ

ABCDEFGHIJKLMNOPQRSTUVWXYZ

ÄÖÜÅÇÈÎÑÓÆØŒ»„«[¶§•†‡]‹¡·¿›...

Old Claude ...

• Roman abcdefghijklmnopqrstuvwxyzABCDEFGHIJKLMNOPQRSTUVWXYZ–$123456

Roman SCLF ABCDEFGHIJKLMNOPQRSTUVWXYZABCDEFGHIJKLMNOPQRSTUVWXYZ–$123

Old Dreadful No. 7

BIT abcdefghijklmnopqrstuvwxyz(".;'!*?':,")

▲24 $1234567890&fiflß-äöüåçèîñóæøœ

ABCDEFGHIJKLMNOPQRSTUVWXYZ

ÄÖÜÅÇÈÎÑÓÆØŒ»„«[¶§•†‡]‹¡·¿›...

Old English
✣ *Agfa Scripts 1*
AGP FAM LET URW abcdefghijklmnopqrstuvwxyz(".;'!*?':,")
▲16 $1234567890&ß-äöüåçèîñó
ABCDEFGHIJKLMNOPQRSTUVWXYZ
ÄÖÜÅÇÈÎ ÑÓ»«[•]‹› ▹I V X st nd rd th ¼ ⅓ ½ ¾ D' c r. 'c 's O' rs. s. & %

Monotype Old English Text
✣ *Monotype Headliners 4*
MCL abcdefghijklmnopqrstuvwxyz(".;'!*?':,")
▲16 $1234567890&fiflß-äöüåçèîñóæøœ
ABCDEFGHIJKLMNOPQRSTUVWXYZ
ÄÖÜÅÇÈÎÑÓÆØŒ»,,«[§•†‡]‹¡·¿›...

Old Fashion Script
✣ *Agfa Scripts 2*
AGP *abcdefghijklmnopqrstuvwxyz(".;'!*?':,")*
▲16 *$1234567890&ß-äöüåçèîñó*
ABCDEFGHIJKLMNOPQRSTUVWXYZ
ÄÖÜÅÇÈÎÑÓ»«[•]‹› ▹I V X st nd rd th ¼ ⅓ ½ ¾ D' c r 'c 's O' rs s & %

MONOTYPE OLD STYLE

✍ *Alexander Phemister • 1860* abcdefghijklmnopqrstuvwxyz(".;'!*?':,")
MCL $1234567890&fiflß-äöüåçèîñóæøœ
ABCDEFGHIJKLMNOPQRSTUVWXYZ
ÄÖÜÅÇÈÎÑÓÆØŒ»,,«[¶§•†‡]‹¡·¿›...

Monotype Old Style ...

• Roman abcdefghijklmnopqrstuvwxyzABCDEFGHIJKLMNOPQRSTUVWXYZ–$12345
Italic *abcdefghijklmnopqrstuvwxyzABCDEFGHIJKLMNOPQRSTUVWXYZ–$123456789*
Bold **abcdefghijklmnopqrstuvwxyzABCDEFGHIJKLMNOPQRSTUVWXYZ–**
Bold Italic ***abcdefghijklmnopqrstuvwxyzABCDEFGHIJKLMNOPQRSTUVWXYZ–$1***

Monotype Old Style Bold Outline
✣ *Monotype Headliners 4*
MCL ADO AGA LIN MAE abcdefghijklmnopqrstuvwxyz(".;'!*?':,")
▲24 $1234567890&fiflß-äöüåçèîñóæøœ
ABCDEFGHIJKLMNOPQRSTUVWX
YZÄÖÜÅÇÈÎÑÓÆØŒ»,,«[§•†‡]‹¡·¿›...

O

....
✣ *Agfa Scripts 1*: Commercial Script, Helinda Rook, Old English, Original Script, Quill Script, Stuyvesant, Wedding Text.
✣ *Monotype Headliners 4*: Inflex Bold, Monotype Old English Text, Monotype Old Style Bold Outline.
✣ *Agfa Scripts 2*: Citadel, Flemish Script 2, Florentine Script 2, French Script, Mahogany Script, Old Fashion Script, Riviera Script.

OLD STYLE NO.7

LIN ADO AGA MAE abcdefghijklmnopqrstuvwxyz(".;'!*?':,")
$1234567890&fiflß-äöüåçèîñóæøœ
ABCDEFGHIJKLMNOPQRSTUVWXYZ
ÄÖÜÅÇÈÎÑÓÆØŒ»„«[¶§•†‡]‹¡·¿›...

Old Style No.7 ...

• Roman abcdefghijklmnopqrstuvwxyzABCDEFGHIJKLMNOPQRSTUVWXYZ–$12345
Italic *abcdefghijklmnopqrstuvwxyzABCDEFGHIJKLMNOPQRSTUVWXYZ–$12345678*
Roman SCOSF ABCDEFGHIJKLMNOPQRSTUVWXYZABCDEFGHIJKLMNOPQRSTUVW...$12345
Italic OSF *abcdefghijklmnopqrstuvwxyzABCDEFGHIJKLMNOPQRSTUVWXYZ–$12345678*

OLYMPIAN

Matthew Carter • 1970 abcdefghijklmnopqrstuvwxyz(".;'!*?':,")
LIN ADO AGA MAE $1234567890&fiflß-äöüåçèîñóæøœ
ABCDEFGHIJKLMNOPQRSTUVWXYZ
ÄÖÜÅÇÈÎÑÓÆØŒ»„«[¶§•†‡]‹¡·¿›...

Olympian ...

• Roman abcdefghijklmnopqrstuvwxyzABCDEFGHIJKLMNOPQRSTUVWXYZ–$
Italic *abcdefghijklmnopqrstuvwxyzABCDEFGHIJKLMNOPQRSTUVWXYZ–$1*
Bold **abcdefghijklmnopqrstuvwxyzABCDEFGHIJKLMNOPQRSTUVWXYZ–$**
Bold Italic ***abcdefghijklmnopqrstuvwxyzABCDEFGHIJKLMNOPQRSTUVWXYZ–$1***

O

Omnia
Type Before Gutenberg 1
Karlgeorg Hoefer • 1990 ABCDEFGHIJKLMNOPQRSTUVWXYZ(".;'!*?':,")
LIN ADO AGA MAE
▲24 $1234567890&-ÄÖÜÅÇÈÎÑÓÆØŒ»„«[§•†‡]‹¡·¿›...

Ondine

Adrian Frutiger • 1954 abcdefghijklmnopqrstuvwxyz(".;'!*?':,")
URW TFC
▲24 $1234567890&fiflß-äöüåçèîñóæøœ
ABCDEFGHIJKLMNOPQRSTUVWXYZ
ÄÖÜÅÇÈÎÑÓÆØŒ»„«[¶§•†‡]‹¡·¿›...

Type Before Gutenberg 1: Duc De Berry, Herculanum, Omnia.

Onyx
Monotype DisplaySet 4
Gerry Powell • 1937
MCL ADO AGA BIT LIN MAE
▲36

abcdefghijklmnopqrstuvwxyz(“.;‘!*?’:,”)
$1234567890&fiflß-äöüåçèîñóæøœ
ABCDEFGHIJKLMNOPQRSTUVWXYZ
ÄÖÜÅÇÈÎÑÓÆØŒ»„«[•]‹¡·¿›...

OPTIMA

Hermann Zapf • 1958
LIN ADO AGA MAE

abcdefghijklmnopqrstuvwxyz(“.;‘!*?’:,”)
$1234567890&fiflß-äöüåçèîñóæøœ
ABCDEFGHIJKLMNOPQRSTUVWXYZ
ÄÖÜÅÇÈÎÑÓÆØŒ»„«[¶§•†‡]‹¡·¿›...

Optima ...

• Regular abcdefghijklmnopqrstuvwxyzABCDEFGHIJKLMNOPQRSTUVWXYZ–$123456789

Oblique *abcdefghijklmnopqrstuvwxyzABCDEFGHIJKLMNOPQRSTUVWXYZ–$123456789*

Bold **abcdefghijklmnopqrstuvwxyzABCDEFGHIJKLMNOPQRSTUVWXYZ–$12345678**

Bold Oblique ***abcdefghijklmnopqrstuvwxyzABCDEFGHIJKLMNOPQRSTUVWXYZ–$12345678***

BITSTREAM ORANDA

Gerard Unger • 1992
BIT

abcdefghijklmnopqrstuvwxyz(“.;‘!*?’:,”)
$1234567890&fiflß-äöüåçèîñóæøœ
ABCDEFGHIJKLMNOPQRSTUVWXYZ
ÄÖÜÅÇÈÎÑÓÆØŒ»„«[¶§•†‡]‹¡·¿›...

Bitstream Oranda ...

• Roman abcdefghijklmnopqrstuvwxyzABCDEFGHIJKLMNOPQRSTUVWXYZ–$1234567890(“.;‘!*?’:,”

Italic *abcdefghijklmnopqrstuvwxyzABCDEFGHIJKLMNOPQRSTUVWXYZ–$1234567890(“.;‘!*?’:,”)&fifl*

Bold **abcdefghijklmnopqrstuvwxyzABCDEFGHIJKLMNOPQRSTUVWXYZ–$1234567890(“.;‘!*?’:,**

Bold Italic ***abcdefghijklmnopqrstuvwxyzABCDEFGHIJKLMNOPQRSTUVWXYZ–$1234567890(“.;‘!*?’:,”)&fi***

Condensed Roman abcdefghijklmnopqrstuvwxyzABCDEFGHIJKLMNOPQRSTUVWXYZ–$1234567890(“.;‘!*?’:,”)&fiflß-äö

Bold Condensed **abcdefghijklmnopqrstuvwxyzABCDEFGHIJKLMNOPQRSTUVWXYZ–$1234567890(“.;‘!*?’:,”)**

O

Monotype DisplaySet 4: Latin Condensed, Onyx, Runic Condensed.
Optima Optima EastA.

ORATOR U&LC

BIT abcdefghijklmnopqrstuvwxyz(".;'!*?':,")
▲12 $1234567890&fiflß-äöüåçèîñóœøæ
ABCDEFGHIJKLMNOPQRSTUVWXYZ
ÄÖÜÅÇÈÎÑÓÆØŒ»„«[¶§·†‡]‹¡·¿›…

Orator U&LC . . .

• 10-Pitch abcdefghijklmnopqrstuvwxyzABCDEFGHIJKLMNOPQRSTUVWXYZ–$1234567890(".;'
15-Pitch abcdefghijklmnopqrstuvwxyzABCDEFGHIJKLMNOPQRSTUVWXYZ–$1234567890(".;'!*?':,")&fiflß-äöüÄÖÜåçèÅÇÈîñóÎÑÓœøæ

ORATOR

ADO AGA LIN MAE ABCDEFGHIJKLMNOPQRSTUVWXYZ(".;'!*?':,")
▲12 $1234567890&-ÄÖÜÅÇÈÎÑÓÆØŒ
ABCDEFGHIJKLMNOPQRSTUVWXYZ
ÄÖÜÅÇÈÎÑÓÆØŒ»„«[¶§•†‡]‹¡·¿›…

Orator . . .

• Regular ABCDEFGHIJKLMNOPQRSTUVWXYZABCDEFGHIJKLMNOPQRSTUVWXYZ–$1234567890(".;'
Slanted *ABCDEFGHIJKLMNOPQRSTUVWXYZABCDEFGHIJKLMNOPQRSTUVWXYZ–$1234567890(".;'*

Oreana

Andy Hullinger • 1993
T26
▲54 ABCDEFGHIJKLMNOPQRSTUVWXYZ

Original Script
Agfa Scripts 1

AGP *abcdefghijklmnopqrstuvwxyz(".;'!*?':,")*
▲18 *$1234567890 &fiß-äöüåçèîñó*
ABCDEFGHIJKLMNOPQRSTUVWXYZ
ÄÖÜÅÇÈÎÑÓ»«/·/‹› >I V X st nd rd th 1/4 1/3 1/2 3/4 D c r c s O rs & %

Osprey

Stephen Farrell • 1993
T26
▲36 ABCDEFGHIJKLMNOPQRS
TUVWXYZ(".;'!*?':,")$123
&-ÄÖÜÅÇÈÎÑÓÆØŒ»„«
[¶§•†‡]‹¡·¿›…

Agfa Scripts 1: Commercial Script, Helinda Rook, Old English, Original Script, Quill Script, Stuyvesant, Wedding Text.

Outhaus
[T-26] FontSet 1
Michael Polydoris • 1993
T26
▲24

abcdefghijklmnopqrstuvwxyz(".;'!*?':,")$1234567890
&-ABCDEFGHIJKLMNOPQRSTUVWXYZ

Oxford
Agfa Baker Calligraphy
Arthur Baker • 1989
AGP ADO AGA LIN MAE
▲18

abcdefghijklmnopqrstuvwxyz(".;'!*?':,")
$1234567890&fiflß-äöüåçèîñóæøœ
ABCDEFGHIJKLMNOPQRSTUVWXYZ
ÄÖÜÅÇÈÎÑÓÆØŒ»„«[¶§•†‡]‹¡·¿›...

A*I OZ BRUSH
A*I OzLand
Robert McCamant • 1991
... Ozwald Cooper, 1930
ALP MTD
▲16

abcdefghijklmnopqrstuvwxyz(".;'!*?':,")
$1234567890&fiflß-äöüåçèîñóæøœ
ABCDEFGHIJKLMNOPQRSTUVWXYZ
ÄÖÜÅÇÈÎÑÓÆØŒ»„«[¶§•†‡]‹¡·¿›... ▷

A*I Oz Brush ...

• Roman abcdefghijklmnopqrstuvwxyzABCDEFGHIJKLMNOPQRSTUVWXYZ-$1234567890(".;'!*?':

Italic abcdefghijklmnopqrstuvwxyzABCDEFGHIJKLMNOPQRSTUVWXYZ-$1234567890(".;'

O

Bitstream Oz Handicraft
George Ryan • 1991
... Ozwald Cooper
BIT
▲24

abcdefghijklmnopqrstuvwxyz(".;'!*?':,")$1234567890&fiflß-äöüåçèîñóæøœ
ABCDEFGHIJKLMNOPQRSTUVWXYZÄÖÜÅÇÈÎÑÓÆØŒ»„«[§•†‡]‹i·¿›...

A*I OZ POSTER
A*I OzLand
Robert McCamant • 1991
... Ozwald Cooper, 1913
ALP MTD
▲30

abcdefghijklmnopqrstuvwxyz(".;'!*?':,")
$1234567890&fiflß-äöüåçèîñóæøœ
ABCDEFGHIJKLMNOPQRSTUVWXYZ
ÄÖÜÅÇÈÎÑÓÆØŒ»„«[¶|§•†‡]‹i-¿›... ▷ct st

A*I Oz Poster ...

• Regular abcdefghijklmnopqrstuvwxyzABCDEFG

Condensed abcdefghijklmnopqrstuvwxyzABCDEFGHIJKLM

[T-26] FontSet 1: Earthquake & Outhaus.
Agfa Baker Calligraphy: Amigo, Marigold, Oxford, Pelican, Visigoth.
A*I OzLand: A*I Oz Brush Roman & Italic, A*I Oz Poster Regular & Condensed.

ITC Ozwald
✥ *ITC Typographica*

✍ *David Farey • 1992*
. . . Ozwald Cooper, c.1928

ADO AGA ITC LIN MAE URW

▲24

abcdefghijklmnopqr
stuvwxyz(“.;‘!*?’:,”)
$1234567890&fiflß-
äöüåçèîñóæøœABCD
EFGHIJKLMNOPQR
STUVWXYZÄÖÜÅÇÈ
ÎÑÓÆØŒ»„«[¢§·†‡]
‹¡·¿›…

O

✥ *ITC Typographica*: ITC Anna, ITC Beesknees, ITC Mona Lisa Recut & Solid, ITC Ozwald.

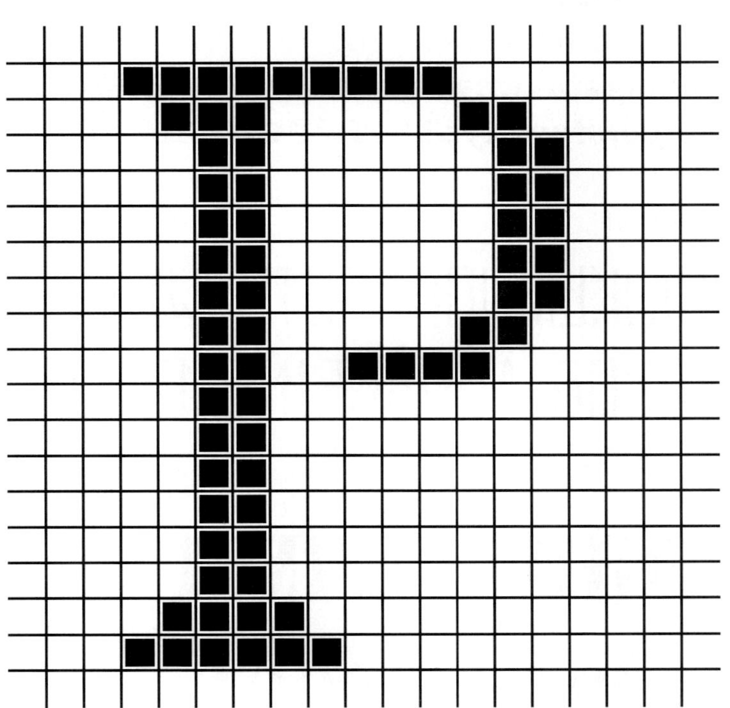

✍ Pierre LeBé, 1601

ITC PACELLA

Vincent Pacella • 1987 abcdefghijklmnopqrstuvwxyz(“.;‘!*?’:,”)

AGP LEF URW $1234567890&ﬁﬂß-äöüåçèîñóæøœ

ABCDEFGHIJKLMNOPQRSTUVWXYZ

ÄÖÜÅÇÈÎÑÓÆØŒ»„«[¶§•†‡]‹¡·¿›…

ITC Pacella …

• Book abcdefghijklmnopqrstuvwxyzABCDEFGHIJKLMNOPQRSTUVWXYZ–$1234567

Book Italic *abcdefghijklmnopqrstuvwxyzABCDEFGHIJKLMNOPQRSTUVWXYZ–$12345678*

Medium abcdefghijklmnopqrstuvwxyzABCDEFGHIJKLMNOPQRSTUVWXYZ–$123456

Medium Italic *abcdefghijklmnopqrstuvwxyzABCDEFGHIJKLMNOPQRSTUVWXYZ–$1234567*

Bold **abcdefghijklmnopqrstuvwxyzABCDEFGHIJKLMNOPQRSTUVWXYZ–$1234**

Bold Italic ***abcdefghijklmnopqrstuvwxyzABCDEFGHIJKLMNOPQRSTUVWXYZ–$1234***

Black **abcdefghijklmnopqrstuvwxyzABCDEFGHIJKLMNOPQRSTUVWXYZ–123**

Black Italic ***abcdefghijklmnopqrstuvwxyzABCDEFGHIJKLMNOPQRSTUVWXYZ–$12***

PACIFICA CONDENSED

IMA ABCDEFGHIJKLMNOPQRSTUVWXYZ(“.;‘!*?’:,”)

▲30 $1234567890&-ÄÖÜÅÇÈÎÑÓÆØŒ»„«[¶§•†]i·¿…

A*I Painter
A*I Wood Type

A*I Design Staff • 1990 ABCDEFGHIJKLMNOPQRSTUVWXYZ

ALP MTD (.;!*?:,)$1234567890&-ABCDEFGHIJK

▲36 LMNOPQRSTUVWXYZ[]

PAISLEY

Noel Rubin & Michael Allard • 1993 abcdefghijklmnopqrstuvwxyz(“.;‘!*?’:,”)

IMA $1234567890&ﬁﬂß-äöüåçèîñóæøœ

▲16 ABCDEFGHIJKLMNOPQRSTUVWXYZ

ÄÖÜÅÇÈÎÑÓÆØŒ»„«[¶§•†‡]‹¡·¿›…

Paisley …

• One abcdefghijklmnopqrstuvwxyzABCDEFGHIJKLMNOPQRSTUVWXYZ–$

A*I Wood Type: A*I Antique Condensed, A*I Barrel, A*I Box Gothic, A*I French XXX Condensed, A*I Painter, A*I Tuscan Egyptian.

P

... Paisley

One Alternate abcdefghijklmnopqrstuvwxyzÅBCDEFGHIJKLMNOPQRSTUVWXYZ

Two abcdefghijklmnopqrstuvwxyzÅBCDEFGHIJKLMNOPQRSTUVWXY

Two Alternate abcdefghijklmnopqrstuvwxyzÅBCDEFGHIJKLMNOPQRSTUVWY

PAJAMAS

FRA ABCDEFGHIJKLMNOPQRSTUVWXYZ

▲24 “.;‘!?’:,”$1234567890¢-ÄÖÜÅÇÈÎÑÓ

Palace Script
Monotype Scripts 2

MCL ADO AGA LIN MAE abcdefghijklmnopqrstuvwxyz(“.;‘!*?’:,”)

▲20 $1234567890&fiflß-äöüåçèîñóæœ

ABCDEFGHIJKLMNOPQRSTUVWXYZ

ÄÖÜÅÇÈÎÑÓÆØŒ»„«[¶§•†‡]‹¡·¿›...

Palace Script ...

• Regular abcdefghijklmnopqrstuvwxyzABCDEFGHIJKLMNOPQRSTUV

Semibold abcdefghijklmnopqrstuvwxyzABCDEFGHIJKLMNOPQRSTUV

PALATINO

Hermann Zapf • 1950 abcdefghijklmnopqrstuvwxyz(“.;‘!*?’:,”)

LIN ADO AGA FAM MAE $1234567890&fiflß-äöüåçèîñóæøœ

ABCDEFGHIJKLMNOPQRSTUVWXYZ

ÄÖÜÅÇÈÎÑÓÆØŒ»„«[¶§•†‡]‹¡·¿›...

Palatino 1 ...

• Roman abcdefghijklmnopqrstuvwxyzABCDEFGHIJKLMNOPQRSTUVWXYZ–$1234567

Italic *abcdefghijklmnopqrstuvwxyzABCDEFGHIJKLMNOPQRSTUVWXYZ–$1234567890*

Bold **abcdefghijklmnopqrstuvwxyzABCDEFGHIJKLMNOPQRSTUVWXYZ–$1234**

Bold Italic ***abcdefghijklmnopqrstuvwxyzABCDEFGHIJKLMNOPQRSTUVWXYZ–$123456***

Palatino 2 ...

Light abcdefghijklmnopqrstuvwxyzABCDEFGHIJKLMNOPQRSTUVWXYZ–$1234567890

Light Italic *abcdefghijklmnopqrstuvwxyzABCDEFGHIJKLMNOPQRSTUVWXYZ–$1234567890(“.;‘!*

Medium **abcdefghijklmnopqrstuvwxyzABCDEFGHIJKLMNOPQRSTUVWXYZ–$12345**

Medium Italic *abcdefghijklmnopqrstuvwxyzABCDEFGHIJKLMNOPQRSTUVWXYZ–$1234567890*

Black **abcdefghijklmnopqrstuvwxyzABCDEFGHIJKLMNOPQRSTUVWXYZ–$1**

Black Italic ***abcdefghijklmnopqrstuvwxyzABCDEFGHIJKLMNOPQRSTUVWXYZ–$12***

P

Monotype Scripts 2: Ashley Script, Monoline Script, New Berolina, Palace Script Regular & Semibold.

PALATINO SCOSF

ABCDEFGHIJKLMNOPQRSTUVWXYZ(".;'!*?':,")

LIN ADO AGA MAE $1234567890&-ÄÖÜÅÇÈÎÑÓÆØŒ

ABCDEFGHIJKLMNOPQRSTUVWXYZ

ÄÖÜÅÇÈÎÑÓÆØŒ»„«[¶§•†‡]‹¡·¿›...

Palatino SCOSF ...

• Roman SCOSF ABCDEFGHIJKLMNOPQRSTUVWXYZABCDEFGHIJKLMNOPQRSTUVWXYZ–$12345

Italic OSF *abcdefghijklmnopqrstuvwxyzABCDEFGHIJKLMNOPQRSTUVWXYZ–$1234567890*

Bold OSF **abcdefghijklmnopqrstuvwxyzABCDEFGHIJKLMNOPQRSTUVWXYZ–$1234**

Bold Italic OSF ***abcdefghijklmnopqrstuvwxyzABCDEFGHIJKLMNOPQRSTUVWXYZ–$123456***

ITC PANACHE

Ed Benguiat • 1988 abcdefghijklmnopqrstuvwxyz(".;'!*?':,")

URW LEF $1234567890&fiflß-äöüåçèîñóæøœ

ABCDEFGHIJKLMNOPQRSTUVWXYZ

ÄÖÜÅÇÈÎÑÓÆØŒ»„«(¶§•†‡)‹¡·¿›...

ITC Panache ...

• Book abcdefghijklmnopqrstuvwxyzABCDEFGHIJKLMNOPQRSTUVWXYZ-$1234567890(".;'!

Book Italic *abcdefghijklmnopqrstuvwxyzABCDEFGHIJKLMNOPQRSTUVWXYZ-$1234567890(".;'!*?*

Bold **abcdefghijklmnopqrstuvwxyzABCDEFGHIJKLMNOPQRSTUVWXYZ–$123456789**

Bold Italic ***abcdefghijklmnopqrstuvwxyzABCDEFGHIJKLMNOPQRSTUVWXYZ–$1234567890***

Black **abcdefghijklmnopqrstuvwxyzABCDEFGHIJKLMNOPQRSTUVWXYZ–$123**

Black Italic ***abcdefghijklmnopqrstuvwxyzABCDEFGHIJKLMNOPQRSTUVWXYZ–$1234***

Papyrus

Chris Costello • 1983 abcdefghijklmnopqrstuvwxyz(".;'!*?':,")

LET $1234567890&fiflß-äöüåçèîñóæøœ

ABCDEFGHIJKLMNOPQRSTUVWXYZ

ÄÖÜÅÇÈÎÑÓÆØŒ»„«[•]‹¡·¿›...▹AABBCCDEEFGHIJK

▹KLLMNOPP QQRRSTUVWXY

Paris Flash

E. Crous-Vidal • 1953 ABCDEFGHIJKLMNOPQRSTUVWXYZ

IMA

▲24 (".;'!*?':,")$1234567890

&-ÄÖÜÅÇÈÎÑÓÆØŒ»„«[•]‹¡·¿›...

Parisian

✍ *Morris Fuller Benton* • 1928 abcdefghijklmnopqrstuvwxyz(“.;‘!*?’:,”)

BIT ADO AGA AGP LIN MAE $1234567890&fiflß-äöüåçèîñóæøœ

▲16 ABCDEFGHIJKLMNOPQRSTUVWXYZ

ÄÖÜÅÇÈÎÑÓÆØŒ»„«[¶§•†‡]‹i·¿›...

Park Avenue

✍ *Robert E. Smith* • 1933 *abcdefghijklmnopqrstuvwxyz(“.;‘!*?’:,”)*

ADO AGA BIT LIN MAE URW *$1234567890&fiflß-äöüåçèîñóæøœ*

▲18 *ABCDEFGHIJKLMNOPQRSTUVWXYZ*

ÄÖÜÅÇÈÎÑÓÆØŒ»„«[¶§•†‡]‹i·¿›...

PARKINSON

✍ *Jim Parkinson* • 1970s – 1980s abcdefghijklmnopqrstuvwxyz(“.;‘!*?’:,”)

FBU $1234567890&fiflß-äöüåçèîñóæøœ

ABCDEFGHIJKLMNOPQRSTUVWXYZ

ÄÖÜÅÇÈÎÑÓÆØŒ»„«[¶§•†‡]‹i·¿›... ▷ ff ffi ffl ∷

Parkinson 1 ...

• Roman abcdefghijklmnopqrstuvwxyzABCDEFGHIJKLMNOPQRSTUVWXYZ–$1234567

Italic *abcdefghijklmnopqrstuvwxyzABCDEFGHIJKLMNOPQRSTUVWXYZ–$12345678*

Bold **abcdefghijklmnopqrstuvwxyzABCDEFGHIJKLMNOPQRSTUVWXYZ–$1**

Bold Italic ***abcdefghijklmnopqrstuvwxyzABCDEFGHIJKLMNOPQRSTUVWXYZ–$1***

Black ▲16 **abcdefghijklmnopqrstuvwxyzABCDEFGHIJKLMNOPQRST**

Bold Condensed ▲18 **abcdefghijklmnopqrstuvwxyzABCDEFGHIJKLMNOPQRSTUVWXYZ-$123456789**

Parkinson 2 ...

Medium abcdefghijklmnopqrstuvwxyzABCDEFGHIJKLMNOPQRSTUVWXYZ–$12345

Medium Italic *abcdefghijklmnopqrstuvwxyzABCDEFGHIJKLMNOPQRSTUVWXYZ–$12345*

Light Condensed ▲18 abcdefghijklmnopqrstuvwxyzABCDEFGHIJKLMNOPQRSTUVWXYZ-$1234567890(“.;‘!*?’:,”)&fiflß

Condensed ▲18 **abcdefghijklmnopqrstuvwxyzABCDEFGHIJKLMNOPQRSTUVWXYZ-$1234567890(“.**

A*I PARMA·PETIT

✍ *Manfred Klein* • 1994 abcdefghijklmnopqrstuvwxyz(“.;‘!*?’:,”)

ALP $1234567890&fiflß-äöüåçèîñóæøœ

▲18 ABCDEFGHIJKLMNOPQRSTUVWXYZ

ÄÖÜÂÇÈÎÑÓÆØŒ »„«[¶§•†]i·¿... ▷1234567890 ❶❷❸❹❺❻❼❽❾❿

A*I ParmaPetit ...

• Roman abcdefghijklmnopqrstuvwxyzABCDEFGHIJKLMNOPQRSTUVWXYZ–$123

Italic *abcdefghijklmnopqrstuvwxyzABCDEFGHIJKLMNOPQRSTUVWXYZ–$123*

A*I PARSONS

Inna Gertsberg • 1994 ... Will Ransom, 1918

abcdefghijklmnopqrstuvwxyz(.;!*?:,)

ALP $1234567890&ffl ß-äöüåçèîñóæøœ

ABCDEFGHIJKLMNOPQRSTUVWXYZ

ÄÖÜÅÇÈÎÑÓÆØŒ [¶·] ¡ ¿ ▷ A N T

A*I Parsons ...

Light abcdefghijklmnopqrstuvwxyzABCDEFGHIJKLMNOPQRSTUVWXYZ–$12345678

• Regular abcdefghijklmnopqrstuvwxyzABCDEFGHIJKLMNOPQRSTUVWXYZ–$1234

Heavy abcdefghijklmnopqrstuvwxyzABCDEFGHIJKLMNOPQRSTUVWXYZ

Party

Carol Kemp • 1993 abcdefghijklmnopqrstuvwxyz(".;'!*?':,")

LET $1234567890&fiflß-äöüåçèîñóæøœ

▲18 ABCDEFGHIJKLMNOPQRSTUVWXYZ

ÄÖÜÅÇÈÎÑÓÆØŒ»„«[•]‹¡·¿›...

▷ a c d e f g i i j k l m n o p q r s t t w y A

PEIGNOT

A. M. Cassandre • 1937 abcdefghijklmnopqrstuvwxyz(".;'!*?':,")

LIN ADO AGA MAE URW $1234567890&fiflß-ÄÖÜÅÇÈÎÑÓÆØŒ

▲16 ABCDEFGHIJKLMNOPQRSTUVWXYZ

ÄÖÜÅÇÈÎÑÓÆØŒ»„«[¶§•†‡]‹¡·¿›...

Peignot ...

Light abcdefghijklmnopqrstuvwxyzABCDEFGHIJKLMNOPQRSTUVWXYZ–$1234567890

• Demi abcdefghijklmnopqrstuvwxyzABCDEFGHIJKLMNOPQRSTUVWXYZ–$123456789

Bold abcdefghijklmnopqrstuvwxyzABCDEFGHIJKLMNOPQRSTUVWXYZ–$12

Pelican

Agfa Baker Calligraphy

Arthur Baker • 1989 abcdefghijklmnopqrstuvwxyz(".;'!*?':,")

AGP ADO AGA LIN MAE $1234567890&fiflß-äöüåçèîñóæøœ

▲18 ABCDEFGHIJKLMNOPQRSTUVWXYZ

ÄÖÜÅÇÈÎÑÓÆØŒ»„«[¶§•†‡]‹¡·¿›...

Pendry Script

Martin Wait • 1981 abcdefghijklmnopqrstuvwxyz(".;'!*?':,")

LET $1234567890&fiflß-äöüåçèîñóæøœ

▲16 ABCDEFGHIJKLMNOPQRSTUVWXYZ

ÄÖÜÅÇÈÎÑÓÆØŒ»„«[•]‹¡·¿›... ▷ g j o r y st

Agfa Baker Calligraphy: Amigo, Marigold, Oxford, Pelican, Visigoth.

Pepita
Monotype Scripts 1
Imre Reiner • 1959
MCL ADO AGA LIN MAE
▲16

abcdefghijklmnopqrstuvwxyz(".;'!*?':,")
$1234567890&fiflß-äöüåçèîñóæøœ
ABCDEFGHIJKLMNOPQRSTUVWXYZ
ÄÖÜÅÇÈÎÑÓÆØŒ»„«[§•†‡]‹¡·¿›...

PEPPERWOOD
Adobe Wood Type 3
Kim Buker Chansler & Carl Crossgrove • 1994
ADO AGA MAE
▲54

ABCDEFGHIJKLMNOPQRSTUVWXYZ
(".;'!*?':,")$1234567890
&-ÄÖÜÅÇÈÎÑÓÆØŒ»„«[•]‹¡·¿›...

Pepperwood ...

Outline ABCDEFGHIJKLMNOPQRSTUVWXYZ–$12345

Fill ABCDEFGHIJKLMNOPQRSTUVWXYZ–$12345

• Regular ABCDEFGHIJKLMNOPQRSTUVWXYZ–$12345

PERKY
Marshall Bohlin • 1994
EMD
▲16

abcdefghijklmnopqrstuvwxyz(".;'!*?':,")
$1234567890&fiflß-äöüåçèîñóæøœ
ABCDEFGHIJKLMNOPQRSTUVWXYZ
ÄÖÜÅÇÈÎÑÓÆØŒ[¶§•†]¡·¿...

Perky ...

• Regular abcdefghijklmnopqrstuvwxyzABCDEFGHIJKLMNOPQRSTUVWXYZ–$1234567890(".;'!*?':,"

Bold abcdefghijklmnopqrstuvwxyzABCDEFGHIJKLMNOPQRSTUVWXYZ–$1234567890(".;'!

P

Monotype Scripts 1: Biffo Script, Dorchester Script, Pepita, Monotype Script Bold, Swing Bold.
Adobe Wood Type 3: Pepperwood Regular, Fill & Outline, Rosewood Regular & Fill, Zebrawood Regular & Fill.

PERPETUA

Eric Gill • 1928 abcdefghijklmnopqrstuvwxyz(“.;‘!*?’:,”)

MCL ADO AGA FAM LIN MAE $1234567890&fiflß-äöüåçèîñóæøœ

▲16 ABCDEFGHIJKLMNOPQRSTUVWXYZ

ÄÖÜÅÇÈÎÑÓÆØŒ»„«[¶§•†‡]‹¡·¿›...

Perpetua ...

• Roman abcdefghijklmnopqrstuvwxyzABCDEFGHIJKLMNOPQRSTUVWXYZ–$123456789

Italic *abcdefghijklmnopqrstuvwxyzABCDEFGHIJKLMNOPQRSTUVWXYZ–$1234567890(“.;‘!*?’:,”*

Bold **abcdefghijklmnopqrstuvwxyzABCDEFGHIJKLMNOPQRSTUVWXYZ–$12**

Bold Italic ***abcdefghijklmnopqrstuvwxyzABCDEFGHIJKLMNOPQRSTUVWXYZ–$123456***

PERPETUA EXPERT

MCL ADO AGA LIN MAE ABCDEFGHIJKLMNOPQRSTUVWXYZ.;!?:,

▲16 1234567890&fffiflffiffl–ÄÖÜÅÇÈÎÑÓÆØŒ

(abdeilmnorst) 1/8 1/4 1/3 3/8 1/2 5/8 2/3 3/4 7/8 $12345/67890¢ ₡Rp

Perpetua Expert ...

• Expert Roman ABCDEFGHIJKLMNOPQRSTUVWXYZ–$1234567890.;!?:,&-fffiflffiffl 1/8 1/4 1/3 3/8 1/2 $12345/67

Expert Italic *$1234567890.;:,–fffiflffiffl 1/8 1/4 1/3 3/8 1/2 $12345/67890¢ (abdeilmnorst) 5/8 2/3 3/4 7/8 ₡Rp*

Expert Bold **$1234567890.;:,–fffiflffiffl 1/8 1/4 1/3 3/8 1/2 $12345/67890¢ (abdeilmnorst) 5/8 2/3 3/4 7/8 ₡Rp**

Expert Bold Italic ***$1234567890.;:,–fffiflffiffl 1/8 1/4 1/3 3/8 1/2 $12345/67890¢ (abdeilmnorst) 5/8 2/3 3/4 7/8 ₡Rp***

PERPETUA TITLING
❖ *Monotype Classic Titling*

MCL ABCDEFGHIJKLMNOPQRST

▲36 UVWXYZ(“.;‘!*?’:,”)$123456789

0&-ÄÖÜÅÇÈÎÑÓÆØŒ»„«[...

P

Perpetua Titling ...

Light ABCDEFGHIJKLMNOPQRSTU

• Regular ABCDEFGHIJKLMNOPQRST

Bold **ABCDEFGHIJKLMNOPQRS**

❖ *Monotype Classic Titling*: Felix Titling, Perpetua Titling Light, Regular & Bold.

PERRYWOOD

✍ *Johannes Birkenbach • 1993* abcdefghijklmnopqrstuvwxyz(“.;‘!*?’:,”)

MCL $1234567890&fiflß-äöüåçèîñóæøœ

ABCDEFGHIJKLMNOPQRSTUVWXYZ

ÄÖÜÅÇÈÎÑÓÆØŒ»„«[¶§•†‡]‹¡·¿›...

Perrywood 1 ...

• Roman abcdefghijklmnopqrstuvwxyzABCDEFGHIJKLMNOPQRSTUVWXYZ–$1234567890(

Italic *abcdefghijklmnopqrstuvwxyzABCDEFGHIJKLMNOPQRSTUVWXYZ–$1234567890(“.;‘!*

Bold **abcdefghijklmnopqrstuvwxyzABCDEFGHIJKLMNOPQRSTUVWXYZ–$123456**

Bold Italic ***abcdefghijklmnopqrstuvwxyzABCDEFGHIJKLMNOPQRSTUVWXYZ–$123456789***

Perrywood 2 ...

Light abcdefghijklmnopqrstuvwxyzABCDEFGHIJKLMNOPQRSTUVWXYZ–$1234567890(“.;‘

Light Italic *abcdefghijklmnopqrstuvwxyzABCDEFGHIJKLMNOPQRSTUVWXYZ–$1234567890(“.;‘!*?*

Semibold abcdefghijklmnopqrstuvwxyzABCDEFGHIJKLMNOPQRSTUVWXYZ–$12345678

Semibold Italic *abcdefghijklmnopqrstuvwxyzABCDEFGHIJKLMNOPQRSTUVWXYZ–$1234567890(“*

Extra Bold **abcdefghijklmnopqrstuvwxyzABCDEFGHIJKLMNOPQRSTUVWXYZ–$12**

Extra Bold Italic ***abcdefghijklmnopqrstuvwxyzABCDEFGHIJKLMNOPQRSTUVWXYZ–$12345***

PHAISTOS

✍ *David Berlow & Just Van Rossum • 1991* abcdefghijklmnopqrstuvwxyz(“.;‘!*?’:,”)

FBU AGP MTD $1234567890&fiflß-äöüåçèîñóæøœ

▲16 ABCDEFGHIJKLMNOPQRSTUVWXYZ

ÄÖÜÅÇÈÎÑÓÆØŒ»„«[¶§•†‡]‹¡·¿›... ▷ Q 3

Phaistos ...

• Roman abcdefghijklmnopqrstuvwxyzABCDEFGHIJKLMNOPQRSTUVWXYZ–$123456

Italic *abcdefghijklmnopqrstuvwxyzABCDEFGHIJKLMNOPQRSTUVWXYZ–$1234567890(*

Bold **abcdefghijklmnopqrstuvwxyzABCDEFGHIJKLMNOPQRSTUVWXYZ–$12**

PHOSPHATE

✍ ... *Jakob Erbar • 1925* ABCDEFGHIJKLMNOPQRSTUVWXYZ

RED (“.;‘!*?’:,”)$1234567890&-ÄÖÜÅÇÈÎÑÓ

▲30 ÆØŒ»„«[¶•]‹¡·¿›...

Phosphate ...

Solid **ABCDEFGHIJKLMNOPQRSTUVWXYZ-$1**

• Inline ABCDEFGHIJKLMNOPQRSTUVWXYZ-$1

P

PHOTINA

José Mendoza y Almeida • 1972
MCL ADO AGA LIN MAE

abcdefghijklmnopqrstuvwxyz(“.;‘!*?’:,”)
$1234567890&fiflß-äöüåçèîñóæøœ
ABCDEFGHIJKLMNOPQRSTUVWXYZ
ÄÖÜÅÇÈÎÑÓÆØŒ»„«[¶§•†‡]‹¡·¿›...

Photina ...

• Roman abcdefghijklmnopqrstuvwxyzABCDEFGHIJKLMNOPQRSTUVWXYZ–$1234567890(
Italic *abcdefghijklmnopqrstuvwxyzABCDEFGHIJKLMNOPQRSTUVWXYZ–$1234567890(“.;*
Bold **abcdefghijklmnopqrstuvwxyzABCDEFGHIJKLMNOPQRSTUVWXYZ–$1234567890**
Bold Italic ***abcdefghijklmnopqrstuvwxyzABCDEFGHIJKLMNOPQRSTUVWXYZ–$123456789***
Semibold **abcdefghijklmnopqrstuvwxyzABCDEFGHIJKLMNOPQRSTUVWXYZ–$12345**
Semibold Italic ***abcdefghijklmnopqrstuvwxyzABCDEFGHIJKLMNOPQRSTUVWXYZ–$12345***
Ultra Bold **abcdefghijklmnopqrstuvwxyzABCDEFGHIJKLMNOPQRSTUVWXYZ–$**
Ultra Bold Italic ***abcdefghijklmnopqrstuvwxyzABCDEFGHIJKLMNOPQRSTUVWXYZ–$12***

Piranesi Italic

Morris Fuller Benton • 1930
... Willard T. Sniffin, 1930
BIT
▲16

abcdefghijklmnopqrstuvwxyz(“.;‘!?’:,”)*
$1234567890&fiflß-äöüåçèîñóæøœ
ABCDEFGHIJKLMNOPQRSTUVWXYZ
ÄÖÜÅÇÈÎÑÓÆØŒ»„«[§•†‡]‹¡·¿›...

PLACARD

Monotype Headliners 2
Monotype Design Staff • 1958
MCL
▲24

abcdefghijklmnopqrstuvwxyz(“.;‘!*?’:,”)$1234567890&fiflß-äöüåçèîñó
œøœABCDEFGHIJKLMNOPQRSTUVWXYZÄÖÜÅÇÈÎÑÓÆØŒ»„«[¶§•†‡]‹¡·¿›...

Placard ...

• Condensed abcdefghijklmnopqrstuvwxyzABCDEFGHIJKLMNOPQRSTUVWXYZ–$123456
Bold Condensed **abcdefghijklmnopqrstuvwxyzABCDEFGHIJKLMNOPQRSTUV**

PLAK

Linotype Headliners
LIN
▲24

abcdefghijklmnopqrstuvwxyz(“.;‘!*?’:,”)$1234567890&fiflß-äöüåçèîñó
æøœABCDEFGHIJKLMNOPQRSTUVWXYZÄÖÜÅÇÈÎÑÓÆØŒ»„«[¶§•†‡...

Plak ...

Black **abcdefghijklmnopqrstuvwxyzABCDEFGHIJKLMNOPQRSTU**

Monotype Headliners 2: Falstaff, Headline Bold, Placard Condensed & Bold Condensed.
Linotype Headliners: Chwast Buffalo Black Condensed, Erbar Light Condensed & Bold Condensed, Metrolite, Metromedium, Metroblack, Plak Black, Black Condensed & Extra Black Condensed, Stop, Times Eighteen Roman & Bold.

. . . Plak

• Black Condensed abcdefghijklmnopqrstuvwxyzABCDEFGHIJKLMNOPQRSTUVWXYZ–$123

Extra Black Condensed abcdefghijklmnopqrstuvwxyzABCDEFGHIJKLMNOPQRSTUVWXYZ–$1234567890(“.;‘!*?’:,”)

PLANTIN

Monotype Design Staff • *1913*
. . . *Robert Granjon, c. 1700*
MCL ADO AGA FAM LIN MAE

abcdefghijklmnopqrstuvwxyz(“.;‘!*?’:,”)
$1234567890&fiflß-äöüåçèîñóæøœ
ABCDEFGHIJKLMNOPQRSTUVWXYZ
ÄÖÜÅÇÈÎÑÓÆØŒ»„«[¶§•†‡]‹¡·¿›…

Plantin 1 . . .

• Roman abcdefghijklmnopqrstuvwxyzABCDEFGHIJKLMNOPQRSTUVWXYZ–$12345

Italic *abcdefghijklmnopqrstuvwxyzABCDEFGHIJKLMNOPQRSTUVWXYZ–$12345678*

Bold **abcdefghijklmnopqrstuvwxyzABCDEFGHIJKLMNOPQRSTUVWXYZ–$1**

Bold Italic ***abcdefghijklmnopqrstuvwxyzABCDEFGHIJKLMNOPQRSTUVWXYZ–$1***

Plantin 2 . . .

Light abcdefghijklmnopqrstuvwxyzABCDEFGHIJKLMNOPQRSTUVWXYZ–$12345

Light Italic *abcdefghijklmnopqrstuvwxyzABCDEFGHIJKLMNOPQRSTUVWXYZ–$12345678*

Semibold **abcdefghijklmnopqrstuvwxyzABCDEFGHIJKLMNOPQRSTUVWXYZ–$12**

Semibold Italic ***abcdefghijklmnopqrstuvwxyzABCDEFGHIJKLMNOPQRSTUVWXYZ–$123***

Bold Condensed ▲16 **abcdefghijklmnopqrstuvwxyzABCDEFGHIJKLMNOPQRSTUVWXYZ–$12345678**

PLANTIN EXPERT

MCL ABCDEFGHIJKLMNOPQRSTUVWXYZ.;!?:,
1234567890&ﬀﬁﬂﬃﬄ–ÄÖÜÅÇÈÎÑÓÆØŒ
(abdeilmnorst) ⅛ ¼ ⅓ ⅜ ½ ⅝ ⅔ ¾ ⅞ $12345/67890¢ ₡Rp

P

Plantin Expert 1 . . .

• Expert Roman ABCDEFGHIJKLMNOPQRSTUVWXYZ–$1234567890.;!?:,&-ﬀﬁﬂﬃﬄ ⅛ ¼ ⅓ ⅜ ½ $12345/67

Expert Roman, Alternate Figures 1234567890 ⅛ ¼ ⅓ ⅜ ½ 12345/67890 ⅝ ⅔ ¾ ⅞

Expert Italic *$1234567890.;:,–ﬀﬁﬂﬃﬄ ⅛ ¼ ⅓ ⅜ ½ $12345/67890¢ (abdeilmnorst) ⅝ ⅔ ¾ ⅞ ₡Rp*

Expert Bold **$1234567890.;:,–ﬀﬁﬂﬃﬄ ⅛ ¼ ⅓ ⅜ ½ $12345/67890¢ (abdeilmnorst) ⅝ ⅔ ¾ ⅞ ₡Rp**

Expert Bold Italic ***$1234567890.;:,–ﬀﬁﬂﬃﬄ ⅛ ¼ ⅓ ⅜ ½ $12345/67890¢ (abdeilmnorst) ⅝ ⅔ ¾ ⅞ ₡Rp***

Plantin Expert 2 . . .

Expert Light ABCDEFGHIJKLMNOPQRSTUVWXYZ–$1234567890.;!?:,&-ﬀﬁﬂﬃﬄ ⅛ ¼ ⅓ ⅜ ½ $12345/6789

Expert Light Italic *$1234567890.;:,–ﬀﬁﬂﬃﬄ ⅛ ¼ ⅓ ⅜ ½ $12345/67890¢ (abdeilmnorst) ⅝ ⅔ ¾ ⅞ ₡Rp*

Expert Semibold **$1234567890.;:,–ﬀﬁﬂﬃﬄ ⅛ ¼ ⅓ ⅜ ½ $12345/67890¢ (abdeilmnorst) ⅝ ⅔ ¾ ⅞ ₡Rp**

Expert Semibold Italic ***$1234567890.;:,–ﬀﬁﬂﬃﬄ ⅛ ¼ ⅓ ⅜ ½ $12345/67890¢ (abdeilmnorst) ⅝ ⅔ ¾ ⅞ ₡Rp***

Playbill

Robert Harling • 1938

BIT URW

▲24

abcdefghijklmnopqrstuvwxyz(".;'!*?':,")$1234567890&fiflß-äöüåçèîñóæøœ

ABCDEFGHIJKLMNOPQRSTUVWXYZÄÖÜÅÇÈÎÑÓÆØŒ»„«[§•†‡]‹¡·¿›...

Plaza

Alan Meeks • 1975

LET FRA URW

▲30

ABCDEFGHIJKLMNOPQRSTUVWXYZ(".;'!*?':,")

$1234567890&-ÄÖÜÅÇÈÎÑÓÆØŒ»„«[•]‹¡·¿›...

▷ AABBCCDDEEFFGGHHIIJJKKLLMMNNOOPPQQRRSTT

Pleasure Bold Shaded

Holger Seeling • 1987

LET

▲42

ABCDEFGHIJKLMNOPQRSTUVWXYZ(".;'!*?':,")

$1234567890&-ÄÖÜÅÇÈÎÑÓÆØŒ»„«[•]‹¡·¿›...

Pneuma

Timothy Donaldson • 1991

LET

▲24

ABCDEFGHIJKLMNOPQRSTUVWXYZ(".;'!*?':,")

$1234567890&-ÄÖÜÅÇÈÎÑÓÆØŒ»„«[•]‹¡·¿›...

POETICA

Robert Slimbach • 1993

ADO AGA LIN MAE

▲16

abcdefghijklmnopqrstuvwxyz(".;'!*?':,")

$1234567890&fiflß-äöüåçèîñóæøœ

ABCDEFGHIJKLMNOPQRSTUVWXYZ

ÄÖÜÅÇÈÎÑÓÆØŒ»„«[¢§•†‡]‹¡·¿›...

Poetica 1 ...

• Chancery I abcdefghijklmnopqrstuvwxyzABCDEFGHIJKLMNOPQRSTUVWXYZ–$1234567890(".;'!*?':,")&fiflß-äöü

Chancery II abcdefghijklmnopqrstuvwxyzABCDEFGHIJKLMNOPQRSTUVWXYZ–$1234567890(".;'!*?':,")&fi

Chancery III abcdefghijklmnopqrstuvwxyzABCDEFGHIJKLMNOPQRSTUVWXYZ–$1234567890(".;'!*?':,"

Chancery IV abcdefghijklmnopqrstuvwxyzABCDEFGHIJKLMNOPQRSTUVWXYZ–$1234567890(".;'!*?':,")&fiflß

Expert Chancery $1234567890.;:,-ffifflffifl ⅛ ¼ ⅓ ⅜ ½ $12345/67890¢ (abdeilmnorst) ⅝ ⅔ ¾ ⅞ ₡Rp

Chancery Roman SC ABCDEFGHIJKLMNOPQRSTUVWXYZABCDEFGHIJKLMNOPQRSTUVWXYZ–$1234567890(

Chancery Roman SC Alternate K K L M N N N Q R R V W X X Z

P

POETICA 2 – SUPPLEMENT

ADO AGA LIN MAE ▲16

Poetica 2 – Supplement . . .

Lowercase Alternates 1

Lowercase Alternates 2

Lowercase Beginnings 1

Lowercase Beginnings 2

Lowercase Endings 1

Lowercase Endings 2

Ampersands

Ligatures

• Inital Swash Capitals

Swash Capitals I ABCDEFGHIJKLMNOPQRSTUVWXYZABCDEFGHIJKLMNOPQRSTUVWXYZ

Swash Capitals II ABCDEFGHIJKLMNOPQRSTUVWXYZABCDEFGHIJKLMNOPQRSTUVW

Swash Capitals III ABCDEFGHIJKLMNOPQRSTUVWXYZABCDEFGHIJKLMNOPQR

Swash Capitals IV ABCDEFGHIJKLMNOPQRSTUVWXYZABCDEFGHIJKLMNO

P

Pointille

Albert Hollenstein • 1975

IMA ▲24

ABCDEFGHIJKLMNOPQRSTUVWXYZ

(".;'!*?':,")$1234567890

€-ÄÖÜÅÇÈÎÑÓÆØŒ»,„«¡¿...

Poliphilus Roman

Monotype AldineDutch

Monotype Design Staff • 1923

. . . Francesco Griffo, c. 1499

MCL ▲16

abcdefghijklmnopqrstuvwxyz(".;'!*?':,")

$1234567890&fifl߬äöüåçèîñóæøœ

ABCDEFGHIJKLMNOPQRSTUVWXYZ

ÄÖÜÅÇÈÎÑÓÆØŒ»,„«[¶§•†‡]‹¡¿›...

Poliphilus Roman Expert

Monotype AldineDutch Expert

MCL ▲16

ABCDEFGHIJKLMNOPQRSTUVWXYZ.;!?:,

1234567890&ffffiffl–ÄÖÜÅÇÈÎÑÓÆØŒ

(abdeilmnorst) 1/8 1/4 1/3 3/8 1/2 5/8 2/3 3/4 7/8 $12345/67890¢ ₡Rp

Poetica 2-Supplement ▶ Poetica Ornaments.

Monotype AldineDutch: Poliphilus Roman, Blado Italic, Van Dijck Roman & Italic.

Monotype AldineDutch Expert: Poliphilus Roman Expert, Blado Italic Expert, Van Dijck Expert Roman & Expert Italic.

FC POLONAISE BOLD

TFC abcdefghijklmnopqrstuvwxyz(“.;‘!*?’:,”)

▲20 $1234567890&fiflß-äöüåçèîñóæøœ

ABCDEFGHIJKLMNOPQRSTUVWXYZ

ÄÖÜÅÇÈÎÑÓÆØŒ„[•]¡·¿...

FC Polonaise Bold . . .

• Regular abcdefghijklmnopqrstuvwxyz ABCDEFGHIJKLMNOPQRSTUVW

Alternate Capitals abcdefghijklmnopqrstuvwxyz ABCDEFGHIJKLMNOPQRSTUV

Pompeijana
Type Before Gutenberg 3
Adrian Frutiger • 1992
LIN ADO AGA MAE
▲16

ABCDEFGHIJKLMNOPQRSTUVWXYZ(“.;‘!*?’:,”)

$1234567890&-ÄÖÜÅÇÈÎÑÓÆØŒ»„«[§•†‡]‹¡·¿›...

Ponderosa
Adobe Wood Type 1
Kim Buker, Barbara Lind & Joy Redick • 1990
ADO AGA LIN MAE
▲90

ABCDEFGHIJKLMNOPQRSTUVWXYZ(“.;‘!*?’:,”)

$1234567890&-ÄÖÜÅÇÈÎÑÓÆØŒ»„«[•]‹¡·¿›...

Poplar
Adobe Wood Type 2
Kim Buker, Barbara Lind & Joy Redick • 1990
ADO AGA LIN MAE
▲36

abcdefghijklmnopqrstuvwxyz(“.;‘!*?’:,”)

$1234567890&fiflß-äöüåçèîñóæøœ

ABCDEFGHIJKLMNOPQRSTUVWXYZ

ÄÖÜÅÇÈÎÑÓÆØŒ»„«[•]‹¡·¿›...

Type Before Gutenberg 3: Notre Dame, Notre Dame Ornaments, Pompeijana, Pompeijana Borders, Rusticana, Rusticana Borders.
Pompeijana ▶ Pompeijana Borders.
Adobe Wood Type 1: Cottonwood, Ironwood, Juniper, Mesquite, Ponderosa, Adobe Wood Type Ornaments 1.

Ponderosa ▶ Adobe Wood Type Ornaments 1.
Adobe Wood Type 2: Birch, Blackoak, Madrone, Poplar, Willow, Adobe Wood Type Ornaments 2.
Poplar ▶ Adobe Wood Type Ornaments 2.

POPPL-LAUDATIO

Friedrich Poppl • 1982 abcdefghijklmnopqrstuvwxyz(".;'!*?':,")
ADO AGA MAE $1234567890&fiflß-äöüåçèîñóæøœ
ABCDEFGHIJKLMNOPQRSTUVWXYZ
ÄÖÜÅÇÈÎÑÓÆØŒ»„«[¶§•†‡]‹i·¿›...

Poppl-Laudatio ...

Light abcdefghijklmnopqrstuvwxyzABCDEFGHIJKLMNOPQRSTUVWXYZ–$1234567890
Light Italic *abcdefghijklmnopqrstuvwxyzABCDEFGHIJKLMNOPQRSTUVWXYZ–$1234567890(".;'*
• Regular abcdefghijklmnopqrstuvwxyzABCDEFGHIJKLMNOPQRSTUVWXYZ–$1234567
Italic *abcdefghijklmnopqrstuvwxyzABCDEFGHIJKLMNOPQRSTUVWXYZ–$1234567890("*
Medium **abcdefghijklmnopqrstuvwxyzABCDEFGHIJKLMNOPQRSTUVWXYZ–$1234**
Medium Italic ***abcdefghijklmnopqrstuvwxyzABCDEFGHIJKLMNOPQRSTUVWXYZ–$1234567***
Bold **abcdefghijklmnopqrstuvwxyzABCDEFGHIJKLMNOPQRSTUVWXYZ–$12**
Bold Italic ***abcdefghijklmnopqrstuvwxyzABCDEFGHIJKLMNOPQRSTUVWXYZ–$1234***

POPPL-LAUDATIO CONDENSED

ADO AGA MAE abcdefghijklmnopqrstuvwxyz(".;'!*?':,")
$1234567890&fiflß-äöüåçèîñóæøœ
ABCDEFGHIJKLMNOPQRSTUVWXYZ
ÄÖÜÅÇÈÎÑÓÆØŒ»„«[¶§•†‡]‹i·¿›...

Poppl-Laudatio Condensed ...

Light Condensed abcdefghijklmnopqrstuvwxyzABCDEFGHIJKLMNOPQRSTUVWXYZ–$1234567890(".;'!*?':,")&fiflß-ä
• Condensed abcdefghijklmnopqrstuvwxyzABCDEFGHIJKLMNOPQRSTUVWXYZ–$1234567890(".;'!*?':,")&fi
Medium Condensed **abcdefghijklmnopqrstuvwxyzABCDEFGHIJKLMNOPQRSTUVWXYZ–$1234567890(".;'!*?'**
Bold Condensed **abcdefghijklmnopqrstuvwxyzABCDEFGHIJKLMNOPQRSTUVWXYZ–$1234567890(".;'!*?**

POPPL-PONTIFEX

Friedrich Poppl • 1976 abcdefghijklmnopqrstuvwxyz(".;'!*?':,")
ADO AGA LIN MAE $1234567890&fiflß-äöüåçèîñóæøœ
ABCDEFGHIJKLMNOPQRSTUVWXYZ
ÄÖÜÅÇÈÎÑÓÆØŒ»„«[¶§•†‡]‹i·¿›...

Poppl-Pontifex ...

• Roman abcdefghijklmnopqrstuvwxyzABCDEFGHIJKLMNOPQRSTUVWXYZ–$1234
Italic *abcdefghijklmnopqrstuvwxyzABCDEFGHIJKLMNOPQRSTUVWXYZ–$123456*
Medium **abcdefghijklmnopqrstuvwxyzABCDEFGHIJKLMNOPQRSTUVWXYZ–$12**
Bold **abcdefghijklmnopqrstuvwxyzABCDEFGHIJKLMNOPQRSTUVWXYZ–$1**
Medium Condensed **abcdefghijklmnopqrstuvwxyzABCDEFGHIJKLMNOPQRSTUVWXYZ–$12345678**

P

POPPL-PONTIFEX
EXPERT & SCOSF

ADO AGA MAE ABCDEFGHIJKLMNOPQRSTUVWXYZ.;!?:,
1234567890&fffiflffiffl–ÄÖÜÅÇÈÎÑÓÆØŒ
(abdeilmnorst) 1/8 1/4 1/3 3/8 1/2 5/8 2/3 3/4 7/8 $12345/67890¢ ₡Rp

Poppl-Pontifex Expert & SCOSF …

• Expert Roman ABCDEFGHIJKLMNOPQRSTUVWXYZ–$1234567890.;!?:,&-fffiflffiffl 1/8 1/4 1/3 3/8 1/2 $123
Expert Italic *$1234567890.;:,–fffiflffiffl 1/8 1/4 1/3 3/8 1/2 $12345/67890¢ (abdeilmnorst) 5/8 2/3 3/4 7/8 ₡Rp*
Expert Medium **ABCDEFGHIJKLMNOPQRSTUVWXYZ–$1234567890.;!?:,&-fffiflffiffl 1/8 1/4 1/3 3/8 1/2**
Expert Bold **$1234567890.;:,–fffiflffiffl 1/8 1/4 1/3 3/8 1/2 $12345/67890¢ (abdeilmnorst) 5/8 2/3 3/4 7/8 ₡Rp**
Expert Medium Condensed **ABCDEFGHIJKLMNOPQRSTUVWXYZ–$1234567890.;!?:,&-fffiflffiffl 1/8 1/4 1/3 3/8 1/2 $12345/67890**
Roman SCOSF ABCDEFGHIJKLMNOPQRSTUVWXYZABCDEFGHIJKLMNOPQRSTUVWXYZ–$123
Italic OSF *abcdefghijklmnopqrstuvwxyzABCDEFGHIJKLMNOPQRSTUVWXYZ–$1234567*
Medium SCOSF **ABCDEFGHIJKLMNOPQRSTUVWXYZABCDEFGHIJKLMNOPQRSTUVW…$123**
Bold OSF **abcdefghijklmnopqrstuvwxyzABCDEFGHIJKLMNOPQRSTUVW…$12345**
Medium Condensed SCOSF **ABCDEFGHIJKLMNOPQRSTUVWXYZABCDEFGHIJKLMNOPQRSTUVWXYZ–$12345678**

POPPL-RESIDENZ

Friedrich Poppl • 1977 *abcdefghijklmnopqrstuvwxyz(“.;‘!*?’:,”)*
ADO AGA MAE *$1234567890&fiflß-äöüåçèîñóæøœ*
▲16 *ABCDEFGHIJKLMNOPQRSTUVWXYZ*
ÄÖÜÅÇÈÎÑÓÆØŒ»„«[•]‹¡·¿›…

Poppl-Residenz …

Light *abcdefghijklmnopqrstuvwxyzABCDEFGHIJKLMNOPQRSTUV*
• Regular *abcdefghijklmnopqrstuvwxyzABCDEFGHIJKLMNOPQRSTUV*

PORTOBELLO

Steve Jackaman • 1992 abcdefghijklmnopqrstuvwxyz(“.;‘!*?’:,”)
RED $1234567890&fiflß-äöüåçèîñóæøœ
▲16 ABCDEFGHIJKLMNOPQRSTUVWXYZ
ÄÖÜÅÇÈÎÑÓÆØŒ»„«[¶§•†‡]‹¡·¿›…

Portobello …

Light abcdefghijklmnopqrstuvwxyzABCDEFGHIJKLMNOPQRSTUVWXYZ–$1234567890(“.;‘!*
• Medium abcdefghijklmnopqrstuvwxyzABCDEFGHIJKLMNOPQRSTUVWXYZ–$1234567890(“.
Demi **abcdefghijklmnopqrstuvwxyzABCDEFGHIJKLMNOPQRSTUVWXYZ–$12345678**
Bold **abcdefghijklmnopqrstuvwxyzABCDEFGHIJKLMNOPQRSTUVWXYZ–$12345**
Extra Bold **abcdefghijklmnopqrstuvwxyzABCDEFGHIJKLMNOPQRSTUVWXYZ–$12**

POSEIDON

Adrian Williams • 1991 abcdefghijklmnopqrstuvwxyz(".;'!*?':,")
MTD $1234567890&fiflß-äöüåçèîñóæøœ
▲16 ABCDEFGHIJKLMNOPQRSTUVWXYZ
ÄÖÜÅÇÈÎÑÓÆØŒ»„«[¶§•†‡]‹i·¿›...

Poseidon ...

• Regular abcdefghijklmnopqrstuvwxyzABCDEFGHIJKLMNOPQRSTUVWXYZ–$1234567890(".;'!*
Italic *abcdefghijklmnopqrstuvwxyzABCDEFGHIJKLMNOPQRSTUVWXYZ–$1234567890(".;'!*?':,")&*
Medium **abcdefghijklmnopqrstuvwxyzABCDEFGHIJKLMNOPQRSTUVWXYZ–$123456**
Medium Italic ***abcdefghijklmnopqrstuvwxyzABCDEFGHIJKLMNOPQRSTUVWXYZ–$123456789***
Bold **abcdefghijklmnopqrstuvwxyzABCDEFGHIJKLMNOPQRSTUVWXYZ–$**
Bold Italic ***abcdefghijklmnopqrstuvwxyzABCDEFGHIJKLMNOPQRSTUVWXYZ–$123***

POST-ANTIQUA

Herbert Post • 1937 abcdefghijklmnopqrstuvwxyz(".;'!*?':,")
LIN ADO AGA MAE $1234567890&fiflß-äöüåçèîñóæøœ
▲16 ABCDEFGHIJKLMNOPQRSTUVWXYZ
ÄÖÜÅÇÈÎÑÓÆØŒ»„«[¶§•†‡]‹¡·¿›...

Post-Antiqua ...

• Regular abcdefghijklmnopqrstuvwxyzABCDEFGHIJKLMNOPQRSTUVWXYZ–$
Bold **abcdefghijklmnopqrstuvwxyzABCDEFGHIJKLMNOPQRSTUVWXYZ–**

P

POST-MEDIÄVAL

Herbert Post • 1951 abcdefghijklmnopqrstuvwxyz(".;'!*?':,")
ADO AGA MAE $1234567890&fiflß-äöüåçèîñóæøœ
ABCDEFGHIJKLMNOPQRSTUVWXYZ
ÄÖÜÅÇÈÎÑÓÆØŒ»„«[¶§•†‡]‹i·¿›...

Post-Mediäval ...

• Roman abcdefghijklmnopqrstuvwxyzABCDEFGHIJKLMNOPQRSTUVWXYZ–$1234567890(
Italic *abcdefghijklmnopqrstuvwxyzABCDEFGHIJKLMNOPQRSTUVWXYZ–$1234567890(".;'!*?':,")&*
Medium **abcdefghijklmnopqrstuvwxyzABCDEFGHIJKLMNOPQRSTUVWXYZ–$1234567**

HF POSTER

Jonathan Macagba • 1991
... Egon Schiele, 1918

HAN MTD

▲30

ABCDEFGHIJKLMNOPQRSTUVWXYZ‹“.;‘!*?’:,”›
$1234567890&-ÄÖÜÅÇÈÎÑÓÆØŒ»‹«•‹¡¿›... ▷ AND

HF Poster ...

Solid ABCDEFGHIJKLMNOPQRSTUVWXYZ-$12345

• Inline ABCDEFGHIJKLMNOPQRSTUVWXYZ-$12345

Poster Black

Jim Parkinson • 1993

FBU

▲24

ABCDEFGHIJKLMNOPQRSTUVWXYZ
(“.;‘!*?’:,”)$1234567890&-ÄÖÜÅÇÈÎÑÓÆ
ØŒABCDEFGHIJKLMNOPQRSTUVWXYZ
ÄÖÜÅÇÈÎÑÓÆØŒ»„«[¶§•]‹¡·¿›... ▷

Prague

Michael Gills • 1991

LET

▲24

ABCDEFGHIJKLMNOPQRSTUVWXYZ
(“.;‘!*?’:,”)$1234567890
&-ÄÖÜÅÇÈÎÑÓÆØŒ»„«[•]‹¡·¿›...

PRAXIS

Gerard Unger • 1977

LEF

abcdefghijklmnopqrstuvwxyz(“.;‘!*?’:,”)
$1234567890&fiflß-äöüåçèîñóæøœ
ABCDEFGHIJKLMNOPQRSTUVWXYZ
ÄÖÜÅÇÈÎÑÓÆØŒ»„«[¶§•†‡]‹¡·¿›...

Praxis 1 ...

• Regular abcdefghijklmnopqrstuvwxyzABCDEFGHIJKLMNOPQRSTUVWXYZ–$1234567890

Regular SCOSF ABCDEFGHIJKLMNOPQRSTUVWXYZABCDEFGHIJKLMNOPQRSTUVWXYZ–$1234567890(

Bold **abcdefghijklmnopqrstuvwxyzABCDEFGHIJKLMNOPQRSTUVWXYZ–$1234567**

Praxis 2 ...

Light abcdefghijklmnopqrstuvwxyzABCDEFGHIJKLMNOPQRSTUVWXYZ–$1234567890(“.;‘!*?’:,”)

Light SCOSF ABCDEFGHIJKLMNOPQRSTUVWXYZABCDEFGHIJKLMNOPQRSTUVWXYZ–$1234567890(“.;‘!*?’:,”)

P

... Praxis 2

Semibold abcdefghijklmnopqrstuvwxyzABCDEFGHIJKLMNOPQRSTUVWXYZ–$12345678

Heavy **abcdefghijklmnopqrstuvwxyzABCDEFGHIJKLMNOPQRSTUVWXYZ–$12345678**

Premier Lightline

Colin Brignall • 1969 abcdefghijklmnopqrstuvwxyz(".;'!*?';")

LET

▲24 $1234567890&fiflß-äöüåçèîñóæøœ

ABCDEFGHIJKLMNOPQRSTUVWXYZ

ÄÖÜÅÇÈÎÑÓÆØŒ»„«[•]‹¡·¿›...

▷ eswAKRSW

Premier Shaded

Colin Brignall • 1970 ABCDEFGHIJKLMNOPQRSTUVWXYZ(".;'!*?';")

LET FRA

▲30 $1234567890&-ÄÖÜÅÇÈÎÑÓÆØŒ»„«[•]‹¡·¿›...

PRESENT SCRIPT

Friedrich Karl Sallwey • 1974 abcdefghijklmnopqrstuvwxyz(".;'!*?';")

ADO AGA LIN MAE $1234567890&fiflß-äöüåçèîñóæøœ

ABCDEFGHIJKLMNOPQRSTUVWXYZ

ÄÖÜÅÇÈÎÑÓÆØŒ»„«[¶§•†‡]‹¡·¿›...

Present Script ...

• Regular abcdefghijklmnopqrstuvwxyzABCDEFGHIJKLMNOPQRSTUVWXYZ–$1234

Bold **abcdefghijklmnopqrstuvwxyzABCDEFGHIJKLMNOPQRSTUVWXYZ**

Black **abcdefghijklmnopqrstuvwxyzABCDEFGHIJKLMNOPQRSTUVWX**

Condensed abcdefghijklmnopqrstuvwxyzABCDEFGHIJKLMNOPQRSTUVWXYZ–$1234567890(".;'!*?'

Bold Condensed **abcdefghijklmnopqrstuvwxyzABCDEFGHIJKLMNOPQRSTUVWXYZ–$1234567890**

Black Condensed **abcdefghijklmnopqrstuvwxyzABCDEFGHIJKLMNOPQRSTUVWXYZ–$1234**

Present Script Regular

✣ *Linotype DisplaySet 1*

LIN ADO AGA MAE abcdefghijklmnopqrstuvwxyz(".;'!*?';")

▲18 $1234567890&fiflß-äöüåçèîñóæøœ

ABCDEFGHIJKLMNOPQRSTUVWXYZ

ÄÖÜÅÇÈÎÑÓÆØŒ»„«[¶§•†‡]‹¡·¿›...

✣ *Linotype DisplaySet 1*: Arnold Böcklin, Fette Fraktur, Helvetica Inserat, Present Script.

P

PRESTIGE ELITE

Clayton Smith • 1953 abcdefghijklmnopqrstuvwxyz(“.;‘!*?’:,”)

ADO AGA LIN MAE URW $1234567890&fiflß-äöüåçèîñóæøœ

▲12 ABCDEFGHIJKLMNOPQRSTUVWXYZ

ÄÖÜÅÇÈÎÑÓÆØŒ»„«[¶§•†‡]‹¡·¿›…

Prestige Elite . . .

• Regular abcdefghijklmnopqrstuvwxyzABCDEFGHIJKLMNOPQRSTUVWXYZ-$1234567890(“.;‘

Slanted *abcdefghijklmnopqrstuvwxyzABCDEFGHIJKLMNOPQRSTUVWXYZ-$1234567890(“.;‘*

Bold **abcdefghijklmnopqrstuvwxyzABCDEFGHIJKLMNOPQRSTUVWXYZ-$1234567890(“.;‘**

Bold Slanted ***abcdefghijklmnopqrstuvwxyzABCDEFGHIJKLMNOPQRSTUVWXYZ-$1234567890(“.;‘***

Pristina

Phill Grimshaw • 1994 abcdefghijklmnopqrstuvwxyz(“.;‘!*?’:,”)

LET $1234567890&fiflß-äöüåçèîñóæøœ

▲16 ABCDEFGHIJKLMNOPQRSTUVWXYZ

ÄÖÜÅÇÈÎÑÓÆØŒ»„«[•]‹¡·¿›…

▷ ∂ ff ffi Th

Pritchard

Martin Wait • 1990 ABCDEFGHIJKLMNOPQRSTUVWXYZ(“.;‘!*?’:,”)

LET $1234567890&-ÄÖÜÅÇÈÎÑÓÆØŒ»„«[•]‹¡·¿›…

▲60

Pritchard Line Out

Martin Wait • 1990 abcdefghijklmnopqrstuvwxyz(“.;‘!*?’:,”)

LET $1234567890&fiflß-äöüåçèîñóæøœ

▲36 ABCDEFGHIJKLMNOPQRSTUVWXYZ

ÄÖÜÅÇÈÎÑÓÆØŒ»„«[•]‹¡·¿›…

P

A*I PROSPERA II

Peter Fraterdeus • 1991 abcdefghijklmnopqrstuvwxyz(".;'!*?':,")

ALP MTD $1234567890&fiflß-äöüåçèîñóæøœ

▲16 ABCDEFGHIJKLMNOPQRSTUVWXYZ

ÄÖÜÅÇÈÎÑÓÆØŒ»,,«[¶§•|‹i·¿›…

▷ ct ff ffi ffl st t Qu Th

A*I Prospera II …

• Roman abcdefghijklmnopqrstuvwxyzABCDEFGHIJKLMNOPQRSTUVWXYZ-$1234567890(".;'!

Italic *abcdefghijklmnopqrstuvwxyzABCDEFGHIJKLMNOPQRSTUVWXYZ-$1234567890(".;'!*?':,")&fifl*

Roman SCLF ABCDEFGHIJKLMNOPQRSTUVWXYZABCDEFGHIJKLMNOPQRSTUVWXYZ-$1234567890(".;'

Bold **abcdefghijklmnopqrstuvwxyzABCDEFGHIJKLMNOPQRSTUVWXYZ-$1234567890(**

Bold Italic ***abcdefghijklmnopqrstuvwxyzABCDEFGHIJKLMNOPQRSTUVWXYZ-$1234567890(".;'!****

P.T. Barnum

BIT abcdefghijklmnopqrstuvwxyz(".;'!*?':,")

▲30 $1234567890&fiflß-äöüåçèîñóæøœ

ABCDEFGHIJKLMNOPQRSTUVWXYZ

ÄÖÜÅÇÈÎÑÓÆØŒ»,,«[§•†‡]‹i·¿›…

PUBLICITY GOTHIC

Sidney Gaunt • 1916 abcdefghijklmnopqrstuvwxyz

IMA TFC

▲24 (".;'!*?':,")$1234567890&fiflß-äöüåçè

îñóæøœABCDEFGHIJKLMNOPQRSTUV

WXYZÄÖÜÅÇÈÎÑÓÆØŒ»,,«[¶§•†‡]‹…

P

Publicity Gothic …

Outline abcdefghijklmnopqrstuvwxyzABCDEF

GHIJKLMNOPQRSTUVWXYZ-$1234567

• Solid abcdefghijklmnopqrstuvwxyzABCDEF

GHIJKLMNOPQRSTUVWXYZ-$1234567

Quadrus
A*I Quanta
Quartz
A*I QuasiModo
ITC Quay Sans
Quill Script
Quixley
ITC Quorum

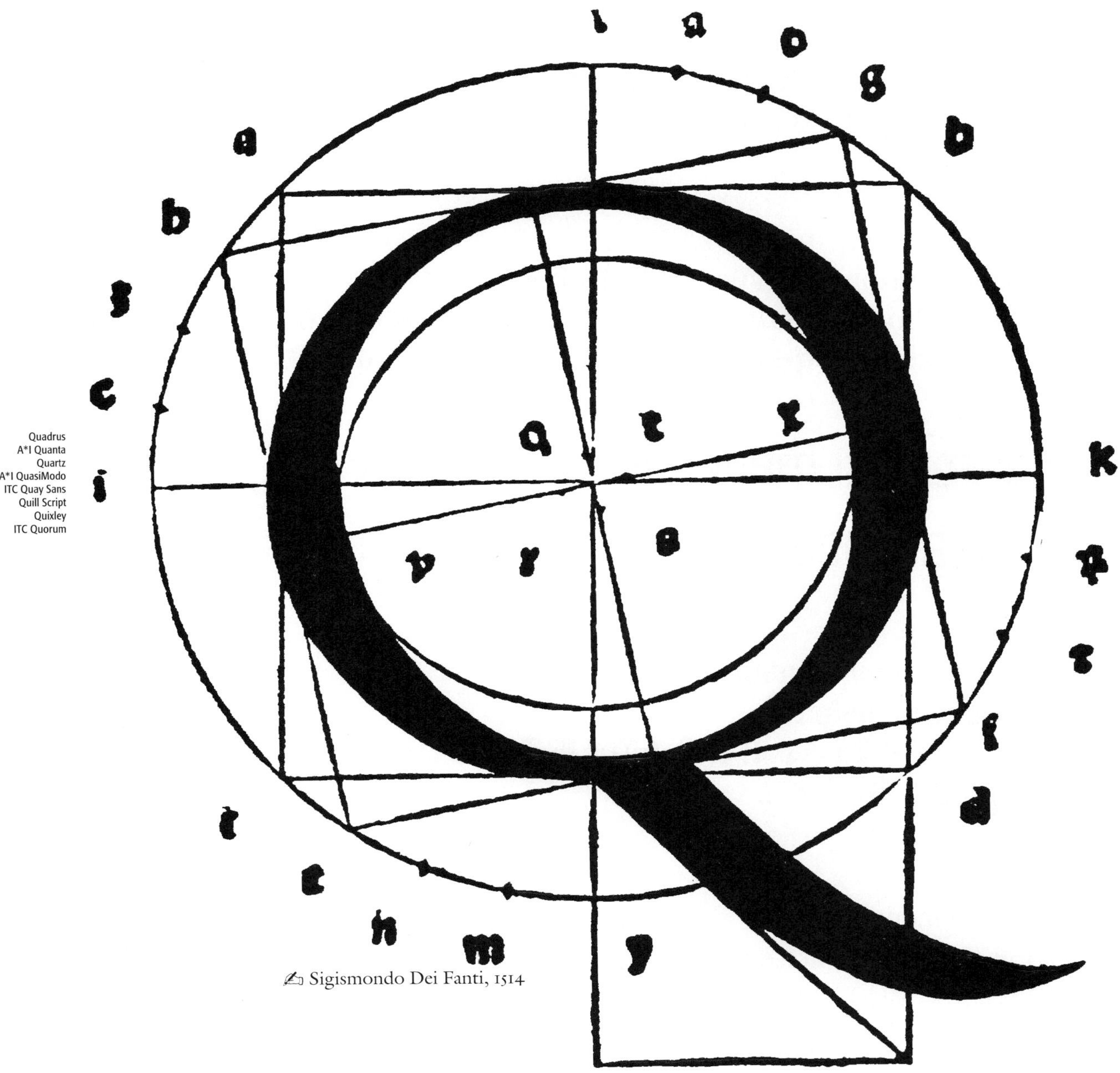

✍ Sigismondo Dei Fanti, 1514

Quadrus
Peter Fahrni • 1990
LET
▲30

ABCDEFGHIJKLMNOPQRSTUVWXYZ[".;'!*?':,"]
$1234567890&-ÄÖÜÅÇÈÎÑÓÆØŒ»„«[•]‹¡·¿›...

A*I QUANTA
Peter Fraterdeus • 1994
ALP

abcdefghijklmnopqrstuvwxyz(".;'!*?':,")
$1234567890&fiflß-äöüåçèîñóæøœ
ABCDEFGHIJKLMNOPQRSTUVWXYZ
ÄÖÜÅÇÈÎÑÓÆØŒ»„«[¶·]‹¡·¿›...

▷ ff

A*I Quanta ...

Thin abcdefghijklmnopqrstuvwxyzABCDEFGHIJKLMNOPQRSTUVWXYZ-$1234567890(".;'!*
Light abcdefghijklmnopqrstuvwxyzABCDEFGHIJKLMNOPQRSTUVWXYZ-$1234567890
• Medium abcdefghijklmnopqrstuvwxyzABCDEFGHIJKLMNOPQRSTUVWXYZ-$1234567
Bold **abcdefghijklmnopqrstuvwxyzABCDEFGHIJKLMNOPQRSTUVWXYZ-$1234**
Black **abcdefghijklmnopqrstuvwxyzABCDEFGHIJKLMNOPQRSTUVWXYZ-$12**

Quartz
URW TFC
▲24

ABCDEFGHIJKLMNOPQRSTUVWXYZ(".;'!*?':,")
$1234567890&-ÄÖÜÅÇÈÎÑÓÆØŒ»„«[¶§•†‡]‹¡·¿›...

A*I QuasiModo
Manfred Klein • 1994
ALP
▲18

abcdefghijklmnopqrstuvwxyz(".;'!?':,")
1234567890&fiflß-äöüçèîñó
ABCDEFGHIJKLMNOPQRSTUVWXYZ
ÄÖÜÇÈÎÑÓ»„« ¢ ...

ITC QUAY SANS
David Quay • 1990
URW AGP LEF FRA

abcdefghijklmnopqrstuvwxyz(".;'!*?':,")
$1234567890&fiflß-äöüåçèîñóæøœ
ABCDEFGHIJKLMNOPQRSTUVWXYZ
ÄÖÜÅÇÈÎÑÓÆØŒ»„«[¶§•†‡]‹¡·¿›...

ITC Quay Sans ...

• Book abcdefghijklmnopqrstuvwxyzABCDEFGHIJKLMNOPQRSTUVWXYZ-$1234567890(".;'!*?':,")&
Book Italic *abcdefghijklmnopqrstuvwxyzABCDEFGHIJKLMNOPQRSTUVWXYZ-$1234567890(".;'!*?':,")&*
Bold **abcdefghijklmnopqrstuvwxyzABCDEFGHIJKLMNOPQRSTUVWXYZ-$1234567890(".;'!*?':,**
Bold Italic ***abcdefghijklmnopqrstuvwxyzABCDEFGHIJKLMNOPQRSTUVWXYZ-$1234567890(".;'!*?':,***

Q

. . . ITC Quay Sans

Black **abcdefghijklmnopqrstuvwxyzABCDEFGHIJKLMNOPQRSTUVWXYZ-$1234567890(**

Black Italic ***abcdefghijklmnopqrstuvwxyzABCDEFGHIJKLMNOPQRSTUVWXYZ-$1234567890(***

Book SCOSF ABCDEFGHIJKLMNOPQRSTUVWXYZABCDEFGHIJKLMNOPQRSTUVWXYZ-$1234567890(".;'!*?':,")&-Ä

Bold SCOSF **ABCDEFGHIJKLMNOPQRSTUVWXYZABCDEFGHIJKLMNOPQRSTUVWXYZ-$1234567890(".;'!*?':,**

Quill Script
Agfa Scripts 1
Tommy Thompson • 1952 *abcdefghijklmnopqrstuvwxyz(".;'!*?':,")*
AGP *$1234567890&-ß-äöüåçèîñó*
▲16 *ABCDEFGHIJKLMNOPQRSTUVWXYZ*
ÄÖÜÅÇÈÎÑÓ»«[·]‹› ▷ *I V X st nd rd th 1/4 1/3 1/2 3/4 D' c r. 'c 's O' rs. s. & c/o*

Quixley
Vince Whitlock • 1991 (Zoltan Nagy) **abcdefghijklmnopqrstuvwxyz(".;'!*?':,")**
LET **$1234567890&fiflß-äöüåçèîñóœøœ**
▲18 **ABCDEFGHIJKLMNOPQRSTUVWXYZ**
ÄÖÜÅÇÈÎÑÓÆØŒ»„«[•]‹i·¿›. . .

ITC QUORUM
Ray Baker • 1977 abcdefghijklmnopqrstuvwxyz(".;'!*?':,")
BIT ADO AGA AGP LEF LIN MAE URW $1234567890&fiflß-äöüåçèîñóæøœ
ABCDEFGHIJKLMNOPQRSTUVWXYZ
ÄÖÜÅÇÈÎÑÓÆØŒ»„«[¶§•†‡]‹i·¿›. . .

ITC Quorum . . .

Light abcdefghijklmnopqrstuvwxyzABCDEFGHIJKLMNOPQRSTUVWXYZ–$1234567890(".;'!*

• Book abcdefghijklmnopqrstuvwxyzABCDEFGHIJKLMNOPQRSTUVWXYZ–$1234567890(".;'

Medium abcdefghijklmnopqrstuvwxyzABCDEFGHIJKLMNOPQRSTUVWXYZ–$1234567890(

Bold **abcdefghijklmnopqrstuvwxyzABCDEFGHIJKLMNOPQRSTUVWXYZ–$123456789**

Black **abcdefghijklmnopqrstuvwxyzABCDEFGHIJKLMNOPQRSTUVWXYZ–$1234567**

Q

Agfa Scripts 1: Commercial Script, Helinda Rook, Old English, Original Script, Quill Script, Stuyvesant, Wedding Text.

Rage Italic
Ragtime
TF Raincheck
Raleigh
Raleigh Gothic
Ramiz
Raphael
Rapier
Rebeca
Recess
Refracta
Regatta Condensed
Reiner Script
Relief
Renault
Reporter No. 2
Retro
Revue
Ribbit
Riot
Ritmo
Riviera Script
Rivoli Initials
NIMX Robust
Robotik
Rockwell
Roman
Sackers Roman
Romeo
Romic
Rosewood
Rotation
Agfa Rotis
Roughedge
Roundy
TF Roux
Roxy
Ru'ach
Rubaya Inline
Rubber Stamp
Ruling Script
Rumble
Rundfunk
Monotype Runic Condensed
A*I Russell Oblique
Russell Square
Rusticana
Ruzicka Freehand

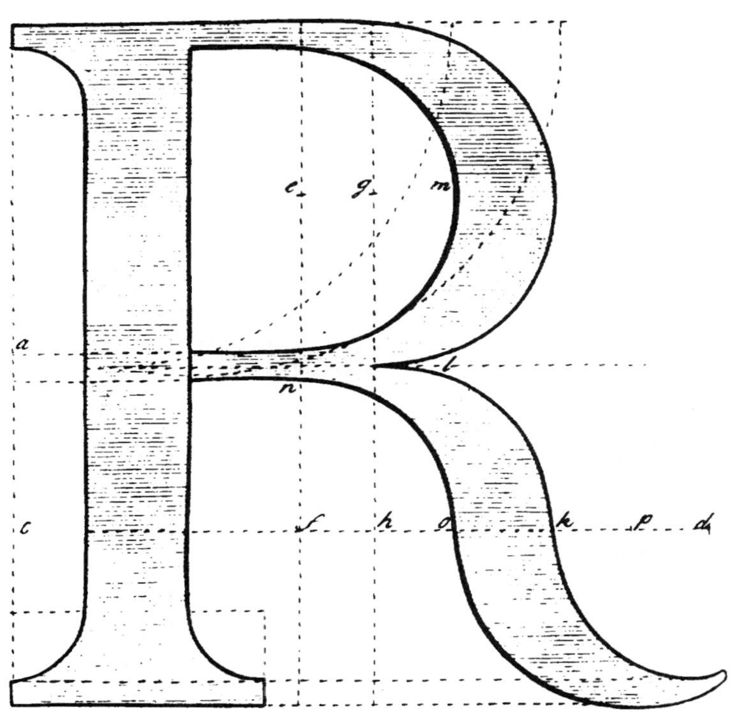
e
g
m
a
n
c
f
h
k
p
d

✍ George Bickham Jr., c.1755

Rage Italic

Ron Zwingelberg • 1984 abcdefghijklmnopqrstuvwxyz(“.;‘!*?’:,”)

LET $1234567890&fiflß-äöüåçèîñóæøœ

▲16 ABCDEFGHIJKLMNOPQRSTUVWXYZÄÖÜÅÇÈÎÑÓÆØŒ»„«[•]‹¡·¿›... ▷ adiotvw&S7

Ragtime

Alan Meeks • 1987 ABCDEFGHIJKLMNOPQRSTUVWXYZ(“.;‘!*?’:,”)

LET $1234567890&-ÄÖÜÅÇÈÎÑÓÆØŒ»„«[•]‹¡·¿›...

▲36

TF RAINCHECK

Joseph Treacy • 1992 abcdefghijklmnopqrstuvwxyz(“.;‘!*?’:,”)$1234567890&fiflß-äöüåçèîñóæøœ

TRE MTD ABCDEFGHIJKLMNOPQRSTUVWXYZÄÖÜÅÇÈÎÑÓÆØŒ»„«[(|§•†‡]‹¡·¿›...▷ 123579/234816 ■□

▲24

TF Raincheck A ...

Light abcdefghijklmnopqrstuvwxyzABCDEFGHIJKLMNOPQRSTUVWXYZ-$1234567890(“.;‘!*?’:”)

Book abcdefghijklmnopqrstuvwxyzABCDEFGHIJKLMNOPQRSTUVWXYZ-$1234567890(“.;‘!*?’:

Demi abcdefghijklmnopqrstuvwxyzABCDEFGHIJKLMNOPQRSTUVWXYZ-$1234567890(“.;‘!*?

Heavy abcdefghijklmnopqrstuvwxyzABCDEFGHIJKLMNOPQRSTUVWXYZ-$1234567890(“.;‘!

R

TF Raincheck B ...

• Regular abcdefghijklmnopqrstuvwxyzABCDEFGHIJKLMNOPQRSTUVWXYZ-$1234567890(“.;‘!*?’:,

Medium abcdefghijklmnopqrstuvwxyzABCDEFGHIJKLMNOPQRSTUVWXYZ-$1234567890(“.;‘!*?’

Bold abcdefghijklmnopqrstuvwxyzABCDEFGHIJKLMNOPQRSTUVWXYZ-$1234567890(“.;‘!*

Ultra abcdefghijklmnopqrstuvwxyzABCDEFGHIJKLMNOPQRSTUVWXYZ-$1234567890(“.;‘!

RALEIGH

✍ *Adrian Williams • 1977*
. . . Carl Dair • 1967
URW ADO AGA AGP BIT LIN MAE

abcdefghijklmnopqrstuvwxyz(".;'!*?':,")
$1234567890&fiflß-äöüåçèîñóæøœ
ABCDEFGHIJKLMNOPQRSTUVWXYZ
ÄÖÜÅÇÈÎÑÓÆØŒ»„«[¶§•†‡]‹¡·¿›...

Raleigh . . .

Light abcdefghijklmnopqrstuvwxyzABCDEFGHIJKLMNOPQRSTUVWXYZ–$1234567890(".;'!*?':,
• Roman abcdefghijklmnopqrstuvwxyzABCDEFGHIJKLMNOPQRSTUVWXYZ–$1234567890(".;'!*
Medium abcdefghijklmnopqrstuvwxyzABCDEFGHIJKLMNOPQRSTUVWXYZ–$1234567890(".;'!
Demibold **abcdefghijklmnopqrstuvwxyzABCDEFGHIJKLMNOPQRSTUVWXYZ–$1234567890(**
Bold **abcdefghijklmnopqrstuvwxyzABCDEFGHIJKLMNOPQRSTUVWXYZ–$123456789**
Extra Bold **abcdefghijklmnopqrstuvwxyzABCDEFGHIJKLMNOPQRSTUVWXYZ–$123456**

RALEIGH GOTHIC

✍ *Morris Fuller Benton • 1932*
RED
▲42

ABCDEFGHIJKLMNOPQRSTUVWXYZ(".;'!*?':,")
$1234567890&-ÄÖÜÅÇÈÎÑÓÆØŒ»„«[¶•]‹¡·¿›... ▷ AKMNSU$Æ

Raleigh Gothic . . .

Light ABCDEFGHIJKLMNOPQRSTUVWXYZ-$1234567890(".;'!*?':,")&-ÄÖÜÅÇÈÎÑÓÆØ
• Medium ABCDEFGHIJKLMNOPQRSTUVWXYZ-$1234567890(".;'!*?':,")&-ÄÖÜÅÇÈÎÑ
Bold **ABCDEFGHIJKLMNOPQRSTUVWXYZ-$1234567890(".;'!*?':,")&-ÄÖ**

RAMIZ

✍ *Greg Samata • 1993*
T26

ABCDEFGHIJKLMNOPQRSTUVWXYZ(.'!*?:,)
$1234567890&–ÄÖÜÅÇÈÎÑÓÆØŒ
ABCDEFGHIJKLMNOPQRSTUVWXYZ»«[]

Ramiz . . .

• Regular ABCDEFGHIJKLMNOPQRSTUVWXYZABCD
Bold **ABCDEFGHIJKLMNOPQRSTUVWXYZAB**
Extended ABCDEFGHIJKLMNOPQRSTU
Bold Extended **ABCDEFGHIJKLMNOPQR**

R

Raphael
Agfa DisplaySet 4
William F. Jackson • ...
AGP
▲18

abcdefghijklmnopqrstuvwxyz(“.;‘!*?’:,”)
$1234567890&fiflß-äöüåçèîñóæøœ
ABCDEFGHIJKLMNOPQRSTUVWXYZ
ÄÖÜÅÇÈÎÑÓÆØŒ»„«[¶§•†‡]‹¡·¿›...

Rapier
Martin Wait • 1989
LET
▲18

abcdefghijklmnopqrstuvwxyz(“.;‘!*?’:,”)
$1234567890&fiflß-äöüåçèîñóæøœ
ABCDEFGHIJKLMNOPQRSTUVWXYZÇ»„«[•]‹¡·¿›...

REBECA
Jack Yan • 1993
JAC

abcdefghijklmnopqrstuvwxyz(“.;‘!*?’:,”)
$1234567890&fiflß-äöüåçèîñóæøœ
ABCDEFGHIJKLMNOPQRSTUVWXYZ
ÄÖÜÅÇÈÎÑÓÆØŒ»„«[¶§•†‡]‹¡·¿›... ▷ ff ffi ffl

Rebeca ...

• Roman abcdefghijklmnopqrstuvwxyzABCDEFGHIJKLMNOPQRSTUVWXYZ–$1234567
Italic *abcdefghijklmnopqrstuvwxyzABCDEFGHIJKLMNOPQRSTUVWXYZ–$1234567890*
Demi abcdefghijklmnopqrstuvwxyzABCDEFGHIJKLMNOPQRSTUVWXYZ–$123
Demi Italic *abcdefghijklmnopqrstuvwxyzABCDEFGHIJKLMNOPQRSTUVWXYZ–$1234567*
Bold **abcdefghijklmnopqrstuvwxyzABCDEFGHIJKLMNOPQRSTUVWXYZ**
Bold Italic ***abcdefghijklmnopqrstuvwxyzABCDEFGHIJKLMNOPQRSTUVWXYZ–$1234***
Roman SCOSF ABCDEFGHIJKLMNOPQRSTUVWXYZABCDEFGHIJKLMNOPQRSTUVWXYZ–$123
Roman LF abcdefghijklmnopqrstuvwxyzABCDEFGHIJKLMNOPQRSTUVWXYZ–$123456
Italic LF *abcdefghijklmnopqrstuvwxyzABCDEFGHIJKLMNOPQRSTUVWXYZ–$12345678*

R

Recess
FTF Chalkboard
FRA
▲18

abcdefghijklmnopqrstuvwxyz(.:!*?:)$1234567890
ABCDEFGHIJKLMNOPQRSTUVWXYZ

Refracta
Martin Wait • 1988
LET
▲36

ABCDEFGHIJKLMNOPQRSTUVWXYZ(“.;‘!*?’:,”)
$1234567890&-ÄÖÜÅÇÈÎÑÓÆØŒ»„«[•]‹¡·¿›...

....
Agfa DisplaySet 4: Branding Iron, Isabella, McCollough, Raphael.
FTF Chalkboard: Blackboard & Recess.

Regatta Condensed
Alan Meeks • 1987
LET
▲36

ABCDEFGHIJKLMNOPQRSTUVWXYZ(“.;‘!*?’:,”)
$1234567890&-ÄÖÜÅÇÈÎÑÓÆØŒ»„«[•]‹¡·¿›...

REINER SCRIPT
Tobias Frere-Jones • 1993
... Imre Reiner, 1951
FBU
▲18

abcdefghijklmnopqrstuvwxyz(“.;‘!*?’:,”)
$1234567890&fifl-äöüåçèîñóæøœ
ABCDEFGHIJKLMNOPQRSTUVWXYZ
ÄÖÜÅÇÈÎÑÓÆØŒ»„«[¶§•†‡]‹¡·¿›...

▷ ct ce cr ee ff ffi ffl fj fr ft kr ne th ti tr tz st &

Reiner Script ...
• Regular abcdefghijklmnopqrstuvwxyzABCDEFGHIJKLMNOPQRSTUVWXYZ-$1234567890(“.;‘!*?’:,”)&fifl-äöüÄÖÜåçè
Bold abcdefghijklmnopqrstuvwxyzABCDEFGHIJKLMNOPQRSTUVWXYZ-$1234567890(“.;‘!*?’:,”)&fifl-

Relief
W. Seifert • 1972
IMA
▲24

ABCDEFGHIJKLMNOPQRSTUVWXYZ
(“.;‘!*?’:,”)$1234567890
&-ÄÖÜÅÇÈÎÑÓÆØŒ„[-]¡-¿...

RENAULT
Wolff Olins • 1968
URW LEF MTD

abcdefghijklmnopqrstuvwxyz(“.;‘!*?’:,”)
$1234567890&fiflß-äöüåçèîñóæøœ
ABCDEFGHIJKLMNOPQRSTUVWXYZ
ÄÖÜÅÇÈÎÑÓÆØŒ»„«[¶§•†‡]‹¡·¿›...

Renault ...
Light abcdefghijklmnopqrstuvwxyzABCDEFGHIJKLMNOPQRSTUVWXYZ–$1234567890(“
Light Italic *abcdefghijklmnopqrstuvwxyzABCDEFGHIJKLMNOPQRSTUVWXYZ-$1234567890(“.;*
• Medium abcdefghijklmnopqrstuvwxyzABCDEFGHIJKLMNOPQRSTUVWXYZ–$12345678
Bold **abcdefghijklmnopqrstuvwxyzABCDEFGHIJKLMNOPQRSTUVWXYZ–$123456**
Bold Italic ***abcdefghijklmnopqrstuvwxyzABCDEFGHIJKLMNOPQRSTUVWXYZ-$12345***

Reporter No. 2
❖ Adobe ScriptSet 1
C. Winkow • 1938
ADO AGA LIN MAE
▲16

abcdefghijklmnopqrstuvwxyz(“.;‘!*?’:,”)
$1234567890&fiflß-äöüåçèîñóæøœ
ABCDEFGHIJKLMNOPQRSTUVWXYZ
ÄÖÜÅÇÈÎÑÓÆØŒ»„«[•]‹¡·¿›...

❖ *Adobe ScriptSet 1*: Mistral & Reporter No. 2.

R

Retro Bold

Colin Brignall & Andrew Smith • 1992

LET

▲18

ABCDEFGHIJKLMNOPQRSTUVWXYZ(".;'!*?':,")
$1234567890&-ÄÖÜÅÇÈÎÑÓÆØŒ»„«[•]‹¡·¿›...

Retro Bold Condensed

Andrew Smith • 1992

LET

▲18

ABCDEFGHIJKLMNOPQRSTUVWXYZ(".;'!*?':,")
$1234567890&-ÄÖÜÅÇÈÎÑÓÆØŒ»„«[•]‹¡·¿›...

Revue

Adobe DisplaySet 1

Colin Brignall • 1968

ADO AGA BIT LIN MAE URW

abcdefghijklmnopqrstuvwxyz(".;'!*?':,")
$1234567890&fiflß-äöüåçèîñóæøœ
ABCDEFGHIJKLMNOPQRSTUVWXYZ
ÄÖÜÅÇÈÎÑÓÆØŒ»„«[•]‹¡·¿›...

Ribbit

Doug Bartow • 1994

RED

▲18

abcdefghijklmnopqrstuvwxyz(".;'!*?':,")
$1234567890&fiflß-äöüåçèîñóæøœ
ABCDEFGHIJKLMNOPQRSTUVWXYZ
ÄÖÜÅÇÈÎÑÓÆØŒ»„«[¶•†‡]‹¡·¿›...

Riot

Mark Allen • 1993

T26

▲24836

Ritmo Bold

Agfa Typographer's Edition 2

Aldo Novarese • 1955

AGP

▲18

abcdefghijklmnopqrstuvwxyz(".;'!*?':,")
$1234567890&ß-äöüåçèîñóæøœ
ABCDEFGHIJKLMNOPQRSTUVWXYZ
ÄÖÜÅÇÈÎÑÓÆØŒ»„«[¶•†‡]‹¡·¿›...

Riviera Script

Agfa Scripts 2

AGP

▲16

abcdefghijklmnopqrstuvwxyz(".;'!*?':,")
$1234567890&ß-äöüåçèîñó
ABCDEFGHIJKLMNOPQRSTUVWXYZ
ÄÖÜÅÇÈÎÑÓ»«[.]‹› I V X ¼ ⅓ ½ ¾ & %

Adobe DisplaySet 1: Aachen Bold, Freestyle Script, Revue, University Roman.
Agfa Typographer's Edition 2: PL Barnum Block, PL Benguiat Frisky Bold, TC Broadway, PL Davison Zip Bold, PL Fiedler Gothic Bold, PL Futura Maxi Book & Bold, Neon Extra Condensed, Ritmo Bold, PL Trophy Oblique.
Agfa Scripts 2: Citadel, Flemish Script 2, Florentine Script 2, French Script, Mahogany Script, Old Fashion Script, Riviera Script.

Rivoli Initials

Willard T. Sniffin • 1928 … Rudolf Koch, 1922

RED ▲30

ABCDEFGHIJKLMNOPQRSTUVWXYZ

(".;'!*?':,")$1234567890

&-ÄÖÜÅÇÈÎÑÓÆØŒ»„«[¶·]‹¡·¿›… ▷Y

NIMX ROBUST

Calvin Glenn • 1993

NIM ▲16

abcdefghijklmnopqrstuvwxyz(".;'!*?':,")

$1234567890&fiflß-äöüåçèîñóæøœ

ABCDEFGHIJKLMNOPQRSTUVWXYZ

ÄÖÜÅÇÈÎÑÓÆØŒ»„«[¶§•†‡]‹¡·¿›…

NIMX Robust …

• Regular abcdefghijklmnopqrstuvwxyzABCDEFGHIJKLMNOPQRSTUVWXYZ–$1234567890(".;'!*?':,")&fifl

Italic *abcdefghijklmnopqrstuvwxyzABCDEFGHIJKLMNOPQRSTUVWXYZ–$1234567890(".;'!*?':,")&fifl*

Bold **abcdefghijklmnopqrstuvwxyzABCDEFGHIJKLMNOPQRSTUVWXYZ–$1234567890(".;'!*?':,")**

Bold Italic ***abcdefghijklmnopqrstuvwxyzABCDEFGHIJKLMNOPQRSTUVWXYZ–$1234567890(".;'!*?':,")***

Robotik

David Quay • 1989

LET ▲30

abcdefghijklmnopqrstuvwxyz(".;'!*?':,")$1234567890&fiflß-äöüåçèîñóæøœ

ABCDEFGHIJKLMNOPQRSTUVWXYZÄÖÜÅÇÈÎÑÓÆØŒ»„«[•]‹¡·¿› . . .

▷ g j k s u w x y A J K M M N N S U W X Y

Robotik Italic

LET ▲30

abcdefghijklmnopqrstuvwxyz(".;'!?':,")$1234567890&fiflß-äöüåçèîñóæøœ*

ABCDEFGHIJKLMNOPQRSTUVWXYZÄÖÜÅÇÈÎÑÓÆØŒ»„«[•]‹¡·¿› . . .

▷ *g j k s u w x y A J K M M N N S U W X Y*

R

ROCKWELL

Monotype Design Staff • 1934

MCL ADO AGA FAM LIN MAE

abcdefghijklmnopqrstuvwxyz(".;'!*?':,")
$1234567890&fiflß-äöüåçèîñóæøœ
ABCDEFGHIJKLMNOPQRSTUVWXYZ
ÄÖÜÅÇÈÎÑÓÆØŒ»,,«[¶§•†‡]‹¡·¿›...

Rockwell 1 ...

Light abcdefghijklmnopqrstuvwxyzABCDEFGHIJKLMNOPQRSTUVWXYZ–$1234567890
Light Italic *abcdefghijklmnopqrstuvwxyzABCDEFGHIJKLMNOPQRSTUVWXYZ–$1234567890("*
• Regular abcdefghijklmnopqrstuvwxyzABCDEFGHIJKLMNOPQRSTUVWXYZ–$1234567
Italic *abcdefghijklmnopqrstuvwxyzABCDEFGHIJKLMNOPQRSTUVWXYZ–$1234567890*
Bold **abcdefghijklmnopqrstuvwxyzABCDEFGHIJKLMNOPQRSTUVWXYZ–$12**
Bold Italic ***abcdefghijklmnopqrstuvwxyzABCDEFGHIJKLMNOPQRSTUVWXYZ–$12345***

Rockwell 2 ...

Condensed ▲18 abcdefghijklmnopqrstuvwxyzABCDEFGHIJKLMNOPQRSTUVWXYZ–$1234567890(".;'!*?':,"
Bold Condensed ▲18 **abcdefghijklmnopqrstuvwxyzABCDEFGHIJKLMNOPQRSTUVWXYZ–$123**
Extra Bold **abcdefghijklmnopqrstuvwxyzABCDEFGHIJKLMNOPQRSTUV**

ROMAN

Agfa Engravers 1

AGP

ABCDEFGHIJKLMNOPQRSTUVWXYZ(".;'!*?':,")
$1234567890&-ÄÖÜÅÇÈÎÑÓ
ABCDEFGHIJKLMNOPQRSTUVWXYZ
ÄÖÜÅÇÈÎÑÓ»«[•]‹›
▷I V X ST ND RD TH 1/4 1/3 1/2 3/4 D' C R. 'C 'S O' RS. S. & %

Roman ...

Light ABCDEFGHIJKLMNOPQRSTUVWXYZABCDEFGHIJKLMNOPQRS
• Medium ABCDEFGHIJKLMNOPQRSTUVWXYZABCDEFGHIJKLMNOPQRST

SACKERS ROMAN

Agfa Engravers 2

AGP

ABCDEFGHIJKLMNOPQRSTUVWXYZ(".;'!*?':,")
$1234567890&-ÄÖÜÅÇÈÎÑÓ
ABCDEFGHIJKLMNOPQRSTUVWXYZ
ÄÖÜÅÇÈÎÑÓ»«[•]‹›
▷I V X ST ND RD TH 1/4 1/3 1/2 3/4 D' C R. 'C 'S O' RS. S. & %

Sackers Roman ...

• Light ABCDEFGHIJKLMNOPQRSTUVWXYZABCDEFGHIJKLMNOP
Heavy ABCDEFGHIJKLMNOPQRSTUVWXYZABCDEFGHIJKLMNOPQ

R

Agfa Engravers 1: Antique Roman Solid & Slanted, Artisan Roman, Burin Roman & Sans, Classic Roman Light & Regular, Handle Oldstyle, Roman Light & Medium.

Agfa Engravers 2: Sackers Antique Roman Open & Solid, Sackers Light Classic Roman, Sackers English Script, Sackers Gothic Light, Medium & Heavy, Sackers Italian Script, Sackers Roman Light & Heavy, Sackers Square Gothic.

ROMEO

Jill Pichotta & David Berlow • 1991

FBU AGP MTD

▲24

abcdefghijklmnopqrstuvwxyz(".;'!*?':,")$1234567890&fiflß-äöüåçèîñóœæøœ

ABCDEFGHIJKLMNOPQRSTUVWXYZÄÖÜÅÇÈÎÑÓÆØŒ»„«[¶§•†‡]‹¡·¿›...

Romeo ...

Skinny Condensed abcdefghijklmnopqrstuvwxyzABCDEFGHIJKLMNOPQRSTUVWXYZ-$1234567890(".:'!*?':,")&fiflß-äöüÄÖ

• Medium Condensed abcdefghijklmnopqrstuvwxyzABCDEFGHIJKLMNOPQRSTUVWXYZ-$1234567890(".;'

ROMIC

Colin Brignall • 1979

URW AGP LET

abcdefghijklmnopqrstuvwxyz(".;'!*?':,")

$1234567890&fiflß-äöüåçèîñóæøœ

ABCDEFGHIJKLMNOPQRSTUVWXYZ

ÄÖÜÅÇÈÎÑÓÆØŒ»„«[¶§•†‡]‹¡·¿›...

Romic ...

Light abcdefghijklmnopqrstuvwxyzABCDEFGHIJKLMNOPQRSTUVWXYZ-$1234567890(".;

Light Italic *abcdefghijklmnopqrstuvwxyzABCDEFGHIJKLMNOPQRSTUVWXYZ-$1234567890("*

• Medium abcdefghijklmnopqrstuvwxyzABCDEFGHIJKLMNOPQRSTUVWXYZ-$1234567890("

Bold **abcdefghijklmnopqrstuvwxyzABCDEFGHIJKLMNOPQRSTUVWXYZ-$1234567890**

Extra Bold **abcdefghijklmnopqrstuvwxyzABCDEFGHIJKLMNOPQRSTUVWXYZ-$12345678**

ROSEWOOD

Adobe Wood Type 3

Kim Buker Chansler & Carl Crossgrove • 1994

ADO AGA MAE

▲30

ABCDEFGHIJKLMNOPQRSTUVWXYZ

(".;'!*?':,")$1234567890

&-ÄÖÜÅÇÈÎÑÓÆØŒ»„«[•]‹¡·¿›...

Rosewood ...

Fill ABCDEFGHIJKLMNOPQRSTUVWXYZ-$1

• Regular ABCDEFGHIJKLMNOPQRSTUVWXYZ-$1

R

Adobe Wood Type 3: Pepperwood Regular, Fill & Outline, Rosewood Regular & Fill, Zebrawood Regular & Fill.

ROTATION

Arthur Ritzel • 1971 abcdefghijklmnopqrstuvwxyz(".;'!*?':,")

LIN ADO AGA MAE $1234567890&fiflß-äöüåçèîñóæøœ
ABCDEFGHIJKLMNOPQRSTUVWXYZ
ÄÖÜÅÇÈÎÑÓÆØŒ»„«[¶§•†‡]‹¡·¿›…

Rotation …

• Roman abcdefghijklmnopqrstuvwxyzABCDEFGHIJKLMNOPQRSTUVWXYZ–$12345

Italic *abcdefghijklmnopqrstuvwxyzABCDEFGHIJKLMNOPQRSTUVWXYZ–$12345*

Bold **abcdefghijklmnopqrstuvwxyzABCDEFGHIJKLMNOPQRSTUVWXYZ–$12345**

AGFA ROTIS SANS SERIF

Otl Aicher • 1989 abcdefghijklmnopqrstuvwxyz(".;'!*?':,")

AGP ADO AGA LIN MAE $1234567890&fiflß-äöüåçèîñóæøœ
ABCDEFGHIJKLMNOPQRSTUVWXYZ
ÄÖÜÅÇÈÎÑÓÆØŒ»„«[¶§•†‡]‹¡·¿›…

Agfa Rotis Sans Serif …

45-Light abcdefghijklmnopqrstuvwxyzABCDEFGHIJKLMNOPQRSTUVWXYZ–$1234567890(".;'!*?':,")&fiflß

46-Light Italic *abcdefghijklmnopqrstuvwxyzABCDEFGHIJKLMNOPQRSTUVWXYZ–$1234567890(".;'!*?':,")&fiflß*

• 55-Regular abcdefghijklmnopqrstuvwxyzABCDEFGHIJKLMNOPQRSTUVWXYZ–$1234567890(".;'!*?':,")&

56-Italic *abcdefghijklmnopqrstuvwxyzABCDEFGHIJKLMNOPQRSTUVWXYZ–$1234567890(".;'!*?':,")&fi*

65-Bold **abcdefghijklmnopqrstuvwxyzABCDEFGHIJKLMNOPQRSTUVWXYZ–$1234567890(".;'!*?':**

75-Extra Bold **abcdefghijklmnopqrstuvwxyzABCDEFGHIJKLMNOPQRSTUVWXYZ–$1234567890(".;'!***

AGFA ROTIS SEMISANS

AGP ADO AGA LIN MAE abcdefghijklmnopqrstuvwxyz(".;'!*?':,")
$1234567890&fiflß-äöüåçèîñóæøœ
ABCDEFGHIJKLMNOPQRSTUVWXYZ
ÄÖÜÅÇÈÎÑÓÆØŒ»„«[¶§•†‡]‹¡·¿›…

R

Agfa Rotis Semisans …

45-Light abcdefghijklmnopqrstuvwxyzABCDEFGHIJKLMNOPQRSTUVWXYZ–$1234567890(".;'!*?':,")&fiflß

46-Light Italic *abcdefghijklmnopqrstuvwxyzABCDEFGHIJKLMNOPQRSTUVWXYZ–$1234567890(".;'!*?':,")&fiflß*

• 55-Regular abcdefghijklmnopqrstuvwxyzABCDEFGHIJKLMNOPQRSTUVWXYZ–$1234567890(".;'!*?':,")&

56-Italic *abcdefghijklmnopqrstuvwxyzABCDEFGHIJKLMNOPQRSTUVWXYZ–$1234567890(".;'!*?':,")*

65-Bold **abcdefghijklmnopqrstuvwxyzABCDEFGHIJKLMNOPQRSTUVWXYZ–$1234567890(".;'!*?'**

75-Extra Bold **abcdefghijklmnopqrstuvwxyzABCDEFGHIJKLMNOPQRSTUVWXYZ–$1234567890(".;'!**

AGFA ROTIS SERIF & SEMISERIF

AGP ADO AGA LIN MAE abcdefghijklmnopqrstuvwxyz(".;'!*?':,")
$1234567890&fiflß-äöüåçèîñóæøœ
ABCDEFGHIJKLMNOPQRSTUVWXYZ
ÄÖÜÅÇÈÎÑÓÆØŒ»„«[¶§•†‡]‹¡·¿›...

Agfa Rotis Serif & Semiserif ...

• Serif, 55-Roman abcdefghijklmnopqrstuvwxyzABCDEFGHIJKLMNOPQRSTUVWXYZ–$1234567890(".;

Serif, 56-Italic *abcdefghijklmnopqrstuvwxyzABCDEFGHIJKLMNOPQRSTUVWXYZ–$1234567890(".*

Serif, 65-Bold **abcdefghijklmnopqrstuvwxyzABCDEFGHIJKLMNOPQRSTUVWXYZ–$1234567890**

Semiserif, 55-Regular abcdefghijklmnopqrstuvwxyzABCDEFGHIJKLMNOPQRSTUVWXYZ–$1234567890(".;'!*?'

Semiserif, 65-Bold **abcdefghijklmnopqrstuvwxyzABCDEFGHIJKLMNOPQRSTUVWXYZ–$1234567890(".**

Roughedge

✍ *Robert J. Howell • 1994* abcdefghijklmnopqrstuvwxyz(.;!*?:,)$1234567890

RJH ▲16 ¢-ABCDEFGHIJKLMNOPQRSTUVWXYZ[]

ROUNDY

❖ *Linotype DisplaySet 4*

LIN abcdefghijklmnopqrstuvwxyz(".;'!*?':,")
$1234567890&fiflß-äöüåçèîñóæøœ
ABCDEFGHIJKLMNOPQRSTUVWXYZ
ÄÖÜÅÇÈÎÑÓÆØŒ»„«[¶§•†‡]‹¡·¿›...

Roundy ...

• Regular abcdefghijklmnopqrstuvwxyzABCDEFGHIJKLMNOPQRSTUVWXYZ–$12

Swash Capitals ABCDEFGHIJKLMNOPQRSTUVWXYZÆŒ

TF ROUX

✍ *Joseph Treacy • 1973* **abcdefghijklmnopqrstuvwxyz(".;'!*?':,")**

TRE MTD ▲22 **$1234567890&fiflß-äöüåçèîñóæøœ**
ABCDEFGHIJKLMNOPQRSTUVWXYZ
ÄÖÜÅÇÈÎÑÓÆØŒ»„«[¶§•†‡]‹¡·¿›... ▷ **123579/23**

❦ TF Roux ...

Shaded abcdefghijklmnopqrstuvwxyzABCDEFG

• Extra Bold **abcdefghijklmnopqrstuvwxyzABCDEFGHIJ**

R

❖ *Linotype DisplaySet 4*: Madame Letters, Numericals & Accents, Roundy Regular & Swash Capitals.
❦ TF Roux ▶ TF Roux Borders.

Roxy

Martin Wait • 1993
LET
▲16

ABCDEFGHIJKLMNOPQRSTUVWXYZ(“.;‘!*?’:,”)
$1234567890&-ÄÖÜÅÇÈÎÑÓÆØŒ»„«[•]‹¡·¿›…

Ru'ach

Tim Donaldson • 1990
LET
▲16

abcdefghijklmnopqrstuvwxyz(“.;‘!*?’:,”)
$1234567890&fifl߬-äöüåçèîñóæøœ
ABCDEFGHIJKLMNOPQRSTUVWXYZ
ÄÖÜÅÇÈÎÑÓÆØŒ»„«[•]‹¡·¿›…

▷ adiqsHK

Rubaya Inline

Andy Hullinger • 1993
T26
▲54

ABCDEFGHIJKLMNOP
QRSTUVWXYZ".;'!':,"

Rubber Stamp

Alan R. Birch • 1983
LET
▲28

ABCDEFGHIJKLMNOPQRSTUVWXYZ
(“.;‘!*?’:,”)$1234567890
&-ÄÖÜÅÇÈÎÑÓÆØŒ»„«[•]‹¡·¿›…

Ruling Script
Calligraphy for Print

Gottfried Pott • 1992
LIN ADO AGA MAE
▲30

abcdefghijklmnopqrstuvwxyz(“.;‘!*?’:,”)
1234567890&ß-äöüåçèîñó
ABCDEFGHIJKLMNOPQRSTUVWXYZ
ÄÖÜÅÇÈÎÑÓ „•‹›

Ruling Script Additions

$fiflæøœÆØŒ»«[¶§†‡]¡·¿…

Rumble

INT
▲24

ABCDEFGHIJKLMNOPQRSTUVWXYZ
“.;‘!?’:,”1234567890&-

Calligraphy for Print: Ruling Script, Sho, Wiesbaden Swing.

Rundfunk

✍ Letraset Design Staff • 1987
... Adolf Behrmann, 1928

LET

▲30

abcdefghijklmnopqrstuvwxyz(".;'!*?':,")$1234567890&fiflß-äöü
åçèîñóæøœABCDEFGHIJKLMNOPQRSTUVWXYZÄÖÜÅÇÈÎÑÓÆØŒ
»„«[•]‹¡·¿›...

▷ w A B K W

Monotype Runic Condensed
Monotype Headliners 5

MCL ADO AGA LIN MAE

▲30

abcdefghijklmnopqrstuvwxyz(".;'!*?':,")$1234567890&fiflß-äöüåçèîñóæøœ
ABCDEFGHIJKLMNOPQRSTUVWXYZÄÖÜÅÇÈÎÑÓÆØŒ»„«[•]‹¡·¿›...

A*I RUSSELL OBLIQUE

✍ K. A. • 1994

ALP

abcdefghijklmnopqrstuvwxyz(".;'!*?':,")
$1234567890&fiflß-äöüåçèîñóæøœ
ABCDEFGHIJKLMNOPQRSTUVWXYZ
ÄÖÜÅÇÈÎÑÓÆØŒ»„«[¶§•†‡]‹¡·¿›...

A*I Russell Oblique ...

• Regular abcdefghijklmnopqrstuvwxyzABCDEFGHIJKLMNOPQRSTUVWXYZ-$1234567890(".;'!*?':,")&

Informal abcdefghijklmnopqrstuvwxyzABCDEFGHIJKLMNOPQRSTUVWXYZ-$1234567890(".;'!*?':,")&fifl

RUSSELL SQUARE

✍ John Russell • 1972

LIN ADO AGA MAE

▲16

abcdefghijklmnopqrstuvwxyz(".;'!*?':,")
$1234567890&fiflß-äöüåçèîñóæøœ
ABCDEFGHIJKLMNOPQRSTUVWXYZ
ÄÖÜÅÇÈÎÑÓÆØŒ»„«[¶§•†‡]‹¡·¿›...

Russell Square ...

• Regular abcdefghijklmnopqrstuvwxyzABCDEFGHIJKLMNOPQRSTUVWXYZ–$

Oblique *abcdefghijklmnopqrstuvwxyzABCDEFGHIJKLMNOPQRSTUVWXYZ–$*

Rusticana
Type Before Gutenberg 3

✍ Adrian Frutiger • 1992

LIN ADO AGA MAE

▲24

ABCDEFGHIJKLMNOPQRSTUVWXYZ
(".;'!*?':,")$1234567890
&-ÄÖÜÅÇÈÎÑÓÆØŒ»„«[•]‹¡·¿›...

Monotype Headliners 5: Monotype Bernhard Condensed, Compacta Bold, Neographik, Monotype Runic Condensed.
Type Before Gutenberg 3: Notre Dame, Notre Dame Ornaments, Pompeijana, Pompeijana Borders, Rusticana, Rusticana Borders.
Rusticana ▶ Rusticana Borders.

R

RUZICKA FREEHAND

Alex Chaisson & Mark Altman • 1993 (Rudolph Ruzicka, 1939)

abcdefghijklmnopqrstuvwxyz(“.;‘!*?’:,”)
$1234567890&fiflß-äöüåçèîñóæøœ

LIN ADO AGA MAE ABCDEFGHIJKLMNOPQRSTUVWXYZ
▲16 ÄÖÜÅÇÈÎÑÓÆØŒ»„«[¶§•†‡]‹¡·¿›...

Ruzicka Freehand ...

• Regular abcdefghijklmnopqrstuvwxyzABCDEFGHIJKLMNOPQRSTUVWXYZ–$1234567890(“.;‘!*?

Regular SCOSF ABCDEFGHIJKLMNOPQRSTUVWXYZABCDEFGHIJKLMNOPQRSTUVWXYZ–$1234567890(“.;‘!*

Bold abcdefghijklmnopqrstuvwxyzABCDEFGHIJKLMNOPQRSTUVWXYZ–$1234567890(“.

Bold SCOSF ABCDEFGHIJKLMNOPQRSTUVWXYZABCDEFGHIJKLMNOPQRSTUVWXYZ–$1234567890(

R

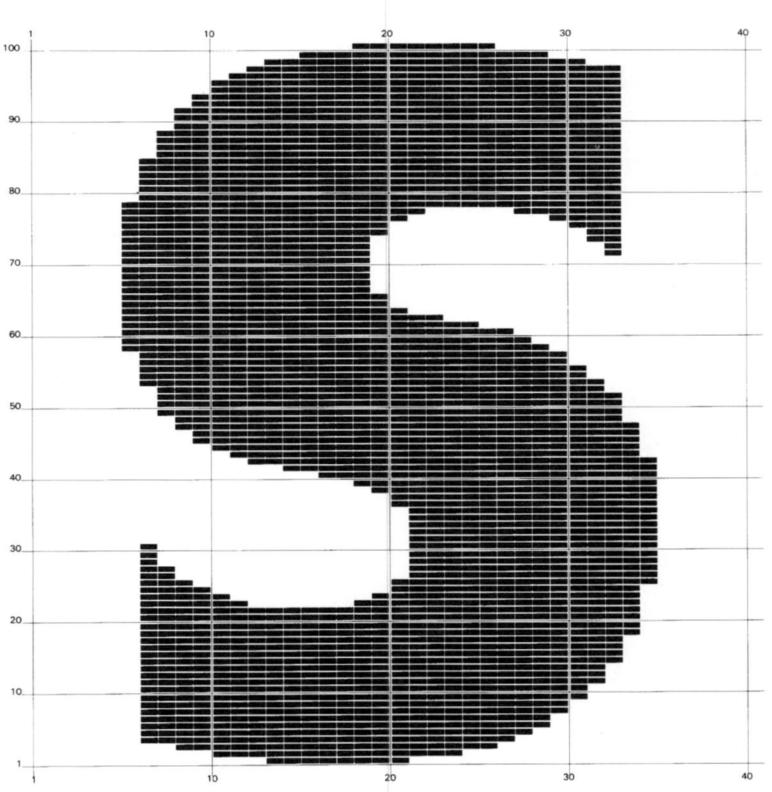
1
10
20
30
40
100
90
80
70
60
50
40
30
20
10
1
1
10
20
30
40

✍ Ladislav Mandel, 1984

SABON

Jan Tschichold • 1964 abcdefghijklmnopqrstuvwxyz(“.;‘!*?’:,”)
LIN ADO AGA MAE $1234567890&fiflß-äöüåçèîñóæøœ
ABCDEFGHIJKLMNOPQRSTUVWXYZ
ÄÖÜÅÇÈÎÑÓÆØŒ»„«[¶§•†‡]‹¡·¿›…

Sabon …

• Roman abcdefghijklmnopqrstuvwxyzABCDEFGHIJKLMNOPQRSTUVWXYZ–$123456
Italic *abcdefghijklmnopqrstuvwxyzABCDEFGHIJKLMNOPQRSTUVWXYZ–$12345*
Bold **abcdefghijklmnopqrstuvwxyzABCDEFGHIJKLMNOPQRSTUVWXYZ–$123456**
Bold Italic ***abcdefghijklmnopqrstuvwxyzABCDEFGHIJKLMNOPQRSTUVWXYZ–$123456***

SABON SCOSF

LIN ADO AGA MAE ABCDEFGHIJKLMNOPQRSTUVWXYZ(“.;‘!*?’:,”)
$1234567890&-ÄÖÜÅÇÈÎÑÓÆØŒ
ABCDEFGHIJKLMNOPQRSTUVWXYZ
ÄÖÜÅÇÈÎÑÓÆØŒ»„«[¶§•†‡]‹¡·¿›…

Sabon SCOSF …

• Roman SCOSF ABCDEFGHIJKLMNOPQRSTUVWXYZABCDEFGHIJKLMNOPQRSTUVWXYZ–$123
Italic OSF *abcdefghijklmnopqrstuvwxyzABCDEFGHIJKLMNOPQRSTUVWXYZ–$12345*
Bold OSF **abcdefghijklmnopqrstuvwxyzABCDEFGHIJKLMNOPQRSTUVWXYZ–$123456**
Bold Italic OSF ***abcdefghijklmnopqrstuvwxyzABCDEFGHIJKLMNOPQRSTUVWXYZ–$123456***

SAGINAW

HEA abcdefghijklmnopqrstuvwxyz(“.;‘!*?’:,”)
▲12 $1234567890&ß-äöüåçèîñóø
ABCDEFGHIJKLMNOPQRSTUVWXYZ
ÄÖÜÅÇÈÎÑÓØ„‹¡¿›… ▷ emnrsalamarataxchclcrchelemen eresetexfffffiilimininitixknllolomonooorос

Saginaw …

Light abcdefghijklmnopqrstuvwxyzABCDEFGHIJKLMNOPQRSTUVWXYZ–
• Medium abcdefghijklmnopqrstuvwxyzABCDEFGHIJKLMNOPQRSTUVWXYZ
Bold **abcdefghijklmnopqrstuvwxyzABCDEFGHIJKLMNOPQRSTUVWXY**

SAM SANS

John Downer • 1993 abcdefghijklmnopqrstuvwxyz(“.;‘!*?’:,”)
FBU $1234567890&fiflß-äöüåçèîñóæøœ
▲18 ABCDEFGHIJKLMNOPQRSTUVWXYZ
ÄÖÜÅÇÈÎÑÓÆØŒ»„«[¶§·†‡]‹¡·¿›… ▷ ff ffi ffl

Sam Sans …

• Thin abcdefghijklmnopqrstuvwxyzABCDEFGHIJKLMNOPQRSTUVWXYZ–$1234567890(“.;‘!*?’:,”

... Sam Sans

Bold abcdefghijklmnopqrstuvwxyzABCDEFGHIJKLMNOPQRSTUVWXYZ–$1234567890(".;

San Marco
✣ *Type Before Gutenberg 2*
Karlgeorg Hoefer • 1990
LIN ADO AGA MAE
▲16

abcdefghijklmnopqrstuvwxyz(".;'!*?':,")
$1234567890&fiflß-äöüåçèîñóæøœ
ABCDEFGHIJKLMNOPQRSTUVWXYZ
ÄÖÜÅÇÈÎÑÓÆØŒ»„«[¶§•†‡]‹¡·¿›... ▷ ch ck ff ft ll ſs ſi ſſ ß – äöüÄÖÜ

Santa Fe
David Quay • 1983
LET
▲18

abcdefghijklmnopqrstuvwxyz(".;'!*?':,")
$1234567890&fiflß-äöüåçèîñóæøœ
ABCDEFGHIJKLMNOPQRSTUVWXYZÇ»„«[•]‹¡·¿›...
▷ abcdefhhhiklmnoopprsstuvwxyzex L J St

SANVITO MULTIPLE-MASTER
(two axes: weight & optical size)
Robert Slimbach • 1993
ADO AGA MAE
▲16

abcdefghijklmnopqrstuvwxyz(".;'!*?':,")
$1234567890&fiflß-äöüåçèîñóæøœ
ABCDEFGHIJKLMNOPQRSTUVWXYZ
ÄÖÜÅÇÈÎÑÓÆØŒ»„«[¶§·†‡]‹¡·¿›...

Sanvito MultipleMaster ...
: 12-point optical size

Light abcdefghijklmnopqrstuvwxyzABCDEFGHIJKLMNOPQRSTUVWXYZ–$1234567890(".;'!*?':,"
• Regular abcdefghijklmnopqrstuvwxyzABCDEFGHIJKLMNOPQRSTUVWXYZ–$1234567890(".;'!
Semibold **abcdefghijklmnopqrstuvwxyzABCDEFGHIJKLMNOPQRSTUVWXYZ–$1234567890(**
Bold **abcdefghijklmnopqrstuvwxyzABCDEFGHIJKLMNOPQRSTUVWXYZ–$12345678**

▲36 abcdefghijklmnopqrstuvwxyz(".;'!*?':,")
$1234567890&fiflß-äöüåçèîñóæøœ
ABCDEFGHIJKLMNOPQRSTUVWXYZ
ÄÖÜÅÇÈÎÑÓÆØŒ»„«[¶§·†‡]‹¡·¿›...

Sanvito MultipleMaster
: 72-point optical size ...

Light abcdefghijklmnopqrstuvwxyzABCDEFGHIJK

S

✣ *Type Before Gutenberg 2*: Carolina, Clairvaux, San Marco.

. . . Sanvito MultipleMaster
: 72-point optical size
• Regular
abcdefghijklmnopqrstuvwxyzABCDEFGHI

Semibold
abcdefghijklmnopqrstuvwxyzABCDEFG

Bold
abcdefghijklmnopqrstuvwxyzABCDEF

Sassoon Primary

Rosemary Sassoon • 1990
ADO AGA LIN MAE

abcdefghijklmnopqrstuvwxyz(“.;‘!*?’:,”)
$1234567890&ﬁﬂß-äöüåçèîñóæøœ
ABCDEFGHIJKLMNOPQRSTUVWXYZ
ÄÖÜÅÇÈÎÑÓÆØŒ»„«[¶§•†‡]‹¡·¿›…

Savoye

Alan Meeks • 1992
LET
▲18

abcdefghijklmnopqrstuvwxyz(“.;‘!*?’:,”)
$1234567890&ﬁﬂß-äöüåçèîñóæøœ
ABCDEFGHIJKLMNOPQRSTUVWXYZÇ»„«[·]‹¡·¿›…

SCAMP

Denise Schmidt • 1992
FBU AGP MTD
▲36

ABCDEFGHIJKLMNOPQRSTUVWXYZ(“.;‘!*?’:,”)$1234567890
&-ÄÖÜÅÇÉÎÑÓÆØŒABCDEFGHIJKLMNOPQRSTUVWXYZ
ÄÖÜÅÇÈÎÑÓÆØŒ»„«[¶§-†‡]‹¡·¿›…

Scamp . . .
• Regular
ABCDEFGHIJKLMNOPQRSTUVWXYZABCDEFGHIJKLMNOPQRSTUVWX

Fat
ABCDEFGHIJKLMNOPQRSTUVWXYZABCDEFGHIJKLMNOPQR

Bold Inline
ABCDEFGHIJKLMNOPQRSTUVWXYZABCDEFGHIJKLMNOPQRSTUVWX

SCHADOW

Georg Trump • 1938
BIT

abcdefghijklmnopqrstuvwxyz(".;'!*?':,")
$1234567890&ﬁﬂß-äöüåçèîñóæøœ
ABCDEFGHIJKLMNOPQRSTUVWXYZ
ÄÖÜÅÇÈÎÑÓÆØŒ»„«[¶§•†‡]‹¡·¿›…

S

. . . Schadow . . .

Light abcdefghijklmnopqrstuvwxyzABCDEFGHIJKLMNOPQRSTUVWXYZ–$1234
Light Cursive *abcdefghijklmnopqrstuvwxyzABCDEFGHIJKLMNOPQRSTUVWXYZ–$123456789*
• Roman abcdefghijklmnopqrstuvwxyzABCDEFGHIJKLMNOPQRSTUVWXYZ–$1234567890(".;
Bold **abcdefghijklmnopqrstuvwxyzABCDEFGHIJKLMNOPQRSTUVWXYZ–$1**
Black **abcdefghijklmnopqrstuvwxyzABCDEFGHIJKLMNOPQRSTUVWXYZ–$1**
Black Condensed ▲18 **abcdefghijklmnopqrstuvwxyzABCDEFGHIJKLMNOPQRSTUVWXYZ–$1234567890("**

STEMPEL SCHNEIDLER

Friedrich Hermann Ernst Schneidler • . . .
LIN ADO AGA MAE

abcdefghijklmnopqrstuvwxyz(".;'!*¿':,")
$1234567890&fiflß-äöüåçèîñóæøœ
ABCDEFGHIJKLMNOPQRSTUVWXYZ
ÄÖÜÅÇÈÎÑÓÆØŒ»„«[¶§•†‡]‹¡·¿›. . .

Stempel Schneidler . . .

Light abcdefghijklmnopqrstuvwxyzABCDEFGHIJKLMNOPQRSTUVWXYZ–$123456789
Light Italic *abcdefghijklmnopqrstuvwxyzABCDEFGHIJKLMNOPQRSTUVWXYZ–$1234567890(".;'!*
• Roman abcdefghijklmnopqrstuvwxyzABCDEFGHIJKLMNOPQRSTUVWXYZ–$12345678
Italic *abcdefghijklmnopqrstuvwxyzABCDEFGHIJKLMNOPQRSTUVWXYZ–$1234567890("*
Medium abcdefghijklmnopqrstuvwxyzABCDEFGHIJKLMNOPQRSTUVWXYZ–$12345
Medium Italic *abcdefghijklmnopqrstuvwxyzABCDEFGHIJKLMNOPQRSTUVWXYZ–$12345678*
Bold **abcdefghijklmnopqrstuvwxyzABCDEFGHIJKLMNOPQRSTUVWXYZ–$12**
Bold Italic ***abcdefghijklmnopqrstuvwxyzABCDEFGHIJKLMNOPQRSTUVWXYZ–$12345***
Black **abcdefghijklmnopqrstuvwxyzABCDEFGHIJKLMNOPQRSTUVWXYZ–**
Black Italic ***abcdefghijklmnopqrstuvwxyzABCDEFGHIJKLMNOPQRSTUVWXYZ–$12***

π Σ Scorpio

Jim Marcus • 1993
T26
▲24

ABCDEFGHIJKLMNOPQRSTUVWXYZ(".;'!*?':,")
$1234567890&ß-ÄÖÜÅÇÈÎÑÓÆØŒ»„«[¶§•†‡]‹¡·¿›. . .

S

MONOTYPE SCOTCH ROMAN
✥ *Monotype TextSet 1*
Monotype Design Staff • 1907
. . . *Richard Austin, c. 1813*
MCL ADO AGA LIN MAE

abcdefghijklmnopqrstuvwxyz(".;'!*?':,")
$1234567890&fiflß-äöüåçèîñóæøœ
ABCDEFGHIJKLMNOPQRSTUVWXYZ
ÄÖÜÅÇÈÎÑÓÆØŒ»„«[¶§•†‡]‹¡·¿›. . .

Monotype Scotch Roman . . .

• Regular abcdefghijklmnopqrstuvwxyzABCDEFGHIJKLMNOPQRSTUVWXYZ–$1234
Italic *abcdefghijklmnopqrstuvwxyzABCDEFGHIJKLMNOPQRSTUVWXYZ–$1234567*

. . .
π Scorpio ▶Scorpio Dingbats.
Σ Scorpio ▶Scorpio Tribal.
✥ *Monotype TextSet 1*: Monotype Goudy Modern Roman & Italic, Monotype Scotch Roman Regular & Italic.

Scotty

Scott Smith • 1993
T26
▲16

abcdefghijklmnopqrstuvwxyz(".;'!*?':,")
$1234567890&fifl-äöüåêîñõ
ABCDEFGHIJKLMNOPQRSTUVWXYZ
ÄÖÜÅÊÎÑ»«[·?]‹›...

Scratch

Greg Samata • 1993
T26
▲24

abcdefghijklmnopqrstuvwxyz.;!?:,$1234567890
&-ABCDEFGHIJKLMNOPQRSTUVWXYZ

Scrawl

Todd Brei • 1993
T26
▲16

abcdefghijklmnopqrstuvwxyz(".;'!*?':,")
$1234567890&fiflß-äöüåçèîñóæøœ
ABCDEFGHIJKLMNOPQRSTUVWXYZ
ÄÖÜÅÇÈÎÑÓÆØŒ»„«[¶§•†‡]›¡·¿‹...

Scriba

Martin Wait • 1992
LET
▲30

ABCDEFGHIJKLMNOPQRSTUVWXYZ
(".;'!*?':,")$1234567890
&-ÄÖÜÅÇÈÎÑÓÆØŒ»„«[•]‹¡·¿›...

Script 12-Pitch

John Schappler • c. 1964
BIT
▲12

abcdefghijklmnopqrstuvwxyz(".;'!*?':,")
$1234567890&fiflß-äöüåçèîñóæœ
ABCDEFGHIJKLMNOPQRSTUVWXYZ
ÄÖÜÅÇÈÎÑÓÆØŒ»„«[¶§·†‡]‹¡·¿›...

Scriptek

David Quay • 1992
LET
▲18

abcdefghijklmnopqrstuvwxyz(".;'!*?':,")
$1234567890&fiflß-äöüåçèîñóæøœ
ABCDEFGHIJKLMNOPQRSTUVWXYZ
ÄÖÜÅÇÈÎÑÓÆØŒ»„«[·]‹¡·¿›...

S

Scriptek Italic

LET abcdefghijklmnopqrstuvwxyz(".;'!*?';,")
▲18 $1234567890&fifl ß-äöüåçèîñóæøœ
ABCDEFGHIJKLMNOPQRSTUVWXYZ
ÄÖÜÅÇÈÎÑÓÆØŒ»„«[·]‹i·¿›...

SEAGULL

Adrian Williams • 1978 abcdefghijklmnopqrstuvwxyz(".;'!*?';,")
BIT $1234567890&fifl ß-äöüåçèîñóæøœ
ABCDEFGHIJKLMNOPQRSTUVWXYZ
ÄÖÜÅÇÈÎÑÓÆØŒ»„«[¶§•†‡]‹i·¿›...

Seagull ...

Light abcdefghijklmnopqrstuvwxyzABCDEFGHIJKLMNOPQRSTUVWXYZ–$1234567890(".;'
• Regular abcdefghijklmnopqrstuvwxyzABCDEFGHIJKLMNOPQRSTUVWXYZ–$1234567890(
Bold **abcdefghijklmnopqrstuvwxyzABCDEFGHIJKLMNOPQRSTUVWXYZ–$12345678**
Heavy **abcdefghijklmnopqrstuvwxyzABCDEFGHIJKLMNOPQRSTUVWXYZ–$123456**

HF SECEDE

Gregory La Vardera • 1993 (Otto Wagner, c. 1900) abcdefghijklmnopqrstuvwxyz(".;'!*?';,")
HAN MTD $1234567890&-fifl ß-äöüåçèîñóæøœ
▲16 ABCDEFGHIJKLMNOPQRSTUVWXYZ
ÄÖÜÅÇÈÎÑÓÆØŒ[·]i¿ ▷g ff ffi ffl fr ft A J M LA LE LO TH TT

HF Secede ...

• Block abcdefghijklmnopqrstuvwxyzABCDEFGHIJKLMNOPQRSTUVWXYZ–$1234567890("
Outline abcdefghijklmnopqrstuvwxyzABCDEFGHIJKLMNOPQRSTUVWXYZ–$1234567890("
Heavy Outline abcdefghijklmnopqrstuvwxyzABCDEFGHIJKLMNOPQRSTUVWXYZ–$1234567890("

S

ITC SERIF GOTHIC

Herb Lubalin & Antonio DiSpigna • 1974 abcdefghijklmnopqrstuvwxyz(".;'!*?';,")
BIT ADO AGA LEF FAM FRA LIN MAE $1234567890&fifl ß-äöüåçèîñóæøœ
ABCDEFGHIJKLMNOPQRSTUVWXYZ
ÄÖÜÅÇÈÎÑÓÆØŒ»„«[¶§•†‡]‹i·¿›...

ITC Serif Gothic ...

Light abcdefghijklmnopqrstuvwxyzABCDEFGHIJKLMNOPQRSTUVWXYZ–$1234567890(".;
• Regular abcdefghijklmnopqrstuvwxyzABCDEFGHIJKLMNOPQRSTUVWXYZ–$1234567890(
Bold **abcdefghijklmnopqrstuvwxyzABCDEFGHIJKLMNOPQRSTUVWXYZ–$1234567890**
Extra Bold **abcdefghijklmnopqrstuvwxyzABCDEFGHIJKLMNOPQRSTUVWXYZ–$123456789**
Heavy **abcdefghijklmnopqrstuvwxyzABCDEFGHIJKLMNOPQRSTUVWXYZ–$12345678**

... ITC Serif Gothic

Black ▲16 abcdefghijklmnopqrstuvwxyzABCDEFGHIJKLMNOPQRSTUVWXYZ

Bold Outline ▲18 abcdefghijklmnopqrstuvwxyzABCDEFGHIJKLMNOPQRSTUVW

SERIFA

Adrian Frutiger • 1967

LIN ADO AGA BIT FAM FRA MAE URW

abcdefghijklmnopqrstuvwxyz(".;'!*?':,")
$1234567890&fiflß-äöüåçèîñóæøœ
ABCDEFGHIJKLMNOPQRSTUVWXYZ
ÄÖÜÅÇÈÎÑÓÆØŒ»„«[¶§•†‡]‹¡·¿›...

Serifa ...

45-Light abcdefghijklmnopqrstuvwxyzABCDEFGHIJKLMNOPQRSTUVWXYZ–$1234567890(

46-Light Italic *abcdefghijklmnopqrstuvwxyzABCDEFGHIJKLMNOPQRSTUVWXYZ–$1234567890(*

• 55-Roman abcdefghijklmnopqrstuvwxyzABCDEFGHIJKLMNOPQRSTUVWXYZ–$1234

56-Italic *abcdefghijklmnopqrstuvwxyzABCDEFGHIJKLMNOPQRSTUVWXYZ–$1234*

65-Bold **abcdefghijklmnopqrstuvwxyzABCDEFGHIJKLMNOPQRSTUVWXYZ–$12**

75-Black **abcdefghijklmnopqrstuvwxyzABCDEFGHIJKLMNOPQRSTUVWXYZ–$**

Serlio

Linotype Engravers Set 1

LIN ADO AGA MAE

▲18

ABCDEFGHIJKLMNOPQRSTUVWXYZ(".;'!*?':,")
$1234567890&-ÄÖÜÅÇÈÎÑÓÆØŒ
ABCDEFGHIJKLMNOPQRSTUVWXYZ
ÄÖÜÅÇÈÎÑÓÆØŒ»„«[¶§•†‡]‹¡·¿›...

SERPENTINE

LIN ADO AGA MAE URW

abcdefghijklmnopqrstuvwxyz(".;'!*?':,")
$1234567890&fiflß-äöüåçèîñóæøœ
ABCDEFGHIJKLMNOPQRSTUVWXYZ
ÄÖÜÅÇÈÎÑÓÆØŒ»„«[¶§•†‡]‹¡·¿›...

Serpentine ...

Light abcdefghijklmnopqrstuvwxyzABCDEFGHIJKLMNOPQRSTUVWXYZ–$1234567

Light Oblique *abcdefghijklmnopqrstuvwxyzABCDEFGHIJKLMNOPQRSTUVWXYZ–$1234567*

• Medium **abcdefghijklmnopqrstuvwxyzABCDEFGHIJKLMNOPQRSTUVWXYZ–$12**

Medium Oblique ***abcdefghijklmnopqrstuvwxyzABCDEFGHIJKLMNOPQRSTUVWXYZ–$12***

Bold **abcdefghijklmnopqrstuvwxyzABCDEFGHIJKLMNOPQRSTUVWXY**

Bold Oblique ***abcdefghijklmnopqrstuvwxyzABCDEFGHIJKLMNOPQRSTUVWXY***

Linotype Engravers Set 1: Engravers Bold Face, Serlio.

Shaman

Phill Grimshaw • 1994

LET

▲24

ABCDEFGHIJKLMNOPQRSTUVWXYZ

("".;'!*?':,"")$1234567890

&-ÄÖÜÅÇÈÎÑÓÆØŒ»„«[•]‹¡·¿›...

▷

SHANNON

Kris Holmes & Janice Prescott • 1982

AGP ADO AGA LIN MAE

abcdefghijklmnopqrstuvwxyz(".;'!*?':,")
$1234567890&fiflß-äöüåçèîñóæøœ
ABCDEFGHIJKLMNOPQRSTUVWXYZ
ÄÖÜÅÇÈÎÑÓÆØŒ»„«[¶§•†‡]‹¡·¿›...

Shannon ...

• Book abcdefghijklmnopqrstuvwxyzABCDEFGHIJKLMNOPQRSTUVWXYZ–$1234567890("

Book Oblique *abcdefghijklmnopqrstuvwxyzABCDEFGHIJKLMNOPQRSTUVWXYZ–$1234567890(".;'!*?'*

Bold **abcdefghijklmnopqrstuvwxyzABCDEFGHIJKLMNOPQRSTUVWXYZ–$123456**

Extra Bold **abcdefghijklmnopqrstuvwxyzABCDEFGHIJKLMNOPQRSTUVWXYZ–$123**

SHANNON PREMIER

AGP ABCDEFGHIJKLMNOPQRSTUVWXYZ.;!?:,
1234567890&ff fi fl ffi ffl –ÄÖÜÅÇÈÎÑÓÆØŒ
(abdeilmnorst) ⅛ ¼ ⅓ ⅜ ½ ⅝ ⅔ ¾ ⅞ $12345/67890¢ ₡Rp

Shannon Premier ...

• Premier Book ABCDEFGHIJKLMNOPQRSTUVWXYZ–$1234567890.;!?:,&-ff fi fl ffi ffl ⅛ ¼ ⅓ ⅜ ½ $12345/67890¢

Premier Book Oblique *$1234567890.;:,–ff fi fl ffi ffl ⅛ ¼ ⅓ ⅜ ½ $12345/67890¢ (abdeilmnorst) ⅝ ⅔ ¾ ⅞ ₡Rp*

Premier Bold **$1234567890.;:,–ff fi fl ffi ffl ⅛ ¼ ⅓ ⅜ ½ $12345/67890¢ (abdeilmnorst) ⅝ ⅔ ¾ ⅞ ₡Rp**

Premier Extra Bold **$1234567890.;:,–ff fi fl ffi ffl ⅛ ¼ ⅓ ⅜ ½ $12345/67890¢ (abdeilmnorst) ⅝ ⅔ ¾**

S

Shatter

Vic Carless • 1973

LET

▲18

abcdefghijklmnopqrstuvwxyz(".;'!*?':,")
$1234567890&fiflß-äöüåçèîñóæøœ
ABCDEFGHIJKLMNOPQRSTUVWXYZ
ÄÖÜÅÇÈÎÑÓÆØŒ»„«[•]‹¡·¿›...

SHELLEY

Matthew Carter • 1972 abcdefghijklmnopqrstuvwxyz(“.;‘!*?’:,”)

LIN ADO AGA BIT MAE URW $1234567890&fiflß-äöüåçèîñóæøœ

▲16 ABCDEFGHIJKLMNOPQRSTUVWXYZ

ÄÖÜÅÇÈÎÑÓÆØŒ»„«[¶§•†‡]‹¡·¿›...

Shelley ...

• Allegro abcdefghijklmnopqrstuvwxyzABCDEFGHIJKLMNOPQRSTUVWX

Andante abcdefghijklmnopqrstuvwxyzABCDEFGHIJKLMNOPQRST

Volante abcdefghijklmnopqrstuvwxyzABCDEFGHIJKLMNOPQRS

Sho

Calligraphy for Print

Karlgeorg Hoefer • 1993 abcdefghijklmnopqrstuvwxyz(“.;‘!*?’:,”)

LIN ADO AGA MAE $1234567890&fiflß-äöüåçèîñóæøœ

▲18 ABCDEFGHIJKLMNOPQRSTUVWXYZ

ÄÖÜÅÇÈÎÑÓÆØŒ»„«[¶§•†‡]‹¡·¿›...

Showcard Gothic

Jim Parkinson • 1993 ABCDEFGHIJKLMNOPQRSTUVWXYZ

FBU

▲30 (“.;‘!*?’:,”)$1234567890Q

&-ÄÖÜÅÇÈÎÑÓÆØŒ»„«[¶§•]‹¡·¿›... ▷▼

SIERRA

Kris Holmes • 1989 abcdefghijklmnopqrstuvwxyz(“.;‘!*?’:,”)

LEF $1234567890&fiflß-äöüåçèîñóæøœ

ABCDEFGHIJKLMNOPQRSTUVWXYZ

ÄÖÜÅÇÈÎÑÓÆØŒ»„«[¶§•†‡]‹¡·¿›...

Sierra ...

• Regular abcdefghijklmnopqrstuvwxyzABCDEFGHIJKLMNOPQRSTUVWXYZ–$12345678

Italic *abcdefghijklmnopqrstuvwxyzABCDEFGHIJKLMNOPQRSTUVWXYZ–$1234567890(*

Bold **abcdefghijklmnopqrstuvwxyzABCDEFGHIJKLMNOPQRSTUVWXYZ–$**

Bold Italic ***abcdefghijklmnopqrstuvwxyzABCDEFGHIJKLMNOPQRSTUVWXYZ–$123***

S

Calligraphy for Print: Ruling Script, Sho, Wiesbaden Swing.

SIGNATURE

Greg Kolodziejzyk • 1987 abcdefghijklmnopqrstuvwxyz(".;'!*?':,")
IMA $1234567890&ß-äöüåçèîñóæøœ
▲16 ABCDEFGHIJKLMNOPQRSTUVWXYZ
ÄÖÜÅÇÈÎÑÓÆØŒ„[•*]¡¿...

Signature ...

Light abcdefghijklmnopqrstuvwxyzABCDEFGHIJKLMNOPQRSTUVWXYZ–$1234567890(".;'!*?':,")&ß-äöü

• Regular abcdefghijklmnopqrstuvwxyzABCDEFGHIJKLMNOPQRSTUVWXYZ–$1234567890(".;'!*?':,")&ß-äö

SILICA

Sumner Stone • 1993 abcdefghijklmnopqrstuvwxyz(".;'!*?':,")
STO $1234567890&fiflß-äöüåçèîñóæøœ
ABCDEFGHIJKLMNOPQRSTUVWXYZ
ÄÖÜÅÇÈÎÑÓÆØŒ»„«[¶§•†‡]‹¡·¿›...

Silica ...

Extra Light abcdefghijklmnopqrstuvwxyzABCDEFGHIJKLMNOPQRSTUVWXYZ–$1234567890(".;'!

Light abcdefghijklmnopqrstuvwxyzABCDEFGHIJKLMNOPQRSTUVWXYZ–$1234567890(".;'

• Regular abcdefghijklmnopqrstuvwxyzABCDEFGHIJKLMNOPQRSTUVWXYZ–$1234567890(".;

Semibold abcdefghijklmnopqrstuvwxyzABCDEFGHIJKLMNOPQRSTUVWXYZ–$1234567890("

Bold abcdefghijklmnopqrstuvwxyzABCDEFGHIJKLMNOPQRSTUVWXYZ–$1234567890

Black abcdefghijklmnopqrstuvwxyzABCDEFGHIJKLMNOPQRSTUVWXYZ–$12345678

TF SIMPER

Joseph Treacy • 1992 abcdefghijklmnopqrstuvwxyz(".;'!*?':,")
TRE MTD $1234567890&fiflß-äöüåçèîñóæøœ
▲16 ABCDEFGHIJKLMNOPQRSTUVWXYZ
ÄÖÜÅÇÈÎÑÓÆØŒ»„«[¶§•†‡]‹¡·¿›...

▷ 123579/234816 ■□

TF Simper ...

• Extra Bold abcdefghijklmnopqrstuvwxyzABCDEFGHIJKLMNOPQRSTUVWXY

Extra Bold Condensed abcdefghijklmnopqrstuvwxyzABCDEFGHIJKLMNOPQRSTUVWXYZ–$1234567

Extra Bold Extra Condensed abcdefghijklmnopqrstuvwxyzABCDEFGHIJKLMNOPQRSTUVWXYZ–$1234567890(".;'!*?':,")&

Serif Extra Bold abcdefghijklmnopqrstuvwxyzABCDEFGHIJKLMNOPQRSTUVW

DV SIMPLIX

Diehl.Volk • 1992 abcdefghijklmnopqrstuvwxyz(".;'!*?':,")

DVT $1234567890&-äöüçèîñó

ABCDEFGHIJKLMNOPQRSTUVWXYZ

ÄÖÜÇÈÎÑÓ»«[¶•†‡]i¿...

▷ ewIQW

DV Simplix . . .

Light abcdefghijklmnopqrstuvwxyzABCDEFGHIJKLMNOPQRSTUVWXYZ–$1234567890(".;'!*?':

Light Oblique *abcdefghijklmnopqrstuvwxyzABCDEFGHIJKLMNOPQRSTUVWXYZ–$1234567890(".;'!*?':*

• Medium abcdefghijklmnopqrstuvwxyzABCDEFGHIJKLMNOPQRSTUVWXYZ–$1234567890(".;'!*

Medium Oblique *abcdefghijklmnopqrstuvwxyzABCDEFGHIJKLMNOPQRSTUVWXYZ–$1234567890(".;'!*?*

Bold **abcdefghijklmnopqrstuvwxyzABCDEFGHIJKLMNOPQRSTUVWXYZ–$1234567890(**

Bold Oblique ***abcdefghijklmnopqrstuvwxyzABCDEFGHIJKLMNOPQRSTUVWXYZ–$1234567890(***

Sinaloa

Rosemarie Tissi • 1974 ABCDEFGHIJKLMNOPQRSTUVWXYZ

LET AGP URW

▲24 (".;'!*?':,")$1234567890

&-ÄÖÜÅÇÈÎÑÓÆØŒ»„«[•]‹i·¿›...

SINCLAIR SCRIPT

Pat Hickson • 1993 abcdefghijklmnopqrstuvwxyz(".;'!*?':,")

RED $1234567890&ß-äöüåçèîñóæøœ

ABCDEFGHIJKLMNOPQRSTUVWXYZ

ÄÖÜÅÇÈÎÑÓÆØŒ»„«[¶•]‹¡·¿›...

Sinclair Script . . .

Light abcdefghijklmnopqrstuvwxyzABCDEFGHIJKLMNOPQRSTUVWXYZ-$1234567890(".;'!*?':,")&

• Medium abcdefghijklmnopqrstuvwxyzABCDEFGHIJKLMNOPQRSTUVWXYZ-$1234567890(".;'!*?

Bold **abcdefghijklmnopqrstuvwxyzABCDEFGHIJKLMNOPQRSTUVWXYZ-$1234567890("**

Skid Row

Akira Kobayashi • 1990 ABCDEFGHIJKLMNOPQRSTUVWXYZ

LET

▲30 (".;'!*?':,")$1234567890

&-ÄÖÜÅÇÈÎÑÓÆØŒ»„«[•]‹i·¿›...

S

NIMX SKINNY

Calvin Glenn • 1993 abcdefghijklmnopqrstuvwxyz(".;'!*?':,")

NIM $1234567890+fiflß-äöüåçèîñóæøœ

▲18 ABCDEFGHIJKLMNOPQRSTUVWXYZ

ÄÖÜÅÇÈÎÑÓÆØŒ»„«[¶§•†‡]<¡·¿>...

NIMX Skinny 1 ...

• Regular abcdefghijklmnopqrstuvwxyzABCDEFGHIJKLMNOPQRSTUVWXYZ–$1234567890(".;'!*?':,")+fiflß-äöüÄÖÜå

Italic *abcdefghijklmnopqrstuvwxyzABCDEFGHIJKLMNOPQRSTUVWXYZ–$1234567890(".;'!*?':,")+fiflß-äöüÄÖÜå*

Bold **abcdefghijklmnopqrstuvwxyzABCDEFGHIJKLMNOPQRSTUVWXYZ–$1234567890(".;'!*?':,")+fiflß-äöüÄÖÜå**

Bold Italic ***abcdefghijklmnopqrstuvwxyzABCDEFGHIJKLMNOPQRSTUVWXYZ–$1234567890(".;'!*?':,")+fiflß-äöüÄÖÜå***

NIMX Skinny 2 ...

Light abcdefghijklmnopqrstuvwxyzABCDEFGHIJKLMNOPQRSTUVWXYZ–$1234567890(".;'!*?':,")+fiflß-äöüÄÖÜå

Light Italic *abcdefghijklmnopqrstuvwxyzABCDEFGHIJKLMNOPQRSTUVWXYZ–$1234567890(".;'!*?':,")+fiflß-äöüÄÖÜå*

Light SC&OSF ABCDEFGHIJKLMNOPQRSTUVWXYZ$1234567890(".;'!*?':,")+-ÄÖÜÅÇÉÎÑÓ[•]¡·¿

Regular SC&OSF ABCDEFGHIJKLMNOPQRSTUVWXYZ$1234567890(".;'!*?':,")+-ÄÖÜÅÇÉÎÑÓ[•]¡·¿

Bold SC&OSF **ABCDEFGHIJKLMNOPQRSTUVWXYZ$1234567890(".;'!*?':,")+-ÄÖÜÅÇÉÎÑÓ[•]¡·¿**

Skreetch Caps

Jim Marcus • 1993 ABCDEFGHIJKLMNO

T26 PQRSTUVWXYZ

▲54 (".;'!*?':,")1234567890

&-ABCDEFGHIJKL

MNOPQRSTUVWXYZ

SKYLINE

Jane Patterson • 1992
... Imre Reiner, 1929

FBU

▲36

abcdefghijklmnopqrstuvwxyz(".;'!*?':,")
$1234567890&fiflß-äöüåçèîñóæøœ
ABCDEFGHIJKLMNOPQRSTUVWXYZ
ÄÖÜÅÇÈÎÑÓÆØŒ»,,«[¶§•†‡]‹¡·¿›... ▷

Skyline ...

• Black abcdefghijklmnopqrstuvwxyzABCDEFGHIJK

Bold Condensed abcdefghijklmnopqrstuvwxyzABCDEFGHIJKLMNOPQRSTUVWXYZ–$1

ITC SLIMBACH

Robert Slimbach • 1987

ADO AGA AGP LEF LIN MAE URW

abcdefghijklmnopqrstuvwxyz(".;'!*?':,")
$1234567890&fiflß-äöüåçèîñóæøœ
ABCDEFGHIJKLMNOPQRSTUVWXYZ
ÄÖÜÅÇÈÎÑÓÆØŒ»,,«[¶§•†‡]‹¡·¿›...

ITC Slimbach ...

• Book abcdefghijklmnopqrstuvwxyzABCDEFGHIJKLMNOPQRSTUVWXYZ–$1234567890

Book Italic *abcdefghijklmnopqrstuvwxyzABCDEFGHIJKLMNOPQRSTUVWXYZ–$1234567890(*

Medium abcdefghijklmnopqrstuvwxyzABCDEFGHIJKLMNOPQRSTUVWXYZ–$12345678

Medium Italic *abcdefghijklmnopqrstuvwxyzABCDEFGHIJKLMNOPQRSTUVWXYZ–$123456789*

Bold **abcdefghijklmnopqrstuvwxyzABCDEFGHIJKLMNOPQRSTUVWXYZ–$123456**

Bold Italic ***abcdefghijklmnopqrstuvwxyzABCDEFGHIJKLMNOPQRSTUVWXYZ–$12345678***

Black **abcdefghijklmnopqrstuvwxyzABCDEFGHIJKLMNOPQRSTUVWXYZ–$1234**

Black Italic ***abcdefghijklmnopqrstuvwxyzABCDEFGHIJKLMNOPQRSTUVWXYZ–$123456***

Slipstream

Letraset Design Studio • 1985

LET FRA

▲24

ABCDEFGHIJKLMNOPQRSTUVWXYZ
(".;'!*?':,")$1234567890
&-ÄÖÜÅÇÈÎÑÓÆØŒ»,,«[•]‹¡-¿›...

S

Slogan

✍ Helmut Matheis • 1959 abcdefghijklmnopqrstuvwxyz(".;'!*?':,")

URW LEF $1234567890&fiflß-äöüåçèîñóæøœ

▲16 ABCDEFGHIJKLMNOPQRSTUVWXYZ

ÄÖÜÅÇÈÎÑÓÆØŒ»„«[¶§•†‡]‹¡·¿›...

SLOOP SCRIPT

✍ Richard Lipton • 1994 abcdefghijklmnopqrstuvwxyz(".;'!*?:,")

FBU $1234567890&fiflß-äöüåçèîñóæøœ

ABCDEFGHIJKLMNOPQRSTUVWXYZ

ÄÖÜÅÇÈÎÑÓÆØŒ»„«[¶§•†‡]‹¡·¿›... ▷ fop pqrrst axy ff fft fll tt Th

Sloop Script ...

• One abcdefghijklmnopqrstuvwxyz ABCDEFGHIJKLMNOPQRSTUVWXYZ

Two abcdefghijklmnopqrstuvwxyz ABCDEFGHIJKLMNOPQRSTUV

Three abcdefghijklmnopqrstuvwxyz ABCDEFGHIJKLMNOPQRSTUVWXYZ

Smaragd
✤ GudrunSchrift
✍ Gudrun Zapf-von Hesse • 1953 ABCDEFGHIJKLMNOPQRSTUVWXYZ

LIN ADO AGA MAE (".;'!?':,")$1234567890

▲24 &-ÄÖÜÅÇÈÎÑÓÆØŒ»„«[•]‹¡·¿› ▷ÄÖÜ

SMUDGER

✍ Andrew Smith • 1994 abcdefghijklmnopqrstuvwxyz(".;'!*?':,")

LET $1234567890¢fiflß-äöüåçèîñóæøœ

▲16 ABCDEFGHIJKLMNOPQRSTUVWXYZ

ÄÖÜÅÇÈÎÑÓÆØŒ»„«[•]‹¡·¿›... ▷ deghklpr sxz ff ft tt & BDEFGHNORTUWXY

SNELL ROUNDHAND

✍ Matthew Carter • 1972 abcdefghijklmnopqrstuvwxyz(".;'!*?':,")

LIN ADO AGA MAE $1234567890&fiflß-äöüåçèîñóæøœ

ABCDEFGHIJKLMNOPQRSTUVWXYZ

ÄÖÜÅÇÈÎÑÓÆØŒ»„«[¶§•†‡]‹¡·¿›...

Snell Roundhand ...

• Regular abcdefghijklmnopqrstuvwxyz ABCDEFGHIJKLMNOPQRSTUVWXYZ–

Bold abcdefghijklmnopqrstuvwxyz ABCDEFGHIJKLMNOPQRSTUVW

Black abcdefghijklmnopqrstuvwxyz ABCDEFGHIJKLMNOPQRSTU

✤ *GudrunSchrift*: Ariadne, Diotima Roman, Italic, Roman SCOSF, Roman OSF, Italic OSF, Smaragd.

Sophia

Matthew Carter • 1993

CAR

▲28

ABCDEFGHIJKLMNOPQRSTUVWXYZ
("․;'!*?':,")$1234567890
&-ÄÖÜÅÇÈÎÑÓÆØŒ»„«[¶§•†‡]‹¡·¿›…
▷ACEEFFGHIKLM°RRTTTXZ<♣♣>4

ITC SOUVENIR

Ed Benguiat • 1970
… Morris Fuller Benton, 1914

ADO AGA BIT LEF FAM LIN MAE URW

abcdefghijklmnopqrstuvwxyz("․;'!*?':,")
$1234567890&fiflß-äöüåçèîñóæøœ
ABCDEFGHIJKLMNOPQRSTUVWXYZ
ÄÖÜÅÇÈÎÑÓÆØŒ»„«[¶§•†‡]‹¡·¿›…

ITC Souvenir 1 …

Light abcdefghijklmnopqrstuvwxyzABCDEFGHIJKLMNOPQRSTUVWXYZ–$1234567

Light Italic *abcdefghijklmnopqrstuvwxyzABCDEFGHIJKLMNOPQRSTUVWXYZ–$12345*

Demi **abcdefghijklmnopqrstuvwxyzABCDEFGHIJKLMNOPQRSTUVWXYZ–$1**

Demi Italic ***abcdefghijklmnopqrstuvwxyzABCDEFGHIJKLMNOPQRSTUVWXYZ–***

ITC Souvenir 2 …

• Medium abcdefghijklmnopqrstuvwxyzABCDEFGHIJKLMNOPQRSTUVWXYZ–$1234

Medium Italic *abcdefghijklmnopqrstuvwxyzABCDEFGHIJKLMNOPQRSTUVWXYZ–$12*

Bold **abcdefghijklmnopqrstuvwxyzABCDEFGHIJKLMNOPQRSTUVWXYZ–**

Bold Italic ***abcdefghijklmnopqrstuvwxyzABCDEFGHIJKLMNOPQRSTUVWX***

SPARTAN CLASSIFIED

S

Linotype Design Staff • 1951

LIN ADO AGA MAE

▲12

abcdefghijklmnopqrstuvwxyz("․;'!*?':,")
$1234567890&fiflß-äöüåçèîñóæøœ
ABCDEFGHIJKLMNOPQRSTUVWXYZ
ÄÖÜÅÇÈÎÑÓÆØŒ»„«[¶§•†‡]‹¡·¿›…

Spartan Classified …

• Book abcdefghijklmnopqrstuvwxyzABCDEFGHIJKLMNOPQRSTUVWXYZ–$1234567890(

Heavy **abcdefghijklmnopqrstuvwxyzABCDEFGHIJKLMNOPQRSTUVWXYZ–$1234567890(**

SPECTRUM + EXPERT & SCOSF

Jan Van Krimpen • 1955 abcdefghijklmnopqrstuvwxyz(".;'!*?':,")

MCL ADO AGA LIN MAE $1234567890&fiflß-äöüåçèîñóæøœ

▲16 ABCDEFGHIJKLMNOPQRSTUVWXYZ

ÄÖÜÅÇÈÎÑÓÆØŒ»„«[¶§•†‡]‹¡·¿›...

Spectrum + Expert & SCOSF ...

• Roman abcdefghijklmnopqrstuvwxyzABCDEFGHIJKLMNOPQRSTUVWXYZ–$1234567890(

Italic *abcdefghijklmnopqrstuvwxyzABCDEFGHIJKLMNOPQRSTUVWXYZ–$1234567890(".;'!*?':,"*

Semibold **abcdefghijklmnopqrstuvwxyzABCDEFGHIJKLMNOPQRSTUVWXYZ–$1234**

Expert Roman ABCDEFGHIJKLMNOPQRSTUVWXYZ–$1234567890.;!?:,&-ff fi fl ffi ffl ⅛ ¼ ⅓ ⅜ ½ $12345/67890¢ (abdeilmnor

Expert Italic *$1234567890.;:,–ff fi fl ffi ffl ⅛ ¼ ⅓ ⅜ ½ $12345/67890¢ (abdeilmnorst) ⅝ ⅔ ¾ ⅞ ₡Rp*

Expert Semibold **$1234567890.;:,–ff fi fl ffi ffl ⅛ ¼ ⅓ ⅜ ½ $12345/67890¢ (abdeilmnorst) ⅝ ⅔ ¾ ⅞ ₡Rp**

Roman SCOSF ABCDEFGHIJKLMNOPQRSTUVWXYZABCDEFGHIJKLMNOPQRSTUVWXYZ–$1234567890(".;

Italic OSF *abcdefghijklmnopqrstuvwxyzABCDEFGHIJKLMNOPQRSTUVWXYZ–$1234567890(".;'!*?':,")*

Semibold OSF **abcdefghijklmnopqrstuvwxyzABCDEFGHIJKLMNOPQRSTUVWXYZ–$12345**

Spike

[T-26] FontSet 3

Greg Samata • 1993 A B C D E F G H I J K L M N O P Q R S T U V W X Y Z (".;'!*?':,")

T26 $ 1 2 3 4 5 6 7 8 9 0 & – Ä Ö Ü Å Ç È Î Ñ Ó Æ Ø

A B C D E F G H I J K L M N O P Q R S T U V W X Y Z

Ä Ö Ü Å Ç È Ñ Æ Ø Œ »«[•]¡¿...

Spotlight

Tony Geddes • 1989 **abcdefghijklmnopqrstuvwxyz(".;'!*?':,")**

LET **$1234567890&fiflß-äöüåçèîñóæøœ**

▲18 **ABCDEFGHIJKLMNOPQRSTUVWXYZ**

ÄÖÜÅÇÈÎÑÓÆØŒ»„«[•]‹¡·¿›...

SPRING

Garrett Boge • 1988 abcdefghijklmnopqrstuvwxyz(".;'!*?':,")

LPT MTD $1234567890&fiflß-äöüåçèîñóæøœ

▲16 ABCDEFGHIJKLMNOPQRSTUVWXYZ

ÄÖÜÅÇÈÎÑÓÆØŒ»„«[•]‹¡·¿›...

Spring ...

Light abcdefghijklmnopqrstuvwxyzABCDEFGHIJKLMNOPQRSTUVWXYZ–$1234

• Regular abcdefghijklmnopqrstuvwxyzABCDEFGHIJKLMNOPQRSTUVWX

S

[T-26] FontSet 3: Spike & Sputnik.

Spumoni
Garrett Boge • 1989
LPT MTD
▲36

abcdefghijklmnopqrstuvwxyz(".;'!*?':,")
$1234567890&fifß-äöüåçèîñóæøœ
ABCDEFGHIJKLMNOPQRSTUVWXYZ
ÄÖÜÅÇÈÎÑÓÆØŒ»,„«[¶§•†‡]‹¡·¿›...

Sputnik
[T-26] FontSet 3
Greg Samata • 1993
T26
▲36

ABCDEFGHIJKLM
NOPQRSTUVWXYZ
(".;'!*?':,")$1234567
890—ÆØŒ»«[/•]¡¿...

Sackers Square Gothic
Agfa Engravers 2
AGP

ABCDEFGHIJKLMNOPQRSTUVWXYZ(".;'!*?':,")
$1234567890&-ÄÖÜÅÇÈÎÑÓ
ABCDEFGHIJKLMNOPQRSTUVWXYZ
ÄÖÜÅÇÈÎÑÓ»«[·]‹›
▷I V X ST ND RD TH — 1/4 1/3 1/2 3/4 ~ D' C R. 'C 'S O' RS. S. & C/O

MN SQUASH
MTD
▲24

ABCDEFGHIJKLMNOPQRSTUVWXYZ
(".;'!*?':,")$1234567890
&-ÄÖÜÅÇÈÎÑÓÆØŒ»,„«[·]‹¡¿›...

MN Squash ...

Outline
ABCDEFGHIJKLMNOPQRSTUVWXYZ$12

• Regular
ABCDEFGHIJKLMNOPQRSTUVWXYZ$12

....
[T-26] FontSet 3: Spike & Sputnik.
Agfa Engravers 2: Sackers Antique Roman Open & Solid, Sackers Light Classic Roman, Sackers English Script, Sackers Gothic Light, Medium & Heavy, Sackers Italian Script, Sackers Roman Light & Heavy, Sackers Square Gothic.

Squire

✍ Michael Neugebauer • 1980 abcdefghijklmnopqrstuvwxyz(".;'!*?':,")

LET URW $1234567890&fiflß-äöüåçèîñóæøœ

▲16 ABCDEFGHIJKLMNOPQRSTUVWXYZ

ÄÖÜÅÇÈÎÑÓÆØŒ»„«[•]‹i·¿›...

▷ f v w z L N Z 2

Squire Extra Bold

LET abcdefghijklmnopqrstuvwxyz(".;'!*?':,")

▲16 $1234567890&fiflß-äöüåçèîñóæøœ

ABCDEFGHIJKLMNOPQRSTUVWXYZ

ÄÖÜÅÇÈÎÑÓÆØŒ»„«[•]‹i·¿›...

▷ f v w z L N Z 2

Staccato 555

✍ Roger Excoffon • 1955 abcdefghijklmnopqrstuvwxyz(".;'!*?':,")

BIT $1234567890&fiflß-äöüåçèîñóæøœ

▲16 ABCDEFGHIJKLMNOPQRSTUVWXYZ

ÄÖÜÅÇÈÎÑÓÆØŒ»„«[¶§•†‡]‹i·¿›...

Stencil

✤ Adobe DisplaySet 4

ADO AGA BIT LIN MAE URW ABCDEFGHIJKLMNOPQRSTUVWXYZ

▲24 (".;'!*?':,")$1234567890

&-ÄÖÜÅÇÈÎÑÓÆØŒ»„«[•]‹¡·¿›...

Stentor

✍ Heinz Schumann • 1964 abcdefghijklmnopqrstuvwxyz(".;'!*?':,")

URW LEF $1234567890&fiflß-äöüåçèîñóæøœ

▲16 ABCDEFGHIJKLMNOPQRSTUVWXYZ

ÄÖÜÅÇÈÎÑÓÆØŒ»„«[¶§•†‡]‹i·¿›...

Stereo

✍ Tobias Frere-Jones • 1993 ABCDEFGHIJKLMNOPQR

FBU

▲30 STUVWXYZ(".;'!*?':,")$123

4567890&-ÄÖÜÅÇÈÎÑÓÆ

ØŒ»„«[¶§•†‡]‹i·¿›... ▷ BPR

✤ *Adobe DisplaySet 4*: Brush Script, Hobo, Stencil.

ITC STONE SERIF

Sumner Stone • 1987 abcdefghijklmnopqrstuvwxyz(".;'!*?':,")

ADO AGA LEF LIN MAE URW $1234567890&fiflß-äöüåçèîñóæøœ

ABCDEFGHIJKLMNOPQRSTUVWXYZ

ÄÖÜÅÇÈÎÑÓÆØŒ»„«[¶§•†‡]‹¡·¿›...

ITC Stone Serif ...

• Medium abcdefghijklmnopqrstuvwxyzABCDEFGHIJKLMNOPQRSTUVWXYZ–$12345

Medium Italic *abcdefghijklmnopqrstuvwxyzABCDEFGHIJKLMNOPQRSTUVWXYZ–$12345678*

Semibold **abcdefghijklmnopqrstuvwxyzABCDEFGHIJKLMNOPQRSTUVWXYZ–$12**

Semibold Italic ***abcdefghijklmnopqrstuvwxyzABCDEFGHIJKLMNOPQRSTUVWXYZ–$123***

Bold **abcdefghijklmnopqrstuvwxyzABCDEFGHIJKLMNOPQRSTUVWXY**

Bold Italic ***abcdefghijklmnopqrstuvwxyzABCDEFGHIJKLMNOPQRSTUVWXYZ–***

ITC STONE SANS

ADO AGA LEF LIN MAE URW abcdefghijklmnopqrstuvwxyz(".;'!*?':,")

$1234567890&fiflß-äöüåçèîñóæøœ

ABCDEFGHIJKLMNOPQRSTUVWXYZ

ÄÖÜÅÇÈÎÑÓÆØŒ»„«[¶§•†‡]‹¡·¿›...

ITC Stone Sans ...

• Medium abcdefghijklmnopqrstuvwxyzABCDEFGHIJKLMNOPQRSTUVWXYZ–$123456789

Medium Italic *abcdefghijklmnopqrstuvwxyzABCDEFGHIJKLMNOPQRSTUVWXYZ–$1234567890(".;*

Semibold **abcdefghijklmnopqrstuvwxyzABCDEFGHIJKLMNOPQRSTUVWXYZ–$123456**

Semibold Italic ***abcdefghijklmnopqrstuvwxyzABCDEFGHIJKLMNOPQRSTUVWXYZ–$1234567890***

Bold **abcdefghijklmnopqrstuvwxyzABCDEFGHIJKLMNOPQRSTUVWXYZ–$12**

Bold Italic ***abcdefghijklmnopqrstuvwxyzABCDEFGHIJKLMNOPQRSTUVWXYZ–$123456***

ITC STONE INFORMAL

ADO AGA LEF LIN MAE URW abcdefghijklmnopqrstuvwxyz(".;'!*?':,")

$1234567890&fiflß-äöüåçèîñóæøœ

ABCDEFGHIJKLMNOPQRSTUVWXYZ

ÄÖÜÅÇÈÎÑÓÆØŒ»„«[¶§•†‡]‹¡·¿›...

ITC Stone Informal ...

• Medium abcdefghijklmnopqrstuvwxyzABCDEFGHIJKLMNOPQRSTUVWXYZ–$12345

Medium Italic *abcdefghijklmnopqrstuvwxyzABCDEFGHIJKLMNOPQRSTUVWXYZ–$1234567890*

Semibold **abcdefghijklmnopqrstuvwxyzABCDEFGHIJKLMNOPQRSTUVWXYZ–$12**

Semibold Italic ***abcdefghijklmnopqrstuvwxyzABCDEFGHIJKLMNOPQRSTUVWXYZ–$12345***

Bold **abcdefghijklmnopqrstuvwxyzABCDEFGHIJKLMNOPQRSTUVWXYZ**

Bold Italic ***abcdefghijklmnopqrstuvwxyzABCDEFGHIJKLMNOPQRSTUVWXYZ–$12***

ITC Stone Serif & Sans · ITC Stone Phonetic Serif & Sans

STONE PRINT

Sumner Stone • 1991 abcdefghijklmnopqrstuvwxyz(".;'!*?':,")

STO $1234567890&fiflß-äöüåçèîñóæøœ

ABCDEFGHIJKLMNOPQRSTUVWXYZ

ÄÖÜÅÇÈÎÑÓÆØŒ»„«[¶§•†‡]‹¡·¿›...

Stone Print ...

• Roman abcdefghijklmnopqrstuvwxyzABCDEFGHIJKLMNOPQRSTUVWXYZ–$1234567890(".;'!*?':,")&

Italic *abcdefghijklmnopqrstuvwxyzABCDEFGHIJKLMNOPQRSTUVWXYZ–$1234567890(".;'!*?':,")&fiflß-*

Semibold **abcdefghijklmnopqrstuvwxyzABCDEFGHIJKLMNOPQRSTUVWXYZ–$1234567890(".;'!*?':,**

Semibold Italic ***abcdefghijklmnopqrstuvwxyzABCDEFGHIJKLMNOPQRSTUVWXYZ–$1234567890(".;'!*?':,")&fiflß***

Bold **abcdefghijklmnopqrstuvwxyzABCDEFGHIJKLMNOPQRSTUVWXYZ–$1234567890(".;'!**

Bold Italic ***abcdefghijklmnopqrstuvwxyzABCDEFGHIJKLMNOPQRSTUVWXYZ–$1234567890(".;'!*?':,")&fi***

STONE PRINT EXTRA

STO ABCDEFGHIJKLMNOPQRSTUVWXYZ(".;'!*?':,")

$1234567890&-ÄÖÜÅÇÈÎÑÓÆØŒ

ABCDEFGHIJKLMNOPQRSTUVWXYZ

ÄÖÜÅÇÈÎÑÓÆØŒ»„«[¶§•†‡]‹¡·¿›...

Stone Print Extra ...

• Roman SCOSF ABCDEFGHIJKLMNOPQRSTUVWXYZABCDEFGHIJKLMNOPQRSTUVWXYZ–$1234567890(".;'!*?':,"

Roman Figures/Fractions 1234567890 1234567890/1234567890 1234567890

Italic SCOSF *ABCDEFGHIJKLMNOPQRSTUVWXYZABCDEFGHIJKLMNOPQRSTUVWXYZ–$1234567890(".;'!*?':,")&-ÄÖ*

Italic Figures/Fractions *1234567890 1234567890/1234567890 1234567890*

Semibold SCOSF **ABCDEFGHIJKLMNOPQRSTUVWXYZABCDEFGHIJKLMNOPQRSTUVWXYZ–$1234567890(".;'!*?**

Semibold Figures/Fractions **1234567890 1234567890/1234567890 1234567890**

Semibold Italic SCOSF ***ABCDEFGHIJKLMNOPQRSTUVWXYZABCDEFGHIJKLMNOPQRSTUVWXYZ–$1234567890(".;'!*?':,")&-ÄÖ***

Semibold Italic Figures/Fractions ***1234567890 1234567890/1234567890 1234567890***

Bold SCOSF **ABCDEFGHIJKLMNOPQRSTUVWXYZABCDEFGHIJKLMNOPQRSTUVWXYZ–$1234567890(".;'!**

Bold Figures/Fractions **1234567890 1234567890/1234567890 1234567890**

Bold Italic SCOSF ***ABCDEFGHIJKLMNOPQRSTUVWXYZABCDEFGHIJKLMNOPQRSTUVWXYZ–$1234567890(".;'!*?':,")&-Ä***

Bold Italic Figures/Fractions ***1234567890 1234567890/1234567890 1234567890***

Stop

✣ *Linotype Headliners*

LIN LEF URW ABCDEFGHIJKLMNOPQRSTUVWXYZ

(".;'!*?':,")$1234567890

▲24 &-ÄÖÜÅÇÈÎÑÓÆØŒ»„«[¶§•†‡]‹¡·¿›...

✣ *Linotype Headliners*: Chwast Buffalo Black Condensed, Erbar Light Condensed & Bold Condensed, Metrolite, Metromedium, Metroblack, Plak Black, Black Condensed & Extra Black Condensed, Stop, Times Eighteen Roman & Bold.

S

STORY

Marshall Bohlin • 1994 abcdefghijklmnopqrstuvwxyz(".;'!*?':,")
EMD $1234567890&fiflß-äöüåçèîñóæøœ
ABCDEFGHIJKLMNOPQRSTUVWXYZ
ÄÖÜÅÇÈÎÑÓÆØŒ[¶§•†];·¿...

Story ...
• Regular abcdefghijklmnopqrstuvwxyzABCDEFGHIJKLMNOPQRSTUVWXYZ–$1234567890(
Bold **abcdefghijklmnopqrstuvwxyzABCDEFGHIJKLMNOPQRSTUVWXYZ–$12345678**

Strobos
Vince Whitlock • 1990 ABCDEFGHIJKLMNOPQRSTUVWXYZ
LET (".;'!*?':,")$1234567890
▲30 &-ÄÖÜÅÇÈÎÑÓÆØŒ»„«[•]‹¡·¿›...

Sturbridge Twisted
INT abcdefghijklmnopqrstuvwxyz.,;!?:,$1234567890&ß–
▲24 ABCDEFGHIJKLMNOPQRSTUVWX
YZÆŒ ▷

Stuyvesant
Agfa Scripts 1
AGP BIT *abcdefghijklmnopqrstuvwxyz(".;'!*?':,")*
▲18 *$1234567890&ß-äöüåçèîñó*
ABCDEFGHIJKLMNOPQRSTUVWXYZ
ÄÖÜÅÇÈÎÑÓ»«[•]« ▷ I V X st nd rd th ¼ ⅓ ½ ¾ D' c r. c s O' rs. s. & %

Stylus
Dennis Pasternak • 1994 abcdefghijklmnopqrstuvwxyz(".;'!*?':,")
GAL $1234567890¢fiflß-äöüåçèîñóæøœ
▲16 ABCDEFGHIJKLMNOPQRSTUVWXYZ
ÄÖÜÅÇÈÎÑÓÆØŒ»„«[¶§•†‡]‹¡·¿›...

Agfa Scripts 1: Commercial Script, Helinda Rook, Old English, Original Script, Quill Script, Stuyvesant, Wedding Text.

S

STYMIE

Morris Fuller Benton • 1931 abcdefghijklmnopqrstuvwxyz(".;'!*?':,")

URW BIT LEF FAM FRA $1234567890&fiflß-äöüåçèîñóæøœ

ABCDEFGHIJKLMNOPQRSTUVWXYZ

ÄÖÜÅÇÈÎÑÓÆØŒ»„«[¶§•†‡]‹¡·¿›...

Stymie ...

Light abcdefghijklmnopqrstuvwxyzABCDEFGHIJKLMNOPQRSTUVWXYZ–$1234567890(".;'!*?

• Regular abcdefghijklmnopqrstuvwxyzABCDEFGHIJKLMNOPQRSTUVWXYZ-$1234567890(".

Medium abcdefghijklmnopqrstuvwxyzABCDEFGHIJKLMNOPQRSTUVWXYZ–$12345678

Black ▲16 abcdefghijklmnopqrstuvwxyzABCDEFGHIJKLMNOPQRSTUVWXYZ–$1

Condensed ▲18 abcdefghijklmnopqrstuvwxyzABCDEFGHIJKLMNOPQRSTUVWXYZ-$1234567890(".;'!*?':,")&fiflß-äöüÄ

Medium Condensed ▲18 abcdefghijklmnopqrstuvwxyzABCDEFGHIJKLMNOPQRSTUVWXYZ-$1234567890(".;'!*?':,")

Light SCOSF ABCDEFGHIJKLMNOPQRSTUVWXYZABCDEFGHIJKLMNOPQRSTUVWXYZ–$1234567890(".;'!

Regular SCOSF ABCDEFGHIJKLMNOPQRSTUVWXYZABCDEFGHIJKLMNOPQRSTUVWXYZ-$1234567890("

MN SULLY JONQUIERES

José Mendoza y Almeida • ... abcdefghijklmnopqrstuvwxyz(".;'!*?':,")

MTD $1234567890&fiflß-äöüåçèîñóæøœ

ABCDEFGHIJKLMNOPQRSTUVWXYZ

ÄÖÜÅÇÈÎÑÓÆØŒ»„«[¶•]‹¡¿›...

MN Sully Jonquieres ...

• Regular abcdefghijklmnopqrstuvwxyzABCDEFGHIJKLMNOPQRSTUVWXYZ$1234567890(".;'!*?'

Bold abcdefghijklmnopqrstuvwxyzABCDEFGHIJKLMNOPQRSTUVWXYZ$1234567890("

SWIFT

Gerard Unger • 1985 abcdefghijklmnopqrstuvwxyz(".;'!*?':,")

LEF $1234567890&fiflß-äöüåçèîñóæøœ

ABCDEFGHIJKLMNOPQRSTUVWXYZ

ÄÖÜÅÇÈÎÑÓÆØŒ»„«[¶§•†‡]‹i·¿›...

Swift 1 ...

Light abcdefghijklmnopqrstuvwxyzABCDEFGHIJKLMNOPQRSTUVWXYZ–$1234567890(

Light Italic *abcdefghijklmnopqrstuvwxyzABCDEFGHIJKLMNOPQRSTUVWXYZ–$1234567890(".;'!*?':,")&fi*

Bold **abcdefghijklmnopqrstuvwxyzABCDEFGHIJKLMNOPQRSTUVWXYZ–$123456789**

Extra Bold **abcdefghijklmnopqrstuvwxyzABCDEFGHIJKLMNOPQRSTUVWXYZ–$12345**

Swift 2 ...

• Roman abcdefghijklmnopqrstuvwxyzABCDEFGHIJKLMNOPQRSTUVWXYZ–$1234567890(

Roman SCOSF ABCDEFGHIJKLMNOPQRSTUVWXYZABCDEFGHIJKLMNOPQRSTUVWXYZ–$123456789

Italic *abcdefghijklmnopqrstuvwxyzABCDEFGHIJKLMNOPQRSTUVWXYZ–$1234567890(".;'!*?':,")&*

S

... Swift 2

Bold Condensed ▲16 **abcdefghijklmnopqrstuvwxyzABCDEFGHIJKLMNOPQRSTUVWXYZ-$1234**

ITC SYMBOL

Aldo Novarese • 1984 abcdefghijklmnopqrstuvwxyz(".;'!*?':,")

URW ADO AGA AGP BIT LEF FAM LIN MAE $1234567890&fiflß-äöüåçèîñóæøœ

ABCDEFGHIJKLMNOPQRSTUVWXYZ

ÄÖÜÅÇÈÎÑÓÆØŒ»„«[¶§•†‡]‹¡·¿›...

ITC Symbol 1 ...

• Book abcdefghijklmnopqrstuvwxyzABCDEFGHIJKLMNOPQRSTUVWXYZ-$1234567890(".;'!

Book Italic *abcdefghijklmnopqrstuvwxyzABCDEFGHIJKLMNOPQRSTUVWXYZ-$1234567890(".;'!*

Book SCOSF ABCDEFGHIJKLMNOPQRSTUVWXYZABCDEFGHIJKLMNOPQRSTUVWXYZ-$1234567890(".;'!*?'

Bold **abcdefghijklmnopqrstuvwxyzABCDEFGHIJKLMNOPQRSTUVWXYZ-$12345678**

Bold Italic ***abcdefghijklmnopqrstuvwxyzABCDEFGHIJKLMNOPQRSTUVWXYZ-$123456789***

ITC Symbol 2 ...

Medium abcdefghijklmnopqrstuvwxyzABCDEFGHIJKLMNOPQRSTUVWXYZ-$1234567890("

Medium Italic *abcdefghijklmnopqrstuvwxyzABCDEFGHIJKLMNOPQRSTUVWXYZ-$1234567890(".*

Medium SCOSF ABCDEFGHIJKLMNOPQRSTUVWXYZABCDEFGHIJKLMNOPQRSTUVWXYZ-$1234567890(".

Black **abcdefghijklmnopqrstuvwxyzABCDEFGHIJKLMNOPQRSTUVWXYZ-$1234**

Black Italic ***abcdefghijklmnopqrstuvwxyzABCDEFGHIJKLMNOPQRSTUVWXYZ-$12345***

Synchro

Alan R. Birch • 1984 ABCDEFGHIJKLMNOPQRSTUVWXYZ

LET FRA

▲24 (".;'!*?':,")$1234567890

ß-ÄÖÜÅÇÈÎÑÓÆØŒ»„«[•]‹¡·¿›...

▷ A C D G O Q W Y 5 6 9

Synchro Reversed

LET ABCDEFGHIJKLMNOPQRSTUVWXYZ

▲24 (".;'!*?':,")$1234567890

ß-ÄÖÜÅÇÈÎÑÓÆØŒ»„«[•]‹¡·¿›...

▷ A C D G O Q W Y 5 6 9

S

ITC SYNDOR

Hans Eduard Meier • 1992 abcdefghijklmnopqrstuvwxyz(".;'!*?':,")

URW LEF $1234567890&fiflß-äöüåçèîñóæøœ

ABCDEFGHIJKLMNOPQRSTUVWXYZ

ÄÖÜÅÇÈÎÑÓÆØŒ»„«[¶§•†‡]‹¡·¿›...

ITC Syndor ...

• Book abcdefghijklmnopqrstuvwxyzABCDEFGHIJKLMNOPQRSTUVWXYZ–$1234567890(".;'!

Book Italic *abcdefghijklmnopqrstuvwxyzABCDEFGHIJKLMNOPQRSTUVWXYZ–$1234567890(".;'!*?':,")*

Book SCOSF ABCDEFGHIJKLMNOPQRSTUVWXYZABCDEFGHIJKLMNOPQRSTUVWXYZ–$1234567890(".;'

Medium abcdefghijklmnopqrstuvwxyzABCDEFGHIJKLMNOPQRSTUVWXYZ–$1234567890

Medium Italic *abcdefghijklmnopqrstuvwxyzABCDEFGHIJKLMNOPQRSTUVWXYZ–$1234567890(".;'!*

Medium SCOSF ABCDEFGHIJKLMNOPQRSTUVWXYZABCDEFGHIJKLMNOPQRSTUVWXYZ–$123456789

Bold **abcdefghijklmnopqrstuvwxyzABCDEFGHIJKLMNOPQRSTUVWXYZ–$123456**

Bold Italic ***abcdefghijklmnopqrstuvwxyzABCDEFGHIJKLMNOPQRSTUVWXYZ–$123456***

SYNTAX

Hans Eduard Meier • 1968 abcdefghijklmnopqrstuvwxyz(".;'!*?':,")

LIN ADO AGA MAE URW $1234567890&fiflß-äöüåçèîñóæøœ

ABCDEFGHIJKLMNOPQRSTUVWXYZ

ÄÖÜÅÇÈÎÑÓÆØŒ»„«[¶§•†‡]‹¡·¿›...

Syntax ...

• Regular abcdefghijklmnopqrstuvwxyzABCDEFGHIJKLMNOPQRSTUVWXYZ–$1234567890

Italic *abcdefghijklmnopqrstuvwxyzABCDEFGHIJKLMNOPQRSTUVWXYZ–$123456789*

Bold **abcdefghijklmnopqrstuvwxyzABCDEFGHIJKLMNOPQRSTUVWXYZ–$123456789**

Black **abcdefghijklmnopqrstuvwxyzABCDEFGHIJKLMNOPQRSTUVWXYZ–$123**

Ultra Black **abcdefghijklmnopqrstuvwxyzABCDEFGHIJKLMNOPQRSTUVWXYZ–$**

A*I Szene

Manfred Klein • 1994 ABCDEFGHIJKLMNOPQRSTUVWXYZ

ALP ".;'!*?':,"1234567890-ÄÖÜÅÇÈÎÑÓ

▲24 ABCDEFGHIJKLMNOPQRSTUVWXYZ

ÄÖÜÅÇÈÎÑÓ„¶§...

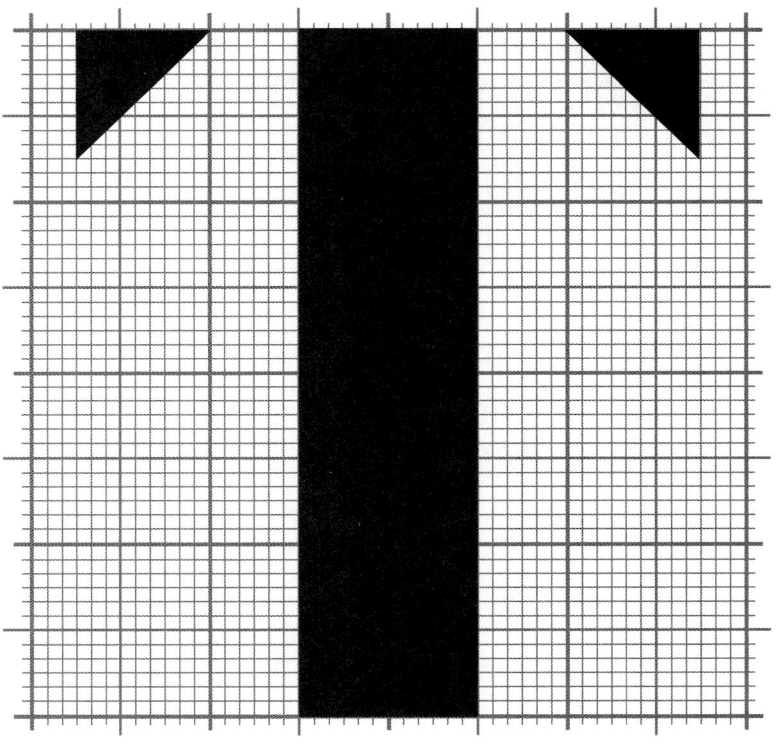

✍ Josef Albers, 1925

Tag

✍ David Sagorski • 1994

LET

▲30

Tangient

✍ Steve Zafarana • 1995

GAL

▲18

abcdefghijklmnopqrstuvwxyz(“.;‘!*?’:,”)
$1234567890&ß-äöüåçèîñóœøœ
ABCDEFGHIJKLMNOPQRSTUVWXYZ
ÄÖÜÅÇÈÎÑÓÆØŒ»„«[¶§†‡]i¿

▷

Tannhäuser

✍ Alan Meeks • 1988

LET

▲16

abcdefghijklmnopqrstuvwxyz(“.;‘!*?’:,”)
$1234567890&fifIß-äöüåçèîñóæøœ
ABCDEFGHIJKLMNOPQRSTUVWXYZ
ÄÖÜÅÇÈÎÑÓÆØŒ»„«[•]‹i·¿›…

▷ d r

Tattoo

✍ Tony Klassen • 1993

T26

▲42

ABCDEFGHIJKLMNO
PQRSTUVWXYZ(!?)
$1234567890ABCDE
FGHIJKLMNOPQ
RSTUVWXYZ

T

Teknik

David Quay • 1989

abcdefghijklmnopqrstuvwxyz("·;'!*?'·,")$1234567890&fifl ß-äöüåçèîñóæøœ

LET

▲30

ABCDEFGHIJKLMNOPQRSTUVWXYZÄÖÜÅÇÈÎÑÓÆØŒ»„«[·]‹¡·¿›. . . ▹ dgυυxAUUWXY

NIMX TEKNO

Calvin Glenn • 1993

abcdefghijklmnopqrstuvwxyz(".;'!*?':,")

NIM $1234567890&fiflß-äöüåçèîñóæøœ

▲16 ABCDEFGHIJKLMNOPQRSTUVWXYZ

ÄÖÜÅÇÈÎÑÓÆØŒ»„«[¶§•†‡]‹¡·¿›...

NIMX Tekno ...

• Regular abcdefghijklmnopqrstuvwxyzABCDEFGHIJKLMNOPQRSTUVWXYZ–$1234567890(".;'!

Bold **abcdefghijklmnopqrstuvwxyzABCDEFGHIJKLMNOPQRSTUVWXYZ–$1234567890(".;'!**

TEKTON

David Siegel • 1989 (Francis Ching)

abcdefghijklmnopqrstuvwxyz(".;'!*?':,")

ADO AGA LIN MAE $1234567890&fiflß-äöüåçèîñóæøœ

ABCDEFGHIJKLMNOPQRSTUVWXYZ

ÄÖÜÅÇÈÎÑÓÆØŒ»„«[¶§•†‡]‹¡·¿›...

Tekton ...

• Regular abcdefghijklmnopqrstuvwxyzABCDEFGHIJKLMNOPQRSTUVWXYZ–$1234567890(".;'!*?':,"

Oblique *abcdefghijklmnopqrstuvwxyzABCDEFGHIJKLMNOPQRSTUVWXYZ–$1234567890(".;'!*?':,"*

Bold **abcdefghijklmnopqrstuvwxyzABCDEFGHIJKLMNOPQRSTUVWXYZ–$1234567890(".;'!***

Bold Oblique ***abcdefghijklmnopqrstuvwxyzABCDEFGHIJKLMNOPQRSTUVWXYZ–$1234567890(".;'!****

TEKTON MULTIPLE-MASTER
(two axes: weight & width)

David Siegel • 1989 (Francis Ching)

abcdefghijklmnopqrstuvwxyz(".;'!*?':,")

ADO AGA MAE $1234567890&fiflß-äöüåçèîñóæøœ

ABCDEFGHIJKLMNOPQRSTUVWXYZ

ÄÖÜÅÇÈÎÑÓÆØŒ»„«[¶§•†‡]‹¡·¿›...

Tekton MultipleMaster ...

Light abcdefghijklmnopqrstuvwxyzABCDEFGHIJKLMNOPQRSTUVWXYZ–$1234567890(".;'!*?':,")&fiflß

Light Oblique *abcdefghijklmnopqrstuvwxyzABCDEFGHIJKLMNOPQRSTUVWXYZ–$1234567890(".;'!*?':,")&fiflß-äöüÄÖ*

• Regular abcdefghijklmnopqrstuvwxyzABCDEFGHIJKLMNOPQRSTUVWXYZ–$1234567890(".;'!*?':,"

Oblique *abcdefghijklmnopqrstuvwxyzABCDEFGHIJKLMNOPQRSTUVWXYZ–$1234567890(".;'!*?':,")&fiflß-*

Bold **abcdefghijklmnopqrstuvwxyzABCDEFGHIJKLMNOPQRSTUVWXYZ–$1234567890(".;'!***

Bold Oblique ***abcdefghijklmnopqrstuvwxyzABCDEFGHIJKLMNOPQRSTUVWXYZ–$1234567890(".;'!*?':,")&fi***

Light Condensed abcdefghijklmnopqrstuvwxyzABCDEFGHIJKLMNOPQRSTUVWXYZ–$1234567890(".;'!*?':,")&fiflß-äöüÄÖÜåçèÅÇÈîñóÎÑÓæøœÆØŒ»„

Light Condensed Oblique *abcdefghijklmnopqrstuvwxyzABCDEFGHIJKLMNOPQRSTUVWXYZ–$1234567890(".;'!*?':,")&fiflß-äöüÄÖÜåçèÅÇÈîñóÎÑÓæøœÆØŒ»„«[¶§•†‡]‹¡·¿*

T

…Tekton MultipleMaster

Condensed abcdefghijklmnopqrstuvwxyzABCDEFGHIJKLMNOPQRSTUVWXYZ–$1234567890(".;'!*?':,")&fiflß-äöüÄÖÜåçèÅÇÈîñóÎÑÓæø

Condensed Oblique *abcdefghijklmnopqrstuvwxyzABCDEFGHIJKLMNOPQRSTUVWXYZ–$1234567890(".;'!*?':,")&fiflß-äöüÄÖÜåçèÅÇÈîñóÎÑÓæøœÆØŒ»„*

Bold Condensed **abcdefghijklmnopqrstuvwxyzABCDEFGHIJKLMNOPQRSTUVWXYZ–$1234567890(".;'!*?':,")&fiflß-äöüÄÖÜåç**

Bold Condensed Oblique ***abcdefghijklmnopqrstuvwxyzABCDEFGHIJKLMNOPQRSTUVWXYZ–$1234567890(".;'!*?':,")&fiflß-äöüÄÖÜåçèÅÇÈîñó***

Light Extended abcdefghijklmnopqrstuvwxyzABCDEFGHIJKLMNOPQRSTUVWXYZ–$12345

Light Extended Oblique *abcdefghijklmnopqrstuvwxyzABCDEFGHIJKLMNOPQRSTUVWXYZ–$123456789*

Extended abcdefghijklmnopqrstuvwxyzABCDEFGHIJKLMNOPQRSTUVWXYZ–$123

Extended Oblique *abcdefghijklmnopqrstuvwxyzABCDEFGHIJKLMNOPQRSTUVWXYZ–$1234567*

Bold Extended **abcdefghijklmnopqrstuvwxyzABCDEFGHIJKLMNOPQRSTUVWXYZ–**

Bold Extended Oblique ***abcdefghijklmnopqrstuvwxyzABCDEFGHIJKLMNOPQRSTUVWXYZ–$123***

TEMPO

Linotype DisplaySet 3

Robert Hunter Middleton • 1930

LIN ADO AGA MAE

▲18

abcdefghijklmnopqrstuvwxyz(".;'!*?':,")
$1234567890&fiflß-äöüåçèîñóæøœ
ABCDEFGHIJKLMNOPQRSTUVWXYZ
ÄÖÜÅÇÈÎÑÓÆØŒ»„«[¶§•†‡]‹¡·¿›…

Tempo …

• Heavy Condensed **abcdefghijklmnopqrstuvwxyzABCDEFGHIJKLMNOPQRSTUVWXYZ–$1234567890(**

Heavy Condensed Italic ***abcdefghijklmnopqrstuvwxyzABCDEFGHIJKLMNOPQRSTUVWXYZ–$12345678***

ITC TIEPOLO

AlphaOmega • 1987

AGP ADO AGA LEF MAE URW

abcdefghijklmnopqrstuvwxyz(".;'!*?':,")
$1234567890&fiflß-äöüåçèîñóæøœ
ABCDEFGHIJKLMNOPQRSTUVWXYZ
ÄÖÜÅÇÈÎÑÓÆØŒ»„«[¶§•†‡]‹¡·¿›…

ITC Tiepolo …

• Book abcdefghijklmnopqrstuvwxyzABCDEFGHIJKLMNOPQRSTUVWXYZ–$1234567890(

Book Italic *abcdefghijklmnopqrstuvwxyzABCDEFGHIJKLMNOPQRSTUVWXYZ–$1234567890(".;'!**

Bold **abcdefghijklmnopqrstuvwxyzABCDEFGHIJKLMNOPQRSTUVWXYZ–$12345678**

Bold Italic ***abcdefghijklmnopqrstuvwxyzABCDEFGHIJKLMNOPQRSTUVWXYZ–$1234567890(***

Black **abcdefghijklmnopqrstuvwxyzABCDEFGHIJKLMNOPQRSTUVWXYZ–$12345**

Black Italic ***abcdefghijklmnopqrstuvwxyzABCDEFGHIJKLMNOPQRSTUVWXYZ–$1234567***

T

Linotype DisplaySet 3: Gothic 13, Tempo Heavy Condensed & Heavy Condensed Italic.

ITC TIFFANY

Ed Benguiat • 1974 ... MacKellar, Smiths & Jordan, c. 1884

abcdefghijklmnopqrstuvwxyz(“.;‘!*?’:,”)
$1234567890&fiflß-äöüåçèîñóæøœ
ABCDEFGHIJKLMNOPQRSTUVWXYZ
ÄÖÜÅÇÈÎÑÓÆØŒ»„«[¶§•†‡]‹¡·¿›...

BIT ADO AGA LEF FAM LIN MAE URW

ITC Tiffany 1 ...

Light abcdefghijklmnopqrstuvwxyzABCDEFGHIJKLMNOPQRSTUVWXYZ–$123

Light Italic *abcdefghijklmnopqrstuvwxyzABCDEFGHIJKLMNOPQRSTUVWXYZ–$1234*

Demi **abcdefghijklmnopqrstuvwxyzABCDEFGHIJKLMNOPQRSTUVWXYZ–$**

Demi Italic ***abcdefghijklmnopqrstuvwxyzABCDEFGHIJKLMNOPQRSTUVWXYZ–$12***

ITC Tiffany 2 ...

• Medium abcdefghijklmnopqrstuvwxyzABCDEFGHIJKLMNOPQRSTUVWXYZ–$12

Medium Italic *abcdefghijklmnopqrstuvwxyzABCDEFGHIJKLMNOPQRSTUVWXYZ–$123*

Heavy **abcdefghijklmnopqrstuvwxyzABCDEFGHIJKLMNOPQRSTUVW**

Heavy Italic ***abcdefghijklmnopqrstuvwxyzABCDEFGHIJKLMNOPQRSTUV***

Tiger Rag

John Viner • 1989

abcdefghijklmnopqrstuvwxyz(“.;‘!*?’:,”)
$1234567890&fiflß-äöüåçèîñóæøœ
ABCDEFGHIJKLMNOPQRSTUVWXYZ
ÄÖÜÅÇÈÎÑÓÆØŒ»„«[•]‹¡·¿›...

LET ▲18

▷ abcdefghijklopqr ACGIKLMNOPRSTTUVWY

FC TIMBRE

abcdefghijklmnopqrstuvwxyz(“.;‘!*?’:,”)
$1234567890&fiflß-äöüåçèîñóæøœ
ABCDEFGHIJKLMNOPQRSTUVWXYZÄÖÜÅÇAÈÎÑÓÆØŒ»„«[•]‹¡•¿›...

TFC ▲18

FC Timbre ...

Open abcdefghijklmnopqrstuvwxyzABCDEFGHIJKLMNOPQRSTUVWXYZ–$1234567890

• Regular **abcdefghijklmnopqrstuvwxyzABCDEFGHIJKLMNOPQRSTUVWXYZ–$1234567890**

TIMES NEW ROMAN 1

Stanley Morison, Victor Lardent & Monotype Design Staff • 1931

abcdefghijklmnopqrstuvwxyz(“.;‘!*?’:,”)
$1234567890&fiflß-äöüåçèîñóæøœ
ABCDEFGHIJKLMNOPQRSTUVWXYZ
ÄÖÜÅÇÈÎÑÓÆØŒ»„«[¶§•†‡]‹¡·¿›...

MCL

Times New Roman 1 ...

• Regular abcdefghijklmnopqrstuvwxyzABCDEFGHIJKLMNOPQRSTUVWXYZ–$123456

Italic *abcdefghijklmnopqrstuvwxyzABCDEFGHIJKLMNOPQRSTUVWXYZ–$12345678*

Times New Roman · Times New Roman Cyrillic, Times New Roman Greek & Dual Greek.

... Times New Roman

Bold **abcdefghijklmnopqrstuvwxyzABCDEFGHIJKLMNOPQRSTUVWXYZ–$1234567**

Bold Italic ***abcdefghijklmnopqrstuvwxyzABCDEFGHIJKLMNOPQRSTUVWXYZ–$12345678***

TIMES NEW ROMAN EXPERT

MCL ABCDEFGHIJKLMNOPQRSTUVWXYZ.;!?:,
1234567890&ff fi fl ffi ffl–ÄÖÜÅÇÈÎÑÓÆØŒ
(abdeilmnorst) 1/8 1/4 1/3 3/8 1/2 5/8 2/3 3/4 7/8 $12345/67890¢ ₡Rp

Times New Roman Expert ...

• Expert Regular ABCDEFGHIJKLMNOPQRSTUVWXYZ–$1234567890.;!?:,&-ff fi fl ffi ffl 1/8 1/4 1/3 3/8 1/2 $12345/67890¢

Expert Italic *$1234567890.;:,–ff fi fl ffi ffl 1/8 1/4 1/3 3/8 1/2 $12345/67890¢ (abdeilmnorst) 5/8 2/3 3/4 7/8 ₡Rp*

Expert Bold **$1234567890.;:,–ff fi fl ffi ffl 1/8 1/4 1/3 3/8 1/2 $12345/67890¢ (abdeilmnorst) 5/8 2/3 3/4 7/8 ₡Rp**

Expert Bold Italic ***$1234567890.;:,–ff fi fl ffi ffl 1/8 1/4 1/3 3/8 1/2 $12345/67890¢ (abdeilmnorst) 5/8 2/3 3/4 7/8 ₡Rp***

TIMES NEW ROMAN 2

MCL abcdefghijklmnopqrstuvwxyz(“.;‘!*?’:,”)
$1234567890&fiflß-äöüåçèîñóæøœ
ABCDEFGHIJKLMNOPQRSTUVWXYZ
ÄÖÜÅÇÈÎÑÓÆØŒ»„«[¶§•†‡]‹¡·¿›...

Times New Roman 2 ...

• Semibold abcdefghijklmnopqrstuvwxyzABCDEFGHIJKLMNOPQRSTUVWXYZ–$1

Semibold Italic *abcdefghijklmnopqrstuvwxyzABCDEFGHIJKLMNOPQRSTUVWXYZ–$123*

Extra Bold ▲16 **abcdefghijklmnopqrstuvwxyzABCDEFGHIJKLMNOPQRSTUVWXYZ**

TIMES NEW ROMAN CONDENSED

MCL ADO AGA LIN MAE abcdefghijklmnopqrstuvwxyz(“.;‘!*?’:,”)
$1234567890&fiflß-äöüåçèîñóæøœ
ABCDEFGHIJKLMNOPQRSTUVWXYZ
ÄÖÜÅÇÈÎÑÓÆØŒ»„«[¶§•†‡]‹¡·¿›...

Times New Roman Condensed ...

• Condensed abcdefghijklmnopqrstuvwxyzABCDEFGHIJKLMNOPQRSTUVWXYZ–$1234567890(“.;‘!*?’:,”)&fi

Condensed Italic *abcdefghijklmnopqrstuvwxyzABCDEFGHIJKLMNOPQRSTUVWXYZ–$1234567890(“.;‘!*?’:,”)&fiflß*

Bold Condensed ▲16 **abcdefghijklmnopqrstuvwxyzABCDEFGHIJKLMNOPQRSTUVWXYZ–$1234567890(**

TIMES NEW ROMAN 3

MCL abcdefghijklmnopqrstuvwxyz(“.;‘!*?’:,”)
$1234567890&fiflß-äöüåçèîñóæøœ
ABCDEFGHIJKLMNOPQRSTUVWXYZ
ÄÖÜÅÇÈÎÑÓÆØŒ»„«[¶§•†‡]‹¡·¿›...

Times New Roman 3 ...

• Small Text ▲12 abcdefghijklmnopqrstuvwxyzABCDEFGHIJKLMNOPQRSTUVWXYZ

Small Text Italic ▲12 *abcdefghijklmnopqrstuvwxyzABCDEFGHIJKLMNOPQRSTUVWXYZ–$*

. . . Times New Roman 3

Small Text Bold ▲12 **abcdefghijklmnopqrstuvwxyzABCDEFGHIJKLMNOPQRSTUVWXYZ–**

Medium abcdefghijklmnopqrstuvwxyzABCDEFGHIJKLMNOPQRSTUVWXYZ–$123456

Medium Italic *abcdefghijklmnopqrstuvwxyzABCDEFGHIJKLMNOPQRSTUVWXYZ–$1234567890*

TIMES NEW ROMAN SEVEN

MCL abcdefghijklmnopqrstuvwxyz(“.;‘!*?’:,”)

▲12 $1234567890&fiflß-äöüåçèîñóæøœ

ABCDEFGHIJKLMNOPQRSTUVWXYZ

ÄÖÜÅÇÈÎÑÓÆØŒ»„«[¶§•†‡]‹¡·¿›...

Times New Roman Seven . . .

• Regular abcdefghijklmnopqrstuvwxyzABCDEFGHIJKLMNOPQRSTUVWXYZ–$12345678

Italic *abcdefghijklmnopqrstuvwxyzABCDEFGHIJKLMNOPQRSTUVWXYZ–$1234567890(“.;‘*

Bold **abcdefghijklmnopqrstuvwxyzABCDEFGHIJKLMNOPQRSTUVWXYZ–$12345678**

Bold Italic ***abcdefghijklmnopqrstuvwxyzABCDEFGHIJKLMNOPQRSTUVWXYZ–$1234567890(“***

TIMES NEW ROMAN PS

Monotype Design Staff • 1989 abcdefghijklmnopqrstuvwxyz(“.;‘!*?’:,”)

MCL ADO AGA LIN MAE $1234567890&fiflß-äöüåçèîñóæøœ

ABCDEFGHIJKLMNOPQRSTUVWXYZ

ÄÖÜÅÇÈÎÑÓÆØŒ»„«[¶§•†‡]‹¡·¿›...

Times New Roman PS . . .

• Regular abcdefghijklmnopqrstuvwxyzABCDEFGHIJKLMNOPQRSTUVWXYZ–$1234567890(

Italic *abcdefghijklmnopqrstuvwxyzABCDEFGHIJKLMNOPQRSTUVWXYZ–$1234567890(“.;*

Bold **abcdefghijklmnopqrstuvwxyzABCDEFGHIJKLMNOPQRSTUVWXYZ–$1234567**

Bold Italic ***abcdefghijklmnopqrstuvwxyzABCDEFGHIJKLMNOPQRSTUVWXYZ–$1234567890***

TIMES NEW ROMAN PS EXPERT

MCL ABCDEFGHIJKLMNOPQRSTUVWXYZ.;!?:,

1234567890&ff fi fl ffi ffl–ÄÖÜÅÇÈÎÑÓÆØŒ

(abdeilmnorst) 1/8 1/4 1/3 3/8 1/2 5/8 2/3 3/4 7/8 $12345/67890¢ ₡Rp

Times New Roman PS Expert . . .

• Expert Regular ABCDEFGHIJKLMNOPQRSTUVWXYZ–$1234567890.;!?:,&-ff fi fl ffi ffl 1/8 1/4 1/3 3/8 1/2 $12345/67890¢ (ab

Expert Italic *$1234567890.;:,–ff fi fl ffi ffl 1/8 1/4 1/3 3/8 1/2 $12345/67890¢ (abdeilmnorst) 5/8 2/3 3/4 7/8 ₡Rp*

Expert Bold **$1234567890.;:,–ff fi fl ffi ffl 1/8 1/4 1/3 3/8 1/2 $12345/67890¢ (abdeilmnorst) 5/8 2/3 3/4 7/8 ₡Rp**

Expert Bold Italic ***$1234567890.;:,–ff fi fl ffi ffl 1/8 1/4 1/3 3/8 1/2 $12345/67890¢ (abdeilmnorst) 5/8 2/3 3/4 7/8 ₡Rp***

T

Times New Roman PS Times New Roman PS Efo.

TIMES SCOSF

Linotype Design Staff • 1932 ... Stanley Morison, et al, 1931
LIN ADO AGA MAE

ABCDEFGHIJKLMNOPQRSTUVWXYZ(“.;‘!*?’:,”)
$1234567890&-ÄÖÜÅÇÈÎÑÓÆØŒ
ABCDEFGHIJKLMNOPQRSTUVWXYZ
ÄÖÜÅÇÈÎÑÓÆØŒ»„«[¶§•†‡]‹¡·¿›...

Times SCOSF ...

• Roman SCOSF ABCDEFGHIJKLMNOPQRSTUVWXYZABCDEFGHIJKLMNOPQRSTUVWXYZ–$1234567
Italic OSF *abcdefghijklmnopqrstuvwxyzABCDEFGHIJKLMNOPQRSTUVWXYZ–$1234567890(“.;*
Bold SCOSF **ABCDEFGHIJKLMNOPQRSTUVWXYZABCDEFGHIJKLMNOPQRSTUVWXYZ–$123**
Bold Italic OSF ***abcdefghijklmnopqrstuvwxyzABCDEFGHIJKLMNOPQRSTUVWXYZ–$1234567890***

TIMES 2

Linotype Design Staff • ... Stanley Morison, et al, 1931
LIN ADO AGA MAE

abcdefghijklmnopqrstuvwxyz(“.;‘!*?’:,”)
$1234567890&fiflß-äöüåçèîñóæøœ
ABCDEFGHIJKLMNOPQRSTUVWXYZ
ÄÖÜÅÇÈÎÑÓÆØŒ»„«[¶§•†‡]‹¡·¿›...

Times 2 ...

• Semibold **abcdefghijklmnopqrstuvwxyzABCDEFGHIJKLMNOPQRSTUVWXYZ–$1234567**
Semibold Italic ***abcdefghijklmnopqrstuvwxyzABCDEFGHIJKLMNOPQRSTUVWXYZ–$123456789***
Extra Bold ▲16 **abcdefghijklmnopqrstuvwxyzABCDEFGHIJKLMNOPQRSTUVWXY**

TIMES TEN

Linotype Design Staff • 1988 ... Stanley Morison, et al, 1931
LIN ADO AGA MAE

abcdefghijklmnopqrstuvwxyz(“.;‘!*?’:,”)
$1234567890&fiflß-äöüåçèîñóæøœ
ABCDEFGHIJKLMNOPQRSTUVWXYZ
ÄÖÜÅÇÈÎÑÓÆØŒ»„«[¶§•†‡]‹¡·¿›...

Times Ten ...

• Roman abcdefghijklmnopqrstuvwxyzABCDEFGHIJKLMNOPQRSTUVWXYZ–$12345
Italic *abcdefghijklmnopqrstuvwxyzABCDEFGHIJKLMNOPQRSTUVWXYZ–$12345*
Bold **abcdefghijklmnopqrstuvwxyzABCDEFGHIJKLMNOPQRSTUVWXYZ–$12345**
Bold Italic ***abcdefghijklmnopqrstuvwxyzABCDEFGHIJKLMNOPQRSTUVWXYZ–$1234***

T

TIMES TEN SCOSF

LIN ADO AGA MAE

ABCDEFGHIJKLMNOPQRSTUVWXYZ(“.;‘!*?’:,”)
$1234567890&-ÄÖÜÅÇÈÎÑÓÆØŒ
ABCDEFGHIJKLMNOPQRSTUVWXYZ
ÄÖÜÅÇÈÎÑÓÆØŒ»„«[¶§•†‡]‹¡·¿›...

Times Ten SCOSF ...

• Roman SCOSF ABCDEFGHIJKLMNOPQRSTUVWXYZABCDEFGHIJKLMNOPQRSTUVWXYZ–$123
Italic OSF *abcdefghijklmnopqrstuvwxyzABCDEFGHIJKLMNOPQRSTUVWXYZ–$12345*
Bold OSF **abcdefghijklmnopqrstuvwxyzABCDEFGHIJKLMNOPQRSTUVWXYZ–$12345**

Times Ten Times Ten Cyrillic, Times Ten EastA, Times Ten Monotonic & Polytonic Greek.

. . . Times Ten SCOSF

Bold Italic OSF ***abcdefghijklmnopqrstuvwxyzABCDEFGHIJKLMNOPQRSTUVWXYZ–$1234***

TIMES EIGHTEEN
✣ *Linotype Headliners*
LIN abcdefghijklmnopqrstuvwxyz(“.;‘!*?’:,”)
▲24 $1234567890&fiflß-äöüåçèîñóæøœ
ABCDEFGHIJKLMNOPQRSTUVWXYZ
ÄÖÜÅÇÈÎÑÓÆØŒ»„«[¶§•†‡]‹¡·¿›...

Times Eighteen . . .

• Roman abcdefghijklmnopqrstuvwxyzABCDEFGHIJKL

Bold **abcdefghijklmnopqrstuvwxyzABCDEFGHIJKL**

TIMES EUROPA

✍ *Walter Tracy • 1971* abcdefghijklmnopqrstuvwxyz(“.;‘!*?’:,”)
LIN ADO AGA MAE $1234567890&fiflß-äöüåçèîñóæøœ
▲12 ABCDEFGHIJKLMNOPQRSTUVWXYZ
ÄÖÜÅÇÈÎÑÓÆØŒ»„«[¶§•†‡]‹¡·¿›...

Times Europa . . .

• Roman abcdefghijklmnopqrstuvwxyzABCDEFGHIJKLMNOPQRSTUVWXYZ–$1234567890(“.;‘

Italic *abcdefghijklmnopqrstuvwxyzABCDEFGHIJKLMNOPQRSTUVWXYZ–$1234567890(“.;‘!*?’:*

Bold **abcdefghijklmnopqrstuvwxyzABCDEFGHIJKLMNOPQRSTUVWXYZ–$1234567890(“.;‘**

Bold Italic ***abcdefghijklmnopqrstuvwxyzABCDEFGHIJKLMNOPQRSTUVWXYZ–$1234567890(“.;‘!****

Tiranti

✍ *Tony Forster • 1993* *abcdefghijklmnopqrstuvwxyz(“.;‘!*?’:,”)*
LET *$1234567890&fiflß-äöüåçèîñóæøœ*
▲16 *ABCDEFGHIJKLMNOPQRSTUVWXYZ*
ÄÖÜÅÇÈÎÑÓ»„«[•]‹¡·¿›... ▹ *bddeghhkklpqrrrrspy& chctffflklldshsttELTh*

T

. . . .
✣ *Linotype Headliners*: Chwast Buffalo Black Condensed, Erbar Light Condensed & Bold Condensed, Metrolite, Metromedium, Metroblack, Plak Black, Black Condensed & Extra Black Condensed, Stop, Times Eighteen Roman & Bold.

TOMBOY

Garrett Boge • 1989 abcdefghijklmnopqrstuvwxyz(".;'!*?':,")

LPT MTD $1234567890&fiflß-äöüåçèîñóæøœ

ABCDEFGHIJKLMNOPQRSTUVWXYZ

ÄÖÜÅÇÈÎÑÓÆØŒ»„«[•]‹¡·¿›...

Tomboy ...

Light abcdefghijklmnopqrstuvwxyzABCDEFGHIJKLMNOPQRSTUVWXYZ-$1234567890(".;'!*?':,")

• Regular abcdefghijklmnopqrstuvwxyzABCDEFGHIJKLMNOPQRSTUVWXYZ-$1234567890(".;'!*

Bold abcdefghijklmnopqrstuvwxyzABCDEFGHIJKLMNOPQRSTUVWXYZ-$1234567890(

Tommy's Type
Group Cats

Judith Sutcliffe • 1993

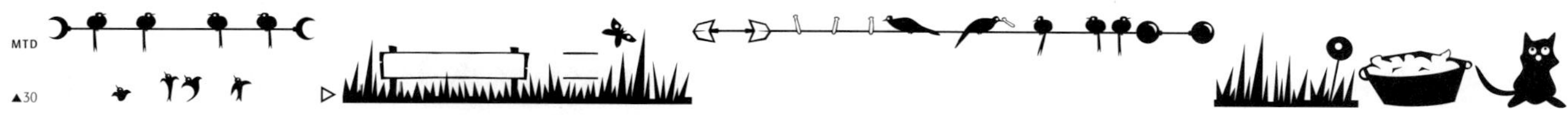

MTD

▲30

PL Torino Open
Agfa Typographer's Edition 3

Ed Benguiat • 1960
... Alessandro Butti, 1908

abcdefghijklmnopqrstuvwxyz(".;'!*?':,")

AGP

▲24 $1234567890&-äöüåçèîñóæøœ

ABCDEFGHIJKLMNOPQRSTUVWXYZ

ÄÖÜÅÇÈÎÑÓÆØŒ»„«[•†‡]‹¡·¿›... ▷2

A*I Toskana

Manfred Klein • 1994 ABCDEFGHIJKLMNOPQRSTUVWXYZ

ALP

▲24 1234567890ÄÖÜÄÖÜ

ABCDEFGHIJKLMNOPQRSTUVWXYZ

TRADE GOTHIC

Jackson Burke • 1948 abcdefghijklmnopqrstuvwxyz(".;'!*?':,")

LIN ADO AGA MAE $1234567890&fiflß-äöüåçèîñóæøœ

ABCDEFGHIJKLMNOPQRSTUVWXYZ

ÄÖÜÅÇÈÎÑÓÆØŒ»„«[¶§•†‡]‹¡·¿›...

....
Group Cats: Catastrophe & Tommy's Type.
Agfa Typographer's Edition 3: Barclay Open, PL Bernhardt Light, Medium & Bold, PL Britannia Bold, Delphian Open, PL Fiorello Condensed, Fluidum Bold, PL Modern Heavy Condensed, PL Torino Open.

... Trade Gothic ...

Light abcdefghijklmnopqrstuvwxyzABCDEFGHIJKLMNOPQRSTUVWXYZ–$1234567890(“

Light Oblique *abcdefghijklmnopqrstuvwxyzABCDEFGHIJKLMNOPQRSTUVWXYZ–$1234567890(“*

• Regular abcdefghijklmnopqrstuvwxyzABCDEFGHIJKLMNOPQRSTUVWXYZ–$123456789

Oblique *abcdefghijklmnopqrstuvwxyzABCDEFGHIJKLMNOPQRSTUVWXYZ–$123456789*

Bold **abcdefghijklmnopqrstuvwxyzABCDEFGHIJKLMNOPQRSTUVWXYZ–$1234567890(“.;‘!*?’**

Bold Oblique ***abcdefghijklmnopqrstuvwxyzABCDEFGHIJKLMNOPQRSTUVWXYZ–$1234567890(“.;‘!*?’***

Bold No. 2 **abcdefghijklmnopqrstuvwxyzABCDEFGHIJKLMNOPQRSTUVWXYZ–$123456789**

Bold No. 2 Oblique ***abcdefghijklmnopqrstuvwxyzABCDEFGHIJKLMNOPQRSTUVWXYZ–$123456789***

TRADE GOTHIC CONDENSED

LIN ADO AGA MAE abcdefghijklmnopqrstuvwxyz(“.;‘!*?’:,”)
▲16 $1234567890&fiflß-äöüåçèîñóæøœ
ABCDEFGHIJKLMNOPQRSTUVWXYZ
ÄÖÜÅÇÈÎÑÓÆØŒ»„«[¶§•†‡]‹¡·¿›...

Trade Gothic Condensed ...

• No.18 Condensed abcdefghijklmnopqrstuvwxyzABCDEFGHIJKLMNOPQRSTUVWXYZ–$1234567890(“.;‘!*?’:,”)

No.18 Condensed Oblique *abcdefghijklmnopqrstuvwxyzABCDEFGHIJKLMNOPQRSTUVWXYZ–$1234567890(“.;‘!*?’:,”)*

No. 20 Bold Condensed **abcdefghijklmnopqrstuvwxyzABCDEFGHIJKLMNOPQRSTUVWXYZ–$1234567890(“.;‘!*?’:,**

No. 20 Bold Condensed Oblique ***abcdefghijklmnopqrstuvwxyzABCDEFGHIJKLMNOPQRSTUVWXYZ–$1234567890(“.;‘!*?’:,***

TRADE GOTHIC EXTENDED

LIN ADO AGA MAE abcdefghijklmnopqrstuvwxyz(“.;‘!*?’:,”)
$1234567890&fiflß-äöüåçèîñóæøœ
ABCDEFGHIJKLMNOPQRSTUVWXYZ
ÄÖÜÅÇÈÎÑÓÆØŒ»„«[¶§•†‡]‹¡·¿›...

Trade Gothic Extended ...

• Extended abcdefghijklmnopqrstuvwxyzABCDEFGHIJKLMNOPQRSTUVW

Bold Extended **abcdefghijklmnopqrstuvwxyzABCDEFGHIJKLMNOPQRSTUVW**

T

TRAJAN
Adobe TitlingSet 1

Carol Twombly • *1989*
ADO AGA LIN MAE
▲30

ABCDEFGHIJKLMNOPQRSTUV
WXYZ(“.;‘!*?’:,”)$1234567890
&-ÄÖÜÅÇÈÎÑÓÆØŒ»„«[·]‹¡·¿›...

Trajan ...

• Roman ABCDEFGHIJKLMNOPQRSTUV

Adobe TitlingSet 1: Charlemagne Roman & Bold, Trajan Roman & Bold.

. . . Trajan
Bold
ABCDEFGHIJKLMNOPQRSTUV

CG TRIUMVIRATE CONDENSED

FAM AGP abcdefghijklmnopqrstuvwxyz(".;'!*?':,")
▲16 $1234567890&fiflß-äöüåçèîñóæøœ
ABCDEFGHIJKLMNOPQRSTUVWXYZ
ÄÖÜÅÇÈÎÑÓÆØŒ»„«[¶§•†‡]‹¡·¿›...

CG Triumvirate Condensed 1 ...

Light Condensed abcdefghijklmnopqrstuvwxyzABCDEFGHIJKLMNOPQRSTUVWXYZ–$1234567890(".;'!*?':,")&fiflß-äöüÄÖÜåçèÅÇ
Light Condensed Italic *abcdefghijklmnopqrstuvwxyzABCDEFGHIJKLMNOPQRSTUVWXYZ–$1234567890(".;'!*?':,")&fiflß-äöüÄÖÜåçèÅÇÈ*

CG Triumvirate Condensed 2 ...

• Condensed abcdefghijklmnopqrstuvwxyzABCDEFGHIJKLMNOPQRSTUVWXYZ–$1234567890(".;'!*?':,")&fiflß-äöü
Condensed Italic *abcdefghijklmnopqrstuvwxyzABCDEFGHIJKLMNOPQRSTUVWXYZ–$1234567890(".;'!*?':,")&fiflß-äöü*
Bold Condensed **abcdefghijklmnopqrstuvwxyzABCDEFGHIJKLMNOPQRSTUVWXYZ–$1234567890(".;'!*?':,")&fiflß-ä**
Bold Condensed Italic ***abcdefghijklmnopqrstuvwxyzABCDEFGHIJKLMNOPQRSTUVWXYZ–$1234567890(".;'!*?':,")&fiflß-ä***

CG Triumvirate Condensed 3 ...

Black Condensed **abcdefghijklmnopqrstuvwxyzABCDEFGHIJKLMNOPQRSTUVWXYZ–$1234567890(".;'!*?':,")&fiflß**
Black Condensed Italic ***abcdefghijklmnopqrstuvwxyzABCDEFGHIJKLMNOPQRSTUVWXYZ–$1234567890(".;'!*?':,")&fifl***

PL Trophy Oblique
Agfa Typographer's Edition 2
Frank Bartuska • 1950 abcdefghijklmnopqrstuvwxyz(".;'!*?':,")
AGP $1234567890&ß-äöüåçèîñóæøœ
▲18 ABCDEFGHIJKLMNOPQRSTUVWXYZ
ÄÖÜÅÇÈÎÑÓÆØŒ»«[•†‡]‹¡¿›...
▷ a c e k l q r s u y G K Y

TRUESDELL

Steve Matteson • 1993
... Frederic W. Goudy, 1930 abcdefghijklmnopqrstuvwxyz(".;'!*?':,")
MTD $1234567890&fiflß-äöüåçèîñóæøœ
▲16 ABCDEFGHIJKLMNOPQRSTUVWXYZ
ÄÖÜÅÇÈÎÑÓÆØŒ»„«[¶§•†‡]‹¡·¿›...
▷ ¶ ♣

Truesdell ...

• Roman abcdefghijklmnopqrstuvwxyzABCDEFGHIJKLMNOPQRSTUVWXYZ–$12345678
Italic *abcdefghijklmnopqrstuvwxyzABCDEFGHIJKLMNOPQRSTUVWXYZ–$1234567890(*
Bold **abcdefghijklmnopqrstuvwxyzABCDEFGHIJKLMNOPQRSTUVWXYZ–$12345**
Bold Italic ***abcdefghijklmnopqrstuvwxyzABCDEFGHIJKLMNOPQRSTUVWXYZ–$1234567***
Roman SCLF & Alternate ABCDEFGHIJKLMNOPQRSTUVWXYZ–$1234567890(".;'!*?':,")&ffifl ffi ffl-ct st ÄÖÜÇÈÎÑÓÆØŒ
Italic LF & Swash Alternate *a d e h b m n v ffffiflffiffl A B C D E F G M P R T U $1234567890.:,ct st Th ä å ç è ñ*

Agfa Typographer's Edition 2: PL Barnum Block, PL Benguiat Frisky Bold, TC Broadway, PL Davison Zip Bold, PL Fiedler Gothic Bold, PL Futura Maxi Book & Bold, Neon Extra Condensed, Ritmo Bold, PL Trophy Oblique.
Truesdell ▶ Truesdell Sorts.

T

... Truesdell

Bold & Bold Italic LF & Alternate **$1234567890.;:,ﬀﬁﬂﬃﬄ ct st** ***h $1234567890.;:,ﬀﬁﬂﬃﬄ ct st***

TRUMP MEDIÄVAL

Georg Trump • 1954 abcdefghijklmnopqrstuvwxyz(".;'!*?':,")

ADO AGA AGP LIN MAE $1234567890&ﬁﬂß-äöüåçèîñóæøœ

ABCDEFGHIJKLMNOPQRSTUVWXYZ

ÄÖÜÅÇÈÎÑÓÆØŒ»,,«[¶§•†‡]‹¡·¿›...

Trump Mediäval ...

• Roman abcdefghijklmnopqrstuvwxyzABCDEFGHIJKLMNOPQRSTUVWXYZ–$1234

Italic *abcdefghijklmnopqrstuvwxyzABCDEFGHIJKLMNOPQRSTUVWXYZ–$123*

Bold **abcdefghijklmnopqrstuvwxyzABCDEFGHIJKLMNOPQRSTUVWXYZ–$123**

Bold Italic ***abcdefghijklmnopqrstuvwxyzABCDEFGHIJKLMNOPQRSTUVWXYZ–$123***

TRUMP MEDIÄVAL SCOSF

ADO AGA LIN MAE ABCDEFGHIJKLMNOPQRSTUVWXYZ(".;'!*?':,")

$1234567890&-ÄÖÜÅÇÈÎÑÓÆØŒ

ABCDEFGHIJKLMNOPQRSTUVWXYZ

ÄÖÜÅÇÈÎÑÓÆØŒ»,,«[¶§•†‡]‹¡·¿›...

Trump Mediäval SCOSF ...

• Roman SCOSF ABCDEFGHIJKLMNOPQRSTUVWXYZABCDEFGHIJKLMNOPQRSTUVWXYZ–$1

Italic OSF *abcdefghijklmnopqrstuvwxyzABCDEFGHIJKLMNOPQRSTUVWXYZ–$123*

Bold OSF **abcdefghijklmnopqrstuvwxyzABCDEFGHIJKLMNOPQRSTUVWXYZ–$123**

Bold Italic OSF ***abcdefghijklmnopqrstuvwxyzABCDEFGHIJKLMNOPQRSTUVWXYZ–$12***

A*I Tuscan Egyptian

A*I Wood Type

A*I Design Staff • 1990

ALP MTD

▲54

ABCDEFGHIJKLMNOPQRSTUVWXYZ

(.:!*?:,)$1234567890&-

ABCDEFGHIJKLMNOPQRSTUVWXYZ[]

A*I Wood Type: A*I Antique Condensed, A*I Barrel, A*I Box Gothic, A*I French XXX Condensed, A*I Painter, A*I Tuscan Egyptian.

T

Twang

Tim Donaldson • 1994 abcdefghijklmnopqrstuvwxyz(“.;‘!*?’:,”)

LET $1234567890+fiflß-äöüåçèîñóæøœ

▲16 ABCDEFGHIJKLMNOPQRSTUVWXYZ

ÄÖÜÅÇÈÎÑÓÆØŒ»„«[•]‹î·¿›... ▷ Aeegnoaa BCDEFGHIJKLMNOPQRRSTU VWXYZ

TWIST

Christian Schwartz • 1993 ABCDEFGHIJKLMNOPQRSTUVWXYZ(“.;‘!*?’:,”)$1234567890&-ÄÖÜÅÇÈÎÑÓÆØŒ

CHR ABCDEFGHIJKLMNOPQRSTUVWXYZÄÖÜÅÇÈÎÑÓÆØŒ»„«•‹¡·¿›...

▲24 ▷

Twist ...

• One ABCDEFGHIJKLMNOPQRSTUVWXYZABCDEFGHIJKLMNOPQRSTUVWXYZ-$1234567

Two ABCDEFGHIJKLMNOPQRSTUVWXYZABCDEFGHIJKLMNOPQRSTUVWXYZ-$123456

Three ABCDEFGHIJKLMNOPQRSTUVWXYZABCDEFGHIJKLMNOPQRSTUVWXYZ-$1

Four ABCDEFGHIJKLMNOPQRSTUVWXYZABCDEFGHIJKLMNOPQRSTUVWXYZ-

Typewriter

Monotype Typewriter Faces

MCL abcdefghijklmnopqrstuvwxyz(“.;‘!*?’:,”)

▲12 $1234567890&fiflß-äöüåçèîñóæøœ

ABCDEFGHIJKLMNOPQRSTUVWXYZ

ÄÖÜÅÇÈÎÑÓÆØŒ»„«[¶§•†‡]‹¡·¿›...

Typewriter Elite

Monotype Typewriter Faces

MCL abcdefghijklmnopqrstuvwxyz(“.;‘!*?’:,”)

▲12 $1234567890&fiflß-äöüåçèîñóæøœ

ABCDEFGHIJKLMNOPQRSTUVWXYZ

ÄÖÜÅÇÈÎÑÓÆØŒ»„«[¶§•†‡]‹¡·¿›...

Typewriter Gothic

Monotype Typewriter Faces

MCL abcdefghijklmnopqrstuvwxyz(“.;‘!*?’:,”)

▲12 $1234567890&fiflß-äöüåçèîñóæøœ

ABCDEFGHIJKLMNOPQRSTUVWXYZ

ÄÖÜÅÇÈÎÑÓÆØŒ»„«[¶§•†‡]‹¡·¿›...

Typo Upright

Morris Fuller Benton • 1905 abcdefghijklmnopqrstuvwxyz(“.;‘!*?’:,”)

BIT $1234567890&fiflß-äöüåçèîñóæøœ

▲18 ABCDEFGHIJKLMNOPQRSTUVWXYZ

ÄÖÜÅÇÈÎÑÓÆØŒ»„«[§•†‡]‹¡·¿›...

Monotype Typewriter Faces: Monotype Courier 12, Typewriter, Typewriter Elite, Typewriter Gothic.

T

Ulysses
Umbra
Uncial
Univers
University Roman
DV Upright
ITC Usherwood
Utopia

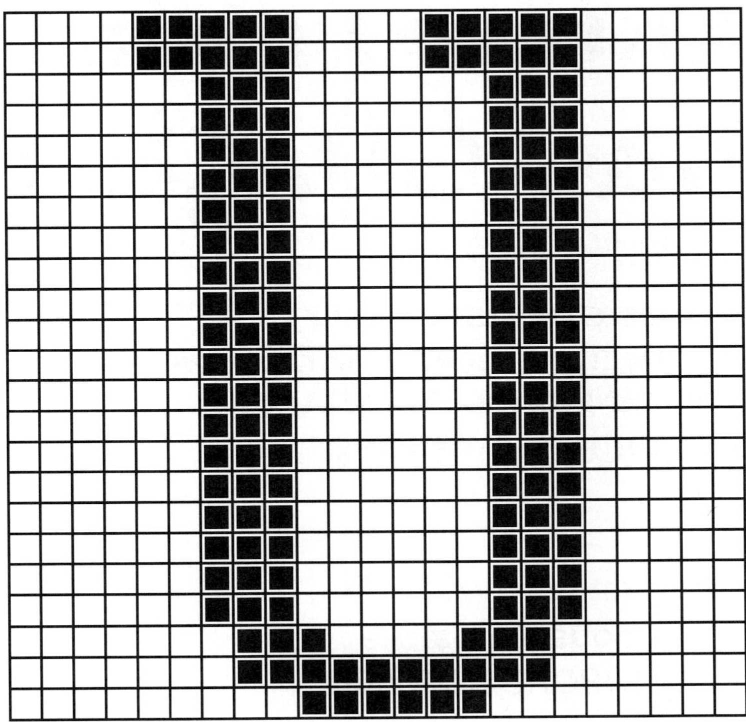

✍ Michael Johnson, 1990

Ulysses

Timothy Donaldson • 1991 abcdefghijklmnopqrstuvwxyz(".;'!*?':,")
LET $1234567890&fifl ß-äöüåçèîñóæøœ
▲16 ABCDEFGHIJKLMNOPQRSTUVWXYZ
ÄÖÜÅÇÈÎÑÓÆØŒ»„«[•]‹¡·¿›...

▷ls

Umbra

Robert Hunter Middleton • 1932 ABCDEFGHIJKLMNOPQRS
BIT ADO AGA TFC LIN MAE TUVWXYZ(".;'!*?':,")$12345
▲42 67890&-ÄÖÜÅÇÈÎÑÓÆØ...

Uncial
Agfa DisplaySet 3
Victor Hammer • 1952 abcdefghijklmnopqrstuvwxyz(".;'!*?':,")
AGP $1234567890&fifl ß-äöüåçèîñóœøœ
▲16 ABCDEFGHIJKLMNOPQRSTUVWXYZ
ÄÖÜÅÇÈÎÑÓÆØŒ»„«[§•†‡]‹¡·¿›...

UNIVERS 1

Adrian Frutiger • 1957 abcdefghijklmnopqrstuvwxyz(".;'!*?':,")
LIN ADO AGA FAM MAE $1234567890&fifl ß-äöüåçèîñóæøœ
ABCDEFGHIJKLMNOPQRSTUVWXYZ
ÄÖÜÅÇÈÎÑÓÆØŒ»„«[¶§•†‡]‹¡·¿›...

Univers 1 ...

45-Light abcdefghijklmnopqrstuvwxyzABCDEFGHIJKLMNOPQRSTUVWXYZ–$12345678
45-Light Oblique *abcdefghijklmnopqrstuvwxyzABCDEFGHIJKLMNOPQRSTUVWXYZ–$12345678*
• 55-Regular abcdefghijklmnopqrstuvwxyzABCDEFGHIJKLMNOPQRSTUVWXYZ–$12345
55-Oblique *abcdefghijklmnopqrstuvwxyzABCDEFGHIJKLMNOPQRSTUVWXYZ–$12345*
65-Bold **abcdefghijklmnopqrstuvwxyzABCDEFGHIJKLMNOPQRSTUVWXYZ–$1234**
65-Bold Oblique ***abcdefghijklmnopqrstuvwxyzABCDEFGHIJKLMNOPQRSTUVWXYZ–$1234***
75-Black **abcdefghijklmnopqrstuvwxyzABCDEFGHIJKLMNOPQRSTUVWXYZ**
75-Black Oblique ***abcdefghijklmnopqrstuvwxyzABCDEFGHIJKLMNOPQRSTUVWXYZ***

U

Agfa DisplaySet 3: Basque, Brophy Script, Chevalier, Uncial.

UNIVERS CONDENSED

LIN ADO AGA FAM MAE abcdefghijklmnopqrstuvwxyz(“.;‘!*?’:,”)
$1234567890&fiflß-äöüåçèîñóæøœ
ABCDEFGHIJKLMNOPQRSTUVWXYZ
ÄÖÜÅÇÈÎÑÓÆØŒ»„«[¶§•†‡]‹¡·¿›...

Univers Condensed ...

47-Light Condensed abcdefghijklmnopqrstuvwxyzABCDEFGHIJKLMNOPQRSTUVWXYZ–$1234567890(“.;‘!*?’:.”)&fiflß-ä

47-Light Condensed Oblique *abcdefghijklmnopqrstuvwxyzABCDEFGHIJKLMNOPQRSTUVWXYZ–$1234567890(“.;‘!*?’:.”)&fiflß-ä*

• 57-Condensed abcdefghijklmnopqrstuvwxyzABCDEFGHIJKLMNOPQRSTUVWXYZ–$1234567890(“.;‘!*?’:,”

57-Condensed Oblique *abcdefghijklmnopqrstuvwxyzABCDEFGHIJKLMNOPQRSTUVWXYZ–$1234567890(“.;‘!*?’:,”*

67-Bold Condensed **abcdefghijklmnopqrstuvwxyzABCDEFGHIJKLMNOPQRSTUVWXYZ–$1234567890(“.;‘!*?’:,**

67-Bold Condensed Oblique ***abcdefghijklmnopqrstuvwxyzABCDEFGHIJKLMNOPQRSTUVWXYZ–$1234567890(“.;‘!*?’:,***

UNIVERS EXTENDED

LIN ADO AGA FAM MAE abcdefghijklmnopqrstuvwxyz(“.;‘!*?’:,”)
$1234567890&fiflß-äöüåçèîñóæøœ
ABCDEFGHIJKLMNOPQRSTUVWXYZ
ÄÖÜÅÇÈÎÑÓÆØŒ»„«[¶§•†‡]‹¡·¿›...

Univers Extended ...

• 53-Extended abcdefghijklmnopqrstuvwxyzABCDEFGHIJKLMNOPQRSTUV

53-Extended Oblique *abcdefghijklmnopqrstuvwxyzABCDEFGHIJKLMNOPQRSTUV*

63-Bold Extended **abcdefghijklmnopqrstuvwxyzABCDEFGHIJKLMNOPQRSTU**

63-Bold Extended Oblique ***abcdefghijklmnopqrstuvwxyzABCDEFGHIJKLMNOPQRSTU***

73-Black Extended **abcdefghijklmnopqrstuvwxyzABCDEFGHIJKLMNOPQRS**

73-Black Extended Oblique ***abcdefghijklmnopqrstuvwxyzABCDEFGHIJKLMNOPQRS***

93-Extra Black Extended **abcdefghijklmnopqrstuvwxyzABCDEFGHIJKLMN**

93-Extra Black Extended Oblique ***abcdefghijklmnopqrstuvwxyzABCDEFGHIJKLMN***

UNIVERS 2

LIN ADO AGA FAM MAE abcdefghijklmnopqrstuvwxyz(“.;‘!*?’:,”)
$1234567890&fiflß-äöüåçèîñóæøœ
ABCDEFGHIJKLMNOPQRSTUVWXYZ
ÄÖÜÅÇÈÎÑÓÆØŒ»„«[¶§•†‡]‹¡·¿›...

Univers 2 ...

39-Thin Ultra Condensed ▲24 abcdefghijklmnopqrstuvwxyzABCDEFGHIJKLMNOPQRSTUVWXYZ–$1234567890(“.;‘!*?’:,”)&fiflß-äöüÄÖÜåçèÅÇÈîñóÎÑÓæøœÆ

49-Light Ultra Condensed No. 2 ▲18 abcdefghijklmnopqrstuvwxyzABCDEFGHIJKLMNOPQRSTUVWXYZ–$1234567890(“.;‘!*?’:,”)&fiflß-äöüÄÖÜåçèÅÇÈîñóÎÑÓæ

• 59-Ultra Condensed ▲18 **abcdefghijklmnopqrstuvwxyzABCDEFGHIJKLMNOPQRSTUVWXYZ–$1234567890(“.;‘!*?’:,”)&fiflß-**

85-Extra Black ▲16 **abcdefghijklmnopqrstuvwxyzABCDEFGHIJKLMNOPQRSTU**

85-Extra Black Oblique ▲16 ***abcdefghijklmnopqrstuvwxyzABCDEFGHIJKLMNOPQRSTU***

University Roman
✤ *Adobe DisplaySet 1*
✍ *Mike Daines & Phillip Kelly • 1972 ... Ross F. George, William Hugh Gordon 1918*
ADO AGA BIT LET LIN MAE URW
▲30

DV Upright
✍ *Diehl.Volk • 1991*
DVT
▲42

abcdefghijklmnopqrstuvwxyz(".;'!*?':,")$1234567890
&-äöüçèîñóABCDEFGHIJKLMNOPQRSTUVWXYZ

ITC USHERWOOD

✍ *Les Usherwood • 1984*
LIN ADO AGA AGP LEF MAE URW

abcdefghijklmnopqrstuvwxyz(".;'!*?':,")
$1234567890&fiflß-äöüåçèîñóæøœ
ABCDEFGHIJKLMNOPQRSTUVWXYZ
ÄÖÜÅÇÈÎÑÓÆØŒ»„«[¶§•†‡]‹¡·¿›...

ITC Usherwood ...

• Book abcdefghijklmnopqrstuvwxyzABCDEFGHIJKLMNOPQRSTUVWXYZ–$1234567890(
Book Italic *abcdefghijklmnopqrstuvwxyzABCDEFGHIJKLMNOPQRSTUVWXYZ–$1234567890(".;'!*
Medium abcdefghijklmnopqrstuvwxyzABCDEFGHIJKLMNOPQRSTUVWXYZ–$123456789
Medium Italic *abcdefghijklmnopqrstuvwxyzABCDEFGHIJKLMNOPQRSTUVWXYZ–$1234567890(".;*
Bold **abcdefghijklmnopqrstuvwxyzABCDEFGHIJKLMNOPQRSTUVWXYZ–$123456789**
Bold Italic ***abcdefghijklmnopqrstuvwxyzABCDEFGHIJKLMNOPQRSTUVWXYZ–$12345678***
Black **abcdefghijklmnopqrstuvwxyzABCDEFGHIJKLMNOPQRSTUVWXYZ–$1234**
Black Italic ***abcdefghijklmnopqrstuvwxyzABCDEFGHIJKLMNOPQRSTUVWXYZ–$123***

U

UTOPIA

✍ *Robert Slimbach • 1989*
ADO AGA LIN MAE

abcdefghijklmnopqrstuvwxyz(".;'!*?':,")
$1234567890&fiflß-äöüåçèîñóæøœ
ABCDEFGHIJKLMNOPQRSTUVWXYZ
ÄÖÜÅÇÈÎÑÓÆØŒ»„«[¶§•†‡]‹¡·¿›...

Utopia ...

• Roman abcdefghijklmnopqrstuvwxyzABCDEFGHIJKLMNOPQRSTUVWXYZ–$1234567
Italic *abcdefghijklmnopqrstuvwxyzABCDEFGHIJKLMNOPQRSTUVWXYZ–$12345678*

✤ *Adobe DisplaySet 1*: Aachen Bold, Freestyle Script, Revue, University Roman.

... Utopia

Semibold abcdefghijklmnopqrstuvwxyzABCDEFGHIJKLMNOPQRSTUVWXYZ–$123456

Semibold Italic *abcdefghijklmnopqrstuvwxyzABCDEFGHIJKLMNOPQRSTUVWXYZ–$123456*

Bold **abcdefghijklmnopqrstuvwxyzABCDEFGHIJKLMNOPQRSTUVWXYZ–$12345**

Bold Italic ***abcdefghijklmnopqrstuvwxyzABCDEFGHIJKLMNOPQRSTUVWXYZ–$123456***

Black ▲16 **abcdefghijklmnopqrstuvwxyzABCDEFGHIJKLMNOPQRSTUV**

UTOPIA EXPERT & SCOSF

ADO AGA LIN MAE ABCDEFGHIJKLMNOPQRSTUVWXYZ.;!?:,
1234567890&ff fi fl ffi ffl - ÄÖÜÅÇÈÎÑÓÆØŒ
(abdeilmnorst) 1/8 1/4 1/3 3/8 1/2 5/8 2/3 3/4 7/8 $12345/67890¢ ₡Rp

❦ Utopia Expert & SCOSF ...

• Expert Roman ABCDEFGHIJKLMNOPQRSTUVWXYZ - $1234567890.;!?:,&-ff fi fl ffi ffl 1/8 1/4 1/3 3/8 1/2 $12345/6

Expert Italic *$1234567890.;:, - ff fi fl ffi ffl 1/8 1/4 1/3 3/8 1/2 $12345/67890¢ (abdeilmnorst) 5/8 2/3 3/4 7/8 ₡Rp*

Expert Semibold ABCDEFGHIJKLMNOPQRSTUVWXYZ - $1234567890.;!?:,&-ff fi fl ffi ffl 1/8 1/4 1/3 3/8 1/2 $1234

Expert Semibold Italic *$1234567890.;:, - ff fi fl ffi ffl 1/8 1/4 1/3 3/8 1/2 $12345/67890¢ (abdeilmnorst) 5/8 2/3 3/4 7/8 ₡Rp*

Expert Bold **$1234567890.;:, - ff fi fl ffi ffl 1/8 1/4 1/3 3/8 1/2 $12345/67890¢ (abdeilmnorst) 5/8 2/3 3/4 7/8 ₡Rp**

Expert Bold Italic ***$1234567890.;:, - ff fi fl ffi ffl 1/8 1/4 1/3 3/8 1/2 $12345/67890¢ (abdeilmnorst) 5/8 2/3 3/4 7/8 ₡Rp***

Expert Black ▲16 **$1234567890.;:, - ff fi fl ffi ffl 1/8 1/4 1/3 3/8 1/2 $12345/67890¢ (abdeilmnorst)**

Roman SCOSF ABCDEFGHIJKLMNOPQRSTUVWXYZABCDEFGHIJKLMNOPQRSTUVWXYZ–$123456

Italic OSF *abcdefghijklmnopqrstuvwxyzABCDEFGHIJKLMNOPQRSTUVWXYZ–$123456789*

Semibold SCOSF ABCDEFGHIJKLMNOPQRSTUVWXYZABCDEFGHIJKLMNOPQRSTUVWXYZ–$12345

Semibold Italic OSF *abcdefghijklmnopqrstuvwxyzABCDEFGHIJKLMNOPQRSTUVWXYZ–$1234567*

Bold OSF **abcdefghijklmnopqrstuvwxyzABCDEFGHIJKLMNOPQRSTUVWXYZ–$123456**

Bold Italic OSF ***abcdefghijklmnopqrstuvwxyzABCDEFGHIJKLMNOPQRSTUVWXYZ–$1234567***

Black OSF ▲16 **abcdefghijklmnopqrstuvwxyzABCDEFGHIJKLMNOP...$12345**

Roman Titling ▲36 ABCDEFGHIJKLMNOPQRST
UVWXYZ(“.;‘!*?’:,”)$123456789
0&-ÄÖÜÅÇÈÎÑÓÆØŒ»„«[•]‹¡·

U

❦ Utopia Expert & SCOSF ▶Utopia Ornaments.

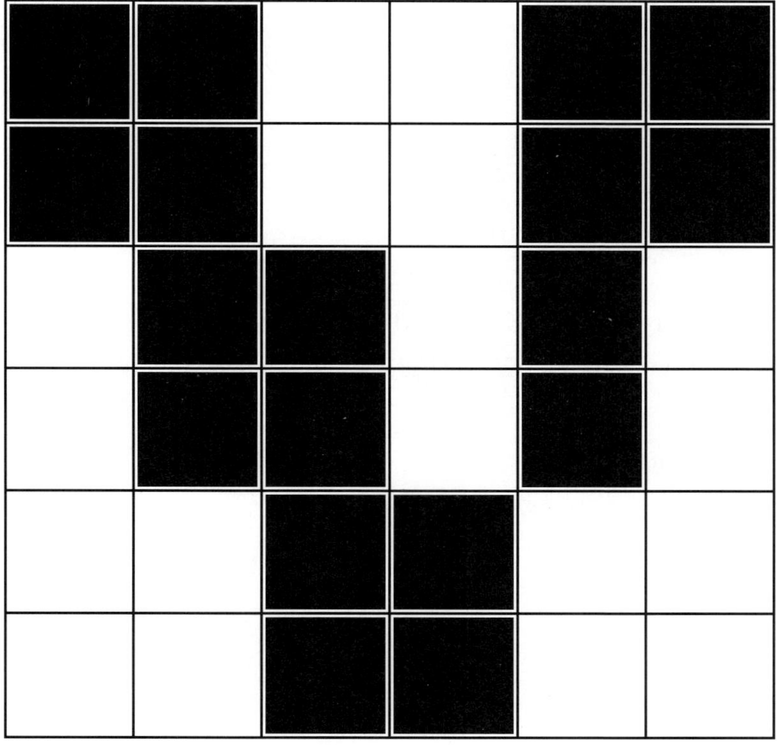

✍ Zuzana Licko, 1988

VAG ROUNDED

LIN ADO AGA BIT LEF MAE URW abcdefghijklmnopqrstuvwxyz(".;'!*?':,")
$1234567890&fiflß-äöüåçèîñóœøœ
ABCDEFGHIJKLMNOPQRSTUVWXYZ
ÄÖÜÅÇÈÎÑÓÆØŒ»„«[¶§•†‡]‹¡·¿›...

VAG Rounded ...

Thin abcdefghijklmnopqrstuvwxyzABCDEFGHIJKLMNOPQRSTUVWXYZ–$1234567890(".;'!*?':,

• Light abcdefghijklmnopqrstuvwxyzABCDEFGHIJKLMNOPQRSTUVWXYZ–$1234567890(".;'!*?'

Bold **abcdefghijklmnopqrstuvwxyzABCDEFGHIJKLMNOPQRSTUVWXYZ–$1234567890("**

Black **abcdefghijklmnopqrstuvwxyzABCDEFGHIJKLMNOPQRSTUVWXYZ–$1234567890("**

VAN DIJCK
✣ *Monotype AldineDutch*

✍ *Monotype Design Staff & Jan Van Krimpen • 1937 ... Christoffel van Dyck, c.1660* abcdefghijklmnopqrstuvwxyz(".;'!★?':,")
$1234567890&fiflß-äöüåçèîñóæøœ

MCL ABCDEFGHIJKLMNOPQRSTUVWXYZ
ÄÖÜÅÇÈÎÑÓÆØŒ»„«[¶§•†‡]‹¡·¿›...

Van Dijck ...

• Roman abcdefghijklmnopqrstuvwxyzABCDEFGHIJKLMNOPQRSTUVWXYZ–$1234567890(".;'!★?'

Italic *abcdefghijklmnopqrstuvwxyzABCDEFGHIJKLMNOPQRSTUVWXYZ–$123456789067890(".;'!★*

VAN DIJCK EXPERT
✣ *Monotype AldineDutch Expert*

MCL ABCDEFGHIJKLMNOPQRSTUVWXYZ.;!?:,
1234567890&ﬀﬁﬂﬃﬄ–ÄÖÜÅÇÈÎÑÓÆØŒ
(abdeilmnorst) 1/8 1/4 1/3 3/8 1/2 5/8 2/3 3/4 7/8 $12345/67890¢ ₡Rp

Van Dijck Expert ...

• Expert Roman ABCDEFGHIJKLMNOPQRSTUVWXYZ–$1234567890.;!?:,&-ﬀﬁﬂﬃﬄ 1/8 1/4 1/3 3/8 1/2 $12345/67890¢ (abdei

Expert Italic *$1234567890.;:,–ﬀﬁﬂﬃﬄ 1/8 1/4 1/3 3/8 1/2 $12345/67890¢ (abdeilmnorst) 5/8 2/3 3/4 7/8 ₡Rp*

Expert Roman & Italic Alternate Oldstyle Figures 1234567890 *1234567890*

Van Dijk

✍ *Jan Van Dijk • 1982* abcdefghijklmnopqrstuvwxyz(".;'!*?':,")

LET LEF URW $1234567890&fiflß-äöüåçèîñóæøœ
ABCDEFGHIJKLMNOPQRSTUVWXYZ
ÄÖÜÅÇÈÎÑÓÆØŒ»„«[•]‹¡·¿›...

Van Dijk Bold

✍ *Peter O'Donnell • 1986 ... Jan Van Dijk, 1982* **abcdefghijklmnopqrstuvwxyz(".;'!*?':,")**

LET **$1234567890&fiflß-äöüåçèîñóæøœ**
ABCDEFGHIJKLMNOPQRSTUVWXYZ
ÄÖÜÅÇÈÎÑÓÆØŒ»„«[•]‹¡·¿›...

V

✣ *Monotype AldineDutch*: Poliphilus, Blado Italic, Van Dijck Roman & Italic.
✣ *Monotype AldineDutch Expert*: Poliphilus Roman Expert, Blado Italic Expert, Van Dijck Expert Roman & Expert Italic.

Varga

✍ Alan Meeks • 1991 abcdefghijklmnopqrstuvwxyz(".;'!*?':,")
LET $1234567890&fiflß-äöüåçèîñóæøœ
▲16 ABCDEFGHIJKLMNOPQRSTUVWXYZ
ÄÖÜÅÇÈÎÑÓÆØŒ»„«[•]‹¡·¿›...

VARIATOR

✍ Jim Marcus • 1993 ABCDEFGHIJKLMNOPQRSTUVWXYZ(.;!*?:,)
T26 ▲20 $1234567890&-ABCDEFGHIJKLMNOPQRSTUVWXYZ

Variator ...

• One ABCDEFGHIJKLMNOPQRSTUVWXYZABCDEFGHIJKLMNOPQRSTUVWX
Two ABCDEFGHIJKLMNOPQRSTUVWXYZABCDEFGHIJKLMNOPQRSTUVWXY
Three abcdefghijklmnopqrstuvwxyzABCDEFGHIJKLMNOPQ

VARIO

✍ Hermann Zapf • 1982 abcdefghijklmnopqrstuvwxyz(".;!*?':,")
LEF $1234567890&ß-äöüåçèîñóæøœ
▲16 ABCDEFGHIJKLMNOPQRSTUVWXYZ
ÄÖÜÅÇÈÎÑÓÆØŒ»„«¡¿

Vario ...

• Regular abcdefghijklmnopqrstuvwxyzABCDEFGHIJKLMNOPQRSTUVWXYZ$123456789
Italic *abcdefghijklmnopqrstuvwxyzABCDEFGHIJKLMNOPQRSTUVWXYZ$123456789*

VECTORA

✍ Adrian Frutiger • 1991 abcdefghijklmnopqrstuvwxyz(".;'!*?':,")
LIN ADO AGA MAE $1234567890&fiflß-äöüåçèîñóæøœ
ABCDEFGHIJKLMNOPQRSTUVWXYZ
ÄÖÜÅÇÈÎÑÓÆØŒ»„«[¶§•†‡]‹¡·¿›...

Vectora ...

45-Light abcdefghijklmnopqrstuvwxyzABCDEFGHIJKLMNOPQRSTUVWXYZ–$1234567890(".;'
46-Light Italic *abcdefghijklmnopqrstuvwxyzABCDEFGHIJKLMNOPQRSTUVWXYZ–$1234567890(".;'*
• 55-Regular abcdefghijklmnopqrstuvwxyzABCDEFGHIJKLMNOPQRSTUVWXYZ–$1234567890
56-Italic *abcdefghijklmnopqrstuvwxyzABCDEFGHIJKLMNOPQRSTUVWXYZ–$1234567890*
75-Bold **abcdefghijklmnopqrstuvwxyzABCDEFGHIJKLMNOPQRSTUVWXYZ–$12345**
76-Bold Italic ***abcdefghijklmnopqrstuvwxyzABCDEFGHIJKLMNOPQRSTUVWXYZ–$12345***
95-Black **abcdefghijklmnopqrstuvwxyzABCDEFGHIJKLMNOPQRSTUVWXYZ–$1**
96-Black Italic ***abcdefghijklmnopqrstuvwxyzABCDEFGHIJKLMNOPQRSTUVWXYZ–$1***

V

ITC VELJOVIC

Jovica Veljovic • 1984 abcdefghijklmnopqrstuvwxyz(“.;‘!*?’:,”)

AGP ADO AGA LEF FRA LIN MAE $1234567890&fiflß-äöüåçèîñóæøœ

ABCDEFGHIJKLMNOPQRSTUVWXYZ

ÄÖÜÅÇÈÎÑÓÆØŒ»„«[¶§•†‡]‹¡·¿›…

ITC Veljovic …

• Book abcdefghijklmnopqrstuvwxyzABCDEFGHIJKLMNOPQRSTUVWXYZ–$1234567

Book Italic *abcdefghijklmnopqrstuvwxyzABCDEFGHIJKLMNOPQRSTUVWXYZ–$1234567890(*

Medium abcdefghijklmnopqrstuvwxyzABCDEFGHIJKLMNOPQRSTUVWXYZ–$12345

Medium Italic *abcdefghijklmnopqrstuvwxyzABCDEFGHIJKLMNOPQRSTUVWXYZ–$1234567*

Bold **abcdefghijklmnopqrstuvwxyzABCDEFGHIJKLMNOPQRSTUVWXYZ–$12**

Bold Italic ***abcdefghijklmnopqrstuvwxyzABCDEFGHIJKLMNOPQRSTUVWXYZ–$123456***

Black **abcdefghijklmnopqrstuvwxyzABCDEFGHIJKLMNOPQRSTUVWXYZ–$**

Black Italic ***abcdefghijklmnopqrstuvwxyzABCDEFGHIJKLMNOPQRSTUVWXYZ–$12***

VENDOME

François Ganeau • 1954 abcdefghijklmnopqrstuvwxyz(“.;‘!*?’):,

URW $123 456 7890&fiflß-äöüåçèîñóæøœ

ABCDEFGHIJKLMNOPQRSTUVWXYZ

ÄÖÜÅÇÈÎÑÓÆØŒ»„«[¶§•†‡]‹¡·¿›…

Vendome …

• Roman abcdefghijklmnopqrstuvwxyzABCDEFGHIJKLMNOPQRSTUVWXYZ–$123 456 78

Italic *abcdefghijklmnopqrstuvwxyzABCDEFGHIJKLMNOPQRSTUVWXYZ–$1234567890(“.*

Medium **abcdefghijklmnopqrstuvwxyzABCDEFGHIJKLMNOPQRSTUVWXYZ–$123**

Medium Italic ***abcdefghijklmnopqrstuvwxyzABCDEFGHIJKLMNOPQRSTUVWXYZ–$1***

Bold ▲16 **abcdefghijklmnopqrstuvwxyzABCDEFGHIJKLMNOPQRS**

Condensed ▲36 abcdefghijklmnopqrstuvwxyzABCDEFGHIJKLMNOPQRS

A*I Venezia

Manfred Klein • 1994 ABCDEFGHIJKLMNOPQRSTUVWXYZ

ALP “.;!:,1234567890ß-ÄÖÜÅÇÈÎÑÓ

▲30 ABCDEFGHIJKLMNOPQRSTUVWXYZ

ÄÖÜÅÇÈÎÑÓ„…

V

Vermont

✍ Freda Sack • 1987 abcdefghijklmnopqrstuvwxyz(".;'!*?':,")

LET $1234567890&fiflß-äöüåçèîñóæøœ

▲18 ABCDEFGHIJKLMNOPQRSTUVWXYZ

ÄÖÜÅÇÈÎÑÓÆØŒ»„«[·]‹i·¿›...

▷a g t

VERSAILLES

✍ Adrian Frutiger • 1982 abcdefghijklmnopqrstuvwxyz(".;'!*?':,")

LIN ADO AGA MAE $1234567890&fiflß-äöüåçèîñóæøœ

ABCDEFGHIJKLMNOPQRSTUVWXYZ

ÄÖÜÅÇÈÎÑÓÆØŒ»„«[¶§•†‡]‹¡·¿›...

Versailles ...

45-Light abcdefghijklmnopqrstuvwxyzABCDEFGHIJKLMNOPQRSTUVWXYZ–$12345

46-Light Italic *abcdefghijklmnopqrstuvwxyzABCDEFGHIJKLMNOPQRSTUVWXYZ–$123456*

• 55-Roman abcdefghijklmnopqrstuvwxyzABCDEFGHIJKLMNOPQRSTUVWXYZ–$12

56-Italic *abcdefghijklmnopqrstuvwxyzABCDEFGHIJKLMNOPQRSTUVWXYZ–$123*

75-Bold **abcdefghijklmnopqrstuvwxyzABCDEFGHIJKLMNOPQRSTUVWXYZ**

76-Bold Italic ***abcdefghijklmnopqrstuvwxyzABCDEFGHIJKLMNOPQRSTUVWXYZ–***

95-Black **abcdefghijklmnopqrstuvwxyzABCDEFGHIJKLMNOPQRSTUVW**

96-Black Italic ***abcdefghijklmnopqrstuvwxyzABCDEFGHIJKLMNOPQRSTUVW***

Victoria Titling Condensed
✣ *Monotype Crazy Headlines*
✍ Monotype Design Staff • 1924 ABCDEFGHIJKLMNOPQRSTUVWXYZ

MCL
▲30 (".;'!*?':,")$1234567890

&-ÄÖÜÅÇÈÎÑÓÆØŒ»„«[•]‹¡·¿›...

Vienna Extended

✍ Anthony De Meester • 1989 ABCDEFGHIJKLMNO

LET
▲24 PQRSTUVWXYZ(".;'!*?':,")

$1234567890&-ÄÖÜ

ÅÇÈÎÑÓÆØŒ»„«[•]‹¡·¿›... ▷J

V

✣ *Monotype Crazy Headlines*: Festival Titling, Kino, Matura, Matura Scriptorial Capitals, Victoria Titling Condensed.

GOUDY VILLAGE NO.2

Frederic W. Goudy • 1932 abcdefghijklmnopqrstuvwxyz (" . ; ' ! * ? ' : , ")

LAN $1234567890&fiflß-äöüåçèîñóæøœ

ABCDEFGHIJKLMNOPQRSTUVWXYZ

ÄÖÜÅÇÈÎÑÓ ÆØŒ » „ « [¶§•†‡] ‹ ¡ ¿ › … ▹ ff ffi ffl fj ct st

Goudy Village No. 2 …

• Roman abcdefghijklmnopqrstuvwxyzABCDEFGHIJKLMNOPQRSTUVWXYZ–$1234567890 (" . ; '

Italic *abcdefghijklmnopqrstuvwxyzABCDEFGHIJKLMNOPQRSTUVWXYZ–$1234567890(" . ; ' ! * ? ' : , ")*

Roman OSF abcdefghijklmnopqrstuvwxyzABCDEFGHIJKLMNOPQRSTUVWXYZ–$1234567890 (" . ; '

Italic OSF *abcdefghijklmnopqrstuvwxyzABCDEFGHIJKLMNOPQRSTUVWXYZ–$1234567890(" . ; ' ! * ? ' : , ")*

Roman SCOSF ABCDEFGHIJKLMNOPQRSTUVWXYZABCDEFGHIJKLMNOPQRSTUVWXYZ–$1234567890 (" . ;

Italic SCOSF *ABCDEFGHIJKLMNOPQRSTUVWXYZABCDEFGHIJKLMNOPQRSTUVWXYZ–$1234567890(" . ; ' ! **

Roman S A/D abcdefghijklmnopqrstuvwxyzABCDEFGHIJKLMNOPQRSTUVWXYZ–$1234567890 (" . ; '

Italic S A/D *abcdefghijklmnopqrstuvwxyzABCDEFGHIJKLMNOPQRSTUVWXYZ–$1234567890(" . ; ' ! * ? ' : , ")*

Roman OSF S A/D abcdefghijklmnopqrstuvwxyzABCDEFGHIJKLMNOPQRSTUVWXYZ–$1234567890 (" . ; '

Italic OSF S A/D *abcdefghijklmnopqrstuvwxyzABCDEFGHIJKLMNOPQRSTUVWXYZ–$1234567890(" . ; ' ! * ? ' : , ")*

VILLAGE

David Berlow • 1992 … Frederic W. Goudy, 1932 abcdefghijklmnopqrstuvwxyz(".;'!*?':,")

FBU $1234567890&fiflß-äöüåçèîñóæøœ

ABCDEFGHIJKLMNOPQRSTUVWXYZ

ÄÖÜÅÇÈÎÑÓÆØŒ»„«[¶§●†‡]‹¡·¿›… ▹ z ff ffi ffl ct st

Village …

• Roman abcdefghijklmnopqrstuvwxyzABCDEFGHIJKLMNOPQRSTUVWXYZ–$123456

Italic *abcdefghijklmnopqrstuvwxyzABCDEFGHIJKLMNOPQRSTUVWXYZ–$1234567890(".;'!*

Bold **abcdefghijklmnopqrstuvwxyzABCDEFGHIJKLMNOPQRSTUVWXYZ–$1234**

Roman SCLF ABCDEFGHIJKLMNOPQRSTUVWXYZABCDEFGHIJKLMNOPQRSTUVWXYZ–$1234

Italic SCLF *ABCDEFGHIJKLMNOPQRSTUVWXYZABCDEFGHIJKLMNOPQRSTUVWXYZ–$123456789*

VILLAGE TITLING

FBU abcdefghijklmnopqrstuvwxyz(".;'!*?':,")

▲24 $1234567890&fiflß-äöüåçèîñóæøœ

ABCDEFGHIJKLMNOPQRSTUVWXYZ

ÄÖÜÅÇÈÎÑÓÆØŒ»„«[¶§●†‡]‹¡·¿›… ▹zffffiffl ct st

V

... Village Titling ...

• Roman Titling abcdefghijklmnopqrstuvwxyzABCDEFGHIJK

Italic Titling *abcdefghijklmnopqrstuvwxyzABCDEFGHIJKLMN*

Bold Titling **abcdefghijklmnopqrstuvwxyzABCDEFGHIJK**

Roman SC Titling ABCDEFGHIJKLMNOPQRSTUVWXYZABCDEFGHIJK

Italic SC Titling *ABCDEFGHIJKLMNOPQRSTUVWXYZABCDEFGHIJKLM*

VISAGE

Garrett Boge • 1990 abcdefghijklmnopqrstuvwxyz(".;'!*?':,")
LPT MTD $1234567890&fiflß-äöüåçèîñóæøœ
ABCDEFGHIJKLMNOPQRSTUVWXYZ
ÄÖÜÅÇÈÎÑÓÆØŒ»„«[¶§•†‡]‹¡·¿›...

Visage 1 ...

• Book abcdefghijklmnopqrstuvwxyzABCDEFGHIJKLMNOPQRSTUVWXYZ–$1234567890
Book Oblique *abcdefghijklmnopqrstuvwxyzABCDEFGHIJKLMNOPQRSTUVWXYZ–$1234567890*
Bold **abcdefghijklmnopqrstuvwxyzABCDEFGHIJKLMNOPQRSTUVWXYZ–$12345**
Bold Oblique ***abcdefghijklmnopqrstuvwxyzABCDEFGHIJKLMNOPQRSTUVWXYZ–$12345***

Visage 2 ...

Light abcdefghijklmnopqrstuvwxyzABCDEFGHIJKLMNOPQRSTUVWXYZ–$1234567890(".;'!
Light Oblique *abcdefghijklmnopqrstuvwxyzABCDEFGHIJKLMNOPQRSTUVWXYZ–$1234567890(".;'!*
Medium **abcdefghijklmnopqrstuvwxyzABCDEFGHIJKLMNOPQRSTUVWXYZ–$12345678**
Medium Oblique ***abcdefghijklmnopqrstuvwxyzABCDEFGHIJKLMNOPQRSTUVWXYZ–$12345678***
Black **abcdefghijklmnopqrstuvwxyzABCDEFGHIJKLMNOPQRSTUVWXYZ–$123**
Black Oblique ***abcdefghijklmnopqrstuvwxyzABCDEFGHIJKLMNOPQRSTUVWXYZ–$123***

Visigoth
Agfa Baker Calligraphy
Arthur Baker • 1988 abcdefghijklmnopqrstuvwxyz(".;'!*?':,")
AGP ADO AGA LIN MAE $1234567890&fiflß-äöüåçèîñóæøœ
▲18 ABCDEFGHIJKLMNOPQRSTUVWXYZ
ÄÖÜÅÇÈÎÑÓÆØŒ»„«[¶§•†‡]‹¡·¿›...

V

Agfa Baker Calligraphy: Amigo, Marigold, Oxford, Pelican, Visigoth.

VIVA MULTIPLE-MASTER
(two axes: weight & width)
Carol Twombly • 1993

ADO AGA MAE
▲24

abcdefghijklmnopqrstuvwxyz(".:;'!*?';,")
$1234567890&fifl ß-äöüåçèîñóæøœ
ABCDEFGHIJKLMNOPQRSTUVWXYZ
ÄÖÜÅÇÈÎÑÓÆØŒ»„«[‹›]‹¡·¿›...

Viva MultipleMaster ...

Light
abcdefghijklmnopqrstuvwxyzABCDEFGHIJK
LMNOPQRSTUVWXYZ–$1234567890(".:;'!*?';,")&

• Regular
abcdefghijklmnopqrstuvwxyzABCDEFGHI
JKLMNOPQRSTUVWXYZ–$1234567890(".:;'!*

Bold
abcdefghijklmnopqrstuvwxyzABCDEF
GHIJKLMNOPQRSTUVWXYZ–$12345678

Light Condensed
abcdefghijklmnopqrstuvwxyzABCDEFGHIJKLMNOPQ
RSTUVWXYZ–$1234567890(".:;'!*?';,")&fifl ß-äöüÄÖÜåçè

Condensed
abcdefghijklmnopqrstuvwxyzABCDEFGHIJKLMNO
PQRSTUVWXYZ–$1234567890(".:;'!*?';,")&fifl ß-äöüÄ

Bold Condensed
abcdefghijklmnopqrstuvwxyzABCDEFGHIJKL
MNOPQRSTUVWXYZ–$1234567890(".:;'!*?';,")&fi

Light Extended
abcdefghijklmnopqrstu
vwxyzABCDEFGHIJKLM

V

... Viva MultipleMaster
Extended

abcdefghijklmnopqrstu
tuvwxyzABCDEFGHIJK

Bold Extended

abcdefghijklmnopqrs
tuvwxyzABCDEFGHIJK

Vivaldi

Fritz Peters • 1970 abcdefghijklmnopqrstuvwxyz(".;'!*?':,")
URW FRA LEF LET MTD $1234567890&fifl ß-äöüåçèîñóæøœ
▲16 ABCDEFGHIJKLMNOPQRSTUVWXYZ
ÄÖÜÅÇÈÎÑÓÆØŒ»,,«[¶§•†‡]‹¡¿›...

Vladimir Script

Vladimir Andrich • .... abcdefghijklmnopqrstuvwxyz(".;'!*?':,")
URW $1234567890&fiflß-äöüåçèîñóæøœ
▲16 ABCDEFGHIJKLMNOPQRSTUVWXYZ
ÄÖÜÅÇÈÎÑÓÆØŒ»,,«[¶§•†‡]‹¡¿›...

V

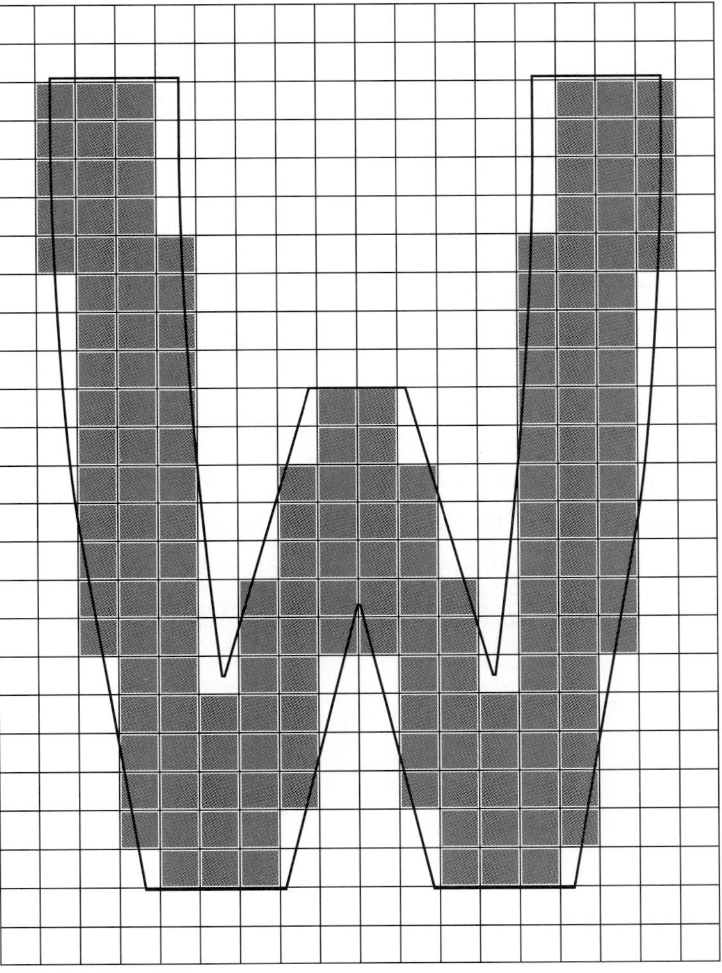

✍ Adrian Frutiger, 1968

Wade Sans

Paul Hickson • 1990 abcdefghijklmnopqrstuvwxyz(".;'!*?':,")
LET $1234567890&fiflß-äöüåçèîñóæøœ
▲18 ABCDEFGHIJKLMNOPQRSTUVWXYZ
ÄÖÜÅÇÈÎÑÓÆØŒ»„«[•]‹¡·¿›... ▷R

Wakefield

Steve Zafarana • 1995 abcdefghijklmnopqrstuvwxyz(".;'!*?':,")
GAL $1234567890&fiflß-äöüåçèîñóæøœ
▲16 ABCDEFGHIJKLMNOPQRSTUVWXYZ
ÄÖÜÅÇÈÎÑÓÆØŒ»„«[¶§•†‡]‹¡·¿›... ▷ ff ffi ffl 1/8 3/8 5/8 2/3 7/8 nd rd st th

MONOTYPE WALBAUM

Monotype Design Staff • 1934 ... Justus Erich Walbaum, c. 1803 abcdefghijklmnopqrstuvwxyz(".;'!*?':,")
MCL FAM $1234567890&fiflß-äöüåçèîñóæøœ
ABCDEFGHIJKLMNOPQRSTUVWXYZ
ÄÖÜÅÇÈÎÑÓÆØŒ»„«[¶§•†‡]‹¡·¿›...

Monotype Walbaum ...

• Roman abcdefghijklmnopqrstuvwxyzABCDEFGHIJKLMNOPQRSTUVWXYZ–$1234567890(".;'!*?'
Italic *abcdefghijklmnopqrstuvwxyzABCDEFGHIJKLMNOPQRSTUVWXYZ–$1234567890(".;'!*?':,'*
Medium **abcdefghijklmnopqrstuvwxyzABCDEFGHIJKLMNOPQRSTUVWXYZ–$1234567890(".;'!**
Medium Italic ***abcdefghijklmnopqrstuvwxyzABCDEFGHIJKLMNOPQRSTUVWXYZ–$1234567890(".;'***

MONOTYPE WALBAUM EXPERT

MCL ABCDEFGHIJKLMNOPQRSTUVWXYZ.;!?:,
1234567890&ff fi fl ffi ffl–ÄÖÜÅÇÈÎÑÓÆØŒ
(abdeilmnorst) 1/8 1/4 1/3 3/8 1/2 5/8 2/3 3/4 7/8 $12345/67890¢ ₡Rp

Monotype Walbaum Expert ...

• Expert Roman ABCDEFGHIJKLMNOPQRSTUVWXYZ–$1234567890.;!?:,&-ff fi fl ffi ffl 1/8 1/4 1/3 3/8 1/2 $12345/67890¢ (abdeilmno
Expert Italic *$1234567890.;:,–ff fi fl ffi ffl 1/8 1/4 1/3 3/8 1/2 $12345/67890¢ (abdeilmnorst) 5/8 2/3 3/4 7/8 ₡Rp*
Expert Medium **$1234567890.;:,–ff fi fl ffi ffl 1/8 1/4 1/3 3/8 1/2 $12345/67890¢ (abdeilmnorst) 5/8 2/3 3/4 7/8 ₡Rp**
Expert Medium Italic ***$1234567890.;:,–ff fi fl ffi ffl 1/8 1/4 1/3 3/8 1/2 $12345/67890¢ (abdeilmnorst) 5/8 2/3 3/4 7/8 ₡Rp***

W

BERTHOLD WALBAUM BOOK

Günter Gerhard Lange • 1975 ... Justus Erich Walbaum, c. 1803 abcdefghijklmnopqrstuvwxyz(".;'!*?':,")
ADO AGA MAE $1234567890&fiflß-äöüåçèîñóæøœ
ABCDEFGHIJKLMNOPQRSTUVWXYZ
ÄÖÜÅÇÈÎÑÓÆØŒ»„«[¶§•†‡]‹¡·¿›...

... Berthold Walbaum Book ...

• Roman abcdefghijklmnopqrstuvwxyzABCDEFGHIJKLMNOPQRSTUVWXYZ–$1234

Italic *abcdefghijklmnopqrstuvwxyzABCDEFGHIJKLMNOPQRSTUVWXYZ–$1234*

Medium **abcdefghijklmnopqrstuvwxyzABCDEFGHIJKLMNOPQRSTUVWXYZ–$**

Medium Italic ***abcdefghijklmnopqrstuvwxyzABCDEFGHIJKLMNOPQRSTUVWXYZ–***

Bold **abcdefghijklmnopqrstuvwxyzABCDEFGHIJKLMNOPQRSTUVWXYZ**

Bold Italic ***abcdefghijklmnopqrstuvwxyzABCDEFGHIJKLMNOPQRSTUVWXYZ–***

BERTHOLD WALBAUM BOOK
EXPERT & SCOSF

ADO AGA MAE ABCDEFGHIJKLMNOPQRSTUVWXYZ.;!?:,

1234567890&fffiflffiffl-ÄÖÜÅÇÈÎÑÓÆØŒ

(abdeilmnorst) 1/8 1/4 1/3 3/8 1/2 5/8 2/3 3/4 7/8 $12345/67890¢ ₡Rp

Berthold Walbaum Book
Expert & SCOSF ...

• Expert Roman ABCDEFGHIJKLMNOPQRSTUVWXYZ–$1234567890.;!?:,&-fffiflffiffl 1/8 1/4 1/3 3/8 1/2 $12345/6

Expert Italic *$1234567890.;:,–fffiflffiffl 1/8 1/4 1/3 3/8 1/2 $12345/67890¢ (abdeilmnorst) 5/8 2/3 3/4 7/8 ₡Rp*

Expert Medium **ABCDEFGHIJKLMNOPQRSTUVWXYZ–$1234567890.;!?:,&-fffiflffiffl 1/8 1/4 1/3 3/8 1/2 $**

Expert Medium Italic ***$1234567890.;:,–fffiflffiffl 1/8 1/4 1/3 3/8 1/2 $12345/67890¢ (abdeilmnorst) 5/8 2/3 3/4 7/8 ₡Rp***

Expert Bold **$1234567890.;:,–fffiflffiffl 1/8 1/4 1/3 3/8 1/2 $12345/67890¢ (abdeilmnorst) 5/8 2/3 3/4 7/8 ₡Rp**

Expert Bold Italic ***$1234567890.;:,–fffiflffiffl 1/8 1/4 1/3 3/8 1/2 $12345/67890¢ (abdeilmnorst) 5/8 2/3 3/4 7/8 ₡Rp***

Roman SCOSF ABCDEFGHIJKLMNOPQRSTUVWXYZABCDEFGHIJKLMNOPQRSTUVWXYZ–$123

Italic OSF *abcdefghijklmnopqrstuvwxyzABCDEFGHIJKLMNOPQRSTUVWXYZ–$123456*

Medium SCOSF **ABCDEFGHIJKLMNOPQRSTUVWXYZABCDEFGHIJKLMNOPQRSTUV...$1234**

Medium Italic OSF ***abcdefghijklmnopqrstuvwxyzABCDEFGHIJKLMNOPQRSTUV...$123456***

Bold OSF **abcdefghijklmnopqrstuvwxyzABCDEFGHIJKLMNOPQRSTUV...$1234**

Bold Italic OSF ***abcdefghijklmnopqrstuvwxyzABCDEFGHIJKLMNOPQRSTUV...$1234***

Wanted

Letraset Design Staff • 1994

LET

▲48

abcdefghijklmnopqrstuvwxyz(".;'!*?':,")

$1234567890&fiflß-äöüåçèîñóæøœ

ABCDEFGHIJKLMNOPQRSTUVWXYZ

ÄÖÜÅÇÈÎÑÓÆØŒ»„«[•]‹¡·¿›...

W

Waterloo Bold

Alan Meeks • 1987 abcdefghijklmnopqrstuvwxyz(“.;‘!*?’:,”)

LET $1234567890&fiflß-äöüåçèîñóæøœ

▲18 ABCDEFGHIJKLMNOPQRSTUVWXYZ

ÄÖÜÅÇÈÎÑÓÆØŒ»„«[•]‹i·¿›...

Wave

Tony Klassen • 1993 abcdefghijklmnopqrstuvwxyz

T26 (“.;‘!*?’:,”)$1234567890&-ABCDEF

▲24 GHIJKLMNOPQRSTUVWXYZ{}

Wedding Text

Agfa Scripts 1

Morris Fuller Benton • 1901 abcdefghijklmnopqrstuvwxyz(“.;‘!*?’:,”)

AGP BIT $1234567890&ß-äöüåçèîñó

▲16 ABCDEFGHIJKLMNOPQRSTUVWXYZ

ÄÖÜÅÇÈÎÑÓ»«[•]‹› ▷I V X st mb rd th ¼ ⅓ ½ ¾ D’ r r. r s O’ rs. s. C c/o

ITC WEIDEMANN

Kurt Weidemann • 1983 abcdefghijklmnopqrstuvwxyz(“.;‘!*?’:,”)

BIT ADO AGA LEF FRA LIN MAE $1234567890&fiflß-äöüåçèîñóæøœ

ABCDEFGHIJKLMNOPQRSTUVWXYZ

ÄÖÜÅÇÈÎÑÓÆØŒ»„«[¶§•†‡]‹i·¿›...

ITC Weidemann 1 ...

• Book abcdefghijklmnopqrstuvwxyzABCDEFGHIJKLMNOPQRSTUVWXYZ–$1234567890(“.;‘!*?’

Book Italic *abcdefghijklmnopqrstuvwxyzABCDEFGHIJKLMNOPQRSTUVWXYZ–$1234567890(“.;‘!*?’:*

Bold **abcdefghijklmnopqrstuvwxyzABCDEFGHIJKLMNOPQRSTUVWXYZ–$123456789**

Bold Italic ***abcdefghijklmnopqrstuvwxyzABCDEFGHIJKLMNOPQRSTUVWXYZ–$123456789***

ITC Weidemann 2 ...

Medium abcdefghijklmnopqrstuvwxyzABCDEFGHIJKLMNOPQRSTUVWXYZ–$1234567890(“.;

Medium Italic *abcdefghijklmnopqrstuvwxyzABCDEFGHIJKLMNOPQRSTUVWXYZ–$1234567890(“.;‘*

Black **abcdefghijklmnopqrstuvwxyzABCDEFGHIJKLMNOPQRSTUVWXYZ–$123456**

Black Italic ***abcdefghijklmnopqrstuvwxyzABCDEFGHIJKLMNOPQRSTUVWXYZ–$12345***

W

Agfa Scripts 1: Commercial Script, Helinda Rook, Old English, Original Script, Quill Script, Stuyvesant, Wedding Text.

WEISS

Emil Rudolf Weiss • 1926 abcdefghijklmnopqrstuvwxyz(".;'!*?':,")

LIN ADO AGA MAE $1234567890&fiflß-äöüåçèîñóæøœ

ABCDEFGHIJKLMNOPQRSTUVWXYZ

ÄÖÜÅÇÈÎÑÓÆØŒ»„«[¶§•†‡]‹¡·¿›...

Weiss ...

• Roman abcdefghijklmnopqrstuvwxyzABCDEFGHIJKLMNOPQRSTUVWXYZ–$1234567890("

Italic *abcdefghijklmnopqrstuvwxyzABCDEFGHIJKLMNOPQRSTUVWXYZ–$1234567890(".;'!*?':,")&fi*

Bold **abcdefghijklmnopqrstuvwxyzABCDEFGHIJKLMNOPQRSTUVWXYZ–$123456789**

Extra Bold **abcdefghijklmnopqrstuvwxyzABCDEFGHIJKLMNOPQRSTUVWXYZ–$123456**

A*I Weissenau

Philip Bouwsma • 1994 abcdefghijklmnopqrstuvwxyz(".;'!*?':,")

ALP $1234567890&fiflß-äöüåçèîñóæøœ

▲18 ABCDEFGHIJKLMNOPQRSTUVWXYZ

ÄÖÜÅÇÈÎÑÓÆØŒ»„«[¶§•†‡]‹¡·¿›...

Wendy

Garrett Boge • 1989 abcdefghijklmnopqrstuvwxyz(".;'!?:,")

LPT MTD $1234567890&fiflß-äöüåçèîñóæøœ

▲18 ABCDEFGHIJKLMNOPQRSTUVWXYZ

ÄÖÜÅÇÈÎÑÓÆØŒ»„«[•]‹¡·¿›...

WERKMAN

Lewis Tsalis • 1993 abcdefghijklmnopqrstuvwxyz(".;'!*?':,")

T26 $1234567890&fiflß-äöüåçèîñóæøœ

▲18 ABCDEFGHIJKLMNOPQRSTUVWXYZ

ÄÖÜÅÇÈÎÑÓÆØŒ»„«[¶·]‹¡·¿›...

Werkman ...

Round abcdefghijklmnopqrstuvwxyzABCDEFGHIJKLMN

• Square abcdefghijklmnopqrstuvwxyzABCDEFGHIJKLMN

W

WESSEX

Matthew Butterick • 1993 abcdefghijklmnopqrstuvwxyz(".;'!*?':,")

FBU $1234567890&fiflß-äöüåçèîñóæøœ

ABCDEFGHIJKLMNOPQRSTUVWXYZ

ÄÖÜÅÇÈÎÑÓÆØŒ»„«[¶§•†‡]‹¡·¿›...

Wessex ...

• Roman abcdefghijklmnopqrstuvwxyzABCDEFGHIJKLMNOPQRSTUVWXYZ–$1234567890(".;'!*?':,

Italic *abcdefghijklmnopqrstuvwxyzABCDEFGHIJKLMNOPQRSTUVWXYZ–$1234567890(".;'!*?':,")*

Semibold **abcdefghijklmnopqrstuvwxyzABCDEFGHIJKLMNOPQRSTUVWXYZ–$1234567890(".;'!***

Roman SCLF ABCDEFGHIJKLMNOPQRSTUVWXYZABCDEFGHIJKLMNOPQRSTUVWXYZ–$1234567890(".;'!*

Roman Titling

▲36 ABCDEFGHIJKLMNOPQRSTUV WXYZ–$1234567890(".;'!*?':,")&-ÄÖÜ

Westwood

David Westwood • 1991 abcdefghijklmnopqrstuvwxyz(".;'!*?':,")

LET $1234567890&fiflß-äöüåçèîñóæøœ

▲28 ABCDEFGHIJKLMNOPQRSTUVWXYZ

ÄÖÜÅÇÈÎÑÓÆØŒ»„«[•]›¡·¿‹...

Wiesbaden Swing
Calligraphy for Print

Rosemarie Kloos-Rau • 1992 abcdefghijklmnopqrstuvwxyz(".;'!*?':,")

LIN ADO AGA MAE $1234567890&fiflß-äöüåçèîñóæøœ

▲24 ABCDEFGHIJKLMNOPQRSTUVWXYZ

ÄÖÜÅÇÈÎÑÓÆØŒ»„«[¶§•†‡]‹¡·¿›...

AGFA WILE ROMAN

AlphaOmega • 1990 abcdefghijklmnopqrstuvwxyz(".;'!*?':,")

AGP $1234567890&fiflß-äöüåçèîñóæøœ

ABCDEFGHIJKLMNOPQRSTUVWXYZ

ÄÖÜÅÇÈÎÑÓÆØŒ»„«[¶§•†‡]‹¡·¿›...

Agfa Wile Roman ...

• Regular abcdefghijklmnopqrstuvwxyzABCDEFGHIJKLMNOPQRSTUVWXYZ–$1234567890(

Italic *abcdefghijklmnopqrstuvwxyzABCDEFGHIJKLMNOPQRSTUVWXYZ–$1234567890(".;'!*?'*

Calligraphy for Print: Ruling Script, Sho, Wiesbaden Swing.

W

... Agfa Wile Roman

Medium abcdefghijklmnopqrstuvwxyzABCDEFGHIJKLMNOPQRSTUVWXYZ–$123456789

Medium Italic *abcdefghijklmnopqrstuvwxyzABCDEFGHIJKLMNOPQRSTUVWXYZ–$1234567890(“.;*

Bold **abcdefghijklmnopqrstuvwxyzABCDEFGHIJKLMNOPQRSTUVWXYZ–$1234567**

Bold Italic ***abcdefghijklmnopqrstuvwxyzABCDEFGHIJKLMNOPQRSTUVWXYZ–$1234567890(***

Black **abcdefghijklmnopqrstuvwxyzABCDEFGHIJKLMNOPQRSTUVWXYZ–$12345**

Black Italic ***abcdefghijklmnopqrstuvwxyzABCDEFGHIJKLMNOPQRSTUVWXYZ–$123456***

Wilhelm Klingspor Gotisch
Linotype DisplaySet 2
Rudolf Koch • 1925
LIN ADO AGA MAE
▲16

abcdefghijklmnopqrstuvwxyz(“.;‘!*?’:,”)
$1234567890&fiflß-äöüåçèîñóæøœ
ABCDEFGHIJKLMNOPQRSTUVWXYZ
ÄÖÜÅÇÈÎÑÓÆØŒ»„«[¶§•†‡]‹¡·¿›...
▷ ch ck ff ft ll ſ s ſi ſſ ß – ä ö ü Ä Ö Ü

WILKE
Martin Wilke • 1988
LIN ADO AGA MAE

abcdefghijklmnopqrstuvwxyz(“.;‘!*?’:,”)
$1234567890&fiflß-äöüåçèîñóæøœ
ABCDEFGHIJKLMNOPQRSTUVWXYZ
ÄÖÜÅÇÈÎÑÓÆØŒ»„«[¶§•†‡]‹¡·¿›...

Wilke ...

• 55-Roman abcdefghijklmnopqrstuvwxyzABCDEFGHIJKLMNOPQRSTUVWXYZ–$12345

56-Italic *abcdefghijklmnopqrstuvwxyzABCDEFGHIJKLMNOPQRSTUVWXYZ–$123456789*

75-Bold **abcdefghijklmnopqrstuvwxyzABCDEFGHIJKLMNOPQRSTUVWXYZ–$1**

76-Bold Italic ***abcdefghijklmnopqrstuvwxyzABCDEFGHIJKLMNOPQRSTUVWXYZ–$123***

95-Black **abcdefghijklmnopqrstuvwxyzABCDEFGHIJKLMNOPQRSTUVWXY**

96-Black Italic ***abcdefghijklmnopqrstuvwxyzABCDEFGHIJKLMNOPQRSTUVWXY***

Willow
Tony Forster • 1990
LET
▲30

ABCDEFGHIJKLMNOPQRSTUVWXYZ(“.;‘!*?’:,”)
$1234567890&-ÄÖÜÅÇÈÎÑÓÆØŒ»„«[•]‹¡·¿›...
▷ A A O o 2 3 4 4 5 7 B B C C C C H H L L L O P
▷ R R R S A S S T T Z N ⁙

W

Linotype DisplaySet 2: Banco, Charme, Flyer Black Condensed & Extra Black Condensed, Wilhelm Klingspor Gotisch.

Willow
Adobe Wood Type 2
Kim Buker, Barbara Lind & Joy Redick • 1990
ADO AGA LIN MAE
▲42

abcdefghijklmnopqrstuvwxyz(“.;‘!*?’:,”)$1234567890&fiflß-äöüåçèîñóæøœ
ABCDEFGHIJKLMNOPQRSTUVWXYZÄÖÜÅÇÈÎÑÓÆØŒ»„«[•]‹¡·¿›…

WINDSOR
Stephenson Blake • 1905
BIT LEF FRA MTD URW

abcdefghijklmnopqrstuvwxyz(“.;‘!*?’:,”)
$1234567890&fiflß-äöüåçèîñóæøœ
ABCDEFGHIJKLMNOPQRSTUVWXYZ
ÄÖÜÅÇÈÎÑÓÆØŒ»„«[¶§•†‡]‹¡·¿›…

Windsor …

Light ▲16 abcdefghijklmnopqrstuvwxyzABCDEFGHIJKLMNOPQRSTUVWXYZ–$
• Regular ▲16 abcdefghijklmnopqrstuvwxyzABCDEFGHIJKLMNOPQRSTUV
Light Condensed ▲16 abcdefghijklmnopqrstuvwxyzABCDEFGHIJKLMNOPQRSTUVWXYZ–$1234567890(“.;‘!
Enlongated ▲18 abcdefghijklmnopqrstuvwxyzABCDEFGHIJKLMNOPQRSTUVWXYZ–$1234567890(“.;‘!*?’:,”)&fifl
• Outline ▲18 abcdefghijklmnopqrstuvwxyzABCDEFGHIJKLMNOPQR

WITTENBERGER FRAKTUR
Monotype Design Staff • c.1903
MCL ADO AGA LIN MAE
▲16

abcdefghijklmnopqrstuvwxyz(“.;‘!*?’:,”)
$1234567890&fiflß-äöüåçèîñóæøœ
ABCDEFGHIJKLMNOPQRSTUVWXYZ
ÄÖÜÅÇÈÎÑÓÆØŒ»„«[¶§•†‡]‹¡·¿›…

Wittenberger Fraktur …

• Regular abcdefghijklmnopqrstuvwxyzABCDEFGHIJKLMNOPQRSTUVWXYZ
Bold abcdefghijklmnopqrstuvwxyzABCDEFGHIJKLMNOPQRSTUVWXY

W

Adobe Wood Type 2: Birch, Blackoak, Madrone, Poplar, Willow, Adobe Wood Type Ornaments 2.
Willow ▶Adobe Wood Type Ornaments 2.

Xylo
Yan Series 333
Young Baroque
MN Zambesi
ITC Zapf Book
ITC Zapf International
ITC Zapf Chancery
Zebrawood
Zeitgeist
Zinjaro
Zombie

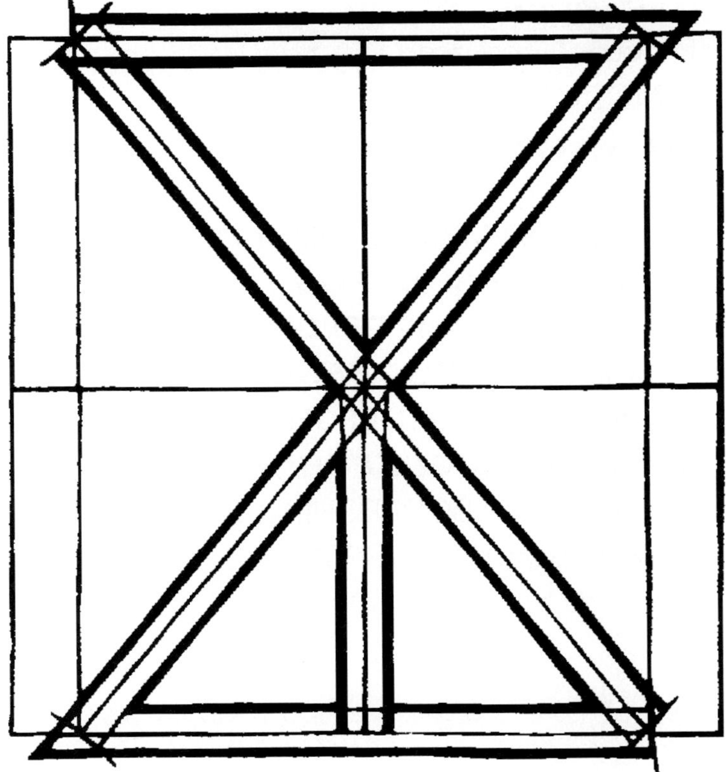

✍ Rudolf Koch, 1928

Xylo

Letraset Design Staff • 1994

LET

▲26

abcdefghijklmnopqrstuvwxyz(“.;‘!*?’:,”)
$1234567890&fiflß-äöüåçèîñóæøœ
ABCDEFGHIJKLMNOPQRSTUVWXYZ
ÄÖÜÅÇÈÎÑÓÆØŒ»„«[•]‹¡·¿›...

YAN SERIES 333

Jack Yan • 1994

JAC

abcdefghijklmnopqrstuvwxyz(“.;‘!*?’:,”)
$1234567890&fiflß-äöüåçèîñóæøœ
ABCDEFGHIJKLMNOPQRSTUVWXYZ
ÄÖÜÅÇÈÎÑÓÆØŒ»„«[¶§• †‡]‹¡·¿›... ▹ff ffi ffl

Yan Series 333 ...

• Roman abcdefghijklmnopqrstuvwxyzABCDEFGHIJKLMNOPQRSTUVWXYZ-$1234567890(“.

Italic *abcdefghijklmnopqrstuvwxyzABCDEFGHIJKLMNOPQRSTUVWXYZ-$12345678*

Bold **abcdefghijklmnopqrstuvwxyzABCDEFGHIJKLMNOPQRSTUVWXYZ-$1234567**

Bold Italic ***abcdefghijklmnopqrstuvwxyzABCDEFGHIJKLMNOPQRSTUVWXYZ-$123456***

Black **abcdefghijklmnopqrstuvwxyzABCDEFGHIJKLMNOPQRSTUVWXYZ-$1234567890**

Black Italic ***abcdefghijklmnopqrstuvwxyzABCDEFGHIJKLMNOPQRSTUVWXYZ-$123456789***

Roman LF abcdefghijklmnopqrstuvwxyzABCDEFGHIJKLMNOPQRSTUVWXYZ-$1234567890(

Italic LF *abcdefghijklmnopqrstuvwxyzABCDEFGHIJKLMNOPQRSTUVWXYZ-$123456789*

Italic Swash Alternate *a d e f k m n t u v w y A B C D E P Q R S Y & fj fr ll sp tt ct ct st Ci Th TT*

Young Baroque

Doyald Young • 1984

LET

▲24

abcdefghijklmnopqrstuvwxyz(“.;‘!?’:,”)$1234567890&fiflß-äöüåçèîñóæøœ*
ABCDEFGHIJKLMNOPQRSTUVW
XYZÇ»„«[·]‹¡·¿›... ▹*ab bcd f gh h hk l b l m n p r r s s ß t u v w y z & ff ff*

MN Zambesi

MTD

▲30

ABCDEFGHIJKLMNOPQRSTUVWXYZ
(“.;‘!*?’:,”)$1234567890
&-ÄÖÜÅÇÈÎÑÓÆØŒ»„«[•]‹¡¿›...

xYz

ITC ZAPF BOOK

Hermann Zapf • 1976 abcdefghijklmnopqrstuvwxyz(“.;‘!*?’:,”)

FRA BIT LEF FAM $1234567890&fifl ß-äöüåçèîñóæøœ

ABCDEFGHIJKLMNOPQRSTUVWXYZ

ÄÖÜÅÇÈÎÑÓÆØŒ»„«[¶§·†‡]‹¡·¿›...

ITC Zapf Book 1 ...

Light abcdefghijklmnopqrstuvwxyzABCDEFGHIJKLMNOPQRSTUVWXYZ$123456789

Light Italic *abcdefghijklmnopqrstuvwxyzABCDEFGHIJKLMNOPQRSTUVWXYZ$12345*

Demi **abcdefghijklmnopqrstuvwxyzABCDEFGHIJKLMNOPQRSTUVWXYZ**

Demi Italic ***abcdefghijklmnopqrstuvwxyzABCDEFGHIJKLMNOPQRSTUVWXYZ***

ITC Zapf Book 2 ...

• Medium abcdefghijklmnopqrstuvwxyzABCDEFGHIJKLMNOPQRSTUVWXYZ$123

Medium Italic *abcdefghijklmnopqrstuvwxyzABCDEFGHIJKLMNOPQRSTUVWXYZ$12*

Heavy **abcdefghijklmnopqrstuvwxyzABCDEFGHIJKLMNOPQRSTUV**

Heavy Italic ***abcdefghijklmnopqrstuvwxyzABCDEFGHIJKLMNOPQRSTUVW***

ITC ZAPF INTERNATIONAL

Hermann Zapf • 1977 abcdefghijklmnopqrstuvwxyz(“.;‘!*?’:,”)

URW AGP BIT LEF FAM $1234567890&fifl ß-äöüåçèîñóæøœ

ABCDEFGHIJKLMNOPQRSTUVWXYZ

ÄÖÜÅÇÈÎÑÓÆØŒ»„«[¶§•†‡]‹¡·¿›...

ITC Zapf International ...

Light abcdefghijklmnopqrstuvwxyzABCDEFGHIJKLMNOPQRSTUVWXYZ–$123

Light Italic *abcdefghijklmnopqrstuvwxyzABCDEFGHIJKLMNOPQRSTUVWXYZ–$12345*

• Medium abcdefghijklmnopqrstuvwxyzABCDEFGHIJKLMNOPQRSTUVWXYZ–$12

Medium Italic *abcdefghijklmnopqrstuvwxyzABCDEFGHIJKLMNOPQRSTUVWXYZ–$1234*

Demi **abcdefghijklmnopqrstuvwxyzABCDEFGHIJKLMNOPQRSTUVWXY**

Demi Italic ***abcdefghijklmnopqrstuvwxyzABCDEFGHIJKLMNOPQRSTUVWXYZ–***

Heavy **abcdefghijklmnopqrstuvwxyzABCDEFGHIJKLMNOPQRSTUV**

Heavy Italic ***abcdefghijklmnopqrstuvwxyzABCDEFGHIJKLMNOPQRSTUVWX***

ITC Zapf Chancery Medium Italic

ITC ZapfSet *abcdefghijklmnopqrstuvwxyz(“.;‘!*?’:,”)*

Hermann Zapf • 1979 *$1234567890&fifl ß-äöüåçèîñóæøœ*

ADO AGA BIT LEF FAM FRA LIN MAE URW *ABCDEFGHIJKLMNOPQRSTUVWXYZ*

▲16 *ÄÖÜÅÇÈÎÑÓÆØŒ»„«[¶§•†‡]‹¡·¿›...*

ITC ZapfSet: ITC Zapf Chancery Medium Italic & ITC Zapf Dingbats.

ITC Zapf Chancery Medium Italic ▶ITC Zapf Dingbats.

XYZ

ITC ZAPF CHANCERY

Hermann Zapf • 1979

ADO AGA BIT LEF FAM FRA LIN MAE URW

▲16

abcdefghijklmnopqrstuvwxyz(".;'!*?':,")
$1234567890&fiflß-äöüåçèîñóæøœ
ABCDEFGHIJKLMNOPQRSTUVWXYZ
ÄÖÜÅÇÈÎÑÓÆØŒ»„«[¶§•†‡]‹¡·¿›...

ITC Zapf Chancery ...

Light abcdefghijklmnopqrstuvwxyzABCDEFGHIJKLMNOPQRSTUVWXYZ–$1234567890(".
Light Italic abcdefghijklmnopqrstuvwxyzABCDEFGHIJKLMNOPQRSTUVWXYZ–$1234
• Regular abcdefghijklmnopqrstuvwxyzABCDEFGHIJKLMNOPQRSTUVWXYZ–$1234567890
Italic abcdefghijklmnopqrstuvwxyzABCDEFGHIJKLMNOPQRSTUVWXYZ–$1234
Demi abcdefghijklmnopqrstuvwxyzABCDEFGHIJKLMNOPQRSTUVWXYZ–$12345
Bold abcdefghijklmnopqrstuvwxyzABCDEFGHIJKLMNOPQRSTUVWXYZ–$1

ZEBRAWOOD

Adobe Wood Type 3

Kim Buker Chansler & Carl Crossgrove • 1994

ADO AGA MAE

▲48

ABCDEFGHIJKLMNOPQ
RSTUVWXYZ(".;'!*?':,")
$1234567890&-ÄÖÜÅÇ
ÈÎÑÓÆØŒ»„«[•]‹¡·¿›...

Zebrawood ...

Fill ABCDEFGHIJKLMNOPQ
• Regular ABCDEFGHIJKLMNOPQ

xyz

Adobe Wood Type 3: Pepperwood Regular, Fill & Outline, Rosewood Regular & Fill, Zebrawood Regular & Fill.

ZEITGEIST

Michael Johnson • 1990 abcdefghijklmnopqrstuvwxyz(“.;‘!*?’:,”)

MCL $1234567890&fifl ß-äöüåçèîñóæøœ

▲18 ABCDEFGHIJKLMNOPQRSTUVWXYZ

ÄÖÜÅÇÈÎÑÓÆØŒ»„«[¶§•†‡]‹¡·¿› . . .

Zeitgeist . . .

• Regular abcdefghijklmnopqrstuvwxyzABCDEFGHIJKLMNOPQRSTUVWXYZ—$1234567890(“.;‘!*?’:,”)&fiflß

Italic *abcdefghijklmnopqrstuvwxyzABCDEFGHIJKLMNOPQRSTUVWXYZ—$1234567890(“.;‘!*?’:,”)&fi*

Bold **abcdefghijklmnopqrstuvwxyzABCDEFGHIJKLMNOPQRSTUVWXYZ—$1234567890(“.;‘!*?’:,”)&**

Condensed abcdefghijklmnopqrstuvwxyzABCDEFGHIJKLMNOPQRSTUVWXYZ—$1234567890(“.;‘!*?’:,”)&fiflß-äöüÄÖÜåçèÅÇÈîñóÎÑÓæ

Cameo abcdefghijklmnopqrstuvwxyzABCDEFGHIJKLMNOPQRSTUVWXYZ—$1234567890(“.;‘!*?’:,”

Crazy Paving abcdefghijklmnopqrstuvwxyzABCDEFGHIJKLMNOPQRSTUVWXYZ—$1234567890(“.;‘!*?’:,”)&fifl

Alternate a b d e i j m n q r t u v w x y ch ck ct gg of sh sp q & ct st A B C D E F G H I J K L M N O P Q R R S T U V W X Y Z oo Qu The 1 2 3 4 5 6 7 8 9 0 ♣ ♠ ♥ ♦

Expert Regular ABCDEFGHIJKLMNOPQRSTUVWXYZ-$1234567890.;!?:,&-ff fi fl ffi ffl 1/8 1/4 1/3 3/8 1/2 $12345/67890¢ (ab

Expert Italic *$1234567890.;:,-ff fi fl ffi ffl 1/8 1/4 1/3 3/8 1/2 $12345/67890¢ (abdeilmnorst) 5/8 2/3 3/4 7/8 ₡Rp*

Expert Bold **$1234567890.;:,-ff fi fl ffi ffl 1/8 1/4 1/3 3/8 1/2 $12345/67890¢ (abdeilmnorst) 5/8 2/3 3/4 7/8 ₡Rp**

Expert Condensed $1234567890.;:,-ff fi fl ffi ffl 1/8 1/4 1/3 3/8 1/2 $12345/67890¢ (abdeilmnorst) 5/8 2/3 3/4 7/8 ₡Rp

Expert Cameo $1234567890.;:,-ff fi fl ffi ffl 1/8 1/4 1/3 3/8 1/2 $12345/67890¢ (abdeilmnorst) 5/8 2/3 3/4 7/8 ₡Rp

Zinjaro

Carol Kemp • 1994 ABCDEFGHIJKLMNOPQRSTUVWXYZ

LET (“.;‘!*?’:,”)$1234567890&-

▲28 ÄÖÜÅÇÈÎÑÓÆØŒ»„«[•]‹¡·¿›. . .

▷

▷

Zombie

Christian Schwartz • 1993 ABCDEFGHIJKLMNOPQRSTUVWXYZ(“.;‘!*?’:,”)

CHR $1234567890&FIFLSS-ÄÖÜÅÇÈÎÑÓÆØŒ

▲24 ABCDEFGHIJKLMNOPQRSTUVWXYZ

ÄÖÜÅÇÈÎÑÓÆØŒ»„«[·]‹¡·¿›. . .

XYZ

PIXymbols ADA Symbols
PolyType Allure
PIXymbols AlphaBox
PIXymbols AlphaCircle
PIXymbols Ameslan
A*I Ampersands
Animals
PolyType Animals
PIXymbols Apothecary
Arabesque Borders & Ornaments
Arrow Dynamic
PolyType ArrowTek
PolyType Art Deco
Mini Pics Art Jam
Artifact
Mini Pics ASL Alphabet
Astrology
Linotype Astrology Pi
PIXymbols Astrology
Attitudes
Linotype Audio Pi
Auriol Flowers
PIXymbols Backstitch
PrintBar Code 39
PrintBar UPC EAN ISBN
PrintBar Interleaved 2 of 5
PrintBar PostNET & FIM
A*I BeforeTheAlphabet-1
Berlin Sans Bold Dingbats
PolyType Birds
Blackfoot
Border Pi
General Glyphics Border Fonts
Key Borders Border Fonts
Borders & Ornaments
PIXymbols Boxkey
PIXymbols BoxnLines
PIXymbols Braille Grade 2

Linotype EEC Pi
European Pi
PIXymbols FabriCare
PIXymbols FARmarks
PIXymbols Flagman
Fleurons : Folio One
Fleurons : Granjon Folio
A*I Flighty
Fontoonies No.1
Fournier Ornaments
Linotype Fraction Pi
PolyType Fruits
Linotype Game Pi
Games & Sports
General Symbols
PIXymbols GridMaker
A*I HeadToHead
PIXymbols Highway Signs
Linotype Holiday Pi
Holidays
PolyType Holidays
PIXymbols Hospital & Safety
Stempel Hot Metal Borders
Incidentals
Industrials
Industry & Engineering
Mini Pics International

Newspaper Pi
Notre Dame Ornaments
Nucleus One
Numerics
PolyType Optyx
Organics
PolyType Ornaments
PIXymbols Passkey
PIXymbols Patchwork
PolyType Patterns
Petroglyph Hawaii
Phonetics
Poetica Ornaments
Pompeijana Borders
Primitives
NIMX Quirks
Radicals
PIXymbols Recycle
Religious
Rococo Borders & Ornaments
TF Roux Borders
Rusticana Borders
Scorpio Dingbats
Scorpio Tribal

David Lance Goines, 1982

π Pi
Σ symbol
λ Logo
❦ ornament
i image

TF Bridgette
BulletsNStuff
Bundebahn Pi
Business & Services
PolyType Business Icons
Calligraphic Ornaments
Caravan Borders & Ornaments
Carta
Adobe Caslon Ornaments
Celebrations
Chemistra Pi
Cheq
PIXymbols Chess
Monotype Christmas Ornaments
City Ornaments
Mini Pics Classic
Colmcille Ornaments
Columbus Ornaments
PIXymbols Command Key
Commercial
Commercial Pi
Commercials
Communications
Monotype Contemporary Ornaments
PolyType Corners
Credit Cards
TF Crossword
PIXymbols Crossword
Deco Numbers
Linotype Decoration Pi
Delectables
Linotype Didot Ornaments
PIXymbols Digits & Clocks
PIXymbols Dingbats
DingBRATS
Dingura
Mini Pics Directional
Diversions
PIXymbols DOSscreen
A*I EclecticOne
Ecology

International Symbols
Interstate Pi
Journeys
Kurusu
PIXymbols LCD
Leaves One
Legal Trademarks
PolyType Leisure
Mini Pics Lil' Critters
Mini Pics Lil' Faces
Logos : Company
Logos : Services
Lucida Math
PIXymbols Luna
Math with Greek Pi
Math & Technical
Mathematical Pi
Medical & Pharmaceutical
PIXymbols Meeting
PIXymbols MenuFonts
MICR
Military & Patriotic
Minion Ornaments
Minion MultipleMaster Ornaments
Mo' Funky Fresh Symbols
Moderns
PIXymbols Morse
PIXymbols Musica
Musical
Naturals

SignPix
Sonata
Monotype Sorts
Special Alphabets
PIXymbols Squared
TF Squiggle
ITC Stone Phonetic
PIXymbols Stylekey
Symbol Monospace
Symbol Proportional
Linotype Technical Pi
Television
Linotype Textile Pi
Thingbat
Thornforms
Times Phonetic
PIXymbols Tolerances
Town Ornaments
Transportation
PIXymbols Travel & Hotel
Truesdell Sorts
PIXymbols TV Listings
Type Embellishments
PIXymbols Unikey
Universal Greek with Math Pi

Universal Math 1
Universal News with Commercial Pi
PIXymbols US Map
Utopia Ornaments
PolyType Vegetables
Village Ornaments
Vine Leaves
Linotype Warning Pi
Water Garden
Wildlifes
Adobe Wood Type Ornaments 1
Adobe Wood Type Ornaments 2
PIXymbols Xcharting
Linotype X-Mas Pi
PIXymbols Xstitch
ITC Zapf Dingbats
Zenzuous Pi

PIXymbols **ADA Symbols**
(Americans with Disabilities Act Signage)
PAG
▲16

POLY·TYPE **ALLURE**
POL

PolyType **Allure** . . .
• One ▲18
Two ▲18

PIX·YMBOLS **ALPHA·BOX**
PAG ABCDEFGHIJKLMNOPQRSTUVWXYZ.,-1234567890 [ ]
▲16 ABCDEFGHIJKLMNOPQRSTUVWXYZ,.-1234567890

PIXymbols **AlphaBox** . . .
No. 1 ABCDEFGHIJKLMNOPQRSTUVWXYZABCDEFGHIJKLMNOPQRSTUVWXYZ-1234
• No. 2 ABCDEFGHIJKLMNOPQRSTUVWXYZABCDEFGHIJKLMNOPQRSTUVWXYZ-1234
No. 2 Bold ABCDEFGHIJKLMNOPQRSTUVWXYZABCDEFGHIJKLMNOPQRSTUVWXYZ-1234

PIX·YMBOLS **ALPHA·CIRCLE** . . .
PAG ABCDEFGHIJKLMNOPQRSTUVWXYZ
▲16 1 2 3 4 5 6 7 8 9 0 10 11 12 13 14 15 16 17 18 19 20 21 31 41 51 61 71 81 91
ABCDEFGHIJKLMNOPQRSTUVWXYZ
1 2 3 4 5 6 7 8 9 0 10 11 12 13 14 15 16 17 18 19 20 21 31 41 51 61 71 81 91

PIXymbols **AlphaCircle** . . .
• A-Regular ABCDEFGHIJKLMNOPQRSTUVWXYZABC
A-Bold ABCDEFGHIJKLMNOPQRSTUVWXYZABC
B-Regular ABCDEFGHIJKLMNOPQRSTUVWXYZABC
B-Bold ABCDEFGHIJKLMNOPQRSTUVWXYZABC

PIX·YMBOLS **AMESLAN**
(American Sign Language)
PAG
▲16

PIXymbols **Ameslan** . . .
• Left Hand
Right Hand

&

A*I Ampersands

Ejaz Syed • 1993
... Ozwald Cooper ....

ALP

Animals
Agfa PiLogoSymbol Fonts
Volume 1
AGL

▲24

PolyType Animals

POL

▲18

PIXymbols Apothecary
One & Two

PAG

▲16

R℞ a□c3fgijm℥øps†x℈(.·!*?,)

$1234567890¢%‰'''<×+=°÷≠±>@□□C3OS℈℥[{•}]

1234567890/1234567890 CDILMVX — — —

ARABESQUE
BORDERS & ORNAMENTS

MCL

▲18

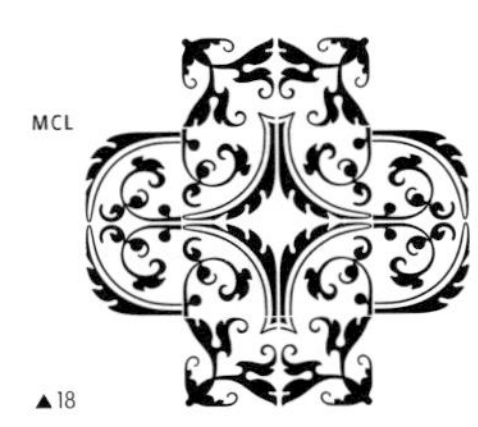

Arabesque Borders & Ornaments ...

• One

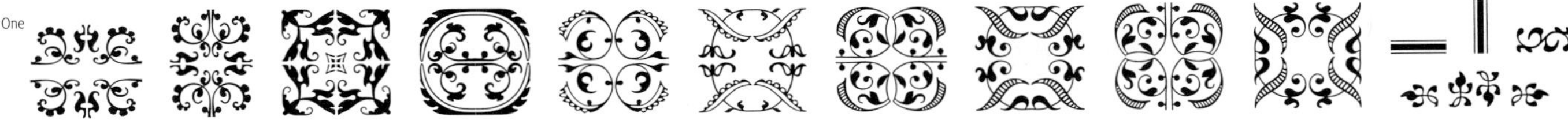

Two

&

... Arabesque Borders & Ornaments Three

ARROW DYNAMIC

EMD

▲16

Arrow Dynamic ...

• Medium

Bold

Heavy

PolyType **ArrowTek**

POL

▲16

PolyType **Art Deco One & Two**

POL

▲16

Mini Pics **Art Jam**

Ty Semaka • 1993

IMA

▲24

ARTIFACT

Carolyn Gibbs • 1993

MTD

Artifact ...

One

▲30

. . . Artifact

• Two

▲30

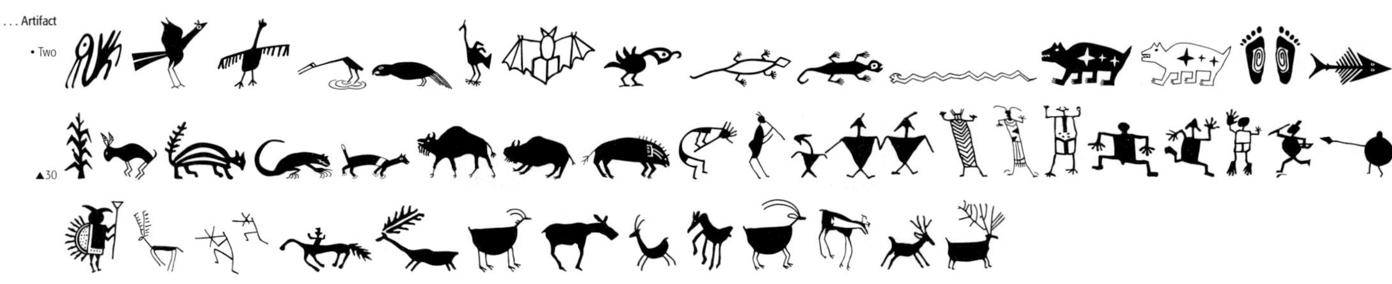

Mini Pics **ASL Alphabet**
(American Sign Language)

IMA

▲18

OPEN HAND CLOSED HAND FLAT HAND CURVED HAND BENT HAND CLAWED HAND AND HAND

1 2 3 4 5 6 7 8 9 0

A B C D E F G H I J K L M N O P Q R S T U V W X Y Z

Astrology 1
Agfa Pi LogoSymbol Fonts
Volume 2
AGL

▲18

Astrology 2
Agfa Pi LogoSymbol Fonts
Volume 3
AGL

▲18

N S

Astrology 3
Agfa Pi LogoSymbol Fonts
Volume 4
AGL

▲18

FULL MOON FIRST QUARTER NEW MOON LAST QUARTER

LINOTYPE ASTROLOGY PI

LIN ADO AGA MAE

Linotype Astrology Pi . . .

One

▲18

• Two

▲18

&

PIX·YMBOLS **ASTROLOGY**

PAG

PIXymbols **Astrology** . . .

One

• Two

Attitudes

✍ *Hugh Whyte • 1993*

LET

▲36

Linotype Audio Pi
❖ *Linotype PiSet 1*

LIN ADO AGA MAE

▲16

AURIOL FLOWERS

LIN

▲18

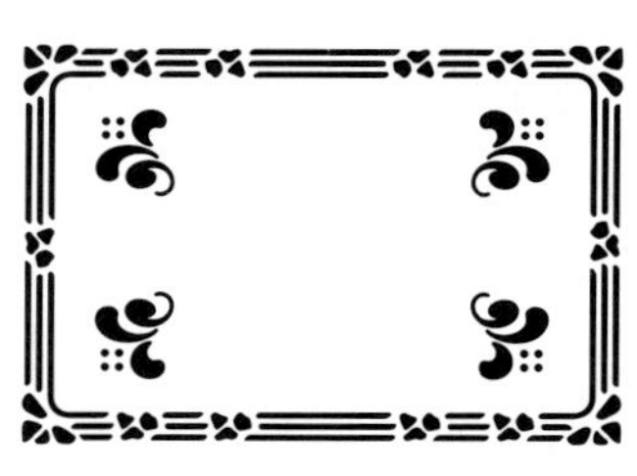

Auriol Flowers . . .

• One

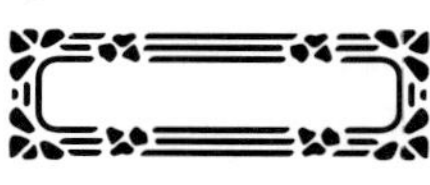

Two

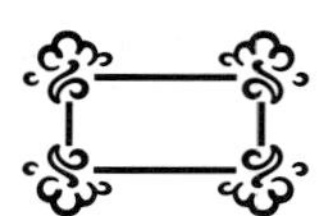

❖ *Linotype PiSet 1*: Linotype Audio Pi & Linotype Warning Pi.

. . . Auriol Flowers

Vignette Sylvie

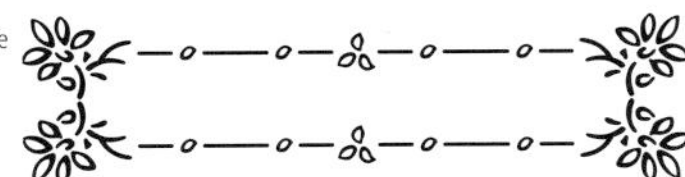

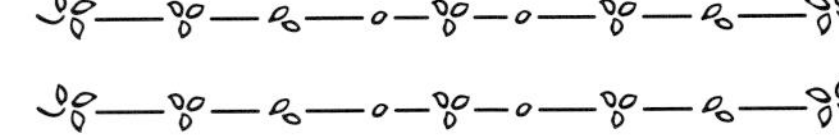

PIXymbols **Backstitch**

PAG

abcdefghijklmnopqrstuvwxyz(;!*?:,)&–1234567890

▲24

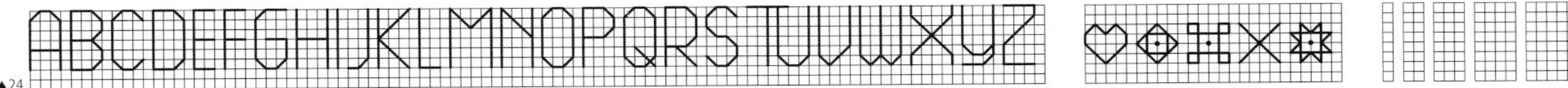

PRINT·BAR **BAR CODE : CODE 39**

BEA

▲24

PRINT BAR-CODE 39

Bar Code : Code 39 . . .

Low Density
Human Readable
& Low Density Normal

4 1 0 1 2 6 5 4 9 5

• Medium Density
Human Readable
& Medium Density Normal

4101265495

High Density
Human Readable
& High Density Normal

4101265495

PRINT·BAR **BAR CODE : UPC EAN ISBN**

BEA

▲24

0 12654 95911 5

Bar Code : UPC EAN ISBN . . .

• UPC-A Normal
& UPC-A with bar width reduction

0 12654 95911 5

0 12654 95911 5

UPC-E Normal
& UPC-E with bar width reduction

0 012654 2 95

0 012654 2 95

EAN-8 Normal
& EAN-8 with bar width reduction

0012 6540 00

0012 6540 00

EAN-13 Normal
& EAN-13 with bar width reduction

4 101265 495412 00

4 101265 495412 00

PRINT·BAR **BAR CODE : INTERLEAVED 2 OF 5**

BEA

▲24

0 4 1 0 1 2 6 5 4 9 5 9 1 1

Bar Code : Interleaved 2 of 5 . . .

Low Density
Human Readable
& Low Density Normal

0 4 1 0 1 2 6 5 4 9 5 9 1 1

• Medium Density
Human Readable
& Medium Density Normal

0 4 1 0 1 2 6 5 4 9 5 9 1 1

&

PRINT·BAR **BAR CODE :** POST·NET & FIM

BEA

▲48, 12, 42

·3090410012·

Bar Code : PostNET & FIM . . .

PostNET High Resolution
Human Readable
& High Resolution Normal

FIM

·3090410012·

A*I BeforeTheAlphabet-1

Manfred Klein • 1994

ALP

▲24

⊕ **Berlin Sans Bold Dingbats**

David Berlow • 1992
. . . Lucian Bernhard . . . .

FBU

▲16

PolyType **Birds**

POL

▲24

BLACKFOOT

Joshua Hadley • 1993

MTD

▲18

Blackfoot . . .

Border

• Composite

Ornaments

⊕ Berlin Sans Bold Dingbats ◀ Berlin Sans 1.

&

Border Pi
❖ *Linotype PiSet 2*

LIN ADA AGA MAE
▲24

GENERAL GLYPHICS
BORDER FONTS

MTD

▲18

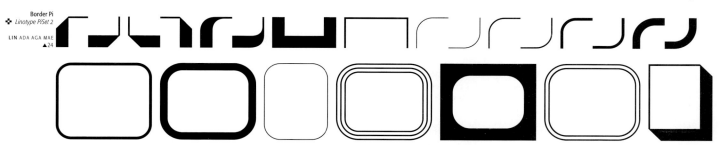

General Glyphics
Border Fonts . . .

Apogee

Argyle

Bourbon Street

Cartographer

Dot Rule

Draughts

Fat Waves

Intersect

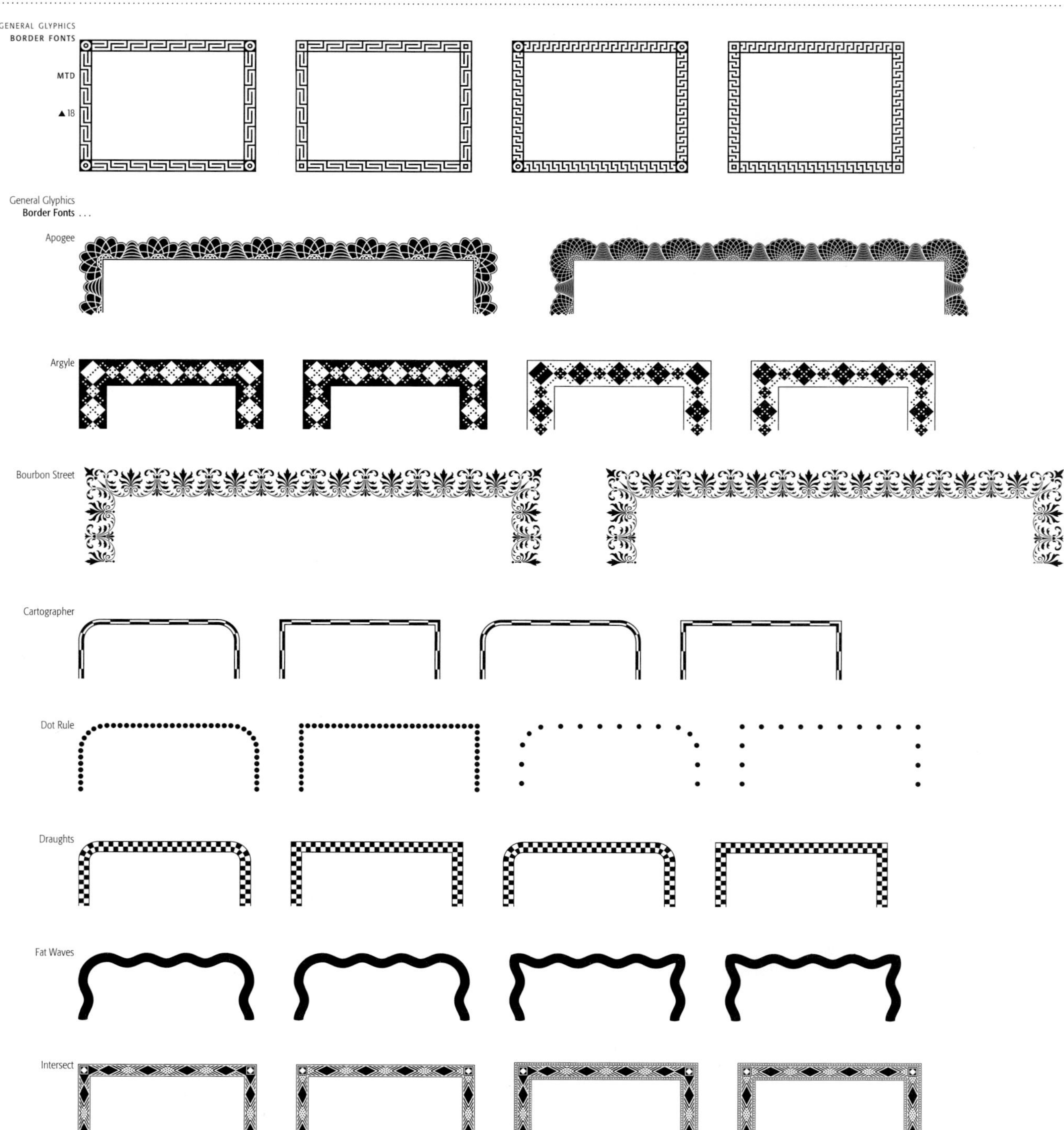

❖ *Linotype PiSet 2*: Border Pi & European Pi.

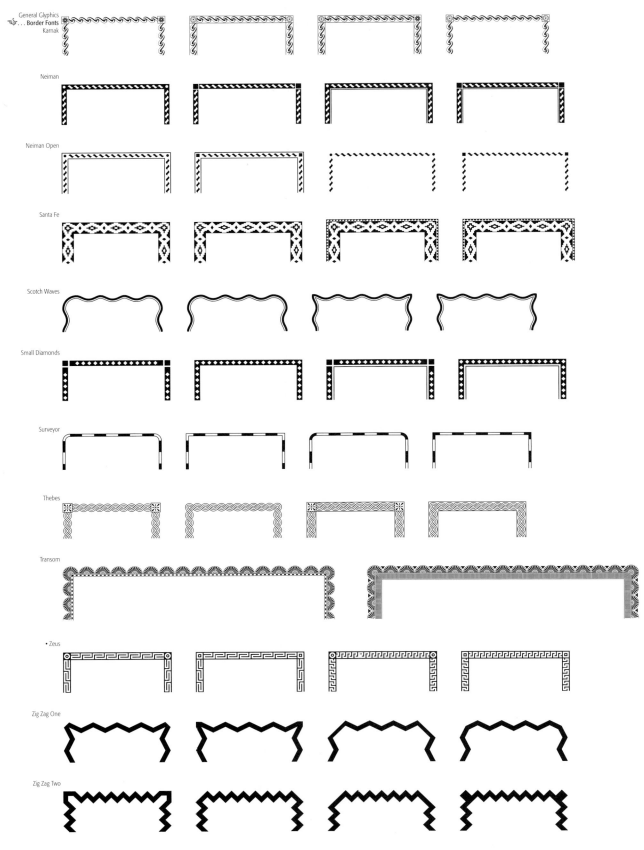

General Glyphics
. . . **Border Fonts**
Karnak

Neiman

Neiman Open

Santa Fe

Scotch Waves

Small Diamonds

Surveyor

Thebes

Transom

• Zeus

Zig Zag One

Zig Zag Two

&

KEY BORDERS
BORDER FONTS
KEY
▲18
Key Borders
Border Fonts . . .
Border A
Border Aaa
Border B
Border Bb
Border Bbb
Border C
Border Cc
Border Ccc
Border D
Border Ddd
Border Ee
Border Eee
Border Ff
Border Fff
Border Ggg
Border Hhh
Border I
Border Iii
Border J
Border Jj
Border Jjj
Border K
Border Kk
Border Kkk
Border L
Border Ll
Border M
Border Nn
Border Nnn
Border O
Border Oo
Border P
Border Pp
Border Q
• Border R
• Border Rr
Border Ss
Border Sss
Border Tt
Borter Ttt

&

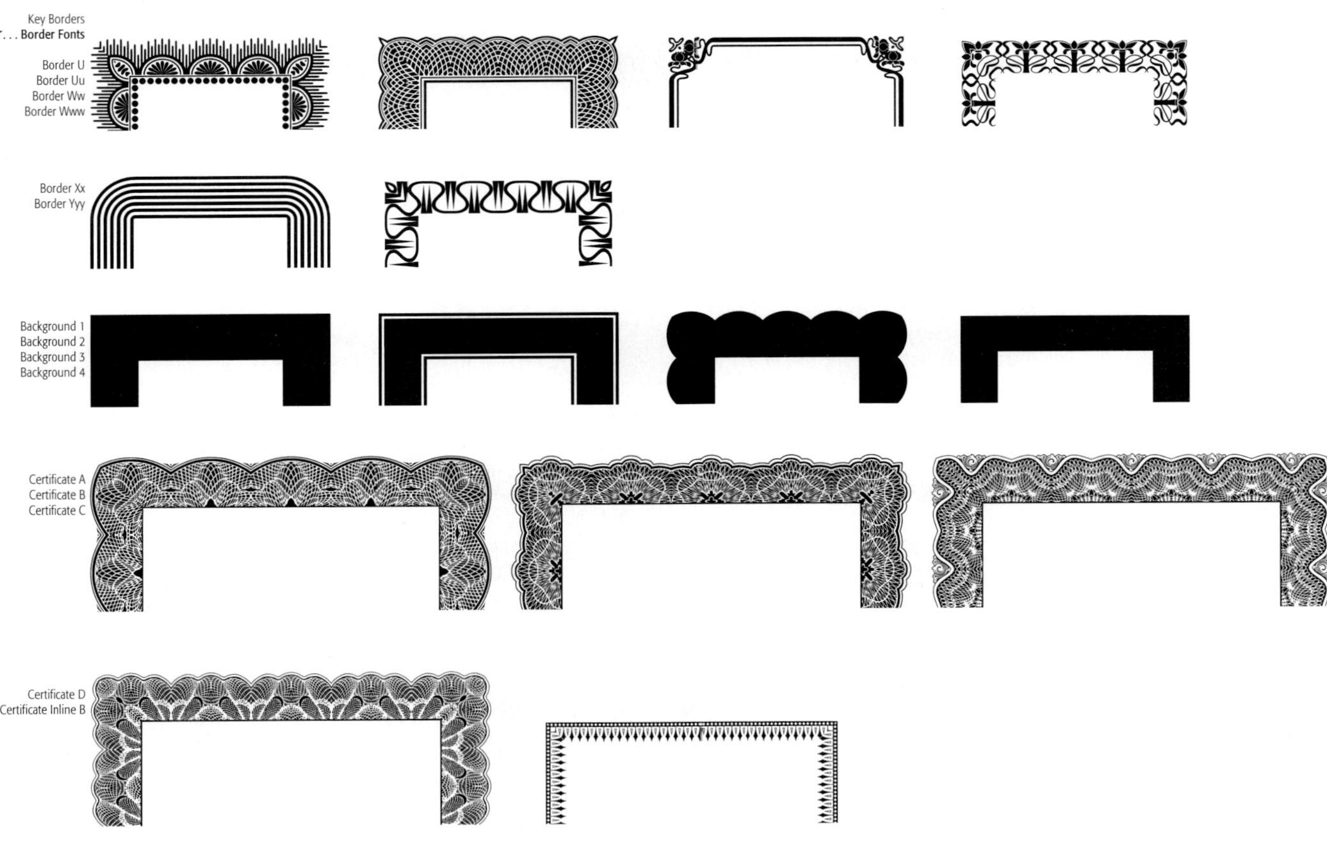

Key Borders
. . . Border Fonts

Border U
Border Uu
Border Ww
Border Www

Border Xx
Border Yyy

Background 1
Background 2
Background 3
Background 4

Certificate A
Certificate B
Certificate C

Certificate D
Certificate Inline B

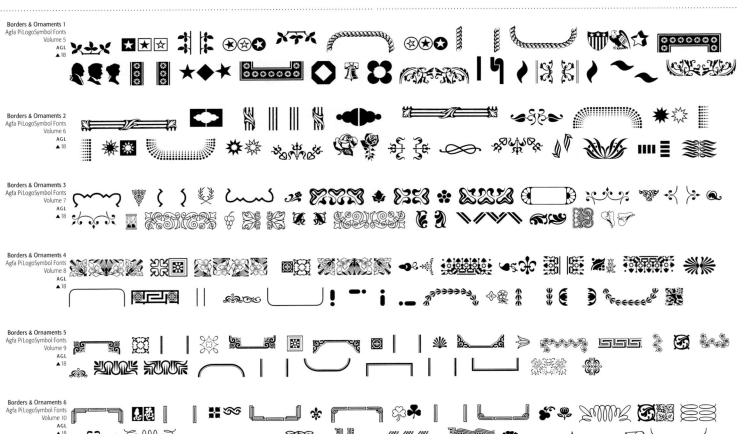

Borders & Ornaments 1
Agfa Pi LogoSymbol Fonts
Volume 5
AGL
▲18

Borders & Ornaments 2
Agfa Pi LogoSymbol Fonts
Volume 6
AGL
▲18

Borders & Ornaments 3
Agfa Pi LogoSymbol Fonts
Volume 7
AGL
▲18

Borders & Ornaments 4
Agfa Pi LogoSymbol Fonts
Volume 8
AGL
▲18

Borders & Ornaments 5
Agfa Pi LogoSymbol Fonts
Volume 9
AGL
▲18

Borders & Ornaments 6
Agfa Pi LogoSymbol Fonts
Volume 10
AGL
▲18

PIX·YMBOLS BOXKEY

PAG a b c d e f g h i j k l m n o p q r s t u v w x y z

▲16 (" . ; ' ! * ? ' : , ")

$ 1 2 3 4 5 6 7 8 9 0 & – [< # % + = { / | \ } ^ _ ` ~ @ >]

A B C D E F G H I J K L M N O P Q R S T U V W X Y Z

PIXymbols **Boxkey** . . .

One A abcdefghijklmnopqrstuvwxyzABCDEFGHIJKLMNOPQRSTUVWXYZ$1234567890(".;"!*?':,")&- <#%+=

One B áàâäãåæçéèêëíìîïñóòôöõøœúùÁÀÂÄÃÅÆÇÉÈÊËÍÌÎÏÑÓÒÔÖÕØŒÚÙ§ Alt

One C ĐđÞþ ß¨¥ ª º º {⌘ }

• Two A a b c d e f g h i j k l m n o p q r s t u v w x y z A B C D E

Two B á à â ä ã å æ ç é è ê ë í ì î ï ñ ó ò ô ö õ ø œ ú ù Á À Â Ä Ã

Two C Đ đ Þ þ ß ¨ ¥ ª º º ⌘

PIXymbols **BoxnLines**

PAG ©℗® SM TM

▲16

©℗® SM TM

PIX·YMBOLS **BRAILLE GRADE 2**

PAG

PIXymbols **Braille Grade 2** . . .

• Touch One •

Touch Two

Reader One •

Reader Two

TF Bridgette
(Bridge Pi)
✤ TF Games
Joseph Treacy • 1994

♡ ♠ ♣ ◇ A 1 2 3 4 5 6 7 8 9 10 J K Q ♡ ◇ ♥ ♠ ♣ ◆ Pass Dbl Void NT

TRE ? NORTH SOUTH EAST WEST PASS DBL VOID NT ?

BulletsNStuff

EMD

▲18

✤ *TF Games*: TF Bridgette, TF Crossword Puzzle & Solution.

BUNDESBAHN PI

LIN ADO AGA MAE

▲18

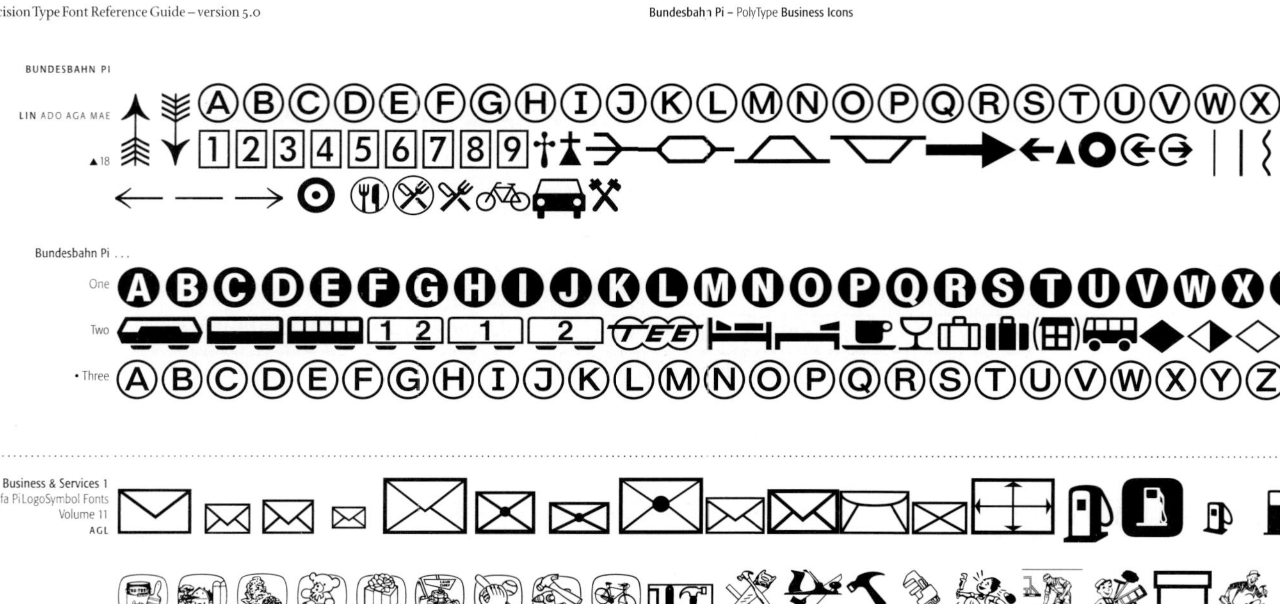

Bundesbahn Pi . . .

One

Two

• Three

Business & Services 1
Agfa Pi LogoSymbol Fonts
Volume 11
AGL

▲24

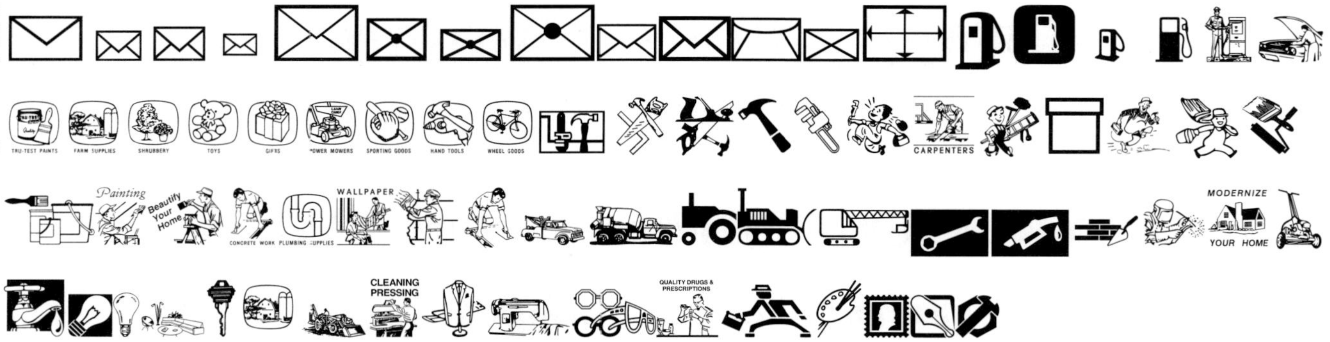

Business & Services 2
Agfa Pi LogoSymbol Fonts
Volume 12
AGL

▲24

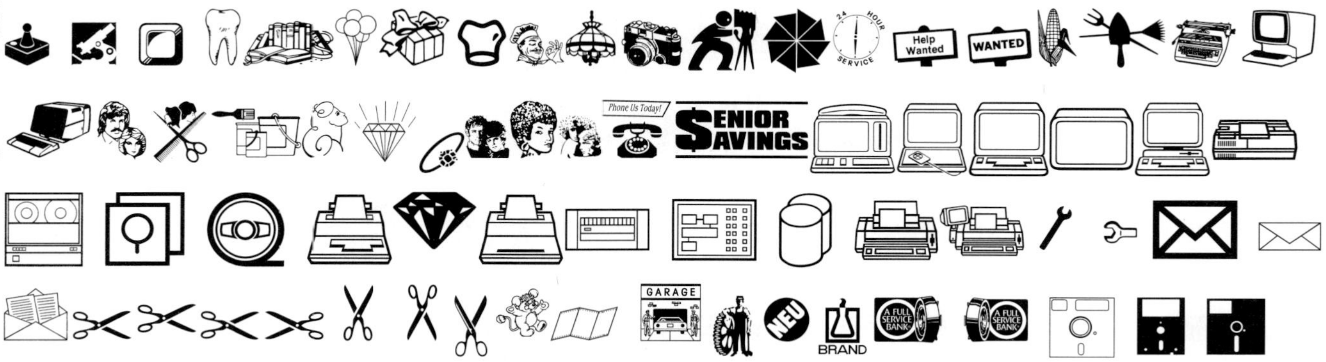

Business & Services 3
Agfa Pi LogoSymbol Fonts
Volume 13
AGL

▲24

POLY-TYPE BUSINESS ICONS

POL

PolyType Business Icons . . .

One
▲18

• Two
▲18

&

VISA

MasterCard

AMERICAN EXPRESS
Cards
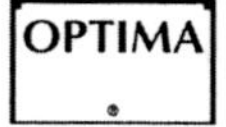
OPTIMA

DISCOVER

DINERS CLUB INTERNATIONAL

Calligraphic Ornaments

Richard Bradley • 1993

LET

▲18

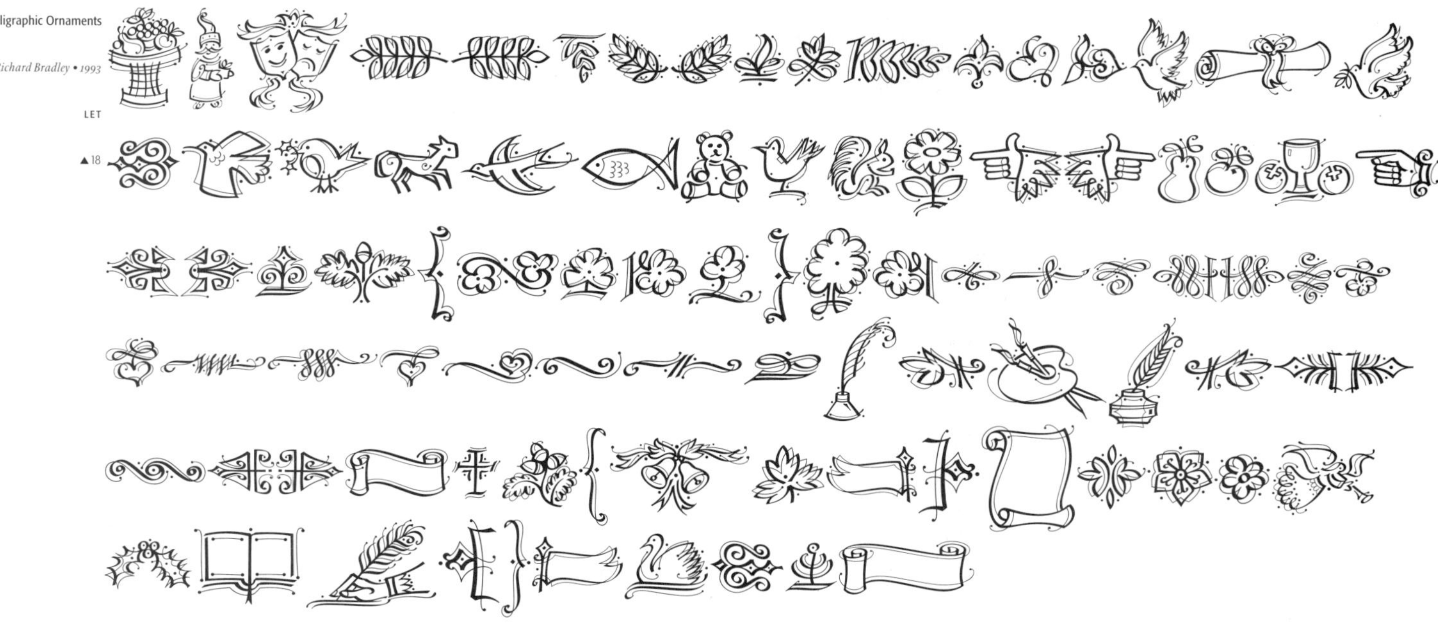

CARAVAN BORDERS & ORNAMENTS

William Addison Dwiggins • 1938

LIN ADO AGA MAE

▲18

Caravan Borders & Ornaments ...

One

• Two

Three

Four

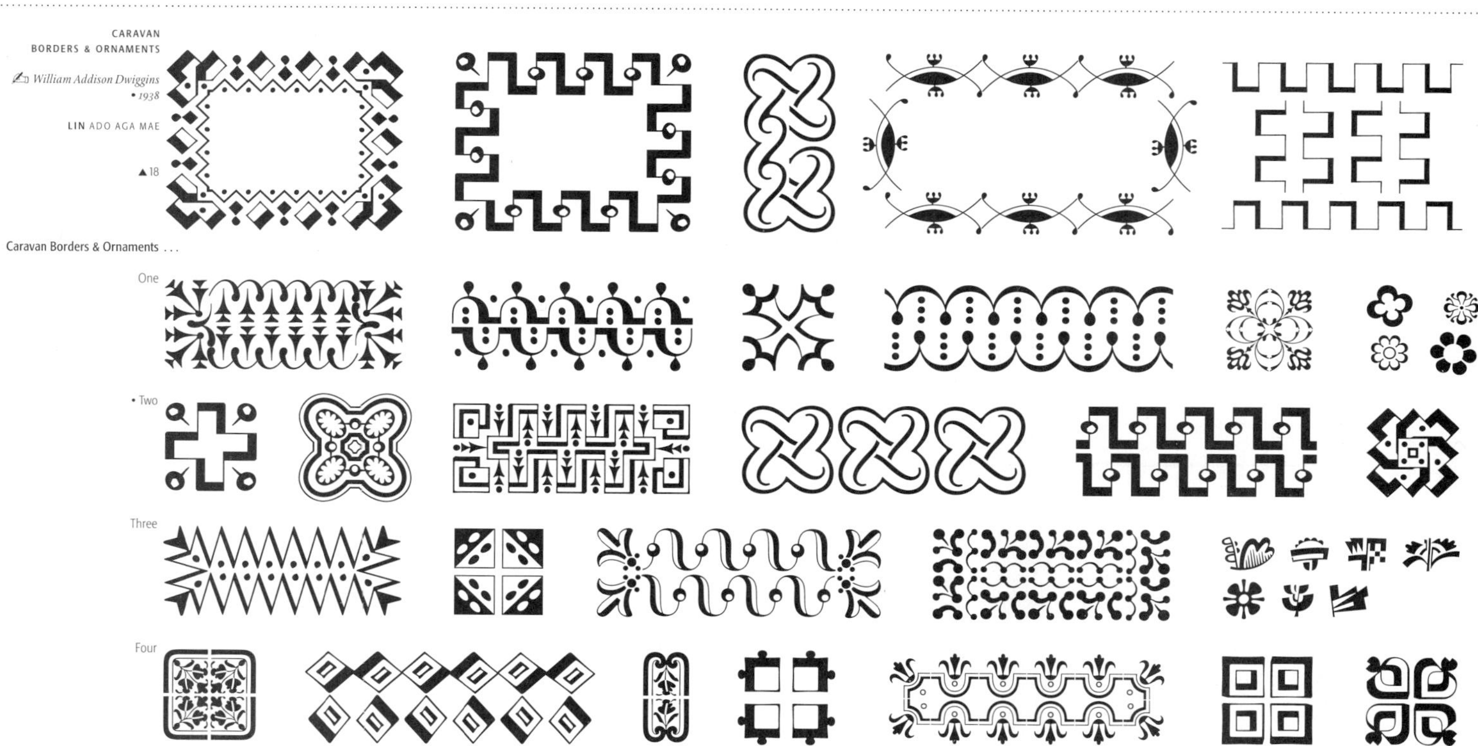

Carta

Lynne Garrell • 1986

ADO AGA LIN MAE

▲18

N
N
W
E
S
1234567890

&

⊕ Adobe Caslon Ornaments

Carol Twombly • *1990*
(William Caslon, 1725)

ADO AGA LIN MAE

▲18

Celebrations

James Wilson • *1994*

LET

▲24

Chemistra Pi

LIN

▲12

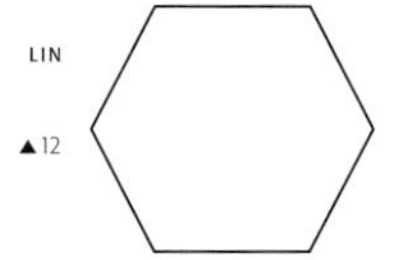
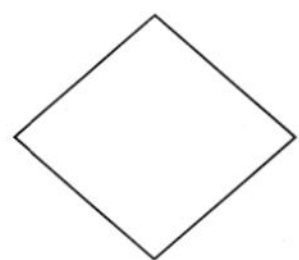
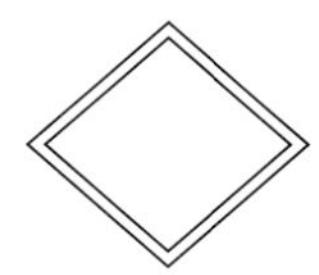
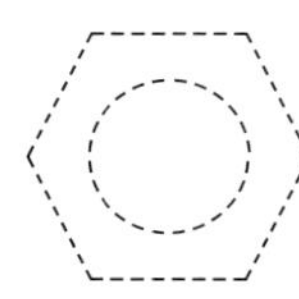
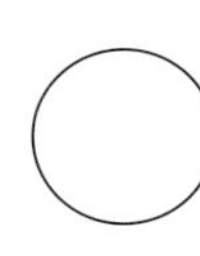

Cheq

John Renner • *1989*

LIN ADO AGA MAE

▲16

PIXymbols **Chess**

PAG

▲18

a b c d e f g h 1 2 3 4 5 6 7 8

MONOTYPE CHRISTMAS ORNAMENTS

MCL

▲18

Monotype Christmas Ornaments ...

One

Two

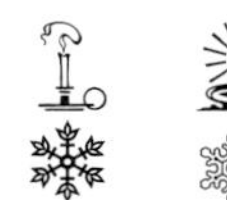

⊕ Adobe Caslon Ornaments ◀ Adobe Caslon Expert & SCOSF.

&

. . . Monotype Christmas Ornaments • Three

Four

Five

Six

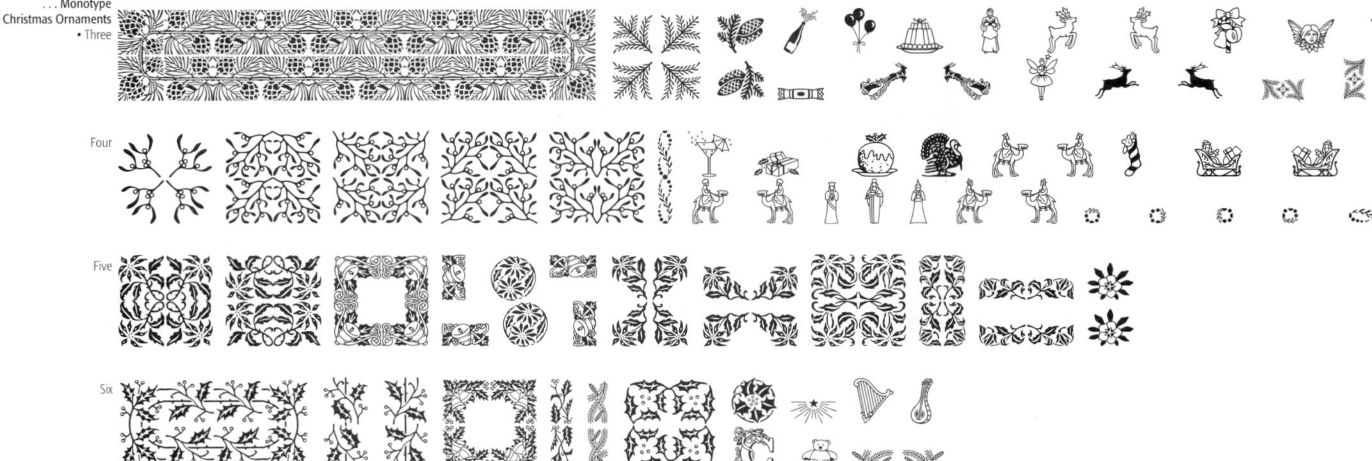

City Ornaments
✣ *Bureau Ornaments*
David Berlow • 1991
FBU AGP MTD
▲18

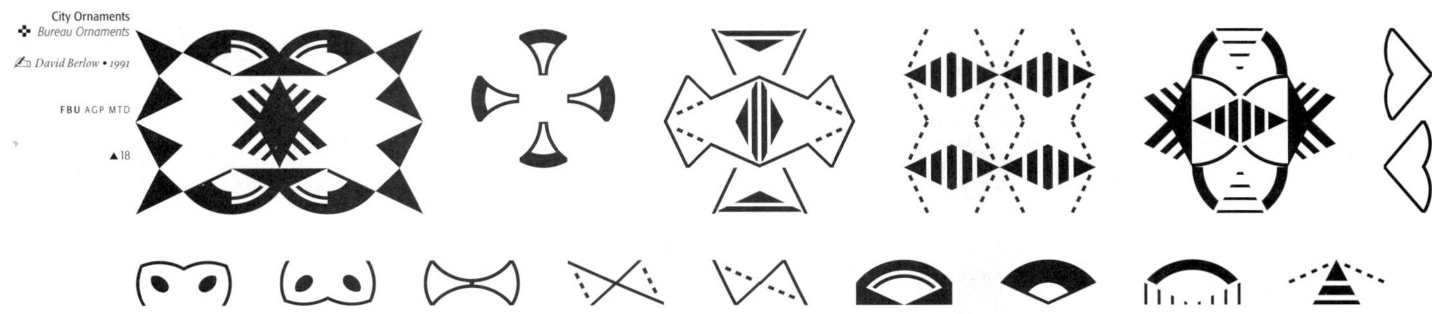

Mini Pics **Classic**
Greg Kolodziejzyk • 1992
IMA
▲24

CLIP & SAVE
COUPON
#✿!@X! OOPS
EXPRESS
AIR MAIL
YES
NO
TOP SECRET
FRAGILE
WHAT?
WOW

⊕ Colmcille Ornaments
MCL
▲18

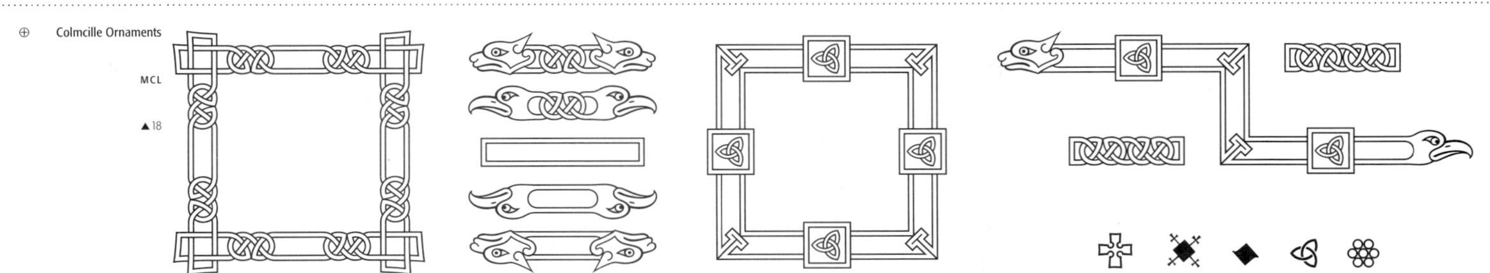

✣ *Bureau Ornaments*: City Ornaments, Town Ornaments, Village Ornaments.
⊕ Colmcille Ornaments ◀ Colmcille.

⊕ COLUMBUS ORNAMENTS
MCL
▲36

Columbus Ornaments . . .

One

• Two

PIX·YMBOLS COMMAND KEY
PAG
▲16

a b c d e f g h i j k l m n o p q r s t u v w x y z

(" . ; ' ! * ? ' : , ")

$ 1 2 3 4 5 6 7 8 9 0 & – [< # % + = { / | \ } ^ _ ` ~ @ >]

A B C D E F G H I J K L M N O P Q R S T U V W X Y Z

PIXymbols Command Key . . .

• One A — a b c d e f g h i j k l m n o p q r s t u v w x y z A B C

One B — Alt Bksp Ctrl Del Enter ⌦ Prt Sc Home Ins Home Break Caps Lock Scroll Lock

Two — ← Cmd 1 Cmd 2 Cmd 3 Cmd 4 Cmd 5 Cmd 6 Cmd 7 Cmd 8 Cmd 9

Commercial 1
Agfa PiLogoSymbol Fonts
Volume 14
AGL
▲18

LBS FOR LBS FOR ¢ lb. PAIRS Viva! NEW NEW % OFF % OFF ¶ ¶ ✓ ✓ % % % % @ @ @ @ @ @

@ @ @ new neu NEW † ℅ ℅ ℅ ℅ ℅ a/c a/c a/c a/c a/c NEW ‰ AVOID ERRORS READ CAREFULLY Getting Started

½ PRICE ea. only

Commercial 2
Agfa PiLogoSymbol Fonts
Volume 15
AGL
▲18

Commercial Pi

BIT

© ® ©®™ ™ @ ℅ a/c ‖ ¶ @ ℅ a/c ‖ © ® ©®™ ™ + – × ÷ = ± °′″ ∅ + _ × ÷ = ± °′″ _ _ _ ... ℞ ♀

♂ • • ● ● ▪ ■ ■ ○ ○ □ □ ★ ★ ○ □ ☒ ☑ ♣ ♠ ♥ ♦ ☎ ✆ ⁂ # ⊗ ☆ ☆ # ♧ ♤ ♡ ◇

☜ ☞ √ ✓ ◀ ▶ ▲ ▼

&

Commercials

✍ *Tom R. Garrett • 1994*

LET

▲24

Communications 1
Agfa PiLogoSymbol Fonts
Volume 16
AGL
▲18

Communications 2
Agfa PiLogoSymbol Fonts
Volume 17
AGL
▲18

Communications 3
Agfa PiLogoSymbol Fonts
Volume 18
AGL
▲18

Communications 4
Agfa PiLogoSymbol Fonts
Volume 19
AGL
▲18

Communications 5
Agfa PiLogoSymbol Fonts
Volume 20
AGL
▲18

Communications 6
Agfa PiLogoSymbol Fonts
Volume 21
AGL
▲18

Communications 8
Agfa PiLogoSymbol Fonts
Volume 23
AGL
▲18

&

MONOTYPE CONTEMPORARY ORNAMENTS

MCL

▲18

Monotype Contemporary Ornaments . . .

• One

Two

Three

Four

Five

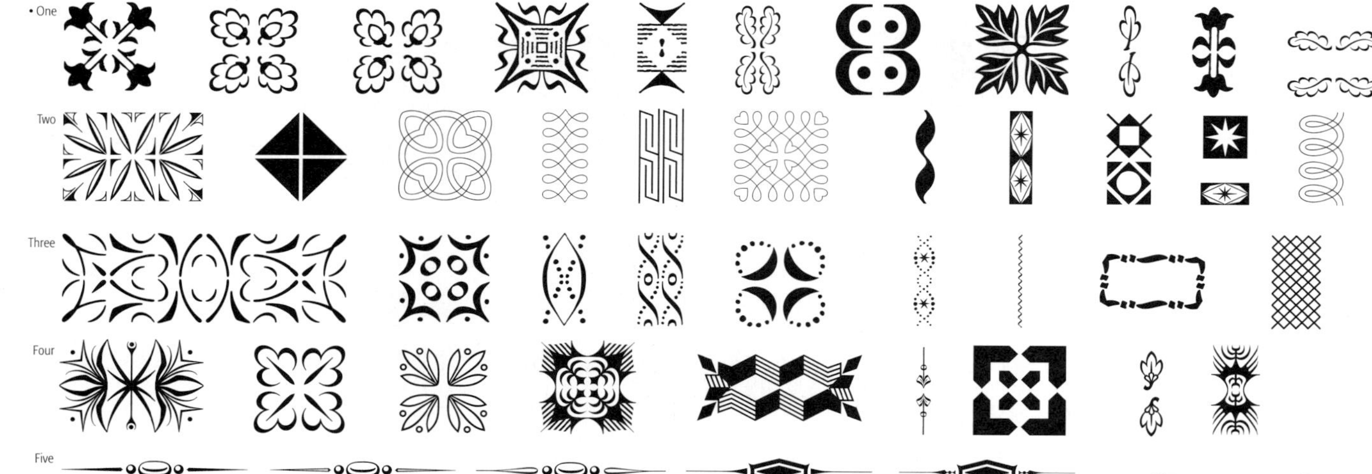

POLY-TYPE CORNERS

POL

▲18

PolyType Corners . . .

• One

Two

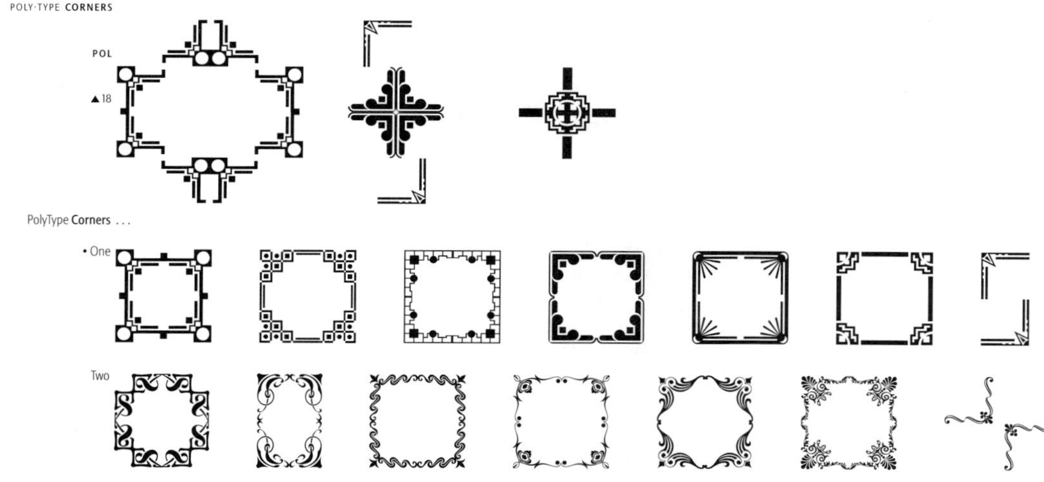

Credit Cards
Agfa PiLogoSymbol Fonts
Volume 24
AGL

▲24

AMERICAN EXPRESS
DISCOVER
VISA
MasterCard
DINERS CLUB
bankcard

TF CROSSWORD
✤ *TF Games*
✍ *Joseph Treacy* • *1989*
TRE MTD
▲18

TF Crossword – Puzzle
TF Crossword – Solution

	1	2	3	4	5	6	7	8	9	10	11	12	13	14	15	16	17	18	19	20	21	22	23	24	25	26
		27	28	29	30	31	32	33	34	35	36	37	38	39	40	41	42	43	44	45	46	47	48	49	50	
	A	B	C	D	E	F	G	H	I	J	K	L	M	N	O	P	Q	R	S	T	U	V	W	X	Y	Z
		1	2	3	4	5	6	7	8	9	0		Ä	Ą	Ă	Ā	Å	Â	Á	Æ	Ç	Ć	Č	Ď	Ď	

PIXymbols **Crossword**

PAG

▲18

1	2	3	4	5	6	7	8	9	10	11	12	13	14	15	16	17	18	19	20	21	22	23	24	25	26	
	A	B	C	D	E	F	G	H	I	J	K	L	M	N	O	P	Q	R	S	T	U	V	W	X	Y	Z

DECO NUMBERS

LIN

1 2 3 4 5 6 7 8 9 0 1234567890 1234567890 1 2 3 4 5 6 7 8 9 0
1234567890 1234567890 1 2 3 4 5 6 7 8 9 0 1 2 3 4 5 6 7 8 9 0

Deco Numbers ...

Circle 1 2 3 4 5 6 7 8 9 0 1 2 3 4 5 6 7 8 9 0 12345678900987654321 1234567890 0

Square 1 2 3 4 5 6 7 8 9 0 1 2 3 4 5 6 7 8 9 0 12345678900987654321 1234567890 0

• Triangle 1 2 3 4 5 6 7 8 9 0 1 2 3 4 5 6 7 8 9 0 1234567890 0 12345

OCR-A 1 2 3 4 5 6 7 8 9 0 1 2 3 4 5 6 7 8 9 0 123456789

Serlio 1 2 3 4 5 6 7 8 9 0 1 2 3 4 5 6 7 8 9 0 1 2 3 4 5 6 7 8 9 0 1
▲20

LINOTYPE DECORATION PI

LIN ADO AGA MAE

▲18

Linotype Decoration Pi ...

• One

Two

Delectables

✍ *Carol Kemp* • *1994*

LET

▲36

&

✤ *TF Games*: TF Bridgette, TF Crossword Puzzle & Solution.

⊕ LINOTYPE DIDOT ORNAMENTS

Adrian Frutiger • 1991
. . . Firmin Didot, 1784

LIN ADO AGA MAE

▲18

Linotype Didot Ornaments . . .

One

• Two

PIX-YMBOLS DIGITS & CLOCKS

PAG

▲18

12345:67890 12:00
1234567890

PIXymbols Digits & Clocks . . .

Digits – Regular ABCDEFGHIJKLMNOPQRSTUVWXYZ$1234567890-(".;'!×?';")[=/+]

Digits – Italic ABCDEFGHIJKLMNOPQRSTUVWXYZ$1234567890-(".;'!×?';")[=/+]

Digits – Bold ABCDEFGHIJKLMNOPQRSTUVWXYZ$1234567890-(".;'!×?';")[=/

Digits – Bold Italic ABCDEFGHIJKLMNOPQRSTUVWXYZ$1234567890-(".;'!×?';")[=/

• Clocks – Regular 12345:678

Clocks – Bold 12345:678

PIX-YMBOLS DINGBATS

PAG

PIXymbols Dingbats . . .

• One

AIR MAIL PAR AVION AIR MAIL

Two

&

⊕ Linotype Didot Ornaments ◀ Linotype Didot.

DingBRATS

✍ *Jake & Scott Scarano • 1993*

MTD

▲24

Dingura

✍ *Carlos Segura • 1993*

T26

▲30

MINI-PICS **DIRECTIONAL**

✍ *Grant Hutchinson • 1993*

IMA

▲18

Mini Pics **Directional** . . .

Arrows

• Triangle Arrows

Circle Arrows

Circle Triangles

Square Arrows

Square Triangles

Diversions

✍ *Ayse Ulay • 1994*

LET

▲36

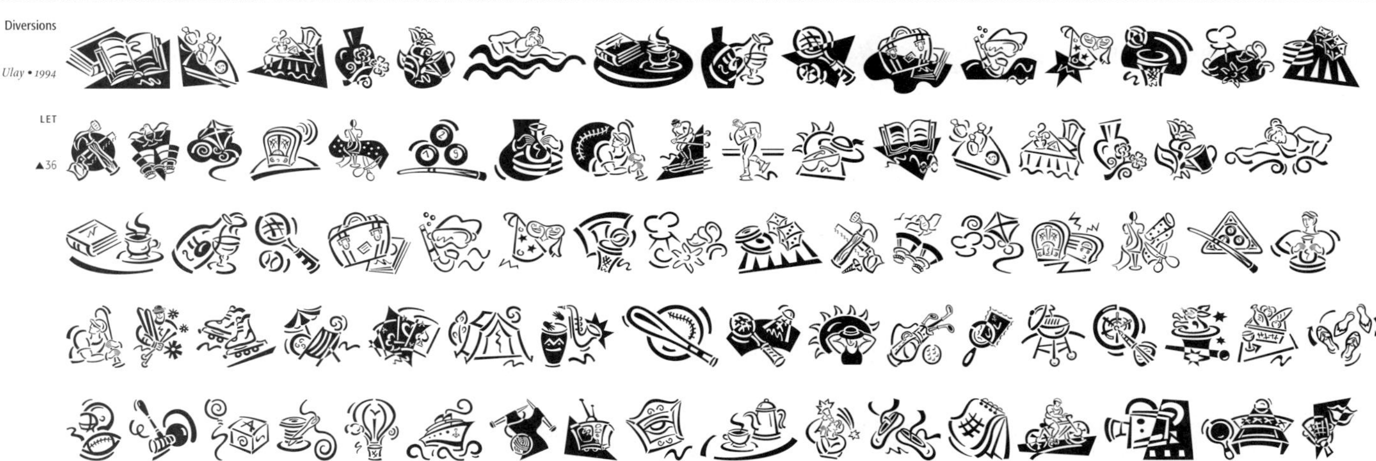

PIXymbols **DOSscreen**
One & Two
PAG
▲18

abcdefghijklmnopqrstuvwxyz(".;'!*?':,")
$1234567890&ß–äöüåçèîñó
ABCDEFGHIJKLMNOPQRSTUVWXYZÄÖÜÅÇÑ»«

A*I EclecticOne
✍ *Brain Sooy • 1994*
ALP
▲30

TM
THE END

Ecology
Agfa PiLogoSymbol Fonts
Volume 25
AGL
▲24

Linotype EEC Pi
LIN
▲30

A B CH D E F GB H I J GR L MC N NL P
PL RO S TR USA SU CY YU YV ZA HK RA CAN BG FL IRL
IS MAL RI RP SF CDN DK CS USA B euro eurostat
EP PE EP PE EUR op EUR op CVRIA CURIA RATIONUM EF EK EG CE EC

&

EUROPEAN PI
Linotype PiSet 2
LIN ADO AGA MAE
▲16

①②③④⑤⑥⑦⑧⑨⑩⑪⑫⑬⑭⑮⑯⑰⑱⑲⑳○○□◇◊☎☆☆☆
❶❷❸❹❺❻❼❽❾❿⓫⓬⓭⓮⓯⓰⓱⓲⓳⓴●●■◆♦☎★★★
1 2 3 4 5 6 7 8 9 0

European Pi ...
• One
Two
Three
Four

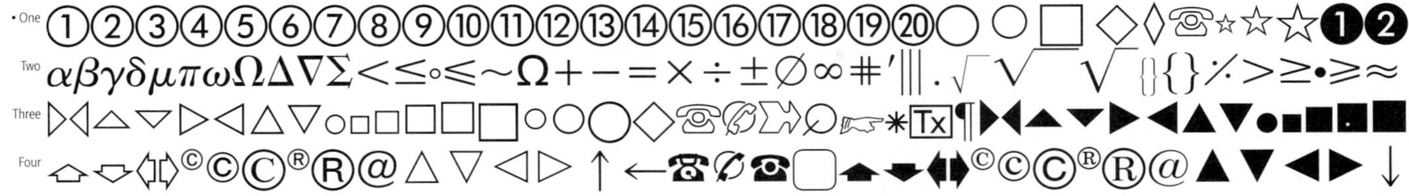

PIXymbols **FabriCare**
PAG

1 2 3 4 5 6 7 8 9
1234567890
F C

PIXymbols **FARmarks**
(Federal Aviation Regulation Markings)
PAG
▲24

ABCDEFGHIJKLMNOPQRSTUVWXYZ
-1234567890 ABCDEFGHIJKLMNOP
QRSTUVWXYZ-1234567890

PIXymbols **Flagman**
PAG
▲24

Fleurons : Folio One
LAN
▲18

Linotype PiSet 2: Border Pi & European Pi.

Fleurons : Granjon Folio

LAN

▲18

A*I Flighty

Manfred Klein • 1994

ALP

▲24

Fontoonies No.1

Steve Zafarana • 1994

GAL

▲30

⊕ Fournier Ornaments

MCL

▲18

&

⊕ Fournier Ornaments ◀ Fournier Expert.

LINOTYPE FRACTION PI
Linotype Fraction Pi
LIN ADO AGA MAE

1 1/64 3/32 5/16 7/8 9/64 11/32 13/16 15/64 17/32 1/8 1/4 1/3 3/8 1/2 5/8 2/3 3/4 7/8 2 1/64 3/32 5/16 7/8 9/64 11/32 13/16 15/64 17/32 1/8 1/4 1/3 3/8 1/2 5/8 2/3 3/4 7/8

Linotype Fraction Pi …

New Century Schoolbook Fractions – Roman & Bold: 12345 12345 67890 12345/67890 67890 **12345 12345 67890 12345/67890 67890**

• Helvetica Fractions – Regular & Bold: 12345 12345 67890 12345/67890 67890 **12345 12345 67890 12345/67890 67890**

PolyType **Fruits**
POL

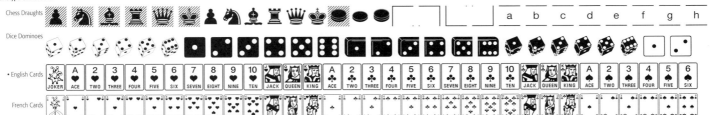

▲20

LINOTYPE GAME PI
LIN ADO AGA MAE

JOKER ACE TWO THREE FOUR FIVE SIX SEVEN EIGHT NINE TEN JACK QUEEN KING ACE TWO THREE FOUR FIVE SIX SEVEN EIGHT NINE TEN JACK QUEEN KING JOKER

JOKER ACE TWO THREE FOUR FIVE SIX SEVEN EIGHT NINE TEN JACK QUEEN KING ACE TWO THREE FOUR FIVE SIX SEVEN EIGHT NINE TEN JACK QUEEN KING JOKER

Linotype Game Pi …

Chess Draughts: a b c d e f g h

Dice Dominoes

• English Cards: JOKER ACE TWO THREE FOUR FIVE SIX SEVEN EIGHT NINE TEN JACK QUEEN KING ACE TWO THREE FOUR FIVE SIX SEVEN EIGHT NINE TEN JACK QUEEN KING ACE TWO THREE FOUR FIVE SIX

French Cards

Games & Sports 1
Agfa PiLogoSymbol Fonts
Volume 26
AGL
▲18

Games & Sports 3
Agfa PiLogoSymbol Fonts
Volume 28
AGL
▲18

Games & Sports 4
Agfa PiLogoSymbol Fonts
Volume 29
AGL
▲18

General Symbols 1
Agfa PiLogoSymbol Fonts
Volume 30
AGL
▲18

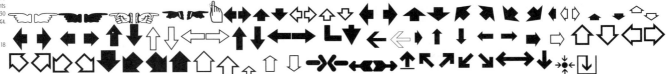

General Symbols 2
Agfa PiLogoSymbol Fonts
Volume 31
AGL
▲18

Linotype Fraction Pi: New Century Schoolbook Roman & Bold Fractions, Helvetica Regular & Bold Fractions.

&

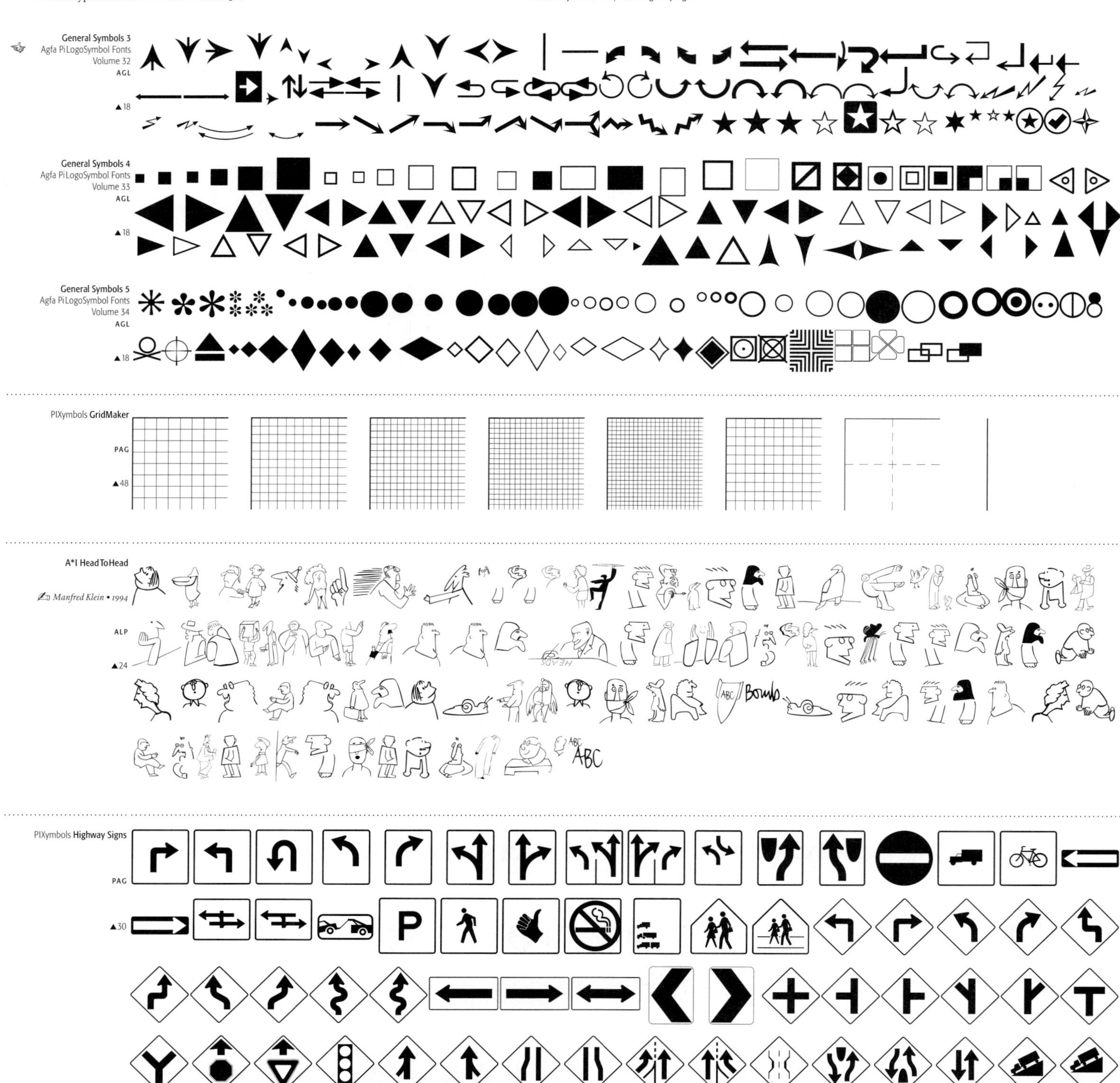
General Symbols 3
Agfa Pi LogoSymbol Fonts
Volume 32
AGL
▲18
General Symbols 4
Agfa Pi LogoSymbol Fonts
Volume 33
AGL
▲18
General Symbols 5
Agfa Pi LogoSymbol Fonts
Volume 34
AGL
▲18
PIXymbols GridMaker
PAG
▲48
A*I HeadToHead
Manfred Klein • 1994
ALP
▲24
PIXymbols Highway Signs
PAG
▲30
STOP

LINOTYPE HOLIDAY PI

LIN ADO AGA MAE

Linotype Holiday Pi . . .

One

▲16

• Two

▲24

Three

▲16

Holidays
Agfa PiLogoSymbol Fonts
Volume 35
AGL

▲18

PolyType Holidays One & Two

POL

▲18

PIX·YMBOLS HOSPITAL & SAFETY

PAG

PIXymbols Hospital & Safety . . .

Hospital Positive

▲16

Hospital Negative

▲16

Safety Positive

▲16

• Safety Negative

▲16

&

STEMPEL HOT METAL BORDERS
LIN
▲18
Stempel Hot Metal Borders . . .
One
Two
• Three
Four

Incidentals

✍ *Frank McShane • 1993*

LET

▲24

Industrials

✍ *Ed Miliano • 1994*

LET

▲30

&

Industry & Engineering 1
Agfa PiLogoSymbol Fonts
Volume 36
AGL
▲16

Industry & Engineering 2
Agfa PiLogoSymbol Fonts
Volume 37
AGL
▲16

Mini Pics **International**
IMA
▲18

International Symbols 1
Agfa PiLogoSymbol Fonts
Volume 38
AGL
▲24

AUS CDN CH DDR DK GB GR BR CO IL IRL E IS NL I P NZ
RCH A S D F SF J SU L TR USA B N

AUS BRD BG CDN CH ČS DDR DK GR IL IRL PL I E IS NL RO P
A D F SF H J SU L TR

International Symbols 2
Agfa PiLogoSymbol Fonts
Volume 39
AGL
▲24

INTERSTATE PI
Guy Jeffrey Nelson • 1993
FBU
▲30

UP
FEDEX-ING
KEYS WALLET
LOOSE CHANGE
CROSS FINGERS
ROAD
IDIOT
ROAD KILL
CHIP ON SHOULDER
DEAD HEAD
TEMPTING CURVES
SLOW ADULTS
DO NOT TURN RED
NO SPEED LIMIT
NO WAY
SASSY
HERE
NO EXIT
NO COP NO STOP
DO NOT LEAVE
TALK
AGE LIMIT
WAY
SULTRY
THERE
DONT TALK

THE END

Interstate Pi . . .
One

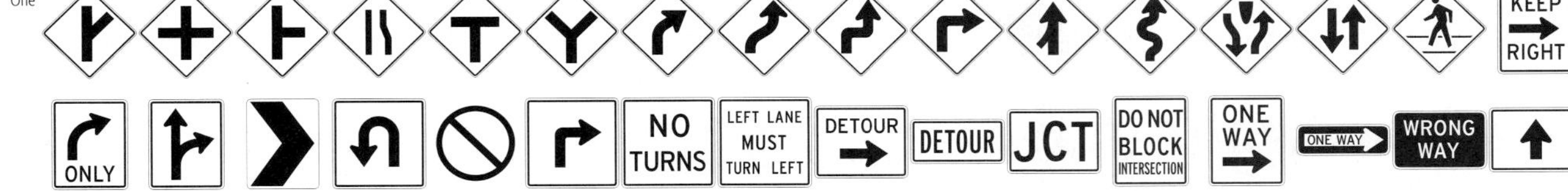
KEEP RIGHT
ONLY
NO TURNS
LEFT LANE MUST TURN LEFT
DETOUR
DETOUR
JCT
DO NOT BLOCK INTERSECTION
ONE WAY
ONE WAY
WRONG WAY

. . . Interstate Pi

Two

Three

• Four

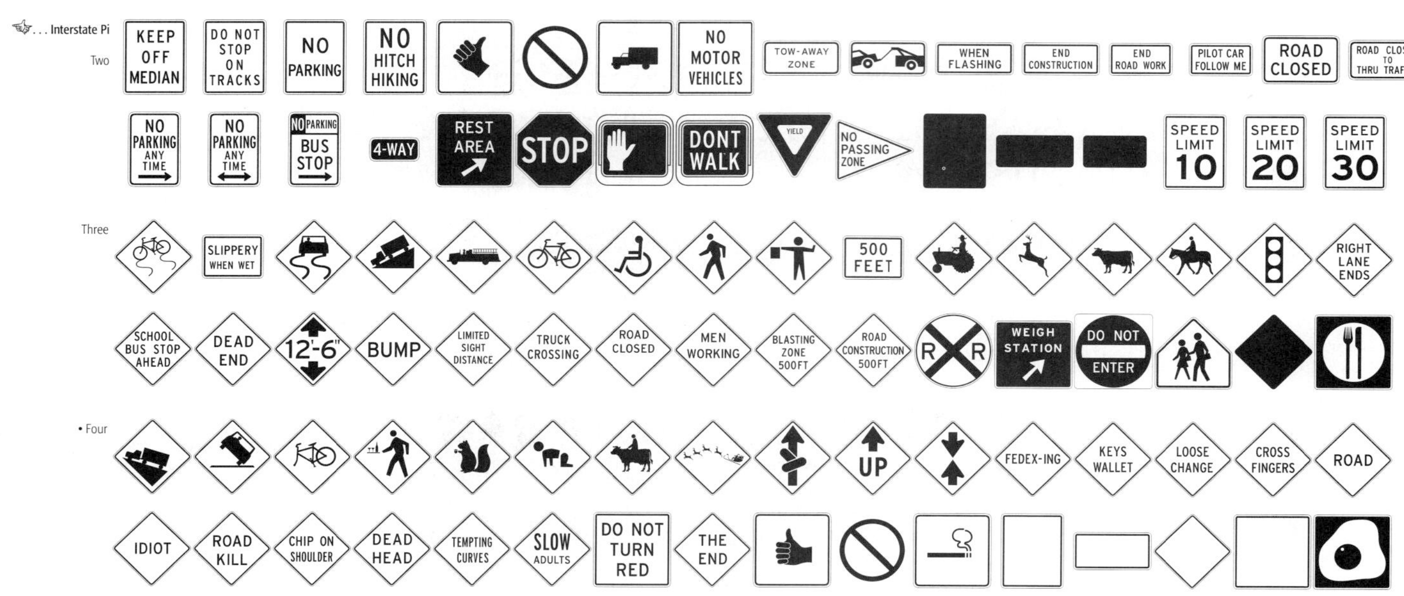
KEEP OFF MEDIAN
DO NOT STOP ON TRACKS
NO PARKING
NO HITCH HIKING
NO MOTOR VEHICLES
TOW-AWAY ZONE
WHEN FLASHING
END CONSTRUCTION
END ROAD WORK
PILOT CAR FOLLOW ME
ROAD CLOSED
ROAD CLOSED TO THRU TRAFFIC
NO PARKING ANY TIME
NO PARKING ANY TIME
NO PARKING BUS STOP
4-WAY
REST AREA
STOP
DONT WALK
YIELD
NO PASSING ZONE
SPEED LIMIT 10
SPEED LIMIT 20
SPEED LIMIT 30
SLIPPERY WHEN WET
500 FEET
RIGHT LANE ENDS
SCHOOL BUS STOP AHEAD
DEAD END
12'-6"
BUMP
LIMITED SIGHT DISTANCE
TRUCK CROSSING
ROAD CLOSED
MEN WORKING
BLASTING ZONE 500FT
ROAD CONSTRUCTION 500FT
R R
WEIGH STATION
DO NOT ENTER
UP
FEDEX-ING
KEYS WALLET
LOOSE CHANGE
CROSS FINGERS
ROAD
IDIOT
ROAD KILL
CHIP ON SHOULDER
DEAD HEAD
TEMPTING CURVES
SLOW ADULTS
DO NOT TURN RED
THE END

Journeys

Eric Hanson • 1994

LET

▲36

GUIDE
MAP
HOLLYWOOD
HOTEL
POST

Kurusu

Jim Marcus • 1993

T26

▲30

&

PIXymbols **LCD**
– AlphaNumerics & Symbols
PAG
▲16

abcdefghijklmnopqrstuvwxyz(".;' !*?' :,")
$1234567890&-[<#={/|\}+%>]^
ABCDEFGHIJKLMNOPQRSTUVWXYZ

Leaves One
LAN
▲30

Legal Trademarks
Agfa PiLogoSymbol Fonts
Volume 40
AGL
▲16

TM TM TM TM TM TM TM TM TM TM TM TM TM SM SM SM SM SM Ⓟ Ⓟ Ⓟ Ⓟ Ⓟ Ⓟ Ⓟ Ⓟ © © © © © © © © © © © ® ® ® ® ®
® ® ® ® ® ® ® ® ® ® © © © © © © © © © © ® ® ® ® ® ® ® ® ® ® © © © © © © ® ® ® ® ® ® ™

PolyType **Leisure One & Two**
POL
▲24

Mini Pics **Lil' Critters**
✍ *Patricia Lillie • 1993*
IMA
▲24

&

Mini Pics **Lil' Faces**

Patricia Lillie • 1993

IMA

▲24

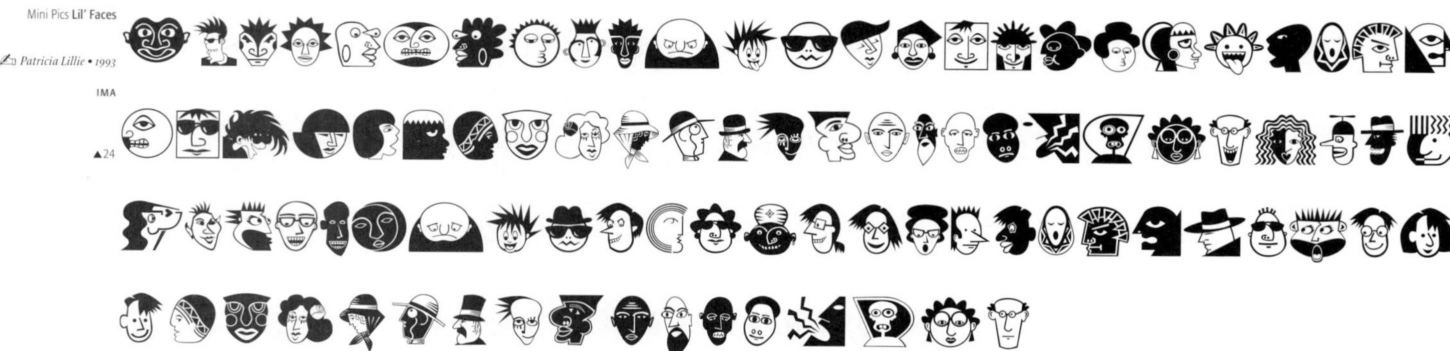

Logos : Company 1
Agfa Pi LogoSymbol Fonts
Volume 41
AGL

Logos : Company 2
Agfa Pi LogoSymbol Fonts
Volume 42
AGL

Logos : Company 3
Agfa Pi LogoSymbol Fonts
Volume 43
AGL

Logos : Company 4
Agfa Pi LogoSymbol Fonts
Volume 44
AGL

Logos : Company 5
Agfa Pi LogoSymbol Fonts
Volume 45
AGL

&

Logos : Company 6
... Agfa PiLogoSymbol Fonts
Volume 46
AGL

Logos : Company 7
Agfa PiLogoSymbol Fonts
Volume 47
AGL

Logos : Company 8
Agfa PiLogoSymbol Fonts
Volume 48
AGL

Logos : Company 9
Agfa PiLogoSymbol Fonts
Volume 49
AGL

Logos : Company 10
Agfa PiLogoSymbol Fonts
Volume 50
AGL

Logos : Company 11
Agfa PiLogoSymbol Fonts
Volume 51
AGL

DATEV
DATEV
DB
Delco
DELTA AIR LINES
Denny's
Denny's
devon
DAKO
DIEHL
digital
digital
DISTILLERIA
DISPO
Do it center
Do it center
Do it best
Dodge
Def Jam recordings
Diakonie in Bayern
DOLBY SYSTEM
DOLBY HX PRO
DOLBY SYSTEM
DOLBY B
DU PONT
DMC
DUNKIN' DONUTS
DUNKIN' DONUTS It's worth the trip.
EF Hutton
EG&G
EATON'S We are. Canada's department store
EATON Nous sommes... le grand magasin du Canada
ECHO First from the start
ELEKTRA
EMA FOODS
EMI AMERICA
EMPEROR INFOBOT
Enchantments
EQUI-NET EQUITABLE REALTY NETWORK
Epic
ENERGIZER
EVEREADY ENERGIZER
ESKOM
ESKOM
ESKOM
Esso
Esso
EVEREADY
EVEREADY
EVEREADY
Executone
EXPRESS STARTS
EXXON
Farmers Petroleum
FAIRCHILD A Schlumberger Company
FEDERAL EXPRESS
FIAT
Fieldcrest
Fieldcrest
FIRSTAR
FLABEG
Flexees
flexnit
FLYING TIGERS
FMC
FMC
food city
FOOD RITE
FORD
FORD
Ford
Ford
FORD TRUCKS
FORD MERCURY
MERCURY LINCOLN
FotoTipoLito Moderna-Ra.
FRANCE TELECOM
FRANCE TELECOM ILE-DE-FRANCE
Friskies
GAB
Gambles
GARRETT
Gazifère
Gazifère Inc.
GEFFEN
galoob
GRACO
GRACO
GM
GM
GM
GMC TRUCKS
GENERAL DYNAMICS
GENERAL TIRE
Georgia Power
Georgia Power
GIANT
GIANT EAGLE
GIANT EAGLE Only the best.
GIANT EAGLE PHARMACY
GIRO
HAMILTON
HUBBARD
Glaxo Inc.
Glaxo
grafi tex
grafi tex
GRESHAM
Gibson
GTE
haas company
HALIFAX URBAN RENEWAL
Gulf
HALIFAX ESTATE AGENTS
HALIFAX
HALIFAX ESTATE AGENCIES
Haeberlein-Metzger AUS TRADITION DAS BESTE
Haeberlein-Metzger AUS TRADITION DAS BESTE
Hallmark
Hallmark Cards
Hanes
Hanes
Hanes
HERITAGE Entertainment Inc.
HEUMANN PHARMA
HELENE CURTIS
HELENE CURTIS
HERTZ RENT A CAR
Hertz
HESS
HICKESON-LANGS
Holiday Inn
Holland
HOLLY HOBBIE
HONDA
HONDA FOLLOW THE LEADER
HOOVER
HUGHES NETWORK SYSTEMS
HUGHES AIRCRAFT COMPANY
HUGHES
hr
hr
HUGHES
Hunt
ICE
HAGGAR
Husky
IBM
IBM
ICI
IDS
IGA
IMAGES
INFOBOT The Information Robot
IM-IT INSURED MUNICIPALS INCOME TRUST
Esso Imperial Oil
Esso L'Impériale
Esso Imperial Oil
Esso L'Impériale
Imperial Oil
Esso L'Impérial
JOCKEY
John Hancock
Jos. Hoover Company
Kellogg's
jpl
JW ROBINSON'S
KAISER'S
KAY BEE TOY STORES
KAY BEE AMERICA'S TOY STORE
Kemper
TOY WORKS
Kemper Mutual Funds
Kemper Financial
KENT
Kmart
KRUPP DRUCK SINZIG
KRUPP VERLAG SINZIG
KRAFT
KRAFT
Kodak
Kodak
Kodak
Kodel polyester
Kroger
Leaf
Lee
Lee
LBS
Lederle
STANDARD Lederle PRODUCTS
L'eggs
liquitex
lettergraphics
Levi's
LINCOLN NATIONAL LIFE INSURANCE COMPANY
Life Stride AFFORDABLES
Lilly
Lockheed
LOSS CONTROL
Lufthansa
MAC TRUCK LINES
Macintosh
Maidenform
3M
makita
MASTER MIX
Marshall
MATRIX
MTX
MaxEPA
Litton
MANUFACTURERS BANK
manutec
MAGIC LINE
Master Teller
MAYTAG
mazda
McCULLOCH
McAlpin's
McAlpin's
McDonald's
McDonald's International
MERCK
mercury
mexicana
midas
Milestone
Printing MINUTEMAN PRESS
MINOLTA
Miss Elaine
MITRE
MITSUBISHI
Monet

&

Logos : Company 12
Agfa Pi LogoSymbol Fonts
Volume 52
AGL

Logos : Company 13
Agfa Pi LogoSymbol Fonts
Volume 53
AGL

Logos : Company 14
Agfa Pi LogoSymbol Fonts
Volume 54
AGL

Logos : Company 15
Agfa Pi LogoSymbol Fonts
Volume 55
AGL

Logos : Company 16
Agfa Pi LogoSymbol Fonts
Volume 56
AGL

Logos : Company 17
Agfa Pi LogoSymbol Fonts
Volume 57
AGL

Logos : Company 18
Agfa Pi LogoSymbol Fonts
Volume 58
AGL

Logos : Company 19
. . . Agfa PiLogoSymbol Fonts
Volume 59
AGL
UNITED
UNITED AIRLINES
UAL INC.
UNITED AIRLINES
U.S. BANCORP
UNITED INSURANCE COMPANY OF AMERICA
UNITED TECHNOLOGIES CHEMICAL SYSTEMS
VHS
UNIVERS
USLIFE
ValuRite
VANITY FAIR
VALVOLINE
VARIG
Vigorena FEEDS
V·A·G
V·A·G
Logos : Company 20
Agfa PiLogoSymbol Fonts
Volume 60
AGL
Whirlpool
WHITE STAG
WWF
WHITE FARM EQUIPMENT
WAYNE ANIMAL HEALTH AIDS
Washburn Laboratories
Wendy's
UK HAMBURG
WA
THE WESTPAC MUSEUM
You can bank on Westpac.
WEIDER
Weiss
Westpac
weyel international
Logos : Company 21
Agfa PiLogoSymbol Fonts
Volume 61
AGL
ALCAN
Audi
ARCO
BAKOLA
BRAUN NÜRNBERG
CNA
CITIBANK
Chicago Board of Trade
Peavey
C&K
DAK
EXXON
IBA
McCORD GASKETS
Style-Rite
USA
XEROX
YMCA
YAMAHA
ZENITH
Logos : Company 22
Agfa PiLogoSymbol Fonts
Volume 62
AGL
DESSERT OF THE MONTH CLUB
EXECUTONE
APICS
A&S
ABN LASALLE Bank
Britannic Assurance
KUBOTA
MAC
LENSPLUS
ББЦ БРОУН БОВЕРИ
MICAFIL
AVIS
AmToy
Kemper America
DataCentral
LEXIS
I.R.S.
LCA
ALLIED VAN LINES
manutec
Logos : Company 23
Agfa PiLogoSymbol Fonts
Volume 63
AGL
VAN KAMPEN MERRITT INC.
intel
Veltra
West Bend
ITT
ITT
HITACHI
Jantzen
Jeep
HAMILTON BEACH
COLECO
COLECO
JOHN DEERE
Logos : Company 24
Agfa PiLogoSymbol Fonts
Volume 64
AGL
commodore
CONNOISSEURS
Corelle LIVINGWARE BY CORNING
CORNING WARE
Counselor
CREST
cristal d'arques
CROSS Lifetime Mechanical Guarantee
CURITY Infant Bedding Collection
Deauville
DēLonghi
DēLonghi America
J. G. DURAND
Dessau
Brass
DOLLY
DP Fit for Life
Dundee
Emerson
Epilady
EVERLAST
FARBERWARE
First Alert
First Class
fisher
Fisher-Price
Fisher-Price Toys
Franklin
French White
Logos : Company 25
Agfa PiLogoSymbol Fonts
Volume 65
AGL
Accent
Acclaim
Algoma
All-Luminum Products
American Harvest
Anchor Hocking
APEX ELECTRONICS
Armitron
Armstrong
AUDIOVOX
BEDTIME ORIGINALS
BIONAIRE
BRAUN
BISSELL
BLACK&DECKER
Broil King
BRITA
BUNN Omatic
Bush
BUSHNELL DIVISION OF BAUSCH & LOMB
CAROUSEL
CASIO Where Miracles Never Cease
Clairol
CONAIR
Dirt Devil
Logos : Company 26
Agfa PiLogoSymbol Fonts
Volume 66
AGL
HASBRO
HASBRO PRESCHOOL
Health o meter
HOOVER
HUFFY MADE IN U*S*A
HUFFY BICYCLES
igloo CORPORATION
JENSEN SOUND LABORATORIES
iSi
Kodak
KIDS COLLECTION
KitchenAid
Lenox Gifts
Lady Remington
Lenoxx Sound
Libbey
LLOYD'S
LORUS QUARTZ
MAGNAVOX
Majestron
MATCHBOX
MATTEL
MATTEL
maxell
melnor
MESSAGE·MINDER
mikasa
MR.COFFEE II
Logos : Company 27
Agfa PiLogoSymbol Fonts
Volume 67
AGL
MB MILTON BRADLEY
MINOLTA
Moulinex
Nikon
Norelco
Ohio Art
Oster
OKIDATA
Oleg Cassini
Oscar de la Renta
PARKER
PARKER GAMES
pierre cardin
Pierre Cardin
PLAYSKOOL
Pollenex
Pressman
PRESTO
Proctor-Silex
PRO-STYLE
PULSAR
Ray-Ban
Regal
Regina
REMCO

&

Logos : Company 28
Agfa Pi LogoSymbol Fonts
Volume 68
AGL

Regent Sheffield
REMINGTON®
REVERE WARE
RIVAL
RONSON
Sango
SANYO
Savant
Sealy
SEIKO
Sergio Valente
SHEAFFER
SHARP
Sunbeam
TEAC
Technics
THERMOS
TIMEX
Tonka
toscany
totes
Unisonic
TYCO
Vivitar
VISIONS
COOKWARE

Logos : Company 29
Agfa Pi LogoSymbol Fonts
Volume 69
AGL

AFFILIATED BANK
AFFILIATED BANK
AMERICAN MOVIE CLASSICS
Galavisión
LIFETIME
TELEVISION
MARTIN MARIETTA
PRISM
UNIVISION
VIDAL SASSOON
Walt Disney
HOME VIDEO
WARING
WaterPik
WELBILT
WELBY
Westclox
WILKINSON
SWORD

Logos : Services 1
Agfa Pi LogoSymbol Fonts
Volume 70
AGL

The Gallery of Homes
MLE
MULTIPLE LISTING SERVICE
MLS
RELO
WORLD LEADER IN RELOCATION
REALTOR® ASSOCIATE
REALTOR®
REALTY WORLD
Realtor
ERA
EQUAL HOUSING OPPORTUNITY
EQUAL OPPORTUNITY LENDER
FSLIC
A FULL SERVICE BANK
A FULL SERVICE BANK
Member
FDIC
Independent Insurance Agent
FARMERS INSURANCE GROUP

Logos : Services 2
Agfa Pi LogoSymbol Fonts
Volume 71
AGL

UL
UL
FARM BUREAU CO-OP
TELEFLORIST
COOP
PERFORMANCE
IMPROVEMENT
drug awareness
national guard

Logos : Services 3
Agfa Pi LogoSymbol Fonts
Volume 72
AGL

                 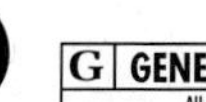 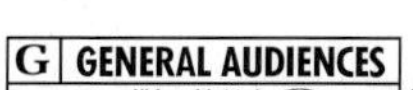            
FARM FINANCIAL SERVICES
Instant banking
Instant cash
Instant update
Instant teller
INSPECTED U.S. DEPARTMENT OF AGRICULTURE
PRINTED IN U.S.A.
CRAFTED WITH PRIDE IN U.S.A.
BANDS OF AMERICA
PRINTED IN CANADA
IMPRIMÉ AU CANADA
GREEN CROSS FOR SAFETY
G GENERAL AUDIENCES
All Ages Admitted
R RESTRICTED
UNDER 17 REQUIRES ACCOMPANYING PARENT OR ADULT GUARDIAN
PG PARENTAL GUIDANCE SUGGESTED
SOME MATERIAL MAY NOT BE SUITABLE FOR CHILDREN
U.S. MAIL
pip
POSTAL INSTANT PRESS
USDA CHOICE
USDA A GRADE

LUCIDA MATH

Charles Bigelow & Kris Holmes • 1989

LIN ADO AGA MAE

Lucida Math
≪ ≤ ± ∓ ≥ ≫

Lucida Math . . .

Italic
abcdefghijklmnopqrstuvwxyz
ABCDEFGHIJKLMNOPQRSTUVWXYZ
1234567890,. ⇀ ⇁ ◁ < ⌣ ⌢ ⋆ / ♭ ♯ ♮
αβψδεφγηιξκλμνπζρστθωφχυ
ΖΨΔΦΓΞΛΠΘΣΩϒ ϵ ϖ ϱ ς ℓ ȷ ı ∂ ϑ ℘

Symbol
𝒜ℬ𝒞𝒟ℰℱ𝒢ℋℐ𝒥𝒦ℒℳ𝒩𝒪𝒫𝒬ℛ𝒮𝒯𝒰𝒱𝒲𝒳𝒴𝒵
§ℜℑ∐ℵ∀∃†‡¶ ⊓ ⊔ ⊑ ⊒ { } ∫ ⊂ ⊃ ⊆ ⊇ ⌈ ⌉ ⌊ ⌋ ⊖ ⊘ ⊙ ≺ ≻ ⪯ ⪰ ⊗ ⊕ ⊘
≪ ≫ ≤ ≥ ± ∓ ÷ × ∗ ↑ ↓ ← → ↔ ↕ ∼ ≈ ⇑ ⇓ ⇐ ⇒ ⇔ ⇕ ‖ | ≡ ⊤ ⊥ ⊢ ⊣
∞ ∝ ∩ ∪ ⊎ ↗ ↖ ↘ ↙ ∈ ∋ △ ▽ ≍ ◇ ♡ ♠ ♣ ○ ∘ ∧ ∨ ⋄ • · − ¬ / / ⊦ \ ≀ √ ∇

. . . Lucida Math

Extension

∏ ∏ ∐ ∐ ∑ ∑ ⋀ ⋀ ∫ ∫ ∮ ∮ ⨂ ⨂ ⨁ ⨁ ⨀ ⨀

PIXymbols Luna One & Two

PAG

▲24

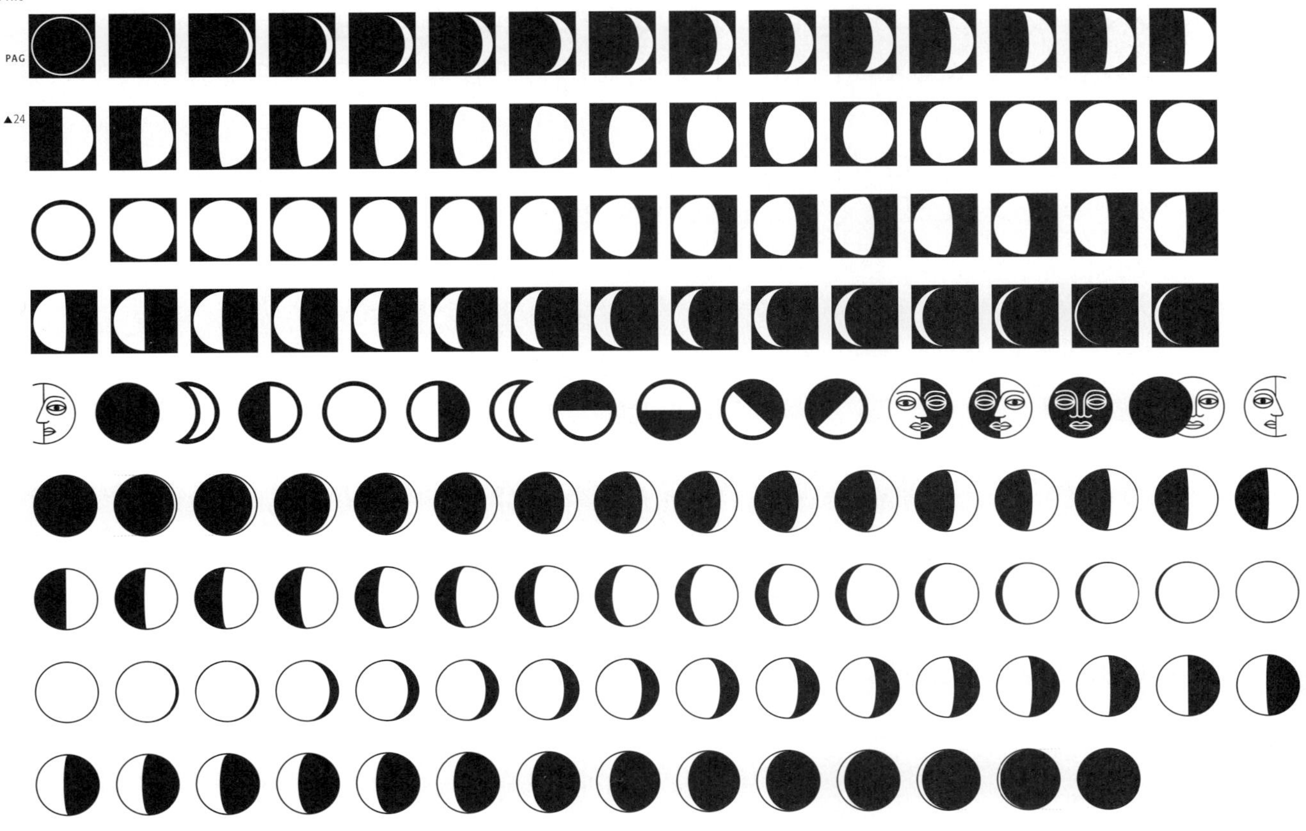

Math with Greek Pi

BIT αβψδεφγηιξκλμνοπϑρστθωφχυζ

ΑΒΨΔΕΦΓΗΙΞΚΛΜΝΟΠΘΡΣΤΘΩϐΧΥΖ

[∼ + − × ÷ = ± ∓ ° ′ ″ ‴] ⟨∞ ∝ ∂ ℏ ƛ ∫⟩

(ε ϖ ∇ √ ‾ Π) {< ⩽ ⩾ ≳ / ≈ ≡ >}

Math & Technical 1
Agfa Pi LogoSymbol Fonts
Volume 73
AGL

Math & Technical 2
Agfa Pi LogoSymbol Fonts
Volume 74
AGL

Math & Technical 3
Agfa Pi LogoSymbol Fonts
Volume 75
AGL

Math & Technical 4
Agfa Pi LogoSymbol Fonts
Volume 76
AGL

Math & Technical 5
Agfa Pi LogoSymbol Fonts
Volume 77
AGL

Math & Technical 6
Agfa Pi LogoSymbol Fonts
Volume 78
AGL

Math & Technical 7
Agfa Pi LogoSymbol Fonts
Volume 79
AGL

Math & Technical 8
Agfa Pi LogoSymbol Fonts
Volume 80
AGL

IVXLCDM **IVXLCDM** I II III IV V VI VII VIII IX X Π ∏ ∩ ∪ ⋂ ⋃ ∩ ∪ ∩ ∪ ∩ ∪ ∩ ∪

⊂ ⊃ ⊂ ⊃ ⊆ ⊇ ⊆ ⊇ ⊆ ⊇ ⊊ ⊋ ⊄ ⊅ ⊈ ⊉ ∈ ∈ ∉ ∈ ∈ ∇ ∇ ∉ ∉ ∋ ∋ ∇ ∇

Math & Technical 9
Agfa Pi LogoSymbol Fonts
Volume 81
AGL

Math & Technical 10
Agfa Pi LogoSymbol Fonts
Volume 82
AGL

αβψδεφγηιξκλμνοπϑϱστθωφχυς ΑΒΨΔΕΦΓΗΙΞΚΛΜΝΟΠΡΣΤΩΥΧΖ—1234567890(+ − = × ÷ #/∇∂)-.,:;

Math & Technical 11
Agfa Pi LogoSymbol Fonts
Volume 83
AGL

αβψδεφγηιξκλμνοπϑϱστθωφχυς ΑΒΨΔΕΦΓΗΙΞΚΛΜΝΟΠΡΣΤΩΥΧΖ—1234567890(+ − = × ÷ #/∇∂)-.,:;

&

Math & Technical 12
Agfa PiLogoSymbol Fonts
Volume 84
AGL

*αβψδεφγηιξκλμνοπϑρστθωφχυζ*ΑΒΨΔΕΦΓΗΙΞΚΛΜΝΟΠΡΣΤΩΥΧΖ

Math & Technical 13
Agfa PiLogoSymbol Fonts
Volume 85
AGL

***αβψδεφγηιξκλμνοπϑρστθωφχυζ*ΑΒΨΔΕΦΓΗΙΞΚΛΜΝΟΠΡΣΤΩΥΧΖ**

Math & Technical 14
Agfa PiLogoSymbol Fonts
Volume 86
AGL

abcdefghijklmnopqrstuvwxyzABCDEFGHIJKLMNOPQRSTUVWXYZ—1234567890(%/*)&-[.,:;!]

Math & Technical 15
Agfa PiLogoSymbol Fonts
Volume 87
AGL

abcdefghijklmnopqrstuvwxyzABCDEFGHIJKLMNOPQRSTUVWXYZ-1234567890(%/*)&[.,:;!]

Math & Technical 16
Agfa PiLogoSymbol Fonts
Volume 88
AGL

abcdefghijklmnopqrstuvwxyzABCDEFGHIJKLMNOPQRSTUVWXYZ—1234567890(%/)&-[.,:;!]*

Math & Technical 17
Agfa PiLogoSymbol Fonts
Volume 89
AGL

abcdefghijklmnopqrstuvwxyzABCDEFGHIJKLMNOPQRSTUVWXYZ—1234567890(%/)&-[.,:;!]*

MATHEMATICAL PI

LIN ADO AGA MAE [MATHEMATICAL PI ↦ ↷ ⤾ ↶ ⤹]

Mathematical Pi ...

One
αβψδεφγηιξκλμνοπϑρστθωφχυζ
ΑΒΨΔΕΦΓΗΙΞΚΛΜΝΟΠΘΡΣΤΘΩ6ΧΥΖ
∞+−×÷=±∓°′″‴∇∅−\∀∃</>
∝≪≫⩽⩾≤≥≦≧≲≳⋜⋝⪋⪌≢≠
-—|ℵℏ·∂εςϖϰƛ ≰≱≮≯≨≩≢≠

Two
𝔞𝔟𝔠𝔡𝔢𝔣𝔤𝔥𝔦𝔧𝔨𝔩𝔪𝔫𝔬𝔭𝔮𝔯𝔰𝔱𝔲𝔳𝔴𝔵𝔶𝔷
𝔄𝔅ℭ𝔇𝔈𝔉𝔊ℌℑ𝔍𝔎𝔏𝔐𝔑𝔒𝔓𝔔ℜ𝔖𝔗𝔘𝔙𝔚𝔛𝔜ℨ
ℓ ℓ g g z z h h ⊏ ⋰ ⋯ ⋱ ⋮ ↦ ↷ ⤾ ↶ ⤹
𝒜ℬ𝒞𝒟ℰℱ𝒢ℋℐ𝒥𝒦ℒℳ𝒩𝒪𝒫𝒬ℛ𝒮𝒯𝒰𝒱𝒲𝒳𝒴𝒵

Three
()()()()()(){}{}{}[][][][][][][][][][]⟨⟩⟨⟩⟨⟩
∫∮∯∫∮∯∫∮∯⋀⋁ΣΠΣΠ∑∏∮ ⋮ ∼ ≃ ≈ ≅ ≌ ≁ ≁
⩓⩔⊼⊻⊼⊻≠#≠=#≠#≡#≢≢≢≢≢≢≢≢≠≄≠≢≠
| | | | ‖ ‖ ‖ / / / / √ √ √))

Four
αβψδεφγηιξκλμνοπϑρστθωφχυζ
ΑΒΨΔΕΦΓΗΙΞΚΛΜΝΟΠΘΡΣΤΘΩ6ΧΥΖ
∞+−×÷=±∓°′″‴∇∈∋∅⊂⊃⊂/⊃
∝⋐⋑∪∩⊆⊇⊊⊋⊏⊐⫅⫆⫋⫌⊄⊅≠≠⊄⊅
∈ ∋ | **∪ ∩ · ∂εςϖϰƛ** ⊄⊅⊈⊉**⊄⊅**∉∌∉∌**⊄⊅**

&

… Mathematical Pi

Five

• Six ABCDEFGHIJKLMNOPQRSTUVWXYZ

Medical & Pharmaceutical 1
Agfa Pi LogoSymbol Fonts
Volume 90
AGL
▲18

Medical & Pharmaceutical 2
Agfa Pi LogoSymbol Fonts
Volume 91
AGL
▲18

PIXymbols Meeting One & Two
PAG
▲24

PIX·YMBOLS MENU·FONTS

PAG

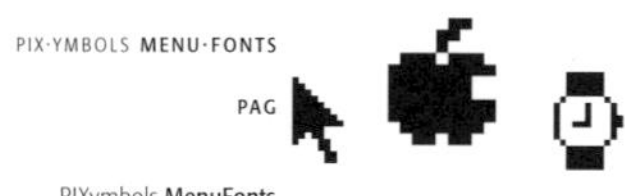

PIXymbols MenuFonts . . .
▲16

MACmenu One abcdefghijklmnopqrstuvwxyz(".;'!*?':,")
$1234567890&fifl-äöüåçèîñóæøœ
ABCDEFGHIJKLMNOPQRSTUVWXYZ
ÄÖÜÅÇÈÎÑÓÆØŒ»„«[§¶°†‡]‹i·¿›...

• MACmenu Two

WINmenu One abcdefghijklmnopqrstuvwxyz(".;'!*?':,")
$1234567890&-äöüåçèîñóæøœ
ABCDEFGHIJKLMNOPQRSTUVWXYZ
ÄÖÜÅÇÈÎÑÓ»„«[¶§°†‡]i·¿

WINmenu Two

WINdialog One abcdefghijklmnopqrstuvwxyz(".;'!*?':,")
$1234567890&-äöüåçèîñóæøœ
ABCDEFGHIJKLMNOPQRSTUVWXYZ
ÄÖÜÅÇÈÎÑÓ»„«[¶§°†‡]i·¿

WINdialog Two

MICR
✣ OCR Set 1
ADO AGA BIT LIN MAE
▲18

1234567890

Military & Patriotic 1
Agfa PiLogoSymbol Fonts
Volume 92
AGL
▲24

Military & Patriotic 2
Agfa PiLogoSymbol Fonts
Volume 93
AGL
▲24

Canada

Ontario

Québec

✣ *OCR Set 1*: MICR, OCR-A, OCR-B.

⊕ **Minion Ornaments**

Robert Slimbach • 1989
ADO AGA LIN MAE

⊕ **Minion MultipleMaster Ornaments**
(one axis: optical size)
Robert Slimbach • 1991
ADO AGA LIN MAE

Regular

Display
▲30

Mo' Funky Fresh Symbols

David Sagorski • 1993

LET

▲24

Moderns

David Sagorski • 1994

LET

▲30

PIXymbols Morse

PAG

•– –••• –•–• –•• • ••–• ––• •••• •• •––– –•– •–•• ––

–• ––– •––• ––•– •–• ••• – ••– •••– •–– –••– –•–– ––••

•–––– ••––– •••–– ••••– ••••• –•••• ––••• –––•• ––––• –––––

–––––• •––––– ••–––– •••––– ••••–– •••••• –••••• ––•••• –––••• –––––

•– –••• –•–• –•• • ••–• ––• •••• •• •––– –•– •–•• ––

–• ––– •––• ––•– •–• ••• – ••– •••– •–– –••– –•–– ––••

&

⊕ Minion Ornaments ◀ Minion Expert & SCOSF.
⊕ Minion MultipleMaster Ornaments ◀ Minion MultipleMaster Expert & SCOSF.

PIX-YMBOLS **MUSICA**
PAG

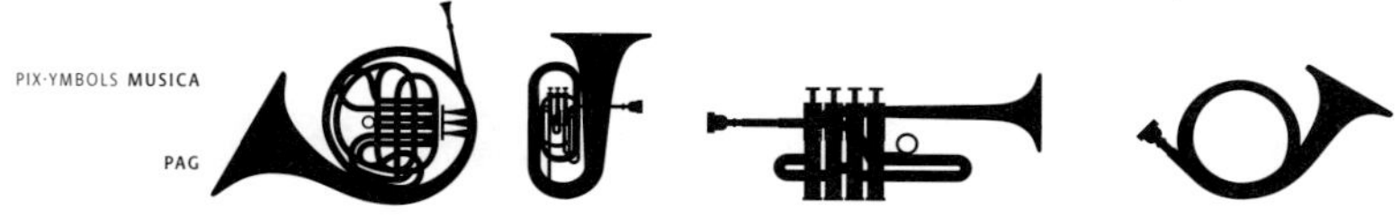

PIXymbols **Musica** . . .
▲12 & 24
Open
• Fill One
Fill Two
Strings
Orchestra

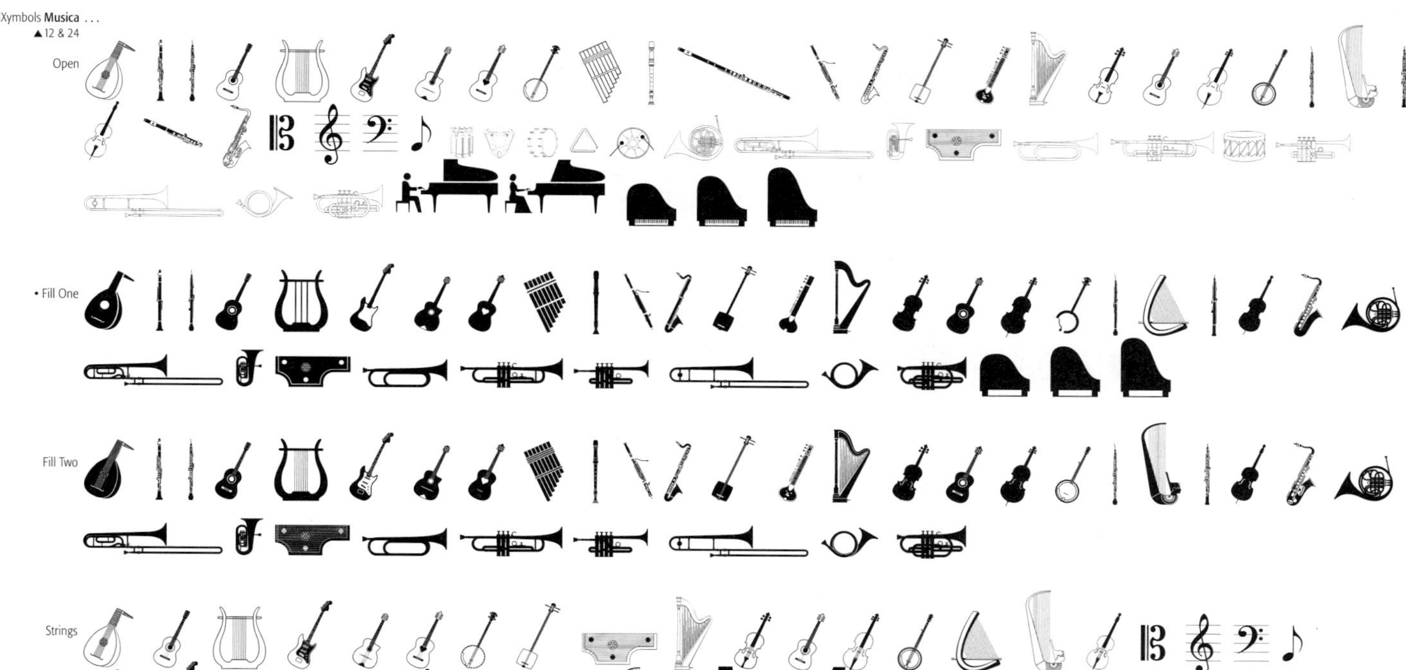

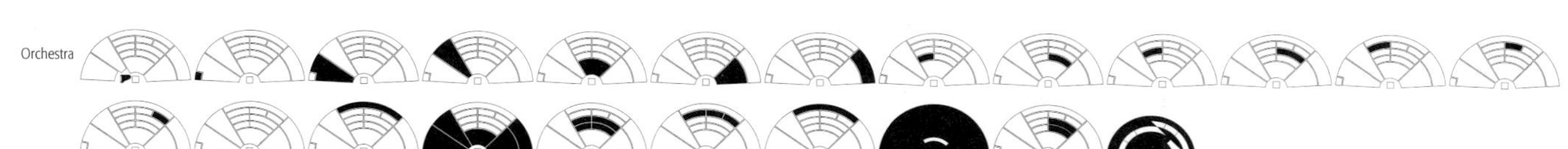

Musical
Agfa PiLogoSymbol Fonts
Volume 94
AGL
▲30

Naturals
✍ *Hugh Whyte • 1993*
LET
▲30

1234567890 1234567890

Newspaper Pi

BIT

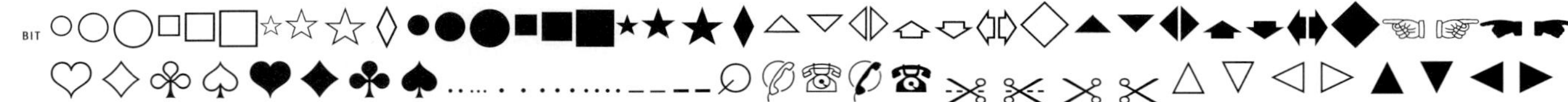

⊕ Notre Dame Ornaments
❖ *Type Before Gutenberg 3*

Karlgeorg Hoefer • 1993

LIN ADO AGA MAE

▲18

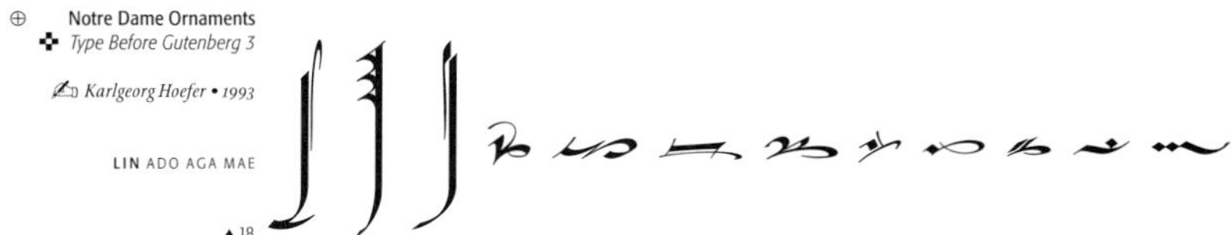

Nucleus One

Joshua Distler & David Nong • 1992

MTD

▲24

Numerics 1
Agfa PiLogoSymbol Fonts
Volume 95
AGL

1 2 3 4 5 6 7 8 9 10 11 12 13 14 15 16 17 18 19 20 1 2 3 4 5 6 7 8 9 10 11 12 13 14 15 16 17 18 19 20
21 22 23 24 25 26 27 28 29 30 31 32 33 34 35 36 37 38 39 40

Numerics 2
Agfa PiLogoSymbol Fonts
Volume 96
AGL

1 2 3 4 5 6 7 8 9 10 1 2 3 4 5 6 7 8 9 10 11 12 13 14 15 16 17 18 19 20 21 22 23 24 25
26 27 28 29 30 31 32 33 34 35 36 37 38 39 40 41 42 43 44 45 46 47 48 49 50

Numerics 3
Agfa PiLogoSymbol Fonts
Volume 97
AGL

1 2 3 4 5 6 7 8 9 10 11 12 13 14 15 16 17 18 19 20 21 22 23 24 25 26 27 28 29 30 31 32 33 34 35
36 37 38 39 40 41 42 43 44 45 46 47 48 49 50 51 52 53 54 55 56 57 58 59 60

Numerics 4
Agfa PiLogoSymbol Fonts
Volume 98
AGL

1 2 3 4 5 6 7 8 9 10 1 2 3 4 5 6 7 8 9 10 11 12 13 14 15 16 17 18 19 20 21 22 23 24 25
26 27 28 29 30 31 32 33 34 35 36 37 38 39 40 41 42 43 44 45 46 47 48 49 50

Numerics 5
Agfa PiLogoSymbol Fonts
Volume 99
AGL

1 2 3 4 5 6 7 8 9 0 1 2 3 4 5 6 7 8 9 0 1 2 3 4 5 6 7 8 9 10
1 2 3 4 5 6 7 8 9 10 1 2 3 4 5 6 7 8 9 10

Numerics 6
Agfa PiLogoSymbol Fonts
Volume 100
AGL

$1234567890 1234567890 1234567890 1234567890/% 1234567890/.,-*

Numerics 7
Agfa PiLogoSymbol Fonts
Volume 101
AGL

1234567890 1234567890 1234567890¢ 1234567890¢ 1234567890 1234567890

⊕ Notre Dame Ornaments ◀ Notre Dame.
❖ *Type Before Gutenberg 3*: Notre Dame, Notre Dame Ornaments, Pompeijana, Pompeijana Borders, Rusticana, Rusticana Borders.

Numerics 8
Agfa PiLogoSymbol Fonts
Volume 102
AGL

1234567890 1234567890 1234567890¢% 1234567890¢ 1234567890 1234567890 *

Numerics 9
Agfa PiLogoSymbol Fonts
Volume 103
AGL

1234567890/1234567890 1234567890/1234567890 12345679 12345679 8 16 32 8 16 32 24679 24679 64 64

Numerics 10
Agfa PiLogoSymbol Fonts
Volume 104
AGL

1234567890 1234567890 1234567890 1234567890 1234567890
1234567890 1 2 3 4 5 6 7 8 9

Numerics 11
Agfa PiLogoSymbol Fonts
Volume 105
AGL

1/2 1/4 3/4 1/5 2/5 3/5 4/5 1/6 5/6 1/8 3/8 5/8 7/8 1/2 1/4 3/4 1/5 2/5 3/5 4/5 1/6 5/6 1/8 3/8 5/8 7/8 1/2 1/4 3/4 1/3 2/3 1/2 1/4 3/4 1/3 2/3 1/10 3/10 7/10 9/10 1/16 3/16 5/16 7/16 9/16 11/16 13/16 15/16
1/32 3/32 5/32 7/32 9/32 11/32 13/32 15/32 17/32 19/32 21/32 23/32 25/32 27/32 29/32 31/32

PolyType **Optyx One & Two**
POL
▲30

Organics
Debbie Hanley • 1993
LET
▲24

PolyType **Ornaments One & Two**
POL
▲18

&

PIX·YMBOLS **PASSKEY**

PAG

▲16

a b c d e f g h i j k l m n o p q r s t u v w x y z

(" . ; ' ! * ? ' : , ")

$ 1 2 3 4 5 6 7 8 9 0 & - [< # % + = { / | \ } ^ _ ` ~ @ >]

A B C D E F G H I J K L M N O P Q R S T U V W X Y Z

PIXymbols **Passkey** . . .

One A abcdefghijklmnopqrstuvwxyzABCDEFGHIJKLMNOPQRSTUVWXYZ$1234567890(".;"!*?':;

One B áàâäãåæçéèêëíìîïñóòôöõøœúùÁÀÂÄÃÅÆÇÉÈÊËÍÌÎÏÑÓÒÔÖÕØŒÚÙ§

One C ĐđÞþ ß ¨ ¥ ← → ↑ ↓ ª ° º { ⌘

• Two A a b c d e f g h i j k l m n o p q r s t u v w x y z A B C D E

Two B á à â ä ã å æ ç é è ê ë í ì î ï ñ ó ò ô ö õ ø œ ú ù Á À Â Ä Ã

Two C Đ đ Þ þ ß ¨ ¥ ← → ↑ ↓ ª ° º ⌘

PIXymbols **Patchwork**

PAG

▲16

PolyType **Patterns Ones & Two**

POL

▲24

⊕ **Petroglyph Hawaii**

❖ *Group Hawaii*

✍ *Judith Sutcliffe • 1993*

MTD

▲24

Phonetics 1

Agfa PiLogoSymbol Fonts

Volume 106

AGL

Phonetics 2

Agfa PiLogoSymbol Fonts

Volume 107

AGL

&

⊕ Petroglyph Hawaii ◀ Hibiscus & Kiilani.

❖ *Group Hawaii:* Hibiscus, Kiilani, Petroglyph Hawaii.

Phonetics 3
Agfa PiLogoSymbol Fonts
Volume 108
AGL

Poetica Ornaments
Robert Slimbach • 1993
ADO AGA LIN MAE
▲16

Pompeijana Borders
Type Before Gutenberg 3
Adrian Frutiger • 1992
LIN ADO AGA MAE
▲18

Primitives
Tom Lulevitch • 1993
LET
▲30

NIMX Quirks
Calvin Glenn • 1993
NIM
▲16

Radicals
Teresa Hopkins • 1993
LET
▲24

&

⊕ Poetica Ornaments ◀ Poetica 2 Supplement.
⊕ Pompeijana Borders ◀ Pompeijana.
Type Before Gutenberg 3: Notre Dame, Notre Dame Ornaments, Pompeijana, Pompeijana Borders, Rusticana, Rusticana Borders.

PIXymbols **Recycle**

PAG

▲16

PETE
HDPE
V
LDPE
PP
PS
Pitch In!

Religious
Agfa Pi LogoSymbol Fonts Volume 109
AGL

▲18

ROCOCO BORDERS & ORNAMENTS
MCL

▲18

Rococo Borders & Ornaments . . .

• One

Two

Three

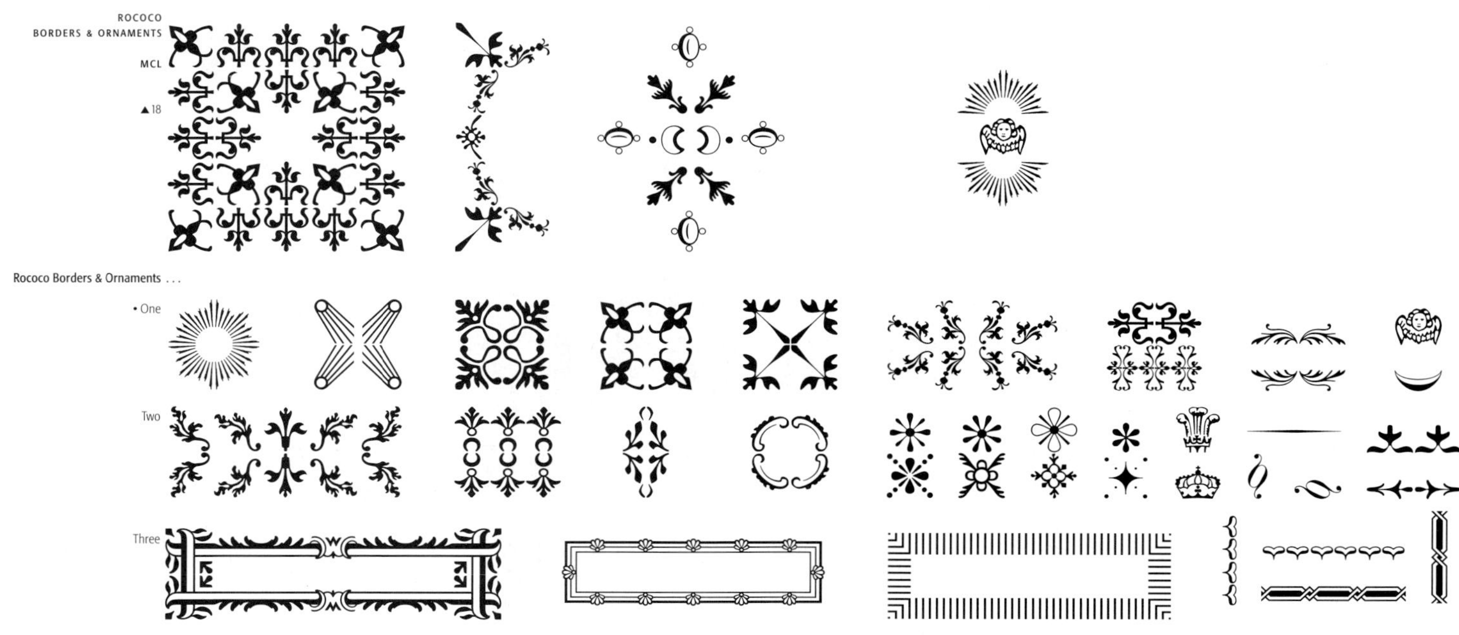

⊕ TF Roux Borders

✍ *Joseph Treacy* • *1994*

TRE MTD

▲15

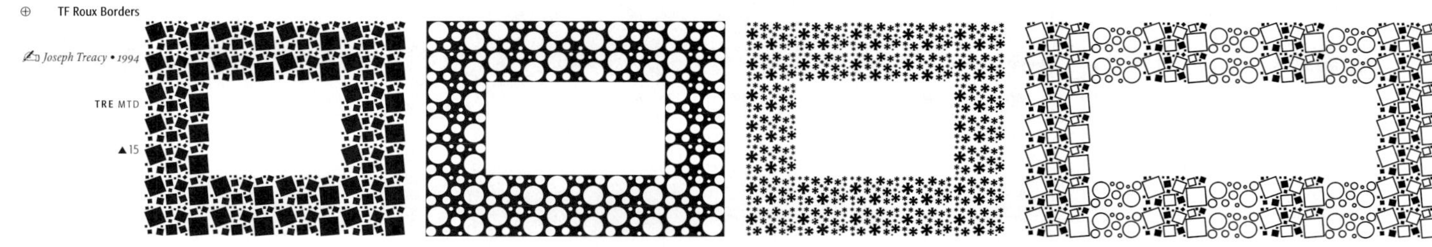

⊕ Rusticana Borders
❖ *Type Before Gutenberg 3*

✍ *Adrian Frutiger* • *1992*

LIN ADO LIN MAE

▲18

⊕ TF Roux Borders ◀ TF Roux.
⊕ Rusticana Borders ◀ Rusticana.
❖ *Type Before Gutenberg 3*: Notre Dame, Notre Dame Ornaments, Pompeijana, Pompeijana Borders, Rusticana, Rusticana Borders.

⊕ **Scorpio Dingbats**

Jim Marcus • 1993

T26

▲18

⊕ **Scorpio Tribal**

Jim Marcus • 1993

T26

▲18

SIGN-PIX

James Harris • 1992

HAR MTD

SignPix ...
▲30
• One

Two

SONATA

Cleo Huggins • 1989

D.C. D.S.

ADO AGA LIN MAE

▲18 1234567890 1234567890 ❄ Ped. tr tr ppp pp p mp m f mf ff fff s sf fz z r 8va 8ab. 8vb

&

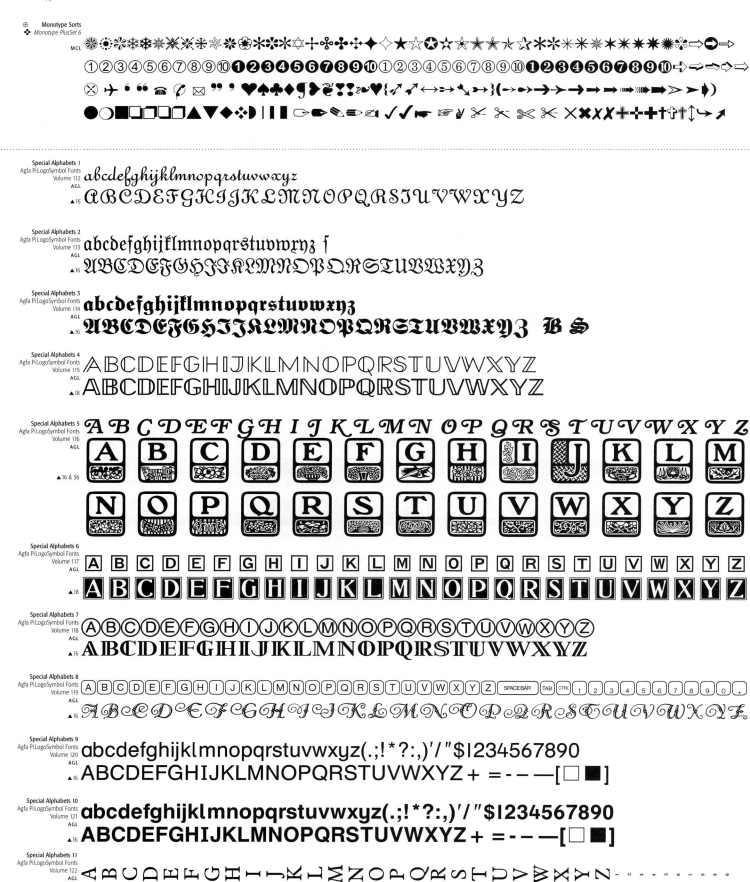

⊕ **Monotype Sorts**
❖ *Monotype PlusSet 6*
MCL

①②③④⑤⑥⑦⑧⑨⑩❶❷❸❹❺❻❼❽❾❿①②③④⑤⑥⑦⑧⑨⑩❶❷❸❹❺❻❼❽❾❿

Special Alphabets 1
Agfa PiLogoSymbol Fonts
Volume 112
AGL
▲16

abcdefghijklmnopqrstuvwxyz
ABCDEFGHIJKLMNOPQRSTUVWXYZ

Special Alphabets 2
Agfa PiLogoSymbol Fonts
Volume 113
AGL
▲16

abcdefghijklmnopqrstuvwxyz ſ
ABCDEFGHIJKLMNOPQRSTUVWXYZ

Special Alphabets 3
Agfa PiLogoSymbol Fonts
Volume 114
AGL
▲16

abcdefghijklmnopqrstuvwxyz
ABCDEFGHIJKLMNOPQRSTUVWXYZ B S

Special Alphabets 4
Agfa PiLogoSymbol Fonts
Volume 115
AGL
▲18

ABCDEFGHIJKLMNOPQRSTUVWXYZ
ABCDEFGHIJKLMNOPQRSTUVWXYZ

Special Alphabets 5
Agfa PiLogoSymbol Fonts
Volume 116
AGL
▲16 & 36

A B C D E F G H I J K L M N O P Q R S T U V W X Y Z
A B C D E F G H I J K L M
N O P Q R S T U V W X Y Z

Special Alphabets 6
Agfa PiLogoSymbol Fonts
Volume 117
AGL
▲18

A B C D E F G H I J K L M N O P Q R S T U V W X Y Z
A B C D E F G H I J K L M N O P Q R S T U V W X Y Z

Special Alphabets 7
Agfa PiLogoSymbol Fonts
Volume 118
AGL
▲16

ⒶⒷⒸⒹⒺⒻⒼⒽⒾⒿⓀⓁⓂⓃⓄⓅⓆⓇⓈⓉⓊⓋⓌⓍⓎⓏ
ABCDEFGHIJKLMNOPQRSTUVWXYZ

Special Alphabets 8
Agfa PiLogoSymbol Fonts
Volume 119
AGL
▲16

A B C D E F G H I J K L M N O P Q R S T U V W X Y Z SPACEBAR TAB CTRL 1 2 3 4 5 6 7 8 9 0 .
ABCDEFGHIJKLMNOPQRSTUVWXYZ

Special Alphabets 9
Agfa PiLogoSymbol Fonts
Volume 120
AGL
▲16

abcdefghijklmnopqrstuvwxyz(.;!*?:,)'/"$1234567890
ABCDEFGHIJKLMNOPQRSTUVWXYZ + = - - — [□ ■]

Special Alphabets 10
Agfa PiLogoSymbol Fonts
Volume 121
AGL
▲16

abcdefghijklmnopqrstuvwxyz(.;!*?:,)'/"$1234567890
ABCDEFGHIJKLMNOPQRSTUVWXYZ + = - - — [□ ■]

Special Alphabets 11
Agfa PiLogoSymbol Fonts
Volume 122
AGL
▲16

ABCDEFGHIJKLMNOPQRSTUVWXYZ 1 2 3 4 5 6 7 8 9 0

&

⊕ Monotype Sorts ◀ Corsiva.
❖ *Monotype PlusSet 6*: Corsiva & Monotype Sorts.

PIX-YMBOLS SQUARED
PAG
▲16

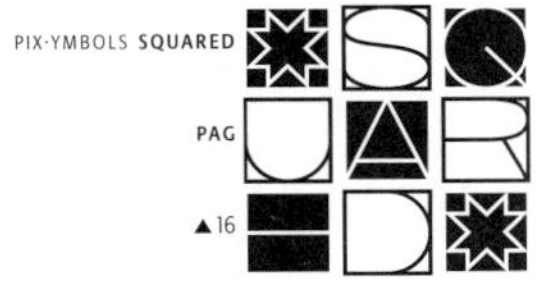

PIXymbols Squared . . .

Light
• Regular
Bold

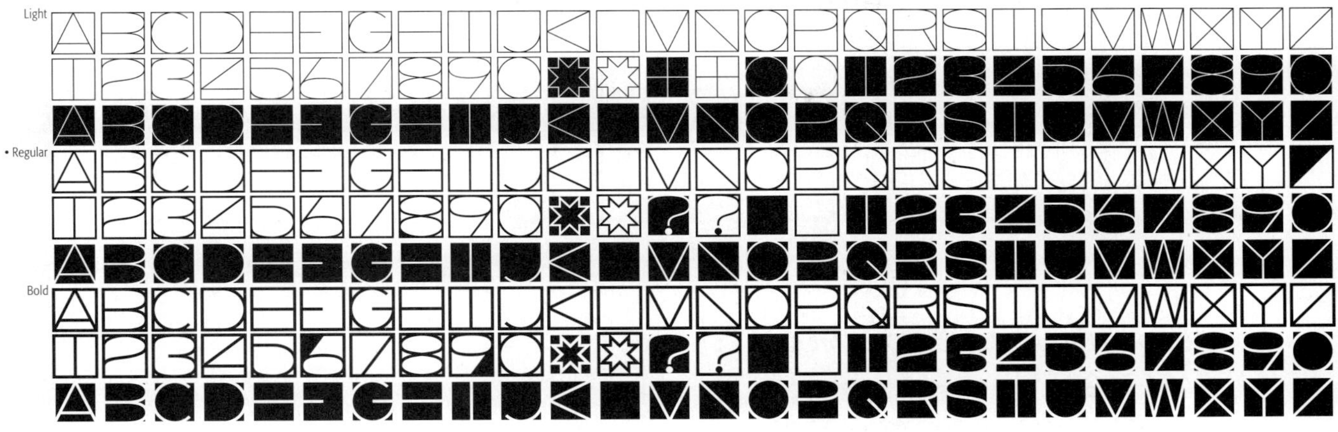

TF SQUIGGLE

Joseph Treacy • 1990

TRE MTD

TF Squiggle . . .

• Serif
Sans
Sans Narrow
Chancery Medium Italic
Typewriter

ITC STONE PHONETIC

John Renner • 1992
(Sumner Stone, 1989)

ADO AGA LIN MAE URW

abcdefghijklmnopqrstuvwxyzɑʙçðɛɸɢʜɪɟʟɰɴɔ’ɾʀʃθʊʋɹχʏʒ

TF Stone Phonetic . . .

• IPA – Serif abcdefghijklmnopqrstuvwxyzɑʙçðɛɸɢʜɪɟʟɰɴɔ’ɾʀʃθʊʋɹχʏʒ

Alternate – Serif

IPA – Sans abcdefghijklmnopqrstuvwxyzɑʙçðɛɸɢʜɪɟʟɰɴɔ’ɾʀʃθʊʋɹχʏʒ

Alternate – Sans

&

PIX·YMBOLS STYLEKEY

PAG

▲16

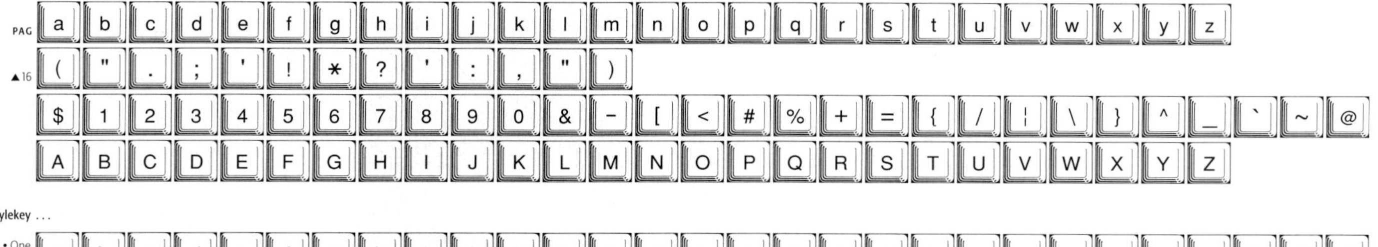

PIXymbols Stylekey . . .

• One
a b c d e f g h i j k l m n o p q r s t u v w x y z A B C

Two
Alt bksp Ctrl Del Enter Delete Print Screen Home Insert Home Break Caps Lock Scroll Lock Num Lock Pause Esc ↵ Shift Tab Page Up ⌦ Roll↓ Cmd Page Down ←Backspace ⇧ Cut Cancel

Function
F1 F2 F3 F4 F5 F6 F7 F8 F9 F10 F11 F12 F13 F14 F15 Cmd 1 Cmd 2 Cmd 3 Cmd 4 Cmd 5 Cmd 6 Cmd 7 Cmd 8 Cmd 9 Cmd 10 Cmd 11 Cmd 12 Cmd 13 Cmd 14

Symbol Monospace

BIT αβχδεφγηιφκλμνοπθρστυϖωξψζ(.;!*?:,)
1234567890[↑|↓←–→⇑⇓⇐⇒⇔⇔⌠}|⌊ |⌊⌉|⌋⌋⌋]
ΑΒΧΔΕΦΓΗΙϑΚΛΜΝΟΠΘΡΣΤΥςΩΞΨΖ
{|⌊⌉||⌋×·÷±≡≈≅≠≤≥∝∞′″°∠√∇∏∑∂∫∈∉∋∩∪}
⟨⊃⊂⊆⊇⊄∅⊥¬ϒℵℑℜ℘⊗⊕♥♠♣♦◊↲®©™®©↔⟩

Symbol Proportional

BIT αβχδεφγηιφκλμνοπθρστυϖωξψζ(.;!*?:,)
1234567890[↑|↓←–→⇑⇓⇐⇒⇔⇔⌠}|⌊ |⌊⌉|⌋⌋⌋]
ΑΒΧΔΕΦΓΗΙϑΚΛΜΝΟΠΘΡΣΤΥςΩΞΨΖ
{|⌊⌉||⌋×·÷±≡≈≅≠≤≥∝∞′″°∠√∇∏∑∂∫∈∉∋∩∪}
⟨⊃⊂⊆⊇⊄∅⊥¬ϒℵℑℜ℘⊗⊕♥♠♣♦◊↲®©™®©↔⟩

LINOTYPE TECHNICAL PI

LIN ─⟨ Tx Ex N K UL ⟩─

▲16

Linotype Technical Pi . . .

One

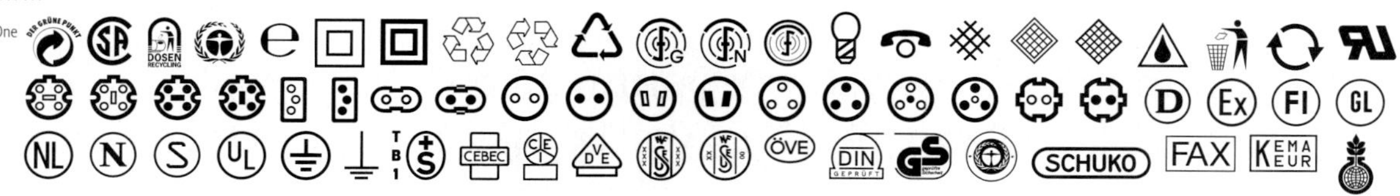

• Two
DIN TÜV Tx KEMA KEUR 220 DIN GS
BEAB BEAB CCA P D S N GL UL UL®

Television 1 & 2
Agfa PiLogoSymbol Fonts
Volumes 123 & 124
AGL

▲18

1 2 3 4 5 6 7 8 9 10 11 12 13 14 15 16 17 18 19 20 21 22 23
26 27 28 29 30 31 32 33 34 35 36 37 38 39 40 41 42 43 44 45 46 47 48
49 50 51 52 53 54 55 56 57 58 59 60 61 62 63 64 65 66 67 68 69 70 71
72 73 74 75 76 77 78 79 80 81 82 83 84 85 86 87 88 89 90 91 92 93 94
95 97 98 99 1 2 3 4 5 6 7 8 9 10 11 12 13 14 15 16 17
BW T.V TV T.V.

LINOTYPE TEXTILE PI
LIN

Linotype Technical Pi . . .
▲16
• One

86°F 104°F 140°F 176°F 203°F 86°F 104°F 140°F 176°F 203°F
30°C 40°C 60°C 80°C 95°C 30°C 40°C 60°C 80°C 95°C 30°C 40°C 60°C 80°C 95°C 30°C 40°C 60°C 80°C 95°C
30 40 50 60 95 30 40 50 60 95 30 40 50 60 95 A F P A F P
95°C 40°C 30°C

Two

86°F 104°F 140°F 203°F 86°F 104°F 140°F 203°F
30° 40° 60° 95° 30° 40° 60° 95° 30° 40° 60° 95° 30° 40° 60° 95° A F P A F P A F P A F P
30 40 50 60 95 30 40 50 60 95 30 40 50 60 95
CL

Thingbat
duckface & John Hersey • 1994
RED
▲18

Thornforms
Marcus Burlile • 1993
T26
▲30

TIMES PHONETIC
LIN ADO AGA MAE

abcdefghijklmnopqrstuvwxyzɑʙçðɛɸɢʜɪɟɪʟɰɴɔ’ɾʀʃθʊʋɹχʏʒ
[̰ ̋ ̤ ̠ ̬ ̂ ̥ ̚ ↓ⁿ⊙ˈˌ,./˜!ə̆ ̧ ̨ ↑ʷæʰ|ː ̝ ̞ ̟ ? ͡ ̏ ̋ ɫ ̼ ̻ ↓ˡœʲ‖ɮ ̩ ɳʔˤ˥˦˧˨˩ ̮ ̙ ̘ ↗ ̟ɶˠǂɬ ˞ ɲʕʢ]
ɐɓɗɖʒɣɠɦɨʄɬɯŋɵβɖɹʂʈʌʌʍˣʌʐɒβɕɖɜɤɢɦɨɉɭɱŋøˀɽʁɧʈʉɻɥʑ

Times Phonetic . . .
• IPA

abcdefghijklmnopqrstuvwxyzɑʙçðɛɸɢʜɪɟɪʟɰɴɔ’ɾʀʃθʊʋɹχʏʒ ̋ ̤ ̠ ̬ ̂ ̥ ̚ ↓ⁿ⊙ˈˌ,./˜!ə̆ ̧

Alternate

ƀčđɘƒ ̰ ɥɩǰƙλᵐɳσþrˡšɩᵛω ̗ʸžᴰʗʤɛˑ ̄ ɰɿ‘ɿᴮˢʧʊ^ω*’ɚ ̤ ̠ ̬ ̂ ̥ ̚ -=ɕ;’,·/˜ə ̈ ̆ ̨ —+ˤˀ ɔː ̝ ̞ ? ‿ ’2 ̥

PIX·YMBOLS TOLERANCES

PAG

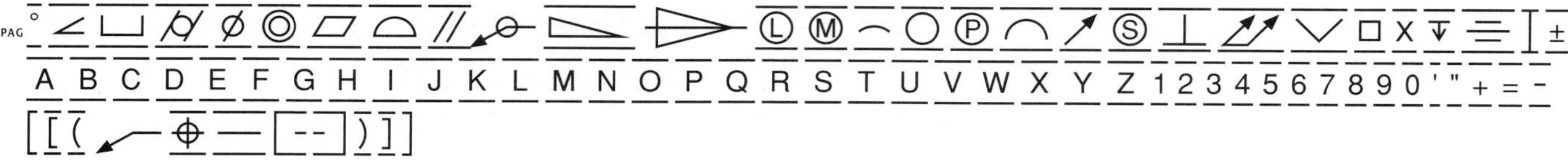

PIXymbols Tolerances . . .

Tolerances One abcdefghijklmnopqrstuvwxyzABCDEFGHIJKLMNOPQRSTUVWXZ-$123456789

Tolerances Two

• Datum One

Datum Two

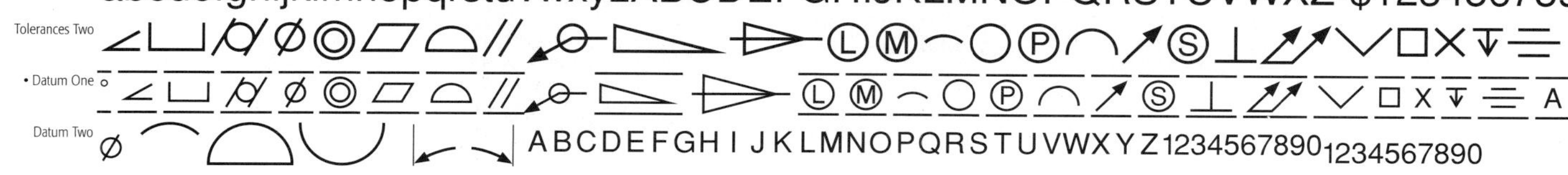

Town Ornaments
Bureau Ornaments
David Berlow • 1991
FBU AGP MTD
▲18

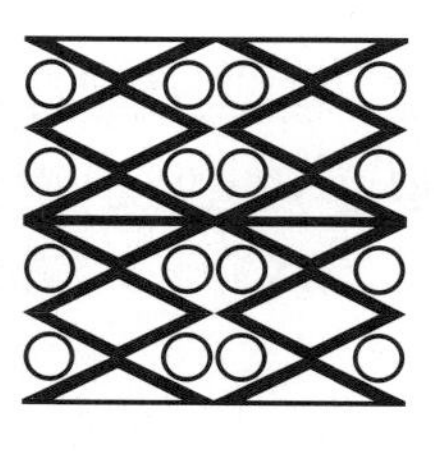

Transportation 1
Agfa PiLogoSymbol Fonts
Volume 125
AGL

▲16

Transportation 2
Agfa PiLogoSymbol Fonts
Volume 126
AGL

▲16

PIX·YMBOLS TRAVEL & HOTEL

PAG

PIXymbols Travel & Hotel . . .
▲16

Travel One Positive

Travel One Negative

Travel Two Positive

Travel Two Negative

Hotel Positive

• Hotel Negative

&

Bureau Ornaments: City Ornaments, Town Ornaments, Village Ornaments.

⊕ Truesdell Sorts

Steve Matteson • 1993
... Frederic W. Goudy, 1930

MTD

PIX-YMBOLS TV LISTINGS

PAG ▲16 TV TYPE

PIXymbols TV Listings ...

• TV Black – Alpha

AB CD EF GH IJ KL MN OP QR ST UV WX YZ ☆ ★
ZY XW VU TS RQ PO NM LK JI HG FE DC BA ♪ *
ABCDEFGHIJKLM&NOPQRSTUVWXYZ ← →

TV Black – Numeric

1234567890 12 34 56 78 90 21 43 65 87 9
1 2 3 4 5 6 7 8 9 10 11 12 13 14 15
16 17 18 19 20 21 31 41 51 61 71 81 91

• TV White – Alpha

AB CD EF GH IJ KL MN OP QR ST UV WX YZ ☆ ★
ZY XW VU TS RQ PO NM LK JI HG FE DC BA ♪ *
ABCDEFGHIJKLM&NOPQRSTUVWXYZ ← →

TV White – Numeric

1234567890 12 34 56 78 90 21 43 65 87 9
1 2 3 4 5 6 7 8 9 10 11 12 13 14 15
16 17 18 19 20 21 31 41 51 61 71 81 91

Type Embellishments One

Michael Gills & Colin Brignall • 1993

LET

▲18

Type Embellishments Two

Michael Gills & Colin Brignall • 1993

LET

▲18

Type Embellishments Three

Michael Gills & Martin Wait • 1994

LET

▲18

&

⊕ Truesdell Sorts ◀ Truesdell.

PIX-YMBOLS **UNIKEY**

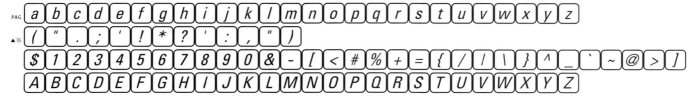

PAG

▲16

PIXymbols **Unikey** . . .

One A

One B

One C

• Two A

Two B

Two C

Universal Greek with Math Pi

✤ *Linotype Universal Pi*

LIN ADO AGA MAE

Universal Math 1

BIT

Universal News with Commercial Pi

✤ *Linotype Universal Pi*

LIN ADO AGA MAE

&

✤ *Linotype Universal Pi*: Universal Greek with Math Pi, Universal News with Commercial Pi.

PIX·YMBOLS US MAP

PAG

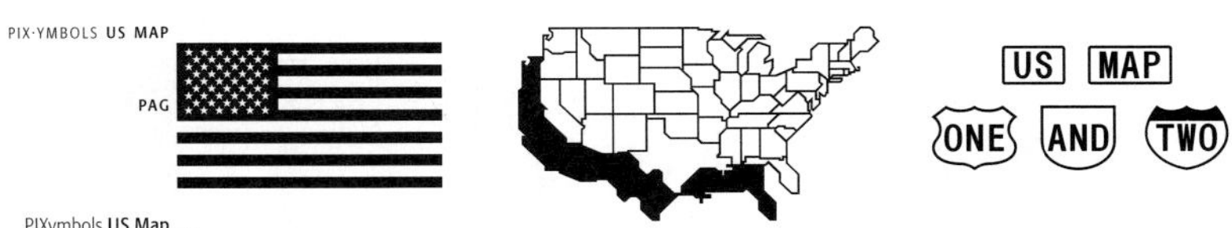
US
MAP
ONE
AND
TWO

PIXymbols US Map . . .
▲16

• One

Two

ABCDEFGHIJKLMNOPQRSTUVWXYZ 1234567890

⊕ Utopia Ornaments

Robert Slimbach • 1989

ADO AGA LIN MAE

PolyType Vegetables

POL

▲18

Village Ornaments
✥ Bureau Ornaments

David Berlow • 1991

FBU AGP MTD

▲18

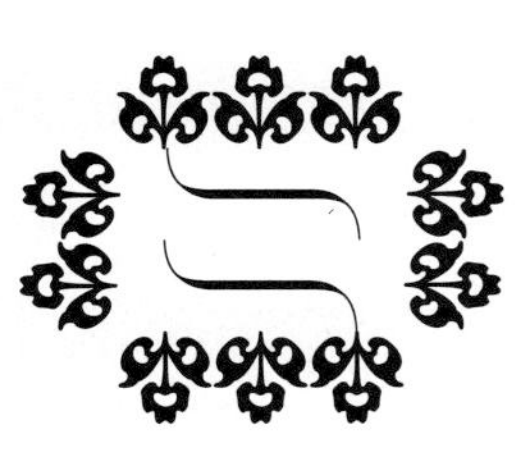

VINE LEAVES

LAN

Vine Leaves . . .

• One

Two

Three

. . . .
⊕ Utopia Ornaments ◀ Utopia Expert & SCOSF.
✥ *Bureau Ornaments*: City Ornaments, Town Ornaments, Village Ornaments.

Linotype Warning Pi
✣ *Linotype PiSet 1*
LIN ADO AGA MAE
▲18

POISON

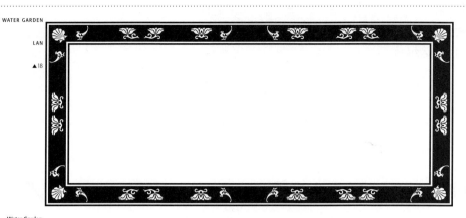

WATER GARDEN
LAN
▲18

Water Garden . . .
• 1-A
1-B
1-C
1-D
1-E
1-F
1-G
1-H
1-I 1-J 1-K
Round

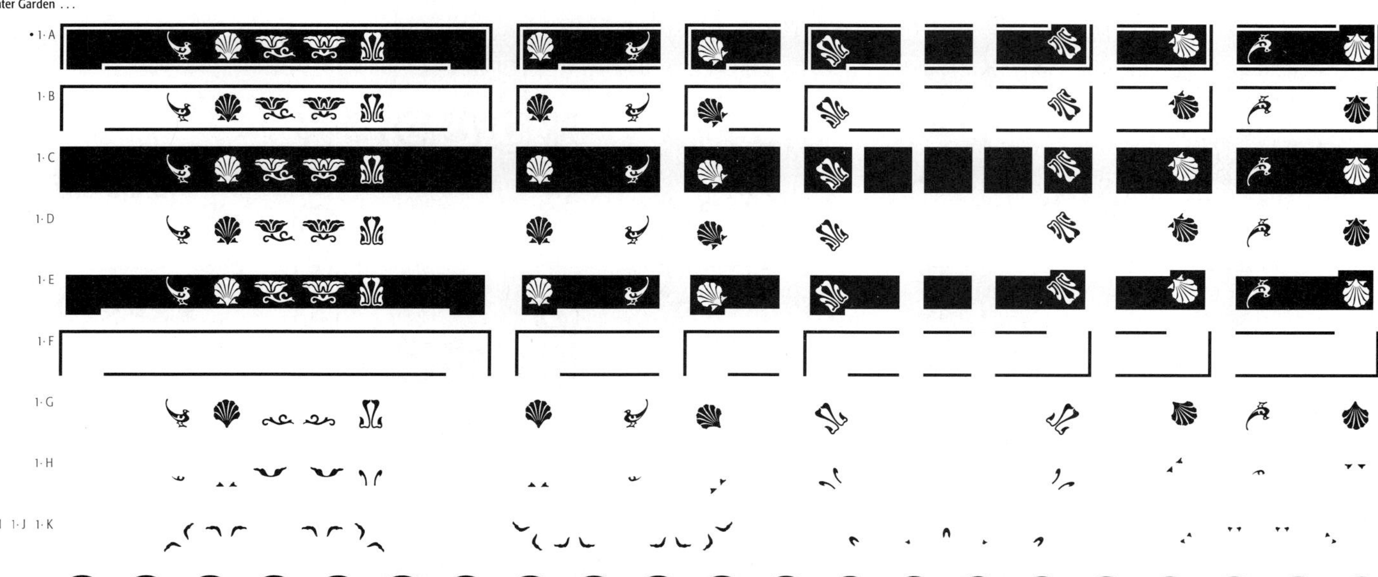

Wildlifes
✍ *David Sagorski • 1994*
LET
▲30

✣ *Linotype PiSet 1*: Linotype Audio Pi & Linotype Warning Pi.

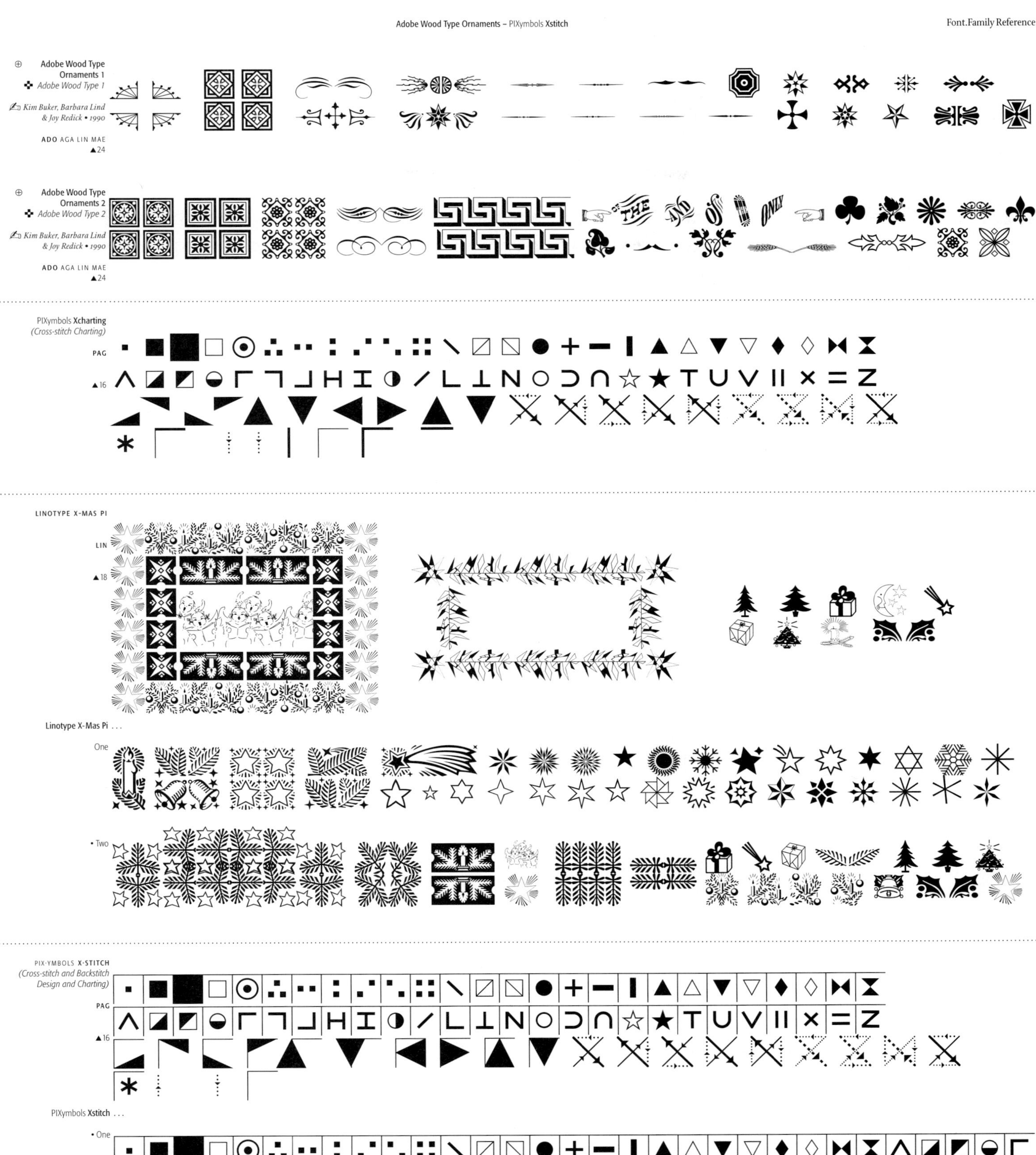
⊕ Adobe Wood Type Ornaments 1
✤ Adobe Wood Type 1
Kim Buker, Barbara Lind & Joy Redick • 1990
ADO AGA LIN MAE
▲24
⊕ Adobe Wood Type Ornaments 2
✤ Adobe Wood Type 2
Kim Buker, Barbara Lind & Joy Redick • 1990
ADO AGA LIN MAE
▲24
PIXymbols Xcharting
(Cross-stitch Charting)
PAG
▲16
LINOTYPE X-MAS PI
LIN
▲18
Linotype X-Mas Pi . . .
One
• Two
PIX·YMBOLS X-STITCH
(Cross-stitch and Backstitch Design and Charting)
PAG
▲16
PIXymbols Xstitch . . .
• One
Two
Xcharting
Backstitch
abcdefghijklmnopqrstuvwxyzABCDEFGHIJKLMNOPQRSTUVWXYZ-1234567890&(;,!*?,)

⊕ Adobe Wood Type Ornaments 1 ◀ Cottonwood, Ironwood, Juniper, Mesquite, Ponderosa.
✤ *Adobe Wood Type 1*: Cottonwood, Ironwood, Juniper, Mesquite, Ponderosa, Adobe Wood Type Ornaments 1.

⊕ Adobe Wood Type Ornaments 2 ◀ Birch, Blackoak, Madrone, Poplar, Willow.
✤ *Adobe Wood Type 2*: Birch, Blackoak, Madrone, Poplar, Willow, Adobe Wood Type Ornaments 2.

. . . PIXymbols **Xstitch**

GridMaker

ITC Zapf Dingbats
ITC ZapfSet 1

Hermann Zapf • 1978

ADO AGA BIT LIN MAE MCL URW

▲24

①②③④⑤⑥⑦⑧⑨⑩❶❷❸❹❺❻❼❽❾❿①②③④⑤⑥⑦⑧⑨⑩❶❷❸❹❺❻❼❽❾❿

Zenzuous Pi
(. . . what is the sound of one font piing? . . .)
Robert Kobodaishi • 1995

K&A

▲00

&

ITC ZapfSet 1: ITC Zapf Chancery Medium Italic & ITC Zapf Dingbats.

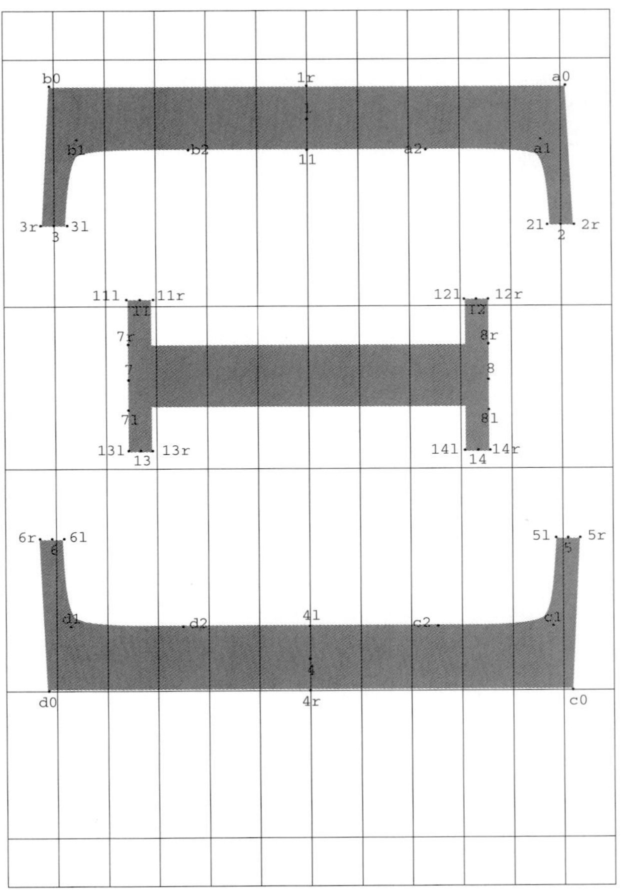
b0
1r
a0
1
b1
b2
1l
a2
a1
3r
3l
3
2l
2
2r
11l
11r
12l
12r
11
12
7r
8r
7
8
7l
8l
13l
13r
14l
14r
13
14
6r
6l
5l
5r
6
5
d1
d2
4l
c2
c1
4
d0
4r
c0

✍ Donald Knuth, 1982

central European and other Roman scripts
• cyrillic
• Greek
• Hebrew
• Korean

Ξ

Fonts for World-wide Languages

This section of the Font Reference Guide displays fonts with specialized character sets and fonts using scripts other than the Latin alphabet. Fonts are grouped and displayed in the categories listed below. Reference codes are used to indicate the languages and/or the script systems supported.

Central European and other Roman Scripts

cern Croatian, Czech, German, Hungarian Lithuanian, Polish, Romanian, Slovakian and English
cerx Albanian, Croatian, Czech, Hungarian Polish, Romanian, Serbian, Slovakian, Slovenian and English
cerz All European languages employing the Latin alphabet, African and American Indian languages, English

Cyrillic

cyrb Russian and Bulgarian
cyrn Russian, Bulgarian, Byelorussian, Macedonian, Serbian, Ukranian
cyro Russian, Bulgarian, Byelorussian, Macedonian, Serbian, Ukranian and English
cyrx Russian, Bulgarian, Byelorussian, Macedonian, Serbian, Ukranian, Moldavian
cyry Russian, Bulgarian, Byelorussian, Macedonian, Serbian, Ukranian, Moldavian and English
cyrz Russian, Bulgarian, Byelorussian, Macedonian, Serbian, Ukranian, Moldavian, Azerbaijani, Kazakh, Kirghiz, Tajik, Turkmen, Uzbek, twenty-five other languages using Cyrillic script and English

Greek

grko Modern/Monotonic Greek and English
grkx Classic/Polytonic Greek
grkz Classic/Polytonic Greek and English

Hebrew

hbrn Contemporary/Secular Hebrew
hbrx Traditional/Rabbinical Hebrew

Korean

krnk Korean (Hangul)

Ą
Ꮛ
Ż
Ж
Ω
N
궤

Note that:

¶ Character sets and keyboard layouts for the fonts in this section differ from foundry to foundry.

¶ Many font packages in this section are supplied with specialized utilities for customizing keyboards, multi-lingual composition, language and/or script sensitive composition, accent placement, phonetic transliteration and other functions ; these packages are indicated by the Ⓚ symbol in the notes for the font display.

ANTIQUE OLIVE EAST·A

K cerx abcdefghijklmnopqrstuvwxyz(“.;‘!*?’:,”)¸ ˛ ¸ ˆ ˚ ˇ ˘ ¨ ´ ˝ ˙

LIN $1234567890&ß-áâăäąćčçďđéěëęíîĺłľńňóôőöŕřśšşťţúűüůýźžż

ABCDEFGHIJKLMNOPQRSTUVWXYZ

»„«[§]‹›ÁÂĂÄĄĆČÇĎĐÉĚËĘÍÎĹŁĽŃŇÓÔŐÖŔŘŚŠŞŤŢÚŰÜŮÝŹŽŻ

Antique Olive EastA ...

Light áâăäąćčçďđéěëęíîĺłľńňóôőöŕřśšşťţúűüůýźžż-ÁÂĂÄĄĆČÇĎĐÉĚËĘÍÎĹŁĽŃŇÓÔŐÖŔŘ

• Regular áâăäąćčçďđéěëęíîĺłľńňóôőöŕřśšşťţúűüůýźžż-ÁÂĂÄĄĆČÇĎĐÉĚËĘÍÎĹĽŁĽŃ

Italic *áâăäąćčçďđéěëęíîĺłľńňóôőöŕřśšşťţúűüůýźžż-ÁÂĂÄĄĆČÇĎĐÉĚËĘÍÎĹŁĽŃŇÓÔ*

Bold **áâăäąćčçďđéěëęíîĺłľńňóôőöŕřśšşťţúűüůýźžż-ÁÂĂÄĄĆČÇĎĐÉĚËĘÍÎĹŁĽŃŇ**

Black **áâăäąćčçďđéěëęíîĺłľńňóôőöŕřśšşťţúűüůýźžż-ÁÂĂÄĄĆČÇĎĐÉĚËĘÍÎĹŁĽŃ**

ARIAL E·FO

cern abcdefghijklmnopqrstuvwxyz(“.;‘!*?’:,”)¸ ˆ ˚ ˇ ˘ ¨ ´

MCL $1234567890&ß-áâăäąćčďđéěęėíîįĺłľńňóôőöŕřśšşťţúűüůūýźžż

ABCDEFGHIJKLMNOPQRSTUVWXYZ

» «[ ]‹›ÁÂĂÄĄĆČĎĐÉĚĘĖÍÎĮĹŁĽŃŇÓÔŐÖŔŘŚŠŞŤŢÚŰÜŮŲŪÝŹŽŻ

Arial Efo ...

• Regular áâăäąćčďđéěęėíîįĺłľńňóôőöŕřśšşťţúűüůūýźžż-ÁÂĂÄĄĆČĎĐÉĚĘĖÍÎĮĹŁĽŃŇÓÔŐ

Italic *áâăäąćčďđéěęėíîįĺłľńňóôőöŕřśšşťţúűüůūýźžż-ÁÂĂÄĄĆČĎĐÉĚĘĖÍÎĮĹŁĽŃŇÓÔŐ*

Bold **áâăäąćčďđéěęėíîįĺłľńňóôőöŕřśšşťţúűüůūýźžż-ÁÂĂÄĄĆČĎĐÉĚĘĖÍÎĮĹŁĽŃŇÓ**

Bold Italic ***áâăäąćčďđéěęėíîįĺłľńňóôőöŕřśšşťţúűüůūýźžż-ÁÂĂÄĄĆČĎĐÉĚĘĖÍÎĮĹŁĽŃŇÓ***

ARIAL NARROW E·FO

cern abcdefghijklmnopqrstuvwxyz(“.;‘!*?’:,”)¸ ˆ ˚ ˇ ˘ ¨ ´

MCL $1234567890&ß-áâăäąćčďđéěęėíîįĺłľńňóôőöŕřśšşťţúűüůūýźžż

ABCDEFGHIJKLMNOPQRSTUVWXYZ

» «[ ]‹›ÁÂĂÄĄĆČĎĐÉĚĘĖÍÎĮĹŁĽŃŇÓÔŐÖŔŘŚŠŞŤŢÚŰÜŮŲŪÝŹŽŻ

Arial Narrow Efo ...

• Regular áâăäąćčďđéěęėíîįĺłľńňóôőöŕřśšşťţúűüůūýźžż-ÁÂĂÄĄĆČĎĐÉĚĘĖÍÎĮĹŁĽŃŇÓÔŐÖŔŘŚŠŞŤŢÚŰÜŮ

Italic *áâăäąćčďđéěęėíîįĺłľńňóôőöŕřśšşťţúűüůūýźžż-ÁÂĂÄĄĆČĎĐÉĚĘĖÍÎĮĹŁĽŃŇÓÔŐÖŔŘŚŠŞŤŢÚŰÜŮ*

Bold **áâăäąćčďđéěęėíîįĺłľńňóôőöŕřśšşťţúűüůūýźžż-ÁÂĂÄĄĆČĎĐÉĚĘĖÍÎĮĹŁĽŃŇÓÔŐÖŔŘŚŠŞŤŢÚ**

Bold Italic ***áâăäąćčďđéěęėíîįĺłľńňóôőöŕřśšşťţúűüůūýźžż-ÁÂĂÄĄĆČĎĐÉĚĘĖÍÎĮĹŁĽŃŇÓÔŐÖŔŘŚŠŞŤŢÚ***

central European • and other Roman scripts

ITC AVANT GARDE GOTHIC PS E-FO

cern abcdefghijklmnopqrstuvwxyz(".;'!*?':,")¸ ˆ ˚ ˇ ˘ ¨ ´

MCL $1234567890&ß-áâăäąćčďđéěęėíîįĺłľńňóôőöŕřśšşťţúűüůūýźžż

ABCDEFGHIJKLMNOPQRSTUVWXYZ

» «( )‹›ÁÂĂÄĄĆČĎĐÉĚĘĖÍÎĮĹŁĽŃŇÓÔŐÖŔŘŚŠŞŤŢÚŰÜŮŲŪÝŹŽŻ

ITC Avant Garde Gothic PS Efo . . .

• Book áâăäąćčďđéěęėíîįĺłľńňóôőöŕřśšşťţúűüůūýźžż-ÁÂĂÄĄĆČĎĐÉĚĘĖÍÎĮĹŁĽŃŇÓ

Book Oblique *áâăäąćčďđéěęėíîįĺłľńňóôőöŕřśšşťţúűüůūýźžż-ÁÂĂÄĄĆČĎĐÉĚĘĖÍÎĮĹŁĽŃŇÓ*

Demi **áâăäąćčďđéěęėíîįĺłľńňóôőöŕřśšşťţúűüůūýźžż-ÁÂĂÄĄĆČĎĐÉĚĘĖÍÎĮĹŁĽŃŇÓ**

Demi Oblique ***áâăäąćčďđéěęėíîįĺłľńňóôőöŕřśšşťţúűüůūýźžż-ÁÂĂÄĄĆČĎĐÉĚĘĖÍÎĮĹŁĽŃŇÓ***

ITC BOOKMAN PS E-FO

cern abcdefghijklmnopqrstuvwxyz(".;'!*?':,")¸ ˆ ˚ ˇ ˘ ¨ ´

MCL $1234567890&ß-áâăäąćčďđéěęėíîįĺłľńňóôőöŕřśšşťţúűüůūýźžż

ABCDEFGHIJKLMNOPQRSTUVWXYZ

» «[ ]‹›ÁÂĂÄĄĆČĎĐÉĚĘĖÍÎĮĹŁĽŃŇÓÔŐÖŔŘŚŠŞŤŢÚŰÜŮŲŪÝŹŽŻ

Ą & Ż

ITC Bookman PS Efo . . .

• Light áâăäąćčďđéěęėíîįĺłľńňóôőöŕřśšşťţúűüůūýźžż-ÁÂĂÄĄĆČĎĐÉĚĘĖÍÎĮĹŁĽŃŇ

Light Italic *áâăäąćčďđéěęėíîįĺłľńňóôőöŕřśšşťţúűüůūýźžż-ÁÂĂÄĄĆČĎĐÉĚĘĖÍÎĮĹŁĽŃŇÓ*

Demi **áâăäąćčďđéěęėíîįĺłľńňóôőöŕřśšşťţúűüůūýźžż-ÁÂĂÄĄĆČĎĐÉĚĘĖÍÎĮĹŁ**

Demi Italic ***áâăäąćčďđéěęėíîįĺłľńňóôőöŕřśšşťţúűüůūýźžż-ÁÂĂÄĄĆČĎĐÉĚĘĖÍÎĮĹŁ***

CENTURY SCHOOLBOOK PS E-FO

cern abcdefghijklmnopqrstuvwxyz(".;'!*?':,")¸ ˆ ˚ ˇ ˘ ¨ ´

MCL $1234567890&ß-áâăäąćčďđéěęėíîįĺłľńňóôőöŕřśšşťţúűüůūýźžż

ABCDEFGHIJKLMNOPQRSTUVWXYZ

» «[ ]‹›ÁÂĂÄĄĆČĎĐÉĚĘĖÍÎĮĹŁĽŃŇÓÔŐÖŔŘŚŠŞŤŢÚŰÜŮŲŪÝŹŽŻ

Century Schoolbook PS Efo . . .

• Roman áâăäąćčďđéěęėíîįĺłľńňóôőöŕřśšşťţúűüůūýźžż-ÁÂĂÄĄĆČĎĐÉĚĘĖÍÎĮĹŁĽŃŇÓ

Italic *áâăäąćčďđéěęėíîįĺłľńňóôőöŕřśšşťţúűüůūýźžż-ÁÂĂÄĄĆČĎĐÉĚĘĖÍÎĮĹŁĽŃŇÓ*

Bold **áâăäąćčďđéěęėíîįĺłľńňóôőöŕřśšşťţúűüůūýźžż-ÁÂĂÄĄĆČĎĐÉĚĘĖÍÎĮĹ**

Bold Italic ***áâăäąćčďđéěęėíîįĺłľńňóôőöŕřśšşťţúűüůūýźžż-ÁÂĂÄĄĆČĎĐÉĚĘĖÍÎĮĹŁ***

COURIER PS E-FO

cern abcdefghijklmnopqrstuvwxyz(".;'!*?':,")¸ ˆ ˚ ˇ ˘ ¨ ´

MCL $1234567890&ß-áâăäąćčďđéěęėíîįĺłľńňóôőöŕřśšşťţúűüůūýźžż

▲12 ABCDEFGHIJKLMNOPQRSTUVWXYZ

»«[]‹ ›ÁÂĂÄĄĆČĎĐÉĚĘĖÍÎĮĹŁĽŃŇÓÔŐÖŔŘŚŠŞŤŢÚŰÜŮŲŪÝŹŽŻ

Ξ

... Courier PS Efo ...

• Regular áâăäąćčďđéěęėíîįĺłľńňóôőöŕřśšşťţúűüůūýźžż-ÁÂĂÄĄĆČĎĐÉĚĘĖÍÎĮĹŁĽŃŇÓÔŐÖŔŘ

Italic *áâăäąćčďđéěęėíîįĺłľńňóôőöŕřśšşťţúűüůūýźžż-ÁÂĂÄĄĆČĎĐÉĚĘĖÍÎĮĹŁĽŃŇÓÔŐÖŔŘ*

Bold **áâăäąćčďđéěęėíîįĺłľńňóôőöŕřśšşťţúűüůūýźžż-ÁÂĂÄĄĆČĎĐÉĚĘĖÍÎĮĹŁĽŃŇÓÔŐÖŔŘ**

Bold Italic ***áâăäąćčďđéěęėíîįĺłľńňóôőöŕřśšşťţúűüůūýźžż-ÁÂĂÄĄĆČĎĐÉĚĘĖÍÎĮĹŁĽŃŇÓÔŐÖŔŘ***

EXCELSIOR EAST-A

Ⓚ cerx abcdefghijklmnopqrstuvwxyz(".;'!*?':,")¸ ˛ ¸ ˆ ˚ ˇ ˘ ¨ ´ ˝ ˙

LIN $1234567890&ß-áâăäąćčçďđéěëęíîĺłľńňóôőöŕřśšşťţúűüůýźžż

ABCDEFGHIJKLMNOPQRSTUVWXYZ

»„«[§]‹›ÁÂĂÄĄĆČÇĎĐÉĚËĘÍÎĹŁĽŃŇÓÔŐÖŔŘŚŠŞŤŢÚŰÜŮÝŹŽŻ

Excelsior EastA ...

• Roman áâăäąćčçďđéěëęíîĺłľńňóôőöŕřśšşťţúűüůýźžż-ÁÂĂÄĄĆČÇĎĐÉĚËĘÍÎĹŁĽŃŇ

Italic *áâăäąćčçďđéěëęíîĺłľńňóôőöŕřśšşťţúűüůýźžż-ÁÂĂÄĄĆČÇĎĐÉĚËĘÍÎĹŁĽŃŇ*

Bold **áâăäąćčçďđéěëęíîĺłľńňóôőöŕřśšşťţúűüůýźžż-ÁÂĂÄĄĆČÇĎĐÉĚËĘÍÎĹŁĽŃŇ**

STEMPEL GARAMOND EAST-A

Ⓚ cerx abcdefghijklmnopqrstuvwxyz(".;'!*?':,")¸ ˛ ¸ ˆ ˚ ˇ ˘ ¨ ´ ˝ ˙

LIN $1234567890&ß-áâăäąćčçďđéěëęíîĺłľńňóôőöŕřśšşťţúűüůýźžż

ABCDEFGHIJKLMNOPQRSTUVWXYZ

»„«[§]‹›ÁÂĂÄĄĆČÇĎĐÉĚËĘÍÎĹŁĽŃŇÓÔŐÖŔŘŚŠŞŤŢÚŰÜŮÝŹŽŻ

central European • and other Roman scripts

Stempel Garamond EastA ...

• Roman áâăäąćčçďđéěëęíîĺłľńňóôőöŕřśšşťţúűüůýźžż-ÁÂĂÄĄĆČÇĎĐÉĚËĘÍÎĹŁĽŃŇÓÔ

Italic *áâăäąćčçďđéěëęíîĺłľńňóôőöŕřśšşťţúűüůýźžż-ÁÂĂÄĄĆČÇĎĐÉĚËĘÍÎĹŁĽŃŇÓÔŐ*

Bold **áâăäąćčçďđéěëęíîĺłľńňóôőöŕřśšşťţúűüůýźžż-ÁÂĂÄĄĆČÇĎĐÉĚËĘÍÎĹŁĽŃŇÓ**

Bold Italic ***áâăäąćčçďđéěëęíîĺłľńňóôőöŕřśšşťţúűüůýźžż-ÁÂĂÄĄĆČÇĎĐÉĚËĘÍÎĹŁĽŃŇÓÔŐ***

NEUE HELVETICA EAST-A

Ⓚ cerx abcdefghijklmnopqrstuvwxyz(".;'!*?':,")¸ ˛ ¸ ˆ ˚ ˇ ˘ ¨ ´ ˝ ˙

LIN $1234567890&ß-áâăäąćčçďđéěëęíîĺłľńňóôőöŕřśšşťţúűüůýźžż

ABCDEFGHIJKLMNOPQRSTUVWXYZ

»„«[§]‹›ÁÂĂÄĄĆČÇĎĐÉĚËĘÍÎĹŁĽŃŇÓÔŐÖŔŘŚŠŞŤŢÚŰÜŮÝŹŽŻ

Neue Helvetica EastA ...

35-Thin áâăäąćčçďđéěëęíîĺłľńňóôőöŕřśšşťţúűüůýźžż-ÁÂĂÄĄĆČÇĎĐÉĚËĘÍÎĹŁĽŃŇÓÔŐÖŔŘŚŠ

35-Thin Oblique *áâăäąćčçďđéěëęíîĺłľńňóôőöŕřśšşťţúűüůýźžż-ÁÂĂÄĄĆČÇĎĐÉĚËĘÍÎĹŁĽŃŇÓÔŐÖŔŘŚŠ*

• 55-Regular áâăäąćčçďđéěëęíîĺłľńňóôőöŕřśšşťţúűüůýźžż-ÁÂĂÄĄĆČÇĎĐÉĚËĘÍÎĹŁĽŃŇÓÔŐÖ

55-Oblique *áâăäąćčçďđéěëęíîĺłľńňóôőöŕřśšşťţúűüůýźžż-ÁÂĂÄĄĆČÇĎĐÉĚËĘÍÎĹŁĽŃŇÓÔŐÖ*

75-Bold **áâăäąćčçďđéěëęíîĺłľńňóôőöŕřśšşťţúűüůýźžż-ÁÂĂÄĄĆČÇĎĐÉĚËĘÍÎĹŁĽŃŇÓ**

☞

... Neue Helvetica EastA

75-Bold Oblique ***áâăäąćčçď đéěëęíîĺľł ňńóôőöŕřśšşťţúűüůýźžż-ÁÂĂÄĄĆČÇĎĐÉĚËĘÍÎĹŁĽŃŇÓ***

OPTIMA EAST-A

K cerx abcdefghijklmnopqrstuvwxyz(".;'!*?':,") ¸ ˛ ˆ ˚ ˇ ˘ ¨ ´ ˝ ˙

LIN $1234567890&ß-áâăäąćčçďđéěëęíîĺľłńňóôőöŕřśšşťţúűüůýźžż

ABCDEFGHIJKLMNOPQRSTUVWXYZ

»„«[§]‹›ÁÂĂÄĄĆČÇĎĐÉĚËĘÍÎĹŁĽŃŇÓÔŐÖŔŘŚŠŞŤŢÚŰÜŮÝŹŽŻ

Optima EastA ...

• Regular áâăäąćčçďđéěëęíîĺľłńňóôőöŕřśšşťţúűüůýźžż-ÁÂĂÄĄĆČÇĎĐÉĚËĘÍÎĹŁĽŃŇÓÔŐÖŔŘ

Oblique *áâăäąćčçďđéěëęíîĺľłńňóôőöŕřśšşťţúűüůýźžż-ÁÂĂÄĄĆČÇĎĐÉĚËĘÍÎĹŁĽŃŇÓÔŐÖŔŘ*

Bold **áâăäąćčçďđéěëęíîĺľłńňóôőöŕřśšşťţúűüůýźžż-ÁÂĂÄĄĆČÇĎĐÉĚËĘÍÎĹŁĽŃŇÓÔŐÖŔ**

Bold Oblique ***áâăäąćčçďđéěëęíîĺľłńňóôőöŕřśšşťţúűüůýźžż-ÁÂĂÄĄĆČÇĎĐÉĚËĘÍÎĹŁĽŃŇÓÔŐÖŔ***

TIMES NEW ROMAN PS E-FO

cern abcdefghijklmnopqrstuvwxyz(".;'!*?':,") ˛ ˆ ˚ ˇ ˘ ¨ ´

MCL $1234567890&ß-áâăäąćčďđéěęėíîįĺľłńňóôőöŕřśšşťţúűüůūýźžż

ABCDEFGHIJKLMNOPQRSTUVWXYZ

» «[ ]‹›ÁÂĂÄĄĆČĎĐÉĚĘĖÍÎĮĹŁĽŃŇÓÔŐÖŔŘŚŠŞŤŢÚŰÜŮŲŪÝŹŽŻ

Times New Roman PS Efo ...

• Regular áâăäąćčďđéěęėíîįĺľłńňóôőöŕřśšşťţúűüůūýźžż-ÁÂĂÄĄĆČĎĐÉĚĘĖÍÎĮĹŁĽŃŇÓÔŐÖŔŘŚ

Italic *áâăäąćčďđéěęėíîįĺľłńňóôőöŕřśšşťţúűüůūýźžż-ÁÂĂÄĄĆČĎĐÉĚĘĖÍÎĮĹŁĽŃŇÓÔŐÖŔŘŚŠ*

Bold **áâăäąćčďđéěęėíîįĺľłńňóôőöŕřśšşťţúűüůūýźžż-ÁÂĂÄĄĆČĎĐÉĚĘĖÍÎĮĹŁĽŃŇÓÔŐ**

Bold Italic ***áâăäąćčďđéěęėíîįĺľłńňóôőöŕřśšşťţúűüůūýźžż-ÁÂĂÄĄĆČĎĐÉĚĘĖÍÎĮĹŁĽŃŇÓÔŐÖŔ***

TIMES TEN EAST-A

K cerx abcdefghijklmnopqrstuvwxyz(".;'!*?':,") ¸ ˛ ˆ ˚ ˇ ˘ ¨ ´ ˝ ˙

LIN $1234567890&ß-áâăäąćčçďđéěëęíîĺľłńňóôőöŕřśšşťţúűüůýźžż

ABCDEFGHIJKLMNOPQRSTUVWXYZ

»„«[§]‹›ÁÂĂÄĄĆČÇĎĐÉĚËĘÍÎĹŁĽŃŇÓÔŐÖŔŘŚŠŞŤŢÚŰÜŮÝŹŽŻ

Times Ten EastA ...

• Roman áâăäąćčçďđéěëęíîĺľłńňóôőöŕřśšşťţúűüůýźžż-ÁÂĂÄĄĆČÇĎĐÉĚËĘÍÎĹŁĽŃŇÓÔ

Italic *áâăäąćčçďđéěëęíîĺľłńňóôőöŕřśšşťţúűüůýźžż-ÁÂĂÄĄĆČÇĎĐÉĚËĘÍÎĹŁĽŃŇÓÔ*

Bold **áâăäąćčçďđéěëęíîĺľłńňóôőöŕřśšşťţúűüůýźžż-ÁÂĂÄĄĆČÇĎĐÉĚËĘÍÎĹŁĽŃŇÓÔ**

Bold Italic ***áâăäąćčçďđéěëęíîĺľłńňóôőöŕřśšşťţúűüůýźžż-ÁÂĂÄĄĆČÇĎĐÉĚËĘÍÎĹŁĽŃŇÓÔ***

TransRoman : Chan

K cerz *abcdefghijklmnopqrstuvwxyz(.;'!*?':,)´ ` ˆ ˇ ˜ ˚ ¨ ¯ ˘ ˝ ˙ ̒ ̦ — ˆ ˜ ⁄ ̦ ̒ ̦ . ˳ ˄ ˌ ̦ ‿ ̑*

LS1 *$1234567890&ß-äöüåçèîñóæøœ*

▲16 *ABCDEFGHIJKLMNOPQRSTUVWXYZ´ ` ˆ ˇ ˜ ˚ ¨ ¯ ˘ ˝ ˙ ̦ — ⁀ ˜ ⁄ ̦ ̒ ̦ . ˳ ˄ ˌ ̦ ‿*

ÄÖÜÅÇÈÎÑÓÆØŒ»«[¶§†]¡¿

āăǎāēąąąąb'ḅčċçḉd'đēĕěėęęęęęęḡğǧġģģgĥḫħīĭįįĵḱǩķkķḱľłļḿńňṅņŋg̃ōŏǒōőǫǫǫǫp̄p̂ŕřŗṡşşş

t̂tsfct'ťţūŭűųųŵẁẍyžẓĀĂǍĀĒḂḄČĊÇḈĐĒĔĚĖĘĘĘĢĠĢĤḤĪĬĨĴḰĶĶĹĻḾŇŅ

ṄŌŎǑŐǪǪP̄ŘŖŖŔŠŞŞŞŞẞŤŢŢŢŪŬŰŲŴÝŽŻ–αειωᵋᴇᴅʙþðŋⁿα̰ε̰ι̰ω̰ÞHſŊ

TRANS·ROMAN : GARA

K cerz abcdefghijklmnopqrstuvwxyz(.;'!*?':,)´ ` ˆ ˇ ˜ ˚ ¨ ¯ ˘ ˝ ˙ ̒ ̦ — ⁀ ˜ ⁄ ̦ ̒ ̦ . ˳ ˄ ˌ ̦ ‿ ̑

LS1 $1234567890&ß-äöüåçèîñóæøœ

ABCDEFGHIJKLMNOPQRSTUVWXYZ´ ` ˆ ˇ ˜ ˚ ¨ ¯ ˘ ˝ ˙ ̦ — ⁀ ˜ ⁄ ̦ ̒ ̦ . ˳ ˄ ˌ ̦ ‿

ÄÖÜÅÇÈÎÑÓÆØŒ»«[¶§†]¡¿

āăǎāēąąąąb'ḅčċçḉd'đēĕěėęęęęęęḡğǧġģģgĥḫħīĭįįĵḱǩķķķĺľłļḿńňṅņŋg̃ōŏǒōőǫǫǫǫp̄

p̂ŕřŗṡşşşt̂tsfct'ťţūŭűųųŵẁẍyžẓĀĂǍĀĒḂḄČĊÇḈĐĒĔĚĖĘĘĘĢĠĢĤḤĪĬĨĴḰĶĶĹĻḾŇŅŅ

ŌŎǑŐǪǪP̄ŘŖŖŔŠŞŞŞŞẞŤŢŢŢŪŬŰŲŴÝŽŻ–αειωᵋᴇᴅʙþðŋⁿα̰ε̰ι̰ω̰ÞHſŊ

TransRoman : Gara …

• Roman ąąąb'ḅčċçḉd'đėęęęęęęḡğǧġģģgĥḫħīĭįįĵḱǩķķĺłļḿńňņőǫǫǫǫp̄p̂ŕŗšşşşşt̂tsfct'ťţūŭűųų

ĀĂǍĀĒḂḄČĊÇḈĐĒĔĚĖĘĘĘĢĠĢĤḤĪĬĨĴḰĶĹĻḾŇṄŌŎǑŐǪǪP̄ŘŖŔŠŞŞŞŤŢŢŢŪŬŰ

Italic *ąąąb'ḅčċçḉd'đėęęęęęęḡğǧġģģgĥḫħīĭįįĵḱǩķķĺłļḿńňņőǫǫǫǫp̄p̂ŕŗšşşşşt̂tsfct'ťţūŭűųų*

ĀĂǍĀĒḂḄČĊÇḈĐĒĔĚĖĘĘĘĢĠĢĤḤĪĬĨĴḰĶĹĻḾŇṄŌŎǑŐǪǪP̄ŘŖŔŠŞŞŞŤŢŢŢŪŬŰŲŴ

Bold **ąąąb'ḅčċçḉd'đėęęęęęęḡğǧġģģgĥḫħīĭįįĵḱǩķķĺłļḿńňņőǫǫǫǫp̄p̂ŕŗšşşşşt̂tsfc**

ĀĂǍĀĒḂḄČĊÇḈĐĒĔĚĖĘĘĘĢĠĢĤḤĪĬĨĴḰĶĹĻḾŇṄŌŎǑŐǪǪP̄ŘŖŔŠŞŞŞŤŢŢŪ

Bold Italic ***ąąąb'ḅčċçḉd'đėęęęęęęḡğǧġģģgĥḫħīĭįįĵḱǩķķĺłļḿńňņőǫǫǫǫp̄p̂ŕŗšşşşşt̂s***

ĀĂǍĀĒḂḄČĊÇḈĐĒĔĚĖĘĘĘĢĠĢĤḤĪĬĨĴḰĶĹĻḾŇṄŌŎǑŐǪǪP̄ŘŖŔŠŞŞŞŤŢŢ

central European and other Roman scripts

TRANS·ROMAN : PALA

K cerz abcdefghijklmnopqrstuvwxyz(.;'!*?':,)´ ` ˆ ˇ ˜ ˚ ¨ ¯ ˘ ˝ ˙ ̒ ̦ — ⁀ ˜ ⁄ ̦ ̒ ̦ . ˳ ˄ ˌ ̦ ‿ ̑

LS1 $1234567890&ß-äöüåçèîñóæøœ

ABCDEFGHIJKLMNOPQRSTUVWXYZ´ ` ˆ ˇ ˜ ˚ ¨ ¯ ˘ ˝ ˙ ̦ — ⁀ ˜ ⁄ ̦ ̒ ̦ . ˳ ˄ ˌ ̦ ‿ ̑

ÄÖÜÅÇÈÎÑÓÆØŒ»«[¶§†]¡¿

āăǎāēąąąąb'ḅčċçḉd'đēĕěėęęęęęęḡğǧġģģgĥḫħīĭįįĵḱǩķķķĺľłļḿńňṅņŋg̃ōŏǒōőǫǫǫǫ

p̄p̂ŕřŗṡşşşt̂tsfct'ťţūŭűųųŵẁẍyžẓĀĂǍĀĒḂḄČĊÇḈĐĒĔĚĖĘĘĘĢĠĢĤḤĪĬĨĴḰĶĶĹ

ŌŎǑŐǪǪP̄ŘŖŖŔŠŞŞŞŞẞŤŢŢŢŪŬŰŲŴÝŽŻ–αειωᵋᴇᴅʙþðŋⁿα̰ε̰ι̰ω̰ÞHſŊ

TransRoman : Pala …

• Roman ąąąb'ḅčċçḉd'đėęęęęęęḡğǧġģģgĥḫħīĭįįĵḱǩķķĺłļḿńňņőǫǫǫǫp̄p̂ŕŗšşşşşt̂tsfct'ťţūŭ

ĀĂǍĀĒḂḄČĊÇḈĐĒĔĚĖĘĘĘĢĠĢĤḤĪĬĨĴḰĶĹĻḾŇṄŌŎǑŐǪǪP̄ŘŖŔŠŞŞŞŤŢ

Italic *ąąąb'ḅčċçḉd'đėęęęęęęḡğǧġģģgĥḫħīĭįįĵḱǩķķĺłļḿńňņőǫǫǫǫp̄p̂ŕŗšşşşşt̂tsfct'ťţūŭűųųŵẁy*

ĀĂǍĀĒḂḄČĊÇḈĐĒĔĚĖĘĘĘĢĠĢĤḤĪĬĨĴḰĶĹĻḾŇṄŌŎǑŐǪǪP̄ŘŖŔŠŞŞŞŤŢŢ

... TransRoman : Pala

Bold ąạąạb̓ḅčċċçḍ'đėęẹęẹęẹęḡğǧġģgħḫḥīĭįịįĵḱǩḳkĺłḷḻḿňṅņőọọọọp̄p̂ŕŗšṡṣṣṣṣt̂tŝt̂cť'ṭţ
ĀĂǍĀĒB̌ḄČĊÇÇĐĐĒĔĚĖĘẸĘĠĢǦḢḤĪĬĨĴĶĶĽĻḾŇṄŌŎǑŐỌỌP̣ŘṘŖŠṠṢṢ

Bold Italic *ąạąạb̓ḅčċċçḍ'đėęẹęẹęẹęḡğǧġģgħḫḥīĭįịįĵḱǩḳkĺłḷḻḿňṅņőọọọọp̄p̂ŕŗšṡṣṣṣṣt̂tŝt̂cť'ṭţūŭ*
ĀĂǍĀĒB̌ḄČĊÇÇĐĐĒĔĚĖĘẸĘĠĢǦḢḤĪĬĨĴĶĶĽĻḾŇṄŌŎǑŐỌỌP̣ŘṘŖŠṠṢṢŤŢ

TRANS-ROMAN : SERIF

cerz abcdefghijklmnopqrstuvwxyz(.;'!*?':,) ´ ` ˆ ˇ ˜ ˚ ¨ ¯ ˘ ˝ ˙ ˛ ̛ — ⁀ ∼ ⁄ ̦ ̉ ̦ ̣ ̥ ̭ ̩ ̬ ̮

LSI $1234567890&ß-äöüåçèîñóæøœ

ABCDEFGHIJKLMNOPQRSTUVWXYZ ´ ` ˆ ˇ ˜ ˚ ¨ ¯ ˘ ˝ ˙ , — ⁀ ∼ ⁄ ̦ ̉ ̦ ̣ ̥ ̭ ̩ ̬ ̮

ÄÖÜÅÇÈÎÑÓÆØŒ»«[¶§†]‹¡¿›

āăǎāēąạąạb̓ḅčċċçḍ'đēĕěėęẹęẹęẹęḡğǧġģgħḫḥīĭįịįĵḱǩḳķkĺłḷḻḿňṅņn͡gōŏǒōōőọọọọp̄p̂ŕŗšṡṣ
ṣṣṣt̂tŝt̂cť'ṭţūŭűųụŵẅẋỵžẓĀĂǍĀĒB̌ḄČĊÇÇĐĐĒĔĚĖĘẸĘĠĢǦḢḤĪĬĨĴĶĶĶĽĻḾŇṄŅŊŌ
ŎǑŐỌỌP̣ŘṘŖŖŠṠṢṢṢṢŤŢŢŢŪŬŰŲŴÝŽŻ–αειωᵋᴇᴅʙþðŋⁿα̰ε̰ι̰ω̰ÞĦŊ

TransRoman : Serif ...

• Roman ąạąạb̓ḅčċċçḍ'đėęẹęẹęẹęḡğǧġģgħḫḥīĭįịįĵḱǩḳkĺłḷḻḿňṅņőọọọọp̄p̂ŕŗšṡṣṣṣṣt̂tŝt̂cť'ṭţūŭűųụŵẅỵ
ĀĂǍĀĒB̌ḄČĊÇÇĐĐĒĔĚĖĘẸĘĠĢǦḢḤĪĬĨĴĶĶĽĻḾŇṄŌŎǑŐỌỌP̣ŘṘŖŠṠṢṢṢŤŢŢŢ

Italic *ąạąạb̓ḅčċċçḍ'đėęẹęẹęẹęḡğǧġģgħḫḥīĭįịįĵḱǩḳkĺłḷḻḿňṅņőọọọọp̄p̂ŕŗšṡṣṣṣṣt̂tŝt̂cť'ṭţūŭűųụŵẅỵ*
ĀĂǍĀĒB̌ḄČĊÇÇĐĐĒĔĚĖĘẸĘĠĢǦḢḤĪĬĨĴĶĶĽĻḾŇṄŌŎǑŐỌỌP̣ŘṘŖŠṠṢṢṢŤŢŢŢŪŰ

Bold **ąạąạb̓ḅčċċçḍ'đėęẹęẹęẹęḡğǧġģgħḫḥīĭįịįĵḱǩḳkĺłḷḻḿňṅņőọọọọp̄p̂ŕŗšṡṣṣṣṣt̂tŝt̂cť'ṭţūŭűų**
ĀĂǍĀĒB̌ḄČĊÇÇĐĐĒĔĚĖĘẸĘĠĢǦḢḤĪĬĨĴĶĶĽĻḾŇṄŌŎǑŐỌỌP̣ŘṘŖŠṠṢṢ

Bold Italic ***ąạąạb̓ḅčċċçḍ'đėęẹęẹęẹęḡğǧġģgħḫḥīĭįịįĵḱǩḳkĺłḷḻḿňṅņőọọọọp̄p̂ŕŗšṡṣṣṣṣt̂tŝt̂cť'ṭţūŭűųụŵ***
ĀĂǍĀĒB̌ḄČĊÇÇĐĐĒĔĚĖĘẸĘĠĢǦḢḤĪĬĨĴĶĶĽĻḾŇṄŌŎǑŐỌỌP̣ŘṘŖŠṠṢṢṢŤŢŢ

TRANS-ROMAN : SANS SERIF

cerz abcdefghijklmnopqrstuvwxyz(.;'!*?':,) ´ ` ˆ ˇ ˜ ˚ ¨ ¯ ˘ ˝ ˙ ˛ ̛ — ⁀ ∼ ⁄ ̦ ̉ ̦ ̣ ̥ ̭ ̩ ̬ ̮

LSI $1234567890&ß-äöüåçèîñóæøœ

ABCDEFGHIJKLMNOPQRSTUVWXYZ ´ ` ˆ ˇ ˜ ˚ ¨ ¯ ˘ ˝ ˙ , — ⁀ ∼ ⁄ ̦ ̉ ̦ ̣ ̥ ̭ ̩ ̬ ̮

ÄÖÜÅÇÈÎÑÓÆØŒ»«[¶§†]‹¡¿›

āăǎāēąạąạb̓ḅčċċçḍ'đēĕěėęẹęẹęẹęḡğǧġģgħḫḥīĭįịįĵḱǩḳķkĺłḷḻḿňṅņn͡gōŏǒōōőọọ
ọp̄p̂ŕŗšṡṣṣṣṣt̂tŝt̂cť'ṭţūŭűųụŵẅẋỵžẓĀĂǍĀĒB̌ḄČĊÇÇĐĐĒĔĚĖĘẸĘĠĢǦḢḤĪĬĨĴĶĶ
ĶĽĻḾŇṄŅŊŌŎǑŐỌỌP̣ŘṘŖŖŠṠṢṢṢṢŤŢŢŢŪŬŰŲŴÝŽŻ-αειωᵋᴇᴅʙþðŋⁿα̰ε̰ι̰ω̰

TransRoman : Sans Serif ...

• Regular ąạąạb̓ḅčċċçḍ'đėęẹęẹęẹęḡğǧġģgħḫḥīĭįịįĵḱǩḳkĺłḷḻḿňṅņőọọọọp̄p̂ŕŗšṡṣṣṣṣt̂tŝt̂cť'ṭţūŭ
ĀĂǍĀĒB̌ḄČĊÇÇĐĐĒĔĚĖĘẸĘĠĢǦḢḤĪĬĨĴĶĶĽĻḾŇṄŌŎǑŐỌỌP̣ŘṘŖŠṠṢṢṢŤ

Oblique *ąạąạb̓ḅčċċçḍ'đėęẹęẹęẹęḡğǧġģgħḫḥīĭįịįĵḱǩḳkĺłḷḻḿňṅņőọọọọp̄p̂ŕŗšṡṣṣṣṣt̂tŝt̂cť'ṭţūŭ*
ĀĂǍĀĒB̌ḄČĊÇÇĐĐĒĔĚĖĘẸĘĠĢǦḢḤĪĬĨĴĶĶĽĻḾŇṄŌŎǑŐỌỌP̣ŘṘŖŠṠṢṢṢŤ

Bold **ąạąạb̓ḅčċċçḍ'đėęẹęẹęẹęḡğǧġģgħḫḥīĭįịįĵḱǩḳkĺłḷḻḿňṅņőọọọọp̄p̂ŕŗšṡṣṣṣṣt̂tŝt̂c**
ĀĂǍĀĒB̌ḄČĊÇÇĐĐĒĔĚĖĘẸĘĠĢǦḢḤĪĬĨĴĶĶĽĻḾŇṄŌŎǑŐỌỌP̣ŘṘŖŠṠṢṢṢŤ

Ą & Ż Ж

Ξ

. . . TransRoman : Sans Serif

Bold Oblique
ąạą̥ą̰b̓ḅčċçç̦ď̓đėęẹę̥ę̰ę̯ę̣ḡğǧġģġḣḫẖī̆įį̰įį̂ḵḱǩķĺłļḷḿňṅṇő̰ọọǫp̄p̑ř̦ŗšṡṣṣṣ̨ṩt̑ts̑c̑
ĀĂǍĀĒB̌ḄČĊÇÇĐĐĒĔĚĖĘȨĘĠĢĢḢḤĪĬǏĴĶĶĽĻḾŇṄŌŎǑŐỌǪṖŘṚŖŠṠṢṢŞŤ

Z-ANTIQUA E-FO

cern abcdefghijklmnopqrstuvwxyz(“.;‘!*?’:,”)¸ ˆ ˚ ˇ ˘ ¨ ˝ ´

MCL $1234567890&ß-áâăäąćčďđéěęėíîįĺľłńňóôőöŕřśšşťţúűüůūýźžż

ABCDEFGHIJKLMNOPQRSTUVWXYZ

» «[ ]‹›ÁÂĂÄĄĆČĎĐÉĚĘĖÍÎĮĹŁĽŃŇÓÔŐÖŔŘŚŠŞŤŢÚŰÜŮŲŪÝŹŽŻ

Z-Antiqua Efo . . .

• Roman áâăäąćčďđéěęėíîįĺľłńňóôőöŕřśšşťţúűüůūýźžż-ÁÂĂÄĄĆČĎĐÉĚĘĖÍÎĮĹŁĽŃŇÓÔ

Italic *áâăäąćčďđéěęėíîįĺľłńňóôőöŕřśšşťţúűüůūýźžż-ÁÂĂÄĄĆČĎĐÉĚĘĖÍÎĮĹŁĽŃŇÓÔŐÖŔŘ*

Bold **áâăäąćčďđéěęėíîįĺľłńňóôőöŕřśšşťţúűüůūýźžż-ÁÂĂÄĄĆČĎĐÉĚĘĖÍÎĮĹŁĽŃŇÓ**

Bold Italic ***áâăäąćčďđéěęėíîįĺľłńňóôőöŕřśšşťţúűüůūýźžż-ÁÂĂÄĄĆČĎĐÉĚĘĖÍÎĮĹŁĽŃŇÓÔ***

ITC Zapf Chancery PS Efo
Medium Italic

cern *abcdefghijklmnopqrstuvwxyz(“.;‘!*?’:,”)¸ ˆ ˚ ˇ ˘ ¨ ˝ ´*

MCL *$1234567890&ß-áâăäąćčďđéěęėíîįĺľłńňóôőöŕřśšşť ţúűüůūýźžż*

▲16 *ABCDEFGHIJKLMNOPQRSTUVWXYZ*

» «[ ]‹›ÁÂĂÄĄĆČĎĐÉĚĘĖÍÎĮĹŁĽŃŇÓÔŐÖŔŘŚŠŞŤŢÚŰÜŮŲŪÝŹŽŻ

central European
• and other Roman scripts

• cyrillic

ARIAL CYRILLIC

cyrn абвгдежзиклмнопрстуфхцчшщъыьэюя

MCL (“.;‘!*?’:,)№1234567890&-áéєйóýэ́я́ю́ы́

АбВГДЕЖЗИКЛМНОПРСТУФХЦЧШЩЪЫЬЭЮЯ

А́Е́ЄЙО́У́Э́Я́Ю́Ы́»„«§…

ѓґєёйќђіїјљњўћџѳѵѕђЃҐЄЁЙЌЂІЇЈЉЊЎЋЏѲѴЅЂ

Arial Cyrillic . . .

• Upright абвгдежзиклмнопрстуфхцчшщъыьэюя-АбВГДЕЖЗИКЛМНОПРСТУФХЦЧШ

Inclined *абвгдежзиклмнопрстуфхцчшщъыьэюя-АбВГДЕЖЗИКЛМНОПРСТУФХЦЧШ*

Bold Upright **абвгдежзиклмнопрстуфхцчшщъыьэюя-АбВГДЕЖЗИКЛМНОПРСТУФХЦ**

Bold Inclined ***абвгдежзиклмнопрстуфхцчшщъыьэюя-АбВГДЕЖЗИКЛМНОПРСТУФХ***

BASKERVILLE CYRILLIC

K cyrx абвгдежзиклмнопрстуфхцчшщъыьэюя

LIN ADO AGA MAE (“.;‘!*?’:,”)№1234567890&-áéєйóýэ́я́ю́ы́ѣ́ї́ї̀ъ́р̀àèйòỳр̀

АБВГДЕЖЗИКЛМНОПРСТУФХЦЧШЩЪЫЬЭЮЯ

ÁÉЄÓÝЭ́Я́Ю́Ы́Ѣ́ЇÍЪ́РÀÈЙÒỲР̀»„«[§]

ґѓєёжйќђїіјљњўћџѳѵѕѫѣҐЃЄЁЖЙЌЂЇІЈЉЊЎЋЏѲѴЅѪѢ

Baskerville Cyrillic . . .

• Upright абвгдежзиклмнопрстуфхцчшщъыьэюя-АБВГДЕЖЗИКЛМНОПРСТУФХ

Inclined *абвгдежзиклмнопрстуфхцчшщъыьэюя-АБВГДЕЖЗИКЛМНОПРСТУФХЦЧШ*

Bold **абвгдежзиклмнопрстуфхцчшщъыьэюя-АБВГДЕЖЗИКЛМНОПРСТУФХ**

BOOK CYRILLIC
✣ *ComboSet 1, ComboSet 2*
cyrb абвгдежзиклмнопрстуфхцчшщъыьэюя

RUS (“.;‘!?’:,“)№1234567890-ёЁйЙV»„«§

АбВГДЕЖЗИКЛМНОПРСТУФХЦЧШЩЪЫЬЭЮЯ

Book Cyrillic . . .

• Upright абвгдежзиклмнопрстуфхцчшщъыьэюя-АбВГДЕЖЗИКЛМНОПРСТУФХ

Oblique *абвгдежзиклмнопрстуфхцчшщъыьэюя-АбВГДЕЖЗИКЛМНОПРСТУФХ*

Bold Upright **абвгдежзиклмнопрстуфхцчшщъыьэюя-АбВГДЕЖЗИКЛМНОПРСТУФ**

Upright Condensed абвгдежзиклмнопрстуфхцчшщъыьэюя-АбВГДЕЖЗИКЛМНОПРСТУФХЦЧШЩЪЫЬ

Upright Extended абвгдежзиклмнопрстуфхцчшщъыьэюя-АбВГДЕЖЗИКЛМНО

Ж

BRUSH CYRILLIC
✣ *DisplaySet 1*
cyrb RUS

Brush A-Inclined *АБВГДЕЖЗИКЛМНОПРСТУФХЦЧШЩЪЫЬЭЮЯ.!,*

▲18

Brush B-Bold Inclined ***АБВГДЕЖЗИКЛМНОПРСТУФХЦЧШЩЪЫЬЭЮЯ.!,***

COURIER CYRILLIC

cyro абвгдежзиклмнопрстуфхцчшщъыьэюя

URW (“.;‘!*?,:,”)№1234567890&-»„«[¶§•†]

▲12 АБВГДЕЖЗИКЛМНОПРСТУФХЦЧШЩЪЫЬЭЮЯ

ґєёйќђіїјљњўћџѵѕҐЄЙЌЂІЇЈЉЊЎЋЏѴЅ

Courier Cyrillic . . .

• Light Upright абвгдежзиклмнопрстуфхцчшщъыьэюя-АБВГДЕЖЗИКЛМНОПРСТУФХЦЧШЩЪЫЬЭЮЯ№123456

Light Oblique *абвгдежзиклмнопрстуфхцчшщъыьэюя-АБВГДЕЖЗИКЛМНОПРСТУФХЦЧШЩЪЫЬЭЮЯ№123456*

Bold Upright **абвгдежзиклмнопрстуфхцчшщъыьэюя-АБВГДЕЖЗИКЛМНОПРСТУФХЦЧШЩЪЫЬЭЮЯ№123456**

Bold Oblique ***абвгдежзиклмнопрстуфхцчшщъыьэюя-АБВГДЕЖЗИКЛМНОПРСТУФХЦЧШЩЪЫЬЭЮЯ№123456***

Ξ

✣ *ComboSet 1*: Book Cyrillic Upright, Oblique, Bold Upright , Upright Condensed & Upright Extended. Mystic Cyrillic Upright, Oblique, Upright Condensed, Condensed Oblique, Upright Extended & Extended Oblique. News Cyrillic Upright, Oblique, Bold Upright, Upright Condensed & Upright Extended. Northern Cyrillic Upright, Oblique, Bold Upright, Upright Condensed & Upright Extended. Oval Upright, Oblique, Upright Condensed & Upright Extended.

✣ *ComboSet 2*: *ComboSet 1* plus Rome Cyrillic Upright, Oblique, Upright Condensed, Condensed Oblique, Upright Extended & Extended Oblique.
✣ *DisplaySet 1*: Brush Cyrillic A-Inclined & B-Bold Inclined, Fat Man Cyrillic Heavy, Osho Cyrillic Script, St. Petersburg Cyrillic Upright & Oblique.

CYRILLIC II : SERIF

K cyry абвгдежзиклмнопрстуфхцчшщъыьэюя

LSI (“.;‘!*?’:,”)№1234567890&-áéєйóýэ́я́ю́ы́ѣ́ъ̀р̀àѐѝòу̀р̀

АБВГДЕЖЗИКЛМНОПРСТУФХЦЧШЩЪЫЬЭЮЯ

А́ЕЄО́У́Э́Я́Ю́Ы́Ѣ́І́Ъ́Р̀А̀ЀЍО̀У̀Р̀

ґѓєёжйќђїїјљњўћџvѵѕѣҐЃЄЁЖЙЌЂІЇЈЉЊЎЋЏVѴЅѢ

Cyrillic II : Serif . . .

• Upright абвгдежзиклмнопрстуфхцчшщъыьэюя-АБВГДЕЖЗИКЛМНОПРСТУФХЦЧШ

Inclined *абвгдежзиклмнопрстуфхцчшщъыьэюя-АБВГДЕЖЗИКЛМНОПРСТУФХЦЧШЩЪ*

Bold Upright **абвгдежзиклмнопрстуфхцчшщъыьэюя-АБВГДЕЖЗИКЛМНОПРСТУФХЦЧ**

Bold Inclined ***абвгдежзиклмнопрстуфхцчшщъыьэюя-АБВГДЕЖЗИКЛМНОПРСТУФХЦЧ***

CYRILLIC II : SANS SERIF

K cyry абвгдежзиклмнопрстуфхцчшщъыьэюя

LSI (“.;‘!*?’:,”)№1234567890&-áéєйóýэ́я́ю́ы́ѣ́ъ̀р̀àѐѝòу̀р̀

АБВГДЕЖЗИКЛМНОПРСТУФХЦЧШЩЪЫЬЭЮЯ

А́ЕЄО́У́Э́Я́Ю́Ы́Ѣ́І́Ъ́Р̀А̀ЀЍО̀У̀Р̀

ґѓєёжйќђїїјљњўћџvѵѕѣҐЃЄЁЖЙЌЂІЇЈЉЊЎЋЏVѴЅѢ

Cyrillic II : Sans Serif . . .

• Regular абвгдежзиклмнопрстуфхцчшщъыьэюя-АБВГДЕЖЗИКЛМНОПРСТУФХЦЧ

Oblique *абвгдежзиклмнопрстуфхцчшщъыьэюя-АБВГДЕЖЗИКЛМНОПРСТУФХЦЧ* • *cyrillic*

Bold **абвгдежзиклмнопрстуфхцчшщъыьэюя-АБВГДЕЖЗИКЛМНОПРСТУФХ**

Bold Oblique ***абвгдежзиклмнопрстуфхцчшщъыьэюя-АБВГДЕЖЗИКЛМНОПРСТУФХ***

CYRILLIC II : MONOSPACED

K cyrx абвгдежзиклмнопрстуфхцчшщъыьэюя

LSI (“.;‘!*?’:,”)№1234567890&-áéєйóýэ́я́ю́ы́ѣ́ъ̀р̀àѐѝòу̀р̀

▲12 АБВГДЕЖЗИКЛМНОПРСТУФХЦЧШЩЪЫЬЭЮЯ

А́ЕЄО́У́Э́Я́Ю́Ы́Ѣ́І́Ъ́Р̀А̀ЀЍО̀У̀Р̀

ґѓєёжйќђїїјљњўћџvѵѕѣҐЃЄЁЖЙЌЂІЇЈЉЊЎЋЏVѴЅѢ

Cyrillic II : Monospaced . . .

• Regular абвгдежзиклмнопрстуфхцчшщъыьэюя-АБВГДЕЖЗИКЛМНОПРСТУФХЦЧШЩЪЫЬЭЮЯ№12345

Inclined *абвгдежзиклмнопрстуфхцчшщъыьэюя-АБВГДЕЖЗИКЛМНОПРСТУФХЦЧШЩЪЫЬЭЮЯ№12345*

Bold **абвгдежзиклмнопрстуфхцчшщъыьэюя-АБВГДЕЖЗИКЛМНОПРСТУФХЦЧШЩЪЫЬЭЮЯ№12345**

Bold Inclined ***абвгдежзиклмнопрстуфхцчшщъыьэюя-АБВГДЕЖЗИКЛМНОПРСТУФХЦЧШЩЪЫЬЭЮЯ№12345***

Ξ

EXCELSIOR CYRILLIC

cyrx абвгдежзиклмнопрстуфхцчшщъыьэюя

LIN ADO AGA MAE (“.;‘!*?’:,”)№1234567890&-áééйóýэ́я́ю́ы́ѣ́ії̈ъ́ра̀ѐй̀о̀у̀р̀

АБВГДЕЖЗИКЛМНОПРСТУФХЦЧШЩЪЫЬЭЮЯ

А́Е́Є́О́У́Э́Я́Ю́Ы́Ѣ́І́Ї́Ъ́Р́А̀Ѐ̀Й̀О̀У̀Р̀»„«[§]

ґѓєёжйќђіїјљњўћџѳѵѕѫѣҐЃЄЁЖЙЌЂІЇЈЉЊЎЋЏѲѴЅѪѢ

Excelsior Cyrillic ...

• Upright абвгдежзиклмнопрстуфхцчшщъыьэюя-АБВГДЕЖЗИКЛМНОПРСТУФ

Inclined *абвгдежзиклмнопрстуфхцчшщъыьэюя-АБВГДЕЖЗИКЛМНОПРСТУ*

Bold Upright **абвгдежзиклмнопрстуфхцчшщъыьэюя-АБВГДЕЖЗИКЛМНОПРСТУФ**

Fat Man Cyrillic Heavy
DisplaySet 1
cyrb
RUS
▲36

АБВГДЕЖЗИКЛМНОПРСТУ
ФХЦЧШЩЪЫЬЭЮЯ.!,

GARAMOND NO.4 CYRILLIC

cyro абвгдежзиклмнопрстуфхцчшщъыьэюя

URW (“.;‘!*?’:,”)№1234567890&-»„«[¶§•†]

АБВГДЕЖЗИКЛМНОПРСТУФХЦЧШЩЪЫЬЭЮЯ

▹ґєёйќђіїјљњўћџѵѕҐЄЙЌЂІЇЈЉЊЎЋЏѴЅ

Ж

Garamond No.4 Cyrillic ...

• Light Upright абвгдежзиклмнопрстуфхцчшщъыьэюя-АБВГДЕЖЗИКЛМНОПРСТУФХЦЧШ

Light Inclined *абвгдежзиклмнопрстуфхцчшщъыьэюя-АБВГДЕЖЗИКЛМНОПРСТУФХЦЧШЩЪЫЬЭ*

Medium Upright **абвгдежзиклмнопрстуфхцчшщъыьэюя-АБВГДЕЖЗИКЛМНОПРСТУФХ**

Medium Upright Alternate **абвгдежзиклмнопрстуфхцчшщъыьэюя-АБВГДЕЖЗИКЛМНОПРСТУФХ**

HELVETICA CYRILLIC

cyrx абвгдежзиклмнопрстуфхцчшщъыьэюя

LIN ADO AGA MAE (“.;‘!*?’:,”)№1234567890&-áééйóýэ́я́ю́ы́ѣ́ії̈ъ́ра̀ѐй̀о̀у̀р̀

АБВГДЕЖЗИКЛМНОПРСТУФХЦЧШЩЪЫЬЭЮЯ

А́Е́Є́О́У́Э́Я́Ю́Ы́Ѣ́І́Ї́Ъ́Р́А̀Ѐ̀Й̀О̀У̀Р̀»„«[§]

ґѓєёжйќђіїјљњўћџѳѵѕѫѣ ҐЃЄЁЖЙЌЂІЇЈЉЊЎЋЏѲѴЅѪѢ

Helvetica Cyrillic ...

• Upright абвгдежзиклмнопрстуфхцчшщъыьэюя-АБВГДЕЖЗИКЛМНОПРСТУФХЦЧШ

Inclined *абвгдежзиклмнопрстуфхцчшщъыьэюя-АБВГДЕЖЗИКЛМНОПРСТУШЩЪЫ*

Bold Upright **абвгдежзиклмнопрстуфхцчшщъыьэюя-АБВГДЕЖЗИКЛМНОПРСТУФХ**

Bold Inclined ***абвгдежзиклмнопрстуфхцчшщъыьэюя-АБВГДЕЖЗИКЛМНОПРСТУФХЦ***

Ξ

DisplaySet 1: Brush Cyrillic A-Inclined & B-Bold Inclined, Fat Man Cyrillic Heavy, Osho Cyrillic Script, St. Petersburg Cyrillic Upright & Oblique.

Helvetica Inserat Cyrillic

K cyrx **абвгдежзиклмнопрстуфхцчшщъыьэюя**

LIN **(“.;‘!*?’:,”)№1234567890&-áééйóýэяюыíйïърàèйòýр**

▲16 **АБВГДЕЖЗИКЛМНОПРСТУФХЦЧШЩЪЫЬЭЮЯ**

ÁÉЄÓЎЭЯЮЫЍЇЪРÀÈЙÒЎР»„«[§]

ґѓєёжйќђіїјљњўћџѳѵѕѫҐЃЄЁЖЙЌЂІЇЈЉЊЎЋЏѲѴЅѪ

Magna Cyrillic Medium

cyro **абвгдежзиклмнопрстуфхцчшщъыьэюя**

URW **(“.;‘!*?’:,”)№1234567890&-»„«[¶§•†]**

АБВГДЕЖЗИКЛМНОПРСТУФХЦЧШЩЪЫЬЭЮЯ

ґєёйќђіїјљњўћџѵѕҐЄЙЌЂІЇЈЉЊЎЋЏѴЅ

MAXIMA CYRILLIC

cyro **абвгдежзиклмнопрстуфхцчшщъыьэюя**

URW **(“.;‘!*?’:,”)№1234567890&-»„«[¶§•†]**

АБВГДЕЖЗИКЛМНОПРСТУФХЦЧШЩЪЫЬЭЮЯ

ґєёйќђіїјљњўћџѵѕҐЄЙЌЂІЇЈЉЊЎЋЏѴЅ

Maxima Cyrillic . . .

Light Upright абвгдежзиклмнопрстуфхцчшщъыьэюя-АБВГДЕЖЗИКЛМНОПРСТУФХЦЧШЩЪЫЬ • *cyrillic*

• Medium Upright **абвгдежзиклмнопрстуфхцчшщъыьэюя-АБВГДЕЖЗИКЛМНОПРСТУФХЦЧШЩЪ**

MINION CYRILLIC

K cyro абвгдежзиклмнопрстуфхцчшщъыьэюя

ADO AGA LIN MAE (“.;‘!*?’:,”)№1234567890&-»„«[¶§•†]•...

АБВГДЕЖЗИКЛМНОПРСТУФХЦЧШЩЪЫЬЭЮЯ

ґѓєёйќђіїјљњџѵѕҐЃЄЁЙЂІЇЈЉЊЏѴЅ

Minion Cyrillic . . .

• Upright абвгдежзиклмнопрстуфхцчшщъыьэюя-АБВГДЕЖЗИКЛМНОПРСТУФХЦЧШЩЪ

Inclined *абвгдежзиклмнопрстуфхцчшщъыьэюя-АБВГДЕЖЗИКЛМНОПРСТУФХЦЧШЩЪЫ*

Semibold Upright **абвгдежзиклмнопрстуфхцчшщъыьэюя-АБВГДЕЖЗИКЛМНОПРСТУФХЦЧШЩ**

Semibold Inclined ***абвгдежзиклмнопрстуфхцчшщъыьэюя-АБВГДЕЖЗИКЛМНОПРСТУФХЦЧШЩЪ***

Bold Upright **абвгдежзиклмнопрстуфхцчшщъыьэюя-АБВГДЕЖЗИКЛМНОПРСТУФХЦЧШ**

Bold Inclined ***абвгдежзиклмнопрстуфхцчшщъыьэюя-АБВГДЕЖЗИКЛМНОПРСТУФХЦЧШЪ***

Ξ

MYSTIC CYRILLIC
ComboSet 1, ComboSet 2
cyrb RUS ▲18

АБВГДЕЖЗИКЛМНОПРСТУФХЦЧШЩЬЫЬЭЮЯ
.!?:, 1234567890 ЁЙ

Mystic Cyrillic ...

• Upright АБВГДЕЖЗИКЛМНОПРСТУФХЦЧШЩЬЫЬЭЮЯ.!?:, 12345678
Oblique *АБВГДЕЖЗИКЛМНОПРСТУФХЦЧШЩЬЫЬЭЮЯ.!?:, 12345678*
Upright Condensed АБВГДЕЖЗИКЛМНОПРСТУФХЦЧШЩЬЫЬЭЮЯ.!?:, 1234567890 ЁЙ
Condensed Oblique *АБВГДЕЖЗИКЛМНОПРСТУФХЦЧШЩЬЫЬЭЮЯ.!?:, 1234567890 ЁЙ*
Upright Extended АБВГДЕЖЗИКЛМНОПРСТУФХЦЧШЩЬЫЬЭЮЯ.!?:, 12
Extended Oblique *АБВГДЕЖЗИКЛМНОПРСТУФХЦЧШЩЬЫЬЭЮЯ.!?:, 12*

NORTHERN CYRILLIC
ComboSet 1, ComboSet 2
cyrb RUS

абвгдежзиклмнопрстуфхцчшщъыьэюя
(".;'!?':,")№1234567890-ёЁйЙV»„«§
АбВГДЕЖЗИКЛМНОПРСТУФХЦЧШЩЪЫЬЭЮЯ

Northern Cyrillic ...

• Upright абвгдежзиклмнопрстуфхцчшщъыьэюя-АбВГДЕЖЗИКЛМНОПРСТ
Oblique *абвгдежзиклмнопрстуфхцчшщъыьэюя-АбВГДЕЖЗИКЛМНОПРСТ*
Bold Upright **абвгдежзиклмнопрстуфхцчшщъыьэюя-АбВГДЕЖЗИКЛМНОП**
Upright Condensed абвгдежзиклмнопрстуфхцчшщъыьэюя-АбВГДЕЖЗИКЛМНОПРСТУФХЦЧШ
Upright Extended абвгдежзиклмнопрстуфхцчшщъыьэюя-АбВГДЕЖЗИКЛМ

Ж

Osho Cyrillic Script
DisplaySet 1
cyrb RUS ▲18

АБВГДЕЖЗИКЛМНОПРСТУФХЦЧШЩЬЫЬЭЮЯ.,

OVAL CYRILLIC
ComboSet 1, Combo Set 2
cyrb RUS

абвгдежзиклмнопрстуфхцчшщъыьэюя
(".;'!?':,")№1234567890-ёЁйЙV»„«§
АбВГДЕЖЗИКЛМНОПРСТУФХЦЧШЩЪЫЬЭЮЯ

Oval Cyrillic ...

• Upright абвгдежзиклмнопрстуфхцчшщъыьэюя-АбВГДЕЖЗИКЛМНОПРСТУФХЦЧШЩЪЫЬЭЮ
Oblique *абвгдежзиклмнопрстуфхцчшщъыьэюя-АбВГДЕЖЗИКЛМНОПРСТУФХЦЧШЩЪЫЬЭЮ*
Upright Condensed абвгдежзиклмнопрстуфхцчшщъыьэюя-АбВГДЕЖЗИКЛМНОПРСТУФХЦЧШЩЪЫЬЭЮЯ№1234567890("
Upright Extended абвгдежзиклмнопрстуфхцчшщъыьэюя-АбВГДЕЖЗИКЛМНОПРСТУФХЦЧШ

ROME CYRILLIC
cyrb RUS ▲42

Upright **АБВГДЕЖЗИКЛМНОПРСТУФХЦЧШЩЪЫЬЭЮЯ**

Ξ

ComboSet 1: Book Cyrillic Upright, Oblique, Bold Upright, Upright Condensed & Upright Extended. Mystic Cyrillic Upright, Oblique, Upright Condensed, Condensed Oblique, Upright Extended & Extended Oblique. News Cyrillic Upright, Oblique, Bold Upright, Upright Condensed & Upright Extended. Northern Cyrillic Upright, Oblique, Bold Upright, Upright Condensed & Upright Extended. Oval Upright, Oblique, Upright Condensed & Upright Extended.

ComboSet 2: ComboSet 1 plus Rome Cyrillic Upright, Oblique, Upright Condensed, Condensed Oblique, Upright Extended & Extended Oblique.
DisplaySet 1: Brush Cyrillic A-Inclined & B-Bold Inclined, Fat Man Cyrillic Heavy, Osho Cyrillic Script, St. Petersburg Cyrillic Upright & Oblique.

. . . ROME CYRILLIC

Oblique АБВГДЕЖЗИКЛМНОПРСТУФХЦЧШЩЪЫЬЭЮЯ

Upright Condensed АБВГДЕЖЗИКЛМНОПРСТУФХЦЧШЩЪЫЬЭЮЯ

Condensed Oblique АБВГДЕЖЗИКЛМНОПРСТУФХЦЧШЩЪЫЬЭЮЯ

Upright Extended АБВГДЕЖЗИКЛМНОПРСТУФХЦЧШЩЪЫ

Extended Oblique АБВГДЕЖЗИКЛМНОПРСТУФХЦЧШЩЪЫ

ROME CYRILLIC SHADED

cyrb RUS ▲42

Upright АБВГДЕЖЗИКЛМНОПРСТУФХЦЧШЩЪ

Oblique АБВГДЕЖЗИКЛМНОПРСТУФХЦЧШЩЪ

Upright Condensed АБВГДЕЖЗИКЛМНОПРСТУФХЦЧШЩЪЫЬЭЮ

Condensed Oblique АБВГДЕЖЗИКЛМНОПРСТУФХЦЧШЩЪЫЬЭЮ

Upright Extended АБВГДЕЖЗИКЛМНОПРСТУФХЦЧШ

• *cyrillic*

Extended Oblique АБВГДЕЖЗИКЛМНОПРСТУФХЦЧШ

SOCRATES CYRILLIC HEAVY

cyrb RUS ▲18

АБВГДЕЖЗИКЛМНОПРСТУФХЦЧШЩЪЫЬЭЮЯ
1234567890.!?:,ЁЙ

Socrates Cyrillic Heavy . . .

• Upright АБВГДЕЖЗИКЛМНОПРСТУФХЦЧШЩЪЫЬЭЮЯ.1234

Oblique АБВГДЕЖЗИКЛМНОПРСТУФХЦЧШЩЪЫЬЭЮЯ.1234

Upright Condensed АБВГДЕЖЗИКЛМНОПРСТУФХЦЧШЩЪЫЬЭЮЯ.1234567890!?:

Condensed Oblique АБВГДЕЖЗИКЛМНОПРСТУФХЦЧШЩЪЫЬЭЮЯ.1234567890!?:

Upright Extended АБВГДЕЖЗИКЛМНОПРСТУФХЦЧШЩЪЫЬЭЮ

Extended Oblique АБВГДЕЖЗИКЛМНОПРСТУФХЦЧШЩЪЫЬЭЮ

ST. PETERSBURG CYRILLIC
✥ *DisplaySet 1*
cyrb АБВГДЕЖЗИКЛМНОПРСТУФХЦЧШЩЪЫЬЭЮЯ
RUS
▲18 1234567890.,ЁЙ

St. Petersburg Cyrillic . . .

• Upright АБВГДЕЖЗИКЛМНОПРСТУФХЦЧШЩЪЫЬЭЮЯ.123456789
Oblique *АБВГДЕЖЗИКЛМНОПРСТУФХЦЧШЩЪЫЬЭЮЯ.123456789*

TIMES NEW ROMAN CYRILLIC

cyrn абвгдежзиклмнопрстуфхцчшщъыьэюя
MCL (“.;‘!*?’:,)№1234567890&-áéє́и́óу́э́я́ю́ы́
АбВГДЕЖЗИКЛМНОПРСТУФХЦЧШЩЪЫЬЭЮЯ
ÁÉЄ́И́ÓУ́Э́Я́Ю́Ы́»„«§…
ґѓєёйќђіїјљњўћџѳѵѕѣҐЃЄЁЙЌЋІЇЈЉЊЎЋЏѲѴЅѢ

Times New Roman Cyrillic . . .

• Upright абвгдежзиклмнопрстуфхцчшщъыьэюя-АбВГДЕЖЗИКЛМНОПРСТУФХЦЧ
Inclined *абвгдежзиклмнопрстуфхцчшщъыьэюя-АбВГДЕЖЗИКЛМНОПРСТУФХЦЧШ*
Bold Upright **абвгдежзиклмнопрстуфхцчшщъыьэюя-АбВГДЕЖЗИКЛМНОПРСТУФХЦЧШ**
Bold Inclined ***абвгдежзиклмнопрстуфхцчшщъыьэюя-АбВГДЕЖЗИКЛМНОПРСТУФХЦЧШ***

TIMES TEN CYRILLIC

Ⓚ cyrx абвгдежзиклмнопрстуфхцчшщъыьэюя
LIN ADO AGA MAE (“.;‘!*?’:,”)№1234567890&-áéє́и́óу́э́я́ю́ы́ѣ́ί̈ї́ъ́р́àèѝòу̀р̀
АБВГДЕЖЗИКЛМНОПРСТУФХЦЧШЩЪЫЬЭЮЯ
ÁÉЄ́ÓУ́Э́Я́Ю́Ы́Ѣ́Ї́Ї́Ъ́Р́ÀÈЍÒУ̀Р̀»„«[§]
ґѓєёжйќђіїјљњўћџѳѵѕѫѣҐЃЄЁЖЙЌЋІЇЈЉЊЎЋЏѲѴЅѪѢ

Times Ten Cyrillic . . .

• Upright абвгдежзиклмнопрстуфхцчшщъыьэюя-АБВГДЕЖЗИКЛМНОПРСТУФХЦ
Inclined *абвгдежзиклмнопрстуфхцчшщъыьэюя-АБВГДЕЖЗИКЛМНОПРСТУФХЦ*
Bold Upright **абвгдежзиклмнопрстуфхцчшщъыьэюя-АБВГДЕЖЗИКЛМНОПРСТУФХЦ**
Bold Inclined ***абвгдежзиклмнопрстуфхцчшщъыьэюя-АБВГДЕЖЗИКЛМНОПРСТУФХ***

Ξ

✥ *DisplaySet 1*: Brush Cyrillic A-Inclined & B-Bold Inclined, Fat Man Cyrillic Heavy, Osho Cyrillic Script, St. Petersburg Cyrillic Upright & Oblique.

TRANS·CYRILLIC : SERIF

cyrz абвгдежзиклмнопрстуфхцчшщъыьюя

LSI (“.;‘!?’:,”)№1234567890-áéєи́óу́э́я́ю́ы́ѣ́ъ́р́

АБВГДЕЖЗИКЛМНОПРСТУФХЦЧШЩЪЫЬЮЯ

ÁÉЄÓУ́Э́Я́Ю́Ы́Ѣ́І́Ъ́Р́»,„«[§]‹•›

ăāäæґѓђд’ҙђєёĕēҗӂӝӟѕіїйӣӥјқќӆӊҥңҥљōöөӫқçћўӳӯӱүүһҳҷӵџ̄әәӛғҡҹѫѭѧѩѩ

ĂĀÄÆҐЃЂД’ҘЂЄЁĔĒҖӁӜӞЅІЇЙӢӤЈҚЌӅӉҤҢҤЉŌÖӨӪҚÇЋЎӲӮӰҮҮҺ

ҲҶӴЏ̄ӘӘӚҒҠҸѪѬѦѨѨ

TransCyrillic : Serif …

• Upright абвгдежзиклмнопрстуфхцчшщъыьюя-АБВГДЕЖЗИКЛМНОПРСТУФХЦЧШ

Inclined *абвгдежзиклмнопрстуфхцчшщъыьюя-АБВГДЕЖЗИКЛМНОПРСТУФХЦЧШЩЪ*

Bold Upright **абвгдежзиклмнопрстуфхцчшщъыьюя-АБВГДЕЖЗИКЛМНОПРСТУФХЦЧ**

Bold Inclined ***абвгдежзиклмнопрстуфхцчшщъыьюя-АБВГДЕЖЗИКЛМНОПРСТУФХЦЧШ***

TRANS·CYRILLIC : SANS SERIF

cyrz абвгдежзиклмнопрстуфхцчшщъыьюя

LSI (“.;‘!?’:,”)№1234567890-áéєи́óу́э́я́ю́ы́ѣ́ъ́р́

АБВГДЕЖЗИКЛМНОПРСТУФХЦЧШЩЪЫЬЮЯ

ÁÉЄÓУ́Э́Я́Ю́Ы́Ѣ́І́Ъ́Р́»,„«[§]‹•›

ăāäæґѓђд’ҙђєёĕēҗӂӝӟѕіїйӣӥјқќӆӊҥңҥљōöөӫқçћўӳӯӱүүһҳҷӵџ̄әәӛғҡҹѫѭѧѩѩ

ĂĀÄÆҐЃЂД’ҘЂЄЁĔĒҖӁӜӞЅІЇЙӢӤЈҚЌӅӉҤҢҤЉŌÖӨӪҚÇЋЎӲӮӰҮҮҺҲ

ҶӴЏ̄ӘӘӚҒҠҸѪѬѦѨѨ

• cyrillic

• Greek

TransCyrillic : Sans Serif …

• Upright абвгдежзиклмнопрстуфхцчшщъыьюя-АБВГДЕЖЗИКЛМНОПРСТУФХЦЧШ

Oblique *абвгдежзиклмнопрстуфхцчшщъыьюя-АБВГДЕЖЗИКЛМНОПРСТУФХЦЧШ*

Bold Upright **абвгдежзиклмнопрстуфхцчшщъыьюя-АБВГДЕЖЗИКЛМНОПРСТУФХЦ**

Bold Oblique ***абвгдежзиклмнопрстуфхцчшщъыьюя-АБВГДЕЖЗИКЛМНОПРСТУФХЦ***

ARIAL GREEK

grko αβγδεζηθικλμνξοπρσυτφχψω ς

MCL (“.‘!*;’•,”)$1234567890&-άέίήύώϊϋΐΰ

ΑΒΓΔΕΖΗΘΙΚΛΜΝΞΟΠΡΣΤΥΦΧΨΩ

ΆΈΉΊΌΎΏΪΫ »΄ ¨ ΅«[§†]…

Arial Greek …

• Upright αβγδεζηθικλμνξοπρσυφχψω-ΑΒΓΔΕΖΗΘΙΚΛΜΝΞΟΠΡΣΤΥΦΧΨΩ–$123456789

Inclined *αβγδεζηθικλμνξοπρσυφχψω-ΑΒΓΔΕΖΗΘΙΚΛΜΝΞΟΠΡΣΤΥΦΧΨΩ–$123456789*

Bold Upright **αβγδεζηθικλμνξοπρσυφχψω-ΑΒΓΔΕΖΗΘΙΚΛΜΝΞΟΠΡΣΤΥΦΧΨΩ–$1234567**

Bold Inclined ***αβγδεζηθικλμνξοπρσυφχψω-ΑΒΓΔΕΖΗΘΙΚΛΜΝΞΟΠΡΣΤΥΦΧΨΩ–$1234567***

BASKERVILLE MONOTONIC GREEK

K grko αβγδεζηθικλμνξοπρσυτφχψω ς

LIN (“.‘!*;’·,”)$1234567890&-άέίήύώϊϋΐΰ

ΑΒΓΔΕΖΗΘΙΚΛΜΝΞΟΠΡΣΤΥΦΧΨΩ

Ά Έ Ή Ί Ό Ύ Ώ Ϊ Ϋ »΄¨΅«[§†]...

Baskerville Monotonic Greek ...

• Upright αβγδεζηθικλμνξοπρσυφχψω-ΑΒΓΔΕΖΗΘΙΚΛΜΝΞΟΠΡΣΤΥΦΧΨΩ–$123456

Inclined *αβγδεζηθικλμνξοπρσυφχψω-ΑΒΓΔΕΖΗΘΙΚΛΜΝΞΟΠΡΣΤΥΦΧΨΩ–$1234567890(“.‘*

Bold Upright **αβγδεζηθικλμνξοπρσυφχψω-ΑΒΓΔΕΖΗΘΙΚΛΜΝΞΟΠΡΣΤΥΦΧΨΩ–$12345**

BASKERVILLE POLYTONIC GREEK

K grkn αβγδεζηθικλμνξοπρστυφχψω ς

LIN (“.‘!*;’·,”)$1234567890&-ϊϋΐΰῒῢ

ΑΒΓΔΕΖΗΘΙΚΛΜΝΞΟΠΡΣΤΥΦΧΨΩ

Ά Έ Ή Ί Ό Ύ Ώ Ϊ Ϋ »«[§†]...

άέήίόύώᾴῄῴὰὲὴὶὸὺὼᾲῂῲἄἔἤἴὄὔὤᾄᾔᾤἂἒἢἲὂὒὢᾂᾒᾢἆἦἶὖὦᾆᾖᾦἇἧἷὗὧᾇᾗᾧ

Baskerville Polytonic Greek ...

• Upright αβγδεζηθικλμνξοπρσυφχψω-ΑΒΓΔΕΖΗΘΙΚΛΜΝΞΟΠΡΣΤΥΦΧΨΩ–$123456

Inclined *αβγδεζηθικλμνξοπρσυφχψω-ΑΒΓΔΕΖΗΘΙΚΛΜΝΞΟΠΡΣΤΥΦΧΨΩ–$1234567890(“.‘*

Bold Upright **αβγδεζηθικλμνξοπρσυφχψω-ΑΒΓΔΕΖΗΘΙΚΛΜΝΞΟΠΡΣΤΥΦΧΨΩ–$12345**

Ω

NEW CENTURY SCHOOLBOOK MONOTONIC GREEK

K grko αβγδεζηθικλμνξοπρσυτφχψω ς

LIN (“.‘!*;’·,”)$1234567890&-άέίήύώϊϋΐ

ΑΒΓΔΕΖΗΘΙΚΛΜΝΞΟΠΡΣΤΥΦΧΨΩ

Ά Έ Ή Ί Ό Ύ Ώ Ϊ Ϋ »΄¨΅«[§†]...

New Century Schoolbook Monotonic Greek ...

• Upright αβγδεζηθικλμνξοπρσυφχψω-ΑΒΓΔΕΖΗΘΙΚΛΜΝΞΟΠΡΣΤΥΦΧΨΩ–$123456

Inclined *αβγδεζηθικλμνξοπρσυφχψω-ΑΒΓΔΕΖΗΘΙΚΛΜΝΞΟΠΡΣΤΥΦΧΨΩ–$1234567*

Bold Upright **αβγδεζηθικλμνξοπρσυφχψω-ΑΒΓΔΕΖΗΘΙΚΛΜΝΞΟΠΡΣΤΥΦΧΨΩ–$**

NEW CENTURY SCHOOLBOOK POLYTONIC GREEK

K grkn αβγδεζηθικλμνξοπρστυφχψω ς

LIN (“.‘!*;’·,”)$1234567890&-ϊϋΐΰῒῢ

ΑΒΓΔΕΖΗΘΙΚΛΜΝΞΟΠΡΣΤΥΦΧΨΩ

Ά Έ Ή Ί Ό Ύ Ώ Ϊ Ϋ »«[§†]...

άέήίόύώᾴῄῴὰὲὴὶὸὺὼᾲῂῲἄἔἤἴὄὔὤᾄᾔᾤἂἒἢἲὂὒὢᾂᾒᾢἆἦἶὖὦᾆᾖᾦἇἧἷὗὧᾇᾗᾧ

New Century Schoolbook Polytonic Greek ...

• Upright αβγδεζηθικλμνξοπρσυφχψω-ΑΒΓΔΕΖΗΘΙΚΛΜΝΞΟΠΡΣΤΥΦΧΨΩ–$123456

Inclined *αβγδεζηθικλμνξοπρσυφχψω-ΑΒΓΔΕΖΗΘΙΚΛΜΝΞΟΠΡΣΤΥΦΧΨΩ–$1234567*

Ξ

. . . New Century Schoolbook Polytonic Greek
Bold Upright **αβγδεζηθικλμνξοπρσυφχψω-ΑΒΓΔΕΖΗΘΙΚΛΜΝΞΟΠΡΣΤΥΦΧΨΩ–$**

COURIER GREEK

grko αβγδεζηθικλμνξοπρσυτφχψω ς
URW (“.’!*;’•,”)$1234567890&-άέίήύώϊϋΐΰ
▲12 ΑΒΓΔΕΖΗΘΙΚΛΜΝΞΟΠΡΣΤΥΦΧΨΩ
ΆΈΉΊΌΎΏΫ»«[§†]…

Courier Greek . . .

• Light Upright αβγδεζηθικλμνξοπρσυφχψω-ΑΒΓΔΕΖΗΘΙΚΛΜΝΞΟΠΡΣΤΥΦΧΨΩ–$1234567890(“.;’!*;’
Light Oblique *αβγδεζηθικλμνξοπρσυφχψω-ΑΒΓΔΕΖΗΘΙΚΛΜΝΞΟΠΡΣΤΥΦΧΨΩ–$1234567890(“.;’!*;’*
Bold Upright **αβγδεζηθικλμνξοπρσυφχψω-ΑΒΓΔΕΖΗΘΙΚΛΜΝΞΟΠΡΣΤΥΦΧΨΩ–$1234567890(“.;’!*;’**
Bold Oblique ***αβγδεζηθικλμνξοπρσυφχψω-ΑΒΓΔΕΖΗΘΙΚΛΜΝΞΟΠΡΣΤΥΦΧΨΩ–$1234567890(“.;’!*;’***

GRAECA
LaserGreek

grkz αβγδεζηθικλμνξοπρστυφχψω ς
LSI (.!*;·,)$1234567890-ϊϋΐΰῒῢ
ΑΒΓΔΕΖΗΘΙΚΛΜΝΞΟΠΡΣΤΥΦΧΨΩ
ΆΈΉΊΌΏ [†] ϡϙϝ ´ ` ῾ ᾿ ῞ ῎ ῝ ῍ ῟ ῏ ᾽ ῾ ͺ ͵ ʹ ῁ ῭ ΅ ῀ ¨
άέήίόύώᾴῄῴὰὲὴὶὸὺὼᾲῂῲᾶῆῖῦῶᾷῇῷ

Graeca . . .

• Upright αβγδεζηθικλμνξοπρστυφχψω-ΑΒΓΔΕΖΗΘΙΚΛΜΝΞΟΠΡΣΤΥΦΧΨΩ–$1234567890(.!*
Inclined *αβγδεζηθικλμνξοπρστυφχψω-ΑΒΓΔΕΖΗΘΙΚΛΜΝΞΟΠΡΣΤΥΦΧΨΩ–$1234567890(.!**
Bold Upright **αβγδεζηθικλμνξοπρστυφχψω-ΑΒΓΔΕΖΗΘΙΚΛΜΝΞΟΠΡΣΤΥΦΧΨΩ–$123456789**
Bold Inclined ***αβγδεζηθικλμνξοπρστυφχψω-ΑΒΓΔΕΖΗΘΙΚΛΜΝΞΟΠΡΣΤΥΦΧΨΩ–$123456789***

• Greek

GREEK SANS
LaserGreek

grkz αβγδεζηθικλμνξοπρστυφχψω ς
LSI (.!*;·,)$1234567890-ϊϋΐΰῒῢ
ΑΒΓΔΕΖΗΘΙΚΛΜΝΞΟΠΡΣΤΥΦΧΨΩ
ΆΈΉΊΌΏ [†] ϡϙϝ ´ ` ῾ ᾿ ῞ ῎ ῝ ῍ ῟ ῏ ᾽ ῾ ͺ ͵ ʹ ῁ ῭ ΅ ῀ ¨
άέήίόύώᾴῄῴὰὲὴὶὸὺὼᾲῂῲᾶῆῖῦῶᾷῇῷ

Greek Sans . . .

• Upright αβγδεζηθικλμνξοπρστυφχψω-ΑΒΓΔΕΖΗΘΙΚΛΜΝΞΟΠΡΣΤΥΦΧΨΩ–$123456789
Oblique *αβγδεζηθικλμνξοπρστυφχψω-ΑΒΓΔΕΖΗΘΙΚΛΜΝΞΟΠΡΣΤΥΦΧΨΩ–$123456789*
Bold Upright **αβγδεζηθικλμνξοπρστυφχψω-ΑΒΓΔΕΖΗΘΙΚΛΜΝΞΟΠΡΣΤΥΦΧΨΩ–$1234567**
Bold Oblique ***αβγδεζηθικλμνξοπρστυφχψω-ΑΒΓΔΕΖΗΘΙΚΛΜΝΞΟΠΡΣΤΥΦΧΨΩ–$1234567***

Ξ

LaserGreek: Graeca Upright, Inclined, Bold & Bold Inclined. Greek Sans Upright, Oblique, Bold Upright & Bold Oblique. Symbol Greek Upright, Inclined, Bold & Bold Inclined. Symbol Greek P Upright, Inclined, Bold & Bold Inclined. Uncial LS.

HELVETICA MONOTONIC GREEK

K grko αβγδεζηθικλμνξοπρσυτφχψω ς

LIN (“.‘!*;’·,”)$1234567890&-άέίήύώϊϋ ΐΰ

ΑΒΓΔΕΖΗΘΙΚΛΜΝΞΟΠΡΣΤΥΦΧΨΩ

ΆΈΉΊΌΎΏΪΫ »΄¨΅«[§†]...

Helvetica Monotonic Greek ...

• Upright αβγδεζηθικλμνξοπρσυφχψω-ΑΒΓΔΕΖΗΘΙΚΛΜΝΞΟΠΡΣΤΥΦΧΨΩ–$12345678

Inclined *αβγδεζηθικλμνξοπρσυφχψω-ΑΒΓΔΕΖΗΘΙΚΛΜΝΞΟΠΡΣΤΥΦΧΨΩ–$12345678*

Bold Upright **αβγδεζηθικλμνξοπρσυφχψω-ΑΒΓΔΕΖΗΘΙΚΛΜΝΞΟΠΡΣΤΥΦΧΨΩ–$12345678**

Bold Inclined ***αβγδεζηθικλμνξοπρσυφχψω-ΑΒΓΔΕΖΗΘΙΚΛΜΝΞΟΠΡΣΤΥΦΧΨΩ–$12345678***

HELVETICA POLYTONIC GREEK

K grkx αβγδεζηθικλμνξοπρστυφχψω ς

LIN (“.‘!*;’·,”)$1234567890&-ϊϋΐΰΐΰ

ΑΒΓΔΕΖΗΘΙΚΛΜΝΞΟΠΡΣΤΥΦΧΨΩ

ΆΈΉΊΌΎΏΪΫ »«[§†]...

άέήίόύώᾴῄῴὰὲὴὶὸὺὼᾲῂῲἅἕἥἵὅὅὥᾅᾕᾥἄἔἤἴὄὄὤᾄᾔᾤἇἧἷὗὧᾇᾗᾧἆἦἶὖὦᾆᾖᾦ

Helvetica Polytonic Greek ...

• Upright αβγδεζηθικλμνξοπρσυφχψω-ΑΒΓΔΕΖΗΘΙΚΛΜΝΞΟΠΡΣΤΥΦΧΨΩ–$12345678

Inclined *αβγδεζηθικλμνξοπρσυφχψω-ΑΒΓΔΕΖΗΘΙΚΛΜΝΞΟΠΡΣΤΥΦΧΨΩ–$12345678*

Bold Upright **αβγδεζηθικλμνξοπρσυφχψω-ΑΒΓΔΕΖΗΘΙΚΛΜΝΞΟΠΡΣΤΥΦΧΨΩ–$12345678**

Bold Inclined ***αβγδεζηθικλμνξοπρσυφχψω-ΑΒΓΔΕΖΗΘΙΚΛΜΝΞΟΠΡΣΤΥΦΧΨΩ–$12345678***

Ω

ITC SOUVENIR MONOTONIC GREEK

K grko αβγδεζηθικλμνξοπρσυτφχψω ς

LIN (“.‘!*;’·,”)$1234567890&-άέίήύώϊϋΐΰ

ΑΒΓΔΕΖΗΘΙΚΛΜΝΞΟΠΡΣΤΥΦΧΨΩ

ΆΈΉΊΌΎΏΪΫ »΄¨΅«[§†]...

ITC Souvenir Monotonic Greek ...

• Light Upright αβγδεζηθικλμνξοπρσυφχψω-ΑΒΓΔΕΖΗΘΙΚΛΜΝΞΟΠΡΣΤΥΦΧΨΩ–$123456789

Demi Upright **αβγδεζηθικλμνξοπρσυφχψω-ΑΒΓΔΕΖΗΘΙΚΛΜΝΞΟΠΡΣΤΥΦΧΨΩ–$123**

ITC SOUVENIR POLYTONIC GREEK

K grkn αβγδεζηθικλμνξοπρστυφχψω ς

LIN (“.‘!*;’·,”)$1234567890&-ϊϋΐΰΐΰ

ΑΒΓΔΕΖΗΘΙΚΛΜΝΞΟΠΡΣΤΥΦΧΨΩ

ΆΈΉΊΌΎΏΪΫ »«[§†]...

άέήίόύώᾴῄῴὰὲὴὶὸὺὼᾲῂῲἅἕἥἵὅὅὥᾅᾕᾥἄἔἤἴὄὄὤᾄᾔᾤἇἧἷὗὧᾇᾗᾧἆἦἶὖὦᾆᾖᾦ

Ξ

ITC Souvenir Polytonic Greek ...

• Light Upright αβγδεζηθικλμνξοπρσυφχψω-ΑΒΓΔΕΖΗΘΙΚΛΜΝΞΟΠΡΣΤΥΦΧΨΩ–$123456789

... ITC Souvenir Polytonic Greek

Demi Upright **αβγδεznθικλμνξοπρσυφχψω-ΑΒΓΔΕΖΗΘΙΚΛΜΝΞΟΠΡΣΤΥΦΧΨΩ–$123**

SYMBOL GREEK

LaserGreek

grkz αβγδεζηθικλμνξοπρστυφχψω ς

LSI (.!*;·,)$1234567890-ϊϋΐΰΐΰ

ΑΒΓΔΕΖΗΘΙΚΛΜΝΞΟΠΡΣΤΥΦΧΨΩ

Ά Έ Ή Ί Ό Ώ [†]

άέήίόύώᾳῃῳὰὲὴὶὸὺὼᾳῃῳᾶ῀ῆῖῦῶᾷῇῷ

Symbol Greek ...

• Upright αβγδεζηθικλμνξοπρστυφχψω-ΑΒΓΔΕΖΗΘΙΚΛΜΝΞΟΠΡΣΤΥΦΧΨΩ-$1234567890(.!*

Inclined *αβγδεζηθικλμνξοπρστυφχψω-ΑΒΓΔΕΖΗΘΙΚΛΜΝΞΟΠΡΣΤΥΦΧΨΩ-$1234567890(.!**

Bold Upright **αβγδεζηθικλμνξοπρστυφχψω-ΑΒΓΔΕΖΗΘΙΚΛΜΝΞΟΠΡΣΤΥΦΧΨΩ-$123456789**

Bold Inclined ***αβγδεζηθικλμνξοπρστυφχψω-ΑΒΓΔΕΖΗΘΙΚΛΜΝΞΟΠΡΣΤΥΦΧΨΩ-$123456789***

TIMES NEW ROMAN GREEK

grko αβγδεζηθικλμνξοπρσυτφχψω ς

MCL ("·'!*;'•,")$1234567890&-άέίήύώϊϋΐΰ

ΑΒΓΔΕΖΗΘΙΚΛΜΝΞΟΠΡΣΤΥΦΧΨΩ

Ά Έ Ή Ί Ό Ύ Ώ Ϊ Ϋ »΄ ¨ ΅«[§†]...

Times New Roman Greek ...

• Upright αβγδεζηθικλμνξοπρσυφχψω-ΑΒΓΔΕΖΗΘΙΚΛΜΝΞΟΠΡΣΤΥΦΧΨΩ–$12345678

Inclined *αβγδεζηθικλμνξοπρσυφχψω-ΑΒΓΔΕΖΗΘΙΚΛΜΝΞΟΠΡΣΤΥΦΧΨΩ–$1234567890*

Bold Upright **αβγδεζηθικλμνξοπρσυφχψω-ΑΒΓΔΕΖΗΘΙΚΛΜΝΞΟΠΡΣΤΥΦΧΨΩ–$12345678**

Bold Inclined ***αβγδεζηθικλμνξοπρσυφχψω-ΑΒΓΔΕΖΗΘΙΚΛΜΝΞΟΠΡΣΤΥΦΧΨΩ–$1234567890***

• Greek

TIMES TEN MONOTONIC GREEK

grko αβγδεζηθικλμνξοπρσυτφχψω ς

LIN ("·'!*;'·,")$1234567890&-άέίήύώϊϋΐΰ

ΑΒΓΔΕΖΗΘΙΚΛΜΝΞΟΠΡΣΤΥΦΧΨΩ

Ά Έ Ή Ί Ό Ύ Ώ Ϊ Ϋ »΄ ¨ ΅«[§†]...

Times Ten Monotonic Greek ...

• Upright αβγδεζηθικλμνξοπρσυφχψω-ΑΒΓΔΕΖΗΘΙΚΛΜΝΞΟΠΡΣΤΥΦΧΨΩ–$1234567

Inclined *αβγδεζηθικλμνξοπρσυφχψω-ΑΒΓΔΕΖΗΘΙΚΛΜΝΞΟΠΡΣΤΥΦΧΨΩ–$1234567*

Bold Upright **αβγδεζηθικλμνξοπρσυφχψω-ΑΒΓΔΕΖΗΘΙΚΛΜΝΞΟΠΡΣΤΥΦΧΨΩ–$123456**

Bold Inclined ***αβγδεζηθικλμνξοπρσυφχψω-ΑΒΓΔΕΖΗΘΙΚΛΜΝΞΟΠΡΣΤΥΦΧΨΩ–$123456***

Ξ

LaserGreek: Graeca Upright, Inclined, Bold & Bold Inclined. Greek Sans Upright, Oblique, Bold Upright & Bold Oblique. Symbol Greek Upright, Inclined, Bold & Bold Inclined. Symbol Greek P Upright, Inclined, Bold & Bold Inclined. Uncial LS.

TIMES TEN POLYTONIC GREEK

grkx αβγδεζηθικλμνξοπρστυφχψω ς

LIN (“.‘!*;’·,”)$1234567890&-ϊϋΐΰΐΰ

ΑΒΓΔΕΖΗΘΙΚΛΜΝΞΟΠΡΣΤΥΦΧΨΩ

Ά Έ Ή Ί Ό Ύ Ώ Ϊ Ϋ »«[§†]…

άέήίόύώᾴῄῴὰὲὴὶὸὺὼᾲῂῲ

Times Ten Polytonic Greek …

• Upright αβγδεζηθικλμνξοπρσυφχψω-ΑΒΓΔΕΖΗΘΙΚΛΜΝΞΟΠΡΣΤΥΦΧΨΩ–$1234567

Inclined *αβγδεζηθικλμνξοπρσυφχψω-ΑΒΓΔΕΖΗΘΙΚΛΜΝΞΟΠΡΣΤΥΦΧΨΩ–$1234567*

Bold Upright **αβγδεζηθικλμνξοπρσυφχψω-ΑΒΓΔΕΖΗΘΙΚΛΜΝΞΟΠΡΣΤΥΦΧΨΩ–$123456**

Bold Inclined ***αβγδεζηθικλμνξοπρσυφχψω-ΑΒΓΔΕΖΗΘΙΚΛΜΝΞΟΠΡΣΤΥΦΧΨΩ–$123456***

Uncial LS
LaserGreek
grkz αβγδεζηθικλμνξοπρστυφχψω ς

LSI (.!*;·,)$1234567890-ϊϋΐΰΐΰ

ΑΒΓΔΕΖΗΘΙΚΛΜΝΞΟΠΡΣΤΥΦΧΨΩ

Ά Έ Ή Ί Ό Ώ [†]

άέήίόύώᾴῄῴὰὲὴὶὸὺὼ

ACHENELI
Designer I Collection
hbrb (.!*?:,’)ץףןםך-תשרקצפעסנמלכיטחזוהדגבא

TOR £1234567890&–$•

▲30

Acheneli …

Medium £1&(.!*?:,’)ץףןםך-תשרקצפעסנמלכיטחזוהדגבא

• Regular £1&(.!*?:,’)ץףןםך-תשרקצפעסנמלכיטחזוהדגבא

Arad Level VI
LaserHebrew
hbrb (“.:!?:,”)

LSI

▲24

AZTOR
Designer II Collection
hbrb (.!*?:,’)ץףןםך-תשרקצפעסנמלכיטחזוהדגבא

TOR £1234567890&–$•

▲30

Aztor …

Outline £(.!*?:,’)ץףןםך-תשרקצפעסנמלכיטחזוהדגבא

• Regular £123456&(.!*?:,’)ץףןםך-תשרקצפעסנמלכיטחזוהדגבא

LaserGreek: Graeca Upright, Inclined, Bold & Bold Inclined. Greek Sans Upright, Oblique, Bold Upright & Bold Oblique. Symbol Greek Upright, Inclined, Bold & Bold Inclined. Symbol Greek P Upright, Inclined, Bold & Bold Inclined. Uncial LS.
LaserHebrew: AradLevelVI, Bethel, Hebraica, ScriptHebrew.

Designer I Collection: Acheneli Regular & Medium, Busoreli Regular & Bold, Careli Regular & Medium, Frizeli Regular & Bold, Gilgal Ultra Bold & Ultra Outline, Ivricana Bold & Outline, Kabelim Bold & Outline, Lublineli Condensed & Extra Bold Condensed, Optwo Regular & Bold, Revieie Regular & Heavy, Yaveneli Regular & Extra Bold.

Bethel
LaserHebrew
hbrx
LSI
18

אבגדהוזחטיכלמנסעפצקרשת/דםןףץ(:?!;.)-1234567890

אבגדהוזטיכלמנספצקרשׁשׂשׁשׂת

BROADWELI
Designer II Collection
hbrb
TOR
30

אבגדהוזחטיכלמנסעפצקרשת-דםןףץ

(.!*?:,’)£1234567890&$–•

Broadweli ...

Engraved אבגדהוזחטיכלמנסעפצקרשת-דםןףץ’(.!*?:,

• Regular אבגדהוזחטיכלמנסעפצקרשת-דםןףץ(.!*?:,

BUSORELI
Designer I Collection
hbrb TOR
30

אבגדהוזחטיכלמנסעפצקרשת-דםןףץ·(.!*?:,’)£1234567890&$–

Busoreli ...

• Regular אבגדהוזחטיכלמנסעפצקרשת-דםןףץ·$–(’,:?*!.)&£1234567890

Bold אבגדהוזחטיכלמנסעפצקרשת-דםןףץ(,:?*!.)£123456

CARELI
Designer I Collection
hbrb
TOR
30

אבגדהוזחטיכלמנסעפצקרשת-דםןףץ(’,:?*!.)

£1234567890&$-·

Careli ...

• Regular אבגדהוזחטיכלמנסעפצקרשת-דםןףץ(’,:?*!.)&£12345

Medium אבגדהוזחטיכלמנסעפצקרשת-דםןףץ(,:?*!.)&£123

COOPERELI
Designer II Collection
hbrb
TOR
24

אבגדהוזחטיכלמנסעפצקרשת-דםןףץ(’,:?*!.)

£1234567890&$–•

Coopereli ...

Outline אבגדהוזחטיכלמנסעפצקרשת-דםןףץ(’,:?*!.)

• Regular אבגדהוזחטיכלמנסעפצקרשת-דםןףץ(,:?*!.)

• Greek
• Hebrew

Ξ

Designer II Collection: Atzor Regular & Outline, Broadweli Engraved & Regular, Coopereli Regular & Outline, Hebras Book & Black, Hobeli Regular & Outline, Lublineli Regular & Extra Bold, Mehandes Regular & Bold, Nekoshet Regular & Bold, Optimeli Regular & Bold, Peigneli Regular & Bold, Uncieli Regular & Outline.

LaserHebrew: AradLevelVI, Bethel, Hebraica, ScriptHebrew.
Classic Collection: David Regular & Bold, Frank Regular & Bold, Galed Regular & Bold, Hadas Regular & Bold, Meiri Regular & Bold, Rashi Regular & Bold, Sofer, Vilna Regular & Bold.

DAVID
❖ *Classic Collection*
hbrb **TOR**
▲18

אבגדהוזחטיכלמנסעפצקרשת-דםןףץ•\$—901234567890£(')',:?*!.

David . . .

• Regular אבגדהוזחטיכלמנסעפצקרשת-דםןףץ•\$—1234567890£(.!*?:,')

Bold **אבגדהוזחטיכלמנסעפצקרשת-דםןףץ•\$—)',:?*!.(1234567890£**

FRANK
❖ *Classic Collection*
hbrb **TOR**
▲18

אבגדהוזחטיכלמנסעפצקרשת-דםןףץ•\$—&1234567890£(.!*?:,')

Frank . . .

• Regular אבגדהוזחטיכלמנסעפצקרשת-דםןףץ•\$—&1234567890£(.!*?:,')

Bold **אבגדהוזחטיכלמנסעפצקרשת-דםןףץ•\$—&1234567890£(.!*?:,')**

FRIZELI
❖ *Designer I Collection*
hbrb

אבגדהוזחטיכלמנסעפצקרשת-דםןףץ(.!*?:,')

TOR
▲24

£1234567890&\$-•

Frizeli . . .

• Regular £1234567890&(.!*?:,')ץףןםד-תשרקצפעסנמלכיטחזהודגבא

Bold **£12345678&(.!*?:,')ץףןםד-תשרקצפעסנמלכיטחזהודגבא**

GALED
❖ *Classic Collection*
hbrb **TOR**
▲18

אבגדהוזחטיכלמנסעפצקרשת-דםןףץ\$—&1234567890£(.!*?:,')

Galed . . .

• Regular £1234567890&(.!*?:,')—ץףןםד-תשרקצפעסנמלכיטחזהודגבא

Bold אבגדהוזחטיכלמנסעפצקרשת-דםןףץ•\$—&1234567890£(.!*?:,')

GILGAL ULTRA
❖ *Designer I Collection*
hbrb

אבגדהוזחטיכלמנסעפצקרשת-דםןףץ

TOR
▲30

(.!*?:,')£1234567890&\$-

Gilgal Ultra . . .

• Bold **אבגדהוזחטיכלמנסעפצקרשת-דםןףץ?*!.**

Outline אבגדהוזחטיכלמנסעפצקרשת-דםןףץ(.!)

❖ *Classic Collection*: David Regular & Bold, Frank Regular & Bold, Galed Regular & Bold, Hadas Regular & Bold, Meiri Regular & Bold, Rashi Regular & Bold, Sofer, Vilna Regular & Bold.

❖ *Designer I Collection*: Acheneli Regular & Medium, Busoreli Regular & Bold, Careli Regular & Medium, Frizeli Regular & Bold, Gilgal Ultra Bold & Ultra Outline, Ivricana Bold & Outline, Kabelim Bold & Outline, Lublineli Condensed & Extra Bold Condensed, Optwo Regular & Bold, Reviele Regular & Heavy, Yaveneli Regular & Extra Bold.

HADAS
❖ *Classic Collection*
hbrb TOR ▲18

(.!*?:,')£1234567890—$• אבגדהוזחטיכלמנסעפצקרשת-ךםןףץ

Hadas …

• Regular £1234567890(.!*?:,')—$• אבגדהוזחטיכלמנסעפצקרשת-ךםןףץ

Bold £1234567890(.!*?:,')—$• אבגדהוזחטיכלמנסעפצקרשת-ךםןףץ

Hebraica
❖ *LaserHebrew*
hbrx

1234567890-(.;!?:) אבגדהוזחטיכלמנסעפצקרשת/ךםןףץ

LSI ▲18

אבגדהוזטיכלמנספצקרשששת ו ו י י

HEBRAS
❖ *Designer II Collection*
hbrb TOR ▲18

(.! *?:,')£1234567890&$– אבגדהוזחטיכלמנסעפצקרשת-ךםןףץ

Hebras …

Book £1234567890&(.! *?:,')–$ אבגדהוזחטיכלמנסעפצקרשת-ךםןףץ

• Black £1234567890&(.! *?:,)–$ אבגדהוזחטיכלמנסעפצקרשת-ךםןףץ

HOBELI
❖ *Designer II Collection*
hbrb

(.!*?:,') אבגדהוזחטיכלמנסעפצקרשת-ךםןףץ

TOR ▲30

£1234567890&$–

Hobeli …

Outline £123456789&(.!*?:,') אבגדהוזחטיכלמנסעפצקרשת-ךםןףץ

• Regular £123456789&(.!*?:,) אבגדהוזחטיכלמנסעפצקרשת-ךםןףץ

• Hebrew

IVRICANA
❖ *Designer I Collection*
hbrb

(.!*?:,') אבגדהוזחטיכלמנסעפצקרשת-ךםןףץ

TOR ▲24

£1234567890&$–

Ivricana …

Bold £12&(.!*?:,') אבגדהוזחטיכלמנסעפצקרשת-ךםןףץ

• Outline &(ץ!*?:,') אבגדהוזחטיכלמנסעפצקרשת-ךםןףץ

KABELIM
❖ *Designer I Collection*
hbrb

(.!*?:,') אבגדהוזחטיכלמנסעפצקרשת-ךםןףץ

TOR ▲24

£1234567890&$–

Kabelim …

Bold £12345678&(.!*?:,') אבגדהוזחטיכלמנסעפצקרשת-ךםןףץ

❖ *Classic Collection*: David Regular & Bold, Frank Regular & Bold, Galed Regular & Bold, Hadas Regular & Bold, Meiri Regular & Bold, Rashi Regular & Bold, Sofer, Vilna Regular & Bold.

❖ *LaserHebrew*: AradLevelVI, Bethel, Hebraica, ScriptHebrew.

❖ *Designer II Collection*: Atzor Regular & Outline, Broadweli Engraved & Regular, Coopereli Regular & Outline, Hebras Book & Black, Hobeli Regular & Outline, Lublineli Regular & Extra Bold, Mehandes Regular & Bold, Nekoshet Regular & Bold, Optimeli Regular & Bold, Peigneli Regular & Bold, Uncieli Regular & Outline.

... Kabelim

• Outline אבגדהוזחטיכלמנסעפצקרשת-ךםןףץ(,:?*!.)&£12345678

LUBLINELI
❖ *Designer II Collection*
hbrb אבגדהוזחטיכלמנסעפצקרשת-ךםןףץ(',:?*!.)
TOR ▲24 £1234567890&$–•

Lublineli ...

• Regular אבגדהוזחטיכלמנסעפצקרשת-ךםןףץ–(',:?*!.)&£1234567890

Extra Bold **אבגדהוזחטיכלמנסעפצקרשת-ךםןףץ(,:?*!.)&£123456789**

LUBLINELI CONDENSED
❖ *Designer I Collection*
hbrb TOR ▲24 אבגדהוזחטיכלמנסעפצקרשת-ךםןףץ•–$&£1234567890(',:?*!.)

Lublineli Condensed ...

• Condensed אבגדהוזחטיכלמנסעפצקרשת-ךםןףץ•$–(',:?*!.)&£1234567890

Extra Bold Condensed **אבגדהוזחטיכלמנסעפצקרשת-ךםןףץ•$–(,:?*!.)&£1234567890**

MEHANDES
❖ *Designer II Collection*
hbrb
TOR ▲42 אבגדהוזחטיכלמנסעפצקרשת-ךםןףץ·–$&£1234567890(′,:?*!.)

Mehandes ...

• Regular אבגדהוזחטיכלמנסעפצקרשת-ךםןףץ·$–(′,:?*!.)&£1234567890

Bold **אבגדהוזחטיכלמנסעפצקרשת-ךםןףץ·$–(,:?*!.)&£1234567890**

MEIRI
❖ *Classic Collection*
hbrb TOR ▲18 אבגדהוזחטיכלמנסעפצקרשת-ךםןףץ•–$&£1234567890(',:?*!.)

Meiri ...

• Regular אבגדהוזחטיכלמנסעפצקרשת-ךםןףץ•$–(',:?*!.)&£1234567890

Bold **אבגדהוזחטיכלמנסעפצקרשת-ךםןףץ•$–(,:?*!.)&£1234567890**

NEKOSHET
❖ *Designer II Collection*
hbrb TOR ▲18 אבגדהוזחטיכלמנסעפצקרשת-ךםןףץ·–$&£1234567890(',:?*!.)

Nekoshet ...

• Regular אבגדהוזחטיכלמנסעפצקרשת-ךםןףץ·$–(',:?*!.)&£1234567890

Bold **אבגדהוזחטיכלמנסעפצקרשת-ךםןףץ·$–(,:?*!.)&£1234567890**

❖ *Designer I Collection*: Acheneli Regular & Medium, Busoreli Regular & Bold, Careli Regular & Medium, Frizeli Regular & Bold, Gilgal Ultra Bold & Ultra Outline, Ivricana Bold & Outline, Kabelim Bold & Outline, Lublineli Condensed & Extra Bold Condensed, Optwo Regular & Bold, Reviele Regular & Heavy, Yaveneli Regular & Extra Bold.

❖ *Designer II Collection*: Atzor Regular & Outline, Broadweli Engraved & Regular, Coopereli Regular & Outline, Hebras Book & Black, Hobeli Regular & Outline, Lublineli Regular & Extra Bold, Mehandes Regular & Bold, Nekoshet Regular & Bold, Optimeli Regular & Bold, Peigneli Regular & Bold, Uncieli Regular & Outline.

OPTIMELI
Designer II Collection
hbrb TOR ▲18 (.!*?:,’)£1234567890&$-· אבגדהוזחטיכלמנסעפצקרשת-ךםןףץ

Optimeli . . .

• Regular £1234567890&(.!*?:,’)-$· אבגדהוזחטיכלמנסעפצקרשת-ךםןףץ

Bold **£1234567890&(.!*?:,)-$· אבגדהוזחטיכלמנסעפצקרשת-ךםןףץ**

OPTWO
Designer I Collection
hbrb TOR ▲18 (.!*?:,’)£1234567890&$-· אבגדהוזחטיכלמנסעפצקרשת-ךםןףץ

Optwo . . .

• Regular £1234567890&(.!*?:,’)-$· אבגדהוזחטיכלמנסעפצקרשת-ךםןףץ

Bold **£1234567890&(.!*?:,)-$· אבגדהוזחטיכלמנסעפצקרשת-ךםןףץ**

PEIGNELI
Designer I Collection
hbrb TOR ▲18 (.!*?:,’)£1234567890&$–· אבגדהוזחטיכלמנסעפצקרשת-ךםןףץ

Peigneli . . .

• Regular £1234567890&(.!*?:,’)–$· אבגדהוזחטיכלמנסעפצקרשת-ךםןףץ

Bold **£1234567890&(.!*?:,)–$· אבגדהוזחטיכלמנסעפצקרשת-ךםןףץ**

RASHI
Classic Collection
hbrb TOR ▲18 (.!*?:,’)£1234567890&$-• אבגדהוזחטיכלמנסעפצקרשת-ךםןףץ

Rashi . . .

• Regular £1234567890&(.!*?:,’)-$• אבגדהוזחטיכלמנסעפצקרשת-ךםןףץ

Bold **£1234567890&(.!*?:,)-$• אבגדהוזחטיכלמנסעפצקרשת-ךםןףץ**

• Hebrew

REVIELI
Designer I Collection
hbrb (.!*?:,’) אבגדהוזחטיכלמנסעפצקרשת-ךםןףץ

TOR ▲30 **£1234567890&$-▪**

Revieli . . .

• Regular **£123456& (.!*?:,’) אבגדהוזחטיכלמנסעפצקרשת-ךםןףץ**

Heavy **£123456& (.!*?:,) אבגדהוזחטיכלמנסעפצקרשת-ךםןףץ**

ScriptHebrew
LaserHebrew
hbrb LSI ▲18 (“.;‘!*?’:,”)1234567890—$• אבגדהוזחטיכלמנסעפצקרשת - ךםןףץ

Classic Collection: David Regular & Bold, Frank Regular & Bold, Galed Regular & Bold, Hadas Regular & Bold, Meiri Regular & Bold, Rashi Regular & Bold, Sofer, Vilna Regular & Bold.
LaserHebrew: AradLevelVI, Bethel, Hebraica, ScriptHebrew.

Sofer
❖ *Classic Collection*
hbrb אבגדהוזחטיכלמנסעפצקרשת-ךםןףץ(.!*?:,')
TOR
▲24 £1234567890&$–•

UNCIELI
❖ *Designer II Collection*
hbrb אבגדהוזחטיכלמנסעפצקרשת-ךםןףץ(.!*?:,')
TOR
▲24 £1234567890&$–•

Uncieli …
Regular אבגדהוזחטיכלמנסעפצקרשת-ךםןףץ(.!*?:,')£123&
• Outline אבגדהוזחטיכלמנסעפצקרשת-ךםןףץ(.!*?:,')£123&

VILNA
❖ *Classic Collection*
hbrb TOR ▲18 (.!*?:,')£1234567890&$–•ץףןםך-אבגדהוזחטיכלמנסעפצקרשת

Vilna …
• Regular £1234567890&(.!*?:,')–$•ץףןםך-אבגדהוזחטיכלמנסעפצקרשת
Bold **£1234567890&(.!*?:,)–$•ץףןםך-אבגדהוזחטיכלמנסעפצקרשת**

YAVANELI
❖ *Designer I Collection*
hbrb אבגדהוזחטיכלמנסעפצקרשת-ךםןףץ(.!*?:,')
TOR
▲30 £1234567890&$–•

Yavaneli …
• Regular £123456&(.!*?:,')אבגדהוזחטיכלמנסעפצקרשת-ךםןףץ
Extra Bold **£123&(.!*?:,)אבגדהוזחטיכלמנסעפצקרשת-ךםןףץ**

HiGwangJu
❖ *LaserKorean*
Ⓚ krnk ㄱ ㄴ ㄷ ㄹ ㅁ ㅂ ㅅ ㅇ ㅈ ㅊ ㅋ ㅌ ㅍ ㅎ ㅏ ㅑ ㅓ ㅕ ㅗ ㅛ ㅜ ㅠ ㅡ ㅣ
LSI ㄲ ㄸ ㅃ ㅆ ㅉ ㅐ ㅒ ㅔ ㅖ ㅚ ㅟ ㅢ ㅘ ㅝ ㅙ ㅞ
▲18 ㄱ ㄴ ㄷ ㄹ ㅁ ㅂ ㅅ ㅇ ㅈ ㅊ ㅋ ㅌ ㅍ ㅎ ㅏ ㅑ ㅓ ㅕ ㅗ ㅛ ㅜ ㅠ ㅡ ㅣ
ㄲ ㄸ ㅃ ㅆ ㅉ ㅐ ㅒ ㅔ ㅖ ㅚ ㅟ ㅢ ㅘ ㅝ ㅙ ㅞ 1234567890(¶.,₱)
아 ㅂ ㅈ ㅉ ㄷ 에 ㄱ ㄲ ㅎ 이 ㅊ ㅋ ㅁ ㄴ ㅇ 오 ㅃ ㅍ ㄹ ㅅ ㅆ ㅌ 우
가 갸 거 계 고 교 구 규 그 각 간 강 갓

❖ *Classic Collection*: David Regular & Bold, Frank Regular & Bold, Galed Regular & Bold, Hadas Regular & Bold, Meiri Regular & Bold, Rashi Regular & Bold, Sofer, Vilna Regular & Bold.
❖ *LaserKorean*: HiGwangJu, HiInchon, NewHiPusan, NewJeju, NewSeoul Regular, Oblique, Bold & Bold Oblique.

❖ *Designer II Collection*: Atzor Regular & Outline, Broadweli Engraved & Regular, Coopereli Regular & Outline, Hebras Book & Black, Hobeli Regular & Outline, Lublineli Regular & Extra Bold, Mehandes Regular & Bold, Nekoshet Regular & Bold, Optimeli Regular & Bold, Peigneli Regular & Bold, Uncieli Regular & Outline.

HiInchon
LaserKorean
krnk
LSI
▲18

ㄱ ㄴ ㄷ ㄹ ㅁ ㅂ ㅅ ㅇ ㅈ ㅊ ㅋ ㅌ ㅍ ㅎ ㅏ ㅑ ㅓ ㅕ ㅗ ㅛ ㅜ ㅠ ㅡ ㅣ
ㄲ ㄸ ㅃ ㅆ ㅉ ㅐ ㅒ ㅔ ㅖ ㅚ ㅟ ㅢ ㅘ ㅝ ㅙ ㅞ
ㄱ ㄴ ㄷ ㄹ ㅁ ㅂ ㅅ ㅇ ㅈ ㅊ ㅋ ㅌ ㅍ ㅎ ㅏ ㅑ ㅓ ㅕ ㅗ ㅛ ㅜ ㅠ ㅡ ㅣ
ㄲ ㄸ ㅃ ㅆ ㅉ ㅐ ㅒ ㅔ ㅖ ㅚ ㅟ ㅢ ㅘ ㅝ ㅙ ㅞ 1234567890(¶.,₱)
아 ㅂ ㅈ ㅉ ㄷ 에 ㄱ ㄲ ㅎ 이 ㅊ ㅋ ㅁ ㄴ ㅇ 오 ㅃ ㅍ ㄹ ㅅ ㅆ ㅌ 우
가 갸 거 계 고 교 구 규 그 각 간 갈 갓

NewHiPusan
LaserKorean
krnk
LSI
▲18

ㄱ ㄴ ㄷ ㄹ ㅁ ㅂ ㅅ ㅇ ㅈ ㅊ ㅋ ㅌ ㅍ ㅎ ㅏ ㅑ ㅓ ㅕ ㅗ ㅛ ㅜ ㅠ ㅡ ㅣ
ㄲ ㄸ ㅃ ㅆ ㅉ ㅐ ㅒ ㅔ ㅖ ㅚ ㅟ ㅢ ㅘ ㅝ ㅙ ㅞ
ㄱ ㄴ ㄷ ㄹ ㅁ ㅂ ㅅ ㅇ ㅈ ㅊ ㅋ ㅌ ㅍ ㅎ ㅏ ㅑ ㅓ ㅕ ㅗ ㅛ ㅜ ㅠ ㅡ ㅣ
ㄲ ㄸ ㅃ ㅆ ㅉ ㅐ ㅒ ㅔ ㅖ ㅚ ㅟ ㅢ ㅘ ㅝ ㅙ ㅞ 1234567890(¶.,₱)
아 ㅂ ㅈ ㅉ ㄷ 에 ㄱ ㄲ ㅎ 이 ㅊ ㅋ ㅁ ㄴ ㅇ 오 ㅃ ㅍ ㄹ ㅅ ㅆ ㅌ 우
가 갸 거 계 고 교 구 규 그 각 간 갈 갓

NewJeju
LaserKorean
krnk
LSI
▲18

ㄱ ㄴ ㄷ ㄹ ㅁ ㅂ ㅅ ㅇ ㅈ ㅊ ㅋ ㅌ ㅍ ㅎ ㅏ ㅑ ㅓ ㅕ ㅗ ㅛ ㅜ ㅠ ㅡ ㅣ
ㄲ ㄸ ㅃ ㅆ ㅉ ㅐ ㅒ ㅔ ㅖ ㅚ ㅟ ㅢ ㅘ ㅝ ㅙ ㅞ
ㄱ ㄴ ㄷ ㄹ ㅁ ㅂ ㅅ ㅇ ㅈ ㅊ ㅋ ㅌ ㅍ ㅎ ㅏ ㅑ ㅓ ㅕ ㅗ ㅛ ㅜ ㅠ ㅡ ㅣ
ㄲ ㄸ ㅃ ㅆ ㅉ ㅐ ㅒ ㅔ ㅖ ㅚ ㅟ ㅢ ㅘ ㅝ ㅙ ㅞ 1234567890(¶.,₱)
아 ㅂ ㅈ ㅉ ㄷ 에 ㄱ ㄲ ㅎ 이 ㅊ ㅋ ㅁ ㄴ ㅇ 오 ㅃ ㅍ ㄹ ㅅ ㅆ ㅌ 우
가 갸 거 계 고 교 구 규 그 각 간 갈 갓

• Hebrew
• Korean

NEW·SEOUL
LaserKorean
krnk
LSI
▲18

ㄱ ㄴ ㄷ ㄹ ㅁ ㅂ ㅅ ㅇ ㅈ ㅊ ㅋ ㅌ ㅍ ㅎ ㅏ ㅑ ㅓ ㅕ ㅗ ㅛ ㅜ ㅠ ㅡ ㅣ
ㄲ ㄸ ㅃ ㅆ ㅉ ㅐ ㅒ ㅔ ㅖ ㅚ ㅟ ㅢ ㅘ ㅝ ㅙ ㅞ
ㄱ ㄴ ㄷ ㄹ ㅁ ㅂ ㅅ ㅇ ㅈ ㅊ ㅋ ㅌ ㅍ ㅎ ㅏ ㅑ ㅓ ㅕ ㅗ ㅛ ㅜ ㅠ ㅡ ㅣ
ㄲ ㄸ ㅃ ㅆ ㅉ ㅐ ㅒ ㅔ ㅖ ㅚ ㅟ ㅢ ㅘ ㅝ ㅙ ㅞ 1234567890(¶.,₱)
아 ㅂ ㅈ ㅉ ㄷ 에 ㄱ ㄲ ㅎ 이 ㅊ ㅋ ㅁ ㄴ ㅇ 오 ㅃ ㅍ ㄹ ㅅ ㅆ ㅌ 우
가 갸 거 계 고 교 구 규 그 각 간 갈 갓

NewSeoul . . .

• Regular

아 ㅂ ㅈ ㅉ ㄷ 에 ㄱ ㄲ ㅎ 이 ㅊ ㅋ ㅁ ㄴ ㅇ 오 ㅃ ㅍ ㄹ ㅅ ㅆ ㅌ 우
가 갸 거 계 고 교 구 규 그 각 간 갈 갓

Oblique

아 ㅂ ㅈ ㅉ ㄷ 에 ㄱ ㄲ ㅎ 이 ㅊ ㅋ ㅁ ㄴ ㅇ 오 ㅃ ㅍ ㄹ ㅅ ㅆ ㅌ 우
가 갸 거 계 고 교 구 규 그 각 간 갈 갓

Designer I Collection: Acheneli Regular & Medium, Busoreli Regular & Bold, Careli Regular & Medium, Frizeli Regular & Bold, Gilgal Ultra Bold & Ultra Outline, Ivricana Bold & Outline, Kabelim Bold & Outline, Lublineli Condensed & Extra Bold Condensed, Optwo Regular & Bold, Revieie Regular & Heavy, Yaveneli Regular & Extra Bold.

LaserKorean: HiGwangJu, HiInchon, NewHiPusan, NewJeju, NewSeoul Regular, Oblique, Bold & Bold Oblique.

. . . NewSeoul

Bold 아 ㅂ ㅈ ㅉ ㄷ 에 ㄱ ㄲ ㅎ 이 ㅊ ㅋ ㅁ ㄴ ㅇ 오 ㅃ ㅍ ㄹ ㅅ ㅆ ㅌ 우
가 갸 거 계 고 교 구 규 그 각 간 갈 갓

Bold Oblique 아 ㅂ ㅈ ㅉ ㄷ 에 ㄱ ㄲ ㅎ 이 ㅊ ㅋ ㅁ ㄴ ㅇ 오 ㅃ ㅍ ㄹ ㅅ ㅆ ㅌ 우
가 갸 거 계 고 교 구 규 그 각 간 갈 갓

Note: *LaserKorean fonts are in single-byte data format for use with English language operating systems.*

궤

ㅌ

LaserKorean: HiGwangJu, HiInchon, NewHiPusan, NewJeju, NewSeoul Regular, Oblique, Bold & Bold Oblique.

- *Korean*

Interlude:

FONT FOUNDRY FOCUS

Information on type
and technology from:

Agfa

Bitstream

The Font Bureau

Galápagos
Design Group

International
Typeface
Corporation

Letraset

Linotype-Hell

Monotype
Typography

Red Rooster
Typefounders

DER
STEMPELSCHNEIDER

✍ Rudolf Koch, 1918

THE AGFATYPE
COLLECTION
HELPS YOU
FACE ANY
CHALLANGE!

...a good face is a letter

THERE IS SOMETHING IN A FACE AN AIR, AND A PECULIAR GRACE, WHICH BOLDEST PAINTERS CANNOT TRACE.
—WILLIAM SOMERVILLE

You look
rather rash
my dear your
colors dont
quite match
your face.

—Daisy Ashford
[Margaret Mary Norman]

I've got to take
under my wing, Tra la,
A most unattractive
old thing, Tra la,
With a caricature of a face.

—Sir William Gilbert, Gilbert & Sullivan, The Mikado

...FACES ARE BUT A GALLERY

In the beginning there was Bitstream

Founded in 1981 by a group of experienced typographic professionals, Bitstream® was the first independent digital type foundry. The term "independent" refers to the fact that the company has no ties to any device, platform, or environment. It was the philosophy of the founders that Bitstream would supply high-quality type to any hardware manufacturer or software developer, regardless of the varied, and often proprietary, technologies that existed in the marketplace.

The Bitstream Typeface Library has become one of the world's great sources of high-quality type for computer-based applications and output devices. In ten years it has grown into a collection of almost 1,100 typefaces offering variety, consistent high quality, and unparalleled typographic authenticity.

The Library is offered in PostScript® Type 1 format for the Macintosh® and IBM® PC platforms, and TrueType® format for Microsoft® Windows™ 3.1. In addition, the Library is currently being finalized in TrueType format for the Macintosh. Also, look for Bitstream to lead the industry in providing type in the newest font technologies, such as TrueType GX.

Building a high-quality type library

The Bitstream Typeface Library was developed under the supervision of Matthew Carter, the creator of such esteemed typefaces as ITC® Galliard,®2 Snell, ITC Charter,®2 and Swiss Compressed. Carter, who also served as Bitstream's Senior Vice President of Design, set uncommonly high standards for the company's highly-skilled design staff. Working from the earliest-generation artwork available, each character of every typeface is hand-digitized on advanced workstations. In building the library, Carter oversaw the licensing of typefaces from such respected international sources as the International Typeface Corporation (ITC), Kingsley-ATF Type Corporation, and Fundicion Tipografica Neufville SA, among others. Bitstream also commissions type designers to create new faces for the Library, such as Gerard Unger;

B
Shelley®3 Allegro

i
Staccato 222

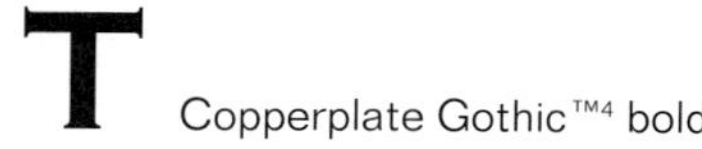
T
Copperplate Gothic™4 bold

S
Gando

t
Folio®5 bold

R

tReAm

ream

or to to oversee the digitization of their world-famous designs, such as Hermann Zapf. In addition, Bitstream's own design staff is always adding its own new designs to the Library. The result is an ever-growing Library, with new releases coming from an exciting variety of sources.

The result of the artist's work culminates as a Bitstream Definitive Outline. Definitive Outlines are the most precise definition of a typeface in the industry, up to five times the resolution of Ikarus or other popular type design processes. Using the Definitive Outlines as the basis for all other type formats is the key to Bitstream's consistent quality, allowing users the closest possible matches and more control of line and page breaks when working with type across platforms and devices.

Bitstream also supplies extensive kerning data for each typeface, and depending on the typeface, the format and the platform, Bitstream supplies the richest character sets available, including ligatures, accented characters, and symbols & dingbats.

Bitstream type on CD-ROM

Bitstream TypeShop™ is the entire Bitstream Typeface Library on an unlocked CD-ROM disc. TypeShop gives users total access to a comprehensive professional-quality type library in PostScript Type 1 format for Macintosh or Windows. Bitstream has also planned for the release of additional CD-ROM products in '95 featuring professional font collections and new typeface designs.

Tradition meets the cutting edge

Bitstream continues to set the pace in the typographic industry. With its innovative new portable font technology, Bitstream brings sophisticated typographic capabilities into the arena of electronic information media. At the same time Bitstream maintains its commitment to a tradition of high-quality font products for users of digital type.

Baskerville roman e Goudy Handtooled™4 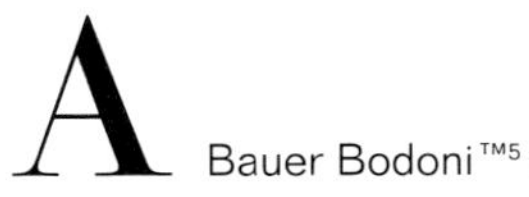 Bauer Bodoni™5 titling 2  Cataneo™1 light

Bitstream

The owners of trademarks and registered trademarks for the typeface names are designated by number and correlate to the following names: 1-Bitstream Inc. 2-International Typeface Corporation 3-Linotype AG and/or its subsidiaries 4-Kingsley ATF Type Corporation 5-Fundicion Tipographica Neufville SA.

IT'S H
IT'S DE

So, type has become a "commodity." That may be so, b
uing about it. We simply add the word "precious" to t
we're kind of, actually we're really picky, come to thin
developing, and the designers we work with. From "o
Jean Evans & David Berlow, to "young guns" like Tobi
"up-n-coming" student prodigies, Font Bureau selects
about how meticulously we design, produce and man
that's the only way we know. If we need better tools,
But most of all, we're snobs about who licenses our fa
you'll hardly need it, we care about good support. Tha

We are Delighted to have Pre
Supporting the Complete Fon

RE AND

AR!

: Font Bureau we're not likely to spend time arg-
ıbel and let it be. So with our precious commodity,
it, we're snobs. Snobs about the faces we spend time
:os" like John Benson, Richard Lipton, John Downer,
rere-Jones, Matthew Butterick, Jill Pichotta, and our
best text and display type available. We're snobs
ture our type. No time or expense is spared in this,
et them. If we see better technologies, we use them.
:o you. We care about good service, and though
vhy we licensed our whole library to Precision Type.

ion Type Marketing &
Bureau Retail Library!

FONT BUREAU

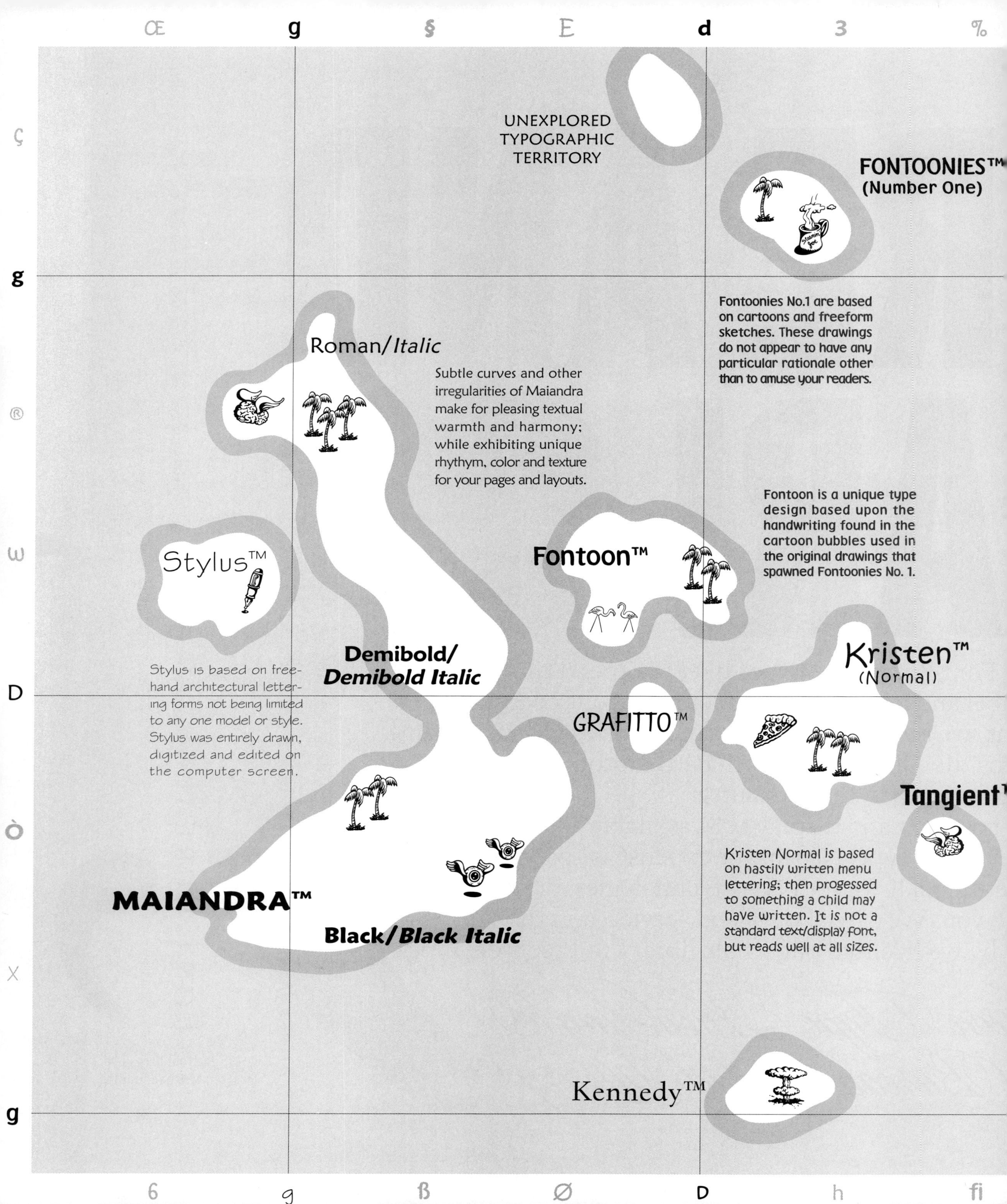
Œ
g
§
E
d
3
%
Ç
g
®
ω
D
Ò
X
g
6
g
ß
Ø
D
h
fi
UNEXPLORED
TYPOGRAPHIC
TERRITORY
FONTOONIES™
(Number One)
Fontoonies No.1 are based on cartoons and freeform sketches. These drawings do not appear to have any particular rationale other than to amuse your readers.
Roman/Italic
Subtle curves and other irregularities of Maiandra make for pleasing textual warmth and harmony; while exhibiting unique rhythym, color and texture for your pages and layouts.
Fontoon is a unique type design based upon the handwriting found in the cartoon bubbles used in the original drawings that spawned Fontoonies No. 1.
Stylus™
Fontoon™
Kristen™
(Normal)
Demibold/
Demibold Italic
Stylus is based on free-hand architectural lettering forms not being limited to any one model or style. Stylus was entirely drawn, digitized and edited on the computer screen.
GRAFITTO™
Tangient
Kristen Normal is based on hastily written menu lettering; then progessed to something a child may have written. It is not a standard text/display font, but reads well at all sizes.
MAIANDRA™
Black/Black Italic
Kennedy™

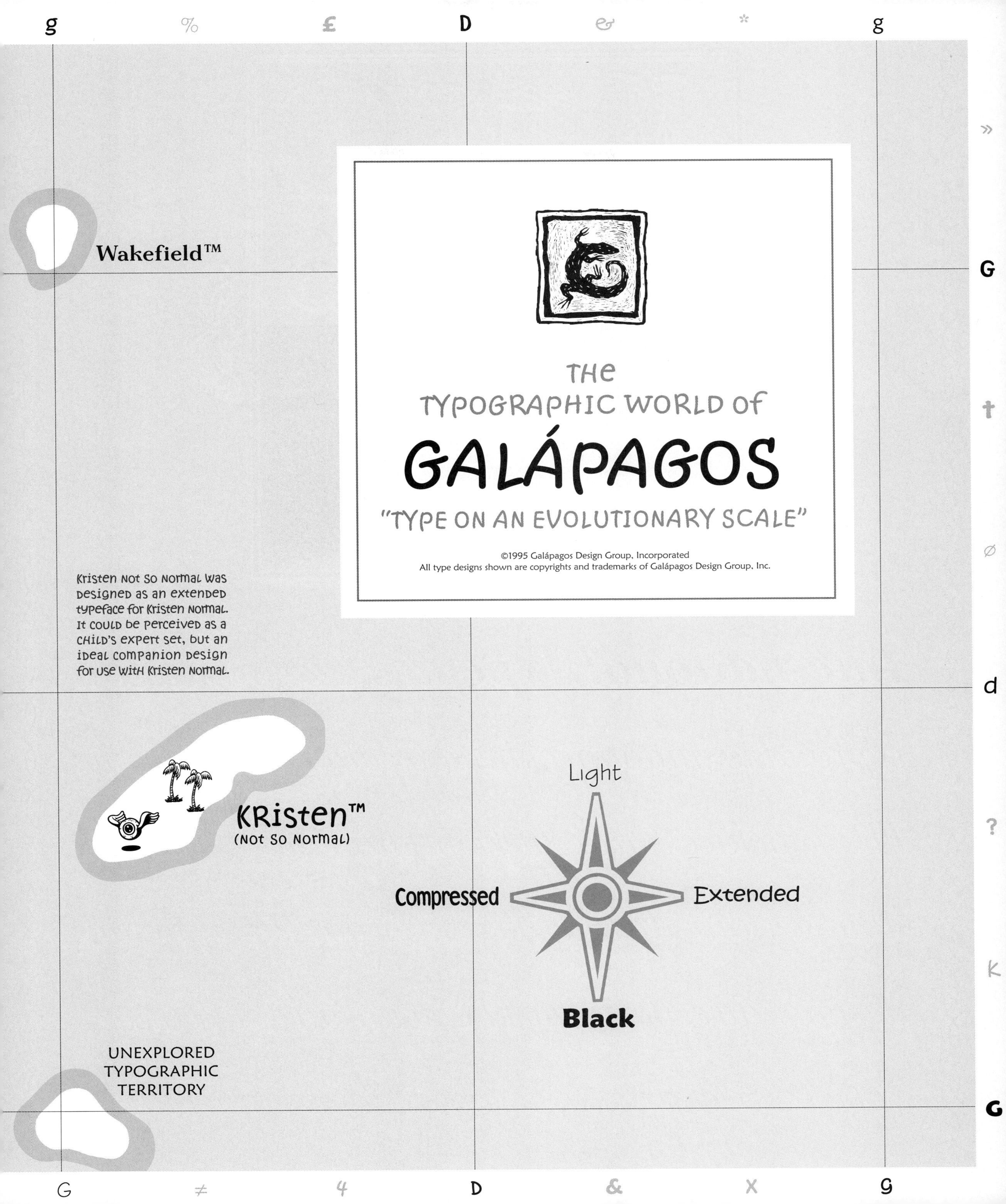

g
%
£
D
&
*
g
Wakefield™
THE
TYPOGRAPHIC WORLD OF
GALÁPAGOS
"TYPE ON AN EVOLUTIONARY SCALE"
©1995 Galápagos Design Group, Incorporated
All type designs shown are copyrights and trademarks of Galápagos Design Group, Inc.
Kristen Not So Normal was designed as an extended typeface for Kristen Normal. It could be perceived as a child's expert set, but an ideal companion design for use with Kristen Normal.
Kristen™
(Not So Normal)
Light
Compressed
Extended
Black
UNEXPLORED
TYPOGRAPHIC
TERRITORY
»
G
t
ø
d
?
k
G
G
≠
4
D
&
X
g

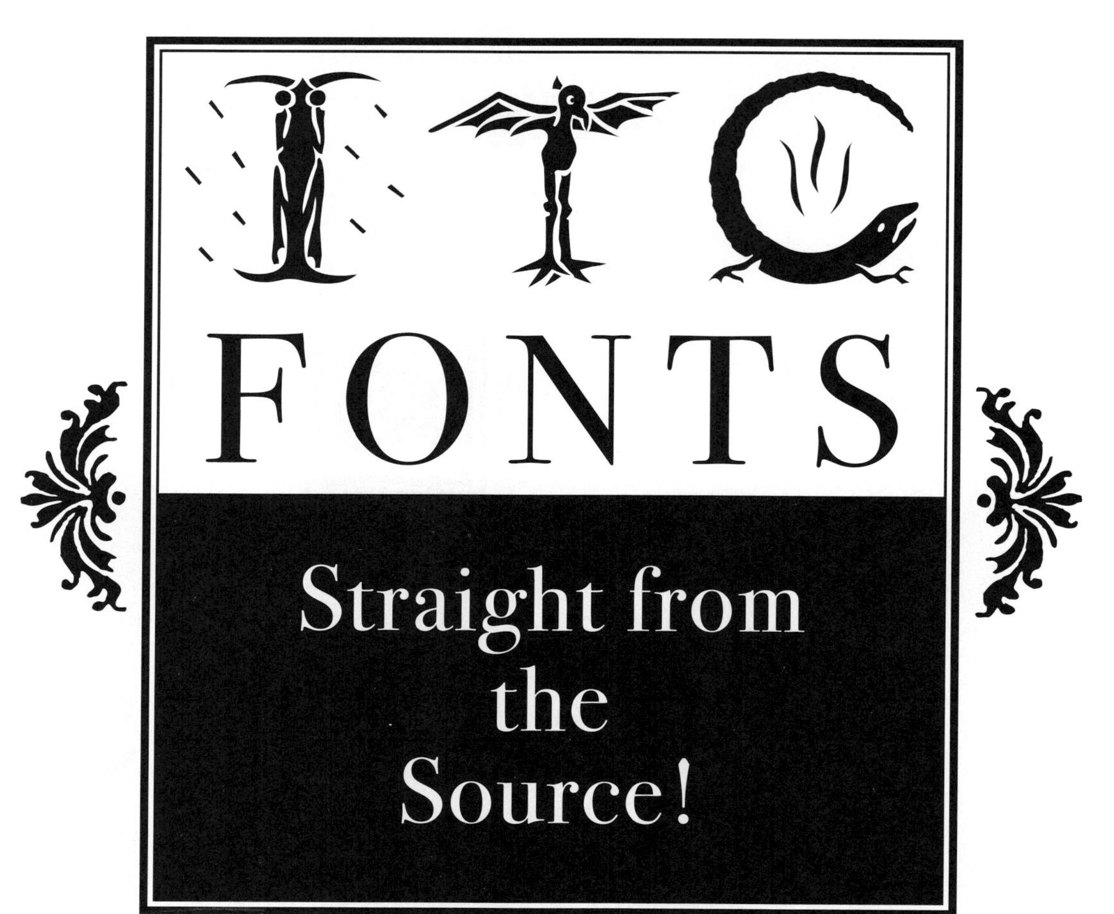
ITC
FONTS
Straight from the Source!

International Typeface Corporation

is proud to announce the availability of our own ITC typefaces straight from the source. You can now get our distinctive, high-quality typeface designs directly from ITC with all the features you'd expect from us at no extra cost, including:

- Oldstyle figures and small caps
- Superior spacing and kerning with up to 1,000 kerning pairs
- Complete character complements, including ligatures, accents and symbols

We at ITC are committed to offering you the highest quality designs from the top typeface designers in the field, such as Matthew Carter, Sumner Stone, Erik Spiekermann, Ed Benguiat and Daniel Pelavin. Every new ITC typeface will be available directly from us, as well as a selection of ITC designs from our existing library. Since our inception in 1969, ITC has been responsible for the creation and refinement of more than 650 typeface designs. The ITC typeface library is a growing resource: new designs are released on a regular basis. ITC works with type designers around the world to create new and original typefaces. While these new designs fill a variety of stylistic categories, every ITC typeface is an endeavor that satisfies today's market and communication needs. ITC was originally formed to meet the new challenges and opportunities of phototypesetting. Now, as then, we seek to work with and reward established type designers, as well as to encourage new talent entering the field. Our goal has always been to produce typefaces of the highest quality using the most advanced technology available. Our firm commitment to excellence in typeface design remains steadfast. One of our best-known vehicles for marketing these designs is *U&lc*® (Upper & Lower Case, the International Journal of Graphic Design and Digital Media) launched in 1974, and reaching more than 110,000 type users and specifiers. Each new ITC typeface release is showcased in *U&lc*. The Journal's award winning editorial and typographic design appeals to communicators on every level, making *U&lc* one of the best-known and influential design publications in the field. ITC

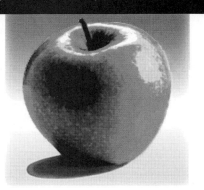

Here's our pick of the crop.

Academy™ Engraved
Aquinas™
Arriba™
Arriba-Arriba™
ARTISTE™
BANG™
Belwe™ Mono
Belwe™ Mono Italic
Bendigo™
Berzell™
BERTRAM™
Bickley™ Script
BITMAX™
Bordeaux™ Roman Bold
Champers™
CITATION™
Claude™ Sans Bold Italic
Coptek™
Digitek™
EMPHASIS™
EPOKHA™
FAITHFUL FLY™
Fashion™ Engraved
Flamme™
FOLLIES™
Greyton™ Script
HAND DRAWN
HARVEY™
HAZEL™
Heliotype™
Indy™ Italic
Informal™ Roman
ISIS™
Jazz™
KANBAN™
Klee™
La Bamba™
Lambada™
Laura™
Lexikos™
Lightnin™
Lino Cut™
Malibu™
Marguerita™
MO' FUNKY FRESH™
Party™
PNEUMA™
PRAGUE™
Pristina™
PITCHARD™
Pitchard™ Line Out
QUADRUS™
Quixley™

Rapier™
RETRO™ BOLD
RETRO™ BOLD CONDENSED
Robotik™
Robotik™ Italic
ROXY™
Ru'ach™
Savoye™
SCRIBA™
Scriptek™
Scriptek™ Italic
SHAMAN™
SKID ROW™
Spotlight™
STROBOS™
TAG™
Teknik™
Tiger Rag™
Tiranti™ Solid
Ulysses™
Varga™
VIENNA™ EXTENDED
Wade™ Sans Light
Westwood™
WILLOW™

And this season's harvest!

Chipper™
Dancin™
Etruscan™
Flight™
Fling™
frances uncial™
Gravura™
John Handy™
Pablo™
Pink™
Scratch™
Scruff™
Twang™
Wanted™
Xylo™

TYPOGRAPERS AND DESIGNERS EVERYWHERE ARE TALKING ABOUT AN EXCITING NEW FONT TECHNOLOGY: GX. APPLE COMPUTER'S NEW QUICKDRAW™ GX TECHNOLOGY OFFERS SOME OF THE RICHEST AND MOST FUNCTIONAL FONTS EVER CREATED. WITH MANY HIGHLY AUTOMATED FEATURES, GX FONTS ARE "SMART," TOO. UNLIKE EXISTING

Join the GX Revolution

FONTS, A GX FONT IS NOT MERELY A COLLECTION OF POINTS THAT DEFINE A CHARACTER OUTLINE. IT CAN HAVE OVER 20 BUILT-IN TYPOGRAPHIC FEATURES. HERE ARE JUST A FEW EXAMPLES:

- **Alternate and swash characters**
- **Ligature sets with automatic insertion capabilities**
- **True drawn small caps (not mathematically altered)**
- **Cap and lowercase numbers**
- **True drawn superior and inferior numbers (not mathematically altered)**
- **Optical edge alignment**
- **Hanging punctuation**
- **Extensive kerning and tracking capabilities**

How can you put GX to work?

- **Choose from extended character sets.**

fi	fi
fl	fl
ft	ft
ff	ff
ffi	ffi
ffl	ffl
fft	fft

Over the centuries, designers have created many additional symbols to improve the readability and attractiveness of documents. Specially designed numerals, fractions, small capitals, decorative initials, ornaments, ligatures, swash and special word endings are just a few examples. Until now, these diverse and versatile characters were not readily available in digital fonts. Designers had to combine alternate symbols from many different font sets. GX restores the ability to build rich, typographically complex fonts.

A GX font can contain thousands of characters. Therefore, the substitution of alternate character forms is as simple as turning a feature on or off via a special menu. It's that easy!

- **Save time.**

One of the most powerful aspects of QuickDraw GX is that the font is electronically embedded within the document so the font information is portable. Embedded fonts make is easy to share document files for viewing and editing, and they provide enhanced communication between the designer and the service bureau.

Lowercase

TO SMALL CAPS

Instantly!

Linotype-Hell

Create refined typography

Sophisticated features give you much greater typographical control. Not only can you improve the quality of your designs, but you can do it automatically. Refined kerning and tracking, optical alignment, and automatic ligature insertion are now simple choices from a pull-down menu. Tracking and kerning can also be adjusted via a simple slider bar, and the users of the Linotype-Hell GX fonts can be confident that kerning values are always perfectly adjusted to the tracking parameters, assuring an even typographic color and maximum levels of readability.

With GX, you can easily transform lowercase letters into true small caps. Or you can experiment by substituting initials with alternate characters. Even the use of superior and inferior numbers and characters is automated. And with some GX fonts you can even structure various weights and proportions of a typestyle. As with Multiple Masters technology, these new master designs can then be used to generate a wide variety of fonts from one typeface while assuring the integrity and readability of the letterforms.

1 2 3 4 5

6 7 8 9 0

GX Core Set CD-ROM

QuickDraw GX supports all existing Macintosh® faces in PostScript™ Type 1 as well as TrueType™ formats, but the extensive typographic functionality which has been incorporated into QuickDraw GX will only work in combination with the new GX fonts and within a GX-savvy application. Linotype-Hell has taken the lead in developing a GX typeface library. The first of these are now available on our GX Core Set CD-ROM, which contains 34 typefaces, including Courier, Helvetica®, Palatino®, ITC Avant Garde Gothic®, ITC Bookman®, New Century Schoolbook™, Times®, ITC Zapf Chancery® and ITC Zapf Dingbats®.

For those not currently working with a GX-savvy application, the CD contains 89 additional fonts that allow users to access extended character sets including Small Caps, Old Style Figures and Expert Sets. These fonts provide an exciting insight into the capabilities of QuickDraw GX and Linotype-Hell's GX fonts.

Tracking
T r a c k i n g
T r a c k i n g

Variation
Variation
Variation

All GX fonts have automatic tracking, which can be easily adjusted using a slider bar. With certain fonts, width and weight can also be adjusted.

The Linotype Library™

GX font development represents our on-going commitment to typographic excellence. For more than 100 years, Linotype-Hell has developed, produced and marketed typefaces which meet the highest standards of quality. The result of these efforts is the world-famous Linotype Library—a collection of more than 2,000 typefaces.

Linotype
LIBRARY

MONOTYPE®

The one word in type

Since 1897, Monotype has been the recognized leader in creating the world's most important typefaces. Since the invention of the original Monotype Type Caster and keyboard, to the first laser typesetters, to PostScript™ &TrueType™ formats, Monotype has evolved its world famous type library with unsurpassed typographic excellence.

A Monotype keyboard circa 1900.

Monotype typefaces have evolved from hot metal, to photo, to digital typesetting formats.

Monotype fonts have been selected for licensing by leading computer, printer, and software companies, and can be found in Apple & HP printers, Windows 3.1, and the Adobe Type Library. Monotype's license with Adobe allows Monotype to sell the Adobe Type Library, in its entirety, as well.

Monotype has facilities in England, USA, and Hong Kong where a staff of typographic experts and talented software engineers are committed to developing the finest crafted typefaces while embracing technological innovation.

MONOTYPE

Headline set in 48 point Dante Titling. Subheads set in 18 point Gill Sans Heavy. Text set in 8, 12 and 14 point Gill Sans Book.

Monotype Delivers on Floppy Disk and CD ROM

2
Monotype CD 4.0

Monotype CD 4.0

- Unrivaled user interface for buying and selecting fonts
  "The best font CD ROM"
- Easy, affordable, and quick
  Unlock fonts in minutes directly from Precision Type
- Cross-platform compatible for Mac & Windows
- The most complete font CD available
  Over 3400 fonts
  Includes the entire Adobe Type Library
  Clip art images
  Font utilities and software

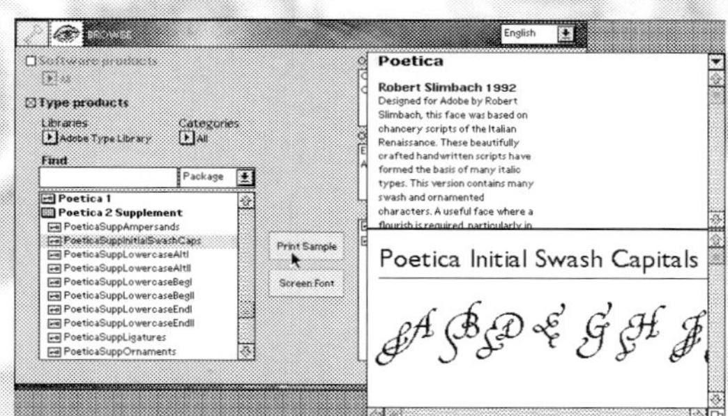

Poetica
Robert Slimbach 1992
Type products
Libraries
Adobe Type Library
Categories
All
Find
Package
Poetica 1
Poetica 2 Supplement
Print Sample
Screen Font
Poetica Initial Swash Capitals

Monotype leads the pack with a user-friendly unlocking and browsing interface.

Monotype Classic Fonts™

- New, cutting edge font development
- Classic typeface revivals
- Expert sets for the highest quality typography

OCEAN · SANS

A Two-Axis Multiple Master Typeface from Monotype Typography

ijklmnopqrs
qrstuvwxyzabcdefghijklm
klmnopqrstuvwxyabcdefghijklm
vwxyzabcdefghijklmnopqrst
defghijklmnopqrstuvwxyzab
hijklmnopqrstuvwxyzabcdefgi
qrstuvwxyzabcdefghijklmnopqrstuv
lmnopqrstuvwxyzabcdefghijklmnopqrstuvwxyzabc
bcdefghijklmnopqrstuvwxyzabcdefghijklmnopqrstuvwxyzabcdefghijklmn
vwxyzabcdefghijklmnopqrstuvwxyzabcdefghijklmnopqrstuvwxyzabcdefghij
qrstuvwxyzabcdefghijklmnopqrstuvwxyzabcdefghijklmnopqrstuvwxyzab

MONOTYPE PRESENTS

Bulmer

Based on the types cut by
William Martin
and used by the printer
William Bulmer

Recent new releases from Monotype include Ocean Sans, a multiple master typeface, and Bulmer, a revival of a late 18th century favorite.

Adobe™ Type Library

- Monotype is the preferred source for Adobe fonts
- Available on CD or Floppy Disk

Type Designers of the World™

- 21 cutting-edge foundries represented including:
  The Font Bureau
  Letter Perfect
  TreacyFaces – and many more!

Administer. Alexon. Alys Script.
Appleyard. Argus. BASSUTO.
Beckenham. Bellini. Badger. Block Gothic.
Byron. Cameo. Canterbury Old Style. Chelsea.
Claremont. Coliseum. COMMANDER. Consort.
Dundee. ELSTON. Equestrienne.
Erasmus. Europa Grotesk. Extension.
Faust. FORUM TITLING.
GILMORE FAHREHHEIT. GILMORE SANS.
Goudy 38. Grove Script. Hancock.
Hess Old Style. HONDURAS.
Javelin. Jubilee. Keyboard. Kingsrow.
Leighton. Lesmore. Pall Mall.
PHOSPHATE. Portobello. QUEST.
RALEIGH GOTHIC. Ribbit. RIVOLI INITIALS.
Saint Louis. Schiller Antiqua. Schindler.

Shinn. Silverado. Sinclair Script.
Sphinx. Stanhope.
Stirling. SYCAMORE. Superba. Titanic.
Veronese. Waverly.

These are the type families from our nearly 300 fonts that have been selected and exclusively licensed from the original designers and foundries, many of them brand-spanking new. (You'll find them all in this Reference Guide.)

Each character is hand digitized and edited to reflect the integrity of the original design. The letterfit on each font is meticulously perfected, and then several thousand hand-tuned kerning pairs are applied.

Every Red Rooster font has a complete character complement that includes European and Scandinavian character sets.

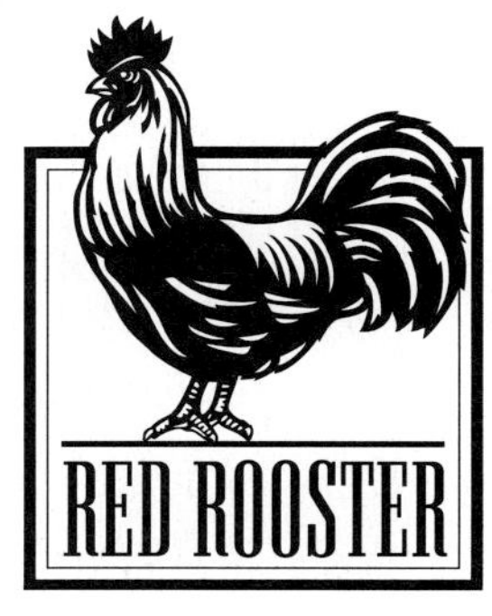
RED ROOSTER

Section Two:

Font Foundry Reference

ff

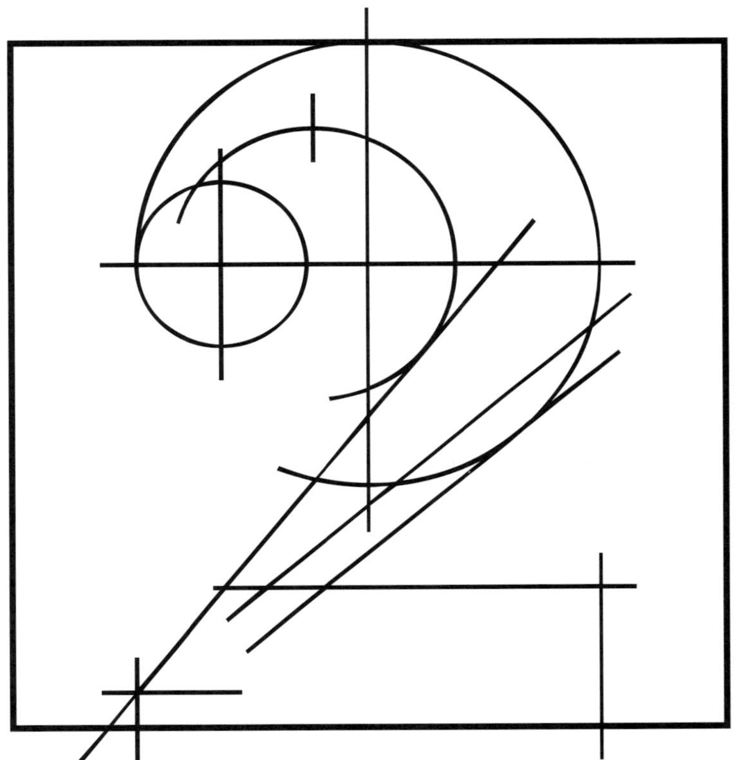

✍ Noel Rubin, 1994

ff

ff

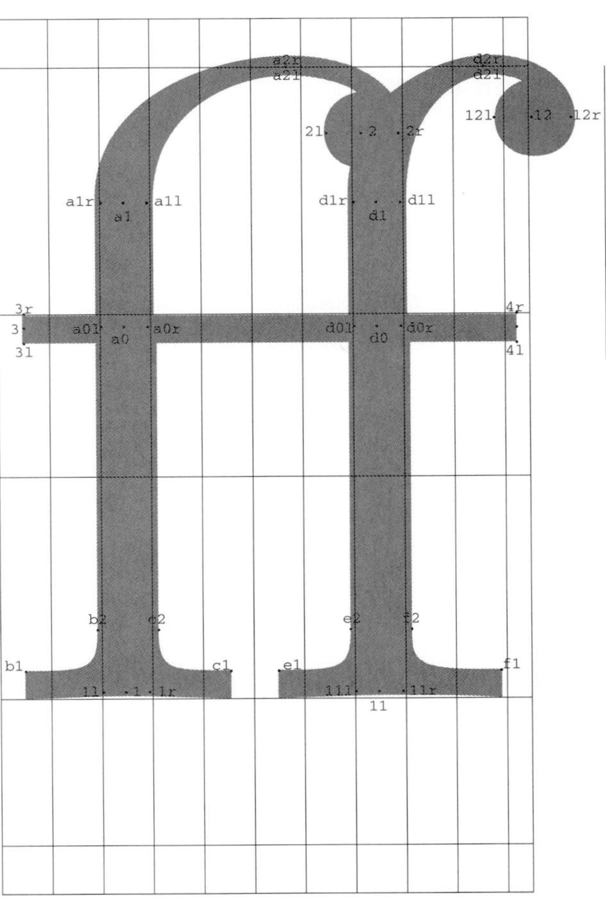
a2r
a2l
d2r
d2l
2l
2
2r
12l
12
12r
a1r
a1
a1l
d1r
d1
d1l
3r
3
3l
a0l
a0
a0r
d0l
d0
d0r
4r
4l
b2
c2
e2
f2
b1
c1
e1
f1
1l
1
1r
11l
11
11r

✍ Donald Knuth, 1982

G :Monotype Typography

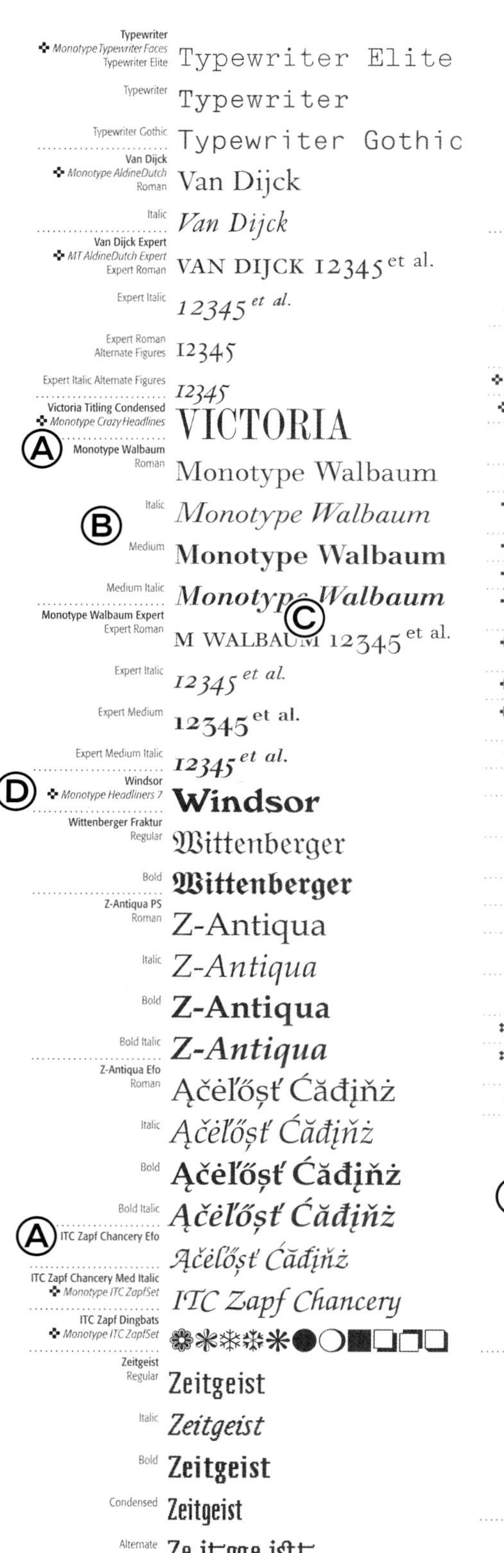
Typewriter
Monotype Typewriter Faces
Typewriter Elite
Typewriter Elite
Typewriter
Typewriter
Typewriter Gothic
Typewriter Gothic
Van Dijck
Monotype AldineDutch
Roman
Van Dijck
Italic
Van Dijck
Van Dijck Expert
MT AldineDutch Expert
Expert Roman
VAN DIJCK 12345 et al.
Expert Italic
12345 et al.
Expert Roman Alternate Figures
12345
Expert Italic Alternate Figures
12345
Victoria Titling Condensed
Monotype Crazy Headlines
VICTORIA
A
Monotype Walbaum
Roman
Monotype Walbaum
Italic
Monotype Walbaum
B
Medium
Monotype Walbaum
Medium Italic
Monotype Walbaum
C
Monotype Walbaum Expert
Expert Roman
M WALBAUM 12345 et al.
Expert Italic
12345 et al.
Expert Medium
12345 et al.
Expert Medium Italic
12345 et al.
D
Windsor
Monotype Headliners 7
Windsor
Wittenberger Fraktur
Regular
Wittenberger
Bold
Wittenberger
Z-Antiqua PS
Roman
Z-Antiqua
Italic
Z-Antiqua
Bold
Z-Antiqua
Bold Italic
Z-Antiqua
Z-Antiqua Efo
Roman
Ąčėľőșť Ćăđįňż
Italic
Ąčėľőșť Ćăđįňż
Bold
Ąčėľőșť Ćăđįňż
Bold Italic
Ąčėľőșť Ćăđįňż
A
ITC Zapf Chancery Efo
Ąčėľőșť Ćăđįňż
ITC Zapf Chancery Med Italic
Monotype ITC ZapfSet
ITC Zapf Chancery
ITC Zapf Dingbats
Monotype ITC ZapfSet
Zeitgeist
Regular
Zeitgeist
Italic
Zeitgeist
Bold
Zeitgeist
Condensed
Zeitgeist
Alternate
Zeitgeist
Crazy Paving
Zeitgeist

. . . Zeitgeist
Cameo & Cameo Expert
Zeitgeist 12345 et al.
Expert Regular
ZEITGEIST 12345 et al.
Expert Italic
12345 et al.
Expert Bold
12345 et al.
Expert Condensed
12345 et al.
Monotype Typography Multi-Font Package Contents
Monotype AldineDutch : Poliphilus Roman & Blado Italic, Van Dijck Roman & Italic.
Monotype AldineDutch Expert : Poliphilus Expert Roman & Blado Expert Italic, Van Dijck Expert Roman & Italic.
Monotype Bodoni & Onyx : Bodoni Book, Book Italic, Ultra Bold, Ultra Bold Italic, MT Onyx.
Monotype Classic Titling : Felix Titling, Perpetua Titling Light, Regular & Bold.
Monotype Crazy Headlines : Festival Titling, Kino, Matura Regular & Scriptorial Capitals, Victoria Titling Condensed.
Monotype Handtooled : Colonna, Imprint Shadow Roman & Italic.
Monotype Headliners 1 : Monotype Clarendon, Monotype New Clarendon Roman & Bold, Monotype Egyptian 72 Extended.
Monotype Headliners 2 : Falstaff, Headline Bold, Placard Condensed & Bold Condensed.
Monotype Headliners 3 : Braggadocio, Klang, Figaro, Forte.
Monotype Headliners 4 : Inflex Bold, Monotype Old English Text, Monotype Old Style Bold Outline.
Monotype Headliners 5 : Monotype Bernard Condensed, Compacta Bold, Neographik, Monotype Runic Condensed.
Monotype Headliners 6 : Albertus Light, Regular & Italic, Castellar.
Monotype Headliners 7 : Binner Gothic, Monotype Franklin Gothic Extra Condensed, Monotype Lightline Gothic, Windsor.
Monotype ITC ZapfSet : ITC Zapf Chancery PS Medium Italic, ITC Zapf Dingbats PS.
Monotype PlusSet 6 : Corsiva & Monotype Sorts.
Monotype Scripts 1 : Biffo Script, Dorchester Script, Pepita, Monotype Script Bold, Swing Bold.
Monotype Scripts 2 : Ashley Script, Monoline Script, New Berolina, Palace Script Regular & Semibold.
Monotype Scripts 3 : Coronet Bold & Mercurius Script.
Monotype Scripts 4 : Script, Commercial Script, French Script.
E
Monotype TextSet 1 : Monotype Goudy Modern Roman & Italic, Monotype Scotch Roman & Italic.
Monotype Typewriter Faces : Monotype Courier 12, Typewriter, Typewriter Elite, Typewriter Gothic.
Monotype DisplaySet 2 : Falstaff, Inflex Bold, Monotype Old Style Bold Outline.
Monotype DisplaySet 4 : Monotype Latin Condensed, Monotype Onyx, Monotype Runic Condensed.
Monotype ScriptSet 3 : Forte, Klang, Mercurius Script.

(F) Monotype Type Designers of the World

foundry: abcdesign

Bijoux
Light Bijoux
Regular Bijoux
Bold Bijoux

Jeunesse
Regular Jeunesse
Italic Jeunesse
Medium Jeunesse
Bold Jeunesse

Jeunesse Sans
Regular Jeunessse
Italic Jeunessse

Font Displays & Information

(A) Font.Family Package Name or Individual Font Name
Identifier for a group of fonts as configured for sale or, identifier for an Individual Font only available in the version shown and/or sold separately.

(B) Font Names
Names for each font in a Font.Family Package identifying the style/weight/width, etc.

(C) One-Line Font Display
Usually, the display is the name of the font. Set with Small Capitals, in all caps, or with swash characters, alternates or other variants where appropriate. (OSF font displays show the Oldstyle Figures rather than repeating the font name.) For those fonts that do not contain the characters necessary to set the font name, a representative character sample is shown.

(D) Multi-Font Package Name
Identifier for a font package that contains two or more individual fonts of different design and/or style. Other fonts in the Multi-Font Package are shown in correct alphabetical order in each foundry's font displays.

(E) Multi-Font Package Contents
The names and complete contents for each foundry's Multi-Font Packages. This listing (when appropriate) will always be found at the end of a foundry's font displays.

Key to Section Two

(F) Additional Font Collections
Some foundries distribute the products of other company's as well as their own. These collections are shown after the font displays of the principal foundry.

(G) Page Contents by Foundry
The name of the foundries whose fonts are displayed on each page.

Symbols & Abbreviations

Multi-Font Package
A font package that contains two or more individual fonts of different design and/or style. Complete contents of Multi-FontPackages are detailed at the end of the font displays for every foundry.

Font display is continued in the next column or on the facing page.

Font display is continued on the following page.

Font display is continued from the preceding page.

MM
MultipleMaster fonts.

SC
Small Capitals character set.

OSF
Oldstyle Figures character set.*

SCOSF
Small Capitals and Oldstyle Figures character set.*

SC&OSF
Small Capitals & Oldstyle Figures character set.

SCLF
Small Capitals and Lining Figures character set.

SCSLF
Small Capitals and Small Lining Figures character set.

SD
Short Descenders.

SA/D
Short Ascenders and Descenders.

Dfr
Dfr (DeutschFraktur) character set.*

*see page xv for examples

foundry: Adobe Systems

The Adobe Type Library offers one of the world's broadest selections of PostScript Type1 fonts including licensed designs from Agfa, Berthold, International Typeface Corporation (ITC), Fundición Tipográfica Neufville, Letraset, Linotype-Hell, Monotype, Nebiolo, Simoncini and Stevenson Blake. ¶ Adobe's own type development program – *Adobe Originals* – is producing a growing collection of fonts that includes contemporary, new type designs as well as revivals of classics from the past.

Aachen Bold — ✤ *Adobe DisplaySet 1* — Aachen

AG Old Face
- Regular — AG Old Face
- Medium — AG Old Face
- Bold — AG Old Face
- Shaded — AG Old Face
- Outline — AG Old Face
- Bold Outline — AG Old Face

AG Old Face Shaded — ✤ *Berthold DisplaySet 1* — AG Old Face

AG Book Stencil — ✤ *Berthold DisplaySet 1* — AG Book

AG Book Rounded
- Regular — AG Book Rounded
- Medium — AG Book Rounded
- Bold — AG BookRounded
- Bold Condensed — AG Book Rounded
- Medium Outline — AG Book Round
- Bold Outline — AG Book Round
- Bold Condensed Outline — AG Book Rounded

AG Schoolbook
- Regular — AG Schoolbook
- Medium — AG Schoolbook
- Regular Alternate — kßtuyGIJKMR
- Medium Alternate — kßtuyGIJKMR

Berthold Akzidenz Grotesk 1
- Light — Akzidenz Grotesk
- Light OSF — osf 12345...
- Regular — Akzidenz Grotesk
- Italic — Akzidenz Grotesk
- Medium — Akzidenz Grotesk
- Medium Italic — Akzidenz Grotesk
- Bold — Akzidenz Grotesk

...Berthold Akzidenz Grotesk 1
- Bold Italic — Akzidenz Grot
- Super — Akzidenz Grot

Berthold Akzidenz Grotesk 2
- Light Condensed — Akzidenz Grotesk
- Condensed — Akzidenz Grotesk
- Medium Condensed — Akzidenz Grotesk
- Medium Condensed Italic — Akzidenz Grotesk
- Bold Condensed — Akzidenz Grotesk
- Extra Bold Condensed — Akzidenz Grotesk
- Extra Bold Condensed Italic — Akzidenz Grotesk
- Extra Bold — Akzidenz Grotesk

Berthold Akzidenz Grotesk Extended
- Light Extended — Akzidenz Grot
- Extended — Akzidenz Grot
- Medium Extended — Akzidenz Grot
- Bold Extended — Akzidenz
- Bold Extended Italic — Akzidenz

Albertus — ✤ *Monotype DisplaySet 1*
- Light — Albertus
- Regular — Albertus
- Italic — Albertus

Aldus + SCOSF
- Roman — Aldus
- Italic — Aldus
- Roman SCOSF — ALDUS 12345...
- Italic OSF — osf 12345...

ITC American Typewriter
- Light — ITC American
- Medium — ITC American
- Bold — ITC American
- Alternates — eR$& eR$& eR$&
- Light Condensed — ITC American Type
- Condensed — ITC American Type
- Bold Condensed — ITC American Type
- Condensed Alternates — eR$& eR$& eR$&

Americana
- Roman — Americana
- Italic — Americana
- Bold — Americana
- Extra Bold — Americana

Amigo — ✤ *Baker Calligraphy* — Amigo

ITC Anna — ✤ *ITC Typographica* — ITC ANNA

Antique Olive 1
- Light — Antique Olive

...Antique Olive 1
- Regular — Antique Olive
- Italic — Antique Olive
- Bold — Antique Olive
- Black — Antique Olive

Antique Olive 2
- Bold Condensed — Antique Olive
- Compact — Antique Olive
- Nord — Antique
- Nord Italic — Antique

Apollo + Expert & SCOSF
- Roman — Apollo
- Italic — Apollo
- Semibold — Apollo
- Expert Roman — APOLLO 12345 et al.
- Expert Italic — 12345 et al.
- Expert Semibold — 12345 et al.
- Roman SCOSF — APOLLO 12345...
- Italic OSF — osf 12345...
- Semibold OSF — osf 12345...

Arcadia — ✤ *Brody DisplaySet 1*
- Regular & Alternate — Arcadia bdhpq

Ariadne — ✤ *GudrunSchrift* — ARIADNE

Arnold Böcklin — ✤ *Linotype DisplaySet 1* — Arnold Böcklin

Ashley Script — ✤ *Monotype ScriptSet 1* — Ashley Script

New Aster
- Roman — New Aster
- Italic — New Aster
- Semibold — New Aster
- Semibold Italic — New Aster
- Bold — New Aster
- Bold Italic — New Aster
- Black — New Aster
- Black Italic — New Aster

Linotype Astrology Pi
- One — ♈ ♉ ♊ ♋ ♌ ♍ ♎ ♏
- Two — [pictorial zodiac symbols]

Linotype Audio Pi — ✤ *Linotype PiSet 1* — [audio logo symbols: ARD, WEST 3, CD, hr, etc.]

Auriol
- Regular — Auriol
- Italic — Auriol
- Bold — Auriol
- Bold Italic — Auriol
- Black — Auriol

ff

✤ *See page 522 for contents of Adobe Systems Multi-Font Packages.*

… Auriol
Black Italic *Auriol*

ITC Avant Garde Gothic 1
Book ITC Avant Garde
Book Oblique *ITC Avant Garde*
Demi **ITC Avant Garde**
Demi Oblique ***ITC Avant Garde***

ITC Avant Garde Gothic 2
Extra Light ITC Avant Garde
Extra Light Oblique *ITC Avant Garde*
Medium ITC Avant Garde
Medium Oblique *ITC Avant Garde*
Bold **ITC Avant Garde**
Bold Oblique ***ITC Avant Garde***

ITC Avant Garde Gothic Condensed
Book Condensed ITC Avant Garde
Medium Condensed ITC Avant Garde
Demi Condensed **ITC Avant Garde**
Bold Condensed **ITC Avant Garde**

ITC Avant Garde Gothic MM
Extra Light ITC Avant Garde
Extra Light Oblique *ITC Avant Garde*
Light ITC Avant Garde
Light Oblique *ITC Avant Garde*
Regular ITC Avant Garde
Regular Oblique *ITC Avant Garde*
Semibold **ITC Avant Garde**
Semibold Oblique ***ITC Avant Garde***
Bold **ITC Avant Garde**
Bold Oblique ***ITC Avant Garde***
Extra Light Condensed ITC Avant Garde Gothic
Extra Light Condensed Oblique *ITC Avant Garde Gothic*
Light Condensed ITC Avant Garde
Light Condensed Oblique *ITC Avant Garde*
Condensed ITC Avant Garde
Condensed Oblique *ITC Avant Garde*
Semibold Condensed **ITC Avant Garde**
Semibold Condensed Oblique ***ITC Avant Garde***
Bold Condensed **ITC Avant Garde**
Bold Condensed Oblique ***ITC Avant Garde***

Avenir 1
35-Light Avenir
35-Light Oblique *Avenir*
55-Regular Avenir
55-Oblique *Avenir*
85-Heavy **Avenir**
85-Heavy Oblique ***Avenir***

Avenir 2
45-Book Avenir
45-Book Oblique *Avenir*
65-Medium Avenir
65-Medium Oblique *Avenir*
95-Black **Avenir**
95-Black Oblique ***Avenir***

Baker Signet
✤ *Adobe DisplaySet 2* Baker Signet

Banco
✤ *Linotype DisplaySet 2* **BANCO**

Barmeno
Regular Barmeno
Medium Barmeno
Bold **Barmeno**
Extra Bold **Barmeno**

Barmeno Extra Bold
✤ *Berthold DisplaySet 1* **Barmeno**

ITC New Baskerville
Roman ITC NewBaskerville
Italic *ITC New Baskerville*
Bold **ITC New Baskervill**
Bold Italic ***ITC New Baskerville***

ITC New Baskerville SCOSF
Roman SCOSF ITC NEW BASKER
Italic OSF *osf 12345…*
Bold SCOSF **ITC NEW BASKER**
Bold Italic OSF ***osf 12345…***

Berthold Baskerville
Roman BertholdBaskerville
Italic *Berthold Baskerville*
Medium **B Baskerville**
Medium Italic ***B Baskerville***
Bold **B Baskerville**

Berthold Baskerville Book
Roman B Baskerville Book
Italic *B Baskerville Book*
Medium **B Baskerville Book**
Medium Italic ***B Baskerville Book***

Baskerville Cyrillic
Upright Абвгдеж Зикл
Inclined *Абвгдеж Зикл*
Bold Upright **Абвгдеж Зикл**

ITC Bauhaus
Light ITC Bauhaus
Medium ITC Bauhaus
Demi **ITC Bauhaus**
Bold **ITC Bauhaus**
Heavy **ITC Bauhaus**

ITC Beesknees
✤ *ITC Typographica* **ITC BEESKNEES**

Bell Gothic
Light Bell Gothic
Bold **Bell Gothic**
Black **Bell Gothic**

Bell Centennial
Name & Number **Bell Centennial**
Address Bell Centennial
Sub Caption Bell Centennial
Bold Listing **BELL CENTENNIAL**
Bold Listing Alternate **BELL CENTENNIAL**

Bellevue
✤ *Berthold ScriptSet 1* *Bellevue*

Belwe
Light Belwe
Medium **Belwe**
Bold **Belwe**
Condensed **Belwe**

Bembo 1
Roman Bembo
Italic *Bembo*
Bold **Bembo**
Bold Italic ***Bembo***

Bembo 2
Semibold Bembo
Semibold Italic *Bembo*
Extra Bold **Bembo**
Extra Bold Italic ***Bembo***

Bembo Expert & SCOSF
Expert Roman BEMBO 12345 et al.
Expert Italic *12345 et al.*
Expert Semibold 12345 et al.
Expert Semibold Italic *12345 et al.*
Expert Bold **12345 et al.**
Expert Bold Italic ***12345 et al.***
Expert Extra Bold **12345 et al.**
Expert Extra Bold Italic ***12345 et al.***
Roman SCOSF BEMBO 12345…
Italic OSF *osf 12345…*
Semibold OSF osf 12345…
Semibold Italic OSF *osf 12345…*
Bold OSF **osf 12345…**

ff

✤ *See page 522 for contents of Adobe Systems Multi-Font Packages.*

...Bembo Expert & SCOSF Bold Italic OSF	osf 12345...
Extra Bold OSF	osf 12345...
Extra Bold Italic OSF	osf 12345...
ITC Benguiat ✣ Adobe DisplaySet 3 Book	ITC Benguiat
Bold	ITC Benguiat
ITC Benguiat Book	ITC Benguiat
Book Italic	ITC Benguiat
Medium	ITC Benguiat
Medium Italic	ITC Benguiat
Bold	ITC Benguiat
Bold Italic	ITC Benguiat
ITC Benguiat Gothic Book	ITC Benguiat
Book Oblique	ITC Benguiat
Medium	ITC Benguiat
Medium Oblique	ITC Benguiat
Bold	ITC Benguiat
Bold Oblique	ITC Benguiat
Heavy	ITC Benguiat
Heavy Oblique	ITC Benguiat
ITC Berkeley Oldstyle Book	ITC Berkeley
Book Italic	ITC Berkeley
Medium	ITC Berkeley
Italic	ITC Berkeley
Bold	ITC Berkeley
Bold Italic	ITC Berkeley
Black	ITC Berkeley
Black Italic	ITC Berkeley
Berliner Grotesk Light	Berliner Grotesk
Medium	Berliner Grotesk
Berling Roman	Berling
Italic	Berling
Bold	Berling
Bold Italic	Berling
Bernhard Modern Roman	Bernhard Modern
Italic	Bernhard Modern
Bold	Bernhard Modern
Bold Italic	Bernhard Modern
Berthold Script ✣ Berthold ScriptSet 1 Regular	Berthold Script
...Berthold Script Medium	Berthold Script
Biffo Script ✣ Monotype ScriptSet 2	Biffo Script
Birch ✣ Adobe Wood Type 2	Birch
Blackoak ✣ Adobe Wood Type 2	Blackoak
Berthold Block Regular	Berthold Block
Italic	Berthold Block
Heavy	Berthold Block
Condensed	Berthold Block
Extra Condensed	Berthold Block
Extra Condensed Italic	Berthold Block
Bodoni 1 Roman	Bodoni
Italic	Bodoni
Bold	Bodoni
Bold Italic	Bodoni
Poster	Bodoni
Bodoni 2 Book	Bodoni
Book Italic	Bodoni
Bold Condensed	Bodoni
Poster Compressed	Bodoni
Poster Italic	Bodoni
Berthold Bodoni Antiqua Light	B Bodoni Antiqua
Light Italic	B Bodoni Antiqua
Roman	B Bodoni Antiqua
Italic	B Bodoni Antiqua
Medium	B Bodoni Antiqua
Medium Italic	B Bodoni Antiqua
Bold	B Bodoni Antiqua
Bold Italic	B Bodoni Antiqua
Berthold Bodoni Antiqua Condensed Condensed	B Bodoni Antiqua
Condensed Italic	B Bodoni Antiqua
Medium Condensed	B Bodoni Antiqua
Medium Condensed Italic	B Bodoni Antiqua
Bold Condensed	B Bodoni Antiqua
Bold Condensed Italic	B Bodoni Antiqua
Berthold Bodoni Antiqua Expert & SCOSF Expert Light	B BODONI 12345 et al.
Expert Light Italic	12345 et al.
Expert Roman	B BODONI 12345 et al.
Expert Italic	12345 et al.
...Berthold Bodoni Antiqua Expert & SCOSF Expert Medium	12345 et al.
Expert Medium Italic	12345 et al.
Expert Bold	12345 et al.
Expert Bold Italic	12345 et al.
Light SCOSF	B Bodoni 12345...
Light Italic OSF	osf 12345...
Roman SCOSF	B Bodoni 12345...
Italic OSF	osf 12345...
Medium SCOSF	B Bodoni 12345...
Medium Italic OSF	osf 12345...
Bold OSF	osf 12345...
Bold Italic OSF	osf 12345...
Bauer Bodoni 1 Roman	Bauer Bodoni
Italic	Bauer Bodoni
Bold	Bauer Bodoni
Bold Italic	Bauer Bodoni
Bauer Bodoni 2 Black	Bauer Bodoni
Black Italic	Bauer Bodoni
Bold Condensed	Bauer Bodoni
Black Condensed	Bauer Bodoni
Bauer Bodoni SCOSF Roman SCOSF	B Bodoni 12345...
Italic OSF	osf 12345...
Bold OSF	osf 12345...
Bold Italic OSF	osf 12345...
Berthold Bodoni Old Face Roman	B Bodoni Old Face
Italic	B Bodoni Old Face
Medium	B Bodoni Old Face
Medium Italic	B Bodoni Old Face
Bold	B Bodoni Old Face
Bold Italic	B Bodoni Old Face
Berthold Bodoni Old Face Expert & SCOSF Expert Roman	B BODONI 12345 et al.
Expert Italic	12345 et al.
Expert Medium	12345 et al.
Expert Medium Italic	12345 et al.
Expert Bold	12345 et al.
Expert Bold Italic	12345 et al.
Roman SCOSF	B Bodoni 12345...
Italic SCOSF	B Bodoni 12345...

... Berthold Bodoni Old Face Expert & SCOSF
Medium SCOSF B Bodoni 12345...
Medium Italic OSF *osf 12345...*
Bold OSF **osf 12345...**
Bold Italic OSF ***osf 12345...***

ITC Bookman 1
Light ITC Bookman
Light Italic *ITC Bookman*
Demi **ITC Bookman**
Demi Italic ***ITC Bookman***

ITC Bookman 2
Medium ITC Bookman
Medium Italic *ITC Bookman*
Bold **ITC Bookman**
Bold Italic ***ITC Bookman***

Border Pi
✣ *Linotype PiSet 2*

Boton
Light Boton
Light Italic *Boton*
Regular Boton
Italic *Boton*
Medium **Boton**
Medium Italic ***Boton***
Bold **Boton**
Bold Italic ***Boton***

Boulevard
✣ *Berthold ScriptSet 1* *Boulevard*

Brush Script
✣ *Adobe DisplaySet 4* ***Brush Script***

Bundesbahn Pi
One B 7 6 32 5 1 4 6 P 95
Two
Three

PMN Caecilia + OSF
45-Light PMN Caecilia
46-Light Italic *PMN Caecilia*
55-Roman PMN Caecilia
56-Italic *PMN Caecilia*
75-Bold **PMN Caecilia**
76-Bold Italic ***PMN Caecilia***
85-Heavy **PMN Caecilia**
86-Heavy Italic ***PMN Caecilia***
45-Light OSF osf 12345...
46-Light Italic OSF *osf 12345...*
55-Roman OSF osf 12345...
56-Italic OSF *osf 12345...*

... PMN Caecilia + OSF
75-Bold OSF **osf 12345...**
76-Bold Italic OSF ***osf 12345...***
85-Heavy OSF **osf 12345...**
86-Heavy Italic OSF ***osf 12345...***

PMN Caecilia SCOSF
45-Light SCOSF Caecilia 12345...
46-Light Italic SCOSF *Caecilia 12345...*
55-Roman SCOSF Caecilia 12345...
56-Italic SCOSF *Caecilia 12345...*
75-Bold SCOSF **Caecilia 12345...**
76-Bold Italic SCOSF ***Caecilia 12345...***
85-Heavy SCOSF **Caecilia 12345...**
86-Heavy Italic SCOSF ***Caecilia 12345...***

Caflisch Script MultipleMaster
Light *Caflisch Script MM*
Light Swash *Caflisch Script MM*
Light Alternate *chckctdffffifflftgkqstftt*
Regular *Caflisch Script MM*
Regular Swash *Caflisch Script MM*
Regular Alternate *chckctdffffifflftgkqstftt*
Semibold *Caflisch Script MM*
Semibold Swash *Caflisch Script MM*
Semibold Alternate *chckctdffffifflftgkqstftt*
Bold *Caflisch Script MM*
Bold Swash *Caflisch Script MM*
Bold Alternate *chckctdffffifflftgkqstftt*

New Caledonia
Roman New Caledonia
Italic *New Caledonia*
Semibold **New Caledonia**
Semibold Italic ***New Caledonia***
Bold **New Caledonia**
Bold Italic ***New Caledonia***
Black **New Caledonia**
Black Italic ***New Caledonia***

New Caledonia SCOSF
Roman SCOSF NCaledonia 123...
Italic OSF *osf 12345...*
Bold SCOSF **NCaledonia 123...**
Bold Italic OSF ***osf 12345...***

Calvert
Light Calvert
Roman Calvert

... Calvert
Bold **Calvert**

Candida
Roman Candida
Italic *Candida*
Bold **Candida**

Cantoria 1
Roman Cantoria
Italic *Cantoria*
Bold **Cantoria**
Bold Italic ***Cantoria***

Cantoria 2
Light Cantoria
Light Italic *Cantoria*
Semibold Cantoria
Semibold Italic *Cantoria*
Extra Bold **Cantoria**
Extra Bold Italic ***Cantoria***

Caravan Borders
✣ *Electra Set 1*
One
Two
Three
Four

Carolina
✣ *Type Before Gutenberg 2*
Regular Carolina
Dfr chckffffllſsſiſſßtzäöü

Carta

Cascade Script
✣ *Linotype ScriptSet 1* ***Cascade Script***

Caslon 540 & Caslon 3
Caslon 540 Roman Caslon 540
Caslon 540 Italic *Caslon 540*
Caslon 3 Roman **Caslon 3**
Caslon 3 Italic ***Caslon 3***

Caslon 540 & Caslon 3 SCOSF
Caslon 540 Roman SCOSF Caslon 540 12345...
Caslon 540 Italic OSF *osf 12345...*
Caslon 3 Roman SCOSF **Caslon 3 12345...**
Caslon 3 Italic OSF ***osf 12345...***

Caslon Open Face
Caslon Open Face

ITC Caslon No. 224
Book ITC Caslon No. 224
Book Italic *ITC Caslon No. 224*
Medium ITC Caslon No.224
Medium Italic *ITC Caslon No.224*
Bold **ITC Caslon No.224**
Bold Italic ***ITC Caslon No.224***
Black **ITC Caslon No.224**

✣ *See page 522 for contents of Adobe Systems Multi-Font Packages.*

. . . ITC Caslon No. 224 Black Italic — ***ITC Caslon No.224***

Adobe Caslon
- Roman — Adobe Caslon
- Italic — *Adobe Caslon*
- Semibold — Adobe Caslon
- Semibold Italic — *Adobe Caslon*
- Bold — **Adobe Caslon**
- Bold Italic — ***Adobe Caslon***

Adobe Caslon Expert & SCOSF
- Expert Roman — A CASLON 12345 et al.
- Expert Italic — *12345 et al.*
- Expert Semibold — 12345 et al.
- Expert Semibold Italic — *12345 et al.*
- Expert Bold — **12345 et al.**
- Expert Bold Italic — ***12345 et al.***
- Roman SCOSF — A CASLON 12345...
- Italic OSF — *osf 12345...*
- Semibold SCOSF — A CASLON 12345...
- Semibold Italic OSF — *osf 12345...*
- Bold OSF — **osf 12345...**
- Bold Italic OSF — ***osf 12345...***
- Alternate Roman — ct k ſh ſi ſl ſſi ſt st v w
- Alternate Italic — *ct k ſh ſi ſl ſſi ſt st v w*
- Alternate Semibold — ct k ſh ſi ſl ſſi ſt st v w
- Alternate Semibold Italic — *ct k ſh ſi ſl ſſi ſt st v w*
- Alternate Bold — **ct ſh ſi k ſl ſſi ſt st v w**
- Alternate Bold Italic — ***ct k ſh ſi ſl ſſi ſt st v w***
- Italic Swash Caps — *ABCDEFGHIJ*
- Semibold Italic Swash Caps — *ABCDEFGHIJ*
- Bold Italic Swash Caps — ***ABCDEFGHIJ***
- Ornaments

Berthold Caslon Book
- Roman — B Caslon Book
- Italic — *B Caslon Book*
- Medium — B Caslon Book
- Bold — **B Caslon Book**

Berthold Caslon Book Expert & SCOSF
- Expert Roman — B CASLON 12345 et al.
- Expert Italic — *12345 et al.*
- Expert Medium — 12345 et al.
- Expert Bold — **12345 et al.**
- Roman SCOSF — B CASLON 12345...

. . . Berthold Caslon Book Expert & SCOSF
- Italic OSF — *osf 12345...*
- Medium SCOSF — B CASLON 12345...
- Bold OSF — **osf 12345...**

Castellar ✜ *Monotype DisplaySet 1* — CASTELLAR

Catull
- Roman — Catull
- Italic — *Catull*
- Medium — Catull
- Bold — **Catull**

Caxton
- Light — Caxton
- Light Italic — *Caxton*
- Book — Caxton
- Book Italic — *Caxton*
- Bold — **Caxton**
- Bold Italic — ***Caxton***

Centaur
- Roman — Centaur
- Italic — *Centaur*
- Bold — **Centaur**
- Bold Italic — ***Centaur***

Centaur Expert & SCOSF
- Expert Roman — CENTAUR 12345 et al.
- Expert Italic — *12345 et al.*
- Expert Bold — **12345 et al.**
- Expert Bold Italic — ***12345 et al.***
- Roman SCOSF — CENTAUR 12345...
- Italic OSF — *osf 12345...*
- Bold OSF — **osf 12345...**
- Bold Italic OSF — ***osf 12345...***
- Italic Swash Capitals — *ABCDEFGHIJKL*

Linotype Centennial
- 45-Light — L Centennial
- 46-Light Italic — *L Centennial*
- 55-Roman — L Centennial
- 56-Italic — *L Centennial*
- 75-Bold — **L Centennial**
- 76-Bold Italic — ***L Centennial***
- 95-Black — **L Centennial**
- 96-Black Italic — ***L Centennial***

Linotype Centennial SCOSF
- 45-Light SCOSF — LCENTENNIAL 123...
- 46-Light Italic OSF — *osf 12345...*
- 55-Roman SCOSF — LCENTENNIAL 123...

. . . Linotype Centennial SCOSF
- 56-Italic OSF — *osf 12345...*
- 75-Bold OSF — **osf 12345...**
- 76–Bold Italic OSF — ***osf 12345...***
- 95-Black OSF — **osf 12345...**
- 96-Black Italic OSF — ***osf 12345...***

Century Expanded
- Roman — Century Expanded
- Italic — *Century Expanded*

Century Old Style
- Roman — Century Old Style
- Italic — *Century Old Style*
- Bold — **Century Old Style**

New Century Schoolbook
- Roman — New Century
- Italic — *New Century*
- Bold — **New Century**
- Bold Italic — ***New Century***

New Century SchBk Fractions ✜ *Linotype Fraction Pi*
- Roman — 1/2 $\frac{1}{2}$ 1/3 $\frac{1}{3}$ 63/64 $\frac{63}{64}$ 22/7 $\frac{22}{7}$
- Bold — **1/2 $\frac{1}{2}$ 1/3 $\frac{1}{3}$ 63/64 $\frac{63}{64}$ 22/7 $\frac{22}{7}$**

ITC Century
- Light — ITC Century
- Light Italic — *ITC Century*
- Book — ITC Century
- Book Italic — *ITC Century*
- Bold — **ITC Century**
- Bold Italic — ***ITC Century***
- Ultra — **ITC Century**
- Ultra Italic — ***ITC Century***

ITC Century Condensed
- Light Condensed — ITC Century
- Light Condensed Italic — *ITC Century*
- Book Condensed — ITC Century
- Book Condensed Italic — *ITC Century*
- Bold Condensed — **ITC Century**
- Bold Condensed Italic — ***ITC Century***
- Ultra Condensed — **ITC Century**
- Ultra Condensed Italic — ***ITC Century***

Charlemagne ✜ *Adobe TitlingSet 1*
- Regular — CHARLEMAGNE
- Bold — **CHARLEMAGNE**

Charme ✜ *Linotype DisplaySet 2* — *Charme*

ITC Cheltenham 1
- Book — ITC Cheltenham
- Book Italic — *ITC Cheltenham*
- Bold — **ITC Cheltenham**

ff

ITC Cheltenham 1
- Bold Italic — *ITC Cheltenham*

ITC Cheltenham 2
- Light — ITC Cheltenham
- Light Italic — *ITC Cheltenham*
- Ultra — **ITC Cheltenham**
- Ultra Italic — ***ITC Cheltenham***

ITC Cheltenham Condensed
- Light Condensed — ITC Cheltenham
- Light Condensed Italic — *ITC Cheltenham*
- Book Condensed — ITC Cheltenham
- Book Condensed Italic — *ITC Cheltenham*
- Bold Condensed — **ITC Cheltenham**
- Bold Condensed Italic — ***ITC Cheltenham***
- Ultra Condensed — **ITC Cheltenham**
- Ultra Condensed Italic — ***ITC Cheltenham***

Cheq
- ♗♕♔♘♙♝♛♚♞♟

Christiana + Expert & SCOSF
- Regular — Christiana
- Italic — *Christiana*
- Medium — Christiana
- Medium Italic — *Christiana*
- Bold — **Christiana**
- Bold Italic — ***Christiana***
- Expert Regular — CHRISTIANA 12345 et al.
- Regular SCOSF — CHRISTIANA 12345

Berthold City
- Light — Berthold City
- Light Italic — *Berthold City*
- Medium — Berthold City
- Medium Italic — *Berthold City*
- Bold — **Berthold City**
- Bold Italic — ***Berthold City***

Clairvaux ❖ *Type Before Gutenberg 2*
- Regular — Clairvaux
- Dfr — chckfffffillſsſiſſßtzäöü

Clarendon
- Light — Clarendon
- Roman — Clarendon
- Bold — **Clarendon**

ITC Clearface
- Roman — ITC Clearface
- Italic — *ITC Clearface*
- Bold — **ITC Clearface**
- Bold Italic — ***ITC Clearface***
- Heavy — **ITC Clearface**
- Heavy Italic — ***ITC Clearface***
- Black — **ITC Clearface**
- Black Italic — ***ITC Clearface***

Clearface Gothic
- 45-Light — Clearface Gothic
- 55-Regular — Clearface Gothic
- 65-Medium — Clearface Gothic
- 75-Bold — **Clearface Gothic**
- 95-Black — **Clearface Gothic**

Cochin
- Roman — Cochin
- Italic — *Cochin*
- Bold — **Cochin**
- Bold Italic — ***Cochin***

Colossalis
- Roman — Colossalis
- Medium — Colossalis
- Bold — **Colossalis**
- Black — **Colossalis**

Comenius Antiqua
- Roman — Comenius Antiqua
- Italic — *Comenius Antiqua*
- Medium — Comenius Antiq
- Bold — **Comenius Anti**

Concorde
- Roman — Concorde
- Italic — *Concorde*
- Medium — Concorde
- Medium Italic — *Concorde*

Concorde Condensed
- Condensed — Concorde
- Medium Condensed — Concorde
- Bold Condensed — **Concorde**
- Bold Condensed Outline — Concorde

Concorde Expert & SCOSF
- Expert Roman — CONCORDE 1234 et al.
- Expert Italic — *12345 et al.*
- Expert Medium — 12345 et al.
- Expert Medium Italic — *12345 et al.*
- Roman SCOSF — CONCORDE 12345...
- Italic OSF — *osf 12345...*
- Medium SCOSF — CONCORDE 1234...
- Medium Italic OSF — *osf 12345...*

Concorde Nova + Expert & SCOSF
- Roman — Concorde Nova
- Italic — *Concorde Nova*
- Medium — Concorde Nova
- Expert Roman — CONCORDE N 12345 et al.
- Expert Italic — *12345 et al.*
- Expert Medium — 12345 et al.
- Roman SCOSF — CONCORDE N 12345...
- Italic OSF — *osf 12345...*
- Medium SCOSF — CONCORDE N 1234...

Cooper Black
- Roman — **Cooper Black**
- Italic — ***Cooper Black***

Copperplate Gothic
- 29 B-C — COPPERPLATE
- 29 A-B — COPPERPLATE
- 30 B-C — COPPERPLATE
- 30 A-B — COPPERPLATE
- 31 B-C — COPPERPLATE
- 31 A-B — COPPERPLATE
- 32 B-C — COPPERPLATE
- 32 A-B — COPPERPLATE
- 33 B-C — COPPERPLATE

Corona
- Roman — Corona
- Italic — *Corona*
- Bold Face No. 2 — **Corona**

Cosmos
- Light — Cosmos
- Light Italic — *Cosmos*
- Medium — Cosmos
- Extra Bold — **Cosmos**

Cosmos Extra Bold ❖ *Berthold DisplaySet 1*
- **Cosmos**

Cottonwood ❖ *Adobe Wood Type 1*
- COTTONWOOD

Cremona
- Roman — Cremona
- Italic — *Cremona*
- Bold — **Cremona**
- Bold Italic — ***Cremona***

ITC Cushing
- Book — ITC Cushing
- Book Italic — *ITC Cushing*
- Medium — ITC Cushing
- Medium Italic — *ITC Cushing*
- Bold — **ITC Cushing**
- Bold Italic — ***ITC Cushing***
- Heavy — **ITC Cushing**

ff

❖ *See page 522 for contents of Adobe Systems Multi-Font Packages.*

. . . ITC Cushing
Heavy Italic — ***ITC Cushing***

Jaeger Daily News
Roman — Jaeger Daily News
Italic — *Jaeger Daily News*
Medium — Jaeger Daily News
Medium Italic — *Jaeger Daily News*
Bold — **Jaeger Daily News**
Bold Italic — ***Jaeger Daily News***
Extra Bold — **J Daily News**
Extra Bold Italic — ***J Daily News***

Linotype Decoration Pi
One
Two

Delta Jaeger
Light — Delta Jaeger
Light Italic — *Delta Jaeger*
Book — Delta Jaeger
Book Italic — *Delta Jaeger*
Medium — Delta Jaeger
Medium Italic — *Delta Jaeger*
Bold — **Delta Jaeger**
Bold Italic — ***Delta Jaeger***
Outline — Delta Jaeger

Linotype Didot + SCOSF
Roman — Linotype Didot
Italic — *Linotype Didot*
Bold — **Linotype Didot**
Roman SCOSF — L DIDOT 12345...
Roman OSF — osf 12345...
Italic OSF — *osf 12345...*
Bold OSF — **osf 12345...**
Headline — Linotype Didot
Headline OSF — osf 12345...
Initials — LINOTYPE DIDOT
Ornaments One
Ornaments Two

DIN Schriften
Engschrift — DIN Schriften
Mittelschrift — DIN Schriften
Neuzeit Grotesk Light — DIN Schriften
Neuzeit Grotesk Bold Condensed — **DIN Schriften**

Diotima + SCOSF
✤ GudrunSchrift
Roman — Diotima
Italic — *Diotima*

. . . Diotima + SCOSF
Roman SCOSF — DIOTIMA 12345...
Roman OSF — osf 12345...
Italic OSF — *osf 12345...*

Dom Casual
Regular — Dom Casual
Bold — **Dom Casual**

Dorchester Script
✤ *Monotype ScriptSet 2* — *Dorchester Script*

Doric Bold
✤ *Linotype ClassAdSet 1* — **Doric Bold**

Duc De Berry
✤ *Type Before Gutenberg 1*
Regular — Duc De Berry
Dfr — chckſſftllſsſiſſßtzäöü

Egyptienne F
55-Roman — Egyptienne F
56-Italic — *Egyptienne F*
65-Bold — **Egyptienne F**
75-Black — **Egyptienne F**

Ehrhardt
Roman — Ehrhardt
Italic — *Ehrhardt*
Semibold — **Ehrhardt**
Semibold Italic — ***Ehrhardt***

Electra 1
✤ *Electra Set 1*
Roman — Electra
Cursive — *Electra*
Bold — **Electra**
Bold Cursive — ***Electra***

Electra 2
Roman SCOSF — ELECTRA 12345...
Roman OSF — osf 12345...
Cursive OSF — *osf 12345...*
Bold SCOSF — **ELECTRA 12345...**
Bold OSF — **osf 12345...**
Bold Cursive OSF — ***osf 12345...***
Display Roman — Electra
Display Cursive — *Electra*
Display Bold — **Electra**
Display Bold Cursive — ***Electra***

Ellington
Light — Ellington
Light Italic — *Ellington*
Roman — Ellington
Italic — *Ellington*
Bold — **Ellington**
Bold Italic — ***Ellington***
Extra Bold — **Ellington**

. . . Ellington
Extra Bold Italic — ***Ellington***

Else NPL
Light — Else NPL
Medium — Else NPL
Semibold — Else NPL
Bold — **Else NPL**

Engravers Bold Face
✤ *Linotype Engravers Set 1* — **ENGRAVERS**

ITC Eras
Light — ITC Eras
Book — ITC Eras
Medium — ITC Eras
Demi — **ITC Eras**
Bold — **ITC Eras**
Ultra — **ITC Eras**

ITC Esprit
Book — ITC Esprit
Book Italic — *ITC Esprit*
Medium — ITC Esprit
Medium Italic — *ITC Esprit*
Bold — **ITC Esprit**
Bold Italic — ***ITC Esprit***
Black — **ITC Esprit**
Black Italic — ***ITC Esprit***

European Pi
✤ *Linotype PiSet 2*
One — ❺❾❹⓯⑯⑤①⑭
Two — √ × + ≤ ~ μ α ∘
Three
Four

Eurostile 1
Regular — Eurostile
Oblique — *Eurostile*
Demi — **Eurostile**
Demi Oblique — ***Eurostile***
Bold — **Eurostile**
Bold Oblique — ***Eurostile***

Eurostile 2
Condensed — Eurostile
Bold Condensed — **Eurostile**
Extended No. Two — Eurostile
Bold Extended No. Two — **Eurostile**

Excelsior
Roman — Excelsior
Italic — *Excelsior*
Bold — **Excelsior**

Excelsior Cyrillic
Upright — Абвгдеж Зикл

ff

. . . Excelsior Cyrillic
- Inclined — *Абвгдеж Зикл*
- Bold Upright — **Абвгдеж Зикл**

Fairfield 1
- 45-Light — Fairfield
- 46-Light Italic — *Fairfield*
- 55-Medium — Fairfield
- 56-Medium Italic — *Fairfield*
- 75-Bold — **Fairfield**
- 76-Bold Italic — ***Fairfield***
- 85-Heavy — **Fairfield**
- 86-Heavy Italic — ***Fairfield***

Fairfield 2
- 45-Light SCOSF — FAIRFIELD 12345...
- 46-Light Italic Swash Caps OSF — *ABCDEF 12345...*
- 55-Medium SCOSF — FAIRFIELD 12345...
- 56-Medium Italic Swash Caps OSF — *ABCDEF 12345...*
- 75-Bold SCOSF — **FAIRFIELD 12345...**
- 76-Bold Italic Swash Caps OSF — ***ABCDEF 1234...***
- 85-Heavy SCOSF — **FAIRFIELD 1234...**
- 86-Heavy Italic Swash Caps OSF — ***ABCDEF 123...***
- 45-Caption Light — *Fairfield*
- 55-Caption Medium — *Fairfield*
- 75-Caption Bold — ***Fairfield***
- 85-Caption Heavy — ***Fairfield***

Falstaff ✜ *Monotype DisplaySet 2* — **Falstaff**

ITC Fenice
- Light — ITC Fenice
- Light Oblique — *ITC Fenice*
- Roman — ITC Fenice
- Oblique — *ITC Fenice*
- Bold — **ITC Fenice**
- Bold Oblique — ***ITC Fenice***
- Ultra — **ITC Fenice**
- Ultra Oblique — ***ITC Fenice***

Fette Fraktur ✜ *Linotype DisplaySet 1*
- Regular — Fette Fraktur
- Dfr — chckfffftllſsſiſſßʒäöü

ITC Flora
- Medium — ITC Flora
- Bold — **ITC Flora**

Flyer Black ✜ *Linotype DisplaySet 2*
- Black Condensed — **Flyer Black**
- Extra Black Condensed — **Flyer Black**

Folio
- Light — Folio

. . . Folio
- Medium — Folio
- Bold — **Folio**
- Extra Bold — **Folio**
- Bold Condensed — **Folio**

Formata
- Light — Formata
- Light Italic — *Formata*
- Regular — Formata
- Italic — *Formata*
- Medium — **Formata**
- Medium Italic — ***Formata***
- Bold — **Formata**
- Bold Italic — ***Formata***

Formata Condensed
- Light Condensed — Formata
- Light Condensed Italic — *Formata*
- Condensed — Formata
- Condensed Italic — *Formata*
- Medium Condensed — **Formata**
- Medium Condensed Italic — ***Formata***
- Bold Condensed — **Formata**
- Bold Condensed Italic — ***Formata***
- Condensed Outline — Formata

Formata Expert & SCOSF
- Expert Light — FORMATA 12345 et al.
- Expert Light Italic — *12345 et al.*
- Expert Regular — **12345 et al.**
- Expert Italic — ***12345 et al.***
- Expert Light Condensed — 12345 et al.
- Expert Light Condensed Italic — *12345 et al.*
- Expert Condensed — **12345 et al.**
- Expert Condensed Italic — ***12345 et al.***
- Light SCOSF — FORMATA 12345...
- Light Italic SCOSF — *FORMATA 12345...*
- Regular SCOSF — FORMATA 12345...
- Italic SCOSF — *FORMATA 12345...*
- Light Condensed SCOSF — FORMATA 12345...
- Light Condensed Italic SCOSF — *FORMATA 12345...*
- Condensed SCOSF — FORMATA 12345...
- Condensed Italic SCOSF — *FORMATA 12345...*

Formata Outline ✜ *Berthold DisplaySet 1* — Formata Outline

Forte ✜ *Monotype ScriptSet 3* — ***Forte***

Franklin Gothic
- No. 2 Roman — **Franklin Gothic**
- Condensed — **Franklin Gothic**
- Extra Condensed — **Franklin Gothic**

ITC Franklin Gothic
- Book — ITC FranklinGothic
- Book Oblique — *ITC FranklinGothic*
- Demi — **ITC FranklinGothic**
- Demi Oblique — ***ITC FranklinGothic***
- Heavy — **ITC FranklinGothic**
- Heavy Oblique — ***ITC FranklinGothic***

Freestyle Script ✜ *Adobe DisplaySet 1* — *Freestyle Script*

Friz Quadrata ✜ *Adobe DisplaySet 3*
- Regular — Friz Quadrata
- Bold — **Friz Quadrata**

Frutiger
- 45-Light — Frutiger
- 46-Light Italic — *Frutiger*
- 55-Regular — Frutiger
- 56-Italic — *Frutiger*
- 65-Bold — **Frutiger**
- 66-Bold Italic — ***Frutiger***
- 75-Black — **Frutiger**
- 76-Black Italic — ***Frutiger***
- 95-Ultra Black — **Frutiger**

Frutiger Condensed
- 47-Light Condensed — Frutiger
- 57-Condensed — Frutiger
- 67-Bold Condensed — **Frutiger**
- 77-Black Condensed — **Frutiger**
- 87-Extra Black Condensed — **Frutiger**

Futura 1
- Light — Futura
- Light Oblique — *Futura*
- Book — Futura
- Book Oblique — *Futura*
- Bold — **Futura**
- Bold Oblique — ***Futura***

Futura 2
- Medium — Futura
- Medium Oblique — *Futura*
- Heavy — **Futura**
- Heavy Oblique — ***Futura***
- Extra Bold — **Futura**

ff

✜ *See page 522 for contents of Adobe Systems Multi-Font Packages.*

Font / Style	Sample
... Futura 2 Extra Bold Oblique	Futura
Futura 3 Light Condensed	Futura
Light Condensed Oblique	Futura
Medium Condensed	Futura
Medium Condensed Oblique	Futura
Bold Condensed	Futura
Bold Condensed Oblique	Futura
Extra Bold Condensed	Futura
Extra Bold Condensed Oblique	Futura
ITC Galliard 1 Roman	ITC Galliard
Italic	ITC Galliard
Bold	ITC Galliard
Bold Italic	ITC Galliard
ITC Galliard 2 Black	ITC Galliard
Black Italic	ITC Galliard
Ultra	ITC Galliard
Ultra Italic	ITC Galliard
Linotype Game Pi Chess/Draughts	
Dice/Dominoes	
English Cards	KING QUEEN JACK 10 TEN 9 NINE JOKER A ACE
French Cards	
Stempel Garamond Roman	Stempel Garamond
Italic	Stempel Garamond
Bold	Stempel Garamond
Bold Italic	Stempel Garamond
Stempel Garamond SCOSF Roman SCOSF	S GARAMOND 123...
Italic OSF	osf 12345...
Bold OSF	osf 12345...
Bold Italic OSF	osf 12345...
Garamond 3 Roman	Garamond 3
Italic	Garamond 3
Bold	Garamond 3
Bold Italic	Garamond 3
Garamond 3 SCOSF Roman SCOSF	GARAMOND 3 1234...
Italic OSF	osf 12345...
Bold SCOSF	GARAMOND 3 1234...
Bold Italic OSF	osf 12345...
Simoncini Garamond Roman	S Garamond

Font / Style	Sample
... Simoncini Garamond Italic	S Garamond
Bold	S Garamond
Berthold Garamond Roman	Berthold Garamond
Italic	Berthold Garamond
Medium	Berthold Garamond
Medium Italic	Berthold Garamond
Bold	Berthold Garamond
Condensed	Berthold Garamond
Medium Condensed	Berthold Garamond
Berthold Garamond Expert & SCOSF Expert Roman	B GARAMOND 1234 et al.
Expert Italic	12345 et al.
Expert Medium	12345 et al.
Expert Medium Italic	12345 et al.
Expert Bold	12345 et al.
Expert Condensed	12345 et al.
Expert Medium Condensed	12345 et al.
Roman SCOSF	B GARAMOND 12345...
Italic OSF	osf 12345...
Medium SCOSF	B GARAMOND 1234...
Medium Italic OSF	osf 12345...
Bold OSF	osf 12345...
Condensed SCOSF	B GARAMOND 12345...
Medium Condensed OSF	osf 12345...
Italic Swash Caps OSF	B Garamond 12345...
ITC Garamond 1 Light	ITC Garamond
Light Italic	ITC Garamond
Bold	ITC Garamond
Bold Italic	ITC Garamond
ITC Garamond 2 Book	ITC Garamond
Book Italic	ITC Garamond
Ultra	ITC Garamond
Ultra Italic	ITC Garamond
ITC Garamond Condensed Light	ITC Garamond
Light Italic	ITC Garamond
Book	ITC Garamond
Book Italic	ITC Garamond
Bold	ITC Garamond
Bold Italic	ITC Garamond

Font / Style	Sample
... ITC Garamond Condensed Ultra	ITC Garamond
Ultra Italic	ITC Garamond
Adobe Garamond Roman	Adobe Garamond
Italic	Adobe Garamond
Semibold	Adobe Garamond
Semibold Italic	Adobe Garamond
Bold	Adobe Garamond
Bold Italic	Adobe Garamond
Adobe Garamond Expert & SCOSF Expert Roman	A GARAMOND 1234 et al.
Expert Italic	12345 et al.
Expert Semibold	A GARAMOND 123 et al.
Expert Semibold Italic	12345 et al.
Expert Bold	12345 et al.
Expert Bold Italic	12345 et al.
Roman SCOSF	A GARAMOND 12345...
Italic OSF	osf 12345...
Semibold SCOSF	A GARAMOND 12345...
Semibold Italic OSF	osf 12345...
Bold OSF	osf 12345...
Bold Italic OSF	osf 12345...
Titling Caps	A GARAMOND
Alternate Roman	
Alternate Italic & Swash Caps	ABCDEF
Garth Graphic Roman	Garth Graphic
Italic	Garth Graphic
Bold	Garth Graphic
Bold Italic	Garth Graphic
Extra Bold	Garth Graphic
Black	Garth Graphic
Condensed	Garth Graphic
Bold Condensed	Garth Graphic
Gazette Roman	Gazette
Italic	Gazette
Bold	Gazette
Gill Sans 1 Light	Gill Sans
Light Italic	Gill Sans
Regular	Gill Sans
Italic	Gill Sans

Font	Style	Specimen
… Gill Sans 1	Bold	Gill Sans
	Bold Italic	*Gill Sans*
Gill Sans 2	Condensed	Gill Sans
	Bold Condensed	Gill Sans
	Extra Bold	Gill Sans
	Ultra Bold	Gill Sans
	Ultra Bold Condensed	Gill Sans
Gill Sans Display	Bold Extra Condensed	Gill Sans
	Display Extra Bold	Gill Sans
	Light Shadowed	Gill Sans
	Shadow	GILL SANS
ITC Giovanni	Book	ITC Giovanni
	Book Italic	*ITC Giovanni*
	Bold	ITC Giovanni
	Bold Italic	*ITC Giovanni*
	Black	ITC Giovanni
	Black Italic	*ITC Giovanni*
Glypha 1	55-Roman	Glypha
	55-Oblique	*Glypha*
	65-Bold	Glypha
	65-Bold Oblique	*Glypha*
Glypha 2	35-Thin	Glypha
	35-Thin Oblique	*Glypha*
	45-Light	Glypha
	45-Light Oblique	*Glypha*
	75-Black	Glypha
	75-Black Oblique	*Glypha*
Gothic 13 ✤ *Linotype DisplaySet 3*		Gothic 13
Goudy 1	Old Style Roman	Goudy
	Old Style Italic	*Goudy*
	Bold	Goudy
	Bold Italic	*Goudy*
Goudy 2	Extra Bold	Goudy
	Heavyface	Goudy
	Heavyface Italic	*Goudy*
Goudy SCOSF	Old Style Roman SCOSF	GOUDY 12345…
	Old Style Italic OSF	*osf 12345…*
	Bold OSF	osf 12345…
… Goudy SCOSF	Bold Italic OSF	*osf 12345…*
Monotype Goudy Modern ✤ *Monotype TextSet 1*	Roman	M Goudy Modern
	Italic	*M Goudy Modern*
Monotype Goudy Text & Lombardic Capitals	Regular	M Goudy Text
	Dfr	chckffftllſsſiſſßäöü
	Lombardic Capitals	LOMBARDIC
Granjon	Roman	Granjon
	Italic	*Granjon*
	Bold	Granjon
Granjon SCOSF	Roman SCOSF	GRANJON 12345…
	Italic OSF	*osf 12345…*
	Bold OSF	osf 12345…
Graphite MultipleMaster	Light Narrow	Graphite MM
	Regular Narrow	Graphite MM
	Bold Narrow	Graphite MM
	Light	Graphite MM
	Regular	Graphite MM
	Bold	Graphite MM
	Light Wide	Graphite MM
	Regular Wide	Graphite MM
	Bold Wide	Graphite MM
Monotype Grotesque 1	Light No. 126	M Grotesque
	Light Italic No. 126	*M Grotesque*
	Regular No. 215	M Grotesque
	Italic No. 215	*M Grotesque*
	Bold No. 216	M Grotesque
	Black No. 216	M Grotesque
Monotype Grotesque 2	Light Condensed No. 126	Monotype Grotesque
	Condensed No. 215	Monotype Grotesque
	Extra Condensed No. 215	Monotype Grotesque
	Bold Extended No. 216	M Grotesque
Guardi	55-Roman	Guardi
	56-Italic	*Guardi*
	75-Bold	Guardi
	76-Bold Italic	*Guardi*
	95-Black	Guardi
	96-Black Italic	*Guardi*
Helvetica	Light	Helvetica
… Helvetica	Light Oblique	*Helvetica*
	Black	Helvetica
	Black Oblique	*Helvetica*
Helvetica Condensed	Light Condensed	Helvetica
	Light Condensed Oblique	*Helvetica*
	Condensed	Helvetica
	Condensed Oblique	*Helvetica*
	Bold Condensed	Helvetica
	Bold Condensed Oblique	*Helvetica*
	Black Condensed	Helvetica
	Black Condensed Oblique	*Helvetica*
Helvetica Compressed	Compressed	Helvetica
	Extra Compressed	Helvetica
	Ultra Compressed	Helvetica
Helvetica Fractions ✤ *Linotype Fraction Pi*	Regular	½ $\frac{1}{2}$ ⅓ $\frac{1}{3}$ 63/64 $\frac{63}{64}$ 22/7 $\frac{22}{7}$
	Bold	½ $\frac{1}{2}$ ⅓ $\frac{1}{3}$ 63/64 $\frac{63}{64}$ 22/7 $\frac{22}{7}$
Helvetica Inserat ✤ *Linotype DisplaySet 1*		Helvetica Inserat
Helvetica Cyrillic	Upright	Абвгдеж Зикл
	Inclined	*Абвгдеж Зикл*
	Bold Upright	Абвгдеж Зикл
	Bold Inclined	*Абвгдеж Зикл*
	Inserat Upright	Абвгдеж Зикл
Helvetica Rounded	Bold	Helvetica Round
	Bold Oblique	*Helvetica Round*
	Black	Helvetica Roun
	Black Oblique	*Helvetica Roun*
	Bold Condensed	Helvetica Rounded
	Bold Condensed Oblique	*Helvetica Rounded*
Neue Helvetica 1	25-Ultra Light	Neue Helvetica
	26-Ultra Light Italic	*Neue Helvetica*
	95-Black	Neue Helvetica
	96-Black Italic	*Neue Helvetica*
Neue Helvetica 2	35-Thin	Neue Helvetica
	36-Thin Italic	*Neue Helvetica*
	55-Roman	Neue Helvetica
	56-Italic	*Neue Helvetica*
	75-Bold	Neue Helvetica
	76-Bold Italic	*Neue Helvetica*

ff

✤ *See page 522 for contents of Adobe Systems Multi-Font Packages.*

Neue Helvetica 3
45-Light Neue Helvetica
46-Light Italic *Neue Helvetica*
65-Medium Neue Helvetica
66-Medium Italic *Neue Helvetica*
85-Heavy **Neue Helvetica**
86-Heavy Italic ***Neue Helvetica***

Neue Helvetica Bold Outline
75-Bold Outline Neue Helvetica

Neue Helvetica Condensed 1
27-Ultra Light Condensed Neue Helvetica
27-Ultra Light Condensed Oblique *Neue Helvetica*
97-Black Condensed **Neue Helvetica**
97-Black Condensed Oblique ***Neue Helvetica***
107-Extra Black Condensed **Neue Helvetica**
107-Extra Black Condensed Oblique ***Neue Helvetica***

Neue Helvetica Condensed 2
37-Thin Condensed Neue Helvetica
37-Thin Condensed Oblique *Neue Helvetica*
57-Condensed Neue Helvetica
57-Condensed Oblique *Neue Helvetica*
77-Bold Condensed **Neue Helvetica**
77-Bold Condensed Oblique ***Neue Helvetica***

Neue Helvetica Condensed 3
47-Light Condensed Neue Helvetica
47-Light Condensed Oblique *Neue Helvetica*
67-Medium Condensed Neue Helvetica
67-Medium Condensed Oblique *Neue Helvetica*
87-Heavy Condensed **Neue Helvetica**
87-Heavy Condensed Oblique ***Neue Helvetica***

Neue Helvetica Extended 1
23-Ultra Light Extended Neue Helvetica
23-Ultra Light Extended Oblique *Neue Helvetica*
93-Black Extended **N Helvetica**
93-Black Extended Oblique ***N Helvetica***

Neue Helvetica Extended 2
33-Thin Extended Neue Helvetica
33-Thin Extended Oblique *Neue Helvetica*
53-Extended Neue Helvetica
53-Extended Oblique *Neue Helvetica*
73-Bold Extended **N Helvetica**
73-Bold Extended Oblique ***N Helvetica***

Neue Helvetica Extended 3
43-Light Extended Neue Helvetica
43-Light Extended Oblique *Neue Helvetica*
63-Medium Extended N Helvetica

...Neue Helvetica Extended 3
63-Medium Extended Oblique *N Helvetica*
83-Heavy Extended **N Helvetica**
83-Heavy Extended Oblique ***N Helvetica***

Herculanum
Type Before Gutenberg 1 HERCULANUM

ITC Highlander
Book ITC Highlander
Book Italic *ITC Highlander*
Medium ITC Highlander
Medium Italic *ITC Highlander*
Bold **ITC Highlander**
Bold Italic ***ITC Highlander***

Hiroshige
Book Hiroshige
Book Italic *Hiroshige*
Medium Hiroshige
Medium Italic *Hiroshige*
Bold **Hiroshige**
Bold Italic ***Hiroshige***
Black **Hiroshige**
Black Italic ***Hiroshige***

Hobo
Adobe DisplaySet 4 Hobo

Linotype Holiday Pi
One
Two
Three TV ROOM

Horley Old Style
Light Horley Old Style
Light Italic *Horley Old Style*
Roman Horley Old Style
Italic *Horley Old Style*
Semibold Horley Old Style
Semibold Italic *Horley Old Style*
Bold **Horley Old Style**
Bold Italic ***Horley Old Style***

Berthold Imago
Light Berthold Imago
Light Italic *Berthold Imago*
Book Berthold Imago
Book Italic *Berthold Imago*
Medium **Berthold Imago**
Medium Italic ***Berthold Imago***
Extra Bold **Berthold Imago**
Extra Bold Italic ***Berthold Imago***

Impact
Adobe DisplaySet 2 **Impact**

Impressum
Roman Impressum
Italic *Impressum*
Bold **Impressum**

Industria
Brody DisplaySet 1
Solid + Alternate Industria qlt
Inline + Alternate Industria qlt

Inflex Bold
Monotype DisplaySet 2 **Inflex Bold**

Insignia
Brody DisplaySet 1
Regular Insignia
Alternate stEJSZ

Ironwood
Adobe Wood Type 1 IRONWOOD

ITC Isadora
Regular *ITC Isadora*
Bold ***ITC Isadora***

Italia
Book Italia
Medium Italia
Bold **Italia**

Monotype Italian Old Style
Roman M Italian Old Style
Italic *M Italian Old Style*
Bold **M Italian Old Style**
Bold Italic ***M Italian Old Style***

Janson Text
55-Roman Janson Text
56-Italic *Janson Text*
75-Bold **Janson Text**
76-Bold Italic ***Janson Text***

Janson Text SCOSF
55-Roman SCOSF JANSON TEXT 12345...
56-Italic OSF *osf 12345...*
75-Bold OSF **osf 12345...**
76-Bold Italic OSF ***osf 12345...***

Joanna
Roman Joanna
Italic *Joanna*
Semibold Joanna
Semibold Italic *Joanna*
Bold **Joanna**
Bold Italic ***Joanna***
Extra Bold **Joanna**

Juniper
Adobe Wood Type 1 JUNIPER

Kabel
Light Kabel
Book Kabel

ff

... Kabel
Heavy Kabel
Black Kabel

ITC Kabel
Book ITC Kabel
Medium ITC Kabel
Demi ITC Kabel
Bold ITC Kabel
Ultra ITC Kabel

Kaufmann
Regular Kaufmann
Bold Kaufmann

Kino
Monotype DisplaySet 3 Kino

Klang
Monotype ScriptSet 3 Klang

ITC Korinna
Roman ITC Korinna
Kursiv ITC Korinna
Bold ITC Korinna
Bold Kursiv ITC Korinna

Künstler Script
Medium Künstler Script
No. 2 Bold Künstler Script
Black Künstler Script

Latin Condensed
Monotype DisplaySet 4 Latin Condensed

ITC Leawood
Book ITC Leawood
Book Italic ITC Leawood
Medium ITC Leawood
Medium Italic ITC Leawood
Bold ITC Leawood
Bold Italic ITC Leawood
Black ITC Leawood
Black Italic ITC Leawood

ITC Legacy Serif
Book ITC Legacy
Book Italic ITC Legacy
Medium ITC Legacy
Medium Italic ITC Legacy
Bold ITC Legacy
Bold Italic ITC Legacy
Ultra ITC Legacy

ITC Legacy Sans
Book ITC Legacy
Book Italic ITC Legacy
Medium ITC Legacy
Medium Italic ITC Legacy

... ITC Legacy Sans
Bold ITC Legacy
Bold Italic ITC Legacy
Ultra ITC Legacy

Letter Gothic
Regular Letter Gothic
Slanted Letter Gothic
Bold Letter Gothic
Bold Slanted Letter Gothic

Life
Roman Life
Italic Life
Bold Life

LinoLetter
Roman LinoLetter
Italic LinoLetter
Medium LinoLetter
Medium Italic LinoLetter
Bold LinoLetter
Bold Italic LinoLetter
Black LinoLetter
Black Italic LinoLetter

LinoLetter SCOSF
Roman SCOSF LinoLetter 1234
Roman OSF osf 12345...
Italic OSF osf 12345...
Medium SCOSF LinoLetter 1234
Medium OSF osf 12345...
Medium Italic OSF osf 12345...
Bold SCOSF LinoLetter 1234
Bold OSF osf 12345...
Bold Italic OSF osf 12345...
Black SCOSF LinoLetter 123
Black OSF osf 12345...
Black Italic OSF osf 12345...

Linoscript
Linotype ScriptSet 2 Linoscript

Linotext
Linotype ScriptSet 2 Linotext

Lithos
Extra Light LITHOS
Light LITHOS
Regular LITHOS
Bold LITHOS
Black LITHOS

Berthold Lo-Type
Light Berthold Lo-Type

... Berthold Lo-Type
Regular Berthold Lo-Type
Medium Berthold Lo-Type
Medium Italic Berthold Lo-Type
Medium Condensed Berthold Lo-Type
Bold Berthold Lo-Ty

ITC Lubalin Graph
Book ITC Lubalin
Book Oblique ITC Lubalin
Demi ITC Lubalin
Demi Oblique ITC Lubalin

Lucida
Roman Lucida
Italic Lucida
Bold Lucida
Bold Italic Lucida

Lucida Sans
Regular Lucida Sans
Italic Lucida Sans
Bold Lucida Sans
Bold Italic Lucida Sans

Lucida Math
Extension ⊙⊕⊗∑√∫∮⨄↓↑
Italic ABCdefΦμΣψξΩ
Symbol ABC∞△▽→♡≤

ITC Machine
Medium ITC MACHINE
Bold ITC MACHINE

Madrone
Adobe Wood Type 2 Madrone

Marigold
Baker Calligraphy Marigold

Mathematical Pi
One ÷ = ± ∓ ≪ ≫ ≤ ≥ ≦ ≧
Two
Three
Four
Five
Six

Matura
Monotype DisplaySet 3
Regular Matura
Scriptorial Caps MATURA

Maximus
Linotype ClassAdSet 1 Maximus

Medici Script
Linotype ScriptSet 1 Medici Script

Melior
Roman Melior
Italic Melior
Bold Melior
Bold Italic Melior

See page 522 for contents of Adobe Systems Multi-Font Packages.

Memphis
Light Memphis
Light Italic *Memphis*
Medium Memphis
Medium Italic *Memphis*
Bold **Memphis**
Bold Italic ***Memphis***
Extra Bold **Memphis**

ITC Mendoza Roman
Book ITC Mendoza
Book Italic *ITC Mendoza*
Medium ITC Mendoza
Medium Italic *ITC Mendoza*
Bold **ITC Mendoza**
Bold Italic ***ITC Mendoza***

Mercurius Bold Script
✜ *Monotype ScriptSet 3* **Mercurius Bold**

Meridien
Roman Meridien
Italic *Meridien*
Medium Meridien
Medium Italic *Meridien*
Bold **Meridien**
Bold Italic ***Meridien***

Mesquite
✜ *Adobe Wood Type 1* MESQUITE

Mezz MultipleMaster
Light Mezz MM
Regular Mezz MM
Semibold Mezz MM
Bold **Mezz MM**
Black **Mezz MM**

MICR
✜ *OCR Set 1* 1234567890

Minion
Roman Minion
Italic *Minion*
Semibold Minion
Semibold Italic *Minion*
Bold **Minion**
Bold Italic ***Minion***
Black **Minion**
Display Roman Minion
Display Italic *Minion*

Minion Expert & SCOSF
Expert Roman MINION 12345 et al.

. . . Minion Expert & SCOSF
Expert Italic *12345 et al.*
Expert Semibold 12345 et al.
Expert Semibold Italic *12345 et al.*
Expert Bold **12345 et al.**
Expert Bold Italic ***12345 et al.***
Expert Black **12345 et al.**
Display Expert Roman MINION 123 et al.
Display Expert Italic *12345 et al.*
Roman SCOSF MINION 12345...
Italic SCOSF *MINION 12345...*
Semibold SCOSF MINION 12345...
Semibold Italic SCOSF *MINION 12345...*
Bold OSF **osf 12345...**
Bold Italic OSF ***osf 12345...***
Black OSF **osf 12345...**
Display Roman SCOSF MINION 123...
Display Italic SCOSF *MINION 123...*
Italic Swash Capitals *MINION*
Semibold Italic Swash Capitals *MINION*
Display Italic Swash Capitals *MINION*
Ornaments

Minion Cyrillic
Upright Абвгдеж Зикл
Inclined *Абвгдеж Зикл*
Semibold Upright Абвгдеж Зикл
Semibold Inclined *Абвгдеж Зикл*
Bold Upright **Абвгдеж Зикл**
Bold Inclined ***Абвгдеж Зикл***

Minion MultipleMaster
Roman Minion MM
Italic *Minion MM*
Semibold Minion MM
Semibold Italic *Minion MM*
Bold **Minion MM**
Bold Italic ***Minion MM***
Display Roman Minion MM
Display Italic *Minion MM*
Condensed Minion MM
Condensed Italic *Minion MM*
Semibold Condensed Minion MM

. . . Minion MultipleMaster
Semibold Condensed Italic *Minion MM*
Bold Condensed **Minion MM**
Bold Condensed Italic ***Minion MM***

Minion MultipleMaster Expert & SCOSF
Expert Roman MINION MM 12345 et al.
Expert Italic *MINION MM 12345 et al.*
Expert Semibold MINION MM 12345 et al.
Expert Semibold Italic *MINION MM 12345 et al.*
Expert Bold **MINION MM 1234 et al.**
Expert Bold Italic ***MINION MM 1234 et al.***
Display Expert Roman MINION MM 123 et al.
Display Expert Italic *MINION MM 123 et al.*
Roman SCOSF MINION MM 12345...
Italic SCOSF *MINION MM 12345...*
Semibold SCOSF MINION MM 12345...
Semibold Italic SCOSF *MINION MM 12345...*
Bold SCOSF **MINION MM 12345...**
Bold Italic SCOSF ***MINION MM 12345...***
Display Roman SCOSF MINIONMM123...
Display Italic SCOSF *MINIONMM123...*
Italic Swash Capitals *MINION MM*
Semibold Italic Swash Capitals *MINION MM*
Bold Italic Swash Capitals ***MINION MM***
Display Italic Swash Capitals *MINION MM*
Expert Condensed MINION MM 12345 et al.
Expert Condensed Italic *MINION MM 12345 et al.*
Expert Semibold Condensed MINION MM 12345 et al.
Expert Semibold Condensed Italic *MINION MM 12345 et al.*
Expert Bold Condensed **MINION MM 12345 et al.**
Expert Bold Condensed Italic ***MINION MM 12345 et al.***
Condensed SCOSF MINION MM 12345...
Condensed Italic SCOSF *MINION MM 12345...*
Semibold Condensed SCOSF MINION MM 12345...
Semibold Condensed Italic SCOSF *MINION MM 12345...*
Bold Condensed SCOSF **MINION MM 12345...**
Bold Condensed Italic SCOSF ***MINION MM 12345...***
Condensed Italic Swash *MINION MM*
Semibold Condensed Italic Swash *MINION MM*
Bold Condensed Italic Swash ***MINION MM***

ff

... **Minion MultipleMaster Expert & SCOSF**
- Ornaments
- Display Ornaments

Minister
- Light — Minister
- Light Italic — *Minister*
- Book — Minister
- Book Italic — *Minister*
- Bold — **Minister**
- Bold Italic — ***Minister***
- Black — **Minister**
- Black Italic — ***Minister***

Mistral (Adobe ScriptSet 1)
- Mistral

Monotype Modern
- Condensed — Monotype Modern
- Condensed Italic — *Monotype Modern*
- Extended — Monotype Modern
- Extended Italic — *Monotype Modern*
- Bold — **Monotype Modern**
- Bold Italic — ***Monotype Modern***
- Wide — M Modern
- Wide Italic — *M Modern*

ITC Mona Lisa (ITC Typographica)
- Recut — ITC Mona Lisa
- Solid — ITC Mona Lisa

Monoline Script (Monotype ScriptSet 1)
- Monoline Script

Myriad MultipleMaster
- Light — Myriad MM
- Light Italic — *Myriad MM*
- Regular — Myriad MM
- Italic — *Myriad MM*
- Semibold — **Myriad MM**
- Semibold Italic — ***Myriad MM***
- Bold — **Myriad MM**
- Bold Italic — ***Myriad MM***
- Black — **Myriad MM**
- Black Italic — ***Myriad MM***
- Light Condensed — Myriad MM
- Light Condensed Italic — *Myriad MM*
- Condensed — Myriad MM
- Condensed Italic — *Myriad MM*
- Semibold Condensed — **Myriad MM**
- Semibold Condensed Italic — ***Myriad MM***

... **Myriad MultipleMaster**
- Bold Condensed — **Myriad MM**
- Bold Condensed Italic — ***Myriad MM***
- Black Condensed — **Myriad MM**
- Black Condensed Italic — ***Myriad MM***
- Light Semi-Extended — Myriad MM
- Light Semi-Extended Italic — *Myriad MM*
- Semi-Extended — Myriad MM
- Semi-Extended Italic — *Myriad MM*
- Semibold Semi-Extended — **Myriad MM**
- Semibold Semi-Extended Italic — ***Myriad MM***
- Bold Semi-Extended — **Myriad MM**
- Bold Semi-Extended Italic — ***Myriad MM***
- Black Semi-Extended — **Myriad MM**
- Black Semi-Extended Italic — ***Myriad MM***

Neuzeit S
- Book — Neuzeit S
- Heavy — **Neuzeit S**

New Berolina (Monotype ScriptSet 1)
- New Berolina

News Gothic
- Regular — News Gothic
- Oblique — *News Gothic*
- Bold — **News Gothic**
- Bold Oblique — ***News Gothic***

Nofret
- Light — Nofret
- Light Italic — *Nofret*
- Roman — Nofret
- Italic — *Nofret*
- Medium — **Nofret**
- Medium Italic — ***Nofret***
- Bold — **Nofret**
- Bold Italic — ***Nofret***

Nofret Expert & SCOSF
- Expert Light — NOFRET 12345 et al.
- Expert Light Italic — *12345 et al.*
- Expert Roman — 12345 et al.
- Expert Italic — *12345 et al.*
- Expert Medium — **NOFRET 12345 et al.**
- Expert Medium Italic — ***12345 et al.***
- Expert Bold — **12345 et al.**
- Expert Bold Italic — ***12345 et al.***
- Light SCOSF — NOFRET 12345...

... **Nofret Expert & SCOSF**
- Light Italic OSF — *osf 12345...*
- Roman SCOSF — NOFRET 12345...
- Italic OSF — *osf 12345...*
- Medium SCOSF — **NOFRET 12345...**
- Medium Italic OSF — ***osf 12345...***
- Bold OSF — **osf 12345...**
- Bold Italic OSF — ***osf 12345...***

Notre Dame (Type Before Gutenberg 3)
- Regular — Notre Dame
- Dfr — chckffftllſsſiſſßtzäöü
- Ornaments

ITC Novarese
- Book — ITC Novarese
- Book Italic — *ITC Novarese*
- Medium — ITC Novarese
- Medium Italic — *ITC Novarese*
- Bold — **ITC Novarese**
- Bold Italic — ***ITC Novarese***
- Ultra — **ITC Novarese**

Nuptial Script (Linotype ScriptSet 1)
- Nuptial Script

OCR-A & Alternate (OCR Set 1)
- OCR-A 123 ä1i¿

OCR-B & Alternate (OCR Set 1)
- OCR-B 123 ä1¡¿

Octavian + Expert & SCOSF
- Roman — Octavian
- Italic — *Octavian*
- Expert Roman — OCTAVIAN 12345 et al.
- Expert Italic — *12345 et al.*
- Roman SCOSF — OCTAVIAN 12345...
- Italic OSF — *osf 12345...*

ITC Officina Serif
- Book — ITC Officina
- Book Italic — *ITC Officina*
- Bold — **ITC Officina**
- Bold Italic — ***ITC Officina***

ITC Officina Sans
- Book — ITC Officina
- Book Italic — *ITC Officina*
- Bold — **ITC Officina**
- Bold Italic — ***ITC Officina***

Old Style No. 7 + SCOSF
- Roman — Old Style No. 7
- Italic — *Old Style No. 7*
- Roman SCOSF — O STYLE NO.7 123...
- Italic OSF — *osf 12345...*

See page 522 for contents of Adobe Systems Multi-Font Packages.

MT Old Style Bold Outline
✣ *Monotype DisplaySet 2* — M Old Style

Olympian
Roman — Olympian
Italic — *Olympian*
Bold — **Olympian**
Bold Italic — ***Olympian***

Omnia
✣ *Type Before Gutenberg 1* — OMNIA

Onyx
✣ *Monotype DisplaySet 4* — Onyx

Optima
Roman — Optima
Oblique — *Optima*
Bold — **Optima**
Bold Oblique — ***Optima***

Orator
Regular — ORATOR
Slanted — *ORATOR*

Oxford
✣ *Baker Calligraphy* — Oxford

ITC Ozwald
✣ *ITC Typographica* — ITC Ozwald

Palace Script
✣ *Monotype ScriptSet 1*
Regular — Palace Script
Semibold — Palace Script

Palatino 1
Roman — Palatino
Italic — *Palatino*
Bold — **Palatino**
Bold Italic — ***Palatino***

Palatino 2
Light — Palatino
Light Italic — *Palatino*
Medium — Palatino
Medium Italic — *Palatino*
Black — **Palatino**
Black Italic — ***Palatino***

Palatino SCOSF
Roman SCOSF — PALATINO 12345...
Italic OSF — *osf 12345...*
Bold OSF — **osf 12345...**
Bold Italic OSF — ***osf 12345...***

Parisian
✣ *Adobe DisplaySet 5* — Parisian

Park Avenue — Park Avenue

Peignot
Light — PEIGNOT
Demi — PEIGNOT
Bold — **PEIGNOT**

Pelican
✣ *Baker Calligraphy* — Pelican

Pepita
✣ *Monotype ScriptSet 2* — Pepita

Pepperwood
✣ *Adobe Wood Type 3*
Regular — PEPPERWOOD
Fill — PEPPERWOOD
Outline — PEPPERWOOD

Perpetua
Roman — Perpetua
Italic — *Perpetua*
Bold — **Perpetua**
Bold Italic — ***Perpetua***

Perpetua Expert & SCOSF
Expert Roman — PERPETUA I 2 3 4 5 et al.
Expert Italic — *12345 et al.*
Expert Bold — **12345 et al.**
Expert Bold Italic — ***12345 et al.***
Roman SCOSF — PERPETUA 12345...
Italic OSF — *osf 12345...*
Bold OSF — **osf 12345...**
Bold Italic OSF — ***osf 12345...***

Photina
Roman — Photina
Italic — *Photina*
Semibold — **Photina**
Semibold Italic — ***Photina***
Bold — **Photina**
Bold Italic — ***Photina***
Ultra Bold — **Photina**
Ultra Bold Italic — ***Photina***

Plantin 1
Roman — Plantin
Italic — *Plantin*
Bold — **Plantin**
Bold Italic — ***Plantin***

Plantin 2
Light — Plantin
Light Italic — *Plantin*
Semibold — **Plantin**
Semibold Italic — ***Plantin***
Bold Condensed — **Plantin**

Poetica 1 + Expert & SCOSF
Chancery I — *Poetica*
Chancery II — *Poetica*
Chancery III — *Poetica*
Chancery IV — *Poetica*
Expert Chancery — *ff fi fl ffi ffl 1 2 3 4 5...*
Chancery SCOSF — POETICA 12345...

... Poetica 1+Expert & SCOSF
Chancery SCOSF Alternate — K K L M N N Q R R V W

Poetica 2 Supplement
LC Alternates I — *b b d d f g g h h j k k l f f s s t*
LC Alternates II — *d g g k k p p s v w y y z z*
LC Beginnings I — *b b e f f h h i j j*
LC Beginnings II — *b b e e f f h h i*
LC Endings I — *a a c d d e g g h i i l*
LC Endings II — *a n d d e h h i i*
Ampersands — & & & & & & & & &
Ligatures — *ch ck ct st*
Initial Swash Caps — *P O E T I C A*
Swash Caps I — *POETICA*
Swash Caps II — *POETICA*
Swash Caps III — *POETICA*
Swash Caps IV — *POETICA*
Ornaments

Pompeijana
✣ *Type Before Gutenberg 3*
Roman — POMPEIJANA
Borders

Ponderosa
✣ *Adobe Wood Type 1* — PONDEROSA

Poplar
✣ *Adobe Wood Type 2* — **Poplar**

Poppl-Laudatio
Light — Poppl-Laudatio
Light Italic — *Poppl-Laudatio*
Regular — Poppl-Laudatio
Italic — *Poppl-Laudatio*
Medium — **Poppl-Laudatio**
Medium Italic — ***Poppl-Laudatio***
Bold — **Poppl-Laudatio**
Bold Italic — ***Poppl-Laudatio***

Poppl-Laudatio Condensed
Light Condensed — Poppl-Laudatio
Regular Condensed — Poppl-Laudatio
Medium Condensed — **Poppl-Laudatio**
Bold Condensed — **Poppl-Laudatio**

Poppl-Pontifex
Roman — Poppl-Pontifex
Italic — *Poppl-Pontifex*
Medium — **Poppl-Pontifex**
Medium Condensed — **Poppl-Pontifex**

Poppl-Pontifex Bold — Poppl-Pontifex
Poppl-Pontifex Expert & SCOSF Expert Roman — P-PONTIFEX 123 et al.
Expert Italic — *12345 et al.*
Expert Medium — P-PONTIFEX 123 et al.
Expert Medium Condensed — P-PONTIFEX 12345 et al.
Expert Bold — **12345 et al.**
Regular SCOSF — P-PONTIFEX 1234…
Italic OSF — *osf 12345…*
Medium SCOSF — P-PONTIFEX 1234…
Medium Condensed SCOSF — P-PONTIFEX 12345…
Bold OSF — **osf 12345…**
Poppl-Residenz Light — Poppl-Residenz
Regular — Poppl-Residenz
Post-Antiqua Regular — Post-Antiqua
Medium — Post-Antiqua
Post-Mediäval Roman — Post-Mediäval
Italic — *Post-Mediäval*
Medium — Post-Mediäval
Present Script Regular — Present Script
Bold — Present Script
Black — Present Script
Condensed — Present Script
Bold Condensed — Present Script
Black Condensed — Present Script
Present Script Regular ✣ Linotype DisplaySet 1 — Present Script
Prestige Elite Roman — Prestige Elite
Slanted — *Prestige Elite*
Bold — **Prestige Elite**
Bold Slanted — ***Prestige Elite***
ITC Quorum Light — ITC Quorum
Book — ITC Quorum
Medium — ITC Quorum
Bold — **ITC Quorum**
Black — **ITC Quorum**
Raleigh Roman — Raleigh
Medium — Raleigh
Demibold — Raleigh
Bold — **Raleigh**

Reporter No. 2 ✣ Adobe ScriptSet 1 — Reporter No. 2
Revue ✣ Adobe DisplaySet 1 — Revue
Rockwell 1 Light — Rockwell
Light Italic — *Rockwell*
Regular — Rockwell
Italic — *Rockwell*
Bold — **Rockwell**
Bold Italic — ***Rockwell***
Rockwell 2 Condensed — Rockwell
Bold Condensed — **Rockwell**
Extra Bold — **Rockwell**
Rosewood ✣ Adobe Wood Type 3 Regular — ROSEWOOD
Fill — ROSEWOOD
Rotation Roman — Rotation
Italic — *Rotation*
Bold — **Rotation**
Agfa Rotis Sans Serif 45-Light — Agfa Rotis
46-Light Italic — *Agfa Rotis*
55-Regular — Agfa Rotis
56-Italic — *Agfa Rotis*
65-Bold — **Agfa Rotis**
75-Extra Bold — **Agfa Rotis**
Agfa Rotis Semisans 45-Light — Agfa Rotis
46-Light Italic — *Agfa Rotis*
55-Regular — Agfa Rotis
56-Italic — *Agfa Rotis*
65-Bold — **Agfa Rotis**
75-Extra Bold — **Agfa Rotis**
Agfa Rotis Serif & Semiserif 55-Roman Serif — Agfa Rotis
56-Italic Serif — *Agfa Rotis*
65-Bold Serif — **Agfa Rotis**
55-Roman Semiserif — Agfa Rotis
65-Bold Semiserif — **Agfa Rotis**
Ruling Script ✣ Calligraphy for Print — Ruling Script
Monotype Runic Condensed ✣ Monotype DisplaySet 4 — Monotype Runic Condensed
Russell Square Regular — Russell Square
Oblique — *Russell Square*
Rusticana ✣ Type Before Gutenberg 3 Regular — RUSTICANA

… Rusticana Borders
Ruzicka Freehand + SCOSF Roman — Ruzicka Freehand
Bold — **Ruzicka Freehand**
Roman SCOSF — R FREEHAND 12345…
Bold SCOSF — **R FREEHAND 12345…**
Sabon Roman — Sabon
Italic — *Sabon*
Bold — **Sabon**
Bold Italic — ***Sabon***
Sabon SCOSF Roman SCOSF — SABON 12345…
Italic OSF — *osf 12345…*
Bold OSF — **osf 12345…**
Bold Italic OSF — ***osf 12345…***
San Marco ✣ Type Before Gutenberg 2 Regular — San Marco
Dfr — chckffftllſsſiſſäöü
Sanvito MultipleMaster Light — Sanvito MM
Regular — Sanvito MM
Semibold — Sanvito MM
Bold — **Sanvito MM**
Display Light — Sanvito MM
Display Regular — Sanvito MM
Display Semibold — Sanvito MM
Display Bold — **Sanvito MM**
Sassoon Primary — Sassoon Primary
Stempel Schneidler Light — S Schneidler
Light Italic — *S Schneidler*
Roman — S Schneidler
Italic — *S Schneidler*
Medium — S Schneidler
Medium Italic — *S Schneidler*
Bold — **S Schneidler**
Bold Italic — ***S Schneidler***
Black — **S Schneidler**
Black Italic — ***S Schneidler***
Monotype Scotch Roman ✣ Monotype TextSet 1 Roman — M Scotch Roman
Italic — *M Scotch Roman*
Monotype Script Bold ✣ Monotype ScriptSet 2 — M Script Bold
ITC Serif Gothic Light — ITC Serif Gothic

✣ See page 522 for contents of Adobe Systems Multi-Font Packages.

... ITC Serif Gothic
- Roman — ITC Serif Gothic
- Bold — ITC Serif Gothic
- Extra Bold — ITC Serif Gothic
- Heavy — ITC Serif Gothic
- Black — ITC Serif Gothic

Serifa
- 45-Light — Serifa
- 46-Light Italic — *Serifa*
- 55-Roman — Serifa
- 56-Italic — *Serifa*
- 65-Bold — **Serifa**
- 75-Black — **Serifa**

Serlio
- ✤ *Linotype Engravers Set 1* — SERLIO

Serpentine
- Light — Serpentine
- Light Oblique — *Serpentine*
- Medium — Serpentine
- Medium Oblique — *Serpentine*
- Bold — **Serpentine**
- Bold Oblique — ***Serpentine***

Shannon
- Book — Shannon
- Book Oblique — *Shannon*
- Bold — **Shannon**
- Extra Bold — **Shannon**

Shelley
- Allegro — Shelley
- Andante — Shelley
- Volante — Shelley

Sho
- ✤ *Calligraphy for Print* — Sho

ITC Slimbach
- Book — ITC Slimbach
- Book Italic — *ITC Slimbach*
- Medium — ITC Slimbach
- Medium Italic — *ITC Slimbach*
- Bold — **ITC Slimbach**
- Bold Italic — ***ITC Slimbach***
- Black — **ITC Slimbach**
- Black Italic — ***ITC Slimbach***

Smaragd
- ✤ *GudrunSchrift* — SMARAGD

Snell Roundhand
- Regular — *Snell Roundhand*
- Bold — *Snell Roundhand*
- Black — *Snell Roundhand*

Sonata
- ♪ ♬ 𝄐 𝄞

ITC Souvenir 1
- Light — ITC Souvenir
- Light Italic — *ITC Souvenir*
- Demi — **ITC Souvenir**
- Demi Italic — ***ITC Souvenir***

ITC Souvenir 2
- Medium — ITC Souvenir
- Medium Italic — *ITC Souvenir*
- Bold — **ITC Souvenir**
- Bold Italic — ***ITC Souvenir***

Spartan Classified
- Book — Spartan
- Heavy — **Spartan**

Spectrum + Expert & SCOSF
- Roman — Spectrum
- Italic — *Spectrum*
- Semibold — **Spectrum**
- Expert Roman — SPECTRUM 12345 et al.
- Expert Italic — *12345 et al.*
- Expert Semibold — **12345 et al.**
- Roman SCOSF — SPECTRUM 12345...
- Italic OSF — *osf 12345...*
- Semibold OSF — **osf 12345...**

Stencil
- ✤ *Adobe DisplaySet 4* — STENCIL

ITC Stone Serif
- Medium — ITC Stone
- Medium Italic — *ITC Stone*
- Semibold — **ITC Stone**
- Semibold Italic — ***ITC Stone***
- Bold — **ITC Stone**
- Bold Italic — ***ITC Stone***

ITC Stone Sans
- Medium — ITC Stone
- Medium Italic — *ITC Stone*
- Semibold — **ITC Stone**
- Semibold Italic — ***ITC Stone***
- Bold — **ITC Stone**
- Bold Italic — ***ITC Stone***

ITC Stone Informal
- Medium — ITC Stone
- Medium Italic — *ITC Stone*
- Semibold — **ITC Stone**
- Semibold Italic — ***ITC Stone***

... ITC Stone Informal
- Bold — **ITC Stone**
- Bold Italic — ***ITC Stone Infor***

ITC Stone Phonetic
- Serif IPA — ɑʙçðɛɸɢʜɪɟɪʟɰɴɔʼ
- Serif Alternate — ƀčđəƒɥǰĸλŋσþɽšŧ
- Sans IPA — ɑʙçðɛɸɢʜɪɟɪʟɰɴɔʼ
- Sans Alternate — ƀčđəƒɥǰĸλŋσþɽšŧω

ITC Symbol
- Book — ITC Symbol
- Book Italic — *ITC Symbol*
- Medium — ITC Symbol
- Medium Italic — *ITC Symbol*
- Bold — **ITC Symbol**
- Bold Italic — ***ITC Symbol***
- Black — **ITC Symbol**
- Black Italic — ***ITC Symbol***

Syntax
- Regular — Syntax
- Italic — *Syntax*
- Bold — **Syntax**
- Black — **Syntax**
- Ultra Black — **Syntax**

Tekton
- Regular — Tekton
- Oblique — *Tekton*
- Bold — **Tekton**
- Bold Oblique — ***Tekton***

Tekton MultipleMaster
- Light — Tekton MultipleMaster
- Light Oblique — *Tekton MultipleMaster*
- Regular — Tekton MultipleMaster
- Oblique — *Tekton MultipleMaster*
- Bold — **Tekton MultipleMaster**
- Bold Oblique — ***Tekton MultipleMaster***
- Light Condensed — Tekton MultipleMaster
- Light Condensed Oblique — *Tekton MultipleMaster*
- Condensed — Tekton MultipleMaster
- Condensed Oblique — *Tekton MultipleMaster*
- Bold Condensed — **Tekton MultipleMaster**
- Bold Condensed Oblique — ***Tekton MultipleMaster***
- Light Extended — Tekton MM
- Light Extended Oblique — *Tekton MM*
- Extended — Tekton MM

ff

. . . Tekton MultipleMaster
- Extended Oblique — *Tekton MM*
- Bold Extended — **Tekton MM**
- Bold Extended Oblique — ***Tekton MM***

Tempo Heavy Condensed ✤ *Linotype DisplaySet 3*
- Heavy Condensed — **Tempo**
- Heavy Condensed Italic — ***Tempo***

ITC Tiepolo
- Book — ITC Tiepolo
- Book Italic — *ITC Tiepolo*
- Bold — **ITC Tiepolo**
- Bold Italic — ***ITC Tiepolo***
- Black — **ITC Tiepolo**
- Black Italic — ***ITC Tiepolo***

ITC Tiffany
- Medium — ITC Tiffany
- Italic — *ITC Tiffany*
- Demi — **ITC Tiffany**
- Demi Italic — ***ITC Tiffany***
- Heavy — **ITC Tiffany**
- Heavy Italic — ***ITC Tiffany***

Times New Roman
- Roman — Times New Roman
- Italic — *Times New Roman*
- Bold — **Times New Roman**
- Bold Italic — ***Times New Roman***

Times New Roman Condensed
- Condensed — Times New Roman
- Condensed Italic — *Times New Roman*
- Bold Condensed — **Times New Roman**

Times 2
- Semibold — **Times**
- Semibold Italic — ***Times***
- Extra Bold — **Times**

Times SCOSF
- Roman SCOSF — TIMES 12345...
- Italic OSF — *osf 12345...*
- Bold SCOSF — **TIMES 12345...**
- Bold Italic OSF — ***osf 12345...***

Times Phonetic
- IPA — ɑβçðɛɸɢʜɪɟʟɰɴɔ’
- Alternate — ƀčđəƒɥǰʞƛɳσþɼšʅω

Times Ten
- Roman — Times Ten
- Italic — *Times Ten*
- Bold — **Times Ten**
- Bold Italic — ***Times Ten***

Times Ten SCOSF
- Roman SCOSF — TIMES 12345...

. . . Times Ten SCOSF
- Italic OSF — *osf 12345...*
- Bold OSF — **osf 12345...**
- Bold Italic OSF — ***osf 12345...***

Times Ten Cyrillic
- Upright — Абвгдеж Зикл
- Inclined — *Абвгдеж Зикл*
- Bold Upright — **Абвгдеж Зикл**
- Bold Inclined — ***Абвгдеж Зикл***

Times Europa
- Roman — Times Europa
- Italic — *Times Europa*
- Bold — **Times Europa**
- Bold Italic — ***Times Europa***

Trade Gothic
- Light — Trade Gothic
- Light Oblique — *Trade Gothic*
- Regular — Trade Gothic
- Oblique — *Trade Gothic*
- Bold — **Trade Gothic**
- Bold Oblique — ***Trade Gothic***
- Bold 2 — **Trade Gothic**
- Bold 2 Oblique — ***Trade Gothic***

Trade Gothic Condensed
- 18 Condensed — Trade Gothic
- 18 Condensed Oblique — *Trade Gothic*
- 20 Bold Condensed — **Trade Gothic**
- 20 Bold Condensed Oblique — ***Trade Gothic***

Trade Gothic Extended
- Extended — Trade Gothic
- Bold Extended — **Trade Gothic**

Trajan ✤ *Adobe TitlingSet 1*
- Regular — TRAJAN
- Bold — **TRAJAN**

Trump Mediäval
- Roman — Trump Mediäval
- Italic — *Trump Mediäval*
- Bold — **Trump Mediäval**
- Bold Italic — ***Trump Mediäval***

Trump Mediäval SCOSF
- Roman SCOSF — T MEDIÄVAL 123...
- Italic OSF — *osf 12345...*
- Bold OSF — **osf 12345...**
- Bold Italic OSF — ***osf 12345...***

Umbra ✤ *Adobe DisplaySet 5* — UMBRA

Univers 1
- 45-Light — Univers

. . . Univers 1
- 45-Light Oblique — *Univers*
- 55-Regular — Univers
- 55-Oblique — *Univers*
- 65-Bold — **Univers**
- 65-Bold Oblique — ***Univers***
- 75-Black — **Univers**
- 75-Black Oblique — ***Univers***

Univers 2
- 85-Extra Black — **Univers**
- 85-Extra Black Oblique — ***Univers***
- 39-Thin Ultra Condensed — Univers
- 49-Light Ultra Condensed — Univers
- 59-Ultra Condensed — **Univers**

Univers Condensed
- 47-Light Condensed — Univers
- 47-Light Condensed Oblique — *Univers*
- 57-Condensed — Univers
- 57-Condensed Oblique — *Univers*
- 67-Bold Condensed — **Univers**
- 67-Bold Condensed Oblique — ***Univers***

Univers Extended
- 53-Extended — Univers
- 53-Extended Oblique — *Univers*
- 63-Bold Extended — **Univers**
- 63-Bold Extended Oblique — ***Univers***
- 73-Black Extended — **Univers**
- 73-Black Extended Oblique — ***Univers***
- 93-Extra Black Extended — **Univers**
- 93-Extra Black Extended Oblique — ***Univers***

Linotype Universal Pi
- Greek with Math Pi — αβΨΔΩΣ+−×÷√
- News with Commercial Pi — ✔ ™ © ♦ # ♦ @ % ® ☎

University Roman ✤ *Adobe DisplaySet 1* — University Roman

ITC Usherwood
- Book — ITC Usherwood
- Book Italic — *ITC Usherwood*
- Medium — ITC Usherwood
- Medium Italic — *ITC Usherwood*
- Bold — **ITC Usherwood**
- Bold Italic — ***ITC Usherwood***
- Black — **ITC Usherwood**
- Black Italic — ***ITC Usherwood***

Utopia
- Roman — Utopia

ff

✤ *See page 522 for contents of Adobe Systems Multi-Font Packages.*

... Utopia
Italic *Utopia*
Semibold **Utopia**
Semibold Italic ***Utopia***
Bold **Utopia**
Bold Italic ***Utopia***
Black **Utopia**

Utopia Expert & SCOSF
Expert Roman UTOPIA 12345 et al.
Expert Italic *12345 et al.*
Expert Semibold **UTOPIA 12345 et al.**
Expert Semibold Italic ***12345 et al.***
Expert Bold **12345 et al.**
Expert Bold Italic ***12345 et al.***
Expert Black **12345 et al.**
Roman SCOSF UTOPIA 12345...
Italic OSF *osf 12345...*
Semibold SCOSF **UTOPIA 12345...**
Semibold Italic OSF ***osf 12345...***
Bold OSF **osf 12345...**
Bold Italic OSF ***osf 12345...***
Black OSF **osf 12345...**
Titling Capitals UTOPIA
Ornaments

VAG Rounded
Thin VAG Rounded
Light VAG Rounded
Bold **VAG Rounded**
Black **VAG Rounded**

Vectora
45-Light Vectora
46-Light Italic *Vectora*
55-Roman Vectora
56-Italic *Vectora*
75-Bold **Vectora**
76-Bold Italic ***Vectora***
95-Black **Vectora**
96-Black Italic ***Vectora***

ITC Veljovic
Book ITC Veljovic
Book Italic *ITC Veljovic*
Medium ITC Veljovic
Medium Italic *ITC Veljovic*

... ITC Veljovic
Bold **ITC Veljovic**
Bold Italic ***ITC Veljovic***
Black **ITC Veljovic**
Black Italic ***ITC Veljovic***

Versailles
45-Light Versailles
46-Light Italic *Versailles*
55-Roman Versailles
56-Italic *Versailles*
75-Bold **Versailles**
76-Bold Italic ***Versailles***
95-Black **Versailles**
96-Black Italic ***Versailles***

Visigoth
Baker Calligraphy Visigoth

Viva MultipleMaster
Light Viva MM
Regular Viva MM
Bold **Viva MM**
Light Condensed Viva MM
Condensed Viva MM
Bold Condensed **Viva MM**
Light Extra-Extended Viva MM
Extra-Extended Viva MM
Bold Extra-Extended **Viva MM**

Berthold Walbaum Book
Roman B Walbaum Book
Italic *B Walbaum Book*
Medium B Walbaum Book
Medium Italic *B Walbaum Book*
Bold **B Walbaum Book**
Bold Italic ***B Walbaum Book***

Berthold Walbaum
Expert & SCOSF
Expert Roman B WALBAUM 1234 et al.
Expert Italic *12345 et al.*
Expert Medium B WALBAUM 123 et al.
Expert Medium Italic *12345 et al.*
Expert Bold **12345 et al.**
Expert Bold Italic ***12345 et al.***
Regular SCOSF B WALBAUM 1234...
Italic OSF *osf 12345...*
Medium SCOSF B WALBAUM 1234...
Medium Italic OSF *osf 12345...*

... Berthold Walbaum
Expert & SCOSF
Bold OSF **osf 12345...**
Bold Italic OSF ***osf 12345...***

Linotype Warning Pi
Linotype PiSet 1

ITC Weidemann
Book ITC Weidemann
Book Italic *ITC Weidemann*
Medium ITC Weidemann
Medium Italic *ITC Weidemann*
Bold **ITC Weidemann**
Bold Italic ***ITC Weidemann***
Black **ITC Weidemann**
Black Italic ***ITC Weidemann***

Weiss
Roman Weiss
Italic *Weiss*
Bold **Weiss**
Extra Bold **Weiss**

Wiesbaden Swing
Calligraphy for Print Wiesbaden Swing

Adobe Wild Type
Birch Birch
Critter CRITTER
Cutout CUTOUT
Giddyup Giddyup
Giddyup Thangs
Myriad Headline **Myriad Headline**
Myriad Sketch Myriad Sketch
Myriad Tilt Myriad Tilt
Mythos MYTHOS
Quake Quake
Rad RAD
Studz STUDZ
Toolbox TOOLBOX
Utopia Headline Utopia Headline

Wilhelm Klingspor Gotisch
Linotype DisplaySet 2
Regular Wilhelm Klingspor
Dfr

Wilke
55-Roman Wilke
56-Italic *Wilke*
75-Bold **Wilke**
76-Bold Italic ***Wilke***
95-Black **Wilke**
96-Black Italic ***Wilke***

ff

Willow
✤ Adobe Wood Type 2 — Willow

Wittenberger Fraktur
✤ Monotype DisplaySet 3
Regular — Wittenberger Fraktur
Dfr — chckffftllſsſiſſßẞäöü
Bold — Wittenberger Fraktur
Bold Dfr — chckffllſsſiſſßẞäöü

AD Wood Type Ornaments 1
✤ Adobe Wood Type 1

AD Wood Type Ornaments 2
✤ Adobe Wood Type 2

ITC Zapf Chancery Med Italic
✤ ITC ZapfSet 1 — ITC Zapf Chancery

ITC Zapf Chancery
Light — ITC Zapf Chancery
Light Italic — ITC Zapf Chancery
Regular — ITC Zapf Chancery
Italic — ITC Zapf Chancery
Demi — ITC Zapf Chancery
Bold — ITC Zapf Chancery

ITC Zapf Dingbats
✤ ITC ZapfSet 1

Zebrawood
✤ Adobe Wood Type 3
Regular — ZEBRAWOOD
Fill — ZEBRAWOOD

Adobe Systems Multi-Font Package Contents

✤ Adobe DisplaySet 1	: Aachen Bold, Freestyle Script, Revue, University Roman.
✤ Adobe DisplaySet 2	: Baker Signet, Impact.
✤ Adobe DisplaySet 3	: ITC Benguiat Book & Bold, Friz Quadrata Regular & Bold.
✤ Adobe DisplaySet 4	: Brush Script, Hobo, Stencil.
✤ Adobe DisplaySet 5	: Parisian, Umbra.
✤ Adobe ScriptSet 1	: Mistral, Reporter No. 2
✤ Adobe TitlingSet 1	: Charlemagne Regular & Bold, Trajan Regular & Bold.
✤ Adobe Wood Type 1	: Cottonwood, Ironwood, Juniper, Mesquite, Ponderosa, Adobe Wood Type Ornaments 1.
✤ Adobe Wood Type 2	: Birch, Blackoak, Madrone, Poplar, Willow, Adobe Wood Type Ornaments 2.
✤ Adobe Wood Type 3	: Rosewood, Pepperwood, Zebrawood.
✤ Baker Calligraphy	: Amigo, Marigold, Oxford, Pelican, Visigoth.
✤ Berthold DisplaySet 1	: AG Book Stencil, AG Old Face Shaded, Barmeno Extra Bold, Cosmos Extra Bold, Formata Outline
✤ Berthold ScriptSet 1	: Bellevue, Berthold Script Regular & Medium, Boulevard.
✤ Brody DisplaySet 1	: Arcadia, Industria Inline & Solid, Insignia.
✤ Calligraphy for Print	: Ruling Script, Sho, Wiesbaden Swing.
✤ Electra Set 1	: Caravan Borders 1, 2, 3, 4, Electra Regular, Cursive, Bold, Bold Cursive.
✤ GudrunSchrift	: Ariadne, Diotima Roman, Italic, Roman SCOSF, Roman OSF, Italic OSF, Smaragd.
✤ ITC Typographica	: ITC Anna, ITC Beesknees, ITC Mona Lisa Recut & Solid, ITC Ozwald.
✤ ITC ZapfSet 1	: ITC Zapf Chancery Medium Italic, ITC Zapf Dingbats.
✤ Linotype ClassAdSet 1	: Doric Bold, Maximus.
✤ Linotype DisplaySet 1	: Arnold Böcklin, Fette Fraktur, Helvetica Inserat, Present Script.
✤ Linotype DisplaySet 2	: Banco, Charme, Flyer Black Condensed & Extra Black Condensed, Wilhelm Klingspor Gotisch.
✤ Linotype DisplaySet 3	: Gothic 13, Tempo Heavy Condensed.
✤ Linotype Engravers Set 1	: Engravers Bold Face, Serlio.
✤ Linotype Fraction Pi	: Helvetica Regular & Bold Fractions, New Century Schoolbook Regular & Bold Fractions
✤ Linotype PiSet 1	: Linotype Audio Pi, Linotype Warning Pi.
✤ Linotype PiSet 2	: Border Pi, European Pi.
✤ Linotype ScriptSet 1	: Cascade Script, Medici Script, Nuptial Script.
✤ Linotype ScriptSet 2	: Linoscript, Linotext.
✤ Linotype Universal Pi	: Universal Greek with Math Pi, Universal News with Commercial Pi.
✤ Monotype DisplaySet 1	: Albertus Light, Regular & Italic, Castellar.
✤ Monotype DisplaySet 2	: Falstaff, Inflex Bold, Monotype Old Style Bold Outline.
✤ Monotype DisplaySet 3	: Kino, Matura Regular & Scriptorial Capitals, Wittenberger Fraktur.
✤ Monotype DisplaySet 4	: Latin Condensed, Onyx, Monotype Runic Condensed.
✤ Monotype ScriptSet 1	: Ashley Script, Monoline Script, New Berolina, Palace Script Regular & Semibold.
✤ Monotype ScriptSet 2	: Biffo Script, Dorchester Script, Pepita, Monotype Script Bold.
✤ Monotype ScriptSet 3	: Forte, Klang, Mercurius Bold Script.
✤ Monotype TextSet 1	: Monotype Goudy Modern Roman & Italic, Monotype Scotch Roman Regular & Italic.
✤ OCR Set 1	: MICR, OCR-A, OCR-B.
✤ Type Before Gutenberg 1	: Duc De Berry, Herculanum, Omnia.
✤ Type Before Gutenberg 2	: Carolina, Clairvaux, San Marco.
✤ Type Before Gutenberg 3	: Notre Dame, Notre Dame Ornaments, Pompeijana, Pompeijana Borders, Rusticana, Rusticana Borders.

foundry: Agfa

The Agfa Type Collection consists of a wide-ranging selection of contemporary standards, originals from Agfa's own design program as well as other sources and – in the Agfa *Typographer's Edition* series – a variety of fonts representative of many different styles, periods and places in typographic history. Agfa also offers an immense number of pi characters, logotypes, dingbats, and pictograms (more than 11,000) in their Pi, Logo & Symbol fonts. ¶ In addition to being a licensed reseller of the complete Adobe Type Library, Agfa also features faces from The Font Bureau Collection.

Accolade
Light — Accolade
Light Italic — Accolade
Medium — Accolade
Bold — Accolade

Administer
Light — Administer
Light Italic — Administer
Book — Administer
Book Italic — Administer
Bold — Administer

Adroit
Light — Adroit
Light Italic — Adroit
Medium — Adroit
Medium Italic — Adroit

Aldous Vertical
✤ Agfa DisplaySet 1 — ALDOUS VERTICAL

Alpin Gothic
No. 1 — Alpin Gothic
No. 2 — Alpin Gothic
No. 2 Italic — Alpin Gothic
No. 3 — Alpin Gothic

American Classic
Roman — American Classic
Italic — American Classic
Bold — American Classi
Extra Bold — American Classi

Amigo
✤ Agfa Baker Calligraphy — Amigo

ITC Anna
✤ Agfa ITC DisplaySet 1 — ITC ANNA

Antique Olive 1
Regular — Antique Olive
Italic — Antique Olive
Medium — Antique Olive
Medium Italic — Antique Olive

Antique Olive 2
Bold — Antique Olive
Compact — Antique Olive
Nord — Antique Olive
Nord Italic — Antique Olive

Antique Roman
✤ Agfa Engravers 1
Solid — Antique Roman
Slanted — Antique Roman

Sackers Antique Roman
✤ Agfa Engravers 2
Open — S Antique Roman
Solid — S Antique Roman

Aquarius No. 8
✤ Agfa DisplaySet 2 — Aquarius

Arta
Light — Arta
Light Italic — Arta
Book — Arta
Book Italic — Arta
Medium — Arta
Medium Italic — Arta
Bold — Arta
Bold Italic — Arta

ff

✤ See this page for contents of Adobe Systems Multi-Font Packages. See page 528 for contents of Agfa Multi-Font Packages.

Artisan Roman ✣ *Agfa Engravers 1* — Artisan Roman

Aura ✣ *Agfa DisplaySet 1* — **Aura**

Basilia
- Roman — Basilia
- Italic — *Basilia*
- Medium — Basilia
- Medium Italic — *Basilia*
- Bold — **Basilia**
- Bold Italic — ***Basilia***
- Black — **Basilia**
- Black Italic — ***Basilia***

Basilica ✣ *Agfa ScriptSet 1* — Basilica

Basque ✣ *Agfa DisplaySet 3* — Basque

ITC Bauhaus
- Light — ITC Bauhaus
- Medium — ITC Bauhaus
- Bold — **ITC Bauhaus**
- Heavy — **ITC Bauhaus**

ITC Beesknees ✣ *Agfa ITC DisplaySet 1* — ITC BEESKNEES

ITC Benguiat Gothic 1
- Book — ITC Benguiat Gothic
- Book Italic — *ITC Benguiat Gothic*
- Bold — **ITC Benguiat Gothic**
- Bold Italic — **ITC Benguiat Gothic**

ITC Benguiat Gothic 2
- Medium — ITC Benguiat Gothic
- Medium Italic — *ITC Benguiat Gothic*
- Heavy — **ITC Benguiat Gothic**
- Heavy Italic — ***ITC Benguiat Gothic***

ITC Berkeley Oldstyle 1
- Book — ITC Berkeley O S
- Book Italic — *ITC Berkeley O S*
- Bold — **ITC Berkeley O S**
- Bold Italic — ***ITC Berkeley O S***

ITC Berkeley Oldstyle 2
- Medium — ITC Berkeley O S
- Medium Italic — *ITC Berkeley O S*
- Black — **ITC Berkeley O S**
- Black Italic — ***ITC Berkeley O S***

Berling
- Book — Berling
- Book Italic — *Berling*
- Bold — **Berling**

Bernhard Modern
- Roman — Bernhard Modern
- Italic — *Bernhard Modern*

. . . Bernhard Modern
- Bold — **Bernhard Modern**
- Bold Italic — ***Bernhard Modern***

Bauer Bodoni
- Roman — Bauer Bodoni
- Italic — *Bauer Bodoni*
- Bold — **Bauer Bodoni**
- Bold Italic — ***Bauer Bodoni***

Bauer Bodoni Black + Condensed
- Black — **Bauer Bodoni**
- Black Italic — ***Bauer Bodoni***
- Bold Condensed — **Bauer Bodoni**
- Black Condensed — **Bauer Bodoni**

CG Poster Bodoni ✣ *Agfa DisplaySet 2*
- Roman — **Poster Bodoni**
- Italic — ***Poster Bodoni***

WTC Our Bodoni
- Light — WTC Our Bodoni
- Light Italic — *WTC Our Bodoni*
- Regular — WTC Our Bodoni
- Italic — *WTC Our Bodoni*
- Medium — **WTC Our Bodoni**
- Medium Italic — ***WTC Our Bodoni***
- Bold — **WTC Our Bodoni**
- Bold Italic — ***WTC Our Bodoni***

Bramley
- Light — Bramley
- Medium — Bramley
- Bold — **Bramley**
- Extra Bold — **Bramley**

Branding Iron ✣ *Agfa DisplaySet 4* — Branding Iron

Brophy Script ✣ *Agfa DisplaySet 3* — Brophy Script

Burin ✣ *Agfa Engravers 1*
- Roman — Burin
- Sans — Burin

ITC Busorama
- Light — ITC BUSORAMA
- Medium — ITC BUSORAMA
- Bold — ITC BUSORAMA

Carmine Tango ✣ *Agfa ScriptSet 2* — Carmine Tango

Cartier ✣ *Agfa TextSet 1*
- Roman — Cartier
- Italic — *Cartier*

ITC Caslon No. 224 One
- Book — ITC Caslon No.224
- Book Italic — *ITC Caslon No.224*
- Bold — **ITC Caslon No.224**
- Bold Italic — ***ITC Caslon No.224***

ITC Caslon No. 224 Two
- Medium — ITC Caslon No.224
- Medium Italic — *ITC Caslon No.224*
- Black — **ITC Caslon No.224**
- Black Italic — ***ITC Caslon No.224***

Caxton
- Light — Caxton
- Light Italic — *Caxton*
- Book — Caxton
- Bold — **Caxton**

Chaplin ✣ *Agfa ScriptSet 2* — Chaplin

Chevalier ✣ *Agfa DisplaySet 3* — CHEVALIER

Citadel ✣ *Agfa Scripts 2* — Citadel

Claire News ✣ *Agfa DisplaySet 5*
- Light — Claire News
- Bold — **Claire News**

Clarendon Book Condensed ✣ *Agfa DisplaySet 2* — Clarendon Book

Claridge
- Roman — Claridge
- Italic — *Claridge*
- Bold — **Claridge**
- Black — **Claridge**

Classic Roman ✣ *Agfa Engravers 1*
- Light — CLASSIC ROMAN
- Regular — CLASSIC ROMAN

Sackers Light Classic Roman ✣ *Agfa Engravers 2* — S CLASSIC ROMAN

ITC Clearface
- Roman — ITC Clearface
- Italic — *ITC Clearface*
- Bold — **ITC Clearface**
- Bold Italic — ***ITC Clearface***

CG Clearface Gothic
- Light — CG Clearface Gothic
- Regular — CG Clearface Gothic
- Medium — **CG Clearface Gothic**
- Bold — **CG Clearface Gothic**
- Black — **CG Clearface Gothic**

CG Cloister ✣ *Agfa TextSet 2*
- Roman — CG Cloister
- Italic — *CG Cloister*

CG Collage
- Roman — CG Collage
- Italic — *CG Collage*
- Bold — **CG Collage**
- Bold Italic — ***CG Collage***

Commercial Script ✣ *Agfa Scripts 1* — Commercial Script

Computer ✣ *Agfa DisplaySet 1* — COMPUTER

ff

Congress
Roman Congress
Italic Congress
Bold Congress
Heavy Congress

Coronet
❖ Agfa ScriptSet 2
Regular Coronet
Bold Coronet

Crillee Italic
Light Italic Crillee Italic
Italic Crillee Italic
Bold Italic Crillee Italic
Extra Bold Italic Crillee Italic

Derek Italic
❖ Agfa DisplaySet 6 Derek Italic

CG DeVinne
❖ Agfa TextSet 2
Roman CG DeVinne
Italic CG DeVinne

Eaglefeather
Light Eaglefeather
Light Italic Eaglefeather
Regular Eaglefeather
Italic Eaglefeather
Bold Eaglefeather
Bold Italic Eaglefeather

Eaglefeather Informal
Informal Light Eaglefeather
Informal Light Italic Eaglefeather
Informal Eaglefeather
Informal Italic Eaglefeather
Informal Bold Eaglefeather
Informal Bold Italic Eaglefeather
Light SCOSF EAGLEFEATHER 12345...

Eaglefeather SCOSF
Regular SCOSF EAGLEFEATHER 12345...
Bold SCOSF EAGLEFEATHER 1234...

Eccentric
❖ Agfa DisplaySet 1 ECCENTRIC

Egyptian 505
Light Egyptian 505
Roman Egyptian 505
Medium Egyptian 505
Bold Egyptian 505

ITC Élan
Book ITC Élan
Book Italic ITC Élan
Medium ITC Élan
Medium Italic ITC Élan
Bold ITC Élan

. . . ITC Élan
Bold Italic ITC Élan
Black ITC Élan
Black Italic ITC Élan

Elante
Roman Elante
Cursive Elante
Bold Elante
Bold Cursive Elante

Sackers English Script
❖ Agfa Engravers 2 S English Script

Engravure
❖ Agfa DisplaySet 6 ENGRAVURE

Erbar Condensed
❖ Agfa DisplaySet 7
Light Condensed Erbar
Medium Condensed Erbar

ITC Esprit
Book ITC Esprit
Book Italic ITC Esprit
Medium ITC Esprit
Medium Italic ITC Esprit
Bold ITC Esprit
Bold Italic ITC Esprit
Black ITC Esprit
Black Italic ITC Esprit

ITC Fenice 1
Roman ITC Fenice
Italic ITC Fenice
Bold ITC Fenice
Bold Italic ITC Fenice

ITC Fenice 2
Light ITC Fenice
Light Italic ITC Fenice
Ultra ITC Fenice
Ultra Italic ITC Fenice

Flemish Script 2
❖ Agfa Scripts 2 Flemish Script 2

ITC Flora
❖ Agfa ITC DisplaySet 2
Medium ITC Flora
Bold ITC Flora

Florentine Script 2
❖ Agfa Scripts 2 Florentine Script 2

Floridian Script
❖ Agfa ScriptSet 1 Floridian Script

Folio
Light Folio
Light Italic Folio
Medium Folio
Bold Folio

French Script
❖ Agfa Scripts 2 French Script

CG Frontiera
45-Light CG Frontiera

. . . CG Frontiera
46-Light Italic CG Frontiera
55-Regular CG Frontiera
56-Italic CG Frontiera
65-Bold CG Frontiera
66-Bold Italic CG Frontiera
75-Extra Bold CG Frontiera
76-Extra Bold Italic CG Frontiera

Garamond Antiqua
Roman Garamond Antiqua
Kursiv Garamond Antiqua
Halbfett Garamond Antiqua
Kursiv Halbfett Garamond Antiqua

Garth Graphic
Roman Garth Graphic
Italic Garth Graphic
Bold Garth Graphic
Bold Italic Garth Graphic
Extra Bold Garth Graphic
Black Garth Graphic
Condensed Garth Graphic
Bold Condensed Garth Graphic

Garth Graphic Premier
Roman G GRAPHIC 1234 et al.
Italic 12345 et al.
Bold 12345 et al.
Bold Italic 12345 et al.
Extra Bold 12345 et al.
Black 12345 et al.
Comdensed 12345 et al.
Bold Condensed 12345 et al.

Geometric
Light Geometric
Light Italic Geometric
Bold Geometric
Bold Italic Geometric

ITC Giovanni
Book ITC Giovanni
Book Italic ITC Giovanni
Bold ITC Giovanni
Bold Italic ITC Giovanni
Black ITC Giovanni
Black Italic ITC Giovanni

Globe Gothic
Light Globe Gothic

ff

❖ See page 528 for contents of Agfa Multi-Font Packages.

... Globe Gothic
- Demi — Globe Gothic
- Bold — Globe Gothic
- Ultra — Globe Gothic

Gothic
- No. 1 — Gothic
- No. 2 — Gothic
- No. 3 — Gothic
- No. 4 — Gothic

Gothic Extralight Extended
- ✜ Agfa DisplaySet 6 — Gothic Extralight

Sackers Gothic
- ✜ Agfa Engravers 2
- Light — S GOTHIC
- Medium — S GOTHIC
- Heavy — S GOTHIC

Goudy Heavyface
- Regular — Goudy Heavy
- Italic — Goudy Heavy
- Condensed — Goudy Heavyface

ITC Goudy Sans
- Book — ITC Goudy Sans
- Book Italic — ITC Goudy Sans
- Medium — ITC Goudy Sans
- Medium Italic — ITC Goudy Sans
- Bold — ITC Goudy Sans
- Bold Italic — ITC Goudy Sans
- Black — ITC Goudy Sans
- Black Italic — ITC Goudy Sans

Graphite
- Light — Graphite
- Regular — Graphite
- Demibold — Graphite
- Bold — Graphite
- Black — Graphite

Graphite Condensed
- Light Condensed — Graphite
- Condensed — Graphite
- Demibold Condensed — Graphite
- Bold Condensed — Graphite
- Black Condensed — Graphite

Graphite Narrow
- Narrow Light — Graphite
- Narrow — Graphite
- Narrow Demibold — Graphite
- Narrow Bold — Graphite
- Narrow Black — Graphite

Graphite Extended
- Light Extended — Graphite

... Graphite Extended
- Extended — Graphite
- Demibold Extended — Graphite
- Bold Extended — Graphite
- Black Extended — Graphite

Graphite Wide
- Wide Light — Graphite
- Wide — Graphite
- Wide Demibold — Graphite
- Wide Bold — Graphite
- Wide Black — Graphite

Hadriano
- Light — Hadriano
- Bold — Hadriano
- Extra Bold — Hadriano
- Extra Bold Condensed — Hadriano

Handle Oldstyle
- ✜ Agfa Engravers 1 — HANDLE OLDSTYLE

Heldustry
- Regular — Heldustry
- Italic — Heldustry
- Demi — Heldustry
- Demi Italic — Heldustry

Helinda Rook
- ✜ Agfa Scripts 1 — Helinda Rook

Holland Seminar
- ✜ Agfa TextSet 1
- Roman — Holland Seminar
- Italic — Holland Seminar

Holland Title
- ✜ Agfa DisplaySet 6 — Holland Title

Hollandse Mediaeval
- ✜ Agfa Text DisplaySet 1
- Roman — Hollandse Mediaeval
- Bold — Hollandse Mediaeval

Impressum
- Roman — Impressum
- Italic — Impressum
- Bold — Impressum
- Bold Italic — Impressum

Isabella
- ✜ Agfa DisplaySet 4 — Isabella

ITC Isadora
- ✜ Agfa ITC DisplaySet 2
- Regular — ITC Isadora
- Bold — ITC Isadora

ITC Isbell
- Book — ITC Isbell
- Book Italic — ITC Isbell
- Bold — ITC Isbell
- Bold Italic — ITC Isbell

Sackers Italian Script
- ✜ Agfa Engravers 2 — S Italian Script

ITC Jamille
- Book — ITC Jamille
- Book Italic — ITC Jamille

... ITC Jamille
- Bold — ITC Jamille
- Bold Italic — ITC Jamille
- Black — ITC Jamille
- Black Italic — ITC Jamille

Jasper
- ✜ Agfa ScriptSet 1 — Jasper

Liberty
- ✜ Agfa ScriptSet 1 — Liberty

Lisbon
- Regular — Lisbon
- Italic — Lisbon
- Bold — Lisbon
- Bold Italic — Lisbon

Mahogany Script
- ✜ Agfa Scripts 2 — Mahogany Script

Marigold
- ✜ Agfa Baker Calligraphy — Marigold

McCollough
- ✜ Agfa DisplaySet 4 — McCollough

ITC Mendoza Roman
- Book — ITC Mendoza
- Book Italic — ITC Mendoza
- Medium — ITC Mendoza
- Medium Italic — ITC Mendoza
- Bold — ITC Mendoza
- Bold Italic — ITC Mendoza

Méridien
- Light — Méridien
- Light Italic — Méridien
- Bold — Méridien
- Black — Méridien

ITC Mona Lisa Recut
- ✜ Agfa ITC DisplaySet 1 — ITC Mona Lisa Recut

Musketeer
- Light — Musketeer
- Regular — Musketeer
- Demibold — Musketeer
- Extra Bold — Musketeer

Agfa Nadianne
- Book — Agfa Nadianne
- Medium — Agfa Nadianne
- Bold — Agfa Nadianne

Agfa Nadianne Condensed
- Book Condensed — Agfa Nadian
- Medium Condensed — Agfa Nadianne
- Bold Condensed — Agfa Nadianne

CG Nashville 1
- Medium — CG Nashville
- Medium Italic — CG Nashville
- Bold — CG Nashville
- Bold Italic — CG Nashville

CG Nashville 2
Light CG Nashville
Light Italic *CG Nashville*
Extra Bold **CG Nashville**
Extra Bold Italic ***CG Nashville***

News
✤ Agfa NewsSet 1
No. 2 News
No. 2 Italic *News*
No. 2 Bold **News**
No. 14 News
No. 14 Italic *News*
No. 14 Bold **News**

ITC Novarese 1
Book ITC Novarese
Book Italic *ITC Novarese*
Bold **ITC Novarese**
Bold Italic ***ITC Novarese***

ITC Novarese 2
Medium ITC Novarese
Medium Italic *ITC Novarese*
Ultra **ITC Novarese**

ITC Officina
Serif Book ITC Officina
Serif Book Italic *ITC Officina*
Serif Bold **ITC Officina**
Serif Bold Italic ***ITC Officina***
Sans Book ITC Officina
Sans Book Italic *ITC Officina*
Sans Bold **ITC Officina**
Sans Bold Italic ***ITC Officina***

Old English
✤ Agfa Scripts 1 Old English

Old Fashion Script
✤ Agfa Scripts 2 *Old Fashion Script*

Original Script
✤ Agfa Scripts 1 *Original Script*

Oxford
✤ Agfa Baker Calligraphy Oxford

ITC Pacella
Book ITC Pacella
Book Italic *ITC Pacella*
Medium ITC Pacella
Medium Italic *ITC Pacella*
Bold **ITC Pacella**
Bold Italic ***ITC Pacella***
Black **ITC Pacella**
Black Italic ***ITC Pacella***

Pasquale
Light Pasquale

. . . Pasquale
Light Italic *Pasquale*
Book Pasquale
Book Italic *Pasquale*
Medium Pasquale
Medium Italic *Pasquale*
Bold **Pasquale**
Bold Italic ***Pasquale***

Pelican
✤ Agfa Baker Calligraphy *Pelican*

ITC Quay Sans
Book ITC Quay Sans
Book Italic *ITC Quay Sans*
Medium ITC Quay Sans
Medium Italic *ITC Quay Sans*
Black **ITC Quay Sans**
Black Italic ***ITC Quay Sans***

Quill Script
✤ Agfa Scripts 1 *Quill Script*

ITC Quorum
Light ITC Quorum
Book ITC Quorum
Bold **ITC Quorum**
Black **ITC Quorum**

Raleigh
Light Raleigh
Medium Raleigh
Bold **Raleigh**
Extra Bold **Raleigh**

Raphael
✤ Agfa DisplaySet 4 Raphael

Riviera Script
✤ Agfa Scripts 2 Riviera Script

Roman
✤ Agfa Engravers 1
Light ROMAN
Medium ROMAN

Sackers Roman
✤ Agfa Engravers 2
Light S ROMAN
Heavy **S ROMAN**

Romic
Light Romic
Light Italic *Romic*
Medium Romic
Bold **Romic**
Extra Bold **Romic**

Agfa Rotis Sans Serif
45-Light Agfa Rotis
46-Light Italic *Agfa Rotis*
55-Regular Agfa Rotis
56-Italic *Agfa Rotis*

. . . Agfa Rotis Sans Serif
65-Bold **Agfa Rotis**
75-Extra Bold **Agfa Rotis**

Agfa Rotis Semisans
45-Light Agfa Rotis
46-Light Italic *Agfa Rotis*
55-Regular Agfa Rotis
56-Italic *Agfa Rotis*
65-Bold **Agfa Rotis**
75-Extra Bold **Agfa Rotis**

Agfa Rotis Serif & Semiserif
55-Roman Serif Agfa Rotis
56-Italic Serif *Agfa Rotis*
65-Bold Serif **Agfa Rotis**
55-Regular Semiserif Agfa Rotis
65-Bold Semiserif **Agfa Rotis**

Sans No. 1
✤ Agfa NewsSet 1
Regular Sans No. 1
Heavy **Sans No. 1**

Schneidler Mediaeval
Roman Schneidler Mediaeval
Italic *Schneidler Mediaeval*
Bold **Schneidler Mediaev**
Bold Italic ***Schneidler Mediaeval***

Shannon
Book Shannon
Book Oblique *Shannon*
Bold **Shannon**
Extra Bold **Shannon**

Shannon Premier
Premier Book SHANNON 12345 et al.
Premier Book Oblique *12345 et al.*
Premier Bold **12345 et al.**
Premier Extra Bold **12345 et al.**

Signature
✤ Agfa TextDisplay Set 1
Light Signature
Black **Signature**

ITC Slimbach
Book ITC Slimbach
Book Italic *ITC Slimbach*
Medium ITC Slimbach
Medium Italic *ITC Slimbach*
Bold **ITC Slimbach**
Bold Italic ***ITC Slimbach***
Black **ITC Slimbach**
Black Italic ***ITC Slimbach***

Souvenir Gothic
Light Souvenir Gothic

✤ See page 528 for contents of Agfa Multi-Font Packages.

... Souvenir Gothic
Light Italic *Souvenir Gothic*
Demibold **Souvenir Gothic**
Demibold Italic ***Souvenir Gothic***

Sackers Square Gothic
❖ *Agfa Engravers 2* S SQUARE GOTHIC

ITC Studio Script
❖ *Agfa ITC DisplaySet 1*
Regular *ITC Studio Script*
Alternate *aabcdefghiiklhnprrpssttv*

Stuyvesant
❖ *Agfa Scripts 1* *Stuyvesant*

ITC Symbol
Book ITC Symbol
Book Italic *ITC Symbol*
Medium ITC Symbol
Medium Italic *ITC Symbol*
Bold **ITC Symbol**
Bold Italic ***ITC Symbol***
Black **ITC Symbol**
Black Italic ***ITC Symbol***

CG Symphony
Regular CG Symphony
Italic *CG Symphony*
Bold **CG Symphony**
Black **CG Symphony**

Symposia
Roman Symposia
Italic *Symposia*
Bold **Symposia**

ITC Tiepolo
Book ITC Tiepolo
Book Italic *ITC Tiepolo*
Bold **ITC Tiepolo**
Bold Italic ***ITC Tiepolo***
Black **ITC Tiepolo**
Black Italic ***ITC Tiepolo***

CG Times
Roman CG Times
Italic *CG Times*
Bold **CG Times**
Bold Italic ***CG Times***

Torino
❖ *Agfa DisplaySet 7*
Bold **Torino**
Condensed Torino

CG Trade
Regular CG Trade
Italic *CG Trade*
Bold No. 2 **CG Trade**
Bold No. 2 Italic ***CG Trade***

CG Trade Condensed
Condensed CG Trade
Condensed Italic *CG Trade*
Bold Condensed **CG Trade**
Bold Condensed Italic ***CG Trade***

Triplett
❖ *Agfa DisplaySet 5*
Light Triplett
Black **Triplett**

CG Triumvirate 1
Light CG Triumvirate
Light Italic *CG Triumvirate*
Black **CG Triumvirate**
Black Italic ***CG Triumvirate***

CG Triumvirate 2
Light CG Triumvirate
Light Italic *CG Triumvirate*
Regular CG Triumvirate
Italic *CG Triumvirate*
Bold **CG Triumvirate**
Bold Italic ***CG Triumvirate***
Heavy **CG Triumvirate**
Heavy Italic ***CG Triumvirate***

CG Triumvirate Condensed
Light Condensed CG Triumvirate
Light Condensed Italic *CG Triumvirate*
Condensed CG Triumvirate
Condensed Italic *CG Triumvirate*
Bold Condensed **CG Triumvirate**
Bold Condensed Italic ***CG Triumvirate***
Black Condensed **CG Triumvirate**
Black Condensed Italic ***CG Triumvirate***

CG Triumvirate 3
Inserat **CG Triumvirate**
Inserat Italic ***CG Triumvirate***
Compressed **CG Triumvirate**
Extra Compressed **CG Triumvirate**

CG Trump Mediaeval
Roman Trump Mediaeval
Italic *Trump Mediaeval*
Bold **Trump Mediaeval**
Bold Italic ***Trump Mediaeval***

Uncial
❖ *Agfa DisplaySet 3* Uncial

ITC Usherwood
Book ITC Usherwood
Book Italic *ITC Usherwood*
Medium ITC Usherwood

... ITC Usherwood
Medium Italic *ITC Usherwood*
Bold **ITC Usherwood**
Bold Italic ***ITC Usherwood***
Black **ITC Usherwood**
Black Italic ***ITC Usherwood***

ITC Veljovic
Book ITC Veljovic
Book Italic *ITC Veljovic*
Medium ITC Veljovic
Medium Italic *ITC Veljovic*
Bold **ITC Veljovic**
Bold Italic ***ITC Veljovic***
Black **ITC Veljovic**
Black Italic ***ITC Veljovic***

Visigoth
❖ *Agfa Baker Calligraphy* **Visigoth**

Wedding Text
❖ *Agfa Scripts 1* Wedding Text

Agfa Wile Roman
Roman Agfa Wile Roman
Italic *Agfa Wile Roman*
Medium Agfa Wile Roman
Medium Italic *Agfa Wile Roman*
Bold **Agfa Wile Roman**
Bold Italic ***Agfa Wile Roman***
Black **Agfa Wile Roman**
Black Italic ***Agfa Wile Roman***

ITC Zapf International
Light ITC Zapf Int'l
Light Italic *ITC Zapf Int'l*
Medium ITC Zapf Int'l
Medium Italic *ITC Zapf Int'l*
Demi **ITC Zapf Int'l**
Demi Italic ***ITC Zapf Int'l***
Heavy **ITC Zapf Int'l**
Heavy Italic ***ITC Zapf Int'l***

Agfa Typographer's Editions

Typographer's Edition 1
PL Behemoth Semi-Condensed **PL Behemoth**
PL Benguiat Frisky PL Benguiat Frisky
Egiziano Black **Egiziano Black**
PL Futura Maxi Light PL Futura Maxi
PL Futura Maxi Demi **PL Futura Maxi**

ff

. . . Typographer's Edition 1

Quirinus Bold — Quirinus

Section Bold Condensed — SECTION BOLD

Stratford Bold — Stratford

PL Tower Condensed — PL Tower

Woodblock — WOODBLOCK

Typographer's Edition 2

PL Barnum Block — PL Barnum

PL Benguiat Frisky Bold — PL Benguiat Frisky

TC Broadway — TC Broadway

PL Davison Zip Bold — PL DAVISON ZIP

PL Fiedler Gothic Bold — PL Fiedler Gothic

PL Futura Maxi Book — PL Futura Maxi

PL Futura Maxi Bold — PL Futura Maxi

Neon Extra Condensed — NEON EXTRA CONDENSED

Ritmo Bold — Ritmo Bold

PL Trophy Oblique — PL Trophy Oblique

Typographer's Edition 3

Barclay Open — Barclay Open

PL Bernhardt Light — PL Bernhardt

PL Bernhardt Medium — PL Bernhardt

PL Bernhardt Bold — PL Bernhardt

PL Britannia Bold — PL Britannia

Delphian Open — DELPHIAN OPEN

PL Fiorello Condensed — PL Fiorello Condensed

Fluidum Bold — Fluidum

PL Modern Heavy Condensed — PL Modern

PL Torino Open — PL Torino Open

Typographer's Edition 4

Bernhard Modern Roman — Bernhard Modern

Beton Extra Bold — Beton Extra Bold

PL Davison Americana — PL Davison

TC Europa Bold — TC Europa Bold

TC Jasper — TC Jasper

Metropolis — Metropolis

Modern Twenty — Modern Twenty

Orlando — ORLANDO

Siena Black — Siena Black

PL Westerveldt — PL Westerveldt

Typographer's Edition 5

Athenaeum Roman — Athenaeum

Athenaeum Italic — *Athenaeum*

Athenaeum Bold — **Athenaeum**

. . . Typographer's Edition 5

Athenaeum Initials Positive — A B C D E

Athenaeum Initials Negative — A B C D E

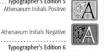

Typographer's Edition 6

Advertiser's Gothic Light — Advertiser's Gothic

Ashley Crawford — ASHLEY CRAWFORD

Capone Light — Capone Light

Dynamo — Dynamo

Modernistic — MODERNISTIC

Typographer's Edition 7

Greeting Monotone — Greeting Monotone

Koloss — Koloss

Phenix American — Phenix American

Phosphor — PHOSPHOR

Zeppelin — Zeppelin

Typographer's Edition 8

PL Brazilia 3 — PL Brazilia

PL Brazilia 7 — PL Brazilia

PL Radiant Bold Extra Condensed — Radiant Bold Extra Condensed

PL Latin Bold — PL Latin Bold

PL Latin Elongated — PL Latin Elongated

Typographer's Edition 9

Miehle Condensed — Miehle

Parisian — Parisian

Phyllis — Phyllis

Phyllis Initials — Phyllis Initials

Sinaloa — SINALOA

Typographer's Edition 10

Bernhard Fashion — Bernhard Fashion

Chic — CHIC

Eclipse — ECLIPSE

Metronome Gothic — Metronome Gothic

Salut — Salut

Typographer's Edition 11

Empire — EMPIRE

Gallia — GALLIA

Gillies Gothic Bold — Gillies Gothic Bold

Quaint Roman — Quaint Roman

Skjald — Skjald

Typographer's Edition 12

Eagle Bold — EAGLE BOLD

Joanna Solotype — Joanna Solotype

Matra — MATRA

Modernique — Modernique

Victorian Silhouette — VICTORIAN

Typographer's Edition 13

Ashley Inline — ASHLEY INLINE

. . . Typographer's Edition 13

Beverly Hills — BEVERLY HILLS

Lotus — LOTUS

Virile — Virile

Virile Open — Virile Open

Typographer's Edition 14

Artistik — Artistik

Futura Black — Futura Black

Yearbook Filler — YEARBOOK

Yearbook Outline — YEARBOOK

Yearbook Solid — YEARBOOK

Agfa Multi-Font Package Contents

Agfa Baker Calligraphy	Amigo, Marigold, Oxford, Pelican, Visigoth.
Agfa DisplaySet 1	Aldous Vertical, Aura, Computer, Eccentric.
Agfa DisplaySet 2	Aquarius No. 8, CG Poster Bodoni, Clarendon Book Condensed.
Agfa DisplaySet 3	Basque, Brophy Script, Chevalier, Uncial.
Agfa DisplaySet 4	Branding Iron, Isabella, McCollough, Raphael.
Agfa DisplaySet 5	Claire News, Light & Bold, Triplett Light & Black.
Agfa DisplaySet 6	Derek Italic, Engravure, Gothic Extra Light Extended, Holland Title.
Agfa DisplaySet 7	Erbar Light Condensed & Medium Condensed, Torino Bold, Torino Condensed.
Agfa Engravers 1	Antique Roman Solid & Slanted, Artisan Roman, Burin Roman, Burin Sans, Classic Roman Light & Regular, Handle Oldstyle, Roman Light & Medium.
Agfa Engravers 2	Sackers Antique Roman Open & Solid, Sackers Light Classic Roman, English Script, Gothic Light, Medium & Heavy, Italian Script, Sackers Roman Light, Square Gothic.
Agfa ITC DisplaySet 1	ITC Anna, ITC Beesknees, ITC Mona Lisa Recut, ITC Studio Script.
Agfa ITC DisplaySet 2	ITC Flora Medium & Bold, ITC Isadora Regular & Bold.
Agfa NewsSet 1	News No. 2 Roman, Italic & Bold, News No. 14 Roman, Italic & Bold, Sans No. 1 Regular & Heavy.
Agfa Scripts 1	Commercial Script, Helinda Rook, Old English, Original Script, Quill Script, Stuyvesant, Wedding Text.
Agfa Scripts 2	Citadel, Flemish Script 2, Florentine Script 2, French Script, Mahogany Script, Old Fashion Script, Riviera Script.
Agfa ScriptSet 1	Basilica, Floridian Script, Jasper, Liberty.
Agfa ScriptSet 2	Carmine Tango, Chaplin, Coronet Regular & Bold.
Agfa TextDisplay Set 1	Hollandse Mediaeval Roman & Bold, Signature Light & Black.
Agfa TextSet 1	Cartier Roman & Italic, Holland Seminar Roman & Italic.
Agfa TextSet 2	CG Cloister Roman & Italic, CG DeVinne Roman & Italic.

Agfa The Font Bureau Collection

Font Bureau 1

BeLucian Book — BeLucian

BeLucian Book Italic — *BeLucian*

BeLucian Demi — BeLucian

BeLucian Ultra — BeLucian

Village Ornaments

Font Bureau 2

Aardvark — AARDVARK

Aardvark Bold — AARDVARK

Commerce Lean — Commerce

Commerce Fat — Commerce

ff

. . . Font Bureau 2
Bureau Grotesque 15 — Bureau Grotesque

Font Bureau 3
Belizio Bold — Belizio
Belizio Bold Italic — *Belizio*
Bureau Agency — Bureau Agency
Bureau Agency Bold — **Bureau Agency**
Numskill Bold — **Numskill**

Font Bureau 4
Bodega Sans — Bodega Sans
Bodega Sans Oldstyle — Bodega Sans
Bodega Sans Black — **Bodega Sans**
Bodega Sans Black Oldstyle — **Bodega Sans**
Town Ornaments

Font Bureau 5
Phaistos Roman — Phaistos
Phaistos Italic — *Phaistos*
Phaistos Bold — **Phaistos**
Romeo Skinny Condensed — Romeo
Romeo Medium Condensed — Romeo

Font Bureau 6
Garage Gothic Regular — Garage Gothic
Garage Gohtic Bold — **Garage Gothic**
Garage Gothic Black — **Garage Gothic**
Ironmonger Black — **IRONMONG'R**
Ironmonger Extended — **IRONMONG'R**

Font Bureau 7
Bureau Eagle Book — Bureau Eagle
Bureau Eagle Bold — **Bureau Eagle**
Bureau Empire — Bureau Empire
Bureau Empire Italic — *Bureau Empire*
City Ornaments

Font Bureau 8
Bureau Roxy Medium — Bureau Roxy
Bureau Roxy Medium Italic — *Bureau Roxy*
Scamp Regular — SCAMP
Scamp Fat — **SCAMP**
Scamp Bold Inline — SCAMP

Font Bureau 9
Bureau Grotesque 13 — Bureau Grotesque
Bureau Grotesque 17 — **Bureau Grotesque**
Bureau Grotesque 37 — **Bureau Grotesque**
Bureau Grotesque 53 — Bureau Grotesque
Bureau Grotesque 79 — **Bureau Grotesq**

Agfa Pi, Logos & Symbols

Animals, Volume 1
Astrology 1, Volume 2
Astrology 2, Volume 3
Astrology 3, Volume 4
Borders & Ornaments 1, Volume 5
Borders & Ornaments 2, Volume 6
Borders & Ornaments 3, Volume 7
Borders & Ornaments 4, Volume 8
Borders & Ornaments 5, Volume 9
Borders & Ornaments 6, Volume 10
Business & Services 1, Volume 11
Business & Services 2, Volume 12
Business & Services 3, Volume 13 — CIRRUS ha YANKEE 24 MONE SUPPL
Commercial 1, Volume 14 — ea. % only RICE
Commercial 2, Volume 15
Communications 1, Volume 16
Communications 2, Volume 17
Communications 3, Volume 18
Communications 4, Volume 19
Communications 5, Volume 20
Communications 6, Volume 21
Communications 8, Volume 23
Credit Cards, Volume 24 — VISA
Ecology, Volume 25
Games & Sports 1, Volume 26
Games & Sports 3, Volume 28
Games & Sports 4, Volume 29
General Symbols 1, Volume 30
General Symbols 2, Volume 31
General Symbols 3, Volume 32
General Symbols 4, Volume 33
General Symbols 5, Volume 34
Holidays, Volume 35
Industry & Engineering 1, Volume 36
Industry & Engineering 2, Volume 37
International Symbols 1, Volume 38 — WAN D E SF SU NL YU USA
International Symbols 2, Volume 39

Legal Trademarks Volume 40
Logos: Company 1 Volume 41
Agfa
ACE
Logos: Company 2 Volume 42
Armstrong
Audi
Arrow
ARCO
Logos: Company 3 Volume 43
BALI
Bass
BIG STAR
BILLY THE KID
Logos: Company 4 Volume 44
Canon CBS
Cooper
Logos: Company 5 Volume 45
DELHAIZE
Consumers
Logos: Company 6 Volume 46
DUPONT
DUNKIN' DONUTS
Logos: Company 7 Volume 47
Ford
FRANCE TELECOM
FMC
FAIRCHILD
A Schlumberger Company
Logos: Company 8 Volume 48
GMC TRUCKS
Logos: Company 9 Volume 49
INFOBOT
The Information Robot
HUGHES
Hertz
HESS
Logos: Company 10 Volume 50
Kodak
KRAFT
ROBINSON'S
Logos: Company 11 Volume 51
McAlpin's
Miss Elaine
3M
Logos: Company 12 Volume 52
MTV
Nature Elle
NYNEX
Logos: Company 13 Volume 53
Panasonic
piggly wiggly
Logos: Company 14 Volume 54
PEPSI
Paramount Pictures
Logos: Company 15 Volume 55
Radio Shack
Logos: Company 16 Volume 56
SQUIBB Diagnostics
SPERRY
SEARS SAVINGS BANK
Logos: Company 17 Volume 57
SEARS SAVINGS BANK
SIEMENS
Logos: Company 18 Volume 58
U-HAUL
UNIFORM
Logos: Company 19 Volume 59
US LIFE
UNITED TECHNOLOGIES
USAA
Logos: Company 20 Volume 60
WENDY'S
Washburn Lab
Logos: Company 21 Volume 61
Chicago Board of Trade
Logos: Company 22 Volume 62
Data Central
valan
Logos: Company 23 Volume 63
Jantzen
Jeep
WANG
Logos: Company 24 Volume 64
FARBERWARE
First Class
CREST
Logos: Company 25 Volume 65
CASIO BOSS
CONAIR
Bissell
Logos: Company 26 Volume 66
melnor
KIDS COLLECTION
Kolcraft
Logos: Company 27 Volume 67
Pressman
Regal
NES MAX
Norelco
Logos: Company 28 Volume 68
TEAC
Vivitar
VISIONS
Logos: Company 29 Volume 69
WPIX NEW YORK ALIVE
Westclox
Logos: Services 1 Volume 70
Member FDIC
Carlyle
Real Estate Limited Partnership-XV
Logos: Services 2 Volume 71
the contact lens center
Logos: Services 3 Volume 72
Télé comptant
Télé services
Télé banque
Télé mise-à-jour
Math & Technical 1 Volume 73
Math & Technical 2 Volume 74
Math & Technical 3 Volume 75
Math & Technical 4 Volume 76
Math & Technical 5 Volume 77

ff

Math & Technical 6 Volume 78
Math & Technical 7 Volume 79
Math & Technical 8 Volume 80
Math & Technical 9 Volume 81
Math & Technical 10 Volume 82
Math & Technical 11 Volume 83
Math & Technical 12 Volume 84
Math & Technical 13 Volume 85
Math & Technical 14 Volume 86
qweadlxbmQERYU123
Math & Technical 15 Volume 87
qweadlxbmQERYU123
Math & Technical 16 Volume 88
qweadlxbmQERYU123
Math & Technical 17 Volume 89
qweadlxbmQERYU123
Medical & Pharmaceutical 1 Volume 90
Medical & Pharmaceutical 2 Volume 91
CAPOTEN captopril tablets
Military & Patriotic 1 Volume 92
Military & Patriotic 2 Volume 93
Québec
Musical Volume 94
Numerics 1 Volume 95
Numerics 2 Volume 96
Numerics 3 Volume 97
Numerics 4 Volume 98
Numerics 5 Volume 99
Numerics 6 Volume 100
Numerics 7 Volume 101
Numerics 8 Volume 102
Numerics 9 Volume 103
Numerics 10 Volume 104
Numerics 11 Volume 105
Phonetics 1 Volume 106
Phonetics 2 Volume 107
Phonetics 3 Volume 108
Religious Volume 109
Seals 1 Volume 110
Seals 2 Volume 111
Special Alphabets 1 Volume 112
abcdefghij ABCDEF
Special Alphabets 2 Volume 113
abcdefghij ABCDEF
Special Alphabets 3 Volume 114
abcdefg ABCDEF
Special Alphabets 4 Volume 115
ABCDE ABCDEF

Special Alphabets 5 Volume 116
ABCD
Special Alphabets 6 Volume 117
ABC ABCDE
Special Alphabets 7 Volume 118
ABCD ABCDE
Special Alphabets 8 Volume 119
ABC ABCDE
Special Alphabets 9 Volume 120
abcdefgh ABCDEF
Special Alphabets 10 Volume 121
abcdefg ABCDEF
Special Alphabets 11 Volume 122
Television 1 Volume 123
1 2 3 63 64 85 86
Television 2 Volume 124
10 11 TV TV T.V. 14 15 7
Transportation 1 Volume 125
Transportation 2 Volume 126

foundry: Alphabets Inc

Alphabets Inc was established by Peter Fraterdeus in 1986 as one of the first of the small, yet dynamic independent digital type foundries taking advantage of the possibilities of Adobe's PostScript technology and Altsys' Fontographer software. From its humble beginnings the foundry has grown to become a notable source for a host of unique designs from Fraterdeus, Robert McCamant, Inna Gertsberg, Manfred Klein, Philip Bouwsma, Randall Jones and others.

A*I Alexia Regular
A*I Alexia
Italic
A*I Alexia
A*I AlphaKid Plain
A*I ALPHAKID
Black
A*I ALPHAKID
Extra Black
A*I ALPHAKID
A*I Ampersands
A*I Antique Condensed A*I Wood Type
A*I ANTIQUE CONDEN
A*I Barrel A*I Wood Type
A*I BARREL
A*I BeforeTheAlphabet-1
A*I Benedict Uncial
A*I B UNCIAL
A*I Bouwsma Script
A*I Bouwsma Script
A*I Box Gothic A*I Wood Type
A*I BOX G
A*I Chaotiqua Regular
A*I Chaotiqua

... A*I Chaotiqua Bold
A*I Chaotiqua
A*I Chevron
A*I Chevron
A*I Dino Heavy
A*I Dino Heavy
A*I EclecticOne
A*I Egyptian Condensed MM Small Light
A*I Egyptian
Small
A*I Egyptian
Small Medium
A*I Egyptian
Small Bold
A*I Egyptian
Small Black
A*I Egyptian
Large Light
A*I Egyptian
Large
A*I Egyptian
Large Medium
A*I Egyptian
Large Bold
A*I Egyptian
Large Black
A*I Egyptian
A*I Flighty
A*I Fragment
A*I FraktKonstruct
A I FRAKT
A*I FranklySpoken
A*I F Spoken
A*I French XXX Condensed A*I Wood Type
A*I FRENCH XXX CONDENSED
A*I Fusion
A*I Fusion
A*I Half
A*I Half
A*I HeadToHeads
A*I Juliana
A*I Juliana
A*I Koch Antiqua Light
A*I Koch Antiqua
Demi
A*I Koch Antiqua
Extra Bold
A*I Koch Antiqua
A*I Neptune Serif
A*I NEPTUNE
A*I Neuland
A*I NEULAND
A*I Oz Brush A*I OzTypes Regular
A*I Oz Brush
Italic
A*I Oz Brush
A*I Oz Poster A*I OzTypes Regular
A*I Oz Poster
Condensed
A*I Oz Poster

A*I Painter A*I Wood Type
A*I PAINT
A*I ParmaPetit Normal
A*I ParmaPetit
Italic
A*I ParmaPetit
A*I Parsons Light
A*I Parsons

See page 531 for contents of Alphabets Inc Multi-Font Packages.

...A*I Parsons
Regular A*I Parsons
Heavy A*I Parsons

A*I Prospera II
Roman A*I Prospera II
Italic *A*I Prospera II*
Bold **A*I Prospera II**
Bold Italic ***A*I Prospera II***
Roman SCLF A*I PROSPERA II 12345...

A*I Quanta
Thin A*I Quanta
Light A*I Quanta
Medium A*I Quanta
Bold **A*I Quanta**
Black **A*I Quanta**

A*I QuasiModo
A*I QuasiModo

A*I Russell Oblique
Regular A*I Russell Oblique
Informal A*I Russell Oblique

A*I Szene
A*I SZENE

A*I Toskana
A*I TOSKANA

A*I Tuscan Egyptian
✤ *A*I Wood Type*
A*I TUSCAN

A*I Venezia
A*I VENEZIA

A*I Weissenau
A*I Weissenau

Alphabets Inc. Multi·Font Package Contents

✤ *A*I OzTypes* : A*I Oz Brush Regular & Italic, A*I Oz Poster Regular & Condensed.

✤ *A*I Wood Type* : A*I Antique Condensed, A*I Barrel, A*I Box Gothic, A*I French XXX Condensed, A*I Painter, A*I Tuscan Egyptian.

foundry: Andersen Agency

A one-man operation and, for the time being, a one-family library. Bill Andersen created Kindergarten to help his schoolteacher wife help her students learn how to write. He plans to produce several other fonts on the same basic theme of handwriting instruction.

Kindergarten
Regular Kindergarten
Bold Kindergarten
Ruled Kindergarten
Teach Ruled Kinder

foundry: Bear Rock Technologies

For the unique reading needs of electronic eyes... Bear Rock Technologies offers a complete suite of bar code labeling fonts for dot matrix, printers, laser printers and high resolution imagesetters.

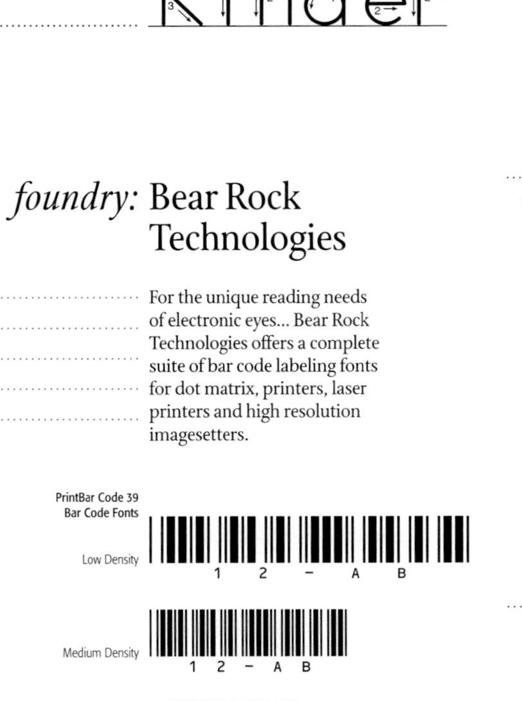

PrintBar Code 39 Bar Code Fonts
Low Density 12-AB
Medium Density 12-AB
High Density 12-AB

For Macintosh
69 fonts for PostScript imagesetters, (1000+ dpi), PostScript and non-PostScript LaserWriters and compatibles.
Sizes from 12 to 72 points in low, medium, and high densities.
31 fonts with human readable characters, 38 fonts without human readable characters.
Includes font utility to add "start" and "stop" characters and calculate optional checksum character.

For Windows & OS/2
29 PostScript fonts for imagesetters (1000+ dpi) and laser printers.
29 TrueType fonts for dot matrix and laser printers.
Sizes from 12 to 72 points in low, medium, and high densities.
26 fonts with human readable characters, 32 fonts without human readable characters.
Includes font utility to add "start" and "stop" characters and calculate optional checksum character.

Also includes 6 USPS Certified POSTNET & FIM fonts.

PrintBar UPC/EAN/ISBN Bar Code Fonts
UPC-A 0 12458 74512 9 11
UPC-E 0 140245 2 11
EAN-13 9 784512 587419 78945
EAN-8 4578 9458

For Macintosh
18 fonts for PostScript imagesetters, (1000+ dpi), PostScript LaserWriters, and compatibles.
Includes 6 fonts with bar width reduction, suitable for flexographic printing.
Human readable OCR-A typeface font used to customize bar code for pharmaceutical, record industry, and other formats.
Font utility to add "start" and "stop" characters and calculate checksum digit.

For Windows & OS/2
26 PostScript fonts for imagesetters (1000+ dpi) and laser printers.
26 TrueType fonts for laser printers.
Includes 12 fonts with bar width reduction, suitable for flexographic printing.
Human readable OCR-A typeface font used to customize bar code for pharmaceutical, record industry, and other formats.
Font utility to add "start" and "stop" characters and calculate checksum digit.

Also includes 6 USPS Certified POSTNET & FIM fonts.

PrintBar Interleaved 2 of 5 Bar Code Fonts
Low Density 1 2 3 8 8 7 9 4 5 6
Medium Density 1 2 3 8 8 7 9 4 5 6

For Macintosh
55 fonts for PostSript imagesetters, (1000+ dpi), PostScript and non-PostScript LaserWriters, ImageWriters and compatibles.
Sizes from 12 to 72 points in low and medium densities.
25 fonts with human readable characters, 30 fonts without human readable characters.
Font utility to add "start" and "stop" characters and calculate optional checksum character.

For Windows & OS/2
22 PostScript fonts for imagesetters (1000+ dpi) and laser printers.
22 TrueType fonts for laser printers and dotmatrix printers.
Font utility to add "start" and "stop" characters and calculate optional checksum digit.

Also includes 6 USPS Certified POSTNET & FIM fonts.

PrintBar PostNET & FIM Bar Code Fonts

For Macintosh
6 USPS certified fonts for PostScript imagesetters, (1000+ dpi), PostScript LaserWriters, and compatibles.
Includes 2 fonts with human readable characters for proofing.
Includes font utility to add "start" and "stop" characters and calculate required checksum digit.

For Windows & OS/2
3 PostScript fonts for imagesetters (1000+ dpi) and laser printers.
3 TrueType fonts for laser printers and dot matrix printers.
Includes 2 fonts with human readable characters for proofing.
Includes font utility to add "start" and "stop" characters and calculate required checksum digit.

StricklyBusiness Plus Special Edition A full-featured label and envelope design program available only to registered PrintBar Macintosh users.

Bear Rock Bar Code Labeler for Windows Professional label design software with full bar code support. Includes Code 39, UPC-A, UPC-E, EAN-8, EAN-13, 2 + 5 supplements, ISBN, Interleaved 2 of 5, Code 128, UCC-128, Codabar, POSTNET, and FIM bar codes.

foundry: Bitstream

Bitstream was founded in 1981 as a company with a new vision: fonts could and should be independent from output technologies. Led by Mike Parker and the noted type designer Matthew Carter, Bitstream went on to become a major source for the supply of fonts and imaging solutions. ¶ Today, the Bitstream Typeface Library contains more than 1,200 fonts, ranging from established standards licensed from International Typeface Corporation, Fundición Tipográfica Neufville and others to original designs from the hands of Gerard Unger, Gudrun Zapf-Von Hesse, John Downer, Richard Lipton, Carol Twombly and Jenny Maestre.

Font	Style	Sample
Aachen	Roman	Aachen
	Bold	Aachen
Ad Lib		Ad Lib
Aldine 401	Roman	Aldine 401
	Italic	*Aldine 401*
	Bold	**Aldine 401**
	Bold Italic	***Aldine 401***
Aldine 721 One	Roman	Aldine 721
	Italic	*Aldine 721*
	Bold	**Aldine 721**
	Bold Italic	***Aldine 721***
Aldine 721 Two	Light	Aldine 721
	Light Italic	*Aldine 721*
	Bold Condensed	**Aldine 721**
Allegro		Allegro
Alternate Gothic No. 2		Alternate Gothic No. 2
Amazone		Amazone
Amelia		Amelia
American Text		American Text
ITC American Typewriter	Light	ITC American
	Medium	ITC American
	Bold	**ITC American**
	Light Condensed	ITC American Type
	Medium Condensed	ITC American Type
	Bold Condensed	**ITC American Type**
Americana	Roman	Americana
	Italic	*Americana*
	Bold	**Americana**
	Extra Bold	**Americana**
	Extra Bold Condensed	**Americana**
Bitstream Amerigo	Roman	Bitstream Amerigo
	Italic	*Bitstream Amerigo*
	Medium	Bitstream Amerigo
	Medium Italic	*Bitstream Amerigo*
	Bold	**Bitstream Amerigo**
	Bold Italic	***Bitstream Amerigo***
Bitstream Arrus	Roman	Bitstream Arrus
	Italic	*Bitstream Arrus*
	Bold	**Bitstream Arrus**
	Bold Italic	***Bitstream Arrus***
	Black	**Bitstream Arrus**
	Black Italic	***Bitstream Arrus***
Aurora Condensed	Condensed	Aurora Condensed
	Bold Condensed	**Aurora Condensed**
ITC Avant Garde Gothic 1	Book	ITC Avant Garde
	Book Oblique	*ITC Avant Garde*
	Demi	**ITC Avant Garde**
	Demi Oblique	***ITC Avant Garde***
ITC Avant Garde Gothic 2	Extra Light	ITC Avant Garde
	Extra Light Oblique	*ITC Avant Garde*
	Medium	ITC Avant Garde
	Medium Oblique	*ITC Avant Garde*
	Bold	**ITC Avant Garde**
	Bold Oblique	***ITC Avant Garde***
ITC Avant Garde Gothic Condensed	Book Condensed	ITC Avant Garde
	Medium Condensed	ITC Avant Garde
	Demi Condensed	**ITC Avant Garde**
	Bold Condensed	**ITC Avant Garde**
Baker Signet		Baker Signet
Balloon	Light	*BALLOON*
	Bold	***BALLOON***
	Extra Bold	***BALLOON***
Bank Gothic	Light	BANK GOTHIC
. . . Bank Gothic	Medium	**BANK GOTHIC**
Baskerville	Roman	Baskerville
	Italic	*Baskerville*
	Bold	**Baskerville**
	Bold Italic	***Baskerville***
Baskerville No. 2	Roman	Baskerville No. 2
	Italic	*Baskerville No. 2*
	Bold	**Baskerville No. 2**
	Bold Italic	***Baskerville No. 2***
Fry's Baskerville		Fry's Baskerville
ITC New Baskerville 1	Roman	ITC New Baskerville
	Italic	*ITC New Baskerville*
	Bold	**ITC New Baskervill**
	Bold Italic	***ITC New Baskerville***
ITC New Baskerville 2	Semibold	ITC New Baskervill
	Semibold Italic	*ITC New Baskerville*
	Black	**ITC New Baskervil**
	Black Italic	***ITC New Baskervill***
ITC Bauhaus	Light	ITC Bauhaus
	Medium	ITC Bauhaus
	Demi	**ITC Bauhaus**
	Bold	**ITC Bauhaus**
	Heavy	**ITC Bauhaus**
Bell Gothic	Regular	Bell Gothic
	Bold	**Bell Gothic**
	Black	**Bell Gothic**
Bell Centennial	Name & Number	Bell Centennial
	Address	Bell Centennial
	Sub-Caption	Bell Centennial
	Bold Listing	**BELL CENTENNIAL**
Belwe	Light	Belwe
	Medium	Belwe
	Bold	**Belwe**
	Condensed	**Belwe**
ITC Benguiat	Book	ITC Benguiat
	Book Italic	*ITC Benguiat*
	Medium	ITC Benguiat
	Medium Italic	*ITC Benguiat*

ff

. . . ITC Benguiat
Bold ITC Benguiat
Bold Italic *ITC Benguiat*

ITC Benguiat Condensed
Book Condensed ITC Benguiat
Book Condensed Italic *ITC Benguiat*
Medium Condensed ITC Benguiat
Medium Condensed Italic *ITC Benguiat*
Bold Condensed ITC Benguiat
Bold Condensed Italic *ITC Benguiat*

ITC Benguiat Gothic 1
Book ITC Benguiat Gothic
Book Italic *ITC Benguiat Gothic*
Bold ITC Benguiat Gothic
Bold Italic *ITCBenguiat Gothic*

ITC Benguiat Gothic 2
Medium ITC Benguiat Gothic
Medium Italic *ITC Benguiat Gothic*
Heavy ITC Benguiat Gothic
Heavy Italic *ITC Benguiat Gothic*

ITC Berkeley Oldstyle 1
Book ITC Berkeley Oldstyle
Book Italic *ITC Berkeley Oldstyle*
Bold ITC Berkeley Oldstyl
Bold Italic *ITC Berkeley Oldstyle*

ITC Berkely Oldstyle 2
Medium ITC Berkeley Oldstyl
Medium Italic *ITC Berkeley Oldstyle*
Black ITC Berkeley Oldsty
Black Italic *ITC Berkeley Oldsty*

Bernhard Bold Condensed
Bernhard Bold Cond

Bernhard Fashion
Bernhard Fashion

Bernhard Modern
Roman Bernhard Modern
Italic *Bernhard Modern*
Bold Bernhard Modern
Bold Italic *Bernhard Modern*

Bernhard Tango
Bernhard Tango

Blackletter 686
Blackletter 686

Blippo Black
Blippo Black

Bodoni 1
Roman Bodoni
Italic *Bodoni*
Bold Bodoni
Bold Italic *Bodoni*

Bodoni 2
Book Bodoni

. . . Bodoni 2
Book Italic *Bodoni*
Bold Condensed Bodoni

Poster Bodoni
Roman Poster Bodoni
Italic *Poster Bodoni*

Bauer Bodoni 1
Roman Bauer Bodoni
Italic *Bauer Bodoni*
Bold Bauer Bodoni
Bold Italic *Bauer Bodoni*

Bauer Bodoni 2
Black Bauer Bodoni
Black Italic *Bauer Bodoni*
Bold Condensed Bauer Bodoni
Black Condensed Bauer Bodoni

Bauer Bodoni Titling
Titling BAUER BODONI
Titling No. 2 BAUER BODONI

ITC Bolt Bold
ITC Bolt Bold

Bookman
Roman Bookman
Italic *Bookman*

Bookman Headline
Roman Bookman
Italic *Bookman*

ITC Bookman 1
Light ITC Bookman
Light Italic *ITC Bookman*
Demi ITC Bookman
Demi Italic *ITC Bookman*

ITC Bookman 2
Medium ITC Bookman
Medium Italic *ITC Bookman*
Bold ITC Bookman
Bold Italic *ITC Bookman*

Bremen
Bold BREMEN
Black BREMEN

Broadway
Regular Broadway
Engraved Broadway

Bruce Old Style
Roman Bruce Old Style
Italic *Bruce Old Style*

Brush 445
Brush 445

Brush 738
Brush 738

Brush Script
Brush Script

Bulmer
Roman Bulmer
Italic *Bulmer*

ITC Busorama
Light ITC BUSORAMA
Medium ITC BUSORAMA
Bold ITC BUSORAMA

Calligraphic 421
Calligraphic 421

Calligraphic 810
Roman Calligraphic 810
Italic *Calligraphic 810*

Candida
Roman Candida
Italic *Candida*
Bold Candida

Bitstream Carmina 1
Medium BT Carmina
Medium Italic *BT Carmina*
Bold BT Carmina
Bold Italic *BT Carmina*

Bitstream Carmina 2
Light BT Carmina
Light Italic *BT Carmina*
Black BT Carmina
Black Italic *BT Carmina*

Caslon Old Face
Roman Caslon Old Face
Italic *Caslon Old Face*
Heavy Caslon Old Face

Caslon 540
Roman Caslon 540
Italic *Caslon 540*

Caslon Bold
Bold Caslon Bold
Bold Italic *Caslon Bold Italic*

Caslon Openface
Caslon Openface

ITC Caslon No.224 One
Book ITC Caslon No. 224
Book Italic *ITC Caslon No. 224*
Bold ITC Caslon No. 224
Bold Italic *ITC Caslon No. 224*

ITC Caslon No.224 Two
Medium ITC Caslon No. 224
Medium Italic *ITC Caslon No. 224*
Black ITC Caslon No. 22
Black Italic *ITC Caslon No. 22*

Bitstream Cataneo 1
Light *Bitstream Cataneo*
Regular *Bitstream Cataneo*
Bold *Bitstream Cataneo*

Bitstream Cataneo 2
Light Swash *a_de-g ABC 12345*
Regular Swash *a_de-g ABC 12345*

ff

... Bitstream Cataneo 2 Bold Swash: a_de-g ABC 12345
Light Extension: Th ct ff sp & a l
Regular Extension: Th ct ff sp & a l
Bold Extension: Th ct ff sp & a l

Caxton Light: Caxton
Light Italic: *Caxton*
Book: Caxton
Book Italic: *Caxton*
Bold: **Caxton**
Bold Italic: ***Caxton***

Century Schoolbook Roman: Century Schoolbook
Italic: *Century Schoolbook*
Bold: **Schoolbook**
Bold Italic: ***Schoolbook***
Bold Condensed: **Century Schoolbook**

Century Expanded Roman: Century Expanded
Italic: *Century Expanded*
Bold: **Century Expanded**
Bold Italic: ***Century Expanded***

Century Oldstyle Roman: Century Oldstyle
Italic: *Century Oldstyle*
Bold: **Century Oldstyle**

Century 731 Roman: Century 731
Italic: *Century 731*
Bold: **Century 731**
Bold Italic: ***Century 731***

Century 725 Roman: Century 725
Italic: *Century 725*
Bold: **Century 725**
Black: **Century 725**
Condensed: Century 725
Bold Condensed: **Century 725**

Century 751 Roman: Century 751
Italic: *Century 751*

ITC Century 1 Book: ITC Century
Book Italic: *ITC Century*
Bold: **ITC Century**
Bold Italic: ***ITC Century***

ITC Century 2 Light: ITC Century
Light Italic: *ITC Century*
Ultra: **ITC Century**
Ultra Italic: ***ITC Century***

ITC Century Condensed 1 Book Condensed: ITC Century
Book Condensed Italic: *ITC Century*
Bold Condensed: **ITC Century**
Bold Condensed Italic: ***ITC Century***

ITC Century Condensed 2 Light Condensed: ITC Century
Light Condensed Italic: *ITC Century*
Ultra Condensed: **ITC Century**
Ultra Condensed Italic: ***ITC Century***

Century Schoolbook Monospaced: Schoolbook

ITC Charter Roman: ITC Charter
Italic: *ITC Charter*
Bold: **ITC Charter**
Bold Italic: ***ITC Charter***
Black: **ITC Charter**
Black Italic: ***ITC Charter***

Cheltenham 1 Roman: Cheltenham
Italic: *Cheltenham*
Bold: **Cheltenham**
Bold Italic: ***Cheltenham***

Cheltenham 2 Bold Condensed: **Cheltenham**
Bold Condensed Italic: ***Cheltenham***
Bold Extra Condensed: **Cheltenham**
Bold Headline: **Cheltenham**
Bold Italic Headline: ***Cheltenham***

ITC Cheltenham 1 Light: ITC Cheltenham
Light Italic: *ITC Cheltenham*
Ultra: **ITC Cheltenham**
Ultra Italic: ***ITC Cheltenham***

ITC Cheltenham 2 Book: ITC Cheltenham
Book Italic: *ITC Cheltenham*
Bold: **ITC Cheltenham**
Bold Italic: ***ITC Cheltenham***

Clarendon 1 Light: Clarendon
Roman: Clarendon
... Clarendon 1 Bold: **Clarendon**

Clarendon 2 Heavy: **Clarendon**
Black: **Clarendon**
Condensed: Clarendon
Bold Condensed: **Clarendon**

ITC Clearface 1 Roman: ITC Clearface
Italic: *ITC Clearface*
Heavy: **ITC Clearface**
Heavy Italic: ***ITC Clearface***

ITC Clearface 2 Bold: ITC Clearface
Bold Italic: *ITC Clearface*
Black: **ITC Clearface**
Black Italic: ***ITC Clearface***
Contour: ITC Clearface

Cloister Black: Cloister Black

Cloister Open Face: Cloister Open

Commercial Pi: ©®™™@%+°×℞♀♂

Commercial Script: *Commercial Script*

Compacta Light: Compacta
Regular: Compacta
Italic: *Compacta*
Bold: **Compacta**
Bold Italic: ***Compacta***
Black: **Compacta**

Bitstream Cooper 1 Light: Bitstream Cooper
Light Italic: *Bitstream Cooper*
Bold: **Bitstream Cooper**
Bold Italic: ***Bitstream Cooper***

Bitstream Cooper 2 Medium: Bitstream Cooper
Medium Italic: *Bitstream Cooper*
Black: **Bitstream Coope**
Black Italic: ***Bitstream Coope***

Bitstream Cooper 3 Black Headline: **BT Cooper**
Black Headline Italic: ***BT Cooper***
Black Outline: BT Cooper

Copperplate Gothic Regular: COPPERPLATE GOTHIC
Bold: **COPPERPLATE GOTH**
Heavy: **COPPERPLATE GOTH**

ff

… Copperplate Gothic Condensed — Copperplate Gothic
Bold Condensed — Copperplate Gothic

Courier 10 Pitch Regular — Courier 10 Pitch
Italic — *Courier 10 Pitch*
Bold — **Courier 10 Pitch**
Bold Italic — ***Courier 10 Pitch***

ITC Cushing 1 Book — ITC Cushing
Book Italic — *ITC Cushing*
Bold — **ITC Cushing**
Bold Italic — ***ITC Cushing***

ITC Cushing 2 Medium — ITC Cushing
Medium Italic — *ITC Cushing*
Heavy — **ITC Cushing**
Heavy Italic — ***ITC Cushing***

Davida Bold — DAVIDA BOLD

Decorated 035 — DECORATED

Della Robbia Roman — Della Robbia
Bold — **Della Robbia**

De Vinne Text Roman — De Vinne
Text Italic — *De Vinne*
Display Roman — De Vinne
Display Italic — *De Vinne*

Dom Regular — Dom
Diagonal — *Dom*
Bold — **Dom**
Bold Diagonal — ***Dom***

Dutch 766 Roman — Dutch 766
Italic — *Dutch 766*
Bold — **Dutch 766**

Dutch 801 One Roman — Dutch 801
Italic — *Dutch 801*
Bold — **Dutch 801**
Bold Italic — ***Dutch 801***

Dutch 801 Two Semibold — Dutch 801
Semibold Italic — *Dutch 801*
Extra Bold — **Dutch 801**
Extra Bold Italic — ***Dutch 801***
Roman Headline — Dutch 801

… Dutch 801 Two Italic Headline — *Dutch 801*

Dutch 823 Roman — Dutch 823
Italic — *Dutch 823*
Bold — **Dutch 823**
Bold Italic — ***Dutch 823***

Dutch 809 Roman — Dutch 809
Italic — *Dutch 809*
Bold — **Dutch 809**

Dutch 811 Roman — Dutch 811
Italic — *Dutch 811*
Bold — **Dutch 811**
Bold Italic — ***Dutch 811***

Egyptian 710 — **Egyptian 710**

Egyptian 505 Light — Egyptian 505
Roman — Egyptian 505
Medium — Egyptian 505
Bold — **Egyptian 505**

Embassy — *Embassy*

Empire — EMPIRE

English 157 — *English 157*

Engravers' Roman Regular — Engravers' Roman
Bold — **Engravers' Roman**

Engravers' Gothic — Engravers' Gothic

Engravers' Old English Regular — Engravers' Old English
Bold — **Engravers' Old Eng**

ITC Eras Light — ITC Eras
Book — ITC Eras
Medium — ITC Eras
Demi — **ITC Eras**
Bold — **ITC Eras**
Ultra — **ITC Eras**
Outline — ITC Eras

Exotic 350 Light — Exotic 350
Demi — **Exotic 350**
Bold — **Exotic 350**

ITC Fenice 1 Roman — ITC Fenice
Italic — *ITC Fenice*

… ITC Fenice 1 Bold — **ITC Fenice**
Bold Italic — ***ITC Fenice***

ITC Fenice 2 Light — ITC Fenice
Light Italic — *ITC Fenice*
Ultra — **ITC Fenice**
Ultra Italic — ***ITC Fenice***

Flareserif 821 Light — Flareserif 821
Roman — Flareserif 821
Bold — **Flareserif 821**

Flemish Script — *Flemish Script*

Folio Light — Folio
Light Italic — *Folio*
Book — Folio
Medium — Folio
Bold — **Folio**
Extra Bold — **Folio**
Bold Condensed — **Folio**

Formal 436 — Formal 436

Formal Script 421 — Formal Script 421

Fraktur — Fraktur

Franklin Gothic Regular — **Franklin Gothic**
Italic — ***Franklin Gothic***
Condensed — **Franklin Gothic**
Extra Condensed — **Franklin Gothic**

ITC Franklin Gothic 1 Book — ITC Franklin Gothic
Book Italic — *ITC Franklin Gothic*
Demi — **Franklin Gothic**
Demi Italic — ***Franklin Gothic***

ITC Franklin Gothic 2 Medium — ITC Franklin Gothic
Medium Italic — *ITC Franklin Gothic*
Heavy — **Franklin Gothic**
Heavy Italic — ***Franklin Gothic***

Freeform 710 — Freeform 710

Freeform 721 Regular — Freeform 721
Italic — *Freeform 721*
Bold — **Freeform 721**
Bold Italic — ***Freeform 721***
Black — **Freeform 721**

ff

Family	Style	Sample
... Freeform 721	Black Italic	Freeform 721
Freehand 471		Freehand 471
Freehand 521		Freehand 521
Freehand 575		Freehand 575
Freehand 591		Freehand 591
Friz Quadrata	Regular	Friz Quadrata
	Bold	Friz Quadrata
Futura 1	Light	Futura
	Light Italic	Futura
	Book	Futura
	Book Italic	Futura
Futura 2	Medium	Futura
	Medium Italic	Futura
	Bold	Futura
	Bold Italic	Futura
Futura 3	Heavy	Futura
	Heavy Italic	Futura
	Extra Black	Futura
	Extra Black Italic	Futura
Futura Condensed	Light Condensed	Futura
	Medium Condensed	Futura
	Bold Condensed	Futura
	Bold Condensed Italic	Futura
	Extra Black Condensed	Futura
	Extra Black Condensed Italic	Futura
Futura Black		Futura
ITC Galliard 1	Roman	ITC Galliard
	Italic	ITC Galliard
	Bold	ITC Galliard
	Bold Italic	ITC Galliard
ITC Galliard 2	Black	ITC Galliard
	Black Italic	ITC Galliard
	Ultra	ITC Galliard
	Ultra Italic	ITC Galliard
Gando		Gando
Original Garamond	Roman	Original Garamond
	Italic	Original Garamond
	Bold	Original Garamond
... Original Garamond	Bold Italic	Original Garamond
American Garamond	Roman	American Garamond
	Italic	American Garamond
	Bold	American Garamond
	Bold Italic	American Garamond
Elegant Garamond	Roman	Elegant Garamond
	Italic	Elegant Garamond
	Bold	Elegant Garamond
Italian Garamond	Roman	Italian Garamond
	Italic	Italian Garamond
	Bold	Italian Garamond
Classical Garamond	Roman	Classical Garamond
	Italic	Classical Garamond
	Bold	Classical Garamon
	Bold Italic	Classical Garamond
ITC Garamond 1	Book	ITC Garamond
	Book Italic	ITC Garamond
	Bold	ITC Garamond
	Bold Italic	ITC Garamond
ITC Garamond 2	Light	ITC Garamond
	Light Italic	ITC Garamond
	Ultra	ITC Garamond
	Ultra Italic	ITC Garamond
ITC Garamond Condensed 1	Book Condensed	ITC Garamond
	Book Condensed Italic	ITC Garamond
	Bold Condensed	ITC Garamond
	Bold Condensed Italic	ITC Garamond
ITC Garamond Condensed 2	Light Condensed	ITC Garamond
	Light Condensed Italic	ITC Garamond
	Ultra Condensed	ITC Garamond
	Ultra Condensed Italic	ITC Garamond
ITC Garamond Narrow	Light Narrow	ITC Garamond
	Light Italic Narrow	ITC Garamond
	Book Narrow	ITC Garamond
	Book Italic Narrow	ITC Garamond
	Bold Narrow	ITC Garamond
	Bold Italic Narrow	ITC Garamond
Geometric 231	Light	Geometric 231
... Geometric 231	Regular	Geometric 231
	Bold	Geometric 231
	Heavy	Geometric 231
Geometric 415	Lite	Geometric 415
	Lite Italic	Geometric 415
	Medium	Geometric 415
	Medium Italic	Geometric 415
	Black	Geometric 415
	Black Italic	Geometric 415
Geometric 706	Medium	Geometric 706
	Black	Geometric 706
	Bold Condensed	Geometric 706
	Black Condensed	Geometric 706
Geometric 212	Book	Geometric 212
	Heavy	Geometric 212
	Book Condensed	Geometric 212
	Heavy Condensed	Geometric 212
Geometric 885		Geometric 885
Geometric Slabserif 703 One	Medium	Geometric 703
	Medium Italic	Geometric 703
	Bold	Geometric 703
	Bold Italic	Geometric 703
Geometric Slabserif 703 Two	Light	Geometric 703
	Light Italic	Geometric 703
	Extra Bold	Geometric 703
	Extra Bold Italic	Geometric 703
Geometric Slabserif 703 Three	Medium Condensed	Geometric Slabserif 703
	Bold Condensed	Geometric Slabserif 703
	Extra Bold Condensed	Geometric Slabserif 703
Geometric Slabserif 712	Light	Geometric 712
	Light Italic	Geometric 712
	Medium	Geometric 712
	Medium Italic	Geometric 712
	Bold	Geometric 712
	Extra Bold	Geometric 712
ITC Gorilla		ITC Gorilla
Gothic 720	Light	Gothic 720
	Light Italic	Gothic 720

. . . Gothic 720
Regular Gothic 720
Italic *Gothic 720*
Bold **Gothic 720**
Bold Italic ***Gothic 720***

Gothic 725
Bold **Gothic 725**
Black **Gothic 725**

Gothic 821 Condensed **Gothic 821**

Gothic No. 13 **Gothic No. 13**

Goudy Old Style
Roman Goudy Old Style
Italic *Goudy Old Style*
Bold **Goudy Old Style**
Bold Italic ***Goudy Old Style***
Extra Bold **Goudy Old Style**

Goudy Catalogue Goudy Catalogue

Goudy Handtooled Goudy Handtool

Goudy Heavyface
Roman **Goudy Heavy**
Condensed **Goudy Heavyface**

ITC Goudy Sans 1
Medium ITC Goudy Sans
Medium Italic *ITC Goudy Sans*
Bold **ITC Goudy Sans**
Bold Italic ***ITC Goudy Sans***

ITC Goudy Sans 2
Light ITC Goudy Sans
Light Italic *ITC Goudy Sans*
Black **ITC Goudy Sans**
Black Italic ***ITC Goudy Sans***

ITC Grizzly **ITC Grizzly**

ITC Grouch **ITC Grouch**

Handel Gothic **Handel Gothic**

Hobo **Hobo**

Humanist 521 One
Regular Humanist 521
Italic *Humanist 521*
Bold **Humanist 521**
Bold Italic ***Humanist 521***

Humanist 521 Two
Light Humanist 521
Light Italic *Humanist 521*
Extra Bold **Humanist 521**
Ultra Bold **Humanist 521**

Humanist 521 Condensed
Condensed Humanist 521

. . . Humanist 521 Condensed
Bold Condensed **Humanist 521**
Extra Bold Condensed **Humanist 521**

Humanist 970
Regular Humanist 970
Bold **Humanist 970**

Humanist 531
Regular Humanist 531
Bold **Humanist 531**
Black **Humanist 531**
Ultra Black **Humanist 531**

Humanist 777 One
Regular Humanist 777
Italic *Humanist 777*
Bold **Humanist 777**
Bold Italic ***Humanist 777***

Humanist 777 Two
Light Humanist 777
Light Italic *Humanist 777*
Black **Humanist 777**
Black Italic ***Humanist 777***

Humanist 777 Three
Light Condensed Humanist 777
Condensed Humanist 777
Bold Condensed **Humanist 777**
Black Condensed **Humanist 777**
Extra Black Condensed **Humanist 777**
Extra Black **Humanist 777**

Humanist Slabserif 712
Roman Humanist 712
Italic *Humanist 712*
Bold **Humanist 712**
Black **Humanist 712**

Huxley Vertical HUXLEY VERTICAL

Imperial
Roman Imperial
Italic *Imperial*
Bold **Imperial**

Impress Impress

Impuls *Impuls*

Incised 901 One
Light Incised 901
Regular Incised 901
Italic *Incised 901*
Black **Incised 901**

Incised 901 Two
Bold **Incised 901**

. . . Incised 901 Two
Compact **Incised 901**
Nord **Incised 901**
Nord Italic ***Incised 901***
Bold Condensed **Incised 901**

Industrial 736
Roman Industrial 736
Italic *Industrial 736*

Informal 011
Regular **INFORMAL 011**
Black **INFORMAL 011**

Bitstream Iowan Old Style
Roman B Iowan Old Style
Italic *B Iowan Old Style*
Bold **B Iowan Old Style**
Bold Italic ***B Iowan Old Style***
Black **B Iowan Old Style**
Black Italic ***B Iowan Old Style***

ITC Isbell 1
Book ITC Isbell
Book Italic *ITC Isbell*
Bold **ITC Isbell**
Bold Italic ***ITC Isbell***

ITC Isbell 2
Medium ITC Isbell
Medium Italic *ITC Isbell*
Heavy **ITC Isbell**
Heavy Italic ***ITC Isbell***

Italia
Book Italia
Medium Italia
Bold **Italia**

ITC Kabel
Book ITC Kabel
Medium ITC Kabel
Demi **ITC Kabel**
Bold **ITC Kabel**
Ultra **ITC Kabel**

Kaufmann
Regular *Kaufmann*
Bold ***Kaufmann***

Kis
Roman Kis
Italic *Kis*

ITC Korinna 1
Regular ITC Korinna
Kursiv *ITC Korinna*
Bold **ITC Korinna**
Bold Kursiv ***ITC Korinna***

ff

Font	Style	Sample
ITC Korinna 2	Heavy	ITC Korinna
	Heavy Kursiv	ITC Korinna
	Extra Bold	ITC Korinna
	Extra Bold Kursiv	ITC Korinna
	Bold Outline	ITC Korinna
Kuenstler 480	Roman	Kuenstler 480
	Italic	Kuenstler 480
	Bold	Kuenstler 480
	Bold Italic	Kuenstler 480
	Black	Kuenstler 480
Lapidary 333	Roman	Lapidary 333
	Italic	Lapidary 333
	Bold	Lapidary 333
	Bold Italic	Lapidary 333
	Black	Lapidary 333
Latin 725	Roman	Latin 725
	Italic	Latin 725
	Medium	Latin 725
	Medium Italic	Latin 725
	Bold	Latin 725
	Bold Italic	Latin 725
Latin Extra Condensed		LATIN EXTRA CONDENSED
ITC Leawood 1	Book	ITC Leawood
	Book Italic	ITC Leawood
	Bold	ITC Leawood
	Bold Italic	ITC Leawood
ITC Leawood 2	Medium	ITC Leawood
	Medium Italic	ITC Leawood
	Black	ITC Leawood
	Black Italic	ITC Leawood
Letter Gothic 12 Pitch	Roman	Letter Gothic 12
	Italic	Letter Gothic 12
	Bold	Letter Gothic 12
	Bold Italic	Letter Gothic 12
Liberty		Liberty
Libra		LIBRA
Life	Roman	Life
	Italic	Life
. . . Life	Bold	Life
	Bold Italic	Life
ITC Lubalin Graph 1	Book	ITC Lubalin
	Book Oblique	ITC Lubalin
	Demi	ITC Lubalin
	Demi Oblique	ITC Lubalin
ITC Lubalin Graph 2	Extra Light	ITC Lubalin
	Extra Light Oblique	ITC Lubalin
	Medium	ITC Lubalin
	Medium Oblique	ITC Lubalin
	Bold	ITC Lubalin
	Bold Oblique	ITC Lubalin
Lucia		Lucia
Bitstream Lucian	Roman	Bitstream Lucian
	Bold	Bitstream Lucian
Lydian	Regular	Lydian
	Italic	Lydian
	Bold	Lydian
	Bold Italic	Lydian
	Cursive	Lydian
ITC Machine		ITC MACHINE
Math Pi with Greek		αβψδεφγΛΜΝΟΠΘ
Matt Antique	Regular	Matt Antique
	Italic	Matt Antique
	Bold	Matt Antique
Maximus Display		MAXIMUS
Mirarae	Regular	Mirarae
	Bold	Mirarae
Mister Earl		Mister Earl
ITC Mixage 1	Book	ITC Mixage
	Book Italic	ITC Mixage
	Bold	ITC Mixage
	Bold Italic	ITC Mixage
ITC Mixage 2	Medium	ITC Mixage
	Medium Italic	ITC Mixage
	Black	ITC Mixage
	Black Italic	ITC Mixage
Modern No. 20	Roman	Modern No. 20
. . . Modern No. 20	Italic	Modern No. 20
Modern 735		Modern 735
Modern 880	Roman	Modern 880
	Italic	Modern 880
	Bold	Modern 880
Monospace 821	Roman	Monospace 821
	Italic	Monospace 821
	Bold	Monospace 821
	Bold Italic	Monospace 821
Monterey		Monterey
Murray Hill	Regular	Murray Hill
	Bold	Murray Hill
News 701	Roman	News 701
	Italic	News 701
	Bold	News 701
News 702	Roman	News 702
	Italic	News 702
	Bold	News 702
	Bold Italic	News 702
News 705	Roman	News 705
	Italic	News 705
	Bold	News 705
	Bold Italic	News 705
News 706	Roman	News 706
	Italic	News 706
	Bold	News 706
News Gothic 1	Regular	News Gothic
	Italic	News Gothic
	Bold	News Gothic
	Bold Italic	News Gothic
News Gothic 2	Light	News Gothic
	Light Italic	News Gothic
	Demi	News Gothic
	Demi Italic	News Gothic
News Gothic Condensed	Condensed	News Gothic
	Condensed Italic	News Gothic
	Bold Condensed	News Gothic
	Bold Condensed Italic	News Gothic

... News Gothic Condensed
- Extra Condensed: News Gothic
- Bold Extra Condensed: News Gothic

Newspaper Pi

ITC Newtext 1
- Book: ITC Newtext
- Book Italic: ITC Newtext
- Demi: ITC Newtext
- Demi Italic: ITC Newtext

ITC Newtext 2
- Light: ITC Newtext
- Light Italic: ITC Newtext
- Regular: ITC Newtext
- Italic: ITC Newtext

Normande
- Roman: Normande
- Italic: Normande

ITC Novarese
- Book: ITC Novarese
- Book Italic: ITC Novarese
- Medium: ITC Novarese
- Medium Italic: ITC Novarese
- Bold: ITC Novarese
- Bold Italic: ITC Novarese
- Ultra: ITC Novarese

Nuptial: Nuptial

OCR
- OCR-A: abcdefg 012345
- OCR-B: abcdefg 012345

OCR 005 MICR
- .010: 01234567890
- .012: 01234567890
- .013: 01234567890

Old Dreadful No. 7: Old Dreadful

Onyx: Onyx

Bitstream Oranda
- Roman: Bitstream Oranda
- Italic: Bitstream Oranda
- Bold: Bitstream Oranda
- Bold Italic: Bitstream Oranda
- Condensed: Bitstream Oranda
- Bold Condensed: Bitstream Oranda

Orator U&LC
- 10 Pitch: Orator U&LC
- 15 Pitch: Orator U&LC

Orbit-B: Orbit-B

Bitstream Oz Handicraft: Bitstream Oz Handicraft

P. T. Barnum: P.T. Barnum

Parisian: Parisian

Park Avenue: Park Avenue

Pica 10 Pitch Roman: Pica 10 Pitch

ITC Pioneer: ITC PIONEER

Piranesi Italic: Piranesi Italic

Playbill: Playbill

Prestige 12 Pitch
- Roman: Prestige 12
- Italic: Prestige 12
- Bold: Prestige 12
- Bold Italic: Prestige 12

ITC Quorum
- Light: ITC Quorum
- Book: ITC Quorum
- Medium: ITC Quorum
- Bold: ITC Quorum
- Black: ITC Quorum

Raleigh
- Light: Raleigh
- Roman: Raleigh
- Medium: Raleigh
- Demi: Raleigh
- Bold: Raleigh
- Extra Bold: Raleigh

Revival 565
- Roman: Revival 565
- Italic: Revival 565
- Bold: Revival 565
- Bold Italic: Revival 565

Revue: Revue

Ribbon
- Regular: Ribbon
- Bold: Ribbon

Romana
- Roman: Romana
- Bold: Romana

ITC Ronda
- Light: ITC Ronda
- Roman: ITC Ronda
- Bold: ITC Ronda

Schadow
- Light: Schadow
- Light Cursive: Schadow
- Regular: Schadow
- Bold: Schadow

... Schadow
- Black: Schadow
- Black Condensed: Schadow

Schneidler 1
- Roman: Schneidler
- Italic: Schneidler
- Bold: Schneidler
- Bold Italic: Schneidler

Schneidler 2
- Light: Schneidler
- Light Italic: Schneidler
- Medium: Schneidler
- Medium Italic: Schneidler
- Black: Schneidler
- Black Italic: Schneidler

Script 12 Pitch: Script 12 Pitch

Seagull
- Light: Seagull
- Meidum: Seagull
- Bold: Seagull
- Heavy: Seagull

ITC Serif Gothic
- Light: ITC Serif Gothic
- Regular: ITC Serif Gothic
- Bold: ITC Serif Gothic
- Extra Bold: ITC Serif Gothic
- Heavy: ITC Serif Gothic
- Black: ITC Serif Gothic
- Bold Outline: ITC Serif Gothic

Serifa 1
- Thin: Serifa
- Thin Italic: Serifa
- Light: Serifa
- Light Italic: Serifa

Serifa 2
- Roman: Serifa
- Italic: Serifa
- Bold: Serifa
- Black: Serifa
- Bold Condensed: Serifa

Shelley
- Allegro: Shelley Allegro
- Andante: Shelley Andante
- Volante: Shelley Volante

Shotgun
- Regular: SHOTGUN
- Blanks: SHOTGUN

ff

Snell
Regular *Snell*
Bold *Snell*
Black *Snell*

ITC Souvenir 1
Light ITC Souvenir
Light Italic *ITC Souvenir*
Demi **ITC Souvenir**
Demi Italic ***ITC Souvenir***

ITC Souvenir 2
Medium ITC Souvenir
Medium Italic *ITC Souvenir*
Bold **ITC Souvenir**
Bold Italic ***ITC Souvenir***
Bold Outline ITC Souvenir

Square 721
Regular Square 721
Bold **Square 721**
Condensed Square 721
Bold Condensed **Square 721**
Extended Square 721
Bold Extended **Square 721**

Square Slabserif 711
Light Square Slabserif 711
Medium Square Slabserif 711
Bold **Square Slabserif**

Staccato 222 *Staccato 222*

Staccato 555 *Staccato 555*

Stencil STENCIL

Stuyvesant *Stuyvesant*

Stymie 1
Light Stymie
Light Italic *Stymie*
Bold **Stymie**
Bold Italic ***Stymie***

Stymie 2
Medium Stymie
Medium Italic *Stymie*
Extra Bold **Stymie**
Extra Bold Condensed **Stymie**

Swiss 721 One
Regular Swiss 721
Italic *Swiss 721*
Bold **Swiss 721**
Bold Italic ***Swiss 721***

Swiss 721 Two
Thin Swiss 721

… Swiss 721 Two
Thin Italic *Swiss 721*
Medium Swiss 721
Medium Italic *Swiss 721*
Heavy **Swiss 721**
Heavy Italic ***Swiss 721***

Swiss 721 Three
Light Swiss 721
Light Italic *Swiss 721*
Black **Swiss 721**
Black Italic ***Swiss 721***
Black No. 2 **Swiss 721**

Swiss 721 Four
Light Condensed Swiss 721
Light Condensed Italic *Swiss 721*
Condensed Swiss 721
Condensed Italic *Swiss 721*
Bold Condensed **Swiss 721**
Bold Condensed Italic ***Swiss 721***

Swiss 721 Five
Light Extended Swiss 721
Extended Swiss 721
Bold Extended **Swiss 721**
Black Extended **Swiss 721**

Swiss 721 Six
Bold Outline Swiss 721
Black Outline Swiss 721
Bold Condensed Outline Swiss 721
Bold Rounded **Swiss 721**
Black Rounded **Swiss 721**

Swiss Seven
911 Compressed **Swiss 911**
911 Extra Compressed **Swiss 911**
911 Ultra Compressed **Swiss 911**
921 **Swiss 921**
924 **Swiss 924**

ITC Symbol 1
Book ITC Symbol
Book Italic *ITC Symbol*
Bold **ITC Symbol**
Bold Italic ***ITC Symbol***

ITC Symbol 2
Medium ITC Symbol
Medium Italic *ITC Symbol*
Black **ITC Symbol**
Black Italic ***ITC Symbol***

Symbol
Monospaced αβχδεφγηΙϑΚΛΜΝ123
Proportional αβχδεΙϑΚΛΜΝ123

Tango **Tango**

Thunderbird THUNDER

ITC Tiffany 1
Light ITC Tiffany
Light Italic *ITC Tiffany*
Demi **ITC Tiffany**
Demi Italic ***ITC Tiffany***

ITC Tiffany 2
Medium ITC Tiffany
Medium Italic *ITC Tiffany*
Heavy **ITC Tiffany**
Heavy Italic ***ITC Tiffany***

ITC Tom's Roman ITC Tom's Roman

Transitional 511
Roman Transitional 511
Italic *Transitional 511*
Bold **Transitional 511**
Bold Italic ***Transitional 511***

Transitional 521
Roman Transitional 521
Cursive *Transitional 521*
Bold **Transitional 521**

Transitional 551
Medium Transitional 551
Medium Italic *Transitional 551*

Typo Upright *TypoUpright*

Umbra UMBRA

Universal Math 1 αβψδεφγηιξκλμν

University Roman
Regular University Roman
Bold **University Roman**

VAG Rounded **VAG Rounded**

Venetian 301
Roman Venetian 301
Italic *Venetian 301*
Demi Venetian 301
Demi Italic *Venetian 301*
Bold **Venetian 301**
Bold Italic ***Venetian 301***

Vineta Vineta

Wedding Text Wedding Text

ITC Weidemann 1
Book ITC Weidemann

ff

... ITC Weidemann 1
Book Italic *ITC Weidemann*
Bold **ITC Weidemann**
Bold Italic ***ITC Weidemann***

ITC Weidemann 2
Medium ITC Weidemann
Medium Italic *ITC Weidemann*
Black **ITC Weidemann**
Black Italic ***ITC Weidemann***

Windsor
Light Windsor
Regular **Windsor**
Light Condensed Windsor
Elongated **Windsor**
Outline Windsor

Zapf Calligraphic 801
Roman ZapfCalligraphic801
Italic *ZapfCalligraphic801*
Bold **ZapfCalligraphic801**
Bold Italic ***Zapf Calligraphic 801***

Zapf Humanist 601 One
Regular Zapf Humanist 601
Italic *Zapf Humanist 601*
Bold **Zapf Humanist 601**
Bold Italic ***Zapf Humanist 601***

Zapf Humanist 601 Two
Demi Zapf Humanist 601
Demi Italic *Zapf Humanist 601*
Ultra **Zapf Humanist 601**
Ultra Italic ***Zapf Humanist 601***

Zapf Elliptical 711
Roman Zapf Elliptical 711
Italic *Zapf Elliptical 711*
Bold **Zapf Elliptical 711**
Bold Italic ***Zapf Elliptical 711***

ITC Zapf Book 1
Light ITC Zapf Book
Light Italic *ITC Zapf Book*
Demi **ITC Zapf Book**
Demi Italic ***ITC Zapf Book***

ITC Zapf Book 2
Medium ITC Zapf Book
Medium Italic *ITC Zapf Book*
Heavy **ITC Zapf Book**
Heavy Italic ***ITC Zapf Book***

ITC Zapf Chancery
Light ITC Zapf Chancery
Light Italic *ITC Zapf Chancery*

... ITC Zapf Chancery
Medium ITC Zapf Chancery
Medium Italic *ITC Zapf Chancery*
Demi ITC Zapf Chancery
Bold **ITC Zapf Chancery**

ITC Zapf International 1
Light ITC Zapf Int'l.
Light Italic *ITC Zapf Int'l.*
Demi **ITC Zapf Int'l.**
Demi Italic ***ITC Zapf Int'l.***

ITC Zapf International 2
Medium ITC Zapf Int'l.
Medium Italic *ITC Zapf Int'l.*
Heavy **ITC Zapf Int'l.**
Heavy Italic ***ITC Zapf Int'l.***

ITC Zapf Dingbats
❀❄✳❒❄✳②♥❻➹

Zurich 1
Regular Zurich
Italic *Zurich*
Bold **Zurich**
Bold Italic ***Zurich***

Zurich 2
Light Zurich
Light Italic *Zurich*
Black **Zurich**
Black Italic ***Zurich***
Extra Black **Zurich**

Zurich 3
Light Condensed Zurich
Light Condensed Italic *Zurich*
Condensed Zurich
Condensed Italic *Zurich*
Bold Condensed **Zurich**
Bold Condensed Italic ***Zurich***

Zurich 4
Light Extra Condensed Zurich
Extra Condensed Zurich
Bold Extra Condensed **Zurich**

Zurich 5
Extended Zurich
Bold Extended **Zurich**
Black Extended Zurich
Ultra Black Extended **Zurich**

foundry: Carter & Cone Type

Matthew Carter is renowned as the designer of some of the most useful and beautiful types in contemporary times: Olympian, Bell Centennial, ITC Charter, Snell Roundhand and ITC Galliard amongst them. ¶ Associated with the Linotype group of companies for many years, Carter was a co-founder of Bitstream in 1981. Some eleven years later he started his own company with another Bitstream pioneer, Cherie Cone. He continues to design useful and beautiful types.

Big Caslon
Roman Big Caslon
Expert Roman BIG CASLON 123
Roman SCOSF BIG CASLON 12
Roman Alternatives ff ff fi fi fj fl ffh

ITC Galliard
Roman ITC Galliard
Italic *ITC Galliard*
Expert Roman ITC GALLIARD 1234 et al
Expert Italic *12345 et al.*
Roman SCOSF GALLIARD 12345...
Roman OSF osf 12345...
Italic OSF *osf 12345...*
Roman Alternatives a ct e h r ff fi &
Italic Alternatives *a ct e ff fi us is as &*
Roman Fractions & Figures 1/8 1/4 1/3 3/8 1/2 12345/67890
Italic Fractions & Figures *1/8 1/4 1/3 3/8 1/2 12345/67890*

Mantinia
MANTINIA

Sophia
SOPHIA

ff

foundry: Diehl.Volk

Mike Diehl and Paul Volk formalized their collaborative design efforts in 1991 with the release of nine fonts under the name of Diehl.Volk Typographics. Their mutually stated goal is to create typefaces that "enthusiastically celebrate and contribute to the ever-burgeoning diversity of the twenty-six letters comprising our alphabet."

DV Boy
Out DV Boy Out
In DV BOY IN
Wide DV B Wide
DV Drukpa
Regular DV Drukpa
Bold DV Drukpa
DV Edition
Serif DV Edition
Sans DV Edition
DV Elevator
Regular DV Elevator
Wide DV Elevator
DV Ellay
Regular DV Ellay
Oblique DV Ellay
DV Radish DV Radish
DV Shaft DV Shaft
DV Simplix
Light DV Simplix
Light Oblique DV Simplix
Medium DV Simplix
Medium Oblique DV Simplix
Bold DV Simplix
Bold Oblique DV Simplix
DV Upright DV Upright

foundry: Elsner+Flake

Founded in 1985 by Veronika Elsner and Gunther Flake. The collection consists of fonts licensed from International Typeface Corporation, Linotype-Hell, Letraset, Fundición Tipográfica Neufville and other sources. Elsner+Flake is based in Hamburg, Germany.

Family	Style	Sample
Alternate Gothic	No. One	Alternate Gothic
	No. Two	Alternate Gothic
	No. Three	Alternate Gothic
ITC American Typewriter	Light	ITC American
	Medium	ITC American
	Bold	ITC American
ITC American Typewriter Italic	Light Italic	ITC American
	Medium Italic	ITC American
	Bold Italic	ITC American
ITC American Typewriter Condensed	Light Condensed	ITC American Type
	Medium Condensed	ITC American Type
	Bold Condensed	ITC American Type
Angro	Light	Angro
	Bold	Angro
ITC Anna ✤ *EF ITC DisplaySet 1*		ITC ANNA
Annlie	Extra Bold	Annlie
	Extra Bold Italic	Annlie
Arsis	Roman	Arsis
	Italic	Arsis
Aurelia	Light	Aurelia
	Light Italic	Aurelia
	Book	Aurelia
	Book Italic	Aurelia
	Bold	Aurelia
ITC Avant Garde Gothic 1	Extra Light	ITC Avant Garde
	Medium	ITC Avant Garde
	Bold	ITC Avant Garde
ITC Avant Garde Gothic 2	Extra Light Oblique	ITC Avant Garde
	Medium Oblique	ITC Avant Garde
	Bold Oblique	ITC Avant Garde
ITC Avant Garde Gothic 3	Book	ITC Avant Garde
	Book Obilque	ITC Avant Garde
	Demibold	ITC Avant Garde
	Demibold Oblique	ITC Avant Garde
ITC Avant Garde Gothic Condensed	Book Condensed	ITC Avant Garde Gothic
	Medium Condensed	ITC Avant Garde Gothic
	Demibold Condensed	ITC Avant Garde Gothic
	Bold Condensed	ITC Avant Garde Gothic
Barbedor 1	Regular	Barbedor
	Italic	Barbedor
	Bold	Barbedor
	Bold Italic	Barbedor
Barbedor 2	Medium	Barbedor
	Medium Italic	Barbedor
	Black	Barbedor
	Black Italic	Barbedor
ITC Barcelona 1	Book	ITC Barcelona
	Book Italic	ITC Barcelona
	Bold	ITC Barcelona
	Bold Italic	ITC Barcelona
ITC Barcelona 2	Medium	ITC Barcelona
	Medium Italic	ITC Barcelona
	Heavy	ITC Barcelona
	Heavy Italic	ITC Barcelona
Baskerville Old Face ✤ *EF DisplaySet 1*		Baskerville Old Face
ITC New Baskerville 1	Roman	ITC New Baskerville
	Italic	ITC New Baskerville
	Bold	ITC New Baskerville
	Bold Italic	ITC New Baskerville
ITC New Baskerville 2	Semibold	ITC New Baskerville
	Semibold Italic	ITC New Baskerville
	Black	ITC New Baskerville
	Black Italic	ITC New Baskerville
ITC Bauhaus	Light	ITC Bauhaus
	Medium	ITC Bauhaus
	Demibold	ITC Bauhaus
	Bold	ITC Bauhaus
	Heavy	ITC Bauhaus

✤ *See page 549 for contents of Elsner+Flake Multi-Font Packages.*

ff

ITC Beesknees
✣ EF ITC DisplaySet 2 ITC BEESKNEES

Belshaw Belshaw

Belwe
Light Belwe
Light Italic *Belwe*
Medium **Belwe**
Bold **Belwe**
Bold Condensed **Belwe**

ITC Benguiat 1
Book ITC Benguiat
Book Italic *ITC Benguiat*
Bold **ITC Benguiat**
Bold Italic ***ITC Benguiat***

ITC Benguiat 2
Medium ITC Benguiat
Medium Italic *ITC Benguiat*

ITC Benguiat Condensed 1
Book Condensed ITC Benguiat
Book Condensed Italic *ITC Benguiat*
Bold Condensed **ITC Benguiat**
Bold Condensed Italic ***ITC Benguiat***

ITC Benguiat Condensed 2
Medium Condensed ITC Benguiat
Medium Condensed Italic *ITC Benguiat*

ITC Benguiat Gothic 1
Book ITC Benguiat Gothic
Book Italic *ITC Benguiat Gothic*
Bold **ITC Benguiat Gothic**
Bold Italic ***ITC Benguiat Gothic***

ITC Benuiat Gothic 2
Medium ITC Benguiat Gothic
Medium Italic *ITC Benguiat Gothic*
Heavy **ITC Benguiat Goth**
Heavy Italic ***ITC Benguiat Goth***

ITC Berkeley Old Style 1
Book ITC Berkeley Old
Book Italic *ITC Berkeley Old*
Bold **ITC Berkeley Old**
Bold Italic ***ITC Berkeley Old***

ITC Berkeley Old Style 2
Medium ITC Berkeley Old
Medium Italic *ITC Berkeley Old*
Black **ITC Berkeley Old**
Black Italic ***ITC Berkeley Old***

Berling
Roman Berling
Italic *Berling*
Bold **Berling**

Bernhard Antique **Bernhard Antique**

Bernhard Fashion Bernhard Fashion

Beton
Light Beton
Demibold Beton
Bold **Beton**
Extra Bold **Beton**
Bold Condensed **Beton**

Bauer Bodoni 1
Roman Bauer Bodoni
Italic *Bauer Bodoni*
Bold **Bauer Bodoni**
Bold Italic ***Bauer Bodoni***

Bauer Bodoni 2
Medium Bauer Bodoni
Medium Italic *Bauer Bodoni*

ITC Bookman 1
Light ITC Bookman
Light Italic *ITC Bookman*
Demibold **ITC Bookman**
Demibold Italic ***ITC Bookman***

ITC Bookman 2
Medium ITC Bookman
Medium Italic *ITC Bookman*
Bold **ITC Bookman**
Bold Italic ***ITC Bookman***

Britannic
Extra Light Britannic
Light Britannic
Medium Britannic
Bold **Britannic**
Ultra **Britannic**

Brody
✣ EF ScriptSet 2 Brody

Cabaret Cabaret

Camellia camellia

Candice Candice

Carousel Carousel

ITC Caslon No. 224 One
Book ITC Caslon No. 224
Book Italic *ITC Caslon No. 224*
Bold **ITC Caslon No. 224**
Bold Italic ***ITC Caslon No. 224***

ITC Caslon No. 224 Two
Medium ITC Caslon No. 224
Medium Italic *ITC Caslon No. 224*
Black **ITC Caslon No. 224**
Black Italic ***ITC Caslon No. 224***

Castle
Light Castle
Book Castle
Bold **Castle**
Ultra **Castle**

ITC Century 1
Light ITC Century
Light Italic *ITC Century*
Bold **ITC Century**
Bold Italic ***ITC Century***

ITC Century 2
Book ITC Century
Book Italic *ITC Century*
Ultra **ITC Century**
Ultra Italic ***ITC Century***

ITC Century Condensed 1
Light Condensed ITC Century
Light Condensed Italic *ITC Century*
Bold Condensed **ITC Century**
Bold Condensed Italic ***ITC Century***

ITC Century Condensed 2
Book Condensed ITC Century
Book Condensed Italic *ITC Century*
Ultra Condensed **ITC Century**
Ultra Condensed Italic ***ITC Century***

ITC Cheltenham 1
Light ITC Cheltenham
Light Italic *ITC Cheltenham*
Bold **ITC Cheltenham**
Bold Italic ***ITC Cheltenham***

ITC Cheltenham 2
Book ITC Cheltenham
Book Italic *ITC Cheltenham*
Ultra **ITC Cheltenham**
Ultra Italic ***ITC Cheltenham***

ITC Cheltenham Condensed 1
Light Condensed ITC Cheltenham
Light Condensed Italic *ITC Cheltenham*
Bold Condensed **ITC Cheltenham**
Bold Condensed Italic ***ITC Cheltenham***

ITC Cheltenham Condensed 2
Book Condensed ITC Cheltenham
Book Condensed Italic *ITC Cheltenham*
Ultra Condensed **ITC Cheltenham**
Ultra Condensed Italic ***ITC Cheltenham***

Cheltenham Old Style
✣ EF DisplaySet 2 Cheltenham O S

Chesterfield Chesterfield

Cirkulus — Cirkulus

ITC Clearface 1
Roman — ITC Clearface
Italic — *ITC Clearface*
Heavy — **ITC Clearface**
Heavy Italic — ***ITC Clearface***

ITC Clearface 2
Bold — ITC Clearface
Bold Italic — *ITC Clearface*
Black — **ITC Clearface**
Black Italic — ***ITC Clearface***

Clearface Gothic
Regular — Clearface Gothic
Bold — **Clearface Gothic**
Extra Bold — **Clearface Gothic**

Commercial Script
✤ EF ScriptSet 2 — *Commercial Script*

Compacta 1
Light — Compacta
Bold — **Compacta**
Bold italic — ***Compacta***
Bold Outline — COMPACTA

Compacta 2
Regular — Compacta
Italic — *Compacta*
Outline — COMPACTA
Black — **Compacta**

Conference — Conference

Cooper Black
Bold — **Cooper Black**
Bold Condensed — **Cooper Black**
Bold Outline — Cooper Black
Bold Condensed Outline — Cooper Black

Cortez — Cortez

Countdown — Countdown

Crillee Italic
Light Italic — *Crillee Italic*
Italic — *Crillee Italic*
Bold Italic — ***Crillee Italic***
Extra Bold Italic — ***Crillee Italic***

Croissant — Croissant

ITC Cushing 1
Book — ITC Cushing
Book Italic — *ITC Cushing*
Bold — **ITC Cushing**
Bold Italic — ***ITC Cushing***

ITC Cushing 2
Medium — ITC Cushing
Medium Italic — *ITC Cushing*
Heavy — **ITC Cushing**
Heavy Italic — ***ITC Cushing***

Data 70 — Data 70

Demos
Medium — Demos
Medium Italic — *Demos*
Semibold — **Demos**
Medium SCOSF — DEMOS 12345...

Digi Grotesk N
Light — Digi Grotesk N
Bold — **Digi Grotesk N**
Semibold Condensed — Digi Grotesk N
Bold Condensed — **Digi Grotesk N**

Digi Grotesk S
Light — Digi Grotesk S
Semibold — **Digi Grotesk S**

DIN 1451
Eng New — DIN 1451
Eng Alternate — DIN 1451
Mittel New — DIN 1451
Mittel Alternate — DIN 1451

Dom Casual
Regular — Dom Casual
Diagonal — *Dom Casual*
Bold — **Dom Casual**
Bold Diagonal — ***Dom Casual***

Dynamo
Medium — Dynamo
Bold — **Dynamo**
Bold Condensed — **Dynamo**
Bold Shadow — Dynamo

Edison
Book — Edison
Book Italic — *Edison*
Semibold — **Edison**
Semibold Italic — ***Edison***
Bold Condensed — **Edison**

Einhorn — Einhorn

ITC Élan 1
Book — ITC Élan
Book Italic — *ITC Élan*
Bold — **ITC Élan**
Bold Italic — ***ITC Élan***

ITC Élan 2
Medium — ITC Élan
Medium Italic — *ITC Élan*
Black — **ITC Élan**
Black Italic — ***ITC Élan***

ITC Élan SCOSF
Book SCOSF — ITC ÉLAN 12345...
Medium SCOSF — ITC ÉLAN 12345...

Elefont — ELEFONT

ITC Eras 1
Light — ITC Eras
Medium — ITC Eras
Bold — **ITC Eras**

ITC Eras 2
Book — ITC Eras
Demi — **ITC Eras**
Ultra — **ITC Eras**

ITC Esprit 1
Book — ITC Esprit
Book Italic — *ITC Esprit*
Bold — **ITC Esprit**
Bold Italic — ***ITC Esprit***

ITC Esprit 2
Medium — ITC Esprit
Medium Italic — *ITC Esprit*
Black — **ITC Esprit**
Black Italic — ***ITC Esprit***

ITC Esprit SCOSF
Book SCOSF — ITC ESPRIT 12345...
Medium SCOSF — ITC ESPRIT 1234...

Eurostile
Regular — Eurostile
Black — **Eurostile**

ITC Fenice 1
Light — ITC Fenice
Light Italic — *ITC Fenice*
Bold — **ITC Fenice**
Bold Italic — ***ITC Fenice***

ITC Fenice 2
Roman — ITC Fenice
Italic — *ITC Fenice*
Ultra — **ITC Fenice**
Ultra Italic — ***ITC Fenice***

ITC Flora
Medium — ITC Flora
Bold — **ITC Flora**

Folio Condensed
Bold Condensed — **Folio Condensed**
Extra Condensed — Folio Condensed

Frankfurter
Medium — Frankfurter
Solid — FRANKFURTER
Highlight — FRANKFURTER

✤ See page 549 for contents of Elsner+Flake Multi-Font Packages.

... Frankfurter
Inline FRANKFURTER

ITC Franklin Gothic 1
Book ITC Franklin Gothic
Book Italic ITC Franklin Gothic
Demi ITC Franklin Gothic
Demi Italic ITC Franklin Gothic

ITC Franklin Gothic 2
Medium ITC Franklin Gothic
Medium Italic ITC Franklin Gothic
Heavy ITC Franklin Goth
Heavy Italic ITC Franklin Goth

ITC Franklin Gothic Condensed 1
Book Condensed ITC Franklin Gothic
Book Condensed Italic ITC Franklin Gothic
Demi Condensed ITC Franklin Gothic
Demi Condensed Italic ITC Franklin Gothic
Book Condensed SCOSF ITC FRANKLIN GOTH 123...

ITC Franklin Gothic Condensed 2
Medium Condensed ITC Franklin Gothic
Medium Condensed Italic ITC Franklin Gothic
Medium Condensed SCOSF ITC FRANKLIN GOTH 123...

ITC Franklin Gothic Compressed
Book Compressed ITC Franklin Gothic
Book Compressed Italic ITC Franklin Gothic
Demi Compressed ITC Franklin Gothic
Demi Compressed Italic ITC Franklin Gothic

ITC Franklin Gothic Extra Compressed
Book Extra Compressed ITC Franklin Gothic
Demi Extra Compressed ITC Franklin Gothic

Franklin Gothic
Regular Franklin Gothic
Condensed Franklin Gothic
Extra Condensed Franklin Gothic

Friz Quadrata
Regular Friz Quadrata
Bold Friz Quadrata

Futura 1
Light Futura
Light Oblique Futura
Bold Futura
Bold Oblique Futura

Futura 2
Book Futura
Book Oblique Futura
Demibold Futura
Demibold Oblique Futura

Futura 3
Medium Futura
Medium Oblique Futura

... Futura 3
Heavy Futura
Extra Bold Futura
Extra Bold Oblique Futura

Futura Condensed 1
Light Condensed Futura
Light Condensed Oblique Futura
Bold Condensed Futura
Bold Condensed Oblique Futura

Futura Condensed 2
Medium Condensed Futura
Medium Condensed Oblique Futura
Extra Bold Condensed Futura
Extra Bold Condensed Oblique Futura

Galadriel
GALADRIEL

ITC Galliard 1
Roman ITC Galliard
Italic ITC Galliard
Black ITC Galliard
Black Italic ITC Galliard

ITC Galliard 2
Bold ITC Galliard
Bold Italic ITC Galliard
Ultra ITC Galliard
Ultra Italic ITC Galliard

ITC Gamma 1
Book ITC Gamma
Book Italic ITC Gamma
Bold ITC Gamma
Bold Italic ITC Gamma

ITC Gamma 2
Medium ITC Gamma
Medium Italic ITC Gamma
Black ITC Gamma
Black Italic ITC Gamma

ITC Gamma SCOSF
Book SCOSF ITC GAMMA 12345...
Medium SCOSF ITC GAMMA 12345...

Garamond No. 5
Light Garamond No. 5
Light Italic Garamond No. 5
Bold Garamond No. 5

ITC Garamond 1
Light ITC Garamond
Light Italic ITC Garamond
Bold ITC Garamond
Bold Italic ITC Garamond

ITC Garamond 2
Book ITC Garamond

... ITC Garamond 2
Book Italic ITC Garamond
Ultra ITC Garamond
Ultra Italic ITC Garamond

ITC Garamond Condensed 1
Light Condensed ITC Garamond
Light Condensed Italic ITC Garamond
Bold Condensed ITC Garamond
Bold Condensed Italic ITC Garamond

ITC Garamond Condensed 2
Book Condensed ITC Garamond
Book Condensed Italic ITC Garamond
Ultra Condensed ITC Garamond
Ultra Condensed Italic ITC Garamond

Gillies Gothic 1
Light Gillies Gothic
Bold Gillies Gothic
Extra Bold Gillies Gothic

Gillies Gothic 2
Extra Bold Gillies Gothic
Extra Bold Shaded Gillies Gothic

ITC Giovanni 1
Book ITC Giovanni
Bold ITC Giovanni
Black ITC Giovanni

ITC Giovanni 2
Book Italic ITC Giovanni
Bold Italic ITC Giovanni
Black Italic ITC Giovanni

ITC Giovanni SCOSF
Book SCOSF ITC GIOVANNI 123...
Bold SCOSF ITC GIOVANNI 123...

Glastonbury
Glastonbury

ITC Golden Type
Original ITC Golden Type
Bold ITC Golden Type
Black ITC Golden Type

ITC Golden Type SCOSF
Original SCOSF ITC GOLDEN 12345...
Bold SCOSF ITC GOLDEN 12345...

Goudy Handtooled
✤ EF DisplaySet 2 Goudy Handtool

ITC Goudy Sans 1
Book ITC Goudy Sans
Book Italic ITC Goudy Sans
Bold ITC Goudy Sans
Bold Italic ITC Goudy Sans

ITC Goudy Sans 2
Medium ITC Goudy Sans
Medium Italic ITC Goudy Sans
Black ITC Goudy Sans

ff

... ITC Goudy Sans 2 Black Italic — ITC Goudy Sans
ITC Goudy Sans SCOSF Book SCOSF — ITC Goudy Sans 123...
Medium SCOSF — ITC Goudy Sans 123...
Hadfield — Hadfield
Handel Gothic Light — Handel Gothic
Medium — Handel Gothic
Bold — Handel Gothic
Harlow Solid — Harlow
Shaded — Harlow
Hawthorn — Hawthorn
Heraldus Extra Bold — Heraldus
Highlight — Highlight
Hogarth Script — Hogarth Script
Hollander Roman — Hollander
Italic — Hollander
Bold — Hollander
Roman SCOSF — Hollander 12345...
Horatio Light — Horatio
Medium — Horatio
Bold — Horatio
Horndon — HORNDON
ITC Isadora Regular — ITC Isadora
Bold — ITC Isadora
ITC Isbell Book — ITC Isbell
Book Italic — ITC Isbell
Bold — ITC Isbell
Bold Italic — ITC Isbell
Italia Book — Italia
Medium — Italia
Bold — Italia
Italia Condensed — Italia
ITC Jamille 1 Book — ITC Jamille
Bold — ITC Jamille
Black — ITC Jamille
ITC Jamille 2 Book Italic — ITC Jamille
Bold Italic — ITC Jamille
Black Italic — ITC Jamille
ITC Jamille SCOSF Book SCOSF — ITC Jamille 12345...

... ITC Jamille SCOSF Bold SCOSF — ITC Jamille 12345...
Jenson Old Style Bold Condensed — Jenson Old Style
Julia Script — Julia Script
ITC Kabel Book — ITC Kabel
Medium — ITC Kabel
Demi — ITC Kabel
Bold — ITC Kabel
Ultra — ITC Kabel
Kapitellia Bold — Kapitellia
Kaufmann ✤ EF DisplaySet 3 — Kaufmann
Knightsbridge Regular — Knightsbridge
Alternate — b d f fi fl h k k r m Th
Koloss — Koloss
ITC Korinna 1 Roman — ITC Korinna
Kursiv — ITC Korinna
Extra Bold — ITC Korinna
Extra Bold Kursiv — ITC Korinna
ITC Korinna 2 Bold — ITC Korinna
Bold Kursiv — ITC Korinna
Heavy — ITC Korinna
Heavy Kursiv — ITC Korinna
Latienne 1 Roman — Latienne
Italic — Latienne
Roman SCOSF — Latienne 12345...
Italic SCOSF — Latienne 12345...
Italic Swash Capitals — LATIENNE
Latienne 2 Medium — Latienne
Medium Italic — Latienne
Medium SCOSF — Latienne 12345...
Medium Italic Swash Capitals — LATIENNE
Latienne 3 Bold — Latienne
Bold Italic — Latienne
Bold Italic Swash Capitals — LATIENNE
Lazybones — Lazybones
LCD — LCD
ITC Leawood 1 Book — ITC Leawood
Book Italic — ITC Leawood
Bold — ITC Leawood

... ITC Leawood 1 Bold Italic — ITC Leawood
ITC Leawood 2 Medium — ITC Leawood
Medium Italic — ITC Leawood
Black — ITC Leawood
Black Italic — ITC Leawood
ITC Leawood SCOSF Book SCOSF — ITC Leawood 1234...
Medium SCOSF — ITC Leawood 123...
Le Griffe Regular — Le Griffe
Alternate One — bdefghaigklmABD
Alternate Two — bdefghijkLABD
Lightline Gothic — Lightline Gothic
Lindsay — Lindsay
ITC Lubalin Graph 1 Extra Light — ITC Lubalin Graph
Extra Light Oblique — ITC Lubalin Graph
Medium — ITC Lubalin Graph
Medium Oblique — ITC Lubalin Graph
ITC Lubalin Graph 2 Book — ITC Lubalin Graph
Book Oblique — ITC Lubalin Graph
Demi — ITC Lubalin Graph
Demi Oblique — ITC Lubalin Graph
ITC Lubalin Graph 3 Bold — ITC Lubalin Graph
Bold Oblique — ITC Lubalin Graph
ITC Lubalin Graph Condensed 1 Book Condensed — ITC Lubalin Graph
Book Condensed Oblique — ITC Lubalin Graph
Demi Condensed — ITC Lubalin Graph
Demi Condensed Oblique — ITC Lubalin Graph
Book Condensed SCOSF — ITC Lubalin 12345...
ITC Lubalin Graph Condensed 2 Medium Condensed — ITC Lubalin Graph
Medium Condensed Oblique — ITC Lubalin Graph
Bold Condensed — ITC Lubalin Graph
Bold Condensed Oblique — ITC Lubalin Graph
Medium Condensed SCOSF — ITC Lubalin 12345...
ITC Machine Regular — ITC MACHINE
Bold — ITC MACHINE
Magnus — Magnus
Marconi Book — Marconi
Book Italic — Marconi
Semibold — Marconi

ff

✤ See page 549 for contents of Elsner+Flake Multi-Font Packages.

... Marconi
Semibold Italic *Marconi*
Book SCOSF MARCONI 12345...

ITC Mendoza Roman 1
Book ITC Mendoza
Book Italic *ITC Mendoza*
Book SCOSF ITC MENDOZA 1234...

ITC Mendoza Roman 2
Medium ITC Mendoza
Medium Italic *ITC Mendoza*
Medium SCOSF ITC MENDOZA 123...

ITC Mendoza Roman 3
Bold **ITC Mendoza**
Bold Italic ***ITC Mendoza***

ITC Mixage 1
Book ITC Mixage
Book Italic *ITC Mixage*
Bold **ITC Mixage**
Bold Italic ***ITC Mixage***

ITC Mixage 2
Medium ITC Mixage
Medium Italic *ITC Mixage*
Black **ITC Mixage**
Black Italic ***ITC Mixage***

ITC Mixage SCOSF
Book SCOSF ITC MIXAGE 12345...
Medium SCOSF ITC MIXAGE 12345...

ITC Modern No. 216 One
Light ITC Modern
Light Italic *ITC Modern*
Bold **ITC Modern**
Bold Italic ***ITC Modern***

ITC Modern No. 216 Two
Medium ITC Modern
Medium Italic *ITC Modern*
Heavy **ITC Modern**
Heavy Italic ***ITC Modern***

ITC Mona Lisa Recut
EF ITC DisplaySet 1 ITC Mona Lisa Recut

Monanti
Roman Monanti
Semibold **Monanti**

Murray Hill
EF DisplaySet 4 Murray Hill

ITC Newtext 1
Light ITC Newtext
Light Italic *ITC Newtext*
Regular **ITC Newtext**
Regular Italic ***ITC Newtext***

ITC Newtext 2
Book ITC Newtext
Book Italic *ITC Newtext*

... ITC Newtext 2
Demi **ITC Newtext**
Demi Italic ***ITC Newtext***

Nikis
Light Nikis
Light Italic *Nikis*
Semibold **Nikis**
Semibold Italic ***Nikis***

ITC Novarese 1
Book ITC Novarese
Book Italic *ITC Novarese*
Bold **ITC Novarese**
Bold Italic ***ITC Novarese***

ITC Novarese 2
Medium ITC Novarese
Medium Italic *ITC Novarese*
Ultra **ITC Novarese**

OCR-B
OCR-B

Octopuss
Regular **Octopuss**
Shaded Octopuss

Odin
Odin

ITC Officina Serif
Book ITC Officina
Book Italic *ITC Officina*
Bold **ITC Officina**
Bold Italic ***ITC Officina***

ITC Officina Sans
Book ITC Officina
Book Italic *ITC Officina*
Bold **ITC Officina**
Bold Italic ***ITC Officina***

Old Towne No. 536
EF DisplaySet 1 Old Towne No. 536

Olympia
Light Olympia
Semibold **Olympia**

ITC Pacella 1
Book ITC Pacella
Book Italic *ITC Pacella*
Bold **ITC Pacella**
Bold Italic ***ITC Pacella***

ITC Pacella 2
Medium ITC Pacella
Medium Italic *ITC Pacella*
Black **ITC Pacella**
Black Italic ***ITC Pacella***

ITC Pacella SCOSF
Book SCOSF ITC PACELLA 12345...
Medium SCOSF ITC PACELLA 12345...

Paddington
Paddington

ITC Panache 1
Book ITC Panache
Bold **ITC Panache**
Black **ITC Panache**

ITC Panache 2
Book Italic *ITC Panache*
Bold Italic ***ITC Panache***
Black Italic ***ITC Panache***

ITC Panache SCOSF
Book SCOSF ITC PANACHE 12345...
Bold SCOSF ITC PANACHE 12345...

Phyllis
Regular *Phyllis*
Initials ABCDEFG

Piccadilly
PICCADILLY

Praxis 1
Light Praxis
Semibold **Praxis**
Heavy **Praxis**
Light SCOSF PRAXIS 12345...

Praxis 2
Regular Praxis
Bold **Praxis**
Regular SCOSF PRAXIS 12345...

Pump
Light Pump
Medium **Pump**
Demi **Pump**
Bold **Pump**
Triline Pump

ITC Quay Sans 1
Book ITC Quay Sans
Book Italic *ITC Quay Sans*
Book SCOSF ITC QUAY SANS 12345...

ITC Quay Sans 2
Medium ITC Quay Sans
Medium Italic *ITC Quay Sans*
Medium SCOSF ITC QUAY SANS 12345...

ITC Quay Sans 3
Black **ITC Quay Sans**
Black Italic ***ITC Quay Sans***

ITC Quorum
Light ITC Quorum
Book ITC Quorum
Medium ITC Quorum
Bold **ITC Quorum**
Black **ITC Quorum**

Radiant EF Text 1
Light Radiant EF

ff

. . . Radiant EF Text 1
Medium Radiant EF
Bold Radiant EF
Radiant EF Text 2
Book Radiant EF
Demibold Radiant EF
Black Radiant EF
Radiant EF Display Condensed 1
Display Condensed No. 1 Radiant EF
Display Condensed No. 3 Radiant EF
Display Condensed No. 5 Radiant EF
Radiant EF Display Condensed 2
Display Condensed No. 2 Radiant EF
Display Condensed No. 4 Radiant EF
Display Condensed No. 6 Radiant EF
Renault
Light Renault
Light Italic Renault
Bold Renault
Bold Italic Renault
Romana 1
Light Romana
Medium Romana
Bold Romana
Romana 2
Book Romana
Demi Romana
Ultra Romana
Schneidler 1
Light Schneidler
Amalthea Light Italic Schneidler
Medium Schneidler
Amalthea Medium Italic Schneidler
Schneidler 2
Roman Schneidler
Amalthea Italic Schneidler
Bold Schneidler
Amalthea Bold Italic Schneidler
Schneidler 3
Black Schneidler
Amalthea Black Italic Schneidler
Schreibmaschine Regular
Schreibmaschine
ITC Serif Gothic 1
Light ITC Serif Gothic
Bold ITC Serif Gothic
Heavy ITC Serif Gothic
ITC Serif Gothic 2
Regular ITC Serif Gothic
Extra Bold ITC Serif Gothic
Black ITC Serif Gothic

Sierra
Roman Sierra
Italic Sierra
Bold Sierra
Bold Italic Sierra
ITC Slimbach 1
Book ITC Slimbach
Book Italic ITC Slimbach
Bold ITC Slimbach
Bold Italic ITC Slimbach
ITC Slimbach 2
Medium ITC Slimbach
Medium Italic ITC Slimbach
Black ITC Slimbach
Black Italic ITC Slimbach
ITC Slimbach SCOSF
Book SCOSF ITC Slimbach 12345...
Medium SCOSF ITC Slimbach 1234...
Slogan
✤ EF DisplaySet 4 Slogan
ITC Souvenir 1
Light ITC Souvenir
Light Italic ITC Souvenir
Demi ITC Souvenir
Demi Italic ITC Souvenir
ITC Souvenir 2
Medium ITC Souvenir
Medium Italic ITC Souvenir
Bold ITC Souvenir
Bold Italic ITC Souvenir
Stentor
Stentor
ITC Stone Serif 1
Medium ITC Stone
Semibold ITC Stone
Bold ITC Stone
ITC Stone Serif 2
Medium Italic ITC Stone
Semibold Italic ITC Stone
Bold Italic ITC Stone
ITC Stone Serif SCOSF
Medium SCOSF ITC Stone 123...
Semibold SCOSF ITC Stone 123...
ITC Stone Sans 1
Medium ITC Stone
Semibold ITC Stone
Bold ITC Stone
ITC Stone Sans 2
Medium Italic ITC Stone
Semibold Italic ITC Stone
Bold Italic ITC Stone

ITC Stone Sans SCOSF
Medium SCOSF ITC Stone 123...
Semibold SCOSF ITC Stone 123...
ITC Stone Informal 1
Medium ITC Stone
Semibold ITC Stone
Bold ITC Stone
ITC Stone Informal 2
Medium Italic ITC Stone
Semibold Italic ITC Stone
Bold Italic ITC Stone
ITC Stone Informal SCOSF
Medium SCOSF ITC Stone 1234...
Semibold SCOSF ITC Stone 123...
Stop
Stop
ITC Studio Script
✤ EF ITC DisplaySet 2 ITC Studio Script
Stymie 1
Light Stymie
Bold Stymie
Bold Condensed Stymie
Stymie 2
Medium Stymie
Black Stymie
Medium Condensed Stymie
Swift 1
Light Swift
Light Italic Swift
Bold Swift
Extra Bold Swift
Swift 2
Roman Swift
Italic Swift
Roman SCOSF Swift 12345...
Bold Condensed Swift
ITC Symbol 1
Book ITC Symbol
Book Italic ITC Symbol
Bold ITC Symbol
Bold Italic ITC Symbol
ITC Symbol 2
Medium ITC Symbol
Medium Italic ITC Symbol
Black ITC Symbol
Black Italic ITC Symbol
ITC Symbol SCOSF
Book SCOSF ITC Symbol 12345...
Medium SCOSF ITC Symbol 12345...
ITC Syndor 1
Book ITC Syndor
Book Italic ITC Syndor

✤ See page 549 for contents of Elsner+Flake Multi-Font Packages.

ff

... ITC Syndor 1 Book SCOSF ITC SYNDOR 12345...
ITC Syndor 2 Medium ITC Syndor
Medium Italic ITC Syndor
Medium SCOSF ITC SYNDOR 12345...
ITC Syndor 3 Bold ITC Syndor
Bold Italic ITC Syndor
Thunderbird Regular THUNDER
Extra Condensed THUNDERBIRD
ITC Tiepolo 1 Book ITC Tiepolo
Bold ITC Tiepolo
Black ITC Tiepolo
ITC Tiepolo 2 Book Italic ITC Tiepolo
Bold Italic ITC Tiepolo
Black Italic ITC Tiepolo
ITC Tiepolo SCOSF Book SCOSF ITC TIEPOLO 12345...
Bold SCOSF ITC TIEPOLO 12345...
ITC Tiffany 1 Light ITC Tiffany
Light Italic ITC Tiffany
Demi ITC Tiffany
Demi Italic ITC Tiffany
ITC Tiffany 2 Medium ITC Tiffany
Medium Italic ITC Tiffany
Heavy ITC Tiffany
Heavy Italic ITC Tiffany
ITC Usherwood 1 Book ITC Usherwood
Book Italic ITC Usherwood
Bold ITC Usherwood
Bold Italic ITC Usherwood
ITC Usherwood 2 Medium ITC Usherwood
Medium Italic ITC Usherwood
Black ITC Usherwood
Black Italic ITC Usherwood
VAG Rundschrift VAG Rundschrift
Van Dijk Van Dijk
Vario Regular Vario
Italic Vario
ITC Veljovic 1 Book ITC Veljovic

... ITC Veljovic 1 Book Italic ITC Veljovic
Bold ITC Veljovic
Bold Italic ITC Veljovic
ITC Veljovic 2 Medium ITC Veljovic
Medium Italic ITC Veljovic
Black ITC Veljovic
Black Italic ITC Veljovic
Vivaldi Vivaldi
Volta Roman Volta
Medium Volta
Medium Italic Volta
Bold Volta
ITC Weidemann 1 Book ITC Weidemann
Book Italic ITC Weidemann
Bold ITC Weidemann
Bold Italic ITC Weidemann
ITC Weidemann 2 Medium ITC Weidemann
Medium Italic ITC Weidemann
Black ITC Weidemann
Black Italic ITC Weidemann
ITC Weidemann SCOSF Book SCOSF ITC WEIDEMANN 1234...
Medium SCOSF ITC WEIDEMANN 123...
Windsor 1 Light Windsor
Bold Windsor
Windsor 2 Ultra Heavy Windsor
Bold Outline Windsor
Windsor 3 Extra Bold Condensed Windsor
Elongated Windsor
Windsor Light Condensed ✣ EF DisplaySet 3 Windsor
ITC Zapf Book 1 Light ITC Zapf Book
Light Italic ITC Zapf Book
Demi ITC Zapf Book
Demi Italic ITC Zapf Book
ITC Zapf Book 2 Medium ITC Zapf Book
Medium Italic ITC Zapf Book
Heavy ITC Zapf Book
Heavy Italic ITC Zapf Book
ITC Zapf Chancery 1 Light ITC Zapf Chancery

... ITC Zapf Chancery 1 Medium ITC Zapf Chancery
Demi ITC Zapf Chancery
Bold ITC Zapf Chancery
ITC Zapf Chancery 2 Light Italic ITC Zapf Chancery
Medium Italic ITC Zapf Chancery
ITC Zapf International 1 Light ITC Zapf Int'l.
Light Italic ITC Zapf Int'l.
Demi ITC Zapf Int'l.
Demi Italic ITC Zapf Int'l.
ITC Zapf International 2 Medium ITC Zapf Int'l.
Medium Italic ITC Zapf Int'l.
Heavy ITC Zapf Int'l.
Heavy Italic ITC Zapf Int'l.

Elsner+Flake Multi·Font Package Contents

✣ EF DisplaySet 1	: Baskerville Old Face & Old Town No. 536.
✣ EF DisplaySet 2	: Cheltenham Old Style & Goudy Handtooled.
✣ EF DisplaySet 3	: Kaufmann & Windsor Light Condensed.
✣ EF ITC DisplaySet 1	: ITC Anna & ITC Mona Lisa Recut.
✣ EF ITC DisplaySet 2	: ITC Beesknees & ITC Studio Script.
✣ EF ScriptSet 1	: Brody & Commercial Script.
✣ EF ScriptSet 2	: Murray Hill & Slogan.

foundry: EmDash

Founded in 1987 by Marshall Bohlin.... EmDash fonts comprise a small yet useful collection of pi characters and assorted informal designs in the style of lettering used for architectural notation.

ArchiText Regular ArchiText
Bold ArchiText
Arrow Dynamic Medium ↖ ↷ ← ⇧ ⇩ ↶ ⇘ ⇗ ⇙
Bold ↖ ↓ ← ⇧ ⇩ ⇙ ⇘ ⇗ ⇙
Heavy ⇧ ⇩ ↙ ⇘ ⇗ ⇦ ⇗ ⇙
BulletsNStuff ↓→▸▸▸▸▸■▶▶▶■■■···■▷▷▷
Gendarme Heavy GENDARME
Hurry Regular Hurry
Bold Hurry
Perky Regular Perky

ff

... Perky
Bold — Perky

Story
Regular — Story
Bold — Story

Upstart
Regular — Upstart
Condensed — Upstart
Extended — Upstart

foundry: Famous Fonts

Founded in 1985 to support the growing need for fonts in PostScript format, the company expanded in 1988 with the acquisiton of Shapes Unlimited, adding a more diversified selection of fonts to their collection. The library is made up largely of fonts licensed from Agfa and from International Typeface Corporation.

ITC American Typewriter
Light — ITC American Type
Medium — ITC American Type
Bold — ITC American Type

ITC American Typewriter Condensed
Light Condensed — ITC American Typewriter
Medium Condensed — ITC American Typewrit
Bold Condensed — ITC American Typewriter

ITC American Typewriter Display
Display Light — ITC American
Display Medium — ITC American
Display Bold — ITC American

ITC American Typewriter Display Condensed
Display Light Condensed — ITC American Type
Display Medium Condensed — ITC American Type
Display Bold Condensed — ITC American Type

ITC American Typewriter Display Bold Outline — ITC American

ITC Avant Garde Gothic 1
Extra Light — ITC Avant Garde
Book — ITC Avant Garde
Medium — ITC Avant Garde
Medium Oblique — ITC Avant Garde

ITC Avant Garde Gothic 2
Demi — ITC Avant Garde
Demi Oblique — ITC Avant Garde
Bold — ITC Avant Garde
Bold Oblique — ITC Avant Garde

ITC Avant Garde Gothic 1 Display
Display Extra Light — ITC Avant Garde

... ITC Avant Garde Gothic 1 Display
Display Extra Light Oblique — ITC Avant Garde

ITC Avant Garde Gothic 2 Display
Display Book — ITC Avant Garde
Display Book Oblique — ITC Avant Garde
Display Medium — ITC Avant Garde
Display Demi — ITC Avant Garde
Display Bold — ITC Avant Garde

ITC Avant Garde Gothic Display Condensed
Display Book Condensed — ITC Avant Garde
Display Medium Condensed — ITC Avant Garde
Display Demi Condensed — ITC Avant Garde
Display Bold Condensed — ITC Avant Garde

Baskerville II
Roman — Baskerville II
Italic — Baskerville II
Bold — Baskerville II
Bold Italic — Baskerville II

ITC New Baskerville 1
Roman — ITC New Baskerville
Italic — ITC New Baskerville
Semibold — ITC New Baskerville

ITC New Baskerville 2
Bold — ITC New Baskerville
Bold Italic — ITC New Baskerville
Black — ITC New Basker
Black Italic — ITC New Baskerville

Belwe
Light — Belwe
Light Italic — Belwe
Medium — Belwe
Condensed — Belwe
Inline — Belwe
Display Bold — Belwe

xxxxxxxxxxxxxxxxxxxx product not available xxxxxxxxxxxxxxxxxxxx

ITC Berkeley Oldstyle 1
Book — ITC Berkeley Oldstyl
Book Italic — ITC Berkeley Oldstyle
Medium — ITC Berkeley Oldsty
Medium Italic — ITC Berkeley Oldstyle

ITC Berkely Oldstyle 2
Bold — ITC Berkeley Oldstyle
Bold Italic — ITC Berkeley Oldstyle
Black — ITC Berkeley Oldstyl
Black Italic — ITC Berkeley Oldstyl

CG Bodoni 1
Book — CG Bodoni
Book Italic — CG Bodoni
Roman — CG Bodoni
Italic — CG Bodoni

CG Bodoni 2
Bold — CG Bodoni
Bold Italic — CG Bodoni
Bold Condensed — CG Bodoni

CG Poster Bodoni
Roman — CG P Bodoni
Italic — CG P Bodoni

Bodoni Extra Bold
Extra Bold — Bodoni
Extra Bold Condensed — Bodoni

ITC Bookman 1
Light — ITC Bookman
Light Italic — ITC Bookman
Medium — ITC Bookman
Medium Italic — ITC Bookman

ITC Bookman 2
Demi — ITC Bookman
Demi Italic — ITC Bookman
Bold — ITC Bookman
Bold Italic — ITC Bookman

C & B Pi — @℞©®™#°▶▷☆◆➪″•†‡{ }

California
Roman — California
Bold — California
Bold Italic — California

CG California
Roman — CG California
Italic — CG California
Bold — CG California
Bold Italic — CG California

Caslon 540
Roman — Caslon 540
Italic — Caslon 540

Caslon No. 3
Roman — Caslon No. 3

ff

... Caslon No. 3
Italic *Caslon No. 3*

Caslon 76
Roman Caslon 76
Italic *Caslon 76*

Caslon Antique
Caslon Antique

ITC Caslon Headline
ITC Caslon Head

Caxton
Light Caxton
Light Italic *Caxton*
Book Caxton
Bold **Caxton**

CG Century
Expanded CG Century
Expanded Italic *CG Century*
Bold **CG Century**
Bold Italic ***CG Century***

Century Old Style
Roman Century Old Style
Italic *Century Old Style*
Bold **Century Old Style**

CG Century Old Style
Roman CG Century Old Style
Italic *CG Century Old Style*
Bold **CG Century Old Style**

CG Century Schoolbook
Roman CG Century School
Italic *CG Century School*
Bold **CGCentury School**

New Century Schoolbook
Roman New Century School
Italic *New Century School*
Bold **New Century**
Bold Italic ***New Century***

Century Textbook
Roman Century Textbook
Italic *Century Textbook*
Bold **Century Textbook**

ITC Century 1
Light ITC Century
Light Italic *ITC Century*
Book ITC Century
Book Italic *ITC Century*

ITC Century 2
Bold **ITC Century**
Bold Italic ***ITC Century***
Ultra **ITC Century**
Ultra Italic ***ITC Century***

ITC Century Condensed 1
Light Condensed ITC Century

... ITC Century Condensed 1
Light Condensed Italic *ITC Century*
Book Condensed ITC Century
Book Condensed Italic *ITC Century*

ITC Century Condensed 2
Bold Condensed **ITC Century**
Bold Condensed Italic ***ITC Century***
Ultra Condensed **ITC Century**
Ultra Condensed Italic ***ITC Century***

ITC Cheltenham 1
Light ITC Cheltenham
Light Italic *ITC Cheltenham*
Book ITC Cheltenham
Book Italic *ITC Cheltenham*

ITC Cheltenham 2
Bold **ITC Cheltenham**
Bold Italic ***ITC Cheltenham***
Ultra **ITC Cheltenham**
Ultra Italic ***ITC Cheltenham***

ITC Cheltenham Condensed 1
Light Condensed ITC Cheltenham
Light Condensed Italic *ITC Cheltenham*
Book Condensed ITC Cheltenham
Book Condensed Italic *ITC Cheltenham*

ITC Cheltenham Condensed 2
Bold Condensed **ITC Cheltenham**
Bold Condensed Italic ***ITC Cheltenham***
Ultra Condensed **ITC Cheltenham**
Ultra Condensed Italic ***ITC Cheltenham***

Cheltenham Display
Display Bold **Cheltenham**
Display Bold Italic ***Cheltenham***

ITC Didi
ITC Didi

English Times
Roman English Times
Italic *English Times*
Bold **English Times**
Bold Italic ***English Times***

English Times Condensed
Condensed English Times
Condensed Italic *English Times*
Bold Condensed **English Times**
Bold Condensed Italic ***English Times***

English Times Display
Display Roman English Times
Display Italic *English Times*
Display Bold **English Times**
Display Bold Italic ***English Times***

ITC Eras 1
Light ITC Eras
Book ITC Eras
Medium ITC Eras

ITC Eras 2
Demi **ITC Eras**
Bold **ITC Eras**
Ultra **ITC Eras**

ITC Fenice 1 Display
Display Light ITC Fenice
Display Light Italic *ITC Fenice*
Display Regular ITC Fenice
Display Regular Italic *ITC Fenice*

ITC Fenice 2 Display
Display Bold **ITC Fenice**
Display Bold Italic ***ITC Fenice***
Display Ultra **ITC Fenice**
Display Ultra Italic ***ITC Fenice***

ITC Franklin Gothic 1
Book ITC Franklin Gothic
Medium ITC Franklin Gothic
Medium Italic *ITC Franklin Gothic*

ITC Franklin Gothic 2
Demi **ITC Franklin Gothic**
Demi Italic ***ITC Franklin Gothic***
Heavy **ITC Franklin Gothic**
Heavy Italic ***ITC Franklin Gothic***

Friz Quadrata
Regular Friz Quadrata
Bold **Friz Quadrata**

Friz Quadrata Display
Display Regular Friz Quadrata
Display Bold **Friz Quadrata**

CG Frontiera 1
45-Light CG Frontiera
46-Light Italic *CG Frontiera*
55-Regular CG Frontiera
56-Italic *CG Frontiera*

CG Frontiera 2
65-Bold **CG Frontiera**
66-Bold Italic ***CG Frontiera***
75-Black **CG Frontiera**
76-Black Italic ***CG Frontiera***

Futura II One
Light Futura II
Light Italic *Futura II*
Book Futura II
Book Italic *Futura II*

Futura II Two
Medium Futura II

ff

... Futura II Two
Medium Italic Futura II
Demi Futura II
Demi Italic Futura II
Futura II Three
Bold Futura II
Bold Italic Futura II
Extra Bold Futura II
Extra Bold Italic Futura II
Futura II Condensed One
Light Condensed Futura II
Medium Condensed Futura II
Futura II Condensed Two
Bold Condensed Futura II
Bold Condensed Italic Futura II
Extra Bold Condensed Futura II
CG Garamond No. 3
Roman CGGaramondNo.3
Italic CG Garamond No. 3
Bold CG Garamond No.3
Bold Italic CG Garamond No. 3
Garamond No. 49
Roman Garamond No. 49
Italic Garamond No. 49
Bold Garamond No. 49
Bold Italic Garamond No. 49
ITC Garamond 1
Light ITC Garamond
Light Italic ITC Garamond
Book ITC Garamond
Book Italic ITC Garamond
ITC Garamond 2
Bold ITC Garamond
Bold Italic ITC Garamond
Ultra ITC Garamond
Ultra Italic ITC Garamond
ITC Garamond Condensed 1
Light Condensed ITC Garamond
Light Condensed Italic ITC Garamond
Book Condensed ITC Garamond
Book Condensed Italic ITC Garamond
ITC Garamond Condensed 2
Bold Condensed ITC Garamond
Bold Condensed Italic ITC Garamond
Ultra Condensed ITC Garamond
Ultra Condensed Italic ITC Garamond
Gill Sans 1
Light Gill Sans
Light Italic Gill Sans

... Gill Sans 1
Medium Gill Sans
Medium Italic Gill Sans
Gill Sans 2
Bold Gill Sans
Extra Bold Gill Sans
Display Ultra Bold Gill Sans
Gill Sans Condensed 1
Light Condensed Gill Sans
Medium Condensed Gill Sans
Gill Sans Condensed 2
Bold Condensed Gill Sans
Display Ultra Bold Outline Gill Sans
Goudy Old Style
Roman Goudy Old Style
Italic Goudy Old Style
Goudy Old Style Condensed
Condensed Goudy Old Style
Condensed Italic Goudy Old Style
Goudy Catalogue
Goudy Catalogue
Goudy 2
Bold Goudy
Bold Italic Goudy
Extra Bold Goudy
Bold Condensed Goudy
Goudy Heavyface Display
Display Roman Goudy Heavy
Display Italic Goudy Heavy
Display Condensed Goudy Heavy
Goudy Display
Display Bold Goudy
Display Handtooled Goudy Handtool
Heldustry
Regular Heldustry
Medium Heldustry
Demi Heldustry
Helios Rounded
Regular Helios Rounded
Semibold Helios Rounded
Bold Helios Rounded
ITC Kabel 1
Book ITC Kabel
Medium ITC Kabel
Demi ITC Kabel
ITC Kabel 2
Bold ITC Kabel
Ultra ITC Kabel
ITC Korinna 1
Regular ITC Korinna
Kursiv ITC Korinna
Bold Kursiv ITC Korinna
ITC Korinna 2
Extra Bold ITC Korinna

... ITC Korinna 2
Extra Bold Kursiv ITC Korinna
Heavy ITC Korinna
Heavy Kursiv ITC Korinna
Mallard II
Italic Mallard II
Bold Mallard II
Meridien 1
Light Meridien
Light Italic Meridien
Medium Meridien
Meridien 2
Bold Meridien
Extra Bold Meridien
Black Meridien
Microstyle 1 Display
Display Regular Microstyle
Display Bold Microstyle
Microstyle 2 Display
Display Extended Microstyle
Display Bold Extended Microstyle
Nimbus Roman
Roman Nimbus
Italic Nimbus
Bold Nimbus
Bold Italic Nimbus
Nimbus Sans
Roman Nimbus
Oblique Nimbus
Bold Nimbus
Bold Oblique Nimbus
Nimbus Mono
Roman Nimbus
Oblique Nimbus
Bold Nimbus
Bold Oblique Nimbus
Nimbus Narrow
Roman Narrow Nimbus
Oblique Narrow Nimbus
Bold Narrow Nimbus
Bold Oblique Narrow Nimbus
ITC Novarese 1
Book ITC Novarese
Book Italic ITC Novarese
Medium ITC Novarese
Medium Italic ITC Novarese
ITC Novarese 2
Bold ITC Novarese
Bold Italic ITC Novarese
Ultra ITC Novarese

ff

Font	Style	Sample
Old English Display		Old English
CG Omega 1	Regular	CG Omega
	Italic	*CG Omega*
	Medium	CG Omega
	Medium Italic	*CG Omega*
CG Omega 2	Bold	**CG Omega**
	Bold Italic	***CG Omega***
	Black	**CG Omega**
	Black Italic	***CG Omega***
Oracle Bold		**Oracle**
Oracle II	Regular	Oracle II
	Italic	*Oracle II*
	Bold	**Oracle II**
	Bold Italic	***Oracle II***
CG Palacio	Roman	CG Palacio
	Italic	*CG Palacio*
	Bold	**CG Palacio**
	Bold Italic	***CG Palacio***
Paladium	Roman	Paladium
	Italic	*Paladium*
	Semibold	**Paladium**
Paladium Display	Display Roman	Paladium
	Display Italic	*Paladium*
	Display Semibold	**Paladium**
Palatino	Roman	Palatino
	Italic	*Palatino*
	Bold	**Palatino**
	Bold Italic	***Palatino***
Perpetua 1	Roman	Perpetua
	Italic	*Perpetua*
	Bold	**Perpetua**
	Bold Italic	***Perpetua***
Perpetua 2	Extra Bold	**Perpetua**
	Black	**Perpetua**
Plantin	Roman	Plantin
	Italic	*Plantin*
	Bold	**Plantin**
	Bold Italic	***Plantin***
CG Plantin 1	Light	CG Plantin
	Light Italic	*CG Plantin*
	Roman	CG Plantin
	Italic	*CG Plantin*
CG Plantin 2	Bold	**CG Plantin**
	Bold Italic	***CG Plantin***
	Bold Condensed	**CG Plantin**
Rockwell 1	Light	Rockwell
	Light Italic	*Rockwell*
	Medium	Rockwell
	Medium Italic	*Rockwell*
Rockwell 2	Bold Italic	***Rockwell***
	Extra Bold	**Rockwell**
Rockwell Condensed	Medium Condensed	Rockwell
	Bold Condensed	**Rockwell**
ITC Serif Gothic	Light	ITC Serif Gothic
	Black	**ITC Serif Gothic**
ITC Serif Gothic Display	Display Bold	ITC Serif Gothic
	Display Heavy	**ITC Serif Gothic**
	Display Bold Outline	ITC Serif Gothic
Serifa 1	35-Thin	Serifa
	36-Thin Italic	*Serifa*
	45-Light	Serifa
	46-Light Italic	*Serifa*
Serifa 2	55-Roman	Serifa
	56-Italic	*Serifa*
	65-Bold	**Serifa**
	75-Black	**Serifa**
ITC Souvenir Display 1	Display Light	ITC Souvenir
	Display Light Italic	*ITC Souvenir*
	Display Medium	ITC Souvenir
	Display Medium Italic	*ITC Souvenir*
ITC Souvenir Display 2	Display Demi	**ITC Souvenir**
	Display Demi Italic	***ITC Souvenir***
	Display Bold	**ITC Souvenir**
	Display Bold Italic	***ITC Souvenir***
Stymie 1	Light	Stymie
	Light Italic	*Stymie*
. . . Stymie 1	Medium	Stymie
	Medium Italic	*Stymie*
Stymie 2	Bold	**Stymie**
	Bold Italic	***Stymie***
	Display Extra Bold	**Stymie**
Stymie Condensed	Light Condensed	Stymie
	Medium Condensed	Stymie
	Display Bold Condensed	**Stymie**
	Display Extra Bold Condensed	**Stymie**
Symbol		123℘%#ΣμΦ∪⇓∈⇔∅
ITC Symbol 1	Book	ITC Symbol
	Book Italic	*ITC Symbol*
	Medium	ITC Symbol
	Medium Italic	*ITC Symbol*
ITC Symbol 2	Bold	**ITC Symbol**
	Bold Italic	***ITC Symbol***
	Black	**ITC Symbol**
	Black Italic	***ITC Symbol***
ITC Tiffany Display	Display Light	ITC Tiffany
	Display Medium	ITC Tiffany
	Display Demi	**ITC Tiffany**
	Display Heavy	**ITC Tiffany**
CG Times 1	Roman	CG Times
	Italic	*CG Times*
	Semibold	**CG Times**
	Semibold Italic	***CG Times***
CG Times 2	Bold	**CG Times**
	Bold Italic	***CG Times***
CG Trade 1	Light	CG Trade
	Light Italic	*CG Trade*
	Regular	CG Trade
	Italic	*CG Trade*
	Bold	**CG Trade**
CG Trade Bold No. 2	Bold	**CG Trade No. 2**
	Bold Italic	***CG Trade No. 2***
CG Trade Condensed 1	Condensed	CG Trade
	Condensed Italic	*CG Trade*
	Bold Condensed	**CG Trade**

Font	Style	Sample
...CG Trade Condensed 1	Bold Condensed Italic	CG Trade
CG Trade Condensed 2	Extra Condensed	CG Trade
	Bold Extra Condensed	CG Trade
CG Trade Extended	Extended	CG Trade
	Bold Extended	CG Trade
CG Triumvirate 1	Ultra Light	CG Triumvirate
	Ultra Light Italic	CG Triumvirate
CG Triumvirate 2	Thin	CG Triumvirate
	Thin Italic	CG Triumvirate
	Light	CG Triumvirate
	Light Italic	CG Triumvirate
CG Triumvirate 3	Regular	CG Triumvirate
	Italic	CG Triumvirate
	Bold	CG Triumvirate
	Bold Italic	CG Triumvirate
CG Triumvirate 4	Heavy	CG Triumvirate
	Heavy Italic	CG Triumvirate
	Black	CG Triumvirate
	Black Italic	CG Triumvirate
CG Triumvirate Condensed 1	Light Condensed	CG Triumvirate
	Light Condensed Italic	CG Triumvirate
CG Triumvirate Condensed 2	Condensed	CG Triumvirate
	Condensed Italic	CG Triumvirate
	Bold Condensed	CG Triumvirate
	Bold Condensed Italic	CG Triumvirate
CG Triumvirate Condensed 3	Black Condensed	CG Triumvirate
	Black Condensed Italic	CG Triumvirate
CG Triumvirate No. 2	Bold	CG Triumvirate No. 2
	Black	CG Triumvirate No. 2
CG Triumvirate Inserat	Regular	CG Triumvirate Inserat
	Italic	CG Triumvirate Inserat
CG Triumvirate Compressed Display	Display Compressed	CG Triumvirate
	Display Extra Compressed	CG Triumvirate
	Ultra Compressed	CG Triumvirate
CG Triumvirate	Light Extended	CG Triumvirate
CG Triumvirate Bold Outline	Display	CG Triumvirate
Univers 1	Light	Univers
	Light Italic	Univers
...Univers 1	Medium	Univers
	Medium Italic	Univers
Univers 2	Bold	Univers
	Bold Italic	Univers
	Extra Bold	Univers
	Extra Bold Italic	Univers
Univers Condensed 1	Light Condensed	Univers
	Light Condensed Italic	Univers
	Medium Condensed	Univers
	Medium Condensed Italic	Univers
Univers Condensed 2	Bold Condensed	Univers
	Bold Condensed Italic	Univers
Univers Condensed 3	49-Light Condensed	Univers
	59-Ultra Condensed	Univers
CG Univers 1	Light	CG Univers
	Light Italic	CG Univers
	Regular	CG Univers
	Italic	CG Univers
CG Univers 2	Bold	CG Univers
	Bold Italic	CG Univers
	Black	CG Univers
	Black Italic	CG Univers
CG Univers Condensed 1	Light Condensed	CG Univers
	Light Condensed Italic	CG Univers
	Condensed	CG Univers
	Condensed Italic	CG Univers
CG Univers Condensed 2	Bold Condensed	CG Univers
Univers Expanded	Medium Expanded	Univers
	Bold Expanded	Univers
	Extra Bold Expanded	Univers
	Ultra Bold Expanded	Univers
ITC Zapf Book	Light	ITC Zapf Book
	Medium	ITC Zapf Book
	Demi	ITC Zapf Book
	Heavy	ITC Zapf Book
ITC Zapf Chancery	Light	ITC Zapf Chancery
	Light Italic	ITC Zapf Chancery
	Medium	ITC Zapf Chancery

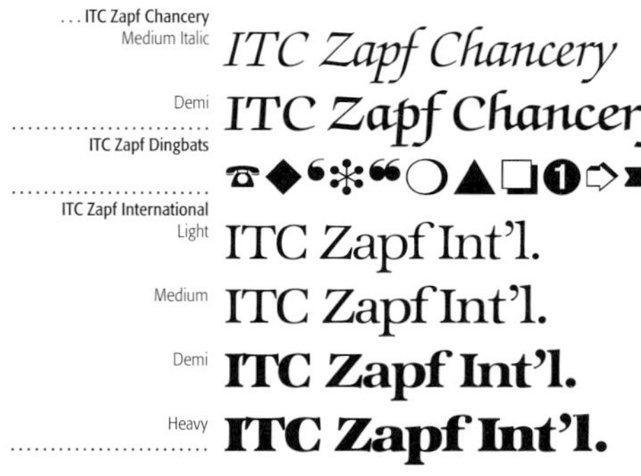

Font	Style	Sample
...ITC Zapf Chancery	Medium Italic	ITC Zapf Chancery
	Demi	ITC Zapf Chancery
ITC Zapf Dingbats		
ITC Zapf International	Light	ITC Zapf Int'l.
	Medium	ITC Zapf Int'l.
	Demi	ITC Zapf Int'l.
	Heavy	ITC Zapf Int'l.

foundry: The Font Bureau

Founded by David Berlow and Roger Black in 1989, the company began as a custom type house designing new fonts and reviving hard-to-find classics for use in newpapers and magazines. The Font Bureau has since evolved into a vital resource for new text and display fonts featuring the work of designers Greg Thompson, John Benson, Richard Lipton, Jill Pichotta, Tobias Frere-Jones, John Downer and others.

Font	Style	Sample
Aardvark	Regular	AARDVARK
	Bold	AARDVARK
Bureau Agency	Regular	Bureau Agency
	Bold	Bureau Agency
Agenda 1	Thin Ultra Condensed	Agenda
	Light	Agenda
	Light Italic	Agenda
	Light Condensed	Agenda
	Light Extra Condensed	Agenda
	Light Ultra Condensed	Agenda
Agenda 2	Medium	Agenda
	Medium Italic	Agenda
	Medium Condensed	Agenda
	Medium Extra Condensed	Agenda
	Medium Ultra Condensed	Agenda
Agenda 3	Bold	Agenda
	Bold Condensed	Agenda
	Bold Extra Condensed	Agenda
	Bold Ultra Condensed	Agenda

ff

... Agenda 3 Black — Agenda
Alhambra — ALHAMBRA
Armada 1 Thin — Armada
Light — Armada
Regular — Armada
Bold — Armada
Black — Armada
Armada 2 Thin Condensed — Armada
Light Condensed — Armada
Condensed — Armada
Bold Condensed — Armada
Black Condensed — Armada
Armada 3 Thin Compressed — Armada
Light Compressed — Armada
Regular Compressed — Armada
Bold Compressed — Armada
Black Compressed — Armada
BadTyp — BADTYP
Belizio Bold — Belizio
Bold Italic — *Belizio*
BeLucian Book — BeLucian
Book Italic — *BeLucian*
Demi — BeLucian
Ultra — BeLucian
Berlin Sans 1 Roman — Berlin Sans
Bold — Berlin Sans
Roman Alternate Caps OSF — BERLIN SANS 12345...
Bold Alternate Caps OSF — BERLIN SANS 123...
Bold Dingbats
Berlins Sans 2 Light — Berlin Sans
Demibold — Berlin Sans
Light Alternate Caps OSF — BERLIN SANS 12345...
Demi Alternate Caps OSF — BERLIN SANS 1234...
Bodega Serif 1 Light — Bodega
Light Oldstyle — Bodega 12345...
Light SCOSF — BODEGA 12345...

Bodega Serif 2 Medium — Bodega
Medium Oldstyle — Bodega 12345...
Medium SCOSF — BODEGA 12345...
Bodega Serif 3 Black — Bodega
Black Oldstyle — Bodega 12345...
Black SCOSF — BODEGA 12345...
Bodega Sans 1 Light — Bodega
Light Oldstyle — Bodega 12345...
Light SCOSF — BODEGA 12345...
Bodega Sans 2 Medium — Bodega
Medium Oldstyle — Bodega 12345...
Medium SCOSF — BODEGA 12345...
Bodega Sans 3 Black — Bodega
Black Oldstyle — Bodega 12345...
Black SCOSF — BODEGA 12345...
Bureau Bodoni Bold Condensed — Bureau Bodoni
Bold Compressed — Bureau Bodoni
Bremen Light — BREMEN
Bold — BREMEN
Black — BREMEN
Cafeteria Light — Cafeteria
Regular — Cafeteria
Bold — Cafeteria
Black — Cafeteria
Bureau Caslon Bold Condensed — Bureau Caslon
Bold Extra Condensed — Bureau Caslon
Bureau Century Bold Condensed — Bureau Century
Bureau Cheltenham Bold Condensed — Bureau Cheltenham
Clicker Regular — Clicker
Extras — 1/3 3/8 ←↓↑→√÷12345
Commerce Lean — Commerce
Fat — Commerce
Bureau Eagle Book — Bureau Eagle
Bold — Bureau Eagle
Ecru — ECRU
ElGrande — ELGRANDE
Elli — Elli

Bureau Empire 1 Regular — Bureau Empire
Italic — *Bureau Empire*
Regular SCOSF — BUREAU EMPIRE 12345...
Bureau Empire 2 Bold — Bureau Empire
Bold SCOSF — BUREAU EMPIRE 12345...
Black — Bureau Empire
Black SCOSF — BUREAU EMPIRE 12345...
Epitaph — EPITAPH
Fobia — fobia
Garage Gothic Regular — Garage Gothic
Bold — Garage Gothic
Black — Garage Gothic
Bureau Garamond Roman — Bureau Garamond
Italic — *Bureau Garamond*
Giza 1 15 — Giza
35 — Giza
55 — Giza
75 — Giza
95 — Giza
Giza 2 11 — Giza
31 — Giza
91 — Giza
13 — Giza
33 — Giza
53 — Giza
73 — Giza
93 — Giza
Giza 3 57 — Giza
77 — Giza
79 — Giza
Graffiti — Graffiti
Bureau Grotesque 1 13 — Bureau Grotesque
15 — Bureau Grotesque
17 — Bureau Grotesque
37 — Bureau Grotesque
53 — Bureau Grotesque
79 — Bureau Grotes
Bureau Grotesque 2 11 — Bureau Grotesque

ff

. . . Bureau Grotesque 2
31 Bureau Grotesque
33 Bureau Grotesque
35 Bureau Grotesque
51 Bureau Grotesque
55 Bureau Grotesqu

Hamilton
Light Hamilton
Medium Hamilton
Bold Hamilton

Herald Gothic
Light HERALD GOTHIC
Medium HERALD GOTHIC
Bold HERALD GOTHIC
Light SC HERALD GOTHIC
Medium SC HERALD GOTHIC
Bold SC HERALD GOTHIC

HipHop
Demi HipHop
Inline HipHop

Hoffmann 1
Light Hoffmann
Light SCOSF HOFFMANN 12345...
Roman Hoffmann
Roman SCOSF HOFFMANN 12345...

Hoffmann 2
Book Hoffmann
Book SCOSF HOFFMANN 12345...
Bold Hoffmann
Bold SCOSF HOFFMANN 1234...
Black Titling HOFFMAN

Interstate
Light Interstate
Regular Interstate
Bold Interstate
Black Interstate

Interstate Condensed
Light Condensed Interstate
Regular Condensed Interstate
Bold Condensed Interstate
Black Condensed Interstate

Interstate Compressed
Light Compressed Interstate
Regular Compressed Interstate
Bold Compressed Interstate
Black Compressed Interstate

Interstate Pi
One ONE WAY JCT KEEP RIGHT ONLY

. . . Interstate Pi
Two PILOT CAR FOLLOW ME ROAD CLOSED TO THRU TRAFFIC NO PARKING NO PARKING ANY TIME NO PARKING BUS STOP NO MOTOR VEHICLES 4-WAY REST AREA STOP
Three SCHOOL BUS STOP AHEAD 500 FEET
Four CHIP ON SHOULDER SLOW ADULTS

Ironmonger
Black IRONMNGR
Extra Condensed IRONMONGER
Extended IRONMNGR
Inlaid IRONMNGR

Ironmonger Three D IRONMNGR

Kniff Kniff

Meno 1
Roman Meno
Italic *Meno*
Bold Meno
Bold Italic *Meno*
Black Meno
Black Italic *Meno*

Meno 2
Roman SCOSF MENO 12345...
Roman OSF & Extras 12345 et al.
Italic OSF & Extras *12345 et al*
Bold OSF & Extras 12345 et al
Bold Italic OSF & Extras *12345 et al*
Black OSF & Extras 12345 et al
Black Italic OSF & Extras *12345 et al*
Italic Swash Capitals *MENO*
Display Roman SCLF MENO 12345...

Munich
Light MUNICH
Bold MUNICH
Black MUNICH

Nobel
Light Nobel
Regular Nobel
Italic *Nobel*
Bold Nobel
Condensed Nobel
Bold Condensed Nobel

Numskill Bold Numskill

Nutcracker Nutcracker

Bureau Ornaments
City Ornaments
Town Ornaments

. . . Bureau Ornaments
Village Ornaments

Parkinson 1
Roman Parkinson
Italic *Parkinson*
Bold Parkinson
Bold Italic *Parkinson*
Black Parkinson
Bold Condensed Parkinson

Parkinson 2
Medium Parkinson
Medium Italic *Parkinson*
Light Condensed Parkinson
Condensed Parkinson

Phaistos
Roman Phaistos
Italic *Phaistos*
Bold Phaistos

Poster Black POSTER

Reiner Script
Regular Reiner Script
Bold Reiner Script

Romeo
Skinny Condensed Romeo
Medium Condensed Romeo

Bureau Roxy
Light Bureau Roxy
Light Italic *Bureau Roxy*
Medium Bureau Roxy
Medium Italic *Bureau Roxy*
Black Bureau Roxy
Black Italic *Bureau Roxy*

Sam Sans
Thin Sam Sans
Bold Sam Sans

Scamp
Regular SCAMP
Bold Inline SCAMP
Fat SCAMP

Showcard Gothic SHOWCARD

Skyline
Bold Condensed Skyline
Black Skyline

Sloop Script
One *Sloop Script*
Two *Sloop Script*
Three *Sloop Script*

Stereo STEREO

ff

Tasse Regular Tasse
Medium Tasse
Bold Tasse
Black Tasse

Tasse Condensed Condensed Tasse
Medium Condensed Tasse
Bold Condensed Tasse
Black Condensed Tasse

Tasse Compressed Compressed Tasse
Medium Compressed Tasse
Bold Compressed Tasse
Black Compressed Tasse

Tasse Extended Extended Tasse
Medium Extended Tasse
Bold Extended Tasse
Black Extended Tasse

Tasse Wide Wide Tasse
Medium Wide Tasse
Bold Wide Tasse
Black Wide Tasse

Village Roman Village
Italic *Village*
Bold **Village**
Roman SCLF Village 12345...
Italic SCLF *Village 12345...*
Roman Titling Village
Italic Titling *Village*
Bold Titling **Village**
Roman SCLF Titling Village 1234...
Italic SCLF Titling *Village 12345...*

Wessex Roman Wessex
Italic *Wessex*
Semibold **Wessex**
Roman SCLF Wessex 12345...
Roman Titling WESSEX

foundry: The Font Company

A diverse selection of about 400 fonts that includes historical revivals as well as contemporary designs. Especially notable is the large selection of fonts licensed from the collections of Alphabet Innovations and TypeSpectra. The Font Company was founded in 1988.

FC Abbey Regular FC Abbey
Medium FC Abbey
Bold FC Abbey

FC Abilene FC Abilene

FC Accent FC Accent

FC Accolade Bold FC Accolade

FC Adelon Extra Bold FC Adelon

FC Adroit 1 Light FC Adroit
Light Italic *FC Adroit*
Medium FC Adroit
Medium Italic *FC Adroit*

FC Adroit 2 Bold FC Adroit
Extra Bold FC Adroit

FC Advertisers Bold FC Advertisers

FC Agenda Light FC Agenda
Medium FC Agenda
Bold FC Agenda
Extra Bold FC Agenda

FC Aggie FC Aggie

FC Amanda FC Amanda

FC Amber FC Amber

FC Amelia FC Amelia

FC American Gothic 1 Light FC American
Light Italic *FC American*
Medium FC American
Medium Italic *FC American*

FC American Gothic 2 Bold FC American

FC American Text FC American Text

FC American Uncial Regular FC American
Bold FC American

FC Annual FC Annual

FC Apache FC Apache

FC April FC April

FC Art Gothic FC Art Gothic

FC Artcraft Regular FC Artcraft
Bold FC Artcraft

FC Ashley FC Ashley

FC Atrax FC Atrax

FC Avalon Light FC Avalon
Medium FC Avalon
Bold FC Avalon

FC Avon FC Avon

FC Baker Signet Regular FC Baker Signet
Medium FC Baker Signet
Bold FC Baker Signet
Black FC Baker Signet

FC Ballantines Regular FC Ballantines
Heavy FC Ballantines

FC Balloon Light FC Balloon
Bold FC Balloon

FC Balzac FC Balzac

FC Barnum FC Barnum

FC Baskerville AI Ad Weight FC Baskerville
Heavy Weight FC Baskerville
Over Weight FC Baskerville

FC Baucher Gothic 1 Normal FC Baucher Gothic
Alternate FC Baucher Gothic

FC Baucher Gothic 2 Medium FC Baucher Gothic
Medium Alternate FC Baucher Gothic
Bold FC Baucher Gothic
Bold Alternate FC Baucher Gothic

FC Baucher Gothic 3 Extended FC Baucher Gothic
Extended Alternate FC Baucher Gothic

FC Baucher Gothic 4 Medium Extended FC Baucher Gothic
Medium Extended Alternate FC Baucher Gothic
Bold Extended FC Baucher Gothic
Bold Extended Alternate FC Baucher Gothic

FC Bauer Topic Medium FC Bauer Topic
Medium Italic *FC Bauer Topic*

... FC Bauer Topic
Bold FC Bauer Topic
Bold Italic FC Bauer Topic

FC Beacon
Light FC Beacon
Medium FC Beacon
Bold FC Beacon

FC Beale
FC Beale

FC Bee 1
One FC Bee
Two FC Bee

FC Bee 2
Three FC Bee
Four FC Bee

FC Benjamin
FC Benjamin

FC Bernhard Bold Condensed
FC Bernhard

FC Bernhard Gothic 1
Extra Light FC Bernhard
Light FC Bernhard
Medium FC Bernhard
Heavy FC Bernhard

FC Bernhard Gothic 2
Extra Heavy FC Bernhard
Ultra FC Bernhard

FC Bernhard Modern
Roman FC Bernhard
Italic FC Bernhard
Bold FC Bernhard
Bold Italic FC Bernhard

FC Bernhard Modern
Headline FC Bernhard

FC Bible
FC Bible

FC Bluejack 1
Light FC Bluejack
Light Italic FC Bluejack
Medium FC Bluejack

FC Bluejack 2
Bold FC Bluejack
Extra Bold FC Bluejack

FC Boa Script
FC Boa Script

FC Bodoni Bold Condensed
FC Bodoni

FC Brittany
FC Brittany

FC Bulmer
Roman FC Bulmer
Italic FC Bulmer
Roman SCOSF FC Bulmer 12345...
Italic OSF FC Bulmer 12345...

FC California Grotesk
Regular FC California Grotesk
Medium FC California Grotesk

... FC California Grotesk
Bold FC California Grotesk
Black FC California Grotesk

FC Cartel 1
Light FC Cartel
Medium FC Cartel
Demi FC Cartel
Bold FC Cartel

FC Cartel 2
Extra Bold FC Cartel

FC Cartoon
FC Cartoon

FC Casablanca 1
Light FC Casablanca
Medium FC Casablanca
Bold FC Casablanca

FC Casablanca 2
Light Condensed FC Casablanca
Medium Condensed FC Casablanca

FC Caslon C 37
Light FC Caslon C 37
Light Italic FC Caslon C 37
Light SCOSF FC Caslon C 37
Light Italic Alternate FC Caslon C 37

FC Caslon C 78
Old Roman FC Caslon C 78
Old Roman Italic FC Caslon C 78

FC Caslon C 79
Bold FC Caslon C 79
Bold Italic FC Caslon C 79
Bold SCLF FC Caslon C 79

FC Caslon C 113
Bold Condensed FC Caslon C 113
Bold Condensed Headline FC Caslon C 113

FC Caslon C 337
Roman FC Caslon C 337
Italic FC Caslon C 337
Roman SCOSF FC Caslon C 337
Italic Swash Capitals OSF FC Caslon C 337

FC Caslon 437
Roman SCLF FC Caslon C 437
Italic Swash Capitals FC Caslon C 437
Roman Headline FC Caslon C 437
Italic Headline FC Caslon C 437

FC Caslon C 637
Medium FC Caslon C 637
Medium Italic FC Caslon C 637

FC Century Expanded
Regular FC Century Expand
Italic FC Century Expand
Bold FC Century Expand

FC O Century
Roman FC O Century

... FC O Century
Italic FC O Century

FC Charter Oak
FC Charter Oak

FC Chevalier
FC Chevalier

FC Chinat
FC CHINAT

FC Cloister 1
Regular FC Cloister
Italic FC Cloister
Bold FC Cloister
Bold Italic FC Cloister

FC Cloister 2
Ad Weight FC Cloister
Heavy Weight FC Cloister
Over Weight FC Cloister
True Condensed FC Cloister

FC Contemporary Brush
Regular FCContemporaryBrush
Bold FCContemporaryBrush
Extra Bold FCContemporaryBrush

FC Continental
Regular FC Continental
Italic FC Continental
Black FC Continental

FC Cooper Old Style 1
Light FC Cooper Old Style
Light Italic FC Cooper Old Style
Demi FC Cooper Old Style
Demi Italic FC Cooper Old Style

FC Cooper Old Style 2
Medium FC Cooper Old Style
Medium Italic FC Cooper Old Style
Bold FC Cooper Old Style

FC Corporate
FC CORPORATE

FC Corvinus Skyline
FC Corvinus Skyline

FC Craw Modern
Regular FCCrawModern
Italic FCCrawModern
Bold FCCrawModer

FC Criterion 1
Light FC Criterion
Light Italic FC Criterion
Regular FC Criterion
Italic FC Criterion

FC Criterion 2
Medium FC Criterion
Bold FC Criterion
Extra Bold FC Criterion

FC Danmark 1
Light FC Danmark

ff

... FC Danmark 1 Medium FC Danmark
Demi FC Danmark
Bold FC Danmark
FC Danmark 2 Extra Bold FC Danmark
Ultra FC Danmark
FC Deepdene Roman FC Deepdene
Italic FC Deepdene
Bold FC Deepdene
Bold Italic FC Deepdene
Roman SCOSF FC DEEPDENE 123...
FC Devinne FC Devinne
FC Diamante Heavy FC Diamante
FC Didoni FC Didoni
FC Digital Light FC Digital
Medium FC Digital
FC DIN 16 Normal FC DIN 16
Italic FC DIN 16
FC Disco FC Disco
FC Egizio Regular FC Egizio
Italic FC Egizio
Bold FC Egizio
Bold Italic FC Egizio
FC Elaine FC Elaine
FC Erbar FC ERBAR
FC Expressa Medium FC Expressa
FC Fanfare Condensed FC Fanfare
FC Firmin Didot Roman FC Firmin Didot
Bold FC Firmin Didot
FC Florentine FC Florentine
FC Frency FC Frency
FC Gatsby Normal FC Gatsby
Italic FC Gatsby
FC Geshexport FC Geshexport
FC Giorgio FC GIORGIO
FC Glamour Light FC Glamour
Medium FC Glamour
Bold FC Glamour
FC Glasgow Extra Bold FC Glasgow

FC Globe Ad Weight FC Globe
Heavy Weight FC Globe
Over Weight FC Globe
True Condensed FC Globe
FC Gorden 1 Normal FC GORDEN
Medium FC GORDEN
FC Gorden 2 Condensed FC GORDEN
FC Goudy 1 Extra Light FC Goudy
Extra Light Italic FC Goudy
FC Goudy 2 Ad Weight FC Goudy
Heavy Weight FC Goudy
Over Weight FC Goudy
True Condensed FC Goudy
FC Handel Gothic FC Handel Gothic
FC Harem FC HAREM
FC Heldustry 1 Regular FC Heldustry
Italic FC Heldustry
Medium FC Heldustry
Medium Italic FC Heldustry
FC Heldustry 2 Demibold FC Heldustry
Demibold Italic FC Heldustry
Bold FC Heldustry
FC Helenic Extended FC Helenic
FC Helium Heavy FC Helium
FC Helserif 1 Light FC Helserif
Light Italic FC Helserif
Medium FC Helserif
FC Helserif 2 Book FC Helserif
Bold FC Helserif
FC Highway Gothic B FC Highway Gothic
C FC Highway Gothic
D FC HIGHWAY GOTHIC
E FC HIGHWAY GOTHIC
FC Highway Gothic EM FC HIGHWAY GOTHIC
FC Hildago FC HILDAGO
FC Hobo Regular FC Hobo
Bold FC Hobo
FC Holly Script FC Holly Script

FC Howland Solid FC Howland
Open FC Howland
FC Hudson FC Hudson
FC Huxley Vertical FC HUXLEY VERTICAL
FC Impact Bold FC Impact
Bold Condensed FC Impact
FC Introspect Book FC Introspect
Bold FC Introspect
Bold Condensed FC Introspect
FC Inverserif FC Inverserif
FC Japanette FC Japanette
FC Jay Gothic Light FC Jay Gothic
Regular FC Jay Gothic
Bold FC Jay Gothic
Extra Bold FC Jay Gothic
FC Kelles FC Kelles
FC Kennerley Regular FC Kennerley
Italic FC Kennerley
Medium FC Kennerley
Medium Italic FC Kennerley
FC Kenneth FC Kenneth
FC Koloss FC Koloss
FC Largo Light FC LARGO
Medium FC LARGO
FC LeAsterix FC LEASTERIX
FC Legothic Light FC Legothic
Medium FC Legothic
Bold FC Legothic
FC Lightline Gothic FC Lightline Gothic
FC Lucida Typewriter Roman FC Lucida Type
Italic FC Lucida Type
Bold FC Lucida Type
Bold Italic FC Lucida Type
FC Marcato FC Marcato
FC Martin Gothic 1 Light FC Martin Gothic
Light Italic FC Martin Gothic
Medium FC Martin Gothic

Font	Sample
... FC Martin Gothic 1 Medium Italic	FC Martin Gothic
FC Martin Gothic 2 Bold	FC Martin Gothic
Bold Italic	FC Martin Gothic
Extra Bold	FC Martin Gothic
FC Martin Gothic 3 Thin	FC Martin Gothic
FC Martinique	FC Martinique
FC Mr. Big	FC Mr. Big
FC Napoli Extra Bold	FC Napoli
FC Nashville Heavy	FCNashville
Heavy Italic	FCNashville
FC Newport Land	FC Newport Land
FC Novel Gothic	FC Novel Gothic
FC Nueland 1	FC NUELAND
FC Nueland 2 Inline	FC NUELAND
FC Ondine	FC Ondine
FC Organ Grinder	FC ORGAN GRINDER
FC Ornitons Heavy	FC Ornitons Heavy
FC Paladin	FC Paladin
FC Pandora Black	FC Pandora Black
FC Parade	FC Parade
FC Pasadena Extra Light	FC Pasadena
Demibold	FC Pasadena
Extra Bold	FC Pasadena
Heavy	FC Pasadena
FC Pekin	FC Pekin
FC Permanent Headline	FC Permanent Headline
FC Philly Sport Script	FC Philly Sport
FC Pinnoccio	FC PINNOCCIO
FC Plakat Light	FC Plakat
Bold	FC Plakat
FC Polonaise Bold	FC Polonaise
Bold Alternate	FC Polonaise
FC Precis Slim	FC Precis
Medium	FC Precis
Bold	FC Precis
Extended	FC Precis
FC Pretoria	FC Pretoria
FC Promoter	FC Promoter

Font	Sample
FC Publicity	FC PUBLICITY
FC Quartz Light	FC QUARTZ
Medium	FC QUARTZ
FC Quint 1 Light	FC Quint
Light Italic	FC Quint
Medium	FC Quint
Medium Italic	FC Quint
FC Quint 2 Bold	FC Quint
Extra Bold	FC Quint
FC Racer	FC Racer
FC Radiant Medium	FC Radiant
Bold	FC Radiant
Heavy	FC Radiant
FC Radiant Condensed Bold Condensed	FC Radiant
Bold Extra Condensed	FC Radiant
F Bold Extra Condensed	FC Radiant F
FC Regency	FC Regency
FC Reiner	FC Reiner
FC Rochester Bold	FC Rochester
Heavy	FC Rochester
FC Roger	FC ROGER
FC Rolling Stone	FC Rolling Stone
FC Roman Shaded Shaded	FC Roman Shaded
Shaded Alternate	FC Roman Shaded
FC Roman Solid Solid	FC Roman Solid
Solid Alternate	FC Roman Solid
FC Roman Stylus Stylus	FC Roman Stylus
Stylus Alternate	FC Roman Stylus
FC Ronda	FC Ronda
FC Roundest Demibold	FC Roundest
Extra Bold	FC Roundest
FC San Serif 1 Light	FC San Serif
Light Italic	FC San Serif
FC San Serif 2 Light H	FC San Serif
Light Alternate H	FC San Serif
FC San Serif 3 Bold	FC San Serif
Bold Italic	FC San Serif

Font	Sample
... FC San Serif 3 Bold Alternate	FC San Serif
Bold Italic Alternate	FC San Serif
FC San Serif 4 Bold H	FC San Serif
Bold Alternate H	FC San Serif
FC San Serif 5 Extra Bold H	FC San Serif
Extra Bold Italic H	FC San Serif
FC Scenario 1 Light	FC Scenario
Light Italic	FC Scenario
Medium	FC Scenario
FC Scenario 2 Bold	FC Scenario
Extra Bold	FC Scenario
FC Sevilla	FC Sevilla
FC Shotgun	FC SHOTGUN
FC Siegfried	FC Siegfried
FC Souvenir Gothic 1 Regular	FC Souvenir Gothic
Italic	FC Souvenir Gothic
Medium	FC Souvenir Gothic
Medium Italic	FC Souvenir Gothic
FC Souvenir Gothic 2 Demibold	FC Souvenir Gothic
Demibold Italic	FC Souvenir Gothic
Bold	FC Souvenir Gothic
FC Spire	FC SPIRE
FC Stanza	FC stanza
FC Stark Semibold	FC Stark
Bold	FC Stark
FC Thor	FC THOR
FC Ticonderoga	FC Ticonderoga
FC Timbre Normal	FC Timbre
Alternate	FC Timbre
FC Toledo Extra Bold	FC Toledo
Extra Bold Italic	FC Toledo
FC Torino	FC Torino
FC Umbra	FC UMBRA
FC Veracruz Extra Bold	FC Veracruz
FC Viant	FC Viant
FC Viking Gothic	FC VIKING GOTHIC

See page 564 for contents of Franklin Type Founders Multi-Font Packages.

FC Village Book — FCVillage
Italic — *FC Village*
Alternate — FCVillage 12345...
FC Vixen — FC Vixen
FC Woodcut — FC Woodcut
FC Wordsworth Medium — FC Wordsworth
Bold — FC Wordsworth
Bold Condensed — FC Wordsworth
FC Yorkshire — FC Yorkshire
FC Zanzibar — FC Zanzibar
FC Zola — FC Zola

foundry: Franklin Type Founders

A library of fonts licensed from International Typeface Corporation and, through the auspices of URW, from a number of smaller foundries world wide. The collection also includes a selection of text and display designs acquired from the Lazy Dog Foundry. ¶ Franklin Type Founders was established by Precision Type in 1994 as a means to market these fonts and others that may otherwise be unavailable or difficult to obtain.

Americana Roman — Americana
Italic — *Americana*
Bold — Americana
Extra Bold — Americana
Amsterdam — Amsterdam
Aster Roman — Aster
Italic — *Aster*
Medium — Aster
Augustea Open — AUGUSTEA
ITC Barcelona 1 Book — ITC Barcelona
Book Italic — *ITC Barcelona*
Bold — ITC Barcelona
Bold Italic — *ITC Barcelona*
ITC Barcelona 2 Medium — ITC Barcelona

... ITC Barcelona 2 Medium Italic — *ITC Barcelona*
Heavy — ITC Barcelona
Heavy Italic — *ITC Barcelona*
Baskerville Handcut Roman — Baskerville Handcut
Italic — *Baskerville Handcut*
Bold — Baskerville Hand
Bold Italic — *Baskerville Hand*
Berliner — Berliner
Beton 1 Light — Beton
Light Italic — *Beton*
Demi — Beton
Demi Italic — *Beton*
Beton 2 Bold — Beton
Bold Italic — *Beton*
Extra Bold — Beton
Extra Bold Italic — *Beton*
Beton 3 Bold Condensed — Beton
Bold Condensed Italic — *Beton*
Big Black — BIG BLACK
Blackboard FTF Chalkboard — Blackboard
Bodoni Ultra — Bodoni
Ultra Italic — *Bodoni*
Bauer Bodoni 1 Black — Bauer Bodoni
Black Italic — *Bauer Bodoni*
Bauer Bodoni 2 Black Headline — Bauer Bodoni
Black Italic Headline — *Bauer Bodoni*
ITC Bolt Bold — ITC Bolt Bold
ITC Bookman 1 Light — ITC Bookman
Light Italic — *ITC Bookman*
Demi — ITC Bookman
Demi Italic — *ITC Bookman*
ITC Bookman 2 Medium — ITC Bookman
Medium Italic — *ITC Bookman*
Bold — ITC Bookman
Bold Italic — *ITC Bookman*
ITC Bookman 3 Medium — ITC Bookman
Medium Italic — *ITC Bookman*
Medium Swash — AOLVT trofipn

... ITC Bookman 3 Medium Italic Swash — *AOLVT trofipn*
Boomerang — Boomerang
Bordeaux Roman — Bordeaux
Italic — *Bordeaux*
Script — Bordeaux
Bostonia — Bostonia
Brody — Brody
Bullfinch Text — Bullfinch
Bullfinch Display — Bullfinch
ITC Busorama Bold — ITC BUSORAMA
Cabaret — Cabaret
Camellia — camellia
Caslon Graphique — Caslon Graph
Castle 1 Light — Castle
Light Italic — *Castle*
Book — Castle
Book Italic — *Castle*
Castle 2 Bold — Castle
Bold Italic — *Castle*
Ultra — Castle
Ultra Italic — *Castle*
Catherine 1 Light — Catherine
Regular — Catherine
Regular Oblique — *Catherine*
Catherine 2 Bold — Catherine
Bold Oblique — *Catherine*
Black — Catherine
Chelmsford 1 Book — Chelmsford
Book Italic — *Chelmsford*
Bold — Chelmsford
Bold Italic — *Chelmsford*
Chelmsford 2 Light — Chelmsford
Light Italic — *Chelmsford*
Medium — Chelmsford
Medium Italic — *Chelmsford*
Chelmsford 3 Ultra — Chelmsford
Ultra Italic — *Chelmsford*
Cheltenham Extra Condensed Bold — Cheltenham

Chieftan Inline CHIEFTAN
Chieftan Solid CHIEFTAN
Chisel Engraved Chisel
Solid Chisel
Choc Choc
Colwell Roman Colwell
Italic Colwell
Courier Regular Courier
Italic Courier
Bold Courier
Bold Italic Courier
Cypress Cypress
DIN 1451 Engschrift DIN 1451
Mittleschrift DIN 1451
Diskus Diskus
Durango Durango
Egyptian 505 Light Egyptian 505
Roman Egyptian 505
Medium Egyptian 505
Bold Egyptian 505
Egyptienne Condensed Bold Condensed Egyptienne
Black Condensed Egyptienne
Egyptienne Extended Black Egyptienne
Einhorn Einhorn
Emporium Emporium
Erin Lynn Erin Lynn
ITC Fat Face Fat Face
Flash Light Flash
Regular Flash
Folio Medium Condensed Folio
Medium Condensed Italic Folio
Bold Condensed Folio
Bold Condensed Italic Folio
Bold Extra Condensed Folio
ITC Galliard 1 Roman ITC Galliard
Italic ITC Galliard
Black ITC Galliard

... ITC Galliard 1 Black Italic ITC Galliard
ITC Galliard 2 Bold ITC Galliard
Bold Italic ITC Galliard
Ultra ITC Galliard
Ultra Italic ITC Galliard
Glastonbury Glastonbury
Glorietta Glorietta
Goudy Light Goudy
Medium Goudy
Bold Goudy
Extra Bold Goudy
Goudy Handtooled Normal Goudy Handtool
Bold Goudy Handtool
Goudy Heavy Face GoudyHeavy
Goudy Heavy Face Condensed Goudy Heavyface
Greco Roman Greco
Italic Greco
Negra Greco
Negra Italic Greco
Bold Greco
Bold Italic Greco
Greco Adornado GRECO
Greco Deco Deco Inline GRECO DECO
Deco Solid GRECO DECO
Harpers Harpers
Harris Harris
Herold HEROLD
Honda Honda
Horndon HORNDON
Ice Age Ice Age
Isadora ISADORA
ITC Isbell 1 Book ITC Isbell
Book Italic ITC Isbell
Medium ITC Isbell
Medium Italic ITC Isbell
ITC Isbell 2 Bold ITC Isbell
Bold Italic ITC Isbell
Heavy ITC Isbell

... ITC Isbell 2 Heavy Italic ITC Isbell
Jensen Old Style Bold Condensed Jensen Old Style
Latin Tall LATIN TALL
Lazy Script Lazy Script
Legriffe Legriffe
Letter Gothic Regular Letter Gothic
Bold Letter Gothic
Liberty LIBERTY
Lindsay Lindsay
Little Louis LITTLE LOUIS
Lucida Roman Lucida
Italic Lucida
Bold Lucida
Bold Italic Lucida
Lucida Sans Regular Lucida Sans
Italic Lucida Sans
Bold Lucida Sans
Bold Italic Lucida Sans
Madison 1 Roman Madison
Italic Madison
Bold Madison
Bold Condensed Madison
Madison 2 Light Madison
Book Madison
Semibold Madison
Ultra Madison
Magna Light Magna
Light Italic Magna
Bold Magna
Magnus Magnus
Manhattan MANHATTAN
Marker Marker
Medina Medina
Messidor Messidor
Microgramma Medium Extended Microgramma
Bold Extended Microgramma
Minneapolis Minneapolis
Mississippi Mississippi

ff

See page 564 for contents of Franklin Type Founders Multi-Font Packages.

ITC Modern No. 216 One
Light ITC Modern
Light Italic ITC Modern
Medium ITC Modern
Medium Italic ITC Modern
ITC Modern No. 216 Two
Bold ITC Modern
Bold Italic ITC Modern
Heavy ITC Modern
Heavy Italic ITC Modern
Nadall NADALL
National Modern
Roman National Modern
Italic National Modern
National Oldstyle
Roman National Oldstyle
Italic National Oldstyle
Neuland
Inline NEULAND
Solid NEULAND
Nevision Casual Nevision Casual
ITC Newtext 1
Light ITC Newtext
Light Italic ITC Newtext
Regular ITC Newtext
Italic ITC Newtext
ITC Newtext 2
Book ITC Newtext
Book Italic ITC Newtext
Demi ITC Newtext
Demi Italic ITC Newtext
Nova Bold Nova
ITC Novarese 1
Book ITC Novarese
Book Italic ITC Novarese
Bold ITC Novarese
Bold Italic ITC Novarese
Novarese 2
Medium ITC Novarese
Medium Italic ITC Novarese
Ultra ITC Novarese
OCR
OCR-A OCR-A
OCR-B OCR-B
Pajamas PAJAMAS
Phyllis Script Phyllis Script
Piccadilly PICCADILLY
Plaza 1
Light PLAZA

... Plaza 1
Bold PLAZA
Plaza 2
Decorative PLAZA
Inline PLAZA
Premier Shadow PREMIER SHADOW
Primus
Light Primus
Bold Primus
Antiqua Bold Primus
Princetown PRINCETOWN
Punch
Regular Punch
Bold Punch
ITC Quay Sans 1
Book ITC Quay Sans
Book Italic ITC Quay Sans
Medium ITC Quay Sans
Medium Italic ITC Quay Sans
Quay Sans 2
Black ITC Quay Sans
Black Italic ITC Quay Sans
Quentin QUENTIN
Railroad Extra Light Railroad
Recess
✤ FTF Chalkboard Recess
Riverboat Riverboat
Rumpus Rumpus
Scaffold SCAFFOLD
Schneidler 1
Roman Schneidler
Italic Schneidler
Bold Schneidler
Bold Italic Schneidler
Schneidler 2
Light Schneidler
Light Italic Schneidler
Medium Schneidler
Medium Italic Schneidler
Schneidler 3
Black Schneidler
Black Italic Schneidler
Schwere Schwere
ITC Serif Gothic 1
Light ITC Serif Gothic
Regular ITC Serif Gothic
Bold ITC Serif Gothic
Extra Bold ITC Serif Gothic

ITC Serif Gothic 2
Heavy ITC Serif Gothic
Black ITC Serif Gothic
Serifa 1
Thin Serifa
Thin Italic Serifa
Light Serifa
Light Italic Serifa
Serifa 2
Roman Serifa
Italic Serifa
Bold Serifa
Black Serifa
Shrifteen SHRIFTEEN
Slipstream SLIPSTREAM
Socrates SOCRATES
Sophie Sophie
Sterling Sterling
Stymie
Light Stymie
Medium Stymie
Bold Stymie
Black Stymie
Stymie Condensed
Medium Condensed Stymie
Bold Condensed Stymie
Superstar Inline SUPERSTAR
Superstar Shadow SUPERSTAR
Synchro SYNCHRO
Thermo THERMO
Timeless
Roman Timeless
Italic Timeless
Bold Timeless
Times Coop Times Coop
Titus Light Titus Light
Tombstone
Solid TOMBSTONE
Outline TOMBSTONE
Uptown UPTOWN
ITC Veljovic 1
Book ITC Veljovic
Book Italic ITC Veljovic
Bold ITC Veljovic
Bold Italic ITC Veljovic
ITC Veljovic 2
Medium ITC Veljovic

ff

ITC Veljovic 2 Medium Italic	ITC Veljovic
Black	ITC Veljovic
Black Italic	ITC Veljovic
Victorian Script	Victorian Script
Vienna Roman	VIENNA
Openface	VIENNA
Vivaldi Script	Vivaldi
ITC Weidemann 1 Book	ITC Weidemann
Book Italic	ITC Weidemann
Bold	ITC Weidemann
Bold Italic	ITC Weidemann
ITC Weidemann 2 Medium	ITC Weidemann
Medium Italic	ITC Weidemann
Black	ITC Weidemann
Black Italic	ITC Weidemann
Weisz Rundschrift	Weiſz Rundſchrift
Windsor 1 Roman	Windsor
Ultra Heavy	Windsor
Windsor 2 Light Condensed	Windsor
Extra Bold Condensed	Windsor
Elongated	Windsor
Worcester Roman	Worcester
Italic	Worcester
Medium	Worcester
Bold	Worcester
Yitsui	Yitsui
ITC Zapf Book 1 Light	ITC Zapf Book
Light Italic	ITC Zapf Book
Demi	ITC Zapf Book
Demi Italic	ITC Zapf Book
ITC Zapf Book 2 Medium	ITC Zapf Book
Medium Italic	ITC Zapf Book
Heavy	ITC Zapf Book
Heavy Italic	ITC Zapf Book
ITC Zapf Chancery 1 Light	ITC Zapf Chancery
Light Italic	ITC Zapf Chancery
Demi	ITC Zapf Chancery
Demi Oblique	ITC Zapf Chancery
ITC Zapf Chancery 2 Medium	ITC Zapf Chancery
Medium Italic	ITC Zapf Chancery
Bold	ITC Zapf Chancery
Bold Oblique	ITC Zapf Chancery

Franklin Type Founders	Multi-Font Package Contents
FTF Chalkboard	: Blackboard & Recess.

foundry: Galápagos Design Group

Founded in 1994 by a group of type design and production experts including Larry Oppenburg, George Ryan, Dennis Pasternak, Steve Zafarana and Mike Leary. The group is focusing on bringing to market a diverse range of new font designs and historical interpretations and revivals in addition to providing custom services and support for an array of type technologies including the Apple TrueTypeGX format.

Fontoon	Fontoon
Fontoonies No. 1	
Kennedy PS	Kennedy
Kristen Normal	Kristen
Not So Normal	Kristen
Maiandra Roman	Maiandra
Bold	Maiandra
Ultra	Maindra
Stylus	Stylus
Tangient	Tangient
Wakefield	Wakefield

foundry: HandcraftedFonts

Jonathan Macagba, founder of HandcraftedFonts, says that one of the company's goals is to "provide display faces with a 'human touch' – handcrafted and often nostalgic." In addition to Macagba's fonts, the collection includes the work of several other designers. Many of the fonts are based on turn-of-the-century poster lettering styles of the Vienna Secession and Weiner Werkstätte movements.

HF AmericanDiner Solid	HF AmericanDiner
Inline	HF AmericanDiner
Narrow	HF AmericanDiner
HF Antique Row Regular	HF Antique Row
HF Doodle Medium	HF Doodle
Medium Italic	HF Doodle
Bold	HF Doodle
Bold Italic	HF Doodle
HF Eden Expanded Light	HF Eden Expanded
HF Exposition One	HF Exposition
Two	HF Exposition
Rounded Medium	HF Exposition
Rounded Demibold	HF Exposition
Rounded Bold	HF Exposition
HF LaVardera Book	HF LaVardera
Bold	HF LaVardera
Extra Bold	HF LaVardera
HF Libris Light	HF LIBRIS
HF Modular Stencil Roman	HF Modular
Italic	HF Modular
Outline	HF Modular
Outline Italic	HF Modular
HF NewGarden Light	HF NewGarden
Bold	HF NewGarden
HF Poster Solid	HF POSTER
Inline	HF POSTER
HF Secede Block	HF Secede
Outline	HF Secede
Outline Heavy	HF Secede

ff

foundry: Harris Design

SignPIX One & Two are the first of a new series of fonts created by James M. Harris. These two fonts contain a useful selection of over 100 signs and symbols used in state and national parks throughout the United States.

SignPix One
Two

foundry: Headliners International

Founded in 1951, Headliners International is one of the oldest names in advertising display type design and typography. The current collection of faces has been chosen from their extensive library of exclusive designs. Each font contains an average of 4,500 kerning pairs.

Armada Light Armada
Light Italic Armada
Medium Armada
Medium Italic Armada
Bold Armada
Extra Bold Armada

Arrow Light Arrow
Medium Arrow
Bold Arrow
Extra Bold Arrow
Black Arrow

Baccarat Light Baccarat
Light Italic Baccarat
Medium Baccarat
Medium Italic Baccarat
Bold Baccarat
Extra Bold Baccarat

Caslon Bold Caslon

Caslon 310 Bold Caslon 310

. . . Caslon 310 Bold Italic Caslon 310

Caslon 1080 Light Caslon 1080
Medium Caslon 1080
Bold Caslon 1080
Extra Bold Caslon 1080

Caslon Display Light Caslon
Medium Caslon
Bold Caslon
Extra Bold Caslon

Cavalier Light Cavalier
Medium Cavalier
Bold Cavalier
Extra Bold Cavalier
Black Cavalier

Empire State Light Empire State
Medium Empire State
Bold Empire State

Grange Light Grange
Medium Grange
Bold Grange
Extra Bold Grange
Black Grange

Huxley High Light Huxley High
Medium Huxley High
Bold Huxley High
Extra Bold Huxley High

Huxley Low Light Huxley Low
Medium Huxley Low
Bold Huxley Low
Extra Bold Huxley Low

Montauk Light Montauk
Medium Montauk
Bold Montauk

Nouveau Riche Light Nouveau Riche
Medium Nouveau Riche
Bold Nouveau Riche

Nouveau Riche Condensed Light Condensed Nouveau Riche
Medium Condensed Nouveau Riche

. . . Nouveau Riche Condensed Bold Condensed Nouveau Riche

Polaris Light Polaris
Light Italic Polaris
Medium Polaris
Medium Italic Polaris
Bold Polaris
Extra Bold Polaris

Poynder Light Poynder
Book Poynder
Medium Poynder
Demibold Poynder
Bold Poynder

Renoir Light Renoir
Medium Renoir
Bold Renoir
Extra Bold Renoir
Black Renoir

Romantique Light Romantique
Medium Romantique
Bold Romantique
Extra Bold Romantique
Black Romantique

Saginaw Light Saginaw
Medium Saginaw
Bold Saginaw

Siena Light Siena
Light Italic Siena
Medium Siena
Medium Italic Siena
Bold Siena
Extra Bold Siena

Trantino Light Trantino
Light Italic Trantino
Medium Trantino
Medium Italic Trantino
Bold Trantino
Extra Bold Trantino

Vignette Light Vignette

ff

Vignette Medium Vignette
Demi Vignette
Bold Vignette
Extra Bold Vignette
Wembley Light Wembley
Light Oblique Wembley

foundry: Image Club

Our selection of fonts from the Image Club Type Library consists mainly of original designs representing the work of Grant Hutchinson, Greg Kolodziejzyk, Ty Semaka, Patricia Lillie and Noel Rubin. Also included are a number of fonts licensed by Image Club from VGC (Visual Graphics Corporation).

Andrich Minerva Roman Andrich Minerva
Italic Andrich Minerva
Antikva Margaret Roman Antikva Margaret
Italic AntikvaMargaret
Arquitectura Arquitectura
Badloc Regular Badloc
Bevel Badloc
Compression Badloc
Beebopp BEEBOPP
Boca Raton Regular Boca Raton
Solid Boca Raton
Caslon Antique Regular Caslon Antique
Italic Caslon Antique
Champagne Champagne
Comic Book One Comic Book
Two Comic Book
Two Outline Comic Book
Decotura Regular DECOTURA
Inline DECOTURA
East Block Open EAST BLOCK
Closed EAST BLOCK

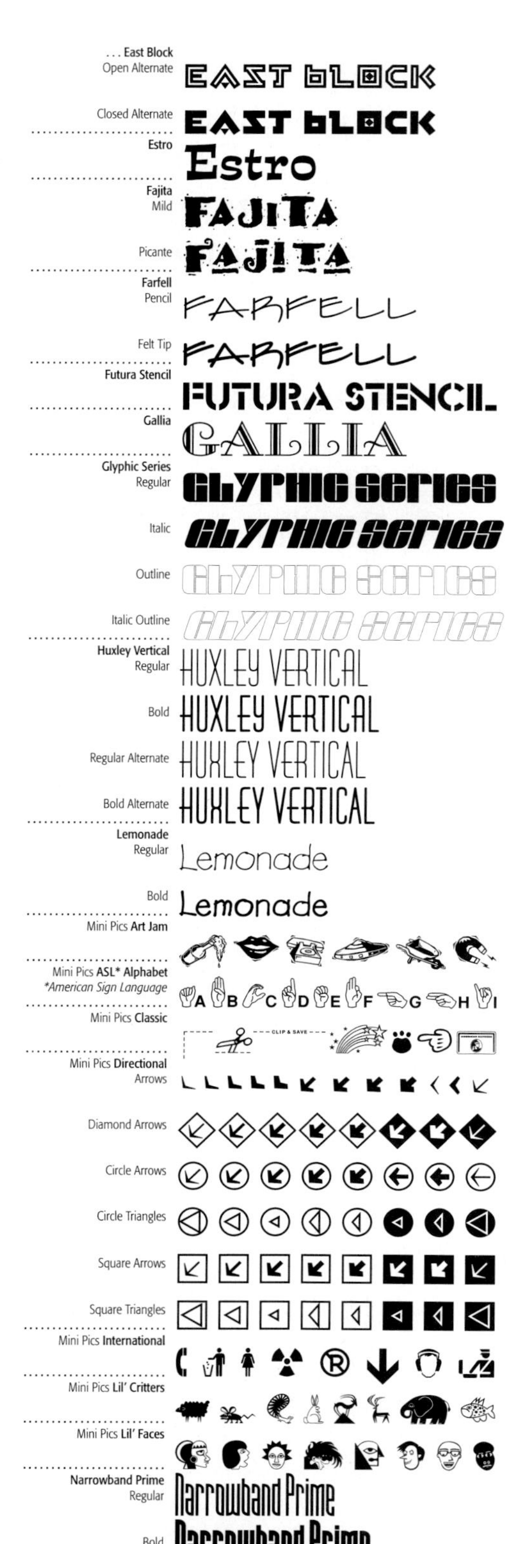
. . . East Block Open Alternate EAST BLOCK
Closed Alternate EAST BLOCK
Estro Estro
Fajita Mild FAJITA
Picante FAJITA
Farfell Pencil FARFELL
Felt Tip FARFELL
Futura Stencil FUTURA STENCIL
Gallia GALLIA
Glyphic Series Regular GLYPHIC SERIES
Italic GLYPHIC SERIES
Outline GLYPHIC SERIES
Italic Outline GLYPHIC SERIES
Huxley Vertical Regular HUXLEY VERTICAL
Bold HUXLEY VERTICAL
Regular Alternate HUXLEY VERTICAL
Bold Alternate HUXLEY VERTICAL
Lemonade Regular Lemonade
Bold Lemonade
Mini Pics Art Jam
Mini Pics ASL* Alphabet
*American Sign Language
A B C D E F G H I
Mini Pics Classic
CLIP & SAVE
Mini Pics Directional Arrows
Diamond Arrows
Circle Arrows
Circle Triangles
Square Arrows
Square Triangles
Mini Pics International
Mini Pics Lil' Critters
Mini Pics Lil' Faces
Narrowband Prime Regular Narrowband Prime
Bold Narrowband Prime

Nevison Casual Script Nevison
New Geneva Nine Nine New Geneva
Nine Point Five New Geneva
Pacifica Condensed PACIFICA CONDENSED
Paisley One Paisley

. . . Paisley Two Paisley
One Alternate Paisley
Two Alternate Paisley
Paris Flash PARIS FLASH
Pointille POINTILLE
Publicity Gothic Solid Publicity Gothic
Outline Publicity Gothic
Relief RELIEF
Signature Light Signature
Regular Signature

foundry: Intecsas

The Intecsas collection is a diverse and eclectic range of display and text fonts, many of them rather obscure designs selected and excavated from the catalogues of early twentieth-century American type foundries.

Aaaaaaaargh Caps AAAAAAAARGH
Aarcover AARCOVER
Adineski Bold ADINESKI
Bold Oblique ADINESKI
Bold Outline ADINESKI
Adine Kernberg Script Adine Kernberg Script
Adriana Davidovsky Adriana
Air Supply Air Supply
Alvin Caps ABC
Aminal Initials
Anderson Script Anderson Script
Anne Stone ANNE
Avery Jean Avery Jean
Beffle Regular BEFFLE
Initials BEFFLE
Bela Drips BELA DRIPS
Belgian Casual Regular Belgian Casual
Italic Belgian Casual

ff

. . . Belgian Casual
- Bold — Belgian Casual
- Bold Italic — Belgian Casual

Bellagio
- Regular — Bellagio
- Bold — Bellagio

Benjamin
- Regular — BENJAMIN
- Bold — BENJAMIN

Bizarro
- I — BIZARRO
- II — BIZARRO
- III — BIZARRO
- IV — BIZARRO

Blasius — BLASIUS

Braille Font

Brandenburger — ABCD

Brookfield
- Light — Brookfield
- Bold — Brookfield

Brooks Initials — BROOKS

Buffalo Bill — BUFFALO BILL

Cardboard Cutout — CARDBOARD

Carrick
- Caps — CARRICK
- Groovy — CARRICK

Chalice — CHALICE

Charlotte Tile — CHARLOTTE

Chinese Menu — Chinese Menu

Christensen Caps
- Regular — ABCD
- Black — ABCD

Command Ment — COMMAND MENT

Constructivist — CONSTRUCT

Corsage — CORSAGE

Crackling Fire — CRACKLING FIRE

Crane Initials — CRANE

Davys Blocks — DAVYS BLOCKS

Davys Dingbats

Davys Key Caps — D alt CONTROL del esc ↑

Davys Big Key Caps — D ALT ↑ DEL ESC

Davys Other Dingbats

Davys Ribbons — DAVYSRIBBONS

DeBellis — DEBELLIS

Deco Twenty Two — DECO TWENTY

Dewhurst — DEWHURST

Dieter Caps — DIETERCAPS

Dilara Caps — DILARA CAPS

Dinderman
- Regular — DINDERMAN
- Heavy — DINDERMAN

Dorothy Initials — ABCD

Dragonwick — Dragonwick

Drawing Pad — DRAWING PAD

Dubiel
- Regular — Dubiel
- Italic — Dubiel
- Bold — Dubiel

Dupuy
- Light — DUPUY
- Regular — DUPUY
- Bold — DUPUY
- Black — DUPUY

Eileen Caps
- Regular — ABCD
- Black — ABCD

Elizabeth Ann — ELIZABETH

Elzevier
- Initials — ABCD
- Initials Black — ABCD

Eraser Dust — Eraser Dust

Even More Face Cuts

Face Cuts

Fetch Scotty — FETCH SCOTTY

Flicker — FLICKER

Forest — FOREST

Frisch Script — Frisch Script

Garton
- Regular — Garton
- Italic — Garton
- Bold — Garton
- Bold Italic — Garton

Gessele Script — Gessele Script

Gouda Old Style

Grab Bag
- Regular
- Junior

Gravestone Rubbing — Gravestone Rubbing

Green Caps — GREEN CAPS

Griffin Dingbats

Ground Hog — Ground Hog

Harting
- I — Harting I
- II — Harting II

Headhunter — HEADHUNTER

Holtzschue — HOLTZSCHUE

Horror Show — HORROR SHOW

Horst Caps — HORST CAPS

Hunan Garden — HUNAN GARDEN

Ian Bent — IAN BENT

Jacobs
- Regular — Jacobs
- Initials — JACOBS

Jeff Nichols — JEFF NICHOLS

Joanna Lee — JOANNA LEE

Judy Finckel — Judy Finckel

Kastner Casual — Kastner Casual

KidStuff

Kinigstein Caps — KINIGSTEIN

Kioko — Kioko

Konanur Caps — KONANUR CAPS

Korf Caps — KORF CAPS

Koshgarian Light — Koshgarian

Kramer
- Light — Kramer
- Initials — KRAMER

Lee Caps — LEE CAPS

Legal Vandal
- Normal — Legal Vandal
- Oblique — Legal Vandal
- Bold — Legal Vandal
- Bold Oblique — Legal Vandal

ff

Lemiesz
LEMIESZ
Lilith Light
Lilith
Heavy
Lilith
Initials
Logger
LOGGER
Lower East Side
Lower East Side
Lucy Script
Lucy Script
MalakaLakaLakaLaka
abcdefghijklmnopqrs
Man About Town
MAN ABOUT
Mary Monroe
Mary Monroe
McGarey Fractured
McGarey Fractured
More Face Cuts
Multiform Regular
MULTIFORM
Solid
MULTIFORM
Munchner Initials
ABCDE
Nauert
Nauert
Nitemare Caps
NITEMARE
No More Face Cuts
Octagon
OCTAGON
Paris Metro
PARIS METRO
Party Down
PARTY DOWN
Pavelle Script
Pavelle
Swash Initials
Pavelle
Phonetic
phonetic aɕɜɛʏɥɪĸɱ
Pixie Font
Pixie Font
Pointage
POINTAGE
Polo Semiscript
Polo Semiscript
Randolph
Randolph
Rechtman Script Regular
Rechtman Script
Bold
Rechtman Script
Handtooled
Rechtman Script
Relief Deco
RELIEF
In Reverse
RELIEF
Reynolds Caps
REYNOLDS CAPS
Rhodes Roman
Rhodes
Rounded Relief
ROUNDED RELIEF
Rudelsberg Regular
Rudelsberg

Rumble
RUMBLE
Saint Albans
Saint Albans
Scratchy Pen
SCRATCHY PEN
Showboat
SHOWBOAT
Sjlausmann Regular
Sjlausmann
Expert Regular
Sjlausmann
Sprecher Initials
ABCD
Starburst
STARBURST
Still More Face Cuts
Sturbridge Twisted
Sturbridge Twisted
Taiga
TAIGA
Tejaratchi Caps
TEJARATCHI CAPS
Thompson Pond
THOMPSON
Toletto
TOLETTO
Travis Brush
Travis Brush
Trench
TRENCH
Trevor Light
Trevor Light
Tucker
Tucker
Tundra
TUNDRA
Upper West Side
UPPER WEST SIDE
Varah Caps
ABCD
Victoria Casual
Victoria Casual
Wedgie
WEDGIE
Wein Initials
WEIN INITIALS
Wharmby
WHARMBY
What A Relief
WHAT A RELIEF
Will Harris
WILL HARRIS
Yasmine Script
Yasmine
Swash
Yasmine
Zaleski Caps
ZALESKI
Caps Inline
ZALESKI
Zallman Caps
ZALLMAN CAPS

foundry: International Typeface Corporation

Since the early 1970s ITC has been commissioning the design of new typefaces and licensing them to the industry at large for use with an immense array of imaging and output technologies. The list of type designers whose work is part of the ITC Collection is lengthy and features some of the best known names in the world of type including Hermann Zapf, Aldo Novarese, Ed Benguiat, Gerard Unger and Sumner Stone to name but a few.¶ Beginning in 1994, ITC began to market their fonts directly – those now available are displayed here.

ITC Anna ✤ *ITC Headliners 1* Regular
ITC ANNA
Regular SC
ITC ANNA
ITC Beesknees ✤ *ITC Headliners 1* Regular
ITC BEESKNEES
Regular SC
ITC BEESKNEES
ITC Bodoni Six + SCOSF Book
ITC Bodoni Six
Book Italic
ITC Bodoni Six
Bold
ITC Bodoni Six
Bold Italic
ITC Bodoni Six
Book SCOSF
ITC BODONI 1234...
Book OSF
osf 12345...
Book Italic OSF
osf 12345...
Bold OSF
osf 12345...
Bold Italic OSF
osf 12345...
ITC Bodoni Twelve + SCOSF Book
ITC Bodoni Twelve
Book Italic
ITC Bodoni Twelve
Bold
ITC Bodoni Twelve
Bold Italic
ITC Bodoni Twelve
Book SCOSF
ITC BODONI 12345...
Book OSF
osf 12345...
Book Italic OSF
osf 12345...
Bold OSF
osf 12345...
Bold Italic OSF
osf 12345...
ITC Bodoni Seventy-Two + SCOSF Book
ITC Bodoni

ff

✤ *See page 570 for contents of ITC Multi-Font Packages.*

... ITC Bodoni Seventy-Two + SCOSF
Book Italic *ITC Bodoni*
Bold **ITC Bodoni**
Bold Italic ***ITC Bodoni***
Book SCOSF ITC BODONI 123...
Book OSF osf 12345...
Book Italic OSF *osf 12345...*
Bold OSF **osf 12345...**
Bold Italic OSF ***osf 12345...***

ITC Century Handtooled + OSF
Bold **ITC Century**
Bold Italic ***ITC Century***
Bold OSF **osf 12345...**
Bold Italic OSF ***osf 12345...***

ITC Charter 1
Roman ITC Charter
Italic *ITC Charter*
Black **ITC Charter**
Black Italic ***ITC Charter***
Roman SCOSF ITC CHARTER 1234...
Roman OSF osf 12345...
Italic OSF *osf 12345...*
Black OSF **osf 12345...**
Black Italic OSF ***osf 12345...***

ITC Charter 2
Bold **ITC Charter**
Bold Italic ***ITC Charter***
Bold SCOSF **ITC CHARTER 123...**
Bold OSF **osf 12345...**
Bold Italic OSF ***osf 12345...***

ITC Cheltenham Handtooled + OSF
Bold **ITC Cheltenham**
Bold Italic ***ITC Cheltenham***
Bold OSF **osf 12345...**
Bold Italic OSF ***osf 12345...***

Friz Quadrata + SCOSF
Regular Friz Quadrata
Italic *Friz Quadrata*
Bold **Friz Quadrata**
Bold Italic ***Friz Quadrata***
Regular SCOSF FRIZ QUADRATA 123...
Regular OSF osf 12345...
Italic OSF *osf 12345...*
Bold OSF **osf 12345...**

... Friz Quadrata + SCOSF
Bold Italic OSF ***osf 12345...***

ITC Garamond Handtooled + OSF
Bold **ITC Garamond**
Bold Italic ***ITC Garamond***
Bold OSF **osf 12345...**
Bold Italic OSF ***osf 12345...***

ITC Highlander 1
Book ITC Highlander
Book Italic *ITC Highlander*
Bold **ITC Highlander**
Bold Italic ***ITC Highlander***
Book SCOSF ITC HIGHLANDER 123...
Book OSF osf 12345...
Book Italic OSF *osf 12345...*
Bold OSF **osf 12345...**
Bold Italic OSF ***osf 12345...***

ITC Highlander 2
Medium ITC Highlander
Medium Italic *ITC Highlander*
Medium SCOSF ITC HIGHLANDER 123...
Medium OSF osf 12345...
Medium Italic OSF *osf 12345...*

ITC Legacy Serif 1
Book ITC Legacy
Book Italic *ITC Legacy*
Bold **ITC Legacy**
Bold Italic ***ITC Legacy***
Book SCOSF ITC LEGACY 12345...
Book OSF osf 12345...
Book Italic OSF *osf 12345...*
Bold OSF **osf 12345...**
Bold Italic OSF ***osf 12345...***

ITC Legacy Serif 2
Medium ITC Legacy
Medium Italic *ITC Legacy*
Ultra **ITC Legacy**
Medium SCOSF ITC LEGACY 12345...
Medium OSF osf 12345...
Medium Italic OSF *osf 12345...*
Ultra OSF **osf 12345...**

ITC Legacy Sans 1
Book ITC Legacy
Book Italic *ITC Legacy*
Bold **ITC Legacy**

... ITC Legacy Sans 1
Bold Italic ***ITC Legacy***
Book SCOSF ITC LEGACY 12345...
Book OSF osf 12345...
Book Italic OSF *osf 12345...*
Bold OSF **osf 12345...**
Bold Italic OSF ***osf 12345...***

ITC Legacy Sans 2
Medium ITC Legacy
Medium Italic *ITC Legacy*
Ultra **ITC Legacy**
Medium SCOSF ITC LEGACY 12345...
Medium OSF osf 12345...
Medium Italic OSF *osf 12345...*
Ultra OSF **osf 12345...**

ITC Mona Lisa
✣ *ITC Headliners 2*
Recut ITC Mona Lisa
Solid ITC Mona Lisa
Recut OSF osf 12345...
Solid OSF osf 12345...

ITC Motter Corpus + OSF
Bold **ITC Motter Corp**
Bold Condensed **ITC Motter Corpus**
Bold OSF **osf 12345...**
Bold Condensed OSF **osf 12345...**

ITC Officina Serif + OSF
Book ITC Officina
Book Italic *ITC Officina*
Bold **ITC Officina**
Bold Italic ***ITC Officina***
Book OSF osf 12345...
Book Italic OSF osf 12345...
Bold OSF **osf 12345...**
Bold Italic OSF ***osf 12345...***

ITC Officina Sans + OSF
Book ITC Officina
Book Italic *ITC Officina*
Bold **ITC Officina**
Bold Italic ***ITC Officina***
Book OSF osf 12345...
Book Italic OSF *osf 12345...*
Bold OSF **osf 12345...**
Bold Italic OSF ***osf 12345...***

ITC Ozwald
✣ *ITC Headliners 2*
Regular **ITC Ozwald**

ff

... ITC Ozwald Regular OSF — osf 123...

ITC Studio Script ✤ ITC Headliners 1
Regular — ITC Studio Script
Alternate — abcdefghijkl ABCDEF
Alternate No. 2 — aefhimnorsFMaenrsssttfft

ITC TrueTypeGX Fonts

ITC Anna GX ✤ ITC GX Headliners 1 — ITC ANNA GX

ITC Charter GX
Roman — ITC Charter GX
Italic — *ITC Charter GX*
Black — **ITC Charter GX**
Black Italic — ***ITC Charter GX***

ITC Highlander GX
Book — ITC Highlander GX
Book Italic — *ITC Highlander GX*
Bold — **ITC Highlander GX**
Bold Italic — ***Highlander GX***

ITC Newtext GX
Light — ITC Newtext GX
Demi — **ITC Newtext GX**

ITC Studio Script GX ✤ ITC GX Headliners 1 — ITC Studio Script

International Typeface Corporation Multi-Font Package Contents

✤ ITC Headliners 1 : ITC Anna, ITC Anna SC, ITC Beesknees, ITC Beesknees SC, ITC Studio Script Regular, Alternate, Alternate No. 2.

✤ ITC Headliners 2 : ITC Mona Lisa Recut, ITC Mona Lisa Recut OSF, ITC Mona Lisa Solid, ITC Mona Lisa Solid OSF, ITC Ozwald Regular, ITC Ozwald Regular OSF.

✤ ITC GX Headliners 1 : ITC Anna GX, ITC Studio Script GX.

foundry: Isis Imaging

Featuring the work of designer Stephen Herron... Midway is based on the architectural lettering of Frank Lloyd Wright used in his Midway Gardens, Chicago project in 1913; the Ohsolong design is a contemporary display face with capitals, small capitals and alternate characters.

Midway
Book — Midway
Book Italic — *Midway*
Bold — **Midway**
Bold Italic — ***Midway***

... Midway
Heavy — Midway
Heavy Italic — *Midway*
Book SCOSF — MIDWAY 12345...
Book Italic OSF — *Midway 12345...*
Bold SCOSF — **MIDWAY 12345...**
Bold Italic OSF — ***Midway 12345...***

Ohsolong — OHSOLONG

foundry: Key Borders

A selection of fonts for the creation of borders and boxes designed by Joseph Dilena. The fonts can be set in multiple color combinations and can also be manipulated and used to follow curves and other shapes in drawing and graphic illustration programs.

Key Borders Border Fonts

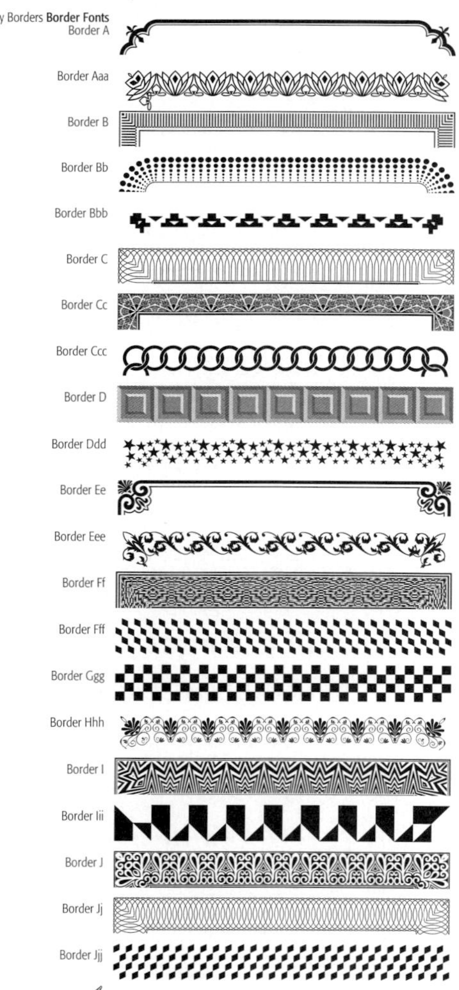

Border A
Border Aaa
Border B
Border Bb
Border Bbb
Border C
Border Cc
Border Ccc
Border D
Border Ddd
Border Ee
Border Eee
Border Ff
Border Fff
Border Ggg
Border Hhh
Border I
Border Iii
Border J
Border Jj
Border Jjj

... Key Borders Border Fonts

Border K
Border Kk
Border Kkk
Border L
Border Ll
Border M
Border Nn
Border Nnn
Border O
Border Oo
Border P
Border Pp
Border Q
Border R
Border Rr
Border Ss
Border Sss
Border Tt
Border Ttt
Border U
Border Uu
Border Ww
Border Www
Border Xx
Border Yyy
Certificate A
Certificate B
Certificate C
Certificate D
Inline B1
Background One
Background Two
Background Three
Background Four

✤ See this page for contents of ITC Multi-Font Packages.

foundry: Lanston Type Co.

The company was founded by Gerald Giampa in the early 1980s after his acquisition of the original pattern matrices and design records of The Lanston Monotype Company of Philadelphia. Since then Lanston Type Company has released a number of fonts that are faithful digital interpretations of Lanston Monotype's hot-metal typefaces including many by the prolific American type designer, Frederic W. Goudy.

Albertan
Roman Albertan
Italic *Albertan*
Roman SCOSF ALBERTAN 12345...
Italic SCOSF *ALBERTAN 12345...*
Roman OSF osf 12345...
Italic OSF *osf 12345...*

Albertan Bold
Bold **Albertan**
Bold Italic ***Albertan***
Bold SD **Albertan**
Bold Italic SD ***Albertan***

Albertan Inline & Titling
Inline ALBERTAN
Inline Italic *ALBERTAN*
Titling ALBERTAN
Titling Italic *ALBERTAN*

Bodoni
Roman Bodoni
Italic *Bodoni*
Roman SCOSF BODONI 12345...
Italic SCOSF *BODONI 12345...*
Roman OSF osf 12345...
Italic OSF *osf 12345...*
Roman SCSLF BODONI 12345...
Italic SCSLF *BODONI 12345...*
Roman SD Bodoni
Italic SD *Bodoni*
Roman SCOSF SD BODONI 12345...
Italic SCOSF SD *BODONI 12345...*
Roman OSF SD osf 12345...
Italic OSF SD *osf 12345...*

... Bodoni
Roman SCSLF SD BODONI 12345...
Italic SCSLF SD *BODONI 12345...*

Bodoni Bold
Bold **Bodoni**
Bold SCOSF **BODONI 12345...**
Bold OSF **osf 12345...**
Bold SCSLF **BODONI 12345...**

Bodoni 26
BODONI 26

Caslon Oldstyle No. 337
Roman Caslon Oldstyle
Italic *Caslon Oldstyle*
Roman SCOSF CASLON 12345...
Italic SCOSF *CASLON 12345...*
Roman OSF osf 12345...
Italic OSF *osf 12345...*
Roman SD Caslon Oldstyle
Italic SD *Caslon Oldstyle*
Roman SCOSF SD CASLON 12345...
Italic SCOSF SD *CASLON 12345...*
Roman OSF SD osf 12345...
Italic OSF SD *osf 12345...*
Roman Quaints ß ſ ſſ ſl ſſl ſt ſt ſh ſb ſk
Italic Quaints *ß ſ ſſ ſl ſſl ſt ſh ſb ſk*
Italic Swash & Quaints *CASLON w ſſ ſſl z v h k*
Italic Swash *CASLON*
Italic Swash OSF *CASLON 12345...*

Caslon Bold 537 & 637
537 Bold **Caslon 537**
537 Bold Italic ***Caslon 537***
537 Bold OSF **537 osf 12345...**
537 Bold Italic OSF ***537 osf 12345...***
637 Bold SD **Caslon 637**
637 Bold Italic SD ***Caslon 637***
637 Bold OSF SD **637 osf 12345...**
637 Bold Italic OSF SD ***637 osf 12345...***

Deepdene
Roman Deepdene
Italic *Deepdene*
Roman SCOSF DEEPDENE 12345...
Italic SCOSF *DEEPDENE 12345...*
Roman OSF osf 12345...
Italic OSF *osf 12345...*

... Deepdene
Italic Swash *Deepdene*
Italic Swash SCOSF *DEEPDENE 12345...*
Italic Swash OSF *osf 12345...*
Italic Swash Alternate *Deepdene 12345...*
Italic Swash SCOSF Alternate *DEEPDENE 12345...*
Italic Swash OSF Alternate *Deepdene 12345...*

Figures Square
012 012 1112

Flash
Flash

Fleurons Folio One

Fleurons Granjon Folio

Forum
Roman Forum
Italic *Forum*

Francis
Francis

Globe Gothic
Roman **Globe Gothic**
Oblique ***Globe Gothic***
Condensed **Globe Gothic**
Condensed Oblique ***Globe Gothic***
Extra Condensed **Globe Gothic**
Extra Condensed Oblique ***Globe Gothic***

Goudy Cloister Initials
A B C

Goudy Oldstyle
Roman Goudy Oldstyle
Italic *Goudy Oldstyle*
Bold **Goudy Oldstyle**
Roman SCOSF GOUDY 12345...
Italic SCOSF *GOUDY 12345...*
Roman OSF osf 12345...
Italic OSF *osf 12345...*
Roman SD Goudy Oldstyle
Italic SD *Goudy Oldstyle*
Roman OSF SD osf 12345...
Italic OSF SD *osf 12345...*

Goudy Thirty
Regular Goudy Thirty
Alternate Goudy Thirty

Goudy Village No. 2
Roman Goudy Village No. 2
Italic *Goudy Village No. 2*
Roman SCOSF GOUDY VILLAGE 123...
Italic SCOSF *GOUDY VILLAGE 123...*

ff

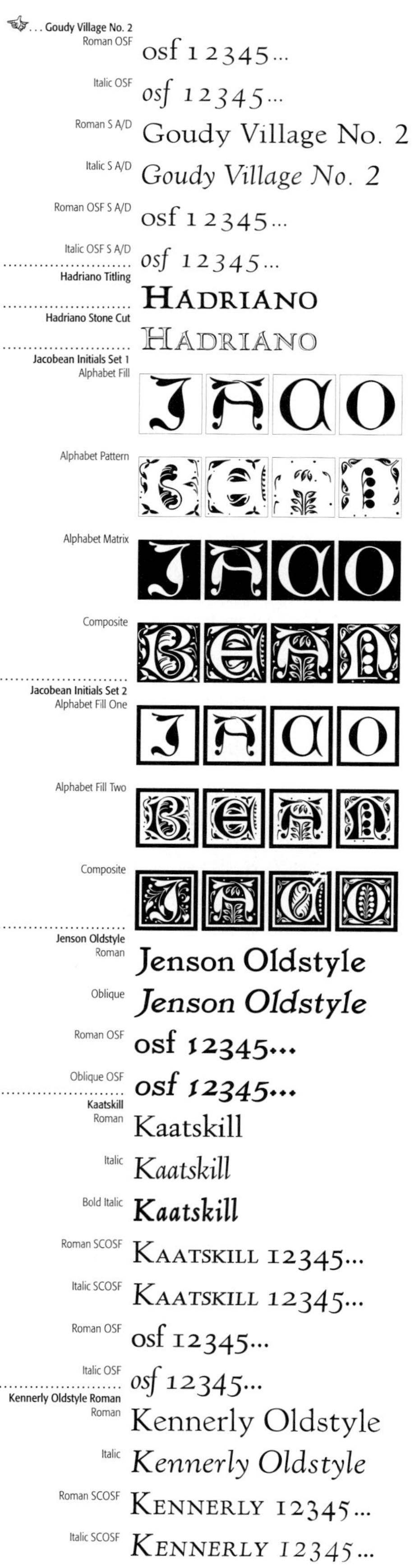
... Goudy Village No. 2
Roman OSF osf 12345...
Italic OSF osf 12345...
Roman S A/D Goudy Village No. 2
Italic S A/D Goudy Village No. 2
Roman OSF S A/D osf 12345...
Italic OSF S A/D osf 12345...
Hadriano Titling
HADRIANO
Hadriano Stone Cut
HADRIANO
Jacobean Initials Set 1
Alphabet Fill
Alphabet Pattern
Alphabet Matrix
Composite
Jacobean Initials Set 2
Alphabet Fill One
Alphabet Fill Two
Composite
Jenson Oldstyle
Roman Jenson Oldstyle
Oblique Jenson Oldstyle
Roman OSF osf 12345...
Oblique OSF osf 12345...
Kaatskill
Roman Kaatskill
Italic Kaatskill
Bold Italic Kaatskill
Roman SCOSF KAATSKILL 12345...
Italic SCOSF KAATSKILL 12345...
Roman OSF osf 12345...
Italic OSF osf 12345...
Kennerly Oldstyle Roman
Roman Kennerly Oldstyle
Italic Kennerly Oldstyle
Roman SCOSF KENNERLY 12345...
Italic SCOSF KENNERLY 12345...
Roman OSF osf 12345...

... Kennerly Oldstyle
Roman
Italic OSF osf 12345...
Italic Swash KENNERLY
Italic Swash OSF osf 12345...
Leaves One
Metropolitan
Roman OSF Metropolitan 12345...
Italic OSF osf 12345...
Roman SCOSF METROPOLITAN 12345...
Italic SCOSF METROPOLITAN 12345...
Obelisk
Titling Capitals & Alternates OBELISK AKMNUW
Titling Capitals & Alternates Oblique OBELISK AKMNUW
Pabst Oldstyle
Pabst Oldstyle
Spire
Titling Capitals & Alternates SPIRE AKMNUW
Titling Capitals & Alternates Italic SPIRE AKMNUW
Twentieth Century
Medium Twentieth Century
Medium Italic Twentieth Century
Vine Leaves
One
Two
Three
Water Garden
A
B
C
D
E
F
G
H
I
J
K
Round

foundry: Letraset

For the past three decades the company has been developing and producing alphabets for graphic communications. Today, Letraset's FONTEK Library of Typefaces is a unique collection of both classic and innovative fonts from designers such as David Quay, Phill Grimshaw, Freda Sacks, Michael Gill, Alan Meeks and many others including Letraset's type director, Colin Brignall. The library also offers the FONTEK DesignFont series, a unique offering of spot illustrations in font format.

Aachen Medium — Aachen

Aachen Bold — Aachen

Academy Engraved — Academy

Agincourt — Agincourt

Algerian Condensed — ALGERIAN

Ambrose — AMBROSE

Aquinas — Aquinas

Aquitaine Initials — AQUITAINE

Aristocrat — Aristocrat

Arriba — Arriba

Arriba-Arriba — Arriba-Arriba

Artiste — ARTISTE

Augustea Open — AUGUSTEA

Avenida — AVENIDA

Balmoral — Balmoral

Bang — BANG

Banner — Banner

Becka Script — Becka Script

Belwe Mono — Belwe Mono

Belwe Mono Italic — Belwe Mono

Bendigo — Bendigo

Bergell — Bergell

Bertie — Bertie

Bertram — BERTRAM

Bible Script — Bible Script

Bickley Script — Bickley Script

Bitmax — BITMAX

ff

Font name	Sample
Blackmoor	Blackmoor
Bluntz	BLUNTZ
Boink	BOINK
Bordeaux Roman	Bordeaux
Bordeaux Italic	Bordeaux
Bordeaux Roman Bold	Bordeaux
Bordeaux Display	Bordeaux
Bordeaux Script	Bordeaux
Brighton Light	Brighton
Brighton Medium	Brighton
Brighton Bold	Brighton
Bronx	Bronx
Burlington	Burlington
Cabaret	Cabaret
Cabarga Cursiva	Cabarga Cursiva
Campaign	CAMPAIGN
Cancellaresca Script	Cancellaresca Script
Carlton	Carlton
Caslon 540 Italic with Swashes	Caslon 540
Caxton Roman Light	Caxton
Caxton Roman Light Italic	Caxton
Caxton Roman Book	Caxton
Caxton Roman Bold	Caxton
Challenge Bold	Challenge
Challenge Extra Bold	Challenge
Champers	Champers
Charlotte Book	Charlotte
Book Italic	Charlotte
Medium	Charlotte
Bold	Charlotte
Book SCOSF	CHARLOTTE 12345...
Charlotte Sans Book	Charlotte
Book Italic	Charlotte
Medium	Charlotte
Bold	Charlotte
Book SCOSF	CHARLOTTE 12345...
Chipper	Chipper
Choc	Choc
Chromium One	CHROMIUM
Citation	CITATION
Claude Sans	Claude Sans
Claude Sans Italic	Claude Sans
Claude Sans Bold Italic	Claude Sans
Commercial Script	Commercial Script
Compacta	Compacta
Compacta Italic	Compacta Italic
Compacta Bold	Compacta Bold
Coptek	Coptek
Corinthian Light	Corinthian
Corinthian Medium	Corinthian
Corinthian Bold	Corinthian
Corinthian Bold Condensed	Corinthian
Crillee Italic	Crillee Italic
Crillee Bold Italic	Crillee Italic
Crillee Extra Bold Italic	Crillee Italic
Crillee Italic Inline Shadow	Crillee Italic
Dancin	Dancin
Data 70	Data 70
Demian	Demian
Demian Bold	Demian
Digitek	Digitek
Dolmen	Dolmen
Dynamo Shadow	Dynamo Shadow
Edwardian Medium	Edwardian
Elysium Book	Elysium
Book Italic	Elysium
Medium	Elysium
Bold	Elysium
Book SCOSF	ELYSIUM 12345...
Emphasis	EMPHASIS
Enviro	ENVIRO
Epokha	EPOKHA
Equinox	Equinox
Etruscan	Etruscan
Faithful Fly	FAITHFUL FLY
Fashion Compressed No. 3	Fashion
Fashion Engraved	Fashion
Figural Book	Figural
Book Italic	Figural
Medium	Figural
Bold	Figural
Book SCOSF	FIGURAL 12345...
Fine Hand	Fine Hand
Flamenco In Line	Flamenco
Flamme	Flamme
Flight	Flight
Fling	Fling
Follies	FOLLIES
Forest Shaded	Forest Shaded
Frances Uncial	frances uncial
Frankfurter Medium	Frankfurter
Frankfurter	FRANKFURTER
Frankfurter Highlight	FRANKFURTER
Frankfurter Inline	FRANKFURTER
Freestyle Script	Freestyle Script
Freestyle Script Bold	Freestyle Script
Gilgamesh Book	Gilgamesh
Book Italic	Gilgamesh
Medium	Gilgamesh
Bold	Gilgamesh
Book SCOSF	GILGAMESH 12345...
Gill Display Compressed	Gill Display
Gill Kayo Condensed	Gill Kayo
Gillies Gothic Extra Bold Shaded	Gillies Gothica
Glastonbury	Glastonbury
Gravura	Gravura
Greyton Script	Greyton Script
Hadfield	Hadfield
Hand Drawn	HAND DRAWN
Harlow	Harlow
Harlow Solid	Harlow
Harvey	HARVEY
Hazel	HAZEL
Heliotype	Heliotype

Font	Sample
Helvetica Medium Condensed	Helvetica
Helvetica Bold Condensed	Helvetica
Highlight	Highlight
Ignatius	Ignatius
Indy Italic	Indy Italic
Informal Roman	Informal Roman
Inscription	Inscription
Iris	IRIS
Isis	ISIS
Jazz	Jazz
John Handy	JOHN HANDY
Kanban	KANBAN
Katfish	Katfish
Klee	Klee
La Bamba	La Bamba
Lambada	Lambada
Laser	Laser
Laser Chrome	Laser Chrome
Latino Elongated	Latino Elongated
Laura	Laura
LCD	LCD
Le Griffe	Le Griffe
Lexikos	Lexikos
Lightnin'	Lightnin'
Limehouse Script	Limehouse Script
Lino Cut	Lino Cut
Locarno Light	Locarno
Locarno Italic	Locarno
Malibu	Malibu
Marguerita	Marguerita
Mastercard	MASTERCARD
Mekanik	Mekanik
Mekanik Italic	Mekanik
Milano	Milano
Mistral	Mistral
Mo' Funky Fresh	MO' FUNKY FRESH

Font	Sample
Oberon	Oberon
Odessa	Odessa
Old English	Old English
One Stroke Script	One Stroke Script
One Stroke Script Bold	One Stroke Script
One Stroke Script Shaded	One Stroke Script
Orlando	ORLANDO
Pablo	Pablo
Papyrus	Papyrus
Party	Party
Pendry Script	Pendry Script
Pink	Pink
Plaza	PLAZA
Pleasure Bold Shaded	PLEASURE
Pneuma	PNEUMA
Prague	PRAGUE
Premier Lightline	Premier Lightline
Premier Shaded	PREMIER
Princetown	PRINCETOWN
Pristina	Pristina
Pritchard	PRITCHARD
Pritchard Line Out	Pritchard
Pump	Pump
Pump Demibold	Pump
Quadrus	QUADRUS
Quixley	Quixley
Rage Italic	Rage Italic
Ragtime	RAGTIME
Rapier	Rapier
Refracta	REFRACTA
Regatta Condensed	Regatta Condensed
Retail Script	Retail Script
Retro Bold	RETRO
Retro Bold Condensed	RETRO
Riva	Riva
Robotik	Robotik

Font	Sample
Robotik Italic	Robotik
Romic Light	Romic
Romic Light Italic	Romic
Roxy	ROXY
Ru'ach	Ru'ach
Rubber Stamp	RUBBER STAMP
Rundfunk	Rundfunk
Santa Fe	Santa Fe
Savoye	Savoye
Scratch	Scratch
Scriba	SCRIBA
Scriptek	Scriptek
Scriptek Italic	Scriptek
Scruff	Scruff
Shaman	SHAMAN
Shatter	Shatter
Sinaloa	SINALOA
Skid Row	SKID ROW
Slipstream	SLIPSTREAM
Smudger	Smudger
Spotlight	Spotlight
Squire	Squire
Squire Extra Bold	Squire
Strobos	STROBOS
Superstar	SUPERSTAR
Synchro	SYNCHRO
Synchro Reversed	SYNCHRO
Tag	TAG
Tannhäuser	Tannhäuser
Teknik	Teknik
Tiger Rag	Tiger Rag
Tiranti Solid	Tiranti
Tropica	Tropica
Twang	Twang
Type Embellishments One	
Type Embellishments Two	
Type Embellishments Three	
Ulysses	Ulysses

Font	Sample
University Roman	University Roman
University Roman Italic	University Roman
University Roman Bold	University Roman
Van Dijk	Van Dijk
Van Dijk Bold	Van Dijk
Varga	Varga
Vegas	Vegas
Vermont	Vermont
Victorian	Victorian
Victorian Inline Shaded	Victorian
Vienna Extended	VIENNA
Vivaldi	Vivaldi
Wade Sans Light	Wade Sans
Wanted	Wanted
Waterloo Bold	Waterloo
Westwood	Westwood
Willow	WILLOW
Xylo	Xylo
Young Baroque	Young Baroque
Zinjaro	ZINJARO

Letraset FONTEK DesignFonts

Attitudes

Calligraphic Ornaments

Celebrations

Commercials

Delectables

Diversions

Incidentals

Industrials

Journeys

Mo' Funky Fresh Symbols

Moderns

Naturals

Organics

Primitives

Radicals

Wildlifes

foundry: Letter Perfect

Garrett Boge founded Leter Perfect in 1988 and since then has produced a range of fonts that reflect his almost twenty years of experience as a calligrapher, lettering artist and type designer. The Letter Perfect collection includes both original works and several revivals.

Font	Sample
DeStijl Regular	DESTIJL
Alternate	DESTIJL
Florens Regular	Florens
Swash OSF	Florens 12345…
Hadrian Bold	Hadrian
Hardwood	Hardwood
Koch Original	Koch Original
Kryptic	KRYPTIC
Manito	MANITO
Old Claude Roman	Old Claude
Roman SCLF	OLD CLAUDE 123…
Roslyn Bold	Roslyn
Silhouette	Silhouette
Spring Light	Spring
Regular	Spring
Spumoni	Spumoni
Tomboy Light	Tomboy
Medium	Tomboy
Bold	Tomboy
Visage Light	Visage
Light Oblique	Visage
Book	Visage
Book Oblique	Visage
Medium	Visage
Medium Oblique	Visage
Bold	Visage
Bold Oblique	Visage
Black	Visage
Black Oblique	Visage
Wendy	Wendy

foundry: Linguist's Software

Founded in 1984 by Philip Payne, Linguist's Software produces fonts and software for many of the world's languages, both living and dead. For most languages, the company's products generate characters in their correct form and placement by translating phonetic equivalents input from a standard keyboard; the font software is also context sensitive. Linguist's Software's products can be used by native speakers of a particular language as well as by occassional users.

Cyrillic Collection: Supports 14 Cyrillic languages and English.

Font	Sample
Cyrillic II : Serif Upright	Абвгдеж Зикл
Inclined	Абвгдеж Зикл
Bold Upright	Абвгдеж Зикл
Bold Inclined	Абвгдеж Зикл
Cyrillic II : Sans Serif Regular	Абвгдеж Зикл
Oblique	Абвгдеж Зикл
Bold	Абвгдеж Зикл
Bold Oblique	Абвгдеж Зикл
Cyrillic II : Monospaced Regular	Абвгдеж Зикл
Inclined	Абвгдеж Зикл
Bold Upright	Абвгдеж Зикл
Bold Inclined	Абвгдеж Зикл

TransCyrillic Collection: Supports all Cyrillic languages.

Font	Sample
TransCyrillic : Serif Upright	Абвгдеж Зикл
Inclined	Абвгдеж Зикл
Bold Upright	Абвгдеж Зикл
Bold Inclined	Абвгдеж Зикл
TransCyrillic : Sans Serif Upright	Абвгдеж Зикл
Oblique	Абвгдеж Зикл
Bold Upright	Абвгдеж Зикл
Bold Oblique	Абвгдеж Зикл

Font	Sample
LaserGreek Graeca Upright	Αβγδε Ζζηθυκ
Graeca Inclined	Αβγδε Ζζηθυκ
Graeca Bold Upright	Αβγδε Ζζηθυκ
Graeca Bold Inclined	Αβγδε Ζζηθυκ
GreekSans Upright	Αβγδε Ζζηθυκ

ff

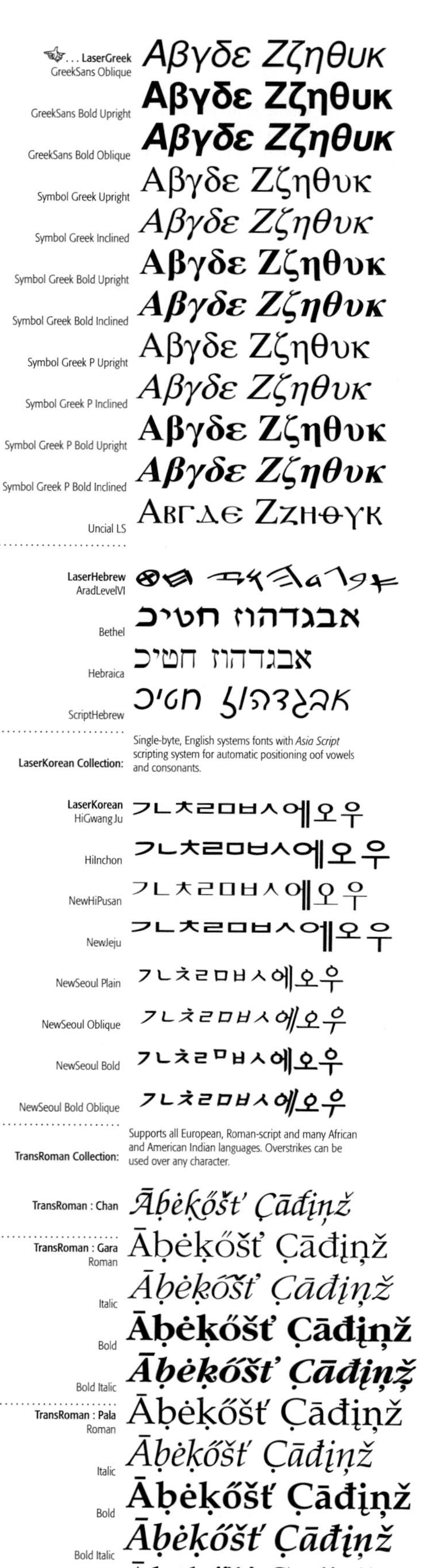
LaserGreek GreekSans Oblique
GreekSans Bold Upright
GreekSans Bold Oblique
Symbol Greek Upright
Symbol Greek Inclined
Symbol Greek Bold Upright
Symbol Greek Bold Inclined
Symbol Greek P Upright
Symbol Greek P Inclined
Symbol Greek P Bold Upright
Symbol Greek P Bold Inclined
Uncial LS
LaserHebrew AradLevelVI
Bethel
Hebraica
ScriptHebrew
LaserKorean Collection: Single-byte, English systems fonts with Asia Script scripting system for automatic positioning oof vowels and consonants.
LaserKorean HiGwangJu
Hilnchon
NewHiPusan
NewJeju
NewSeoul Plain
NewSeoul Oblique
NewSeoul Bold
NewSeoul Bold Oblique
TransRoman Collection: Supports all European, Roman-script and many African and American Indian languages. Overstrikes can be used over any character.
TransRoman : Chan
TransRoman : Gara Roman
Italic
Bold
Bold Italic
TransRoman : Pala Roman
Italic
Bold
Bold Italic
TransRoman : Serif Roman

... TransRoman : Serif Italic — Āḅėķőšť Çāđįņž
Bold — Āḅėķőšť Çāđįņž
Bold Italic — Āḅėķőšť Çāđįņž
TransRoman : Sans Serif Regular — Āḅėķőšť Çāđįņž
Oblique — Āḅėķőšť Çāđįņž
Bold — Āḅėķőšť Çāđįņž
Bold Oblique — Āḅėķőšť Çāđįņž

TransSlavic Collection: Supports all European, Roman-script and many African and American Indian languages. Overstrikes can be used over any character.

TransSlavic : Chan — Āḅėķőşť Çāđįņž
TransSlavic : Gara Roman — Āḅèķőşť Çāđįņž
Italic — Āḅèķőşť Çāđįņž
Bold — Āḅèķőşť Çāđįņž
Bold Italic — Āḅèķőşť Çāđįņ
TransSlavic : Pala Roman — Āḅèķőşť Çāđįņž
Italic — Āḅèķőşť Çāđįņž
Bold — Āḅèķőşť Çāđįņž
Bold Italic — Āḅèķőşť Çāđįņž
TransSlavic : Serif Roman — Āḅèķőşť Çāđįņž
Italic — Āḅèķőşť Çāđįņž
Bold — Āḅèķőşť Çāđįņž
Bold Italic — Āḅèķőşť Çāđįņž
TransSlavic : Sans Serif Regular — Āḅèķőşť Çāđįņž
Oblique — Āḅèķőşť Çāđįņž
Bold — Āḅèķőşť Çāđįņ
Bold Oblique — Āḅèķőşť Çāđįņ

foundry: Linotype-Hell

Since 1888, the name Linotype has been synonymous with innovative technology and type development. In the late 1920s, the company established itself as a leader in the design of type with a successful program managed by C.H. Griffith which produced many types which are still well-known and popular. The type designers whose work can be found in the Linotype Library includes some of the best known and respected names in the field: Adrian Frutiger, Hermann Zapf, Matthew Carter, Walter Tracy, William Addison Dwiggins and many, many others.

Aachen Bold ✤ *Adobe DisplaySet 1* — Aachen
Akzidenz Grotesk Light — Akzidenz Grotesk
Regular — Akzidenz Grotesk
Bold — Akzidenz Grotesk
Black — Akzidenz Grotesk
Albertus ✤ *Monotype DisplaySet 1* Light — Albertus
Regular — Albertus
Italic — Albertus
Aldus + SCOSF Roman — Aldus
Italic — Aldus
Roman SCOSF — ALDUS 12345...
Italic OSF — osf 12345...
ITC American Typewriter Light — ITC American
Medium — ITC American
Bold — ITC American
Alternates — eR$& eR$& eR$&
Light Condensed — ITC American Type
Condensed — ITC American Type
Bold Condensed — ITC American Type
Condensed Alternates — eR$& eR$& eR$&
Americana Roman — Americana
Italic — Americana
Bold — Americana
Extra Bold — Americana
Amigo ✤ *Baker Calligraphy* — Amigo
ITC Anna ✤ *ITC Typographica* — ITC ANNA

✤ *See page 592 for contents of Linotype-Hell Multi-Font Packages.*

Antique Olive 1
Light Antique Olive
Regular Antique Olive
Italic Antique Olive
Bold Antique Olive
Black Antique Olive

Antique Olive 2
Bold Condensed Antique Olive
Compact Antique Olive
Nord Antique
Nord Italic Antique

Antique Olive EastA
Light Áćęłőşť Čąďíňż
Regular Áćęłőşť Čąďíňż
Italic Áćęłőşť Čąďíňż
Bold Áćęłőşť Čąďíňż
Black Áćęłőşť Čąďíňż

Apollo + Expert & SCOSF
Roman Apollo
Italic Apollo
Semibold Apollo
Expert Roman APOLLO 12345 et al.
Expert Italic 12345 et al.
Expert Semibold 12345 et al.
Roman SCOSF APOLLO 12345...
Italic OSF osf 12345...
Semibold OSF osf 12345...

Arcadia
❖ Brody DisplaySet 1
Regular & Alternate Arcadia bdhpq

Ariadne
❖ GudrunSchrift
ARIADNE

Arnold Böcklin
❖ Linotype DisplaySet 1
Arnold Böcklin

Ashley Script
❖ Monotype ScriptSet 1
Ashley Script

New Aster
Roman New Aster
Italic New Aster
Semibold New Aster
Semibold Italic New Aster
Bold New Aster
Bold Italic New Aster
Black New Aster
Black Italic New Aster

Linotype Astrology Pi
One ♈♉♊♋♌♍♎♏
Two

Linotype Audio Pi
❖ Linotype PiSet 1
ARD ... CD hr

Auriol
Regular Auriol
Italic Auriol
Bold Auriol
Bold Italic Auriol
Black Auriol
Black Italic Auriol

Auriol Flowers
One
Two
Vignette Style

ITC Avant Garde Gothic 1
Book ITC Avant Garde
Book Oblique ITC Avant Garde
Demi ITC Avant Garde
Demi Oblique ITC Avant Garde

ITC Avant Garde Gothic 2
Extra Light ITC Avant Garde
Extra Light Oblique ITC Avant Garde
Medium ITC Avant Garde
Medium Oblique ITC Avant Garde
Bold ITC Avant Garde
Bold Oblique ITC Avant Garde

ITC Avant Garde Gothic Condensed
Book Condensed ITC Avant Garde
Medium Condensed ITC Avant Garde
Demi Condensed ITC Avant Garde
Bold Condensed ITC Avant Garde

Avenir 1
35-Light Avenir
35-Light Oblique Avenir
55-Regular Avenir
55-Oblique Avenir
85-Heavy Avenir
85-Heavy Oblique Avenir

Avenir 2
45-Book Avenir
45-Book Oblique Avenir
65-Medium Avenir
65-Medium Oblique Avenir
95-Black Avenir
95-Black Oblique Avenir

Baker Signet
❖ Adobe DisplaySet 2
Baker Signet

Banco
❖ Linotype DisplaySet 2
BANCO

ITC New Baskerville
Roman ITC New Baskerville
Italic ITC New Baskerville
Bold ITC New Baskerville
Bold Italic ITC New Baskerville

ITC New Baskerville SCOSF
Roman SCOSF ITC NEW BASKER
Italic OSF osf 12345...
Bold SCOSF ITC NEW BASKER
Bold Italic OSF osf 12345...

Baskerville Cyrillic
Upright Абвгдеж Зикл
Inclined Абвгдеж Зикл
Bold Upright Абвгдеж Зикл

Baskerville Monotonic Greek
Upright Αβγδε Ζζηθικ
Inclined Αβγδε Ζζηθικ
Bold Upright Αβγδε Ζζηθικ

Baskerville Polytonic Greek
Upright Αβγδἕ Ζζῆθΐκ
Inclined Αβγδἕ Ζζῆθΐκ
Bold Upright Αβγδἕ Ζζῆθΐκ

ITC Bauhaus
Light ITC Bauhaus
Medium ITC Bauhaus
Demi ITC Bauhaus
Bold ITC Bauhaus
Heavy ITC Bauhaus

ITC Beesknees
❖ ITC Typographica
ITC BEESKNEES

Bell Gothic
Light Bell Gothic
Bold Bell Gothic
Black Bell Gothic

Bell Centennial
Name & Number Bell Centennial
Address Bell Centennial
Sub Caption Bell Centennial
Bold Listing BELL CENTENNIAL
Bold Listing Alternate BELL CENTENNIAL

Belwe
Light Belwe
Medium Belwe
Bold Belwe
Condensed Belwe

Bembo 1
Roman Bembo
Italic Bembo
Bold Bembo

ff

... **Bembo 1**
- Bold Italic — *Bembo*

Bembo 2
- Semibold — Bembo
- Semibold Italic — *Bembo*
- Extra Bold — **Bembo**
- Extra Bold Italic — ***Bembo***

Bembo Expert & SCOSF
- Expert Roman — BEMBO 12345 et al.
- Expert Italic — *12345 et al.*
- Expert Semibold — 12345 et al.
- Expert Semibold Italic — *12345 et al.*
- Expert Bold — **12345 et al.**
- Expert Bold Italic — ***12345 et al.***
- Expert Extra Bold — **12345 et al.**
- Expert Extra Bold Italic — ***12345 et al.***
- Roman SCOSF — Bembo 12345...
- Italic OSF — *osf 12345...*
- Semibold OSF — osf 12345...
- Semibold Italic OSF — *osf 12345...*
- Bold OSF — **osf 12345...**
- Bold Italic OSF — ***osf 12345...***
- Extra Bold OSF — **osf 12345...**
- Extra Bold Italic OSF — ***osf 12345...***

ITC Benguiat ✤ *Adobe DisplaySet 3*
- Book — ITC Benguiat
- Bold — **ITC Benguiat**

ITC Benguiat
- Book — ITC Benguiat
- Book Italic — *ITC Benguiat*
- Medium — ITC Benguiat
- Medium Italic — *ITC Benguiat*
- Bold — **ITC Benguiat**
- Bold Italic — ***ITC Benguiat***

ITC Benguiat Gothic
- Book — ITC Benguiat
- Book Oblique — *ITC Benguiat*
- Medium — ITC Benguiat
- Medium Oblique — *ITC Benguiat*
- Bold — **ITC Benguiat**
- Bold Oblique — ***ITC Benguiat***
- Heavy — **ITC Benguiat**
- Heavy Oblique — ***ITC Benguiat***

ITC Berkeley Oldstyle
- Book — ITC Berkeley

... **ITC Berkeley Oldstyle**
- Book Italic — *ITC Berkeley*
- Medium — ITC Berkeley
- Medium Italic — *ITC Berkeley*
- Bold — **ITC Berkeley**
- Bold Italic — ***ITC Berkeley***
- Black — **ITC Berkeley**
- Black Italic — ***ITC Berkeley***

Berling
- Roman — Berling
- Italic — *Berling*
- Bold — **Berling**
- Bold Italic — ***Berling***

Bernhard Modern
- Roman — Bernhard Modern
- Italic — *Bernhard Modern*
- Bold — **Bernhard Modern**
- Bold Italic — ***Bernhard Modern***

Biffo Script ✤ *Monotype ScriptSet 2* — Biffo Script

Birch ✤ *Adobe Wood Type 2* — Birch

Blackoak ✤ *Adobe Wood Type 2* — **Blackoak**

Bodoni 1
- Roman — Bodoni
- Italic — *Bodoni*
- Bold — **Bodoni**
- Bold Italic — ***Bodoni***
- Poster — **Bodoni**

Bodoni 2
- Book — Bodoni
- Book Italic — *Bodoni*
- Bold Condensed — **Bodoni**
- Poster Compressed — **Bodoni**
- Poster Italic — ***Bodoni***

Bauer Bodoni 1
- Roman — Bauer Bodoni
- Italic — *Bauer Bodoni*
- Bold — **Bauer Bodoni**
- Bold Italic — ***Bauer Bodoni***

Bauer Bodoni 2
- Black — **Bauer Bodoni**
- Black Italic — ***Bauer Bodoni***
- Bold Condensed — **Bauer Bodoni**
- Black Condensed — **Bauer Bodoni**

Bauer Bodoni SCOSF
- Roman SCOSF — B Bodoni 12345...
- Roman OSF — osf 12345...

... **Bauer Bodoni SCOSF**
- Italic OSF — *osf 12345...*
- Bold OSF — **osf 12345...**
- Bold Italic OSF — ***osf 12345...***

ITC Bookman 1
- Light — ITC Bookman
- Light Italic — *ITC Bookman*
- Demi — **ITC Bookman**
- Demi Italic — ***ITC Bookman***

ITC Bookman 2
- Medium — ITC Bookman
- Medium Italic — *ITC Bookman*
- Bold — **ITC Bookman**
- Bold Italic — ***ITC Bookman***

Border Pi ✤ *Linotype PiSet 2*

Brush Script ✤ *Adobe DisplaySet 4* — Brush Script

Bundesbahn Pi
- One
- Two
- Three

PMN Caecilia + OSF
- 45-Light — PMN Caecilia
- 46-Light Italic — *PMN Caecilia*
- 55-Roman — PMN Caecilia
- 56-Italic — *PMN Caecilia*
- 75-Bold — **PMN Caecilia**
- 76-Bold Italic — ***PMN Caecilia***
- 85-Heavy — **PMN Caecilia**
- 86-Heavy Italic — ***PMN Caecilia***
- 45-Light OSF — osf 12345...
- 46-Light Italic OSF — *osf 12345...*
- 55-Roman OSF — osf 12345...
- 56-Italic OSF — *osf 12345...*
- 75-Bold OSF — **osf 12345...**
- 76-Bold Italic OSF — ***osf 12345...***
- 85-Heavy OSF — **osf 12345...**
- 86-Heavy Italic OSF — ***osf 12345...***

PMN Ceacilia SCOSF
- 45-Light SCOSF — Caecilia 12345...
- 46-Light Italic SCOSF — *Caecilia 12345...*
- 55-Roman SCOSF — Caecilia 12345...
- 56-Italic SCOSF — *Caecilia 12345...*
- 75-Bold SCOSF — **Caecilia 12345...**
- 76-Bold Italic SCOSF — ***Caecilia 12345...***

ff

✤ *See page 592 for contents of Linotype-Hell Multi-Font Packages.*

... PMN Caecilia SCOSF
85-Heavy SCOSF CAECILIA 12345...
86-Heavy Italic SCOSF *CAECILIA 12345...*

New Caledonia
Roman New Caledonia
Italic *New Caledonia*
Semibold **New Caledonia**
Semibold Italic ***New Caledonia***
Bold **New Caledonia**
Bold Italic ***New Caledonia***
Black **New Caledonia**
Black Italic ***New Caledonia***

New Caledonia SCOSF
Roman SCOSF N CALEDONIA 12...
Italic OSF *osf 12345...*
Bold SCOSF **N CALEDONIA 12...**
Bold Italic OSF ***osf 12345...***

Calvert
Light Calvert
Roman Calvert
Bold **Calvert**

Candida
Roman Candida
Italic *Candida*
Bold **Candida**

Cantoria 1
Roman Cantoria
Italic *Cantoria*
Bold **Cantoria**
Bold Italic ***Cantoria***

Cantoria 2
Light Cantoria
Light Italic *Cantoria*
Semibold **Cantoria**
Semibold Italic ***Cantoria***
Extra Bold **Cantoria**
Extra Bold Italic ***Cantoria***

Caravan Borders
One
Two
Three
Four

Carolina
✣ *Type Before Gutenberg 2*
Regular Carolina
Dfr chckfffftllſsſiſſßtzäöü

Carta

Cascade Script
✣ *Linotype ScriptSet 1* ***Cascade Script***

Caslon 540 & Caslon 3
Caslon 540 Roman Caslon 540
Caslon 540 Italic *Caslon 540*
Caslon 3 Roman **Caslon 3**
Caslon 3 Italic ***Caslon 3***

Caslon 540 & Caslon 3 SCOSF
Caslon 540 Roman SCOSF CASLON 540 1234...
Caslon 540 Italic OSF *osf 12345...*
Caslon 3 Roman SCOSF **CASLON 3 1234...**
Caslon 3 Italic OSF ***osf 12345...***

Caslon Open Face
Caslon Open Face

ITC Caslon No. 224
Book ITCCaslon No.224
Book Italic *ITCCaslon No.224*
Medium ITC Caslon No.224
Medium Italic *ITC Caslon No.224*
Bold **ITC Caslon No.224**
Bold Italic ***ITC Caslon No.224***
Black **ITC Caslon No.224**
Black Italic ***ITC Caslon No.224***

Adobe Caslon
Roman Adobe Caslon
Italic *Adobe Caslon*
Semibold **Adobe Caslon**
Semibold Italic ***Adobe Caslon***
Bold **Adobe Caslon**
Bold Italic ***Adobe Caslon***

Adobe Caslon Expert & SCOSF
Expert Roman A CASLON 12345 et al.
Expert Italic *12345 et al.*
Expert Semibold **12345 et al.**
Expert Semibold Italic ***12345 et al.***
Expert Bold **12345 et al.**
Expert Bold Italic ***12345 et al.***
Roman SCOSF A CASLON 12345...
Italic OSF *osf 12345...*
Semibold SCOSF **A CASLON 12345...**
Semibold Italic OSF ***osf 12345...***
Bold OSF **osf 12345...**
Bold Italic OSF ***osf 12345...***
Alternate Roman ctkſhfiflffſtstvw
Alternate Italic *ctkſſhſiſlſſſtſtvw*
Alternate Semibold **ctkſhfiflffſtstvw**

... Adobe Caslon
Expert & SCOSF
Alternate Semibold Italic ***ctkſſhſiſlſſſtſtvw***
Alternate Bold **ctkſhfiflffſtstvw**
Alternate Bold Italic ***ctkſſhſiſlſſſtſtvw***
Italic Swash Caps *ABCDEFGHIJ*
Semibold Italic Swash Caps ***ABCDEFGHIJ***
Bold Italic Swash Caps ***ABCDEFGHIJ***
Ornaments

Castellar
✣ *Monotype DisplaySet 1* CASTELLAR

Caxton
Light Caxton
Light Italic *Caxton*
Book Caxton
Book Italic *Caxton*
Bold **Caxton**
Bold Italic ***Caxton***

Centaur
Roman Centaur
Italic *Centaur*
Italic Alternate z *Centaur z*
Bold **Centaur**
Bold Italic ***Centaur***

Centaur Expert & SCOSF
Expert Roman CENTAUR 12345 et al.
Expert Italic *12345 et al.*
Expert Bold **12345 et al.**
Expert Bold Italic ***12345 et al.***
Roman SCOSF CENTAUR 12345...
Italic OSF *osf 12345...*
Bold OSF **osf 12345...**
Bold Italic OSF ***osf 12345...***
Italic Swash *Centaur*
Expert Italic Alternate *a e k r g t z v & w*

Linotype Centennial
45-Light L Centennial
46-Light Italic *L Centennial*
55-Roman L Centennial
56-Italic *L Centennial*
75-Bold **L Centennial**
76-Bold Italic ***L Centennial***
95-Black **L Centennial**
96-Black Italic ***L Centennial***

Linotype Centennial SCOSF
45-Light SCOSF L CENTENNIAL 123...

ff

… Linotype Centennial SCOSF
- 46-Light Italic OSF — *osf 12345…*
- 55-Roman SCOSF — L CENTENNIAL 123…
- 56-Italic OSF — *osf 12345…*
- 75-Bold OSF — **osf 12345…**
- 76-Bold Italic OSF — ***osf 12345…***
- 95-Black OSF — **osf 12345…**
- 96-Black Italic OSF — ***osf 12345…***

Century Expanded
- Roman — Century Expanded
- Italic — *Century Expanded*

Century Old Style
- Roman — Century Old Style
- Italic — *Century Old Style*
- Bold — **Century Old Style**

New Century Schoolbook
- Roman — New Century
- Italic — *New Century*
- Bold — **New Century**
- Bold Italic — ***New Century***

New Century Schoolbook Greek Monotonic
- Upright — Αβγδε Ζζηθικ
- Inclined — *Αβγδε Ζζηθικ*
- Bold Upright — **Αβγδε Ζζηθικ**

New Century Schoolbook Greek Polytonic
- Upright — Αβγδἕ Ζζἥθΐκ
- Inclined — *Αβγδἕ Ζζἥθΐκ*
- Bold Upright — **Αβγδἕ Ζζἥθΐκ**

New Century SchBk Fractions
✤ *Linotype Fraction Pi*
- Roman — 1/2 $\frac{1}{2}$ 1/3 $\frac{1}{3}$ 63/64 $\frac{63}{64}$ 22/7 $\frac{22}{7}$
- Bold — **1/2 $\frac{1}{2}$ 1/3 $\frac{1}{3}$ 63/64 $\frac{63}{64}$ 22/7 $\frac{22}{7}$**

ITC Century
- Light — ITC Century
- Light Italic — *ITC Century*
- Book — ITC Century
- Book Italic — *ITC Century*
- Bold — **ITC Century**
- Bold Italic — ***ITC Century***
- Ultra — **ITC Century**
- Ultra Italic — ***ITC Century***

ITC Century Condensed
- Light Condensed — ITC Century
- Light Condensed Italic — *ITC Century*
- Book Condensed — ITC Century
- Book Condensed Italic — *ITC Century*
- Bold Condensed — **ITC Century**
- Bold Condensed Italic — ***ITC Century***

… ITC Century Condensed
- Ultra Condensed — **ITC Century**
- Ultra Condensed Italic — ***ITC Century***

Charlemagne
✤ *Adobe TitlingSet 1*
- Regular — CHARLEMAGNE
- Bold — **CHARLEMAGNE**

Charme
✤ *Linotype DisplaySet 2*
- *Charme*

ITC Cheltenham 1
- Book — ITC Cheltenham
- Book Italic — *ITC Cheltenham*
- Bold — **ITC Cheltenham**
- Bold Italic — ***ITC Cheltenham***

ITC Cheltenham 2
- Light — ITC Cheltenham
- Light Italic — *ITC Cheltenham*
- Ultra — **ITC Cheltenham**
- Ultra Italic — ***ITC Cheltenham***

ITC Cheltenham Condensed
- Light Condensed — ITC Cheltenham
- Light Condensed Italic — *ITC Cheltenham*
- Book Condensed — ITC Cheltenham
- Book Condensed Italic — *ITC Cheltenham*
- Bold Condensed — **ITC Cheltenham**
- Bold Condensed Italic — ***ITC Cheltenham***
- Ultra Condensed — **ITC Cheltenham**
- Ultra Condensed Italic — ***ITC Cheltenham***

Cheq
- ♔♕♔♘♙♚♛♚♞♟

Chemstra Pi
- H H H N

Chwast Buffalo Black Cond
✤ *Linotype Headliners*
- **Chwast Buffalo**

Clairvaux
✤ *Type Before Gutenberg 2*
- Regular — Clairvaux
- Dfr — chckfffftllſsſiſſßtzäöü

Clarendon
- Light — Clarendon
- Roman — Clarendon
- Bold — **Clarendon**

ITC Clearface
- Roman — ITC Clearface
- Italic — *ITC Clearface*
- Bold — **ITC Clearface**
- Bold Italic — ***ITC Clearface***
- Heavy — **ITC Clearface**
- Heavy Italic — ***ITC Clearface***
- Black — **ITC Clearface**
- Black Italic — ***ITC Clearface***

Clearface Gothic
- 45-Light — Clearface Gothic
- 55-Regular — Clearface Gothic
- 65-Medium — Clearface Gothic
- 75-Bold — **Clearface Gothic**
- 95-Black — **Clearface Gothic**

Cochin
- Roman — Cochin
- Italic — *Cochin*
- Bold — **Cochin**
- Bold Italic — ***Cochin***

Concorde
- Roman — Concorde
- Italic — *Concorde*
- Bold — **Concorde**
- Bold Italic — ***Concorde***

Cooper Black
- Roman — **Cooper Black**
- Italic — ***Cooper Black***

Copperplate Gothic
- 29 B-C — COPPERPLATE
- 29 A-B — COPPERPLATE
- 30 B-C — COPPERPLATE
- 30 A-B — COPPERPLATE
- 31 B-C — COPPERPLATE
- 31 A-B — COPPERPLATE
- 32 B-C — COPPERPLATE
- 32 A-B — COPPERPLATE
- 33 B-C — COPPERPLATE

Corona
- Roman — Corona
- Italic — *Corona*
- Bold Face No. 2 — **Corona**

Cottonwood
✤ *Adobe Wood Type 1*
- COTTONWOOD

ITC Cushing
- Book — ITC Cushing
- Book Italic — *ITC Cushing*
- Medium — ITC Cushing
- Medium Italic — *ITC Cushing*
- Bold — **ITC Cushing**
- Bold Italic — ***ITC Cushing***
- Heavy — **ITC Cushing**
- Heavy Italic — ***ITC Cushing***

Deco Numbers
- Circle — 1 2 3 19 75 ● 4 6 1
- Square — 1 2 3 19 75 ■ 4 6 1

ff

✤ See page 592 for contents of Linotype-Hell Multi-Font Packages.

Family	Style	Sample
. . . Deco Numbers	Triangle	1 19 75 4 6 1
	OCR A	1 2 19 75 4 6 1
	Serlio	1 2 3 4 1 7 9 2 5 9
Linotype Decoration Pi	One	
	Two	
Linotype Didot + SCOSF	Roman	Linotype Didot
	Italic	*Linotype Didot*
	Bold	**Linotype Didot**
	Roman SCOSF	L Didot 12345...
	Roman OSF	osf 12345...
	Italic OSF	*osf 12345...*
	Bold OSF	**osf 12345...**
	Headline	Linotype Didot
	Headline OSF	osf 12345...
	Initials	LINOTYPE DIDOT
	Ornaments One	
	Ornaments Two	
DIN Schriften	Engschrift	DIN Schriften
	Mittelschrift	DIN Schriften
	Neuzeit Grotesk Light	DIN Schriften
	Neuzeit Grotesk Bold Condensed	**DIN Schriften**
Diotima + SCOSF ❖ *GudrunSchrift*	Roman	Diotima
	Italic	*Diotima*
	Roman SCOSF	DIOTIMA 12345...
	Roman OSF	osf 12345...
	Italic OSF	*osf 12345...*
Dom Casual	Regular	Dom Casual
	Bold	**Dom Casual**
Dorchester Script ❖ *Monotype ScriptSet 2*		*Dorchester Script*
Doric Bold ❖ *Linotype ClassAdSet 1*		**Doric Bold**
Duc De Berry ❖ *Type Before Gutenberg 1*	Regular	Duc De Berry
	Dfr	chckfffftllſsſiſſßtzäöü
Linotype EEC Pi		euro
Egyptienne F	55-Roman	Egyptienne F
	56-Italic	*Egyptienne F*
	65-Bold	**Egyptienne F**
	75-Black	**Egyptienne F**
Ehrhardt	Roman	Ehrhardt
. . . Ehrhardt	Italic	*Ehrhardt*
	Semibold	**Ehrhardt**
	Semibold Italic	***Ehrhardt***
Electra 1	Roman	Electra
	Cursive	*Electra*
	Bold	**Electra**
	Bold Cursive	***Electra***
Electra 2	Roman SCOSF	ELECTRA 12345...
	Roman OSF	osf 12345...
	Cursive OSF	*osf 12345...*
	Bold SCOSF	**ELECTRA 12345...**
	Bold OSF	**osf 12345...**
	Bold Cursive OSF	***osf 12345...***
	Display	Electra
	Display Cursive	*Electra*
	Display Bold	**Electra**
	Display Bold Cursive	***Electra***
Ellington	Light	Ellington
	Light Italic	*Ellington*
	Roman	Ellington
	Italic	*Ellington*
	Bold	**Ellington**
	Bold Italic	***Ellington***
	Extra Bold	**Ellington**
	Extra Bold Italic	***Ellington***
Else NPL	Light	Else NPL
	Medium	Else NPL
	Semibold	Else NPL
	Bold	**Else NPL**
Engravers Bold Face ❖ *Linotype Engravers Set 1*		**ENGRAVERS**
ITC Eras	Light	ITC Eras
	Book	ITC Eras
	Medium	ITC Eras
	Demi	**ITC Eras**
	Bold	**ITC Eras**
	Ultra	**ITC Eras**
Erbar Condensed ❖ *Linotype Headliners*	Light Condensed	Erbar Condensed
	Bold Condensed	**Erbar Condensed**
ITC Esprit	Book	ITC Esprit
	Book Italic	*ITC Esprit*
	Medium	ITC Esprit
	Medium Italic	*ITC Esprit*
	Bold	**ITC Esprit**
	Bold Italic	***ITC Esprit***
	Black	**ITC Esprit**
	Black Italic	***ITC Esprit***
European Pi ❖ *Linotype PiSet 2*	One	5 9 4 15 16 5 1 14
	Two	√ × + ≤ ~ μ α °
	Three	
	Four	© ← ©
Eurostile 1	Medium	Eurostile
	Medium Oblique	*Eurostile*
	Demi	**Eurostile**
	Demi Oblique	***Eurostile***
	Bold	**Eurostile**
	Bold Oblique	***Eurostile***
Eurostile 2	Condensed	Eurostile
	Bold Condensed	**Eurostile**
	Extended No. Two	Eurostile
	Bold Extended No. Two	**Eurostile**
Excelsior	Roman	Excelsior
	Italic	*Excelsior*
	Bold	**Excelsior**
Excelsior Cyrillic	Upright	Абвгдеж Зикл
	Inclined	*Абвгдеж Зикл*
	Bold Upright	**Абвгдеж Зикл**
Excelsior EastA	Roman	Áćęłőşť Čąďíňż
	Italic	*Áćęłőşť Čąďíňż*
	Bold	**Áćęłőşť Čąďíňż**
Fairfield 1	45-Light	Fairfield
	46-Light Italic	*Fairfield*
	55-Medium	Fairfield
	56-Medium Italic	*Fairfield*
	75-Bold	**Fairfield**
	76-Bold Italic	***Fairfield***
	85-Heavy	**Fairfield**

. . . Fairfield 1
86-Heavy Italic Fairfield

Fairfield 2
45-Light SCOSF FAIRFIELD 12345...
46-Light Italic Swash Caps OSF ABCDEF 12345...
55-Medium SCOSF FAIRFIELD 12345...
56-Medium Italic Swash Caps OSF ABCDEF 12345...
75-Bold SCOSF FAIRFIELD 12345...
76-Bold Italic Swash Caps OSF ABCDEF 1234...
85-Heavy SCOSF FAIRFIELD 1234...
86-Heavy Italic Swash Caps OSF ABCDEF 123...
45-Caption Light Fairfield
55-Caption Medium Fairfield
75-Caption Bold Fairfield
85-Caption Heavy Fairfield

Falstaff
✤ Monotype DisplaySet 2 Falstaff

ITC Fenice
Light ITC Fenice
Light Oblique ITC Fenice
Roman ITC Fenice
Oblique ITC Fenice
Bold ITC Fenice
Bold Oblique ITC Fenice
Ultra ITC Fenice
Ultra Oblique ITC Fenice

Fette Fraktur
✤ Linotype DisplaySet 1
Regular Fette Fraktur
Dfr chckfffftllſsſiſſßʒäöü

ITC Flora
Medium ITC Flora
Bold ITC Flora

Flyer Black
✤ Linotype DisplaySet 2
Black Condensed Flyer Black
Extra Black Condensed Flyer Black

Folio
Light Folio
Medium Folio
Bold Folio
Extra Bold Folio
Bold Condensed Folio

Forte
✤ Monotype ScriptSet 3 Forte

Franklin Gothic
No. 2 Roman Franklin Gothic
Condensed Franklin Gothic
Extra Condensed Franklin Gothic

ITC Franklin Gothic
Book ITC Franklin Gothic

. . . ITC Franklin Gothic
Book Oblique ITC Franklin Gothic
Demi ITC Franklin Gothic
Demi Oblique ITC Franklin Gothic
Heavy ITC Franklin Gothic
Heavy Oblique ITC Franklin Gothic

Freestyle Script
✤ Adobe DisplaySet 1 Freestyle Script

Friz Quadrata
✤ Adobe DisplaySet 3
Regular Friz Quadrata
Bold Friz Quadrata

Frutiger 1
45-Light Frutiger
46-Light Italic Frutiger
65-Bold Frutiger
66-Bold Italic Frutiger

Frutiger 2
55-Regular Frutiger
56-Italic Frutiger
75-Black Frutiger
76-Black Italic Frutiger
95-Ultra Black Frutiger

Frutiger Condensed
47-Light Condensed Frutiger
57-Condensed Frutiger
67-Bold Condensed Frutiger
77-Black Condensed Frutiger
87-Extra Black Condensed Frutiger

Futura 1
Light Futura
Light Oblique Futura
Book Futura
Book Oblique Futura
Bold Futura
Bold Oblique Futura

Futura 2
Medium Futura
Medium Oblique Futura
Heavy Futura
Heavy Oblique Futura
Extra Bold Futura
Extra Bold Oblique Futura

Futura 3
Light Condensed Futura
Light Condensed Oblique Futura
Condensed Futura
Condensed Oblique Futura

. . . Futura 3
Bold Condensed Futura
Bold Condensed Oblique Futura
Extra Bold Condensed Futura
Extra Bold Condensed Oblique Futura

ITC Galliard 1
Roman ITC Galliard
Italic ITC Galliard
Bold ITC Galliard
Bold Italic ITC Galliard

ITC Galliard 2
Black ITC Galliard
Black Italic ITC Galliard
Ultra ITC Galliard
Ultra Italic ITC Galliard

Linotype Game Pi
Chess Draughts
Dice Dominoes
English Cards KING QUEEN JACK 10 TEN 9 NINE JOKER A ACE
French Cards

Stempel Garamond
Roman Stempel Garamond
Italic Stempel Garamond
Bold Stempel Garamond
Bold Italic Stempel Garamond

Stempel Garamond SCOSF
Roman SCOSF S GARAMOND 123...
Roman OSF osf 12345...
Italic OSF osf 12345...
Bold OSF osf 12345...
Bold Italic OSF osf 12345...

Stempel Garamond EastA
Roman Áćęłőşť Čąđíňż
Italic Áćęłőşť Čąđíňż
Bold Áćęłőşť Čąđíňż
Bold Italic Áćęłőşť Čąđíňż

Garamond 3
Roman Garamond 3
Italic Garamond 3
Bold Garamond 3
Bold Italic Garamond 3

Garamond 3 SCOSF
Roman SCOSF GARAMOND 3 1234...
Italic OSF osf 12345...
Bold SCOSF GARAMOND 3 1234...
Bold Italic OSF osf 12345...

Simoncini Garamond
Roman S Garamond

✤ See page 592 for contents of Linotype-Hell Multi-Font Packages.

ff

Family	Style	Sample
... Simoncini Garamond	Italic	*S Garamond*
	Bold	**S Garamond**
ITC Garamond 1	Light	ITC Garamond
	Light Italic	*ITC Garamond*
	Bold	**ITC Garamond**
	Bold Italic	***ITC Garamond***
ITC Garamond 2	Book	ITC Garamond
	Book Italic	*ITC Garamond*
	Ultra	**ITC Garamond**
	Ultra Italic	***ITC Garamond***
ITC Garamond Condensed	Light Condensed	ITC Garamond
	Light Condensed Italic	*ITC Garamond*
	Book Condensed	ITC Garamond
	Book Condensed Italic	*ITC Garamond*
	Bold Condensed	**ITC Garamond**
	Bold Condensed Italic	***ITC Garamond***
	Ultra Condensed	**ITC Garamond**
	Ultra Condensed Italic	***ITC Garamond***
Adobe Garamond	Roman	Adobe Garamond
	Italic	*Adobe Garamond*
	Semibold	**Adobe Garamond**
	Semibold Italic	***Adobe Garamond***
	Bold	**Adobe Garamond**
	Bold Italic	***Adobe Garamond***
Adobe Garamond Expert & SCOSF	Expert Roman	A GARAMOND 1234 et al.
	Expert Italic	*12345 et al.*
	Expert Semibold	**12345 et al.**
	Expert Semibold Italic	***12345 et al.***
	Expert Bold	**12345 et al.**
	Expert Bold Italic	***12345 et al.***
	Roman SCOSF	A Garamond 12345...
	Italic OSF	*osf 12345...*
	Semibold SCOSF	**A Garamond 12345...**
	Semibold Italic OSF	***osf 12345...***
	Bold OSF	**osf 12345...**
	Bold Italic OSF	***osf 12345...***
	Titling Caps	A GARAMOND
	Alternate Roman	aenrrtctzQ
... Adobe Garamond Expert & SCOSF	Alternate Italic	*v&ct st ABCDEF*
Garth Graphic	Roman	Garth Graphic
	Italic	*Garth Graphic*
	Bold	**Garth Graphic**
	Bold Italic	***Garth Graphic***
	Extra Bold	**Garth Graphic**
	Black	**Garth Graphic**
	Condensed	Garth Graphic
	Bold Condensed	**Garth Graphic**
Gazette	Roman	Gazette
	Italic	*Gazette*
	Bold	**Gazette**
Gill Sans 1	Light	Gill Sans
	Light Italic	*Gill Sans*
	Regular	Gill Sans
	Italic	*Gill Sans*
	Bold	**Gill Sans**
	Bold Italic	***Gill Sans***
Gill Sans 2	Condensed	Gill Sans
	Bold Condensed	**Gill Sans**
	Extra Bold	**Gill Sans**
	Ultra Bold	**Gill Sans**
	Ultra Bold Condensed	**Gill Sans**
Gill Sans Display	Bold Extra Condensed	**Gill Sans**
	Display Extra Bold	**Gill Sans**
	Light Shadowed	Gill Sans
	Shadow	GILL SANS
ITC Giovanni	Book	ITC Giovanni
	Book Italic	*ITC Giovanni*
	Bold	**ITC Giovanni**
	Bold Italic	***ITC Giovanni***
	Black	**ITC Giovanni**
	Black Italic	***ITC Giovanni***
Glypha 1	55-Roman	Glypha
	55-Oblique	*Glypha*
	65-Bold	**Glypha**
	65-Bold Oblique	***Glypha***
Glypha 2	35-Thin	Glypha
... Glypha 2	35-Thin Oblique	*Glypha*
	45-Light	Glypha
	45-Light Oblique	*Glypha*
	75-Black	**Glypha**
	75-Black Oblique	***Glypha***
Gothic 13 ✤ *Linotype DisplaySet 3*		**Gothic 13**
Goudy Old Style	Roman	Goudy Old Style
	Italic	*Goudy Old Style*
	Bold	**Goudy Old Style**
	Bold Italic	***Goudy Old Style***
Goudy SCOSF	Old Style Roman SCOSF	Goudy 12345...
	Old Style Italic OSF	*osf 12345...*
	Bold OSF	**osf 12345...**
	Bold Italic OSF	***osf 12345...***
Goudy	Extra Bold	**Goudy**
	Heavyface	**Goudy Heavy**
	Heavyface Italic	***Goudy Heavy***
Monotype Goudy Modern ✤ *Monotype TextSet 1*	Roman	M Goudy Modern
	Italic	*M Goudy Modern*
Goudy Text & Lombardic Capitals	Regular	Goudy Text
	Dfr	chckfffftllſsſiſſßtzäöü
	Alternate	ff fi fl ffi ffl G T J B T
	Lombardic Capitals	LOMBARDIC
Granjon	Roman	Granjon
	Italic	*Granjon*
	Bold	**Granjon**
Granjon SCOSF	Roman SCOSF	Granjon 12345...
	Italic OSF	*osf 12345...*
	Bold OSF	**osf 12345...**
Monotype Grotesque 1	Light No. 126	M Grotesque
	Light Italic No. 126	*M Grotesque*
	Regular No. 215	M Grotesque
	Italic No. 215	*M Grotesque*
	Bold No. 216	**M Grotesque**
	Black No. 216	**M Grotesque**
Monotype Grotesque 2	Light Condensed No. 126	M Grotesque
	Condensed No. 215	M Grotesque
	Extra Condensed No. 215	M Grotesque

ff

Font	Style	Sample
. . . Monotype Grotesque 2	Bold Extended No. 216	M Grotesque
Guardi	55-Roman	Guardi
	56-Italic	*Guardi*
	75-Bold	**Guardi**
	76-Bold Italic	***Guardi***
	95-Black	**Guardi**
	96-Black Italic	***Guardi***
Helvetica	Light	Helvetica
	Light Oblique	*Helvetica*
	Black	**Helvetica**
	Black Oblique	***Helvetica***
Helvetica Condensed	Light Condensed	Helvetica
	Light Condensed Oblique	*Helvetica*
	Condensed	Helvetica
	Condensed Oblique	*Helvetica*
	Bold Condensed	**Helvetica**
	Bold Condensed Oblique	***Helvetica***
	Black Condensed	**Helvetica**
	Black Condensed Oblique	***Helvetica***
Helvetica Compressed	Compressed	Helvetica
	Extra Compressed	Helvetica
	Ultra Compressed	Helvetica
Helvetica Inserat ❖ *Linotype DisplaySet 1*		Helvetica Inserat
Helvetica Fractions ❖ *Linotype Fraction Pi*	Regular	½ ½ ⅓ ⅓ 63/64 $\frac{63}{64}$ 22/7 $\frac{22}{7}$
	Bold	**½ ½ ⅓ ⅓ 63/64 $\frac{63}{64}$ 22/7 $\frac{22}{7}$**
Helvetica Cyrillic	Upright	Абвгдеж Зикл
	Inclined	*Абвгдеж Зикл*
	Bold Upright	**Абвгдеж Зикл**
	Bold Inclined	***Абвгдеж Зикл***
Helvetica Monotonic Greek	Upright	Αβγδε Ζζηθικ
	Inclined	*Αβγδε Ζζηθικ*
	Bold Upright	**Αβγδε Ζζηθικ**
	Bold Inclined	***Αβγδε Ζζηθικ***
Helvetica Polytonic Greek	Upright	Αβγδἕ Ζζῆθΐκ
	Inclined	*Αβγδἕ Ζζῆθΐκ*
	Bold Upright	**Αβγδἕ Ζζῆθΐκ**
	Bold Inclined	***Αβγδἕ Ζζῆθΐκ***
Helvetica Inserat Cyrillic	Upright	Абвгдеж Зикл

Font	Style	Sample
Helvetica Rounded	Bold	**Helvetica Round**
	Bold Oblique	***Helvetica Round***
	Black	**Helvetica Roun**
	Black Oblique	***Helvetica Roun***
	Bold Condensed	**Helvetica Rounded**
	Bold Condensed Oblique	***Helvetica Rounded***
Neue Helvetica 1	25-Ultra Light	Neue Helvetica
	26-Ultra Light Italic	*Neue Helvetica*
	95-Black	**Neue Helvetica**
	96-Black Italic	***Neue Helvetica***
Neue Helvetica 2	35-Thin	Neue Helvetica
	36-Thin Italic	*Neue Helvetica*
	55-Regular	Neue Helvetica
	56-Italic	*Neue Helvetica*
	75-Bold	**Neue Helvetica**
	76-Bold Italic	***Neue Helvetica***
Neue Helvetica 3	45-Light	Neue Helvetica
	46-Light Italic	*Neue Helvetica*
	65-Medium	Neue Helvetica
	66-Medium Italic	*Neue Helvetica*
	85-Heavy	**Neue Helvetica**
	86-Heavy Italic	***Neue Helvetica***
Neue Helvetica Condensed 1	27-Ultra Light Condensed	Neue Helvetica
	27-Ultra Light Condensed Oblique	*Neue Helvetica*
	97-Black Condensed	**Neue Helvetica**
	97-Black Condensed Oblique	***Neue Helvetica***
	107-Extra Black Condensed	**Neue Helvetica**
	107-Extra Black Condensed Oblique	***Neue Helvetica***
Neue Helvetica Condensed 2	37-Thin Condensed	Neue Helvetica
	37-Thin Condensed Oblique	*Neue Helvetica*
	57-Condensed	Neue Helvetica
	57-Condensed Oblique	*Neue Helvetica*
	77-Bold Condensed	**Neue Helvetica**
	77-Bold Condensed Oblique	***Neue Helvetica***
Neue Helvetica Condensed 3	47-Light Condensed	Neue Helvetica
	47-Light Condensed Oblique	*Neue Helvetica*
	67-Medium Condensed	Neue Helvetica
	67-Medium Condensed Oblique	*Neue Helvetica*

Font	Style	Sample
. . . Neue Helvetica Condensed 3	87-Heavy Condensed	**Neue Helvetica**
	87-Heavy Condensed Oblique	***Neue Helvetica***
Neue Helvetica Extended 1	23-Ultra Light Extended	Neue Helvetica
	23-Ultra Light Extended Oblique	*Neue Helvetica*
	93-Black Extended	**N Helvetica**
	93-Black Extended Oblique	***N Helvetica***
Neue Helvetica Extended 2	33-Thin Extended	Neue Helvetica
	33-Thin Extended Oblique	*Neue Helvetica*
	53-Extended	Neue Helvetica
	53-Extended Oblique	*Neue Helvetica*
	73-Bold Extended	**NeueHelvetica**
	73-Bold Extended Oblique	***NeueHelvetica***
Neue Helvetica Extended 3	43-Light Extended	Neue Helvetica
	43-Light Extended Oblique	*Neue Helvetica*
	63-Medium Extended	Neue Helvetica
	63-Medium Extended Oblique	*Neue Helvetica*
	83-Heavy Extended	**N Helvetica**
	83-Heavy Extended Oblique	***N Helvetica***
Neue Helvetica Bold Outline	75-Bold Outline	Neue Helvetica
Neue Helvetica EastA	35-Thin	Áćęłőşť Čąđíňż
	35-Thin Oblique	*Áćęłőşť Čąđíňż*
	55-Regular	Áćęłőşť Čąđíňż
	55-Oblique	*Áćęłőşť Čąđíňż*
	75-Bold	**Áćęłőşť Čąđíňż**
	75-Bold Oblique	***Áćęłőşť Čąđíňż***
Herculanum ❖ *Type Before Gutenberg 1*		HERCULANUM
Hiroshige	Book	Hiroshige
	Book Italic	*Hiroshige*
	Medium	Hiroshige
	Medium Italic	*Hiroshige*
	Bold	**Hiroshige**
	Bold Italic	***Hiroshige***
	Black	**Hiroshige**
	Black Italic	***Hiroshige***
Hobo ❖ *Adobe DisplaySet 4*		Hobo
Linotype Holiday Pi	One	[pictograms]
	Two	[pictograms]
	Three	[pictograms] GAS … TV ROOM

ff

❖ *See page 592 for contents of Linotype-Hell Multi-Font Packages.*

Horley Old Style
Light Horley Old Style
Light Italic *Horley Old Style*
Roman Horley Old Style
Italic *Horley Old Style*
Semibold Horley Old Style
Semibold Italic *Horley Old Style*
Bold **Horley Old Style**
Bold Italic ***Horley Old Style***

Stempel Hot Metal Borders
One
Two
Three
Four

Impact
✤ *Adobe DisplaySet 2* **Impact**

Impressum
Roman Impressum
Italic *Impressum*
Bold **Impressum**

Industria
✤ *Brody DisplaySet 1*
Solid + Alternate Industria qlt
Inline + Alternate Industria qlt

Inflex Bold
✤ *Monotype DisplaySet 2* **Inflex Bold**

Insignia
✤ *Brody DisplaySet 1*
Regular Insignia
Alternate stEJSZ

Ironwood
✤ *Adobe Wood Type 1* IRONWOOD

ITC Isadora
Regular ITC Isadora
Bold **ITC Isadora**

Italia
Book Italia
Medium Italia
Bold **Italia**

Monotype Italian Old Style
Roman M Italian Old Style
Italic *M Italian Old Style*
Bold **M Italian Old Style**
Bold Italic ***M Italian Old Style***

Janson Text
55-Roman Janson Text
56-Italic *Janson Text*
75-Bold **Janson Text**
76-Bold Italic ***Janson Text***

Janson Text SCOSF
55-Roman SCOSF JANSON TEXT 1234...
56-Italic OSF *osf 12345...*

. . . **Janson Text SCOSF**
75-Bold OSF **osf 12345...**
76-Bold Italic OSF ***osf 12345...***

Joanna
Roman Joanna
Italic *Joanna*
Semibold Joanna
Semibold Italic *Joanna*
Bold **Joanna**
Bold Italic ***Joanna***
Extra Bold **Joanna**

Juniper
✤ *Adobe Wood Type 1* JUNIPER

Kabel
Light Kabel
Book Kabel
Heavy Kabel
Black **Kabel**

ITC Kabel
Book ITC Kabel
Medium ITC Kabel
Demi ITC Kabel
Bold **ITC Kabel**
Ultra **ITC Kabel**

Kaufmann
Regular *Kaufmann*
Bold ***Kaufmann***

Kino
✤ *Monotype DisplaySet 3* Kino

Klang
✤ *Monotype ScriptSet 3* Klang

ITC Korinna
Roman ITC Korinna
Kursiv *ITC Korinna*
Bold **ITC Korinna**
Bold Kursiv ***ITC Korinna***

Künstler Script
Medium *Künstler Script*
No. 2 Bold *Künstler Script*
Black ***Künstler Script***

Latin Condensed
✤ *Monotype DisplaySet 4* Latin Condensed

ITC Leawood
Book ITC Leawood
Book Italic *ITC Leawood*
Medium ITC Leawood
Medium Italic *ITC Leawood*
Bold **ITC Leawood**
Bold Italic ***ITC Leawood***
Black **ITC Leawood**

. . . **ITC Leawood**
Black Italic ***ITC Leawood***

ITC Legacy Serif
Book ITC Legacy
Book Italic *ITC Legacy*
Medium ITC Legacy
Medium Italic *ITC Legacy*
Bold **ITC Legacy**
Bold Italic ***ITC Legacy***
Ultra **ITC Legacy**

ITC Legacy Sans
Book ITC Legacy
Book Italic *ITC Legacy*
Medium ITC Legacy
Medium Italic *ITC Legacy*
Bold **ITC Legacy**
Bold Italic ***ITC Legacy***
Ultra **ITC Legacy**

Letter Gothic
Regular Letter Gothic
Slanted *Letter Gothic*
Bold Letter Gothic
Bold Slanted *Letter Gothic*

Life
Roman Life
Italic *Life*
Bold **Life**

LinoLetter
Roman LinoLetter
Italic *LinoLetter*
Medium LinoLetter
Medium Italic *LinoLetter*
Bold **LinoLetter**
Bold Italic ***LinoLetter***
Black **LinoLetter**
Black Italic ***LinoLetter***

LinoLetter SCOSF
Roman SCOSF LINOLETTER 1234
Roman OSF osf 12345...
Italic OSF *osf 12345...*
Medium SCOSF LINOLETTER 1234
Medium OSF osf 12345...
Medium Italic OSF *osf 12345...*
Bold SCOSF **LINOLETTER 1234**
Bold OSF **osf 12345...**

. . . LinoLetter SCOSF	Bold Italic OSF	*osf 12345...*
	Black SCOSF	**LinoLetter 123**
	Black OSF	**osf 12345...**
	Black Italic OSF	***osf 12345...***
Linoscript ✤ *Linotype ScriptSet 2*		Linoscript
Linotext ✤ *Linotype ScriptSet 2*	Regular	Linotext
	Dfr	ch ck ff ft ll ſs ſi ſſ tz tz ä ö ü
Lithos	Extra Light	LITHOS
	Light	LITHOS
	Regular	LITHOS
	Bold	**LITHOS**
	Black	**LITHOS**
ITC Lubalin Graph	Book	ITC Lubalin
	Book Oblique	*ITC Lubalin*
	Demi	**ITC Lubalin**
	Demi Oblique	***ITC Lubalin***
Lucida	Roman	Lucida
	Italic	*Lucida*
	Bold	**Lucida**
	Bold Italic	***Lucida***
Lucida Sans	Regular	Lucida Sans
	Italic	*Lucida Sans*
	Bold	**Lucida Sans**
	Bold Italic	***Lucida Sans***
Lucida Math	Italic	*ABCdefΦμΣψξΩ*
	Symbol	ABC∞△▽→♡≤
	Extension	⊙⊕⊗∑√∫∮⊎↓↑
ITC Machine	Medium	ITC MACHINE
	Bold	**ITC MACHINE**
Madame ✤ *Linotype DisplaySet 4*	Letters	MADAME
	Numericals	1 2 3 4 5 6 7 $!
	Accents	Á Ò Ł Š Ñ Ă Ž Ù
Madrone ✤ *Adobe Wood Type 2*		Madrone
Marigold ✤ *Baker Calligraphy*		Marigold
Mathematical Pi	One	÷ = ± ∓ ≪ ≫ ≤ ≥ ≦ ≧
	Two	↶ ↷ ↵ ↷ ↦ ¦ ---- a b c d
	Three	{∲⟧∫}⟨Σ⟩∯⟩⟦Π√⟧ ⩓ ⩔ ⊼
	Four	⊄ ⊆ ⊊ ⊇ ⊋ ⋐ ⋑ ∝ ≠ ∈
. . . Mathematical Pi	Five	⌒ < ⋚ ≈ < ≦ < ⋛ ≶ ⋚
	Six	◫ ◭ □ ◇ ◪ ▶ ◨ ☆ ≟
Matura ✤ *Monotype DisplaySet 3*	Regular	**Matura**
	Scriptorial Caps	MATURA
Maximus ✤ *Linotype ClassAdSet 1*		Maximus
Medici Script ✤ *Linotype ScriptSet 1*		*Medici Script*
Melior	Roman	Melior
	Italic	*Melior*
	Bold	**Melior**
	Bold Italic	***Melior***
Memphis	Light	Memphis
	Light Italic	*Memphis*
	Medium	Memphis
	Medium Italic	*Memphis*
	Bold	**Memphis**
	Bold Italic	***Memphis***
	Extra Bold	**Memphis**
ITC Mendoza Roman	Book	ITC Mendoza
	Book Italic	*ITC Mendoza*
	Medium	ITC Mendoza
	Medium Italic	*ITC Mendoza*
	Bold	**ITC Mendoza**
	Bold Italic	***ITC Mendoza***
Mercurius Bold Script ✤ *Monotype ScriptSet 3*		***Mercurius Bold***
Meridien	Roman	Meridien
	Italic	*Meridien*
	Medium	Meridien
	Medium Italic	*Meridien*
	Bold	**Meridien**
	Bold Italic	***Meridien***
Mesquite ✤ *Adobe Wood Type 1*		MESQUITE
Metro ✤ *Linotype Headliners*	Metrolite	Metro
	Metromedium	Metro
	Metroblack	**Metro**
MICR ✤ *OCR Set 1*		⑆ 1 2 3 4 5 6 7 8 9 0
Minion	Roman	Minion
	Italic	*Minion*
. . . Minion	Semibold	Minion
	Semibold Italic	*Minion*
	Bold	**Minion**
	Bold Italic	***Minion***
	Black	**Minion**
	Display Roman	Minion
	Display Italic	*Minion*
Minion Expert & SCOSF	Expert Roman	MINION 12345 et al.
	Expert Italic	*12345 et al.*
	Expert Semibold	12345 et al.
	Expert Semibold Italic	*12345 et al.*
	Expert Bold	**12345 et al.**
	Expert Bold Italic	***12345 et al.***
	Expert Black	**12345 et al.**
	Expert Display Roman	MINION 1234...
	Expert Display Italic	*12345 et al.*
	Roman SCOSF	Minion 12345...
	Italic SCOSF	*Minion 12345...*
	Semibold SCOSF	Minion 12345...
	Semibold Italic SCOSF	*Minion 12345...*
	Bold OSF	**osf 12345...**
	Bold Italic OSF	***osf 12345...***
	Black OSF	**osf 12345...**
	Display Roman SCOSF	Minion 123...
	Display Italic SCOSF	*Minion 123...*
	Italic Swash Capitals	*MINION*
	Semibold Italic Swash Capitals	*MINION*
	Display Italic Swash Capitals	*MINION*
	Ornaments	❧ ❦ ❧ ✿ ~ ~
Minion Cyrillic	Upright	Абвгдеж Зикл
	Inclined	*Абвгдеж Зикл*
	Semibold Upright	Абвгдеж Зикл
	Semibold Inclined	*Абвгдеж Зикл*
	Bold Upright	**Абвгдеж Зикл**
	Bold Inclined	***Абвгдеж Зикл***
Minister	Light	Minister
	Light Italic	*Minister*
	Book	Minister

ff

✤ *See page 592 for contents of Linotype-Hell Multi-Font Packages.*

... Minister Book Italic — *Minister*
Bold — **Minister**
Bold Italic — ***Minister***
Black — **Minister**
Black Italic — ***Minister***

Mistral ✣ Adobe ScriptSet 1 — Mistral

ITC Mona Lisa ✣ ITC Typographica Recut — ITC Mona Lisa
Solid — ITC Mona Lisa

Monoline Script ✣ Monotype ScriptSet 1 — Monoline Script

Monotype Modern Condensed — Monotype Modern
Condensed Italic — *Monotype Modern*
Extended — Monotype Modern
Extended Italic — *Monotype Modern*
Bold — **Monotype Modern**
Bold Italic — ***Monotype Modern***
Wide — M Modern
Wide Italic — *M Modern*

Neuzeit S Book — Neuzeit S
Heavy — **Neuzeit S**

New Berolina ✣ Monotype ScriptSet 1 — New Berolina

News Gothic Regular — News Gothic
Oblique — *News Gothic*
Bold — **News Gothic**
Bold Oblique — ***News Gothic***

Notre Dame ✣ Type Before Gutenberg 3 Regular — Notre Dame
Dfr — chckffftllſsſiſſäöü
Ornaments

ITC Novarese Book — ITC Novarese
Book Italic — *ITC Novarese*
Medium — ITC Novarese
Medium Italic — *ITC Novarese*
Bold — **ITC Novarese**
Bold Italic — ***ITC Novarese***
Ultra — **ITC Novarese**

Nuptial Script ✣ Linotype ScriptSet 1 — Nuptial Script

OCR-A & Alternate ✣ OCR Set 1 — OCR-A

OCR-B & Alternate ✣ OCR Set 1 — OCR-B

Octavian + Expert & SCOSF Roman — Octavian

... Octavian + Expert & SCOSF Italic — *Octavian*
Expert Roman — OCTAVIAN 12345 et al.
Expert Italic — *12345 et al.*
Roman SCOSF — OCTAVIAN 12345...
Italic OSF — *osf 12345...*

ITC Officina Serif Book — ITC Officina
Book Italic — *ITC Officina*
Bold — **ITC Officina**
Bold Italic — ***ITC Officina***

ITC Officina Sans Book — ITC Officina
Book Italic — *ITC Officina*
Bold — **ITC Officina**
Bold Italic — ***ITC Officina***

Old Style No. 7 + SCOSF Roman — Old Style No. 7
Italic — *Old Style No. 7*
Roman SCOSF — OLD STYLE NO. 7 123...
Italic OSF — *osf 12345...*

MT Old Style Bold Outline ✣ Monotype DisplaySet 2 — M Old Style

Olympian Roman — Olympian
Italic — *Olympian*
Bold — **Olympian**
Bold Italic — ***Olympian***

Omnia ✣ Type Before Gutenberg 1 — OMNIA

Onyx ✣ Monotype DisplaySet 4 — Onyx

Optima Roman — Optima
Oblique — *Optima*
Bold — **Optima**
Bold Oblique — ***Optima***

Optima EastA Roman — Áćęłőșť Čąđíňż
Oblique — *Áćęłőșť Čąđíňż*
Bold — **Áćęłőșť Čąđíňż**
Bold Oblique — ***Áćęłőșť Čąđíňż***

Orator Regular — ORATOR
Slanted — *ORATOR*

Oxford ✣ Baker Calligraphy — Oxford

ITC Ozwald ✣ ITC Typographica — ITC Ozwald

Palace Script ✣ Monotype ScriptSet 1 Regular — Palace Script
Semibold — Palace Script

Palatino 1 Roman — Palatino
Italic — *Palatino*
Bold — **Palatino**
Bold Italic — ***Palatino***

Palatino 2 Light — Palatino
Light Italic — *Palatino*
Medium — Palatino
Medium Italic — *Palatino*
Black — **Palatino**
Black Italic — ***Palatino***

Palatino SCOSF Roman SCOSF — PALATINO 12345...
Italic OSF — *osf 12345...*
Bold OSF — **osf 12345...**
Bold Italic OSF — ***osf 12345...***

Parisian ✣ Adobe DisplaySet 5 — Parisian

Park Avenue — Park Avenue

Peignot Light — PEIGNOT
Demi — PEIGNOT
Bold — **PEIGNOT**

Pelican ✣ Baker Calligraphy — Pelican

Pepita ✣ Monotype ScriptSet 2 — Pepita

Perpetua Roman — Perpetua
Italic — *Perpetua*
Bold — **Perpetua**
Bold Italic — ***Perpetua***

Perpetua Expert & SCOSF Expert Roman — PERPETUA 12345 et al.
Expert Italic — *12345 et al.*
Expert Bold — **12345 et al.**
Expert Bold Italic — ***12345 et al.***
Roman SCOSF — PERPETUA 12345...
Italic OSF — *osf 12345...*
Bold OSF — **osf 12345...**
Bold Italic OSF — ***osf 12345...***

Photina Roman — Photina
Italic — *Photina*
Semibold — **Photina**
Semibold Italic — ***Photina***
Bold — **Photina**

ff

. . . Photina
Bold Italic Photina
Ultra Bold Photina
Ultra Bold Italic Photina
Plak
Linotype Headliners
Black Plak
Black Condensed Plak
Black Extra Condensed Plak
Plantin 1
Roman Plantin
Italic Plantin
Bold Plantin
Bold Italic Plantin
Plantin 2
Light Plantin
Light Italic Plantin
Semibold Plantin
Semibold Italic Plantin
Bold Condensed Plantin
Poetica 1 + Expert & SCOSF
Chancery I Poetica
Chancery II Poetica
Chancery III Poetica
Chancery IV Poetica
Expert Chancery 12345...
Chancery SCOSF POETICA 12345...
Chancery SCOSF Alternate
Poetica 2 Supplement
LC Alternates I
LC Alternates II
LC Beginnings I
LC Beginnings II
LC Endings I
LC Endings II
Ampersands
Ligatures
Initial Swash Caps
Swash Caps I POETICA
Swash Caps II POETICA
Swash Caps III POETICA
Swash Caps IV POETICA
Ornaments
Pompeijana
Type Before Gutenberg 3
Regular POMPEIJANA
Borders

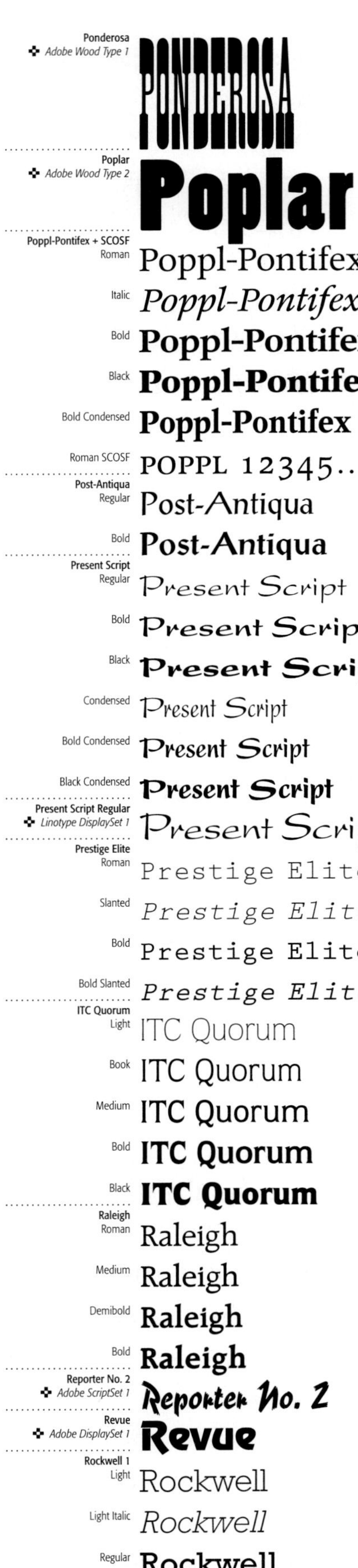
Ponderosa
Adobe Wood Type 1
PONDEROSA
Poplar
Adobe Wood Type 2
Poplar
Poppl-Pontifex + SCOSF
Roman Poppl-Pontifex
Italic Poppl-Pontifex
Bold Poppl-Pontifex
Black Poppl-Pontifex
Bold Condensed Poppl-Pontifex
Roman SCOSF POPPL 12345...
Post-Antiqua
Regular Post-Antiqua
Bold Post-Antiqua
Present Script
Regular Present Script
Bold Present Script
Black Present Script
Condensed Present Script
Bold Condensed Present Script
Black Condensed Present Script
Present Script Regular
Linotype DisplaySet 1
Present Script
Prestige Elite
Roman Prestige Elite
Slanted Prestige Elite
Bold Prestige Elite
Bold Slanted Prestige Elite
ITC Quorum
Light ITC Quorum
Book ITC Quorum
Medium ITC Quorum
Bold ITC Quorum
Black ITC Quorum
Raleigh
Roman Raleigh
Medium Raleigh
Demibold Raleigh
Bold Raleigh
Reporter No. 2
Adobe ScriptSet 1
Reporter No. 2
Revue
Adobe DisplaySet 1
Revue
Rockwell 1
Light Rockwell
Light Italic Rockwell
Regular Rockwell

. . . Rockwell 1
Italic Rockwell
Bold Rockwell
Bold Italic Rockwell
Rockwell 2
Condensed Rockwell
Bold Condensed Rockwell
Extra Bold Rockwell
Rotation
Roman Rotation
Italic Rotation
Bold Rotation
Agfa Rotis Sans Serif
45-Light Agfa Rotis
46-Light Italic Agfa Rotis
55-Regular Agfa Rotis
56-Italic Agfa Rotis
65-Bold Agfa Rotis
75-Extra Bold Agfa Rotis
Agfa Rotis Semisans
45-Light Agfa Rotis
46-Light Italic Agfa Rotis
55-Regular Agfa Rotis
56-Italic Agfa Rotis
65-Bold Agfa Rotis
75-Extra Bold Agfa Rotis
Agfa Rotis Semiserif & Serif
55-Roman Semiserif Agfa Rotis
65-Bold Semiserif Agfa Rotis
55-Roman Serif Agfa Rotis
56-Italic Serif Agfa Rotis
65-Bold Serif Agfa Rotis
Roundy
Linotype DisplaySet 4
Regular Roundy
Swash Capitals ROUNDY
Ruling Script
Calligraphy for Print
Regular RulingScript
Addition ꝏæœÆŒ$fifl
Runic Condensed
Monotype DisplaySet 4
Runic Condensed
Russell Square
Regular Russell Square
Oblique Russell Square
Rusticana
Type Before Gutenberg 3
Regular RUSTICANA
Borders
Ruzicka Freehand + SCOSF
Roman Ruzicka Freehand
Bold Ruzicka Freehand
Roman SCOSF R FREEHAND 12345...

See page 592 for contents of Linotype-Hell Multi-Font Packages.

. . . Ruzicka Freehand + SCOSF Bold SCOSF	R FREEHAND 12345...
Sabon Roman	Sabon
Italic	*Sabon*
Bold	**Sabon**
Bold Italic	***Sabon***
Sabon SCOSF Roman SCOSF	SABON 12345...
Italic OSF	*osf 12345...*
Bold OSF	**osf 12345...**
Bold Italic OSF	***osf 12345...***
San Marco ✤ *Type Before Gutenberg 2* Regular	San Marco
Dfr	chckfftllſsſiſſäöü
Sassoon Primary	Sassoon Primary
Stempel Schneidler Light	S Schneidler
Light Italic	*S Schneidler*
Roman	S Schneidler
Italic	*S Schneidler*
Medium	S Schneidler
Medium Italic	*S Schneidler*
Bold	**S Schneidler**
Bold Italic	***S Schneidler***
Black	**S Schneidler**
Black Italic	***S Schneidler***
Monotype Scotch Roman ✤ *Monotype TextSet 1* Roman	M Scotch Roman
Italic	*M Scotch Roman*
Monotype Script Bold ✤ *Monotype ScriptSet 2*	***Monotype Script***
ITC Serif Gothic Light	ITC Serif Gothic
Roman	ITC Serif Gothic
Bold	**ITC Serif Gothic**
Extra Bold	**ITC Serif Gothic**
Heavy	**ITC Serif Gothic**
Black	**ITC Serif Gothic**
Serifa 45-Light	Serifa
46-Light Italic	*Serifa*
55-Roman	Serifa
56-Italic	*Serifa*
65-Bold	**Serifa**
75-Black	**Serifa**
Serlio ✤ *Linotype Engravers Set 1*	SERLIO

Serpentine Light	Serpentine
Light Oblique	*Serpentine*
Medium	**Serpentine**
Medium Oblique	***Serpentine***
Bold	**Serpentine**
Bold Oblique	***Serpentine***
Shannon Book	Shannon
Book Oblique	*Shannon*
Bold	**Shannon**
Extra Bold	**Shannon**
Shelley Allegro	*Shelley*
Andante	*Shelley*
Volante	*Shelley*
Sho ✤ *Calligraphy for Print*	**Sho**
ITC Slimbach Book	ITC Slimbach
Book Italic	*ITC Slimbach*
Medium	ITC Slimbach
Medium Italic	*ITC Slimbach*
Bold	**ITC Slimbach**
Bold Italic	***ITC Slimbach***
Black	**ITC Slimbach**
Black Italic	***ITC Slimbach***
Smaragd ✤ *GudrunSchrift* Roman	SMARAGD
Alternate	ÄÖÜ
Snell Roundhand Regular	*Snell Roundhand*
Bold	***Snell Roundhand***
Black	***Snell Roundhand***
Sonata	
ITC Souvenir 1 Light	ITC Souvenir
Light Italic	*ITC Souvenir*
Demi	**ITC Souvenir**
Demi Italic	***ITC Souvenir***
ITC Souvenir 2 Medium	ITC Souvenir
Medium Italic	*ITC Souvenir*
Bold	**ITC Souvenir**
Bold Italic	***ITC Souvenir***
ITC Souvenir Monotonic Greek Light Upright	Αβγδε Ζζηθικ
Demi Upright	**Αβγδε Ζζηθικ**

ITC Souvenir Polytonic Greek Light Upright	Αβγδἕ Ζζῆθΐκ
Demi Upright	**Αβγδἕ Ζζῆθΐκ**
Spartan Classified Book	Spartan
Heavy	**Spartan**
Spectrum + Expert & SCOSF Roman	Spectrum
Italic	*Spectrum*
Semibold	**Spectrum**
Expert Roman	SPECTRUM 12345 et al.
Expert Italic	*12345 et al.*
Expert Semibold	**12345 et al.**
Roman SCOSF	SPECTRUM 12345...
Italic OSF	*osf 12345...*
Semibold OSF	**osf 12345...**
Stencil ✤ *Adobe DisplaySet 4*	**STENCIL**
ITC Stone Serif Medium	ITC Stone
Medium Italic	*ITC Stone*
Semibold	**ITC Stone**
Semibold Italic	***ITC Stone***
Bold	**ITC Stone**
Bold Italic	***ITC Stone***
ITC Stone Sans Medium	ITC Stone
Medium Italic	*ITC Stone*
Semibold	**ITC Stone**
Semibold Italic	***ITC Stone***
Bold	**ITC Stone**
Bold Italic	***ITC Stone***
ITC Stone Informal Medium	ITC Stone
Medium Italic	*ITC Stone*
Semibold	**ITC Stone**
Semibold Italic	***ITC Stone***
Bold	**ITC Stone**
Bold Italic	***ITC Stone***
ITC Stone Phonetic Serif IPA	ɑβçðɛɸɢʜɪɟʟɰɴɔ'
Serif Alternate	ƀčđɘƒɥǰʞλŋσþŗšɬ
Sans IPA	ɑβçðɛɸɢʜɪɟʟɰɴɔ'
Sans Alternate	ƀčđɘƒɥǰʞλŋσþŗšɬω
Stop ✤ *Linotype Headliners*	**STOP**
ITC Symbol Book	ITC Symbol

ff

ITC Symbol
Book Italic — *ITC Symbol*
Medium — ITC Symbol
Medium Italic — *ITC Symbol*
Bold — **ITC Symbol**
Bold Italic — ***ITC Symbol***
Black — **ITC Symbol**
Black Italic — ***ITC Symbol***

Syntax
Regular — Syntax
Italic — *Syntax*
Bold — **Syntax**
Black — **Syntax**
Ultra Black — **Syntax**

Linotype Technical Pi
One — SA CEBEC D Ex FI GL FA X
Two — SA D P D Ex GL Tx PTB ÖVE

Tekton
Regular — Tekton
Oblique — *Tekton*
Bold — **Tekton**
Bold Oblique — ***Tekton***

Tempo Heavy Condensed
✤ *Linotype DisplaySet 3*
Heavy Condensed — **Tempo**
Heavy Condensed Italic — ***Tempo***

Linotype Textile Pi
One — 30°C 40°C 60°C 80°C 30°C 86°F 30°C 140°F 60°C 203°F 95°C
Two — 30 40 60 30 86°F 30 140°F 60 203°F 95

ITC Tiffany
Medium — ITC Tiffany
Italic — *ITC Tiffany*
Demi — **ITC Tiffany**
Demi Italic — ***ITC Tiffany***
Heavy — **ITC Tiffany**
Heavy Italic — ***ITC Tiffany***

Times New Roman
Roman — Times New Roman
Italic — *Times New Roman*
Bold — **Times New Roman**
Bold Italic — ***Times New Roman***

Times New Roman Condensed
Roman — Times New Roman
Italic — *Times New Roman*
Bold — **Times New Roman**

Times 2
Semibold — **Times**
Semibold Italic — ***Times***
Extra Bold — **Times**

Times SCOSF
Roman SCOSF — TIMES 12345…
Italic OSF — *osf 12345…*
Bold SCOSF — **TIMES 12345…**
Bold Italic OSF — ***osf 12345…***

Times Phonetic
IPA — ɑʙçðɛɸɢʜɪɟɪʟɰɴɔ’
Alternate — ƀčđəʃɥǰʞλɳσþɼšɪω

Times Ten
Roman — Times Ten
Italic — *Times Ten*
Bold — **Times Ten**
Bold Italic — ***Times Ten***

Times Ten SCOSF
Roman SCOSF — TIMES 12345…
Roman OSF — osf 12345…
Italic OSF — *osf 12345…*
Bold OSF — **osf 12345…**
Bold Italic OSF — ***osf 12345…***

Times Ten Cyrillic
Upright — Абвгдеж Зикл
Inclined — *Абвгдеж Зикл*
Bold — **Абвгдеж Зикл**
Bold Inclined — ***Абвгдеж Зикл***

Times Eighteen
✤ *Linotype Headliners*
Roman — Times 18
Bold — **Times 18**

Times Ten East A
Roman — Áćęłőșť Čąđíňż
Italic — *Áćęłőșť Čąđíňż*
Bold — **Áćęłőșť Čąđíňż**
Bold Italic — ***Áćęłőșť Čąđíňż***

Times Ten Monotonic Greek
Upright — Αβγδε Ζζηθικ
Inclined — *Αβγδε Ζζηθικ*
Bold Upright — **Αβγδε Ζζηθικ**
Bold Inclined — ***Αβγδε Ζζηθικ***

Times Ten Polytonic Greek
Upright — Αβγδἕ Ζζῆθΐκ
Inclined — *Αβγδἕ Ζζῆθΐκ*
Bold Upright — **Αβγδἕ Ζζῆθΐκ**
Bold Inclined — ***Αβγδἕ Ζζῆθΐκ***

Times Europa
Roman — Times Europa
Italic — *Times Europa*
Bold — **Times Europa**
Bold Italic — ***Times Europa***

Trade Gothic
Light — Trade Gothic
Light Oblique — *Trade Gothic*
Regular — Trade Gothic
Oblique — *Trade Gothic*
Bold — **Trade Gothic**
Bold Oblique — ***Trade Gothic***
Bold No. 2 — **Trade Gothic**
Bold No. 2 Oblique — ***Trade Gothic***

Trade Gothic Condensed
18 Condensed — Trade Gothic
18 Condensed Oblique — *Trade Gothic*
20 Condensed Bold — **Trade Gothic**
20 Condensed Bold Oblique — ***Trade Gothic***

Trade Gothic Extended
Extended — Trade Gothic
Bold Extended — **Trade Gothic**

Trajan
✤ *Adobe TitlingSet 1*
Regular — TRAJAN
Bold — **TRAJAN**

Trump Mediäval
Roman — Trump Mediäval
Italic — *Trump Mediäval*
Bold — **Trump Mediäval**
Bold Italic — ***Trump Mediäval***

Trump Mediäval SCOSF
Roman SCOSF — T MEDIÄVAL 12345…
Italic OSF — *osf 12345…*
Bold OSF — **osf 12345…**
Bold Italic OSF — ***osf 12345…***

Umbra
✤ *Adobe DisplaySet 5*
UMBRA

Univers 1
45-Light — Univers
45-Light Oblique — *Univers*
55-Regular — Univers
55-Oblique — *Univers*
65-Bold — **Univers**
65-Bold Oblique — ***Univers***
75-Black — **Univers**
75-Black Oblique — ***Univers***

Univers 2
85-Extra Black — **Univers**
85-Extra Black Oblique — ***Univers***
39-Thin Ultra Condensed — Univers
49-Light Ultra Condensed — Univers
59-Ultra Condensed — **Univers**

ff

✤ *See page 592 for contents of Linotype-Hell Multi-Font Packages.*

Univers Condensed
47-Light Condensed Univers
47-Light Condensed Oblique *Univers*
57-Condensed Univers
57-Condensed Oblique *Univers*
67-Bold Condensed **Univers**
67-Bold Condensed Oblique ***Univers***

Univers Extended
53-Extended Univers
53-Extended Oblique *Univers*
63-Bold Extended **Univers**
63-Bold Extended Oblique ***Univers***
73-Black Extended **Univers**
73-Black Extended Oblique ***Univers***
93-Extra Black Extended **Univers**
93-Extra Black Extended Oblique ***Univers***

Linotype Universal Pi
✤ *Linotype Universal Pi*
Greek with Math Pi αβΨΔΩΣ+−×÷√
News with Commercial Pi ™ © # ♦ @ % ® ☎

University Roman
✤ *Adobe DisplaySet 1* University Roman

ITC Usherwood
Book ITC Usherwood
Book Italic *ITC Usherwood*
Medium ITC Usherwood
Medium Italic *ITC Usherwood*
Bold **ITC Usherwood**
Bold Italic ***ITC Usherwood***
Black **ITC Usherwood**
Black Italic ***ITC Usherwood***

Utopia
Roman Utopia
Italic *Utopia*
Semibold **Utopia**
Semibold Italic ***Utopia***
Bold **Utopia**
Bold Italic ***Utopia***
Black **Utopia**

Utopia Expert
Expert Roman UTOPIA 12345 et al.
Expert Italic *12345 et al.*
Expert Semibold **UTOPIA 12345 et al.**
Expert Semibold Italic ***12345 et al.***
Expert Bold **12345 et al.**
Expert Bold Italic ***12345 et al.***

. . . Utopia Expert
Expert Black ***12345 et al.***
Roman SCOSF UTOPIA 12345...
Italic OSF *osf 12345...*
Semibold SCOSF **UTOPIA 12345...**
Semibold Italic OSF ***osf 12345...***
Bold OSF **osf 12345...**
Bold Italic OSF ***osf 12345...***
Black OSF **osf 12345...**
Titling Capitals UTOPIA
Ornaments

VAG Rounded
Thin VAG Rounded
Light VAG Rounded
Bold **VAG Rounded**
Black **VAG Rounded**

Vectora
45-Light Vectora
46-Light Italic *Vectora*
55-Roman Vectora
56-Italic *Vectora*
75-Bold **Vectora**
76-Bold Italic ***Vectora***
95-Black **Vectora**
96-Black Italic ***Vectora***

ITC Veljovic
Book ITC Veljovic
Book Italic *ITC Veljovic*
Medium ITC Veljovic
Medium Italic *ITC Veljovic*
Bold **ITC Veljovic**
Bold Italic ***ITC Veljovic***
Black **ITC Veljovic**
Black Italic ***ITC Veljovic***

Versailles
45-Light Versailles
46-Light Italic *Versailles*
55-Roman Versailles
56-Italic *Versailles*
75-Bold **Versailles**
76-Bold Italic ***Versailles***
95-Black **Versailles**
96-Black Italic ***Versailles***

Visigoth
✤ *Baker Calligraphy* Visigoth

Walbaum Book
Roman Walbaum Book
Italic *Walbaum Book*
Bold **Walbaum Book**
Bold Italic ***Walbaum Book***

Walbaum SCOSF
Roman SCOSF WALBAUM 12345...
Roman OSF osf 12345...
Italic OSF *osf 12345...*
Bold OSF **osf 12345...**
Bold Italic OSF ***osf 12345...***

Linotype Warning Pi
✤ *Linotype PiSet 1*

ITC Weidemann
Book ITC Weidemann
Book Italic *ITC Weidemann*
Medium ITC Weidemann
Medium Italic *ITC Weidemann*
Bold **ITC Weidemann**
Bold Italic ***ITC Weidemann***
Black **ITC Weidemann**
Black Italic ***ITC Weidemann***

Weiss
Roman Weiss
Italic *Weiss*
Bold **Weiss**
Extra Bold **Weiss**

Wiesbaden Swing
✤ *Calligraphy for Print* Wiesbaden Swing

Wilhelm Klingspor Gotisch
✤ *Linotype DisplaySet 2*
Regular Wilhelm Klingspor
Dfr chckffffillſſiſſäöü

Wilke
55-Roman Wilke
56-Italic *Wilke*
75-Bold **Wilke**
76-Bold Italic ***Wilke***
95-Black **Wilke**
96-Black Italic ***Wilke***

Willow
✤ *Adobe Wood Type 2* Willow

Wittenberger Fraktur
✤ *Monotype DisplaySet 3*
Regular Wittenberger Fraktur
Dfr chckffllſsſiſſäöü
Bold **Wittenberger Fraktur**
Bold Dfr **chckffllſsſiſſäöü**

ff

AD Wood Type Ornaments 1 ✤ *Adobe Wood Type 1*	
AD Wood Type Ornaments 2 ✤ *Adobe Wood Type 2*	
Linotype Xmas Pi One	
Two	
ITC Zapf Chancery Medium Italic ✤ *ITC ZapfSet 1*	*ITC Zapf Chancery*
ITC Zapf Chancery Light	ITC Zapf Chancery
Light Italic	*ITC Zapf Chancery*
Regular	ITC Zapf Chancery
Italic	*ITC Zapf Chancery*
Demi	ITC Zapf Chancery
Bold	**ITC Zapf Chancery**
ITC Zapf Dingbats ✤ *ITC ZapfSet 1*	

Linotype-Hell Multi-Font Package Contents

✤ *Adobe DisplaySet 1*	: Aachen Bold, Freestyle Script, Revue, University Roman.
✤ *Adobe DisplaySet 2*	: Baker Signet, Impact.
✤ *Adobe DisplaySet 3*	: ITC Benguiat Book & Bold, Friz Quadrata Regular & Bold.
✤ *Adobe DisplaySet 4*	: Brush Script, Hobo, Stencil.
✤ *Adobe DisplaySet 5*	: Parisian, Umbra.
✤ *Adobe ScriptSet 1*	: Mistral, Reporter No. 2
✤ *Adobe TitlingSet 1*	: Charlemagne Regular & Bold, Trajan Regular & Bold.
✤ *Adobe Wood Type 1*	: Cottonwood, Ironwood, Juniper, Mesquite, Ponderosa, Adobe Wood Type Ornaments 1.
✤ *Adobe Wood Type 2*	: Birch, Blackoak, Madrone, Poplar, Willow, Adobe Wood Type Ornaments 2.
✤ *Baker Calligraphy*	: Amigo, Marigold, Oxford, Pelican, Visigoth.
✤ *Brody DisplaySet 1*	: Arcadia, Industria Inline & Solid, Insignia.
✤ *Calligraphy for Print*	: Ruling Script, Sho, Wiesbaden Swing.
✤ *GudrunSchrift*	: Ariadne, Diotima Roman, Italic, Roman SCOSF, Roman OSF, Italic OSF, Smaragd.
✤ *ITC Typographica*	: ITC Anna, ITC Beesknees, ITC Mona Lisa Recut & Solid, ITC Ozwald.
✤ *ITC ZapfSet 1*	: ITC Zapf Chancery Medium Italic, ITC Zapf Dingbats.
✤ *Linotype ClassAdSet 1*	: Doric Bold, Maximus.
✤ *Linotype DisplaySet 1*	: Arnold Böcklin, Fette Fraktur, Helvetica Inserat, Present Script.
✤ *Linotype DisplaySet 2*	: Banco, Charme, Flyer Black Condensed & Extra Black Condensed, Wilhelm Klingspor Gotisch.
✤ *Linotype DisplaySet 3*	: Gothic 13, Tempo Heavy Condensed.
✤ *Linotype DisplaySet 4*	: Madame Letters, Accents, Numericals, Roundy Regular, Swash Caps.
✤ *Linotype Engravers Set 1*	: Engravers Bold Face, Serlio.
✤ *Linotype Fraction Pi*	: Helvetica Regular & Bold Fractions, New Century Schoolbook Regular & Bold Fractions
✤ *Linotype Headliners*	: Chwast Buffalo Black Condensed, Erbar Condensed & Bold Condensed, Metrolite, Metromedium, Metroblack, Plak Black, Black Condensed & Extra Black Condensed, Stop, Times Eighteen Roman & Bold.
✤ *Linotype PiSet 1*	: Linotype Audio Pi, Linotype Warning Pi..
✤ *Linotype PiSet 2*	: Border Pi, European Pi.
✤ *Linotype ScriptSet 1*	: Cascade Script, Medici Script, Nuptial Script.
✤ *Linotype ScriptSet 2*	: Linoscript, Linotext, Linotext Dfr.
✤ *Linotype Universal Pi*	: Universal Greek with Math Pi, Universal News with Commercial Pi.
✤ *Monotype DisplaySet 1*	: Albertus Light, Regular & Italic, Castellar.
✤ *Monotype DisplaySet 2*	: Falstaff, Inflex Bold, Monotype Old Style Bold Outline.
✤ *Monotype DisplaySet 3*	: Kino, Matura Regular & Script Capitals, Wittenberger Fraktur.
✤ *Monotype DisplaySet 4*	: Latin Condensed, Onyx, Monotype Runic Condensed.
✤ *Monotype ScriptSet 1*	: Ashley Script, Monoline Script, New Berolina, Palace Script Regular & Semibold.
✤ *Monotype ScriptSet 2*	: Biffo Script, Dorchester Script, Pepita, Monotype Script Bold.
✤ *Monotype ScriptSet 3*	: Forte, Klang, Mercurius Bold Script.
✤ *Monotype TextSet 1*	: Monotype Goudy Modern Roman & Italic, Monotype Scotch Roman Regular & Italic.
✤ *OCR Set 1*	: MICR, OCR-A, OCR-B.
✤ *Type Before Gutenberg 1*	: Duc De Berry, Herculanum, Omnia.
✤ *Type Before Gutenberg 2*	: Carolina, Clairvaux, San Marco.
✤ *Type Before Gutenberg 3*	: Notre Dame, Notre Dame Ornaments, Pompeijana, Pompeijana Borders, Rusticana, Rusticana Borders.

foundry: Monotype Typography

In the late 1920s Stanley Morison became typographic advisor to the Monotype Corporation and initiated a program of design and development which produced a number of typefaces that have become classics – Gill Sans, Times New Roman, Perpetua, Ehrhardt and Fournier to mention a few. Today, Monotype Typography continues this tradition with the introduction of original, new fonts and the ongoing revival of typefaces from their archive of designs for hot-metal setting. ¶ Monotype also offers a collection of typefaces from independent designers and foundries – *Type Designers of the World* – and is a licensed reseller of the complete Adobe Type Library.

Abadi 1 Extra Light	Abadi
Extra Light Italic	*Abadi*
Regular	Abadi
Italic	*Abadi*
Bold	**Abadi**
Bold Italic	***Abadi***
Abadi 2 Light	Abadi
Light Italic	*Abadi*
Extra Bold	**Abadi**
Extra Bold Italic	***Abadi***
Abadi 3 Light Condensed	Abadi
Condensed	Abadi
... Abadi 3 Bold Condensed	**Abadi**
Extra Bold Condensed	**Abadi**
Albertus ✤ *Monotype Headlinders 6* Light	Albertus
Regular	Albertus
Italic	*Albertus*
Amasis 1 Roman	Amasis
Italic	*Amasis*
Bold	**Amasis**
Bold Italic	***Amasis***
Amasis 2 Light	Amasis
Light Italic	*Amasis*
Medium	Amasis
Medium Italic	*Amasis*
Black	**Amasis**
Black Italic	***Amasis***
Apollo Roman	Apollo
Italic	*Apollo*
Semibold	**Apollo**
Arabesque Borders & Ornaments One	
Two	
Three	
Arial 1 Regular	Arial
Italic	*Arial*
Bold	**Arial**
Bold Italic	***Arial***
Arial 2 Light	Arial
Light Italic	*Arial*
Black	**Arial**
Black Italic	***Arial***
Arial 3 Medium	Arial
Medium Italic	*Arial*
Bold	**Arial**
Bold Italic	***Arial***
Arial 4 Light Condensed	Arial
Condensed	Arial
Bold Condensed	**Arial**
Extra Bold Condensed	**Arial**
Arial Rounded Light	Arial Rounded

✤ *See this page for contents of Linotype-Hell Multi-Font Packages. See page 599 for contents of Monotype Typography Multi-Font Packages.*

. . . Arial Rounded
Regular Arial Rounded
Bold Arial Rounded
Extra Bold Arial Rounded

Arial Narrow
Regular Arial
Italic *Arial*
Bold Arial
Bold Italic *Arial*

Arial Cyrillic
Upright Абвгдеж Зикл
Inclined *Абвгдеж Зикл*
Bold Upright Абвгдеж Зикл
Bold Inclined *Абвгдеж Зикл*

Arial Efo
Regular Ąčėľőșť Ćăđįňż
Italic *Ąčėľőșť Ćăđįňż*
Bold Ąčėľőșť Ćăđįňż
Bold Italic *Ąčėľőșť Ćăđįňż*

Arial Greek
Upright Αβγδε Ζζηθικ
Inclined *Αβγδε Ζζηθικ*
Bold Upright Αβγδε Ζζηθικ
Bold Inclined *Αβγδε Ζζηθικ*

Arial Dual Greek
Upright Αβγδε Ζζηθικ
Inclined *Αβγδε Ζζηθικ*
Bold Upright Αβγδε Ζζηθικ
Bold Inclined *Αβγδε Ζζηθικ*

Arial Narrow Efo
Regular Ąčėľőșť Ćăđįňż
Italic *Ąčėľőșť Ćăđįňż*
Bold Ąčėľőșť Ćăđįňż
Bold Italic *Ąčėľőșť Ćăđįňż*

Ashley Script
❖ *Monotype Scripts 2* Ashley Script

ITC Avant Garde Gothic PS
Book ITC Avant Garde
Book Oblique *ITC Avant Garde*
Demi ITC Avant Garde
Demi Oblique *ITC Avant Garde*

ITC Avant Garde Gothic PS Efo
Book Ąčėľőșť Ćăđįňż
Book Oblique *Ąčėľőșť Ćăđįňż*
Demi Ąčėľőșť Ćăđįňż
Demi Oblique *Ąčėľőșť Ćăđįňż*

Monotype Baskerville
Roman M Baskerville
Italic *M Baskerville*

. . . Monotype Baskerville
Semibold M Baskerville
Semibold Italic *M Baskerville*
Bold M Baskerville
Bold Italic *M Baskerville*

Monotype Baskerville Expert
Expert Roman M BASKERVILLE 123 et al.
Expert Italic *12345 et al.*
Expert Semibold 12345 et al.
Expert Semibold Italic *12345 et al.*
Expert Bold 12345 et al.
Expert Bold Italic *12345 et al.*

Bell
Roman Bell
Italic *Bell*
Semibold Bell
Semibold Italic *Bell*
Bold Bell
Bold Italic *Bell*

Bell Expert
Expert Roman BELL 12345 et al.
Expert Italic *12345 et al.*
Expert Semibold 12345 et al.
Expert Semibold Italic *12345 et al.*
Expert Bold 12345 et al.
Expert Bold Italic *12345 et al.*
Expert Roman Alternate JKQRk
Expert Italic Alternate *AJ KQRTVbkÆ*
Expert Semibold Alternate JKQRk
Expert Semibold Italic Alternate *AJ KQRTVbkÆ*
Expert Roman Alternate JKQR
Expert Semibold Alternate JKQR

Bembo 1
Roman Bembo
Italic *Bembo*
Bold Bembo
Bold Italic *Bembo*

Bembo 2
Semibold Bembo
Semibold Italic *Bembo*
Extra Bold Bembo
Extra Bold Italic *Bembo*

Bembo Expert 1
Expert Roman BEMBO 12345 et al.
Expert Italic *12345 et al.*

. . . Bembo Expert 1
Expert Bold 12345 et al.
Expert Bold Italic *12345 et al.*
Expert Roman, Italic, Bold, Bold Italic Alternates R *R* R *R*

Bembo Expert 2
Expert Semibold BEMBO 12345 et al.
Expert Semibold Italic *12345 et al.*
Expert Extra Bold 12345 et al.
Expert Extra Bold Italic *12345 et al.*
Expert Semibold, Semibold Italic, Extra Bold Alternates R *R* R

Monotype Bernard Condensed
❖ *Monotype Headliners 5* Monotype Bernard

Biffo Script
❖ *Monotype Scripts 1* Biffo Script

Binner Gothic
❖ *Monotype Headliners 7* Binner Gothic

Binny Old Style
Roman Binny Old Style
Italic *Binny Old Style*

Blado Italic
❖ *Monotype AldineDutch* *Blado Italic*

Blado Italic Expert
❖ *MT AldineDutch Expert* *12345 et al.*

Blueprint
Regular Blueprint
Italic *Blueprint*
Bold Blueprint
Bold Italic *Blueprint*

Monotype Bodoni 1
Roman Monotype Bodoni
Italic *Monotype Bodoni*
Bold Monotype Bodoni
Bold Italic *Monotype Bodoni*

Monotype Bodoni 2
❖ *Monotype Bodoni & Onyx*
Book Monotype Bodoni
Book Italic *Monotype Bodoni*
Ultra Bold M Bodoni
Ultra Bold Italic *M Bodoni*

Monotype Bodoni 3
Bold Condensed Monotype Bodoni
Bold Condensed Italic *Monotype Bodoni*
Black M Bodoni
Black Italic *M Bodoni*

Book Antiqua
Roman Book Antiqua
Italic *Book Antiqua*
Bold Book Antiqua
Bold Italic *Book Antiqua*

Bookman Old Style
Roman Bookman Old
Italic *Bookman Old*
Bold Bookman Old

ff

... Bookman Old Style Bold Italic — Bookman Old
ITC Bookman PS Light — ITC Bookman
Light Italic — ITC Bookman
Demi — ITC Bookman
Demi Italic — ITC Bookman
ITC Bookman PS Efo Light — Ąčėľőşț Ćăđįňż
Light Italic — Ąčėľőşț Ćăđįňż
Demi — Ąčėľőşț Ćăđįňż
Demi Italic — Ąčėľőşț Ćăđįňż
Braggadocio ✤ Monotype Headliners 3 — Braggadocio
Brush Script ✤ Monotype Scripts 4 — Brush Script
Monotype Bulmer Roman — Bulmer
Italic — Bulmer
Semibold — Bulmer
Semibold Italic — Bulmer
Bold — Bulmer
Bold Italic — Bulmer
Display Roman — Bulmer
Display Italic — Bulmer
Display Bold — Bulmer
Display Bold Italic — Bulmer
Monotype Bulmer Expert Expert Roman — BULMER 12345 et al.
Expert Italic — 12345 et al.
Expert Semibold — 12345 et al.
Expert Semibold Italic — 12345 et al.
Expert Bold — 12345 et al.
Expert Bold Italic — 12345 et al.
Roman SCOSF — BULMER 12345...
Semibold SCOSF — BULMER 12345...
Roman Alternates — J$ 01234567890
Italic Alternates — JKNOQTY$012345678
Semibold Alternates — J$ 01234567890
Semibold Italic Alternates — JKNOQTY$012345678
Bold Alternates — J$ 01234567890
Bold Italic Alternates — JKNOQTY$012345678
Display Roman Alternates — Jfffiflffi$ 0123456789
Display Italic Alternates — JKNOQTfifl$012345
Display Bold Alternates — J$fifl 01234567890

... Monotype Bulmer Expert Display Bold Italic Alternates — JKNOQTfifl$0123
Calisto Roman — Calisto
Italic — Calisto
Bold — Calisto
Bold Italic — Calisto
Calvert Light — Calvert
Medium — Calvert
Bold — Calvert
Cantoria 1 Roman — Cantoria
Italic — Cantoria
Bold — Cantoria
Bold Italic — Cantoria
Cantoria 2 Light — Cantoria
Light Italic — Cantoria
Semibold — Cantoria
Semibold Italic — Cantoria
Extra Bold — Cantoria
Extra Bold Italic — Cantoria
Castellar ✤ Monotype Headliners 6 — CASTELLAR
Centaur Roman — Centaur
Italic — Centaur
Bold — Centaur
Bold Italic — Centaur
Centaur Expert Expert Roman — CENTAUR 12345 et al.
Expert Italic — 12345 et al.
Expert Bold — 12345 et al.
Expert Bold Italic — 12345 et al.
Expert Roman & Italic Alternates — QRQR Q
Expert Bold & Bold Italic Alternates — QR Q
Expert Swash Italic — C e N t a U r g k w &
Century Expanded Expanded — Century Expanded
Expanded Italic — Century Expanded
Bold — Century Expanded
Bold Italic — Century Expanded
Century Gothic Regular — Century Gothic
Italic — Century Gothic
Bold — Century Gothic
Bold Italic — Century Gothic

Monotype Century Old Style Roman — M Century Old Style
Italic — M Century Old Style
Bold — M Century Old Sty
Bold Italic — M Century Old Sty
Monotype Century Schoolbook Roman — M C Schoolbook
Italic — M C Schoolbook
Bold — M C Schoolbook
Bold Italic — M C Schoolbook
Century Schoolbook PS Efo Regular — Ąčėľőşț Ćăđįňż
Italic — Ąčėľőşț Ćăđįňż
Bold — Ąčėľőşț Ćăđįňż
Bold Italic — Ąčėľőşț Ćăđįňż
Christmas Ornaments One
Two
Three
Four
Five
Six
Clarendon ✤ Monotype Headliners 1 Monotype Clarendon — Monotype Clarendon
New Clarendon Roman — New Clarendon
New Clarendon Bold — New Clarendon
Clarion Roman — Clarion
Italic — Clarion
Bold — Clarion
Monotype Clearface Bold — Monotype Clearface
Clearface Gothic Demibold — M Clearface Gothic
Clearface Gothic Bold — M Clearface Cothic
Colmcille Regular — Colmcille
Italic — Colmcille
Bold — Colmcille
Bold Italic — Colmcille
Regular Alternate — ÁḂĊ ꝺꞅꝣċꞇṁꝑꞃꞅċꞇ
Italic Alternate — ÁḂĊ ꝺꞅꝣċꞇṁꝑꞃꞅċꞇ
Bold Alternate — ÁḂĊ ꝺꞅꝣċꞇṁꝑꞃꞅċꞇ
Bold Italic Alternate — ÁḂĊ ꝺꞅꝣċꞇṁꝑꞃꞅċꞇ
Ornaments
Colonna ✤ Monotype Handtooled — Colonna
Columbus Roman — Columbus

✤ ✤ See page 599 for contents of Monotype Typography Multi-Font Packages.

ff

. . . Columbus Italic	Columbus
Semibold	Columbus
Semibold Italic	Columbus
Bold	Columbus
Bold Italic	Columbus
Columbus Expert Expert Roman	COLUMBUS 12345 et al.
Expert Italic	12345 et al.
Expert Semibold	12345 et al.
Expert Semibold Italic	12345 et al.
Expert Bold	12345 et al.
Expert Bold Italic	12345 et al.
Ornaments One	
Ornaments Two	
Commercial Script ✤ Monotype Scripts 4	Commercial Script
Compacta Bold ✤ Monotype Headliners 5	Compacta
Contemporary Ornaments One	
Two	
Three	
Four	
Coronet Bold ✤ Monotype Scripts 3	Coronet
Corsiva ✤ Monotype PlusSet 6	Corsiva
Monotype Courier Twelve ✤ Monotype Typewriter Faces	M Courier Twelve
Courier PS Regular	Courier PS
Oblique	Courier PS
Bold	Courier PS
Bold Oblique	Courier PS
Courier PS Efo Regular	Ąčėľőşţ Ćăđįňż
Italic	Ąčėľőşţ Ćăđįňż
Bold	Ąčėľőşţ Ćăđįňż
Bold Italic	Ąčėľőşţ Ćăđįňż
Dante Roman	Dante
Italic	Dante
Medium	Dante
Medium Italic	Dante
Bold	Dante
Bold Italic	Dante
Dante Expert Expert Roman	DANTE 12345 et al.
Expert Italic	12345 et al.
. . . Dante Expert Expert Medium	12345 et al.
Expert Medium Italic	12345 et al.
Expert Bold	12345 et al.
Expert Bold Italic	12345 et al.
Expert Alternate	1£
Expert Italic Alternate	ʒ ʒy g gg gg , ; £
Expert Medium Alternate	1£
Expert Medium Italic Alternate	ʒ ʒy g gg gg , ; £
Expert Bold Alternate	1£
Expert Bold Italic Alternate	ʒ ʒy g gg gg , ; £
Titling	DANTE
Delima 1 Light	Delima
Light Italic	Delima
Roman	Delima
Italic	Delima
Bold	Delima
Bold Italic	Delima
Delima 2 Semibold	Delima
Semibold Italic	Delima
Extra Bold	Delima
Extra Bold Italic	Delima
Dorchester Script ✤ Monotype Scripts 1	Dorchester Script
MT Egyptian 72 Extended ✤ Monotype Headliners 1	M Egyptian 72
Ehrhardt Roman	Ehrhardt
Italic	Ehrhardt
Semibold	Ehrhardt
Semibold Italic	Ehrhardt
Ehrhardt Expert Expert Roman	EHRHARDT 12345 et al.
Expert Italic	12345 et al.
Expert Semibold	12345 et al.
Expert Semibold Italic	12345 et al.
Ellington Light	Ellington
Light Italic	Ellington
Roman	Ellington
Italic	Ellington
Bold	Ellington
Bold Italic	Ellington
. . . Ellington Extra Bold	Ellington
Extra Bold Italic	Ellington
Engravers Roman	ENGRAVERS
Bold	ENGRAVERS
Monotype Engravers Old English	M Engravers Old English
Falstaff ✤ ⌗ Monotype Headliners 2	Falstaff
Felix Titling ✤ Monotype Classic Titling	FELIX
Festival Titling ✤ Monotype Crazy Headlines	FESTIVAL
Figaro ✤ Monotype Headliners 3	Figaro
Footlight 1 Roman	Footlight
Italic	Footlight
Bold	Footlight
Bold Italic	Footlight
Footlight 2 Light	Footlight
Light Italic	Footlight
Extra Bold	Footlight
Extra Bold Italic	Footlight
Forte ✤ ⌗ Monotype Headliners 3	Forte
Fournier + Expert Roman	Fournier
Italic	Fournier
Tall Capitals	Fournier
Tall Capitals Italic	Fournier
Expert Roman	FOURNIER 12345 et al.
Expert Italic	12345 et al.
Alternate	ct fb fh fj fk J st w £ $ Q
Italic Alternate	ct fb fh fj fk st £ $ Q
Ornaments	
MT Franklin Gothic Ex Cond ✤ Monotype Headliners 7	M Franklin Gothic
French Script ✤ Monotype Scripts 4	French Script
Monotype Garamond Roman	Monotype Garamond
No. 156 Italic	Monotype Garamond
No. 174 Italic	Monotype Garamond
Bold	Monotype Garamond
Bold Italic	Monotype Garamond
Monotype Garamond Expert Expert Roman	M GARAMOND 12345 et al.
Expert Italic	12345 et al.

ff

Family	Style	Sample
. . . Monotype Garamond Expert	Expert Bold	12345 et al.
	Expert Bold Italic	*12345 et al.*
Gill Sans 1	Light	Gill Sans
	Light Italic	*Gill Sans*
	Regular	Gill Sans
	Italic	*Gill Sans*
	Bold	**Gill Sans**
	Bold Italic	***Gill Sans***
Gill Sans 2	Extra Bold	**Gill Sans**
	Ultra Bold	**Gill Sans**
	Condensed	Gill Sans
	Bold Condensed	**Gill Sans**
	Ultra Bold Condensed	**Gill Sans**
Gill Sans 3	Book	Gill Sans
	Book Italic	*Gill Sans*
	Heavy	**Gill Sans**
	Heavy Italic	***Gill Sans***
Gill Sans 1 Alternate *(alternate figure 1)*	Light	Gill Sans
	Light Italic	*Gill Sans*
	Regular	Gill Sans
	Italic	*Gill Sans*
	Bold	**Gill Sans**
	Bold Italic	***Gill Sans***
Gill Sans 3 Alternate *(alternate figure 1)*	Book	Gill Sans
	Book Italic	*Gill Sans*
	Heavy	**Gill Sans**
	Heavy Italic	***Gill Sans***
Gill Sans Display 1	Bold	**Gill Sans**
	Extra Bold	**Gill Sans**
	Bold Condensed	**Gill Sans**
Gill Sans Display 2	Bold Extra Condensed	**Gill Sans**
	Light Shadowed	Gill Sans
	Shadow	GILL SANS
Gloucester	Oldstyle	Gloucester
	Bold	**Gloucester**
	Bold Condensed	**Gloucester**
	Bold Extra Condensed	**Gloucester**
	Bold Extended	**Gloucester**
Goudy 1	Monotype Goudy Old Style	M Goudy Old Style
	Monotype Goudy Old Style Italic	*M Goudy Old Style*
	Bold	**Goudy**
	Bold Italic	***Goudy***
	Catalogue	Goudy
	Catalogue Italic	*Goudy*
Goudy 2	Modern	Goudy Modern
	Modern Italic	*Goudy Modern*
	Extra Bold	**Goudy**
	Monotype Goudy Text	Monotype Goudy Text
Monotype Goudy Modern ✣ *Monotype TextSet 1*	Roman	M Goudy Modern
	Italic	*M Goudy Modern*
Monotype Goudy Text & Lombardic Caps	Text	Monotype Goudy Text
	Dfr	ch ck ff ft ll f ſſ ß ſtz ÄÖL
	Alternate	BGT Jſtctffififlffl
	Lombardic Capitals	LOMBARDIC
Monotype Grotesque 1	Light No. 126	Monotype Grotesque
	Light Italic No. 126	*Monotype Grotesque*
	Regular No. 215	Monotype Grotesque
	Italic No. 215	*Monotype Grotesque*
	Bold No. 216	**M Grotesque**
	Black No. 216	**Monotype Grotesque**
Monotype Grotesque 2	Light Condensed No. 126	Monotype Grotesque
	Condensed No. 215	Monotype Grotesque
	Extra Condensed No. 215	Monotype Grotesque
	Black No. 216	**Monotype Grotesque**
	Bold Extended No. 216	**M Grotesque**
Headline Bold ✣ *Monotype Headliners 2*		**Headline Bold**
Horley Old Style 1	Roman	Horley Old Style
	Italic	*Horley Old Style*
	Bold	**Horley Old Style**
	Bold Italic	***Horley Old Style***
Horley Old Style 2	Light	Horley Old Style
	Light Italic	*Horley Old Style*
	Semibold	Horley Old Style
	Semibold Italic	*Horley Old Style*
Imprint	Roman	Imprint
	Italic	*Imprint*
. . . Imprint	Bold	**Imprint**
	Bold Italic	***Imprint***
Imprint Expert	Expert Roman	IMPRINT 12345 et al.
	Expert Italic	*12345 et al.*
	Expert Bold	**12345 et al.**
	Expert Bold Italic	***12345 et al.***
Imprint Shadow ✣ *Monotype Handtooled*	Roman	Imprint
	Italic	*Imprint*
Inflex Bold ✣ ⌘ *Monotype Headliners 4*		**Inflex Bold**
Monotype Ionic	Roman	Monotype Ionic
	Italic	*Monotype Ionic*
	Bold	**Monotype Ionic**
Monotype Italian Old Style	Roman	M Italian Old Style
	Italic	*M Italian Old Style*
	Bold	**M Italian Old Style**
	Bold Italic	***M Italian Old Style***
Monotype Janson	Roman	Monotype Janson
	Italic	*Monotype Janson*
	Bold	**Monotype Janson**
	Bold Italic	***Monotype Janson***
Monotype Janson Expert	Expert Roman	M JANSON 12345 et al.
	Expert Italic	*12345 et al.*
	Expert Bold	**12345 et al.**
	Expert Bold Italic	***12345 et al.***
Joanna	Roman	Joanna
	Italic	*Joanna*
	Semibold	Joanna
	Semibold Italic	*Joanna*
	Bold	**Joanna**
	Bold Italic	***Joanna***
	Extra Bold	**Joanna**
Joanna OSF	Roman OSF	Joanna 12345...
	Italic OSF	*osf 12345...*
	Bold OSF	**osf 12345...**
	Bold Italic OSF	***osf 12345...***
Kino ✣ *Monotype Crazy Headlines*		Kino
Klang ✣ ⌘ *Monotype Headliners 3*		*Klang*
Monotype Latin Condensed ⌘ *Monotype DisplaySet 4*		M Latin Condensed

ff

✣ ⌘ *See page 599 for contents of Monotype Typography Multi-Font Packages.*

Letter Gothic
- Regular — Letter Gothic
- Oblique — *Letter Gothic*
- Bold — **Letter Gothic**
- Bold Oblique — ***Letter Gothic***

Monotype Lightline Gothic
❖ *Monotype Headliners 7* — M Lightline Gothic

Lydian
- Regular — **Lydian**
- Cursive — *Lydian*

Matura
❖ *Monotype Crazy Headlines*
- Regular — **Matura**
- Script Capitals — Matura ABC

Mercurius Script Bold
❖ ⁘ *Monotype Scripts 3* — ***Mercurius Script***

Monotype Modern 1
- Bold — **Monotype Modern**
- Bold Italic — ***Monotype Modern***
- Extended — Monotype Modern
- Extended Italic — *Monotype Modern*

Monotype Modern 2
- Bold — **Monotype Modern**
- Bold Italic — ***Monotype Modern***
- Condensed — Monotype Modern
- Condensed Italic — *Monotype Modern*
- Extended — Monotype Modern
- Extended Italic — *Monotype Modern*
- Wide — M Modern
- Wide Italic — *M Modern*

Monoline Script
❖ *Monotype Scripts 2* — Monoline Script

Neographik
❖ *Monotype Headliners 5* — **Neographik**

New Berolina
❖ *Monotype Scripts 2* — *New Berolina*

Monotype News Gothic
- Regular — M News Gothic
- Italic — *M News Gothic*
- Bold — **M News Gothic**
- Condensed — M News Gothic
- Bold Condensed — **M News Gothic**

News Plantin
- Roman — News Plantin
- Italic — *News Plantin*
- Bold — **News Plantin**
- Bold Italic — ***News Plantin***

Nimrod
- Roman — Nimrod
- Italic — *Nimrod*
- Bold — **Nimrod**
- Bold Italic — ***Nimrod***

Ocean Sans MultipleMaster
- Light — Ocean Sans MM
- Light Italic — *Ocean Sans MM*
- Book — Ocean Sans MM
- Book Italic — *Ocean Sans MM*
- Semibold — **Ocean Sans MM**
- Semibold Italic — ***Ocean Sans MM***
- Bold — **Ocean Sans MM**
- Bold Italic — ***Ocean Sans MM***
- Extra Bold — **Ocean Sans MM**
- Extra Bold Italic — ***Ocean Sans MM***

Octavian + Expert & SCOSF
- Roman — Octavian
- Italic — *Octavian*
- Expert Roman — OCTAVIAN 12345 et al.
- Expert Italic — *12345 et al.*
- Roman SCOSF — OCTAVIAN 12345...
- Italic OSF — *osf 12345...*

Monotype Old English Text
❖ ⁘ *Monotype Headliners 4* — M Old English Text

Monotype Old Style
- Roman — Monotype Old Style
- Italic — *Monotype Old Style*
- Bold — **M Old Style**
- Bold Italic — ***M Old Style***

MT Old Style Bold Outline
❖ ⁘ *Monotype Headliners 4* — M Old Style

Monotype Onyx
❖ ⁘ *Monotype Bodoni & Onyx* — Monotype Onyx

Palace Script
❖ *Monotype Scripts 2*
- Regular — *Palace Script*
- Semibold — *Palace Script*

Pepita
❖ *Monotype Scripts 1* — *Pepita*

Perpetua
- Roman — Perpetua
- Italic — *Perpetua*
- Bold — **Perpetua**
- Bold Italic — ***Perpetua***

Perpetua Expert
- Expert Roman — PERPETUA 12345 et al.
- Expert Italic — *12345 et al.*
- Expert Bold — **12345 et al.**
- Expert Bold Italic — ***12345 et al.***

Perpetua
❖ *Monotype Classic Titling*
- Titling Light — PERPETUA
- Titling — PERPETUA
- Titling Bold — **PERPETUA**

Perrywood 1
- Roman — Perrywood

... Perrywood 1
- Italic — *Perrywood*
- Bold — **Perrywood**
- Bold Italic — ***Perrywood***

Perrywood 2
- Light — Perrywood
- Light Italic — *Perrywood*
- Semibold — **Perrywood**
- Semibold Italic — *Perrywood*
- Extra Bold — **Perrywood**
- Extra Bold Italic — ***Perrywood***

Photina
- Roman — Photina
- Italic — *Photina*
- Semibold — **Photina**
- Semibold Italic — ***Photina***
- Bold — **Photina**
- Bold Italic — ***Photina***
- Ultra Bold — **Photina**
- Ultra Bold Italic — ***Photina***

Placard
❖ *Monotype Headliners 2*
- Condensed — **Placard**
- Bold Condensed — **Placard**

Plantin 1
- Roman — Plantin
- Italic — *Plantin*
- Bold — **Plantin**
- Bold Italic — ***Plantin***

Plantin 2
- Light — Plantin
- Light Italic — *Plantin*
- Semibold — **Plantin**
- Semibold Italic — ***Plantin***
- Bold Condensed — **Plantin**

Plantin Expert 1
- Expert Roman — PLANTIN 12345 et al.
- Expert Italic — *12345 et al.*
- Expert Bold — **12345 et al.**
- Expert Bold Italic — ***12345 et al.***
- Expert Alternate Figures — 12345

Plantin Expert 2
- Expert Light — PLANTIN 12345 et al.
- Expert Light Italic — *12345 et al.*
- Expert Semibold — **12345 et al.**
- Expert Semibold Italic — ***12345 et al.***

Poliphilus Roman
❖ *Monotype AldineDutch* — Poliphilus Roman

ff

Poliphilus Roman Expert
❖ MT AldineDutch Expert — POLIPHILUS 12345 et al.

Rockwell 1
Light — Rockwell
Light Italic — *Rockwell*
Roman — Rockwell
Italic — *Rockwell*
Bold — **Rockwell**
Bold Italic — ***Rockwell***

Rockwell 2
Condensed — Rockwell
Bold Condensed — **Rockwell**
Extra Bold — **Rockwell**

Rococo Borders & Ornaments
One
Two
Three

Monotype Runic Condensed
❖ ∷ Monotype Headliners 5 — Monotype Runic

Sabon
Roman — Sabon
Italic — *Sabon*
Semibold — **Sabon**

Sabon OSF
Roman OSF — Sabon 12345...
Italic OSF — *osf 12345...*
Semibold OSF — **osf 12345...**

Monotype Scotch Roman
❖ Monotype TextSet 1
Roman — M Scotch Roman
Italic — *Monotype Scotch*

Monotype Script Bold
❖ Monotype Scripts 1 — ***Monotype Script***

Monotype Sorts
❖ Monotype PlusSet 6

Monotype Spartan
One Two — M SPARTAN
One Three — M SPARTAN
Two Four — MONOTYPE SPARTAN
Three Four — MONOTYPE SPARTAN
Four — MONOTYPE SPARTAN

Monotype Spartan Italic
One Two Italic — *M SPARTAN*
One Three Italic — *M SPARTAN*
Two Four Italic — *MONOTYPE SPARTAN*
Three Four Italic — *MONOTYPE SPARTAN*
Four Italic — *MONOTYPE SPARTAN*

Monotype Spartan Bold
One Two Bold — **M SPARTAN**
One Three Bold — **M SPARTAN**
Two Four Bold — **MONOTYPE SPARTAN**

... Monotype Spartan Bold
Three Four Bold — **MONOTYPE SPARTAN**
Four Bold — **MONOTYPE SPARTAN**

Spectrum + Expert & SCOSF
Roman — Spectrum
Italic — *Spectrum*
Semibold — **Spectrum**
Expert Roman — SPECTRUM 12345 et al.
Expert Italic — *12345 et al.*
Expert Semibold — **12345 et al.**
Roman SCOSF — SPECTRUM 12345...
Italic OSF — *osf 12345...*
Semibold OSF — **osf 12345...**

Swing Bold
❖ Monotype Scripts 1 — ***Swing Bold***

Symbol PS — ΑΒΧΔΕΦΓαβχδεφγ

Times New Roman 1
Roman — Times New Roman
Italic — *Times New Roman*
Bold — **Times New Roman**
Bold Italic — ***Times New Roman***

Times New Roman Expert
Expert Roman — T N ROMAN 12345 et al.
Expert Italic — *12345 et al.*
Expert Bold — **12345 et al.**
Expert Bold Italic — ***12345 et al.***

Times New Roman 2
Semibold — **Times New Roman**
Semibold Italic — ***Times New Roman***
Extra Bold — **Times New Roman**

Times New Roman Condensed
Condensed — Times New Roman
Condensed Italic — *Times New Roman*
Bold Condensed — **Times New Roman**

Times New Roman 3
Medium — Times New Roman
Medium Italic — *Times New Roman*
Small Text Roman — Times New Roman
Small Text Italic — *Times New Roman*
Small Text Bold — **Times New Roman**

Times New Roman Seven
Roman — Times New Roman
Italic — *Times New Roman*
Bold — **Times New Roman**
Bold Italic — ***Times New Roman***

Times New Roman PS
Roman — Times N Roman PS
Italic — *Times New Roman PS*

... Times New Roman PS
Bold — **Times N Roman PS**
Bold Italic — ***Times N Roman PS***

Times New Roman PS Expert
Expert Roman — T N ROMAN PS 123 et al.
Expert Italic — *12345 et al.*
Expert Bold — **12345 et al.**
Expert Bold Italic — ***12345 et al.***

Times New Roman Cyrillic
Upright — Абвгдеж Зикл
Inclined — *Абвгдеж Зикл*
Bold Upright — **Абвгдеж Зикл**
Bold Inclined — ***Абвгдеж Зикл***

Times New Roman Greek
Upright — Αβγδε Ζζηθικ
Inclined — *Αβγδε Ζζηθικ*
Bold Upright — **Αβγδε Ζζηθικ**
Bold Inclined — ***Αβγδε Ζζηθικ***

Times New Roman Dual Greek
Dual Greek Upright — Αβγδε Ζζηθικ
Dual Greek Inclined — *Αβγδε Ζζηθικ*
Dual Greek Bold Upright — **Αβγδε Ζζηθικ**
Dual Greek Bold Inclined — ***Αβγδε Ζζηθικ***

Times New Roman PS Efo
Roman — Ąčėľőşť Ćăđįňż
Italic — *Ąčėľőşť Ćăđįňż*
Bold — **Ąčėľőşť Ćăđįňż**
Bold Italic — ***Ąčėľőşť Ćăđįňż***

20th Century 1
Light — 20th Century
Light Italic — *20th Century*
Medium — 20th Century
Medium Italic — *20th Century*
Bold — **20th Century**
Bold Italic — ***20th Century***

20th Century 2
Semimedium — 20th Century
Semibold — **20th Century**
Medium Condensed — 20th Century
Bold Condensed — **20th Century**

20th Century 3
Extra Bold — **20th Century**
Extra Bold Italic — ***20th Century***
Ultra Bold — **20th Century**
Ultra Bold Italic — ***20th Century***
Extra Bold Condensed — **20th Century**
Ultra Bold Condensed — **20th Century**

❖ ∷ See page 599 for contents of Monotype Typography Multi-Font Packages.

Typewriter
❖ *Monotype Typewriter Faces*
Typewriter Elite — Typewriter Elite
Typewriter — Typewriter
Typewriter Gothic — Typewriter Gothic

Van Dijck
❖ *Monotype AldineDutch*
Roman — Van Dijck
Italic — *Van Dijck Italic*

Van Dijck Expert
❖ *MT AldineDutch Expert*
Expert Roman — VAN DIJCK 12345 et al.
Expert Italic — *fi ff fl 12345 et al.*
Expert Roman Alternate Figures — 12345
Expert Italic Alternate Figures — *12345*

Victoria Titling Condensed
❖ *Monotype Crazy Headlines* — VICTORIA

Monotype Walbaum
Roman — Monotype Walbaum
Italic — *Monotype Walbaum*
Medium — Monotype Walbaum
Medium Italic — *Monotype Walbaum*

Monotype Walbaum Expert
Expert Roman — M WALBAUM 12345 et al.
Expert Italic — *12345 et al.*
Expert Medium — 12345 et al.
Expert Medium Italic — *12345 et al.*

Windsor
❖ *Monotype Headliners 7* — Windsor

Wittenberger Fraktur
Regular — Wittenberger
Bold — **Wittenberger**

Z-Antiqua PS
Roman — Z-Antiqua
Italic — *Z-Antiqua*
Bold — **Z-Antiqua**
Bold Italic — ***Z-Antiqua***

Z-Antiqua Efo
Roman — Ąčėľőșť Čăđįňż
Italic — *Ąčėľőșť Čăđįňż*
Bold — **Ąčėľőșť Čăđįňż**
Bold Italic — ***Ąčėľőșť Čăđįňż***

ITC Zapf Chancery PS Efo
Medium Italic — *Ąčėľőșť Čăđįňż*

ITC Zapf Chancery Med Italic
❖ *Monotype ITC ZapfSet* — *ITC Zapf Chancery*

ITC Zapf Dingbats
❖ *Monotype ITC ZapfSet* — ❁❄❅❆✱●❍■❏❐❑

Zeitgeist
Regular — Zeitgeist
Italic — *Zeitgeist*
Bold — **Zeitgeist**
Condensed — Zeitgeist
Alternate — Zeitgeist
Crazy Paving — Zeitgeist

. . . Zeitgeist
Cameo & Expert Cameo — Zeitgeist 12345 et al.
Expert Regular — ZEITGEIST 12345 et al.
Expert Italic — *12345 et al.*
Expert Bold — **12345 et al.**
Expert Condensed — 12345 et al.

Monotype Typography Multi·Font Package Contents

❖ *Monotype AldineDutch*	: Poliphilus Roman & Blado Italic, Van Dijck Roman & Italic.
❖ *MT AldineDutch Expert*	: Poliphilus Roman Expert & Blado Italic Expert, Van Dijck Expert Roman & Italic.
❖ *Monotype Bodoni & Onyx*	: Bodoni Book, Book Italic, Ultra Bold, Ultra Bold Italic, MT Onyx.
❖ *Monotype Classic Titling*	: Felix Titling, Perpetua Titling Light, Regular & Bold.
❖ *Monotype Crazy Headlines*	: Festival Titling, Kino, Matura Regular & Scriptorial Capitals, Victoria Titling Condensed.
❖ *Monotype Handtooled*	: Colonna, Imprint Shadow Roman & Italic.
❖ *Monotype Headliners 1*	: Monotype Clarendon, Monotype New Clarendon Roman & Bold, Monotype Egyptian 72 Extended.
❖ *Monotype Headliners 2*	: Falstaff, Headline Bold, Placard Condensed & Bold Condensed.
❖ *Monotype Healinders 3*	: Braggadocio, Klang, Figaro, Forte.
❖ *Monotype Headliners 4*	: Inflex Bold, Monotype Old English Text, Monotype Old Style Bold Outline.
❖ *Montotype Headliners 5*	: Monotype Bernard Condensed, Compacta Bold, Neographik, Monotype Runic Condensed.
❖ *Monotype Headliners 6*	: Albertus Light, Regular & Italic, Castellar.
❖ *Monotype Headliners 7*	: Binner Gothic, Monotype Franklin Gothic Extra Condensed, Monotype Lightline Gothic, Windsor.
❖ *Monotype ITC ZapfSet*	: ITC Zapf Chancery Medium Italic & ITC Zapf Dingbats.
❖ *Monotype PlusSet 6*	: Corsiva & Monotype Sorts.
❖ *Monotype Scripts 1*	: Biffo Script, Dorchester Script, Pepita, Monotype Script Bold, Swing Bold.
❖ *Monotype Scripts 2*	: Ashley Script, Monoline Script, New Berolina, Palace Script Regular & Semibold.
❖ *Monotype Scripts 3*	: Coronet Bold & Mercurius Script.
❖ *Monotype Scripts 4*	: Brush Script, Commercial Script, French Script.
❖ *Monotype TextSet 1*	: Monotype Goudy Modern Roman & Italic, Monotype Scotch Roman & Italic.
❖ *Monotype Typewriter Faces*	: Monotype Courier 12, Typewriter, Typewriter Elite, Typewriter Gothic.
⌘ *Monotype DisplaySet 2*	: Falstaff, Inflex, Monotype Old Style Bold Outline.
⌘ *Monotype DisplaySet 4*	: Monotype Latin Condensed, Monotype Onyx, Monotype Runic Condensed.
⌘ *Monotype ScriptSet 3*	: Forte, Klang, Mercurius Script.

Monotype Type Designers of the World

foundry: abcdesign

Bijoux
Light — Bijoux
Regular — Bijoux
Bold — **Bijoux**

Jeunesse
Regular — Jeunesse
Italic — *Jeunesse*
Medium — Jeunesse
Bold — **Jeunesse**

Jeunesse Sans
Regular — Jeunesse
Italic — *Jeunesse*

Jeunesse Slab
Regular — Jeunesse
Italic — *Jeunesse*

Jocelyn
Light — Jocelyn
Regular — Jocelyn
Semibold — Jocelyn
Bold — **Jocelyn**

Jonas
Body — Jonas
Head — Jonas

Ulissa
Regular — Ulissa
Italic — *Ulissa*
Bold — **Ulissa**
Bold Italic — ***Ulissa***

Ulissa Condensed
Light Condensed — Ulissa Condensed
Book Condensed — Ulissa Condensed
Medium Condensed — Ulissa Condensed
Bold Condensed — **Ulissa Condensed**

foundry: Alphabets Inc

A*I Font Sampler
A*I Antique Condensed — A*I ANTIQUE
A*I French XXX Condensed — A*I FRENCH XXX CONDENSED
A*I Neuland — A*I NEULAND
A*I Oz Brush — A*I Oz Brush
A*I Oz Poster — A*I Oz Poster
A*I Prospera II-Roman — A*I Prospera II

A*I Egyptian Bold Condensed
Text — A*I Egyptian
Display — A*I Egyptian

A*I Koch Antiqua
Light — A*I Koch Antiqua
Demi — A*I Koch Antiqua
Extra Bold — A*I Koch Antiqua

A*I Neuland — A*I NEULAND

A*I Oz Brush
Regular — A*I Oz Brush
Italic — *A*I Oz Brush*

A*I Oz Poster
Regular — A*I Oz Poster
Condensed — A*I Oz Poster

A*I Prospera II
Roman — A*I Prospera II
Italic — *A*I Prospera II*
Bold — **A*I Prospera II**

ff

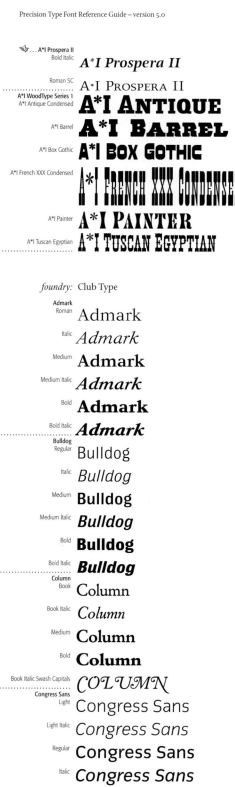

... A*I Prospera II
Bold Italic A*I Prospera II
Roman SC A*I PROSPERA II

A*I WoodType Series 1
A*I Antique Condensed A*I ANTIQUE
A*I Barrel A*I BARREL
A*I Box Gothic A*I BOX GOTHIC
A*I French XXX Condensed A*I FRENCH XXX CONDENSED
A*I Painter A*I PAINTER
A*I Tuscan Egyptian A*I TUSCAN EGYPTIAN

foundry: Club Type

Admark
Roman Admark
Italic Admark
Medium Admark
Medium Italic Admark
Bold Admark
Bold Italic Admark

Bulldog
Regular Bulldog
Italic Bulldog
Medium Bulldog
Medium Italic Bulldog
Bold Bulldog
Bold Italic Bulldog

Column
Book Column
Book Italic Column
Medium Column
Bold Column
Book Italic Swash Capitals COLUMN

Congress Sans
Light Congress Sans
Light Italic Congress Sans
Regular Congress Sans
Italic Congress Sans
Bold Congress Sans
Bold Italic Congress Sans
Extra Bold Congress Sans
Extra Bold Italic Congress Sans

Eurocrat
Regular Eurocrat
Italic Eurocrat

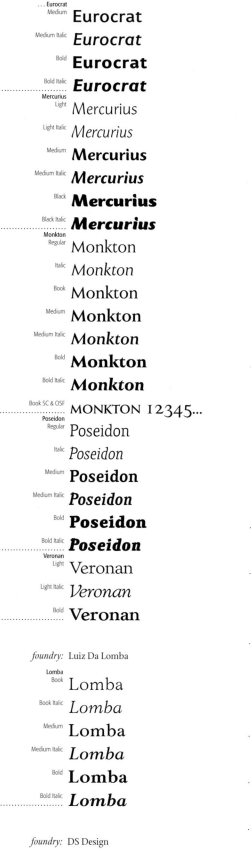

... Eurocrat
Medium Eurocrat
Medium Italic Eurocrat
Bold Eurocrat
Bold Italic Eurocrat

Mercurius
Light Mercurius
Light Italic Mercurius
Medium Mercurius
Medium Italic Mercurius
Black Mercurius
Black Italic Mercurius

Monkton
Regular Monkton
Italic Monkton
Book Monkton
Medium Monkton
Medium Italic Monkton
Bold Monkton
Bold Italic Monkton
Book SC & OSF MONKTON 12345...

Poseidon
Regular Poseidon
Italic Poseidon
Medium Poseidon
Medium Italic Poseidon
Bold Poseidon
Bold Italic Poseidon

Veronan
Light Veronan
Light Italic Veronan
Bold Veronan

foundry: Luiz Da Lomba

Lomba
Book Lomba
Book Italic Lomba
Medium Lomba
Medium Italic Lomba
Bold Lomba
Bold Italic Lomba

foundry: DS Design

DingBRATS

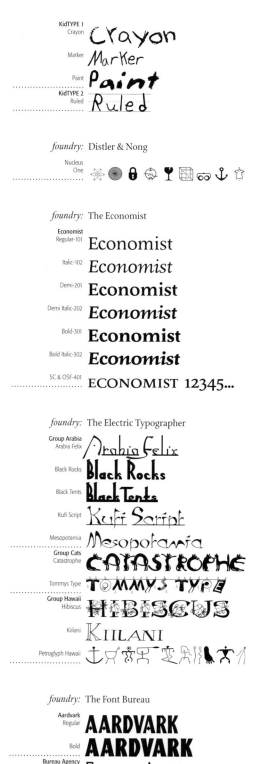

KidTYPE 1
Crayon Crayon
Marker Marker
Paint Paint

KidTYPE 2
Ruled Ruled

foundry: Distler & Nong

Nucleus
One

foundry: The Economist

Economist
Regular-101 Economist
Italic-102 Economist
Demi-201 Economist
Demi Italic-202 Economist
Bold-301 Economist
Bold Italic-302 Economist
SC & OSF-401 ECONOMIST 12345...

foundry: The Electric Typographer

Group Arabia
Arabia Felix Arabia Felix
Black Rocks Black Rocks
Black Tents Black Tents
Kufi Script Kufi Script
Mesopotamia Mesopotamia

Group Cats
Catastrophe CATASTROPHE
Tommys Type TOMMYS TYPE

Group Hawaii
Hibiscus HIBISCUS
Kiilani KIILANI
Petroglyph Hawaii

foundry: The Font Bureau

Aardvark
Regular AARDVARK
Bold AARDVARK

Bureau Agency
Regular Bureau Agency
Bold Bureau Agency

Belizio
Bold Belizio
Bold Italic Belizio

BeLucian
Book BeLucian
Book Italic BeLucian

See page 605 for contents of Monotype Type Designers of the World Multi-Font Packages.

...BeLucian Demi
BeLucian
Ultra
BeLucian
Bodega Sans Light
Bodega Sans
Light Oldstyle
Bodega Sans
Black
Bodega Sans
Black Oldstyle
Bodega Sans
Commerce Lean
Commerce
Fat
Commerce
Bureau Eagle Book
Bureau Eagle
Bold
Bureau Eagle
Bureau Empire Regular
Bureau Empire
Italic
Bureau Empire
Garage Gothic Regular
Garage Gothic
Bold
Garage Gothic
Black
Garage Gothic
Bureau Grotesque 13
Bureau Grotesque
15
Bureau Grotesque
17
Bureau Grotesque
37
Bureau Grotesque
53
Bureau Grotesque
79
B Grotesque
Ironmonger Black
IRONMNGR
Extended
IRONMNGR
Numskill Bold
Numskill
Bureau Ornaments City
Town
Village
Phaistos Roman
Phaistos
Italic
Phaistos
Bold
Phaistos
Romeo Skinny Condensed
Romeo
Medium Condensed
Romeo
Bureau Roxy Medium
Bureau Roxy
Medium Italic
Bureau Roxy
Scamp Regular
SCAMP
...Scamp Bold Inline
SCAMP
Fat
SCAMP
foundry: General Glyphics
General Glyphics Border Fonts Apogee
Argyle
Bourbon Street
Cartographer
Dot Rule
Draughts
Fat Waves
Intersect
Karnak
Neiman
Neiman Open
Santa Fe
Scotch Waves
Small Diamonds
Surveyor
Thebes
Transom
Zeus
Zig Zag One
Zig Zag Two
foundry: Carolyn Gibbs
Artifact 1
2
foundry: Joshua Hadley
Blackfoot Border
Composite
Ornaments
foundry: HandcraftedFonts
HF AmericanDiner Solid
HF AmericanDiner
Inline
HF AmericanDiner
Narrow
HF AmericanDiner
HF Antique Row
HF DisplaySet 1
HF Antique Row
HF Doodle Medium
HF Doodle
Medium Italic
HF Doodle
Bold
HF Doodle
Bold Italic
HF Doodle
HF Eden Expanded Light
HF DisplaySet 1
HF Eden Expanded
HF Exposition Plain One
HF Exposition
Two
HF Exposition
HF Exposition Rounded Medium
HF Exposition
Demibold
HF Exposition
Bold
HF Exposition
HF LaVardera Book
HF LaVardera
Bold
HF LaVardera
Extra Bold
HF LaVardera
HF Libris Light
HF LIBRIS
HF Modular Stencil Regular
HF Modular
Italic
HF Modular
Outline
HF Modular
Italic Outline
HF Modular
HF NewGarden Light
HF NewGarden
Bold
HF NewGarden
HF Poster Solid
HF POSTER
Inline
HF POSTER
HF Secede Block
HF Secede
Outline
HF Secede
Outline Heavy
HF Secede
foundry: Harris Design
Sign Pix One
Two
foundry: Paul Lang
Langer Regular
Langer
Italic
Langer
Bold
Langer
Bold Italic
Langer
Regular Alternate
Langer
Italic Alternate
Langer
ff

Langer Bold Alternate — Langer
Bold Italic Alternate — Langer

foundry: Letter Perfect

DeStijl Regular — DeStijl
Alternate — DeStijl
Florens Regular — Florens
Swash OSF — Florens 12345
Hadrian Bold — Hadrian
Hardwood — Hardwood
Koch Original — Koch Original
Kryptic — Kryptic
Manito — Manito
Old Claude Roman — Old Claude
Roman SCLF — Old Claude
Roslyn Bold — Roslyn
Silhouette — Silhouette
Spring Light — Spring
Regular — Spring
Spumoni — Spumoni
Tomboy Light — Tomboy
Medium — Tomboy
Bold — Tomboy
Visage Light — Visage Light
Wendy — Wendy

foundry: Steve Matteson

Mead Regular — Mead
Bold — Mead
Truesdell Roman — Truesdell
Italic — Truesdell
Bold — Truesdell
Bold Italic — Truesdell
Roman Alternate — TRUESDELL
Italic Alternate — a&d e ABC ffi fi fl 123…
Bold Alternate — ct st ff fi fl ffi ffl 123…
Bold Italic Alternate — ct st ff fi fl ffi ffl 123…
Sorts

foundry: Mecanorma

MN Access Medium — MN ACCESS
Bold — MN ACCESS
MN American Uncial — MN A Uncial
MN Anatol — mn anatol
Arnold Böcklin — Arnold Böcklin
MN Art Deco — MN ART DECO
MN Art World — MN ART WORLD
Aster Roman — Aster
Demi — Aster
Balloon Bold — BALLOON
Extra Bold — BALLOON
Blippo Black — Blippo Black
MN Brio — MN Brio
British Inserat Regular — British Inserat
Condensed — British Inserat
Brush — Brush
MN Bulletin Typewriter — MN Bulletin Type
MN Caligra — MN Caligra
MN Campus — MN CAMPUS
MN Card Camio — MN CARD CAMIO
MN Carplate — MN CARPLATE
Caslon Antique — Caslon Antique
Celtic Regular — Celtic
Italic — Celtic
Bold — Celtic
MN Chinon — MN Chinon
MN Choc — MN Choc
MN Circus — MN Circus
MN Classic Script — MN Classic Script
MN Comic Strip — MN COMIC
Commercial Script — Commercial Script
MN Compacta Bold — MN Compacta
MN Contest — MN CONTEST
Cooper Black Roman — Cooper Black
Italic — Cooper Black
Outline — Cooper Black
MN Dubbeldik — mn dubbeldik

Dynamo Medium — Dynamo
Bold — Dynamo
Shadow — Dynamo
Egyptienne Bold Condensed — Egyptienne
MN Enroute — MN Enroute
Estro — Estro
Eurostile Medium — Eurostile
Extended — Eurostile
Bold Extended — Eurostile
MN Fidelio — MN Fidelio
Folio Bold — Folio
Extra Bold — Folio
MN Fumo Dropshadow — MN Fumo Drop
Futura Black — Futura Black
MN Galba — MN GALBA
MN Gillies Gothic 1 Light — MN Gillies Gothic
Bold — MN Gillies Gothic
MN Gillies Gothic 2 Ultra — MN Gillies Gothic
Ultra Shaded — MN Gillies Gothic
MN Globe Gothic Bold — MN Globe Gothic
Bold Condensed — MN Globe Gothic
Outline — MN Globe Gothic
MN Gloworm Regular — MN Gloworm
Compressed — MN Gloworm
MN Gothique — MN Gothique
MN Hansson Stencil Bold — MN HANSSON
MN Hotel — MN HOTEL
MN Isonorm — MN Isonorm
MN Jackson — MN JACKSON
MN Latina — MN Latina
MN Leopard — MN LEOPARD
Milton Demibold — Milton
MN Mistral — MN Mistral
MN Normalise DIN — MN Normalise DIN
Olive Bold — Olive
Compact — Olive
Nord — Olive
Orator — Orator

See page 605 for contents of Monotype Type Designers of the World Multi-Font Packages.

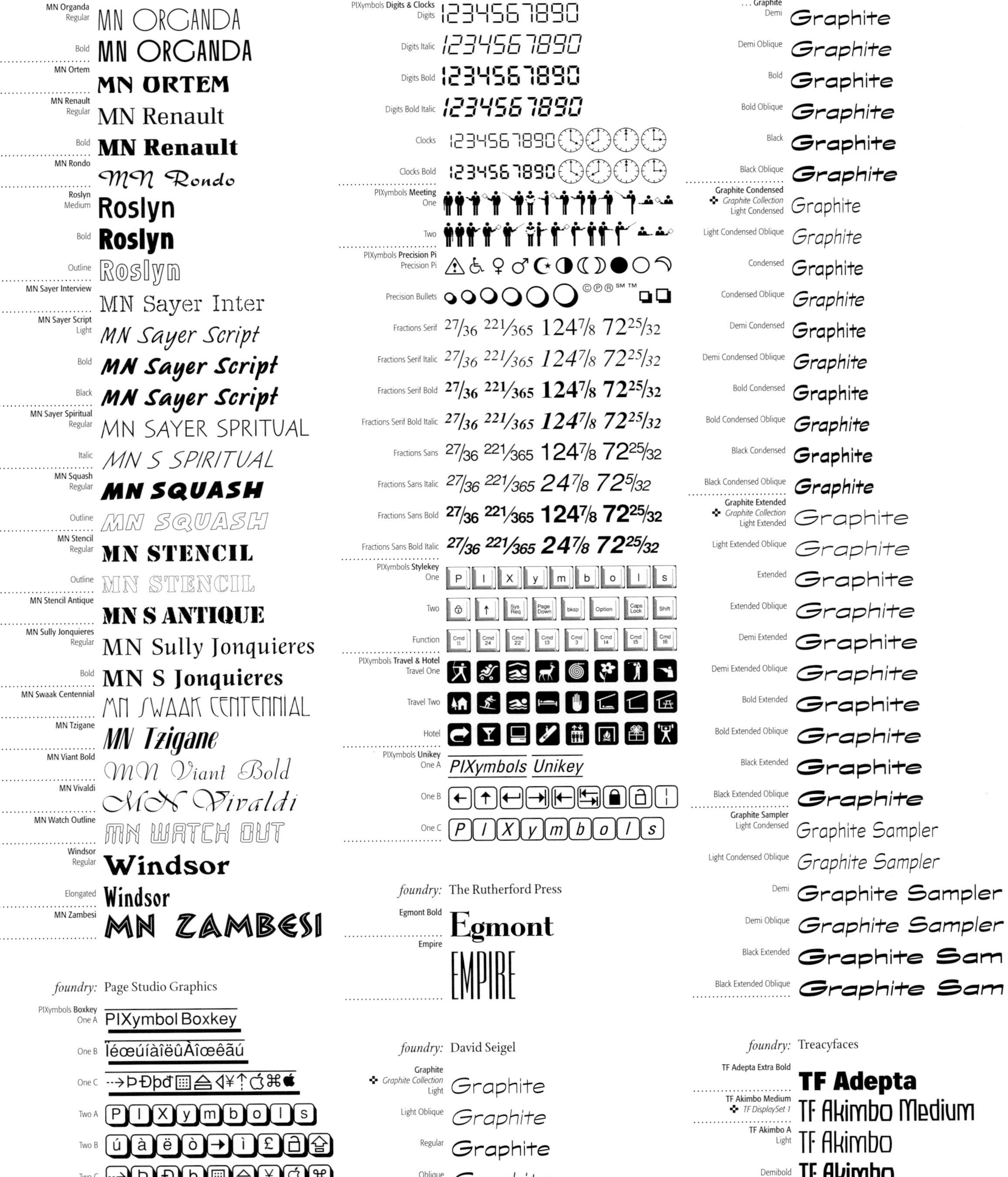

MN Organda Regular — MN ORGANDA
Bold — MN ORGANDA
MN Ortem — MN ORTEM
MN Renault Regular — MN Renault
Bold — MN Renault
MN Rondo — MN Rondo
Roslyn Medium — Roslyn
Bold — Roslyn
Outline — Roslyn
MN Sayer Interview — MN Sayer Inter
MN Sayer Script Light — MN Sayer Script
Bold — MN Sayer Script
Black — MN Sayer Script
MN Sayer Spiritual Regular — MN SAYER SPRITUAL
Italic — MN S SPIRITUAL
MN Squash Regular — MN SQUASH
Outline — MN SQUASH
MN Stencil Regular — MN STENCIL
Outline — MN STENCIL
MN Stencil Antique — MN S ANTIQUE
MN Sully Jonquieres Regular — MN Sully Jonquieres
Bold — MN S Jonquieres
MN Swaak Centennial — MN SWAAK CENTENNIAL
MN Tzigane — MN Tzigane
MN Viant Bold — MN Viant Bold
MN Vivaldi — MN Vivaldi
MN Watch Outline — MN WATCH OUT
Windsor Regular — Windsor
Elongated — Windsor
MN Zambesi — MN ZAMBESI

foundry: Page Studio Graphics

PIXymbols Boxkey One A — PIXymbol Boxkey
One B — Iéœúíàîëû Àîœêãú
One C
Two A — P I X y m b o l s
Two B — ú à ë ò ì £
Two C — Þ Ð þ ¥ ⌘

PIXymbols Digits & Clocks Digits — 1234567890
Digits Italic — 1234567890
Digits Bold — 1234567890
Digits Bold Italic — 1234567890
Clocks — 1234567890
Clocks Bold — 1234567890
PIXymbols Meeting One
Two
PIXymbols Precision Pi Precision Pi
Precision Bullets — © ℗ ® SM TM
Fractions Serif — 27/36 221/365 124 7/8 72 25/32
Fractions Serif Italic — 27/36 221/365 124 7/8 72 25/32
Fractions Serif Bold — 27/36 221/365 124 7/8 72 25/32
Fractions Serif Bold Italic — 27/36 221/365 124 7/8 72 25/32
Fractions Sans — 27/36 221/365 124 7/8 72 25/32
Fractions Sans Italic — 27/36 221/365 24 7/8 72 5/32
Fractions Sans Bold — 27/36 221/365 124 7/8 72 25/32
Fractions Sans Bold Italic — 27/36 221/365 24 7/8 72 25/32
PIXymbols Stylekey One — P I X y m b o l s
Two — Sys Req, Page Down, bksp, Option, Caps Lock, Shift
Function — Cmd 11, Cmd 24, Cmd 22, Cmd 13, Cmd 3, Cmd 14, Cmd 15, Cmd 16
PIXymbols Travel & Hotel Travel One
Travel Two
Hotel
PIXymbols Unikey One A — PIXymbols Unikey
One B
One C — P I X y m b o l s

foundry: The Rutherford Press

Egmont Bold — Egmont
Empire — EMPIRE

foundry: David Seigel

Graphite ✥ Graphite Collection Light — Graphite
Light Oblique — Graphite
Regular — Graphite
Oblique — Graphite

. . . Graphite Demi — Graphite
Demi Oblique — Graphite
Bold — Graphite
Bold Oblique — Graphite
Black — Graphite
Black Oblique — Graphite
Graphite Condensed ✥ Graphite Collection Light Condensed — Graphite
Light Condensed Oblique — Graphite
Condensed — Graphite
Condensed Oblique — Graphite
Demi Condensed — Graphite
Demi Condensed Oblique — Graphite
Bold Condensed — Graphite
Bold Condensed Oblique — Graphite
Black Condensed — Graphite
Black Condensed Oblique — Graphite
Graphite Extended ✥ Graphite Collection Light Extended — Graphite
Light Extended Oblique — Graphite
Extended — Graphite
Extended Oblique — Graphite
Demi Extended — Graphite
Demi Extended Oblique — Graphite
Bold Extended — Graphite
Bold Extended Oblique — Graphite
Black Extended — Graphite
Black Extended Oblique — Graphite
Graphite Sampler Light Condensed — Graphite Sampler
Light Condensed Oblique — Graphite Sampler
Demi — Graphite Sampler
Demi Oblique — Graphite Sampler
Black Extended — Graphite Sam
Black Extended Oblique — Graphite Sam

foundry: Treacyfaces

TF Adepta Extra Bold — TF Adepta
TF Akimbo Medium ✥ TF DisplaySet 1 — TF Akimbo Medium
TF Akimbo A Light — TF Akimbo
Demibold — TF Akimbo

ff

:Monotype Typography

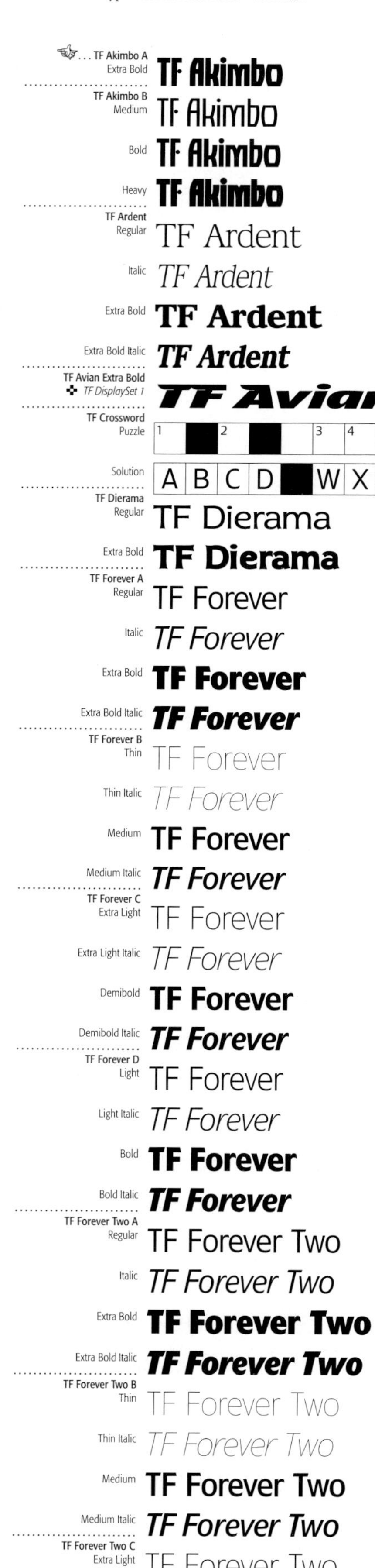

TF Akimbo A Extra Bold TF Akimbo
TF Akimbo B Medium TF Akimbo
Bold TF Akimbo
Heavy TF Akimbo
TF Ardent Regular TF Ardent
Italic TF Ardent
Extra Bold TF Ardent
Extra Bold Italic TF Ardent
TF Avian Extra Bold TF DisplaySet 1 TF Avian
TF Crossword Puzzle 1 2 3 4
Solution A B C D W X
TF Dierama Regular TF Dierama
Extra Bold TF Dierama
TF Forever A Regular TF Forever
Italic TF Forever
Extra Bold TF Forever
Extra Bold Italic TF Forever
TF Forever B Thin TF Forever
Thin Italic TF Forever
Medium TF Forever
Medium Italic TF Forever
TF Forever C Extra Light TF Forever
Extra Light Italic TF Forever
Demibold TF Forever
Demibold Italic TF Forever
TF Forever D Light TF Forever
Light Italic TF Forever
Bold TF Forever
Bold Italic TF Forever
TF Forever Two A Regular TF Forever Two
Italic TF Forever Two
Extra Bold TF Forever Two
Extra Bold Italic TF Forever Two
TF Forever Two B Thin TF Forever Two
Thin Italic TF Forever Two
Medium TF Forever Two
Medium Italic TF Forever Two
TF Forever Two C Extra Light TF Forever Two

... TF Forever Two C Extra Light Italic *TF Forever Two*
Demibold **TF Forever Two**
Demibold Italic ***TF Forever Two***
TF Forever Two D Light TF Forever Two
Light Italic *TF Forever Two*
Bold **TF Forever Two**
Bold Italic ***TF Forever Two***
TF Guest Check Heavy **TF G Check**
TF Habitat A Roman TF Habitat
Italic *TF Habitat*
Bold **TF Habitat**
Bold Italic ***TF Habitat***
TF Habitat B Book TF Habitat
Book Italic *TF Habitat*
Demibold **TF Habitat**
Demibold Italic ***TF Habitat***
TF Habitat Condensed A Condensed TF Habitat
Condensed Italic *TF Habitat*
Bold Condensed **TF Habitat**
Bold Condensed Italic ***TF Habitat***
TF Habitat Bold Contour A TF Habitat
TF Habitat Bold Contour B TF Habitat
TF Habitat Intials Cameo Initials A B C D E F G H I
Cameo Large A B C D E F G H I
TF Hôtelmoderne A Medium TF Hôtelmoderne
Demi TF Hôtelmoderne
Bold TF Hôtelmoderne
Heavy TF Hôtelmoderne
TF Hôtelmoderne Two A Medium TF Hôtelmoderne Two
Demi TF Hôtelmoderne Two
Bold TF Hôtelmoderne Two
Heavy TF Hôtelmoderne Two
TF Hôtelmoderne Serif Heavy TF Hôtelmoderne Serif
Heavy Shaded TF Hôtelmoderne Serif
TF Maltby Antique A Regular TF Maltby Antique
Medium TF Maltby Antique
Extra Bold **TF Maltby Antique**
Heavy **TF Maltby Antique**

TF Maltby Antique B Book TF Maltby Antique
Bold **TF Maltby Antique**
Black **TF Maltby Antique**
Heavy Ragged TF Maltby Antique
TF Maltby Ragged Initials TF MALTBY
TF Raincheck A Light TF Raincheck
Book TF Raincheck
Demibold TF Raincheck
Heavy TF Raincheck
TF Raincheck B Regular TF Raincheck
Medium TF Raincheck
Bold TF Raincheck
Ultra TF Raincheck
TF Roux Extra Bold **TF Roux**
Shaded TF Roux
Borders
TF Simper Extra Bold **TF Simper**
TF Simper Extra Bold Condensed **TF Simper**
TF Simper Extra Bold Extra Condensed **TF Simper**
TF Simper Serif Extra Bold **TF Simper**
TF Squiggle Serif
Sans
Sans Narrow
Typewriter
Chancery Medium Italic

foundry: U-Design Type Foundry

Bill's Cast 'O Characters
Bill's Fat Freddy's Caps B FAT FRED
Bill's Hand Chiseled Bill's Hand Chiseled

foundry: Peter von Zezschwitz

Zeta Fonts Collection 1 Campanula Companula
Mahlua MAHLUA
Odilia Odilia

See page 605 for contents of Monotype Type Designers of the World Multi-Font Packages.

ff

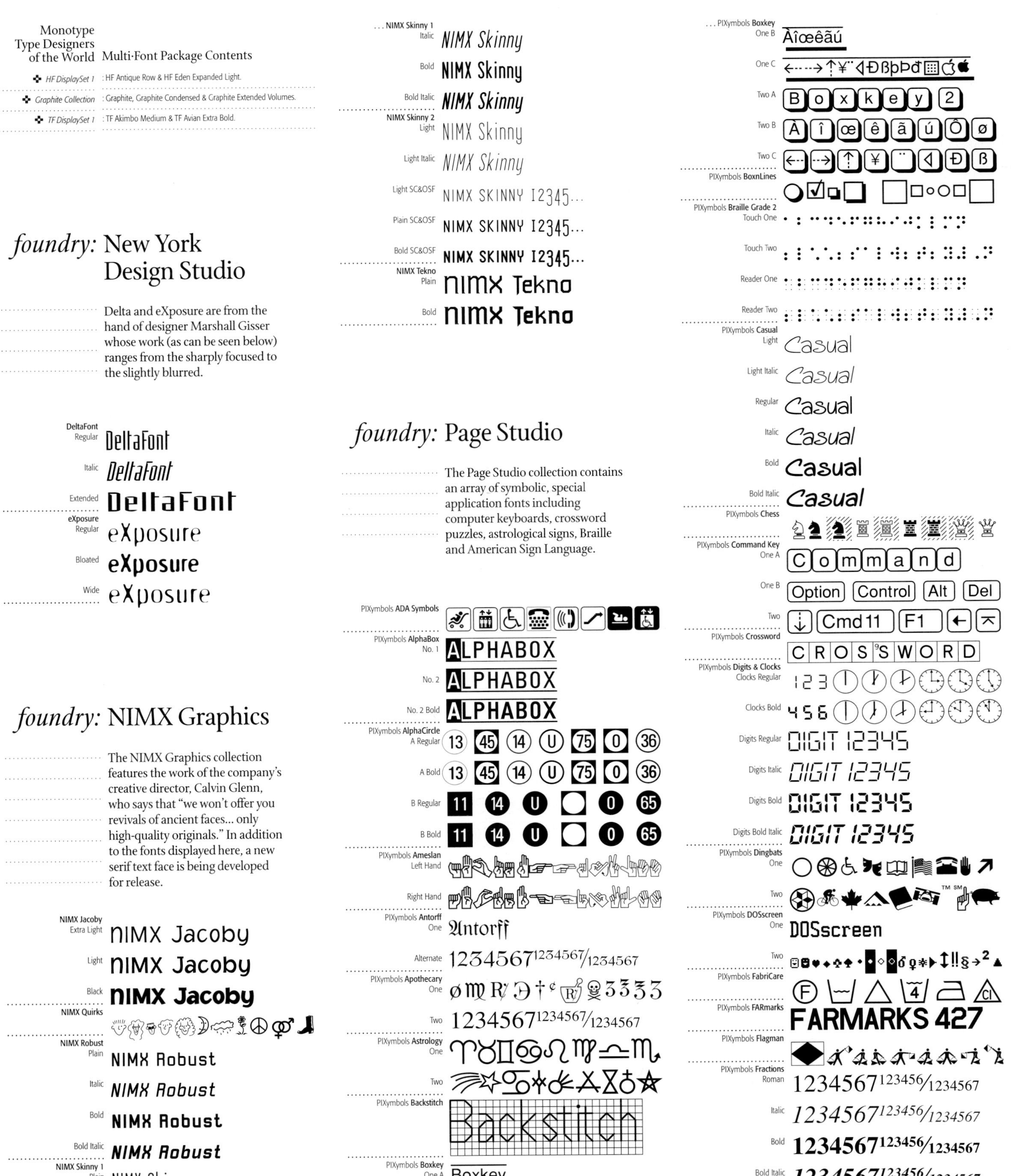

Monotype Type Designers of the World — Multi·Font Package Contents

- HF DisplaySet 1 : HF Antique Row & HF Eden Expanded Light.
- Graphite Collection : Graphite, Graphite Condensed & Graphite Extended Volumes.
- TF DisplaySet 1 : TF Akimbo Medium & TF Avian Extra Bold.

foundry: New York Design Studio

Delta and eXposure are from the hand of designer Marshall Gisser whose work (as can be seen below) ranges from the sharply focused to the slightly blurred.

DeltaFont Regular, Italic, Extended
eXposure Regular, Bloated, Wide

foundry: NIMX Graphics

The NIMX Graphics collection features the work of the company's creative director, Calvin Glenn, who says that "we won't offer you revivals of ancient faces... only high-quality originals." In addition to the fonts displayed here, a new serif text face is being developed for release.

NIMX Jacoby Extra Light, Light, Black
NIMX Quirks
NIMX Robust Plain, Italic, Bold, Bold Italic
NIMX Skinny 1 Plain, Italic, Bold, Bold Italic
NIMX Skinny 2 Light, Light Italic, Light SC&OSF, Plain SC&OSF, Bold SC&OSF
NIMX Tekno Plain, Bold

foundry: Page Studio

The Page Studio collection contains an array of symbolic, special application fonts including computer keyboards, crossword puzzles, astrological signs, Braille and American Sign Language.

PIXymbols ADA Symbols
PIXymbols AlphaBox No. 1, No. 2, No. 2 Bold
PIXymbols AlphaCircle A Regular, A Bold, B Regular, B Bold
PIXymbols Ameslan Left Hand, Right Hand
PIXymbols Antorff One, Alternate
PIXymbols Apothecary One, Two
PIXymbols Astrology One, Two
PIXymbols Backstitch
PIXymbols Boxkey One A, One B, One C, Two A, Two B, Two C
PIXymbols BoxnLines
PIXymbols Braille Grade 2 Touch One, Touch Two, Reader One, Reader Two
PIXymbols Casual Light, Light Italic, Regular, Italic, Bold, Bold Italic
PIXymbols Chess
PIXymbols Command Key One A, One B, Two
PIXymbols Crossword
PIXymbols Digits & Clocks Clocks Regular, Clocks Bold, Digits Regular, Digits Italic, Digits Bold, Digits Bold Italic
PIXymbols Dingbats One, Two
PIXymbols DOSscreen One, Two
PIXymbols FabriCare
PIXymbols FARmarks
PIXymbols Flagman
PIXymbols Fractions Roman, Italic, Bold, Bold Italic

ff

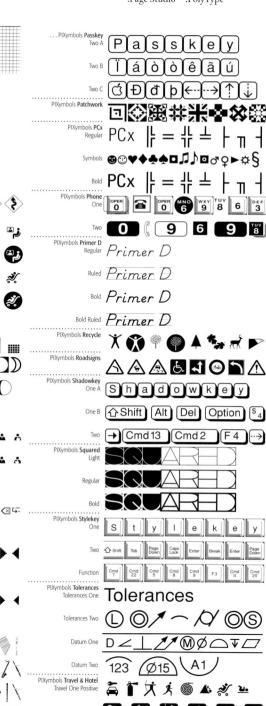

PIXymbols GridMaker

PIXymbols Highway Gothic B — Highway Gothic

PIXymbols Highway Gothic C — Highway Gothic

PIXymbols Highway Gothic D — Highway Gothic

PIXymbols Highway Gothic E — Highway Gothic

PIXymbols Highway Gothic E(M) — Highway Gothic

PIXymbols Highway Signs

PIXymbols Hospital & Safety
Hospital Positive
Hospital Negative
Safety Positive
Safety Negative

PIXymbols LCD
Alphanumerics — LCD
Symbols

PIXymbols Luna
One
Two

PIXymbols Malkoff — Malkoff

PIXymbols Meeting
One
Two

PIXymbols MenuFonts
MACmenu One — MenuFonts
MACmenu Two
WINmenu One — WINmenu
WINmenu Two
WINdialog One — WINdialog
WINdialog Two

PIXymbols Morse

PIXymbols Musica
Open
Fill One
Fill Two
Strings
Orchestra

PIXymbols Newsdot
Regular — Newsdot
Italic — Newsdot
Bold — Newsdot
Bold Italic — Newsdot

PIXymbols Passkey
One A — Passkey
One B — Ïáòòêãú
One C — ĆĐđÞþ←---→↑↓

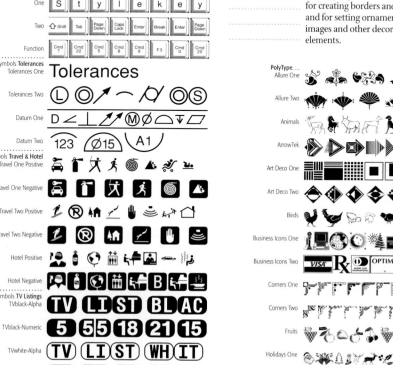

. . . PIXymbols Passkey
Two A — P a s s k e y
Two B — Ï á ò ò ê ã ú
Two C

PIXymbols Patchwork

PIXymbols PCx
Regular — PCx
Symbols
Bold — PCx

PIXymbols Phone
One — OPER 0, OPER 0, MNO 6, WXY 9, TUV 8, 6, DEF 3
Two — 0, 9, 6, 9, TUV 8

PIXymbols Primer D
Regular — Primer D
Ruled — Primer D
Bold — Primer D
Bold Ruled — Primer D

PIXymbols Recycle

PIXymbols Roadsigns

PIXymbols Shadowkey
One A — S h a d o w k e y
One B — Shift Alt Del Option $4
Two — Cmd 13 Cmd 2 F 4

PIXymbols Squared
Light — SQUARED
Regular — SQUARED
Bold — SQUARED

PIXymbols Stylekey
One — S t y l e k e y
Two — Shift Tab Page Down Caps Lock Enter Break Enter Page Down
Function — Cmd 7 Cmd 22 Cmd 5 Cmd 8 Cmd 9 F3 Cmd 11 Cmd 20

PIXymbols Tolerances
Tolerances One — Tolerances
Tolerances Two

Datum One
Datum Two — 123 Ø15 A1

PIXymbols Travel & Hotel
Travel One Positive
Travel One Negative
Travel Two Positive
Travel Two Negative
Hotel Positive
Hotel Negative

PIXymbols TV Listings
TVblack-Alpha — TV LIST BLAC
TVblack-Numeric — 5 55 18 21 15
TVwhite-Alpha — TV LIST WHIT
TVwhite-Numeric — 5 55 18 21 15

PIXymbols Unikey
One A — Unikey UNIKEY
One B
One C
Two A — U n i k e y 2
Two B
Two C

PIXymbols US Map
One
Two — USA US NY 95 495

PIXymbols Xcharting

PIXymbols Xstitch
Xstitch
Xcharting One
Xcharting Two
Backstitch — Backstitch
GridMaker

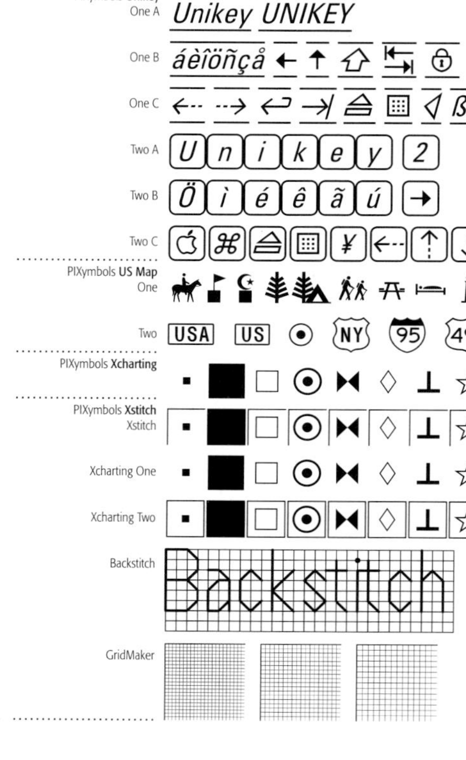

foundry: PolyType

Poly Type specializes in fonts used for creating borders and patterns and for setting ornaments, graphic images and other decorative elements.

PolyType. . .
Allure One
Allure Two
Animals
ArrowTek
Art Deco One
Art Deco Two
Birds
Business Icons One
Business Icons Two
Corners One
Corners Two
Fruits
Holidays One
Holidays Two

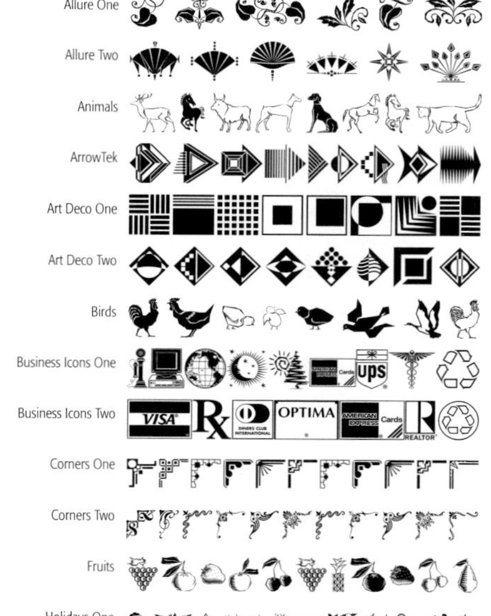
UPS
VISA
OPTIMA
REALTOR

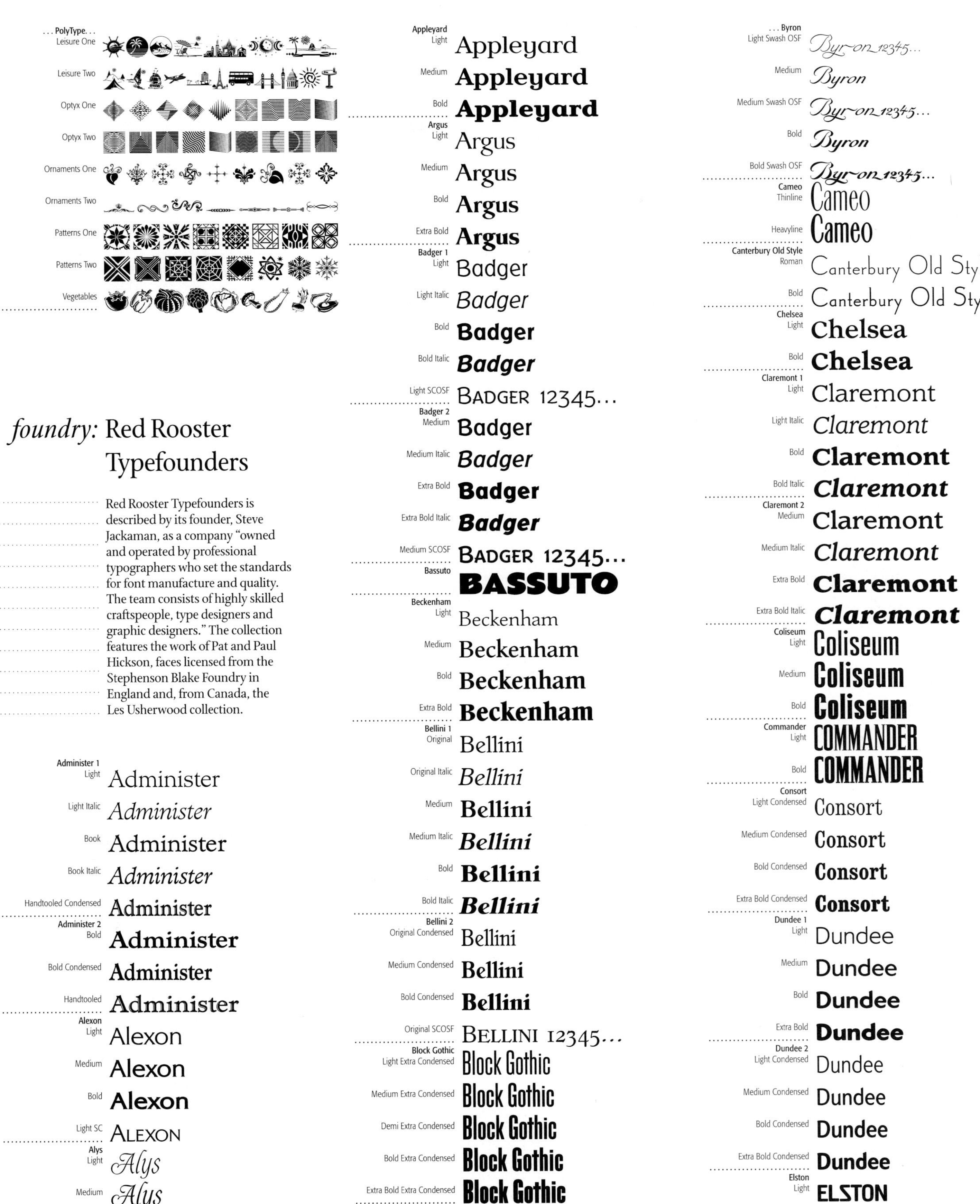
...PolyType... Leisure One
Leisure Two
Optyx One
Optyx Two
Ornaments One
Ornaments Two
Patterns One
Patterns Two
Vegetables
Administer 1 Light Administer
Light Italic Administer
Book Administer
Book Italic Administer
Handtooled Condensed Administer
Administer 2 Bold Administer
Bold Condensed Administer
Handtooled Administer
Alexon Light Alexon
Medium Alexon
Bold Alexon
Light SC Alexon
Alys Light Alys
Medium Alys
Bold Alys
Appleyard Light Appleyard
Medium Appleyard
Bold Appleyard
Argus Light Argus
Medium Argus
Bold Argus
Extra Bold Argus
Badger 1 Light Badger
Light Italic Badger
Bold Badger
Bold Italic Badger
Light SCOSF Badger 12345...
Badger 2 Medium Badger
Medium Italic Badger
Extra Bold Badger
Extra Bold Italic Badger
Medium SCOSF Badger 12345...
Bassuto BASSUTO
Beckenham Light Beckenham
Medium Beckenham
Bold Beckenham
Extra Bold Beckenham
Bellini 1 Original Bellini
Original Italic Bellini
Medium Bellini
Medium Italic Bellini
Bold Bellini
Bold Italic Bellini
Bellini 2 Original Condensed Bellini
Medium Condensed Bellini
Bold Condensed Bellini
Original SCOSF Bellini 12345...
Block Gothic Light Extra Condensed Block Gothic
Medium Extra Condensed Block Gothic
Demi Extra Condensed Block Gothic
Bold Extra Condensed Block Gothic
Extra Bold Extra Condensed Block Gothic
Byron Light Byron
...Byron Light Swash OSF Byron 12345...
Medium Byron
Medium Swash OSF Byron 12345...
Bold Byron
Bold Swash OSF Byron 12345...
Cameo Thinline Cameo
Heavyline Cameo
Canterbury Old Style Roman Canterbury Old Style
Bold Canterbury Old Style
Chelsea Light Chelsea
Bold Chelsea
Claremont 1 Light Claremont
Light Italic Claremont
Bold Claremont
Bold Italic Claremont
Claremont 2 Medium Claremont
Medium Italic Claremont
Extra Bold Claremont
Extra Bold Italic Claremont
Coliseum Light Coliseum
Medium Coliseum
Bold Coliseum
Commander Light COMMANDER
Bold COMMANDER
Consort Light Condensed Consort
Medium Condensed Consort
Bold Condensed Consort
Extra Bold Condensed Consort
Dundee 1 Light Dundee
Medium Dundee
Bold Dundee
Extra Bold Dundee
Dundee 2 Light Condensed Dundee
Medium Condensed Dundee
Bold Condensed Dundee
Extra Bold Condensed Dundee
Elston Light ELSTON
Bold ELSTON

foundry: Red Rooster Typefounders

Red Rooster Typefounders is described by its founder, Steve Jackaman, as a company "owned and operated by professional typographers who set the standards for font manufacture and quality. The team consists of highly skilled craftspeople, type designers and graphic designers." The collection features the work of Pat and Paul Hickson, faces licensed from the Stephenson Blake Foundry in England and, from Canada, the Les Usherwood collection.

ff

Equestrienne 1
Light Equestrienne
Light Italic *Equestrienne*
Bold **Equestrienne**
Bold Italic ***Equestrienne***
Light SCLF EQUESTRIENNE 123...

Equestrienne 2
Book Equestrienne
Book Italic *Equestrienne*
Medium **Equestrienne**
Medium Italic ***Equestrienne***
Book SCLF EQUESTRIENNE 12...

Erasmus
Light Erasmus
Medium Erasmus
Bold **Erasmus**
Extra Bold **Erasmus**
Light SCOSF ERASMUS 12345...
Medium SCOSF ERASMUS 12345...

Europa Grotesque
Light Europa Grotesque
Medium Europa Grotesque
Bold **Europa Grotesque**
Extra Bold **Europa Grotesque**

Extension 1
Light Extension
Light Italic *Extension*
Medium **Extension**
Medium Italic ***Extension***
Extra Bold **Extension**
Extra Bold Italic ***Extension***

Extension 2
Book Extension
Book Italic *Extension*
Bold **Extension**
Bold Italic ***Extension***

Faust
Light Faust
Light Italic *Faust*
Medium Faust
Bold **Faust**
Extra Bold **Faust**
Light SCOSF FAUST 12345...

Forum
Light FORUM
Medium FORUM

... Forum
Bold **FORUM**
Light OSF OSF 12345...
Medium OSF OSF 12345...
Bold OSF **OSF 12345...**

Gilmore Fahrenheit
GILMORE FAHRENHEIT

Gilmore Sans Extra Bold Extra Condensed Titling
GILMORE SANS

Goudy 38 One
Light Goudy 38
Light Italic *Goudy 38*
Medium Goudy 38
Extra Bold **Goudy 38**

Goudy 38 Two
Book Goudy 38
Book Italic *Goudy 38*
Bold **Goudy 38**

Grove Script
Light *Grove Script*
Medium *Grove Script*
Bold ***Grove Script***

Hancock Bold Condensed
Hancock

Hess Old Style
Roman Hess Old Style
Medium Hess Old Style
Bold **Hess Old Style**
Extra Bold **Hess Old Style**
Roman SCLF HESS OLD STYLE 12...

Honduras
Inline HONDURAS
Solid **HONDURAS**

Javelin
Light *Javelin*
Medium *Javelin*
Bold ***Javelin***
Extra Bold ***Javelin***

Jubilee
Light Jubilee
Medium Jubilee
Bold **Jubilee**

Keyboard
Light Keyboard
Medium Keyboard
Bold **Keyboard**

Kingsrow
Light Kingsrow
Medium Kingsrow
Bold **Kingsrow**
Extra Bold **Kingsrow**

Leighton
Light Leighton
Light Italic *Leighton*
Bold **Leighton**
Bold Condensed **Leighton**

Lesmore 1
Light Lesmore
Light Italic *Lesmore*
Medium **Lesmore**
Medium Italic ***Lesmore***

Lesmore 2
Book Lesmore
Book Italic *Lesmore*
Bold **Lesmore**
Bold Italic ***Lesmore***

Lesmore 3
Light Condensed Lesmore
Light Condensed Italic *Lesmore*
Medium Condensed **Lesmore**
Medium Condensed Italic ***Lesmore***

Lesmore 4
Book Condensed Lesmore
Book Condensed Italic *Lesmore*
Bold Condensed **Lesmore**
Bold Condensed Italic ***Lesmore***

Pall Mall
Light Pall Mall
Bold **Pall Mall**
Light Titling SC PALL MALL
Bold Titling SC **PALL MALL**

Phosphate
Inline PHOSPHATE
Solid **PHOSPHATE**

Portobello
Light Portobello
Medium Portobello
Demi **Portobello**
Bold **Portobello**
Extra Bold **Portobello**

Quest
Light QUEST
Medium QUEST
Bold **QUEST**

Raleigh Gothic
Extra Light Condensed RALEIGH GOTHIC
Medium Condensed RALEIGH GOTHIC
Extra Bold Condensed **RALEIGH GOTHIC**

Ribbit
Ribbit

ff

See page 610 for contents of Russian Type Foundry Multi-Font Packages.

Rivoli Initials — RIVOLI

Saint Louis
- Light — Saint Louis
- Bold — Saint Louis
- Extra Bold — Saint Louis

Schiller Antiqua
- Light — Schiller Antiqua
- Medium — Schiller Antiqua
- Bold — Schiller Antiqua
- Extra Bold — Schiller Antiqua

Schindler
- Light — Schindler
- Book — Schindler
- Medium — Schindler
- Bold — Schindler
- Extra Bold — Schindler

Shinn 1
- Light — Shinn
- Light Italic — *Shinn*
- Medium — Shinn
- Medium Italic — *Shinn*
- Extra Bold — Shinn
- Extra Bold Italic — *Shinn*

Shinn 2
- Book — Shinn
- Book Italic — *Shinn*
- Bold — Shinn
- Bold Italic — *Shinn*

Silverado 1
- Light — Silverado
- Medium — Silverado
- Bold — Silverado
- Extra Bold — Silverado

Silverado 2
- Light Condensed — Silverado
- Medium Condensed — Silverado
- Bold Condensed — Silverado
- Extra Bold Condensed — Silverado

Sinclair Script
- Light — Sinclair Script
- Medium — Sinclair Script
- Bold — Sinclair Script

Sphinx
- Inline — Sphinx
- Solid — Sphinx

Stanhope
- Light — Stanhope
- Light Italic — *Stanhope*

. . . Stanhope
- Medium — Stanhope
- Medium Italic — *Stanhope*
- Bold — Stanhope
- Bold Italic — *Stanhope*

Stirling 1
- Light — Stirling
- Light Italic — *Stirling*
- Bold — Stirling
- Bold Italic — *Stirling*

Stirling 2
- Medium — Stirling
- Medium Italic — *Stirling*
- Extra Bold — Stirling
- Extra Bold Italic — *Stirling*

Superba Bold — Superba

Sycamore
- Light — SYCAMORE
- Bold — SYCAMORE

Thingbat

Titanic Condensed — Titanic

Veronese 1
- Book — Veronese
- Medium — Veronese
- Bold — Veronese
- Extra Bold — Veronese

Veronese 2
- Book Condensed — Veronese
- Medium Condensed — Veronese
- Bold Condensed — Veronese
- Extra Bold Condensed — Veronese

Waverly 1
- Light — Waverly
- Light Italic — *Waverly*
- Bold — Waverly
- Bold Italic — *Waverly*

Waverly 2
- Medium — Waverly
- Medium Italic — *Waverly*
- Extra Bold — Waverly
- Extra Bold Italic — *Waverly*

Waverly 3
- Light Condensed — Waverly
- Medium Condensed — Waverly
- Bold Condensed — Waverly
- Extra Bold Condensed — Waverly

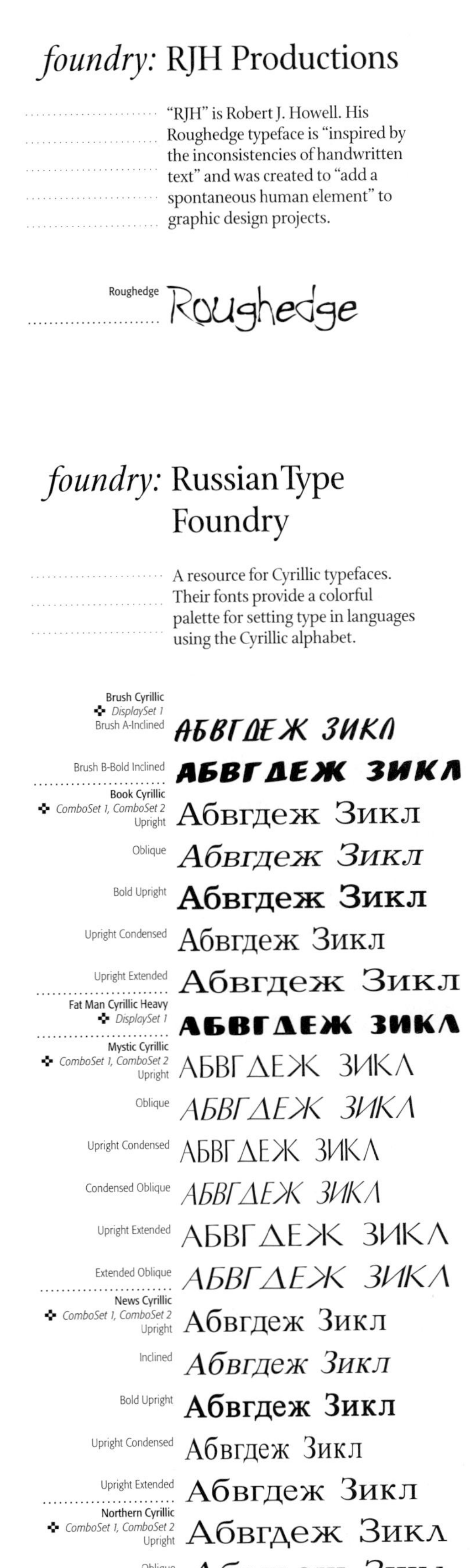

foundry: RJH Productions

"RJH" is Robert J. Howell. His Roughedge typeface is "inspired by the inconsistencies of handwritten text" and was created to "add a spontaneous human element" to graphic design projects.

Roughedge — Roughedge

foundry: Russian Type Foundry

A resource for Cyrillic typefaces. Their fonts provide a colorful palette for setting type in languages using the Cyrillic alphabet.

Brush Cyrillic
DisplaySet 1
- Brush A-Inclined — АБВГДЕЖ ЗИКЛ
- Brush B-Bold Inclined — АБВГДЕЖ ЗИКЛ

Book Cyrillic
ComboSet 1, ComboSet 2
- Upright — Абвгдеж Зикл
- Oblique — *Абвгдеж Зикл*
- Bold Upright — Абвгдеж Зикл
- Upright Condensed — Абвгдеж Зикл
- Upright Extended — Абвгдеж Зикл

Fat Man Cyrillic Heavy
DisplaySet 1 — АБВГДЕЖ ЗИКЛ

Mystic Cyrillic
ComboSet 1, ComboSet 2
- Upright — АБВГДЕЖ ЗИКЛ
- Oblique — *АБВГДЕЖ ЗИКЛ*
- Upright Condensed — АБВГДЕЖ ЗИКЛ
- Condensed Oblique — *АБВГДЕЖ ЗИКЛ*
- Upright Extended — АБВГДЕЖ ЗИКЛ
- Extended Oblique — *АБВГДЕЖ ЗИКЛ*

News Cyrillic
ComboSet 1, ComboSet 2
- Upright — Абвгдеж Зикл
- Inclined — *Абвгдеж Зикл*
- Bold Upright — Абвгдеж Зикл
- Upright Condensed — Абвгдеж Зикл
- Upright Extended — Абвгдеж Зикл

Northern Cyrillic
ComboSet 1, ComboSet 2
- Upright — Абвгдеж Зикл
- Oblique — *Абвгдеж Зикл*
- Bold Upright — Абвгдеж Зикл

ff

Northern Cyrillic
- Upright Condensed: Абвгдеж Зикл
- Upright Extended: Абвгдеж Зик

Osho Cyrillic Script ✤ *DisplaySet 1*: АБВГДЕЖ З

Oval Cyrillic ✤ *ComboSet 1, ComboSet 2*
- Upright: Абвгдеж Зикл
- Oblique: Абвгдеж Зикл
- Upright Condensed: Абвгдеж Зикл
- Upright Extended: Абвгдеж Зикл

Rome Cyrillic ✤ *ComboSet 2*
- Upright: АБВГДЕЖ ЗИКЛ
- Oblique: АБВГДЕЖ ЗИКЛ
- Upright Condensed: АБВГДЕЖ ЗИКЛ
- Condensed Oblique: АБВГДЕЖ ЗИКЛ
- Upright Extended: АБВГДЕЖ ЗИКЛ
- Extended Oblique: АБВГДЕЖ ЗИКЛ

Rome Cyrillic Shaded
- Upright: АБВГДЕЖ ЗИКЛ
- Oblique: АБВГДЕЖ ЗИКЛ
- Upright Condensed: АБВГДЕЖ ЗИКЛ
- Condensed Oblique: АБВГДЕЖ ЗИКЛ
- Upright Extended: АБВГДЕЖ ЗИКЛ
- Extended Oblique: АБВГДЕЖ ЗИКЛ

Socrates Cyrillic Heavy
- Upright: АБВГДЕЖ ЗИК
- Oblique: АБВГДЕЖ ЗИК
- Upright Condensed: АБВГДЕЖ ЗИКЛ
- Condensed Oblique: АБВГДЕЖ ЗИКЛ
- Upright Extended: АБВГДЕЖ ЗИ
- Extended Oblique: АБВГДЕЖ ЗИ

St. Petersburg Cyrillic ✤ *DisplaySet 1*
- Upright: АБВГДЕЖ ЗИКЛ
- Oblique: АБВГДЕЖ ЗИКЛ

Sunny Cyrillic
- Upright: Абвгдеж Зикл
- Oblique: Абвгдеж Зикл
- Bold Upright: Абвгдеж Зикл
- Upright Condensed: Абвгдеж Зикл
- Upright Extended: Абвгдеж Зикл

Sunny Cyrillic Thin
- Upright: Абвгдеж Зикл
- Oblique: Абвгдеж Зикл
- Upright Condensed: Абвгдеж Зикл
- Condensed Oblique: Абвгдеж Зикл
- Upright Extended: Абвгдеж Зикл
- Extended Oblique: Абвгдеж Зикл

Sunny Cyrillic Light & Heavy
- Light Upright: Абвгдеж Зикл
- Light Oblique: Абвгдеж Зикл
- Light Condensed Upright: Абвгдеж Зикл
- Light Condensed Oblique: Абвгдеж Зикл
- Light Extended Upright: Абвгдеж Зикл
- Light Extended Oblique: Абвгдеж Зикл
- Heavy Upright: Абвгдеж Зикл
- Heavy Oblique: Абвгдеж Зикл
- Heavy Condensed Upright: Абвгдеж Зикл
- Heavy Condensed Oblique: Абвгдеж Зикл
- Heavy Extended Upright: Абвгдеж Зикл
- Heavy Extended Oblique: Абвгдеж Зикл

Russian Type Foundry Multi·Font Package Contents

✤ *ComboSet 1*: Book Cyrillic Upright, Oblique, Bold Upright, Upright Condensed & Upright Extended. Mystic Cyrillic Upright, Oblique, Upright Condensed, Condensed Oblique, Upright Extended & Extended Oblique. News Cyrillic Upright, Inclined, Bold Upright, Upright Condensed, & Upright Extended. Northern Cyrillic Upright, Oblique, Bold Upright, Upright Condensed & Upright Extended. Oval Cyrillic Upright, Oblique, Upright Condensed & Upright Extended.

✤ *ComboSet 2*: Book Cyrillic Upright, Oblique, Bold Upright, Upright Condensed & Upright Extended. Mystic Cyrillic Upright, Oblique, Upright Condensed, Condensed Oblique, Upright Extended & Extended Oblique. News Cyrillic Upright, Inclined, Bold Upright, Upright Condensed, & Upright Extended. Northern Cyrillic Upright, Oblique, Bold Upright, Upright Condensed & Upright Extended. Oval Cyrillic Upright, Oblique, Upright Condensed & Upright Extended. Rome Cyrillic Upright, Oblique, Upright Condensed, Condensed Oblique, Upright Extended & Extended Oblique.

✤ *DisplaySet 1*: Brush Cyrillic A Inclined & B Bold Inclined, Fat Man Cyrillic Heavy, Osho Cyrillic Script, St. Petersburg Cyrillic.

foundry: Christian Schwartz Design

We currently offer two faces from this young and talented designer. Zombie was inspired by hand lettering on the B-52's 1989 album, *Cosmic Thing.* Of it, Schwartz says, "It's completely inevitable. If you've seen Zombie once, you're under its power forever. It will cast its spell, and then appear everywhere you look – ... Don't try to fight it. It's unstoppable."

Twist One & Two
- One: TWIST ONE
- Two: TWIST TWO

Twist Three & Four
- Three: TWIST THREE
- Four: TWIST FOUR

Zombie: ZOMBIE

foundry: Stone Type Foundry

Sumner Stone notes that "Stone Type Foundry is a small independent company that designs, manufactures and markets new type designs. It is an old kind of business with a new kind of equipment. Small, independent type foundries are what made type happen from the first days of printing until the early twentieth century. Now we are back."

EndsMeansMends
- Ends
- Means: MEANS
- Mends: MENDS

Silica
- Extra Light: Silica
- Light: Silica
- Regular: Silica
- Semibold: Silica
- Bold: Silica
- Black: Silica

Stone Print
- Roman: Stone Print
- Italic: Stone Print
- Semibold: Stone Print
- Semibold Italic: Stone Print
- Bold: Stone Print
- Bold Italic: Stone Print

Stone Print Extra
- Roman SCOSF: STONE PRINT 12345...
- Italic SCOSF: STONE PRINT 12345...
- Semibold SCOSF: STONE PRINT 12345...
- Semibold Italic SCOSF: STONE PRINT 12345...
- Bold SCOSF: STONE PRINT 12345...
- Bold Italic SCOSF: STONE PRINT 12345...
- Figures/Fractions: 27/36 42 3/8 427 35/64 12345
- Italic Figures/Fractions: 27/36 42 3/8 427 35/64 12345
- Semibold Figures/Fractions: 27/36 42 3/8 427 35/64 1234
- Semibold Italic Figures/Fractions: 27/36 42 3/8 427 35/64 1234
- Bold Figures/Fractions: 27/36 42 3/8 427 35/64 123
- Bold Italic Figures/Fractions: 27/36 42 3/8 427 35/64 12345

ff

✤ *See this page for contents of Russian Type Foundry Multi-Font Packages.*

foundry: Torah

Torah is an Israeli company founded in 1988. In addition to creating Hebrew fonts, Torah also produces digital translations of religious writings. In its broadest sense, the Hebrew word *Torah* refers to the entire body of Jewish teaching incorporated in the Talmud, the Old Testament and later religious commentaries.

Classic Collection

- David — אבגדהוז חטיכ
- David Bold — אבגדהוז חטיכ
- Frank — אבגדהוז חטיכ
- Frank Bold — אבגדהוז חטיכ
- Galed — אבגדהוז חטיכ
- Galed Bold — אבגדהוז חטיכ
- Hadas — אבגדהוז חטיכ
- Hadas Bold — אבגדהוז חטיכ
- Meiri — אבגדהוז חטיכ
- Meiri Bold — אבגדהוז חטיכ
- Rashi — אבגדהוז חטיכ
- Rashi Bold — אבגדהוז חטיכ
- Sofer — אבגדהוז חטיכ
- Vilna — אבגדהוז חטיכ
- Vilna Bold — אבגדהוז חטיכ

Designer I Collection

- Acheneli Medium — אבגדהוז חטיכ
- Acheneli — אבגדהוז חטיכ
- Busoreli — אבגדהוז חטיכ
- Busoreli Bold — אבגדהוז חטיכ
- Careli — אבגדהוז חטיכ
- Careli Medium — אבגדהוז חטיכ
- Frizeli — אבגדהוז חטיכ
- Frizeli Bold — אבגדהוז חטיכ
- Gilgal Ultra Bold — אבגדהוז חטיכ
- Gilgal Ultra Outline — אבגדהוז חטיכ
- Ivricana Bold — אבגדהוז חטיכ
- Ivricana Outline — אבגדהוז חטיכ
- Kabelim Bold — אבגדהוז חטיכ
- Kabelim Outline — אבגדהוז חטיכ
- Lublineli Condensed — אבגדהוז חטיכ

. . . Designer I Collection

- Lublineli Extra Bold Condensed — אבגדהוז חטיכ
- Optwo — אבגדהוז חטיכ
- Optwo Bold — אבגדהוז חטיכ
- Revieli — אבגדהוז חטיכ
- Revieli Heavy — אבגדהוז חטיכ
- Yavaneli — אבגדהוז חטיכ
- Yavaneli Extra Bold — אבגדהוז חטיכ

Designer II Collection

- Atzor — אבגדהוז חטיכ
- Atzor Outline — אבגדהוז חטיכ
- Broadweli — אבגדהוז חטיכ
- Broadweli Engraved — אבגדהוז חטיכ
- Coopereli — אבגדהוז חטיכ
- Coopereli Outline — אבגדהוז חטיכ
- Hebras Book — אבגדהוז חטיכ
- Hebras Black — אבגדהוז חטיכ
- Hobeli — אבגדהוז חטיכ
- Hobeli Outline — אבגדהוז חטיכ
- Lublineli — אבגדהוז חטיכ
- Lublineli Extra Bold — אבגדהוז חטיכ
- Mehandes — אבגדהוז חטיכ
- Mehandes Bold — אבגדהוז חטיכ
- Nekoshet — אבגדהוז חטיכ
- Nekoshet Bold — אבגדהוז חטיכ
- Optimeli — אבגדהוז חטיכ
- Optimeli Bold — אבגדהוז חטיכ
- Peigneli — אבגדהוז חטיכ
- Peigneli Bold — אבגדהוז חטיכ
- Uncieli — אבגדהוז חטיכ
- Uncieli Outline — אבגדהוז חטיכ

foundry: Treacyfaces

An independent type foundry founded by Joe Treacy, a completely self-taught calligrapher and letterform designer. His first typeface – Bryn Mawr – was released by Linotype in 1984. The collection features innovative and unique designs for text and display, all with meticulous letter fitting and extensive kerning.

- **TF Adepta A Extra Bold** ❖ *TF DisplaySet 2* — TF Adepta
- **TF Akimbo A** Akimbo A Light — TF Akimbo
- Akimbo A Demibold — TF Akimbo
- Akimbo A Extra Bold — TF Akimbo
- **TF Akimbo B** Medium — TF Akimbo
- Bold — TF Akimbo
- Heavy — TF Akimbo
- **TF Akimbo Medium** ❖ *TF DisplaySet 1* — TF Akimbo
- **TF Ardent A** Regular — TF Ardent
- Italic — *TF Ardent*
- Extra Bold — TF Ardent
- Extra Bold Italic — *TF Ardent*
- **TF Avian Extra Bold** ❖ *TF DisplaySet 1* — TF Avian
- **TF Bryn Mawr A** Light — TF Bryn Mawr
- Light Italic — *TF Bryn Mawr*
- Medium — TF Bryn Mawr
- Medium Italic — *TF Bryn Mawr*
- **TF Bryn Mawr B** Book — TF Bryn Mawr
- Book Italic — *TF Bryn Mawr*
- Bold — TF Bryn Mawr
- Bold Italic — *TF Bryn Mawr*
- **TF Dierama** Regular — TF Dierama
- Extra Bold — TF Dierama
- **TF Forever A** Regular — TF Forever
- Italic — *TF Forever*
- Extra Bold — TF Forever
- Extra Bold Italic — *TF Forever*
- **TF Forever B** Thin — TF Forever
- Thin Italic — *TF Forever*
- Medium — TF Forever

ff

... TF Forever B Medium Italic — TF Forever
TF Forever C Extra Light — TF Forever
Extra Light Italic — TF Forever
Demibold — TF Forever
Demibold Italic — TF Forever
TF Forever D Light — TF Forever
Light Italic — TF Forever
Bold — TF Forever
Bold Italic — TF Forever
TF Forever Two A Regular — TF Forever Two
Italic — TF Forever Two
Extra Bold — TF Forever Two
Extra Bold Italic — TF Forever Two
TF Forever Two B Thin — TF Forever Two
Thin Italic — TF Forever Two
Medium — TF Forever Two
Medium Italic — TF Forever Two
TF Forever Two C Extra Light — TF Forever Two
Extra Light Italic — TF Forever Two
Demibold — TF Forever Two
Demibold Italic — TF Forever Two
TF Forever Two D Light — TF Forever Two
Light Italic — TF Forever Two
Bold — TF Forever Two
Bold Italic — TF Forever Two
TF Games TF Bridgette Bridge Pi — QKA♡◇♠♣123DBL
TF Crossword-Puzzle — 1 2 3 4
TF Crossword-Solution — A B C D W X
TF Guestcheck Heavy ✤ TF DisplaySet 2 — TF Guest
TF Habitat A Regular — TF Habitat
Italic — TF Habitat
Bold — TF Habitat
Bold Italic — TF Habitat
TF Habitat B Book — TF Habitat
Book Italic — TF Habitat
Demi — TF Habitat
Demi Italic — TF Habitat
TF Habitat Condensed A Condensed — TF Habitat Condensed

... TF Habitat Condensed A Condensed Italic — TF Habitat Condensed
Bold Condensed — TF Habitat Condensed
Bold Condensed Italic — TF Habitat Condensed
TF Habitat Bold Contour A — TF Habitat
TF Habitat Bold Contour B — TF Habitat
TF Habitat Bold Cameo Initials Cameo Initials One — A B C D E F G H I
Cameo Initials Two — A B C D E F G H I
TF Hôtelmoderne A Medium — TF Hôtelmoderne
Demi — TF Hôtelmoderne
Bold — TF Hôtelmoderne
Heavy — TF Hôtelmoderne
TF Hôtelmoderne Two A Medium — TF Hôtelmoderne
Demi — TF Hôtelmoderne
Bold — TF Hôtelmoderne
Heavy — TF Hôtelmoderne
TF Hôtelmoderne Serif Heavy — TF Hôtelmoderne Serif
Heavy Shaded — TF Hôtelmoderne Serif
TF Maltby Antique A Regular — TF Maltby Antique
Medium — TF Maltby Antique
Extra Bold — TF Maltby Antique
Heavy — TF Maltby Antique
TF Maltby Antique B Book — TF Maltby Antique
Bold — TF Maltby Antique
Heavy Ragged — TF Maltby Antique
Black — TF Maltby Antique
TF Maltby Antique Ragged Initials — TF MALTBY
TF Raincheck A Light — TF Raincheck
Book — TF Raincheck
Demi — TF Raincheck
Heavy — TF Raincheck
TF Raincheck B Regular — TF Raincheck
Medium — TF Raincheck
Bold — TF Raincheck
Ultra — TF Raincheck
TF Roux Extra Bold — TF Roux
Extra Bold Shaded One — TF Roux
Borders
TF Simper Extra Bold — TF Simper

... TF Simper Extra Bold Condensed — TF Simper
Extra Bold Extra Condensed — TFSimper
Serif Extra Bold — TF Simper
TF Squiggle Serif
Sans
Sans Narrow
Chancery Medium
Typewriter

Treacyfaces Multi-Font Package Contents

✤ TF DisplaySet 1	: TF Akimbo Medium & TF Avian Extra Bold.
✤ TF DisplaySet 2	: TF Adepta A Extra Bold & TF Guestcheck Heavy.
✤ TF Games	: TF Bridgette Bridge Pi, TF Crossword-Puzzle, TF Crossword-Solution.

foundry: [T-26]

A new digital type foundry "representing today's typographic forms of expression and experimentation." Based in Chicago, [T-26] was founded by Carlos Segura and Scott Smith in 1993. The collection features their work as well as that of other designers from around the world.

Aleksei Solid — Aleksei
Disturbed — Aleksei
Inline — Aleksei
Baluster — BALUSTER
Blast-o-rama Regular — Blast-o-rama
Beat — Blast-o-rama
Bold — Blast-o-rama
Bubbalove Light — Bubbalove
Medium — Bubbalove
Bold — Bubbalove
Carnival — Carnival
Chasline Regular — Chasline
Italic — Chasline
Bold — Chasline
Bold Italic — Chasline

✤ See this page for contents of Treacyfaces Multi-Font Packages. See page 613 for contents of [T-26] Multi-Font Packages.

ff

Christmas Gift Script Regular — Christmas Gift Script
Bold — Christmas Gift Script
Cirruss — Cirruss
Decco Modern Normal — Decco Modern
Organic — Decco Modern
Devit — DEVIT
Dingura
Earthquake ✣ [T-26] FontSet 1 — Earthquake
Entropy — ENTROPY
Euphoria — Euphoria
Escalido Gothico — Escalido
Streak — Escalido
Flaco Solid — FLACO
Inline — FLACO
Flexure — Flexure
Freakshow Scary — Freakshow
Real Scary — Freakshow
FreeBe Caps ✣ [T-26] FontSet 2 — FREEBE
FreeDom ✣ [T-26] FontSet 2 — FreeDom
Gadzooks Regular — Gadz
Sans — Gadz
Squared — Gadz
Garbage Normal — Garbage
Italic — Garbage
Gothic Blond Slim — Gothic Blond
Husky — Gothic Blond
Handwrite Inkblot — Handwrite Inkblot
Janaki Regular — Janaki
Italic — Janaki
Bold — Janaki
Bold Italic — Janaki
Black — Janaki
Kurusu
Mata Regular — MATA
Bold — MATA
Condensed — MATA
... Mata Bold Condensed — MATA
Mill Harrow Regular — mill harrow
Knob
Missive — Missive
Neo Bold — NEO BOLD
Oreana — OREANA
Osprey — OSPREY
Outhaus ✣ [T-26] FontSet 1 — Outhaus
Ramiz Regular — RAMIZ
Bold — RAMIZ
Extended — RAMIZ
Bold Extended — RAMIZ
Revolution — revolution
Riot — riot
Rubaya Inline — RUBAYA INLINE
Scorpio Regular — SCORPIO
Dingbats
Tribal
Scotty — Scotty
Scratch — Scratch
Scrawl — Scrawl
Skreetch Caps — SKREETCH
Spike ✣ [T-26] FontSet 3 — SPIKE
Sputnik ✣ [T-26] FontSet 3 — SPUTNIK
Square 40 Regular — SQUARE
Inline — SQUARE
Tattoo — TATTOO
Thornforms
Union Round — Union Round
Square — Union Square
Variator One — VARIATOR
Two — VARIATOR
Three — Variator
Wave — Wave
Werkman Round — Werkman
Square — Werkman

[T-26] Multi-Font Package Contents

✣ [T-26] FontSet 1 : Earthquake & Outhaus.
✣ [T-26] FontSet 2 : FreeDom & FreeBe Caps.
✣ [T-26] FontSet 3 : Spike & Sputnik.

foundry: URW

Many years before the Macintosh and Fontographer, URW created *Ikarus:* the first viable software product for the production of digital fonts; it is still widely used by many typeface manufacturers. The URW typeface collection offers a vast selection of fonts including original designs by Herman Zapf and his wife Gudrun and licensed fonts from ITC, Letraset, WTC and other sources.

Aachen Display Medium — Aachen
Bold — Aachen
Aachen Poster Bold — Aachen
Outline Bold — Aachen
Accius Light — Accius
Regular — Accius
Italic — Accius
Medium — Accius
Medium Italic — Accius
Bold — Accius
Bold Italic — Accius
Accius Condensed Light Condensed — Accius
Medium Condensed — Accius
Bold Condensed — Accius
Heavy Condensed — Accius
Heavy Condensed Italic — Accius
Black Condensed — Accius
Accius Extended Light Extended — Accius
Extended — Accius
Medium Extended — Accius
Bold Extended — Accius
Bold Extended Italic — Accius

ff

Accius Narrow		Accius Narrow
Accius Ultra		Accius Ultra
Accius Buch Ultra Light	Ultra Light	Accius Buch
	Ultra Light Italic	Accius Buch
Accius Buch	Light	Accius Buch
	Regular	Accius Buch
	Italic	Accius Buch
	Medium	Accius Buch
	Medium Italic	Accius Buch
	Bold	Accius Buch
	Bold Italic	Accius Buch
Accius Buch Condensed	Light Condensed	Accius Buch
	Light Condensed Italic	Accius Buch
	Condensed	Accius Buch
	Medium Condensed	Accius Buch
	Bold Condensed	Accius Buch
Accius Buch Extended	Light Extended	Accius Buch
	Extended	Accius Buch
	Medium Extended	Accius Buch
	Bold Extended	Accius Buch
Accius Buch Outline	Medium	Accius Buch
	Bold	Accius Buch
Accius Buch Rounded	Regular	Accius Buch
	Medium	Accius Buch
	Bold	Accius Buch
	Bold Condensed	Accius Buch
URW Alcuin 1	Light	URW Alcuin
	Light SCOSF	URW ALCUIN 1234...
	Bold	URW Alcuin
	Bold SCOSF	URW ALCUIN 123...
URW Alcuin 2	Regular	URW Alcuin
	Regular SCOSF	URW ALCUIN 1234...
	Extra Bold	URW Alcuin
	Extra Bold SCOSF	URW ALCUIN 123...
Algerian		ALGERIAN
Alternate Gothic	No. 1	Alternate Gothic
	No. 2	Alternate Gothic
	No. 3	Alternate Gothic
Alte Schwabacher		Alte Schwabacher
ITC American Typewriter	Light	ITC AmericanType
	Light Italic	ITC AmericanType
	Medium	ITC AmericanType
	Medium Italic	ITC AmericanType
	Bold	ITC AmericanType
	Bold Italic	ITC AmericanType
ITC American Typewriter Display	Light	ITC American
	Medium	ITC American
	Bold	ITC American
ITC American Typewriter Condensed	Light Condensed	ITC American Type
	Medium Condensed	ITC American Type
	Bold Condensed	ITC American Type
American Uncial		american uncial
Anglius Regular		Anglius
ITC Anna		ITC ANNA
Annlie	Extra Bold	Annlie
	Extra Bold Italic	Annlie
URW Antiqua 1	Regular	URW Antiqua
	Italic	URW Antiqua
	Medium	URW Antiqua
	Medium Italic	URW Antiqua
	Bold	URW Antiqua
	Bold Italic	URW Antiqua
	Condensed	URW Antiqua
URW Antiqua 2	Extra Bold	URW Antiqua
	Extra Bold Italic	URW Antiqua
	Ultra Bold	URW Antiqua
	Ultra Bold Italic	URW Antiqua
	Super	URW Antiqua
	Super Italic	URW Antiqua
URW Antiqua Alternative	Super Alternative	URW Antiqua
	Super Alternative Italic	URW Antiqua
URW Antiqua SCOSF	Regular SCOSF	U ANTIQUA 12345...
	Medium SCOSF	U ANTIQUA 1234...
	Condensed SCOSF	U ANTIQUA 12345...
Antique Olive	Light	Antique Olive
... Antique Olive	Regular	Antique Olive
	Italic	Antique Olive
	Medium	Antique Olive
	Bold	Antique Olive
Antique Olive Compact	Regular	Antique Olive
	Italic	Antique Olive
Antique Olive Condensed	Condensed	Antique Olive
	Bold Condensed	Antique Olive
Antique Olive Nord	Regular	Antique Olive
	Outline	Antique Olive
Antique Olive SCOSF	Regular SCOSF	ANT OLIVE 12345...
	Medium SCOSF	ANT OLIVE 12345...
Anzeigen Grotesk	Text	Anzeigen Grotesk
	Display	Anzeigen Grotesk
Aritus	Regular	Aritus
	Bold	Aritus
	Extra Bold	Aritus
Arnold Böcklin		Arnold Böcklin
Arsis	Regular	Arsis
	Italic	Arsis
Augius Open		AUGIUS
ITC Avant Garde Gothic	Extra Light	ITC Avant Garde
	Extra Light Oblique	ITC Avant Garde
	Book	ITC Avant Garde
	Book Oblique	ITC Avant Garde
	Medium	ITC Avant Garde
	Medium Oblique	ITC Avant Garde
	Demi	ITC Avant Garde
	Demi Oblique	ITC Avant Garde
	Bold	ITC Avant Garde
	Bold Oblique	ITC Avant Garde
ITC Avant Garde Gothic Condensed	Book Condensed	ITC Avant Garde
	Medium Condensed	ITC Avant Garde
	Demi Condensed	ITC Avant Garde
	Bold Condensed	ITC Avant Garde
ITC Avant Garde Gothic Laser	Book	ITC Avant Garde
	Book Oblique	ITC Avant Garde
	Demi	ITC Avant Garde

ff

. . . ITC Avant Garde Gothic Laser
- Demi Oblique — ITC Avant Garde

Balloon Display
- Extra Bold — BALLOON
- Shadow — BALLOON

Balloon Poster
- Extra Bold — BALLOON
- Extra Bold Outline — BALLOON

Balmoral
- Balmoral

Barbedor 1
- Regular — Barbedor
- Italic — Barbedor
- Regular SCOSF — BARBEDOR 12345...
- Medium — Barbedor
- Medium Italic — Barbedor
- Medium SCOSF — BARBEDOR 12345...

Barbedor 2
- Bold — Barbedor
- Bold Italic — Barbedor
- Heavy — Barbedor
- Heavy Italic — Barbedor

Baskerville
- Medium Italic — Baskerville
- Old Face — Baskerville
- Old Face SCOSF — BASKERVILLE 1234...

ITC New Baskerville 1
- Roman — ITC New Baskerville
- Italic — ITC New Baskerville
- Bold — ITC NewBaskerville
- Bold Italic — ITC New Baskerville

ITC New Baskerville 2
- Semibold — ITC NewBaskerville
- Semibold Italic — ITC New Baskerville
- Black — ITC NewBaskervill
- Black Italic — ITC NewBaskervill

ITC Bauhaus
- Light — ITC Bauhaus
- Medium — ITC Bauhaus
- Demi — ITC Bauhaus
- Bold — ITC Bauhaus
- Heavy — ITC Bauhaus
- Poster Heavy — ITC Bauhaus

ITC Beesknees
- Poster — ITC BEESKNEES
- Display — ITC BEESKNEES

Bell
- Medium — Bell
- Italic — Bell

Bellevue
- Bellevue

Belshaw
- Belshaw

Belwe
- Light — Belwe
- Light Italic — Belwe
- Medium — Belwe
- Bold — Belwe
- Bold Condensed — Belwe

product not available

ITC Benguiat
- Book — ITC Benguiat
- Book Italic — ITC Benguiat
- Medium — ITC Benguiat
- Medium Italic — ITC Benguiat
- Bold — ITC Benguiat
- Bold Italic — ITC Benguiat

ITC Benguiat Condensed
- Book Condensed — ITC Benguiat
- Book Condensed Italic — ITC Benguiat
- Medium Condensed — ITC Benguiat
- Medium Condensed Italic — ITC Benguiat
- Bold Condensed — ITC Benguiat
- Bold Condensed Italic — ITC Benguiat

ITC Benguiat Gothic
- Book — ITC Benguiat Gothic
- Book Italic — ITC Benguiat Gothic
- Medium — ITC Benguiat Gothic
- Medium Italic — ITC Benguiat Gothic
- Bold — ITC Benguiat Gothic
- Bold Italic — ITC Benguiat Gothic
- Heavy — ITC BenguiatGothic
- Heavy Italic — ITC BenguiatGothic

ITC Berkeley Old Style
- Book — ITC Berkeley Old Style
- Book Italic — ITC Berkeley Old Style

. . . ITC Berkeley Old Style
- Medium — ITC Berkeley Old Style
- Medium Italic — ITC Berkeley Old Style
- Bold — ITCBerkeley Old Style
- Bold Italic — ITC Berkeley Old Style
- Black — ITCBerkeleyOldStyle
- Black Italic — ITCBerkeley OldStyle

Berliner Grotesk Display
- Light — Berliner Grotesk
- Demibold — Berliner Grotesk

Berling
- Roman — Berling
- Italic — Berling
- Bold — Berling

Bernhard Antique
- Bold Condensed — Bernhard Antique

Bernhard Fashion
- Bernhard Fashion

Beton
- Light — Beton
- Demi — Beton
- Bold — Beton
- Extra Bold — Beton
- Bold Condensed — Beton

Beton Poster
- Extra Bold — Beton
- Extra Bold Outline — Beton

Binner
- Display — BINNER
- Poster — BINNER
- Outline — BINNER

Blippo Black
- Display — Blippo Black
- Poster — Blippo Black
- Outline — Blippo Black

Block
- Regular — Block
- Italic — Block
- Heavy — Block
- Condensed — Block
- Extra Condensed — Block

Bauer Bodoni
- Roman — Bauer Bodoni
- Italic — Bauer Bodoni
- Demibold — Bauer Bodoni
- Demibold Italic — Bauer Bodoni
- Bold — Bauer Bodoni
- Bold Italic — BauerBodoni

Bauer Bodoni SCOSF
- Roman SCOSF — BAUER BODONI 123...

. . . Bauer Bodoni SCOSF
Demibold SCOSF BauerBodoni 123…

Bauer Bodoni Display
Roman Bauer Bodoni
Italic *Bauer Bodoni*
Demibold **Bauer Bodoni**
Demibold Italic ***Bauer Bodoni***
Bold **Bauer Bodoni**
Bold Italic ***Bauer Bodoni***

Bodoni Antiqua
Light Bodoni Antiqua
Light Italic *Bodoni Antiqua*
Roman Bodoni Antiqua
Italic *Bodoni Antiqua*
Demibold **Bodoni Antiqua**
Demibold Italic ***Bodoni Antiqua***
Bold **Bodoni Antiqua**
Bold Italic ***Bodoni Antiqua***

Bodoni Antiqua Black
Black **B Antiqua Black**
Italic ***B Antiqua Black***

Bodoni Antiqua Condensed
Condensed Bodoni Antiqua Condensed
Condensed Italic *Bodoni Antiqua Condensed*
Demibold Condensed **B Antiqua Condensed**
Demibold Condensed Italic ***B Antiqua Condensed***
Bold Condensed **B Antiqua Condensed**
Bold Condensed Italic ***B Antiqua Condensed***

Bodoni Antiqua SCOSF
Light SCOSF Bodoni Antiqua 123…
Roman SCOSF Bodoni Antiqua 123…

IBM Bodoni
Roman IBM Bodoni
Italic *IBM Bodoni*
Medium IBM Bodoni

Bodoni No. 2 Ultra **Bodoni No. 2**

ITC Bookman
Light ITC Bookman
Light Italic *ITC Bookman*
Medium ITC Bookman
Medium Italic *ITC Bookman*
Demibold **ITC Bookman**
Demibold Italic ***ITC Bookman***
Bold **ITC Bookman**
Bold Italic ***ITC Bookman***

ITC Bookman Laser
Light ITC Bookman

. . . ITC Bookman Laser
Light Italic *ITC Bookman*
Demibold **ITC Bookman**
Demibold Italic ***ITC Bookman***

Bottleneck
Display **Bottleneck**
Poster **Bottleneck**
Outline Bottleneck

Bramley
Light Bramley
Light SCOSF Bramley 12345…
Medium Bramley
Medium SCOSF Bramley 12345…
Bold **Bramley**
Extra Bold **Bramley**

Breughel
Roman Breughel
Italic *Breughel*
Bold **Breughel**
Bold Italic ***Breughel***
Black **Breughel**
Black Italic ***Breughel***

Brighton
Light Brighton
Light Italic *Brighton*
Medium Brighton
Bold **Brighton**

Britannic
Extra Light Britannic
Light Britannic
Medium Britannic
Bold **Britannic**
Ultra **Britannic**

Broadway Display
Regular **Broadway**
Engraved BROADWAY

Broadway Poster
Regular **Broadway**
Outline Broadway

Brush Script *Brush Script*

Buster BUSTER

Buxom BUXOM

Candice *Candice*

Candida
Roman Candida
Italic *Candida*
Medium Candida

Cargo **Cargo**

Carousel **Carousel**

Caslon Black **Caslon Black**

ITC Caslon No. 224
Book ITC Caslon No. 224
Book Italic *ITC Caslon No. 224*
Medium ITC Caslon No. 224
Medium Italic *ITC Caslon No. 224*
Bold **ITC Caslon No. 224**
Bold Italic ***ITC Caslon No. 224***
Black **ITC Caslon No. 224**
Black Italic ***ITC Caslon No. 224***

Castle
Light Castle
Book Castle
Bold **Castle**
Ultra **Castle**

Caxton 1
Book Caxton
Book Italic *Caxton*
Bold **Caxton**
Bold Italic ***Caxton***
Bold Condensed **Caxton**

Caxton 2
Light Caxton
Light Italic *Caxton*
Extra Bold **Caxton**
Extra Bold Italic ***Caxton***
Extra Bold Condensed **Caxton**

Caxton Display 1
Book Caxton
Book Italic *Caxton*
Bold **Caxton**
Bold Italic ***Caxton***
Bold Condensed **Caxton**

Caxton Display 2
Light Caxton
Light Italic *Caxton*
Extra Bold **Caxton**
Extra Bold Italic ***Caxton***
Extra Bold Condensed **Caxton**

Century Expanded
Roman Century Expanded
Italic *Century Expanded*

Century Old Style
Roman Century Old Style

ff

Family	Style	Sample
. . . Century Old Style	Italic	*Century Old Style*
	Bold	**Century Old Style**
	Roman SCOSF	CENTURY 12345...
Century Schoolbook	Roman	C Schoolbook
	Italic	*C Schoolbook*
	Bold	**C Schoolbook**
	Bold Italic	***C Schoolbook***
Century Schoolbook Laser	Roman	C Schoolbook
	Italic	*C Schoolbook*
	Bold	**C Schoolbook**
	Bold Italic	***C Schoolbook***
ITC Century	Light	ITC Century
	Light Italic	*ITC Century*
	Book	ITC Century
	Book Italic	*ITC Century*
	Bold	**ITC Century**
	Bold Italic	***ITC Century***
ITC Century Ultra	Ultra	**ITC Century**
	Ultra Italic	***ITC Century***
	Ultra Condensed	**ITC Century**
	Ultra Condensed Italic	***ITC Century***
ITC Century Condensed	Light Condensed	ITC Century
	Light Condensed Italic	*ITC Century*
	Book Condensed	ITC Century
	Book Condensed Italic	*ITC Century*
	Bold Condensed	**ITC Century**
	Bold Condensed Italic	***ITC Century***
ITC Century Handtooled	Regular	**ITC Century**
	Italic	***ITC Century***
ITC Cerigo	Book	ITC Cerigo
	Book Italic	*ITC Cerigo*
	Book Swash Caps	*ITC Cerigo*
	Book Italic Swash Caps	*ITC Cerigo*
	Medium	ITC Cerigo
	Medium Italic	*ITC Cerigo*
	Bold	**ITC Cerigo**
	Bold Italic	***ITC Cerigo***
ITC Charter	Roman	ITC Charter
. . . ITC Charter	Italic	*ITC Charter*
	Bold	**ITC Charter**
	Bold Italic	***ITC Charter***
	Black	**ITC Charter**
	Black Italic	***ITC Charter***
Chelmsford	Light	Chelmsford
	Book	Chelmsford
	Book Italic	*Chelmsford*
	Medium	Chelmsford
	Bold	**Chelmsford**
	Ultra	**Chelmsford**
Cheltenham Old Style	Old Style	Cheltenham Old Style
	Old Style No. 2	Cheltenham Old Style
ITC Cheltenham	Light	ITC Cheltenham
	Light Italic	*ITC Cheltenham*
	Book	ITC Cheltenham
	Book Italic	*ITC Cheltenham*
	Bold	**ITC Cheltenham**
	Bold Italic	***ITC Cheltenham***
ITC Cheltenham Condensed	Light Condensed	ITC Cheltenham
	Light Condensed Italic	*ITC Cheltenham*
	Book Condensed	ITC Cheltenham
	Book Condensed Italic	*ITC Cheltenham*
	Bold Condensed	**ITC Cheltenham**
	Bold Condensed Italic	***ITC Cheltenham***
ITC Cheltenham Handtooled	Regular	**ITC Cheltenham**
	Italic	***ITC Cheltenham***
ITC Cheltenham Ultra	Ultra	**ITC Cheltenham**
	Ultra Italic	***ITC Cheltenham***
	Ultra Condensed	**ITC Cheltenham**
	Ultra Condensed Italic	***ITC Cheltenham***
Chesterfield		Chesterfield
Chevalier SC	Open SC	CHEVALIER
	Stripes SC	CHEVALIER
Chisel		Chisel
Churchward Brush	Regular	**Churchward Brush**
	Italic	***Churchward Brush***
Cirkulus		cirkulus
City	Bold	**City**
	Bold Outline	City
Clarendon	Light	Clarendon
	Medium	Clarendon
	Bold	**Clarendon**
	Extra Bold	**Clarendon**
	Bold Expanded	**Clarendon**
URW Classico	Regular	URW Classico
	Italic	*URW Classico*
	Medium	URW Classico
	Medium Italic	*URW Classico*
	Bold	**URW Classico**
	Bold Italic	***URW Classico***
	Black	**URW Classico**
ITC Clearface	Regular	ITC Clearface
	Italic	*ITC Clearface*
	Bold	**ITC Clearface**
	Bold Italic	***ITC Clearface***
	Heavy	**ITC Clearface**
	Heavy Italic	***ITC Clearface***
	Black	**ITC Clearface**
	Black Italic	***ITC Clearface***
Clearface Gothic	Regular	Clearface Gothic
	Bold	**Clearface Gothic**
	Extra Bold	**Clearface Gothic**
Columna Solid		COLUMNA
Commercial Script	Text	*Commercial Script*
	Display	*Commercial Script*
Compacta	Light	Compacta
	Regular	Compacta
	Italic	*Compacta*
	Bold	**Compacta**
	Bold Italic	***Compacta***
	Black	**Compacta**
Compacta Display	Light	Compacta
	Regular	Compacta
	Italic	*Compacta*
	Bold	**Compacta**

ff

… Compacta Display	Bold Italic	Compacta
	Black	Compacta
Compacta Poster	Black	Compacta
	Black Outline	Compacta
Conference		Conference
Congress	Light	Congress
	Regular	Congress
	Italic	Congress
	Medium	Congress
	Bold	Congress
	Black	Congress
Contus	Roman	Contus
	Italic	Contus
	Medium	Contus
	Medium Italic	Contus
	Roman SCOSF	CONTUS 12345…
Contus Condensed	Condensed	Contus Condensed
	Medium Condensed	Contus Condensed
	Bold Condensed	Contus Condensed
Cooper Black Display	Roman	Cooper Black
	Italic	Cooper Black
	Condensed	Cooper Black
	Outline	Cooper Black
	Condensed Outline	Cooper Black
Cooper Black Poster	Black	Cooper Black
	Black Outline	Cooper Black
Copperplate	Light	COPPERPLATE
	Medium	COPPERPLATE
	Bold	COPPERPLATE
Copperplate Condensed	Light Condensed	COPPERPLATE
	Medium Condensed	COPPERPLATE
	Bold Condensed	COPPERPLATE
Corinthian	Light	Corinthian
	Medium	Corinthian
	Bold	Corinthian
	Extra Bold	Corinthian
Cortez		Cortez
Countdown		Countdown
Courier	Light	Courier
	Light Oblique	Courier
	Bold	Courier
	Bold Oblique	Courier
Courier Cyrillic	Light Upright	Абвгдеж Зикл
	Light Oblique	Абвгдеж Зикл
	Bold Upright	Абвгдеж Зикл
	Bold Oblique	Абвгдеж Зикл
Courier Greek	Light Upright	Αβγδε Ζζηθικ
	Light Oblique	Αβγδε Ζζηθικ
	Bold Upright	Αβγδε Ζζηθικ
	Bold Oblique	Αβγδε Ζζηθικ
Crillee Italic	Light	Crillee Italic
	Regular	Crillee Italic
	Bold	Crillee Italic
	Extra Bold	Crillee Italic
Croissant		Croissant
ITC Cushing	Book	ITC Cushing
	Medium	ITC Cushing
	Heavy	ITC Cushing
	Bold	ITC Cushing
Data		Data
Davida		DAVIDA
De Vinne Ornamented		De Vinne
Dex Gothic		DEX GOTHIC
Dextor		DEXTOR
Diskus Medium		Diskus Medium
Dom Casual	Regular	Dom Casual
	Italic	Dom Casual
	Bold	Dom Casual
	Bold Italic	Dom Casual
Dynamo	Medium	Dynamo
	Bold	Dynamo
	Bold Condensed	Dynamo
	Bold Shadow	Dynamo
Eckmann		Eckmann
Edwardian 1	Medium	Edwardian
	Medium Italic	Edwardian
… Edwardian 1	Bold	Edwardian
	Bold Italic	Edwardian
Edwardian 2	Light	Edwardian
	Light Italic	Edwardian
	Extra Bold	Edwardian
	Extra Bold Italic	Edwardian
Egizio Condensed		Egizio
Egyptienne Display	Medium Condensed	Egyptienne
	Bold Condensed	Egyptienne
	Bold Extended	Egyptienne
Einhorn		Einhorn
ITC Élan 1	Book	ITC Élan
	Book Italic	ITC Élan
	Book SCOSF	ITC ÉLAN 12345…
	Bold	ITC Élan
	Bold Italic	ITC Élan
ITC Élan 2	Medium	ITC Élan
	Medium Italic	ITC Élan
	Medium SCOSF	ITC ÉLAN 12345…
	Black	ITC Élan
	Black Italic	ITC Élan
Elefont	Regular	ELEFONT
	Outline	ELEFONT
Englische Schreibschrift	Regular	Englische Schreibschrift
	Demibold	Englische Schreibschrift
	Bold	Englische Schreibschrift
Engravers	Roman	ENGRAVERS
	Bold	ENGRAVERS
ITC Eras	Light	ITC Eras
	Book	ITC Eras
	Medium	ITC Eras
	Demi	ITC Eras
	Bold	ITC Eras
	Ultra	ITC Eras
	Poster Ultra	ITC Eras
ITC Esprit 1	Book	ITC Esprit
	Book Italic	ITC Esprit
	Book SCOSF	ITC ESPRIT 12345…

. . . ITC Esprit 1
Bold ITC Esprit
Bold Italic *ITC Esprit*

ITC Esprit 2
Medium ITC Esprit
Medium Italic *ITC Esprit*
Medium SCOSF ITC ESPRIT 1234...
Black ITC Esprit
Black Italic *ITC Esprit*

Eurostile
Regular Eurostile
Medium Eurostile
Bold Eurostile
Heavy Eurostile
Black Eurostile

Eurostile Extended
Extended Eurostile
Black Extended Eurostile

Eurostile SCOSF
Regular SCOSF EUROSTILE 12345...
Bold SCOSF EUROSTILE 12345...

Ewie Ewie

Excius
Roman Excius
Italic *Excius*
Medium Excius
No. 2 Excius

ITC Fenice 1
Roman ITC Fenice
Italic *ITC Fenice*
Bold ITC Fenice
Bold Italic *ITC Fenice*

ITC Fenice 2
Light ITC Fenice
Light Italic *ITC Fenice*
Ultra ITC Fenice
Ultra Italic *ITC Fenice*

Fette Fraktur Fette Fraktur

Fette Gotisch Fette Gotisch

Fina Medium Condensed Fina

Flash Display
Light *Flash*
Bold *Flash*

Flash Poster
Bold *Flash*
Outline Bold *Flash*

Flatus
Light Flatus
Light Italic *Flatus*

. . . Flatus
Regular Flatus
Italic *Flatus*
Medium Flatus
Medium Italic *Flatus*
Bold Flatus

ITC Flora
Regular ITC Flora
Bold ITC Flora

Flytus
Bold Flytus
Bold Condensed Flytus

Folio
Light Folio
Light Italic *Folio*
Medium Folio

Frankfurter Display
Regular FRANKFURTER
Medium FRANKFURTER
Highlight FRANKFURTER
Inline FRANKFURTER

Frankfurter Poster
Regular FRANKFURTER
Outline FRANKFURTER

Franklin Gothic
Regular Franklin Gothic
Condensed Franklin Gothic
Extra Condensed Franklin Gothic

ITC Franklin Gothic
Book ITC Franklin Gothic
Book Italic *ITC Franklin Gothic*
Medium ITC Franklin Gothic
Medium Italic *ITC Franklin Gothic*
Demi ITC Franklin Gothic
Demi Italic *ITC Franklin Gothic*
Heavy ITC Franklin Goth
Heavy Italic *ITC Franklin Goth*

ITC Franklin Gothic Condensed
Book Condensed ITC Franklin Gothic
Book Condensed Italic *ITC Franklin Gothic*
Book Condensed SCOSF ITC F GOTHIC 12345...
Medium Condensed ITC Franklin Gothic
Medium Condensed Italic *ITC Franklin Gothic*
Medium Condensed SCOSF ITC F GOTHIC 12345...
Demi Condensed ITC Franklin Gothic
Demi Condensed Italic *ITC Franklin Gothic*

ITC Franklin Gothic Compressed
Book Compressed ITC Franklin Gothic

. . . ITC Franklin Gothic Compressed
Book Compressed Italic *ITC Franklin Gothic*
Demi Compressed ITC Franklin Gothic
Demi Compressed Italic *ITC Franklin Gothic*

ITC Franklin Gothic Extra Compressed
Book Extra Compressed ITC Franklin Gothic
Demi Extra Compressed ITC Franklin Gothic

Freestyle Script
Regular Freestyle Script
Bold Freestyle Script

Friz Quadrata
Regular Friz Quadrata
Italic *Friz Quadrata*
Bold Friz Quadrata
Bold Italic *Friz Quadrata*

Frutus
Light Frutus
Light Italic *Frutus*
Regular Frutus
Italic *Frutus*
Medium Frutus
Medium Italic *Frutus*
Bold Frutus
Bold Italic *Frutus*

Frutus SCOSF
Light SCOSF FRUTUS 12345...
Regular SCOSF FRUTUS 12345...

Futura
Light Futura
Light Oblique *Futura*
Book Futura
Book Oblique *Futura*
Medium Futura
Medium Oblique *Futura*
Demibold Futura
Demibold Oblique *Futura*
Bold Futura
Bold Oblique *Futura*
Extra Bold Futura
Extra Bold Oblique *Futura*

Futura Condensed
Light Condensed Futura Condensed
Light Condensed Oblique *Futura Condensed*
Medium Condensed Futura Condensed
Medium Condensed Oblique *Futura Condensed*
Bold Condensed Futura Condensed

ff

Futura Condensed
Bold Condensed Oblique — Futura Condensed
Extra Bold Condensed — Futura Condensed
Extra Bold Condensed Oblique — Futura Condensed

Futura SCOSF
Light SCOSF — FUTURA 12345...
Book SCOSF — FUTURA 12345...

Futura Black — Futura Black

Futura Display
Display — Futura
Poster — Futura
Poster Outline — Futura

Futura No. 2 Display
Book — Futura
Medium — Futura
Demibold — Futura
Bold — Futura
Bold Italic — Futura
Extra Bold — Futura
Extra Bold Condensed — Futura
Extra Bold Condensed Italic — Futura

Futura No. 2 Display SCOSF
Book SCOSF — FUTURA 12345...
Medium SCOSF — FUTURA 12345...

Futura No. 3 Bold — Futura

Futura No. 7 Medium — Futura

Futura No. 8 Display — FUTURA

Futura Poster
Extra Bold — Futura
Extra Bold Oblique — Futura
Extra Bold Outline — Futura
Extra Bold Outline Oblique — Futura

Futura Shadowed Extra Bold — Futura

Galadriel — GALADRIEL

ITC Gamma
Book — ITC Gamma
Book Italic — ITC Gamma
Book SCOSF — ITC GAMMA 12345...
Bold — ITC Gamma
Bold Italic — ITC Gamma
Medium — ITC Gamma
Medium Italic — ITC Gamma
Medium SCOSF — ITC GAMMA 12345...
Black — ITC Gamma
Black Italic — ITC Gamma

Garamond No. 2
Roman — Garamond No. 2
Medium — Garamond No. 2
Roman SCOSF — GARAMOND NO. 12345...
Medium SCOSF — GARAMOND NO. 1234...

Garamond No. 3
Roman — Garamond No. 3
Italic — Garamond No. 3
Medium — Garamond No. 3
Medium Italic — Garamond No. 3
Bold — Garamond No. 3

Garamond No. 9
Roman — Garamond No. 9
Italic — Garamond No. 9
Medium — Garamond No. 9
Extra Bold — Garamond No. 9

ITC Garamond
Light — ITC Garamond
Light Italic — ITC Garamond
Book — ITC Garamond
Book Italic — ITC Garamond
Bold — ITC Garamond
Bold Italic — ITC Garamond
Ultra — ITC Garamond
Ultra Italic — ITC Garamond

ITC Garamond Condensed
Light Condensed — ITC Garamond
Light Condensed Italic — ITC Garamond
Book Condensed — ITC Garamond
Book Condensed Italic — ITC Garamond
Bold Condensed — ITC Garamond
Bold Condensed Italic — ITC Garamond
Ultra Condensed — ITC Garamond
Ultra Condensed Italic — ITC Garamond

ITC Garamond Handtooled
Regular — ITC Garamond
Italic — ITC Garamond

Garamond No. 4 Cyrillic
Light Upright — Абвгдеж Зикл
Light Inclined — Абвгдеж Зикл
Medium Upright — Абвгдеж Зикл
Medium Upright Alternate — Абвгдеж Зикл

product not available

product not available

Gillies Gothic
Light — Gillies Gothic
Bold — Gillies Gothic
Extra Bold — Gillies Gothic
Shaded — Gillies Gothic

product not available

ITC Giovanni
Book — ITC Giovanni
Book Italic — ITC Giovanni
Bold — ITC Giovanni
Bold Italic — ITC Giovanni
Black — ITC Giovanni
Black Italic — ITC Giovanni

Glaser Stencil — GLASER STENCIL

Glytus Light — Glytus Light

ITC Golden Type
Original — ITC Golden Type
Original SCOSF — ITC GOLDEN 12345...
Bold — ITC Golden Type
Bold SCOSF — ITC GOLDEN 12345...
Black — ITC Golden Type

Gothic Outline Title — GOTHIC OUTLINE TITLE

Goudy Catalogue
Roman — Goudy Catalogue
Italic — Goudy Catalogue
Roman SCOSF — G CATALOGUE 1234...

Goudy Handtooled
Regular — Goudy Handtool

ff

… Goudy Handtooled Regular SCOSF	G HAND 12345…
Goudy Heavyface Display	G Heavyface
Poster	G Heavyface
Outline Poster	G Heavyface
Goudy Old Style Roman	Goudy Old Style
Italic	*Goudy Old Style*
Bold	**Goudy Old Style**
Extra Bold	**Goudy Old Style**
ITC Goudy Sans Book	ITC Goudy Sans
Book Italic	*ITC Goudy Sans*
Medium	ITC Goudy Sans
Medium Italic	*ITC Goudy Sans*
Bold	**ITC Goudy Sans**
Bold Italic	***ITC Goudy Sans***
Black	**ITC Goudy Sans**
Black Italic	***ITC Goudy Sans***
WTC Goudy Light	WTC Goudy
Light Italic	*WTC Goudy*
Roman	WTC Goudy
Italic	*WTC Goudy*
Medium	WTC Goudy
Medium Italic	*WTC Goudy*
Bold	**WTC Goudy**
Bold Italic	***WTC Goudy***
Grotesque No. 9	**Grotesque No. 9**
URW Grotesk Light	URW Grotesk
Light Italic	*URW Grotesk*
Regular	URW Grotesk
Italic	*URW Grotesk*
Medium	URW Grotesk
Medium Italic	*URW Grotesk*
Bold	**URW Grotesk**
Bold Italic	***URW Grotesk***
URW Grotesk Condensed Light Condensed	URW Grotesk
Bold Condensed	**URW Grotesk**
URW Grotesk SCOSF Light SCOSF	U GROTESK 12345…
Regular SCOSF	U GROTESK 12345…
URW Grotesk Z Light Condensed	URW Grotesk Z

Hadfield	Hadfield
Handel Gothic Light	Handel Gothic
Medium	Handel Gothic
Bold	**Handel Gothic**
Harlow Regular	Harlow
Solid	Harlow
Hawthorn	Hawthorn
ITC Highlander Book	ITC Highlander
Book Italic	*ITC Highlander*
Medium	ITC Highlander
Medium Italic	*ITC Highlander*
Bold	**ITC Highlander**
Bold Italic	***ITC Highlander***
Highlight	Highlight
Hiroshige 1 Book	Hiroshige
Book Italic	*Hiroshige*
Bold	**Hiroshige**
Bold Italic	***Hiroshige***
Hiroshige 2 Medium	Hiroshige
Medium Italic	*Hiroshige*
Black	**Hiroshige**
Black Italic	***Hiroshige***
Hobo	Hobo
Hogarth Script	Hogarth Script
Horatio Light	Horatio
Medium	Horatio
Bold	**Horatio**
Ice Age	Ice Age
Impressum Light	Impressum
Light Italic	*Impressum*
Medium	Impressum
Impressum SCOSF Light SCOSF	IMPRESSUM 12345…
Medium SCOSF	IMPRESSUM 1234…
ITC Isadora Regular	ITC Isadora
Bold	**ITC Isadora**
Italia Book	Italia
Medium	Italia
Bold	**Italia**

… Italia Poster Bold	**Italia**
Medium Condensed	Italia
ITC Jamille Book	ITC Jamille
Book Italic	*ITC Jamille*
Bold	**ITC Jamille**
Bold Italic	***ITC Jamille***
Black	**ITC Jamille**
Black Italic	***ITC Jamille***
Bold SCOSF	ITC JAMILLE 12345…
Jenson Old Style Bold Condensed	**Jenson Old Style**
Julia Script	Julia Script
ITC Kabel Book	ITC Kabel
Medium	ITC Kabel
Demi	ITC Kabel
Bold	**ITC Kabel**
Ultra	**ITC Kabel**
Kalligraphia	Kalligraphia
Kaufmann Bold	Kaufmann Bold
Knightsbridge	Knightsbridge
ITC Korinna Regular	ITC Korinna
Kursiv	*ITC Korinna*
Bold	**ITC Korinna**
Bold Kursiv	***ITC Korinna***
Extra Bold	**ITC Korinna**
Extra Bold Kursiv	***ITC Korinna***
Heavy	**ITC Korinna**
Heavy Kursiv	***ITC Korinna***
Künstlerschreibschrift Medium	Künstlerschreibschrift
Bold	**Künstlerschreibschrift**
Latienne 1 Roman	Latienne
Italic	*Latienne*
Roman SCOSF	LATIENNE 12345…
Italic SCOSF	*LATIENNE 12345…*
Roman Swash Caps	LATIENNE
Italic Swash Caps	*LATIENNE*
Latienne 2 Medium	Latienne
Medium Italic	*Latienne*
Medium SCOSF	LATIENNE 12345…

ff

Latienne 2 Medium Swash Caps	LATIENNE
Medium Italic Swash Caps	LATIENNE
Latienne 3 Bold	Latienne
Bold Italic	Latienne
Bold Swash Caps	LATIENNE
Bold Italic Swash Caps	LATIENNE
URW Latino Roman	URW Latino
Italic	URW Latino
Medium	URW Latino
Medium Italic	URW Latino
Bold	URW Latino
Bold Italic	URW Latino
Black	URW Latino
Latin Wide	Latin
Lazybones	Lazybones
LCD	LCD
ITC Leawood Book	ITC Leawood
Book Italic	ITC Leawood
Medium	ITC Leawood
Medium Italic	ITC Leawood
Bold	ITC Leawood
Bold Italic	ITC Leawood
Black	ITC Leawood
Black Italic	ITC Leawood
ITC Legacy Serif Book	ITC Legacy
Book Italic	ITC Legacy
Medium	ITC Legacy
Medium Italic	ITC Legacy
Bold	ITC Legacy
Bold Italic	ITC Legacy
Ultra	ITC Legacy
ITC Legacy Sans Book	ITC Legacy
Book Italic	ITC Legacy
Medium	ITC Legacy
Medium Italic	ITC Legacy
Bold	ITC Legacy
Bold Italic	ITC Legacy
Ultra	ITC Legacy
Letter Gothic	Letter Gothic
Life Roman	Life
Italic	Life
Bold	Life
Roman SCOSF	LIFE 12345…
Lindsay	Lindsay
Litera Light	Litera
Regular	Litera
Medium	Litera
Heavy	Litera
Litera Display Light	Litera
Regular	Litera
Medium	Litera
Heavy	Litera
ITC Lubalin Graph 1 Book	ITC Lubalin Graph
Book Oblique	ITC Lubalin Graph
Demi	ITC Lubalin Graph
Demi Oblique	ITC Lubalin Graph
ITC Lubalin Graph 2 Light	ITC Lubalin Graph
Light Oblique	ITC Lubalin Graph
Medium	ITC Lubalin Graph
Medium Oblique	ITC Lubalin Graph
Bold	ITCLubalin Graph
Bold Oblique	ITCLubalin Graph
ITC Lubalin Graph Condensed 1 Book Condensed	ITC Lubalin Graph
Book Condensed Oblique	ITC Lubalin Graph
Demi Condensed	ITC Lubalin Graph
Demi Condensed Oblique	ITC Lubalin Graph
ITC Lubalin Graph Condensed 2 Medium Condensed	ITC Lubalin Graph
Medium Condensed Oblique	ITC Lubalin Graph
Bold Condensed	ITC Lubalin Graph
Bold Condensed Oblique	ITC Lubalin Graph
Lucida Roman	Lucida
Roman SCOSF	LUCIDA 12345…
Sans Typewriter Regular	Lucida
Sans Typewriter Demi	Lucida
ITC Machine Regular	ITC MACHINE
Medium	ITC MACHINE
ITC Machine Bold	ITC MACHINE
Poster Bold	ITC MACHINE
Madius No. 3 Roman	Madius No. 3
Italic	Madius No. 3
Medium	Madius No. 3
Medium Condensed	Madius No. 3
Magna Cyrillic Medium Upright	Абвгдеж Зикл
Magnus Bold	Magnus
Mandarin	MANDARIN
ITC/LSC Manhattan	ITC/LSC Manhattan
Mariage	Mariage
Marlboro	Marlboro
Maxima Cyrillic Light Upright	Абвгдеж Зикл
Medium Upright	Абвгдеж Зикл
Memphis Extra Light	Memphis
Light	Memphis
Medium	Memphis
Bold	Memphis
ITC Mendoza Roman Book	ITC Mendoza
Book Italic	ITC Mendoza
Medium	ITC Mendoza
Medium Italic	ITC Mendoza
Bold	ITC Mendoza
Bold Italic	ITC Mendoza
Book SCOSF	ITC MENDOZA 12345…
Book Italic OSF	osf 12345…
Medium SCOSF	ITC MENDOZA 1234…
Metropolitaines Display	METROPOLITAINES
Poster	METROPOLITAINES
Outlines	METROPOLITAINES
Minister Light	Minister
Light Italic	Minister
Book	Minister
Book Italic	Minister
Bold	Minister
Mistral	Mistral
ITC Mixage Book	ITC Mixage
Book Italic	ITC Mixage

ff

Family	Style	Sample
… ITC Mixage	Medium	ITC Mixage
	Medium Italic	*ITC Mixage*
	Bold	**ITC Mixage**
	Bold Italic	***ITC Mixage***
	Black	**ITC Mixage**
	Black Italic	***ITC Mixage***
ITC Mona Lisa	Recut	ITC Mona Lisa
	Solid	ITC Mona Lisa
ITC Motter Corpus	Bold	**ITC Motter**
	Bold Condensed	**ITC Motter Corpus**
Motter Femina		***Motter Femina***
Murray Hill		*Murray Hill*
Neuzeit Grotesk	Light	Neuzeit Grotesk
	Regular	Neuzeit Grotesk
	Bold	**Neuzeit Grotesk**
	Black	**Neuzeit Grotesk**
	Black Condensed	**Neuzeit Grotesk**
	Black Extra Condensed	**Neuzeit Grotesk**
News Gothic	Light	News Gothic
	Regular	News Gothic
	Medium	News Gothic
	Demi	**News Gothic**
	Bold	**News Gothic**
News Gothic No. 2		News Gothic No. 2
News Gothic SCOSF	Light SCOSF	NEWS GOTHIC 12345…
	Regular SCOSF	NEWS GOTHIC 12345…
Nimbus Roman	Roman	Nimbus
	Italic	*Nimbus*
	Bold	**Nimbus**
	Bold Italic	***Nimbus***
	Extra Bold	**Nimbus**
	Extra Bold Italic	***Nimbus***
Nimbus Roman No. 2		Nimbus
Nimbus Roman No. 9	Roman	Nimbus
	Italic	*Nimbus*
	Medium	Nimbus
	Medium Italic	*Nimbus*
	Bold	**Nimbus**
… Nimbus Roman No. 9	Bold Italic	***Nimbus***
	Extra Bold	**Nimbus**
	Regular SCOSF	NIMBUS 12345…
Nimbus Roman No. 9 Condensed	Condensed	Nimbus
	Condensed Italic	*Nimbus*
	Bold Condensed	**Nimbus**
Nimbus Roman No. 9 Laser	Roman	Nimbus
	Italic	*Nimbus*
	Medium	Nimbus
	Medium Italic	*Nimbus*
Nimbus Sans	Regular	Nimbus
	Italic	*Nimbus*
	Bold	**Nimbus**
	Bold Italic	***Nimbus***
	Condensed	Nimbus
	Condensed Italic	*Nimbus*
	Bold Condensed	**Nimbus**
	Bold Condensed Italic	***Nimbus***
Nimbus Sans Display	Ultra Light	Nimbus
	Light	Nimbus
	Light Italic	*Nimbus*
	Regular	Nimbus
	Italic	*Nimbus*
	Bold	**Nimbus**
	Bold Italic	***Nimbus***
	Black	**Nimbus**
	Black Italic	***Nimbus***
Nimbus Sans Display Black	Black	**Nimbus**
	Black Condensed	**Nimbus**
Nimbus Sans Display Condensed	Light Condensed	Nimbus
	Light Condensed Italic	*Nimbus*
	Condensed	Nimbus
	Condensed Italic	*Nimbus*
	Bold Condensed	**Nimbus**
	Bold Condensed Italic	***Nimbus***
	Black Condensed	**Nimbus**
	Black Condensed Italic	***Nimbus***
Nimbus Sans Display Extended	Light Extended	Nimbus
… Nimbus Sans Display Extended	Extended	Nimbus
	Bold Extended	**Nimbus**
	Black Extended	**Nimbus**
Nimbus Sans Display Outline	Bold Outline	Nimbus
	Black Extended Outline	Nimbus
Nimbus Sans No. 4 Medium	Condensed	Nimbus No. 4
Nimbus Sans Novus 1	Light	Nimbus
	Light Italic	*Nimbus*
	Regular	Nimbus
	Italic	*Nimbus*
	Bold	**Nimbus**
	Bold Italic	***Nimbus***
Nimbus Sans Novus 2	Medium	Nimbus
	Medium Italic	*Nimbus*
	Semibold	Nimbus
	Semibold Italic	*Nimbus*
	Heavy	**Nimbus**
	Heavy Italic	***Nimbus***
	Black	**Nimbus**
	Black Italic	***Nimbus***
Nimbus Sans Novus Black	Black	**Nimbus**
	Black Italic	***Nimbus***
Nimbus Sans Novus Condensed	Light Condensed	Nimbus
	Condensed	Nimbus
	Medium Condensed	Nimbus
	Semibold Condensed	Nimbus
	Bold Condensed	**Nimbus**
	Heavy Condensed	**Nimbus**
	Black Condensed	**Nimbus**
Nimbus Sans Novus Outline		Nimbus
Nimbus Sans Novus Ultra	Ultra Light	Nimbus
	Ultra Light Italic	*Nimbus*
	Ultra Light Condensed	Nimbus
	Ultra Condensed	**Nimbus**
Nimbus Mono	Regular	Nimbus Mono
	Oblique	*Nimbus Mono*
	Bold	**Nimbus Mono**
	Bold Oblique	***Nimbus Mono***

Nimbus Sans Cyrillic
Upright Абвгдеж Зикл
Oblique Абвгдеж Зикл
Bold Upright Абвгдеж Зикл
Bold Oblique Абвгдеж Зикл

Nimbus Sans Greek
Upright Αβγδε Ζζηθικ
Oblique Αβγδε Ζζηθικ
Bold Upright Αβγδε Ζζηθικ
Bold Oblique Αβγδε Ζζηθικ

Nissan Nissan

ITC Novarese
Book ITC Novarese
Book Italic ITC Novarese
Medium ITC Novarese
Medium Italic ITC Novarese
Bold ITC Novarese
Bold Italic ITC Novarese
Ultra ITC Novarese

OCR B Letterpress OCRBLetterpress

Octopuss
Display Octopuss
Display Shadow Octopuss
Poster Octopuss
Poster Outline Octopuss

Odin
Display Odin
Poster Odin
Outline Odin

ITC Officina
Serif Book ITC Officina
Serif Book Italic ITC Officina
Serif Bold ITC Officina
Serif Bold Italic ITC Officina
Sans Book ITC Officina
Sans Book Italic ITC Officina
Sans Bold ITC Officina
Sans Bold Italic ITC Officina

Okay Okay

Old English Old English

Old Towne No. 536 Old Towne No. 536

Ondine Ondine

ITC Ozwald ITCOzwald

ITC Pacella
Book ITC Pacella

... ITC Pacella
Book Italic ITC Pacella
Medium ITC Pacella
Medium Italic ITC Pacella
Bold ITC Pacella
Bold Italic ITC Pacella
Black ITC Pacella
Black Italic ITC Pacella

ITC Pacella SCOSF
Book SCOSF ITC Pacella 12345...
Medium SCOSF ITC Pacella 12345...

Paddington Paddington

URW Palladio
Regular URW Palladio
Italic URW Palladio
Medium URW Palladio
Medium Italic URW Palladio
Bold URW Palladio
Bold Italic URW Palladio

Pallus
Regular Pallus
No. 2 Pallus

Paltus Antiqua
No. 2 Medium Italic Paltus Antiqua
No. 3 Roman Paltus Antiqua
No. 3 Italic Paltus Antiqua
No. 3 Bold Paltus Antiqua
No. 3 Bold Italic Paltus Antiqua

ITC Panache
Book ITC Panache
Book Italic ITC Panache
Bold ITC Panache
Bold Italic ITC Panache
Black ITC Panache
Black Italic ITC Panache

Park Avenue Park Avenue

Peignot Medium Peignot

product not available

product not available

Phyllis
Regular Phyllis
Initials PHYLLIS

ITC Pioneer ITC PIONEER

Playbill Playbill

Plaza
Regular PLAZA
Ultra PLAZA
Swash PLAZA

Plaza Initials
Regular PLAZA
Ultra PLAZA

Plaza Ultra
Poster Ultra PLAZA
Poster Ultra Outline PLAZA

Prestige Elite
Regular Prestige Elite
Oblique Prestige Elite
Bold Prestige Elite
Bold Oblique Prestige Elite

Princetown PRINCETOWN

Proteus
Light Proteus
Book Proteus
Medium Proteus
Bold Proteus

Pump
Light Pump
Medium Pump
Demi Pump
Bold Pump
Triline Pump Bold

Quartz Bold QUARTZ BOLD

ITC Quay Sans
Book ITC Quay Sans
Book Italic ITC Quay Sans
Bold ITC Quay Sans
Bold Italic ITC Quay Sans
Black ITC Quay Sans
Black Italic ITC Quay Sans
Book SCOSF ITC Quay Sans 12345...

ff

Family	Style	Sample
… ITC Quay Sans	Bold SCOSF	ITC QUAY SANS 1234…
ITC Quorum	Light	ITC Quorum
	Book	ITC Quorum
	Medium	ITC Quorum
	Bold	ITC Quorum
	Black	ITC Quorum
Raleigh	Light	Raleigh
	Regular	Raleigh
	Medium	Raleigh
	Demibold	Raleigh
	Bold	Raleigh
	Extra Bold	Raleigh
Raleigh Display	Light	Raleigh
	Regular	Raleigh
	Medium	Raleigh
	Demibold	Raleigh
	Bold	Raleigh
	Extra Bold	Raleigh
Renault	Light	Renault
	Light Italic	Renault
	Medium	Renault
	Bold	Renault
	Bold Italic	Renault
Revue	Display	Revue
	Poster	Revue
	Outline	Revue
Rialto		Rialto
		product not available
Roman Script		Roman Script
Romana	Light	Romana
	Book	Romana
	Medium	Romana
	Demi	Romana
	Bold	Romana
	Ultra	Romana
Romic	Light	Romic
	Light Italic	Romic
	Medium	Romic
	Bold	Romic
	Extra Bold	Romic
Sabius	Roman	Sabius
	Italic	Sabius
	Medium	Sabius
	Roman SCOSF	SABIUS 12345…
	Medium SCOSF	SABIUS 12345…
Schneidler Mediaeval	Light	Schneidler Mediaeval
	Regular	Schneidler Mediaeval
	Medium	Schneidler Mediaeval
	Bold	Schneidler Mediaeval
	Black	S Mediaeval
Schneidler Mediaeval SCOSF	Light SCOSF	S MEDIAEVAL 12345…
	Regular SCOSF	S MEDIAEVAL 12345…
	Medium SCOSF	S MEDIAEVAL 1234…
Schneidler Amalthea	Light	Schneidler Amalthea
	Regular	Schneidler Amalthea
	Medium	Schneidler Amalthea
	Bold	Schneidler Amalthea
	Black	Schneidler Amalthea
Serifa	Thin	Serifa
	Light	Serifa
	Regular	Serifa
	Medium	Serifa
	Bold	Serifa
Serifa Display	Thin	Serifa
	Light	Serifa
	Regular	Serifa
	Medium	Serifa
	Bold	Serifa
Serpentine	Bold	Serpentine
	Bold Italic	Serpentine
Shamrock		Shamrock
Shelley		Shelley
Sinaloa		SINALOA
Skidoos	Display	Skidoos
	Poster	Skidoos
	Outline	Skidoos
ITC Slimbach	Book	ITC Slimbach
	Book Italic	ITC Slimbach
	Medium	ITC Slimbach
	Medium Italic	ITC Slimbach
	Bold	ITC Slimbach
	Bold Italic	ITC Slimbach
	Black	ITC Slimbach
	Black Italic	ITC Slimbach
ITC Slimbach SCOSF	Book SCOSF	ITC SLIMBACH 123…
	Medium SCOSF	ITC SLIMBACH 123…
Slogan		Slogan
Snv	Regular	Snv
	Condensed	Snv
	Extra Condensed	Snv
ITC Souvenir 1	Light	ITC Souvenir
	Light Italic	ITC Souvenir
	Demi	ITC Souvenir
	Demi Italic	ITC Souvenir
ITC Souvenir 2	Medium	ITC Souvenir
	Medium Italic	ITC Souvenir
	Bold	ITC Souvenir
	Bold Italic	ITC Souvenir
Springfield		Springfield
Squire	Regular	Squire
	Bold	Squire
Standard Symbols		αβχδεφγιφμ®℘∂∞⇓∨∉
Stencil		STENCIL
Stentor		Stentor
Stilla		Stilla

ff

ITC Stone Serif
Medium ITC Stone
Medium Italic *ITC Stone*
Semibold **ITC Stone**
Semibold Italic ***ITC Stone***
Bold **ITC Stone**
Bold Italic ***ITC Stone***

ITC Stone Serif SCOSF
Medium SCOSF ITC STONE 12345…
Semibold SCOSF **ITC STONE 12345…**

ITC Stone Sans
Medium ITC Stone
Medium Italic *ITC Stone*
Semibold **ITC Stone**
Semibold Italic ***ITC Stone***
Bold **ITC Stone**
Bold Italic ***ITC Stone***

ITC Stone Sans SCOSF
Medium SCOSF ITC STONE 12345…
Semibold SCOSF **ITC STONE 12345…**

ITC Stone Informal
Medium ITC Stone
Medium Italic *ITC Stone*
Semibold **ITC Stone**
Semibold Italic ***ITC Stone***
Bold **ITC Stone**
Bold Italic ***ITC Stone***

ITC Stone Informal SCOSF
Medium SCOSF ITC STONE 12345…
Semibold SCOSF **ITC STONE 12345…**

ITC Stone Phonetic Sans
Medium ɪθç ʃθɔnɛ ʃanʃ hɔnɛ

Stop
STOP

ITC Studio Script
ITC Studio Script

Stymie
Light Stymie
Regular Stymie
Medium **Stymie**
Black **Stymie**
Condensed Stymie
Medium Condensed **Stymie**
Light SCOSF STYMIE 12345…
Regular SCOSF STYMIE 12345…

Superstar
Regular SUPERSTAR
Shadow SUPERSTAR

ITC Symbol 1
Book ITC Symbol
Book Italic *ITC Symbol*
Book SCOSF ITC SYMBOL 12345…
Bold **ITC Symbol**
Bold Italic ***ITC Symbol***

ITC Symbol 2
Medium ITC Symbol
Medium Italic *ITC Symbol*
Medium SCOSF ITC SYMBOL 12345…
Black **ITC Symbol**
Black Italic ***ITC Symbol***

ITC Syndor
Book ITC Syndor
Book Italic *ITC Syndor*
Book SCOSF ITC SYNDOR 12345…
Medium ITC Syndor
Medium Italic *ITC Syndor*
Medium SCOSF ITC SYNDOR 12345…
Bold **ITC Syndor**
Bold Italic ***ITC Syndor***

Syntax
Regular Syntax
Italic *Syntax*
Medium Syntax
Bold **Syntax**

Syntax Display
Regular Syntax
Italic *Syntax*
Medium Syntax
Bold **Syntax**

Tango
Tango

Tarragon
Tarragon

Thorowgood
Regular **Thorowgood**
Italic ***Thorowgood***

Thunderbird
Regular THUNDER
Extra Condensed THUNDERBIRD

ITC Tiepolo
Book ITC Tiepolo
Book Italic *ITC Tiepolo*
Medium ITC Tiepolo
Medium Italic *ITC Tiepolo*
Black **ITC Tiepolo**
Black Italic ***ITC Tiepolo***

ITC Tiepolo SCOSF
Book SCOSF ITC TIEPOLO 12345…
Medium SCOSF **ITC TIEPOLO 1234…**

ITC Tiffany 1
Demi **ITC Tiffany**
Demi Italic ***ITC Tiffany***
Heavy **ITC Tiffany**
Heavy Italic ***ITC Tiffany***

ITC Tiffany 2
Light ITC Tiffany
Light Italic *ITC Tiffany*
Medium ITC Tiffany
Medium Italic *ITC Tiffany*

Timeless
Light Timeless
Light Italic *Timeless*

Timeless Cyrillic
Light Upright Абвгдеж Зикл
Light Oblique *Абвгдеж Зикл*
Medium Upright **Абвгдеж Зикл**

Timeless Greek
Light Upright Αβγδε Ζζηθικ
Light Oblique *Αβγδε Ζζηθικ*
Medium Upright **Αβγδε Ζζηθικ**

Timeless Phonetic
Standard Light θιɰɛʟɛʃʃ ʼнɔɴɛθɪç ʃθa

Time Script
Light Time Script
Medium **Time Script**
Bold **Time Script**

Unitus
Light Unitus
Light Italic *Unitus*
Regular Unitus
Italic *Unitus*
Bold **Unitus**
Bold Italic ***Unitus***
Black **Unitus**
Black Italic ***Unitus***
Ultra Bold **Unitus**

Unitus Condensed
Light Condensed Unitus
Light Condensed Italic *Unitus*
Condensed Unitus
Condensed Italic *Unitus*
Bold Condensed **Unitus**
Bold Condensed Italic ***Unitus***

Unitus Display
Light Unitus
Light Italic *Unitus*

ff

. . . Unitus Display Regular	Unitus
Italic	Unitus
Bold	Unitus
Bold Italic	Unitus
Black	Unitus
Ultra Bold	Unitus
Unitus Display Condensed Light Condensed	Unitus
Light Condensed Italic	Unitus
Condensed	Unitus
Bold Condensed	Unitus
Unitus Expanded Expanded	Unitus
Bold Expanded	Unitus
Black Expanded	Unitus
Ultra Bold Expanded	Unitus
Unitus Narrow Light Narrow	Unitus
Narrow	Unitus
University Roman	University
Italic	University
Bold	University
University Swash Italic	University
ITC Usherwood Book	ITC Usherwood
Book Italic	ITC Usherwood
Medium	ITC Usherwood
Medium Italic	ITC Usherwood
Bold	ITC Usherwood
Bold Italic	ITC Usherwood
Black	ITC Usherwood
Black Italic	ITC Usherwood
VAG Rundschrift Text	VAG Rundschrift
Display	VAG Rundschrift
Van Dijk	Van Dijk
Vegas	Vegas
Vendome Roman	Vendome
Italic	Vendome
Medium	Vendome
Medium Italic	Vendome
Bold	Vendome
Condensed	Vendome
Vivaldi	Vivaldi
Vladimir Script	Vladimir Script
Volta Roman	Volta
Medium	Volta
Medium Italic	Volta
Bold	Volta
Walbaum Buch Roman	Walbaum Buch
Medium	Walbaum Buch
Bold	Walbaum Buch
Washington Extra Light	Washington
Light	Washington
Regular	Washington
Bold	Washington
Black	Washington
Weiss Rundgotisch	Weiſſ Rundgotiſch
Windsor Regular	Windsor
Bold	Windsor
Ultra Heavy	Windsor
Extra Bold Condensed	Windsor
Windsor Elongated	Windsor
Windsor Outline	Windsor
Worcester Round Regular	Worcester Round
Italic	Worcester Round
Medium	Worcester Round
Bold	Worcester Round
Worcester Round Outline	Worcester Round
ITC Zapf Chancery Light	ITC Zapf Chancery
Light Italic	ITC Zapf Chancery
Medium	ITC Zapf Chancery
Medium Italic	ITC Zapf Chancery
Demi	ITCZapf Chancery
Bold	ITCZapf Chancery
ITC Zapf Laser ITC Zapf Chancery Medium Italic	ITC Zapf Chancery
ITC Zapf Dingbats	✰❀❍✷❊●✲❄▲
ITC Zapf International Light	ITC Zapf Int'l
Light Italic	ITC Zapf Int'l
Medium	ITC Zapf Int'l
Medium Italic	ITC Zapf Int'l
. . . ITC Zapf International Demi	ITC Zapf Int'l
Demi Italic	ITC Zapf Int'l
Heavy	ITC Zapf Int'l
Heavy Italic	ITC Zapf Int'l
Zipper	Zipper
Zirkus	ZIRKUS

foundry: Vanguard Media

Vanguard Media is "owned and operated by three young art school grads who decided to break into the software industry. The Comicbook font has been used on the PBS television show *Where in the World is Carmen San Diego?* and on MTV's Liquid Television series *Autoguard 2000.*

Comicbook Book	COMICBOOK
Book Italic	COMICBOOK
Demi	COMICBOOK
Demi Italic	COMICBOOK
Bold	COMICBOOK
Bold Italic	COMICBOOK

foundry: Jack Yan & Associates

Jack Yan began working with lettering and calligraphy in 1987, producing over 100 designs. In 1993 he and his company began translating some of those designs into digital font formats. The first offerings – JY Rebeca and Yan Series 333 – are shown here. The company, based in Wellington, New Zealand, plans to release new fonts on a continuing basis.

Rebeca Roman	Rebeca
Italic	Rebeca
Demi	Rebeca
Demi Italic	Rebeca

ff

... Rebeca

Bold	Rebeca
Bold Italic	*Rebeca*
Roman SCOSF	REBECA 12345...
Roman LF	Rebeca 12345...
Italic LF	*Rebeca 12345...*

Yan Series 333

Roman	Yan Series 333
Italic	*Yan Series 333*
Bold	**Yan Series 333**
Bold Italic	***Yan Series 333***
Black	**Yan Series 333**
Black Italic	***Yan Series 333***
Roman LF	Yan Series 333 123...
Italic LF	*Yan Series 333 123...*
Italic Swash Alternate	*Aa C C & Dd Ee*

font foundry codes

Adobe Systems ADO
Agfa AGP AGA AGL
Alphabets Inc ALP
Andersen Agency AND
Bear Rock Technologies BEA
Bitstream BIT
Carter & Cone Type CAR
Diehl.Volk DVT
Elsner+Flake LEF
EmDash EMD
Famous Fonts FAM
The Font Bureau FBU
The Font Company TFC
Franklin Type Founders FRA
Galápagos Design Group GAL
Handcrafted Fonts HAN
Harris Design HAR
Headliners International HEA
Image Club IMA
Intecsas INT

Font Index

International Typeface Corporation ITC
Isis Imaging ISI
Key Borders KEY
Lanston Type Company LAN
Letraset LET
Letter Perfect LPT
Linguist's Software LSI
Linotype-Hell LIN
Monotype Typography MCL MAE MTD
New York Design Studio NYD
NIMX Graphics NIM
Page Studio PAG
PolyType POL
Red Rooster Typefounders RED
RJH Productions RJH
Russian Type Foundry RUS
Christian Schwartz Design CHR
Stone Type Foundry STO
Torah TOR
Treacyfaces TRE
[T-26] T26
URW URW
Vanguard Media VAN
Jack Yan & Associates JAC

font foundry codes

✍ Albert Hollenstein, 1975

?

Font Index

Primary, bold reference following font names indicates source foundry and page number for comprehensive font displays in SECTION 1; secondary references indicate source foundry and page number for one-line font displays and/or notes in SECTION 2. *Note*: Pi, Symbol, Logo, Ornament & Image fonts and fonts for World-wide Languages are also indexed separately beginning on page 643.

A…

B...

Bookman Headline
BIT533

Bookman Old Style MCL67
MCL593

ITC Bookman ADO67
ADO506 BIT533 FAM550 FRA561 LEF543 LIN578 URW616

ITC Bookman Laser
URW616

ITC Bookman PS
MCL594

ITC Bookman PS Efo MCL470
MCL594

Boomerang
FRA561

Bordeaux LET67
FRA561 LET573

Border Pi LIN413
ADO506 LIN578

Agfa PLS Borders & Ornaments AGL416
AGL529

General Glyphics Border Fonts MTD413
MTD601

Key Borders Border Fonts KEY415
KEY570

Bostonia
FRA561

Boton ADO68
ADO506

Bottleneck
URW616

Boulevard ADO69
ADO506

A*I Bouwsma Script ALP69
ALP530

A*I Box Gothic ALP69
ALP530 MTD600

PIXymbols Boxkey PAG417
MTD603 PAG605

PIXymbols BoxnLines PAG417
PAG605

DV Boy DVT69
DVT542

Braggadocio MCL70
MCL594

Braille Font
INT567

PIXymbols Braille Grade 2 PAG417
PAG605

Bramley URW70
AGP523 URW616

Brandenburger
INT567

Branding Iron AGP70
AGP523

PL Brazilia
AGP528

Bremen FBU71
BIT533 FBU555

Breughel
URW616

TF Bridgette TRE417
TRE612

Brighton LET71
LET573 URW616

MN Brio MTD71
MTD602

PL Britannia Bold AGP72
AGP528

British Inserat
MTD602

Brittanic
LEF543 URW616

FC Brittany
TFC558

Broadway BIT72
BIT533 URW616

TC Broadway AGP72
AGP528

Broadweli TOR489
TOR611

Brody
FRA561 LEF543

Brody DisplaySet 1
ADO522 LIN592

Bronx LET72
LET573

Brookfield
INT567

Brooks Initials
INT567

Brophy Script AGP72
AGP523

Bruce Old Style BIT73
BIT533

Brush 445 BIT73
BIT533

Brush 738
BIT533

Brush Cyrillic RUS476
RUS609

Brush Script ADO73
ADO506 BIT533 LIN578 MCL594 MTD602 URW616

TF Bryn Mawr TRE73
TRE611

Bubbalove T26·74
T26·612

Buffalo Bill
INT567

Bulldog
MTD600

MN Bulletin Typewriter
MTD602

BulletsNStuff EMD417
EMD549

Bullfinch
FRA561

Bulmer
BIT533

FC Bulmer TFC74
TFC558

Monotype Bulmer MCL74
MCL594

Bundesbahn Pi LIN418
ADO506 LIN578

Burin AGP76
AGP523

Burlington LET76
LET573

Agfa PLS Business & Services AGL418
AGL529

PolyType Business Icons POL418
POL606

ITC Busorama
AGP523 BIT533 FRA561

Busoreli TOR489
TOR611

Buster
URW616

Buxom
URW616

Byron RED76
RED607

C...

C & B Pi
FAM550

Cabaret LET78
FRA561 LEF543 LET573

Cabarga Cursiva LET78
LET573

PMN Caecilia LIN78
ADO506 LIN578

Cafeteria FBU79
FBU555

Caflisch Script MultipleMaster ADO79
ADO506

New Caledonia LIN80
ADO506 LIN579

California
FAM550

CG California
FAM550

FC California Grotesk
TFC558

MN Caligra
MTD602

Calisto MCL80
MCL594

Calligraphic 421 BIT81
BIT533

Calligraphic 810
BIT533

Calligraphic Ornaments LET419
LET575

Calligraphy for Print
ADO522 LIN592

Calvert MCL81
ADO506 LIN579 MCL594

Camellia
FRA561 LEF543

Cameo
RED607

Campaign LET81
LET573

Campanula
MTD604

MN Campus
MTD602

Cancellaresca Script LET81
LET573

Candice
LEF543 URW616

Candida BIT82
ADO506 BIT533 LIN579 URW616

Canterbury Old Style RED82
RED607

Cantoria MCL82
ADO506 LIN579 MCL594

Capone Light
AGP528

Caravan Borders & Ornaments LIN419
ADO506 LIN579

MN Card Camio
MTD602

Cardboard Cutout INT83
INT567

Careli TOR489
TOR611

Cargo
URW616

Carlton
LET573

Bitstream Carmina BIT83
BIT533

Carmine Tango
AGP523

Carnival T26·83
T26·612

Carolina LET83
ADO506 LIN579

Carousel
LEF543 URW616

MN Carplate
MTD602

Carrick
INT567

Carta ADO419
ADO506 LIN579

FC Cartel
TFC558

Cartier AGP84
AGP523

FC Cartoon TFC84
TFC558

FC Casablanca
TFC558

Cascade Script LIN84
ADO506 LIN579

Adobe Caslon ADO87
ADO507 LIN579

Adobe Caslon Ornaments ADO420
ADO507 LIN579

Berthold Caslon Book ADO89
ADO507

Big Caslon CAR88
CAR541

Bureau Caslon
FBU555

Caslon 1080
HEA565

Caslon 3 LIN84
ADO506 BIT533 FAM550 LIN579

Caslon 310
HEA565

Caslon 540 LIN84
ADO506 BIT533 FAM550 LIN579

Caslon 540 Italic with Swashes LET85
LET573

Caslon 76
FAM551

Caslon Antique IMA86
FAM551 IMA566 MTD602

Caslon Black
URW616

Caslon Bold
BIT533 HEA565

Caslon Bold No. 537 LAN86
LAN571

Caslon Bold No. 637 LAN86
LAN571

Caslon Display
HEA565

Caslon Graphique
FRA561

Caslon Open Face LIN85
ADO506 BIT533 LIN579

Caslon Old Face
BIT533

Caslon Oldstyle No. 337 LAN85
LAN571

FC Caslon C 37
TFC558

FC Caslon C78
TFC558

FC Caslon C79
TFC558

FC Caslon C 113
TFC558

FC Caslon C 337
TFC558

FC Caslon C 437
TFC558

FC Caslon C 637
TFC558

ITC Caslon Headline FAM87
FAM551

ITC Caslon No. 224 BIT87
ADO506 AGP523 BIT533 LEF543 LIN579 URW616

Castellar MCL89
ADO507 LIN579 MCL594

Castle URW90
FRA561 LEF543 URW616

PIXymbols Casual
PAG605

Bitstream Cataneo BIT90
BIT533

Catastrophe MTD90
MTD600

Catherine
FRA561

Group Cats
MTD600

Catull ADO91
ADO507

Cavalier HEA91
HEA565

Caxton URW91
ADO507 AGP523 BIT534 FAM551 LET573 LIN579 URW616

Caxton Condensed URW91
URW616

Celebrations LET420
LET575

Celtic
MTD602

Centaur MCL92
ADO507 LIN579 MCL594

Linotype Centennial LIN92
ADO507 LIN579

Bureau Century
FBU555

Century 725 BIT95
BIT534

Century 731
BIT534

Century 751
BIT534

Century Expanded BIT93
ADO507 BIT534 LIN580 MCL594 URW616

CG Century Expanded
FAM551

FC Century Expanded
TFC558

Century Gothic MCL96
MCL594

Century Old Style ADO93
ADO507 BIT534 FAM551 LIN580 URW616

Monotype Century Old Style
MCL594

Century Schoolbook
BIT534 MCL594 URW617

Century Schoolbook PS Efo MCL470
MCL594

Century Schoolbook Laser
URW617

Century Schoolbook Monospaced
BIT534

Century Textbook
FAM551

CG Century
FAM551

CG Century Old Style
FAM551

CG Century Schoolbook
FAM551

FC Century Expanded
TFC558

FC O Century
TFC558

ITC Century BIT94
ADO507 BIT534 LEF543 FAM551 LIN580 URW617

ITC Century Handtooled ITC95
ITC569 URW617

New Century Schoolbook LIN94
ADO507 FAM551 LIN580

New Century Schoolbook Fractions
ADO507 LIN580

New Century Schoolbook Greek LIN484
LIN580

ITC Cerigo URW96
URW617

Chalice
INT567

Challenge LET96
LET573

Champagne IMA97
IMA566

Champers LET97
LET573

D...

?

De Vinne BIT125
BIT535 URW618

CG De Vinne
AGP524

FC Devinne
TFC559

Devit T26·126
T26·613

Dewhurst
INT567

Dex Gothic
URW618

Dextor
URW618

FC Diamante
TFC559

ITC Didi FAM126
FAM551

FC Didoni
TFC559

FC Firmin Didot TFC127
TFC559

Linotype Didot LIN126
ADO509 LIN581

Linotype Didot Ornaments LIN426
ADO509 LIN581

TF Dierama TRE127
MTD604 TRE611

Dieter Caps
INT567

Digi Grotesk
LEF544

FC Digital
TFC559

Digitek LET127
LET573

PIXymbols Digits & Clocks PAG426
MTD603 PAG605

Dilara Caps
INT567

DIN 1451
FRA562 LEF544

FC DIN 16
TFC559

DIN Schriften LIN127
ADO509 LIN581

Dinderman
INT567

PIXymbols Dingbats PAG426
PAG605

DingBRATS MTD427
MTD600

Dingura T26·427
T26·613

A*I Dino Heavy
ALP530

Diotima LIN128
ADO509 LIN581

Mini Pics Directional IMA427
IMA566

FC Disco TFC128
TFC559

Diskus
FRA562 URW618

RTF DisplaySet 1
RUS610

Diversions LET427
LET575

Dolmen LET128
LET573

Dom Casual LIN129
ADO509 BIT535 LEF544 LIN581 URW618

HF Doodle HAN129
HAN564 MTD601

Dorchester Script MCL129
ADO509 LIN581 MCL595

Doric Bold LIN129
ADO509 LIN581

Dorothy Initials
INT567

PIXymbols DOSscreen PAG428
PAG605

Dragonwick
INT567

Drawing Pad
INT567

DV Drukpa DVT130
DVT542

MN Dubbeldik
MTD602

Dubiel
INT567

Duc De Berry LIN130
ADO509 LIN581

Dundee
RED607

Dupuy
INT567

Durango FRA130
FRA562

Dutch 766
BIT535

Dutch 801
BIT535

Dutch 809
BIT535

Dutch 811
BIT535

Dutch 823
BIT535

Dynamo URW130
AGP528 LEF544 LET573 MTD602 URW618

E...

Bureau Eagle FBU134
AGP529 FBU555 MTD601

Eagle Bold
AGP528

Eaglefeather AGP134
AGP524

Earthquake T26·135
T26·613

East Bloc IMA135
IMA566

Eccentric
AGP524

Eckmann URW135
URW618

A*I Eclectic One ALP428
ALP530

Eclipse
AGP528

Agfa PLS Ecology AGL428
AGL529

Economist MTD135
MTD600

Ecru FBU135
FBU555

HF Eden Expanded Light
HAN564 MTD601

Edison LEF135
LEF544

DV Edition
DVT542

Edwardian URW136
LET573 URW618

Linotype EEC Pi LIN428
LIN581

EF DisplaySets 1, 2, 3
LEF549

EF ITC DisplaySets 1 & 2
LEF549

EF ScriptSets 1 & 2
LEF549

Egiziano Black
AGP527

FC Egizio
TFC559

Egizio Condensed URW137
URW618

Egmont Bold
MTD603

Monotype Egyptian 72 Extended MCL137
MCL595

Egyptian 505 BIT137
AGP524 BIT535 FRA562

Egyptian 710
BIT535

A*I Egyptian Bold Condensed ALP137
MTD599

A*I Egyptian Condensed MultipleMaster
ALP530

Egyptienne
FRA562 MTD602 URW618

Egyptienne F LIN138
ADO509 LIN581

Ehrhardt MCL138
ADO509 LIN581 MCL595

Eileen Caps
INT567

Einhorn URW138
FRA562 LEF544 URW618

El Grande FBU139
FBU555

FC Elaine
TFC559

ITC Élan URW139
AGP524 LEF544 URW618

Elante
AGP524

Electra LIN139
ADO509 LIN581

Electra Set 1
ADO522

Elefont URW141
LEF544 URW618

DV Elevator DVT141
DVT542

DV Ellay
DVT542

Elli FBU141
FBU555

Ellington MCL141
ADO509 LIN581 MCL595

Else NPL LIN142
ADO509 LIN581

Elizabeth Ann
INT567

Elston
RED607

Elysium LET142
LET573

Elzevier
INT567

Embassy BIT142
BIT535

Emphasis LET143
LET573

Bureau Empire FBU143
AGP529 FBU555 MTD601

Empire
AGP528 BIT535 MTD603

Empire State
HEA565

Emporium
FRA562

EndsMeansMends STO144
STO610

Englische Schreibschrift
URW618

English 157
BIT535

Sackers English Script AGP144
AGP524

English Times
FAM551

Engravers
URW618

Engravers Bold Face LIN145
ADO509 LIN581

Engravers' Gothic BIT145
BIT535

Engravers' Old English BIT144
BIT535

Monotype Engravers Old English MCL144
MCL595

Engravers' Roman BIT145
BIT535

Monotype Engravers MCL145
MCL595

Engravure
AGP524

MN Enroute
MTD602

Entropy T26·145
T26·613

Enviro
LET573

Epitaph FBU146
FBU555

Epokha LET146
LET573

Equestrienne
RED608

Equinox LET146
LET573

ITC Eras BIT146
ADO509 BIT535 FAM551 LEF544 LIN581 URW618

Eraser Dust
INT567

Erasmus RED147
RED608

Erbar LIN147
AGP524 LIN581

FC Erbar
TFC559

Erin Lynn
FRA562

Escalido T26·147
T26·613

ITC Esprit URW148
ADO509 AGP524 LEF544 LIN581 URW618

Estro IMA148
IMA566 MTD602

Etruscan LET148
LET573

Euphoria
T26·613

Eurocrat
MTD600

TC Europa Bold
AGP528

Europa Grotesque
RED608

European Pi LIN429
ADO509 LIN581

Eurostile LIN148
ADO509 LEF544 LIN581 MTD602 URW619

Eurostile Extended
URW619

Even More Face Cuts
INT567

Ewie
URW619

Excelsior LIN149
ADO509 LIN581

Excelsior Cyrillic LIN478
ADO509 LIN581

Excelsior EastA LIN471
LIN581

Excius
URW619

Exotic 350
BIT535

HF Exposition HAN149
HAN564 MTD601

eXposure NYD150
NYD605

FC Expressa
TFC559

Extension
RED608

F...

PIXymbols FabriCare PAG429
PAG605

Face Cuts
INT567

Fairfield LIN152
ADO510 LIN581

Faithful Fly LET153
LET573

Fajita IMA153
IMA566

Falstaff MCL153
ADO510 LIN582 MCL595

FC Fanfare Condensed TFC153
TFC559

Farfell IMA153
IMA566

PIXymbols FARmarks PAG429
PAG605

Fashion LET154
LET573

ITC Fat Face
FRA562

Fat Man Cyrillic Heavy RUS478
RUS609

Faust RED154
RED608

Felix Titling MCL155
MCL595

ITC Fenice URW155
ADO510 AGP524 BIT535 FAM551 LEF544 LIN582 URW619

Festival Titling MCL155
MCL595

Fetch Scotty
INT567

Fette Fraktur LIN155
ADO510 LIN582 URW619

Fette Gotisch
URW619

MN Fidelio
MTD602

PL Fiedler Gothic AGP156
AGP528

Figaro MCL156
MCL595

Figural LET156
LET573

Figures Square
LAN571

Fina Medium Condensed
URW619

Fine Hand LET156
LET573

PL Fiorello Condensed AGP156
AGP528

Flaco T26·157
T26·613

PIXymbols Flagman PAG429
PAG605

Flamenco
LET573

G...

?

ITC Goudy Sans **AGP192**
AGP525 BIT537 LEF545 URW621

Monotype Goudy Modern **MCL190**
ADO512 LIN583 MCL596

Monotype Goudy Old Style
MCL596

Monotype Goudy Text **MCL191**
ADO512 LIN583 MCL596

WTC Goudy
URW621

Grab Bag
INT567

Graeca **LSI485**
LSI575

Graffiti **FBU192**
FBU555

Grange
HEA565

Granjon **LIN192**
ADO512 LIN583

Graphite **MTD193**
AGP525 MTD603

Graphite Collection
MTD605

Graphite MultipleMaster
ADO512

Graphite Sampler
MTD603

Gravestone Rubbing
INT567

Gravura
LET573

Greco **FRA194**
FRA562

Greco Adornado **FRA194**
FRA562

Greco Deco
FRA562

Greek Sans **LSI485**
LSI575

Green Caps
INT567

Greeting Monotone
AGP528

Greyton Script **LET195**
LET573

PIXymbols GridMaker **PAG432**
PAG606

Griffin Dingbats
INT567

ITC Grizzly
BIT537

Bureau Grotesque **FBU195**
AGP529 FBU555 MTD601

Grotesque No. 9
URW621

Monotype Grotesque **MCL195**
ADO512 LIN583 MCL596

URW Grotesque
URW621

ITC Grouch
BIT537

Ground Hog
INT567

Group Arabia
MTD600

Group Cats
MTD600

Group Hawaii
MTD600

Grove Script **RED196**
RED608

Guardi **LIN196**
ADO512 LIN584

GudrunSchrift
LIN592

TF Guestcheck **TRE196**
MTD604 TRE612

H...

TF Habitat **TRE198**
MTD604 TRE612

Hadas **TOR491**
TOR611

Hadfield **LET199**
LEF546 LET573 URW621

Hadrian
LPT575 MTD602

Hadriano
AGP525

Hadriano Stonecut **LAN199**
LAN572

Hadriano Titling **LAN200**
LAN572

A*I Half
ALP530

Hamilton **FBU200**
FBU556

Hancock Bold Condensed
RED608

Hand Drawn
LET573

FC Handel Gothic
TFC559

Handel Gothic
BIT537 LEF546 URW621

Handle Oldstyle **AGP200**
AGP525

Handwrite Inkblot **T26·200**
T26·613

MN Hansson Stencil Bold
MTD602

Hardwood
LPT575 MTD602

FC Harem
TFC559

Harlow
LEF546 LET573 URW621

Harpers
FRA562

Harris
FRA562

Harting **INT201**
INT567

Harvey **LET201**
LET573

Group Hawaii
MTD600

Hawthorn
LEF546 URW621

Hazel **LET201**
LET573

Headhunter
INT567

Headline Bold **MCL201**
MCL596

A*I HeadToHeads **ALP432**
ALP530

Hebraica **LSI491**
LSI576

Hebras **TOR491**
TOR611

FC Heldustry
TFC559

Heldustry
AGP525 FAM552

FC Helenic
TFC559

Helinda Rook **AGP201**
AGP525

Helios Rounded **FAM202**
FAM552

Heliotype **LET202**
LET573

FC Helium
TFC559

FC Helserif
TFC559

Helvetica **LIN202**
ADO512 LET574 LIN584

Helvetica Condensed **LIN202**
ADO512 LIN584

Helvetica Cyrillic **LIN478**
ADO512 LIN584

Helvetica Fractions
ADO512 LIN584

Helvetica Greek **LIN486**
LIN584

Helvetica Inserat **LIN203**
ADO512 LIN584

Helvetica Inserat Cyrillic **LIN479**
LIN584

Helvetica Rounded **LIN203**
ADO512 LIN584

Neue Helvetica **LIN204**
ADO512 LIN584

Neue Helvetica EastA **LIN471**
LIN584

Heraldus Extra Bold
LEF546

Herculanum **LIN206**
ADO513 LIN584

Herold
FRA562

Herold Gothic
FBU556

Hess Old Style
RED608

HF DisplaySet 1
MTD605

Hibiscus **MTD206**
MTD600

ITC Highlander **ITC206**
ADO513 ITC569 URW621

ITC Highlander GX
ITC570

Highlight
LEF546 LET574 URW621

FC Highway Gothic
TFC559

PIXymbols Highway Gothic
PAG606

PIXymbols Highway Signs **PAG432**
PAG606

HiGwangJu **LSI494**
LSI576

HiInchon **LSI495**
LSI576

FC Hildago
TFC559

HipHop **FBU207**
FBU556

Hiroshige **URW207**
ADO513 LIN584 URW621

Hobeli **TOR491**
TOR611

FC Hobo
TFC559

Hobo **ADO207**
ADO513 BIT537 LIN584 URW621

Hoffmann **FBU208**
FBU203

Hogarth Script **URW208**
LEF546 URW621

Linotype Holiday Pi **LIN433**
ADO513 LIN584

Agfa PLS Holidays **AGL433**
AGL529

PolyType Holidays **POL433**
POL606

Holland Seminar **AGP208**
AGP525

Holland Title
AGP525

Hollander **LEF209**
LEF546

Hollandse Mediaeval
AGP525

FC Holly Script
TFC559

Holtzschue
INT567

Honda
FRA562

Honduras **RED209**
RED608

Horatio
LEF546 URW621

Horley Old Style **MCL209**
ADO513 LIN585 MCL596

Horndon
FRA562 LEF546

Horror Show
INT567

Horst Caps
INT567

PIXymbols Hospital & Safety **PAG433**
PAG606

Stempel Hot Metal Borders **LIN434**
LIN585

MN Hotel
MTD602

TF Hôtelmoderne **TRE210**
MTD604 TRE612

FC Howland
TFC559

FC Hudson
TFC559

Humanist 521
BIT537

Humanist 531
BIT537

Humanist 777
BIT537

Humanist 970
BIT537

Humanist Slabserif 712
BIT537

Hunan Garden
INT567

Hurry **EMD211**
EMD549

Huxley **HEA211**
HEA565

FC Huxley Vertical
TFC559

Huxley Vertical **IMA212**
BIT537 IMA566

I...

Ian Bent
INT567

Ice Age **URW214**
FRA562 URW621

Ignatius **LET214**
LET574

Berthold Imago **ADO214**
ADO513

FC Impact
TFC559

Impact **ADO214**
ADO513 LIN585

Imperial **BIT215**
BIT537

Impress
BIT537

Impressum **LIN215**
ADO513 AGP525 LIN585 URW621

Imprint **MCL215**
MCL596

Impuls **BIT216**
BIT537

Incidentals **LET434**
LET575

Incised 901
BIT537

Industria **LIN216**
ADO513 LIN585

Industrial 736
BIT537

Industrials **LET434**
LET575

Agfa PLS Industry & Engineering **AGL435**
AGL529

Indy Italic **LET217**
LET574

Inflex
ADO513 LIN585 MCL596

Informal 011
BIT537

Informal Roman **LET217**
LET574

Inscription **LET217**
LET574

Insignia **LIN217**
ADO513 LIN585

PrintBar Interleaved 2 of 5 **BEA411**
BEA531

Mini Pics International **IMA435**
IMA566

Agfa PLS International Symbols **AGL435**
AGL529

Interstate **FBU217**
FBU556

Interstate Pi **FBU435**
FBU556

FC Introspect
TFC559

FC Inverserif
TFC559

Monotype Ionic **MCL218**
MCL596

Bitstream Iowan Old Style **BIT218**
BIT537

Iris **LET219**
LET574

Ironmonger **FBU219**
AGP529 FBU556 MTD601

Ironmonger 3-D **FBU319**
FBU556

Ironwood **ADO220**
ADO513 LIN585

Isabella **AGP220**
AGP525

Isadora
FRA562

ITC Isadora **LIN220**
ADO513 AGP525 LEF546 LIN585 URW621

ITC Isbell **BIT220**
AGP525 BIT537 FRA562 LEF546

Isis **LET221**
LET574

MN Isonorm
MTD602

Italia **BIT221**
ADO513 BIT537 LEF546 LIN585 URW621

Monotype Italian Old Style **MCL221**
ADO513 LIN585 MCL596

Sackers Italian Script **AGP221**
AGP525

ITC Headliners 1 & 2
ITC570

ITC GX Headliners
ITC570

J...

K...

L...

M...

?

N...

O...

P...

Q...

R...

S...

?

T...

?

U...

V...

W...

X...

Y...

Z...

Pi, Symbol, Logo, Ornament & Image Font Index

A...

B...

C...

D...

E...

F...

G...

H...

I...

J...

K...

?

L...

M...

N...

O...

P...

Q...

R...

S...

T...

U...

V...

W...

X...

Z...

World-wide Languages Font Index

A...

B...

C...

?

?

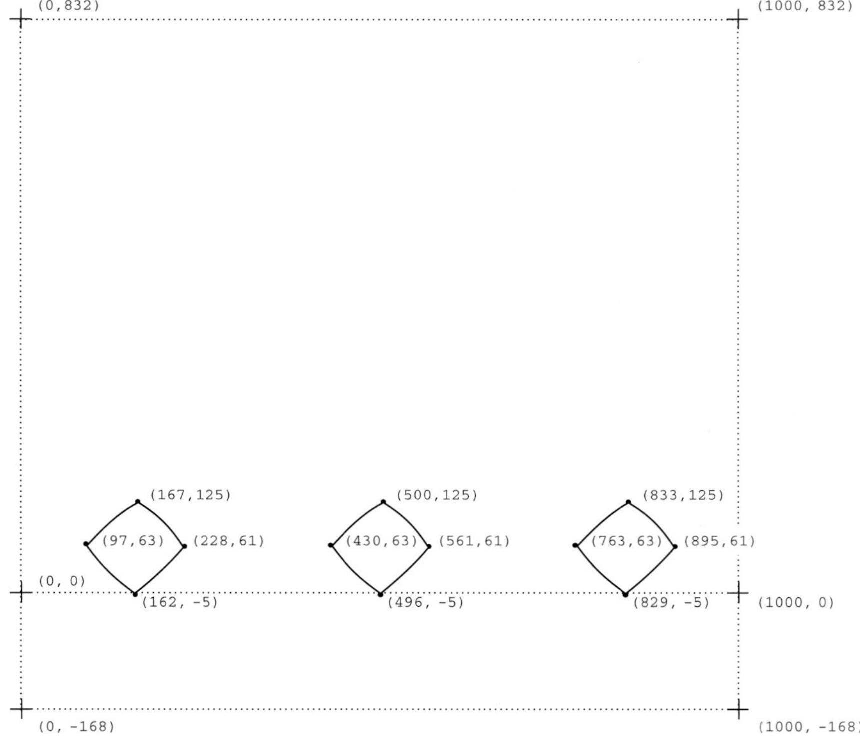
(0,832)
(1000, 832)
(167,125)
(500,125)
(833,125)
(97,63)
(228,61)
(430,63)
(561,61)
(763,63)
(895,61)
(0, 0)
(162, -5)
(496, -5)
(829, -5)
(1000, 0)
(0, -168)
(1000, -168)

✍ Adrian Frutiger, 1992

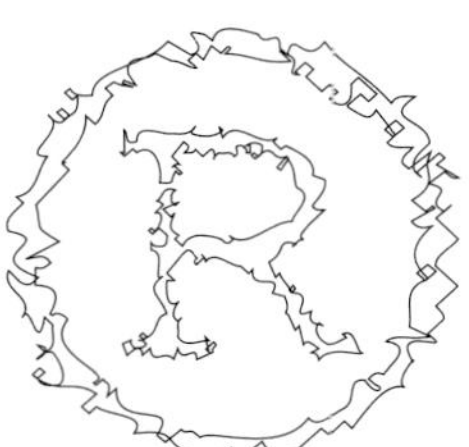

Trademarks

Adobe, Adobe Garamond, Adobe Caslon, Adobe Expert Collection, Adobe Originals, Adobe Wood Type, Birch, Blackoak, Caflisch Script, Carta, Charlemagne, Cheq, Cottonwood, Critter, Cutout, Giddyup, Giddyup Thangs, Ironwood, Juniper, Lithos, Madrone, Mesquite, Mezz, Minion, Myriad, Mythos, Pepperwood, Poetica, Ponderosa, Poplar, PostScript, Quake, Rad, Rosewood, Sanvito, Sonata, Studz, Trajan, Tekton, Viva, Utopia, Wild Type, Willow and Zebrawood are trademarks of Adobe Systems Incorporated which may be registered in certain jurisdictions.

Garth Graphic and Rotis are registered trademarks and Agfa Nadianne, Agfa Wile, CG Triumvirate, Hadriano, and Shannon are trademarks of Agfa Division, Miles Inc.

Beacon, Baskerville Ad Weight, Baskerville Heavy Weight, Baskerville Over Weight, FC Bluejack, Legothic and Polonaise are trademarks of Alphabet Innovations, Inc.

A*I Antique, A*I Barrel, A*I Box Gothic, A*I Egyptian, A*I French XXX, A*I Koch Antiqua, A*I Neuland, A*I Oz Brush, A*I Painter, A*I Poster, A*I Prospera II, A*I Tuscan Egyptian and A*I Wood Type are trademarks of Alphabets Inc.

Amigo, Hiroshige, Marigold, Oxford, Pelican and Visigoth are trademarks of Alpha Omega Typography Inc.

Kindergarten is a trademark of Andersen Agency.

Apple and Macintosh are registered trademarks and TrueType is a trademark of Apple Computer Inc.

Kaufmann and Park Avenue are registered trademarks and Ad Lib, American Text, Americana, Balloon, Bank Gothic, Bernhard Fashion, Bernhard Modern, Bernhard Tango, Bookman, Broadway, Brody, Brush Script, Bulmer, Caslon 540, Caslon Antique, Caslon Bold, Caslon Openface, Century Expanded, Century Oldstyle, Century Schoolbook, Cheltenham, Cloister Black, Cloister Open Face, Commercial Script, Cooper Black, Copperplate Gothic, Craw Modern, Dom, Egyptian 505, Estro, Franklin Gothic, Gallia, Gold Rush, Goudy Catalogue, Goudy, Goudy Handtooled, Goudy Old Style, Hobo, Latin Extra Condensed, Liberty, Lydian, Murray Hill, News Gothic, Onyx, PT Barnum, Parisian, Piranesi Italic, Romana, Steelplate, Stencil, Stymie, Thunderbird, Typo Upright and Wedding Text are trademarks of Kingsley/ATF Type Corporation.

Danmark is a trademark of Arthur Baker.

PrintBar is a trademark of Bear Rock Technologies Corporation.

Akzidenz Grotesk, Berthold, Berthold Baskerville Book, Berthold Bodoni, Berthold Caslon Book, Berthold City, Berthold Garamond, Berthold Imago, Block Berthold, Boton, Catull, Christiana, Colossalis, Comenius, Concorde, Delta Jaeger, Formata, Jaeger Daily News, Lo-Type, and Nofret are registered trademarks and AG Book, AG Old Face, AG Schoolbook, Barmeno, Bellevue, Berliner Grotesk, Berthold Baskerville, Berthold Bodoni Old Face, Berthold Script, Berthold Walbaum, Berthold Walbaum Book, Boulevard, Concorde Nova, Cosmos, Cremona, Poppl-Laudatio, Poppl-Pontifex, Poppl-Residenz, Post-Antiqua and Post-Mediäval are trademarks of H. Berthold AG.

Lucida is a registered trademark of Bigelow & Holmes.

Bijoux, Jeunesse, Jocelyn, Jonas, and Ulissa are trademarks of Johannes Birkenbach.

Bitstream Amerigo, Bitstream Carmina and Bitstream Charter are registered trademarks and Old Dreadful No. 7 and Swiss are trademarks of Bitstream Inc.

Impact and Windsor are trademarks of Stevenson Blake (holdings) Ltd.

Big Caslon, Mantinia and Sophia are trademarks of Carter & Cone Type Inc.

DV Boy Out, DV Boy In, DV Boy Wide, DV Drukpa, DV Edition, DV Elevator, DV Ellay, DV Radish, DV Shaft, DV Simplix and DV Upright are trademarks of Diehl.Volk Typographics.

Econotype and Economist are trademarks of The Economist.

ArchiText is a registered trademark and ArrowDynamic, BulletsNStuff, Gendarme and Upstart are trademarks of EmDash.

The Font Bureau is a registered trademark and Aardvark, BadTyp, Belizio, BeLucian, Bodega Sans, Bodega Serif, Bureau Agency, Bureau Eagle, Bureau Empire, Bureau Grotesque, Bureau Roxy, Cafeteria, Commerce, Ecru, Garage Gothic, Graffiti, Bureau Garamond, Ironmonger, Hamilton, HipHop, Hoffmann, Nobel, Numskill, Nutcracker, Ornaments City, Ornaments Town, Ornaments Village, Phaistos, Romeo, Roxy, Sam Sans, Scamp, Skyline and Wessex are trademarks of The Font Bureau, Inc.

Elli is a trademark of The Font Bureau and Harvard University.

FC Abbey, FC Abilene, FC Accent, FC Accolade, FC Adelon, FC Advertisers, FC Agenda, FC Aggie, FC Amanda, FC Amber, FC Amelia, FC American Gothic, FC American Text, FC American Uncial, FC Annual, FC Apache, FC April, FC Art Gothic, FC Artcraft, FC Ashley, FC Atrax, FC Avalon, FC Avon, FC Ballantines, FC Balloon, FC Balzac, FC Barnum, FC Baucher Gothic, FC Bauer Topic, FC Beale, FC Bee, FC Benjamin, FC Bernhard, FC Bernhard Gothic, FC Bernhard Modern, FC Bible, FC Boa Script, FC Bodoni Bold Condened, FC Brittany, FC Bulmer, FC California Grotesk, FC Cartel, FC Cartoon, FC Casablanca, FC CaslonC113, FC CaslonC337, FC CaslonC37, FC CaslonC437, FC CaslonC637, FC CaslonC78, FC CaslonC79, FC Century Expanded, FC Charter Oak, FC Chevalier, FC Chinat, FC Cloister, FC Contemporary Brush, FC Continental, FC Cooper Old Style, FC Corporate, FC Corvinus Skyline, FC Craw Modern, FC Deepdene, FC Devinne, FC Diamante Heavy, FC Didoni, FC Digital, FC Din16, FC Disco, FC Egizio, FC Elaine, FC Erbar, FC Expressa, Fanfare, FC Firmin Didot, FC Florentine, FC Frency, FC Gatsby, FC Geshexport, FC Glamour, FC Glasgow, FC Gordon, FC Goudy, FC Handel Gothic, FC Harem, FC Helenic, FC Helium, FC Highway Gothic, FC Hildago, FC Hobo, FC Holly Script, FC Howland, FC Hudson, FC Huxley Vertical, FC Impact, FC Introspect, FC Inverserif, FC Japanette, FC Jay Gothic, FC Kelles, FC Kennerley, FC Kenneth, FC Koloss, FC Largo, FC LeAsterix, FC Lightline Gothic, FC Marcato, FC Martinique, FC Mr. Big, FC Napoli, FC Nashville, FC Newport Land, FC Novel Gothic, FC Nueland, FC O Century, FC Ondine, FC Organ Grinder, FC Paladin, FC Pandora Black, FC Parade, FC Pasadena, FC Pekin, FC Permanent Headline, FC Philly Sport Script, FC Pinnoccio, FC Plakat, FC Precis, FC Pretoria, FC Publicity, FC Quartz, FC Racer, FC Radiant, FC Regency, FC Reiner, FC Rochester, FC Roger, FC Rolling Stone, FC Roman Shaded, FC Roman Solid, FC Roman Stylus, FC Ronda, FC Roundest, FC San Serif, FC Sevilla, FC Shotgun, FC Siegfried, FC Souvenir Gothic, FC Spire, FC Stanza, FC Stark, FC Thor, FC Ticonderoga, FC Timbre, FC Toledo, FC Torino, FC Umbra, FC Veracruz, FC Viant, FC Viking Gothic, FC Village, FC Vixen, FC Woodcut, FC Wordsworth, FC Yorkshire, FC Zanzibar and FC Zola are trademarks of The Font Company.

Blippo and Handel Gothic are trademarks of FotoStar International.

Charme, Folio, Futura, Impressum, Serifa, Simoncini Garamond, Stempel Schneidler and Weiss are registered trademarks and Bauer Bodoni and Candida are trademarks of Fundicion Tipografica Neufville S.A.

Fontoon, Fontoonies, Kennedy, Kristen, Maiandra, Stylus, Tangient and Wakefield are trademarks of Galápagos Design Group.

BorderFonts is a trademark of General Glyphics.

Artifact is a trademark of Carolyn Gibbs.

Auriol is a trademark of Haas.

Blackfoot is a trademark of Joshua Hadley.

HF AmericanDiner, HF Antique Row, HF Doodle, HF Eden Expanded, HF Exposition, HF LaVardera, HF Libris Light, HF Modular Stencil, HF NewGarden, HF Poster and HF Secede are trademarks of HandcraftedFonts Co.

SignPix is a trademark of Harris Design.

Headliners and Preset are trademarks of Headliners International, Inc.

Arquitectura, Badloc, Beebopp, Champagne, Image Club, Lemonade, Pacifica Condensed and Signature are tradmarks of Image Club Graphics.

Raleigh and Seagull are trademarks of Ingrama S.A.

IBM and OS/2 are registered trademarks and IBM PC and PS/2 are trademarks of International Business Machines Corporation.

ITC American Typewriter, ITC Anna, ITC Avant Garde Gothic, ITC Barcelona, ITC Bauhaus, ITC Beesknees, ITC Benguiat, ITC Benguiat Gothic, ITC Berkeley Old Style, ITC Bookman, ITC Busorama, ITC Caslon No. 224, ITC Century, ITC Cheltenham, ITC Clearface, ITC Cushing, ITC Élan, ITC Eras, ITC Esprit, ITC Fenice, ITC Flora, ITC Franklin Gothic, ITC Galliard, ITC Garamond, ITC Giovanni, ITC Isadora, ITC Isbell, ITC Kabel, ITC Korinna, ITC Leawood, ITC Legacy, ITC Lubalin Graph, ITC Machine, ITC Mendoza Roman, ITC Modern No. 216, ITC Mona Lisa, ITC New Baskerville, ITC Newtext, ITC Novarese, ITC Officina, ITC Ozwald, ITC Quay Sans, ITC Quorum, ITC Serif Gothic, ITC Slimbach, ITC Stone, ITC Studio Script, ITC Souvenir, ITC Symbol, ITC Syndor, ITC Tiepolo, ITC Usherwood, ITC Veljovic, ITC Weidemann, ITC Zapf Book, ITC Zapf Chancery, ITC Zapf International and ITC Zapf Dingbats are registered trademarks and ITC Bodoni, ITC Cerigo, ITC Charter, ITC Highlander and ITC Motter Corpus are trademarks of International Typeface Corporation.

Aurora, Impuls, Reporter and Schadow are trademarks of Johannes Wagner.

Nucleus is a trademark of Joshua Distler.

Key Borders is a trademark of Joseph Dilena.

Langer is a trademark of Paul M. Lang.

Albertan, Bodoni No. 175, Bodoni 26, Bodoni No. 175, Caslon Oldstyle No. 337, Caslon Bold No. 637, American Caslon, New Caslon, Deepdene, Figures Square, Flash, Fleurons, Folio One, Forum, Francis, Globe Gothic, Goudy Oldstyle No. 394, Goudy Thirty, Hadriano, Jenson Oldstyle, Kaatskill, Kennerly, Metropolitan, Obelisk, Pabst Oldstyle No. 45, Spire, Swing Bold, Vine Leaves, 20th Century 604, 20th Century 605, and 20th Century 606 are trademarks of Lanston Type Co. Ltd.

Aachen, Academy, Agincourt, Ambrose, Aquinas, Aquitaine, Aristocrat, Arriba, Arriba-Arriba, Artiste, Avenida, Balmoral, Bang, Banner, Becka, Belwe, Bendigo, Bergell, Bertie, Bertram, Bible, Bickley, Bitmax, Blackmoor, Bluntz, Boink, Bordeaux, Brighton, Bronx, Burlington, Cabaret, Campaign, Cancellaresca, Carlton, Caxton, Challenge, Champers, Charlotte, Chromium, Citation, Claude, Compacta, Coptek, Corinthian, Crillee, Data 70, Demian, Digitek, Dolmen, Edwardian, Elysium, Emphasis, Enviro, Epokha, Equinox, Faithful Fly, Fashion, Figural, Fine Hand, Flamenco, Flamme, Follies, Forest, Frankfurter, Freestyle, Gilgamesh, Glastonbury, Greyton, Hadfield, Harlow, Harvey, Hazel, Heliotype, Highlight, Ignatius, Indy, Informal, Inscription, Isis, Jazz, Kanban, Katfish, Klee, La Bamba, Lambada, Laser,

Latino, Laura, LCD, Le Griffe, Lexikos, Lightnin', Limehouse, Lino Cut, Malibu, Marguerita, MasterCard, Mekanik, Milano, Mo' Funky Fresh, Oberon, Odessa, One Stroke, Orlando, Papyrus, Party, Pendry, Pink, Plaza, Pleasure, Pneuma, Prague, Premier, Princetown, Pristina, Pritchard, Pump, Quadrus, Quixley, Rage, Ragtime, Rapier, Refracta, Regatta, Retail, Retro, Riva, Robotik, Romic, Roxy, Ru'ach, Rubber Stamp, Rundfunk, Santa Fe, Savoye, Scriba, Scriptek, Shaman, Shatter, Sinaloa, Skid Row, Slipstream, Smudger, Spotlight, Squire, Strobos, Superstar, Synchro, Tannhäuser, Teknik, Tiger Rag, Tiranti, Tropica, Ulysses, University, Van Dijk, Varga, Vegas, Vermont, Victorian, Vienna, Wade, Waterloo, Westwood, Willow, Young Baroque, Zinjaro, DesignFonts and Letraset are trademarks of Esselte Pendaflex Corpration in the United States, of Letraset Canada Limited in Canada, and of Esselte Letraset Limited elsewhere.

DeStijl, Florens, Hadrian, Hardwood, Koch Original, Kryptic, Manito, Old Claude, Silhouette, Spring, Spring Light, Spumoni, Tomboy, Visage and Wendy are trademarks of Letter Perfect.

Cyrillic II, Cyrillic II Sans Serif, Cyrillic II Mono, TransCyrillic and TransSlavic are trademarks and LaserGreek, LaserHebrew and LaserKorean are registered trademarks of Linguist's Software.

Aldus, Arcadia, Auriol, Avenir, PMN Caecilia, New Caledonia, Linotype Centennial, Cochin, Doric, Electra, Excelsior, Frutiger, Stempel Garamond, Garamond 3, Gazette, Glypha, Granjon, Guardi, Helvetica, Industria, Insignia, Janson Text, Linoscript, Linotext, Linotype, Maximus, Melior, Memphis, Meridien, Metrolite, Olympia, Olympian, Optima, Palatino, Peignot, Present, Raleigh, Rotation, Sabon, Shelley, Snell Roundhand, Syntax, Times, Trump Mediäval, Univers, Vectora, Versailles, Westside and Wilke are registered trademarks and Ariadne, Arnold Böcklin, Linotype Astrology Pi, Poster Bodoni, Bodoni, Caravan Borders, Carolina, Cascade, New Century Schoolbook, Chwast Buffalo, Clairvaux, Clarendon, Clearface Gothic, Corona, Dalcora, Linotype Decoration Pi, Linotype Didot, Diotima, Duc De Berry, Eckmann, Egyptienne F, Fairfield, Flyer, Linotype Game Pi, Gothic 13, Herculanum, Kabel, Künstler Script, LinoLetter, Madame, Medici, Metroblack, Metromedium, MICR, Neuland, Neuzeit S, News Gothic, Notre Dame, Nuptial, Omnia, Plak, Pompeijana, Roundy, Ruling, Rusticana, Ruzicka Freehand, Salto, San Marco, Sho, Smaragd, Times Phonetic, Trade Gothic, Type Before Gutenberg, Wiesbaden Swing, and Wilhelm-Klingspor-Gotisch are trademarks of Linotype-Hell AG and/or its subsidiaries which may be registered in certain jurisdictions.

Lomba is a trademark of Luiz Da Lomba.

Tempo and Umbra are trademarks of Ludlow Industries (UK) Ltd.

Dynamo is a trademark of Ludwig & Mayer.

Antique Olive, Banco and Mistral are registered trademarks of Marcel Olive.

Heldustry, Helserif and Martin Gothic are trademarks of Phil Martin, Inc.

Mead and Truesdell are trademarks of Steve Matteson.

MN Access, MN American Uncial, MN Anatol, MN Art Deco, MN Art World, MN Brio, MN Bulletin Typewriter, MN Caligra, MN Campus, MN Card Camio, MN Carplate, MN Chinon, MN Choc, MN Circus, MN Classic Script, MN Comic Strip, MN Contest, MN Duddeldik, MN Enroute, MN Fidelio, MN Fumo Dropshadow, MN Galba, MN Gillies Gothic, MN Globe Gothic, MN Glowworm, MN Gothic, MN Hansson Stencil, MN Hotel, MN Isonorm, MN Jackson, MN Latina, MN Leopard, MN Mistral, MN Normalise Din, MN Renault, MN Rondo, MN Organda, MN Ortem, MN Sayer, MN Squash, MN Stencil, MN Sully Junquires, MN Swaak, MN Tzigane, MN Viant, MN Vivaldi, MN Watch and MN Zambesi are trademarks of Mecanorma.

Microsoft is a registered trademark and Windows is a trademark of Microsoft Corporation.

Monotype is a registered trademark of Monotype Typography Ltd registered in the U.S. Patent and Trademark Office. Monotype Baskerville, Monotype Bernard, Monotype Bodoni, Monotype Century Old Style, Monotype Century Schoolbook, Monotype Clarendon, Monotype Clearface, Monotype Courier 12, Monotype Egyptian 72, Monotype Engraver's Old English, Monotype Franklin Gothic, Monotype Garamond, Monotype Goudy Modern, Monotype Goudy Oldstyle, Monotype Goudy Text, Monotype Italian Old Style, Monotype Janson, Monotype Latin, Monotype Lightline Gothic, Monotype Modern, Monotype News Gothic, Monotype Old Style, Monotype Onyx, Monotype Runic, Monotype Scotch Roman, Monotype Script, Monotype Sorts, Monotype Spartan and Monotype Walbaum are trademarks of Monotype Typography Ltd. Abadi, Albertus, Amasis, Apollo, Arial, Ashley Script, Bell, Bembo, Bernard, Biffo, Binner Gothic, Binny Old Style, Blado, Blueprint, Book Antiqua, Bookman Old Style, Braggadocio, Calisto, Calvert, Cantoria, Castellar, Centaur, Century Gothic, Clarion, Colmcille, Columbus, Cooper Black, Coronet, Corsiva, Dante, Delima, Dorchester Script, Ehrhardt, Ellington, Falstaff, Felix, Festival, Figaro, Forte, Fournier, Gill Sans, Grotesque 126, Headline, Horley Old Style, Imprint, Inflex, Ionic, Joanna, Kino, Klang, Matura, Mercurius Script, New Berolina, Neographic, New Clarendon, News Plantin, Nimrod, Ocean Sans, Octavian, Palace Script, Pepita, Perpetua, Perrywood, Photina, Placard, Plantin, Poliphilus, Rockwell, Sabon, Spectrum, Symbol PS, Swing, Times New Roman, 20th Century, Typewriter Elite, Van Dijck, Z-Antiqua PS and Zeitgeist are trademarks of The Monotype Corporation some of which are registered in certain countries.

Estro and Eurostile are trademarks of Nebiolo.

DeltaFont and eXposure are trademarks of New York Design Studio.

NIMX Jacoby, NIMX Quirks, NIMX Robust, NIMX Skinny and NIMX Tekno are trademarks of NIMX Graphics.

Else is a trademark of Norton Photosetting, Ltd.

PIXymbols is a tradmark of Page Studio Graphics.

British Inserat is a trademark of P.L.I.

Amsterdam, ARRMS, Berliner, Big Black, Blackboard, Boomerang, Bostonia, Bullfinch Display, Bullfinch Text, Catherine Black, Catherine Bold, Catherine Bold Oblique, Catherine Light, Catherine Regular, Catherine Regular Oblique, Chieftan Inline, Chieftan Solid, Colwell Hand, Colwell Italic, Cypress, Durango, Emporium, Erin Lynn, FontBuyer, FontLink, Franklin Type Founders, Glorietta, Greco Adornado, Greco Bold, Greco Bold Italic, Greco Deco Inline, Greco Deco Solid, Greco Negra, Greco Negra Italic, Greco Roman, Greco Roman Italic, Harpers, Harris, Herold, Isadora, Latin Tall, Lazy Script, Little Louis, Manhattan, Marker, Medina, Minneapolis, Mississippi, Nadall, National Modern, National Modern Italic, National Oldstyle, National Oldstyle Italic, Neuland Inline, Neuland Solid, Nova Bold, Pajamas, Precision Type, Punch, Punch Bold, Railroad Light, Recess, Riverboat, Rumpus, Scaffold, Schwere, Shrifteen, Socrates, Sophie, Sterling, The Complete Font Software Resource, The Precision Type Font Reference Guide, The White Book, Thermo, Tombstone Outline, Tombstone Solid, TypeOnSite, Uptown, Vienna Openface, Vienna Regular and Yitsui are trademarks of Precision Type Inc.

Milton is a trademark of Q.B.F.

Roughedge is a trademark of RJH Productions.

Book, Fatman, News, Northern, Osho, Oval, St. Petersburg and Sunny are trademarks of Russian Type Foundry.

Egmont and Empire are trademarks of Rutherford Press.

Twist and Zombie are trademarks of Christian Schwartz Design.

Graphite is a trademark of David Siegel.

New Aster is a trademark and Life is a registered trademark of Simoncini S.A.

Stone and Stone Phonetic are trademarks of Stone Type Foundry.

Arabia Felix, Black Rocks, BlackTents, Catastrophe, Hibiscus, Kiilani, Kufi Script, Mesopotamia, Petroglyph Hawaii and Tommy's Type are trademarks of Judith Sutcliffe.

Amazone and Libra are trademarks of Tetterode Nederland (Lettergieterij Amsterdam).

Agenda, Bodega and Clicker are trademarks of Greg Thompson and Commerce is a trademark of Greg Thompson and Rick Valicenti.

Treacyfaces, TF Bryn Mawr, TF Crossword, TF Forever and TFHabitat are registered trademarks and TF Adepta, TF Akimbo, TF Ardent, TF Avian, TF Dierama, TF Guestcheck, TF Habitat, TF Habitat Contour, TF Hôtelmoderne, TF Maltby, TF Raincheck, TF Roux, TF Simper and TF Squiggle are trademarks of Treacyfaces, Inc.

Adroit, Criterion, Quint and Scenario are trademarks of TypeSpectra, Inc.

Ikarus and URW are registered trademarks of URW Unternehmensberatung, Karow Rubow Weber GmbH.

Berling is a trademark of Verbum A.B. Stockholm.

Amelia, Andrich Minerva, Antikva Margaret, Aquarius, Arrow, Baker Signet, Basilea, Bisque, Broadway, Copperplate Gothic, Davida, Egyptian 505, Friz Quadrata, Global, Glyphic Series, Maximus, Nevision Casual Script, Orbit-B, Organda, Pointille, Relief, Reporter, Russell Square, Serpentine, Thor and Vivaldi are trademarks of Visual Graphics Corporation.

Admark, Bulldog, Column, Congress, Eurocrat, Mercurius, Monkton, Poseidon and Veronan are trademarks of Adrian Williams Design Ltd.

Campanula, Mahlau and Odilia are trademarks of Zeta Fonts.

All other brand and product names are trademarks of their respective holders.

Precision Type is not responsible for typographical errorz. . .

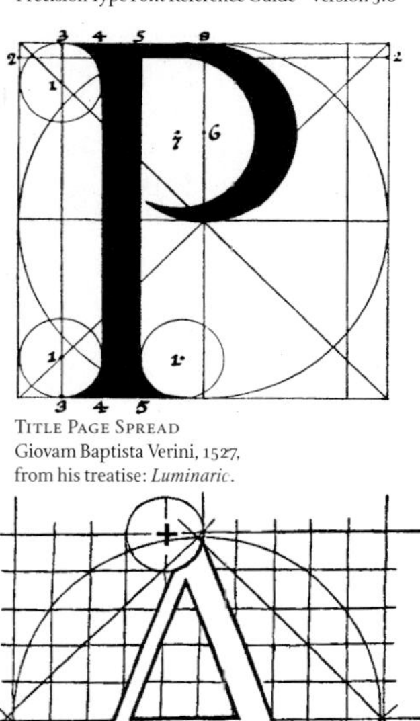

Title Page Spread
Giovam Baptista Verini, 1527,
from his treatise: *Luminario.*

Cover Letter
Geofroy Tory, 1527,
from his book: *Champ Fleury.*

Letters of Introduction

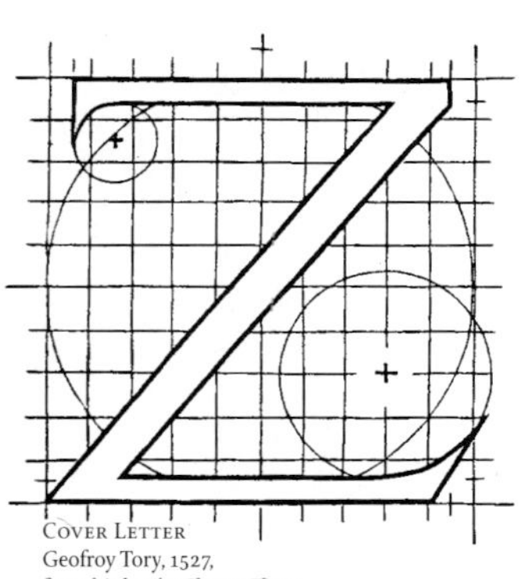

Cover Letter
Geofroy Tory, 1527,
from his book: *Champ Fleury.*

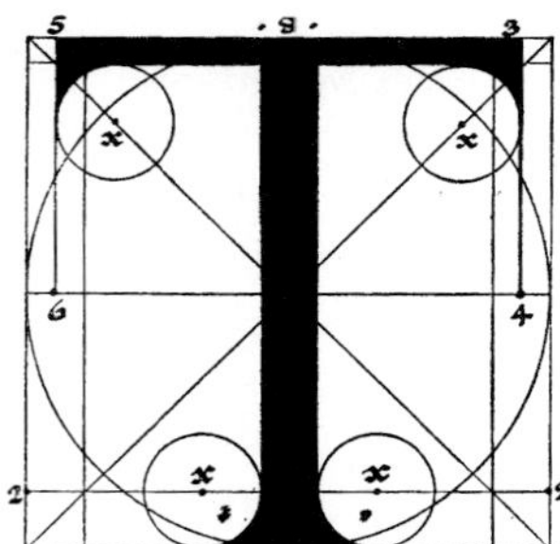

Title Page Spread
Giovam Baptista Verini, 1527,
from his treatise: *Luminario.*

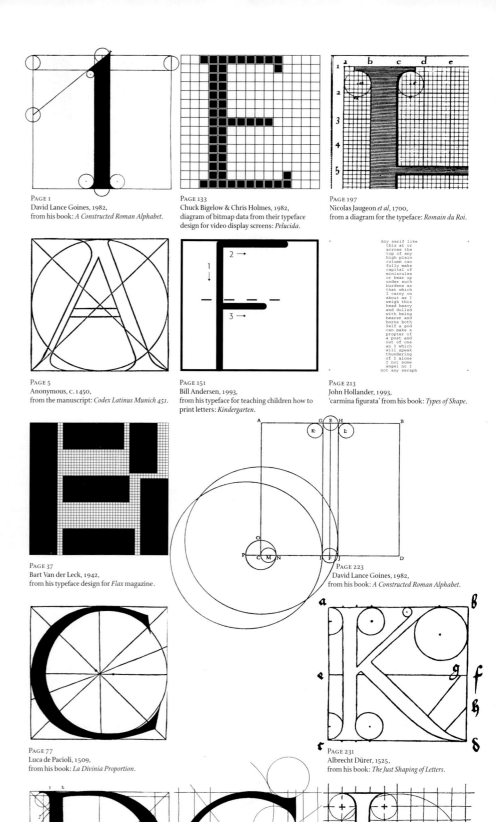

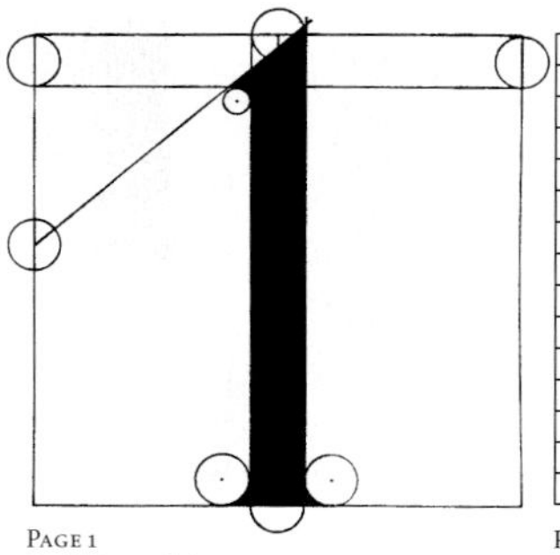

Page 1
David Lance Goines, 1982,
from his book: *A Constructed Roman Alphabet.*

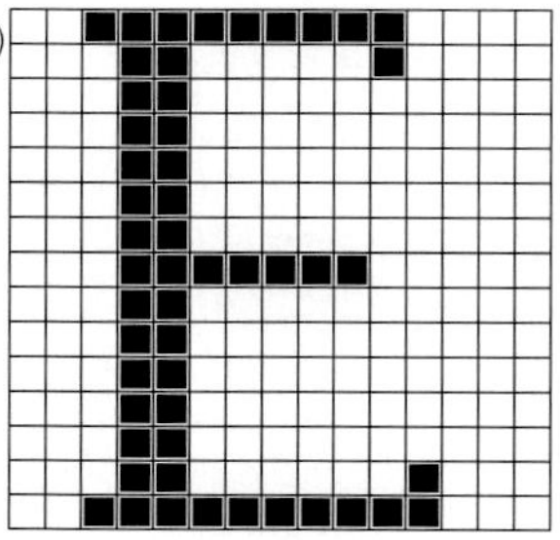

Page 133
Chuck Bigelow & Chris Holmes, 1982,
diagram of bitmap data from their typeface design for video display screens: *Pelucida.*

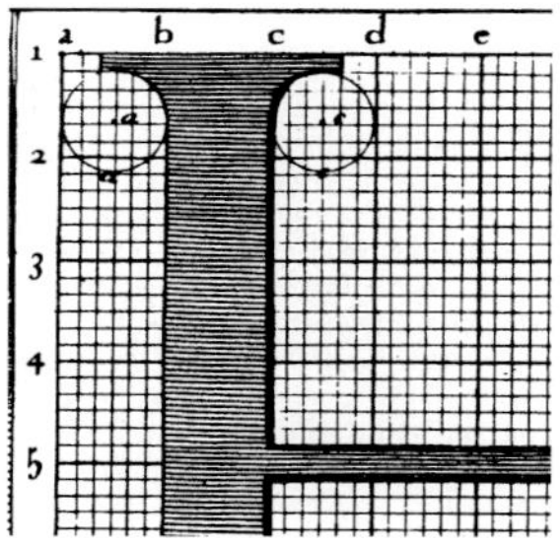

Page 197
Nicolas Jaugeon *et al*, 1700,
from a diagram for the typeface: *Romain du Roi.*

Page 5
Anonymous, c. 1450,
from the manuscript: *Codex Latinus Munich 451.*

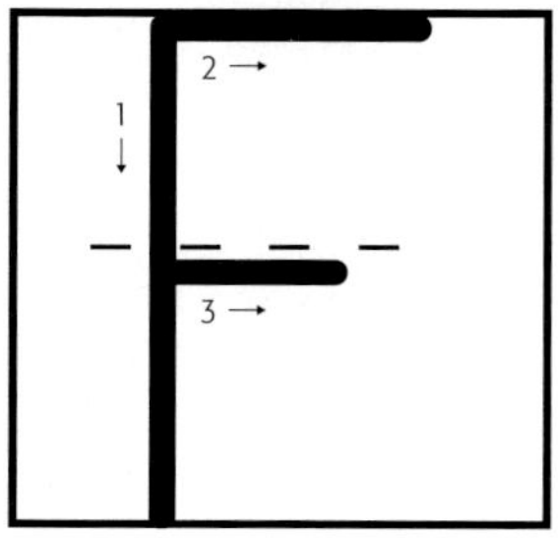

Page 151
Bill Andersen, 1993,
from his typeface for teaching children how to print letters: *Kindergarten.*

Any serif like
this at or
across the
top of any
high plain
column can
fully make
capital of
miniscules
or bear up
under such
burdens as
that which
I carry on
about as I
weigh this
head heavy
and dulled
with being
bearer and
borne both
Self a god
can make a
propter of
a post and
out of one
an I which
will speak
thundering
of I alone
I not some
angel no I
not any seraph

Page 213
John Hollander, 1993,
'carmina figurata' from his book: *Types of Shape.*

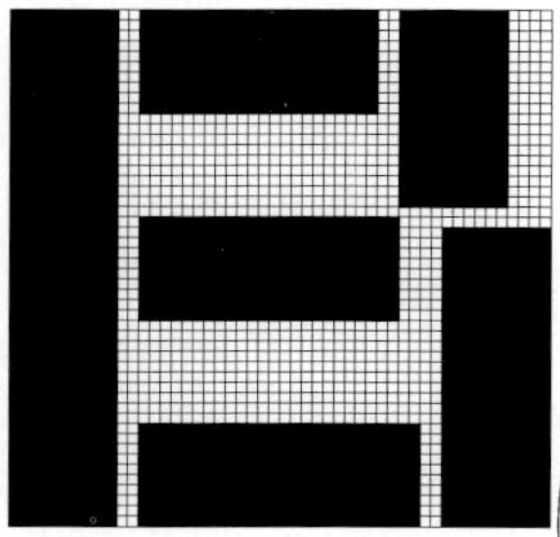

Page 37
Bart Van der Leck, 1942,
from his typeface design for *Flax* magazine.

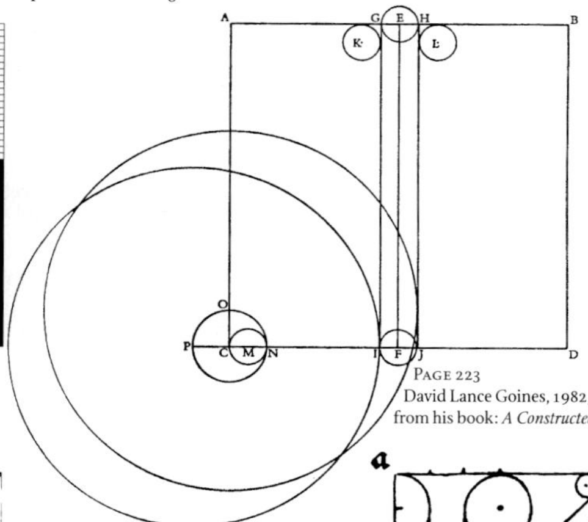

Page 223
David Lance Goines, 1982,
from his book: *A Constructed Roman Alphabet.*

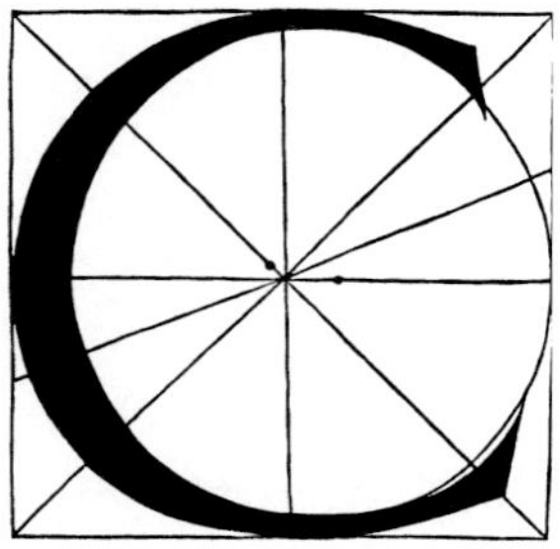

Page 77
Luca de Pacioli, 1509,
from his book: *La Divinia Proportion.*

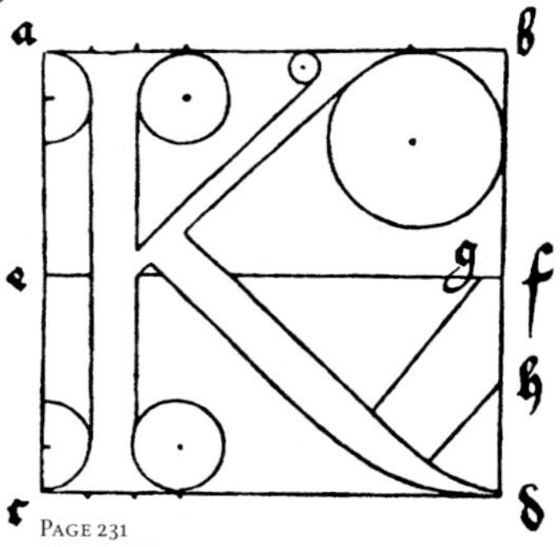

Page 231
Albrecht Dürer, 1525,
from his book: *The Just Shaping of Letters.*

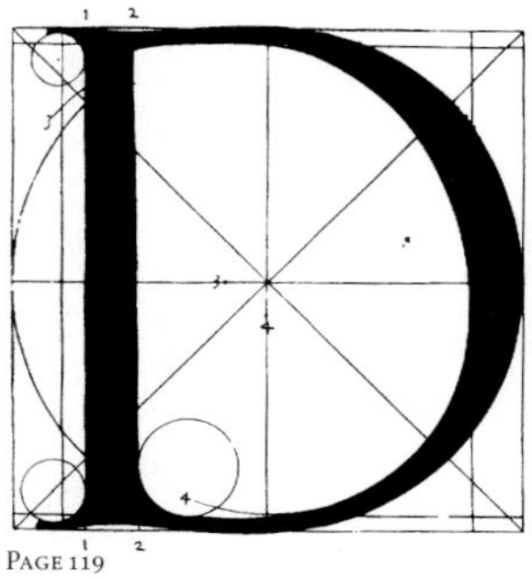

Page 119
Marco Antonio Rossi, 1598,
from his book: *Giardino de scrittori.*

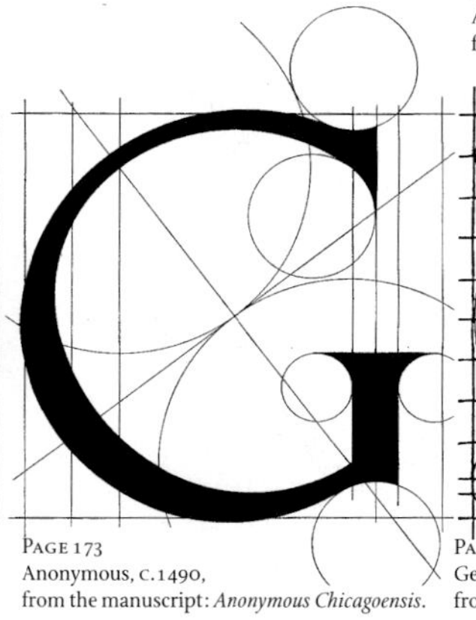

Page 173
Anonymous, c. 1490,
from the manuscript: *Anonymous Chicagoensis.*

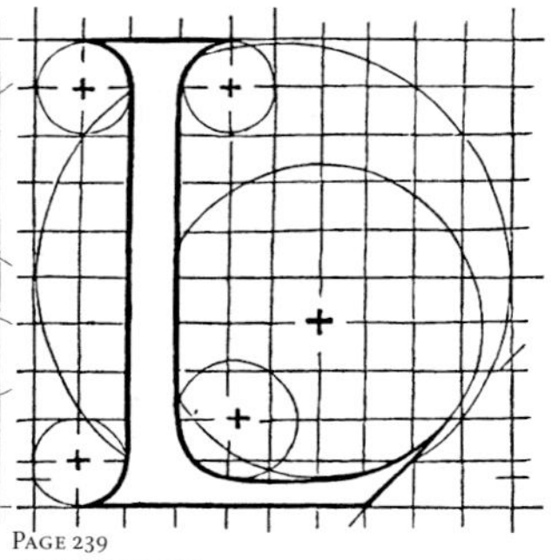

Page 239
Geofroy Tory, 1527,
from his book: *Champ Fleury.*

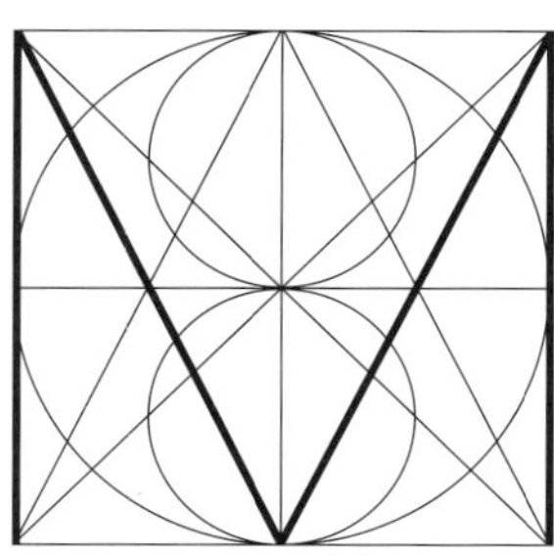

Page 253
John Howard Benson & Arthur Graham Cary, 1940, from their book: *The Elements of Lettering.*

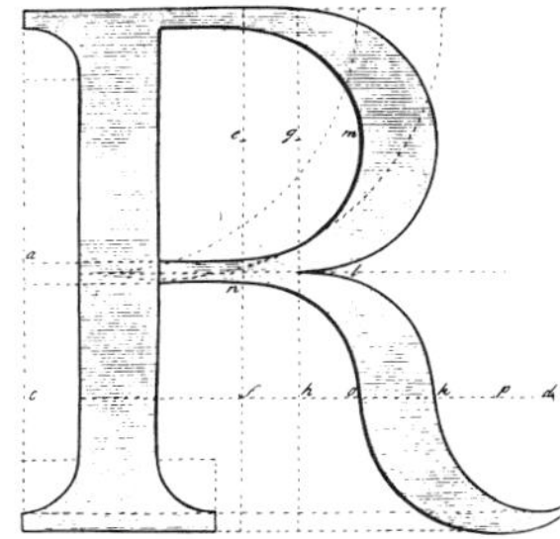

Page 321
George Bickham Jr., c.1755, from his book: *Geometrical Constuction to form the Twenty-four Letters of the Alphabet.*

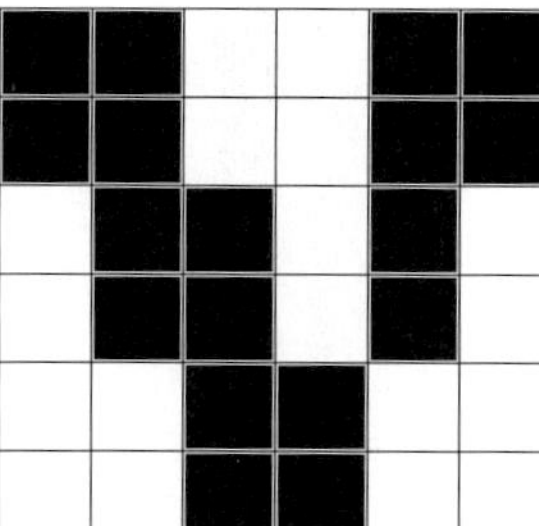

Page 381
Zuzana Licko, 1988, from her typeface design: *Oakland Six.*

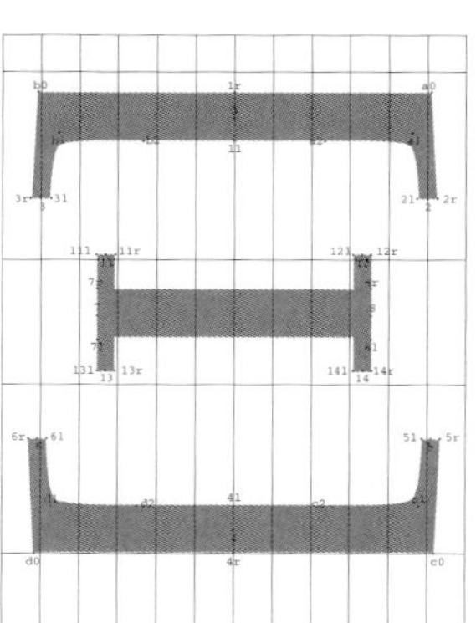

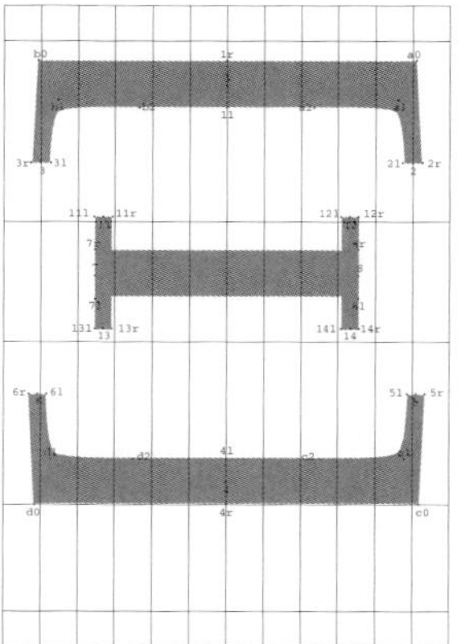

Page 467
Donald Knuth, 1982, diagram of Metafont outline data from his typeface: *Computer Modern.*

Page 499
Noel Rubin, 1994, from his typeface design: *Rubino Serif.*

Page 275
Juan Yciar, 1548, from his writing manual: *Arte subtilissima.*

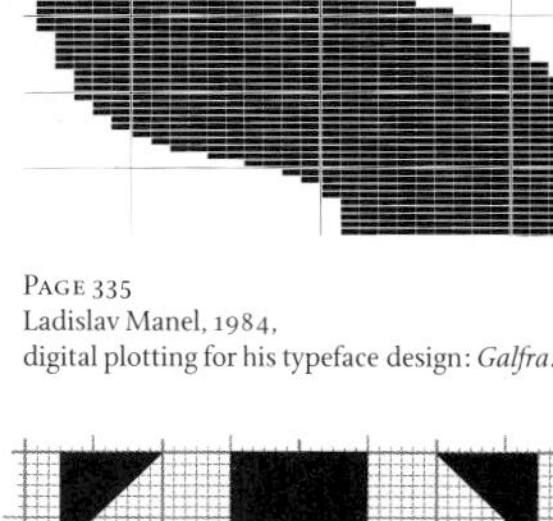

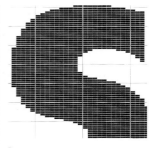

Page 335
Ladislav Manel, 1984, digital plotting for his typeface design: *Galfra.*

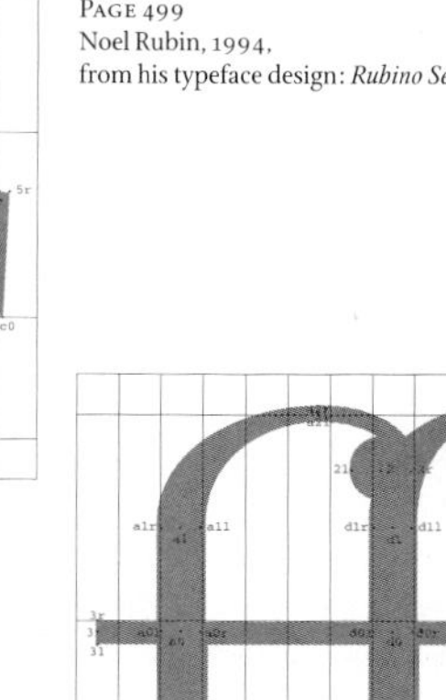

Page 501
Donald Knuth, 1982, diagram of Metafont outline data from his typeface: *Computer Modern.*

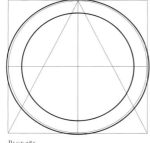

Page 285
Paul Renner, 1927, from a diagram for his typeface design: *Futura.*

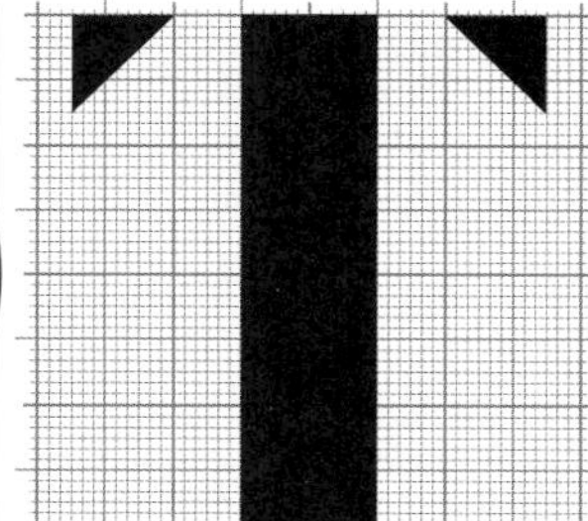

Page 361
Josef Albers, 1925, design for geometrical stencil lettering.

Page 391
Adrian Frutiger, 1968, design grid/matrix, character design, character fit to grid. . . from his typeface design: *OCR-B.*

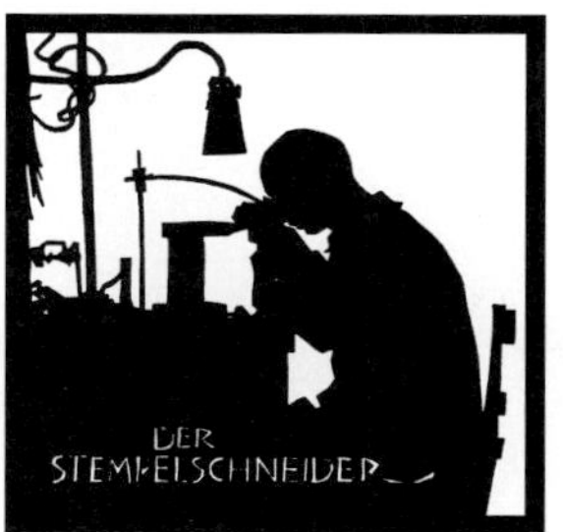
DER
STEMPELSCHNEIDER

Recto following Page 497
Rudolf Koch, 1918, 'Der Stempelschneider' (The Punchcutter) from his portfolio of woodcuts: *The Typefoundry in Silhouette.*

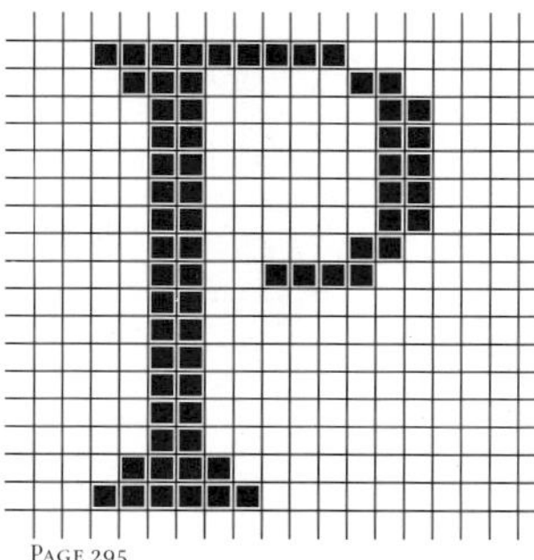

Page 295
Pierre LeBé, 1601, from his diagram for a needlepoint alphabet.

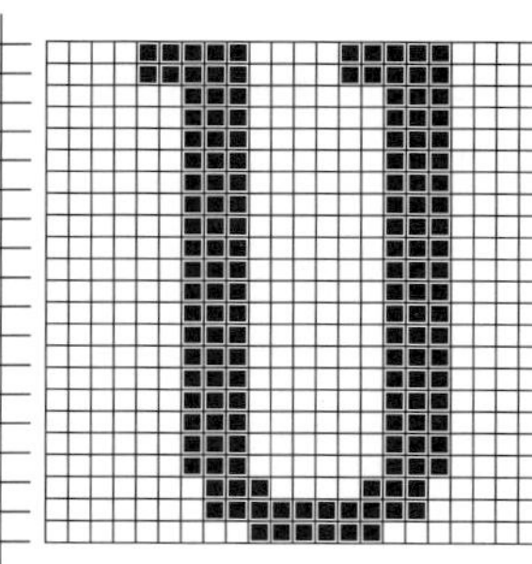

Page 375
Michael Johnston, 1990, from his typeface design: *Zeitgeist.*

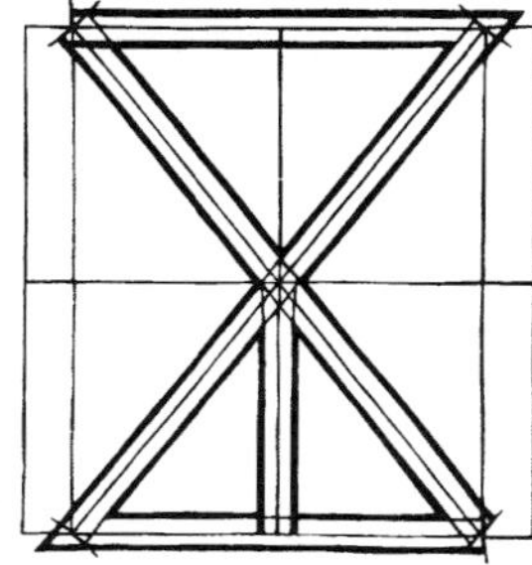

Page 399
Rudolf Koch, 1928, 'diagram of contruction' for his typeface design: *Kabel.*

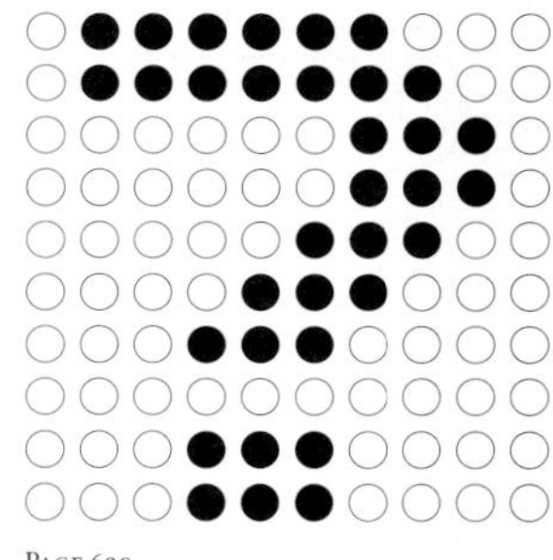

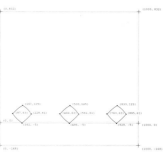

Page 629
Albert Hollenstein, 1975, from his typeface design: *Pointelle.*

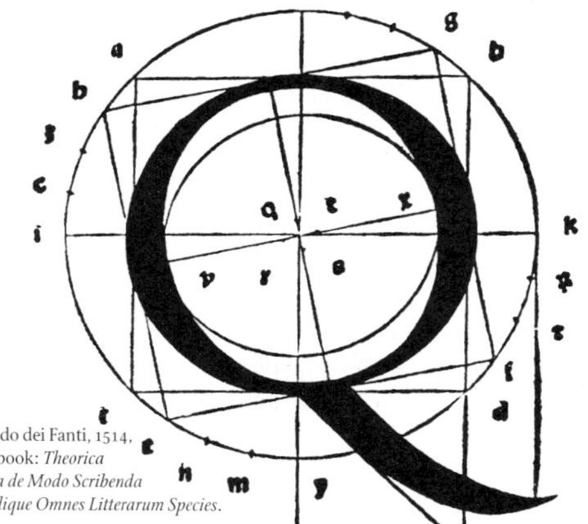

Page 317
Sigismondo dei Fanti, 1514, from his book: *Theorica et Practica de Modo Scribenda Fabricandique Omnes Litterarum Species.*

Page 405
David Lance Goines, 1982, from his book: *A Constructed Roman Alphabet.*

Page 647
Adrian Frutiger, 1992, diagram of PostScript outline data from his typeface design: *Rusticana.*

The Faces. . .

THE PRECISION TYPE FONT REFERENCE GUIDE, VERSION 5.0. . .

would not have been possible without the assistance, contributions and patience of many people; some of them are:

Larry Bernstein
Michael Blumenthal
Scott Brennan
Adam Cevallos
Tracy Esposito
Eric Finder
Edward Hopkins
Lydia Inglett
Ellen Kaufman
Jerry Kaufman
Jeff Meyer
Kay Meyer
Carl Meyer
Pam Newman
Steven Newman
Helen Parisi
Tina Pelliccione
Michael Polesky
Bonnie Schmidt
Mitchell Sirlin
Lenny Strober
Kirk Walton
Alice Wang

research, organization, planning & production — Jeff Level, Bruce Newman, Brenda Newman, George Romaka

typography & design — Jeff Level

typographic research & texts — Kobodaishi & Associates

pre-press production — Island Litho, Farmingdale New York

printing, binding & fulfilment — Quebecor Printing, Kingsport Tennessee

Thanks to David Lance Goines for the use of the figure 1, *the letter* J, *and, of course, the* & *from his book:* A Constructed Roman Alphabet; *used herein with his kind permission.*

behind the Faces.

BRUCE NEWMAN

President and CEO of Precision Type.

Mr. Newman has over 15 years of technology related management experience. Prior to co-founding Precision Type in 1992, he served as the president of Precision Type & Form Inc, a commercial typography and pre-press service company. Previously, he was vice-president of sales for the typography division of William Graphics, a commerical printer based in New York.

BRENDA NEWMAN

Executive Vice-President of Precision Type.

A co-founder of Precision Type, Ms. Newman previously served as vice-president of Precision Type & Form Inc where she was responsible for all aspects of the computer pre-press services division. Earlier, she was group manager for Abrew Typographers of New York.

JEFF LEVEL

Type Consultant and Graphic Designer.

Jeff Level has been professionally involved in the fields of type development and font software marketing since 1982. He has held positions as manager of type development for Autologic Incorporated and type director for Monotype Typography.

Typophon

Of the thousands of typeface designs to be found in this book, several must be singled out for particular mention. Matthew Carter's *Mantinia* is the principal type used on the cover and his *ITC Galliard* is used on the cover and for text & display. Sumner Stone's *Stone Print* family of types is used throughout for text and for notes on the font displays. And, last (certainly not least), Bernd Möllenstädts *Formata Condensed* types are used extensively for notes and information on the font displays.